The **Rough Guide** to

The Greek Islands

written and researched by

**Andrew Benson, Lance Chilton, Marc Dubin,
Nick Edwards, Mark Ellingham, John Fisher,
Geoff Garvey, Natania Jansz**

with additional contributions by

Sarah Gear, Michael Haag

ROUGH GUIDES

NEW YORK • LONDON • DELHI

www.roughguides.com

Contents

Beach life colour
section following p.264

Greek cuisine colour
section following p.472

◁◁ Santoríni ◁ Wild flowers in Crete

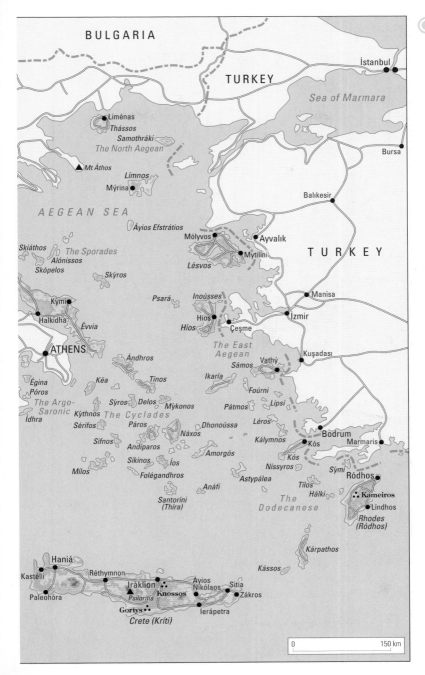

BULGARIA

TURKEY

İstanbul

Sea of Marmara

Liménas
Thássos
Samothráki
The North Aegean

Bursa

Mt Áthos
Límnos
Mýrina

Balıkesir

AEGEAN SEA

Áyios Efstrátios

Mólyvos
Ayvalık

Mytilíni

Lésvos

TURKEY

Skiáthos
The Sporades
Alónissos
Skópelos
Skýros

Psará
Inoússes
Manisa

Kými
Hios
Halkídha
Évvia
Híos
Çeşme
İzmir

ATHENS

The East
Aegean

Vathý

Ándhros
Sámos
Kuşadası

Égina
Kéa
Tínos
Ikaría

Póros
Foúrni

The Argo-
Saronic
Sýros
Delos
Mýkonos
Pátmos
Lipsí

Ídhra
Kýthnos
The Cyclades
Léros

Sérifos
Páros
Dhonoússa

Sífnos
Náxos
Kálymnos
Bódrum

Andíparos
Kós
Marmaris

Síkinos
Íos
Amorgós
Kós

Mílos
Folégandhros
Nissyros
Sými

Anáfi
Astypálea
Tílos
Ródhos

Santoríni
(Thíra)
The
Dodecanese
Hálki

Kameiros

Lindhos

Rhodes
(Ródhos)

Kárpathos

Kássos

Haniá

Kastélli
Réthymnon
Áyios
Nikólaos
Sitía

Iráklion
Zákros

Psilorítis
Knossos

Paleohóra
Gortys
Ierápetra

Crete (Kríti)

0   150 km

Introduction to

The Greek Islands

It would take a lifetime of island-hopping to really get to know the sixty-plus permanently inhabited Greek islands, let alone the countless smaller gull-roosts which dot the Aegean and Ionian seas. At the right time of year or day, they conform remarkably well to their fantastic travel-poster image; any tourist board would give its eye-teeth for the commonplace vision of purple-shadowed island silhouettes floating on a cobalt-and-rose horizon.

Closer to hand, island **beaches** come in all shapes, sizes and consistencies, from discrete crescents framed by tree-fringed cliffs straight out of a Japanese screen painting, to deserted, mile-long gifts deposited by small streams, where you could imagine enacting Crusoe-esque scenarios among the dunes. But inland there is always civilization, whether the tiny cubist villages of the remoter outposts or burgeoning resorts as cosmopolitan – and brazen – as any in the Mediterranean.

What amazes most first-time visitors is the islands' relative **lack of pollution**. If you're used to the murky waters of the open Mediterranean as sampled in Spain, Israel or much of Italy, the Aegean will come as a revelation, with forty-foot visibility the norm, and all manner of sea creatures visible, from starfish and octopuses on the bottom, to vast schools of fish.

The sea is also a **watersports** paradise: the joys of snorkelling and kayaking are on offer to novices, and some of the best windsurfing areas in the world beckon. Yacht charter, whether bare-boat or skippered, is big business, particularly out of Rhodes, Kálymnos, Kós, Lefkádha, Póros and Pireás; indeed, the Greek islands are rated on a par with the Caribbean for quality sailing itineraries. And during the months when the sea is too cold or the weather too blustery, many islands – not necessarily the largest ones – offer superb **hiking** on surviving mule-trails between hill villages, or up the highest summits.

Although more protected than the Greek mainland from invasions, the various archipelagos have been subject to a staggering variety of **foreign influences**. Romans, Arabs, Byzantines, crusading Knights of Saint John, Genoese, Venetians, French, English, Italians and Ottomans have all controlled different islands since the time of Alexander the Great. The high tide of empire has left behind countless **monuments**: frescoed Byzantine churches and monasteries, the fortified Venetian towns of the Cyclades and the Ionians, the more conventional castles of the Genoese and Knights in the northern and eastern Aegean and Dodecanese, Ottoman bridges and mosques, and the Art Deco or Rationalist edifices of the Italian Fascist administration.

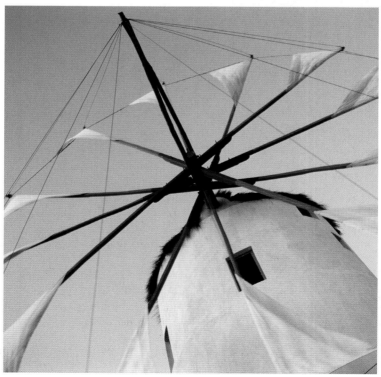

△ Windmill on Santoríni

Constructions from many of these eras are often juxtaposed with – or even superimposed on – the cities and temples of ancient Greece, which provide the foundation in all senses for claims of an enduring Hellenic **cultural identity** down the centuries; museums, particularly on Crete, Corfu, Rhodes, Sámos, Híos, Lésvos and Límnos, amply document the archeological evidence. But it was medieval Greek peasants, fishermen and shepherds, working without an indigenous ruling class or formal Renaissance to impose models of taste or patronize the arts, who most tangibly contributed to our idea of Greekness with their songs and dances, costumes, weaving and vernacular architecture. Much of this has vanished in recent decades, replaced by an avalanche of electric-*bouzoúki*-instrumental cassettes, "genuine museum copies" and tacky souvenir shops, but enough remains in isolated pockets for visitors to marvel at Greek popular culture's combination of form and function.

Of course, most Greek-island visits are devoted to more hedonistic pursuits: going lightly dressed, swimming in balmy waters at dusk, talking and drinking under the stars until 3am. Such pleasures amply compensate for certain enduring weaknesses in the Greek **tourism "product"**: don't go expecting orthopedic mattresses, state-of-the-art plumbing, Cordon-Bleu cuisine or attentive service. Except at a limited number of upmarket facilities in new or restored buildings, hotel and pension rooms can be box-like, wine (unless you're willing to pay dearly for top labels) is pot-luck, and the food at its best is fresh, abundant and simply presented.

Boatyards

Even in the more touristy islands, a remarkable number of traditional boatyards (*karnáyia*) still survive. Small craft are built in the time-honoured way, with the keel and framework assembled first from seasoned pine – which abounds in Greek coastal regions – and then overlaid with planking. You can often spot karnáyia from some distance by the bright-orange mínio, or red-lead paint, applied to the exposed wood – long illegal in most of the EU but still the preservative of choice in Greece. Equipment can be low-tech and most techniques unchanged over centuries, with wooden trellising and launching rollers the rule; serious accidents caused by hulls lurching the wrong way at the wrong time are not unheard of.

The Greek islanders

To attempt an understanding of the islanders, it's useful to realize how recent and traumatic were the events that created the modern Greek state and **national character** – the latter a blend of extroversion and pessimism which is partly due to Greece's strategic position between the West and the Middle East.

Until the early 1900s, Crete, the east Aegean and the Dodecanese – nearly half the islands described in this book – remained under Ottoman or Italian rule. Meanwhile, many people from these "unredeemed" territories lived in Asia Minor, Egypt, western Europe or the northern Balkans. The Balkan Wars of 1912–13, Greece's 1917–18 World War I involvement fighting Bulgaria, the Greco-Turkish war of 1919–22 and the organized **population exchanges** which followed each of these conflicts had profound, brutal effects. Orthodox refugees from Turkey suddenly made up a noticeable proportion of the population of Crete and the northeast Aegean (especially Límnos, Lésvos and Sámos), and with the forced or voluntary departure of their Levantines, Muslims and (during World War II) Jews, these islands lost their multicultural traits.

> The advent of mass tourism in the 1960s arguably saved a number of islands from complete desolation, though local attitudes towards this deliverance have been decidedly ambivalent.

9

△ Fish stall in Crete

Even before the last world war, the Italian occupation of the Dodecanese was characterized by progressively stricter suppression of Greek Orthodox identity, but in general the war years in most other island groups were not quite so dire as on the mainland. Neither was the 1946–49 civil war that followed, nor the 1967–74 dictatorship, so keenly felt out in the Aegean, though benign neglect was about the best many islands could expect until the 1960s. Given the chance to emigrate to Australia, North America or Africa, many entrepreneurial islanders did so, continuing a trend of **depopulation** which ironically had accelerated earlier in the twentieth century, following political union of the northeast Aegean and Dodecanese with the Greek mainland. The uncomfortably close memory of catastrophe, continuing misrule and scarce opportunity at home spurred yet another diaspora.

The advent of **mass tourism** in the 1960s arguably saved a number of islands from complete desolation, though local attitudes towards this deliverance have been decidedly ambivalent. It galls local pride to have become a class of seasonal service personnel, and the encounter between outsiders and villagers has often been corrosive to a deeply conservative rural society. Though younger Greeks are happily adaptable as they rake in the proceeds at resort areas, tourists still need to be sensitive in their behaviour towards the older generation. The mind boggles imagining the reaction of black-clad elders to nude bathing, or even scanty apparel, in a country where – despite being now thoroughly out of step with majority sentiment in the wake of some ludicrous scandals – the Orthodox church was, until the 1990s, an all-but-established faith and self-appointed guardian of national identity. In the presence of ubiquitous Italian-style espresso bars, Internet cafés and ATMs, it's easy to be lulled into thinking that Greece became thoroughly European the moment it joined the EU – until a flock of sheep is paraded along the main street at high noon, and the 1pm ferry shows up at 3pm, or not at all.

Where to go

There is no such thing as a "typical" Greek island; each has its distinctive personality, history, architecture, flora – even a unique tourist clientele. Landscapes vary from the lush cypress-and-olive-swathed Ionians to the bare, wind-scoured ridges of the Cyclades and Dodecanese, by way of subtle gradations between these extremes in the Sporades and northeast Aegean. Setting aside the scars from a few unfortunate man-made developments, it would be difficult to single out an irredeemably ugly island; all have their adherents and individual appeal, described in their account introductions.

Perhaps the best strategy for initial visits is to sample assorted islands from contiguous archipelagos – Crete, the Dodecanese, the Cyclades and the northeast Aegean are all reasonably well connected with each other,

The Evil Eye

Belief in the Evil Eye (in Greek, simply *tó Máti* or "the Eye") is pan-Mediterranean and goes at least as far back as Roman times, but nowhere has it hung on so tenaciously as in Greece (and neighbouring coastal Turkey). In a nutshell, whenever something attractive, valuable or unusual – an infant, a new car, a prized animal – becomes suddenly, inexplicably indisposed, it is assumed to be *matiasméno* or "eyed". Blue-eyed individuals are thought most capable of casting this spell, always unintentionally or at least unconsciously (unlike *máyia*, wilful black magic). The diagnosis is confirmed by discreet referral to a "wise woman", who is also versed in the proper counter-spell. But prevention is always better than cure, and this involves two main strategies. When admiring something or someone, the admirer – blue-eyed or otherwise – must mock-spit (*"phtoo, phtoo, phtoo!"*) to counteract any stirrings of envy which, according to anthropologists, are the root-cause of the Eye. And the proud owners or parents will protect the object of admiration in advance with a blue amulet, hung about the baby's/ animal's neck or the car's rear-view mirror, or even painted directly onto a boat-bow.

Wayside shrines

Throughout Greece you'll see, by the side of the road, small shrines or *proskynitária* which usually hold a saint's icon, an oil lamp, a few floatable wicks and a box of matches. Unlike in Latin America, they don't necessarily mark the spot where someone met their end in a motoring accident (though just occasionally they do); typically they were erected by a family or even one individual in fulfilment of a vow, or *támma*, to a specific saint to reciprocate for any favours granted, in particular being spared death in a road mishap. *Proskynitária* come in various sizes and designs, from spindly, derrick-like metal constructions to sumptuous, gaily painted models of small cathedrals in marble and plaster which you can practically walk into. Often they indicate the presence of a larger but less convenient (and often locked) church off in the countryside nearby, dedicated to the same saint, and act as a substitute shrine where the devout wayfarer can pay reverence to the icon it contains.

though the Sporades, Argo-Saronic and Ionian groups offer limited (or no) possibilities for island-hopping, and usually involve a long traipse across the mainland to get to. If time and money are short, the best place to visit is well-preserved **Ídhra** in the Argo-Saronic Gulf, just a short ride from Pireás (the main port of Athens), but an utterly different place once the day-cruises have gone; neighbouring **Spétses** has similar architectural charm and more accessible beaches. Of the Sporades, **Skýros** and **Skópelos** remain the most traditional and aesthetic, with forests, pale-sand beaches and well-preserved capitals. Among the Cyclades, cataclysmically volcanic **Santoríni (Thíra)** and **Mýkonos** with its perfectly preserved harbour-town rank as must-see spectacles, but fertile, mountainous **Náxos** and gently rolling **Sífnos** have life more independent of cruise-ship tourism and seem more amenable to long stays. For true aficionados, dramatically cliff-girt **Amorgós** or **Folégandhros**, rocky **Sýros** with its UNESCO-recognized harbour town, artistic **Tínos** or lonely **Anáfi** and its balmy, south-facing beaches are less obvious but equally satisfying choices. Crete could (and does) fill an entire Rough Guide to itself, but the highlights have to be **Knossos** and the nearby **archeological museum** in Iráklion, the other Minoan palaces at **Phaestos** and **Ayía Triádha**, and the west in general – Réthymnon with its intact old town, the proud city of **Haniá**, with its hinterland extending to the relatively unspoiled southwest coast, reachable via the fabled **Samarian gorge**. **Rhodes**, with its unique old town, is capital of the Dodecanese, but picturesque,

△ Lefkádha beach

Neoclassical **Sými** opposite and austere **Pátmos**, the island of Revelation, are far more manageable. **Kárpathos**, marooned between Rhodes and Crete, has some of the best beaches and walking in the Dodecanese, while **Léros** and **Níssyros** will appeal to those looking for characterful, unspoilt islands that don't necessarily have superb coastlines. From Pátmos or Léros, it's easy to continue north via **Sámos** – still one of the most attractive islands despite recent fires – and **Híos**, with striking medieval architecture, to balmy, olive-cloaked **Lésvos**, perhaps the most traditional of all islands in its way of life. The Ionian islands are, probably more than any other region except Crete and Rhodes, package-holiday territory, but if you're exiting Greece towards Italy, by all means stop at **Corfu** to savour the Venetian-style main town, which along with neighbouring **Paxí** islet escaped damage from the 1953 earthquake which devasted the southern Ionians. Little **Itháki**, most easily reached from the mainland, is relatively untouristy, given a lack of beaches, though big brother **Kefalloniá** is now well and truly in the spotlight owing to spectacular scenery – and (over)exposure in Louis de Bernière's blockbuster novel, *Captain Corelli's Mandolin*.

When to go

Most islands and their inhabitants are far more agreeable, and resolutely Greek, outside the **busiest period** of early July to late August, when crowds of foreigners or locals, soaring temperatures and the effects of the infamous **meltémi** can detract considerably from enjoyment. The meltémi is a cool, fair-weather wind which originates in high-pressure systems over the far north Aegean, gathering momentum as it travels southwards and assuming near-gale magnitude by the time it reaches Crete. North-facing coasts there, and throughout the Cyclades and Dodecanese, bear the full brunt; its howling is less pronounced in the north or east Aegean, where continental landmasses provide some shelter for the islands just offshore. In the Ionian archipelago, an analogous northwest wind off the Adriatic is called the **maïstros**.

You won't miss out on **warm weather** if you come between late May (half-term week in the UK, thus busy) and mid-June – when a wide variety of garden produce and fish is still available – or in September, when the sea is warmest for swimming, though at these times you'll find little activity on the northernmost islands of Thássos, Límnos and Samothráki. During October you'll probably hit a week's stormy spell, but for much of that month the "little summer of Áyios Dhimítrios", the Greek equivalent of **Indian summer**, prevails. While autumn choice in restaurants and nightlife can be limited, the light is softer, and going out at midday becomes a pleasure rather than an ordeal. The only black spot on visits from late August through September are swarms of **flies** and a few aggressive **wasps**, especially in districts with an appreciable grape harvest. The most reliable venues for late-autumn or early-winter breaks are Rhodes and relatively balmy southeastern Crete, where swimming in December is not unheard of.

> **The most reliable venues for late-autumn or early-winter breaks are Rhodes and relatively balmy southeastern Crete.**

December to March are the **coldest** and least reliably sunny months, particularly on the Ionian islands, typically the rainiest patch in Greece from November onwards (though global warming has meant recent wet summers as well). The high peaks of northerly or lofty islands wear a brief mantle of **snow** around the turn of the year, with Crete's mountainous spine staying partly covered into April. Between January and April the glorious lowland wildflowers start to bloom, beginning in the southeast Aegean. April weather is notoriously unreliable, though the air is crystal-clear and

14

the landscape **green** – a photographer's dream. May is more settled, though the sea is still a bit cool for prolonged dips.

Other factors that affect the timing of a Greek-island visit have to do with the level of tourism and the related **amenities** provided. Service standards, particularly in tavernas, invariably slip under peak-season pressure, and room rates are at their highest from mid-July to August 23. If you can only visit during midsummer, reserve a package well in advance, or plan an itinerary off the beaten track. Between November and April, you have to contend with pared-back ferry and plane schedules (and almost non-existent hydrofoil or catamaran departures), plus skeletal facilities when you arrive. However, you will find adequate services to the more populated islands, and at least one hotel and taverna open in the port or main town of all but the tiniest isles.

Average temperatures (°F) and rainfall (days)

	Jan Max | Min	March Max | Min	May Max | Min	July Max | Min	Sept Max | Min	Nov Max | Min
Crete (Haniá)	60 | 46	64 | 48	76 | 56	86 | 68	82 | 64	70 | 54
rainfall	17	11	5	0	3	10
Cyclades (Mýkonos)	58 | 50	62 | 52	72 | 62	82 | 72	78 | 68	66 | 58
rainfall	14	8	5	0.5	1	9
Ionian (Corfu)	56 | 44	62 | 46	74 | 58	88 | 70	82 | 64	66 | 52
rainfall	13	10	6	2	5	12
Dodecanese (Rhodes)	58 | 50	62 | 48	74 | 58	86 | 70	82 | 72	68 | 60
rainfall	15	7	2	0	1	7
Sporades (Skiáthos)	55 | 45	58 | 47	71 | 58	82 | 71	75 | 64	62 | 53
rainfall	12	10	3	0	8	12
East Aegean (Lésvos)	54 | 42	60 | 46	76 | 60	88 | 70	82 | 66	64 | 50
rainfall	11	7	6	2	2	9

29

things not to miss

It's not possible to see everything that the Greek Islands have to offer in one trip – and we don't suggest you try. What follows is a selective taste of the islands' highlights: outstanding buildings, superb ancient sites and natural wonders. They're arranged in five colour-coded categories, which you can browse through to find the very best things to see, and experience. All highlights have a page reference to take you straight into the Guide, where you can find out more.

01 **Harbour, Sými** Page **335** • The mansions of Sými's picturesque harbour, built with wealth from the sponge trade, are part of an architecturally protected area.

02 Lindos acropolis, Rhodes Page **322** • From the Hellenistic acropolis of Lindos, high above the modern village, you look north along the length of Rhodes island.

03 Kérkyra (Corfu) old town Page **495** • With its elegant Venetian architecture and fine museums, Corfu's capital is the cultural heart of the Ionians.

04 Hiking in the Samariá Gorge Page **285** • The magnificent Samariá Gorge is the longest in Europe.

05 **Chapel of Metamórfosis, Dhíkeos peak, Kós** Page **359** • A hike up 846-metre Dhíkeos peak to the Metamórfosis chapel rewards you with excellent panoramic views.

06 **View over Firá** Page **205** • The island capital of Firá is one of several villages that teeter at the edge of Santoríni caldera cliff.

07 **Beaches and watersports** See *Beach life* **colour section** • Greece's expansive coast provides a multitude of opportunities for getting into the water, or just lying next to it.

08 Knossos palace, Crete Page **233** • The most restored, vividly coloured and ultimately the most exciting of Crete's Minoan palaces.

10 Mólyvos, Lésvos Page **444** • The castle-crowned village of Mólyvos ranks as one of the most beautiful on Lésvos.

09 Sámos Page **395** • Despite recent fires, Sámos remains arguably the most verdant and beautiful of the east Aegean islands.

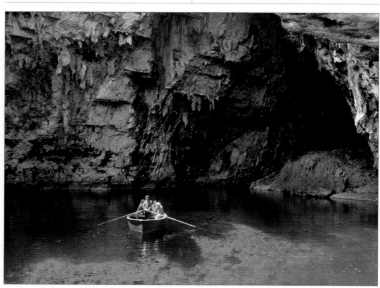

11 Melissáni Cave, Kefalloniá Page **546** • Take a boat trip to the underwater Melissáni Cave, and admire the rock formations and play of light on the cave walls.

12 Tomatoes drying, Pyrgí Page **423** • Strings of sun-drying tomatoes are a common sight during autumn in Híos's mastic villages.

13 Getting out on the water Page **81** • The Greek archipelagos are an excellent place to sail, island-hop or simply spend a day on a boat.

14 Andípaxi Page **535** • With its aquamarine waters and idyllic beaches, Paxí's satellite islet makes a perfect daytrip destination.

15 Náoussa harbour, Páros Page **173** • Páros's second port, Naoússa is still very much a traditional working harbour.

16 **Loggerhead sea turtle** Page **563** • The Ionian islands harbour one of the Mediterranean's main concentrations of the endangered loggerhead sea turtle.

18 **Ídhra** Page **107** • Ídhra's perfect horseshoe-shaped harbour is surrounded by grand eighteenth-century mansions.

17 **Haniá old town, Crete** Page **277** • Haniá displays haunting vestiges of its Venetian and Ottoman past.

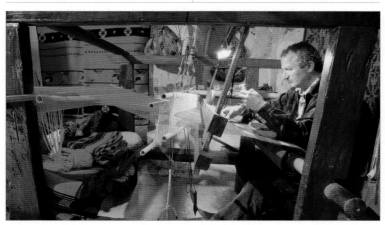

19 **Village weaver, Crete** Page **257** • Traditional crafts, such as weaving and embroidery, still flourish on Greece's largest island.

20 **Ápella beach, Kárpathos** Page **307** • One of the most scenic of Kárpathos's east-coast beaches.

21 **Váï beach, Crete** Page **261** • A superb beach, fringed by a wild date-palm grove.

22 **Nightlife** Page **71** • The after-dark scene in the most popular island resorts is lively, varied and long.

23 **Dovecotes on Tínos** Page **149** • Distinctive, ornate dovecotes, introduced by the Venetians, punctuate the island of Tínos.

24 **Kárpathos: view south from Ólymbos village** Page **308** • The view south from windswept, remote Ólymbos gives a good idea of the rugged coast of unspoilt northern Kárpathos.

25 **Windsurfing off Vassilikí, Lefkádha** Page **540** • Located in a vast, cliff-flanked bay, Vassilikí is one of Europe's biggest windsurf centres.

26 Monastery of Ayíou Ioánnou Theológou, Pátmos

Page **383** • Built in honour of St John the Divine, this huge monastery is a warren of interconnecting courtyards, chapels, stairways, arcades, galleries and roof terraces.

27 Stéfanos crater floor, Níssyros

Page **349** • No stay on Níssyros would be complete without a visit to the island's dormant volcano.

28 Hozoviotíssas monastery, Amorgós

Page **194** • With its vast walls gleaming white at the base of a sheer orange cliff, the Hozoviotíssas monastery is a dramatic sight.

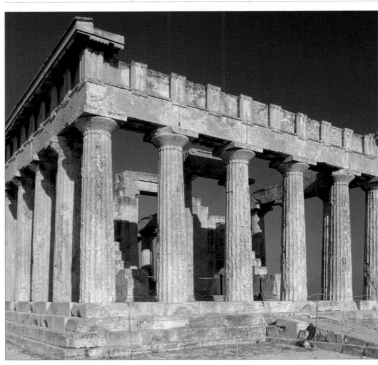

29 Temple of Aphaea, Égina

Page **99** • The beautiful fifth-century-BC Temple of Aphaea is one of the most complete and visually complex ancient buildings in Greece.

Basics

Basics

Getting there

It's two thousand miles or more from the UK and Ireland to the Greek islands, so for most visitors flying is the only viable option. There are direct flights to a variety of Greek island destinations from all major British airports; journey time is three-and-a-half to four-and-a-half hours. Road or rail alternatives from the UK take a minimum of three days, and are only worth considering if you plan to visit Greece as part of an extended trip through Europe.

Only two carriers currently fly direct to Greece from North America, so most North Americans travel via a European hub for the onward connecting flight. You may discover that it's cheaper to arrange the final leg of the journey yourself; such onward flights from the UK are detailed on pp.28-30. It's fairly easy to track down flights from Australia to Athens, less so from New Zealand.

Airfares to Greece from Europe and North America depend on the **season**, with the highest applicable from June to early September (plus Easter week); fares drop during the "shoulder" seasons – April/May and late September/October – and you'll get the best prices during the low season, November to March (excluding Christmas and New Year weeks which count as peak season). Australian and New Zealand fares have their low season from mid-January to the end of February and October/November; high season is mid-May to August, plus December to mid-January; and shoulder season the rest of the year.

You can often cut costs by going through a **specialist/discount flight agent**, who may also offer a range of other travel-related services such as travel insurance, car rentals, tours and the like. From the UK, you may find it more cost-effective to pick up a **package deal**, with accommodation included, from one of the tour operators listed on p.31.

Booking flights online

Even if you don't end up actually buying your ticket online, a web search will clue you up on what the prevailing published economy fares are. However the airlines' websites themselves tend to give you a choice of only nonchangeable/ nonrefundable and full economy fares – for the numerous options in between, you'll have to ring them, or consult a general discount travel site. The cheapest fares require a minimum stay of three days away, and over a Saturday night, with a typical maximum period of thirty or sixty days. They also make you liable to penalties (including total loss of ticket value) if you miss your outbound departure or change your return date. Sometimes student/youth tickets are available to those under 26, as are "Senior" or "Golden" fares available for those over 60.

Some general travel sites like Expedia or Travelocity offer "special bargain" fares – the problem with some of these is you don't get to see the scheduling, or the airlines used, until after you've bought the ticket. There have also been reported instances of so-called "fare loading" – where you irrevocably pay for a promised fare only to be told it is "no longer available" and end up with a more expensive ticket.

Online booking agents and general travel sites

ⓦ **www.cheapflights.co.uk** (UK & Ireland), ⓦ www.cheapflights.com (US), ⓦ www.cheapflights.ca (Canada) or ⓦ www.cheapflights.com.au (Australia & New Zealand) Not a booking site itself, but maintains links to the travel agents offering the deals.
ⓦ **www.cheaptickets.com** Discount flight specialists (US only).
ⓦ **www.etn.nl/discount.htm** A hub of consolidator and discount agent web links,

maintained by the nonprofit European Travel Network.

ⓦ**www.expedia.co.uk** (UK & Ireland), ⓦwww .expedia.com (US) or ⓦwww.expedia.ca (Canada) Discount airfares, all-airline search engine and daily deals.

ⓦ**www.geocities.com/thavery2000** An extensive list of airline websites and US toll-free numbers.

ⓦ**www.kelkoo.co.uk** Useful UK-only price-comparison site, checking several sources of low-cost flights (and other goods and services) according to specific criteria.

ⓦ**www.lastminute.com** (UK & Ireland), ⓦwww.lastminute.com.au (Australia) or ⓦwww .lastminute.co.nz (New Zealand) Good holiday-package and flight-only deals available at very short notice.

ⓦ**www.opodo.co.uk** Popular and reliable source of cheap UK airfares. Owned by, and run in conjunction with, nine major European airlines.

ⓦ**www.orbitz.com** (US only) Comprehensive web travel source, with the usual flight, car rental and hotel deals but also great follow-up customer service.

ⓦ**www.priceline.co.uk** or ⓦwww .priceline.com Bookings from the UK/US only. Name-your-own-price auction website that can knock around forty percent off standard website fares. You can't choose the airline or flight times (although you do specify dates) and the tickets are nonrefundable, nontransferable and nonchangeable.

ⓦ**www.skyauction.com** Bookings from the US only. Auctions tickets and travel packages using a "second bid" scheme. The best strategy is to bid the maximum you're willing to pay, since if you win you'll pay just enough to beat the runner-up regardless of your maximum bid.

ⓦ**www.travel.co.nz** Comprehensive online travel company, with discounted fares.

ⓦ**www.travelocity.co.uk** (UK & Ireland), ⓦwww.travelocity.com (US) or ⓦwww. travelocity.ca (Canada) Destination guides, hot web fares and deals for car rental, accommodation and lodging as well as fares.

ⓦ**www.travelselect.com** A subsidiary of lastminute.com (see opposite) that is useful and fairly easy to use, but without most of the guff and banner adverts of the better-known sites.

ⓦ**www.travelshop.com.au** Australian website offering discounted flights, packages, insurance and online bookings.

ⓦ**www.zuji.com.au** Destination guides, hot fares and great deals for car rental, accommodation and lodging.

From the UK and Ireland

Increasingly, there is little difference between charter and scheduled flights to Greece in terms of penalties and prices; the main suriviving distinctions are that it's difficult to get more than a four-week travel period for charters, and in winter only scheduled flights are available. So far the only no-frills airlines serving Greece are easyJet and Air Scotland; the main advantage in using them is the ability to secure economical one-way fares.

Although **Athens** remains the prime destination for cheap fares, there are also direct flights from Britain to (on the mainland) **Thessaloníki** (for Thássos and the Sporades), **Kavála** (for Thássos and the northeast Aegean), and **Préveza** (Áktio; for Lefkádha) and direct to the islands of **Crete, Rhodes, Kós, Corfu, Mýkonos, Zákynthos, Kefalloniá, Skiáthos, Sámos, Santoríni, Lésvos** and **Límnos**. With any

---

Connections at Athens airport

Missing connections at Athens Airport is a distinct possibility, due to the airport's enormous size (though a few well-concealed lifts for luggage trolleys between arrival and departure levels help reduce stress). Airport rules stipulate a **minimum of 55 minutes** between your incoming flight's arrival and onward flight's departure, but some airlines insist on a minimum leeway of **90 minutes**. Given late arrivals (especially on Olympic) and lengthy security checks, try to observe this rule when buying tickets. Some, but not all, ticketing systems won't let you book an itinerary if the layover is too short.

Check your luggage through to your final Greek destination. Even if your inbound international flight is hideously late, you then stand a good chance of getting yourself to the end of your itinerary that day, even if your checked baggage only shows up the next day.

Fly less – stay longer! Travel and climate change

Climate change is a serious threat to the ecosystems that humans rely upon, and air travel is the fastest-growing contributor to the problem. Rough Guides regard travel, overall, as a global benefit, and feel strongly that the advantages to developing economies are important, as is the opportunity of greater contact and awareness among peoples. But we all have a responsibility to limit our personal impact on global warming, and that means giving thought to how often we fly, and what we can do to redress the harm that our trips create.

Flying and climate change

Pretty much every form of motorized travel generates CO_2 (the main cause of human-induced climate change) but planes are far and away the worst offenders, not just because of the sheer distances they allow us to travel, but because they release a selection of greenhouse gases high into the atmosphere. The statistics are frightening: two people taking a return flight between Europe and the US will contribute as much to climate change as an average household's gas and electricity over a whole year.

Fuel-cell and other less harmful types of plane may emerge eventually. But until then, there are really just two options for concerned travellers: to reduce the amount we travel by air (take fewer trips – stay for longer!), and to make the trips we do take "climate neutral" via a carbon offset scheme.

Carbon offset schemes

Offset schemes run by climatecare.org, carbonneutral.com and others allow you to make up for some or all of the greenhouse gases that you are responsible for releasing. To do this, they provide "carbon calculators" for working out the global-warming contribution of a specific flight (or even your entire existence), and then let you contribute an appropriate amount of money to fund offsetting measures. These include rainforest and other indigenous reforestation, and initiatives to reduce future energy demand – often run in conjunction with sustainable development schemes.

Rough Guides, together with Lonely Planet and other concerned partners in the travel industry, are supporting a carbon offset scheme run by climatecare.org. Please take the time to view our website and see how you can help to make your trip climate neutral.

ⓦ **www.roughguides.com/climatechange**

---

flight to Athens, you can buy a **domestic connecting flight** on Olympic or Aegean to one of almost three dozen additional Greek mainland and island airports.

The **charter flight season** for Greece operates most years from early May to late October. The main charter airlines which offer flight-only to Greece are Excel, Thomas Cook and TUI, though flight-only deals are rare at peak season.

You can pay dearly for direct services to the island of your choice, and for many destinations you may well find two-stop scheduled services via Athens are much cheaper. **Sample return fares** at high season range from a reasonable £160–210 (Gatwick to Rhodes, Skiáthos or Corfu) up to a hefty

£300 (Manchester to Kefalloniá, Gatwick to Lésvos).

The greatest variety of **flight destinations** tends to be from London Gatwick and Manchester, from where you should have a choice of most of the Greek regional airports listed opposite. Flying from elsewhere in Britain, or looking for last-minute discounts, you'll find options more limited, most commonly to Athens, Corfu, Rhodes, Kós and Crete.

Summer charters operate **from Dublin** to Rhodes, Crete, Corfu and often Zákynthos. A high-season flight-only charter from Dublin to an island costs upwards of €320 return.

The main advantages of **scheduled flights** are that they can usually be issued as e-tickets and can be valid for up to a year. The Greek national carrier Olympic Airlines, notorious as the least punctual airline in the skies and threatened with drastic restructuring as of writing, plus British Airways, currently constitute a duopoly in terms of direct "full service" to Greece from Britain. From Ireland, there's just Malev, which offers direct service to Athens from Dublin during summer only; otherwise you have to juggle various combinations from Belfast or Dublin via London on the likes of Aerlingus, bmibaby, or Ryanair.

Specimen **return fares** between the UK and Athens range from £130 or so in the pit of winter to as much as £350 in August or at Easter (add £60 for Manchester departures) – and this range will only drift upward as fuel costs rise, with easyJet fares being as high or higher than those on the "real" airlines in peak season. From the Irish Republic, fares range from €100 to €500 depending on time of year. If cost is an overriding factor, at peak travel seasons you may have little choice but to **go indirectly to Athens**, via intervening European cities. Travel websites will pick the cheapest routes and carriers on the day, but experience has shown that Alitalia, Lufthansa, Maersk Air and Air France have the most congenial schedules from the UK. All should get you to Athens in time for the last onward flight of the day to the largest islands.

Don't overlook the possibility of using **Frequent Flyer miles** to reach Athens. From the UK, direct flights on Olympic or BA require 25,000 points, while many indirect carriers (such as Swiss/Lufthansa) only need in the region of 20,000 miles. From North America, most airlines require 70,000–80,000 miles. You'll still have to pay all taxes and charges (around £55 from Britain), but a major advantage is that these types of tickets are usually date-changeable for a small fee.

Scheduled airlines and routes

Aer Lingus UK ☎ 0845/084 4444, Republic of Ireland ☎ 0818 365 000, ⓦ www.aerlingus.com. Connecting service to major UK airports.
Air Scotland (Grecian Airways) ☎ 0141/222 2363, ⓦ www.air-scotland.com. Two flights weekly from Glasgow to Athens, March–Oct.
bmi ☎ 0870/607 0555, ⓦ www.flybmi.com. Code-share service with Olympic from Scotland and north of England to major UK airports.

bmibaby Republic of Ireland ☎ 01/435 0011, ⓦ www.bmibaby.com. Connecting service from Ireland to major UK airports.
British Airways UK ☎ 0870/850 9850, Republic of Ireland ☎ 1800 626 747, ⓦ www.ba.com. Up to three flights daily Heathrow to Athens; four weekly from Gatwick to Thessaloníki, and two weekly year-round from Gatwick to Iráklion (Crete).
easyJet ☎ 0870/000 000, ⓦ www.easyjet.com. One flight daily from both Luton and Gatwick to Athens.
Malev Republic of Ireland ⓦ www.malev.com. malev.com. Three weekly to Athens from Dublin, May–Sept only.
Olympic Airlines ☎ 0870/606 0460, ⓦ www .olympic-airways.gr. Three daily from Heathrow to Athens, six weekly (morning) from Gatwick to Athens; five evenings weekly Gatwick to Thessaloníki; one to two weekly Manchester to Athens.
Ryanair Republic of Ireland ☎ 0818/303 030, ⓦ www.ryanair.com. Connecting service to London Stansted.

Flight and travel agents in the UK and Republic of Ireland

Avro ☎ 0870/458 2841, ⓦ www.avro.co.uk. Seat-only sales on flights to major holiday islands from most UK airports, on Monarch Airlines; easy-to-use website.
Excel Airways ☎ 0870/998 9898, ⓦ www.xl.com. Flights to almost every major charter-served airport in Greece, mostly from Gatwick and Manchester but often Glasgow, Birmingham and East Midlands; competitive fares, easy-to-use site.
Greece & Cyprus Travel Centre ☎ 0121/355 6955, ⓦ www.greece-cyprus.co.uk. Competent flight consolidator for Olympic in particular; myriad fares to suit every need, including one-ways.
Joe Walsh Tours Dublin ☎ 01/676 0991, ⓦ www .joewalshtours.ie. General budget fares and holidays agent.
McCarthys Travel Republic of Ireland ☎ 021/427 0127, ⓦ www.mccarthystravel.ie. Established Irish travel agent now part of the Worldchoice chain of travel shops.
North South Travel ☎ 01245/608291, ⓦ www .northsouthtravel.co.uk. Friendly, competitive flight agency, offering discounted fares worldwide – profits are used to support projects in the developing world, especially the promotion of sustainable tourism.
Rosetta Travel Belfast ☎ 028/9064 4996, ⓦ www.rosettatravel.com. Flight and holiday agent, specializing in deals direct from Belfast.

STA Travel ☏ 0870/160 0599, ⊛ www.statravel
.co.uk. Worldwide specialists in low-cost flights and
tours for students and under-26s.
Thomas Cook ☏ 0870/750 5711, ⊛ www
.thomascook.com. Good selection of flight-onlys to
the biggest holiday islands from a half-dozen UK
airports, though difficult to find in this dense site.
Thomson Flights ☏ 0800/000 747, ⊛ www
.thomsonflights.com. Limited flight-only deals to
major holiday centres on TUI, its parent-company
airline.
Trailfinders UK ☏ 020/7938 3939, ⊛ www
.trailfinders.com, Republic of Ireland ☏ 01/677
7888, ⊛ www.trailfinders.ie. One of the best-
informed and most efficient agents for independent
travellers; branches in all the UK's largest cities,
plus Dublin.

Packages and tours

Virtually every British mainstream **tour
operator** includes Greece in its programme,
though with many of the larger, cheap-and-
cheerful outfits you'll find choices limited to
the established resorts – notably the islands
of Rhodes, Kós, Lésvos, Crete, Skiáthos,
Zákynthos and Corfu. If you buy one of
these at a last-minute discount, especially
in spring or autumn, you may find it costs
little more than a flight – and you can use the
accommodation included as much or as little
as you want.

For a more low-key and genuinely Greek
resort, however, book your holiday through
one of the **specialist agencies** listed
below. Most of these are fairly small-scale
operations, providing competitively priced
packages with flights (unless otherwise
stated) and often more traditional village-
based accommodation. They also make an
effort to offer islands without overdeveloped
tourist resorts. Such agencies tend to divide
into two types: those which, like the major
chains, contract a block of accommodation
and flight seats (or even their own plane) for
a full season; and an increasing number of
bespoke agencies who tailor holidays at your
request, making all transport and accommodation arrangements on the spot. These can
work out somewhat more expensive, but the
quality of flights and lodging is often correspondingly higher.

The **walking** holiday operators listed
either run treks of ten to fifteen people plus

guide, or provide customers with a printed,
self-guiding itinerary, and arranged accommodation each day. Of late there are outfits
organizing **other physical activities**, most
notably swimming between the islands.

Sailing holidays involve small flotillas of
four-to-eight-berth yachts, with changing
anchorages each night, or are shore-based
schools. Prices start at around £415 per
person, flights included, in a group of four
on a thirty-foot boat for a one-week flotilla.
Alternatively, confident sailors can arrange to
charter a "bare boat".

Villa or village accommodation holidays

Cachet Travel ☏ 020/8847 8700, ⊛ www
.cachet-travel.co.uk. Attractive range of villas and
apartments, in the more unspoilt south and west of
Crete, plus remote corners of Sámos.
CV Travel ☏ 0870/606 0013, ⊛ www.cvtravel
.co.uk. Quality villas, mostly on Corfu and Paxí but
also Spétses, Lefkáda and Crete.
Direct Greece ☏ 0870/191 9244, ⊛ www.direct
-greece.co.uk. Moderately priced villas, apartments
and restored houses on Rhodes, Hálki, Zákynthos,
Kefalloniá, Lésvos, Corfu, Lefkáda and Crete.
Greek Islands Club ☏ 020/8232 9780, ⊛ www
.greekislandsclub.com. Extremely high-quality villas
throughout the Ionian and Sporades islands; also
Pátmos, Thíra and Crete.
Greek Sun Holidays ☏ 01732/740317 ⊛ www
.greeksun.co.uk. Good-value package holidays in
the Dodecanese, northeast Aegean and Cyclades;
also tailor-made island-hopping itineraries.
Hidden Greece ☏ 020/7839 2553 ⊛ www
.hidden-greece.co.uk. Two bespoke agencies, each
running for forty-plus years, have joined forces,
arranging accommodation on and transport to
32 less-visited islands in the Cyclades, northeast
Aegean and Dodecanese, as well as much of Crete.
Island Wandering ☏ 0870/777 9944, ⊛ www
.islandwandering.com. Tailor-made island-hopping
itineraries between most Greek archipelagos; deals
range from prebooked accommodation only (this
tends to be on the basic side) to mini-tours, with
local ferry or air transfers arranged.
Laskarina Holidays ☏ 01444/880380, ⊛ www
.laskarina.co.uk. Top-end villas, quality hotels and
restored houses on Skópelos, Alónissos, Hálki, Skmi,
Tílos, Kálymnos, Télendhos, Léros, Lipsí, Pátmos,
Ikaría and Sámos; excellent customer service.
Pure Crete ☏ 020/8760 0879, ⊛ www.pure
-crete.com. Characterful, converted cottages and
farmhouses in western Crete.

Simpson Travel ☎020/8392 5852, ⓦwww
.simpson-travel.com. Villas, upmarket hotels and
village "hideaways" on Crete, Corfu, Paxí and
Meganíssi.
Sunvil Holidays ☎020/8568 4499, ⓦwww
.sunvil.co.uk/greece. Durable and consistently high-
quality outfit specializing in upmarket hotels and
villas in the Ionian islands, the Sporades, western
Crete, Lésvos, Límnos, Sámos, Ikaría and Pátmos.
Also walking holidays on Amorgós.
Tapestry Holidays ☎020/8235 7788, ⓦwww
.tapestryholidays.com. Quality villas, hotels and
restoration inns on Kefalloniá, Corfu, Paxí, Skópelos
and Itháki.
Travel à la Carte ☎01635/201250, ⓦwww.
travelalacarte.co.uk. Established Corfu specialist,
now diversified into beach and rural villas on
Skiáthos, Hálki, Paxí and Sými as well.

Walking, wildlife and swimming holidays

ATG Oxford ☎01865/315678, ⓦwww.atg
-oxford.co.uk. Somewhat pricey but high-standard
guided walks on Crete and select Cyclades.
Exodus ☎0870/240 5550, ⓦwww.exodus.co.uk.
One-week treks on Évvia or the White Mountains of
Crete; also sail-walk two-week tours through the
Cyclades and one week multi-activity trips.
Explore Worldwide ☎01252/760 000, ⓦwww
.exploreworldwide.com. Treks on Crete and
Kefalloniá; also island-wanderer trips, mostly in the
Cyclades, mixing kaïki-sailing with light walking
ashore.
Jonathan's Tours ☎00 33 561046447,
ⓦwww.jonathanstours.com. Family-run walking
holidays on Crete (where Jonathan has 17 years'
experience), Lésvos and Lefkádha; spring and
autumn departures.
Marengo Guided Walks ☎01485/532710,
ⓦwww.marengowalks.com. Annually changing
programme of easy walks guided by ace botanist
Lance Chilton; typical one-week offerings may
include Sámos, Skmi, northern Lésvos, Crete and
Thássos.
Ramblers Holidays ☎01707/331133, ⓦwww
.ramblersholidays.co.uk. Spring in Crete, Easter
on Sámos.
Swim Trek ☎020/8696 6220, ⓦwww.swimtrek
.com. 6-day swimming tours between and around
Náxos, Páros and the minor Cyclades, the brainchild
of Aussie cross-channel swimmer Simon Murie;
May–Oct except Aug.
Walking Plus ☎020/8835 8303 ⓦwww
.walkingplus.co.uk. Enthusiastic Gilly and Robin
Cameron Cooper offer guided and self-guided off-
season walks on Náxos and Tínos.

Sailing holidays

Nautilus Yachting ☎01732/867445, ⓦwww
.nautilus-yachting.co.uk Bareboat yacht charter out
of just about every marina in the country, including
some unusual choices like Sámos and Kalamáta.
Seafarer Cruising & Sailing ☎0870/442 2447,
ⓦwww.seafarercruises.com. Argo-Saronic flotilla
specialists, also a Póros-based school.
Setsail Holidays ☎01787/310445, ⓦwww
.setsail.co.uk. Bareboat charters across the
country, flotillas from Skiáthos, and a sail-and-stay
programme based on Póros.
Sportif ☎01273/844919, ⓦwww.sportif
-uk.com. Windsurfing packages on Kós, Rhodes and
Kárpathos. Instruction clinics in conjunction with
nearby accommodation.
Sunsail ☎0870/777 0313, ⓦwww.sunsail.com.
Resort-based tuition in dinghy sailing, yachting
and windsurfing at three locations in Greece,
mostly the Ionians but including southern Pílio; also
one- or two-week flotilla sailings in the Ionians and
Sporades and good facilities for nonsailing children.
Templecraft ☎01732/867445, ⓦwww
.templecraft.com. Bareboat charters and flotilla
holidays in the Ionian archipelago.

Special-interest holidays

Peligoni Club ☎01243/511499, ⓦwww.peligoni
.com. Painting, yoga, Pilates and photography
workshops based in a scattered cluster of villas and
cottages in northern Zákynthos.
Saga Holidays ☎0800/096 0074, ⓦwww.saga
.co.uk. The UK's biggest and most established
specialist in tours and holidays aimed at older people.
Skyros Holidays ☎020/7267 4424, ⓦwww
.skyros.co.uk. Holistic health, fitness, crafts and
"personal growth" holidays at two centres on the
island of Skkros, as well as prestigious writers'
workshops tutored by big names.

By rail

Travelling **by train** from Britain or Ireland to
Greece takes two-and-a-half to three-and-
a-half days and fares work out vastly more
expensive than flights. It is not even possible
to buy a through rail ticket; however, with an
InterRail or Eurail Pass you can take in Greece
as part of a wider train trip around Europe.

The most practical route from Britain
crosses France and Italy before embarking
on the ferry from Bari or Brindisi to Pátra
(Patras). Book seats well in advance, especially in summer (for ferry information, see
the box on p.34).

Rail passes

An **InterRail pass** offers unlimited travel (except for express-train supplements and reservation fees) on a zonal basis with 28 European rail networks. These passes are only available to **European residents**, and come in over-26 and (cheaper) under-26 versions; you can save £5 by booking via the InterRail website ⓦwww.inter-rail.co.uk

To reach Greece from the UK you'll need a one-month pass valid for at least two zones; Greece falls in Zone G, together with Italy, Turkey and Slovenia, plus many of the Italy–Greece ferries (though not out of Venice).

For **North Americans, Australians and New Zealanders, a Eurail Pass** (which must be purchased before arrival in Europe) will not pay for itself if you're planning to stick to Greece. You stand a better chance of getting your money's worth out of a Eurail Flexipass, good for ten or fifteen days' travel within a two-month period. Like the normal pass, this comes in first-class, under-26/ second-class (Eurorail Youth Flexipass) and group (Eurail Saver Flexipass) versions.

Rail contacts

UK and Ireland
The Man in Seat 61 ⓦwww.seat61.com. Named after British rail buff Mark Smith's favourite seat on the Eurostar, this noncommercial site expertly offers practical advice for planning a train journey from the UK to just about anywhere in Eurasia. You can't buy tickets here, but all the necessary links are provided.
Rail Europe UK ☎0870/584 8848, ⓦwww .raileurope.co.uk. Discounted rail fares for under-26s on a variety of European routes; also agents for InterRail and Eurostar.

North America
DER Travel ☎1-888 337-7350, ⓦwww .dertravel.com/rail. Eurail and many individual country passes.
European Rail Services Canada ☎1-800 205-5800 or 416/695-1211, ⓦwww .europeanrailservices.com. Eurail and many individual country passes.
Rail Europe US ☎1-877 257-2887, Canada ☎1-800 361-RAIL, ⓦwww.raileurope.com. Official North American Eurail Pass agent; also sells most single-country passes.

Australia and New Zealand
CIT World Travel Australia ☎02/9267 1255 or 03/9650 5510, ⓦwww.cittravel.com.au. Eurail passes.
Rail Plus Australia ☎1300 555 003 or 03/9642 8644, ⓦwww.railplus.com.au. Sells Eurail passes.
Trailfinders Australia ☎02/9247 7666, ⓦwww. trailfinder.com.au. All European passes.

By car

If you have the time and inclination, **driving to Greece** can be a pleasant proposition. The most popular **route** is down through France and Italy to catch one of the Adriatic ferries; alternatives via Hungary, Romania and Bulgaria are to be avoided.

The fastest way to get across **to the continent** is the **Eurotunnel** service via the Channel Tunnel; the alternative is one of the time-honoured **ferry** crossings (see below). Eurotunnel operates shuttle trains 24 hours a day, for cars, motorcycles, buses and their passengers. **Rates** depend on the time of year, time of day and length of stay; it's cheaper to travel between 10pm and 6am, while the highest fares are reserved for weekend departures and returns in July and August. For current information, contact the **Eurotunnel Customer Services Centre** at ☎0870/535 3535, ⓦwww.eurotunnel. com.

The traditional cross-Channel options for most travellers are the **ferry or hovercraft** links between Dover and Calais or Boulogne (the quickest and cheapest routes), Ramsgate and Dunkerque, or Newhaven and Dieppe. Irish drivers will prefer routes bypassing Britain, direct to Roscoff or Cherbourg, or from the southwest of England to St-Malo or Caen.

Ferry **prices** vary according to the time of year and, for motorists, the size of your car. The Dover–Calais/Boulogne runs, for example, start at about £245–340 open return for a car with up to five passengers, though prices can nearly double in peak season.

Via Italy

For motorists heading for western Greece or the Ionian islands, it has always made most sense to drive **via Italy** – and whatever your final destination, taking a ferry on the final leg makes for a more relaxed journey. Initial routes down to Italy through

Italy–Greece ferries

From Ancona ANEK to Pátra (21hr) usually via Igoumenítsa (15hr), 6 weekly most of year; Minoan to Pátra (20hr 30min) via Igoumenítsa (14hr 30min), 5–6 weekly year-round; Superfast daily year-round to Igoumenítsa (15hr) and Pátra (21hr), or direct to Pátra (19hr 30min). All sailings afternoon/early evening.

From Bari Superfast daily year-round to Igoumenítsa (9hr 30min) and Pátra (15hr 30min), also Corfu direct June–Aug (8hr); Ventouris to Igoumenítsa (11hr 30min) via Corfu (10hr), almost daily most of year; Agoudimos daily July–Aug only to Igoumenítsa (9hr) and Pátra (15hr 30min). Most sailings early evening.

From Brindisi Agoudimos to Corfu/Igoumenítsa, 6 weekly July–Aug (5hr 30min/6hr 30min); Fragline to Corfu/Igoumenítsa (8–9hr) almost daily April–Sept; Maritime Way to Igoumenítsa/Pátra (7hr/13hr), daily except Jan. Most departures in evening, except Agoudimos usually about noon.

From Venice ANEK to Igoumenítsa (24hr 30min), Corfu (26hr 30min) and Pátra (34hr), 6 weekly March–Oct, Igoumenítsa and Pátra only Oct–March 4 weekly; Minoan to Igoumenítsa (20hr), Corfu (21hr 30min) and Pátra (28hr 30min) daily March–Oct, 4 weekly Oct–March. Departures vary from noon to early evening.

Sample fares

Seasonal/company price ranges below are one-way, port taxes included; fares to Pátra are the same as those to Corfu/Igoumenítsa. Substantial reductions apply on many lines for both InterRail and Eurail pass-holders, and for those under 26. Discounts of 20–35 percent are usually available on return tickets, even in peak season. A few companies allow you to sleep in your van on board; ask about reduced "camping" fares.

Igoumenítsa from Bari or Brindisi: pullman seat €36–73; car €25–70.
Pátra from Ancona: pullman seat €75–103; car €68–118.
Pátra from Bári: pullman seat €67–81; car €49–79.
Pátra from Venice: pullman seat €72–106; car €71–121.

Italian agents

The dialling code for Italy is ☎39; when ringing from overseas you must include the initial '0' of the local area code.

Agoudimos Brindisi: c/o Hellas Ferry Lines, ☎0831/550180; Bari: c/o Morfimare, ☎080/5789815.
ANEK Ancona: Anek Italia, ☎071/207 2346; Venice: Anek Italia, ☎041/5286522.
Fragline Brindisi: ☎0831/548 318.
Maritime Way Brindisi: c/o Euromare ☎0831/573800.
Minoan Lines Ancona: ☎071/201 708; Venice: ☎041/2407177.
Superfast Ferries Ancona: ☎071/202 033; Bari: ☎080/521 1416.
Ventouris Bari: c/o P. Lorusso & Co ☎080/5217609; Brindisi: c/o Adriatico ☎0831/548340.
NB Viamare Travel Ltd (☎020/7431 4560, ⊛www.viamare.com) is the UK agent for most of these companies.

Ferries on the Internet

Agoudimos Lines ⊛www.agoudimos-lines.com
ANEK ⊛www.anek.gr
Fragline ⊛www.fragline.gr
Maritime Way ⊛www.maritimeway.com
Minoan Lines ⊛www.minoan.gr
Superfast ⊛www.superfast.com
Ventouris ⊛www.ventouris.gr

France and Switzerland are a question of personal taste. One of the most direct is Calais–Reims–Geneva–Milan and then down the Adriatic coast to one of the four Italian ports available. Even on the quickest autoroutes the journey will involve two overnight stops.

Most departures from Italy sail via the island of **Corfu**; you can stop over at no extra charge if you get this specified on your ticket. Generally, ferries run year-round, but with reduced frequencies from December to April. For more details see the box opposite.

From any Italian port, a crossing to Pátra costs the same as to Igoumenítsa or Corfu; the **cheapest** of all the crossings is from Brindisi to Igoumenítsa. Drivers will discover that the extra cost in Italian motorway tolls and fuel exactly offsets the Brindisi or Bari route's savings over those from Ancona or Venice.

In summer, it is essential to **book tickets** a few weeks ahead. During the winter you can just turn up at the main ports (Brindisi and Ancona have the most reliable departures then), but it's still wise to book a few days in advance if you want a cabin. A few phone calls or internet searches before leaving home are, in any case, advisable, as the range of fares is considerable.

From North America

The Greek national airline, Olympic Airways, flies direct to Athens out of New York (JFK; 3–7 weekly), Montréal and Toronto. Olympic – and its domestic competitor Aegean – offers reasonably priced add-on flights within Greece, especially to the Greek islands. Delta is the only North American carrier currently offering any direct service to Athens (daily from New York-JFK), though through fares with code-sharing airlines are quoted from Atlanta, Boston, Calgary, Chicago, Dallas/Fort Worth, Los Angeles, Miami, San Francisco, Vancouver, Winnipeg and Washington DC (National).

Nonstop flights **to Athens out of New York-JFK** cost US$600–1200 depending on season for a thirty-day ticket; one-stop flights via other European hubs can yield significant savings, especially in peak season. Common-rating (ie price-fixing) agreements between airlines means that fares to **Athens** from the **Midwest, Deep South or the West Coast** don't vary much: US$650–750 low season, US$1100–1300 high season.

Such tickets typically involve the use of American Airlines, BA, United, Air France, Alitalia, Iberia, KLM and Swiss, via their European gateway cities. With little to distinguish itineraries price-wise, you might examine the stopover time at their respective European hubs, as these often differ by several hours. You may be better off getting a domestic add-on to New York and heading directly to Athens from there.

As with the US, airfares **from Canada** vary depending on where you start your journey, and whether you take a direct service. Olympic flies out of Toronto, with a stop in Montréal, three to four times weekly **to Athens**; they're rarely the cheapest option, though. Most of the time you'll have to choose among one- or two-stop itineraries on a variety of European carriers or perhaps Delta via New York; costs run from CDN$1300 in low season from Toronto to over CDN$3000 from Vancouver in high season.

Airlines

Air Canada ☎ 1-888/247–2262, 🌐 www .aircanada.com.
Air France ☎ 1-800/237-2747, Canada ☎ 1-800/667-2747, 🌐 www.airfrance.com.
Alitalia ☎ 1-800/223-5730, Canada ☎ 1-800/361-8336, 🌐 www.alitalia.com.
American Airlines ☎ 1-800/433-7300, 🌐 www .aa.com.
British Airways ☎ 1-800/AIRWAYS, 🌐 www .ba.com.
Continental Airlines domestic ☎ 1-800/523-FARE, international ☎ 1-800/231-0856, 🌐 www .continental.com.
Delta Air Lines domestic ☎ 1-800-221-1212, international ☎ 1-800/241-4141, 🌐 www.delta .com.
Iberia ☎ 1-800/772-4642, 🌐 www.iberia.com.
Lufthansa US ☎ 1-800/645-3880, Canada ☎ 1-800/563-5954, 🌐 www.lufthansa.com.
Northwest/KLM US domestic ☎ 1-800/225-2525, international ☎ 1-800/447-4747. 🌐 www.nwa.com, 🌐 www.klm.com.
Olympic Airways ☎ 1-800/223-1226 or 718/896-7393, 🌐 www.olympicairlines.com.
Swiss ☎ 1-877 FLY-SWISS, 🌐 www.swiss.com.
United Airlines Domestic ☎ 1-800/241-6522, international ☎ 1-800/538-2929, 🌐 www.united .com.
Virgin Atlantic ☎ 1-800/862-8621, 🌐 www .virgin-atlantic.com.

Travel agents

Air Brokers International ☏1-800 883-3273 or 415/397-1383, ⓦwww.airbrokers.com. Consolidator and specialist in RTW tickets.

Airtech ☏212/219-7000, ⓦwww.airtech.com. Standby seat broker; also deals in consolidator fares.

Educational Travel Center ☏1-800 747-5551 or 608/256-5551, ⓦwww.edtrav.com. Low-cost fares worldwide, student/youth discount offers, Eurail passes.

Flightcentre US ☏1-866 WORLD-51, ⓦwww .flightcentre.us, Canada ☏1-888 WORLD-55, ⓦwww.flightcentre.ca. Rock-bottom fares worldwide.

New Frontiers US ☏1-800 677-0720 or 212/986-6006, ⓦwww.newfrontiers.com. Discount firm, specializing in travel from the US to Europe.

STA Travel US ☏1-800 329-9537, Canada ☏1-888/427-5639, ⓦwww.statravel.com. Worldwide specialists in independent travel; also student IDs, travel insurance, car rental, rail passes, etc.

Student Flights ☏1-800 255-8000 or 480/951-1177, ⓦwww.isecard.com/studentflights. Student/youth fares, plus student IDs and European rail and bus passes.

TFI Tours ☏1-800 745-8000 or 212/736-1140, ⓦwww.lowestairprice.com. Consolidator with global fares.

Travel Avenue ☏1-800 333-3335, ⓦwww .travelavenue.com. Full-service travel agent that offers discounts in the form of rebates.

Travel Cuts US ☏1-800 592-CUTS, Canada ☏1-888 246-9762, ⓦwww.travelcuts.com. Popular, long-established student-travel organization, with worldwide offers.

Travelers Advantage ☏1-877 259-2691, ⓦwww.travelersadvantage.com. Discount travel club, with cashback deals and discounted car rental. Membership required ($1 for 3 month trial).

Travelosophy US ☏1-800 332-2687, ⓦwww .itravelosophy.com. Good range of discounted and student fares worldwide.

Tour operators

Classic Adventures ☏1-800 777-8090, ⓦwww .classicadventures.com. Two good offerings: spring or autumn rural cycling tours of "classical Greece", crossing the north Peloponnese to Zákynthos in eleven days, or a pedal through the archeological sites and medieval towns of Crete, in twelve days.

Hellenic Adventures ☏1-800 851-6349 or 612/827-0937, ⓦwww.hellenicadventures.com. Small-group (14 pax max), customized tours (generally 3 per season), led by enthusiastic expert guides. Good info on the website for independent travellers too.

Saga Holidays ☏1-800/343-0273, ⓦwww. sagaholidays.com. Specializes in worldwide group travel for seniors.

Valef Yachts ☏1-800 223-3845, ⓦwww .valefyachts.com. North American reps for Zeus Cruises, offering a choice of fixed, seven-day motor-yacht cruises around the Dodecanese, the Sporades, the Cyclades, the Argo-Saronics or the Ionian islands; a bit rushed, but affordable at $850–1500 per person. Also very expensive bareboat charter (yachts, mostly over 60ft); pick your craft from the online brochure.

From Australia and New Zealand

As of writing, there are no direct flights from Australia or New Zealand to Greece; you'll have to get yourself to Southeast Asia or North America for onward travel.

Tickets purchased direct from the airlines tend to be expensive; travel agents or Australia-based websites offer much better deals on fares and have the latest information on limited specials and stopovers.

For a **simple return fare**, you may have to buy an add-on internal flight to reach the international gateways of Sydney or Melbourne. Tickets are generally **valid for one year**; high-season departures can typically be had for A$2300–2500 for multi-stop itineraries via Southeast Asia, the Middle East and a European hub. A 180-day, two-stop ticket on might run A$2300, while for about the same price you could fly east-bound via North America. Low-season fares cost A$1600–1800.

From New Zealand, the usual routes to Athens are either westbound several times weekly via Bangkok, Sydney or Singapore, or eastbound almost daily via Los Angeles with Air New Zealand on the first leg. At **high season** count on paying NZ$2500–2800 in either direction; **low season** prices aren't much different at NZ$2200–2500.

Airlines

Aeroflot ☏02/9262 2233, ⓦwww.aeroflot.com .au.

Air New Zealand Australia ☏13 24 76, ⓦwww .airnz.com.au, New Zealand ☏0800 737 000, ⓦwww.airnz.co.nz.

Alitalia Australia ☎ 02/9244 2445, New Zealand ☎ 09/308 3357, ⊛ www.alitalia.com.
British Airways Australia ☎ 1300 767 177, New Zealand ☎ 0800 274 847, ⊛ www.ba.com.
Egyptair Australia ☎ 02/9241 5696, ⊛ www .egyptair.com.eg.
Emirates Australia ☎ 1300 303 777 or 02/9290 9700, New Zealand ☎ 09/377 6004, ⊛ www .emirates.com.
Gulf Air Australia ☎ 02/9244 2199, New Zealand ☎ 09/308 3366, ⊛ www.gulfairco.com.
Lufthansa Australia ☎ 1300 655 727, New Zealand ☎ 0800 945 220, ⊛ www.lufthansa.com.
Qantas Australia ☎ 13 13 13, New Zealand ☎ 0800 808 767 or 09/357 8900, ⊛ www.qantas .com.
Royal Jordanian Australia ☎ 02/9244 2701, New Zealand ☎ 03/365 3910, ⊛ www.rja.com.jo.
Singapore Airlines Australia ☎ 13 10 11, New Zealand ☎ 0800 808 909, ⊛ www.singaporeair .com.
Thai Airways Australia ☎ 1300 651 960, New Zealand ☎ 09/377 3886, ⊛ www.thaiair.com.

Travel agents

Flight Centre Australia ☎ 13 31 33, ⊛ www .flightcentre.com.au, New Zealand ☎ 0800 243 544, ⊛ www.flightcentre.co.nz.
STA Travel Australia ☎ 1300 733 035, New Zealand ☎ 0508/782 872, ⊛ www.statravel.com.
Student Uni Travel Australia ☎ 02/9232 8444, ⊛ www.sut.com.au, New Zealand ☎ 09/379 4224, ⊛ www.sut.co.nz.
Trailfinders Australia ☎ 02/9247 7666, ⊛ www .trailfinders.com.au.

Tour operators

Sun Island Tours Australia ☎ 02/9283 3840, ⊛ www.sunislandtours.com.au. An assortment of island-hopping, fly-drives, cruises and guided land-tour options, as well as upscale accommodation on big-name islands such as Rhodes, Kós and Sámos.

Departure points: Athens, Pireás and main ports

As noted in the "Getting there" section, you may well find yourself travelling to or from the islands via Athens. This is a great opportunity to check out the revived Greek capital and to take in some of its unique cultural attractions. With its sprawling 1960s and 1970s concrete architecture, Athens may not be the most attractive of cities, but the centre has been transformed since the 2004 Olympics: there's excellent public transportation between the airport and the port via the centre of town, an unrivalled Classical Greek heritage, great restaurants and a lively street life. A couple of nights' stopover will allow you to take in the Acropolis and the other major ancient sites and museums, wander around the old quarter of Pláka and the bazaar area, and sample some of the country's best food and nightlife. Even in a single day, a morning arrival would give you time for a look at the Acropolis and Pláka before heading down to the port of Pireás (Piraeus) to catch an overnight ferry.

Not all of the islands are accessible from Pireás, so we've given brief accounts of other useful mainland ports below.

Athens

Athens' Eleftheríos Venizélos airport is at Spáta, some 33km southeast of the city.

It has excellent facilities including several ATMs, bureaux de change, luggage storage and a tourist office. **Public transportation** from the airport is excellent. The **Metro** (€6 single, €10 return, discounts for multiple tickets) is usually more convenient, taking you straight into the heart of the city where you can change to the other metro lines at either Monastiráki (for Pireás) or Sýndagma: trains run every half hour from 6.30am to 11.30pm and take around thirty minutes. The **suburban train** to Laríssis station is not quite so handy for the centre of town but it runs longer hours (5.50am–1.20am) for identical fares.

Buses are much slower, especially at rush hours, but they're also much cheaper, run all night and offer direct links to other parts of the city including Pireás. The most useful are the #X95 to Sýndagma square (at least three an hour, day and night) and #X96 to the port at Pireás via Glyfádha and the beach suburbs (at least two an hour, day and night). **Tickets** cost €2.90, and are valid for a single airport trip plus all central Athens public transport for 24 hours after being validated (including the metro or bus to Pireás). Buy them from a booth beside the stops or on the bus: make sure you have small change.

Taxis are subject to the vagaries of traffic and can take anything from forty minutes (at night) to an hour and forty minutes (at rush hour) to reach the centre; the fare should be roughly €18–25 to central Athens or Pireás.

The main **Tourist Office** is at Amalías 26, just off Sýndagma square (Mon-Fri 9am–7pm, Sat & Sun 10am–4pm).

Accommodation

Finding accommodation in Athens is only likely to be a problem during the midsummer peak – even so it's always best to phone ahead or book online. On the whole, it's expensive. The small selection below covers a range of the cheaper options, from hostels to mid-range hotels.

For a quick stay you want to be right in the centre, and most of those included are in Pláka, the oldest quarter of the city, in the shadow of the Acropolis with lots of outdoor restaurants and cafés.

Acropolis House Kódhrou 6 ☏210 32 22 344, ehtlacrhs@otenet.gr. Metro Sýndagma. A rambling, slightly dilapidated 150-year-old mansion much loved by its regulars – mostly students and academics. B & B. ❹

Athos Patröou 3 ☏210 32 21 977, ⓦathoshotel .gr. Metro Sýndagma. Small hotel with comfortable en-suite rooms with TV, a/c, mini-bar etc. Also a rooftop bar with Acropolis views. B & B. ❺

Central Apóllonos 21 ☏210 32 34 357, ⓦwww .centralhotel.gr. Metro Sýndagma. Designer-style rooms with marble bathrooms and excellent soundproofing. Family and interconnecting rooms also available; all with a/c, TV, fridge and everything you'd expect. Large roof terrace with Acropolis views and hot tub. B & B. ❻

Evropi Satovriándhou 7 ☏210 52 23 081. Metro Omónia. Very, very basic but great value old-fashioned hotel. Reasonably quiet, despite being only a block from Platía Omonías; inexpensive single rooms. ❷

Marble House Cul-de-sac off A. Zínni 35A, Koukáki ☏210 92 34 058, ⓦwww.marblehouse .gr. Metro Syngroú-Fix. Family-run, friendly and not far from the action. Simple rooms with and without private bath, some with a/c (for extra charge). ❸

Phaedra Herefóndos 16, corner Adhrianoú ☏210 32 38 461, ⓕ210 32 27 795. Metro Akrópoli. Simple rooms with bare tile floors, TV and a/c, not all en suite (but you get a private bathroom). Friendly management and one of the best deals in Pláka. ❹

Student & Traveller's Inn Kydhathinéon 16 ☏210 32 44 808, ⓦwww.studenttravellersinn .com. Metro Akrópolí/Sýndagma. Perennially popular travellers' meeting place. Dorm beds from €16 to €26; private quads, triples and doubles, en-suite or shared bath. Clean and comfortable, though not always the quietest. ❹

Tempi Eólou 29 ☏210 32 13 175, ⓦwww .travelling.gr/tempihotel. Metro Monastiráki. Budget backpackers with tiny rooms, most with shared facilities, and shared kitchen. Good location in market area. ❸–❹

Thission Apostólou Pávlou 25, Thissío ☏210 34 67 634, wwww.hotel-thissio.gr. Metro Thissío. Threadbare rooms (with a/c and TV), but virtually every one has a magnificent view of the Acropolis and there's a pleasant roof-terrace café. In a lively, newly fashionable area. ❹

Eating

Pláka is bursting with touristy restaurants, most of them poor value despite their great locations. Among the best of these, with tables outside on a stepped street beneath the Acropolis, is the *Mezedopolio Palio Tetradhio* at Mnisikléous 26, often with live music. For more authentic and cheaper fare head towards Monastiráki or its trendy neighbour Psyrrí: *Baïraktaris* on Platía Monastirakíou serves great Greek classics and kebabs; *Café Abysinia* on nearby Platía Avysinnías offers a more modern (and more expensive) take on traditional Greek cooking - always busy with a young local crowd; *Taverna tou Psyrrí*, Eskhýlou 12, in the midst of the lively Psyrrí nightlife, is another that's always packed.

The city and sights

The centre of Athens is compact, and anything not in walking distance is well served by the metro, bus or inexpensive taxis. Finding your bearings is generally pretty easy: the **Acropolis** is visible, around a corner, from almost any part of the city centre. Beneath it to the east lies **Pláka**, with **Monastiráki** curling around to the north. **Sýndagma** (Platía Syndágmatos), the traditional centre of the city and home to the Greek Parliament, lies to the northeast of these two, midway between the Acropolis and the hill of **Lykavitós**. The ritzy **Kolonáki** quarter curls up the hill's slopes above Sýndagma, with a funicular to save you the final climb to the summit and its famous views. Below Kolonáki many of the city's major museums can be found along the broad avenue of Leofóros Vassilísis Sofías. On the other side of the avenue, behind the Parliament, lie the jungly **National Gardens**.

To the north, broad avenues lead to **Omónia** (Platía Omonías), the heart of commercial and business Athens. The **market and bazaar** area lies en route, while beyond to the north are the **National Archeological Museum** and the slightly alternative, studenty neighbourhoods of **Exárhia** and **Neápoli**, with a concentration of lively tavernas and bars. Close to the market you'll find the thriving nightlife of **Psyrrí**, whose modernizing influence spreads to the west in **Keramikós**, **Gázi** and **Metaxouryío**.

The inevitable focus of any visit to Athens, however brief, is the **Acropolis** (daily April–Sept 8am–7.30pm; Oct–March 8am–4.30pm; €12 ticket includes most other major Classical sites; metro Akrópoli). The complex of temples on top, rebuilt by Pericles in the "Golden Age" of the fifth century BC, is focused on the famed **Parthenon**. A small museum houses some of the original sculptures.

Other outstanding Classical sites are those on the south slope of the Acropolis, including the **Theatre of Dionysos** (daily: summer 8am–7pm; winter 8.30am–3pm; €2); the

Ancient Agora or market area (daily: summer 8am–7pm; winter 8.30am–3pm; €4; metro Monastiráki) on the opposite side of the Acropolis; the nearby **Roman Forum** (daily: summer 8.30am–7.30pm; winter 8.30am–3pm; €2; metro Monastiráki); and the ancient cemetery, the **Kerameikos** (daily 8.30am–3pm; €2; metro Thissío). Entrance to all of these is included in the Acropolis ticket.

Also unmissable is the refurbished **National Archeological Museum** (Summer Mon 1–7.30pm, Tues–Sun 8.30am–7.30pm; Winter Mon 10.30am–5pm, Tues–Sun 8.30am–3pm; €7; metro Viktorías or any bus labelled *Mousseio*) at 28 Oktovríou 44. Quite simply the finest collection of Greek antiquities anywhere in the world, its highlights include *Odyssey*-era gold treasures from Mycenae and a vast collection of wonderful sculpture.

Other excellent museums include the **Benáki** (Mon, Wed, Fri & Sat 9am–5pm, Thurs 9am–midnight, Sun 9am–3pm; €6; metro Evangelismós), at Koumbári 1, cnr Vassilísis Sofías, a fascinating personal collection of ancient and folk treasures; the nearby **Goulandhrís Museum of Cycladic Art** (Mon & Wed–Fri 10am–4pm, Sat 10am–3pm; €5; metro Evangelismós), with wonderful figurines from the third millennium BC; the **Byzantine and Christian Museum** (Tues–Sun 8.30am–3pm; €4; metro Evangelismós) at Vassilísis Sofías 22, for icons and religious architecture; and the **Folk Art Museum** (Tues–Sun 10am–2pm; €2), Kydhathinéon 17 in Pláka, for weaving, pottery, regional costumes and other traditional Greek arts and crafts.

Pireás

The ferry port at **Pireás** is around 9km from the city centre. The metro takes about 25 minutes (Line 1 via Omónia and Monastiráki); taxis should cost €7–10; or buses (#40 from Sýndagma, #49 from Omónia) run all night. If you're travelling by rail from Pátra, the train continues through Athens down to Pireás.

The tourist office publishes a weekly **schedule of ferry departures** giving approximate journey times and costs to all the most popular island destinations, and there's a similar schedule in the weekly *Athens News*.

The majority of the ships – for the Argo-Saronic, Ikaría or Sámos, and the popular Cyclades – leave between 7 and 9am. There is then another burst of activity between noon and 3pm towards the Cyclades and Dodecanese, and a final battery of departures in the evening, bound for a wide variety of ports, but especially night sailings to Crete, the northeast Aegean, the western Cyclades and Dodecanese.

There's no need to **buy tickets** for conventional ferries before you get here, unless you want a berth in a cabin or are taking a car on board; at Greek holiday times (August and Easter especially) these can be hard to get and it's worth booking in advance – the big companies all have Internet booking. Flying Dolphin hydrofoil reservations are also a good idea at busy times. In general, though, the best plan is simply to turn up at Pireás early and check with some of the dozens of **shipping agents** around the metro station and along the quayside Platía Karaïskáki (agents in central Athens also sell tickets). Bear in mind that most of these act only for particular lines, so for a full picture you will need to ask at three or four outlets. Prices for domestic boat journeys vary little, but the quality of the craft and circuitousness of routes vary greatly.

Boats for different destinations leave from a variety of points around the main harbour, some of them a significant distance away (some of the big ferries have airport-style buses to get you there). All the ferries display signs showing their destination and departure time; you can't buy tickets on the boat, but there's often a ticket hut on the quayside nearby.

For **food**, you'll find numerous take-away places, bakeries and *souvláki* joints around the market area and near the metro station, as well as all along the waterfront.

Other mainland ports

Although Pireás has a wide choice of ferry, catamaran and hydrofoil connections, certain islands can (or must) be reached from other ports on the mainland. Below is a quick run-through of the more important and useful.

Note also that there are two islands – Évvia (northeast of Athens) and Lefkádha in the Ionian islands – that require no ferry, and can be reached by bus, and in Évvia's case also by train.

Alexandhróupoli

The third northern port (6hr by bus from Thessaloníki) has daily ferries and summer-only hydrofoils to Samothráki, plus at least two weekly departures to Límnos and other northeast Aegean isles. It's a somewhat unenticing place to stay, though if you get stuck the *Lido* at Paleológou 15 (☎25510 28808) represents by far the best budget-hotel value.

Igoumenítsa

Many ferries from Italy call at Igoumenítsa, stopping at Corfu en route. There are regular shuttles across to Corfu, to both the main town and also Lefkími in the south, plus one or two daily services to Paxí. Hotel vacancies are plentiful as nobody stays more than a night; the *Stavrodhromi* (☎26650 22343) is a reliable, friendly cheapie, 500m inland at Soulíou 14.

Kavála

The second port of northern Greece (3hr by bus from Thessaloníki) offers fast access to Thássos, either direct by hydrofoil, or from the nearby roll-on-roll-off shuttle point at Keramotí. There are also links to Límnos and other northeast Aegean islands, as well as (only in summer) to Samothráki. The city has a line of good tavernas in the old quarter below the castle, but pleasant, affordable hotels are in short supply. In ascending order of comfort and price, try the *Akropolis* (☎2510 223 543) at Venizélou 29, the *Nefeli* at Erythroú Stavroú 50 (☎2510 227 441) or the *Esperia* (☎2510 229 621) at Erythroú Stavroú 42, opposite the archeological museum.

Kyllíni

This small port, south of Pátra (buses), is the main departure point for the Ionian island of Zákynthos, and in summer has boats to Póros on Kefalloniá. Little point in staying, if you time things right.

Kými

This is technically an island port – on Évvia (see Chapter Six) – but is mentioned here as it is the main port for Skýros in the Sporades.

Kými can be reached from Athens by bus, which should be timed to dovetail with ferry departures. If you miss the connection, staying options are limited to two fairly expensive hotels.

Lávrio

This tiny port, south of Athens (and reachable by bus from the Mavromatéon terminal; 1hr 15min) has several daily ferries to Kéa, the closest of the Cyclades, less often to Kýthnos, Kéa's neighbour, as well as two to three weekly departures to Híos, Lésvos, Áyios Efstrátios and Límnos. In high summer there are also a few services.

Neápoli

A small, undistinguished port at the southern foot of the Peloponnese, with occasional ferry connections to Dhiakoftí on Kýthira, and frequent local boats to the islet of Elafónissos.

Astakós

This small port on the western mainland has daily ferries to Itháki and Kefalloniá in the Ionian. Astakós is rarely busy but has few places to stay – buses from Athens tend to dovetail with ferry departures, currently just once daily around noon.

Pátra (Patras)

Pátra is the major port of the Peloponnese, and the main jump-off for Italy and most of the Ionian islands. Easiest access from Athens is on the train (Stathmós Peloponíssou terminal; 4hr), since the Pátra station is right by the boat terminals. The city itself is uninteresting, so plan on moving out the same day, if possible. Reasonable budget hotels include the *El Greco*, Ayíou Andhréou 145 (☎2610 272 931) or the *Atlanta* at Zaïmi 10 (☎2610 220 098).

Ráfina

Another small port near Athens (again reachable by bus from the Mavromatéon terminal; 40min). Connections are to most of the Cyclades or nearby Évvia.

Thessaloníki

The northern capital is a busy mainland port. There are useful long-haul ferries to Kós and Rhodes via Sámos; to the northeastern Aegean islands; and to Crete via select Sporades and Cyclades. In summer only there are departures to Skíathos, Skópelos and Alónissos in the Sporades. It's worth exploring the Byzantine churches, especially the Áyios Yeóryios Rotónda and tiny Ósios Dhavíd, as well as the Archeological Museum. Hotels are plentiful if mostly uninspiring, noisy and often vastly overpriced; worthwhile exceptions include the *Tourist* on Mitropóleos 21 (☎2310 270 501); the *Nea Mitropolis* at Syngroú 22 (☎2310 525 540); the *Pella* at Íonos Dhragoúmi 63 (☎2310 524 221); and the *Orestias Castorias* at Agnóstou Stratiótou 14 (☎2310 276 517).

Vólos and Áyios Konstandínos

Vólos is the major port city of Thessaly, in central Greece. It is most easily reached from Athens by bus (Mavromatéon terminal; 4hr), though there's also a through express train daily, via Lárissa. Ferries and hydrofoils run regularly to the Sporades – Skiáthos, Skópelos and Alónissos. Try to complete your journey the same day; failing that, pleasantly situated budget hotels include the *Roussas* (☎24210 21732) at Iatroú Tzánou, 1km east of the dock, or the *Iasson* right by the dock (☎24210 26075). Áyios Konstandínos is an alternative but less active port for the Sporades, again with buses from Athens (Mavromatéon terminal; 2hr 30min).

Yíthio

This elegant Peloponnese town has daily ferries to the island of Kýthira, plus twice or thrice weekly to Kíssamos in western Crete. It's a 4–5hr haul here by bus from Athens (Kifissoú 100 terminal), changing at Spárti. Budget hotels or pensions in town include the *Matina*, Vassiléos Pávlou 19 (☎27330 22518); the *Saga* on Tzanetáki, opposite Kranae islet (☎27330 23220); and the *Kranai*, Vassiléos Pávlou 17 (☎27330 24394).

Visas and red tape

UK and all other EU nationals need only a valid passport to enter Greece, and are no longer stamped in on arrival or out upon departure. US, Australian, New Zealand, Canadian and most non-EU Europeans receive mandatory entry and exit stamps in their passports and can stay, as tourists, for ninety days (cumulative) in any six-month period. Such nationals arriving by flight or boat from another EU state not party to the Schengen Agreement may not be stamped in routinely at minor Greek ports, so make sure this is done in order to avoid unpleasantness on exit. Your passport must be valid for three months after your arrival date.

Unless of Greek descent, or married to an EU national, visitors from **non-EU** countries are currently not, in practice, being given extensions to tourist visas by the various Aliens' Bureaux in Greece. You must leave not just Greece but the entire Schengen Group – essentially the entire EU as it was before May 2004, minus Britain and Eire, plus Norway and Iceland – and stay out until the maximum-90-days-in-180 rule as set forth above is satisfied. If you **overstay** your time and then leave under your own power – ie are not deported – you'll be hit with a huge fine upon departure, ranging from €587 to €1174, and possibly be banned from re-entering for a period of time; no excuses will be entertained except (just maybe) a doctor's certificate

stating you were immobilized in hospital. It cannot be overemphasized just how exigent Greek immigration officials have become on this issue.

Greek embassies abroad

Australia 9 Turrana St, Yarralumla, Canberra, ACT 2600 ☎ 02/6273 3011.
Britain 1A Holland Park, London W11 3TP ☎ 020/7221 6467, ⓦ www.greekembassy.org.uk.
Canada 80 Maclaren St, Ottawa, ON K2P 0K6 ☎ 613/238-6271.
Ireland 1 Upper Pembroke St, Dublin 2 ☎ 01/676 7254.
New Zealand 5–7 Willeston St, Wellington ☎ 04/473 7775.
USA 2221 Massachusetts Ave NW, Washington, DC 20008 ☎ 202/939-5800, ⓦ www.greekembassy.org.

Information, maps and websites

The National Tourist Organization of Greece (Ellinikós Organismós Tourismoú, or EOT; GNTO abroad, ⓦ www.gnto.gr) maintains offices in most European capitals, plus major cities in North America and Australia (see opposite for addresses). It publishes an array of free, glossy, regional pamphlets, invariably five to ten years out of date, which are okay for getting an idea of where you want to go, even if the actual text should be taken with a spoonful of salt. Also available from the EOT are a reasonable foldout map of the country and a number of (equally outdated) brochures on special interests and festivals.

Tourist offices

In Greece, you will find official **EOT offices** in many of the larger island capitals and resorts where, in addition to the usual leaflets, you can find weekly **schedules** for the inter-island **ferries** – hardly one-hundred-percent reliable, but useful as a guideline. EOT staff should be able to advise on **bus** departures as well as current opening hours for local sites and museums, and occasionally can give assistance with accommodation.

Where there is no EOT office, you can get information (and often a range of leaflets) from **municipally run** tourist offices, for example those in Kós and Rhodes – these can be highly motivated and better than the EOT branches. In the absence of any of these, you can visit the **Tourist Police**, essentially a division (often just a single room) of the local police. They can sometimes provide you with lists of rooms to let, which they regulate, but they're really where you go if you have a **serious complaint** about a taxi, accommodation or an eating establishment.

Greek national tourist offices abroad

Australia 51 Pitt St, Sydney, NSW 2000 ☎02/9241 1663, ⓔhto@tpg.com.au.
Canada 91 Scollard St, 2nd Floor, Toronto, ON M5R 1GR, ☎416/968-2220, ⓔgrnto.tor@ sympatico.ca.
UK 4 Conduit St, London W1R 0DJ ☎020/7495 4300, ⓔEOT-greektouristoffice@btinternet.com.
USA 645 5th Ave, New York, NY 10022 ☎212/421-5777.

Maps

Maps in Greece are an endless source of confusion and often outright misinformation. Each cartographic company seems to have its own peculiar system of transcribing Greek letters into the Roman alphabet – and these, as often as not, do not match the semi-official transliterations on the road signs, which again may not match, even in the same region.

The most reliable **general touring maps** of the Greek islands are those published by Athens-based Road Editions (ⓦwww .road.gr) and rivals Anavasi ⓦwww .mountains.gr/anavasi), both based on large-scale military maps not easily available

to the public. Road Editions products, at scales of 1:25,000 to 1:100,000, are widely available in Greece at selected bookstores and kiosks, including their own retail outlets in Athens (Ippokrátous 39), Thessaloníki (Proxénou Koromilá 41), Pátra (Zaïmi 20) and Iráklion (Hándhakos 29), as well as at petrol stations and general tourist shops country-wide. Anavasi products are available in better Athens bookstores, at their own shop-front at Stoá Arsakíou 6A in central Athens, as well as on the islands they cover, which include most of the Cyclades and Sporades at scales of 1:25,000–1:40,000. Anavasi maps are waterproof and almost rip-proof, and tend to be newer than Road – they're almost always the top choice for the islands they cover. In Britain both brands are found at Stanfords (see p.44) and the Hellenic Book Service (see p.44). In the US, they're sold exclusively through Map Link or Omni Resources (☎910/227-8300, ⓦwww.omni-map.com). A third choice for the islands, with good coverage of Crete, Skýros and a handful of others, is Emvelia Editions (ⓦwww. emvelia.gr). They have just one retail outlet in Athens – Ellinoekdhotiki at Navarínou 12 – and very sporadic sales points overseas.

Where individual Road, Emvelia or Anavasi products are unavailable, good second choices are the GeoCenter maps *Greece and the Islands* and *Greek Islands/Aegean Sea*, which together cover the country at a scale of 1:300,000. These are widely available in Britain and North America (see the list of map outlets on p.44), though much less easily in Greece.

Hiking/topographical maps

Hiking/topographical maps are steadily improving in quality and availability, with both **Road Editions** and **Anavasi** loosening the stranglehold which the Army long excercised on detailed information. Anavasi's GPS-compatible, CD-ROM-available series is considered more accurate than Road – with better-verified road and path networks – and their larger-scale products for the islands they cover are detailed enough to walk with.

A German company, **Harms**, has five maps at 1:80,000 scale which cover Crete from west to east and show, with about fifty percent accuracy, many hiking routes. Finally, for hiking in particular areas of Crete, Corfu, Kálymnos, Sámos, Rhodes, Sými, Thássos and Lésvos, map-and-guide booklets published by **Marengo Publications** in England also prove very useful. Stanfords keeps a good stock of these, or order from Marengo direct on ☏01485/532710, ⓦwww.marengo walks.com.

Map outlets

In the UK and Ireland

Blackwell's Map Centre 53 Broad St, Oxford OX1 3BQ ☏01865/792792, ⓦwww.maps .blackwell.co.uk. Branches in Bristol, Cambridge, Cardiff, Leeds, Liverpool, Newcastle, Reading and Sheffield.
The Map Shop 30A Belvoir St, Leicester LE1 6QH ☏0116/247 1400, ⓦwww.mapshopleicester.co.uk.
National Map Centre 22–24 Caxton St, London SW1H 0QU ☏020/7222 2466, ⓦwww.mapsnmc .co.uk.
National Map Centre Ireland 34 Aungier St, Dublin ☏01/476 0471, ⓦwww.mapcentre.ie.
Newcastle Map Centre 55 Grey St, Newcastle upon Tyne NE1 6EF ☏0191/261 5622, ⓦwww .traveller.ltd.uk.
Stanfords 12–14 Long Acre, London WC2 ☏020/7836 1321, ⓦwww.stanfords.co.uk. Also at 39 Spring Gardens, Manchester ☏0161/831 0250, and 29 Corn St, Bristol ☏0117/929 9966.
The Travel Bookshop 13–15 Blenheim Crescent, London W11 2EE ☏020/7229 5260, ⓦwww. thetravelbookshop.co.uk.
Traveller 55 Grey St, Newcastle upon Tyne ☏0191/261 5622, ⓦwww.newtraveller.com.

In the US and Canada

110 North Latitude US ☏336/369-4171, ⓦwww.110nlatitude.com.
Book Passage 51 Tamal Vista Blvd, Corte Madera, CA 94925, plus in the San Francisco Ferry Building ☏1-800/999-7909 or 1-415/927-0960, ⓦwww. bookpassage.com.
Distant Lands 56 S Raymond Ave, Pasadena, CA 91105 ☏1-800 310-3220, ⓦwww.distantlands.com.
Globe Corner Bookstore 28 Church St, Cambridge, MA 02138 ☏1-800 358-6013, ⓦwww.globecorner.com.
Longitude Books 115 W 30th St #1206, New York, NY 10001 ☏1-800 342-2164, ⓦwww .longitudebooks.com.
Map Town 400 5 Ave SW #100, Calgary, AB, T2P 0L6 ☏1-877/921-6277, ⓦwww.maptown.com.
Travel Bug Bookstore 3065 W Broadway,

Vancouver, BC, V6K 2G9 ☏604/737-1122, ⓦwww .travelbugbooks.ca.
World of Maps 1235 Wellington St, Ottawa, ON, K1Y 3A3 ☏1-800 214-8524, ⓦwww.worldofmaps.com.

In Australia and New Zealand

Map Centre ⓦwww.mapcentre.co.nz.
Mapland 372 Little Bourke St, Melbourne ☏03/9670 4383, ⓦwww.mapland.com.au.
Map Shop 6–10 Peel St, Adelaide ☏08/8231 2033, ⓦwww.mapshop.net.au.
Map World 371 Pitt St, Sydney t02/9261 3601, ⓦwww.mapworld.net.au. Also in Perth, Canberra and Brisbane.
Map World 173 Gloucester St, Christchurch ☏0800 627 967, ⓦwww.mapworld.co.nz.

Greece on the Internet

Greece is strongly represented on the **Internet**, though some websites are little more than propaganda and/or polemics – anything to do with Macedonia, for example. Almost every heavily visited island will have its own site, often in bizarre, barely readable "Gringlish", though others – mastered by expatriate residents – are fluent but either obsolete or vague on specifics. Country-wide and regional sites recommended below are reasonably balanced, current and literate.

News, views and printed matter

ⓦaegeantimes.net A good digest of current Greece-, Turkey- and Cyprus-related news stories from around the world.
ⓦwww.athensnews.gr The online edition of the *Athens News*, Greece's longest-running quality English-language newspaper, with the day's top stories.
ⓦwww.ekathimerini.com The online edition of the abridged English-translation of *Kathimerini*, one of Greece's most respected dailies. It's fully archived for years back, and has an excellent search facility.
ⓦwww.hellenicbooks.com The website of the UK's premier Greek bookstore. It posts full, opinionated reviews of its stock, offers the possibility of buying online, and has witty descriptions of every island.

Greek culture

ⓦwww.culture.gr The Greek Ministry of Culture's website. Good alphabetical gazetteer to monuments, archeological sites and museums; lots of info about the more obscure sites.

ⓦ**www.geocities.com/rebetology** Basically the site of an annual *rebétika*-related conference and festive gathering on Ídhra, but also posts interesting papers and snippets in its archive.

ⓦ**www.kemo.gr** The last word on Greece's minority communities, without the usual ranting polemics – many academic but readable papers posted for free download.

Travel in Greece

ⓦ**www.gtp.gr** The website of *Greek Travel Pages*, the fat (and expensive) printed manual on every Greek travel agent's desk. Mostly used for its ferry schedules (also kept on a separate site, ⓦ**www .gtpweb.com**), this has improved no end but is still not one-hundred-percent reliable or complete, omitting some minor local ferries and hydrofoils.

ⓦ**www.ktel.org** Bilingual website of the KTEL, or national bus syndicate, which posts fairly reliable schedules. Coverage includes the entire mainland and larger (but not smaller) islands.

Greek destinations

ⓦ**www.foi.org.uk** The site of Friends of the Ionian, which encourages sustainable, off-the-beach tourism; lots on the environment, natural history and local walks.

ⓦ**www.ionian-islands.com** A good if rather commercial site with lots of links to accommodation, travel and eating establishments.

ⓦ**www.island-ikaria.com** Literate, interesting, well-organized and fairly current, covering everything from hot springs to festivals.

ⓦ**www.kalymnos-isl.gr** The island's official website, last updated early 2004.

ⓦ**www.leros.org** A bit of "Gringlish" to contend with, but clearly devised with love, giving a fun, thorough flavour of the island's landscapes, people and traditional architecture.

ⓦ**www.parosweb.com** Good all-purpose site for

the island, with plenty of news on and for visitors and expats, an events calendar and the usual accommodation, property and dining info.

ⓦ**www.saronicnet.com** Accommodation (hotels and villas) and activities (diving, donkey-trekking) on Ídhra, Spétses and Póros – three separate sites best accessed through this portal.

ⓦ**www.skiathosinfo.com** Excellent info on getting to Skiáthos and what you'll find on arrival, as well as literally hundreds of useful links to sites on the Sporades specifically and Greece in general.

ⓦ**stigmes.gr/br** An English-summary online edition of what's claimed to be Crete's leading monthly magazine, plus lots of links to other Crete-related sites.

ⓦ**www.symivisitor.com** Current news for aficionados; a range of accommodation, restaurant and beach profiles, presented by the publishers of the monthly island newspaper.

ⓦ**www.west-crete.com** Cretophiles' favourite site, with all travel/cultural topics (including trekking and naturist beaches) and links to helpful businesses; not restricted to the west of the island.

Greek weather

ⓦ**forecast.uoa.gr** A good one-stop site, maintained by the University of Athens physics faculty. A limited selection of reporting stations, however; for much of Greece you click on a thumbnail image of the entire country, which must be enlarged to read conditions at specific places.

ⓦ**www.poseidon.ncmr.gr** Greek oceanographer's site maintained by the National Centre for Marine Research which profiles Aegean weather meticulously, including graphics of sea currents and surface winds, based on satellite imaging. It's slowish but sophisticated, good for yachties, and reports one topic (rain, temperature, wind-speed, etc) at a time.

Insurance

Even though EU health care privileges apply in Greece (see opposite for details), you should consider taking out an insurance policy before travelling to cover against theft, loss, illness or injury. Before paying for a whole new policy, however, it's worth checking whether you are already covered: some all-risks homeowners' or renters' insurance policies may cover your possessions when overseas, and many private medical schemes (such as BUPA or WPA in the UK) offer coverage extensions for abroad.

In Canada, provincial health plans usually provide partial cover for medical mishaps overseas, while holders of official student/ teacher/ youth cards in Canada and the US are entitled to meagre accident coverage and hospital inpatient benefits. **Students** will often find that their student health coverage extends during the vacations and for one term beyond the date of last enrolment. Most **credit-card issuers** also offer some sort of vacation insurance, which is often automatic if you pay for the holiday with their card. However, it's vital to check just what these policies cover – frequently only death or dismemberment in the UK.

After exhausting the possibilities above, you might want to contact a **specialist travel insurance** company, or consider the travel insurance deal we offer (see below). A typical travel insurance policy usually provides cover for the **loss** of baggage, tickets and – up to a certain limit – cash, cards or cheques, as well as **cancellation** or curtailment of your journey. Most of them exclude so-called **dangerous sports** unless an extra premium is paid: in the Greek islands this means motorbiking, windsurfing and possibly sailing. Many policies can be chopped and changed to exclude coverage you don't need – for example, sickness and accident benefits can often be excluded or included at will. They do not pay out for medical treatment necessary for injuries incurred whilst under the influence of alcohol or drugs. If you do take medical coverage, ascertain whether benefits will be paid as treatment proceeds or only after return home, whether there is a **24-hour medical emergency number**, and how much the deductible excess is (sometimes negotiable). When securing baggage cover, make sure that the **per-article limit** – typically under £500 in the UK – will cover your most valuable possession. Travel agents and tour operators in the UK are likely to **require travel insurance** when you book a package holiday, though they can no longer insist that you buy their own – however, you will be required to sign a declaration saying that you have a policy with a particular company.

Rough Guides Travel Insurance

Rough Guides has teamed up with Columbus Direct to offer you travel insurance that can be tailored to suit your needs.

Readers can choose from many different travel insurance products, including a low-cost backpacker option for long stays; a short break option for city getaways; a typical package holiday option; and many others. There are also annual multi-trip policies for those who travel regularly, with variable levels of cover available. Different sports and activities (trekking, skiing, etc) can be covered if required on most policies.

Rough Guides travel insurance is available to the residents of 36 different countries with different language options to choose from via our website – ⓦwww .roughguidesinsurance.com – where you can also purchase the insurance. Alternatively, UK residents should call 0800 083 9507; US citizens should call 1-800 749-4922; Australians should call 1 300 669 999. All other nationalities should call +44 870 890 2843.

If you need to make a **medical claim**, you should keep all receipts for medicines and treatment, and in the event you have anything stolen or lost, you must obtain an **official statement** from the police or the air-line which lost your bags. With a rise in the number of fraudulent claims, most insurers won't even consider one unless you have a police report. There is usually also a **time limit** for submitting claims after the end of your journey.

Health

British and other EU nationals are officially entitled to free medical care in Greece upon presentation of an E111 form, available from most post offices. By the start of 2006, this and most other E-forms are set to be replaced by a Europe-wide benefits "European Health Insurance Card". "Free", however, means admittance only to the lowest grade of state hospital (known as a yenikó nosokomío), and does not include nursing care, special tests or the cost of medication. If you need prolonged medical care, you should make use of private treatment, which is slightly less expensive than elsewhere in western Europe – this is where your travel insurance policy (see opposite) comes in handy. The US, Canada, Australia and New Zealand have no formal healthcare agreements with Greece (other than allowing for free emergency trauma treatment).

There are no required **inoculations** for Greece, though it's wise to ensure that you are up to date on tetanus and polio. The **drinking water** is safe pretty much everywhere, though you will come across shortages or brackish supplies on some of the drier and more remote islands, and nitrate levels exceed the advised limits in some agricultural areas, in particular Thessalía and Argolídha. Bottled water is widely available if you're feeling cautious.

Specific hazards

The main health problems experienced by visitors – including many blamed on the food – have to do with **overexposure to the sun**. To avoid these, don't spend too long in the sun, cover up, wear a hat, and drink plenty of fluids in the hot months to avoid any danger of **sunstroke**; remember that even hazy sun can burn. To avoid hazards by the sea, goggles or a dive mask for swimming and footwear for walking over wet or rough rocks are useful.

Hazards of the deep

In the sea, you may have the bad luck to meet an armada of **jellyfish** (*tsoúkhtres*), especially in late summer; they come in various colours and sizes ranging from purple "pizzas" to invisible, minute creatures. Various over-the-counter remedies for jellyfish stings are sold in resort pharmacies; baking soda or diluted ammonia (including urine) also help to lessen the sting. The welts and burning usually subside of their own accord within a few hours; there are no deadly man-of-war species in Greek waters.

Less vicious but more common are black, spiky **sea urchins** (*ahíni*), which infest rocky shorelines year-round; if you step on or graze one, a sewing needle (you can crudely sterilize it by heat from a cigarette lighter) and olive oil or toothpaste are effective for removing spines; if you don't extract them they'll fester.

Stingrays and skates (Greek names include *platý, seláhi, vátos* or *trígona*) can injure with their barbed tail: they mainly frequent bays with sandy bottoms where they can camouflage themselves.

When snorkelling in deeper water, especially around Crete, the Dodecanese, or the east Aegean, you may happen upon a brightly coloured **moray eel** (*smérna*) sliding back and forth out of its rocky lair. Keep a respectful distance – their slightly comical air and clown-colours belie an irritable temper and the ability to inflict nasty bites or even sever fingers.

Sandflies, dogs, mosquitoes, wasps and ticks

If you are sleeping on or near a **beach**, it's wise to use insect repellent, either lotion or wrist/ankle bands, and/or a tent with a screen to guard against **sandflies**. Their bites are potentially dangerous, as these insects spread two forms of leishmaniasis, parasitic infections characterized in one form by ulcerated skin and scarring, in the other by chronic fever, anaemia, weight loss, and death if untreated. These can be difficult to diagnose, and may require long courses of medication.

In Greece, the main reservoirs for leishmaniasis are **dogs**. Transmission of the disease to humans by fleas has not been proven, but it's wisest not to befriend strays as they also carry echinococcosis, a debilitating liver fluke transmitted by stroking their fur. In humans these form nodules and cysts requiring surgical removal. If bitten by a dog (or any other mammal) you should seek medical advice – **rabies** still occurs in Greece.

Mosquitoes (*kounóupia*) in Greece carry nothing worse than a vicious bite, but they can be infuriating. The most widespread solution are the small plug-in electrical devices that vaporize a semi-odourless insecticide tablet; many accommodation proprietors supply them routinely, and if you see them supplied on your night-table it's a good bet they'll be needed. Insect repellents such as Autan are available from most general stores and kiosks. Small electronic ultrasound generators are available that supposedly repel mosquitoes, but scientific tests have shown them to be ineffective. Some modern accommodation rooms have pull-down mosquito nets fitted to the external doors and windows.

Wasps and **hornets** (*sfigónes*, *sfíkes*) are common, particularly during the wine-making season (Aug–Oct) when they're attracted by all the fermenting grape-mess. Some mind their own business, others are very aggressive, even dive-bombing swimmers some distance out to sea. One of the best repellent measures (used by tavernas) is coffee grounds set alight. Domestic **bees** (*mélisses*) can be aggressive when near their hives – particularly if you are wearing new denim or wool – and individuals that decide to attack will be suicidally persistent; scrape the detached, embedded sting from your skin with a finger nail to prevent the injection of more venom.

Ticks mostly feed on sheep, but wait on vegetation for new hosts, including passing dogs and humans. Check your legs after walking through long grass near flocks. If one finds you and has started to feed, you should detach it carefully by rocking or twisting, rather than pulling it off; do not use traditional methods such as oil or a lighted match. Ticks can spread Lyme disease or typhus, and any tick bite that results in a rash or other symptoms should always be examined medically.

Creepy-crawlies

Adders (*ohiés*) and **scorpions** (*skorpií*) are found throughout Greece; both creatures are shy – scorpions in particular are nocturnal – but take care when climbing over dry-stone walls where snakes like to sun themselves, and don't put hands or feet in places, like shoes, where you haven't looked first. Wiggly, fast-moving, six-inch **centipedes** which look like a rubber toy should also be treated with respect, as they pack a nasty bite.

The number of annual deaths from **snakebite** in Europe is very small. Many snakes will bite if threatened, whether they are venomous or not – shock is a likely result of any bite. If a bite injects venom, then swelling will normally occur within thirty minutes. If this happens, get medical attention, keep the bitten part still, and make sure all body movements are as gentle as possible. If medical attention is not nearby then bind the limb firmly to slow the blood circulation, but not so tightly as to stop the blood flow.

In addition to munching its way through a

fair fraction of Greece's surviving pine forests, the **pine processionary caterpillar** – taking this name from the long, nose-to-tail convoys which individuals form at certain points in their life cycle – sports highly irritating hairs, with a poison worse than a scorpion's. If you touch one, or even a tree-trunk they've been on recently, you'll know all about it for a week, and the welts may require antihistamine lotion or pills to heal.

Plants

If you snap a **wild-fig** shoot while walking in the countryside, take care not to come in contact with the highly irritant **sap**. The immediate antidote to this alkaloid is a mild acid – lemon juice or vinegar; left unneutralized, fig "milk" raises welts which take a month to heal. Severe allergic reactions have to be treated with strong steroids, either topical cream (available from pharmacies) or intravenously in hospital casualty wards. Other plants, such as euphorbia, sumach and rue, may have similar effects on sensitive skins.

Pharmacies, drugs and contraception

For **minor complaints** it's enough to go to the local **farmakío**. Greek pharmacists are highly trained and dispense a number of medicines which elsewhere could only be prescribed by a doctor. In the larger towns and resorts there'll usually be one who speaks good English. Pharmacies are usually closed evenings and Saturday mornings, but all should have a monthly schedule (in both English and Greek) on their door showing the complete roster of night and weekend duty pharmacists in town.

Greeks are famously hypochondriac, so pharmacies are veritable Aladdin's caves of **arcane drugs and sundry formulas** – just about everything available in North America and northern Europe is here, and then some. **Homeopathic** and **herbal** remedies are quite widely available, too, now sold in most larger pharmacies alongside more conventional products.

If you regularly use any form of **prescription drug**, you should bring along a copy of the prescription, together with the generic name of the drug; this will help should you need to replace it, and also avoids possible problems with customs officials. In this regard, you should be aware that **codeine is banned** in Greece. If you import any you might find yourself in serious trouble, so check labels carefully; it's the core ingredient of Panadeine, Veganin, Solpadeine, Codis and Nurofen Plus, to name just a few common compounds.

Hayfever sufferers should be prepared for the early Greek pollen season, at its height from April to June. Pollen from Aleppo and Calabrian pine in April/May can be particularly noxious. If you are taken by surprise, you'll be able to get tablets at a pharmacy, but best to come prepared.

Contraceptive pills are more readily available every year, but don't count on getting these – or spermicidal jelly/foam – outside of a few large island towns, over-the-counter at the larger pharmacies; Greek women tend not to use any sort of birth control systematically, and have an average of four abortions during their adult life. **Condoms**, however, are inexpensive and ubiquitous at supermarkets – or just ask for *profylaktiká* (the slangy terms *plastiká* or *kapótes* are even better understood) at any pharmacy or corner *períptero* (kiosk). **Women's hygienic supplies** are sold sometimes in pharmacies, much more often in supermarkets. Napkins ("Always" brand) are ubiquitous; tampons can be trickier to find in remoter spots, especially on the smaller islands.

Doctors and hospitals

You'll find English-speaking **doctors** in any of the bigger towns or resorts. For an **ambulance**, phone ☏166. In **emergencies**, treatment is given free – apart from a €3 appointment fee – in **state hospitals** (ask for the *epígonda peristatiká* – casualty ward). You will only get the most basic nursing care, and food and changes of bedding are not provided. Somewhat better are the ordinary state-run **outpatient clinics** (*yiatría*) attached to most public hospitals and also found in rural locales. These operate on a first-come, first-served basis, so go early; usual hours are 8am to noon, though it's sometimes possible to get seen by someone between 1 and 5pm.

Travellers with disabilities

Unfortunately, many of the wonders of Greece such as stepped alleys and ancient monuments are potential hazards for anyone who has difficulty in walking, is wheelchair-bound or suffers from other **disabilities**. Access to all but the newest public buildings and hotels can also be problematic. It is possible, however, to enjoy an inexpensive and trauma-free holiday in Greece with a little forward planning. The Greek National Tourist Office is a help as long as you have specific questions to put to them; they publish a useful questionnaire that you could send to hotels or owners of apartment and villa accommodation.

Before purchasing **travel insurance**, ensure that people with a pre-existing medical condition are not excluded. A **medical certificate** of your fitness to travel, provided by your doctor, is also extremely useful; some airlines or insurance companies may insist on it.

You should also carry extra supplies of any required **drugs** and a prescription including the generic name in case of emergency. It's probably best to assume that any special equipment, drugs or clothing you may require is unavailable in Greece and will need to be brought with you.

Costs, money and banks

The cost of living in Greece has increased astronomically since it joined the EU, subsequently adopted the euro, and raised its VAT rate in early 2005. Food prices in shops, or the tariff for a coffee, now match or exceed those of many other EU member countries (including the UK). However, outside the established resorts, travel remains affordable, with the aggregate cost of restaurant meals, short-term accommodation and public transport falling somewhere in between that of cheaper Spain or France and pricier Italy.

Prices depend on where and when you go. Larger tourist resorts and the trendier small islands (such as Sými, Sífnos, Ídhra, Paxí and Pátmos) are more expensive, and costs everywhere increase sharply during July, August, Christmas, New Year and Easter.

Some basic costs

On most islands a **daily per-person budget** of £32/US$58/€46 will get you basic accommodation, breakfast, picnic lunch, a short ferry or bus ride and a simple evening meal, as one of a couple. Camping would cut costs marginally. On £56/US$101/€81 a day you could be living quite well, plus sharing the cost of renting a large motorbike or small car.

Inter-island **ferry fares**, a main unavoidable expense, are subsidized by the government (until 2007, anyway) in an effort to preserve remote island communities. To give you some idea of prices, the cheapest cabin for the overnight journey from Athens to Sámos, a twelve-hour trip, costs about €45, while a deck-class ticket for the four-hour trip from Rhodes to Kós costs about €13. For €7–14 you can catch a conventional ferry or high-speed craft to numerous small islands that lie closer to Rhodes, Kós and Sámos, the most likely touchdown points if you're flying to the Dodecanese or east Aegean on a direct charter; a cheap cabin from Pireás to Rhodes, one of the longest single ferry journeys in Greece, will set you back about

€60. Local ferries in the Cyclades are a bit pricier for the sea miles travelled; Páros or Náxos to Thíra costs about €11.

The simplest double **room** generally costs €30–35 a night, depending on the location and the plumbing arrangements. Bona fide single rooms are rare, and cost about seventy percent of double rates. Organized **campsites** are little more than €5 per person, with similar charges per tent and perhaps 25 percent more for a camper van. With discretion you can camp for free in the remotest rural areas.

A basic taverna **meal** with bulk wine or a beer can be had for around €11–15 per person. Add a better bottle of wine, seafood or more careful cooking, and it could be up to €18–24 a head; you'll rarely pay more than that. Sharing seafood, Greek salads and dips is a good way to keep costs down in the better restaurants, and even in the most developed of resorts, with inflated "international" menus, you'll often be able to find a more earthy but decent taverna where the locals eat.

Youth and student discounts

Various official and quasi-official **youth, student and teacher ID cards** soon pay for themselves in savings; they all cost $US22 or local equivalent for a year. Full-time students are eligible for the **International Student ID Card** (ISIC; ⓦ www.isiccard.com), which entitles the bearer to special air, rail and ferry fares and discounts at museums, theatres and other attractions. For Americans there's also a health benefit, providing token medical coverage and a per-day stipend for hospital stays up to two months. You only have to be 26 or younger to qualify for the **International Youth Travel Card**, which provides much the same benefits as the ISIC. Teachers qualify for the **International Teacher Identity Card (ITIC)**, offering similar insurance benefits but more limited travel discounts. Consult the website of the International Student Travel Confederation (ⓦ www.istc.org) for the nearest retail outlet for any of these cards. A university photo ID might open some doors, but is not as easily recognizable as the ISIC cards, although the latter are often not accepted as valid proof of age.

Senior discounts

Seniors are entitled to discounts at state-run attractions of 25 to 30 percent; long-term bus passes in the major cities are similarly discounted; and, without making much effort to publicize the fact, Olympic Airways (and quite possibly its new private competitors) also offer discounts on full fares on domestic flights. Keep proof of age to hand for all these benefits.

Currency

Greece is one of twelve EU countries that changed over to a single currency, the **euro** (€), in February 2002. The fixed conversion rate used was 340.75 dhrachmas (*dhrakhmés*) to one euro; people still commonly quote prices in dhrachmas, and many till receipts continue to show the value in both currencies. Greek shopkeepers do not bother much with shortfalls of 10 cents or less, whether in their favour (especially) or yours. You will be able to exchange any leftover drachma paper notes until March 2012, at branches of the Bank of Greece.

For the most up-to-date **exchange rates** of the US dollar or the pound sterling against the euro, consult the very useful currency speculators' website, ⓦ www.oanda.com.

Euro notes exist in denominations of 5, 10, 20, 50, 100, 200 and 500 euro, and coins in denominations of 1, 2, 5, 10, 20 and 50 cents and 1 and 2 euro. Each country in the euro-zone strikes its own coins (just one face is distinctive), but the other side – and all notes – are uniform throughout Europe. Avoid getting stuck with **counterfeit euro notes** (€100 and €200 ones abound). The best tests are done by the naked eye: genuine notes all have a hologram strip or (if over €50) patch at one end, there's a watermark at the other, plus a security thread embedded in the middle. If you end up being given such a note, you'll have to lump it – if you unwittingly try to pass it on, or report it in good faith to the police, you'll still be assumed party to the scam, and face a session of interrogation at the very least.

Banks and exchange

Greek banks are normally open Monday to Thursday 8.30am–2.30pm and Friday

8.30am–2pm. Always take your passport with you as proof of identity and allow time for at least one long queue. Outside these hours, the largest hotels and travel agencies provide an exchange service, albeit with hefty commissions. On small islands with no full-service bank, "authorized" bank agents will charge yet another extra fee to cover the cost of posting a travellers' cheque to a proper branch.

A number of authorized brokers for exchanging foreign cash have emerged in major tourist centres. When changing small amounts, choose those bureaux that charge a flat percentage commission (usually one percent) rather than a high minimum. There's also a small number of 24-hour automatic **foreign-note-changing machines** in a few resorts, but a high minimum commission tends to be deducted. There is no need to **purchase euro** beforehand unless you're arriving at some ungodly hour at one of the remoter frontier posts. All major airports have an ATM or banking booth for incoming international flights.

Travellers' cheques

The safest, though most fiddly, way to carry money is as **travellers' cheques**. You can cash the cheques at most banks, though rarely elsewhere. Each travellers' cheque encashment in Greece will incur a minimum commission charge of €1.20–2.40 depending on the bank, so you won't want to make too many small-value transactions. For larger amounts, a set percentage will apply.

Credit cards and ATMs

Major **credit cards** are not usually accepted by cheaper tavernas or hotels, but they're almost essential for renting cars or buying airline tickets. Major travel agents may also accept them, though a **three-percent surcharge** is often levied on the purchase of ferry (as opposed to air) tickets.

Credit/debit cards are also likely to be your main source of funds while travelling, by withdrawing money (using your usual PIN) from the vast network of Greek **ATMs**. Larger airports have at least one ATM in the arrivals hall, and any town or island with a population larger than a few thousand (or a substantial tourist traffic) also has them. The best distrib-

uted are those of the National Bank/Ethniki Trapeza, the Trapeza Pireos/Bank of Piraeus, the Commercial Bank/Emboriki Trapeza and the Alpha Bank, which happily and interchangeably accept Visa, MasterCard, Visa Electron, Plus and Cirrus cards; American Express holders are restricted to the ATMs of Alpha and National Bank.

ATM transactions with **debit cards** linked to a current (checking) account attract **charges** of 2.25 percent on the sterling/dollar transaction value, plus a commission fee of 2.65 percent; the "tourist" (rather than the more favourable "interbank" rate) will be applied. A few banks or building societies waive some or all of these fees. Using **credit cards** at an ATM costs roughly the same – 2 percent plus a 2.75-percent "overseas transaction fee", moreover with typically inflated "cash advance" interest accruing from the minute the funds are drawn down.

Wiring money

In an emergency you can arrange to have substantial amounts of money wired from your home bank to a bank in Greece. Receiving funds by SWIFT transfer takes anywhere from two to ten working days. From the UK, a bank charge of 0.03 percent, with a minimum of £17, maximum £35, is typically levied for two-day service; some building societies charge a £20 flat fee irrespective of the amount. If you choose this method, your home bank will need the IBAN (international bank account number) for the account to which funds are being sent or, failing that, the bank name and branch code. It's unwise to transfer more than the equivalent of €10,000; above that limit, as part of measures to combat money-laundering, the receiving Greek bank will begin asking awkward questions and imposing punitive commissions.

Having money wired from home using one of the **companies** listed opposite is less convenient and even more expensive than using a bank; local affiliate offices are thin on the ground in Greece, although you may find that main post offices are the designated receiving points for Western Union. However, the funds should be available for collection at Amex's or Western Union's local representative office within hours – sometimes minutes – of being sent.

Money-wiring companies

Travelers Express MoneyGram US ☎ 1-800/444-3010, Canada ☎ 1-800 933-3278, UK, Republic of Ireland and New Zealand ☎ 00800 6663 9472, Australia ☎ 001 1800 230 100, ⓦ www.moneygram.com.

Western Union US and Canada ☎ 1-800/CALL-CASH, Australia ☎ 1800 501 500, New Zealand ☎ 0800 005 253, UK ☎ 0800 833 833, Republic of Ireland ☎ 66/947 5603, ⓦ www.westernunion.com (those in the US or Canada can send money online).

Getting around

Island-hopping is an essential feature of a Greek holiday; the ferry network – supplemented in season by hydrofoils and catamarans – is extensive, and will eventually get you to any of the sixty-plus inhabited isles. Planes are relatively expensive, at three to four times the cost of a deck-class ferry ticket and about twice as much as the cheapest cabin berth. They are, however, useful for saving time at the start or finish of a visit, providing critical links between smaller islands and Athens, Thessaloníki, Rhodes and Crete. On the islands themselves, buses provide skeletal connections, which most tourists choose to supplement by renting a scooter, motorbike or car.

Sea transport

There are several different varieties of vessel for sea travel: **roll-on-roll-off** (ro-ro) short-haul barge-ferries, nicknamed *pondófles* or "slippers" in Greek, designed to shuttle mostly vehicles short distances; medium-sized-to-large **ordinary ferries**, which, stretching the definition, include a new generation of **"high-speed"** boats (*tahyplóö*), about thirty percent faster than conventional ferries; **catamarans**, also medium-sized to large, which match hydrofoils in speed but carry a certain number of cars; **hydrofoils**, which carry only passengers; and local **kaïkia**, small boats which do short hops and excursions in season. Costs are very reasonable on the longer journeys, though proportionately more expensive for shorter, inter-island connections, or baldly overpriced for monopoly crossings (eg Alexandhroúpoli–Samothráki).

We've indicated most of the **ferry, catamaran and hydrofoil connections**, both on the map (see p.90 for a general pattern) and in the "Travel details" at the end of each chapter. Don't take our listings as gospel, however, as schedules are notoriously erratic, and must be verified each year; details given are for departures between late June and mid-September. **Out-of-season** departure frequencies are severely reduced, with many islands connected only once or twice a week.

The most reliable, up-to-date information is available from the local **port police** (*limenarhío*), which on the Attic peninsula maintains offices at Pireás (☎ 210 45 11 310), Rafína (☎ 22940 28888) and Lávrio (☎ 22920 25249), as well as at the harbours of all fair-sized islands. Smaller places may only have a *limenikós stathmós* (marine station), often just a single room with a VHF radio. Their officers keep complete schedules posted – and, meteorological report in hand, are the final arbiters of whether a ship will sail or not in stormy weather conditions.

Many companies produce regular **schedule** booklets, which may not be adhered to as the season wears on – check websites (if any) for current information. The only attempt at an all-inclusive ferry guide is the Greek travel agents' monthly manual *Greek*

Travel Pages, often outdated by the time it's printed; again you're better off referring to their website (see p.45).

Regular ferries

On most **ferry** routes, your only consideration will be getting a boat that leaves on the day, and for the island, that you want. However, when sailing from **Pireás**, the main port of Athens, to the Cyclades or Dodecanese islands, you should have a choice of at least two, often three, sailings and may want to bear in mind a few of the factors below.

Spanking-new **boats** are still a rarity; you will more often than not encounter a former English Channel or Scandinavian fjord ferry, rechristened and enjoying a new lease of life in the Aegean. **Routes** and speed of the boats can vary enormously. A journey from Pireás to Santoríni, for instance, can take anything from five (high-speed boat) to ten ("milk-run" conventional ferry) hours. Prior to buying a ticket, establish how many stops there will be, and the estimated time of arrival.

Regular ferry **tickets** are, in general, best bought a day before departure, unless you need to reserve a cabin berth or space for a car. (If a boat fails to sail for mechanical or bad-weather reasons, the ticket price is refunded.) There are only three periods of the year – March 23–25, the week before and after Easter, and late July to early September – when ferries need to be booked at least a week in advance. Around the times of elections – whether national, municipal, or European – there will also be a crunch for the best cabins, as Greeks are required to return to their home precinct to vote.

You cannot buy your ticket on board; in many cases there may not even be a last-minute sales booth at the quayside. Staff at the gangway will bar you from embarking if you don't have a ticket (the only furtive exceptions may be the short-haul, ro-ro services, for example from Igoumenítsa to Corfu, or the central mainland to Évvia). All ticket sales are now computerized, and supposedly have accurate seat/berth allocations that preclude **overbookings**. The only company that has provision for phone or Internet sales is Hellenic Seaways, which controls over half the Aegean ferry traffic;

tickets must be picked up at the port at least thirty minutes before departure. **Fares** for each route are currently set by the transport ministry and should not differ among ships or agencies (though they're minutely more *towards* Pireás as opposed to *from*).

The cheapest class of ticket, which you'll probably automatically be sold, is **deck class**, variously called *tríti* or *ikonomikí thési*. This gives you the run of most boats except for the upper-class restaurant and bar.

Newly acquired boats seem, with their glaring overhead lights and plastic bucket seats, expressly designed to frustrate summertime travellers attempting to sleep on deck. In such cases it's worth the few extra euro for a **cabin bunk** (second-class cabins are usually quadruple, occasionally triple or double). **First-class** cabins usually cost scarcely less than a plane flight; the main difference between first and second being the presence of a bathroom in the cabin, and a better location. Most cabins are overheated or overchilled, and pretty airless; ask for an *exoterikí* (outer) cabin if you want a porthole (though these are always bolted shut).

Motorbikes and cars get issued extra tickets, in the latter case four to five times the passenger deck-class fare, depending on size. Car fees are roughly proportionate to distance: for example Sámos–Ikaría cost €26–30 depending on port and direction, while Sámos–Pireás is about €80. This limits the number of islands you'll want to drag a car to – it's really only worth it for the larger ones like Crete, Rhodes, Híos, Lésvos, Sámos, Corfu or Kefalloniá, and even then for a stay of more than four days. Elsewhere, you may find it cheaper to leave your car on the mainland and rent another on arrival. Technically, written permission is required to take rental motorbikes and cars on ferries, though in practice few crew will quiz you on this.

Ferries sell a limited range (biscuits, greasy pizzas) of overpriced, mediocre **food on board**; honourable exceptions are the meals served on overnight sailings to Crete. On the short, daytime hops between the various islands of the Argo-Saronic, Cyclades and Sporades, stock up beforehand with your own snacks.

Hydrofoils and catamarans

Hydrofoils – commonly known as *dhelfínia* or "Flying Dolphins" – are roughly twice as fast (and at least twice as expensive) as ordinary ferries. On the plus side, their network neatly fills gaps in ferry scheduling, with more convenient departure times. Their main drawback (aside from frequent engine breakdowns) is that they were originally designed for cruising on placid Russian or Polish rivers, and are quite literally out of their depth on the open sea; thus they are extremely sensitive to bad weather, and even in moderate seas are not for the seasick-prone. Most of these services don't operate – or are heavily reduced – from October to June. Hydrofoils are not allowed to carry scooters or bicycles.

At present, hydrofoils operate among the **Argo-Saronic** islands close to Athens, between Kavála and **Thássos**, between Alexandhroúpoli and **Samothráki**, and in the **Dodecanese** and east Aegean among Rhodes, Sými, Tílos, Níssyros, Kós, Kálymnos, Léros, Lipsí and Pátmos, with regular forays up to Sámos, Agathoníssi, Ikaría and Foúrni. The principal mainland ports are Aktí Tselépi in Pireás, Vólos and Áyios Konstandínos, as well as Igoumenítsa, Kavála and (some years) Alexandhroúpoli. Services in the Argo-Saronic are run by Hellenic Seaways and Vasilopoulos Flying Dolphins, and in the Dodecanese by Aegean Flying Dolphins and Samos Flying Dolphins. You may see craft with other livery, but we have excluded them from "Travel details", as they are chartered by tour agencies and do not offer scheduled services.

Catamarans attempt to combine the speed of hydrofoils with the (relative) reliability and vehicle-carrying capacity of larger ferries. The fact that they are new and sleek, purpose-built in France or Scandinavia, has not prevented numerous breakdowns, since they are constantly playing catch-up to fill in weather-cancelled itineraries and thus miss necessary maintenance. **Inside** they are ruthlessly air-conditioned, with no deck seating and with Greek TV blaring at you from numerous screens; paying a few euro extra for *dhiakikriméni thési* (upper class) gets you a better view and less crowding, but there's no escaping the TV. Cabins are non-existent and food facilities even more unappetizing than on conventional ferries. Car fares are normal, though passenger **tickets** are at least double a comparable ferry journey, ie similar to hydrofoil rates. Their stratospheric fuel costs mean that they haven't become as ubiquitous as anticipated, but they're still found serving the Pireás–Híos–Lésvos–Límnos–north mainland line, routes to Crete, the Argo-Saronics, the Sporades, and the most popular Cyclades.

Small ferries, kaïkia and taxi boats

In season, **kaïkia** and **small ferries** of a few hundred tonnes' displacement sail between adjacent islands and to a few of the more obscure ones. These can be extremely useful and often very pleasant, but are no cheaper than mainline services – in fact, more expensive if classified as a tourist-agency charter rather than a scheduled service. The more consistent *kaïki* links are summarized in the "Travel details" section of each chapter, though the only firm information is to be had on the quayside. *Kaïkia* and small ferries, despite appearances, have a good safety record. Swarms of **taxi boats** are a feature of Sými, Rhodes, Hálki and Itháki, among other spots; these exist to shuttle clients on set routes to remote beaches or ports which can only be reached arduously, if at all, overland. Costs on these can be pretty stiff, usually per person but occasionally per boat.

Domestic flights

State-run Olympic Airlines and its subsidiary Olympic Aviation at present operate most of the **domestic flights** within Greece, though they were teetering at the brink of closure as of writing. They (or any successor) cover a fairly wide network of islands and larger mainland towns, and while most routes are to and from Athens or Thessaloníki, there are some very useful peripheral ones centred on Rhodes, Corfu and Crete. Privately run Aegean Airlines has cherry-picked the high-volume, high-profit routes from Athens and Thessaloníki to Crete (Haniá and Iráklion), Thíra, Mytilíni, Mýkonos, Rhodes, Kós, Híos, Corfu, Kavála, Ioánnina and Alexandhroúpoli. **Tickets** for both airlines are most easily obtained from travel agents (their own high-street outlets are thin on the ground). Aegean often undercuts Olympic with price specials, and surpasses it service-wise, though flight frequencies tend to be sparse.

Olympic **schedules** can be picked up at their offices abroad (see "Getting there" for contact details in the relevant countries) or through their branch offices and representatives in Greece, which are maintained in almost every town or island of any size. Aegean's are easiest to get from their desks at major airports. Both airlines publish English-language schedules at least twice yearly (spring and autumn).

Fares for flights to and between the islands, including the domestic airport tax, work out around three to four times the cost of a deck-class ferry journey, but on certain inter-island hauls poorly served by boat (Rhodes–Kárpathos or Corfu–Kefaloniá, for example), you should consider this time well bought, and indeed some of these subsidized peripheral routes cost less than a hydrofoil/catamaran journey would.

Island flights are often full in peak season; if they're an essential part of your plans, it is worth trying to make a **reservation** at least two weeks in advance. If a flight you've set your heart on is full, **waiting lists** exist – and are worth signing on to; experience has shown that there are almost always one or two booking cancellations. Domestic air tickets are nonrefundable, but you can change your flight, space permitting, without penalty as late as 24 hours before your original departure.

Like ferries, flights are subject to **cancellation** in very bad weather, since many services are on small 46- or 74-seat ATR turboprop planes, smaller "Dash 8" (De Havilland 37-seaters), or the tiny Dornier 18-seaters, none of which will fly in strong winds or (depending on the destination airport) after dark. Size restrictions also mean that the 15-kilo baggage weight limit can be fairly strictly enforced, especially on the Dorniers; if, however, you've just arrived from overseas or purchased your ticket outside Greece, you are allowed the standard international limit (20–23 kilos depending on carrier). All services operated on the domestic network are **non-smoking**.

Contacts for Greek domestic airlines

Aegean Countrywide ☏ 801 11 20 000, 🌐 www .aegeanair.com.
Olympic Airlines/Aviation Countrywide ☏ 801 11 44 444, 🌐 www.olympicairlines.com.

Island ground transport

Most islands have some kind of bus service, but many visitors prefer to rent a two- or four-wheeler. Even if you just do this for a day, you can get the measure of a small or medium-sized island and work out where you'd like to be based.

Buses

Bus services on the **major routes** are highly efficient and frequent. On **secondary roads** they're less regular, with long gaps, but even the remotest villages will be connected a few days weekly by a school or market bus to the island (or in Crete, provincial) capital. These often depart for the capital shortly before dawn, returning there between 1.30 and 3pm. On the islands there are usually buses to connect the port and main town for ferry arrivals or departures.

The network is nationally run by a single syndicate known as the **KTEL** (Kratikó Tamío Ellinikón Leoforíon). However, in the larger island towns there can be several scattered terminals for services in different directions, so make sure you have the right station for your departure.

Buses are traditionally two-toned cream-and-green, being slowly replaced by hi-tech, navy-and-green models. They are amazingly prompt as a rule, so be there in plenty of time for scheduled departures. On small island routes, it's generally first come, first served, with some standing allowed, and tickets dispensed on the spot by an *ispráktoros* or conductor.

Motorbikes, scooters and bicycles

The cult of the **motorcycle** is highly developed in Greece, presided over by a jealous deity apparently requiring regular human sacrifice; accidents among both foreign and local bikers are routine occurrences, with annual fatalities edging into two figures on the busier islands. But with caution and common sense – and an eye to increasingly enforced regulations – riding a two-wheeler through a resort should be a lot safer than piloting one through London or New York.

Many tourists come to grief on rutted dirt tracks or astride mechanically dodgy machines. In other cases **accidents** are due to attempts to cut corners, in all senses, or by riding two to an underpowered scooter simply not designed to propel such a load. Don't be tempted by this apparent economy – you won't regret getting two separate automatic scooters, or one powerful manual bike to share – and remember that you're likely to be charged an exorbitant sum for any repairs if you do have a wipeout. Also, verify that your travel insurance policy covers motorcycle accidents.

One worthwhile precaution is to wear a **crash helmet** (*krános*); many rental outfits will offer you (an admittedly ill-fitting) one, and some will make you sign a waiver of liability if you refuse it. Helmet-wearing is in fact required by law, with a €78 fine levied for failure to do so; on some smaller islands (eg Léros) the rule is laxly enforced, on others (eg Sámos and Corfu) random police roadblocks do a brisk commerce in citations, and foreign renters are most definitely not exempt.

Reputable establishments demand a full motorcycle driving licence for any engine over 80cc (Greek law actually stipulates "over 50cc"), and you will usually have to leave your passport as security. For smaller models, any driving licence will do. Failure to carry the correct licence on your person attracts an €86 fine.

Fines of any sort are to be paid within ten working days at the municipal cashier's (*dhimotikó tamío*); proof of payment then needs to be taken to the police station to have the citation cancelled. Non-payment will be followed by a court date being set, and the Greek authorities – so dilatory in other respects – are amazingly efficient at translating summons into foreign languages and forwarding them to your overseas address. No-shows are automatically convicted, and a conviction will make re-entry to Greece awkward at best.

Small **motor scooters** with automatic transmission, known in Greek as *papákia* (little ducks) after their characteristic noise, are good transport for all but the hilliest islands. They're available for rent on many islands for €10–18 per day. Prices can be bargained down out of peak season, or if you negotiate for a longer period of rental.

Before riding off, make sure you check the bike's **mechanical state**, since many are only cosmetically maintained. Bad brakes, non-functioning electrics and worn or oil-fouled spark plugs are the most common defects; dealers often keep the front brakes far too loose, with the commendable intention of preventing you going over the handlebars. If you break down it's your responsibility to return the machine; better outlets offer a free retrieval service.

The latest models of **scooters**, generally Honda, Piaggio, Vespa or Peugeot make, are practical enough, but thirsty on fuel; make sure there's a kick-start as backups to the battery, since ignition switches commonly fail. The new Haojin 125cc automatic scooter is the only model really powerful enough for two riders. Bungee cords (a *khtapódi*, or "octopus", in slang) for tying down bundles are supplied on request, while capacious baskets are also often a feature. The ultra-trendy, low-slung models with fat, small-radius tyres, however, are unstable on anything other than the smoothest, flattest island roads. Especially if you intend to go off-road, always choose traditionally designed bikes with large-radius, nobbly, narrow tyres, if available. Again, if you're going to spend every day of your vacation astride a scooter, consider bringing or buying cyclists' or motorcyclists' **gloves**; they may look stupid during summer, but if you lose all the skin off your hands when you go for a spill, the wounds can take months to heal, and leave huge scars.

In the family of true **motorbikes** with manual transmissions (*mihanákia*), and safer tyres (as described above), the favourites, in descending order of reliability, are the Honda 50, Yamaha Townmate and Suzuki FB Birdie; gears are shifted with an easy-to-learn left-foot pedal action, and (very important) these can all be push-started in second gear if the starting crank fails. For two riders, the least powerful safe model at nominal extra cost is the Honda Cub 90cc or Yamaha 80 Townmate. Best of all is the attractive Honda

Astrea 100 and its rival-brand clones (eg Kawasaki Kaze), very powerful but scarcely bigger than older models. With the proper licence and off-road experience, dirt-bikes of 125cc and up can also be found in most resorts. **Quads** are also increasingly offered in many resorts – silly-looking, and a nuisance on beaches, but undoubtedly safer for two riders.

Cycling

Cycling in Greece is not such hard going as you might imagine (except in midsummer), especially on one of the mountain bikes that are now the rule at rental outfits; they rarely cost more than €7 a day. You do, however, need steady nerves, as roads are generally narrow with no verges or bike lanes (except on Kós), and many Greek drivers consider cyclists a lower form of life, on a par with the snakes regularly found run over.

If you have your own mountain or touring bike (the latter not rented in Greece), you might consider taking it along by **train** or **plane** (it's free if within your 20–23kg international air allowance, but always arrange it in writing with the airline beforehand to avoid huge charges at check-in). Once in Greece you should be able to take a bike for free on most of the ferries, in the guard's van on most trains (for a small fee – it goes on a later goods train otherwise), and with a little persuasion in the luggage bays of buses. Any small spare parts you might need, however, are best brought along, since specialist bike shops are only found in the largest island towns.

Driving and car rental

Automobiles have obvious advantages for getting to the more inaccessible parts of larger islands, but this is not an especially cheap Mediterranean country in which to **rent a car**. If you intend to drive **your own vehicle** to and through Greece, via EU member states, it's worth knowing that insurance contracted in any EU member state is valid in any other, but in many cases this is only third-party cover – the statutory legal minimum. Competition in the industry is so intense, however, that many UK insurers will throw in full, pan-European cover for free

or for a nominal sum, up to sixty days; shop around if necessary.

EU citizens bringing their own cars are, in theory, free to circulate in the country for six months, or until their home-based road tax or insurance expires, whichever happens first; see remarks on p.84 for keeping a car in Greece for longer. Other nationalities will get a **non-EU car** entered in their passport; the carnet normally allows you to keep a vehicle in Greece for up to six months, exempt from road tax.

Car rental

Car rental within Greece starts at around €300 a week in high season for the smallest, A-group vehicle from a one-off outlet or local chain, including unlimited mileage, tax and insurance. Overseas tour operators' and international chains' brochures threaten alarming rates of nearly €400 for the same period but, except in August, no rental company expects to fetch that price for a car. Outside peak season, at the smaller local outfits, you can often get terms of €30–35 per day, all inclusive, with even better rates for three days or more. **Comparison shopping** among agencies in the larger resorts can yield a variation in quotes of up to twenty percent for the same conditions over a four to seven-day period; the most negotiable variable is whether or not kilometres in excess of one hundred per day (a common hidden catch) are free. Open **jeeps**, which are increasingly popular, begin at about €65 per day, rising to as much as €100 at busy times and places.

Brochure prices in Greece almost never include VAT at 19 percent, **collision damage waiver** (CDW) and personal insurance. The CDW typically has a deductible of €400–600, some or all of which can be levied for even the tiniest scratch or missing mud-flap. To avoid this, it is strongly recommended that you pay the €5–7 extra per a day for Super Collision Damage Waiver, Franchise Waiver or Liability Waiver Surcharge, as it is variously called. Even better, frequent travellers should take out **annual excess insurance** through Insurance 4 Car Hire (℡020/7012 6300, 🌐www.insurance4carhire.com), which will cover all UK- and North America-based drivers.

All agencies will want a blank **credit card** slip as a deposit up front (destroyed when you return the vehicle safely); minimum age requirements vary from 21 to 23. **Driving licences** issued by any EU state are honoured, but an International Driving Permit is required by all other drivers, including Australians, New Zealanders and North Americans. This must be arranged before departure in your home country. Some unscrupulous agencies still rent to these nationals on production of just a home licence, but you can be arrested and charged if caught by the traffic police without an IDP if you require one.

In peak season, you may get a better price through one of the **overseas booking companies** that deal with local firms than if you negotiate for rental in Greece itself. One of the most competitive companies in Britain is Transhire; the website ⓦ www. rentacar-uk.com also comes recommended. Autorent, Budget, Payless, EuroHire, European, Kosmos, National/Alamo, Reliable, Eurodollar and Just are dependable Greek, or smaller international, chains with branches in many towns; all are considerably cheaper than the biggest international operators such as Hertz or Avis but it is always worthwhile visiting all the international chains' websites for a quote, and with a Frequent Flyer discount code you may well match prices of the discount booking companies noted above. Specific local recommendations are given in the guide.

In terms of **models**, the more reputable companies tend to offer the Citroën Saxo, Kia Pikanto, Chevrolet Matiz or Fiat Cinquecento or Seisento as A-group cars, and Opel (Vauxhall) Corsa 1.2, Fiat Uno or Punto, Peugeot 106, Hyundai Atos or Getz, Renault Clio or Twingo or Nissan Micra in the B group. Any more than two adults, with luggage, will generally require B category, in which the Atos and the Clio are the most robust models. In the C or D categories, suitable for two adults and two kids, Renault Mègane or Peugeot 307 are preferable to the Seat Cordoba/Ibiza. The standard four-wheel-drive option is a Suzuki jeep (1.3- or 1.6-litre), mostly open – great for bashing down steep, rutted tracks to remote beaches.

Car-rental agencies

Britain

Avis ☎0870 606 0100, ⓦwww.avis.com.
Budget ☎0800 181 181,
ⓦwww.budget.com.
Hertz ☎0870 844 8844, ⓦwww.hertz.com.
National ☎0870 536 5365, ⓦwww.nationalcar .co.uk.
Sixt ⓦwww.e-sixt.com.
Thrifty ☎01494/751 600, ⓦwww.thrifty.com.
Transhire ☎0870 789 8000, ⓦwww.transhire .com.

Ireland

Avis Northern Ireland ☎028/9024 0404, Republic of Ireland ☎01/605 7500, ⓦwww.avis.ie.
Budget Republic of Ireland ☎0903/277 11, ⓦwww.budget.ie.
Cosmo Thrifty Northern Ireland ☎028/9445 2565, ⓦwww.thrifty.com.
Hertz Republic of Ireland ☎01/676 7476, ⓦwww .hertz.ie.
Sixt Republic of Ireland ☎1850 206 088, ⓦwww .irishcarrentals.ie.
Thrifty Republic of Ireland ☎1800 515 800, ⓦwww.thrifty.ie.

North America

Alamo ☎1-800/462-5266, ⓦwww.alamo.com.
Auto Europe ☎1-800/223-555, ⓦwww .autoeurope.com.
Avis US ☎1-800/230-4898, Canada ☎1-800 272-5871, ⓦwww.avis.com.
Budget t1-800/527-0700, ⓦwww.budgetrentacar .com.
Dollar US ☎1-800/800-3665, ⓦwww.dollar.com.
Europe by Car ☎1-80/ 223-1516, ⓦwww .europebycar.com.
Hertz US ☎1-800/654-3131, Canada ☎1-800 263-0600, ⓦwww.hertz.com.
National ☎1-800/962-7070, ⓦwww.nationalcar .com.
Thrifty ☎1-800/847-4389, ⓦwww.thrifty.com.

Australia

Avis ☎13 63 33 or 02/9353 9000, ⓦwww.avis .com.au.
Budget ☎1300 362 848, ⓦwww.budget.com.au.
Hertz ☎13 30 39 or 03/9698 2555, ⓦwww.hertz .com.au.
National ☎13 10 45, ⓦwww.nationalcar.com.au.
Thrifty ☎1300 367 227, ⓦwww.thrifty.com.au.

New Zealand

Apex ☎0800 93 95 97 or 03/379 6897, ⓦwww
.apexrentals.co.nz.
Avis ☎09/526 2847 or 0800 655 111, ⓦwww
.avis.co.nz.
Budget ☎080/652 227, ⓦwww.budget.co.nz.
Hertz ☎0800 654 321, ⓦwww.hertz.co.nz.
National ☎0800 800 115, ⓦwww.nationalcar
.co.nz.
Thrifty ☎09/309 0111, ⓦwww.thrifty.co.nz.

Driving in Greece

As in all of continental Europe, you drive **on
the right** in Greece. The country has one of
the highest (fatal) **accident rates** in Europe,
and on the larger tourist islands it's easy to
see why. Driving habits amongst locals can
be atrocious: overtaking is erratic, tailgat-
ing and barging out from side-roads are
preferred pastimes, lane lines go unheeded,
turn signals go unused and motorbikes hog
the road or weave from side to side. **Drunk
driving** is also a major problem; Sunday
afternoons in rural areas are particularly bad,
and for the same reason you should be extra
vigilant driving late at night at weekends or
on holidays. Well-publicized police campaigns are addressing the problem, with
radar guns being deployed against speeders
as well.

Matters are made worse by poor **road
conditions**: signposting is absent or badly
placed, pavement markings are faded,
curves are invariably banked the wrong way
and slick with olive-blossom drop in May,
asphalt can turn into a one-lane surface or
a dirt track without warning on secondary
routes, railway crossings are rarely guarded,
and you're heavily dependent on magnifying
mirrors at blind intersections in congested
villages. Uphill drivers insist on their **right of
way**, as do those first to approach a one-
lane bridge; **flashed headlights** usually
mean the opposite of what they do in the
UK or North America, here signifying that
the other driver insists on coming through
or overtaking. However, this gesture rapidly
repeated from someone approaching means
they're warning you of a police control-point
ahead. **Parking** in the biggest island towns
is uniformly a nightmare owing to congestion
and demand. **Pay-and-display** systems

(plus residents-only schemes) as in the UK
are the rule, and it's not always clear where
you obtain tickets (sometimes from a kiosk,
sometimes from a machine).

Wearing a **seatbelt** is compulsory – you
will be fined for non-observance at the many
checkpoints – as is keeping a first-aid kit in
the boot (many rental companies skimp on
this), and children under the age of 10 are
not allowed to sit in the front seats. It's illegal to drive away from any kind of **accident**
– or to move the vehicles before the police
appear – and in cases where serious injury
has resulted you can be held at a police
station for up to 24 hours. For any substantial property damage, you wait for the police
to arrive; they will take down the details of
all drivers, note the time and place of the
incident, give copies of the statement to
all involved for insurance purposes (or forward one to the rental company if your car
is rented), and then give you permission to
go on your way if the car hasn't been crip-
pled. Though forensics aren't their long suit,
they're generally a lot more civil and calm
than the Greek drivers actually involved in
the accident.

Tourists with proof of AA/RAC/AAA membership are given free road assistance from
ELPA, the Greek equivalent, which runs
breakdown services on several of the
larger islands; in an emergency ring their
road assistance service on ☎10400. Many
car rental companies have an agreement
with ELPA's equally widespread competitors Hellas Service (☎1057), Interamerican
(☎1168) and Express Service (☎1154).
However, you will always get a faster
response if you dial the local number for the
province you're stranded in (ask for these in
advance).

Running a vehicle

Fuel, whether regular unleaded (*amólyvdhi*),
super unleaded, super lead-replacement or
diesel, is currently cresting the one-euro-per-
litre barrier in most of the country, and could
well have reached €1.25 by the time you
read this. Lead-replacement fuel for older
cars without catalytic converters is called
"Neo Super" or "Super LRP". Most scooters
and motorbikes run better on super, even if
they nominally take regular.

It is easy to run short of fuel **after dark or at weekends** in both rural and urban Greece; most stations close at 7 or 8pm, and nearly as many are shut all day Sunday. One pump per district will always remain open, but interpreting the Greek-only pharmacy-type-rota lists posted at shut stations is another matter. This is not so much of a problem on the major highways, but it is a factor everywhere else. So always fill up, or insist on full rental vehicles at the outset, and if you've brought your own car, keep a full petrol can at all times.

Some stations, which claim to be open around the clock, are in fact **automated-only at night** – you have to use bill-taking machines, which don't give change. If you fill your tank without having exhausted your credit, punch the button for a receipt and get change the next day during attended hours (assuming you're still in the area). Petrol stations run by multinational companies (BP, Shell) usually take **credit cards**; Greek chains like Aegean, EKO, Elda, Eteka, Jetoil, Revoil and Elinoil usually don't (except in tourist areas or along main highways). The tiny, generic-petrol stations of the EP (Elefthero Pratirio) chain are always the cheapest around.

In terms of **maintenance**, the easiest car models to have serviced and buy parts for in Greece are VWs (including old microbuses and Transporter vans), Mercedes, BMWs, Audis, Opels, Ladas, Skodas and virtually all French, Italian, Korean and Japanese makes. British models are a bit more difficult, but you should be fine as long as you haven't brought anything too esoteric like a Hillman Minx – the Mini is, for example, still a cult vehicle in Greece, Fords are present (though not common), and the Opel is of course the continental brand of Vauxhall.

Taxis

Greek **taxis** are among the cheapest in western Europe – so long as you get an honest driver who switches the meter on and doesn't use high-tech devices to doctor the reading. Use of the meter is mandatory within city or town limits, where Tariff 1 applies, while in rural areas or between midnight and 5am, Tariff 2 is in effect. On certain islands, set rates apply on specific fixed routes for collective taxis – these only depart when full. Otherwise, throughout Greece the meter starts at €0.75, though the minimum fare is €1.50; any baggage not actually on your lap is charged at €0.30 a piece. Additionally, there are surcharges of €2 for leaving or entering an airport (€3 for Athens), and €0.80 for leaving a harbour area. If you summon a taxi by phone on spec, there's a €1.50 charge, while a prearranged rendezvous is €2.10 extra; in either case the meter starts running from the moment the driver begins heading towards you. All categories of supplemental charges must be set out on a laminated card affixed to the dashboard. For a week or so before and after Orthodox Easter, and Christmas, a *filodhórima* or gratuity of about ten percent is levied. Any or all of these extras will legitimately bump up the basic rate of about €8 per ten rural kilometres.

Accommodation

There are huge numbers of beds for tourists in Greece, so most of the season you can rely on turning up pretty much anywhere and finding a room – if not in a hotel, then in a private house or block of rooms (the standard island accommodation). Only from late July to early September, and around Easter, the country's high season, are you likely to experience problems. At these times, if you don't have accommodation reserved well in advance, you'd be wise to keep well off the main tourist trails, turning up at each new place early in the day and taking whatever is available – you may be able to exchange it for something better later on.

Out of season, you face a slightly different problem: most private rooms and campsites operate only from late April or early May to October, leaving hotels as your only option. During winter you may have no choice but to stay in the main towns or ports. There will often be very little life outside these places anyway, with all the seasonal beach bars and restaurants closed. On many smaller islands, you will often find just one hotel – and perhaps one taverna – staying open year-round. Be warned also that any resort or harbour hotels which do operate through the winter are likely to have a certain number of **prostitutes** as long-term guests; licensed prostitution is legal in Greece, and the management at many places consider this the most painless way to keep the bills paid.

Hotels

Hotels and self-catering complexes in the larger resorts are often contracted out on a seasonal basis by foreign package-holiday companies, though there are often vacancies available (especially in spring or autumn) for walk-in trade. The tourist police set official **categories** for hotels, which range from L (Luxury) down to the rarely encountered E class; all except the top category have to keep within set price limits. The letter system is supposed to be replaced with a star grading system as in other countries, but the process, while begun, is being resisted; L is five-star, E is no-star, etc. While they last, letter ratings are supposed to correspond to **facilities** available, though in practice categorization often depends on location within a resort, number of rooms and influence with the tourism authorities – there are so-called E-class hotels with under nine rooms which are plusher than nearby C-class outfits. It is mandatory for D-class hotels to have all rooms with attached baths; C-class must additionally have a bar or designated breakfast area. The presence of a pool or tennis court will attract a B-class rating, while A-category hotels should have a restaurant, bar, business facilities and extensive common areas. Often these, and the L outfits (essentially self-contained complexes), back onto a quasi-private beach.

In terms of **food**, C-class hotels are only required to provide the most rudimentary

of continental breakfasts – you may often choose not to take, or pay, for it – while B-class and above will usually offer some sort of buffet breakfast including cheese, cold cuts, sausages, eggs and so on. With some exceptions, hotel restaurants are rarely memorable.

Private rooms

The most common island accommodation is **privately let rooms** (*dhomátia*). Like hotels, these are regulated and officially divided into three classes (A to C), according to facilities. These days the bulk of them are in new, purpose-built, low-rise buildings, but a few are still actually in people's homes, where you may be treated to disarming hospitality.

Licensed rooms are mostly scrupulously clean, however limited their other amenities. At their (now all-but-vanished) **simplest**, you'll get a bare, concrete-floored room, with a hook on the back of the door and toilet facilities outside in the courtyard. At the **fancier** end of the scale, they are modern, fully furnished places with en-suite bathroom, TV, air-conditioning, and a fridge, if not a fully equipped kitchen shared by guests. Between these extremes there will be a choice of rooms at various prices – owners will usually show you the most expensive first. Some of the cheap places will also have more expensive rooms with en-suite facilities – and vice versa, with rare singles often tucked under stairways or other less desirable corners of the building. Price and quality are not necessarily directly linked, so always ask to see the room before agreeing to take it.

Areas to **look for rooms**, along with recommendations of the best places, are included in the Guide. However, the rooms may find you: owners descend on ferry or bus arrivals to fill any space they have, sometimes waving photos of the premises. Many island municipalities are acting, to outlaw this practice, owing to widespread bait-and-switch tactics and the pitching of unlicensed rooms. Rooms can often be a longer journey from the initial meeting than you had expected. In smaller places you'll often see rooms advertised, sometimes in German (*Zimmer*); the Greek signs to look out for are "ENIKIAZÓMENA DHOMÁTIA"

Accommodation price codes

Throughout the book we've categorized accommodation according to the following **price codes**, which denote the **cheapest available double room in high season**. All prices are for the room only, except where otherwise indicated in accounts. Many hotels, especially those in category ❹ and over, include breakfast in the price; we indicate this by including "B & B" in the listing, but you should check when booking. During low season, rates can drop by more than fifty percent, especially if you are staying for three or more nights. Exceptions are during the Christmas and Easter weeks when you'll pay high-season prices. Single rooms, where available, cost around seventy percent of the price of a double.

❶ Up to €25
❷ €26–35
❸ €36–50

❹ €51–70
❺ €71–90
❻ €91–120

❼ €121–170
❽ € 171 plus and upwards

Youth hostels and **mountain refuges** typically charge €7–9 for a dormitory bed.

or "ENIKIÁZONTEH DHOMÁTIA". In the more developed island resorts, where package holiday-makers predominate, *dhomátia* owners will often require you to stay for at least three days, or even a week.

It has become standard practice for rooms proprietors, like hotel staff, to ask to keep your **passport** – ostensibly for the tourist police, who require customer particulars – but in reality to prevent you skipping out with an unpaid bill. Some owners may be satisfied with just taking down your details, as is done in most hotels, and they'll almost always return the documents once you get to know them, or if you need them for another purpose.

If you are **stranded**, or arrive very late in a remote island village, you may very well find that there is someone with an unlicensed room prepared to earn extra money by putting you up. This should not be counted on, but things work out more often than not.

Old-fashioned, 1970s-vintage rooms on the remoter islets, occasionally still without private bath, tend to fall into the ❶ price category. Basic en-suite rooms without cooking facilities weigh in at ❷; newer, well-amenitied rooms, self-catering studios, and modest C-class hotels occupy the top end of the ❸ niche, the better among these edging into ❹. Category ❺ corresponds fairly well to the better-value B-class hotels and the humbler designer inns in popular centres like the trendy Cyclades, while ❻ tallies with most of B-class and the state-of-the-art restoration projects. ❼–❽ means A- and L-class, and the sky's the limit here – €300 is by no means unheard of these days.

Prices and supplements in any establishment should by law be displayed on the back of the door of your room, or over the reception desk. If you feel you're being overcharged at a place that is officially registered, threaten to report it to the tourist office or police, who will generally adopt your side in such cases. A hotelier is free to offer a room at any amount under the official rate, but it's an offence to charge one euro-cent over the permitted price for the **current season**. Depending on location, there are up to three of these: typically October to May (low), June to mid-July, and September (mid) and mid-July through August (high). Small amounts over the posted price may be legitimately explained by municipal tax or out-of-date forms, but usually you will pay less than the maximum.

In **winter**, officially from November 1 until early April, private rooms – except in Ródhos Old Town and the biggest towns of Crete – are closed pretty much across the board to keep the few open hotels in business. There's no point in traipsing about hoping to find exceptions; most owners obey the system very strictly. If they don't, the room-owners will find you themselves, watching out for hotel rivals, guide you back to their place.

A fair number of hotels, and rather fewer apartments and rooms, have **websites** – but often these are run by agencies rather than the owner, and have little useful information. Be warned that some proprietors only check their email at infrequent intervals, if at all, and phoning may be essential for advance booking.

Villas and long-term rentals

The easiest – and usually most economical – way to arrange a **villa rental** is through one of the package-holiday companies detailed on p.31. They represent some superb places, from fairly simple to luxurious, and costs can be very reasonable, especially if shared between a few people. Several of the companies we list will arrange **twin-centre** stays on two islands over two weeks.

On the islands, a few local travel agents arrange villa rentals, though they are often places the overseas companies gave a miss on or could not fill. **Out of season**, you can sometimes get a good deal on villa or apartment rental for a month or more by asking around locally, though in these days of EU convergence and the increasing desirability of the islands as year-round residences, "good deal" means anything under €180 per month for a large studio (*garsoniéra*) or €250 for a small one-bedroom flat.

Youth hostels

Greece is not exactly packed with **youth hostels**, and those that do exist tend, with few exceptions, to be pretty run-down and filthy, and thus a far cry from similar north European institutions. Competition from inexpensive rooms and unofficial "student hostels", open to all, means they are simply not as cost-effective as elsewhere in Europe. It's best to have a valid IYHF card, but you can often buy one on the spot, or maybe just pay a little extra for your bed. Extra payment for sheets, towels and the like can bump up the price. Dorms tend to have four to six beds; most hostels have a curfew of 11pm or midnight, and many places only open in spring and summer.

The only surviving hostels on the **islands** are on Thíra, Corfu, Rhodes and Crete. Few of these are officially recognized by the IYHF.

Monasteries

Greek **monasteries** and **convents** have a tradition of putting up travellers (of the appropriate sex). On the islands, monastic hospitality is not common, so you should always ask locally before heading out to a monastery or convent for the night. Also, dress modestly – no shorts or short skirts – and try to arrive early in the evening, not later than 8pm or sunset (whichever is earlier).

Camping

Officially recognized campsites range from ramshackle compounds on the islands to highly organized and rather soulless complexes, formerly run by EOT prior to privatization. Most places cost about €5–7 a night per person, slightly less per tent and €6–8 per camper van, but at the fanciest sites, rates for two people plus a tent can almost equal the price of a basic room. The Panhellenic Camping Association regularly (but not annually) publishes a booklet covering most officially recognized Greek campsites and the facilities they offer; it's available from many EOT offices.

Freelance camping, as the EOT calls it, was forbidden under a law originally enacted to harass gypsies, but regulations are increasingly enforced against tourists. Another drawback is the increased prevalence of theft in rural areas. You will feel less vulnerable inside a tent, camper van or even a rock-cave – not that rain is likely during the long Greek summer, but some protection is essential from wind, sun, insects and stray animals raiding your food. You will always need at least a light sleeping bag, since even summer nights can get cool and damp; a foam pad is also recommended for pitching on harder ground.

If you do camp rough, it's vital to exercise sensitivity and discretion. Police will crack down on people camping (and especially littering) around popular tourist beaches, particularly when a large community of campers develops. Off the beaten track, however, nobody is very bothered, though it is always best to ask permission locally in the village taverna or café. During high season, when everything – even the authorized campsites – may be full, attitudes towards freelance camping are more relaxed, even in the most touristed places. At such times the best strategy is to find a sympathetic taverna, which in exchange for regular patronage will probably be willing to guard small valuables and let you use their facilities.

Eating and drinking

Greeks spend a lot of time socializing outside their homes, and sharing a meal is one of the chief ways of doing it. The atmosphere is always relaxed and informal, with pretensions rare outside of certain major resorts. Greeks are not prodigious drinkers – tippling is traditionally meant to accompany food – though since the mid-1990s a range of bars and clubs has sprung up.

Breakfast

Greeks don't generally eat **breakfast**, something reflected in the abysmal quality of most hotel "continental" offerings; the choice of juice tends to be orange, orange and orange, with fresh fruit rare, at any place below 'B' category. *Méli me voútyro* is syrupy, commercial honey and prepacked pats of butter (or margarine) to slather on bread or *friganiés* (melba-toast slivers). Confusingly, jam is called *marmeládha* in Greek; ask for *portokáli* – orange – if you want proper marmalade. Tea means obscure Sri Lankan or Madagascan brands of bag, often left to stew in a metal pot. The only egg-and-bacon kind of places are in resorts where foreigners congregate, or where there are returned North American- or Australian-Greeks. Such spots can sometimes be good value (€5.50–8 for the works, including "French" filter coffee or a cappuccino), especially if there's competition.

Picnics and snacks

Picnic fare is easily available at bakeries and *manávika* (fruit-and-veg stalls). **Bread**, alas, is often of minimal nutritional value and inedible within a day of purchase. It's worth paying extra at the bakery (*foúrnos* or *psomádhiko*) for *olikís* (wholemeal), *sikalísio* (rye bread), *oktásporo* (eight-grain) or even *enneásporo* (nine-grain), the latter types most commonly baked where large numbers of Germans or Scandinavians are about. When buying **olives**, go for the fat Kalamáta or Ámfissa ones; they're more expensive, but tastier. However, locally gathered olives – especially the slightly shrivelled *hamádhes* or fully ripened, ground-gathered olives – often have a distinctive nutty taste, compensating

for large kernels. The best **honey** is reckoned to be the pure-thyme variety from the more barren islands (such as Límnos, Náxos, Kálymnos and Astypálea).

Honey is an ideal topping for the famous local **yogurt**. All larger towns have at least one dairy shop where locally produced yogurts are sold in plastic or (better) clay containers of various sizes. Sheep-milk yogurt is richer and sweeter, scarcely requiring honey; cows-milk yogurt is tarter but more widely available. Side by side with these will be *krémes* (custards) and *ryzógala* (rice puddings) in one-serving plastic containers. **Feta** cheese is ubiquitous, often with up to a dozen varieties to choose from, made from goat-, sheep- or cow-milk, or varying proportions thereof. You're encouraged to taste before buying; this sampling advice goes for other indigenous cheeses as well, the most palatable of which are the expensive gruyère-type *graviéra*.

Despite EU membership, growing personal incomes and exotic tastes, Greece imports very little garden produce from abroad, aside from bananas, the odd pineapple and a few mangoes. **Fruit** in particular is relatively expensive and available only by season, though in the more cosmopolitan spots it is possible to find such things as avocados (the light-green Fuerte variety from Crete are excellent) for much of the year. Reliable picnic fruits include several types of cherries (June–July); *yiarmádhes*, a variety of giant peach available from August to mid-September (after which they go mealy and should be avoided); *krystália*, tiny, hard green pears that ripen a month or two later and are heavenly; *vaniliés*, orange- or red-fleshed plums whose season lasts from late August through

October; and the *himoniátiko* melon (called casava in North America) which appears in September, in its yellow, puckered skin with green flecks. Greece also has a burgeoning kiwi industry, and while the first crop in October coincides with the end of the tourist season, availability continues into the following May. Less portable, but succulent, are figs; there's a crop of small fruits in May, followed by larger ones in August and September. Salad **vegetables** are more reasonably priced; besides the famous, enormous tomatoes (June–Sept), there is a bewildering variety of springtime greens, including rocket, dill, enormous spring onions and lettuces. Useful expressions for shopping are *éna tétarto* (250g) and *misó kiló* (500g).

Traditional **snacks** can be one of the distinctive pleasures of Greek eating, though they are being increasingly edged out by an obsession with Western fast food at nationwide chains such as *Goody's* (above-average burgers, pasta and salad bar), *Everest* and *Grigoris Mikroyevmata* (assorted turnovers), *Roma Pizza* and *Theios Vanias* (baked pastries) – somewhat less insipid for being home-grown. However, independently produced kebabs (*souvlákia*) are widely available, and in most larger resorts and towns you'll find *yíros* – doner kebab with garnish in thick, doughy *píta* bread.

Other common snacks include *tyrópites* (cheese pies – the best are the *striftés* or *kouroú* if available) and *spanokópites* (spinach pies), which can usually be found at the baker's, as can *voutímata* (dark biscuits heavy on the molasses, cinnamon and butter). Pizza can be very good as well, sold *al metro* (by the piece).

Restaurants

Greek cuisine and **restaurants** are usually simple and straightforward, with no snobbery attached to eating out; most people do it regularly, and it's still affordable – typically €11–16 per person for a substantial (non-seafood) meal with a measure of house wine. But even if preparation is basic, you should expect it to be wholesome – Greeks are fussy about freshness and provenance, shunning prefried chips and frozen New Zealand chops. That said, there's a lot of

lazy cooking in resorts, where menus are dominated by bad pizza, spaghetti bolognese, chops and "tourist moussaká": a dish heavy with cheap potato slices, and nary a crumb of mince. There are, moreover, growing numbers of what the Greeks call "**koultouriárika**" restaurants, often pretentious attempts at Greek nouvelle cuisine with speciality wine lists, which tend to be long on airs and graces, and (at €20–30 a head) short on value. The exceptions which succeed have been singled out in the text.

In the absence of recommendations, a good strategy is to go where the Greeks go. And, despite increasing EU labour regulations limiting staff hours, they go late: 2 to 3.30pm for **lunch**, 9 to 11pm for **supper**. You can eat earlier, but you're likely to get indifferent service and doctored cuisine if you frequent establishments catering to the tourist schedule. One good omen is the waiter bringing a carafe of refrigerated water, unbidden, rather than pushing you to order bottled stuff.

Waiters are generally inclined to urge you into ordering more than you want, then bring things you haven't ordered. Although cash-register receipts are required in all establishments, these are often only for the grand total, and itemized **bills** will be in Greek script. With hard times for many popular destinations, bill-padding has become endemic, as a few unwarranted euro extra per party adds up by month's end; even without reading Greek, make sure that the number and cost of items tallies with what you ordered. Though printed menu prices are supposedly inclusive of all taxes and service, a small extra tip of 7–10 percent directly to the waiter is hugely appreciated.

Bread is generally assessed as part of the "cover" charge (€0.40–0.90 per person), so you have to pay for it even if (as so often) it's barely edible. Good bread is so remarkable as to warrant mention in the restaurant accounts. **Children** are always welcome, day or night, at family tavernas, and they are quickly socialized into the Greek routine of late hours. Kids are expected to be kids – playing tag around the tables – but at the same time they are not allowed to cramp adults' style.

Estiatória

The two basic types of restaurant are the **estiatório** and the taverna. Distinctions are slight, though the former is more commonly found in the largest island towns and tends to have the more complicated, oven-baked casserole dishes termed **mayireftá** (literally, "cooked"). With their long hours, old-fashioned-tradesmen's clientele and tiny profit margins, *estiatória* (sometimes known as *inomayiría*, "wine-and-cook-houses") are, alas, something of a vanishing breed. An *estiatório* will generally feature a variety of *mayireftá* as moussakas, macaroni pie, meat or game stews, stuffed tomatoes or peppers, the oily vegetable casseroles called *ladherá* and oven-baked meat and fish. Usually you go into the kitchen and point at the desired steam trays to choose these dishes.

Batches are cooked in the morning and then left to stand, which is why *mayireftá* food is often **lukewarm**. Greeks don't mind this (most actually believe that hot food is bad for you), and most such dishes are actually enhanced by being allowed to steep in their own juice. Similarly, you have to specify if you want your food with little or no oil (*horís ládhi*), but you will be considered a little strange since Greeks regard olive oil as essential to digestion. **Desserts** (*epidhórpia* in formal Greek) of the pudding-and-pie variety don't exist at *estiatória*, though yogurt is occasionally served. Fruit, however, is always available in season; watermelon (often on the house), melon and grapes are the summer standards. Autumn treats worth asking after include *kydhóni* or *akhládhi stó foúrno*, baked quince or pear with some sort of syrup or nut topping. Sometimes you may be offered a complimentary slice of sweet semolina halva (*smigdhalísios halvás*).

Tavernas and psistariés

Tavernas range from the glitzy and fashionable to rough-and-ready ones with seating under a reed canopy, behind a beach. Really primitive ones have a very limited (often unwritten) menu, but the more established will offer some of the main *mayireftá* dishes mentioned above, as well as standard taverna fare. This essentially means **mezédhes** (hors-d'oeuvres) or **orektiká** (appetizers)

and **tís óras** (meat and fish, fried or grilled to order). **Psistariés** or grill-houses serve spit-roasted lamb, pork or goat (generically termed *kondosoúvli*), grilled chicken or *kokorétsi* (grilled offal roulade). They will usually have a limited selection of *mezédhes* and salads (*salátes*), but no *mayireftá* at all.

Since the idea of courses is foreign to Greek cuisine, starters, main dishes and salads often arrive together unless you request otherwise. The best thing is to order a selection of *mezédhes* and salads to share, in true Greek fashion. Waiters encourage you to take the *horiátiki saláta* – the so-called Greek **salad**, including *féta* cheese – because it is the most expensive. If you only want tomato, or tomato and cucumber, ask for *domatosaláta* or *angourodomáta*. *Láhano-karóto* (cabbage-carrot) and *maroúli* (lettuce) are the typical winter and spring salads respectively.

The most common **mezédhes** are *tzatzíki* (yogurt, garlic and cucumber dip), *melitzanosaláta* (aubergine/eggplant dip), fried courgette/zucchini or aubergine/eggplant slices, *yígandes* (white haricot beans in vinaigrette or hot tomato sauce), *tyropitákia* or *spanakópites* (small cheese and spinach pies), *revythókeftedhes* or *pittaroúdhia* (chickpea patties similar to falafel), octopus salad and *mavromátika* (black-eyed peas).

Among **meats**, souvlaki and chops are reliable choices, often locally produced. In both cases, pork is usually better and cheaper than veal. The best souvlaki, though not always available, is lamb; more commonly encountered are rib chops called *païdhákia*, while roast lamb (*arní psitó*) is considered *estiatório* fare. *Keftédhes* (breadcrumbed meatballs), *biftékia* (similar, but meatier) and the spicy, coarse-grain sausages called *loukánika* are cheap and good. Chicken, especially grilled, is widely available but typically battery-farmed in Ípiros or on Évia. Other dishes worth trying are stewed goat (*gídha vrastí*) or baked goat (*katsíki stó foúrno*) – goat in general is a wonderfully healthy meat, typically free-range and undosed with antibiotics or hormones.

Fish and seafood

Seaside *psarotavérnes* offer **fish**, though for the inexperienced, ordering can be fraught with peril. Summer visitors get a relatively

Vegetarians

If you are **vegetarian**, you may be in for a hard time, and will often have to assemble a meal from various *mezédhes*. Even the excellent standbys of yoghurt with honey, *tzatzíki* and Greek salad begin to pall after a while, and many of the supposed "vegetable" dishes on menus are cooked in stock or have pieces of meat added to liven them up. Wholly or largely vegetarian restaurants, however, are slowly on the increase in touristy areas; they are highlighted in the Guide where appropriate.

poor choice of fish, most of it frozen, farmed or imported from Egypt and North Africa. Drag-net trawling is prohibited from the end of May until the beginning of October, when only lamp-lure, trident, "doughnut" trap and multihook line methods are allowed. During these warmer months, such few fish as are caught tend to be smaller and dry-textured, and are served with *ladholémono* (oil and lemon juice) sauce. Taverna owners often comply only minimally with the requirement to indicate when seafood is **frozen** (look for the abbreviation "kat.", "k" or just an asterisk on the Greek-language side of the menu).

Given these considerations, it's often best to set your sights on the **humbler**, seasonally migrating or perennially local species. The cheapest consistently available fish are *gópes* (bogue), *atherína* (sand smelts) and *marídhes* (picarel), the latter two eaten head and all. In the Dodecanese, *yermanós* (same as Australian leatherback) is a good frying fish which appears in spring; a more universal, inexpensive May–June treat is fresh, grilled or fried *bakaliáros* (hake), the classic UK fish-and-chip shop species. *Gávros* (anchovy) and *sardhélles* (sardines) are late summer fixtures, at their best in the northeast Aegean. In the north Aegean or around Pílio, *pandelís* or *sykiós* (in French *corb*) is caught in early summer, and highly esteemed since it's a rock-dweller, not a bottom feeder – and therefore a bit pricier. *Koliós* (mackerel) is excellent either grilled or baked in sauce. In autumn especially you may encounter *psarósoupa* (fish broth) or *kakaviá* (a bouillabaisse-like stew).

Less esteemed species tend to **cost** about €20–30 per kilo; choicer varieties of fish, such as red mullet, *tsipoúra* (gilt-head bream), seabass or *fangrí* (common bream), will be expensive if wild – €40–50 per kilo, depending on what the market will bear. If the price seems too good to be true, it's

almost certainly **farmed**. Prices are usually quoted by the kilo (less often by the portion; standard procedure is to go to the glass-fronted cooler and pick your specimen, then have it weighed (uncleaned) in your presence. If you are concerned that you may be later overcharged, which sometimes happens, have the amount confirmed orally or on a slip of paper.

Cheaper **seafood** (*thalassiná*) such as fried baby squid (usually frozen) and octopus are a summer staple of most seaside tavernas, and often mussels, cockles and small prawns will be on offer at reasonable prices.

Wines

All sorts of eateries will offer you a choice of bottled **wines**, and many still have their own house variety: kept in barrels, sold in bulk by the quarter-, half- or full litre, and served either in glass flagons or the brightly coloured tin "monkey-cups" called *kantária*. You should ask whether they have wine *varelísio* (barrelled) or *hýma* (in bulk). Per-litre prices depend on locale and quality, ranging from €5 (Ikaría) to €9 or even €10 (Corfu, Rhodes), with smaller measures priced (more or less) proportionately. Non-resinated wine is almost always more than decent; if in doubt, order a bottle or can of soda water, which can render even the sourest wine drinkable when used to dilute it. **Retsina** – pine-resinated wine, a slightly acquired taste – is also available straight from the barrel, though the bottled brands Yeoryiadhi from Thessaloníki, Liokri from Ahaïa, Malamatina from central Greece, and that prepared by the co-ops on Sámos and Límnos are all quaffable and likely to be more consistent in quality.

Among the **bottled wines** available **nationwide**, Cambas Attikos, Zítsa and the Rhodian CAIR products (especially the Moulin and 2400 range) are good, inexpensive whites, while Boutari Naoussa and Kourtakis

Apelia are decent, mid-range reds. If you want a better but still moderately priced red, go for the Merlot of either Boutari and Tsantali, or Averof Katoï from Epirus.

If you're travelling around **wine-producing islands**, however, you may as well choose **local bottlings**; the best available guides to the emerging Greek domaines and vintners are Nico Manessis' *The Illustrated Greek Wine Book* or Konstantinos Lazarakis' *The Wines of Greece*. Almost anything produced on Límnos is decent; the Alexandrine muscat is now used for whites, the local *límnio* grape for reds and rosés. Thíra, another volcanic island, has a number of premium white products such as Ktima Arghyrou and Boutari Nykhteri, and the Gentilini Robola white of Kefalloniá is justly esteemed. Páros (Moraïtis), Náxos and Ikaria (Ktima Karimali Ikariotikos) all have acceptable local vintages, while Crete is now beginning to have labels superior to the bog-standard Logado, such as Economou (Sitía) and Lyrarakis (Iráklion). On Rhodes, Alexandhris products from Émbonas are well thought of, as is the Emery label with its Villaré white, and products of the Triandafyllou winery near Ialyssós.

Curiously, island red wines are almost uniformly mediocre, except for Hatzemmanouil from Kos; in this respect you're better off choosing **reds from the mainland**. Carras from Halkidhikí does the excellent Porto Carras, while Ktima Tselepou offers a very palatable Cabernet-Merlot blend. Andonopoulou (Pátra, including an organic line), Ktima Papaïoannou Nemea (Peloponnese), and Tsantali Rapsani (Thessaly) are all superb, velvety reds – and likely to be found only in the better *koultouriárika* tavernas or *káves* (bottle shops). Antonopoulos, Tselepos (Mantinía domaine), Spyropoulos (again Mantinía) and Papaïoannou also do excellent **mainland whites**, especially the Spyropoulos Orino Mantinia, sometimes found organically produced.

Other **premium microwineries** on the mainland whose products have long been fashionable, in both red and white, include the vastly overrated Hatzimihali (Atalánti, central Greece); the outstanding Dhiamandakou (near Náoussa, red and white), Athanasiadhi (central Greece), Skouras (Argolid) and the two rival Lazaridhi vintners (Dhráma,

east Macedonia), especially their superb Merlots. For any of these you can expect to pay €8–11 per bottle in a shop, double that at a taverna.

Last but not least, CAIR on Rhodes makes its very own **"champagne"** ("naturally sparkling wine fermented en boteille", says the label), in both brut and demi-sec versions. It's not Moët & Chandon quality by any means, but at less than €6 per bottle, who's complaining?

Cafés, cake shops and bars

A venerable Greek institution, likely to survive the onslaught of mass global culture, is the **kafenío**, found in every town, village and hamlet in the country. In addition, you'll come across **ouzerís**, **zaharoplastía** (Greek patisseries) and **barákia**.

The kafenío

The **kafenío** (plural *kafenía*) is the traditional Greek coffeehouse or café. Although its main business is "Greek" (Middle Eastern) coffee – prepared *skéto* or *pikró* (unsweetened), *métrio* (medium) or *glykó* (sweet) – it also serves spirits such as ouzo (see p.70), brandy (usually Metaxa or Botrys brand, in three grades), beer, the sage-based tea known variously as *alisfakiá* (isles) or *tsáï vounoú* (mainland), soft drinks and juices. Another refreshing drink sold in cafés is *kafés frappé*, iced instant coffee with or without milk and sugar – uniquely Greek despite its French-sounding name. Like Greek coffee, it is always accompanied by a welcome glass of cold water. One quality fizzy soft drink to single out is the Vólos-based Epsa, with its Orangina-like bottles and high juice content. A refreshing curiosity – confined to Corfu and Paxí – is *tsitsibýra* (ginger beer), a holdover from the nineteenth-century British occupation of the Ionian islands; cloudy, greyish-white and fizzy, it tastes vaguely of lemon and the sour beginnings of fermentation.

Usually the only **edibles** available at kafenia are "spoon sweets" or *glyká koutalioú* (sticky, syrupy preserves of quince, grape, fig, citrus fruit or cherry) and the traditional, now-vanishing *ipovrýhio*, a piece of mastic submerged in a glass of water like a submarine – which is what the word means in Greek.

Like tavernas, *kafenía* range from the plastic, chrome and sophisticated to the old-fashioned, spit-on-the-floor or mock-retro variety, with marble or brightly painted metal tables and straw-bottomed chairs. They still form the pivot of life in remoter villages, and you get the impression that many men spend most of their waking hours there. Greek women are rarely to be seen in the more traditional places; even in holiday resorts, you will find that there is at least one coffeehouse that the local men have reserved for themselves.

Some *kafenía* close at siesta time, but many remain open from early in the morning until late at night. The chief summer socializing time is 6–8pm, immediately after the afternoon nap. This is the time to take your pre-dinner ouzo, as the sun begins to sink and the air cools down.

Ouzo, tsípouro, mezédhes, ouzerís and mezedhopolía

Ouzo, *tsípouro* (confined to Thássos and the Sporades) and *tsikoudhiá* (Crete) are simple spirits of up to 48 percent alcohol, distilled from grape-mash residue left over from wine-making, and then usually flavoured with herbs such as anise or fennel. There are nearly thirty name brands of ouzo or *tsípouro*, with the best reckoned to be from Lésvos and Sámos islands, or Zítsa and Týrnavos on the mainland.

When you order, you will be served two glasses: one with the ouzo, and one full of water to be tipped into your ouzo until it turns a milky white. You can drink it straight, but the strong, burning taste is hardly refreshing if you do. It is also the norm to add **ice cubes**, a bowl of which will be provided upon request. The next measure up from a glass is a *karafáki* – a deceptively small 200-millilitre vial, and the favourite means of delivery for *tsípouro* – which will very rapidly render you legless if you don't alternate tippling with snacks. A much smoother, unflavoured variant of ouzo is **soúma**, found chiefly on Rhodes and Sámos, but in theory anywhere grapes are grown. The smoothness is deceptive – as with *tsípouro*, two or three glasses of it and you had better not

have any other firm plans for the afternoon.

Formerly every ouzo you ordered was automatically accompanied by a small plate of **mezédhes** on the house: bits of cheese, cucumber, tomato, a few olives, sometimes octopus or even a couple of small fish. Nowadays "*ouzomezés*" is a separate, more expensive option on the price list. Often, however, they are not featured on any formal menu, but if you order a *karafáki* you will automatically be offered a small selection of snacks.

One kind of drinking establishment, found in the better resorts and select neighbourhoods of the larger islands and towns, specializes in ouzo and *mezédhes*. These are called **ouzerí** (same in the Greek plural, but we've added 's' through the Guide) or *tsipourádhika* (plural) wherever vacationers from the north mainland congregate. In some towns you may also come across *mezedhopolía*, basically a bigger, more upmarket kind of ouzerí. Ouzerís, *tsipourádhika* and *mezedhopolía* are well worth trying for the marvellous variety of *mezédhes* they serve (though some mediocre tavernas have counterfeited the name). At the genuine article, several plates of *mezédhes* plus drinks will effectively substitute for a more involved meal at a taverna (though it usually works out more expensive if you have a healthy appetite). Faced with an often bewilderingly varied menu, you might opt for the *pikilía* (medley, assortment) available in several sizes, the largest and most expensive one usually heavy on the seafood. At other ouzerís or *tsipourádhika* the language barrier may be overcome by the waiter wielding an enormous tray laden with all the current cold offerings – you pick the ones you like the look of.

Sweets and coffee

The **zaharoplastío**, a cross between café and patisserie, serves coffee, a limited range of alcohol, yogurt with honey and sticky cakes. The better establishments offer an amazing variety of pastries, cream-and-chocolate confections, honey-soaked Greco–Turkish sweets like *baklavás*, *kataïfi* (honey-drenched "shredded wheat"), *loukoumádhes* (deep-fried batter puffs dusted with cinnamon and dipped in syrup), *galak-*

toboúreko (custard pie) and so on. If you want a stronger slant towards the dairy products and away from the pure sugar, seek out a **galaktopolío**, where you'll often find *ryzógalo* (rice pudding), *kréma* (custard) and locally made *yiaoúrti* (yogurt), best if it's *próvio* (from sheep's milk). Both *zaharoplastía* and *galaktopolía* are more family-oriented places than a *kafenío*.

Ice cream, sold principally at the *gelaterie*, which have swept across Greece of late (*Dhodhoni* is the posh home-grown chain, Haägen-Dazs is the competition), can be very good and almost indistinguishable from Italian prototypes. A scoop (*baláki*) costs €1.10–1.50; you'll be asked if you want it in a cup (*kypelláki*) or a cone (*konáki*), and whether you want toppings like *santí* (whipped cream) or nuts. By contrast, the mass-produced brands like Delta or Evga are pretty unremarkable, with the exception of Skandalo and Nirvana labels.

"Nes"(café) has become the generic term for all instant **coffee**, regardless of brand; it's generally pretty vile, and since the mid-1990s there's been a nationwide reaction against it. Even in the smallest island town or resort there will be at least one trendy café that does a range of foreign-style coffees – filter, dubbed *fíltros* or *gallikós* (French); cappuccino; and espresso – at overseas prices. A more enticing, recent innovation is *freddoccino*, a cappuccino-based alternative to the traditional cold frappé. Outside of the largest towns, properly made versions of these drinks will be harder to find – and may come from instant packets.

Bars, beer and water

Bars (*barákia* in the plural) are found all over Greece. They range from clones of Parisian cafés or Spanish bodegas to seaside cocktail bars, with music or TV running all day. At their most sophisticated, however, they are well-executed theme venues in ex-industrial premises or Neoclassical houses, with Western (currently techno, dub or ambient) soundtracks. Although we give recommendations in the Guide, most Greek bars have a half-life of about one year; the best way to find the current hot spots, especially if they're more club than bar, is to watch for fly-posters in the neighbourhood, advertising bar-hosted events.

Bar drinks are invariably more expensive than in a café – count on €5–8. Bars are, however, most likely to stock a range of **beers**, mostly foreign labels made locally under licence at just a handful of breweries on the central mainland. **Local brews** include Alfa, a hoppy lager brewed in Athens that's the best and most consistent of the mainstream labels; Mythos, a mild lager in a green bottle, put out by the Boutari vintners; Veryina, brewed in Komotiní and common in the northeastern mainland and isles; Pils Hellas, a sharp pilsner; and last but not least, the resurrected Fix, for years until its demise in 1980 Greece's only beer. Greece also has a **microbrewery**, the Athens-based Craft: they make a tasty pilsner and an amber lager, but distribution is not wide.

Kronenberg 1664 and Kaiser are two of the more common quality **foreign-licence** varieties, with the latter available in both light and dark. Bland, inoffensive Amstel is the standard cheapie, claimed by some Dutch to be better than the one available in Holland; Amstel also makes a very palatable, strong (seven percent) **bock**. Heineken, still referred to as a "*prássini*" by bar and taverna staff after its green bottle, despite the advent of Mythos, is too sharp for many. Genuinely imported German beers, such as Bitburger, Fisher and Warsteiner (plus a few British ones), are on offer in the fancier resorts.

Mineral water, mostly still, typically comes as half-litre and one-and-a-half litre plastic bottles. The ubiquitous Loutraki brand is not esteemed by the Greeks themselves, who prefer various brands from Crete and Epirus. In the better tavernas there has been a backlash against plastic bottles – which constitute a tremendous litter problem – and you can now get it in one-litre glass bottles. Souroti is the principal brand of sparkling (*aerioúho* in Greek) water, in small bottles, though Tuborg club soda is ubiquitous.

Communications

Greece's postal system is adequate, especially for outgoing mail. Service provided by OTE (Organismós Tiliepikinoníon tís Elládhos, the telecoms entity) is improving drastically under the twin threats of privatization and competition from thriving local mobile networks. All land-line exchanges are digital, and you should have few problems reaching any number from either overseas or within Greece. Mobile phone users are well looked after, with a signal even in the Athens metro. At least one Internet facility is found in any major towns or resort, while most business-class hotels will have Internet access from the room, and many resort-class hotels have a phone socket for plugging in your laptop.

Postal services

Post offices, recognizable by their stylized Hermes-head on a blue background, are open Monday to Friday from 7.30am to 2pm, though certain main branches have hours until the evening and on Saturday morning. **Airmail letters** take three to seven days to reach the rest of Europe, five to twelve days to get to North America, and a bit longer for Australia and New Zealand. Generally, the larger the island (and the planes serving its airport), the quicker the service. Postal rates for up to 20g are a uniform €0.65 to all overseas destinations. For a modest fee (about €3) you can shave a day or two off delivery time to any destination by using the **express service** (*katepígonda*). **Registered** (*systiméno*) delivery is also available for a similar amount, but proves quite slow unless coupled with express service. For a simple letter or card, a stamp (*grammatósimo*) can also be purchased at an authorized postal agency (usually a stationery store).

Parcels should (and often can) only be handled in the main provincial or county capitals; this way, your bundle will be in Athens, and on an international flight, within a day or so. For non-EU/EEA destinations, always present your box open for inspection, and come prepared with tape and scissors – most post offices will sell cardboard boxes, but nothing to actually close the package. An array of services are available: air parcel (fast and expensive), surface-air lift (a couple of weeks slower but much cheaper), insured, and proof of delivery among others.

Ordinary **post boxes** are bright yellow, express boxes dark red, but it's best to use only those by the door of an actual post office, since days may pass between collections at other street-corner or wall-mounted boxes. If you are confronted by two slots, "ESOTERIKÓ" is for domestic mail, "EXO-TERIKÓ" for overseas. Often there are more: one box or slot for mail into Athens and suburbs, one for your local province, one for "other" parts of Greece, and one for overseas; if in doubt, ask someone.

The **poste-restante** system is reasonably efficient, especially at the post offices of larger towns. Mail should be clearly addressed and marked "poste restante", with your surname underlined, to the main post office of whichever town you choose. It will be held for a month and you'll need your passport to collect it.

Phones

During 2002, all Greek phone numbers changed to a system resembling the French one, in which you are obliged to dial all ten numbers of a subscriber, including the former area code, wherever you may be. All land lines begin with 2, all mobiles begin with 6.

Call boxes, poorly maintained and invariably sited at the noisiest street corners, work only with phonecards (*tilekártes*); these come in various denominations starting at €4, available from kiosks and newsagents. Despite numbers hopefully scribbled on the appropriate tabs, call boxes cannot be rung back; however, green, **countertop cardphones** kept by many hotels can be rung.

Useful phone codes and numbers

Phoning abroad from Greece
Dial the country code (given below) + area code (minus any initial 0) + number
Australia ☏0061
New Zealand ☏0064
Canada ☏001
UK ☏0044
Ireland ☏00353
USA ☏001

Specialty Greek phone prefixes
Local call rate ☏0801
Toll-free/Freefone ☏0800

Useful Greek telephone numbers
Ambulance ☏166
Police/Emergency ☏100
Fire brigade, urban ☏199
Speaking clock ☏141
Forest fire reporting ☏191
Tourist police ☏171 (Athens); ☏210 171 (elsewhere)
Operator ☏132 (Domestic)
Operator ☏139 (International)

Other options for local calls include **counter coin-op phones** in bars, *kafenía* and hotel lobbies; these take small euro coins and also can be rung back as a rule. Most of them are made in northern Europe and bear instructions in English.

Local or intercity calls to land lines are cheap on OTE *tilekártes*, but if you plan on making lots of international calls, you'll want a **calling card**, all of which involve calling a free access number from either a phone box or fixed line (not a mobile) and then entering a twelve-digit code. OTE has its own scheme, Khronokarta, but competitors generally prove cheaper. Always tell the card vendor where you intend to call, to get the card best suited for you (Ya!-Q for the UK). Avoid making calls **from hotel rooms**, as a minimum one-hundred-percent surcharge will be slapped on.

Mobile phones

Mobile phones are an essential fashion accessory in Greece – in a population of roughly 11 million, there are claimed to be nearly 7 million mobile handsets in use. Four **networks** operate at present: Vodafone, TIM, Cosmote and Q-Telecom. Calling any

of their numbers from Britain, you will find that costs are exactly the same as calling a fixed phone, though of course such numbers are pricey when rung locally. **Coverage** countrywide is good, though there are a few "dead" zones in the mountains, or on really remote islets. Contract-free plans are heavily promoted in Greece, and if you're here for more than a week or so, buying a Greek **pay-as-you-go** SIM card (for €15–20) from any of the numerous mobile phone outlets will pay for itself very quickly, and you can re-use the same number on your next visit. Top-up calling cards – starting from €8–10 depending on the network – are available at all *períptera*. UK providers may tell you that another SIM can't be fitted without a hefty surcharge to unlock your phone, but you are legally entitled to the unblock code from the manufacturer after (usually) six months of use. Otherwise, have a mobile shop in Greece unblock the phone for a small charge with a simple computer procedure. North American users will only be able to use tri-band phones in Greece. Roaming with your home provider will land you with outrageous charges of over €1 equivalent per minute minimum (UK providers – far more for North American ones), no matter where you're calling, plus almost as much to have incoming calls forwarded to you. Text messaging is a far cheaper alternative if you choose not to get a Greek SIM.

Email and Internet

Internet cafés are the easiest places to check web-based email accounts; locations are noted throughout the Guide. Rates tend to be about €6 per hour maximum, often less, with shorter increments always available. Few are smoke-free – ones that host many young computer gamers are particularly bad – so check the environment and the speed of the machines before you settle

down to an hour or so of email-checking.

If you are travelling with your own **laptop**, you may well be able to roam in Greece depending on what agreement your home ISP has with any Greek partners. Check with your ISP, and get the local dial-up number, before you leave. **Piggybacking charges** tend to be fairly high, but for a modest number of minutes per day, still work out much less than patronizing an Internet café. Alternatively, you can take out a **temporary Internet account** with one of the half-dozen Greek ISPs (minimum period one month, cost €10–14/month plus very modest hourly charges).

The media

Although the Greek press and airwaves have been ostensibly free since the fall of the colonels' dictatorship in 1974, nobody would ever propose the Greek media as a paradigm of responsible or objective journalism. Many papers are sensational, state-run radio and TV often biased in favour of the ruling party, and private channels imitative of the worst American programming.

British **newspapers** are fairly widely available in Greece at a cost of €1.75–2.50 for dailies, or €4 for Sunday editions. You'll find one-to-two-day-old copies (same day by noon in Athens) of *The Times*, the *Telegraph*, the *Independent* and the *Guardian*'s European edition, plus a few of the tabloids, in all the resorts as well as in major towns and airports. American and international alternatives include the turgid *USA Today* and the more readable *International Herald Tribune*, the latter including as a major bonus a free though abridged English translation of the respected Greek daily *Kathimerini* (online at Ⓦwww.ekathimerini.com; also see opposite). Among foreign **magazines**, *Time* and *Newsweek* are widely available.

There are few surviving **locally produced** English-language magazines or papers. Glossy *Odyssey* (€5) is produced every other month by and for wealthy diaspora

Greeks; it has excellent book reviews in particular. The main English-language newspaper is the *Athens News* (weekly every Friday, online at Ⓦwww.athensnews.gr; €2) in colour with good features and Balkan news, plus entertainment and arts listings, available in most resorts.

Greek publications

Many papers have ties (including funding) with specific **political groups**, with only a bare handful of quality dailies. Among these, the **centrist** *Kathimerini* – whose former proprietress Helen Vlahos attained heroic status for her defiance of the junta – approaches the standards of France's *Le Monde*, while *Eleftherotypia*, especially its Sunday edition, is the local equivalent of the *Guardian*/the *Observer*. *Avriani* and *To Vima* (with its excellent *Vimagazino* supplement) stake out pro-PASOK territory, whilst *Ta Nea* is a popular, MOR tabloid, much loved for its extensive small ads and its Saturday magazine, *Takhydhromos*. On the far **Left**, *Avyi* is the Eurocommunist/Synaspismós forum with literary leanings, while *Rizospastis* acts as the organ of the KKE (unreconstructed Communists). *Ethnos* became notorious some years back for receiving covert funding from the KGB to act as a disinformation bulletin. At the other end of the political spectrum, *Apoyevmatini* generally supports the **centre-right** Néa Dhimokratía party, while *Estia's* no-photo format and reactionary politics are both stuck somewhere at the beginning of the twentieth century.

Among **magazines** that are not merely translations of overseas titles, *To Pondiki* (The Mouse) is a satirical weekly review in the same vein as Britain's *Private Eye*; its famous covers are spot-on and accessible to anyone with minimal Greek. More specialized niches are occupied by low-circulation titles such as *Adhesmeftos Typos* (a slightly rightist, muckraking journal) and *Andi*, an intelligent analytical fortnightly going since 1974 (its first issue confiscated by the junta), with reviews and cultural critiques, somewhat in the mould of Britain's *New Statesman*.

Radio

Greek **radio** music programmes are always accessible (if variable in quality), and since abolition of the government's monopoly of wavelengths, regional stations have mushroomed; indeed the airwaves are positively cluttered as every island town sets up its own studio and transmitter. The two state-run channels are ER1 (a mix of news, talk and popular music) and ER2 (strictly popular music).

On heavily touristed islands like Rhodes, Corfu and Crete, there will usually be at least one station on the FM band trying its luck at English-moderated programming by and for foreigners. The Turkish state radio's Third Channel is also widely (if unpatriotically) listened to on east Aegean islands for its classical, jazz and blues programmes. The **BBC World Service** broadcasts on short wave throughout Greece; 6.18, 9.41, 15.07 and 12.09 MHz are the most common frequencies. However, short-wave services are being phased out in many parts of the world, so consult Ⓦ www.bbc.co.uk/worldservice, for current frequencies.

Television

Greece's state-funded **TV stations**, ET1, NET and (from Thessaloníki) ET3, nowadays lag behind private channels – Antenna, Star, Alpha, Alter and Makedonia TV – in the ratings, though not necessarily in quality of offerings. Programming tends to be a mix of soaps (especially Italian, Spanish and Latin American), game shows, movies and sports, with lately a leavening of natural history documentaries, costume dramas and today-in-history features. All foreign films and serials are broadcast in their original language, with Greek subtitles. Most private channels operate around the clock; public stations broadcast from around 5.30am until 3am. Numerous **cable and satellite** channels are received, including CNN, MTV, Filmnet, BBC World, French TV5 and Italian Rai Due. The range available depends on the area (and hotel) you're in.

Opening hours, public holidays and visitor attractions

It's difficult to generalize about Greek opening hours, especially museum and site schedules, which change constantly. The traditional timetable starts with shops opening between 8.30 and 9am, then runs through until lunchtime, when there is a long break for the hottest part of the day. Most places, except banks and government offices, may then reopen in the mid- to late afternoon. Tourist areas tend to adopt a more northern European timetable, with shops, travel agencies and offices, as well as the most important archeological sites and museums, usually open throughout the day.

Business and shopping hours

Private businesses, or anyone providing a service, frequently operate a straight 9am-to-5 or 6pm schedule. If someone is actually selling something, then they are more likely to follow a split shift as detailed below.

Shopping hours during the hottest months are theoretically Monday, Wednesday and Saturday from approximately 9am to 2.30pm, and Tuesday, Thursday and Friday from 8.30am to 2pm and 6 to 9pm. During the cooler months the morning schedule shifts slightly forward, the evening session a half or even a full hour back. There are so many exceptions to rules by virtue of holidays and professional idiosyncrasy that you can't count on getting anything done except from Monday to Friday, 9.30am and 1pm. **Delis** and **butchers** are not allowed to sell fresh meat during summer afternoons (though some flout this rule); similarly **fishmongers** are only open in the morning until they sell out (usually by noon), as are **pharmacies**, which additionally are shut on Saturday (except for the duty pharmacist).

Travel agencies at the busiest resorts are open continuously from about 9am to 10pm Monday to Saturday, with some Sunday hours as well.

Public holidays

January 1
January 6
March 25
First Monday of Lent (48 days before Easter; see below)
Good Friday (variable April/May; see below)
Easter Sunday (variable April/May; see below)
May 1
Pentecost or Whit Monday (50 days after Easter; see below)
August 15
October 28
December 25 and 26

Variable religious feasts

Lenten Monday	Easter Sunday	Whit Monday
2006 March 6	2006 April 23	2006 June 12
2007 February 19	2007 April 8	2007 May 28
2008 March 10	2008 April 27	2008 June 16

Most **government agencies** are open to the public on weekdays from 8am to 2pm. In general, however, you'd be optimistic to show up after 1pm expecting to be served the same day, as queues can be long, and many services cease at that hour.

All of the above will be regularly thrown out of sync by the numerous public holidays and festivals – or the equally numerous strikes, which can be general or profession-specific. The most important holidays, when almost everything will be closed, are listed opposite.

Ancient sites and monasteries

All the major **ancient sites** are fenced off and, like most **museums**, charge **admission fees** ranging from €2 to €12, with an average fee of around €3. Entrance to all state-run sites and museums is **free** on Sundays and public holidays from November to March, although they will be shut on the dates of public holidays shown opposite.

Opening hours vary between the major **ancient sites**. As far as possible, individual times are quoted in the text, but bear in mind that these change with exasperating frequency, and at smaller sites may be subject to the whim of a local site guard. Unless specified, the times quoted are generally summer hours, in effect from around late May to the end of September. Reckon on similar days but later opening and earlier closing in winter. Usually, the **last admission ticket** is sold fifteen to twenty minutes before the cited closing time.

Along with your ticket most sites and museums will provide a little colour **folding pamphlet** prepared by the Tamío Arheoloyikón Porón (Archeological Receipts Fund); they usually include an accurate if potted history and site or gallery plan, and we've found them to be uniformly excellent, in stark contrast to the often miserable labelling of the sites or galleries themselves. Serious students will therefore want to invest in **site guides** or **museum catalogues**, which have often been expertly compiled by the excavating archeologists or curators.

Monasteries are generally open from approximately 9am to 1pm and 5 to 8pm (3.30 to 6.30pm in winter) for limited visits. Most impose a fairly strict **dress code** for visitors: no shorts on either sex, with women expected to cover their arms and wear skirts; the necessary wraps are sometimes provided on the spot.

It's free to take **photos** of open-air sites, though museum photography and the use of videos or tripods anywhere requires an extra fee and written permit. This usually has to be arranged in writing from the nearest Department of Antiquities (Eforía Arheotíton). It's also worth knowing that Classical studies students can get a free annual pass to all Greek museums and sites by presenting themselves at the office on the rear corner (Tossítsa/Bouboulínas) of the National Archeological Museum in Athens – take documentation and two passport-sized photographs.

Festivals and cultural events

Many of the big Greek popular festivals have a religious basis, so they're observed in accordance with the Orthodox calendar. Give or take a few saints, this is similar to the regular Catholic liturgical year, except for Easter, which can fall as many as four (but usually one or two) weeks to either side of the Western festival – though in 2001 and again in 2004 the two coincided (usually a rare occurrence). Summer cultural festivals are tied firmly to the weather and tourist traffic, with most resorts laying on events at atmospheric outdoor venues from July to September.

Easter

Easter is by far the most important festival of the Greek year – infinitely more so than Christmas – and taken much more seriously than it is anywhere in western Europe, aside from Spain. From Palm Sunday until the following Monday, the state radio and TV networks are given over primarily to religious programmes.

The **festival** is an excellent time to be in Greece, both for its beautiful religious ceremonies and for the days of feasting and celebration that follow, though you'll need to book accommodation months in advance. The mountainous island of **Ídhra** with its alleged 360 churches and monasteries is the prime Easter resort; other famous Easter celebrations are held at Corfu, Pyrgí on Híos, Ólymbos on Kárpathos and St John's monastery on Pátmos, where on Holy Thursday the abbot washes the feet of twelve monks in the village square, in imitation of Christ doing the same for his disciples.

The first great public ceremony takes place on **Good Friday** evening as the Deposition from the Cross is lamented in church. At dusk the Epitáfios, Christ's funeral bier (in large villages there will be more than one, from each church), lavishly decorated by the women of the parish leaves the sanctuary and is paraded solemnly through the streets. On Ídhra, the Epitáfios of Ayíou Ioánni (the fishermen's parish) is taken into the water at Kamíni to bless the boats and calm the sea; on Sámos, the various biers are taken to the village cemeteries to bless the dead. In Kérkyra Town, the Epitáfios procession takes place on Saturday morning, while special crockery rains down from upper storeys of houses to banish the evil. In many places, Crete especially, this is accompanied by the burning of effigies of Judas Iscariot.

Late **Saturday** evening sees the climax in a majestic *Anástasis* mass to celebrate Christ's triumphant return. At the stroke of midnight all the lights in every crowded church are extinguished, and the congregation plunged into the darkness which envelops Christ as He passes through the underworld. Then there's a faint glimmer of light behind the altar screen before the priest appears, holding aloft a lighted taper and chanting *Avtó to Fós . . .* ("This is the Light of the World"). Stepping down to the level of the parishioners, he touches his flame to the unlit candles of the nearest worshippers, intoning *Dévte, lévete Fós* ("Come, take the Light"). Those at the front of the congregation and on the aisles do the same for their neighbours until the entire church – and the outer courtyard, standing room only for latecomers – is ablaze with burning candles and the miracle reaffirmed.

The traditional greeting, as dynamite explodes all around you in the street, is *Khristós Anésti* ("Christ is risen"), to which the response is *Alithós Anésti* ("Truly He is risen"). In the week up to Easter Sunday you should wish people *Kaló Páskha* ("Happy Easter"); on or after the day, you say *Khrónia Pollá* ("Many happy returns").

If you have the inclination to listen, the chanting from midnight to 2am in the half-empty churches is actually the most beautiful part of the Resurrection liturgy, unmarred by high explosives. Most worshippers, however, have long since taken the burning **candles** home through the streets; they are said to bring good fortune to the house if they arrive still burning. On reaching the front door it is common practice to make the sign of the cross on the lintel with the flame, leaving a black smudge visible for the rest of the year. The forty-day **Lenten fast** from all animal products – still observed by the devout and in rural areas – is traditionally broken early on Sunday morning with a meal of *mayerítsa*, a soup made from lamb tripe, rice, dill and lemon. The rest of the lamb will be roasted on a spit for Sunday lunch, and festivities often take place through the rest of the day.

The Greek equivalent of **Easter eggs** are hard-boiled eggs (painted red on Holy Thursday), which are baked into twisted, sweet bread-loaves (*tsourékia*) or distributed on Easter Sunday. People rap their eggs against their friends' eggs, and the owner of the last uncracked egg is considered lucky. In many remote locales, the most revered local icons spend the week after Easter in a slow procession around the district or icon, "visiting" each church (and sometimes each house) to bring luck.

The festival calendar

Most of the other Greek festivals are celebrations of one or other of a multitude of **saints**; the most important are detailed below, though there are literally scores of **local festivals**, or *paniyíria*, celebrating the patron saint of every parish church. With hundreds of possible name-saints' days (calendars list two or three, often obscure, for each day) you're unlikely to travel around Greece for long without stumbling on some sort of observance – sometimes right across the town or island, otherwise quiet, local and consisting of little more than a special liturgy and banners adorning the chapel in question. Saints' days are also celebrated as **name days**; if you learn that it's an acquaintance's name day, you wish them *Khrónia Pollá* ("Many years", as in "Many happy returns"). Also listed are a few more pagan or secular holidays, most enjoyable of which are the pre-Lenten carnivals.

It is important to remember the concept of the *paramoní*, or **eve of the festival**. Most of the events listed below are celebrated on the night before, so if you show up on the morning of the date given you will very probably have missed any music, dancing or drinking.

January 1
New Year's Day (*Protokhroniá*) in Greece is the feast day of Áyios Vassílios (St Basil). The traditional New Year greeting is "*Kalí Khroniá*".

January 6
Epiphany (*Theofánia*, or *Tón Fóton*), when the *kalikántzari* (hobgoblins) who run riot on earth during the twelve days of Christmas are rebanished to the netherworld by various rites of the Church. The most important of these is the blessing of baptismal fonts and all outdoor bodies of water. At seaside or riverside locations, the priest traditionally casts a crucifix into the deep, with local youths competing for the privilege of recovering it.

Pre-Lenten carnivals
These – known in Greek as **Apokriátika** – span three weeks, climaxing during the seventh weekend before Easter. *Katharí Dheftéra* (Lenten Monday) of the first carnival week is always 48 days before Easter Sunday. The Ionian islands, especially Kefalloniá, are also good for carnival, as is Ayiássos on Lésvos, while the outrageous Goat Dance is enacted on Skýros in the Sporades.

March 25
Independence Day and the feast of the **Annunciation** (*Evangelismós* in Greek) is both a religious and a national holiday, with, on the one hand, military parades and dancing to celebrate the beginning of the revolt against Ottoman rule in 1821, and on the other church services to honour the news given to Mary that she was to become the Mother of Christ. There are major festivities on Tínos, Ídhra (Hydra) and any locality with a monastery or church named Evangelístria or Evangelismós.

April 23
The feast of **Áyios Yeóryios** (St George), the patron of shepherds, is a big rural celebration, with much feasting and dancing at associated shrines and towns. If April 23 falls before Easter, ie during Lent, the festivities are postponed until the Monday after Easter.

May 1
May Day (*Protomayiá*) is the great urban holiday when townspeople traditionally make for the countryside to picnic, returning with bunches of wild flowers. Wreaths are hung on their doorways or balconies until they are burnt in bonfires on St John's eve (June 23). There are also large demonstrations by the Left, claiming the *Ergatikí Protomayiá* (Working-Class First of May) as their own.

May 21
The feast of **Áyios Konstandínos** (St Constantine) and his mother, **Ayía Eléni** (St Helen), the first pro-Orthodox Byzantine rulers. It's widely celebrated as the name day for two of the more popular Christian names in Greece.

May–June
The Monday of **Áyio Pnévma** (the Holy Spirit, Whit Monday in UK) marks the descent of same to the assembled disciples, fifty days after Easter. Usually a modest liturgy is celebrated at rural chapels of the Holy Spirit, gaily decked out with pennants; at Pagóndas village on Sámos, there's a musical festival.

June 29–30
The joint feast of **Áyios Pétros** and **Áyios Pávlos** (SS Peter and Paul), two of the more widely celebrated name days, is on the 29th. Celebrations often run together with that for the Gathering of (all) the **Holy Apostles** (Áyii Apóstoli), on the 30th.

July 17
The feast of Ayía Marína: a big event in rural areas, as she's an important protector of crops. Ayía Marína village on Kássos will be en fête, as will countless small mainland villages. Between mid-July and mid-September there are religious holidays every few days, especially in the rural areas, and what with these, the summer heat and a mass exodus from the big cities, ordinary business slows or even halts.

July 20
The feast of Profítis Ilías (the Prophet Elijah) is widely celebrated at the countless hill- or mountain-top shrines of Profítis Ilías – nowadays, as on Sámos, with a 4WD trip up to the mountain of the same name with sound systems cranked up and barbecue spits turning on arrival.

July 26
Ayía Paraskeví is celebrated in parishes or villages bearing that name.

August 6
Metamórfosis toú Sotíros (Transfiguration of the Saviour) provides another excuse for celebrations, particularly at Khristós Ráhon village on Ikaría, and at Plátanos on Léros. On Hálki the date is marked by messy food fights with flour, eggs and squid ink.

August 15
Apokímisis tís Panayías (Assumption or Dormition of the Blessed Virgin Mary). This is the day when people traditionally return to their home village, and in most places there will be no accommodation available on any terms. Even some Greeks will resort to sleeping in the streets at the great pilgrimage to Tínos; also major festivities at Páros, at Ayiássos on Lésvos, and at Ólymbos on Kárpathos.

August 29
Apokefálisis toú Prodhrómou (Beheading of John the Baptist). Popular pilgrimages and celebrations at Vrykoúnda on Kárpathos.

September 8
Yénnisis tís Panayías (Birth of the Virgin Mary) sees special services in churches dedicated to the event, and a double cause for rejoicing on Spétses where they also celebrate the anniversary of the battle of the straits of Spétses, which took place on September 8, 1822. A re-enactment of the battle takes place in the harbour, followed by fireworks and feasting well into the night. Elsewhere, there's a pilgrimage of childless women to the monastery at Tsambíka, Rhodes.

September 14
A last major summer festival, the Ípsosis toú Stavroú (Exaltation of the Cross), keenly observed on Hálki.

September 24
The feast of Áyios Ioánnis Theológos (St John the Divine), observed on Níssyros and Pátmos, where at the saint's monastery there are solemn, beautiful liturgies the night before and early on the morning.

October 26
The feast of Áyios Dhimítrios (St Demetrios), another popular name day. In rural areas the new wine is traditionally broached on this day, a good excuse for general inebriation.

October 28
Óhi Day, the year's major patriotic shindig, is a national holiday with parades, folk-dancing and speeches to commemorate Metaxas's apocryphal one-word reply to Mussolini's 1940 ultimatum: *Ohi!* ("No!").

November 8
Another popular name day, the feast of the Archangels Michael and Gabriel (Mihaíl and Gavriíl, or *tón Taxiárhon*), marked by rites at the numerous churches named after them, particularly at the rural monastery of Taxiárhis on Sými, and the big monastery of Mandamádhos, Lésvos.

December 6
The feast of Áyios Nikólaos (St Nicholas), the patron of seafarers, who has many chapels dedicated to him.

December 25
If less all-encompassing than Greek Easter, Christmas (*Khristoúyenna*) is still an important religious feast celebrating the birth of Christ; since the early 1990s it has taken on all the usual commercial trappings, with decorations, gifts and alarming outbreaks of plastic Santas on house-eaves. December 26 is *Sýnaxis tis Panayías*, or Gathering of the Virgin's Entourage, *not* Boxing Day as in Britain.

December 31
New Year's Eve (*Paramoní Protohroniá*), when, as on the other twelve days of Christmas, a few children still go door-to-door singing the traditional *kálanda* (carols), receiving money in return. Adults tend to sit around playing cards, often for money. A special baked loaf, the *vassilópitta*, in which a coin is concealed to bring its finder good luck throughout the year, is cut at midnight.

Cultural festivals

As well as religious festivals, Greece has a full range of cultural festivals, including a few on the more popular islands. The most durable are listed below:

Astypálea Municipal Festival (July–Aug)
Itháki Music Festival (July)
Ippokrateia Festival Kós (July–Aug)
Lesviakó Kalokéri Lésvos (July–Aug)
Manolis Kalomiris Festival, Sámos (July–Aug)
Réthymnon Renaissance Festival (July–Aug)
Sými Festival (late June–early Sept)
Lefkádha Arts Jamboree (Aug)
Iráklion Festival (early Aug)
Santoríni Music Festival (Aug–Sept)
Rhodes Festival (Aug–Oct)

Cinema

Greek **cinemas** show a large number of American and British movies, always in the original soundtrack with Greek subtitles, though fly-posters tend to be Greek-only. **Indoor** screenings are affordable, currently €6–8 depending on location and plushness of facilities; cinemas shut from mid-May to late September unless they have air conditioning or a roll-back roof. Accordingly, in summer, vast numbers of **outdoor** cinemas operate; an outdoor movie (same prices) is worth catching at least once for the experience alone; there are usually two screenings, at about 9pm and 11pm, with the sound at the latter turned down slightly to avoid complaints of noise from adjacent residences.

Sports and outdoor pursuits

The Greek seashore offers endless scope for watersports, with windsurfing-boards for rent in most resorts and, less frequently, waterskiing and parasailing facilities. On land, the greatest attraction lies in hiking; often the smaller, less developed islands are better for this than the larger ones criss-crossed by roads.

In terms of spectating, the twin Greek obsessions are **football** (soccer) and **basketball**, with **volleyball** a close third in popularity.

Watersports

Windsurfing is massively popular around Greece, with Greek gold or silver medalists at the last two Olympics. The country's bays and coves are ideal for beginners, and boards can be rented in literally hundreds of resorts. Particularly good areas, with established schools, include Vassilikí on Lefkádha island, Kéfalos on Kós, Zákynthos, western Náxos, Kokkári on Sámos, several spots on Lésvos, Corfu's west coast, numerous locales on Crete and Methóni in the Peloponnese. Board rental rates are very reasonable – about €10–15 an hour, with good dis-

counts for longer periods – and instruction is generally also available.

Waterskiing is available at a number of the larger resorts, and a fair few of the smaller ones too. By the crippling rental standards of the ritzier parts of the Mediterranean it is a bargain, with twenty minutes' instruction often available for around €25–30. At many resorts, **parasailing** (*parapént* in Greek) is also possible; rates start at €30 a go.

A combination of steady winds, appealing seascapes and numerous natural harbours have long made Greece a tremendous place for **sailing**. Holiday companies offer all sorts of packaged and tailor-made cruises (see p.32 in "Getting there"). In Greece, small boats and motorized dinghies are rented out by the day at many resorts. Spring and autumn are the most pleasant and least expensive seasons; *meltémi* winds make for pretty nauseous sailing between late June and early September, and summer rates for the same craft can be three times as high as shoulder-season prices.

Because of the potential for pilfering submerged antiquities, **scuba-diving** is still fairly restricted, though the government has relaxed its controls of late and there are now over one hundred dive centres spread throughout parts of the mainland, the Dodecanese, the Ionians, the Cyclades and Crete. Single dives start around €40 and various courses are available. For more information and an update on new, approved sites, contact the Union of Greek Diving Centres (☏210 92 29 532 or 210 41 18 909) or the Hellenic Federation of Underwater Activities (☏210 98 19 961).

Walking

If you have the time and stamina **walking** is probably the single best way to see the quieter islands. This guide includes descriptions of a number of the more accessible island hikes. For more detail, you may want to acquire specific hiking guidebooks; see p.667 in Contexts. See also p.43 for details of hiking maps available, and p.32 for details of companies offering walking holidays on the islands.

Football and basketball

Football (soccer) is far and away the most popular sport in Greece – both in terms of participating and watching, its status strengthened still further by Greece's heroic and unlikely emergence as champions of Euro 2004 in Portugal. The most important teams are Panathanaïkós and AEK of Athens, Olympiakós of Pireás and PAOK of Thessaloníki. Other major teams in the provinces include Xánthi and the Cretan Ofí. If you're interested, matches (usually played on Wed nights and Sun afternoons) are easy enough to coincide with from September to May. In mid-autumn you could catch one of the Greek teams playing European competition – their performances in the Champions League of late have been very creditable.

The nation's **basketball** team is one of the continent's strongest and won the European Championship in 1987 – cheered all the way with enormous enthusiasm. At club level, many of the football teams maintain basketball squads – Panathanaïkós were European champions in 1996, 2000 and 2002, and Olympiakós back in 1997.

Living in Greece

Many habitual visitors fall in love with Greece to the extent that they take up part- or full-time residence there, more likely buying property than renting it, and most probably retired or self-employed rather than working at relatively low Greek wage scales for employees or casual labour. Beyond the first hurdle of obtaining a residence permit, there are a number of other issues to consider: working, keeping a vehicle, Internet connection and animal welfare. For the full scoop on real estate, consult *Buying a Property: Greece* (Navigator Guides, UK).

Residence Permits and Voting

EU (and EEA) nationals are allowed to stay indefinitely in any EU state, but to avoid any problems – eg in setting up a bank account – (and to be entitled to vote locally in Euro and municipal elections), get a five-year **residence permit** (*ádhia dhiamonís*). If you're not employed (self- or otherwise), you may be required to prove that you have sufficient resources to support yourself. If you are not contributing to one of the Greek social

Greek-language courses

The longest established outlet is The Athens Centre, Arhimídhous 48, 116 36 Athens (☎210 70 12 268, ⌘www.athenscentre.gr). One to try on Crete is Lexis, 48 Dhaskaloyiánni, 73100 Haniá (☎28210 55673, ⌘lexis.edu.gr). There are always adverts in the *Athens News* for other schools, which come and go.

insurance schemes, you will require a letter (translated into Greek) from the Department of Works and Pensions in the UK stating that your home contributions are current. In the largest towns, you apply for a residence permit at the Alien's Bureau (*Ypiresía Allodhapón*) or, in its absence, the central police station. You will need to bring your passport, several photographs, revenue stamps (*hartósima*, available from the local tax office or some kiosks) and a stable address (not a hotel). Permits are given for terms of five years.

You should allow four to six weeks for all the formalities to be completed; the bottleneck is usually a required **health examination** at the nearest public hospital. Once you've assembled all the results, you trot these over yourself to the local public health office, where its administrative council will vet and endorse these, and issue you with a certificate of approval. Finally you take this to the local police or Aliens' Bureau, which should have your permit ready, free of charge, within three working days. Renewals are much more straightforward; there's no health examination, you just leave your old permit with the police who apply an update stamp within a few weeks.

EU nationals with a residence permit become eligible to **vote** in municipal elections (every four years, in October, next in 2006 and 2010) and Euro elections, though in the latter case they must choose a country – you can't vote in both the UK and Greece. Bring your passport and residence permit to the nearest town hall and you will be entered onto the computerized voter registration rolls in a matter of minutes.

Residence/work permits for **non-EU/non-EEA nationals** can only be obtained on application to a Greek embassy or consulate outside of Greece; you have a much better chance of securing one if you are married to a Greek, are of Greek background by birth (an *omoyenís*), or have permanent-resident

status in another EU state, but even then expect wrangles and delays.

Many non-EU nationals working illegally in Greece still resort to the pre-Schengen ploy of heading off to Bulgaria or Turkey for a few days every three months and re-entering at a different border post for a new passport stamp; this usually works, but if not, penalties as described on p.42 potentially apply.

Working

EU membership notwithstanding, **short-term unskilled work** in Greece is often badly paid and undocumented, with employers skimping on the requirement to pay IKA (social insurance contributions) for their employees. The influx, since 1990, of over a million immigrants from various countries – chiefly Albania and central Europe – has resulted in a surplus of unskilled labour and severely depressed wages. Undocumented, **non-EU/non-EEA nationals** who wish to work in Greece do so surreptitiously, with the ever-present risk of denunciation to the police and instant deportation. In a climate of rising unemployment, Greek immigration authorities are cracking down hard on any suitable targets, be they Albanian, African, South African or North American. That old foreigners' standby, teaching English, is now available only to TEFL certificate-holders – preferably Greeks, non-EU nationals of Greek descent and EU/EEA nationals in that order. If you are a non-EU/EEA foreign national of Greek descent you are termed *omoyenís* (returned Greek diaspora member) and in fact have tremendous employment, taxation and residence rights and privileges. Similarly, that other long-standing fallback of long-haul backpackers, picking fruit or greenhouse vegetables, is now the exclusive province of semi-permanent immigrants.

You may prefer to engage in **tourism-related work**, where your language skills or specialist training put you at some advantage. Most women working casually in Greece find waiting jobs in **bars** or **restaurants** around the main resorts; men, unless they are trained chefs, will probably find it much harder to secure any position, even washing up. Corfu, with its big British slant, is an obvious choice for bar work; Rhodes, Kós, Crete, Skiáthos, Páros, Íos and Santoríni are also promising. Start looking, if you can, around April or May; you'll get better rates at this time if you're taken on for a season. If you've the expertise, you might staff one of the **windsurfing** schools or **scuba** operations that have sprung up on several islands.

Perhaps the best tourism-related work, however, is being a **rep for a package holiday company**. All you need is EU nationality and language proficiency compatible with the clientele, though knowledge of Greek is a big plus. English-only speakers are pretty well restricted to places with a big British package trade, namely Crete, Rhodes, Skiáthos, Sámos, Lésvos and the Ionian islands – or English-speaking hotels and complexes elsewhere. Many such staff are recruited from Britain, but it's also common to be hired on the spot through local affiliates in April or May. A big plus, however you're taken on, is that you're guaranteed about six months of steady work, often with use of a car thrown in.

Keeping a car or motorcycle

Both tourist visitors and residents, of any nationality, are only allowed to **keep a vehicle in Greece** with foreign number plates for a maximum of six months, or until the current road-tax sticker and/or insurance from your home country expires, whichever comes first. After that you face a number of inconvenient choices: mandatorily re-exporting the car, storing it for six months, or obtaining local registration. Many holiday home-owners long used the six-on, six-off system, storing their EU-plated car off-road under customs seal, but this has become difficult now that one must pay a full year's insurance locally anyway, and most Greek companies will no longer insure a foreign car. Especially on isolated islands, many foreigners just drive along for years on foreign plates with no road tax, but if you're caught – either by ordinary traffic police or

plainclothes customs inspectors, especially vigilant at busy ferry docks – these personnel are empowered to impound the vehicle concerned immediately, and the "ransom" (basically a fine plus arbitrary import duty) is prohibitive. If a car is circulating with foreign plates, you must always be able to prove that the car has been in Greece for less than six months (the dated ticket for any ferry you may have arrived on from Turkey or Italy is considered sufficient evidence).

Should you decide to import your beloved buggy, **import duties** run anywhere from 30 to 120 percent of the value of the car, depending on its age and engine displacement; the nearest Greek embassy overseas will provide you with a current table of fees charged. You take your car or motorcycle to the nearest customs compound, where personnel will go over it and make a written application to headquarters in Pireás; within ten working days you (or rather your designated *ektelonistís* or customs agent) will receive an assessment of duty, against which there is no appeal, and which must be paid immediately. For EU-plated cars at least this is blatantly illegal – their drivers should get Greek plates at little or no cost on demand – but despite being referred to the European Court several times on this (and always losing) the Greek state shows no sign of stopping this practice. The only way out is to make a declaration at your nearest Greek embassy or consulate that you intend to take up full-time residence in Greece (ie you are not just a holiday-home owner); apparently such an official document should satisfy the most exigent Greek official and get you a pair of Greek plates in a few weeks. In any case, you will immediately begin to save massive amounts of money by paying insurance at local rates rather than the inflated Athens-equivalent rates levied on all foreign-registered cars.

If this all sounds too much hassle, remember that the **cost of cars** has plunged in Greece and for many models is much less than Britain – a Korean-made compact runabout starts at around €6000, plus tax. A nice new scooter can be had for €1000–1500, but remember that there are stiff fines for being caught driving even an 80cc scooter on a car licence (for which the limit is 50cc); budget €450 for a licence course, and enough facility in reading Greek to pass the written test.

Internet connection

Along with most other utilties, Greek telecoms are in the process of being deregulated; there are now two fixed-telephony providers (set to grow) and a myriad of internet packages and providers. Many rural exchanges still won't support broadband (or ADSL as it's universally referred to in Greece); **dial-up** subscriptions cost from €9 per month if you pre-pay for a year, plus modest hourly charges for on-line time. The Yermanos chain of electronic widgets is one of the most impartial outlets for all the providers, or visit ⓦ www.otenet.gr – but *not* OTE premises themselves, whose poorly trained personnel disavow all knowledge of advantageous offers on their subsidiary's website. **ADSL** is vastly overpriced by north European standards – getting on for €50 a month at the lowest speeds – but there is pressure from the EU to push these rates down; watch out for specials (ie free connection and router box).

Pets and Animal Welfare

No single issue potentially pits foreign residents (especially English ones) in Greece against their locally born neighbours more than the status of pets and animal welfare in general. Abuse, especially in the rural areas, is rife: many islands have a remote valley where it was customary to set old donkeys loose to starve; hunting dogs are kept chained to outdoor stakes in all weathers, without enough water or food; and surplus kittens are routinely drowned in a weighted sack. Strychnine poisoning of "extra" or annoying animals is the rule (especially in winter when there are no longer soft-hearted foreigners around to leave food out for strays) – so never let your dog run loose. There is also a stubborn resistance at all social levels to neutering, or to spending money on an animal beyond a handful of cat food. Most Greek animal-lovers and pet-owners are urban and/or foreign-educated, as are veterinary practices and pet-supply shops, and they have thus far made little headway against deeply engrained attitudes. It is also deeply offensive to many Greeks (especially taverna owners) for foreigners to feed scraps to the under-table cats running in mendicant packs, as signs often warn you.

Under both European and Greek law it's an offence to poison, torture, abandon or otherwise mistreat an animal, but in the deep country you are just wasting your breath, and raising the blood pressure of everyone concerned, by proselytizing to change opinions. If you feel strongly about the foregoing, support an animal welfare organization, which will be found anywhere large numbers of expats are resident – Rhodes, Corfu, Ídhra and Sámos are prime examples. These groups organize mass neuterings by visiting vets, maintain feeding stations and organize the adoption of strays by overseas families. In the latter instance, they are always looking for air passengers returning to northern Europe willing to accompany a caged animal to the destination airport, where it will be met by representatives of the eventual owner.

Crime and personal safety

Greece is one of Europe's safest countries, with a low crime rate and a deserved reputation for honesty. If you leave a bag or wallet at a café, you'll probably find it scrupulously looked after, pending your return. Similarly, Greeks are relatively relaxed about leaving possessions unattended on the beach or on campsites. The biggest hazards on beaches, oddly, are free-ranging goats – who will eat just about anything left accessible – and the wake of passing cruise ships or ferries, which can wash all your possessions out to sea with little or no warning.

Recent years, however, have seen a large increase in **theft** and **crimes against persons** at archeological sites, in towns, remote villages and resorts, so it's wise to lock rooms and cars securely, treating Greece like any other European destination. In particular, there has been a huge rise in pickpocketing on the old section of the **Athens metro** (not the new extension, which is heavily policed). See p.73 for **emergency phone numbers**.

Thousands of **women** travel independently in Greece without being **harassed** or feeling intimidated. With the sea-change in local mores since the 1980s – specifically, a vast increase in the "availability" of young Greek women to young local men, up to and including living together before marriage – almost all of the traditional Mediterranean-macho impetus for trying one's luck with foreign girls has faded. Any hassle you do get is from a nearly extinct species of professionally single Greek men, known as *kamákia* (fish harpoons), who haunt beach bars and dance clubs. Sadly, foreign women stand more chance of being **sexually assaulted** at certain notorious resorts (Kávos, Corfu; Laganás, Zákynthos; Faliráki, Rhodes) by northern European men than they do by ill-intentioned locals. With too many people seemingly checking their common sense in at the departing airport along with their luggage, the UK Foreign Office has been obliged to remind them in print not to go out bar-crawling alone, to go home alone, or to accept late-night rides from strangers (indeed **hitching** at any time of the day is not advisable for lone female travellers). In the more remote mountains and islands women may feel slightly uncomfortable travelling **alone**. The intensely traditional villagers may have trouble understanding why you are unaccompanied, and might not welcome your presence in their exclusively male *kafenía* – often the only place where you can get a drink. Travelling with a man, you're more likely to be treated as a *xéni*, a word meaning both (female) stranger and guest.

Lone men need to be wary of one long-established racket in the largest island ports. You may be approached by dubious gents asking the time, or your origins, and then offering to take you for a drink in a nearby bar. This is invariably staffed with hostesses (who may also be prostitutes), whose main job is to convince you to treat them to drinks. At the end of the night you'll be landed with an outrageous bill, some of which goes towards the hostess's "commission"; physical threats are brought to bear on reluctant payers.

Cultural hints and etiquette

It's more likely that you'll (inadvertently or otherwise) give offence than receive it; accordingly a summary of the most common misdemeanours is provided, along with some positive cultural etiquette to observe. Attitudes towards the disabled, the elderly, gays and children will also be different to what you're used to at home.

Police and specific offences

There is a single, nationwide **police force**, the *Elliniki Astynomia*, rather than the division into urban corps and rural gendarmerie normal in most of Europe. Greek cops can be gruff at the best of times, and many have little regard for foreigners. Police practice often falls short of northern European norms, and fit-ups or beatings in custody are not unknown.

You are required to **carry suitable ID** on you at all times (except when in bathing costume) – either a passport or a driving licence. Otherwise, the most common causes of a brush with authority are nude bathing or sunbathing, camping outside an authorized site, public inebriation or lewd behaviour, and taking photos in forbidden areas.

Nude bathing is explicitly legal on only a very few beaches (most famously on Mýkonos), and is deeply offensive to the more traditional Greeks – exercise considerable sensitivity to local feeling and the kind of place you're in. It is, for example, very bad etiquette to swim or sunbathe nude within sight of a church, of which there are many along the Greek coast. Generally, if a beach has become fairly well established as naturist, or is well secluded, laws go unenenforced. Police will only be summoned if nudity is getting too overt on mainstream tourist stretches. Most of the time, the only action will be a warning, but you can officially be arrested straight off – facing up to three days in jail and a stiff fine. **Topless (sun)bathing** for women is technically legal nationwide, but specific locales often opt out of the "liberation" by posting signs, which should be heeded.

Very similar guidelines apply to **camping rough**, which has been ostensibly illegal nationwide since 1977. Even for this you're still unlikely to incur anything more than a warning to move on. The only real risk of arrest is if you are told to clear off and fail to do so. In either of the above cases, even if the police do take any action against you, it's more likely to be a brief spell in their cells than any official prosecution.

The **hours between 3 and 5pm**, the midday *mikró ípno* (siesta), are sacrosanct – one does not make phone calls to strangers or any sort of noise (especially with motorcycles) at this time. **Quiet** is also mandated by law **between midnight and 8am** in residential areas, though Greek construction crews frequently violate this by starting up at 7.30am or so.

The well-publicized ordeal of twelve British plane-spotters who processed slowly through Greek jails and courts in 2001–02 on espionage charges (they had, however, received warnings on prior occasions) should be ample incentive to **take no pictures** at all in and **around airports or military installations**. The latter are usually well festooned with signs of a bellows camera with a red "x" through it. "No pictures at all" includes farewell snaps on the runway; most civilian airports double as air-force bases.

Any sort of **disrespect** towards the Greek state or Orthodox Church in general, or Greek civil servants in particular, may be construed as actionable, so it's best to keep your comments on how things are working (or not) to yourself. Every year a few foreign louts find themselves in deep trouble over a drunken indiscretion. This is a society where verbal injuries count, with a backlog of court cases dealing with the alleged public utterance of *malákas* (wanker).

In the non-verbal field, ripped or soiled clothes and untucked-in shirts are considered nearly as insulting. Don't expect a uniformly civil reception if dressed in **grunge attire**, since Greeks will interpret this in one of two possible ways, neither reflecting well on you. Poverty is an uncomfortably close memory for many, and they may consider that you're making light of hard times. More to the point, fashion victim-hood is developed to near-Italian levels in Greece; if you clearly have so little self-respect as to appear slovenly and dishevelled in public, why should any Greek respect you?

Public drunkenness of the sort which fuelled the much-publicized crimes at Faliráki in 2003 (see p.320) has always been held in contempt in Greece, where the inability to hold one's liquor is considered unmanly and shameful. Inebriation will be considered an aggravating factor if you're busted for something else, not an excuse.

Drug offences are treated as major crimes, particularly since there's a mushrooming local use and addiction problem. The maximum penalty for "causing the use of drugs by someone under 18", for example, is life imprisonment and an astronomical fine. Theory is by no means practice, but foreigners caught in possession of even small amounts of marijuana do get long jail sentences if there's evidence that they've been supplying the drug to others. Moreover, you could be inside on remand for well over a year awaiting a trial date, with little or no chance of bail being granted.

If you get arrested for any offence, you have a right to contact your **consulate**, which will arrange a lawyer for your defence. Beyond this, there is little they can, or in most cases will, do. Full-ranking consulates are only found in Athens and Thessaloníki; there are honorary British consulates on Rhodes, Crete and Corfu.

Disabled and senior travellers

The **disabled**, except notably on Kós, are not especially well catered to in Greece. Few street-corners have wheelchair ramps, beeps for the sight-impaired are rare at pedestrian crossings, and buses are not generally of the "kneeling" type. Only Athens airport, and airline staff in general (who are used to handling wheelchairs), are disabled-friendly. However, as EU-wide legislation on the subject is implemented, the situation should improve.

Senior travellers by contrast fare well in Greece, which has a deeply ingrained tradition of respect for one's elders; you are, for example, rather less likely to be grumbled or shouted at by bus drivers or harbour officials.

Travelling with children

Children are worshipped and indulged, demonstrably to excess, and present few problems when travelling. As elsewhere in the Mediterranean, they are not segregated from adults at meal times, and early on in life are inducted into the typical late-night routine. Thus you'll see plenty of kids at tavernas, expected to eat (and up to their capabilities, talk) like adults. Outside of certain all-inclusive resorts, however, there are very few amusements specifically for kids – certainly nothing like Disney World Paris – though luxury hotels are more likely to offer some kind of **babysitting or crèche service** than mid-range, C-class hotels.

Most ferry-boat lines and airlines in Greece offer some sort of **discount** for children, ranging from fifty to one hundred percent depending on their age; hotels and rooms won't charge extra for infants, and levy a modest supplement for "third" beds which the child occupies by him/herself.

Gay and lesbian travellers

Greece is deeply ambivalent about **homosexuality**: ghettoised as "to be expected" in the arts, theatre and music scenes, but apt to be closeted elsewhere – though the rampant 2004–05 sex scandals amongst the Orthodox clergy have blown the door wide open on the prevalent hypocrisy. Homosexuality is legal over the age of 17, and (male) bisexual behaviour common but rarely admitted; the legal code itself, however, still contains perjorative references to passive partners. Greek men are terrible flirts, but cruising them is a semiotic minefield and definitely at your own risk – references in (often obsolete) gay guides to "known" male cruising grounds should be treated sceptically. "Out" gay Greeks are rare, and "out" local lesbians rarer still; foreign same-sex couples will be regarded in the provinces with some bemusement but accorded the standard courtesy as foreigners – as long as they refrain from indulging in displays of affection in public, which remains taboo in rural areas. There is, however, a fairly obvious scene at resorts like Ídhra, Rhodes and Mýkonos. Skála Eressoü on Lésvos, the birthplace of Sappho, is (appropriately) an international mecca for lesbians.

Directory

Addresses In Greece streets are cited in the genitive case, usually with no tag like "Street" or "Avenue"; the number always follows. Thus 36 Venizelos Avenue is written as Venizélou 36, and it's this convention which we've adopted throughout the book. The practice is different with platía (square, plaza) and *leofóros* (avenue), which always appear before the name. Postcodes are five-digit, nationwide, and precede the municipality concerned, eg 831 00 Sámos.

Bargaining This isn't a regular feature of touristic life, though you'll find it possible with private rooms and certain hotels out of season. Similarly, you should be able to negotiate discounted rates for vehicle rental, especially for longer periods. Services such as shoe, watch and camera repair don't have iron-clad rates, so use common sense when assessing charges (advance written estimates are not routine practice).

Departure tax This is levied on all international ferries – currently €5–8 per person and per car or motorbike, usually (but not always) included within the quoted price of the ticket. To non-EU states (such as Turkey) it's €12–15 per person, sometimes arbitrarily levied twice (on entry and exit). There's also an airport departure tax of €12 for all EU/EEA destinations, €22 for all non-EU destinations, but this is always included in the price of the ticket. Many small regional flights (eg Léros–Astypálea) are exempt from this. Additionally, a special tax, nicknamed the *spatósima* locally, is levied within the ticket price of all flights leaving Athens: €7.79 for Greek destinations, €10.30 for non-Greek ones.

Electricity Voltage is 220 volt AC throughout the country. Wall outlets – rarely abundant enough – take double round-pin plugs as in the rest of continental Europe. Three-to-two-pin adapters should be purchased beforehand in the UK, as they can be difficult to find locally; standard 5-, 6- or 7-amp models permit operation of a hair dryer or travel iron. Unless they're dual voltage, North American appliances will require both a step-down transformer and a plug adapter (the latter easy to find in Greece).

Films Fuji and Kodak print films are reasonably priced and easy to have processed – "One Hour Foto" places abound in resorts. APS film is also widely sold and processed.

Laundries *Plindíria*, as they're known in Greek, are prominent in the main resort towns; sometimes an attended service wash is available for little or no extra charge over the basic cost of €6–7 per wash and dry. Self-catering villas or *dhomátia* will usually be furnished with a drying line and a selection of plastic wash-tubs (*skáfes*) or a bucket (*kouvás*). In hotels, laundering should be done in a more circumspect manner; management can object if you use bathroom washbasins, Greek wall-mounting being what it is, or do more than a few socks and undies. It's best to use the flat pans of showers for both washing and hanging up to dry.

Períptera These are street-corner kiosks, or sometimes a hole-in-the-wall shopfront. They sell everything from pens to disposable razors, stationery to soap, sweets to condoms, cigarettes to plastic crucifixes, yogurts to milk-in-cartons – and are often open when nothing else is.

Time As throughout the EU, Greek summer time begins at 2am on the last Sunday in March, when the clocks go forward one hour, and ends at 2am the last Sunday in October when they go back. Be alert to this, as the change is not well publicized, leading scores of visitors to miss planes and ferries every year. Greek time is thus always two hours ahead of Britain. For North America, the difference is seven hours for Eastern Standard Time, ten hours for Pacific Standard Time, with an extra hour plus or minus for those weeks in April when one place is on daylight saving and the other isn't. A recorded time message (in distinctly slow Greek, 24-hour convention) is available by dialling ☎141.

GREEK FERRIES, CATAMARANS, HYDROFOILS & FLIGHTS

⊕ Scheduled flights
⊕ Charter arrivals only

Shading of lines indicates
frequency of sailings in summer

Daily
4 to 6 per week
1 to 3 per week

Adapted from an original drawing by Phil Green

1

The Argo-Saronic

CHAPTER 1 **Highlights**

* **Faneroménis Monastery, Salamína** Admire the post-Byzantine frescoes at the oldest monastery in this archipelago. See p.95

* **Temple of Aphaea, Égina** The best-preserved Archaic temple on any island, set on a pretty pine-wooded hill. See p.99

* **Póros Town** Climb up the clocktower for a view over the Argo-Saronic Gulf and the Peloponnese. See p.103

* **Ídhra Town** A perfect horseshoe-shaped harbour surrounded by grand eighteenth-century mansions. See p.107

* **Spétses** Enjoy some of the most alluring beaches in the Argo-Saronics along Spétses' pine-speckled coastline. See p.115

△ Ídhra Town

The Argo-Saronic

The rocky, partly volcanic **Argo–Saronic** islands, most of them barely an olive's throw from the Argolid, differ to a surprising extent not just from that peninsula but also from one another. Less surprising – given their proximity to the mainland – is their massive popularity, with Égina (Aegina) almost becoming an Athenian suburb at weekends. Ídhra (Hydra), Póros and Spétses are scarcely different in summer, though their visitors include a higher proportion of foreign tourists. More than any other group, these islands are best out of season, when transient populations fall dramatically and the port towns return to a quieter, more provincial pace.

The northernmost island of the Argo-Saronic group, **Salamína**, is effectively a suburb of Pireás, just over 1km offshore to the east; it is as much a dormitory for those commuting to the capital as it is a weekend retreat, but sees very few foreign visitors. **Égina**, important in antiquity and more or less continually inhabited since then, is the most fertile of the group, famous for its pistachio nuts, as well as for one of the finest ancient temples in Greece. Like Salamína, it's just feasible as a commuter base, though Égina's main problem – crowds – can be avoided by visiting at midweek, advice that applies equally to its pine-cloaked satellite isle, **Angístri**.

The three southerly islands, **Spétses**, **Ídhra** and **Póros**, are piney to various degrees, comparatively infertile, and (like Égina and Angístri) have only a single natural spring between them (on Póros), all of them relying on water-tankers or pipes from the mainland. Accordingly, they were not extensively settled until medieval times, when refugees from the mainland – principally Albanian Christians – established themselves here. In response to the barrenness and dryness of their new homes the islanders adopted seagoing commerce (and piracy) as livelihoods. The seamanship and huge fleets thus acquired were placed at the disposal of the Greek insurgents during the War of Independence. Today, foreigners and Athenians have replaced locals in the depopulated harbour towns; windsurfers, water-taxis and yachts are faint echoes of the massed warships, schooners and *kaïkia* once at anchor.

Salamína

Salamína (Salamís; popularly called Kouloúri) is the quickest possible island-hop from Athens. Take the metro to Pireás and then one of the green buses to the shipyard port of Pérama, 5km west of Pireás, and a roll-on-roll-off ferry

THE ARGO-SARONIC

will whisk you across to the little harbour of **Paloúkia** in a matter of minutes. The craft crosses the narrow strait where, in 480 BC, the Greek navy trounced the Persian fleet, despite being outnumbered three to one; this battle is said by some to be more significant than the battle of Marathon, ten years earlier.

On arrival, you won't be rewarded by unspoilt beaches or a poster-picturesque island, but you will find a slow-paced, lived-in place with some surprisingly large bays supporting rural communities, as well as distinct, *Arvanítika*-influenced folk dances and costumes at festival times. Saronic Gulf water quality has improved markedly since the 1990s and pockets of bathers splash happily about, especially on the less exposed western side of the island. Despite Athenian reticence about (or outright disparagement of) Salamína, it makes an excellent escape from the capital's pollution and frenetic pace.

Paloúkia, Selínia, Salamína Town and Faneroméni

The **bus station** by the **ferry dock** in **PALOÚKIA** has services to the nearby capital Salamína Town (3km) and beyond, though the large selection of signed destinations can be confusing. Around 6km to the south of Paloúkia (direct buses) is the popular local town of **SELÍNIA**, which supports a fairly lively tourist scene. This is the main summer resort, with a pleasant waterfront, a bank, several tavernas and two inexpensive but quite pleasant hotels, the *Akroyali* (☎210 46 73 263; ❸) and the *Votsalakia* (☎210 46 71 334; ❸).

SALAMÍNA TOWN (also known, like the island, as Kouloúri) is home to 26,000 of the island's 31,000 population. It's a busy, functional place, with a couple of banks, a fish market and a long palm-tree laced promenade facing Salamína Bay. Pretty much uniquely for an island town – and emphasizing the absence of tourists – there is no bike or scooter rental outlet, and also no hotel. However, the locals throng several decent **ouzerís** on the shore esplanade, and such full-on **tavernas** as *O Lakis* (in Katástima district near the town hall), or adjacent *O Thanasis* and the small but impressive *O Kakias* (*Nikolakakias*). **Iliaktí beach**, some 5km to the west, is innocuous enough, as is the coastal strip running through the resorts of **Áyios Ioánnis** and **Résti** to the south of Salamína Town.

Buses marked for Faneroméni run to the port at the northwest tip of the island, Stenó, from where there are frequent ferries across to Néa Péramos, near Mégara on the Athens–Kórinthos road. En route, the road passes the frescoed **monastery of Faneroméni** (6km from Salamína; daily 8.30am–12.30pm & 4pm–sunset), majestically sited above the gulf amidst pine woods and working as a convent (25 nuns) since 1944. Founded in the thirteenth century, its unusual *katholikón* was restored in 1670 by Osios Lavrendios of Mégara and subsequently decorated by Yeoryios Markos of Árgos with frescoes so vivid that their painter, stepping back to admire his finished creation, supposedly died of amazement. Near the monastery, occupying its former boathouse, is the so-called **Kellí Sikelianoú**, which the local archbishop granted to the prominent modern Greek poet Angelos Sikelianos as a retreat from 1941 until the latter's death in 1952. Sikelianos wrote some of his finest poetry here in between bouts of entertaining various literati, and plans are afoot to restore the *kellí* ("cell") as a museum.

Eándio and the south

South from Salamína Town, the road edges the coast towards Eándio (6km; regular buses). There are a few tavernas along the way and opportunities to swim, though a well-organized, fenced-off public beach lies just outside Eándio. **EÁNDIO** (also known as Moúlki) itself is quite a pleasant village, with a little pebble beach and the island's best **hotel**, the *Gabriel* (☎210 46 62 275; ❹), overlooking the bay.

Several roads continue beyond Eándio. The most interesting route heads southwest towards Kanákia (8km from Eándio; two buses daily), over the island's main pine-covered mountain, passing (at around 5km) the photogenic monastery of **Ayíou Nikoláou tón Lemoníon**. Another road runs more or less due south to **Peráni** coastal resort (4km along) before emerging at the small-scale resort of **Peristéria** (5km). This is much more attractive than the littered, exposed beach and scruffy huts of **Kanákia**, which has an end-of-the-world feel.

Égina (Aegina)

Ancient **Aegina** was a major power in Classical times, rivalling Athens. It traded to the limits of the known world, maintained a sophisticated silver coinage system (the first in Greece) and had prominent athletes and craftsmen. During the fifth century BC, however, the islanders made the political mistake of siding with their fellow Dorians, the Spartans. Athens used this as a pretext to act on long-standing jealousy; her fleets defeated those of the islanders in two separate sea battles and, after the second, the population was expelled and replaced by more tractable colonists.

Subsequent history was less distinguished, with a pattern of occupation familiar to central Greece – by Romans, Franks, Venetians, Catalans and Ottomans – before the War of Independence brought a brief period as seat of government for the fledgling Greek nation. For many decades thereafter it was a penal island, and you can still see the **enormous jail** at the top of Odhós Faneroménis (it is now being restored to house a museum); the building was originally an **orphanage**, founded by first president Kapodhistrias in 1828. Only since the 1980s has Égina shaken off its consequently dour reputation and begun to attract significant numbers of expatriate residents.

These days, the island is most famous for its **pistachio orchards**, whose thirsty trees lower the water table a foot or so around – hence the bags of nuts for sale in the main town, and the notices warning you of the perennial water crisis. In common with other Argo-Saronics, there are also a surprising number of pine trees, especially in the north and east. Athenians regard Égina mainly as a beach/weekend annexe, being the closest place to the capital most of them would swim, though for foreign visitors an added draw is its beautiful fifth-century BC **Temple of Aphaea**. This is located on the northeast coast, close to the resort-port of **Ayía Marína**.

Hydrofoil services are more frequent than ferries, run from the same quay in Pireás as the conventional boats, and cost hardly any more. Make sure your boat docks at **Égina Town**, the island capital, rather than at **Souvála**, an Athenian bolthole on Égina's north coast and generally devoid of interest to outsiders. If you bring a car over for the weekend, reserve your Sunday return trip well in advance – spots sell out quickly year-round and you could find yourself trapped on the island until Monday midday.

Égina Town

ÉGINA TOWN, the island's capital, makes an attractive base, with some grand old buildings dating from when it served as the first capital of Greece (1826–28) during the War of Independence. The Neoclassical architecture is matched by a sophisticated ethos, with a semi-permanent yacht-dwelling contingent, special events and a well-stocked bazaar which remains lively even at weekends.

Arrival and information

The **bus station** is on the spacious Platía Ethneyersías, just north of the ferry arrival point, with excellent services to most villages; buy your tickets beforehand at the little booth. The **taxi** rank is at the base of the jetty, opposite the row of **booths** selling tickets for various catamarans, ferries and hydrofoils, including the Keravnos catamaran for Angístri (☎22970 91163); Vasilopoulos Flying Dolphins (☎22970 29027); the slow Ayios Nektarios Eginas ferry (☎22970 25625); and Hellenic Seaways (conventional ferries ☎22970 22945; hydrofoils ☎22970 24456). The **post office** is at the rear of the square, and

Pireás ▲   ▲ Pireás

▼ Méthana, Póros & Ídhra

*Map labels:*
Souvála
Mousío Khristou Kaprálou
LIVÁDHI
Kolóna
ÉGINA TOWN
Angístri
Ómorfi Ekklisía
Áyios Nektários
Paleohóra
Temple of Aphaea
Mesagrós
Ayía Marína
Alónes
Fáros
Theotókou Khryssoleondísis
Yiannákidhes
Marathónas
Pahiá Ráhi
Lazáridhes
Pórtes
Anitséou
Ellaníou Dhiós
Eyinítissa
Mt Óros 532m
Vláhidhes
Pérdhika
Sfendoúri
Kípi
Moní Islet
N
0   3 km
ÉGINA (AEGINA)

numerous **banks** have ATMs. Several premises on and behind the main water-front, touting assiduously, rent cars, scooters, motorbikes and mountain bikes – Égina is large and hilly enough to make a motor worthwhile for anything other than a pedal to the beaches towards Pérdhika. Aegina Island Holidays (☎22970 26430), on the waterfront near the church of Panayítsa, offers excursions to the Epidaurus theatre festival. **Internet** access is available at Prestige, on Eákou at the corner of Spýrou Ródhi. **Foreign-language papers** are stocked by Kalezis, midway along the waterfront.

Accommodation

As on most of the Argo-Saronics, **accommodation** is at a premium at weekends but, out of season, discounts apply Monday to Thursday nights. With the exceptions noted, most lodgings are subject to a certain amount of traffic noise. Bathrooms, curiously, are rudimentary just about everywhere, including our top-rated listings.

Artemis Kanári 20 ☎22970 25195, ⓦwww .pipinis-travel.com. Basic 1960s hotel, but rooms (with fridges and air conditioning) are adequate and it's probably the quietest location in town; views from the front rooms over a pistachio orchard are second to none. **❸**

Brown Southern waterfront, past Panayítsa church ☎22970 22271, ⓦwww.hotel brown.gr. The town's top offering, this B-class/3-star hotel opposite the southerly town beach, housed in a former sponge factory dating from 1886, earns its rating from its vast common areas (terrace bar, buffet-breakfast salon). The best and

calmest units are the garden bungalows; there are also galleried family suites sleeping four. B&B **❻**

Eginitiko Arhontiko Corner Thomaïdhou and Ayíou Nikólaou, by giant church ☎22970 24968, ⓦwww.aeginitikoarchontiko.gr. Well-appointed rooms, all with double beds, fridges and air conditioning, at this converted ochre- and-orange Neoclassical mansion. The *pièce de resistance* is the suite (**❺**) with painted ceilings; breakfast is served in a coloured-glass conservatory. B&B **❹**

House of Peace Corner Afrodhítis and Kanári ☎22970 23790, ⓔthehouseofpeace@can.gr. Slightly airless bungalow-studios set in a garden studded with palm and pistachio trees; the stand-ard rooms in the main house were recently reno-vated. Breakfast by arrangement. ❹

Ilektra Leonárdhou Ladhá 25, northwest of the square ☏ 22970 26715 or 693 87 26 441. Quiet *dhomátia* establishment with smallish rooms and equally small balconies. ❷

Pavlou Behind Panayítsa church at Eyinítou 21 ☏ 22970 22795. A good budget hotel with air

conditioning and sometimes double beds in the mosaic-floored rooms; because it was retrofitted to en-suite status, some rooms have their baths across the hall. ❸

Plaza Seafront just south of town beach ☏ 22970 25600. Great sea views from this hotel's front rooms with mosaic floors, fridges and air condi-tioning, though of course they will be a bit noisy. ❸

The Town

The long harbour **waterfront** combines the workaday with the picturesque, but is nonetheless appealing: fishermen talk and tend their nets, *kaïkia* sell produce from the mainland, and there's one of the finest seascapes in Greece, comprising other Argo-Saronic isles and Peloponnesian mountains. North of the port, beyond the tiny but popular town beach, a lone column on a promontory, known logically enough as **Kolóna** (column), marks the remains of the Temple of Apollo and the ancient acropolis. Near the entrance to the ruins (Tues–Sun 8.30am–3pm; €3), a small but worthwhile **archeological museum**, houses finds from the extensive excavations that revealed 2500 years and ten layers of settlement, which dwarf the actual temple precincts. Highlights of the display, some of it labelled in Greek or German only, include a room of Middle Bronze Age pottery, rescued from a nearby building site, with renowned squid/octopus motifs and less common checkerboard patterns.

On the north flank of Kolóna hill there's an attractive bay with a small, sandy **beach** – the best swimming spot in the immediate vicinity of the town, where clean water belies an often seaweed-strewn shore. The other town beaches, south of Kolóna and south of the yacht marina respectively, are smaller and markedly less clean, if more popular.

Other sights include the restored (1802) **Pýrgos Markéllou**, seat of the first Greek government, dominating a park near the large church of Áyios Nikólaos whose landmark square belfries pierce the skyline from every vantage point. In the suburb of Livádhi, just to the north, a plaque marks **Nikos Kazantzakis'** 1940s–1950s residence, where he wrote his most celebrated book, *Zorba the Greek*. Three kilometres out of town in the same direction, admirably sign-posted, is the **Mousío Khrístou Kaprálou/Christos Kapralos Museum** (June–Oct Tues–Sun 10am–2pm & 6–8pm; Nov–May Fri–Sun 10am–2pm; €2), housed in several ateliers in which the prominent Greek sculptor and painter spent his summers for three decades up to his death in 1993. The influ-ence of Henry Moore is evident in the wood, terracotta and bronze pieces on display; there's a whole wing of canvases, often startlingly elongated nudes, and a replica of his famous frieze *Monument of the Battle of the Pindus*, the original of which now adorns a hall in the Greek Parliament building.

Eating, drinking and entertainment

There are several recommendable **ouzerís** and **tavernas**, particularly at the south end of pedestrianized Panayióti Irióti behind the fish market, and at opposite ends of the waterfront – fussy Athenian patronage keeps the standards up (for the most part). By contrast, the obvious central-waterfront cafés near the ferry jetty are poor value, charging Kolonáki (Athens) prices; as well as our more moderate recommendations below, there are two normal-priced sea-view *kafenía* to either side of the fish-market entrance, where the locals go. Athenians are also partly responsible for surprisingly ample choice in **nightlife** given a town of about nine thousand souls. There are three summer **cinemas** – Anesis on Eákou towards the Pýrgos Markéllou beginning in June, joined later on by the Olympia on Faneroménis opposite the football grounds, and the Akroyiali beyond the football grounds on the Pérdhika road – all showing high-quality foreign films; the winter cinema Titina stands opposite the Pýrgos Markéllou. There are two good places for **live music**: the *En Egini*, Spýrou Ródhi 44 (☎22970 22922), and *Kyvernio*, Mitropóleos 4 (☎22970 25801); both kick off at midnight on Fridays and Saturdays and feature live Greek acts. Reservations are recommended at both places if you want to secure a table.

Avli Panayióti Irióti 17. Some of the least expensive sit-down breakfasts in town, but the place later becomes a full-service taverna and low-key bar with Latin/jazz sounds. Summer seating is in the *avlí* (courtyard), but it also has a cosy interior with fireplace for winter.

Flisvos North waterfront by town beach. The best spot for grilled fresh fish and a few meat dishes, at fair prices.

Ippokambos Faneromenis 9, south of town near the football stadium and the ex-orphanage. A *mezedhopolío* run by Lebanese George, with rich, slightly bumped-up fare (allow €18–20 each), including dishes such as pork roulade and stuffed squid. Evenings only, 7.30pm–1am.

Lekkas Kazantzáki 4, adjacent to *Flisvos*. Renowned for good vegetable platters and well-sourced meat grills, washed down by excellent bulk sherry-style wine. Very inexpensive for Égina; two can eat for about €20.

Pelaïsos Waterfront between fish market and Panayítsa. The best value of a cluster of Greek-patronized taverna-ouzerís in this area, with a good mix of platters, but limited seating. Opens 8.15am for breakfast too.

🏃 **Yeladhakis** (also known as *tou Steliou* or *Iy Agora*) Rear of fish market. Much the best, and least expensive, of three rival seafood ouzerís here; accordingly it's usually mobbed and you may have to wait for a table. The stock-in-trade is octopus, sardines, shrimp, plus a few vegetarian starters; summer seating in the cobbled lane, winter up in the loft inside.

Áyios Nektários and Paleohóra

Áyios Nektários, a whitewashed modern convent situated around 6km east of Égina Town, was named in honour of the Greek Orthodox Church's most recent and controversial saint (born Anastasios Kefalas), a rather high-living monk who died in 1920 and was canonized in 1962. An oversized church – supposedly the largest in Greece – looms beside the convent.

A kilometre or so further east is **Paleohóra**, which was established as the island's capital in the ninth century as a refuge against piracy, but failed singularly in this capacity during Barbarossa's 1537 raid. Abandoned in 1826–27, Paleohóra is now utterly deserted, but possesses the romantic appeal of a ghost village. You can drive right up to the site (unenclosed, free): take the turning left after passing Áyios Nektários and keep going about 400m. Some thirty of Paleohóra's churches and monasteries remain in a recognizable state (there's a helpful map-placard at the north entrance to the site), but only those of Áyios Dhionýsios, Episkopí (both usually locked), Áyios Yeóryios Katholikós and Metamórfosis (on the lower of the two trails, both open) and Ayía Kyriakí/ Zoödhóhou Piyís (the remotest) retain frescoes of any merit and in recognizable condition. Little remains of the town itself – when the islanders left, they simply dismantled their houses and moved the masonry to newly founded Égina Town.

The Temple of Aphaea

The Doric **Temple of Aphaea** (Tues–Sun 8am–5pm; €4) lies 12km east of Égina Town, among pines, which are tapped to flavour the local retsina, and beside a less aesthetic radio mast. It is one of the most complete and visually complex ancient buildings in Greece, its superimposed arrays of columns and lintels evocative of an Escher drawing. Built between 500 and 480 BC to replace two destroyed sixth-century predecessors, it slightly predates the Parthenon. The dedication is unusual: Aphaea was a Cretan nymph who, fleeing from the lust of King Minos, fell into the sea, was caught by some fishermen and brought to ancient Aegina, the only known locus of her cult, and one observed here since 1300 BC. As recently as two centuries ago, the temple's pediments were intact and essentially in perfect condition, depicting two battles at Troy. However, like the Elgin marbles, they were "purchased" from the Turks – this time by Ludwig I of Bavaria, and they currently reside in Munich's Glyptothek museum.

Nine daily **buses** from Égina Town to Ayía Marína stop at the temple, or you can walk up from Ayía Marína along a path.

The east: Ayía Marína to Mount Óros

The island's major beach resort **AYÍA MARÍNA**, another 3km on, sits on the east coast of the island, south of the Aphaea temple ridge. The demise of most foreign package holidays here in the past five years has sent the place into a tailspin, with one out of three commercial premises dustily vacant. The beach is still packed, though, overlooked by an abandoned, half-built hotel; the water, while now adequately clean, is rather shallow and more suited to children than adults.

Beyond the resort, the paved road continues south 8km to **PÓRTES**, a low-key shore hamlet. Among the mix of modern summer villas and old basalt cottages are scattered several tiny fish **tavernas**: *Galinopetra*, overlooking the northerly anchorage, is the most basic, *Thanasis* next up is the most ambitious, whilst *Akroyiali* to the south falls somewhere in-between, all offering fish and *mezédhes*. Beyond *Akroyiali*, towards the south anchorage, stretches a functional but partly sandy beach with decent snorkelling offshore.

The road climbs to the village of Anitséou (with a taverna), just below a major saddle on the flank of Mount Óros, and then forges west towards the scenic village of **Pahiá Ráhi**, almost entirely rebuilt in traditional style by foreign and Athenian owners. From here a rough, single-lane, winding track leads down to the main west-coast road at Marathónas (see below), passable to any scooter and – with care – a compact car, though large vehicles should stick to the longer, paved, tree-lined route back to Égina Town, and then loop back to Marathónas along the coastal road.

Mount Óros

South of the saddle between Pahiá Ráhi and Anitséou, signposted 400m off the paved road, are the foundations of the shrine of **Ellaníou Dhiós**, with the monastery of Taxiárhis squatting amid the massive masonry. The 532-metre summit cone of **Mount Óros**, an hour's walk from the highest point of the road, is capped by the modern chapel of Análipsi (Ascension) and has views across the entire island and much of the Argo-Saronic Gulf.

Gerald Thompson's *A Walking Guide to Aegina*, available locally, details a series of walks across the range of mountains and wooded valleys between Mount Óros and the Aphaea temple and down to the port of Souvála, all avoiding main roads.

The west: Marathónas to Pérdhika

The road southeast of Égina Town, along the west coast of the island, is served by regular buses (8–9 daily). Sprawling **MARATHÓNAS**, 5km from Égina, has the biggest of the west coast's rather scruffy sand beaches, and is tolerable enough, with a scattering of rooms, tavernas and cafés along the shore. The next settlement, **EYINÍTISSA**, has a popular, sheltered cove backed by eucalypts and a beach bar.

PÉRDHIKA, 9km along at the end of the coastal road, scenically set on a little bay packed with yachts, is the most picturesque village on the island; the back streets of this elongated village may be rather characterless, but its pedestrianized, southerly waterfront esplanade reveals a relaxed, seaside-holiday atmosphere. It also has the best range of non-package holiday **accommodation** outside Égina Town: there are rooms on the main road, and just off it. Immediately before the waterfront you'll find the *Hotel Hippocampus* (℡22970 61363; ❸), and nearer the harbour are the *Antzi Studios* (℡22970 61233; ❷), distinguishable in high summer by the bougainvillea draped over the blue-and-white painted facade.

On the quay, overlooking Moní islet and the Peloponnese, are a half-dozen or so **tavernas**, among which *Saronis* is a little cheaper and gets considerable local patronage; *Tò Proreon*, with its potted-plant decor, has the most attractive atmosphere; while *Andonis*, an Athenian hangout, is the most popular fish taverna of the bunch. Among several **café-bars**, mostly at the far end, *Ermis* is the main late-night spot.

The only other diversion at Pérdhika is a trip to the pale-limestone offshore islet of **Moní** (10min; several departures daily; €5 return). There are no facilities on the island, most of which is fenced off as a nature conservation area, but it's worth the trip for a swim in wonderfully clear water, since Pérdhika Bay itself is shallow and yacht-tainted.

Angístri

Angístri, fifteen minutes by catamaran from Égina, is small enough to be overlooked by most island-hoppers, though the visitors it does have are a diverse mix: Athenian and German old-timers who bought and restored property here years ago, plus British or Swedish short-termers on package trips. Beaches are cleaner and less crowded (if not hugely better) than on Égina, and out of season pine-covered Angístri lapses into a leisurely village pace, with many islanders still making a living from fishing and farming. Headscarves worn by the old women indicate the islanders' Albanian ancestry, and until the mid-1990s they still spoke *Arvanítika* – a dialect of medieval Albanian with Greek accretions – amongst themselves.

Skála, Metóhi and Mýlos

The contemporary resort of **SKÁLA**, built over vineyards during the 1970s, is dominated by modern apartment buildings and hotels with little to distinguish them, spreading west halfway along the north shore of the island. The popular town beach, Angístri's only sandy one, nestles against the protected east shore of this headland, between the landmark church of Áyii Anáryiri and the car-ferry jetty. At slow times arriving craft will probably be met by **accommodation** touts, including those affiliated with the *Aktaion Hotel* (℡22970 91222; ❹), the best option on the main strip, a few paces up the beach, with a swimming pool, restaurant and standard rooms. Continuing in the same direction, then about 200m along the street leading west from the church, you'll find the large studios of *Ilios* (℡22970 91029; ❸), above the namesake giftshop, with a pleasant managing family and partial sea views. For an unobstructed view of the water and much the best position in Skála, head ten minutes left (south) from the jetty to reach the *Alkyoni Hotel* (☎22970 91377; ❸), with large stone-floored rooms and a lovely coffee/breakfast bar. When **eating out**, choose from among *Yiorgos*, long-running seafood specialist just above the jetty; shed-like *Gionis* (no sign), the original 1970s taverna under some trees, at the north end of the beach opposite Áyii Anáryiri; and *Plori*, a few steps west by the bus stop, a decent ouzerí with locals in attendance and acoustic music some nights. Other **nightlife** takes place in the various bars along the north-shore road, for example at *Copacabana*, which also does breakfasts, coffees, waffles and desserts.

From the paved road's end just beyond the *Alkyoni Hotel*, a marked path leads within ten minutes to secluded **Halikiádha**, a pebble beach backed by crumbling cliffs and pine-covered hills; this is Angístri's best beach, and is clothing-optional.

METÓHI, the hillside hamlet just above Skála, was once the main village, but during the 1980s was completely bought up and restored by foreigners and Athenians. The only native islanders dwelling here now run the reasonably priced *Taverna Parnassos*, which offers its own cheese, a few *mayireftá* per day and good bulk wine in addition to the usual grills and *mezédhes*.

Ever-spreading Skála threatens in the future to merge with **MÝLOS** (Megalohóri), just 1.5km west along the north coast. Once you penetrate a husk of new construction, you find an attractive, traditional Argo-Saronic-style village centre with a church and platía. Although there's no decent beach nearby, it makes a good alternative base, with plenty of rented **rooms**, **studios** and a hotel or two, though the place has a more limited season (June–Aug) than Skála. **Tavernas** include *Sailor*, top for meat grills, and *Yiannis*, a cavernous spot with sea views and live music at weekends.

The rest of the island

Scooters and **mountain bikes** are available for rent from several outlets in Skála and Mýlos; it is less than 8km to Limenária, near the end of the trans-island road, so in cooler weather you can comfortably cross Angístri by pedal power, or on foot from Metóhi along a winding dirt track through the pines. In summer only, four daily departures of a box-like **minibus** connect Skála and Mýlos with Limenária. The broad, paved west-coast road takes you past the turning for **Dhragonéra**, a smallish, pine-fringed pebble beach with a dramatic panorama across to the mainland; there's a summer *kantína*, and more secluded, well-attended covelets to the right.

LIMENÁRIA, a small farming community at the edge of a fertile plateau in the southeast corner of the island, is still largely unaffected by tourism. The single, central **taverna** − *O Tasos* − is adequate and popular at weekends, but pricier than you'd expect for the location, functioning also as a *kafenío* and general store selling local farm products such as honey, retsina, pickled capers and olive oil. The closest good swimming is a few hundred metres east down a cement drive, then steps, at **Máriza**, where a cement lido gives access to deep, crystalline water. A broader paved road leads 2km west, past a shallow salt marsh, to the little anchorage of **Apónissos**, connected via a small causeway to an eponymous islet (private, off limits), with the larger island of **Dhoroússa** looming beyond. The *Aponisos Taverna* (summer only) is the single **eating** option here, but swimming opportunities (minuscule sand patches, stagnant water) are even more limited.

Póros

Separated from the mainland by a 450-metre strait, **Póros** ("the ford") barely qualifies as an island, and more than any other Argo-Saronic island it remains a (mostly Swedish) package-tour venue despite a marked slump in the trade in recent years; proximity to Pireás − and storm-proof access from the Argolid opposite − also guarantees a weekend Athenian invasion. The port town retains character, however, and the topography is interesting: Póros is in fact two islands, **Sferiá** (Póros Town) and the far larger **Kalávria**, separated from each other by a shallow engineered canal, now silting up, and spanned by a bridge.

In addition to regular ferry and hydrofoil connections with Pireás and the other Argo-Saronics, Póros has frequent, almost round-the-clock boats shuttling across from the workaday mainland port of **Galatás** in the Peloponnese (5 min; €0.50, €0.80 after midnight), plus there's a car ferry every half hour from the north end of the quay. These permit interesting excursions − locally to ancient Troezen near Trizína, and the nearby Devil's Bridge. Further afield, day-trips to Náfplio or nocturnal ones to performances of ancient drama at the great theatre of Epidaurus (Epídhavros) are possible by car, or by taking an excursion provided by travel agents in Póros Town.

Póros Town

Ferries from other Argo-Saronics or from Galatás drop you at **PÓROS TOWN**, the only proper settlement on the island, which rises steeply on the western half of tiny volcanic Sferiá to its landmark clocktower at the summit, with great views of the tiled rooftops and straits. The cafés and waterfront lined with fishing and pleasure craft are lively until late − which means it's inadvisable to stay nearby. The only real sight is a two-room **archeological museum** about halfway along the southeast quay (Tues–Sun 8.30am–3pm; €2), with items from Troezen, Méthana, Hermione, Kalaureia and Galatás; there are no real knock-out exhibits, but the assortment of grave finds, jewellery, painted

Méthana, Égina & Pireás

Trizína ◄ Méthana, Náfplio ◄ & Epidaurus

POROS

Rossikós
Navstathmós

Vayioniá

Megálo Neório

"Love Bay"

•• Temple of
Poseidon

Mikró
Neório

Kalávria

Profitis Ilías
303m

Kanálli

Póros
Town

Askélli

Vígla
358m

Zoödhóhou Piyís

Galatás

Monastiríou

Sferiá

N

0   2 km

Ídhra & Spétses

pottery, loom weights, oil lamps and grave *stelae*, from Mycenaean to Byzantine times, is well worth a half-hour perusal.

Practicalities

Drivers must use the public **car park** next to the Galatás ferry dock; the local **bus stop** is on the quay, near the foot passengers' water-taxi to Galatás. Strung along the waterfront, on either side of the separate car-ferry and hydrofoil moorings, are several **travel agents**, including Marinos Tours (⌀22980 23423), main sales point for Hellenic Seaways hydrofoil tickets and with well-priced local **maps**; Askeli Travel (⌀22980 24900), handling conventional ferries; and the Euroseas agent (⌀22980 25902). These, and other agencies such as Family Tours (⌀22980 23743) and Saronic Gulf Travel (⌀22980 24555), deal in tours to the Argolid and most notably as **accommodation** bureaux for various apartments and hotels on Kalávria; touts can be persistent here and are worth avoiding.

Additional facilities around the waterfront include **scooter**, **car** and **bicycle** rental outlets (you can take all of them across to the mainland; thus scooters are surprisingly expensive at €15–20 per day), four **banks** (with ATMs) and a **post office**. **Internet** access and foreign-language newspapers are available at the Kendro Typou, opposite the long-haul ferry berthing.

Accommodation

Hotels on Sferiá are scarce, and mostly found in the area around the Galatás car-ferry dock: two options are the adequate if bland *Dimitra* (⌀22980 25981 or 22980 25901; ❸) a bit inland, and the more distinguished *Dionysos* (⌀22980 23511; ❹–❺), a converted mansion immediately opposite the dock, but with potential noise problems and unwelcoming management. **Rooms** or studios in the town tend to be unmarked; one conspicuous exception is *Villa Tryfon* (⌀22980 25854; ❹), with 1970s rooms, mostly with bay-view balconies and cheerful blue-and-white decor. Even quieter places to stay are up on the hill behind the clocktower, although prices are high for what you get; the budget-conscious should seriously consider staying across the way in Galatás, where equivalent facilities are pitched a category lower.

Eating, drinking and nightlife

Down on the quay amongst the cafés, bars and souvenir shops facing Galatás are a few full-service **tavernas**, of which *Poseidon* on the north promenade is one of the few open at lunchtime, making a decent fist of seafood dishes in particular, though you'll have more choice and quality up the hill and on Kalávria. Beside the summer Cinema Diana above the small shopping centre, signs point up to ⚓ *Karavolos* ("snail"; dinner only), which unsurprisingly has snails on the menu along with other typical ouzerí fare; portions are large and prices (for Póros anyway) fair. On or just off of Platía Ayíou Yeoryíou (the way up is well marked from the northern promenade) is a cluster of evening-only tavernas, the most atmospheric (set under a plane tree) being *O Platanos* (dinner only), run by a local butcher and offering excellent meat grills washed down by the oddity of rosé retsina. For seafood, *Kathestos*, on the front between the town hall and the museum, is about the best.

As you head further southeast along the front, cafés serving **breakfast** or **light snacks** become quieter and better value; two to single out are *Mostra*, at the rear of Platía Dhimarhíou, and *Iy Platía*, next to the archeological museum. A cluster of noisy music-bars on the quay provides the main **nightlife** options, though the island's top venue (in all senses) is hillside day-and-night-club *Poseidonio*, 3km above town (1pm until small hours), with a pool and DJ.

Kalávria

Most of Póros' accommodation is found on Kalávria, the main body of the island, along the couple of kilometres to either side of the bridged canal beyond

△ Póros Town

the Naval Cadets' Training School. Some of the hotels to the west in **Kanálli** and **Mikró Neório** are ideally situated to catch the dawn chorus – the Navy's marching band – though Mikró does have a worthwhile independent **taverna**, *Petros*. If you'd rather sleep in, head 2km beyond the bridge to **Megálo Neório**, where the pleasant *Pavlou* **hotel-taverna** (T 22980 22734, F 22980 22735; ④–⑤) fronts a larger beach and a watersports centre offering water-skiing. The paved road – and westerly **bus** service from Póros Town – continues past small, scenic but hopelessly overcrowded **"Love Bay"** before reaching the **Rossikós Navstathmós**, a crumbling Russian naval base dating from the late eighteenth century and Count Orloff's protracted but ultimately failed attempt to coordinate a Greek anti-Ottoman revolt. There's a hard-packed, mostly shadeless beach here, with lots of small craft anchored offshore; in general beaches west of the canal are more protected but the water can be stagnant.

Beach resorts east of the canal are comparatively exposed to the open sea but by the same token the water is often cleaner. **Askélli**, with its strip of hotels and villas, is long but crowded, with another motorized watersports centre; **Monastiríou**, about 4km from town, is more peaceful and fills last, with two **tavernas** – the more Greek-feeling and affordable being *Kalavria* – dividing the sunbed trade between them.

Zoödhóhou Piyís, the Temple of Poseidon and Vayioniá

The easterly bus route, and the paved road in this direction, end at the eighteenth-century **monastery of Zoödhóhou Piyís**, next to the island's only spring. The present buildings, dating from 1804, are currently inhabited by four monks; there's an expensive but pleasant snack café outside by the fountain.

Initially, Kalávria appears to be mostly pine forest, but the northern side of the island has fertile plateaus (especially Foússa, where wine is made), olive terraces and magnificent panoramic views. The loop road beyond Askélli leads you to a saddle between the island's two highest peaks and the well-signed foundations of a sixth-century BC **Temple of Poseidon** (enclosed but gate always open; free), the major item of Kalaureia, the ancient name for Póros. It was here that Demosthenes, fleeing from the Macedonians after taking part in the last-ditch resistance of the Athenians, took poison rather than surrender. Since 1997 the Swedish Institute of Archeology has reprised its nineteenth-century excavations of the surprisingly extensive site, though this means that the most interesting bits are roped off. Beyond the temple a road leads down to **Vayioniá**, port of the ancient shrine and the best of several beaches on the island's north shore, with a seasonal snack bar.

Ídhra (Hydra)

The island of **Ídhra** is treated as a preserved national monument, blessedly free of wheeled traffic and modern construction, making it one of the most peaceful and refreshing destinations in Greece. The island became established as a fashionable venue during the 1950s, when Sophia Loren appeared in *Boy on a Dolphin* (filmed here in 1957) and characters ranging from Greek painter Nikos Hatzikyriakos-Ghikas to Canadian songster Leonard Cohen bought and restored grand old houses. Since then Ídhra has experienced a predictable metamorphosis into one of the more popular resorts in Greece, despite a very limited number of good beaches. The town's busy from Easter until October, although the "three islands in one day" cruises that used to disgorge hundreds of trippers per liner have dwindled to just one or two arrivals per day. Weekends still see Ídhra packed to the gills, when the front becomes one long outdoor café and souvenir stall, though it's easy enough to leave all this behind on foot or by excursion boat.

Ídhra Town

ÍDHRA TOWN and port, with tiers of substantial grey-stone mansions and humbler white-walled, red-tiled houses climbing up from a perfect horseshoe harbour, form a beautiful spectacle. The waterfront mansions were built mostly during the eighteenth century on the accumulated wealth of a remarkable merchant fleet of 160 ships, which traded as far afield as America and – during the Napoleonic Wars – broke the British blockade to sell grain to France. Fortunes were made and the island also enjoyed a special relationship with the Ottoman Porte, governing itself and paying no tax, but providing sailors for the sultan's navy. These conditions naturally attracted Greek immigrants from the less privileged mainland, and by the 1820s the town's population was nearly 20,000 – an incredible figure when you reflect that today it is under 3000. During the War of Independence, Hydriot merchants provided many of the ships for the Greek forces and consequently many of the commanders.

Arrival and information

The town is fairly compact, but away from the waterfront, streets and alleyways are steep and labyrinthine; the best **map** is that issued by Saitis Tours next to the Alpha Bank (℗22980 52184), also agents for the Euroseas **catamaran**. Tickets for Hellenic Seaways **hydrofoils** and conventional ferries (which do not unload cars here) are sold on the eastern front, upstairs right opposite their anchorage (℗22980 54007). Several **banks** (**ATMs**) line the waterfront; the **post office** is on the market-*halle* square just inland, while a **laundry** is found on the lane opposite the telecoms building and next to the state clinic. Hydra Divers, at the entrance to the market-*halle* square (℗22980 53900, Ⓦwww.divingteam.gr), offers round-the-island cruises as well as **dive trips** year-round by arrangement, PADI courses and Nitrox-Trimix tanks.

Accommodation

Because of the preservation order affecting the entire town, construction of new accommodation is banned, private balconies are rare (though air conditioning is almost universal) and the limited number of beds are in restored premises, all priced accordingly. There are no street addresses per se, and signage can be inconspicuous – ask for further directions when booking. Unless otherwise specified, establishments are open all year; high-season prices also apply to weekends in any season.

Alkionides Same lane as summer cinema ☎22980 54055, ⓦwww.alkionideshydra.com. Peaceful yet central pension with a pleasant courtyard and helpful management; all rooms have hot plates and fridges. **❹**

Amaryllis 100m inland from the hydrofoil dock, take the right fork ☎22980 53611, ☏22980 52249. Nondescript 1960s building that somehow evaded the preservation code, yet it proves a decent small hotel and has small balconies. **❹**

🏃 **Bratsera** 150m inland from the hydrofoil dock, past the *Amaryllis* ☎22980 53971 ⓦwww.greekhotel.com/saronic/hydra/bratsera. Easily the best available on the island, this A-class/4-star hotel occupies a former sponge factory, and the extensive common areas (including bar, restaurant, conference room and medium-sized pool) serve as a de facto museum of the industry with photos and artefacts. Five grades of rooms, even the lowest two having flagstone floors and proper shower stalls. Open mid-March to Oct. **❼–❽**

🏃 **Miranda** 200m inland along main lane from mid-quay ☎22980 52230, ⓦwww.mirandahotel.gr. An 1810 mansion converted into one of the most popular hotels here, with wood floors and fridges. Rooms vary; best are nos. 2 and

3, both with painted, coffered ceilings and large sea-view terraces. Large breakfasts in the shaded courtyard are another big plus; there is a basement bar for winter. B&B **❻**

Nikos Botsis About 100m inland along main lane from mid-quay ☎22980 52395, ⓦwww.hydra-island.gr/botsis. Clean, plain white rooms in a four-storey building, most with balconies – and potentially street noise out front. Fri–Sun **❹**, Mon–Thurs **❸**

Orloff On largest inland square, near pharmacy ☎22980 52564, ⓦwww.orloff.gr. Another restored mansion hotel, with blue-curtained and -carpeted, high-ceilinged, variable rooms. High enough in town for partial sea views, with a very secluded courtyard where a superior buffet breakfast is served. B&B **❽**

Pityoussa Main lane heading southeast out of town; info at Stavento shop. ☎22980 52810, ⓦwww.piteoussa.com. Named after the three giant pines out front, this inn has just five ground-floor, recently refurbished units, with cutting-edge facilities, including CD and DVD players and designer baths; quietest – though none is especially noisy – is no. 5 facing the garden. If full, there is co-managed, more basic *Theodoros* (**❸**) next door, upstairs. **❺**

The Town

The **mansions** (*arhondiká*) of the eighteenth-century merchant families, designed by Venetian and Genoese architects, are still the great monuments of the town; some are labelled at the entrance with "*Oikía*" (Residence of...) followed by the family name. On the western waterfront stands the **Voulgaris** mansion, with its interesting interior, and on the hill behind it is the **Tombazis** mansion, used as a holiday hostel for arts students. Set among pines above the restored windmill on the western point, the sumptuous **Koundouriotis** mansion (Tues–Sun 10am–5pm; €4), with panelled ceilings and a collection of paintings, was the home of George Koundouriotis, a wealthy shipowner who fought in the War of Independence and whose great-grandson, Pavlos Koundouriotis, was president of republican Greece during the 1920s. On the eastern waterfront are the **Kriezis**, the **Spiliopoulos** and the **Tsamadhos** mansions – the latter now the national merchant navy college, which you can sometimes visit between lectures. The **historical archives museum** is also on the eastern waterfront (Tues–Sun 9.30am–5pm; €3), with a museum wing containing costumes, period engravings, plus ships' prows and sidearms from the independence struggle.

Ídhra also reputedly has no fewer than 365 churches – a total claimed by many a Greek island, but here with some justice. The most important is the church of **Kímisis tís Theotókou**, set in a monastic courtyard by the port, with a distinctive clocktower and an **Ecclesiastical Museum** (Tues–Sun 10am–5pm; €2).

Eating, drinking and nightlife

The obvious quayside cafés are fine for people-watching, but you pay for this – €4 coffees are the norm – and there are few bona-fide restaurants on the harbour. For better **eating** (and **drinking**) opportunities you'll have to head either inland or around the promontory just to the west.

Tavernas and ouzerís

Annita's 70m in from mid-quay, lane leading to *Miranda Hotel*. Never mind the silly numbered tourist menus and the occasional touting, the food – a mix of *mayireftá* and grills – is good and reasonably priced, with locals in attendance. Good rosé bulk wine; seating indoors or on the cobbles.

Barba Dhimas About 125m inland, on the same lane as the summer cinema. A small, well-priced taverna with decent *mezédhes*, small fish and even snail casserole.

Gitoniko (Manolis & Christina's) Inland, near Áyios Konstandínos church. Very friendly, durable taverna with excellent, well-priced *mayireftá* at lunch – which runs out early – plus grills (including succulent fish) in the evening; extensive roof-terrace seating or indoors according to time of year.

Iliovasilema (Sunset) Behind the cannons, west promontory. The place for an end-of-holiday treat or romantic tryst; upmarket, continental-style cooking that will set you back about €30 per person with (bottled) wine.

To Koutouki tis Agoras Rear of market-*halle*. Doesn't look like much with its rickety tables, but this inexpensive tradesmen's ouzerí can be inspired, with titbits ranging from *pastourmás*

(cured meat) to octopus. At its best in the early evening.

Paradhosiako 80m inland on lane leading up from the hydrofoil dock. All the standard platters at this heaving, popular ouzerí – so service often suffers; €20 per person with drink.

To Steki Inland lane between *Nikos Botsis* rooms and *Miranda Hotel*. Consistently good-value if slightly oily *mayireftá* (tempered by strong retsina) served by welcoming staff, at either the street-side terrace or a lovely shady courtyard that's an extension of the main inland square.

O Thanasis Same lane as *Annita's*, closer to the water. Ídhra's best *souvláki* stall, providing takeaways or sit-down meals at a handful of outdoor tables with water-views you'd pay twice as much for elsewhere.

Bars and cafés

Amalour 150m straight inland from the hydrofoil dock. Laid-back bar with an eclectic play list and thirty-to-forty-something crowd; sometimes hosts special events or theme nights.

Apangio 90m inland on lane leading up from the hydrofoil dock, opposite *Amaryllis* Hotel. A favourite morning spot, with some of the least expensive breakfasts in town, though

---

Ídhra festivals

On the second or third weekend in June, Ídhra Town celebrates the **Miaoulia**, in honour of Admiral Andreas Miaoulis whose **fire boats**, packed with explosives, were set adrift upwind of the Turkish fleet during the War of Independence. The highlight of the celebrations is the burning of a boat at sea as a tribute to the sailors who risked their lives in this dangerous enterprise.

Easter is a particularly colourful and moving experience, especially on Friday evening when the fishermen's parish of Áyios Ioánnnis at Kamíni carries its *Epitáfios* or symbolic bier of Christ into the shallows to bless the boats and ensure calm seas. On the second full weekend in October, the town hosts the annual, four-day **Rebétiko Conference**, with academic seminars by day and performances in this musical genre (see p.643) at various venues after dark. Indeed the calendar is punctuated by conferences and seminars; if you learn of any that coincide with your travel plans, move quickly to secure hydrofoil seats and hotel beds.

coffees can taste peculiar owing to the island's water supply.

Hydronetta Tucked under the cannons on the west side of the promontory. The classic sunset-watching venue, with appropriate soundtrack, though it carries on into the small hours. Limited seating gives it an exclusive, chill-out vibe.

Pirate Corner of waterfront by clocktower. Going since the 1970s, this is a more lively venue, with a younger crowd and Western music.

Beaches around Ídhra Town

The only sandy beach near town is at **MANDHRÁKI**, 1.5km east of the harbour along a concrete road; it's dominated by the *Miramare Hotel* (☎22980 52300, Ⓦ www.miramare.gr; ⓺), whose garden bungalows are not quite up to the standard of some in-town digs, though the bar-restaurant occupies an imposing former shipyard of independence war hero Admiral Miaoulis. Weekday (Mon–Thurs) specials reduce the price to ⓸–⓹, and there are also non-motorized watersports, open to all, and frequent boat-shuttles to town for guests. At the shingly public bathing cove a few paces west, *Mandraki 1800* (also known as *tou Lazarou*; Easter–Oct) is one of the better rural **tavernas** on the island, with slightly pricey ouzerí fare.

Around the westerly harbour promontory in the opposite direction, a paved coastal path leads around to **KAMÍNI**, about a twenty-minute walk. Just as you reach Kamíni, on the right is a small pension, *Antonia* (☎22980 52481; ⓷); Eleni Petrolekka has a popular rival pension and apartments (☎22980 52701; ⓷) across the street. Arrival at Kamíni fishing anchorage proper is signalled by the 🍴 *Taverna tis Kondylenias*, famous for its seafood – the grilled *thrápsalo* (giant squid) is very good – and wonderful sunset views. About 50m up the dry, paved stream bed from the anchorage there's a less expensive alternative, *Christina's*, with a more limited, daily-changing menu – again including some fish – and partial sea view.

Thirty minutes' walk beyond Kamíni, past the popular swimming cove at **Kastéllo**, brings you to **VLYHÓS**, a small hamlet with a rebuilt nineteenth-century bridge and a shingle beach; swimming in the lee of an offshore islet is decent. In peak season three taverna-cafés function – stronger at drinks than food – while there's a single rooms establishment, *Antigone* (☎22980 53228, Ⓕ 22980 53042; ⓸). **Water-buses** ferry passengers (€1.50 one way) to Ídhra port every half hour. Out of season you'll have to **charter** a craft at the port, which ranges from €9 (Kamíni) to €50 (Bísti) per boat, depending on destination.

The rest of the island

There are no motor vehicles on Ídhra, except for a few trucks to transport supplies and rubbish or do trench-works, and just one surfaced road (from the port to Mandhráki); the island is mountainous and its interior accessible only by foot or hoof. Accordingly, most tourists don't venture beyond the town, so with a little walking you can find a dramatically different kind of island – one of rural cottages, terraces of grain to feed the donkeys, hilltop monasteries and pine forest, mostly recovered from a devastating 1985 blaze.

Following the streets of the town upwards and inland behind the *Miranda*, you reach a path that winds up the mountain for about an hour's walk to either the **monastery of Profítis Ilías** or (slightly lower) the **convent of Ayía Efpraxía**, the only inhabited and open rural monasteries on Ídhra. What must be the longest stairway in Greece (or alternatively a zigzag path) constitutes the final approach to the former (closed noon–4pm, but water and *loukoúm* are hospitably left at the gate to revive you from the climb up). A trail continues left behind Profítis Ilías to a saddle overlooking the south coast, from where a path-less scramble brings you within twenty minutes to the 590-metre summit of **Mount Éros**, the Argo-Saronic islands' highest viewpoint. Otherwise, the path continues as an initially revetted *kalderími* descending the deserted backside of Ídhra to scattered houses and locked chapels near the sea at Klimáki, before climbing again as a trail, past Áyios Pétros chapel and some spectacular coast, to a stretch of bulldozer track ending (1hr 15min from Profítis Ilías) at **Áyios Nikólaos** monastery. This is more usually reached directly from town on a well-marked (with multicoloured paint stripes) and obvious path, threading between Ayía Matróna and Ayía Triádha (both locked); at Áyios Nikólaos' saddle, flanked by a namesake hamlet, the trail drops to **Limnióniza** (1hr 15min from town), the best and most scenic cove on the south coast, with a pebble beach and pines on the slopes above – though no facilities, and no water-buses out. Committed walkers can continue east of Áyios Nikólaos to **Panayía Zoúrvas**, near the eastern tip of the island (2hr each way from town).

Southwest of Vlyhós, a broad dirt donkey-track continues past a busy boat-repair yard to **Episkopí**, a high plateau planted with olives and vineyards and dotted by a scattering of homes (no facilities), and then climbs above Mólos Bay. Beyond Episkopí itself, paths towards the southwestern tip of Ídhra are overgrown and should not be attempted without local guidance. The idyllic coves of **Bísti** (Áyios Yeóryios) and **Áyios Nikólaos** to either side of the cape are normally reached by **water-buses** provided by Hydra Divers (hourly 11am–3pm, mid-May to early Oct; €10 return). Bísti has a pebble beach with a snack bar; Áyios Nikólaos has a fair-sized, partly sandy beach, and there are kayaks to rent at both.

Spétses

Spétses was the island where the author John Fowles lived during the early 1950s and which he used, thinly disguised as Phraxos, as the setting for *The Magus*. Since the 1890s, it has been a favourite resort for well-to-do Athenians, with foreigners following after World War II; the island seems to have risen above a bad 1980s reputation earned by cheap package tours and lager louts. The architecture of Spétses Town is distinct and distinguished, though less photogenic (and less regulated) than that of Ídhra; various concrete monsters were allowed to creep in during the 1960s, but all buildings now must be roofed with the traditional Byzantine canal-tiles rather than the hideous flanged "*Romaïká*" tiles used in much of Greece. Despite two devastating forest fires in 1990 and 2001, which together burnt over half of Spétses' area, hints of the landscape described by Fowles are still to be seen: "away from its inhabited corner [it is] truly haunted . . . its pine forests uncanny". Haunted perhaps, and certainly all but empty; even at Áyii Anáryiri, Spétses' largest of several excellent beaches, there are only scattered holiday villas on the slopes inland.

Spétses Town

SPÉTSES TOWN is the island's port – and the only proper settlement apart from a private villa estate at Ligonéri just west. It shares with Ídhra the same history of late eighteenth-century mercantile adventure and prosperity, and the same leading role in the War of Independence, which made its foremost citizens the aristocrats of the newly independent Greek state. Pebble-mosaic courtyards and pavements sprawl around 200-year-old mansions, whose architecture is quite distinct from the Peloponnesian styles across the water. Though homeowners may bring private cars onto the island, their movement inside town limits is prohibited. A few conventional taxis supplement (expensive) horse-drawn buggies, whose bells jingle cheerfully night and day along the long waterfront. Hundreds of scooters, three-wheeled trikes and minivans are the preferred mode of transport, careering continuously through the town streets and making life almost as difficult for pedestrians as if cars had been completely unrestricted.

Arrival and information

Bus services are limited to two summer-only lines: from the *Hotel Poseidonion* to Ligonéri, and from Áyios Mámas beach to Áyii Anáryiri. A better way to get around is by rented **mountain bike** (at least 4 outlets), and despite many hills you can make the 25-kilometre paved circuit without too much exertion. Otherwise, avail yourself of up to ten **scooter-rental** outlets scattered across town – the going rate is €15 per day – and fill up at one of just two **petrol stations** (at the Dápia (main harbour) and at Ayía Marína). Spétses is also a great place to tour by sea, as many tempting coves aren't accessible overland: the Yachting Club (see opposite) rents **small boats** by the day. At the Dápia, *kaïkia* advertise set routes or round-the-island trips, while **water-taxis** are a pricey alternative (€15–60 per boatload depending on destination). The two **ticket agencies** are Bardakos (☏22980 73141), on the Dápia, for hydrofoils, and Mimoza Travel (☏22980 75170), 100m east, for the Eurofast catamaran. The **post office** is just inland from Áyios Mámas beach, while several **banks** (all with ATMs) surround the Dápia. **Internet** access is provided by Delfinia Net Café, behind Áyios Mámas beach.

Accommodation

Town **accommodation** ranges from relatively basic, 1970s-vintage rooms to jaw-droppingly expensive luxury complexes by way of self-catering studios. At slow times, proprietors meet arriving seacraft, and it might not be a bad idea to consider their (sometimes remote) offerings – anywhere central is apt to be noisy. If you don't fancy pounding the streets yourself, contact the Dápia travel agencies Alasia Travel (☎ 22980 74098) and the Yachting Club (☎ 22980 73400), which between them control bookings for a half-dozen lodgings.

Economou Mansion Kounoupítsa shoreline ☎ 22980 73400. Spetses' premier restored inn, occupying part of an 1851 property. The ground floor of the main house has six well-converted rooms retaining period features (€175); an outbuilding hosts two luxury sea-view suites (€235). Breakfast (included) is served by the fair-sized pool. ⑥

Klimis Waterfront 200m east of the Dápia ☎ 22980 72334. Not exactly bags of character here, but it's convenient, theoretically open all year and the most congenial of a few adjacent, similar 1960s box-hotels; direct or oblique sea views from all the balconied rooms. ❸

Nissia Kounoupítsa shoreline ☎ 22980 75000, ⓦ www.nissia.gr. Built on the grounds of an early twentieth-century factory (of which only the Art Nouveau facade remains), and arrayed around a large pool, this is Spétses' *poseur* address. Units range from two-person studios at the back (€230), through four-person maisonettes with two bedrooms, living room and kitchen (€450), to luxury four-person units with sea-view salons (€570). Rates include breakfast, though kitchens are fully equipped. ❽

Poseidonion Waterfront 50m west of Dápia ☎ 22980 72308, ⓦ www.poseidonion.com. Kings and presidents once slept at this now slightly faded Edwardian period piece. Wood-floored, high-ceilinged rooms, with antique furniture and tubs in the bathrooms, and the extensive common areas, are better kept than the neglected hotel exterior suggests. Open daily June–early Sept, only weekends otherwise. ❺

Villa Christina 200m inland from the Dapia ☎ 22980 72218, Ⓔvillachristina@hol.gr. Restored inn occupying a rambling old building with two courtyards, though no sea views. Air-conditioned rooms are basic but adequate; top-floor units are vastly preferable. ❹

Villa Orizondes 500m inland from the Dápia, via Platía Oroloyíou ("Clocktower square") ☎ 22980 72509 or 697 44 69 893. Spartan hotel in a quiet spot, with variable-sized rooms with fridges, air conditioning and TVs; more than half have knock-out sea views over a bucolic orchard. ❹

The Town

The town's sights are principally its majestic old houses and gardens, the grandest of which is the well-signposted Hatziyannis Mexis family mansion, built in 1795 and now used as the **local museum** (Tues–Sun 8.30am–2pm; €3). Exhibit highlights, well labelled in English, include magnificent polychrome-wooden ships' prows from the revolutionary fleet, as well as its flag, plus (out of sight in a plain wooden ossuary) the bones of Spetsiot admiral-heroine Laskarina Bouboulina, a wealthy widow who commanded her own ship (the *Agamemnon*), reputedly seduced her lovers at gunpoint, and was shot in 1825 by the father of a girl her son had eloped with. One of Bouboulina's homes, behind the cannon-studded main harbour known as the **Dápia**, has been made into a **museum** by her descendants and is well worth visiting. Guided tours (30min; €5) – the only admission permitted – are given in English up to ten times daily.

Just outside the town, Fowles aficionados will notice **Anáryiros Koryalénos College**, a curious Greek recreation of an English public school where the author was employed and set part of his tale; it is now vacant, save for the occasional conference or kids' holiday programme. Like the massive waterfront **Hotel Poseidonion**, the college was endowed by Sotirios Anaryiros, the island's great nineteenth-century benefactor. An enormously rich self-made man who made his fortune in America, he was also responsible for replanting the island's pine forests, depleted by generations of shipbuilders. His former **residence**, one block inland from the Dápia and signposted inconspicuously in Greek only, is a colossus of Neoclassical kitsch, complete with two sculpted sphinxes out front.

Walking east from the Dápia, after 1500m you reach the entrance to the **Palió Limáni**, still a well-protected anchorage used by overnighting water-tankers and roll-on-roll-off ferries. It's overlooked by the monastic church of **Áyios Nikólaos** with its graceful belfry and some vast pebble mosaics out front; inside, Paul-Marie Bonaparte, nephew of Napoleon and casualty of the Greek War of Independence in 1827, was embalmed for five years in a barrel of rum until his body could be repatriated to France. End of the road is **Baltíza** inlet where, among the sardine-packed yachts and excursion craft, a few boatyards continue to build *kaïkia* in the traditional manner.

Eating, drinking and nightlife

Brace yourself for the steepest **food** and **drink** prices in the Greek islands outside of Mýkonos and Rhodes – decades of Athenian patronage ensure that they're 25–30 percent higher than usual. That said, a number of fair-value, reasonable-quality spots are listed below. The perennial centres for **nightlife** are Baltíza, where over half-a-dozen clubs and bars try their luck in any given season – most durable are *Tsitsiano*, for Greek sounds, and *Baltiza*, a vaulted structure on the north shore, given to theme nights – and Áyios Mámas beach, where there are several bars, including *Rendez Vouz*. Just behind the Bouboulina mansion, *Titania* is a summer **cinema**.

Exedra (tou Siora) Palió Limáni. High-quality standard dishes like *moussakás* and *anginéres ala políta*, and unbeatable waterside seating, make it worth the higher prices.

Kafeneion Dápia, by Alpha Bank. Pebble mosaics underfoot and sepia photos indicate that this was the island's first watering hole; start the day with well-priced English breakfast, and tame sparrows begging for crumbs, progressing later to a full range of *mezédhes*, or just a drink whilst waiting for a hydrofoil.

Lazaros 500m inland from the Dápia, starting from the newsagent. Cavernous interior with an old jukebox, dangling gourds and wine barrels; it serves a limited but savoury menu of grills, goat in lemon sauce, superior *taramás* and decent bulk wine – shame about the prefab oven chips. Dinner only, late March–early Oct.

Nykhthimeron (To Amoni) Baltíza. The alias means "the forge", and chef Nektarios' father and grandfather ran the local smithy out of this characterful building, which is now an eminently reasonable ouzerí. Seasonal fresh seafood titbits, vegetarian appetizers, a few grills and home-made *tyropitákia* are the simple but well-executed specialities. Despite the name ("night-and-day" in ancient Greek), open dinner only.

Patralis Kounoupítsa waterfront, 300m before the *Spetses Hotel*. The most upmarket, white-tablecloth venue on this side of town, with excellent service. Their *psári ala Spetsióta* (fish in ratatouille sauce) is made with tuna or amberjack, not low-quality *pérka* as elsewhere, there's good bulk wine if your wallet doesn't stretch to the startlingly priced wine list, and baked-apple dessert rounds off the experience.

Roussos Áyios Mámas beach. A shrine of unfussy *mayireftá* – courgettes au gratin, *yiouvétsi*, baked fish – and about the least expensive taverna in town; tellingly popular with locals.

Around the island

Some people **swim** happily enough at the **Áyios Mámas** town beach, though most will prefer to get clear of the built-up areas. The most popular beaches within twenty-minute walking distance are (east of town) the long, one with amenities at **Ligonéri**, between the *Spetses* and *Lefka Palace* hotels, and (west of town) more cramped **Ayía Marína**, with watersports, a popular bar and the first views offshore towards the tempting but off-limits islet of **Spetsopoúla**, the private property of the heirs of shipping magnate Stavros Niarchos.

Beyond these in either direction a paved road loops around the island in sinuous bends. The pine forest that survived the 1990 and 2001 blazes is mostly in

△ Ayía Paraskeví bay, Spétses

the far southwest, close to the coastline of little coves and rocky promontories. Heading anticlockwise beyond Ligonéri, the first beach you reach is **Vréllos** (no facilities), with just a single surviving copse of trees in a fire-denuded landscape. Next up is **Zoyeriá**, where forest resumes and sculpted rocks make up for the small beach. Naturists will appreciate secluded **Kórbi**, accessible only by a steep, ten-minute path starting from beside a concrete roadside water-tank, but **Ayía Paraskeví** just beyond is arguably the island's best beach, a 600-metre arc of pebbles backed by a chapel, an attractive *kantína* and a full-service taverna (May–Oct).

Áyii Anáryiri, on the south side of Spétses halfway around from town, is the island's most popular beach, a long, sheltered, mostly sandy bay. Gorgeous first thing in the morning, it fills up later with bathers, windsurfers and, at one corner, speedboats driving water-skiers. There's a good seafront taverna, *Manolis* (open all season), and another, *Tasos*, just behind (summer only). If it's all too much, carry on a bit to unheralded **Xylokériza** beach, reached by a 500-metre access drive signed merely for its snack bar (June–Sept); the protected bay itself is mixed sand and white pebbles.

Walkers might want to go directly over the top of the island to Áyii Anáryiri; the 1990 blaze ravaged most of the forest between Ayía Marína and Áyii Anáryiri, though happily new trees are now growing back. Routes out of town start from beyond the *Lazaros* taverna, and pass various rural chapels, a hunting lodge, and a forest service lookout tower – as well as the island's summit, with fine views. Scooter-riders will find the track optimistically marked ("Profítis Ilías 5") from the Áyii Anáryiri end to be in fact impassable on two wheels.

Travel details

All services to the Argo-Saronic islands from the Athens area, whether conventional ferry, catamaran or hydrofoil, depart from Aktí Tselépi in Pireás – slower craft from the Posidhónos side of Tselépi, faster conveyances from the Miaoúli side. There are always more at weekends (Fri–Sun) and fewer from October to June; hydrofoils or catamarans are twice as fast, and about twice as expensive, as conventional craft. Égina, not surprisingly, has the most frequent departures over the longest time range (hourly in season 7am–9.45pm *to* Pireás, 6am–9pm *from* Pireás). Car ferries on the Égina–Póros–Ídhra route also stop in both directions at Méthana on the Peloponnesian mainland, where it is possible to board; hydrofoils or catamarans also link Póros, Ídhra and Spétses two to four times daily with Pórto Héli or Emióni on the Argolid mainland opposite. At the time of writing there is no conventional ferry service between Spétses and Pireás, nor are there any hydrofoil or catamaran links between Égina/Angístri and the other Argo-Saronic islands.

Company contact details for Pireás (local island agencies are given in the island accounts):

Hellenic Seaways (ferries, hydrofoils and Flying Cat to all points) ☎210 41 99 000, ⊛www.hellenicseaways.gr

Vasilopoulos Flying Dolphins (to Égina) ☎210 41 19 500

Ayios Nektarios Eginas (ferry to Égina) ☎210 42 25 625

Euroseas (Eurofast catamaran to Póros, Ídhra, Spétses) ☎210 41 13 108

Ferries

All conventional ferry services are operated by Hellenic Seaways unless otherwise stated.

Égina (Égina Town) to: Pireás (9–12 daily with Hellenic Seaways; 1hr 30min; 3 daily with Ayios Nektarios Eginas; 2hr); Angístri (2 daily Mon–Thurs, 3 daily Fri–Sun; 30min); Póros (4 daily Mon–Thurs, 5 daily Fri–Sun; 1hr 15min); Ídhra (4 weekly; 2hr 15min).

Égina (Souvála) to: Pireás (3–4 daily; 1hr 15min).

Póros to: Pireás (4 daily Mon–Thurs & Sun, 5–6 Fri & Sat; 3hr); Égina (4 daily Mon–Thurs & Sun, 5–6 daily Fri & Sat; 1hr 20min); Galatás, Argolid mainland (roll-on-roll-off barge every 30min 6am–10.40pm; 5min).

Ídhra to: Pireás (4 weekly, Fri–Sun afternoon only, calling at Póros and Égina Town; 3hr 45min for full journey).

Salamina (Paloúkia) to: Pérama (every 60min 1–5am, every 15min 5am–10pm, every 30min 10pm–1am; 15min).

Spétses to: Kósta (Almost hourly roll-on-roll-off barges; 15min).

Keravnos catamaran

Angístri (Mýlos and/or Skála) to: Égina Town (4–5 daily Mon–Fri, 2 daily Sat & Sun; 7.30am–8.30pm; 15–20min); Pireás (4–5 daily Mon–Fri, 2 daily Sat & Sun; 65–70min).

Égina to: Pireás (4–5 daily Mon–Fri, 2 daily Sat & Sun; 50min).

NB The Keravnos berth in Égina Town is at mid-quay, in front of three banks.

Eurofast catamaran

Runs twice daily between Spétses, Ídhra, Póros and Pireás in each direction, often omitting Póros on the evening run back to Pireás. Typical departures from Pireás at 9.30am and 3pm, from Spétses noon and 5.30pm.

Hydrofoils and Flying Cat

Égina to: Pireás (16 Hellenic Seaways hydrofoils and 6–7 Vasilopoulos Flying Dolphins daily; 45min).

Póros to: Pireás (5 daily Mon–Sat, 7 daily Sun; 1hr); Ídhra (6 daily Mon–Sat, 7 daily Sun; 40min); Spétses (4–5 daily; 1hr 30min).

Ídhra to: Pireás (8 daily Mon–Sat, 10 daily Sun; 1hr 40min); Póros (4 daily Mon–Sat, 6 daily Sun; 40min); Spétses (6 daily Mon–Thurs, 7–8 daily Fri–Sun; 45min).

Spétses to: Pireás (6 daily Mon–Thurs, 7–8 daily Fri–Sun; 2hr 25min); Ídhra (6 daily Mon–Thurs, 7–8 daily Fri–Sun; 45min); Póros (3 daily Mon–Sat, 5 daily Sun; 1hr 25min).

2

The Cyclades

CHAPTER 2 # Highlights

❉ **Boat tour around Mílos**
The best way to take in the geological diversity of this volcanic island. See p.138

❉ **Mýkonos Town** Labyrinthine lanes filled with restaurants, boutiques and nightlife.
See p.155

❉ **Delos** The Cyclades' sacred centre and holiest ancient site, birthplace of Apollo and Artemis. See p.161

❉ **Ermoúpoli, Sýros** Once Greece's busiest port, the elegant capital of the Cyclades is now a UNESCO heritage site. See p.163

❉ **Church of Ekatondapylianí, Parikía, Páros** An imposing and ornate Byzantine church incorporating an impressive number of architectural styles.
See p.171

❉ **Tragéa, Náxos** This fertile inland plain, covered with orchards, shelters most of the villages on the Cyclades' largest island. See p.184

❉ **Hóra, Folégandhros** Free of traffic and sitting atop a spectacular cliff, this capital has a handsome old kástro.
See p.202

❉ **Caldera of Santoríni** A geographical wonder, this crater left by a colossal volcanic explosion averages five miles in diameter.
See p.205

△ Church of Ekatondapylianí, Parikía, Páros

The Cyclades

N
amed, most probably, after the circle they form around the sacred island of Delos, the **Cyclades** (Kykládhes) is the most satisfying Greek archipelago for island-hopping. On no other group do you get quite such a strong feeling of each island as a microcosm, each with its own distinct traditions, customs and path of modern development. Most of these self-contained realms are compact enough to explore in a few days, giving you a sense of completeness and identity impossible on, say, Crete or most of the Ionian islands.

The islands do share some features, with the majority of them (Ándhros, Náxos, Sérifos and Kéa excepted) being arid and rocky; most also share the "Cycladic" style of brilliant-white Cubist architecture. The extent and impact of tourism, though, is markedly haphazard, so that although some English is spoken on most islands, a slight detour from the beaten track – from Íos to Síkinos, for example – can have you groping for your Greek phrasebook.

But whatever the level of tourist development, there are only three islands where it completely dominates their character in season: **Íos**, the original hippie-island and still a paradise for hard-drinking backpackers, **Thíra**, the major island in the volcanic cluster of **Santoríni** and a dramatic natural back-drop for luxury cruise liners, and **Mýkonos**, by far the most popular of the group, with its teeming old town, selection of nude beaches and sophisticated restaurants, clubs and hotels. After these, **Páros**, **Náxos** and **Mílos** are the most popular, with their beaches and main towns packed at the height of the season, which in the Cyclades is late July to late August. The once-tranquil **Minor Cyclades** around Náxos have become fashionable destinations for well-heeled Athenians in recent years, as have nearby **Amorgós**, and **Folégandhros** to the west, with its unspoilt hóra. To avoid the hordes altogether – except in August, when escape is impossible – the most promising islands are **Síkinos**, **Kímolos** or **Anáfi**. For a different view of the Cyclades, visit **Tínos** and its imposing pilgrimage church, a major spiritual centre of Greek Orthodoxy, or **Sýros** with its elegant townscape and (like Tínos) large Catholic minority. Due to their closeness to Athens, adjacent **Ándhros**, **Kéa**, **Kýhnos** and **Sérifos** are predict-ably popular – and relatively expensive – weekend havens for Greeks, while **Sífnos** remains a popular destination for upmarket tourists of all nationalities. The one major ancient site is **Delos** (Dhílos), certainly worth making time for; the commercial and religious centre of the Classical Greek world, it's visited most easily on a day-trip, by *kaïki* or jet-boat from Mýkonos. When it comes to **moving on**, many of the islands – in particular Mílos, Páros, Náxos and Thíra – are handily connected with Crete (easier in late July and August), while from Tínos, Mýkonos, Sýros, Páros, Náxos, Thíra or Amorgós, you can reach many of

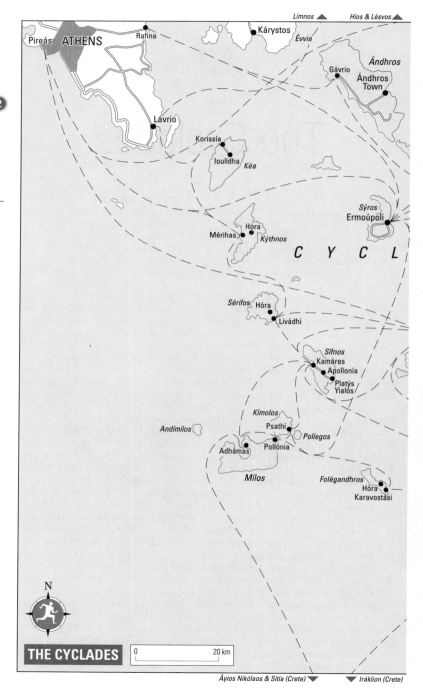

Pireás ATHENS Rafína

Kárystos

Évvia

Ándhros

Gávrio

Ándhros
Town

Lávrio

Korissía

Ioulídha Kéa

Sýros
Ermoúpoli

Hóra

Mérihas Kýthnos

C Y C L

Sérifos Hóra

Livádhi

Sífnos

Kamáres

Apollonía

Platýs
Yialós

Kímolos

Andímilos

Psathí

Políegos

Adhámas Pollónia

Mílos

Folégandhros

Hóra

Karavostási

N

THE CYCLADES

0   20 km

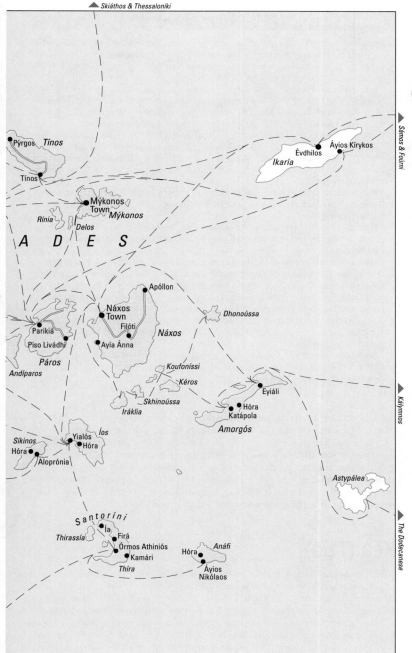

Skiáthos & Thessaloníki

Sámos & Foúrni

Kálymnos

The Dodecanese

Pýrgos · *Tínos*

Tínos

Évdhilos · Áyios Kírykos

Ikaría

Mýkonos Town

Mýkonos

Rínia

Delos

A   D   E   S

Apóllon

Náxos Town

Filóti

Náxos

Dhonoússa

Parikiá

Píso Livádhi

Ayía Ánna

Páros

Andíparos

Koufoníssi

Kéros

Skhinoússa

Iráklia

Eyiáli

Hóra

Katápola

Amorgós

Íos

Yialós

Hóra

Síkinos

Hóra

Aloprónia

Astypálea

Santoríni

Thirassía

Ía · Firá

Órmos Athiniós

Kamári

Thíra

Hóra

Anáfi

Áyios Nikólaos

Watersports in the Cyclades

More and more watersports facilities are opening up across the islands, offering a generally good level of teaching and equipment to rent. Prices start from around €20 for an hour's windsurfing lesson and equipment rental, to around €70 for a day's diving course, and €250 for a full week's training.

Íos: Meltemi Extreme Watersports, outlets on Mylopótamos and Manganári beaches ☎693 21 53 912, ⓦwww.meltemiwatersports.com. Rental and waterskiing, windsurfing and wakeboarding lessons. Also hire canoes, pedaloes, snorkelling equipment and sailboats. Ten percent discount for Rough Guide readers.

Mílos: Apollon Diving Centre, *Apollon Hotel*, Pollónia ☎22870 41347, ⓦwww.apollon-diving.com. Diving courses for beginners and snorkelling trips; Sea Kayak Mílos ☎22870 23597, ⓦwww.seakayakgreece.com, or book through Brau Kat travel on the waterfront in Adhámas. Guided kayak trips around the island, with the chance to stop for a swim.

Mýkonos: Mykonos Diving Center, Psaroú Beach ☎22890 24808, ⓦwww.dive.gr. Diving courses from beginner to advanced, including night dives for certified divers and snorkelling trips.

Náxos: Flisvos Sportsclub, Áyios Yeóryios beach ☎22850 22935, ⓦwww.flisvos-sportclub.com. Arranges and teaches kitesurfing and windsurfing, and rents catamarans.

Páros and Andíparos: Blue Island Divers, main street, Andíparos ☎22840 61493, ⓦwww.blueisland-divers.gr. Diving courses around Andíparos, including snorkelling trips; Fly Under Diving Club, Sánta Maria beach, Páros ☎22840 52491. Courses from beginners to advanced, including kids' lessons and wreck and reef diving; Páros Kite Pro Center, Poúnda, Páros ☎22840 42757, ⓦwww.paroskite-procenter.com. All levels of kite surfing, from beginner courses upwards, and equipment rental; Surfistas, Sánta Maria beach, Páros ☎694 65 06 340. Board rental and windsurfing taught by professionals.

Santoríni: Santoríni Diving Centre, outlets on Kamári and Périssa beaches ☎22860 31006. Diving courses for beginners, as well as volcanic reef diving for certified divers and snorkelling trips.

the Dodecanese by direct boat. Similarly, you can regularly get from Mýkonos, Náxos, Sýros and Páros to Ikaría and Sámos (in the eastern Aegean).

One consideration for the timing of your visit is that the Cyclades often get frustratingly **stormy**, particularly in early spring or late autumn, and it's also the group worst affected by the *meltémi*, which blows sand and tables about with ease throughout much of July and August. Delayed or cancelled ferries (even in the height of tourist season) are not uncommon, so if you're heading back to Athens to catch a flight, leave yourself a day or two's leeway.

Kéa (Tziá)

Kéa, the closest of the Cyclades to the mainland, is extremely popular in August and on weekends year-round with Athenian families. Their impact is mostly confined to certain small coastal resorts, leaving most of the interior quiet, although there is a preponderance of expensive apartments and villas and not as many good tavernas as you might expect (and virtually no nightlife) because so many visitors self-cater. Midweek or outside August, Kéa is a more enticing destination for those who enjoy a rural ramble, with its rocky, forbidding perimeter and inland oak and almond groves.

As ancient Keos, the island and its strategic, well-placed harbour supported four cities – a pre-eminence that continued until the nineteenth century when Sýros became the main Greek port. Tourists account for the bulk of the sea traffic with regular (in season) **ferry/speed boat connections** to and from Lávrio on the mainland (only a ninety-minute bus ride from Athens), plus sporadic catamarans and ferries to and from Sýros and Kýthnos. Frequency of these services should improve as Lávrio port capacity is expanded, but for details you'll have to check directly with its port police as agents in Athens usually won't sell tickets to Kéa.

The northwest coast: Korissía to Otziás

The small northern ferry and hydrofoil port of **KORISSÍA** has fallen victim to uneven expansion; if you don't like its looks upon disembarking, try to get a bus to Písses (16km), Otziás (6km) or Ioulídha (6km). **Buses** usually meet the boats; during July and August there's a regular fixed schedule around the island, but at other times public transport can be very elusive. There are a few **taxis** on Kéa and several **motorbike-rental** outfits at the port, all more expensive than on neighbouring islands.

The ill-equipped seafront **tourist information** office is only sporadically open, but *To Stegadhi*, agents for any hydrofoils or catamarans operating, sell maps and guides, and can phone around in search of **accommodation**. The best year-round choices at the port are the very friendly *Nikitas* pension (☎22880 21193; ❸), with plain, comfortable en-suite rooms, *Hotel Korissia* (☎22880 21484; ❹), well inland along the stream bed with decent air-conditioned rooms, and the somewhat noisy *Karthea* (☎22880 21222; ❹) which does, however, boast single rooms. For **eating**, a series of nondescript tavernas along the waterfront serves standard Greek fare, though the only standout is *Apothiki*, a great place to splurge on hearty dishes like chicken *souvláki* wrapped in bacon. There's good swimming at **Yialiskári**, a small, eucalyptus-fringed beach between Korissía and Vourkári; along the way, at the northern edge of Korissía, cool, contemporary *Keos Katoikies* (☎22880 84002, ⓦwww.keos.gr; ❼), and the swanky, more traditional *Hotel Brillante Zoi* (☎22880 22685; ❻), offer plush amenities and a peaceful setting. The *Yialiskari* rooms (☎22880 21197; ❸), not far from the beach, are basic, but far better value. The nearby *Tastra* beach bar-café is something of a hub for nightlife on the island, having lured revellers from now more residential Korissía and Ioulídha.

VOURKÁRI, a couple of kilometres to the northeast, is more compact and arguably more attractive than Korissía, serving as the favourite hangout of the yachting set. A few expensive **tavernas**, including the nationally renowned *Giannis Maroulis* and *Konstantina Marouli*, serve up fresh seafood, and there's a very good ouzerí – *Strofi tou Mimi* – located where the road cuts inland towards Otziás. Despite a few nondescript bars, the nightlife here, as on the rest of the island, consists primarily of hanging out in tavernas long after plates have been cleared.

Another 4km on, past the picked-over ruins of the Minoan palace **Ayía Iríni** that lie virtually unnoticed on the peninsula north of the island's main harbour, **OTZIÁS** has a small beach that's a bit better than the one at Korissía, though more exposed to prevailing winds; facilities are limited to a couple of tavernas and a fair number of apartments for rent. Kéa's only functioning monastery, the eighteenth-century **Panayía Kastrianí**, is an hour's walk along a dirt road from Otziás. Although more remarkable for its fine setting on a high bluff than for any intrinsic interest, the hostel at the monastery (☎22880 24348) is the cheapest accommodation on the island, albeit rather basic, isolated and not dependably open. From here you can take the pleasant walk on to the island's capital, Ioulídha, in another two hours.

Ioulídha

IOULÍDHA (ancient Ioulis), also known as Hóra, was the birthplace of the renowned early fifth-century BC poets Simonides and Bacchylides. With its numerous red-tiled roofs, Neoclassical buildings and winding flagstoned paths, it is by no means a typical Cycladic village, but, beautifully situated in an amphitheatric fold in the hills, it is architecturally the most interesting settlement on the island, and the best base for exploring it. Accordingly Ioulídha has "arrived" in recent years, with numerous bars and bistros, much patronized in August and on weekends, but during other times it's quiet, its narrow lanes excluding vehicles. It's accessible from Korissía by paved road or on foot over the ancient stone paths that connected the towns during the island's heyday.

The **archeological museum** (Tues–Sun 8.30am–3pm; free) displays surprisingly extensive finds from the four ancient city-states of Kéa, although the best items were long ago spirited away to Athens. The lower reaches of the town stretch across a spur to the **kástro**, a tumbledown Venetian fortress incorporating stones from an ancient temple of Apollo. Fifteen minutes' walk northeast, on the path toward Panayía Kastrianí, you pass the **Lion of Kéa**, a sixth-century BC sculpture carved out of an outcrop of rock, 6m long and 3m high. There are steps right down to the lion, but the effect is most striking from a distance.

Along with a **post office** and **bank agent**, there are a couple of **pensions**, the best of which is the comfortable *Ioulis* (☎22880 22177; ❺), with its own terrace restaurant, up in the *kástro*. Choices for **eating** and **drinking** tend to be of a generally higher quality than in Korissía; however, unless you arrive during a busy season, you may find many places closed. *Iy Piatsa*, just as you enter the lower town from the car park, has a variety of tasty dishes, while up on the platía, *Rolando's* serves a full range of fish plates best enjoyed with the ubiquitous ouzo; neighbouring *To Kalofagadhon* is the best place for a full-blown meat feast. The aptly named *Panorama* serves up pastries and coffee and is a good place to watch the sun set. Once a hub of nightlife, the central town shuts down early these days, though the mayor, Antonakis Zoulos, happens to be one of the most accomplished traditional musicians in Greece, so you could stop at the town hall to ask where he'll be performing next. Full-on *bouzoúki* nights occur regularly at bars, cafés and tavernas in town or back at the port.

Southern Kéa

About 8km southwest of Ioulídha, reached via a mix of tracks and paths, or by mostly paved road, the crumbling Hellenistic watchtower of **Ayía Marína** sprouts dramatically from the grounds of a small nineteenth-century monastery. Beyond, the paved main road twists around the startling scenic head of the lovely agricultural valley at **PÍSSES**, emerging at a large and little-developed beach. There are two tavernas, plus a pleasant **campsite**, *Camping Kea*, which has good turfy ground and also runs the studios (☎22880 31302; ❸) further inland. Of the tavernas, the best is *To Akroyiali*, with a good range of dishes and some decent house wine, as well as rooms to rent upstairs (☎22880 31301 or 22880 31327; ❸).

Beyond Písses, the asphalt peters out along the five-kilometre road south to **KOÚNDOUROS**, a sheltered bay popular with yachters; there's a taverna behind the largest of several sandy coves, none cleaner or bigger than the beach at Písses. The luxury *Kea Beach* hotel (☎22880 31230; ❻) sits out on its own promontory with tennis courts, pool, and a hamlet of dummy windmills built as holiday homes. At the south end of the bay, *St George Bungalows* (☎22880 31277; ❸) has well-kept rooms at very reasonable prices, as well as its own taverna which is recommended. A further 2km south at **Kambí**, there's a nice little beach and a good taverna, *To Kambi*.

Besides the very scant ruins of ancient Poiessa near Písses, the only remains of any real significance from Kéa's past are fragments of a temple of Apollo at **ancient Karthaia**, tucked away on the southeastern edge of the island above Póles Bay, with an excellent deserted twin beach that's easiest reached by boat. Otherwise, it's a good three-hour round-trip walk from the hamlet of Stavroudháki, some way off the track road linking Koúndouros, Hávouna and Káto Meriá. Travelling by motorbike, the road between Písses and Káto Meriá is worth following along the island's summit to Ioulídha; it's paved between Ioulídha and Káto Meriá, and the entire way affords fine views over the thousands of magnificent oaks which are Kéa's most distinctive feature.

Kýthnos (Thermiá)

Though one of the duller and most barren of the Cyclades, a short stay on **Kýthnos**, which owes its alternative name, Thermiá, to its renowned hot springs, is a good antidote to the exploitation likely to be encountered elsewhere. Few foreigners bother to visit, and the island is even quieter than Kéa, particularly to the south where hikes from Dhryopídha, with its colourfully tiled roofs, to coastal coves are the primary diversion. It's a place where Athenians come to buy land for villas, go spear-fishing and sprawl on generally mediocre beaches without having to jostle for space. You could use it as a first or last island stop; in August there are several **ferry connections** a week with Kéa and Lávrio, and frequent ferry and catamaran services to and from Sérifos, Sífnos, Pireás, Mílos and Kímolos.

Mérihas and around

In good weather, boats dock on the west coast at **MÉRIHAS**, a rather functional ferry and fishing port with most of the island's facilities. This fact almost obliges you to stay here, and makes Mérihas more touristy than other spots on the island, but it's redeemed by proximity to the island's best beaches. The nearest is Martinákia, which has a taverna of the same name, but the closest beach of any repute is **Episkopí**, a 500-metre stretch of averagely clean grey sand with a single taverna, thirty minutes' walk north of the town; you can shorten this considerably by sticking to coast-hugging trails and tracks below the road. Far better are the adjacent beaches of **Apókroussi**, which has a canteen, and **Kolóna**, the latter essentially a sand spit joining the islet of Áyios Loukás to Kýthnos. These lie about an hour's walk northwest of Episkopí, and are easiest reached by boat trip from the harbour. Between the first two beaches lie the sparse ruins of the tenth-century fortified town of **Vryókastro**.

Owners of **accommodation** often meet the ferries in high season. There are numerous rooms to let, but they tend to be large and equipped for visiting families, so they can be on the expensive side – although with some opportunity for bargaining during the week. Out of season, owners are often not on the premises, but a contact phone number is usually posted. Few places have sea views, one exception being the rooms maintained by Yannoulis Larentzakis (☎22810 32247; ❸), near the ferry dock. A little inland, behind the small bridge on the seafront, *Panayiota* (☎22810 32268; May–Oct; ❸) and *Studios Panorama* (☎22810 32184; May–Oct; ❹) are decent choices; and there are plenty of other rooms and studios of similar price and quality along the same road. The Milos Express agency near the dock may be able to help you find a room (☎22810 32104, ℱ22810 32291). Camping is generally tolerated, even on Martinákia beach.

The best **restaurants** are *Ostria*, a classic fish taverna on the waterfront, *Gialos*, specializing in lamb dishes, and *To Kandouni*, furthest from the ferry, a tasty grill with specialities such as *sfougáto* ("Cretan omelette"). There's also a bakery on the road to Dhryopídha.

The **bus service**, principally to Loutrá, Hóra, Dhryopídha and Kanála, is reasonably reliable, running around six times daily in season; the only motorbike rental is through the main Milos Express agency and is noticeably more expensive than on many islands. The Cava Kythnos shop doubles as the official **National Bank** outlet (exchange all day, credit cards accepted for a three-percent fee), and is the agent for hydrofoil tickets and the boat to Kéa.

Hóra and Loutrá

HÓRA lies 6km northeast of Mérihas, in the middle of the island. Tilting south off an east–west ridge, and laid out to an approximate grid plan, it's an awkward blend of Kéa-style gabled roofs, Cycladic churches with dunce-cap cupolas, and concrete monsters. There is a **post office** (open only until noon); the closest accommodation at present is at Loutrá. You can **eat** at the friendly *To Kentro* taverna near the small, central square, at the folksy *To Steki tou Detzi* grill, or at *Messaria*, whose specialities include rabbit in wine sauce.

The much-vaunted resort of **LOUTRÁ** (3km north of Hóra and named after its thermal baths) is scruffy, its nineteenth-century spa long since replaced by a sterile modern construction. The best **taverna**, *Katerini*, is a little out on a limb in the neighbouring bay to the west. Otherwise there are a few seafront bars and tavernas offering basic services, such as showers, to yachting crews. There is no shortage of places to sleep: **pensions** such as *Delfini* (☎22810 31430; ❸), *Meltemi* (☎22810 31271, ⓦwww.meltemihotel-kythnos.gr; ❸, apartments ❺), where the owners run walking trips around the island, and *Porto Klaras* (☎22810 31276, ⓦwww.porto-klaras.gr; ❹), with lovely sea views, are acceptable choices. The new *Kythnos Bay* (☎22810 31218; ❻), meanwhile, is probably the most comfortable option. You can also stay in the state-run *Xenia* baths complex (☎ 22810 31217; ④), where a twenty-minute bath plus basic check-up – blood pressure, heart rate and weight – costs about €5. The small bay of Ayía Iríni, just 1km east of Loutrá, and north of the church from which it takes its name, is a more pleasant place to swim and boasts the decent *Trehandíri* taverna on the hill above the bay. About a ninety-minute walk from Loutrá, on Cape Kéfalos, lie the picturesque ruins of the medieval **Kástro toú Áï Yióryi**, abandoned in the mid-seventeenth century.

Dhryopídha and southern Kýthnos

You're handily placed in Hóra to tackle the most interesting thing to do on Kýthnos: the beautiful **walk** south to Dhryopídha. It takes about ninety minutes, initially following the old cobbled way that leaves Hóra heading due south; critical junctions in the first few minutes are marked by red paint dots. The only reliable water source is a well in the valley bottom, reached after thirty minutes, just before a side trail to the triple-naved **chapel of Áyios Spyrídhon** which has recycled Byzantine columns. Just beyond this, you collide with a bulldozed track between Dhryopídha and Áyios Stéfanos, but purists can avoid it by bearing west towards some ruined ridgetop windmills and picking up secondary paths for the final forty minutes of the hike.

More appealing than Hóra by virtue of spanning a ravine, **DHRYOPÍDHA**, with its pleasing tiled roofs, is reminiscent of Spain or Tuscany. A surprisingly large place, it was once the island's capital, built around a famous cave, the Katafíki, at the head of a well-watered valley. Tucked away behind the cathedral is a tiny **folklore museum** that opens erratically in high season. Beside the cathedral is a cheap *psistariá*, *To Steki*. Some people let rooms in their houses, but the nearest official accommodation is 6km south at Kanála.

KANÁLA is a good alternative to Loutrá. There are some rooms in the older settlement up on the promontory and a good taverna, *Louloudhas*, with a huge terrace overlooking the larger western beach, **Megáli Ámmos**, which also has rooms and a combination snack-bar and taverna. Three of the nicer **pensions** in the area are *Nikos Bouritis* (☎ 22810 32195; ④), *Nikos Filippaios* (☎ 22810 32653; ④) and the *Margarita* (☎ 22810 32265; B&B ④), which has a home-like atmosphere. From Kanála, a succession of small coves extends up the east coast as far as **ÁYIOS STÉFANOS**, a small coastal hamlet.

Southwest of Dhryopídha, reached by a turning off the road to Kanála, **Flamboúri** is the most presentable beach on the west coast. The double bay of **Ayíou Dhimitríou** further south, although not too exciting, has a couple of tavernas and rooms to rent in high season.

Sérifos

Sérifos has long languished outside the mainstream of history and modern tourism. Little has happened here since the legendary Perseus returned with Medusa's head, in time to save his mother, Danaë, from being ravished by the local king Polydectes – turning him, his court and the green island into stone. Many would-be visitors are deterred by the apparently barren, hilly interior, which, with the stark, rocky coastline, makes Sérifos appear uninhabited until the ferry turns into Livádhi bay. Though newly paved roads have made the interior more accessible in recent years, the island is best recommended for serious **walkers**, who can head for several small villages in the under-explored interior, plus some isolated coves. Modern Serifots love seclusion, and here, more than anywhere else in the Cyclades, you will find farmsteads miles from anywhere, with only a donkey path to their door. Many people still keep livestock and produce their own wines, and many also cultivate the wild narcissus for export.

Few islanders speak much English; even a few select words of amateur Greek will come in handy and will be warmly received.

Livádhi and the main beaches

Most visitors stay in the port, **LIVÁDHI**, set in a wide greenery-fringed bay and handy for most of the island's beaches. The usually calm bay here is a magnet for island-hopping yachts, whose crews chug to and fro in dinghies all day and night to take on fresh water which, despite appearances, Sérifos has in abundance. It's not the most attractive place on Sérifos and mosquitoes abound, but Livádhi and the neighbouring cove of Livadhákia are certainly the easiest places to find rooms and any amenities you might need, all of which are very scarce elsewhere.

Unfortunately, the long **beach** at Livádhi is nothing to write home about; the sand is hard-packed and muddy, and the water weedy and prone to intermittent jellyfish flotillas – only the far northeastern end is at all usable. Heading away from the dock, turn left up the main business street, or climb over the southerly headland from the cemetery, to reach the neighbouring, far superior, **Livadhákia**, a golden-sand beach, shaded by tamarisk trees, with an acceptable taverna. If you prefer more seclusion, five minutes' stroll across the headland to the south brings you to the smaller **Karávi** beach, which is cleaner and almost totally naturist, but has no shade or facilities.

A 45-minute walk north of the port along a bumpy track leads to **Psilí Ámmos**, a sheltered, white-sand beach considered the best on the island. Accordingly it's popular, with two rival tavernas that tend to be full in high season. Naturists are pointed – via a ten-minute walk across the headland – towards the larger and often deserted **Áyios Ioánnis** beach, but this is rather exposed with no facilities at all, and only the far south end is inviting. Both beaches are theoretically visited by *kaïkia* from Livádhi, as are two nearby sea caves, but don't count on it. Additionally, and plainly visible from arriving ferries, two more sandy coves hide at the far eastern flank of the island opposite an islet; they are accessible on foot only, by a variation of the track to Psilí Ámmos. The more northerly of the two, **Áyios Sóstis**, has a well with fresh water and is the most commonly used beach for secluded camping.

Practicalities

The helpful Krinas Travel (☎ 22810 51448, ⓦ www.serifos-travel.com), near the jetty, sells **boat** tickets. The **bus stop** and posted schedule are at the base of the yacht and fishing-boat jetty; **buses** connect Livádhi with Hóra, 2km away, every half hour in season, but only manage one or two daily trips to Megálo Livádhi, Galaní and Kállitsos. You can rent a **bike** or **car** from Blue Bird (☎ 22810 51511), next to the filling station on the main street, or from Krinas Travel. There are a couple of **ATM**s along the seafront, and **Internet** access on a sole computer is available at the Malabar pub, inside the shopping arcade.

Accommodation

Proprietors don't always meet ferries, with the exception of the excellent *Coralli Camping* (see below), complete with pool and restaurant, by the beach in Livadhákia, which regularly sends a minibus. In high season you'll have to step lively off the boat to get a decent bed; the most rewarding hunting grounds are on the headland above the ferry dock in Livádhi itself, or the more peaceful Livadhákia, a ten-minute walk away. Unlike many other islands, most of the accommodation is open year-round.

Livádhi

Anna's Rooms On the seafront ☎ 22810 51263. Comfortable doubles with shared veranda. ❹

Margaritas On the beach at the other end of the bay away from the main town ☎ 22810 51321. Basic, family-run rooms with verandas in a peaceful spot. ❷

Naias Hotel Near the ferry dock ☎ 22810 51749, ⓦ www.naiasserifos.gr. Slightly dated, but comfortable, good-value hotel. All rooms come with balconies, and some with sea views. Breakfast €5 extra. ❹

Pension Cristi On the headland overlooking the bay ☎ 22810 51775. Beautiful, cool modern pension in great location. Rooms are large and airy, sharing an enormous veranda with sea views. ❹

Livadhákia

Alexandros Vassilea On the beach, behind the taverna of the same name ☎ 22810 51119. Cluster of spotless, balconied doubles (❸) and apartments (❹). April–Oct.

Coralli Camping Bungalows On the beach ☎ 22810 51500, ⓦ www.coralli.gr. Excellent bungalows (❹) on the campsite, with communal pool and bar. Also run the brand-new 4–6-person *Coralli Studios* (❺) closer to town.

Helios Main road through Livádhakia ☎ & ⓕ 22810 51066. Welcoming bougainvillea-draped pension with homely doubles and all mod cons. ❹

Vaso Rooms Close to the beach ☎ 22810 51346. Spacious doubles and triples, some with kitchens, and all with balconies. ❸

Eating and nightlife

As on most islands, **tavernas** near the quay tend to be slightly pricier; walk up the beach and meals get less expensive. The new bar-restaurant *Passaggio* does some good trans-European fare, although it's not the cheapest spot, and it is popular later in the evening, whilst a little further along the bay, the more traditional *Takis* is another good choice. Cheaper options include *Stamatis*, a local favourite, and, at the extreme northeast end of the beach, *Margarita's* with a homely feel and courtyard seating. For crêpes, ice cream, and *loukoumádhes* try *Meli*, in the commercial centre by the port police.

Nightlife is surprisingly lively, and most of it is clustered in or near a mini-mall on the seafront just up from the yacht jetty, so you should be able to quickly find something to suit your taste. As well as *Passaggio*, *Karnayio* next door is a popular night-time spot; both play excellent and varied music. One street back, *Metalleio* is a more full-on dance bar that gets into the swing after midnight. For something more Greek, try *Alter Ego* behind the shopping arcade, or the fiercely local *Edem Music Club* on the road up to Hóra.

Hóra

HÓRA is a pleasant if steep forty-minute walk up a cobbled way (if you're travelling light), with the *kalderími* leading off from a bend in the road about 300m out of Livádhi. By late September, you'll have no choice but to walk, since the bus – like nearly everything else – ceases operation for the winter.

Quiet and atmospheric, Hóra teeters precariously above the harbour and is one of the least spoilt villages of the Cyclades. The best sights are on the town's borders; tiny churches cling to the cliff-edge, and there are breathtaking views across the valleys below. At odd intervals along its alleyways, you'll find part of the old castle making up the wall of a house, or a marble statue leaning incongruously in one corner.

The central platía is home to a couple of atmospheric tavernas, which make a nice alternative to eating on the rowdier seafront down below, whilst *Aerino* bar, nearby, offers a romantic spot for an evening drink. Near the bus stop, the *Petros* and *Stavros* tavernas are also good choices. The latter, also known as the *Panorama Restaurant* for its view, can arrange **rooms** (☎22810 51303; ❷). The island's **post office** is found in the lowest quarter, and a few more expensive rooms for rent lie about 200m north of town, on the street above the track to the cemetery.

From Hóra, a pleasant diversion is the hour-long **walk** down to **Psilí Ámmos**: start from beside Hóra's cemetery and aim for the lower of two visible pigeon towers, and then keep close to the phone wires, which will guide you towards the continuation of the double-walled path descending to a bend in the road just above the beach.

Northern Sérifos

North of Hóra, the island's high water table sometimes breaks the surface to run in delightful rivulets swarming with turtles and frogs, though in recent years many of the open streams seem to have dried up. Reeds, orchards and even the occasional palm tree still take advantage of the unexpected moisture, even if it's no longer visible. This is especially true at **KÁLLITSOS** (Kéndarhos), reached by a ninety-minute path from Hóra, marked by fading red paint splodges along a donkey track above the cemetery. Once at Kállitsos (no facilities), a paved road leads west for 3km to the fifteenth- to seventeenth-century **monastery of Taxiarhón**, designed for sixty monks but presently home only to one of the island's two parish priests – part of a dying breed of farmer-fisherman monks. If he's about, the priest will show you treasures in the monastic church, such as an ivory-inlaid bishop's throne, silver lamps from Egypt (to where many Serifots emigrated during the nineteenth century) and the finely carved *témblon*.

As you loop back towards Hóra from Kállitsos on the asphalt, the fine villages of Galaní and Panayía (named after its tenth-century church) make convenient stops. In **GALANÍ** you can sometimes get simple **meals** at the central store, which also sells excellent, tawny-pink, sherry-like wine; its small-scale production in the west of the island is highly uneconomic, so you'll find it at few other places. Below the village, trails lead to the remote and often windswept beach of **Sykaminiá**, with no facilities and no camping allowed; a better bet for a local swim is the more sheltered cove of **Platýs Yialós** at the extreme northern tip of the island, reached by a partly paved track (negotiable by scooter) that branches off just east of Taxiarhón. The neighbouring beach has a taverna that may have a couple of very basic rooms available in season. The church at **Panayía** is usually locked, but comes alive on its feast day of Xilopanayía (August 16). Traditionally, the first couple to dance around the adjacent olive tree would be the first to marry that year, but this led to unseemly brawls so the priest always goes first these days.

Southwestern Sérifos

A little way south of Panayía, you reach a junction in the road. Turn left to return to Hóra, or continue straight towards **Megálo Horió** – the site of ancient Seriphos, but with little else to recommend it. A few kilometres' detour off this road, **Avéssalos** is one of the island's least explored beaches, making up for its relatively uninspiring landscape with sheer peace and quiet. **Megálo Livádhi**, further on from Megálo Horió, is a remote and quiet beach resort 8km west of Hóra, with two lovely tavernas whose tables are practically on the beach. *Iy Marditsa* taverna has some simple rooms behind the beach (☎22810 51003; ➋). Iron and copper ore were once exported from here, but cheaper African deposits sent the mines into decline and today most of the idle machinery rusts away, though some gravel-crushing still goes on. At the north end of the beach, there's a monument to four workers killed during a protest against unfair conditions in 1916. An alternative turning just below Megálo Horió leads to the small mining and fishing port of **Koutalás**, a pretty sweep of bay with a church-tipped rock, and a long if narrow beach. It has become rather a ghost settlement and the workers' restaurants have all closed down, but there is one snack-bar/taverna, catering mainly to yachting crews. Above the port are the scant ruins of a medieval **kástro**. The winding track above the village leads to Livádhi, and apart from the pleasant **Gánema** beach, which has a taverna of the same name, there are no places to rest or buy refreshments on the two-hour journey back.

Sífnos

Sífnos is a more immediately appealing island than its northern neighbours since it's prettier, more cultivated and has some fine architecture. This means that it's also much more popular; be aware that in July and August, rooms are very difficult to find. Take any you can find as you arrive, or come armed with a reservation. In keeping with the island's somewhat upmarket clientele, signalled by new luxury hotels springing up across the island, camping rough is forbidden, while nudity is tolerated only in isolated coves.

The island's modest size – no bigger than Kýthnos or Sérifos – makes it eminently explorable. The **bus service** is excellent, most of the roads quite decent, and there's a network of paths that is fairly easy to follow. Sífnos has a strong tradition of pottery (as early as the third century BC) and has long been esteemed for its distinctive cuisine, intrinsically linked to the development of pottery, which allowed for the more sophisticated preparation of baked dishes. The island is perhaps best appreciated today, however, for its many beautifully situated **churches** and **monasteries**.

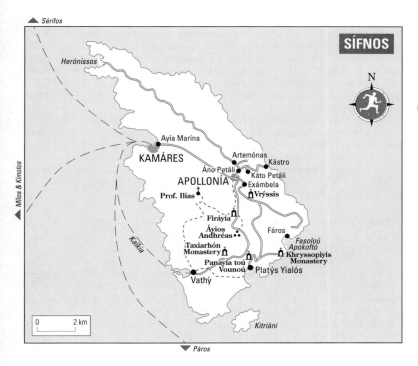

Ferry connections are more frequent to Sífnos than to the other more northerly islands. In season, the *Express Milos* and *Express Pegasus* ply a regular shuttle via Kýthnos and Sérifos, then on to Mílos and Kímolos before heading east to Folégandhros, Síkinos, Íos and Thíra, from where the course is reversed back to Pireás, whilst the new Speedrunner (operated by the family who run *Elies*; see p.137) links Sífnos with Kýthnos, Sérifos, Páros and Mílos on an almost daily basis in season. Links with the central Cyclades are far less frequent, with twice-weekly high-season ferries to Páros or Sýros, as well as a high-speed service to Thíra.

Kamáres

KAMÁRES, the island's port, is tucked away at the foot of high, bare cliffs in the west, which enclose a beach. A compact resort with concrete blocks of villas edging up to the base of the cliffs, Kamáres' seafront road is crammed with bars, travel agencies, ice-cream shops and restaurants. Proprietors tend not to meet boats; while hunting for a room, you can store luggage at the Aegean Thesaurus **travel agency** (☎22840 33151) right by the ferry dock, who also book accommodation across the island, and sell a worthwhile package consisting of an accurate topographical map, bus/boat schedules and a short text on Sífnos (€2). They can also book you on hiking tours or Greek cookery lessons.

Accommodation is relatively expensive, though bargaining can be productive outside peak season. Try the reasonable *Hotel Stavros* (☎22840 33383, ⓦwww.sifnostravel.com; ❹), who have a decent book exchange in their reception, or, further along above the town beach, the friendly *Boulis Hotel* (☎22840

32122, ⓦwww.hotelboulis.gr; ❺). Above the *Boulis*, the welcoming *Makis* **campsite** (☎22840 32366, ⓦwww.makiscamping.gr) has good facilities and good-value air-conditioned rooms (❸). Continue past the *Makis* and turn right up from the end of the beach to find newer, quieter accommodation in a cluster of houses known as Ayía Marína, including the *Mosha Pension* (☎22840 31719, ⓕ22840 33719; ❸), and the *Delphini Hotel* (☎22840 33740 ⓕ22840 33741; ❼), which has its own pool.

The best **restaurants** are *Meropi Kambourakis*, ideal for a pre-ferry lunch; the *Boulis* on the waterfront with its collection of huge retsina barrels; *O Argyris* fish taverna; ⍝ *Camaron*, serving great pastas and pizzas; the cosy *Kamares* ouzerí and good-value *Kyra Margena* at the far end of the beach in Ayía Marína. Kamáres also has a little **nightlife**; try *Yamas*, good for a sunset cocktail and **Internet** access, and *Follie-Follie*. The best place to **rent a scooter or car** is at *No. 1*, on the road to Apollonía.

Apollonía and Artemónas

A steep twenty-minute bus ride (hourly service until late at night) takes you up to **APOLLONÍA**, the centre of Hóra, an amalgam of three hilltop villages which have merged over the years into one continuous community. With white buildings, flower-draped balconies, belfries and pretty squares, it is eminently scenic, though not self-consciously so. On the central platía, Iroöon, the **folk museum** (daily 9.30am–2pm & 6–10pm; €1), with its collection of textiles, lace, costumes and weaponry, is worth a visit.

Radiating out from the platía is a network of stepped marble footways and the main pedestrian street, flagstoned Odhós Stylianoú Prókou, which leads off to the south, lined with shops, restaurants, bars and churches, including the cakebox cathedral, **Áyios Spyrídhon**, and the eighteenth-century church of **Panayía Ouranoforía** (commonly transliterated as Yeraniofórou and many variations thereof), which stands in the highest quarter of town, incorporating fragments of a seventh-century BC temple of Apollo and a relief of St George over the door. Nearby, **Áyios Athanásios**, next to Platía Kleánthi Triandafýlou, has frescoes and a wooden *témblon*. Some 3km southeast, a short distance from the village of Exámbela, you'll find the active monastery of **Vrýssis** which dates from 1612 and is home to a good collection of religious artefacts and manuscripts.

ARTEMÓNAS, fifteen minutes north of Apollonía on foot and served by frequent buses, is worth a morning's exploration for its churches and elegant Venetian and Neoclassical houses. **Panayía Gourniá** (the key is kept at the house next door) has vivid frescoes; the clustered-dome church of **Kohí** was built over an ancient temple of Artemis (also the basis of the village's name); and seventeenth-century **Áyios Yeóryios** contains fine icons. Artemónas is also the point of departure for **Herónissos**, an isolated hamlet with a few tavernas and potteries behind a deeply indented, rather bleak bay at the northwestern tip of the island. The road is paved, and you may find occasional boat trips from Kamáres, though these are only worth the effort on calm days.

Practicalities

The **post office** and **bus stop** edge onto Apollonía's central platía. The **bank** and **police station** are located on the main road leading north out of town, and there's an **Internet** café on the road to Fáros. You can rent **bikes** at Moto Apollo, beside the petrol station on the road to Fáros, but the island is best explored on foot. There are **rooms** scattered all over the village, making them hard to find; *Giamaki Rooms* (T 22840 33973, F 22840 33923; ❸) just off the main pedestrian street is an excellent choice. Your best bet is to look on the square for the main branch of the excellent Aegean Thesaurus travel agency (T 22840 33151, W www.thesaurus.gr), or try the nearby Room Rental Association (T 22840 31333). The very friendly *Hotel Sifnos* (T 22840 31624, W www.sifnoshotel.com; ❺), on the main pedestrian street, is the most traditional in its architecture and furnishing. A bit further along, *Patriarca* (T 22840 32400, W www.patriarca.gr; ❼) is a stunning new boutique hotel just below the cathedral. All the central hotels are sure to be noisy when the nearby clubs are open during the summer, but if you want quieter premises with a better view, be prepared to pay more: *Margarita Kouki* (T 22840 31894; ❸), above the luxurious *Petali Village* (T 22840 33024, W www.hotelpetali.gr; ❼), north of the square on the pedestrian lane, is a welcome exception.

There are a number of **restaurants** in Apollonía, including *Iy Orea Sifnos*, with good food despite its kitsch decor, on the central square. On the main pedestrian street, the charmingly decorated *Odos Oneiron* offers eclectic upscale dishes, while the more reasonably priced *Adiexodos* offers great *mezédhes* on its terrace with a view; *Cafe Sifnos* does something for nearly every taste and is open all day. There are several tavernas up in the backstreets: *To Apostoli to Koutouki* is quite good for standard Greek fare and very reasonable. Probably the best and most famous place to eat on the island, owing to its highly rated chef, is ⚘ *Liotrivi (Manganas)* (T 22840 31246) on the square up in Artemónas, where there's also an excellent bakery.

Most of the **nightlife** can be found on the main pedestrian street south of the square, where you'll find *Botsi*, *Volto* and the long-standing *Argo*. The *Camel Club*, on the road to Fáros, is another popular place for late-night action. For *rebétika* music there's the *Aloni*, just above the crossroad to Kástro.

The east coast

Most of Sífnos's coastal settlements are along the less precipitous eastern shore, within a modest distance of Apollonía and its surrounding cultivated plateau. These all have good bus services, and a certain amount of food and accommodation, **Kástro** being far more appealing than the resorts of **Platýs Yialós** and **Fáros** which can get very overcrowded in July and August.

Kástro

KÁSTRO seems the last place on Sífnos to fill up in season, and can be reached on foot from Apollonía in 45 minutes, all but the last ten on a clear path threading its way east via the hamlet of Káto Petáli. Built on a rocky outcrop with an almost sheer drop to the sea on three sides, the ancient capital of the island retains much of its medieval character. Parts of its boundary walls survive, along with a full complement of sinuous, narrow streets graced by balconied, two-storey houses and some fine sixteenth- and seventeenth-century churches with ornamental floors. Venetian coats of arms and ancient wall fragments can still be seen on some of the older dwellings; there are the remains of the ancient acropolis (including a ram's-head sarcophagus by one of the medieval gates), as well as a small **archeological museum** (Tues–Sun 8am–2.30pm; free), which does not always stick closely to the official opening hours, installed in a former Catholic church in the higher part of the village.

Among the several **rooms**, the modernized *Aris Rafeletos* apartments (T & F 22840 31161; ❺) are open all year. More basic, but boasting gorgeous views, *Maximos* (T 22840 33692; ❸) has a couple of rooms next to his jewellery shop.

Nationally renowned, but disarmingly shabby, ⚓ *To Astro* is an obvious taverna to try, as is the slightly more orderly *Leonidas*, while the *Kavos Sunrise* café-bar is laid-back and has a fantastic view. On the edge of town, the *Castello* disco-bar is a livelier hangout.

There's nothing approximating a beach in Kástro; for a swim you have to walk to the nearby rocky coves of **Serália** (to the southeast, and with more rooms) and **Paláti**. You can also hike – from the windmills on the approach road near Káto Petáli – to either the sixteenth-century monastery of **Khryssostómou** or along a track opposite the cliff face that overlooks the picture-postcard-perfect church of the **Eptá Martýres** (Seven Martyrs) which juts out into the sea; nudists sun themselves and snorkel on and around the flat rocks below.

Platýs Yialós

From Apollonía, there are almost hourly buses to the resort of **PLATÝS YIALÓS**, 12km away, near the southern tip of the island. Despite claims to be the longest beach in the Cyclades, the sand can get very crowded. Diversions include a pottery workshop, but many are put off by the continuous row of snack-bars and rooms to rent, which line the entire stretch of beach, and also the strong winds that plague it. **Rooms** are generally expensive; the welcoming *Pension Aggeliki* (℡22840 71288, ⓦwww.sifnosageliki.com; ❹), near the bus stop, has reasonably priced doubles (❹) however, as well as some stunning apartments (❼); *Hotel Efrossyni* (℡22840 71353, ⓦwww.hotel-efrosini.gr; B&B ❺), next door, is comfortable. The local **campsite** (℡22840 71286) is rather uninspiring – a stiff hike inland, shadeless and on sloping, stony ground. Among several fairly pricey **tavernas** are *Ariadne*, with a nicely shaded verandah, *Foni*, a friendly fish taverna that hosts live music acts some evenings, and *Kalimera*, with French-influenced Greek cuisine, whilst a five-minute walk over the headland brings you to Lazarou Beach, a tiny bay entirely occupied by a bar and restaurant stretching right the way down to the water's edge.

A more rewarding half-hour walk uphill from Platýs Yialós brings you to the convent of **Panayía toú Vounoú** (though it's easy to get lost on the way without the locally sold map); the caretaker should let you in if she's about.

Fáros and around

There are less crowded beaches just to the northeast of Platýs Yialós (though unfortunately not directly accessible along the coast). **FÁROS**, with regular bus links to Apollonía, makes an excellent fall-back base. A small and friendly resort, it has some of the cheapest **accommodation** on the island, as well as a couple of more upmarket places, including Fabrica (℡22840 71427, ⓦwww .fabrica-sifnos.com; ❻), which maintains comfortable rooms in two charming properties; one a historic eighteenth-century stone structure. *To Kyma* is a pleasant seafront **taverna**, and the smart *On the Rocks*, perched on the headland at the far end of **Fasoloú beach**, serves a tasty selection of snacks as well as full meals. The chef at *Zambelis,* meanwhile, claims to have served as personal chef to Christina Onassis. The closest beaches are not up to much: the town strand itself is muddy, shadeless and crowded, and the one to the northeast past the headland is not much better. Head off in the opposite direction, however, through the older part of the village, and things improve at **Glyfó**, a longer, wider family beach about twenty minutes away.

Continuing from Glyfó, a fifteen-minute cliffside path leads to the beach of **Apokoftó**, with a couple of good tavernas, and, up an access road, to the *Hotel Flora* (℡22840 71278; ❺), which has superb views. The shore itself tends to collect seaweed, however, and a rock reef must be negotiated to get into the water. Flanking Apokoftó to the south, marooned on a sea-washed spit and featuring on every EOT poster of the island, is the disestablished, seventeenth-century **Khryssopiyís monastery**. According to legend, the cleft in the rock appeared when two village girls, fleeing to the spit to escape the attentions of menacing pirates, prayed to the Virgin to defend their virtue. The friendly nearby **taverna** bearing the name of the monastery and known locally as *Lebesis* specializes in reasonably priced lamb dishes and has a lovely, shaded terrace.

The interior and Vathý

Apollonía is a good base from which to start your explorations of more remote Sífnos. Taking the path out from Katavatí (the district south of Apollonía) you'll pass, after a few minutes, the beautiful empty **monastery of Firáyia** and – fifteen minutes along the ugly modern road – the path climbing up to **Áyios Andhréas**, where you'll be rewarded with tremendous views over the islands of Sýros, Páros, Íos, Folégandhros and Síkinos. Just below the church is an enormous Bronze Age archeological site.

Even better is the all-trail walk to Vathý, around three hours from Katavatí. Bear right at a signed junction; part way along, you can detour on a conspicuous side trail to the **monastery of Profítis Ilías**, on the very summit of the island, with a vaulted refectory and extensive views.

Vathý

A fishing village on the shore of a stunning funnel-shaped bay, **VATHÝ** is the most attractive and remote base on the island. However, with the opening of a brand-new luxury hotel, frequented by celebrities and politicians, *Elies Resorts* (☎22840 34000, ⓦwww.eliesresorts.com), the character of this previously remote spot is certainly beginning to change. There are an increasing number of **rooms**, the best deals probably being at *Marana Rooms* (☎22840 71120;❷), at the opposite end of the bay to *Elies*, or those attached to the tiny **monastery of the Archangel Gabriel**. For **food**, *Manolis* does excellent grills and has a fascinating gyrating clay oven in the courtyard; *Okeanida* has good *mezédhes* such as chickpea balls and cheesy aubergine patties, while *Tò Tsikali* behind the monastery has farm-fresh cheese and rabbit dishes.

There are regular **buses** (8 daily in high season, 2 daily at other times), and *kaïkia* run daily in season from Kamáres. It is possible to walk to Platýs Yiálos in ninety minutes, but the path is not well marked.

Mílos

Volcanic **Mílos** is geologically diverse with weird rock formations, hot springs, good beaches and sensational views. Minoan settlers were attracted by obsidian, and other products of its volcanic soil made the island one of the most impor-tant of the Cyclades in the ancient world. Today, the quarrying of barite, perlite and porcelain has left deep scars on the landscape but given the island a relative prosperity and independence. With more **beaches** than any other island in the Cyclades, Mílos hasn't had to tart itself up to court tourism – in itself a good reason to stay several days.

You get a good preview of the island's **geological wonders** as your ferry enters Mílos Bay, one of the world's most striking natural harbours, shaped by a series of ancient explosions. Off the north coast, accessible only by excursion boat, the Glaroníssia (Seagull Isles) are shaped like massed organ pipes, and there are more strange formations on the southwest coast at Kléftiko. Inland, too, you frequently come across odd, volcanic outcrops, and thermal springs burst forth.

Like most volcanic islands, Mílos is quite fertile; away from the summits of **Profítis Ilías** in the southwest and lower hills in the east, a gently undulating countryside is intensively cultivated to produce grain, hay and orchard fruits. The island's domestic architecture, with its lava-built, two-up-two-down houses, isn't as immediately impressive as its more pristine neighbours, but is charming nonetheless.

Adhámas

The main, lively port of **ADHÁMAS**, known as Adhámandas to locals, was founded by Cretan refugees fleeing a failed rebellion in 1841. With a handsome marble-paved esplanade around its natural headland, it's now among the most attractive ports in the Cyclades.

Towards the south beach, the **Mining Museum of Mílos** (summer daily 9am–2pm & 6–9pm; free) houses an extensive collection of mining tools, minerals and geological maps of Mílos. Near the quayside, the small but interesting **Ecclesiastical Museum** (sporadically open in summer; free) is housed in the century-old Áyia Triádha church. Highly recommended is one of the **boat tours** around the island, which make several stops at otherwise inaccessible swimming spots like the magnificent Kléftiko, continuing along the bizarre coastline and passing the Glaroníssia on the way to Kímolos (see p.143) where they often stop for a late lunch. Weather permitting, the boats normally leave at 9am from the quayside, and return at 6pm. Tickets cost around €30 per person, including lunch.

Practicalities

There are several **banks**, a **post office** and an **Internet café** near the Ecclesiastical Museum, as well as the hub of the island's **bus services**, which run hourly to Pláka, nine times daily in high season to Pollónia, seven times daily to Provatás and Paleohóri via Zefyría. The taxi rank is nearby – call ⓣ22870 22219 to book. Some visitors arrive by plane from Athens; most seats, however, are reserved by the local mining industry. Olympic Airways is located near the National Bank, near Adhámas port; the **airport** is 5km southeast of the port, close to Zefyría.

During high season, the highly organized **tourist office** opposite the ferry dock (ⓣ22870 22445, ⓦwww.milos-island.gr) has a daily updated list of available rooms around the island and a handy brochure, while Milos Travel, also on the waterfront (ⓣ22870 22000, ⓦwww.milostravel.gr), is another good resource for finding somewhere to stay, and also offers coastal boat trips, car rental, maps and ferry tickets; next door, the Brau Kat agency can book sea kayaking trips.

Accommodation

Most accommodation is concentrated on the hill above the harbour and on or just off the main road to Pláka, and ranges from moderately priced addresses with shared facilities, such as the rooms of *Anna Gozadinou* (ⓣ22870 22364; ❸), to smart rooms with TV and all mod cons, such as *Mimosa* (ⓣ22870 21688, ⓔmimosa@panafonet.gr; ❹), and the spacious, elegant studios of ⚡ *Villa Notos* (ⓣ22870 21943, ⓦwww.villanotos.gr; ❺), run by a charming family, in a peaceful spot by the town beach left of the ferry landing. Some of the best hotels include the *Delfini* (ⓣ22870 22001; ❹), one block behind the town beach; the stylish, central, double-glazed *Portiani Hotel* (ⓣ22870 22940, ⓔsirmalen@otenet.gr; ❻) and the luxury *Santa Maria Village* (ⓣ22870 21949, ⓦwww.santamaria-milos .gr; ❼), 300m behind the beach. The **campsite** (ⓣ22870 31410, ⓦwww .miloscamping.gr) at Hivadholímni beach (see p.142) on the south shore of the bay also has bungalows (❺); its minibus meets ferries.

Eating and nightlife

⚡ *Flisvos*, near the jetty, is a good place to **eat**, with a varied menu, and excellent people-watching potential. Of the three adjacent tavernas along the seafront towards the long tamarisk-lined beach south of town, *Navagio*, specializing in fish, is the best value. Just off the main street inland, *Pitsounakia* is a good, cheap *psistariá* with a pleasant courtyard. For **nightlife**, apart from the obvious string of cafés along the main seafront drag, *Akri* and *Aragosta* above the jetty are trendy **bars**, with pleasant views. *Vibera La Betina* next door, and *Malion*, behind the beach, are other current hot spots where the music ranges from loud rock or techno (usually at the former) to Greek pop or the odd live *bouzoukí* night (often at the latter).

Pláka and Trypití

The main appeal of Mílos is in an area that has been the island's focus of habitation since Classical times, where a cluster of villages huddles in the lee of a crag, 4km northwest of the harbour.

PLÁKA (MÍLOS) is the largest of these communities and the official capital of the island. Behind the lower car park, at the top of the approach boulevard through the newer district, the **archeological museum** (Tues–Sun 8.30am–3pm; €3) contains numerous obsidian implements, plus a whole wing of finds from ancient Phylakope (see p.142), whose highlights include a votive lamp in the form of a bull and a rather Minoan-looking terracotta goddess. Labelling is scant, but you'll no doubt recognize the plaster-cast copy of the *Venus de Milo*, the original of which was found on the island in 1820. The statue was promptly delivered to the French consul for "safekeeping" from the Turks; her arms were knocked off in the melee surrounding her abduction. This was the last the Greeks saw of *Venus* until a copy was belatedly sent from the Louvre in Paris. Up in a mansion of the old quarter, the newly renovated **folk museum** (Tues–Sat 10am–2pm & 6–9pm, Sun 10am–2pm; €3) has a well-presented array of artefacts related to the history of arts, crafts and daily life on Mílos.

A stairway beginning near the police station leads up to the old Venetian **kástro**, its slopes clad in stone and cement to channel precious rainwater into cisterns. The enormous chapel of **Panayía Thalassítra** looms near the summit, where the ancient Melians made their last stand against the Athenians before the massacre of 416 BC. It offers one of the best views in the Aegean, particularly at sunset in clear conditions.

Pláka has a **post office** and a **motorbike–rental** outfit near the archeological museum. There are **rooms** available scattered around the village, with those on the west side offering spectacular views. Among the nicest of these are the pretty studios of Stratis Vourakis (☎22870 21702;❹). Dimitri Moraitis (☎22870 41353;❺) has newly refurbished rooms in the house where the *Venus de Milo* was allegedly hidden following its discovery, and *Maria's Rooms* (☎22870 21572; ❸) are charming, if basic, studios close to the archeological museum. There are also three or four blocks of modern accommodation overlooking the busy approach road. A number of ouzerís make Pláka a good base for **eating**: highly recommended are *Arhondoula*, serving excellent seafood dishes, and slightly more upscale *Alisachni*, offering classic Greek dishes with a modern flair.

△ Roman amphitheatre and Mílos Bay

The attractive village of **TRYPITÍ** (meaning "perforated"), which takes its name from the cliffside tombs nearby and covers a long ridge 1km south of Pláka, is another good base. There are a few modest **rooms**, two of which are just down the steep street from the tiny platía below the main church. The best places to **eat** are rustic *Glaronisia* serving up traditional taverna fare, and *Ergina*, which features oven-roasted goat and cuttlefish; for coffee and evening drinks, the stylish *Remvi Café* just past the bus stop has great views. From Trypití, it's a pleasant 45-minute walk down to Adhámas via Skinópi on the winding old *kalderími*, which begins on the saddle linking Trypití with the hamlet of Klimatovoúni.

Catacombs, Ancient Melos and the coast

From Pláka's archeological museum, signs point you towards the **early Christian catacombs** (Tues–Sun 8am–5pm; free), 1km south of Pláka and just 400m from Trypití village; steps lead down from the road to the inconspicuous entrance. Some 5000 bodies were buried in tomb-lined corridors stretching some 200m into the soft volcanic rock, making them the largest catacombs in Greece; only the first 50m is illuminated and accessible by boardwalk. Don't miss the ruins of **ancient Melos**, located just above the catacombs, which extend down from Pláka almost to the sea. There are huge Dorian walls, the usual column fragments lying around and, best of all, a well-preserved Roman **amphitheatre** (unrestricted access). Only seven rows of seats remain intact, but these look out evocatively over Klíma to the bay. En route to the theatre from the cement road is the signposted spot where the *Venus de Milo* was found in what may have been the compound's gymnasium.

At the very bottom of the vale, **KLÍMA** is the most photogenic of several fishing hamlets on the island, with its picturesque boathouses tucked underneath the principal living areas. There's no beach to speak of, and only one place to stay – the impeccably sited, if a little basic, *Panorama* (☎22870 21623, ⊕22870 22112; ❹), with an acceptable balcony taverna.

Pláthiena, 45 minutes' walk northwest of Pláka, is the closest proper beach, and thus is extremely popular in summer. There are no facilities, but the beach is fairly well protected and partly shaded by tamarisks.

Southern Mílos

The main road to the south of the island splits at **Kánava junction**, a dreary place at first glance owing to the large power plant. But opposite this, indicated by a rusty sign pointing seaward, is the first of Mílos's **hot springs**, which bubble up in the shallows and are much enjoyed by the locals.

The left or easterly fork leads to **ZEFYRÍA**, hidden among olive groves below the bare hills; it was briefly the medieval capital until an eighteenth-century epidemic drove out the population. Much of the old town is still deserted, though some life has returned, and there's a magnificent seventeenth-century church.

South of here it's a further 8km down a winding road to the coarse-sand beach of **Paleohóri**. Actually a triple strand totalling 800m in length, it's indisputably the island's best; clothing's optional at the westerly cove, where steam vents heat the shallow water and the rock overhangs onshore. There are a number of **places to stay**, such as the inland *Paleochori Studios* (☎22870 31267, ⓔpaleochori@in.gr; ❹), the purpose-built rooms at the *Vihos Artemis* restaurant (☎22870 31222, ⊕22870 23386; ❹) nearer the beach, and the rooms of Maria Tsirigotaki (☎22870 31231; ❸) and at *Panayiota Vikeli* (☎22870 31228; ❹). The best place to **eat** is *Pelagos*, which has a large raised patio.

The westerly road from Kánava junction leads past the airport gate to **Hivad-holímni**, the best beach on Mílos bay itself. Not that this is saying much: Hivadholímni is north-facing and thus garbage-prone, with shallow, grubby water offshore, although there is a taverna, a disco-bar and a sizeable community of campers during the summer. It's better to veer south to **Provatás**, a short but tidy beach, closed off by colourful cliffs to the east. Being so easy to get to, it hasn't escaped some development: there are two rooms establishments plus, closer to the shore, a newer, luxury complex, *Golden Mílos Beach* (☎22870 31307, ✉gmilosbe@otenet.gr; ➐). The best value for food and accommodation is the *Maïstrali* (☎22870 31420, ℻22870 31164; ➎), with private rooms and restaurant right on the beach.

Several kilometres before Provatás, a road forks east through a dusty white quarry to the trendy and popular beach of **Firipláka**. Further east, **Tsigrádho** beach is accessible by boat, or by the novel means of a rope hanging down a crevice in the cliff face. Two kilometres west of Provatás, you'll see a highway sign directing you below and to the left of the road for the village of **Kípos**, home to a small **medieval chapel** dedicated to the Kímisis (Assumption). It sits atop foundations far older – as evidenced by the early Christian reliefs stacked along the west wall and a carved, cruciform baptismal font in the *ierón* behind the altar screen. At one time a spring gushed from the low-tunnel cave beside the font – sufficiently miraculous in itself on arid Mílos. A few minutes to the west, unspoilt **Yérondas** beach is easily accessed, though seldom visited by tourists.

For the most part **Hálakas**, the southwestern peninsula centred on the wilderness of 748-metre Profítis Ilías, is uninhabited and little built upon, with the exception of the **monastery of Sidherianós**. The roads are memorable, if a little tiring, and several spots are worth making the effort to see. **Emboriós** on the east side of the peninsula has a fine little beach and a great local taverna with a few cheap rooms run by Manoulis Koliarkis (☎22870 21389; ➌). On the mostly rugged west coast, **Triádhes** is one of the finest and least spoilt beaches in the Cyclades, but you'll have to bring your own provisions. **Kléftiko** in the southwest corner is only reachable by boat (from Kípos via Yérondas or from Adhámas, see p.138), but repays the effort to get there with its stunning rock formations, semi-submerged rock tunnels and colourful coral.

The north coast

From either Adhámas or the Pláka area, good roads run roughly parallel to the **north coast** which, despite being windswept and largely uninhabited, is not devoid of interest. **Mandhrákia**, reached from Triovássalos, is another boathouse settlement, and **Sarakíniko**, to the east, is a sculpted inlet with a sandy sea bed and a summer beach café. Nearby **Mitakás** is difficult to find along an unmarked trail from the main road but worth the search for its secluded beach. A few kilometres further east, the little hamlet of **Páhena** is not shown on many maps, though it has another lovely beach. For **rooms** in the area try Terry's Travel, based in Adhámas (☎22870 22640, ⓦwww.terrysmilostravel.com; ➌). Still heading east, the remains of three superimposed Neolithic settlements crown a small knoll at **Fylakopí** (ancient Phylakope); the site was important archeologically, but hasn't been maintained and is difficult to interpret. Just before the site is another of Mílos's coastal wonders: the deep-sea inlet of **Papáfranga**, set in a ravine and accessible through a gap in the cliffs.

Pollónia

POLLÓNIA, 12km northeast of Adhámas, is immensely popular with wind-surfers, and a diving centre has further increased its popularity among water-sports enthusiasts. Pollónia is essentially a small harbour protected by a storm-lashed spit of land on the northeast, where self-catering units are multiplying rapidly, fringed by a long, but narrow, tamarisk-lined beach to the rear, and closed off on the south by a smaller promontory on which the tiny original settlement huddles. Besides the town beach, the only other convenient, half-decent beach is at **Voúdhia**, 3km east, where you will find more of the island's hot springs, although it is effectively spoilt by its proximity to huge mining works, which lend it the desolate air of a *Mad Max* location.

On the quay are several **tavernas** and a couple of very mediocre café/snack-bars. Inland and south of here you'll find a concentration of **accommodation**, more simple rooms and apartments, most with the slight drawback of occasional noise and dust from quarry trucks. Among the highest-quality units are *Kapetan Tasos Studios* (T 22870 41287 W www.kapetantasos.gr; ❺), with good views of the straits between Mílos and Kímolos, and the nearby *Kostantakis Studios* (T 22870 041357, W www.kostantakis.gr; ❺), which allows children to help out on the farm. ✠ *Flora* (T 22870 41249, E roulamix@hotmail.com; ❸), with a few cute rooms arranged around a courtyard, and breakfast on the beach, on the road towards the spit, is another option, as are *Efi* rooms (T 22870 41396, E milos2233@yahoo.gr; ❹), above the far end of the beach. *Andreas* (T 22870 41262, E brigitte-milos@bluewin.ch; ❹) has triple studios with stunning views and easy access to the quiet neighbouring bay. Pollónia has no bank or post office, but the friendly Axios Rent A Car office (T & F 22870 41234) can change money and advise you on accommodation matters. They also sell second-hand English books.

Taking the ferry to Kímolos may be the main reason you're here. The *Levkas* car ferry makes the trip about four times daily year-round, although it tends not to sail in high winds; call the port authority (T 22870 28860) to check.

Kímolos

Of the three islets off the coast of Mílos, only **Kímolos** is inhabited. Volcanic like Mílos, with the same little lava-built rural cottages, it profits from its geology and used to export chalk (kimolía in Greek) until the supply was exhausted. Fuller's earth is still extracted locally, and the fine dust of this clay is a familiar sight on the island, where mining still outstrips fishing and farming as an occupation. Rugged and barren in the interior, it has some fertile land on the southeast coast where wells provide water, and this is where the population of about eight hundred is concentrated.

Kímolos is sleepy from September to June, and even in August sees few visitors, just as well since there are fewer than a hundred beds on the whole island, and little in the way of other amenities. This, however, may be about to change as rumours spread of plans to build a geothermic spa on the island.

Psathí, Hóra and Goúpa

Whether you arrive by ferry, or by *kaïki* from Pollónia, you'll dock at the hamlet of **PSATHÍ**, which is pretty much a nonevent except for the excellent *To Kyma* ("The Wave") **taverna** midway along the beach, specializing in fried octopus.

The laissez-faire attitude towards tourism on the island is demonstrated by the fact that **ferry tickets** are only sold outside the expensive café at the end of the jetty, an hour or so before the anticipated arrival of the boat. The *Levkas* comes and goes from Pollónia on Mílos from the base of the jetty four times a day, whilst some of the larger ferries call in on their way to and from Mílos. A minibus runs from the port to the capital, which can also be reached by foot in about fifteen minutes.

Around the bay, there are a few old windmills and dazzlingly white **HÓRA** perched on the ridge above them. The magnificent, two-gated sixteenth-century **kástro** is one of the best preserved of such fortresses, built against marauding pirates in the Cyclades; the perimeter houses are intact and inhabited, though its heart is a jumble of romantic ruins. Just outside the *kástro* to the north stands the conspicuously unwhitewashed, late sixteenth-century church of **Khryssóstomos**, the oldest and most beautiful on the island. Near the church is the new **archeological museum** (irregular hours) with pottery from the Geometric to the Roman period.

There are a few adequate **rooms** near the port, most reserved through the same number (☎22870/51392; ②–④) at which you can also inquire about other rooms around Kímolos. Better situated **accommodation** options include Margaro Petraki's rooms (☎22870 51314;②), tucked away in the rather unglamorous maze of backstreets, or try those of Apostolos Ventouris (☎22870 51329;②) above his *kafenío* nearby. Sofia Ventouris (☎22870 51219; ⑤) has a few new studios with sea views, close to the church. For **meals**, aside from a couple of basic *psistariés* and a café-bar, the aptly named *Panorama*, near the east gate of the *kástro*, is the most elaborate and consistently open taverna. *Meltemi*, to the west of the village, is another good taverna, which also has some rooms (☎22870 51360; ③). Finally, there are a couple of boat agencies, and a **post office** in the west of the village, as well as an **ATM**.

East of Hóra, a ten-minute walk brings you to **GOÚPA**, a traditional fishing village with a few **tavernas**. At its base, **Rémma** beach remains unspoilt, as does **Klíma**, just off the main dirt road to Prássa to the north.

Around the island

During summer at least, the hamlet of **ALYKÍ** on the south coast is a better bet for staying than Psathí and Hóra; it only takes about thirty minutes to walk there on the paved road that forks left from the port. Alykí is named after the saltpan that sprawls between a rather mediocre beach offering no shade or shelter, but where you'll find the **rooms** of Sardi (☎22870 51458; ③) and Pasamichalis (☎22870 51340; ③), as well as a few simple **tavernas**. You can stroll west one cove to **Bonátsa** for better sand and shallow water, though you won't escape the winds. Passing another cove you come to the even more attractive beach of **Kalamítsi**, with better shade and a decent taverna. To the east, between Alykí and Psathí, the smaller, more secluded beach of **Skála** is better for camping, which is generally tolerated here.

The 700 metre coarse-sand beach of **Elliniká** is a 45-minute walk west of Alykí; starting on the road, bear left – just before two chapels on a slope – onto a narrower track which runs through the fields at the bottom of the valley. Divided by a low bluff, the beach is bracketed by two capes and looks out over Dhaskalió islet and across to harder-to-reach Kambána beach, home of nesting turtles. Elliniká tends to catch heavy weather in the afternoon, and there are no facilities here.

Another road leads northeast from Hóra to a beach and radioactive springs at **Prássa**, 7km away. The route takes in impressive views across the straits to

Κávo Dóro Channel

ÁNDHROS

Cape Fássa

Makroyiáli Bay

Hártes

Amolohós Vitáli

Apáno Fellós

Fellós Bay

Áyios Pétros Aténi Vorí

Áyios Nikólaos Monastery

GÁVRIO

Khryssí Ammos

Káto Katákilos

Vourkotí

Yiália Nimborió

Batsí

Ano Katákilos Arnás

Steniés

HÓRA (ÁNDHROS TOWN)

Delavóyias

Káto Apróvato

Apikía

Áno Apróvato Strapouríes

Messariá

Paleópolis Ménites

Aladino

Sinéti

Falliká

Panakhrándoú Monastery

Stavrópedha

Yerónikas Paleókastro

Zagorá

Kapariá

Korthí

Aïdhónia

N

Epátia

Profítis Ilías

Ayía Moní

0   5 km

Rafína

▼ Tínos, Mýkonos, Sýros

Políegos, and there are several shady peaceful coves where it's possible to camp out. Innumerable goat tracks invite exploration of the rest of the island; in the northwest, on Kímolos's summit, are the ruins of an imposing Venetian fortress known as **Paleókastro**.

Ándhros

Ándhros, the second largest and northernmost of the Cyclades, is also one of the most verdant, making it a great place for serious walkers. Thinly populated but prosperous, its fertile, well-watered valleys and gorges have sprouted scores of Athenian holiday villas whose red-tiled roofs and white walls stand out among the greenery. Some of the more recent of these have robbed many of the villages of life and atmosphere, turning them into scattered settlements with no nucleus, and creating a weekender mentality manifest in noisy Friday- and Sunday-evening traffic jams at the ferry dock. The island doesn't cater to independent travellers, and it can be difficult to find a bed during August, especially at weekends. On the positive side, the permanent population is distinctly hospitable; traditionally working on ships, they are only too happy to try out their English on you. Together with some of the more idiosyncratic reminders of the Venetian period, such as the *peristereónes* (pigeon towers) and the *frákhtes* (dry-stone walls, here raised to the status of an art form), it is this friendliness that lends Ándhros its charm.

Ferries connect the island with Rafina on the mainland, only an hour from Athens or fifteen minutes from the airport by bus, and, in season, you can loop back onto the central Cycladic routes via Mýkonos, Tínos or Sýros. A bus usually meets arriving ferries and runs to Batsí and on to Hóra at least six times a day in high season.

Northern and western Ándhros

All ferries and catamarans arrive at the main port, **GÁVRIO**, a moderately attractive holiday resort. Few venture onto the adjacent windswept beach, although there are plenty more attractive alternatives just to the south, where you'll find some of the area's better accommodation. A converted dovecote houses a sporadically functioning **tourist office**, and there are half-a-dozen ferry **ticket agents**, a **bank**, and a **post office** on the waterfront.

The cheapest **accommodation** is in the basic *Galaxias* (T 22820 71228; ❸), which serves as a late-arrival fall-back. There are more rooms and studios along and above the main coastal road to Batsí: *Aktio* (T 22820 71607, W www .aktiostudios.gr; ❹) is fairly representative, while *Andros Holiday Hotel* (T 22820 71384, W www.androsholiday.com; ❼) is a good upmarket choice. **Restaurants** worth trying include the good if basic *Estiatorio o Valmas*, *Tria Asteria*, and the popular *En Gavrio* ouzerí. **Nightlife** revolves around a string of nondescript cafés and bars along the harbourfront and at Áyios Pétros beach several kilometres south. Along the same stretch the excellent *Yiannouli* taverna is worth checking out for lunch.

Around 3km northwest of the port are two beaches, the first with holiday villas and a taverna, the second hidden beyond the headland and popular with rough campers. Beyond the village of Apáno Fellós, the countryside is empty except for a few hamlets inhabited by the descendants of Albanians who settled here and in southern Évvia some six hundred years ago.

Most visitors head 8km south down the coast, past the lively Khryssí Ámmos beach and the upmarket *Perrakis Hotel* above it (T 22820 71456, W www .hotelperrakis.gr; ❼), to **BATSÍ**, the island's main resort, with large hotels and bars around its fine natural harbour. The beautiful though often crowded beach curves round the port, and the sea is cold, calm and clean (except near the taxi park). **Hotels** range from the central, comfortable *Chryssi Akti* (T 22820 41236, F 22820 41628; ❺) to the upmarket *Aneroussa Beach Hotel* (T 22820 41044, F 22820 41045; ❼), south of town past the Stivári area towards **Ayía Marína beach** – a picturesque cove with *Yiannoulis Mastrozannes* fish taverna and studios (T 22820 41963; ❸). Besides these there are plenty of other rooms and **restaurants**: *Sirocco* (on the steps above the port) serves a range of international dishes, while *Stamatis* is an established taverna with a nice atmosphere, and *Delfinia* has a pleasant, sheltered balcony. There are several **café-bars**, such as *Capriccio* and *Nameless*, a half-a-dozen or so loud indoor bars featuring the standard foreign/Greek musical mix, and even an outdoor cinema with a different film every night in the summer. For information on walking tours, free local brochures or other travel needs, go to Greek Sun Travel (☎22820 41190, ⓔgreeksun@traveling.gr), upstairs near the taxi park. Two **banks** have ATMs.

Inland villages and Delavóyias beach

From Batsí you're within easy walking distance of some beautiful inland villages. At **KÁTO KATÁKILOS**, one hour inland, there are a couple of seasonal **tavernas**; a rough track leads after another hour to **ATÉNI**, a hamlet in a lush, remote valley. **ÁNO KATÁKILOS**, also reached from Batsí, has a couple of under-visited tavernas with fine views across the village. A right-hand turning out of Ano Katákilos heads up the mountain to **ARNÁS** after about an hour, whose lone taverna is often shrouded in mist. A long, three-hour rough hike down from Arnás to the eastern coast of the island brings you to the secluded, sheltered beach of **Vorí** with its clean, course sand and romantic landscape featuring several shipwrecks. Another rewarding trip is to a well-preserved, twenty-metre-high tower at **Áyios Pétros**, a mystery even to locals, 5km from Gávrio and 9km from Batsí.

South of Batsí along the main road are **Káto** and **Áno Apróvato**. Káto has rooms, including *Galini* (☎22820 41472; ❷), a taverna and a path to a quiet beach, while nearby is the largely unexplored archeological site of **Paleópolis**. Áno has the excellent taverna *Balkoni tou Aigaiou* (or "Aegean Balcony"). Along the shore here, though just as easily accessed on the road beginning in Batsí, **Delavóyias** beach is something of a haven for naturists. Within walking distance, the *Blue Bay Village* (☎22820 41150, ⓦwww.blue-bay.gr; ❺) has simple, comfortable rooms as well as a pool.

Hóra

A bus service links the west-coast Gávrio and Batsí with **HÓRA** (also known as **ÁNDHROS TOWN**), 35km from Gávrio. With its setting on a rocky spur cutting across a huge bay, the capital is the most attractive place on the island. Paved in marble and schist from the still-active local quarries, the buildings around the bus station are grand nineteenth-century affairs, and the squares with their ornate wall fountains and gateways are equally elegant. The hill quarters are modern and rather exclusive, while the small port on the west side of the headland has a yacht supply station and ferry landing. There are beaches on both sides of the headland, the better of which is Parapórti, to the east, though it's somewhat exposed to the *meltémi* winds in summer.

From the square right at the end of town you pass through an archway and down to windswept **Platía Ríva**, with its statue of the unknown sailor scanning the sea. Beyond lies the thirteenth-century Venetian **kástro**, precariously joined to the mainland by a narrow-arched bridge, which was damaged by German munitions in World War II. Inside the stark modern **archeological museum** (Tues–Sun 8.30am–2.30pm; €2), on the main street – are well laid out and labelled displays, with instructive models. Its prize item is the fourth-century *Hermes of Andros*, reclaimed from a prominent position in the Athens archeological museum. Behind it, the **Modern Art Museum** (Mon, Wed–Sun 8am–2.30pm, also 6–8pm in summer; €3) has a sculpture garden and a permanent collection with works by Picasso, Matisse, Kandinsky, Chagall and others, as well as temporary shows.

The few **hotels** in town are on the expensive side and tend to be busy with holidaying Greeks, although you could try the traditional *Aegli* (☎22820 22303;

❸), opposite the big church on the main walkway. Most rooms are clustered behind the long **Nimborió beach** northwest of town, and range from good clean rooms like those of *Villa Stella* (☎22820 22471; ❸) to modern apartments such as the *Alcioni Inn* (☎22820 23652, ℉22820 24522; ❺). The *Paradise Hotel* (☎22820 22187, Ⓦwww.paradiseandros.gr; ❼), with its swimming pool and tennis court, is the best upmarket choice, while the hillside *Stagira* (☎22820 23525, ℉22820 24502; ❼), just outside of town, is the best spot for a romantic retreat. For **eating**, *Plátanos* has a generous *mezédhes* selection that can be enjoyed with an ouzo under the plane trees, and *O Stathmos*, right by the bus station, is good with reasonable prices. The nicest fish taverna is *Nona*, tucked away at the town end of Nimborió at the old Plakoura harbour, while *Cabo del Mar* is pricey but good, with an unsurpassed view.

Nimborió beach is the epicentre of the island's **nightlife**, such as it is, with a few thumping discos that start with Western music and shift into Greek pop into the wee hours of the morning. There's a **post office** and **bank** around town, a couple of **travel agents** and three **motorbike rentals** behind the beach.

Villages around Hóra

Hiking is particularly inviting south and west from Hóra, where there are lush little river valleys. One obvious destination is **MÉNITES**, a hill village 6km up a green valley choked with trees and straddled by stone walls. The church of the **Panayía** may have been the location of a temple of Dionysos, where water was turned into wine; water still flows continuously from the local rocks. Heading from here back to Hóra, you pass the medieval village of **MESSARIÁ**, with the deserted twelfth-century Byzantine church of **Taxiárhis** below, the picturesque setting for a nine-day festival of the Virgin Mary that begins on August 15. The finest monastery on the island, **Panakhrándou**, is only an hour's (steep) walk away, via the village of Falliká: reputedly tenth-century, it's still defended by massive walls but occupied these days by just three monks. It clings to an iron-stained cliff southwest of Hóra, to which you can return directly with a healthy two- to three-hour walk down the creek valley, guided by red dots.

Hidden by the ridge directly north of Hóra, the prosperous nineteenth-century village of **STENIÉS**, an hour's hike away, was built by the vanguard of today's shipping magnates; just below, at **Yialiá**, there's a small pebble beach with a taverna and *Paraskeyi Tsoumezi* rooms (☎22820 23130; ❸) nearby. On the road to Strapouriés is a wonderful taverna, *Bozakis*, which boasts a view all the way down to the coast and excellent food. Beyond Steniés is **APIKÍA**, a tidy little village, which bottles Sariza-brand mineral water for a living; there are a few **tavernas**, including *O Tassos*, which has a lovely garden setting and specialities such as goat and rabbit. There are a very limited number of **rooms** here, including *Pighi Sariza Hotel*, Apikía (☎22820 23799, ℉22820 22476; ❺). The road is now asphalted up to Vourkotí and even past this point is quite negotiable via Arnás to the west coast. There are some stunning views all along this road but bike-riders need to take care when the *meltémi* is blowing – it can get dangerously windy.

With your own transport, the sheltered cove of **Sinéti** south of Hóra is also worth a detour.

Southern Ándhros

If you're exploring the south of the island from Gávrio or Batsí, you might head first to **Zagorá**, a fortified Geometric town – unique in having never been built over – that was excavated in the early 1970s. Located on a desolate, flat-topped promontory with cliffs falling away on three sides, it's worth a visit for the view alone.

Alternatively, from Hóra, **PALEÓKASTRO** is one of the first stops, a tumbledown village with a ruined Venetian castle and a legend about an old woman who betrayed the stronghold to the Turks, then jumped off the walls in remorse, landing on a rock now known as "Old Lady's Leap". Further south, the village of **KORTHÍ** is a friendly place which is slowly waking up to its tourist potential. Set on a large sandy bay, cut off from the rest of the island by a high ridge and so relatively unspoilt, it is pleasant enough to merit spending the night at the austere-looking *Hotel Korthion* (T22820 61218; ❸). There are also several good **tavernas**, including *To Vintsi tis Yitsas* at the waterfront. You could also take in the nearby convent (about half an hour's walk away) of **Zoöd-hóhou Piyís** (open to visitors before noon), with illuminated manuscripts and a disused weaving factory.

Tínos

Tínos still feels like one of the most Greek of the larger islands in the Cyclades. A few foreigners have discovered its beaches and unspoilt villages, but most visitors are Greek, here to see the church of **Panayía Evangelístria**, a grandiose shrine erected on the spot where a miraculous icon with healing powers was found in 1822. A local nun, now canonized as Ayía Pelayía, was directed in a vision to unearth the relic just as the War of Independence was getting underway, a timely coincidence that served to underscore the links between the Orthodox Church and Greek nationalism. Today, there are two major annual pilgrimages, on March 25 and August 15, when, at 11am, the icon bearing the Virgin's image is carried in state down to the harbour over the heads of the faithful.

The Ottoman tenure here was the most fleeting in the Aegean. **Exóbourgo**, the craggy mount dominating southern Tínos and surrounded by most of the island's sixty-odd villages, is studded with the ruins of a Venetian citadel that defied the Turks until 1715, long after the rest of Greece had fallen. An enduring legacy of the long Venetian rule is a persistent **Catholic minority**, which accounts for almost half the population, and a sectarian rivalry said to be responsible for the numerous graceful belfries scattered throughout the island – Orthodox and Catholic parishes vying to build the tallest. The sky is pierced, too, by distinctive and ornate **dovecotes**, even more in evidence here than on Ándhros. Aside from all this, the inland village architecture is striking and there's a flourishing folk-art tradition that finds expression in the abundant local marble. The islanders have remained open and hospitable to the relatively few foreigners and the steady stream of Greek visitors who touch down here, and any mercenary inclinations seem to be satisfied by booming sales in religious paraphernalia to the faithful.

Tínos Town

At **TÍNOS TOWN**, trafficking in devotional articles certainly dominates the streets leading up from the busy waterfront to the Neoclassical church **Panayía Evangelístria** (daily 8am–8pm) that towers above. Evangelistrías in particular overflows with holy-water vessels, votive candles and plastic icons, while parallel Megaloháris, which points a slightly more direct approach to

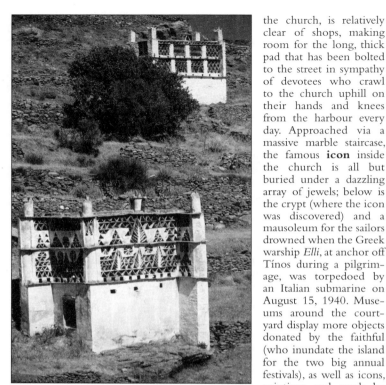

the church, is relatively clear of shops, making room for the long, thick pad that has been bolted to the street in sympathy of devotees who crawl to the church uphill on their hands and knees from the harbour every day. Approached via a massive marble staircase, the famous **icon** inside the church is all but buried under a dazzling array of jewels; below is the crypt (where the icon was discovered) and a mausoleum for the sailors drowned when the Greek warship *Elli*, at anchor off Tínos during a pilgrimage, was torpedoed by an Italian submarine on August 15, 1940. Museums around the courtyard display more objects donated by the faithful (who inundate the island for the two big annual festivals), as well as icons, paintings and work by local marble sculptors.

△ Venetian dovecotes on Tínos

The shrine aside – and all the attendant stalls, shops and bustle – the port is none too exciting, with just scattered inland patches of nineteenth-century buildings. You might make time for the **archeological museum** (Tues–Sun 8.30am–3pm; €2) on the way up to the church, whose collection includes a fascinating sundial from the local Roman sanctuary of Poseidon and Amphitrite (see p.152).

Practicalities

Ferries dock at any of three different **jetties**; which one depends on weather conditions. There are at least four boats a day from Pireás via Sýros going on to Mýkonos, and several from Rafína via Ándhros, as well as a useful catamaran, and less frequent ferry connections to Páros, Náxos and Thíra. When you're leaving, ask your ticket agent which jetty to head for. **Buses** leave from a small parking area in front of a cubbyhole-office on the quay, to Pánormos, Kallóni, Stení, Pórto and Kiónia (timetables available here; no buses after 7.30pm). A **motorbike** is perhaps a more reliable means of exploring – Vidalis at Zanáki Alavánou 16 is a good rental agency.

Windmills Travel (☎ & ⓕ 22830 23398, ⓦ www.windmillstravel.com), on the front towards the new jetty, can help with information as well as **tour bookings** and hotel bookings both here and on Mýkonos; they even have a book exchange. In season an excursion boat does day-trips taking in Delos (see p.161) and Mýkonos (Tues–Sun; €20 round trip); this makes it possible to see Delos without the expense of staying overnight in Mýkonos, but only allows you two-and-a-half hours at the site. The **tourist police** are located on the road to the west of the new jetty.

Accommodation

To have any chance of securing a reasonably priced **room** around the pilgrimage day of March 25 (August 15 is hopeless), you must arrive several days in advance. At other times, there's plenty of choice, though you'll still be competing with out-of-season pilgrims, Athenian tourists and the ill and disabled seeking a miracle cure. The accommodation listed below is open from mid-April to October only, unless stated otherwise.

Anna's Rooms Road to Kionia ☎ 22830 22877, ⓦ www.tinos.nl. Excellent, family-run apartments set in a large garden just ten minutes' walk out of town. ❹

Avra On waterfront ☎ 22830 22242, ⓔ georgegerardis@yahoo.co.uk. Neoclassical relic with spacious rooms and attractive plant-filled communal area. B&B ❸

Eleana 200m inland from the Commercial bank ☎ 22830 22461. A good, if basic, budget option hotel, with clean rooms and breakfast included in the price. ❸

Hotel Tinion On waterfront ☎ 22830 22261, ⓦ www.tinionhotel.gr. Stylish 1920s hotel just back from the waterfront. Spacious rooms, some with balconies. Breakfast €9. ❹

Meltémi Near Megaloháris ☎ 22830 22881, ⓕ 22830 22884. Basic, dated hotel useful if you're here out of season. Open all year. ❸

Tinos Camping Ten-minute walk south of port ☎ 22830 22344. Popular, comfortable en-suite rooms with air conditioning and kitchens, set on one of the nicest campsites in the Cyclades. Follow the signs from the port. ❸

As usual, most seafront **restaurants** are rather overpriced and indifferent, with the exception of a friendly *psitopolió* right opposite the bus station, and the smarter Lymposion on Evangelistrías, serving coffees, pastas and *mezédhes*, and also with a fast **Internet** connection. About midway along the port near the *Leto Hotel*, behind the dolphin fountain, there is a cluster of excellent tavernas, one of the best being ⚓ *Epineio* with good-value, tasty Greek dishes and excellent seafood. A small vine-covered alleyway leads from here to Palládha, a public square with a farmers' **market** every morning with local fruit and vegetables, and lined with yet more good choices: *Metaxi Mas*, a pricey *mezedopolío* that has a remarkably varied menu, including delicious *hortokeftédhes* (vegetable croquettes); and *Palea Palladha*, justifiably proud of its grilled *loukániko* (spicy sausage), sharp local feta and smooth house wine. At the end of the alleyway there's a small traditional bakery, *Psomi Horiatiko*. For late-night snacks, try *Edesma* (meaning "food") just off Palládha, which stays open till 5am.

There are a few **bars**, mostly in a huddle near the new quay. Sleek *Fevgatos* has sophisticated decor, *Koursaros* on the corner plays rock music, and *Pyrsos* is pretty lively with a mixture of international hits and Greek music. *Kaktos*, meanwhile, has dancing on a terrace with ocean views, while *Sivilla* blends Greek and world music in a cosy setting. At 3am all the bars in Tínos Town close, but for those not ready to hit the sack, *Paradise* up past *Anna's Rooms* (see p.151), stays open until dawn playing mainly Greek music.

Southern beaches

Kiónia, 3km northwest of Tínos Town (hourly buses in summer), is the site of the **Sanctuary of Poseidon and Amphitrite** (Tues–Sun 8.30am–3pm; free), which was discovered in 1902; the excavations yielded principally columns (*kiónia* in Greek), but also a temple, baths, a fountain and hostels for the ancient pilgrims. The **beach** is functional enough, lined with rooms to rent and snack-bars, but it's better to walk past the large *Tinos Beach Hotel* (☎22830 22626, ⓦ www.tinosbeach.gr; ❼), the last stop for the bus, and follow an unpaved road to a series of sandy coves beyond.

The beach beyond the headland east of town starts off rocky but improves if you walk 500m further along. Further east, **Pórto** (six buses daily) boasts two good beaches, with a couple of good tavernas as well as family-friendly **apartments** with a pool at the reasonably priced restaurant *Akti Aegeou* (☎22830 24248, ⓦ www.aktiaegeou.gr; ❺), on the first beach of Áyios Pandelímon, as well as the smart studios *Porto Raphael* (☎22830 23913, ⓦ www.portoraphael .gr; ❸), above Áyios Ioánnis beach. ⚓ *Porto Tango* (☎22830 24411, ⓦ www .portotango.gr; ❼) is an excellent upmarket hotel here, with a lovely pool setting, luxurious rooms and its own spa.

Northern Tínos

A good beginning to a foray into the interior is to take the stone stairway – the continuation of Odhós Ayíou Nikoláou – that passes behind and to the left of the Evangelistrías. This climbs for ninety minutes through appealing countryside to **KTIKÁDHOS**, a fine village with a good sea-view taverna, *Drosia*. You can either flag down a bus on the main road or stay with the trail until Xinára (see opposite).

Heading northwest from the junction flanked by Ktikádhos, Tripótamos and Xinára, there's little to stop for – except the fine **dovecotes** around Tarambádhos – until you reach **KARDHIANÍ**, 8km along, one of the most strikingly set and beautiful villages on the island, with its views across to Sýros from amid a dense oasis. The cliff-hugging *O Dinos* here serves shellfish with a prime sunset view. The *Tavsternia* taverna also commands stunning panoramic views and there are a few café-bars perched above the turning for **Órmos Isterníon**, a comparatively small but overdeveloped beach.

Five daily buses along this route finish up at **PÝRGOS**, a few kilometres further north and smack in the middle of the island's marble-quarrying district. A beautiful village, its local artisans are renowned throughout Greece for their skill in producing marble ornamentation; ornate fanlights and bas-relief plaques crafted here adorn houses throughout Tínos. Pýrgos is also home to the School of Arts, and the **museum of Tinian artists** (daily 10.30am–1.30pm & 5.30–7pm; €2, ticket also valid for Yiannoulis Halepas Museum) contains numerous representative works from some of the island's finest artists. Nearby, the **Yiannoulis Halepas Museum** (same hours and ticket) is devoted exclusively to the work of the artist who was born in this home and who is generally recognized as the most important Neoclassical Greek sculptor. There are two *kafenía* and the excellent *Ta Myronia* **taverna** on the attractive shady platía. Pýrgos is popular in summer, and if you want to stay there are some new **studios** for rent on the main road coming into the village; alternatively, ask the locals on the platía.

The marble products were once exported from **PÁNORMOS** harbour, 4km northeast, which has a tiny, commercialized beach, a few tavernas and cafés, and some good-value accommodation at *Elena* (℡22830 31694; ❸) right on the waterfront. Better is **Rohári** beach on the northwest side of the bay, accessible by foot or *kaïki*, with its deep clear waters and massive waves. The tiny island it faces is called Planítis, "the Planet".

Around Exóbourgo

The ring of villages around **Exóbourgo** mountain is another focus of interest on Tínos. The fortified pinnacle itself (570m), with ancient foundations as well as the ruins of three Venetian churches and a fountain, is reached by steep steps from **XINÁRA** (near the island's major road junction), the seat of the island's Roman Catholic bishop. Most villages in north central Tínos have mixed populations, but Xinára and its immediate neighbours are purely Catholic; the inland villages also tend to have a more sheltered position, with better farmland nearby – the Venetians' way of rewarding converts and their descendants. Yet **TRIPÓTAMOS**, just south of Xinára, is a completely Orthodox village with possibly the finest architecture in this region – and has accordingly been pounced on by foreigners keen to restore its historic properties.

At **LOUTRÁ**, the next community north of Xinára, there's an Ursuline convent and a good **folk art museum** (summer only, daily 10.30am–3.30pm; free) in the old Jesuit monastery; to visit, leave the bus at the turning for Skaládho. From Krókos, 1km northwest of Loutrá, which has a scenically situated taverna, it's a forty-minute walk via Skaládho to **VÓLAKAS** (also transliterated as Vólax), one of the most remote villages on the island, a windswept oasis surrounded by bony rocks. Here, half a dozen elderly Catholic basketweavers fashion some of the best examples in Greece. There is a small **folklore museum** (free) which you have to ask the lady living in the house opposite the entrance to open, and the charming outdoor Fontaine Theatre which in August hosts visiting theatre groups from all over Greece. Accommodation is hard to come by, but there are a couple of places to eat, including the recommended *O Rokos* and *I Volax* **tavernas**.

At Kómi, 5km beyond Krókos, you can take a detour for **KOLYMBÍTHRA**, a magnificent double beach: one part wild, huge and windswept (temporary residence to pink flamingos migrating to Africa during May), the other sheltered and with a couple of tavernas including *Kolibithra Beach* (☎22830 51213), which also has rooms (❹). The bus to Kallóni goes on to Kolymbíthra twice a day in season; out of season you'll have to get off at Kómi and walk 4km.

From either Skaládho or Vólakas you go on to Koúmaros, where another long stairway leads up to Exóbourgo, or skirt the pinnacle towards the agricultural villages of **FALATÁDHOS** and **STENÍ**, which appear as white speckles against the fertile Livádha valley. Falatádhos has a number of whitewashed churches, the most notable of which is **Áyios Ioánnis** for its marble decoration. There is also a **house of exhibitions** (changing hours; free), which shows contemporary art in summer. The village has a number of excellent restaurants including *Lefkes* taverna and *To Katoï*, specializing in grilled dishes. From Stení, which has fewer amenities but plenty of postcard-perfect whitewashed buildings to admire, you can catch the bus back to the harbour (7 daily). On the way down, try to stop off at one of the beautiful settlements just below the important twelfth-century **convent of Kekhrovouníou**, where Ayía Pelayía had her vision. Particularly worth visiting are **Triandáros** and **Dhýo Horiá**, which has a fine main square where cave-fountains burble. If you have your own transport, there are quite wide and fairly negotiable tracks down to some lovely secluded bays on the east of the island from the area of Stení. One such is **Sánta Margaríta**; given the lack of tourist development here, it's a good idea to take something to drink.

This is hardly an exhaustive list of Tiniot villages; armed with a map and good walking shoes for tackling the many old trails that still exist, you could spend days within sight of Exóbourgo and never pass through the same hamlets twice. Take warm clothing out of season, especially if you're on a scooter, since the forbidding mountains behind Vólakas and the Livadhéri plain keep things noticeably cool.

Mýkonos

Originally visited only as a stop on the way to ancient Delos, **Mýkonos** has become easily the most popular (and the most expensive) of the Cyclades. Boosted by direct air links with Britain and domestic flights from Athens, it sees more than a million tourists pass through in a good year (half of them in August alone), producing some spectacular overcrowding in high summer on Mýkonos's 75 square kilometres. But if you don't mind the crowds, or you come in the shoulder season, the prosperous capital is still one of the most beautiful of all island towns, its immaculately whitewashed houses concealing hundreds of little churches, shrines and chapels.

The sophisticated nightlife is pretty hectic, amply stimulated by Mýkonos's former reputation as *the* gay resort of the Mediterranean – a title that has been surrendered to Sitges in Spain. Today, gay tourists are well in the minority on the island until September, when the gay clientele is present in full force. The locals (more than 10,000 at last estimate, more than half of them Albanian immigrants) take it all in their stride, ever conscious of the important revenue generated by their laissez-faire attitude. When islanders first opened up to the artsy tourists who began appearing on Mýkonos in the 1960s, they assumed their eccentric visitors were sharing cigarettes due to lack of funds. Since then, a lot of the innocence has evaporated, and the island certainly isn't unspoilt, but Mýkonos does offer excellent (if busy) beaches, picturesque windmills and a rolling arid interior. Best of all, the well-organized local tourist industry does everything in its power to see that beaches are more cared for and that transportation runs more frequently than on most neighbouring islands. A local ban on the construction of large international chain restaurants and hotels has done much to preserve the landscape, as does the presence of the second-largest biological cleaning plant in Greece.

Mýkonos Town and around

Don't let the crowds put you off exploring **MÝKONOS TOWN**, the archetypal postcard image of the Cyclades. Its sugar-cube buildings are stacked around a cluster of seafront fishermen's dwellings, with every nook and cranny scrubbed and shown off. Most people head out to the beaches during the day, so early morning or late afternoon are the best times to wander the maze of narrow streets. The labyrinthine design was intended to confuse the pirates who plagued Mýkonos in the eighteenth and early nineteenth centuries, and it still has the desired effect.

Arrival, information and accommodation

There is some accommodation information at the recently expanded **airport** (3km southeast of town) and at the **new port** where large cruise ships dock (a few kilometres north of town in Toúrlos), but unless you know where you're going it's easier to take a bus or taxi into town, and sort things out there. The vast majority of visitors arrive by ferry at the **jetty** at the north end of town, where a veritable horde of room-owners pounces on the newly arrived. The scene is actually quite intimidating, so it is far better to go 100m further,

New Port, Toúrlos & Áyios Stéfanos

MÝKONOS TOWN

0   100 m

Accommodation Centre

Island Ferries

North Bus Station

Archeological Museum

AYIOU STÉFANOU

@

A

RESTAURANTS & BARS

Aigli	12	Kavos	1	Pierros	3
Astra	11	Kostas	14	Porta	8
Caprice	9	Nikos Taverna	7	Ramrod	3
El Pecado	4	Pasta Fresca Barkia	5	Sea Satin Market	16
Icarus	3	Piano Bar	9	Skandinavian Bar	6
Kalua	2	Pelican	10	Space	17
Kastro	9	Philippi Garden		Toy	13
Katerina's	9	Restaurant	D	Yiavroutas Estiatorio	15

POLYKANDHRIOTI

B

Boats to Delos

KAMBANI

2

Folklore Museum

National Bank & Port Police

PLATIA M. MAVROYÉNOUS

3

Kástro

Paraportianí

KAMBANI

5

KAMBANI

Áno Méra

AYIOU IOANNOU

9

7 8

AYION ANARYIRON

DHRAKOPOULOU

THITOU

ANDHRONIKOU MATOYANNI

ZOUGANELI

MAVROYENI

LITTLE VENICE

TRIOBUTA

N

AY. KERASMOU

KALOYERA

10

ALEFKÁNDHRA

C
D

11 12

LITOU

13

Maritime Museum

Mýkonos Accommodation Center

TOURLIANIS

14 15

MITROPOLIS

ENOPLON DHYNAMEON

ROHARI

Windmills

AY. EFTHIMIOU

TRIROU

LÁKKA

Car Park

17

XENIAS

E
F

16

Laundry

@

South Bus Station

G

AYIOU IOANNOU

VÍDHA

Scooter Rental

Scooter Rental

Scooter Rental

Scooter Rental

I

H

J

ACCOMMODATION

Adonis	H
Belvedere	F
Elysium	I
Geranium	J
La Veranda	B
Pension Marina	G
Philippi	D
Semeli	E
Stelios Pension	A
Terra Maria	C

Megáli Ammos   Órnós & Airport

where a row of offices deals with official hotels, rented rooms and camping information, or go into the heart of town to the extremely helpful Mykonos Accommodation Center (℡22890 23160, ⓦwww.mykonos-accommodation .com) on Énóplon Dhynaméon near the Maritime Museum.

The **north bus station** for Toúrlos, Áyios Stéfanos, Eliá and Áno Méra is located by the old ferry landing, whilst past the dull central Polikandhrioti beach, at the other end of town, the **south bus station** serves the beaches to the south. Also here is the **post office**, Olympic Airways office and several **motorbike rental** agencies, along with a host of **Internet** cafés, among the best being Internet World. Buses to all the most popular beaches and resorts run frequently until the early hours. **Taxis**, of which there are only 32 on the island, run from Platía Mavroyénous on the seafront and from the south bus station, and their rates are fixed and quite reasonable; try Mykonos Radio Taxi (℡22890 22400). Be aware that some taxi drivers may try and get you to pay the full fare per person; this is not legal, and you should refuse. There are countless advertiser-based tourist **publications** circulating throughout Mýkonos during high season, the best of which is the free *Mykonos Sky Map*, available from most agents and hotels.

Catamaran and ferry tickets are sold at several separate and uncooperative **travel agencies** on the harbour front. Check out the various possibilities, and if your boat leaves from the new port, catch the bus up from the old ferry landing across from the Eurobank.

Accommodation

Accommodation prices in Mýkonos rocket in the high season to a greater degree than almost anywhere else in Greece. For this reason, it may well be worth considering **camping** in high season – there are two campsites; both will rent out tents, or even sell them for €25, should you get stuck. *Mykonos Camping* (℡22890 24578, ⓦwww.mycamp.gr) above Paránga beach is smaller and has a more pleasant setting than nearby *Paradise Camping* on Paradise Beach (℡22890 22129, ⓦwww.paradisemykonos.com). However, the latter also has bungalows (❺). Both are packed in season, and dance music from the 24-hour bars on Paradise beach makes sleep difficult. Hourly bus services to Paránga and Paradise beaches continue into the early hours but can get overcrowded.

Adonis Near the waterfront, south of town ℡22890 22434, ⓦwww.mykonosadonis.gr. Beautiful hotel in the Vídha area, with views of the windmills from some of its nicely appointed rooms. ❼

Belvedere Off Ayíou Ioánnou ℡22890 25122, ⓦwww.belvederehotel.com. Upmarket hotel with stunning rooms, views and a pool, in a quiet area of town. It even has its own swanky Japanese restaurant, *Matsuhisa*. ❼

Elysium On hillside south of town ℡22890 23952, ⓦwww.elysiumhotel.com. Almost exclusively gay hotel with beautiful views, boasting a poolside bar that's also a popular setting for a late-afternoon cocktail. ❼

Geranium On hillside south of town ℡22890 24620, ⓦwww.geraniumhotel.com. Very stylish gay hotel with rooms, studios and a villa. Pool and

bar with nude sunbathing area if you're beautiful enough. ❼

La Veranda On hillside east of town. ℡22890 23670, ⓔlaveranda@panafonet.gr. A laid-back, upmarket hotel with rooms set around a small pool. ❼

Pension Marina Off Ayíou Ioánnou ℡22890 24960, ⓔmarina@mykonos-web.com. Nice neat rooms arranged around courtyard in a quiet spot to the south of town. ❺

Philippi Kaloyéra 25 ℡22890 22294, ⓔchriko@otenet.gr. Clean, comfortable en-suite rooms set around a quiet garden right in the middle of the bustling old town. ❺

Semeli Off Ayíou Ioánnou ℡22890 27466, ⓦwww.semelihotel.gr. Pricey, luxurious hotel above town with pool, whirlpool and very tastefully decorated rooms. ❽

Stelios Pension Above the old port ☎ 22890 24641, ℗ 22890 26779. Excellent-value en-suite rooms in prime location, but still away from the bustle of town. Take the steps leading up from the OTE office. ❺

Terra Maria Kaloyéra 18 ☎ 22890 24212, ⓔ tertaxma@otenet.gr. Contemporary hotel with cool, clean rooms with balconies. Central, but remains nice and peaceful. ❻

The Town

Getting lost in the convoluted streets and alleys of town is half the fun of exploring Mýkonos, although there are a few places worth seeking out. Coming from the ferry quay you'll pass the **archeological museum** (Tues–Sun 8.30am–3pm; €2) on your way into town, which displays some good Delos pottery; the town also boasts a **maritime museum** displaying various nautical artefacts, including a lighthouse re-erected in the back garden (Tues–Sun 10.30am–1pm & 6.30–9pm; €3). Next door is **Lena's House** (Mon–Sat 6–9pm, Sun 5–7pm; free), a completely restored and furnished middle-class home from the nineteenth century. At the base of the Delos jetty, the **folklore museum** (Mon–Sat 5.30–8.30pm, Sun 6.30–8.30pm; free), housed in an eighteenth-century mansion, crams in a larger-than-usual collection of bric-a-brac, including a vast four-poster bed. The museum shares the same promontory as the old Venetian *kástro*, the entrance to which is marked by Mýkonos's oldest and best-known church, **Paraportianí**, which is a fascinating asymmetrical hodgepodge of four chapels amalgamated into one.

The shore leads to the area known as **Little Venice** because of its high, arcaded Venetian houses built right up to the water's edge. Together with the adjoining **Alefkándhra** district, this is a dense area packed with art galleries, trendy bars and discos. Away from the seafront, behind Platía Alefkándhra, are Mýkonos's two **cathedrals**: Roman Catholic and Greek Orthodox. Beyond, the famous **windmills** look over the area, a little shabby but ripe for photo opportunities. South of here, sleepier **Vídha**, which runs along a tiny beach, has seen the recent arrival of accommodation spilling over from the rest of town.

Eating

Even **light meals** and **snacks** are expensive in Mýkonos, but there are several bakeries, supermarkets and fruit stalls, some concentrated near the south bus station. The area around Alefkándhra is a promising place to head for a full **meal**, whilst if you're looking for late-night coffee, try *Kavos*, open 24 hours right by the town beach.

Kostas Mitropoleos. Friendly taverna near Little Venice, with competitive prices, and a good wine list including barrelled wine (not easily found on Mýkonos).

Nikos Taverna near the port at Little Venice. One of the most famous restaurants on the island. Every inch of its terrace is packed with customers, which can have a detrimental effect on service.

Pasta Fresca Barkia near the beach. Lively pizzeria on the waterfront; a great spot for people-watching.

Pelican off Kaloyera. Popular taverna serving Greek staples and good pasta dishes. Not the cheapest, but has one of the nicest settings on a vine-covered platía.

Philippi Garden Restaurant Kaloyera. Exclusive restaurant in romantic setting serving home-grown vegetarian food, as well as superb seafood and traditional local dishes.

Sea Satin Market below the windmills. Expensive, beautifully located restaurant right on the water with excellent seafood and grills, and a clubby vibe after midnight.

Yiavroutas Estiatorio Mitropoleos. Small, unpretentious, family-run place serving excellent-value Greek dishes and good barrelled wine. Also open most of the night, if you're in need of fuel.

Gay nightlife

Although there are no huge gay clubs on Mýkonos, there is a good batch of excellent, comparatively laid-back bars, both for dancing and drinking, in town, and bar-hopping is definitely the way to go. The *Piano Bar*, with fun cabaret acts, is a very good place to warm up, as is nearby *Toy*, which has great drinks. *Porta*, near *Nikos Taverna*, is a lively place to head to as the evening gets going. Things inevitably end up on the other side of town on the platía where seemingly hundreds of men gather outside around dancing bars *Ramrod*, *Icarus*, and the legendary *Pierros*, that's been on the go here since the 1960s.

Nightlife

Nightlife in town is every bit as good as it's cracked up to be – and every bit as pricey. Those looking for a cheap drink should head for to the *Skandinavian Bar* which thumps out dance music and good cocktails until the early hours. For something a bit more sophisticated, try *Aigli* and *Astra*, two chic cafés by day that turn clubby by night; or head to the bars that line Andhroníkou Matoyiánni and Enóplon Dhynaméon, collectively referred to by some as "Fifth Avenue" for the nightly fashion parade along its cobblestone catwalk. A slightly more low-key vibe happens in Little Venice's *Katerina's*, *Caprice*, *Piano Bar* and *Kastro*; or you could try the stylish lounge-style clubs along the waterfront including *El Pecado* and *Kalua*.

For out-and-out dancing, *Space*, on Lákka square, is the largest club on the island. *Cavo Paradiso* (W www.cavoparadiso.gr), near *Paradise Camping*, however, is the after-hours club where die-hard party animals of all persuasions come together, often united by world-famous DJs.

The beaches

The closest **beaches** to town are those to the north, at **Toúrlos** (only 2km away but horrid) and **Áyios Stéfanos** (3km, much better), both developed resorts and connected by a very regular bus service to Mýkonos Town. There are tavernas and rooms to let (as well as package hotels) at Áyios Stéfanos, away from the beach; *Mocambo Lido* taverna at the far end of the bay has a pleasant setting and good food.

Other nearby destinations include southwest peninsula resorts, with undistinguished beaches tucked into pretty bays. The nearest to town, 1km away, is **Megáli Ámmos**, a good beach backed by flat rocks and pricey rooms, but nearby Kórfos bay is disgusting, thanks to the town dump and machine noise. Buses serve **Ornós**, an average beach, and **Áyios Ioánnis**, a dramatic bay with the new super-deluxe *St John Hotel* (T 22890 28752, W www.saintjohn.gr; ❽) and a tiny, stony beach, which achieved its moment of fame as a location for the film *Shirley Valentine*.

The south coast is the busiest part of the island. *Kaïkia* ply from town to all of its beaches, which are still regarded to some extent as family strands by the Greeks. You might begin with **Platýs Yialós**, 4km south of town, though you won't be alone: one of the longest-established resorts on the island, it's not remotely Greek any more, the sand is monopolized by hotels, and you won't get a room to save your life between June and September. **Psaroú**, next door to the west, is very pretty – 150m of white sand backed by foliage and calamus reeds, crowded with sunbathers. Here you'll find *N'Ammos*, an elegant fish **restaurant** on the waterfront. Other beach facilities include a diving club, waterskiing and windsurfer rental, but again you'll need to reserve well in advance to secure **rooms** between mid-June and mid-September. Try *Soula Rooms* (T22890 22006, Wwww.soula-rooms.gr; ❺), a surprisingly calm property on the beach.

Just over the headland to the east of Platýs Yialós is **Paránga beach**, actually two beaches separated by a smaller headland, the first of which has a decent taverna with some basic rooms and is quieter than its noisy neighbour, which is home to a loud beach bar and *Mykonos Camping* (see p.157). A dusty footpath beyond Platýs Yialós crosses the fields and caves of the headland across the clifftops past Paránga, and drops down to **Paradise beach**, a crescent of golden sand that is packed in season. Here, as on many of Mýkonos's most popular beaches, it can be difficult to find an opening big enough to fit a towel, and what little space you manage to find clear of people is likely to be taken up by straw umbrellas, which can be rented (usually along with two accompanying loungers) for about €5. Behind the beach are shops, self-service restaurants and the noisy 24-hour beach bars of *Paradise Camping*. The next bay east contains **Super Paradise** (officially "Plindhrí") beach, accessible by footpath or by *kaïki*. One of the most fun beaches on the island, it has a decent taverna and two bars at opposite ends of the beach pumping out cheesy summer hits. One half of the beach is very mixed, getting progressively more gay as you walk away from where the *kaïkia* dock towards the beach bar perched in the hills, below which the beach is almost exclusively gay and nudist.

One of the best beaches on Mýkonos is **Eliá**, the last port of call for the *kaïkia*. A broad, sandy stretch with a verdant backdrop, it's the longest beach on the island, though split in two by a rocky area, and almost exclusively gay late in the season. To retreat from the crowds, follow the bare rock footpath over the spur (look for the white house) at the end of the beach that cuts upwards for grand views east and west and then winds down to **Kaló Livádhi** (seasonal bus service), a stunning beach adjoining an agricultural valley scattered with little farmhouses; even here there's a restaurant (a good one at that) at the far end of the beach. **Ayía Ánna**, further on, boasts a shingle beach and taverna, with the cliffs above granting some fine vistas. **Kalafáti**, still further east, is more of a tourist community, its white-sand beach supporting a few hotels, restaurants and a disco. There's a local bus service from here to Áno Méra (see below), or you can jump on an excursion boat to **Tragoníssi**, the islet just offshore, for spectacular coastal scenery, seals and wild birds. The rest of the east coast is more difficult to reach: there are some small beaches, really only worth the effort if you crave solitude, and the region is dominated by the peak of Profitis Ilías, sadly spoilt by a huge radar dome and military establishment. **Liá**, roughly 12km east of Eliá, is smaller but delightful, with bamboo windbreaks and clear water, plus another good taverna.

The **north coast** suffers persistent battering from the *meltémi*, plus tar and litter pollution, and for the most part is bare, brown and exposed. **Pánormos Bay** is the exception to this, with the lovely, relatively sheltered beaches of **Pánormos** and **Áyios Sóstis** along its western edge. Despite a good restaurant, a relaxed beach bar and the rather conspicuous *Albatros Club Hotel* (T22890 25130, Wwww.albatros-mykonos.com; ❻) on Pánormos, these beaches remain the least crowded on the island, and although they are not served by buses, they are becoming increasingly popular.

Áno Méra

From Pánormos Bay, it's an easy walk to the only other settlement of any size on the island, **ÁNO MÉRA**, where you should be able to find a **room**. The village prides itself on striving to maintain a traditional way of life, although the result is rather pseudo and wishy-washy: the so-called traditional *kafenío* has long since ditched Greek coffee for cappuccino and traditional sweets for "ice-cream special". There are, however, several acceptable **restaurants** on the platía, of which *Daniele at Basoulas* is currently the most popular for its wide range of Mediterranean dishes; you'll also find a large **hotel** here, the upmarket, if ageing, *Ano Mera* (☎22890 71215, ℱ22890 71276; ❼). The red-roofed church near the square is the sixteenth-century **monastery of Panayía Tourlianí**, where a collection of Cretan icons and the unusual eighteenth-century marble baptismal font are worth seeing. It's not far, either, to the late twelfth-century **Paleokástro monastery** (also known as **Dárga**), just north of the village, in a magnificent green setting on an otherwise barren slope. To the northwest are more of the same dry and wind-buffeted landscapes, though they do provide some enjoyable, rocky walking with expansive views across to neighbouring islands.

Delos (Dhílos)

The remains of **ancient Delos**, Pindar's "unmoved marvel of the wide world", though skeletal and swarming now with lizards and tourists, give some idea of the past grandeur of this sacred isle a few sea-miles west of Mýkonos. The ancient town lies on the west coast on flat, sometimes marshy ground that rises in the south to **Mount Kýnthos**. From the summit – an easy walk – there's a magnificent view across the Cyclades.

The first excursion boats to Delos leave the small port near the west end of Mýkonos harbour daily at 8.30am (€7 round trip), except Mondays when the site is closed. You have to return on the same boat, but in season each does the trip several times and you can choose what time you leave. The last return is usually about 3pm, and you'll need to arrive early if you want to make a thorough tour of the site. In season a daily *kaïki* makes return trips from the beaches (€10) with pick-up points at Platýs Yialós and Órnos, but only allows you three hours on the island. Check ahead with operators of Delos excursion boats or look for posters advertising evening concerts and other special performances that occasionally animate the ancient site in season.

Some history

Delos's ancient fame was due to the fact that Leto gave birth to the divine twins Artemis and Apollo on the island, although its fine harbour and central position did nothing to hamper development. When the Ionians colonized the island around 1000 BC it was already a cult centre, and by the seventh century BC it had become the commercial and religious centre of the **Amphictionic League**. Unfortunately Delos also attracted the attention of Athens, which sought dominion over this prestigious island; the wealth of the Delian Confederacy, founded after the Persian Wars to protect the Aegean cities, was harnessed to Athenian ends, and for a while Athens controlled the Sanctuary of Apollo. Athenian attempts to "purify" the island began with a decree that no one could die or give birth on Delos – the sick and the pregnant were taken to the islet of Rínia – and culminated in the simple expedient of banishing the native population.

Delos reached its peak in the third and second centuries BC, after being declared a free port by its Roman overlords. In the end, though, its undefended wealth brought ruin: first Mithridates (88 BC) then Athenodorus (69 BC) plundered the treasures and the island never recovered. By the third century AD, Athens could not even sell it, and for centuries every passing seafarer stopped to collect a few prizes.

The site

As you land at **the site** (Tues–Sun 8.30am–3pm; €5), the Sacred Harbour is on your left, the Commercial Harbour on your right and straight ahead lies the **Agora of the Competialists**. Competialists were Roman merchants or freed slaves who worshipped the Lares Competales, the guardian spirits of crossroads; offerings to Hermes would once have been placed in the middle of the agora, their position now marked by a round and a square base. The **Sacred Way** leads north from the far left corner; it used to be lined with statues and the grandiose monuments of rival kings. Along it you reach three marble steps leading into the **Sanctuary of Apollo**; much was lavished on the god, but the forest of offerings has been plundered over the years. On your left is the Stoa of the Naxians, while against the north wall of the House of the Naxians, to the right, a huge statue of Apollo stood in ancient times. In 417 BC the Athenian general Nikias led a procession of priests across a bridge of boats from Rínia to dedicate a bronze palm tree; when it was later blown over in a gale it took the statue with it. Three **Temples of Apollo** stand in a row to the right along the Sacred Way: the Delian Temple, that of the Athenians and the Porinos Naos, the earliest of them, dating from the sixth century BC. To the east towards the museum you pass the **Sanctuary of Dionysos**, with its marble phalluses on tall pillars.

The best finds from the site are in Athens, but the **museum** (same hours; included in the price) still justifies a visit, if only to see the famous **lions**, their lean bodies masterfully executed by Naxians in the seventh century BC to ward off intruders who would have been unfamiliar with the fearful creatures. Of the original nine, three have disappeared and one – captured by Venetians in the seventeenth century – adorns the Arsenale in Venice. To the north stands a wall that marks the site of the **Sacred Lake** where Leto gave birth, clinging to a palm tree, guarded by excellent reproductions of the lions. On the other side of the lake is the City Wall, built in 69 BC – too late to protect the treasures.

Set out in the other direction from the Agora of the Competialists and you enter the residential area, known as the **Theatre Quarter**. Many of the walls and roads remain, but there is none of the domestic detail that brings other such sites to life. Some colour is added by the mosaics: one in the House of the Trident, and better ones in the House of the Masks, most notably a vigorous portrayal of Dionysos riding on a panther's back. The theatre itself seated 5500 spectators, and, though much ravaged, offers some fine views. Behind the theatre, a steep path leads past the Sanctuaries of the Foreign Gods and up Mount Kýnthos for spectacular views back down over the ruins and out to the surrounding Cyclades.

Sýros

Don't be put off by first impressions of **Sýros**. From the ferry it can seem vaguely industrial, but away from the Neório shipyard things improve quickly. Very much a working island with only a relatively recent history of tourism, it is among the most Greek of the Cyclades and the most populous island in the group. It might also come as a refreshing change from its more touristic neighbours. Of course, outsiders do come to the island – in fact there's a thriving permanent foreign community – and the beaches are hardly undeveloped, but everywhere there's the underlying assumption that you're a guest of an inherently private people.

Ermoúpoli

The main town and port of **ERMOÚPOLI** is one of the most striking in the Cyclades. A UNESCO World Heritage Site, it possesses an elegant collection of grand town houses which rise majestically from the bustling, café-lined

SÝROS

N

Liá   Kámbos   **Kastrí**

Syríngas   **Halandhrianí**

Plátos

Mýtikas

Dhelfíni   Fínikas

Kíni   Áno Sýros

ERMOÚPOLI

Dhanakós

Galissás

Armeós Beach

Máni   ✈ Airport

Faneroméni

Parakopí   Azólimno

Fínikas   Khroussá

Posidhonía

Agathopés   Mégas   Vári

Yialós   Vári Beach

Akhládhi

Komitó

Tínos ▶

Sámos ▶

Mýkonos ▶

0   2 km

▼ Páros

waterfront. The town was founded during the War of Independence by refugees from Psará and Híos, and grew in importance to become Greece's chief port in the nineteenth century. Although Pireás outstripped it long ago, Ermoúpoli is still the largest town in the Cyclades, and the archipelago's capital. Medieval Sýros was largely a Catholic island, but an influx of Orthodox refugees during the War of Independence created two distinct communities; now almost equal in numbers, the two groups today still live in their respective quarters occupying two hills that rise up from the sea. They do, however, commonly celebrate each others' festivals, lending a vibrant mix of culture that gives the island its colour.

Arrival, information and accommodation

Sýros is a major crossover point on the ferry-boat routes, and most people arrive by boat to be met by the usual horde of locals offering rooms. There is no bus service from the airport, and you will have to take a taxi (☎22810 86222). On the waterfront there are several **travel agencies** that sell boat tickets, and you'll also find the **bus station**, **tourist police** and **banks** here. Of the several

motorbike-rental places, Apollon on Andipárou, one block behind the seafront, is recommended. The town's only **Internet café**, *Bizanas*, is on Platía Miaoúli in the base of the town hall.

Accommodation

TeamWork agency (☎ 22810 83400, ⓦ www.teamwork.gr), on the waterfront, is a useful source of information and is able to help with your accommodation needs. In the summer you might try one of the accommodation kiosks on the waterfront. The accommodation listed overleaf is open all year, unless stated otherwise.

Anemomilos Áno Sýros ☎6944 515366. Deluxe apartment-style lodging in a renovated windmill up in Áno Sýros. **❼**

Dream Off Naxou ☎22810 84356, ⓕ22810 86452. Decent, basic rooms, some with balconies, run by a charming family and situated just back from the waterfront. **❸**

Hotel Hermes Platía Kanári ☎22810 88011, ⓦwww.hermes-syros.com. Smart hotel in a prime location, overlooking the port. All rooms have sea views, and the hotel is also home to a very popular seafront restaurant. **❻**

Hotel Nisaki Papadhám (behind the port authority) ☎22810 88200, ⓦwww.hotelnisaki.gr. Bright, airy, modern hotel with sea views. **❺**

Kastro Rooms Kalomenopóulou 12 ☎22810 88064. Spacious rooms in a beautiful old mansion house near the main square, with access to a communal kitchen. If you're lucky, you'll be treated to some traditional music from owner Markos. **❸**

Omiros Karga, past Mitropolis ☎22810 84910, ⓔomirosho@otenet.gr. One of the most romantic options on Sýros, on a quiet road in the direction of Áno Sýros. Classically styled rooms set in an elegant nineteenth-century mansion built for Tinoan sculptor Vitalis. **❺**

Paradise Omirou ☎22810 83204, ⓦwww .hotel-paradise-syros.com. Clean basic en-suite rooms in a quiet part of town. All rooms have access to a pleasant shaded courtyard, whilst rooms on the top floor have good views. **❸**

Sea Colours Apartments Athinas (book through TeamWork Agency; see p.165). Traditionally decorated apartments for 2–6 people, right next to the peaceful Áyios Nikólaos beach, 5min walk from the main platía. **❹**

Syrou Melathron Babagiotou ☎22810 86495, ⓔsyroumel@otenet.gr. Rather regal hotel set in restored nineteenth-century mansion in a quiet area of town. Has suites as well as spacious rooms, some with sea views. **❼**

The Town

Ermoúpoli itself is worth at least a night's stay, with grandiose buildings a relic of its days as a major port. The long, central **Platía Miaoúli** is named after an admiral of the War of Independence whose statue stands there, and in the evenings the population parades in front of its arcades, while children ride the mechanical animals. Up the stairs to the left of the town hall is the small **archeological museum** (Tues–Sun 8.30am–3pm; free), with three rooms of finds from Sýros, Páros and Amorgós. To the left of the clocktower more stairs climb up to **Vrondádho**, the hill that hosts the Orthodox quarter. The wonderful church of the **Anástasis** stands atop the hill, with its domed roof and great views over Tínos and Mýkonos – if it's locked, ask for the key at the priest's house.

Up from the right of the square you'll find the **Apollon Theatre**, a copy of Milan's La Scala, which occasionally hosts performances. Further on up is the handsome Orthodox church of **Áyios Nikólaos**, and beyond it to the right is **Vapória**, where the island's wealthiest shipowners, merchants and bankers built their mansions.

On the taller hill to the left is the intricate medieval quarter of **Áno Sýros**, with a clutch of Catholic churches below the cathedral of St George. It takes about 45 minutes of tough walking up Omírou, which becomes Karga, to reach this quarter (or a rare bus from the main station), passing the Orthodox and Catholic cemeteries on the way – the former full of grand shipowners' mausoleums, the latter with more modest monuments and French and Italian inscriptions (you can halve the walking time by taking a shortcut onto the stair-street named Andhréa Kárga, part of the way along). There are fine views of the town below, and, close by, the **Cappuchin monastery of St Jean**, founded in 1535 to do duty as a poorhouse. Once up here it's worth visiting the local art and church exhibitions at the Markos **Vamvakaris museum** (daily 10.30am–1pm & 7–10pm; €1.50), and the **Byzantine museum** attached to the monastery.

Heading west from Ermoúpoli, on the road leading from the ferry quay to Kíni, accessible by bus, the **industrial museum** (Mon & Wed–Sun 10am–2pm, also Thurs–Sun 6–9pm; €2.50, Wed free) traces the history of the island's

△ Áyios Nikólaos, Ermoúpoli

ship-building, mining and many other industries through a well-labelled series of artefacts and exhibitions.

Eating

As well as being home to a number of excellent restaurants, there are numerous shops along the waterfront selling *loukoúmia* (Turkish delight), *madoláta* (nougats) and *halvadhópita* (sweetmeat pie) for which the island is famed.

Ais Ithoki Kyr Stefanou. Welcoming taverna on small bougainvillea-covered street, serving traditional local dishes such as fried tomatoes, as well as a good *souvláki*.

Archontariki One block east of main platía. Very popular rustic taverna tucked away on a side street behind the port. Serves local specialities, including a special casserole of mushrooms and ham baked in cheese.

Artemision Áno Sýros. Romantically situated restaurant with some of the best views in town, and a tasty, traditional menu.

La Dolce Vita Filini. One of the best, though not the cheapest, restaurants on the island, it occupies a nice spot on steps leading up Filini near where

the ferries dock. Serves creative Greek fusion cooking; try the chicken and ouzo dish. Closed Sun.

Lilis Áno Sýros. Legendary taverna much beloved by locals, and once frequented by Markos Vamvakaris himself (see below).

Retro Taverna Vorotopoulou. Excellent-value taverna near the main platía serving Greek food with some decent vegetarian options. You'll be treated to *bouzoúki* music most nights too.

Thalami On waterfront off Apollonos. Top-notch seafood restaurant in a splendid nineteenth-century villa right on the water's edge.

Yiannena Estiatorio Platía Kanári. Popular, friendly spot by the water with a French bistro feel. Serves great seafood and other Greek standards.

Nightlife

Sýros still honours its contribution to the development of **rebétika**; *bouzoúki*-great Markos Vamvakaris hailed from here, and a platía in Áno Sýros has been named after him on which there is a tiny, sporadically open **museum** in his honour. **Taverna–clubs**, with music at weekends, now take their place beside a batch of more conventional disco–clubs, and there are several other (often expensive) *bouzoúki* bars scattered around the island, mostly strung along routes to beach resorts (see posters and local press for details). The seafront has a rash of lively **bars** in apparent competition for the title of trendiest, but with little to choose between them.

Aegean Casino Opposite ferry dock. Large casino open till 6am for those who have money to burn (and are sufficiently well dressed).

Agora Platía Miaoúli. Pleasant, relaxed bar and club with garden. Plays an eclectic, ethnic mix of music to a chilled-out crowd.

Bitter and Sweet On waterfront past Platía Kanári. Intimate little club in the old Port Authority building. Open 7 days a week in summer, when a live DJ plays a good range of music to dressed-up people.

Bizanas Platía Miaoúli. Cavernous pool hall right on the platía. Also open for Internet access during the day.

Boheme del Mar On waterfront. Trendy, laid-back bar playing everything from reggae to jazz. A great spot for coffee during the day too.

Piramatiko Platía Miaoúli. Busy, sophisticated bar, playing a loud and varied mix from indie to house.

Vento On road to the airport. Huge dance club about 3km out of town, which gets going with trance and European hits around 4am. Take a taxi or find a friend with a scooter.

Southern Sýros

Buses ply the main loop road south (to Gallissás, Fínikas, Mégas Yialós and Vári) hourly in season, and run until late. First stop, **GALISSÁS**, is fundamentally an agricultural village, but has been taken over since the mid-1980s by backpackers attracted by the island's best **campsite**, *Two Hearts* (☏ 22810 42052, ⓦ www .twohearts-camping.com). The site has good facilities and sends minibuses to most boats. There is also a surplus of **rooms**, which makes bargaining possible, and a few bona fide hotels, of which the cheapest are *Semiramis* (☏ 22810 42067, Ⓕ 22810 43000; ❹) and the excellent *Françoise* (☏ 22810 42000, ⓦ www.francoise-hotel.com; ❹), though the *Benois* (☏ 22810 42833, ⓦ www .benois.gr; B&B ❹) is decent value. Among the many **eating** choices, *To Iliovasilema*, next to *Benois*, is an acceptable fish taverna, and *Cavos*, part of a luxury complex, the *Dolphin Bay* Hotel (☏ 22810 42924, Ⓕ 22810 42843; ❼), has impressive views overlooking the bay. *Argo* is a great place for live Greek music. Galissás's identity crisis is exemplified by the proximity of bemused, grazing dairy cattle, a heavy-metal music **pub** and upmarket handicraft shops. Still, the locals are welcoming, and if you feel the urge to escape, you can rent a scooter, or walk ten minutes past the headland to the nudist beach of **Armeós**, where there's fresh spring water. Note that buses out can be erratically routed out of season; to be sure of making your connection you must wait at the high-road stop, not down by the beach.

A pleasant forty-minute walk or a ten-minute bus ride south from Galissás brings you to the more mainstream resort of **FÍNIKAS**, purported to have been settled originally by the Phoenicians (although an alternative derivation could be from *fínikas*, meaning "palm tree" in Greek). The **beach** is narrow and gritty, right next to the road but protected to some extent by a row of tamarisk trees; the pick of the **hotels** is the *Cyclades* (☏ 22810 42255, ⓦ www .hotelcyclades.com; B&B ❹), with an acceptable restaurant just in front, while the *Amaryllis* **rooms** (☏ 22810 42894, Ⓕ 22810 43681; ❹) are slightly cheaper. The fish taverna *Barbalias* on the seafront is recommended. *Maistrali Marine*, near the bus stop, has **Internet** access.

Fínikas is separated by a tiny headland from its neighbour **POSIDHONÍA** (or Delagrazzia), a nicer spot with some idiosyncratically ornate mansions and a bright-blue church right on the edge of the village. It's worth walking ten minutes further south, past the naval yacht club and its patrol boat, to **Agathopés**, with a sandy beach and a little islet just offshore. **Komitó**, at the end of the road leading south from Agathopés, is little more than a stony beach fronting an olive grove. **Accommodation** around Posidhonía ranges from the smart *Possidonion* hotel (☎22810 42100, ✉posidonion@syr.forthnet.gr; ❹) on the seafront to basic rooms inland. *Meltemi*, on the road to Agathopés, is a good seafood **taverna**.

From Posidhonía the road swings east to **MÉGAS YIALÓS**, a small resort below a hillside festooned with brightly painted houses. The long, narrow beach is lined with shady trees and there are pedal boats for hire. Of the **room** set-ups, *Mike and Bill's* (☎22810 43531, ⓦwww.syrosmikeandbill.gr; ❹) is clean and comfortable, whilst the nearby *Alexandra Hotel* (☎22810 42540, ⓦwww .hotelalexandra.gr; ❹), on the bay, enjoys lovely views, and includes breakfast in the price. **VÁRI** is more – though not much more – of a town, with its own small fishing fleet. Beach-goers, generally a younger crowd than on the other beaches, are in a goldfish bowl as it were, with tavernas and **rooms** looming right overhead, but it is the most sheltered of the island's bays, something to remember when the *meltémi* is up. The *Kamelo* hotel (☎22810 61217, ☏22810 61117; ❹) provides the best value, while the *En Plo* beach **bar** is a fun spot in season. The adjacent cove of **AKHLÁDHI** is far more pleasant and family-friendly and boasts a small good-value hotel, *Hotel Emily* (☎22810 61400; ❹), on the seafront, and one taverna.

Northen Sýros

Closest to the capital, and a few kilometres north of Galissás, and reached by bus in fifteen minutes (hourly in season), is the twin-beach coastal settlement of **KÍNI**. Good accommodation can be found at the *Sunset Hotel* (☎22810 71211, ✉enxensyr@otenet.gr; ❹), with the excellent *Zalounis* taverna just below. **Dhelfíni**, just to the north, is also a fine pebbly beach, dramatically accessed on a rather awkward footpath.

Elsewhere, expect potholes, especially further to the north where the land is barren and high, with few villages. The main route north from Áno Sýros is quite easily negotiable by bike, provided you don't mind the hills; en route, the village of **Mýtikas** has a decent taverna just off the road. A few kilometres further on, the road forks, with the left turn leading, after another left, to the small settlement of **Sýringas**, where there's an interesting cave to explore. Straight on leads to **Kámbos**, from where a path leads down to Liá beach; the right fork eventually descends to the northeast coast and the early-Cycladic cemetery at **Halandhrianí**. Most of the finds from the nineteenth-century excavation of the site are now in Athens, though there is still an unexcavated settlement here. On **Kastrí** hill, to the north, are the remains of one of the Cyclades' most ancient fortified habitations dating from the third millennium BC.

Páros and Andíparos

Gently and undramatically furled around the single peak of Profitis Ilías, **Páros** has a little of everything one expects from a Greek island: old villages, monasteries, fishing harbours, a labyrinthine capital, nice beaches and varied nightlife. Parikía, the hóra, is the major hub of inter-island ferry services, so that if you wait long enough you can get to just about any island in the Aegean. However, the island can be touristy and expensive, so it's touch and go when it comes to finding rooms and beach space in August, when the more attractive inland settlements, the port of **Náoussa** and the satellite island of **Andíparos** handle

▲ Sýros   ▲ Mýkonos & Tínos   ▲ Ikaría & Sámos

PÁROS & ANDÍPAROS

▶ Dhonoússa & Amorgós

▶ Náxos, Íos & Santoríni

▶ Ayía Ánna (Náxos)

Platiá Ámmos

Monastíri
Kolymbíthres   Langéri   Sánta María

Delion   Náoussa
                                    Ambelás
Krýos   Longovárdhas
               Monastery
PARIKÍA   Maráthi   Glyfádha

Ayii Anaryiri   Kóstos
Paraspóros   Áyios
          Thapsaná   Minás
Ayía   Convent   Léfkes   Mármara Mólos
Irini   Kristoú stoú   Pródhromos   Áy. Andónios
          Dhássous   Píso Livádhi
Andíparos   Petaloúdhes ▲ Profítis Ilías Márpissa
          Poúnda Kamári   Logarás
Psaralíki   Poúnda
Kalóyeros
     Glýfa   Ayii Theodhóri
          Alykí Angeriá   Dhryós   Khryssí Aktí
                                      (Golden Beach)
                                      Dhryónissi
Áyios
Yeóryios   Sorós

Dhespotikó

N

0   5 km

the overflow. The August 15 festival here is one of the best such observances in
Greece, with a parade of flare-lit fishing boats and fireworks delighting as many
Greeks as foreigners, though it's a real feat to secure accommodation around
this time.

Parikía and around

Bustling **PARIKÍA** sets the tone architecturally for the rest of Páros, with its
ranks of typically Cycladic white houses punctuated by the occasional Venetian-
style building and church domes.

Arrival, information and accommodation

Ferries dock in Parikía by the windmill; the **bus stop** is 100m or so to the
right. Bus routes extend to Náoussa in the north, Poúnda (for Andíparos) in
the west, Alykí in the south and Dhryós on the island's east coast (with another
very useful service between Dhryós and Náoussa). Be aware that there are two
places called Poúnda on Páros, one being the west-coast port, the other a beach
on the way to Dhryós on the east coast (see p.177). Buses to Náoussa carry on
running hourly through the night, while other services stop around midnight.

The **airport** is around 12km south of town, close to Alykí – from where ten daily buses run to Parikía.

Most of the island is flat enough for cycling, though you'll be hard pressed to find any bicycles. **Motorbikes** are more common and are available for rent at several places in town; Forget-Me-Not, along the seafront west of the bus stop, offers a professional and friendly service. Polos Tours, left of the windmill, is one of the more together and friendly **travel agencies**, issuing air tickets when Olympic is shut, and acting as agents for virtually all the boats. Luggage can be left at various travel agents (look for the signs) along the waterfront. There is an excellent **Internet** café, *Memphis*, on the waterfront where you can also burn digital photos to CD.

Continue inland from the **windmill** past the taxi station to reach **Mavroyénous Square**, around which you'll find a maze of houses designed to thwart both the wind and pirates, and the telephone office, police station (and tourist police), banks and Olympic Airways office.

Accommodation

You'll be met off the ferry by locals offering accommodation, even at the most unlikely hours, although you'll have to be quick to grab a room in summer. Most rooms and hotels are to the left of the windmill, and some can be a long walk. Of the two **campsites** nearest to town, *Koula Camping* (☎22840 22081, ⓦwww.campingkoula.gr), along the seafront east of the bus stop, is an acceptable choice for a night or two, whilst *Krios Camping* (☎22840 21705, ⓦwww.krios-camping.gr), across the bay to the north, has a nice beach, a pool and a regular minibus into town. There is a good **hostel**, the *Young Inn*, in Alykí (see p.176).

Argonauta Back of Platía Mavroyénous near the National Bank ☎22840 21440, ⓦwww.argonauta.gr. Friendly hotel with smart, simple rooms arranged around a beautiful courtyard. One of the best deals in town. April–Oct. ❹

Dina just off the old market street ☎22840 21325, ⓦwww.hoteldina.com. Pleasant, central little hotel set in its own gardens in a quiet spot near the market. Open May–Oct. ❹

Festos West of Ekatondapyliani ☎22840 21635, Ⓔconsolas@hol.gr. Excellent pension with clean doubles and communal courtyard on a quiet back-street inland. B&B ❸

Hotel Anna Platanou 500m west of the port ☎22840 21751, ⓦwww.annaplatanou.gr. Smart, family-run property with clean, spacious rooms, on the road towards Cinema Rex. Ten-percent discount for Rough Guide readers. April–Oct. ❺

Kypreou Opposite ferry dock ☎22840 21383. Small family-run hotel with basic en-suite rooms in a prime location across from Ekatondapyliani church. ❹

Mike's Rooms Opposite ferry dock ☎22840 22856. Backpacker-friendly place near the port with clean, comfortable rooms and hospitable staff. ❹

Rena Rooms Behind ancient cemetery ☎22840 22220, ⓦwww.cycladesnet.gr/rena. Spacious doubles and family rooms on a quiet street near the post office. Sea views from the top floor. ❸

Villa Katerina 10 minutes' walk out of town towards Cinema Rex ☎22840 21864, ⓦwww.villakaterina.gr. Bright, family-friendly doubles, studios and apartments in a peaceful location. ❹

The Town

Just beyond the central clutter of the ferry port, to the left (southeast) of the windmill, Parikía has one of the most architecturally interesting churches in the Aegean – the **Ekatondapyliani**, or "The One Hundred Gated". What's visible today was designed and supervised by Isidore of Miletus in the sixth century, but construction was actually carried out by his pupil Ignatius. Legend tells that it was so beautiful on completion that the master, consumed with jealousy, grappled with his apprentice on the rooftop and both of them fell to their deaths. They are portrayed kneeling at the column bases across the courtyard, the old master tugging at his beard in repentance and his rueful pupil clutching a broken head. The church was substantially altered after a severe earthquake in the eighth century, but its essentially Byzantine aspect remains, its shape an imperfect Greek cross. Enclosed by a great wall to protect its icons from pirates, it is in fact three interlocking churches; the oldest, the chapel of Áyios Nikólaos to the left of the apse, is an adaptation of a pagan building dating from the early fourth century BC. To the right of the courtyard, the **Byzantine museum** (daily 9am–9pm; €1.50) displays a collection of icons. Behind Ekatondapylianí, the **archeological museum** (Tues–Sun 8am–3pm; €2) has a fair collection of antique bits and pieces, its prize exhibits being a fifth-century winged Nike and a piece of the Parian Chronicle, a social and cultural history of Greece up to 264 BC engraved in marble. Nearby are the exposed, excavated ruins of an **ancient cemetery** used from the eighth century BC until the second century AD, and a few hundred metres east of town lies a smattering of **archeological sites** including the ruins of a sculpture and pottery workshop from the Hellenistic period as well as an ancient sanctuary.

These sights apart, the real attraction of Parikía is simply to wander the town itself, especially along the meandering **old market street**. Arcaded lanes lead past Venetian-influenced villas, traditional island dwellings and ornate wall-fountains. The town culminates in a seaward Venetian **kástro**, whose surviving east wall incorporates a fifth-century BC round tower and is constructed using masonry pillaged from a temple of Athena. Part of the temple's base is still visible next to the beautiful, arcaded church of Áyios Konstandínos and Ayía Eléni which crowns the highest point, from where the fortified hill drops sharply to the quay in a series of hanging gardens.

Eating

Most of the **eating** establishments in Parikía are along the waterfront to the right of the windmill. The Parian Products Farmers' Union, near the police station, is a lovely wine and cheese shop perfect for stocking up for a beach picnic, while the Ragousis Bakery, behind the National Bank, is a good place for sandwiches and pastries. For snacks, there is a cluster of fast-food outlets near the ferry dock, whilst hidden in the backstreets, and along the seafront to the west, there are plenty of small crêperies and cafés.

Apollon Off old market street. Set in a converted 1920s olive press on the tiny backstreets near the market, this is one of the island's best restaurants. Considering its popularity, its prices aren't bad.

Cavo D'Oro Livádhia. Italian restaurant with a large choice of pizza and pasta near *Koula Camping*. They also do takeaway.

Ephessus Inland past *Mike's Rooms* (see p.171). Good, bustling taverna serving excellent grills and seafood, and with good meal deals for couples.

Happy Green Cow On side street behind National Bank. Fantastically eclectic vegetarian restaurant. Not cheap, but some of the most imaginative vegetarian cooking around.

Hibiscus On waterfront south of windmill. One of the oldest restaurants on the island, it serves generous-sized, wood-oven-baked pizzas in a great spot overlooking the sea.

Ippocrates On seafront away from ancient cemetery. Great-value taverna specializing in fresh seafood.

Trata Behind ancient cemetery. Family-run taverna serving tasty seafood and grilled meats on a vine-covered patio.

Nightlife

Parikía has a wealth of **pubs**, **bars** and low-key **discos**. The most popular cocktail bars extend along the seafront, mostly to the south of the windmill, tucked into a series of open squares and offering staggered "happy hours", so that you can drink cheaply for much of the evening. There's also a thriving cultural centre, Arhilohos (near Ekatondapylianí), which caters mostly to locals, but which has occasional **film** screenings – there are also two open-air cinemas, Neo Rex and Paros, where foreign films are shown in season.

Alexandros Café Southern end of quay. One of the more grown-up choices for a sophisticated evening drink in a fabulously romantic spot around the base of a windmill.

Alga Quay south of windmill. Hip dance bar further along the bay with outdoor seating and live DJ playing anything from R&B to house to 1970s music.

Black Dog Serenade Quay south of windmill. French-owned bar on the waterfront playing quietly hip music and serving a good gin fizz.

Dubliner/Paros Rock Just off quay. Large, brash dance complex set back from the main drag, comprising four loud bars, a snack section, disco and seating area.

Pebbles Quay south of windmill. Upstairs bar playing classical and lounge music, with good sunset views.

Pirate Bar One block inland from quay. Popular, established jazz and blues bar near the town hall.

Saloon D'Or Quay south of windmill. Rowdy but fun spot on the main drag, with cheap drinks and mainstream music.

Around Parikía

If you're staying in Parikía, you'll want to get out into the surroundings at some stage, if only to the beach. The most rewarding **excursion** is the hour's walk along the road starting just past the museum up to the **Áyii Anáryiri** monastery. Perched on the bluff above town, this makes a great picnic spot, with cypress groves, a gushing fountain and some splendid views.

There are **beaches** immediately north and south of the harbour, though none is particularly attractive when compared with Páros's best. In fact, you might prefer to avoid the northern stretch altogether and head **south** along the asphalt road instead. The first unsurfaced side-track you come to leads to a small, sheltered beach; fifteen minutes further on is **PARASPÓROS**, with an attractively landscaped and relatively quiet **campsite** (☎22840 21100) and beach near the remains of an ancient temple to Asklepios, the god of healing and son of Apollo. Continuing for 45 minutes (or a short hop by bus) brings you to arguably the best of the bunch, **AYÍA IRÍNI**, with good sand and a taverna next to a farm and shady olive grove.

In the same direction, but a much longer two-hour haul each way, is **PETA-LOÚDHES**, the so-called "Valley of the Butterflies", a walled-in oasis where millions of Jersey tiger moths perch on the foliage during early summer (June–Sept 9am–8pm; €2). The trip pays more dividends when combined with a visit to the eighteenth-century nunnery of **Khristoú stoú Dhássous**, at the crest of a ridge twenty minutes to the north. Only women are allowed in the sanctuary, although men can get as far as the courtyard. The succession of narrow drives and donkey paths linking both places begins just south of Parikía. Petaloúdhes can be reached from Parikía by bus (in summer), by scooter or on an overpriced excursion by mule.

Náoussa and around

The second port of Páros, **NÁOUSSA**, is a far more attractive choice than Parikía. Although a major resort town, with modern concrete hotels and attendant trappings, it's developed around a charming little port where fishermen still tenderize octopuses by thrashing them against the walls, and you can wander among winding, narrow alleys and simple Cycladic houses. The local **festivals** – an annual Fish and Wine Festival on July 2, and an August 23 shindig celebrating an old naval victory over the Turks – are still celebrated with enthusiasm; the latter tends to be brought forward to coincide with the August 15 festival of the Panayía. Most people are here for the local beaches (see opposite) and the relaxed nightlife; there's really only one attraction, a **museum** (daily 9am–1.30pm & 7–9pm; free) in the monastery of Áyios Athanásios, with an interesting collection of Byzantine and post-Byzantine icons from the churches and monasteries around Náoussa.

The town is noted for its nearby beaches and is a good place to head for as soon as you reach Páros. Because it's newer and more fashionable than Parikía, accommodation is more expensive. Nissiotissa Tours (☎22840 51480), off the left side of the main square, can help you find a room, though it specializes in transport. The *Sea House* (☎22840 52198; ❺) on the rocks above Pipéri beach was the first place in Náoussa to let **rooms** and has one of the best locations. Out of season you should haggle for reduced prices at the basic but well-located *Stella* (☎22840 51317, ⓦwww.hotelstella.gr; ❸), with rooms arranged around its own garden, several blocks inland from the old harbour. If you don't mind a five-minute climb, family-run *Katerina Rooms* (☎22840 51642, ⓦwww.katerinastudios.gr; ❹) have beautiful uninterrupted sea views. Most elegant is the spotlessly cool boutique **hotel** *Heaven* (☎22840 51549, ⓦwww.heaven-naoussa.gr; ❼), which is also set back away from the harbour. Further along the bay is the peaceful *Captain Dounas* (☎22840 52525, ⓦwww.dounas.com; B&B ❼), with large family-friendly apartments and pool. There are two **campsites** in the vicinity: the relaxed and friendly *Naoussa* (☎22840 51565), out of town towards Kolymbíthres (see p. 000), and the newer *Surfing Beach* complex (☎22840 52491-6, ⓦwww.surfbeach.gr) at Sánta María, northeast of Náoussa, with bungalows as well as a popular beach bar, beach and watersports facilities; both run courtesy minibuses to and from Parikía.

Most of the harbour **tavernas** are decent, specializing in fresh fish and seafood, though there are more interesting places to eat at along the main road leading inland from just beside the little bridge over the canal. *Glaros*, with good barrelled unresinated wine, and the *Vengera* opposite, stay open until the early hours. There are some excellent **bars** clustered around the old harbour, making bar-hopping easy: *Linardo* and *Agosta* play dance music, whilst *Café del Mar* has

△ Fishermen in Náoussa, Páros

one of the best settings with its busy tables stretching out to the edge of the sea. Nearby *Shark* is another recommended spot. There are several big clubs up from the bus station, including *Vareladikos,* popular with a younger, late-night crowd. Once a week in summer, hordes of people take the 3.30am bus to the Beach Bar at Sánta María Camping for a weekly beach party – keep an eye out for flyers.

Local beaches

Pipéri beach is a couple of minutes' walk west of Náoussa's harbour; there are other good-to-excellent beaches within walking distance, and a summer *kaïki* service to connect them for about €4 round trip. To the west, an hour's hike brings you to **Kolymbíthres** ("Basins"), where there are three tavernas and the wind- and sea-sculpted rock formations from which the place draws its name. A few minutes beyond, **Monastíri** beach, below the abandoned Pródhromos monastery, is similarly attractive, and partly nudist. If you go up the hill after Monastíri onto the rocky promontory, the island gradually shelves into the sea via a series of flattish rock ledges, making a fine secluded spot for diving and snorkelling, as long as the sea is calm. Go northeast and the sands are better still, the barren headland spangled with good surfing beaches. **Langéri** is backed by dunes; the best surfing is at **Sánta María**, a trendy beach connected with Náoussa by road, which also has a couple of tavernas, including the pleasant Aristofanes; and **Platiá Ámmos** perches on the northeastern tip of the island.

The northeast coast and inland

AMBELÁS hamlet marks the start of a longer trek down the **east coast**. Ambelás itself has a good beach, a small taverna and some rooms and hotels, of which the *Hotel Christiana* (☎22840 51573, ⓕ22840 52503; ❸) is good value, with great fresh fish and local wine in the restaurant and extremely friendly proprietors. From here a rough track leads south, passing several undeveloped stretches on the way; after about an hour you reach **Mólos beach**, impressive and not particularly crowded. **MÁRMARA**, twenty minutes further on, has rooms to let and makes an attractive place to stay, though the marble that the village is built from and named after has largely been whitewashed over.

If Mármara doesn't appeal, then serene **MÁRPISSA**, just to the south, might – a maze of winding alleys and ageing archways overhung by floral balconies, all clinging precariously to the hillside. *Afendakis* (☎ & ⓕ22840 41141; ❷) has clean and modern rooms and furnished apartments (❻), and you can while away a spare hour climbing up the conical Kéfalos hill, on whose fortified summit the last Venetian lords of Páros were overpowered by the Ottomans in 1537. Today the monastery of **Áyios Andónios** occupies the site, but the grounds are locked; to enjoy the views over eastern Páros and the straits of Náxos fully, pick up the key from the priest in Márpissa before setting out (ask in the minimarket of his whereabouts). On the shore nearby, **PÍSO LIVÁDHI** was once a quiet fishing village, but is now dominated by package-holiday facilities; the main reason to visit is to catch a (seasonal) *kaïki* to Ayía Ánna on Náxos. *Hotel Andromache* (☎22840 41387, ⓕ22840 41733; ❺) is a good place behind the beach, as is the *Akteon Hotel* (☎22840 41873, ⓕ22840 41733; ❺) at the tamarisk-shaded **Logarás beach** next door, or ask at the friendly Perantinos Travel Agency (☎22840 41135) near the bus stop. For a meal try *Vrochas* **taverna**, and head to the *Anchorage* café/bar for afternoon snacks or night-time cocktails. You can catch a (seasonal) *kaïki* to Ayía Ánna on Náxos from here.

Inland

The road runs west from Píso Livádhi back to the capital. A **medieval flag-stoned path** once linked both sides of the island, and parts of it survive in the east between Mármara and the villages around Léfkes. **PRÓDHROMOS**, encountered first, is an old fortified farming settlement with defensive walls girding its nearby monastery, while **LÉFKES** itself, an hour up the track, is perhaps the most beautiful and unspoilt settlement on Páros. The town, whose name means "poplars", flourished from the seventeenth century on, its population swollen by refugees fleeing from coastal piracy; indeed it was the island's hóra during most of the Ottoman period. Léfkes's marbled alleyways and amphitheatrical setting are unparalleled, and also undisturbed by motor-bikes, which are forbidden in the middle of town. The central **church** that dominates the town's landscape is made largely of local marble and contains an impressive collection of icons, though it is most often closed; the views over the hill-hugging cemetery behind it and across the interior to the sea are the most remarkable on the island. Despite the few rooms, a disco (Akrovatis), a taverna on the outskirts and the presence of two oversized hotels – the *Hotel Pantheon* (T 22840 41646, F 22840 41700; ⑤), a large 1970s hotel at the top of the village, and *Lefkes Village* (T 22840 41827, W www.lefkesvillage.gr; ⑦), a beautiful hotel on the outskirts, with stunning views – the area around the main square has steadfastly resisted change; the central *kafenío* and bakery observe their siestas religiously, and reserved local residents seem to prefer that tourists remain along the coastal resorts.

Thirty minutes further on, through olive groves, the path reaches **KÓSTOS**, a simple village and a good place for lunch in a taverna. Any traces of path disappear at **MARÁTHI**, on the site of the ancient marble quarries which once supplied much of Europe. Considered second only to Carrara marble, the last slabs were mined here by the French in the nineteenth century for Napoleon's tomb. From Maráthi, it's easy enough to pick up the bus on to Parikía, but if you want to continue hiking, strike south for the monastery of **Áyios Minás**, twenty minutes away. Various Classical and Byzantine masonry fragments are worked into the walls of this sixteenth-century foundation, and the friendly custodians can put you on the right path up to the convent of **Thapsaná**, 4km from Parikía. From here, other paths lead either back to Parikía (two hours altogether from Áyios Minás), or on up to the island's summit for the last word in views over the Cyclades.

The south of the island

There's little to stop for south of Parikía until **POÚNDA**, 6km away, and then only to catch the ferry to Andíparos (see opposite). What used to be a sleepy hamlet is now a concrete jungle, and neighbouring **ALYKÍ** appears to be permanently under construction. The **airport** is close by, making for lots of unwelcome noise; redeeming features include a good-value **hostel**, the *Young Inn* (T 697 64 15 232, W www.young-inn.com; €8 per bed), and an excellent beachside restaurant, by the large tamarisk tree. The end of the southern bus route is at Angeriá, about 3km inland of which is the **convent of Áyii Theodhóri**. Its nuns specialize in weaving locally commissioned articles and are further distinguished as *paleomeroloyítes*, or old-calendarites, meaning that they follow the medieval Orthodox (Julian) calendar, rather than the Gregorian one.

Working your way around the **south coast** on foot, there are two routes east to Dhryós. Either retrace your steps to Angeriá and follow the (slightly inland) coastal road, which skirts a succession of isolated coves and small beaches, or keep on across the foothills from Áyii Theodhóri – a shorter walk. Aside from an abundant water supply (including a duck pond) and surrounding orchards, **DHRYÓS** village is mostly modern and characterless, lacking even a well-defined platía. You'd do better to follow the signs to the attractive, and relatively quiet, **Dhryós** beach.

Between here and Píso Livádhi to the north are several sandy coves – Khryssí Aktí ("Golden Beach"), Tzirdhákia, Mezádha, Poúnda (not to be confused with the port of the same name on the opposite coast) and Logarás – prone to pummelling by the *meltémi*, yet all favoured to varying degrees by campers and windsurfers. **KHRYSSÍ AKTÍ** now has many tavernas, room complexes and hotels, such as the *Amaryllis Hotel* right on the beach (T22840 41410, Wwww .amaryllis-hotel-paros.com; ●); it also offers the whole range of watersports. In addition, there are tavernas at Logarás, but other facilities are concentrated in Dhryós, which is still the focal point of this part of the island.

Andíparos

The secret is definitely out about **Andíparos**. The waterfront is lined with new hotels and apartments, and in high season it can be full, though in recent years families seem to be displacing the young, international crowd. However, the island has managed to hold on to a friendly small-island atmosphere and still has a lot going for it, including good sandy beaches and an impressive cave, and the rooms and hotels are less expensive than on Páros.

Most of the population of eight hundred live in the large low-lying northern **village**, across the narrow straits from Páros, the new development on the outskirts concealing an attractive traditional settlement around the *kástro*. A long, flagstoned pedestrian street forms its backbone, leading from the jetty to the Cycladic houses around the outer wall of the *kástro*, which was built by Leonardo Loredano in the 1440s as a fortified settlement safe from pirate raids – the Loredano coat of arms can still be seen on a house in the courtyard. The only way into the courtyard is through a pointed archway from the platía, where several cafés are shaded by a giant eucalyptus. Inside, more whitewashed houses surround two churches and a cistern built into the surviving base of the central tower.

Andíparos's **beaches** begin right outside central town: **Psaralíki**, just to the south with golden sand and tamarisks for shade, is much better than Sifnéïko (aka "Sunset") on the opposite side of the island. Villa development is starting to follow the newly paved road down the east coast, but has yet to get out of hand. **Glýfa**, 4km down, is another good beach and, further south, **Sorós** has rooms and tavernas. On the west coast there are some fine small sandy coves at **Áyios Yeóryios**, the end of the road, and another long stretch of sand at **Kalóyeros**. *Kaïkia* make daily trips round the island and, less frequently, to the uninhabited islet of Dhespotikó, opposite Áyios Yeóryios.

The great **cave** (summer daily 10.45am–3.45pm; €3) in the south of the island is the chief attraction for day-trippers. In these eerie chambers the Marquis de Nointel, Louis XIV's ambassador to Constantinople, celebrated Christmas Mass in 1673 while a retinue of five hundred, including painters, pirates, Jesuits and Turks, looked on; at the exact moment of midnight explosives were detonated to emphasize the enormity of the event. Although electric light and cement steps have diminished its mystery and grandeur, the cave remains impressive. Tour buses (€3 round trip) and public buses (€1 one way) run from the port every hour in season; bus services and opening hours are reduced out of season, and in winter you'll have to fetch the key for the cave from the mayor or village council (T22840 61218).

Practicalities

To get here, you have a choice of **boats** from Parikía (hourly in season, weather permitting; 40min), arriving at the jetty opposite the main street, or the car ferry from Poúnda (every 30min; 10min), arriving 150m to the south.

There are plenty of **hotels** along the waterfront, including *Anargyros* (☎22840 61204; ❸), which has good, basic rooms. More upmarket places to the north of the jetty include *Mantalena* (☎22840 61206, ◍www.hotelmantalena.gr; ❹) with large rooms and balconies, and spotless, contemporary *Artemis* (☎22840 61460, ◍www.artemisantiparos.com; ❹), while inland there are some cheaper rooms as well as the *Hotel Galini* (☎22840 61420; ❺) to the left of the main street. The popular **campsite** (☎22840 61221) is a ten-minute walk northeast along a track, next to its own nudist beach; the water here is shallow enough for campers to wade across to the neighbouring islet of Dhipló. For peace and quiet with a degree of comfort try *Oliaros* (☎22840 25305, ◍www.oliaros.gr; ❹) at Áyios Yeóryios, a long stretch of beach with several tavernas, of which *Captain Pipinos* is recommended.

The best of the waterfront **tavernas** is *Anargyros*, below the hotel of the same name. The main street leads up beside it; *Klimataria*, 100m inland off to the left, has tables in a pleasant garden, though it's only open at night. *The Internet Cafe*, also on the main street, has excellent coffee, as does *Romvi's* on the waterfront. There are plenty of **bars** around the eucalyptus-filled platía, where a festive atmosphere prevails at night. *Café Margarita* is a pleasant street-side hangout on the way up to the platía, while the *Nautica* is probably the liveliest of the waterfront spots. For quiet music and views of the mountains try *Yam*, an outdoor restaurant and bar near the *Klimataria*. A **bank**, a **post office**, a cinema and several **travel agents** cluster around the waterfront, and there's a launderette near the windmill. You can rent scooters and **bicycles** at Europcar near the ferry dock.

Náxos

Náxos is the largest and most fertile of the Cyclades, and, with its green and mountainous highland scenery, seems immediately distinct from many of its neighbours. The difference is accentuated by the **unique architecture** of many of the interior villages: the Venetian Duchy of the Aegean, which ruled from the thirteenth to the sixteenth century, left towers and fortified mansions scattered throughout the island, while medieval Cretan refugees bestowed a singular character upon Náxos's eastern settlements.

Today Náxos could easily support itself without tourists by relying on its production of potatoes, olives, grapes and lemons, but it has thrown in its lot with mass tourism, so that parts of the island are now almost as busy as Páros in season. The island certainly has plenty to see if you know where to look: the highest mountains in the Cyclades, intriguing central valleys, a spectacular north coast and marvellously sandy beaches in the southwest. It is also renowned for its wines, cheese – sharp *kefalotýri* and milder *graviéra* – and *kítron*, a sweet liqueur distilled from the fruit of this citrus tree.

Náxos Town

A long causeway, built to protect the harbour to the north, connects the town with the islet of Palátia – the place where, according to legend, Theseus abandoned Ariadne on his way home from Crete. The famous stone **Portára** that has greeted visitors for 2500 years is the portal of a temple of Apollo, built on the orders of the tyrant Lygdamis in the sixth century BC, but never completed.

Most of the town's life goes on down by the crowded port esplanade or just behind it; backstreets and alleys lead up through low arches of the old town, Bourgos, to the fortified **kástro** from where Marco Sanudo, the thirteenth-century Venetian who established the Duchy of Archipelago, and his successors ruled over the Cyclades.

Arrival, information and accommodation

Náxos is served by a tiny **airport**, located just a few minutes' bus ride from Náxos Town. Large **ferries** dock along the northerly harbour causeway; all small boats and the very useful Express Skopelitis ferry use the jetty in the fishing harbour, not the main car-ferry dock. The **bus station** is at its landward end; buses run five times a day to Apóllon, with one of the morning services going via Engarés and Abrámi, which is much slower though not any cheaper. There are six buses a day to Apíranthos via Filóti, two of these going on to Moutsoúna

NÁXOS TOWN

0   100 m

Portára
(Temple of Apollo) ❶

GRÓTTA

RING ROAD

RING ROAD

NEOFYTOU

Naxos Tourist Information ⓘ ❸

Bus Station

❷ ❻ ❼ ❹ ❺

❾ ❽ BOÚRGOS

❿

Port Police

PARALIA

Ferry Jetty

Small Ferry Jetty

Archeological Museum

KÁSTRO

⓫

⓬

ACCOMMODATION

Anixis	D
Apollon	C
Chateau Zevgoli	F
Flisvos Sportclub Hotel	L
Galaxy	M
Glaros	I
Hotel Grotta	B
Iliada Studios	A
Panorama	E
Pension Irene I	H
Pension Irene II	J
Pension Kastell	G

RESTAURANTS & BARS

Babylonia	9
Bikini	3
Cafe Picasso	16
Coco's Café	10
Day & Night	13
Escoba	13
Irini's	6
Katerina's Grill	14
Lakridi	8
Lucullus	7
Manolis Garden	5
Metaxi Mas	4
Palatia	1
Popi's	11
Portokali	17
Rendezvous	12
Scirocco	15
Super Island	2

PRANTOUNA

⓭

⓮ PAPAVASSILIOU

ARISTIDI PROTOPAPADAKI

ARIADNIS

Road to interior

MAIN SQUARE ⓯

⓰

AG. ARSENIOU

N

Police

⓱

Áyios Yeóryios

▼ 🄚 & 🄛

Airport ▼

on the east coast. Buses run (every 30min 8am–midnight) to Áyios Prokópios, Ayía Ánna and as far as the Pláka campsite on Pláka beach, and four times a day to Pyrgáki. Printed timetables are available from the bus station. More convenient are the **day-tours** of Náxos (€20) that can be booked at **Naxos Tourist Information** (℡22850 25201, ℻22850 25200), on the seafront near the jetty, which offers a wealth of information, and somewhere to leave your bags (€1.50). It's also the best place to book special tours to the Minor Cyclades as well as accommodation, since the proprietor maintains some of the finest properties on the island. German-run **Naxos Horse Riding** (℡694 88 09 142) organizes daily trips in the area for all levels for around €40 per person.

Accommodation

There's plenty of accommodation in Náxos and you should have no problem finding somewhere to stay. Once you've run the gauntlet of touts on the jetty, you would do well to head straight to Naxos Tourist Information (see above) who can book **rooms** for you. There are three basic areas to look: the old quarter near the *kástro*, where they are hard to find and relatively expensive; up to the left (north) of town in Grótta; and south of town near Áyios Yeóryios beach, where they are most abundant and less expensive, but with significant night-time noise from clubs and discos.

Anixis Bourgos ℡22850 22932, ⊕www.hotel-anixis.gr. Pleasant, simply decorated rooms set around a garden near the *kástro*. March–Oct. ❸

Apollon South of Grótta ℡22850 22468, ⊕www.naxostownhotels.com. Comfortable, modern doubles, all with balconies, in a good location near Grótta beach. ❻

Chateau Zevgoli Bourgos ℡22850 22993, ⊕www.naxostownhotels.com. Charming, traditional hotel near the *kástro*, with nice views and antique-furnished rooms. March–Nov. ❺

Flisvos Sportclub Hotel Áyios Yeóryios ℡22850 24308, ⊕www.flisvos-sportclub.com. Self-contained mini-resort with hotel and restaurant. Also home to a watersports centre (see box p.122), and can organize walking tours of the island and mountain bike rental. ❻

Galaxy Southern part of Áyios Yeóryios ℡22850 22422, ⊕www.hotel-galaxy.com. Upmarket hotel with pool and large modern rooms and studios with sea views and balconies. ❼

Glaros Áyios Yeóryios ℡22850 23101, ⊕www.hotelglaros.com. Comfortable, stylish hotel practically on the beach. Most rooms come

with sea views, and all have verandas. March–Oct. ❹

Hotel Grotta Grótta ℡22850 22215, ⊕www.hotelgrotta.gr. Welcoming hotel in good location, only a 5min walk from the waterfront. Offers comfortable rooms, a Jacuzzi and a generous breakfast. B&B ❺

Iliada Studios Grótta ℡22850 23303, ✉iliada@otenet.gr. Quiet studio complex in Grótta on the cliff beyond town, with good views out to sea. Feb–Nov. ❹

Panorama Bourgos ℡22850 24404, ✉panoramanaxos@in.gr. Spotless family-run hotel near the *kástro*, with airy rooms and sea views. May–Oct. ❸

Pension Irene I & II Both near the main square ℡22850 23169 or 69733 37782, ⊕www.irenepension-naxos.com. Clean, spacious pension with two locations, one with a nice pool. The friendly proprietors will meet guests at the ferry jetty. ❸

Pension Kastell Just south of *kástro* ℡22850 23082, ⊕www.kastell.gr. Friendly pension offering large rooms with balconies and a nice roof garden. €5 extra for a hearty breakfast. March–Oct. ❸

The Town

Only two of the *kástro*'s original seven towers remain, though the **north gate** (approached from Apóllon and known as the Traní Portá or "Great Gate") survives as a splendid example of a medieval fort entrance. The Venetians' Catholic descendants, now dwindled to a few old ladies, still live in the old mansions that encircle the site, many with ancient coats of arms above crumbling doorways. One of these, the **Domus Della-Rocca-Barozzi** (daily 10am–3pm & 7.30–10.30pm; €5), is open to the public and offers the best views from the *kástro*; the guided tour even includes a tasting from the family's wine cellar, and live classical concerts often animate the adjoining courtyard on summer evenings. Other brooding relics survive in the same area: a seventeenth-century Ursuline convent and the Roman Catholic cathedral, restored in questionable taste in the 1950s, though still displaying a thirteenth-century crest inside. Nearby was one of Ottoman Greece's first schools, the French School; opened in 1627 for Catholic and Orthodox students alike, its pupils included, briefly, Nikos Kazantzakis (see p.663). The school building now houses an excellent **archeological museum** (Tues–Sun 8.30am–3pm; €3), with finds from Náxos, Koufoníssi, Kéros and Dhonoússa, including an important collection of Early Cycladic figurines. Archaic and Classical sculpture and pottery dating from Neolithic through to Roman times are also on display. On the roof terrace, a Hellenistic mosaic floor shows a nereid (sea nymph) surrounded by deer and peacocks.

Eating

The waterfront is crammed with places to eat, most of them decent. For picnics, there's a good bakery about midway along the harbour front, while for local cheese, wine, *kítron*, spices and other dried comestibles, head for Tirokomika Proionia Naxou, a delightful old store on Papavassilíou.

Bikini Opposite ferry dock. This popular crêperie also serves good breakfasts and snacks. Ideal if you're waiting for a ferry.

Cafe Picasso Main square. Excellent Mexican restaurant, with some good vegetarian options, and another branch on Pláka beach. Evenings only.

Irini's Paralia. One of the best of the simple oven-food tavernas on the waterfront.

Katerina's Grill Papavassiliou. Good choice for cheap breakfasts, grills and wood-oven baked pizzas. Also a good spot for people-watching.

Lucullus Bourgos. Romantic restaurant serving home-made local specialities in an intimate setting in the old town.

Manolis Garden Bourgos. Popular taverna with small but excellent menu both in taste and value for money. Located in a large garden in the old town.

Metaxi Mas Bourgos. No-fuss ouzerí serving excellent food on a little street heading up to the *kástro*.

Palatia Below Portára. Fish taverna, which, despite its location, is surprisingly reasonable and serves great food.

Popi's Paralia. A veritable institution, specializing in lamb raised on the proprietor's own land. Inside there's also a wine, *kítron* and cheese shop.

Portokali Overlooking Áyios Yeóryios. Perched on the headland to the south of town with good views, this is an excellent spot for watching the sunset, although the international and Greek dishes are accordingly overpriced.

Rendezvous Paralia. Busy waterfront café serving excellent cakes and coffee.

Scirocco Main square. Well-known restaurant popular with locals and tourists alike for its good-value traditional meals, hence the occasional long queue to get in.

Nightlife

Much of the evening action goes on at the south end of the waterfront, where you'll find **café-bars** and **clubs** jostling for business, luring people in with staggeringly huge menus of cheap cocktails. Should that fail to tempt, there's also an open-air **cinema**, the Cine Astra, on the road to the airport at the southern end of town; it's a fair walk out, but the Ayía Ánna bus stops here.

Babylonia Náxos's first and currently only gay bar, discreetly situated on an upper-level building on the waterfront.

Coco's Café Good little cocktail spot on the waterfront, playing South American music and serving breakfast through the day.

Day & Night Popular bar turning out European, and later on Greek, music every weekend on its packed veranda.

Escoba Just behind *Day & Night*, this place serves yet more great cocktails, and is a little larger, so less of a crush.

Lakridi A tiny jazz bar, which sometimes plays classical music, tucked away on a street behind the port police.

Super Island The town's biggest club, with dancing to European hits split over two floors.

The southwestern beaches

The **beaches** around Náxos Town are worth sampling. For some unusual swimming just to the **north** of the port, beyond the causeway, **Grótta** is easiest to reach. Besides the caves after which the place is named, the remains of submerged Cycladic buildings are visible, though only when you're out in the water. The finest spots, though, are all **south** of town, the entire southwestern coastline boasting a series of excellent **beaches** accessible by regular bus. **ÁYIOS YEÓRYIOS**, a long sandy bay fringed by the southern extension of the hotel area, is within walking distance. There's a line of cafés and tavernas at the northern end of the beach, and a windsurfing school, plus a campsite, although there are far more attractive places to camp on Pláka beach (see below).

Buses take you to **ÁYIOS PROKÓPIOS** beach, with plenty of reasonably priced hotels, rooms and basic tavernas, plus the upmarket *Hotel Lianos Village* (T22850 26366, W www.lianosvillage.com; ⑥), with its pleasant pool setting. Two excellent, traditional restaurants are *Anessio* and *Colosseo*, while the younger, funkier *Kahlua* and *Splash* are good cafés. Rapid development along this stretch means that this resort has blended into the next one of **AYÍA ÁNNA**, further along the busy road, with accommodation of a similar price and quality. The seaview *Iria Beach Hotel* (T22850 42600, W www.iriabeach-naxos.com; ⑤) and the nearby *Kouros Hotel* (Tt22850 29151, W www.kouros-naxos.com; ③) are comfortable options. The best food in Ayía Anna is at the *Gorgona* taverna, family run and with excellent prices. *Gorgona* also offers rooms, studios and apartments, all newly refurbished with en-suite bathrooms and air conditioning (T 22850 41007; ③). Moving along the coast, away from the built-up area, the beach here is nudist.

Beyond the headland, **PLÁKA** beach, a vegetation-fringed expanse of white sand, stretches for 5km. Things are not so built up here, and parts of the beach are nudist (past *Plaka* campsite). There are two suitably laid-back and friendly **campsites** here: *Maragas* (T22850 24552, W www.maragascamping .gr), which also has double rooms (③) and studios (③), and the newer *Plaka* (T22850 42700, W www.plakacamping.gr), a little further along, which is small and quiet with a few inexpensive bungalows (②), and a hotel (③). The *Hotel Orkos Village* (T22850 75321, W www.orkoshotel.gr; ④) has apartments in an attractive location, on a hillside above the coast between Pláka beach and Mikrí Vígla, and the *Plaza Beach Hotel* T22850 29400, W www.plazabeachhotel.gr; ⑦) is a glittering new mega-resort at the southern end of the beach that is likely to push the nudists further out. Good **tavernas** in the vicinity of Pláka are the equally good *Golden Beach*, *Paradiso* and *Galini*, while *Amore Mio* is the most romantic spot for dining, with views of the coast. The nearby *Waffle House* has a tasty range of home-made ice cream.

For real isolation, go to the other side of the Mikrí Vígla headland which begins at the southern edge of Pláka beach, along a narrow footpath across the cliff-edge, to **KASTRÁKI** beach; towards the middle of the beach, *Areti* (T22850 75292; ⑤) has apartments and a restaurant, but the fresh food at nearby *Axiotissa* **taverna** is unbeatable. A few people camp around the taverna on the small headland a little further down. In summer, this stretch – all the way from Mikrí Vígla down to Pyrgáki – attracts camper vans and windsurfers from all over Europe. On the **Alíko** promontory to the south of Kastráki there is a small nudist beach, known locally as "Hawaii Beach" for the vibrant blue colour of its waters.

From Kastráki, it's a couple of hours' walk up to the Byzantine castle of **Apalírou**, which held out for two months against the besieging Marco Sanudo.

The fortifications are relatively intact and the views magnificent. Picturesque **Pyrgáki** beach has a couple of tavernas and a few rooms; 4km further on is the slightly larger **Ayiássos** beach.

The rest of the **southern coast** – virtually the whole of the southeast of the island – is remote and mountain-studded; you'd have to be a dedicated and well-equipped camper and hiker to get much out of the region.

Central Náxos and the Tragéa

Although buses bound for Apóllon (in the north) link up the central Naxian villages, the core of the island – between Náxos Town and Apíranthos – is best explored by moped or on foot. Much of the region is well off the beaten track, and can be a rewarding excursion if you've had your fill of beaches; Christian Ucke's *Walking Tours on Naxos*, available from bookshops in Náxos Town, is a useful guide for hikers.

Once out of Náxos Town, you quickly arrive at the neighbouring villages of **GLINÁDHO** and **GALANÁDHO**, both scruffy market centres, forking right and left respectively. Glinádho is built on a rocky outcrop above the Livádhi plain, while Galanádho displays the first of Náxos's fortified mansions and an unusual double church. A combined Orthodox chapel and Catholic sanctuary separated by a double arch, the church reflects the tolerance of the Venetians during their rule, and the locals, to each other's religions. Continue beyond Glinádho to **TRÍPODHES** (ancient Biblos), 9km from Náxos Town. Noted by Homer for its wines, this old-fashioned agricultural village has no sights as such, but you can enjoy a coffee at the shaded *kafenío*. The start of a long but rewarding walk is a rough road (past the parish church) which leads down the colourful Pláka valley, past an old watchtower and the Byzantine church of **Áyios Matthéos** ("mosaic pavement"), and ends at the glorious Pláka beach (see p.183).

To the east, the twin villages of **SANGRÍ**, on a vast plateau at the head of a long valley, can be reached by continuing to follow the left-hand fork past Galanádho, a route which allows a look at the domed eighth-century church of **Áyios Mámas** (on the left), once the Byzantine cathedral of the island but neglected during the Venetian period and now a sorry sight. **Káto Sangrí** boasts the remains of a Venetian castle, while **Áno Sangrí** is an attractive little place, all cobbled streets and fragrant courtyards. Thirty minutes' stroll away, on a path leading south out of the village, are the partially reconstructed remains of a Classical temple of Demeter.

The Tragéa

From Sangrí, the road twists northeast into the **Tragéa** region, scattered with olive trees and occupying a vast highland valley. It's a good jumping-off point for all sorts of exploratory rambling, and **HALKÍ** is a fine introduction to what is to come. Set high up, 16km from Náxos Town, it's a noble and quiet town with some lovely churches, including the **Panayía Protóthronis** church, with its eleventh- to thirteenth-century frescoes; it only opens to visitors in the morning. Nearby are the romantic ruins of the seventeenth-century Venetian **Grazia-Barozzi Tower**. Tourists wanting to stay here are still something of a rarity, although you can usually get a **room** in someone's house by asking at the store. *Yiannis* **taverna** is the focal point of village activity and has a good selection of fresh *mezédhes* to enjoy with a glass of ouzo. Nearby is the distillery and shop of Vallindras Naxos Citron, whose charming proprietors explain the process of producing *kítron* followed by a little tasting session. The olive and citrus plantations surrounding Halkí are crisscrossed by paths and tracks, the groves dotted with numerous Byzantine chapels and the ruins of fortified *pýrgi* or Venetian mansions.

The road from Halkí heads 2km north to **MONÍ**. Just before the village, you pass the sixth-century monastery of **Panayía Dhrossianí**, a group of stark, grey-stone buildings with some excellent frescoes; the monks allow visits at any time, though you may have to contend with coach tours from Náxos Town. Moní itself enjoys an outstanding view of the Tragéa and surrounding mountains, and has four traditional **tavernas**, plus some **rooms** (ask at the tavernas; ❷). The main road leads on to Kinídharos, with an old marble quarry above the village; a few kilometres beyond, a signpost points you down a rough track to the left, to **FLÉRIO** (commonly called Melanés). The most interesting of the ancient marble quarries on Náxos, this is home to two famous **kouri**, dating from the sixth century BC, that were left recumbent and unfinished because of flaws in the material. Even so, they're finely detailed figures, over 5m in length. One of the statues lies in a private, irrigated orchard; the other is up a hillside some distance above, and you will need local guidance to find it.

From Flério you could retrace your steps to the road and head back to Hóra via Mýli and the ruined Venetian castle at Kouronohóri, both pretty hamlets connected by footpaths (9km). If you're feeling more adventurous, ask to be directed south to the footpath that leads over the hill to the Potamiá villages. The first of these, **ÁNO POTAMIÁ**, has a fine taverna and a rocky track back towards the Tragéa. Once past the valley, the landscape becomes craggy and barren, the forbidding Venetian fortress of **Apáno Kástro** perched on a peak just south of the path. This is believed to have been Sanudo's summer home, but the fortified site goes back further, if the Mycenaean tombs found nearby are any indication. From the fort, paths lead back to Halkí in around an hour. Alternatively, you can continue further northwest down the Potamiá valley towards Hóra, passing first the ruined **Cocco Pýrgos** – said to be haunted by one Constantine Cocco, the victim of a seventeenth-century clan feud – on the way to **MÉSO POTAMIÁ**, joined by some isolated dwellings with its twin village **KÁTO POTAMIÁ** nestling almost invisibly among the greenery flanking the creek. From here you can follow the road back to Náxos Town, about a six-kilometre trek.

At the far end of the gorgeous Tragéa valley, **FILÓTI**, the largest village in the region, lies on the slopes of Mount Zás (or Zeus) which, at 1000m, is the highest point in the Cyclades. Under the shade of the plane trees on the main platía are several pleasant *kafenía*, as well as *Babulas Grill-Restaurant* (☎22850 31426; ❷), which has the best rooms in the village. To get an idea of the old village, climb the steps up the hill starting at the platía. A turning at the southern end of the village is signposted to the **Pýrgos Himárou**, a remote twenty-metre Hellenistic watchtower, and also to **Kalándou** beach, 25km away on the south coast; beyond the turning the road is unpaved. There are no villages in this part of the island, so bring supplies if you're planning to camp. From the village, it's a round-trip walk of three to four hours on mostly unmarked trails to the summit of **Zás**, a climb which rewards you with an astounding panorama of virtually the whole of Náxos and its Cycladic neighbours. Save yourself the rather tedious walk along the main Filóti–Apóllon road by taking the bus towards Apóllon and asking the driver to let you off at the Dhánakos turning, where the waymarked final approach trail begins just beside a small chapel on your right. There is also a marked turn-off to the Zás Cave, a pleasant place for a picnic, but not the best point from which to tackle the steep ascent to the summit.

Apíranthos

APÍRANTHOS (Apérathos in local dialect), a hilly, winding 10km beyond the cave, shows the most Cretan influence of all the interior villages. It is a good quiet place to stay for a few days, and being high in the mountains is noticeably cooler and greener than the coast. There are two Venetian fortified mansions, and the square contains a miniature church with a three-tiered bell tower. Ask to be pointed to the start of the spectacular **path** up over the ridge behind; this ends either in Moní or Kalóxilos, depending on whether you fork right or left respectively at the top. Cafés and tavernas on the main street look out over a terraced valley below; the nationally renowned **taverna** *Leftheri*, here, is generally regarded as one of the best restaurants on the island, serving up carefully prepared local dishes. **Rooms** are available but are not advertised – ask in the cafés or in the embroidery shop.

Apíranthos has a beach annexe of sorts at **Moutsoúna**, 12km east. Emery mined near Apíranthos used to be transported here by means of an aerial funicular and then shipped out of the port. The industry collapsed in the 1980s, and the sandy cove beyond the dock now features a growing colony of holiday villas and the excellent *Ostria* taverna. An unpaved road heads south along the coast to a remote sandy beach at **Psilí Ámmos** – ideal for self-sufficient campers, but you must take enough water. From here a track carries on to relatively secluded **Pánormos** beach in the southeastern corner of the island.

Northern Náxos

The route through the mountains from Apíranthos to Apóllon is very scenic, and the road surface is in good condition all the way. Jagged ranges and hairpin bends confront you before reaching Kóronos, the halfway point, where a road off to the right threads through a wooded valley to **Liónas**, a tiny and very Greek port with a pebble beach. You'd do better to continue, past Skadhó, to the remote, emery-miners' village of **KORONÍDHA** which is a pleasing, vine-covered settlement – the highest village on the island and the original home of *kítron* liqueur.

Back on the main road, a series of slightly less hairy bends leads down a long valley to **APÓLLON**, a small resort with two beaches: a tiny and crowded stretch of sand backed by cafés and restaurants, and a longer and quieter stretch of shingle, popular mainly with Greek families. The only major attraction is a **kouros**, approached by a path from the main road just above the village. Lying *in situ* at a former marble quarry, this largest of Náxos's abandoned stone figures is just over 10m long, but, compared with those at Flério, disappointingly lacking in detail. Here since 600 BC, it serves as a singular reminder of the Naxians' traditional skill; the famous Delian lions (see p.163) are also made of Apollonian marble. Not surprisingly, bus tours descend upon the village during the day, and Apóllon is now quite a popular little place. The local festival, celebrated on August 28–29, is one of Náxos's best.

It's easy to make a round trip of the north coast and inland villages by bus from Náxos Town. The coastal road is spectacularly beautiful, going high above the sea for most of the way, making it more like parts of Crete or the mainland than other islands. Ten kilometres past the northern cape sprouts the beautiful **Ayiá** *pýrgos*, or tower, another foundation (in 1717) of the Cocco family. There's a tiny hamlet nearby, and, 7km further along, a track leads off to **Abrámi** beach, an idyllic spot with a highly recommended family-run **taverna** with **rooms** to let, *Pension and Restaurant Efthimios* (☎22850 63244, 📧abram@can .gr; ❷). Just beyond the hamlet of Hília Výssi is the abandoned **monastery of**

Faneroménis, built in 1606. Carrying on along the coastal road you will reach the Engarés valley, at the foot of which is another quiet beach, **Amití**, accessed via one of two dirt tracks, the most obvious being the one leading down from Galíni, only 6km from Náxos Town. Inland from Galíni, the unspoilt town of **Engarés** is home to the excellent *Haris* taverna; *Vasilis* in equally undervisited **Melanés** (reachable by road from Engarés) serves chickens and game raised on site. On the final stretch back to the port, you pass a unique eighteenth-century Turkish fountain-house and the fortified monastery of **Ayíou Ioánnou Khryssostómou**, where a couple of aged nuns are still in residence. A footpath from the monastery and the road below lead straight back to town.

Minor Cyclades

Four of the six small islands in the patch of the Aegean between Náxos and Amorgós have slid from obscurity into fashion in recent years. The group is known commonly as the Minor Cyclades and includes **Áno Koufoníssi**, **Skhinoússa**, **Iráklia** and **Dhonoússa**. The islands' new popularity is hastening the development of better facilities and higher prices, but with little room for expansion and only limited ferry service, they've managed to avoid the mass tourism of the rest of the Cyclades. You can even find peace and quiet – what the Greeks call *isykhiá* – here in August, when you should make the crossing from Áno Koufoníssi to **Kéros**, with no permanent population but an important archeological site, or **Káto Koufoníssi**, inhabited only by goatherds.

Though a Pireás-based **ferry** has been known to call at the islands – linking them with Náxos and Amorgós and (sometimes) Páros and Sýros – the small, local *Express Skopelitis* is a more frequent fixture, leaving the little ferry quay in Náxos almost daily in August to head to most of the islets. At other times of year, don't arrive unless you're in no hurry to push on.

Áno Koufoníssi, Káto Koufoníssi and Kéros

Áno Koufoníssi (usually referred to simply as Koufoníssi) is the most populous island of the group, and is reachable by ferries from Náxos several times per week in high season, outside of which you might better use the private vessel of Prasinos Excursions from Pánormos (T22850 71438; €20–50 per person depending on size of group). With some of the least-spoilt beaches in the Cyclades, the island is attracting increasing numbers of Greek and foreign holidaymakers. Small enough to walk round in a morning, the island can actually feel overcrowded in July and August.

The old single-street village of **HÓRA**, on a low hill behind the harbour, is being engulfed by new room and hotel development, but still has a friendly, small-island atmosphere. A map by the jetty shows where to find all the island's **rooms**: the popular restaurant and pension *Melissa* (T22850 71454, F22850 71732; ❸) is a good, family-run choice, just inland from the beach. The most upmarket options include *Hotel Aegeon* (T22850 74050, W www.hotel-aigaion .gr; B&B ❺), with clean, modern rooms, right by the village beach; friendly *Katerina Studios* (T22850 71670, F22850 71455 ; ❸), complete with kitchens, nearby; and the newer *Ermes Rooms* (T22850 71693, F22850 74214; ❹), all with balconies, behind the post office. The more basic *Akroyiali* (T22850 71685; ❹), on the front just beyond the beach, is open all year. Yeoryia Kouveou has beautifully situated rooms at *Hondros Kavos* (T22850 71707, F22850 71441; ❹), located over an equally popular seafood taverna outside the village to the east.

MINOR CYCLADES

Amorgós

Dhonoússa (see inset)

Áno Koufoníssi

114m

Pori

Harakópou

Finikas

Hóra

Kéros

Dhaskalió

Andíkéri

Panayia

Káto Koufoníssi

Neró

Skhinoússa

Almyrós

Hóra

Mersini

Tsigoúri

N

3 km

Dhonoússa

Skyloníssi

Papás 383m

Haravyí

Mersini

Kalotarítissa

Stavrós

Kéndros

Livádhi

Iráklia

Livádhi

Áyios Yeóryios

Panayia (Hóra)

Papás 419m

Áyios Athanásios

Áyios Ioánnis Cave

Vourkária

Alimiá

Karvounólakos

Pigádhi

Náxos

Koufoníssi is noted for its fish **tavernas**; *Remezzo*, up in Hóra, has excellent food and a cosy atmosphere, while *Captain Nicola* at the bay is cheaper than most and has a fine array of seafood. Nearby *To Steki Tis Marias* is a good breakfast place with a few rooms (❷), and has views over the narrow channel to Káto Koufoníssi. The most popular nightspot is *Soroccos*, a lively **café–bar** on the front, while good alternatives include *Ta Kalamia*, with a quieter choice of music, and *Nikitas*, which has excellent views. *To Palio Fanari*, to the west of the village, is the club favoured by locals, playing a mix of dance and Greek music. The ticket agency is on the main street, and there is a **post office** (limited hours) just north of the town hall, with an **ATM** installed outside.

All the good beaches are in the southeast of the island, getting better as you go east along a dirt path that skirts the coastline along the edge of low cliffs. **Fínikas**, a ten-minute walk from the village, is the first of four wide coves with gently shelving golden sand, where there are rooms and a good taverna. Further east is **Harakópou**, which has a windswept **campsite** (☎22850 71683) with cane shade and rather poor facilities, on the headland before the next beach **Thános**; the owners may meet the boat to collect your luggage, but you may have to walk. Next is **Platiá Poúnda**, where caves have been hollowed out of the cliffs. Further east, the path rounds a rocky headland to **Porí**, a much longer and wilder beach, backed by dunes and set in a deep bay. It can be reached more easily from the village by following a track heading inland through the low scrub-covered hills.

Káto Koufoníssi, the practically uninhabited island to the southwest, has a seasonal taverna and some more secluded beaches; a *kaïki* shuttles people across until late in the evening. A festival is held here on August 15, at the church of the Panayía. The island of **Kéros** is harder to reach, but if there is a willing group of people keen to visit the ancient site, a boat and boatmen can be hired for around €50 for the day.

Skhinoússa

A little to the southwest, the island of **Skhinoússa** is just beginning to awaken to its tourist potential. Boats dock at the small port of Mersíni, which has one pension (☎22850 71159; ❹) and a couple of cafés; a road leads up to **HÓRA** (also called Panayía), the walk taking just over fifteen minutes. As you enter the village, the well-stocked **tourist centre**, which is also the main ferry agent, is one of the first buildings you'll come across; it has a metred phone and sells Greek and foreign press. There is also another, newer tourist office at the other end of town, which is just as helpful, and also sells locally made produce, and burns digital photos onto CDs.

Accommodation is mostly in fairly simple rooms, such as *Agnadema* (☎22850 71987, ✉agnadema@nax.forthnet.gr; ❸), with basic rooms ten minutes' walk from town, and the pleasant *Pension Galini* (☎22850 71983; ❸), set in a quiet garden, and with sea views. The rooms belonging to Anna (☎22850 71161; ❷) are quiet and comfortable, whilst nearby the *Iliovasilema Hotel* (☎22850 71948, ✉iliovasilema@schinousa.gr; ❸) enjoys stunning views of the harbour. The main concentration of **restaurants**, cafés and bars is along the main thoroughfare. Traditional *Panorama* and *Margarita* offer diners some of the best views on the island.

There are no fewer than sixteen **beaches** dotted around the island, accessible by a network of trails. **Tsigoúri** is a ten-minute walk southwest from Hóra; largely undeveloped except for *Grispos Villas* (☎22850 71930, ⓦwww.grisposvillas.com; B&B ❺), which has a good taverna with great views. The only other beach with any refreshments is **Almyrós**, a half-hour southeast of Hóra, which has a simple canteen.

Iráklia

Iráklia (pronounced Iraklía by locals), the westernmost of the Minor Cyclades, has just over 100 permanent residents. As the first stop on the ferry service from Náxos, the island is hardly undiscovered by tourists, but with fewer amenities than some of its neighbours it retains the romantic, ramshackle feel of a more secluded retreat.

Ferries call at **ÁYIOS YEÓRYIOS**, a small but sprawling settlement behind a sandy tamarisk-backed beach. ⚲ *Anna's Place* (☎ & Ⓕ 22850 71145; ❸) has some excellent rooms with shared cooking facilities and great views. Nearby, friendly Alexandra Tournaki (☎ 22850 71482; ❷) also has decent rooms. Other accommodation options dotted around the town include; *Maïstrali* (☎ 22850 71807, Ⓔ nickmaistrali@in.gr; ❸), closer to the port, Dhimitrios Stefanidhis (☎ 22850 71484; ❷), *Sohoro Rooms* (☎ 22850 71565; ❷), and *Anthi & Angelo's* (☎ 22850 71486; ❷). Up on the top of the hillside, the brand-new *Aiolos* hotel (☎ 693 26 32 050, Ⓔ mroussos@hol.gr; ❻) is a sign of things to come; it currently has only two suites, but should grow over the next two years into a fully fledged upmarket hotel. For eating, *O Pefkos* is a pleasant **taverna**, with tables shaded by a large pine tree. Two agencies sell tickets for **ferries**, but there are no banks in town, nor are there bus or taxi services. The *Perigiali* taverna also has a small shop selling maps showing the mule path to a fine **cave** of Áyios Ioánnis on the west side of the island.

Livádhi, the best beach on the island, is a fifteen-minute walk southeast of town. There is shade, but bring refreshments, as the taverna, whose owner allows **campers** to pitch their tents on his land, might not be open. The village of Livádhi, deserted since 1940, stands on the hillside above, its houses ruined and overgrown; among the remains are Hellenistic walls incorporated into a later building, and fortifications from the time of Marco Sanudo. Marietta Markoyianni (☎ 22850 71252; ❷) has rooms on the beach; *Zografos Rooms* (☎ 22850 71946, Ⓕ 22850 71956; ❹), above the road to Panayía, has fine views but is rather remote.

PANAYÍA or **HÓRA**, an unspoilt one-street village at the foot of Mount Papás, is another hour's walk inland along the paved road. It has a bakery and mini-market, two café-shops and an excellent ouzerí, but no rooms. A track to the east heads down to Pigádhi, a rocky beach with sea urchins, at the head of a narrow inlet. To the west, a track from the near-deserted hamlet of **Áyios Athanásios** leads back to the port.

The **cave of Áyios Ioánnis** lies behind the mountain, at the head of a valley leading to Vourkária bay. From Panayía, follow a signposted track west before zigzagging up to a saddle well to the north of the summit, with views over Skhinoússa, Koufoníssi, Kéros, Náxos and Amorgós; the path drops down to the south around the back of the mountain. A painted red arrow on the left indicates the turning to the cave, just over an hour's walk from Panayía. A church bell hangs from a cypress tree above the whitewashed entrance; inside there's a shrine, and the cave opens up into a large chamber with stalactites and stalagmites. It can be explored to a depth of 120m and is thought to be part of a much larger cave system, yet to be opened up; a festival is held here every year on August 18.

The main trail continues beyond the cave to a small sandy beach at **Alimiá** but this can be reached more easily with the beach-boat from Áyios Yeóryios.

In season, the boat sails daily to either Skhinoússa, Alimiá or the nearby pebble beach of Karvounólakos.

Dhonoússa

Dhonoússa is a little out on a limb compared with the other Minor Cyclades, and ferries call less frequently. Island life centres on the pleasant port settlement of **STAVRÓS**, spread out behind the harbour and the village beach.

Rooms, most without signs, tend to be booked up by Greek holiday-makers in August; try Maria Prasinos (☎22850 51578; ❹), with rooms along a lane behind the church; *Iliovasilema* (☎22850 51570, ℻22850 51607; ❹), which also has a decent restaurant; or *Firoa* (☎22850 51658; ❸), 150m away from the centre. There are a few **tavernas** in town, all of them reasonable and good. The **ticket agency** above the harbour changes money at astronomically high rates and has been known to be less than accommodating, so you would be wise to bring enough with you.

The hills around Stavrós are low and barren and scarred by bulldozed tracks, but a little walking is repaid with dramatic scenery and a couple of fine beaches. Campers and nudists head for **Kéndros**, a long and attractive stretch of sand fifteen minutes to the east, although shade is limited and there are no facilities. A road on the hillside above leads to the farming hamlets of Haravyí and Mersíni; these have more hens and goats in the streets than people, and there are no cafés, shops or rooms. **Mersíni** is an hour's walk from Stavrós and has a welcome spring beneath a plane tree, the island's only running water. A nearby path leads down to Livádhi, an idyllic white-sand beach with tamarisks for shade. In July and August, there's often a beach-boat from the port.

The road to **Kalotarítissa**, on the northeast coast, is paved and not an especially attractive walk. You might want to head inland from Stavrós toward Papás, the island's highest point, from where a valley drops down rapidly to the tiny village with a simple taverna that sometimes has a room to rent. There are two small pebble beaches and a path that continues above the coast to Mersíni. It takes four to five hours to walk round the island.

Amorgós

Amorgós, with its dramatic mountain scenery and laid-back atmosphere, is attracting visitors in increasing numbers; most ferries and catamarans call at both Katápola in the southwest and Aegiali (Eyiáli) in the north – with these destinations, rather than Amorgós, on schedules – and there is a regular bus service (6 daily in summer) between both ports. The island can get extremely crowded in midsummer, the numbers swollen by French people paying their respects to the film location of Luc Besson's *The Big Blue*, although few actually venture out to the wreck of the *Olympia*, at the island's west end, which figured so prominently in the movie. In general it's a low-key, escapist clientele, happy to have found a relatively large, interesting and uncommercialized island with excellent walking.

Katápola and around

KATÁPOLA, set at the head of a deep bay, is actually three separate hamlets: **Katápola** proper on the south flank, **Rahídhi** on the ridge at the head of the gulf and **Xilokeratídhi** along the north shore. There is a beach in front of

Rahídhi, but the beach to the west of Katápola is better, though not up to the standards of Aegiali in the northeast. In season there is also a regular *kaïki* to nearby beaches at **Maltézi** and **Plákes** (€3 return) and a daily *kaïki* to the islet of **Gramvoússa** off the western end of Amorgós (€6–8 return).

Prekas in Katápola, just along from the ferry dock, is the one-stop **boat-ticket agency**, and there are several **motorbike-rental** outlets – the best is Thomas Auto Moto – though the local bus service is more than adequate and the walking trails are delightful. There are walking maps on sale throughout the island, the maps published by Anavasi being the most useful. The **bus** shuttles almost hourly until 11pm between Katápola and Hóra, the island capital; several times daily it continues to Ayía Ánna via Hozoviotíssas monastery, and once a day (9.45am) out to the "Káto Meriá", made up of the hamlets of Kamári, Arkessíni and Kolofána.

There are plenty of small **hotels** and **pensions** and, except in high summer when rooms are almost impossible to find, proprietors tend to meet those boats arriving around sunset – though not necessarily those that show up in the small hours. A good clean place next to the beach at the western end of Katápola is *Eleni Rooms* (☎22850 71628, ✉roomseleni@hack-box.net; ❹); *Dimitri's Place* in Rahídhi (☎22850 71309; ❷) is a compound of interconnecting buildings in an orchard with shared cooking facilities. The smart traditional *Hotel Minoa* (☎22850 71480, ✉hotelminoalanderis@yahoo.com; ❺), on the waterfront, has clean rooms and also offers **Internet** access. South of the port you'll find *Anna Studios* (☎22850 71218, ℻22850 71084; ❸), in a garden setting and with basic cooking facilities. There are several similarly priced pensions further east, including *Sofia* (☎22850 71493, ℻22850 71494; ❸) in its own garden. The town **campsite** (☎ & ℻22850 71257) is just off the beach well signed between Rahídhi and Xilokeratídhi. There's also a newer one, *Camping Kastanis* (☎22850 71277, ⓦwww.kastanis.com), a ten-minute walk uphill towards Hóra.

In Katápola proper, *Mourayio* is the most popular **taverna** in town; alternatively, try the *Psaropoula* or *Minos*. There are four tavernas close to the campsite near Xilokeratídhi, of which the first is a friendly fish taverna, and of the others around the corner *Vitzentzos* is by far the best. What **nightlife** there is focuses on a handful of cafés and pubs. The bar *Le Grand Bleu* in Xilokeratídhi regularly shows *The Big Blue* on video, but there are other less obvious and less expensive places to drink, such as *The Blue Moon Bar* next door.

A signed surfaced road runs past the church in Rahídhi and south out of Katápola to the remains of **ancient Minoa**, about a half-hour's walk uphill. The site is in the process of being excavated, and is impressive for its size, and the views it commands over the bay, Hóra and ancient Arkessíni, as much as anything else. Your walk is rewarded by fragments of polygonal wall, four or five courses high, the foundations of an Apollo temple, a crumbled Roman structure and bushels of unsorted pottery shards. Beyond Minoa, the road dwindles to a jeep trail, continuing within a few hours on foot to Arkessíni (see p.195) via several hamlets – a wonderful **excursion** with the possibility of catching the bus back.

Hóra and around

HÓRA, accessible by an hour-long walk along the path beginning from behind the Rahídhi campsite, is one of the best-preserved settlements in the Cyclades, with a scattering of tourist shops, cafés, tavernas and rooms. Dominated by a volcanic rock plug, wrapped with a chapel or two, the thirteenth-century Venetian fortifications look down on countless other bulbous churches including the tiny **Áyios Fanoúrios**, and a line of decapitated windmills beyond. Of the half-dozen or so **places to stay**, the rooms belonging to Maria Theologitou (☏22850 71542; ④) are recommended, as is the stunning 🎄 *Traditional Guest House* (☏22850 71814, Ⓦwww.amorgos-studios.amorgos.net; ④), one of the most beautiful boutique hotels in the Cyclades. Hóra is littered with atmospheric little places to **eat** and **drink**: *Liotrivi* restaurant, down the steps from the bus stop, is probably the best place for a meal, whilst *To Tsagaradiko* on the platía is another excellent choice. Of the several café-bars, *Kallisto* and *Zygos* are good, whilst *Bayoko*, by the bus stop, does a hearty breakfast. Also in the upper square is the island's main **post office**.

From the top of Hóra, near the upper telecoms tower, a wide cobbled *kalderími* drops down to two major attractions, effectively short-cutting the road and taking little longer than the bus to reach them. Bearing left at an inconspicuous fork after fifteen minutes, you'll come to the spectacular **monastery of Hozoviotíssas** (daily 8am–1pm; donation expected, modest dress required; skirts are not supplied for women – bring your own), which appears suddenly as you round a bend, its vast wall gleaming white at the base of a towering orange cliff. Only four monks occupy the fifty rooms now, but they are quite welcoming considering the number of visitors who file through; you can see the eleventh-century icon around which the monastery was founded, along with a stack of other treasures. Legend has it that during the Iconoclastic period, a precious icon of the Virgin was committed to the sea by beleaguered monks at Hózova, in the Middle East, and it washed up safely at the base of the palisade here. The view from the *katholikón*'s terrace is the highlight for most visitors, and to round off the experience, you are ushered into a comfy reception room and treated to a sugary lump of *loukoúmi*, a warming shot of *rakomelo* (raki made with honey) and a cool glass of water.

The right-hand trail leads down, within forty minutes, to the pebble **beaches** at **Ayía Ánna**. Skip the first batch of tiny coves in favour of the path to the westernmost bay, where naturists cavort, almost in scandalous sight of the monastery far above. As yet there are no tavernas here, nor a spring, so bring food and water for the day.

Southwestern Amorgós

For alternatives to Ayía Ánna, take the morning bus out toward modern Arkessíni, alighting at **Kamári** hamlet (where there's a single taverna) for the twenty-minute path down to the adjacent beaches of **Notiná**, **Moúros** and **Poulopódhi**. Like most of Amorgós's south-facing beaches, they're clean, with calm water, and a freshwater spring dribbles most of the year. The road is paved as far as **Kolofána**, where there is one place with **rooms**. From here unpaved roads lead to the western tip of the island, and remote beaches at Káto Kámbos and at Paradhísa, facing the islet of Gramvoússa.

△ Monastery of Hozoviotíssas, Amorgós

Archeology buffs will want to head north from Kamári to Vroútsi, start of the overgrown hour-long route to **ancient Arkessini**, a collection of tombs, six-metre-high walls and houses out on the cape of Kastrí. The main path from Minoa also passes through Vroútsi, ending next to the well-preserved Hellenistic fort known locally as the "Pýrgos", just outside modern **ARKESSÍNI**. The village has a single taverna with rooms, and, more importantly, an afternoon bus back to Hóra and Katápola.

Northeastern Amorgós

The energetically inclined can walk the four to five hours from Hóra to Eyiáli, continuing on the faint trail just beyond Hozoviotíssas; remember to take along water, as there is nowhere to fill up on the way. Along most of the route, you're treated to amazing views of **Nikouriá islet**, nearly joined to the main island, and in former times a leper colony. The only habitations en route are the summer hamlet of **Asfodhilítis**, and **Potamós**, a double village with a café.

EΫIALI (AEGIALI) is smaller and more picturesque than Katápola, and so tends to be more popular. For **boat tickets** and money exchange try Nautilus, just back from the water; there's also an **ATM** right by the ferry dock. **Accommodation** is scattered around the backstreets and is easy to find; friendly _Pension Christine_ (☎22850 73236, ⊛www.christina-pension.amorgos.net; ❸) has bright, cheerful rooms, whilst for something a bit more upmarket, _Filoxenia_ (☎22850 73453, ⊛www.amorgosfiloxenia.gr; ❹) has a lovely, peaceful position perched on the hillside at the edge of town. Stretching along the beach, the _Lakki Village_ (☎22850 73253, ⊛www.lakkivillage.gr; ❹) complex offers family-friendly rooms and studios, and behind this sits the flower-draped _Pension Askas_ (☎22850 73333, ⊛www.askaspension.gr; ❹); both have their own shaded tavernas. Next to _Pension Askas_ is the friendly official **campsite**, _Aegiali Camping_ (☎22850 73500, ⊛www.aegialicamping.gr), usually busier than the one in Katápola. Overlooking the bay on the road up to Tholária is a luxury hotel with a swimming pool, the _Aegialis_ (☎22850 73393, ⊛www.amorgos-aegialis.com; ❼). For **eating out**, Limani (also called _Katina's_) is packed until midnight by virtue of its excellent food and barrel wine. Other places tend to be pricier and of inferior quality, with the exception of the tiny _12 Acropolis_ restaurant. Besides a few seasonal music **bars**, nightlife is focused around the _Corte Club_ at the _Egialis_ hotel and the strip of bars along the beach, with evenings inevitably ending up at _The Que_.

The main Eyiáli **beach** is more than serviceable, getting less weedy and reefy as you stroll further north, the sand interrupted by the remains of a Roman building jutting into the sea. A trail here leads over various headlands to three bays: the first sandy, the second mixed sand and gravel, the last shingle, where naturism is just about tolerated. There are no facilities anywhere so bring along what you need.

There is a **bus service** up to each of the two villages visible above and east of Eyiáli, with eight departures daily up and down (a timetable is posted by the harbour bus stop), but it would be a shame to miss out on the beautiful **loop walk** linking them with the port (2hrs). A path starting at the far end of the beach heads inland and crosses the road before climbing steeply to **THOLÁRIA**, named after vaulted Roman tombs found around Vígla, the site of ancient Aegiale. Vígla is on a hill opposite the village but there is little to see beyond the bases of statues and traces of city walls incorporated into later terracing. Another path winds down behind the hill to a tiny pebble beach at Mikrí Vlihádha far below. There are a few **taverna-cafés**, including the handsome wooden-floored *Iy Kali Kardhia* near the church, and several places to stay, including some comfortable **rooms** (reserve through *Lakki Village* in Aegiali), the large and upmarket *Vigla* (℡ 22850 73288, Ⓕ 22850 73332; ➏) and the *Thalassino Oneiro* (℡ 22850 73345; ➌), which has a fine restaurant and an extremely friendly owner.

   LANGÁDHA is another hour's walk along a path starting below Tholária; to the left of the trail is the chapel of Astrátios with an altar supported by the capital of a Corinthian column. Past here there are views down to the inlet of Megáli Vlihádha and, on a clear day, across to Ikaría in the north. The path descends through the village of Stroúmbos, abandoned apart from a few houses restored as holiday homes, and into a small gorge before climbing the steps up to Langádha. The *Artemis Pension* (℡ 22850 73315, ⓦ www.artemis-pension.gr; ➍) is a good place to stay here, and runs a decent taverna nearby.

   Beyond Langádha, another rocky path travels around the base of the island's highest peak, the 821-metre-high **Kríkellos**, passing the fascinating church of **Theológos** on the way, with lower walls and ground plan dating to the fifth century. Somewhat easier to reach, by a slight detour off the main Tholária–Langádha trail, are the church and festival grounds of **Panayía Panohorianí** – not so architecturally distinguished but a fine spot nonetheless.

Íos

Though not terribly different – geographically or architecturally – from its immediate neighbours, no other island attracts the same vast crowds of young people as **Íos**. Attempts are being made, however, to move the island's tourism upmarket; buildings are now painted white with blue trim, instead of garish psychedelic hues, camping rough is discouraged, and Greece's early closing laws (3am except Fri & Sat) are enforced, so bars no longer stay open all night. The island is still extremely popular with the young backpacker set, who take over the island with a vengeance in the high season, although the rest of the year a large number of young families are choosing to holiday here.

   The only real villages – **Yialós**, **Hóra** and **Mylopótamos** – are in one small corner of the island, and development elsewhere is somewhat restricted by poor roads. As a result there are still some very quiet beaches with just a few rooms to rent. Yialós has one of the best and safest natural harbours in the Cyclades, with a paved esplanade.

   Most visitors stay along the arc delineated by the port – at Yialós, where you'll arrive (there's no airport), in Hóra above it or at the beach at Mylopótamos; it's a small area, and you soon get to know your way around. **Buses** constantly shuttle between Koumbára, Yialós, Hóra and Mylopótamos, with a daily service running roughly from 8am to midnight; you should never have to wait more than fifteen minutes during high season, but at least once try the short walk up (or down) the stepped path between Yialós and Hóra. Various travel offices run their own buses to the beaches at Manganári and Ayía Theodhóti; they sell return tickets only and are a bit expensive (€6). To rent your **own transport**, try Jacob's Car and Bike Rental (℡ 22860 91047) in Yialós or Vangelis Bike Rental (℡ 22860 91919) in Hóra; unlike most of the other islands, here you'll need a valid motorcycle licence. For a motorboat, head to Mylopótamos where Ios Boat Rental (℡ 22860 91301, ⓦ www.iosboat.com) requires no licence, just a credit card. For a quick escape from the party atmosphere at the height of the season, try one of the daily excursions around quiet nearby beaches on the beautiful *Leigh Browne* sailing vessel parked in the harbour (€20).

Despite its past popularity, **sleeping on the beach** on Íos is discouraged these days; given the problem of theft, it's best to stick to the official campsites.

Yialós

From **YIALÓS** quayside, **buses** turn around just to the left, while Yialós **beach** – surprisingly peaceful and uncrowded – is another five minutes' walk in the same direction. You might be tempted to grab a room in Yiálos as you arrive: owners meet the ferries, hustling the town's **accommodation**, and there are also a couple of kiosks by the jetty that will book rooms for you. In shoulder season you can bargain for prices considerably lower than those listed below. *Hotel Mare Monte* (☎22860 91585, ✉maremonte@otenet.gr; ⑤), about halfway down the beach, has clean spacious rooms, a small pool, and includes breakfast; *Galini Rooms* (☎22860 91115, ✉galiniios@yahoo.com; ④), down a lane behind the beach, is a good quiet choice; whilst further down the same road, the *Brother's Hotel* (☎22860 91508, ⓦwww.brothershotel.com; ⑤) is a relaxed family option with comfortable rooms and pool. One of the best choices is the family-owned *Golden Sun* (☎22860 91110, ⓦwww.goldensun. gr; ④), about 300m up the road to Hóra, which has a large pool, and the newly revamped *Yialos Beach* (☎22860 91421, ⓦwww.yialosbeach.gr; ⑤) with smart doubles and studios set around yet another pool, just behind the hospital. There are more rooms on the stepped path from Yialós to Hóra, although they can be noisy at night. *Ios Camping* (☎22860 91329) is friendly and clean and has a rather luxurious swimming pool. Yialós has other essentials, including a reasonable supermarket and a few **tavernas**. The *Octopus Tree*, a small *kafenío* by the fishing boats, serves cheap fresh seafood caught by the owner, while on the front heading towards the beach, the *Waves Restaurant* does good Indian food; *Enigma* is a warm, intimate space serving cuisine from Cyprus, and *Café Cyclades* is a good spot for a snack. A twenty-minute stroll over the headland at **KOUMBÁRA**, there's a smaller and less crowded beach, with a rocky islet to explore, and the *Polydoros* taverna, one of the better places to eat on Íos – well worth the walk or bus ride; here you'll also find the excellent *Filippos* fish taverna and the lively *La Luna* café-bar on the beach.

Hóra

HÓRA (also called Íos Town), a twenty-minute walk up behind the port, is one of the most picturesque towns in the Cyclades, filled with meandering arcaded lanes and whitewashed chapels, though it's not exactly quiet when the younger crowd moves in for the high season. It divides naturally into two parts: the old town climbing the hillside to the left as you arrive, and the newer development to the right.

The **archeological museum** (Tues–Sun 8.30am–3pm; €2), in the yellow town hall, is part of an attempt to attract a more diverse range of visitors to the island. The **outdoor theatre** of Odysseus Elytis, behind the windmills, provides a beautiful setting in which to enjoy concerts and plays, details of which can be found at the **travel agent** and information booth next to the archeological museum.

There are plenty of basic **rooms** in the old part, although the bars can make it noisy. Your best strategy for a modicum of quiet is to wend your way up to the left where you find several establishments, including the excellent ⚐ *Francesco's* (☎22860 91223, ⓦ www.francescos.net; ❸) which offers the best value on the island, with clean doubles, a small number of dorms (€12 per person) and spectacular views from its bar. Near the bus stop, there's the new, more grown-up, *Mediterraneo* (☎22860 91521, ⓦ www.mediterraneo-ios.com; ❺), with nice balconied rooms overlooking a pool. In the new quarter *Lofos Pension* (☎22860 91481, ⓔ lofosvillagehotel@yahoo.com; ❸), to the right up from the Rollan supermarket, is a good bet, and also runs the swanky new *Lofos Village* hotel (❸) further up the hill (contact details as above). The friendly *Four Seasons Pension* (☎22860 91308, ⓕ22860 91136; ❹), up from Vangelis Bike Rental, is another quiet, but still central, choice.

Every evening in summer, Hóra is the centre of the island's **nightlife**, its streets throbbing with music from ranks of competing discos and clubs – mostly free, or with a nominal entrance charge, and inexpensive drinks. (Do, however, be wary of drinks that are overly cheap, as a few unscrupulous bars still resort to selling *bomba*, a cheap local drink that gets you drunk fast and makes you sick. If in doubt, ask for spirits by brand name.) Most of the smaller **bars** and pubs are tucked into the thronging narrow streets of the old village on the hill, offering something for everyone, and you'll have no trouble finding them. A welcome exception to the techno-pop dancing fodder can be found at the *Ios Club*, perched right up on the hill, which plays quieter music, has reasonable food and is a good place to watch the sunset. Evenings tend to start out in places like the *Fun Pub*, which also plays free films and has a pool table, and then progress around midnight to the bars up in the old town where *Rehab*, *Flames* and the *Red Bull Bar* are popular choices. Those looking to carry on, eventually stagger down to the main road, where the larger **dance clubs** such as *Star Club*, *Scorpion* and the somewhat kitsch *Sweet Irish Dream* are clustered near the bus stop.

Eating is a secondary consideration, but there are plenty of cheap and cheerful *psistariés* and takeaway joints: sound choices include the Italian restaurant

Pinocchio, *The Nest* taverna, and the *Lord Byron mezedhopolíon* in an alley up to the left in the old quarter – it's open year round and tries hard to recreate a traditional atmosphere, with old rebétika music and some good, unusual Greek food. ✈ *Ali Baba's*, meanwhile, is an excellent place to start the evening, with good food deals on a range of international choices and a free film most nights.

Around the island

The most popular stop on the island's bus routes is **MYLOPÓTAMOS** (universally abbreviated to Mylópotas), the site of a magnificent beach with watersport facilities (see box on p.122) and a mini-resort. Due to the large number of young travellers in Íos, **camping** is a popular option. *Far Out Beach Club* (℡ 22860 91468, ⓦ www.faroutclub.com) is the larger of the campsites, with excellent facilities, including a good-value cafeteria and bar (where you may well end up even if you're not staying). It is, however, very popular and can get noisy and crowded in August. *Purple Pig Stars* (℡ 22860 91302, ⓦ www .purplepigstars.com) is a friendly, laid-back complex by the road up to Hóra, with clean bungalows (❷) and good camping facilities, including its own club and poolside bar. Up the road at the far end of the beach, *Gorgona* (℡ & ⓕ 22860 91307; ❹), *Dracos* (℡ 22860 91281; ❹) and *Hotel Ios Plage* (℡ 22860 91301, ⓦ www.iosplage.com; ❺) have reasonable rooms, the last with an excellent restaurant on its terrace. *Hotel Katerina* (℡ 22860 91614, ⓦ www.ioskaterina .com; ❺), nicely situated by a pool looking over the bay, and the luxurious *Ios Palace Hotel* (℡ 22860 91269, ⓦ www.iospalacehotel.com; ❻), above the near end of the beach, are among the most upmarket choices besides the two expensive hotels maintained by *Far Out* (℡ 22860 91468, ⓦ www.faroutclub.com; ❻), the *Far Out Village Hotel*, next to the *Far Out Beach Club*, and the *Far Out Hotel* (❻), up on the hill on the road approaching Mylopótamos. On the rocks, beyond the *Ios Palace*, the *Harmony Restaurant* is one of the better places to eat, serving pizzas and Mexican food. The restaurants and self-service cafés behind the beach are uninspiring, and only the *Faros Café* rates a mention for staying open through the night to cater for the crowds returning from Hóra in the early hours. Mylopótamos itself has surprisingly little in the way of nightlife.

From Yialós, daily boats depart at around 10am (returning in the late afternoon; €12 return) to **Manganári** on the south coast, where there's a beach and a swanky hotel; you can also get there by scooter. Most people go from Yialós to Manganári by private buses run by travel agencies (€6 return), which leave Yialós about 11am, calling at Hóra and Mylopótamos and returning later in the afternoon; the condition of the road, however, makes the boat a much more pleasant option. Once predominantly nudist, shedding clothes here is now officially discouraged though still very much in practice. There's more to see, and a better atmosphere, **Ayía Theodhóti** up on the east coast. You can get there on a paved road across the island – the daily excursion bus costs €3 return. A couple of kilometres south of Ayía Theodhóti is **Paleókastro**, a ruined Venetian castle which encompasses the remains of a marble-finished town and a Byzantine church. In the unlikely event that the beach – a good one and mainly nudist – is too crowded, try the one at **Psathí**, 14km to the southeast, although you'll need your own transport. Frequented by wealthy Athenians, this small resort has a couple of average, but pricey, tavernas, although *Alonistra* fish taverna is a cheaper, excellent exception. Another decent beach is at **Kálamos**: get off the Manganári bus at the turning for Kálamos, which leaves you with a four-kilometre walk.

"**Homer's**" **tomb** can be reached by motorbike along a safe unpaved road (turning left from the paved road to Ayía Theodhóti 4.5km from Hóra). The town itself has long since slipped down the side of the cliff, but the rocky ruins of the entrance to a tomb remain, as well as some graves – one of which is claimed to be Homer's, but which in reality probably dates only to the Byzantine era.

Síkinos

Síkinos has so small a population that the mule ride or walk up from the port to the village was only replaced by a bus late in the 1980s and, until the new jetty was completed at roughly the same time, it was the last major Greek island where ferry passengers were still taken ashore in launches. With no dramatic characteristics, nor any nightlife to speak of, few foreigners make the short trip over here from neighbouring Íos and Folégandhros or from sporadically connected Páros, Náxos or Thíra. There is now a **bank** with an ATM on the island as well as a **post office** up in Kástro-Hóra, and you can sometimes change cash at the store in Aloprónia.

Aloprónia and Kástro-Hóra

Such tourist facilities as exist are concentrated in the little harbour of **ALOPRÓNIA**, with its long sandy beach and extended breakwater and jetty. More and more formal **accommodation** is being built, but it's still possible to camp or just sleep out under the tamarisks behind the beach. Try *Flora* (☎22860 51214; ❸), with comfortable rooms near the main road leading to Hóra, or the popular *The Rock* (☎22860 51186; ❸), above the *Rock Café*. Alternatively, the comfortable and traditional *Hotel Kamares* (☎22860 51234, ☎22860 51281; ❸) has a nicer setting than the pricier, but luxurious, *Porto Sikinos* complex (☎22860 51220, ⓦwww.portosikinos.gr; ❻). The handful of **tavernas** and

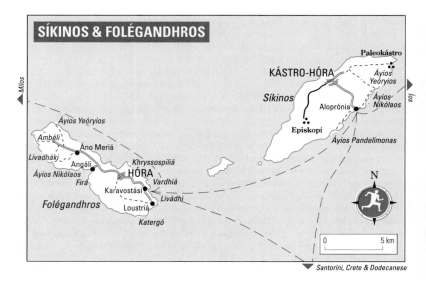

SÍKINOS & FOLÉGANDHROS

Paleokástro

KÁSTRO-HÓRA

Áyios Yeóryios

Síkinos

Aloprónia

Áyios Nikólaos

Íos

Milos

Episkopí

Áyios Yeóryios

Ambéli

Áno Meriá

Livadháki

Angáli

Khryssospiliá

Áyios Nikólaos

HÓRA

Firá

Vardhiá

Karavostási

Livádhi

Folégandhros

Loustriá

Áyios Pandelímonas

Katergó

N

0   5 km

▼ *Santoríni, Crete & Dodecanese*

café-bars in town are virtually all affiliated with the properties listed above and bear the same names, *Loukas* taverna being the most affordable if the most standard option.

The double village of **KÁSTRO-HÓRA** is served by the single island bus, which shuttles regularly from early morning till quite late in the evening between the harbour and here, though the route should soon be extended to Episkopí with the completion of the new road. On the ride up, the scenery turns out to be less desolate than initial impressions suggest. Draped across a ridge overlooking the sea, Kástro-Hóra makes for a charming day-trip, and the lovely oil-press **museum** (summer 5–7pm; free), run privately by a Greek-American, is highly recommended. A partly ruined monastery, **Zoödhóhou Piyís** ("Life-giving Spring", a frequent name in the Cyclades), crowns the rock above. The architectural highlight of the place, though, is the central quadrangle of **Kástro**, a series of ornate eighteenth-century houses arrayed defensively around a chapel square, their backs to the exterior of the village. There are only a few basic **rooms** in town, reserved through the Divoli family (T 22860 51263 or 22860 51212; ❷) or Antonios Margetis (T 22860 51253; ❸). A good selection of **food** is available, along with fine local wine, at *Klimataria* and *To Steki tou Garbi* next door. The *kafenía* up here are very traditional affairs and you might feel more welcome at the café-bars *Kastro* or *Platía*.

Around the island

West of Kástro-Hóra, an hour-plus walk takes you through a landscape lush with olive trees to **Episkopí**, where elements of an ancient temple-tomb have been ingeniously incorporated into a seventh-century church – the structure is known formally as the Iróön, though it's now thought to have been a Roman mausoleum rather than a temple of Hera. Ninety minutes from Kástro-Hóra, in the opposite direction, lies **Paleókastro**, the patchy remains of an ancient fortress. The beaches of **Áyios Yeóryios** and **Áyios Nikólaos** are reachable by a regular *kaïki* from Aloprónia; the former is a better option because it has the daytime *Almira* restaurant. It is possible to walk to them, but there is no real path at the later stages. A more feasible journey by foot is to the pebble beach at **Áyios Pandelímonas**: just under an hour's trail walk southwest of Aloprónia, it is the most scenic and sheltered on the island, and is also served by a *kaïki* in season.

Folégandhros

The cliffs of **Folégandhros** rise sheer over 300m from the sea in places, and until the early 1980s they were as effective a deterrent to tourists as they always were to pirates. Folégandhros was used as an island of political exile right up until 1974, but life in the high, barren interior has been eased since the junta years by the arrival of electricity and the construction of a road running lengthways from the harbour to Hóra and beyond. Development has been given further impetus by the recent increase in tourism and the mild commercialization this has brought.

A veritable explosion in accommodation for most budgets, and improvement in ferry arrival times, means there is no longer much need for – or local tolerance of – sleeping rough on the beaches. The increased wealth and trendiness of the heterogeneous clientele are reflected in fancy jewellery shops, an arty postcard gallery and a helipad. Yet away from the showcase Hóra and the beaches, the countryside remains mostly pristine, and is largely devoted to the spring and summer cultivation of barley, the mainstay of many of the Cyclades before the advent of tourism. Donkeys and donkey paths are also still very much in evidence, since the terrain on much of the island is too steep for vehicle roads.

Karavostási and around

KARAVOSTÁSI, the rather unprepossessing port whose name simply means "ferry stop", serves as a last-resort base; it has several **hotels** but little atmosphere. Best value is *Hotel Aeolos* (T 22860 41205, W www.aeolos-folegandros .gr; **④**), while *Vardia Bay* (T 22860 41277, W www.vardiabay.com; **⑥**, out of season **①**) has a great location and is open all year. The modern *Vrahos Hotel* (T 22860 41450, W www.hotel-vrahos.gr; **⑤**) has some nice rooms on the far side of the bay. *Iy Kali Kardhia* **taverna** above the harbour has an excellent traditional menu, and there are a couple of pleasant beach **bars** including the *Smyrna Ouzeri*, housed in a converted boathouse. There are many buses a day in summer to Hóra, three continuing to Áno Meriá; Jimmy's **motorbike rental** (T 22860 41448) is cheaper than its counterparts in Hóra.

The closest **beach** is the smallish, but attractive enough, sand-and-pebble **Vardhiá**, signposted just north over the headland. Some fifteen minutes' walk south lies **Livádhi**, a rather average beach with tamarisk trees and the island's official **campsite**, *Livadhi Camping* (T & F 22860 41204), which is good and friendly, although the hot water supply can be erratic.

Easily the most scenic beach on Folégandros, a 300-metre stretch of pea-gravel with an offshore islet, is at **Katergó**, on the southeastern tip of the island. Most people visit on a boat excursion from Karavostási or Angáli, but you can also get there on foot from the hamlet of Livádhi, a short walk inland from Loustriá. Be warned, though, that it's a rather arduous trek, with some nasty trail-less slithering in the final moments.

Hóra

The island's real character and appeal are to be found in the spectacular **HÓRA**, perched on a clifftop plateau some 45 minutes' walk from the dock; an hourly high-season **bus** service (6 daily spring & autumn) runs from morning until late at night. Locals and foreigners – hundreds of them in high season – mingle at the cafés and tavernas under the almond, flowering Judas and pepper trees of the two main platíes, passing the time undisturbed by traffic, which is banned from the village centre. Towards the cliff-edge, and entered through two arcades, the defensive core of the medieval **kástro** is marked by ranks of two-storey houses, whose repetitive, almost identical stairways and slightly recessed doors are very appealing.

From the square where the bus stops, a zigzag path with views down to both coastlines climbs to the cragtop, wedding-cake church of **Kímisis Theotókou**, nocturnally illuminated to grand effect. Beyond and below it hides the **Khryssospiliá**, a large cave with stalactites, accessible only to proficient climbers; the necessary steps and railings have crumbled away into the sea, although a minor, lower grotto can still be visited by *kaïki* from the port.

Practicalities

Accommodation in and around Hóra seems slightly weighted to favour hotels over rooms, with concentrations around the bus plaza at the eastern entrance to the village and at the western edge. Many of the tavernas and shops advertise rooms in their windows; otherwise try the basic but comfortable *Nikos Rooms* (☏ 22860 41055; ❹) in the centre. Of the hotels, the *Polikandia* (☏ 22860 41322, 🅕 22860 41323; ❹), just below the bus stop, is one of the best choices. The most luxurious facilities are at the cliff-edge *Anemomilos Apartments* (☏ 22860 41309, 🆆 www.anemomilosapartments.com; ❻), immaculately appointed, with stunning views and a romantic cocktail bar from which to watch the sunset. They also have a room specially adapted for wheelchair users. The new *Meltemi* (☏ 22860 41328, 🅔 meltemihotel@yahoo.gr; ❹), just opposite, has clean, beautiful rooms. The only hotel actually within Hóra is the traditional *Castro* (☏ 22860 41230, 🆆 www.hotel-castro.com; ❻), built in 1212, with three rather dramatic rooms looking directly out on an alarming drop to the sea. At the western edge of Hóra near the police station, a dense cluster of rooms tend to block each other's views. By the roadside on the way to Áno Meriá, the *Fani-Vevis* (☏ 22860 41237; ❹), in a Neoclassical mansion overlooking the sea, functions only in high season.

Hóra's dozen or so **restaurants** are surprisingly varied. The *Folegandhros* ouzerí in the first plaza is fun, if a bit eccentrically run. Breakfast can be enjoyed on the adjacent Platía Kondaríni at *Iy Melissa*, which does good fruit and yoghurt, omelettes and juices. *Iy Piatsa* has a nightly changing menu of well-executed Greek dishes, while their neighbour and local hangout *O Kritikos* is notable only for its grills. *Iy Pounda* near the bus stop is the most traditional place and has a small garden. Hóra is inevitably beginning to sprawl at the edges, and the burgeoning **nightlife** – a few dance bars along with a number of music pubs and ouzerís – is to the north, away from most accommodation. *Avissos* and *Patitiri* are two hip, lively bars, while *Avli* offers use of its hubbly bubbly pipes, and *Kellari* is a rustic and charming wine bar where the atmosphere is more relaxed. A **post office**, **ATM**, and **Internet** access in the travel agency by the bus station, completes the list of amenities, though the single **ferry agent** also does money exchange, as does the friendly and competent Italian-run Sottovento agency on the other side of town (☏ 22860 41444, 🅔 sottovento94@hotmail .com), which also offers a wide range of other services.

The rest of the island

Northwest of Hóra, a narrow, paved road threads its way towards **ÁNO MERIÁ**, the other village of the island; after 4km you pass its first houses, clustered around the three churches of Áyios Pandelímonas, Áyios Yeóryios and Áyios Andhréas. The **folk museum** (daily 5–8pm; donation requested), on a nineteenth-century farm near the town's entrance, traces the history of the island's people. **Tavernas**, which operate in high season only, include the traditional *O Mimis*, *Tou Mitsaki* and *Iliovasilema*.

Up to seven times a day in high season, a **bus** trundles out here to drop people off at the footpaths down to the various sheltered beaches on the southwest shore of the island. Busiest of these is **Angáli** (also called Vathý), where there are a few simple summer-only tavernas, reached by a fifteen-minute walk along a dirt road from the bus stop. Near to Angáli are the better of the few basic **rooms** available in the northern part of the island: *Irini* (☏ 22860 41190; ❸) and *Panagiotis* (☏ 22860 41301; ❸).

Nudists should take the paths which lead twenty minutes east or west to **Firá** or **Áyios Nikólaos** beaches respectively; the latter in particular, with its many tamarisks, coarse sand and view back over the island, is Katergó's only serious rival in the best-beach stakes. At Áyios Nikólaos, a lone taverna operates up by the namesake chapel; Firá has no facilities at all. From the *Iliovasilema* taverna, a motorable track continues north to a point from where a 500-metre path takes you down to the pleasant little bay of **Ambéli**.

Santoríni (Thíra)

As the ferry manoeuvres into the great caldera of **Santoríni**, the land seems to rise up and clamp around it. Gaunt, sheer cliffs loom hundreds of metres above, nothing grows or grazes to soften the awesome view, and the only colours are the reddish-brown, black and grey pumice striations layering the cliff face of **Thíra**, the largest island in this mini-archipelago, and the location of all but the smallest of its modern settlements. The landscape tells of a history so dramatic and turbulent that legend hangs as fact upon it.

From as early as 3000 BC, the island developed as a sophisticated outpost of Minoan civilization, until sometime between 1647 and 1628 BC (according to latest estimates) when catastrophe struck: the volcano-island erupted, its heart sank below the sea, leaving a crater (**caldera**) 10km in diameter, and earthquakes reverberated across the Aegean. Thíra was destroyed and the great Minoan civilization on Crete was dealt a severe blow. At this point, the island's history became linked with legends of Atlantis, the "Happy Isles Submerged by Sea". Plato insisted that the legend was true, and Solon dated the cataclysm to 9000 years before his time – if you're willing to accept a mistake and knock off the final zero, a highly plausible date.

These apocalyptic events, though, scarcely concern modern tourists, who come here to take in the spectacular views, stretch out on the island's dark-sand beaches and absorb the peculiar, infernal geographic features; as recently as a century ago, Thíra was still reckoned to be infested with vampires. The tourism industry has changed traditional island life, creating a rather expensive playground, which on the plus side makes this one of the most tourist-friendly islands in the Cyclades. There is one time-honoured local industry, however, that has benefited from all the outside attention: **wine**. Santoríni is one of Greece's most important producers, and the fresh, dry white wines it is known for (most from the *assýrtiko* grape for which the region is known) are the perfect accompaniment to the seafood served in the many restaurants and tavernas that hug the island's postcard-perfect cliffs.

Arrival

Ferries dock at the somewhat grim port of **Órmos Athiniós**; **Skála Firás** and **Ía** in the north are reserved for local ferries, excursion *kaïkia* and cruise ships. **Buses**, astonishingly crammed, connect Athiniós with the island capital Firá, and, less frequently, with Ía and the main beaches at Kamári and Périssa. Disembark quickly and take whatever bus is going, if you want to avoid a long wait or a tedious hike up. You'll be accosted at Athiniós by people offering rooms all over the island; in the summer it might be a good idea to pay attention to them, given the scramble for beds, in Firá especially. There have been reports, though, of various scams involving the promise of beds in Firá which turn out to be elsewhere; keep your wits about you, and if in doubt, ask someone else. From Skála Firás, you have the traditional route of 580 steps (about 45 minutes) up to Firá – not too difficult a walk, if you don't mind mule manure – or you can go by mule (€3.50, negotiable off-season) or cable car (summer only 6.40am–10pm, every 20min; €3), so exhilarating a ride that you may want to take it for fun. The **airport** is on the east side of the island, near Monólithos; there is a regular shuttle-bus service to the Firá bus station, which runs until 10pm.

Firá

Half-rebuilt after a devastating earthquake in 1956, **FIRÁ** (also known as Thíra or Hóra) still clings precariously to the edge of the enormous caldera. The rising and setting of the sun are especially beautiful when seen here against the whites of the Cycladic buildings clinging to the clifftop, and are even enough to make battling through the high-season crowds worthwhile.

Arrival, information and accommodation

Buses leave Firá from just south of Platía Theotokopoúlou to Périssa, Perívolos, Kamári, Monólithos, Akrotíri, Órmos Athiniós and the airport. **Taxis** go from near the bus station, within steps of the main square. If you want to see the whole island in a couple of days, a rented **motorbike** might do, though you must be very careful – especially since local drivers seem to enjoy antagonizing tourists on difficult and precipitous roads. Try Moto Chris at the top of the road that leads down to *Santorini Camping* (see below), while Ancient Thira Tours (℗22860 23915) on the main street in Firá, hire out **mountain bikes** and quads. The Firá branch of Nomikos Travel, opposite the OTE, is friendly and organizes **excursions** and trips to ancient Thíra and Thirassía in conjunction with Kamari Tours (℗22860 31390). The state-run **tourist office** (daily 9am–midnight in season; ℗22860 25490), on the main street near the bus station, may also be able to help you out. There are several **Internet cafés** gathered on the main square, and a number of **launderettes** dotted around town, the best being We do Laundry, just above the road to the campsite.

Accommodation

Santoríni certainly isn't cheap, and properties in Firá with a view of the caldera tend to be expensive. **Firostefáni**, between Firá and Imerovígli, has slightly less expensive rooms with equally stunning views, though as the area gets trendier by the minute, it's hardly a bargain destination. Another good location, where you don't have to pay as much for the view, is **Karterádhos**, a small village about twenty minutes' walk southeast of Firá. The official **youth hostel** was closed for renovation at the time of writing, but plans to reopen in 2006; contact the hostel in Ía (see p.208) to find out. The only other option for budget accommodation is *Santorini Camping* (℗22860 22944, www.santorinicamping .gr), the nearest **campsite** to town. (The best campsite on the island is near Akrotíri village; see p.211.) Considering Santoríni's popularity, it's definitely worth phoning for accommodation in advance.

Firá

Archontiko Apartments Off Agiou Mina ℗22860 24376, archontikoapartments@hotmail.com. Stunning antique-furnished apartments perched in a quiet spot over the caldera. May–Oct. **5**

Hotel New Haroula On road to the campsite ℗22860 24226, www.newharoula.com. Stylish but laid-back family-run hotel with pool and smart doubles. April–Oct. **5**

Loucas Off Ypapantis ℗22860 22480, www .loucashotel.com. Traditional caldera-side hotel with rooms in barrel-ceilinged caves carved into the cliffside to prevent collapse during an earthquake, and a beautiful new pool. Feb–Oct. **7**

Pelican Hotel On road to campsite ℗22860 23113, www.pelican.gr. Large hotel with spacious rooms near the centre. B&B **6**

San Giorgio Opposite fast-food restaurant *Goody's* on the main square ℗22860 23516, www.sangiorgiovilla.gr. Excellent value, clean en-suite rooms, all with balconies (ten percent discount for Rough Guide readers). April–Oct. **4**

Theoxenia Ypapantis ℗22860 22740, www .theoxenia.net. Stylish boutique hotel with large rooms right in the old town. Guests can also use the caldera-side pool at the nearby *Arisanna* hotel. **7**

Villa Rena 10 minutes' walk from town towards the folklore museum ℗22860 28130. Comfortable hotel with a large pool in a quiet spot near the open-air cinema (ten percent discount for Rough Guide readers). April–Oct. **5**

Firostefáni

Hotel Galini On waterfront ℗22860 22095, www.hotelgalini.gr. Good-value, friendly hotel carved into the cliff face in a relatively quiet spot 10 minutes' walk from Firá. March–Nov. **6**

Hotel Mylos On main street ℗22860 23884. One of the cheaper options in Firostefáni; rooms come with all mod cons and balconies. April–Oct. **5**

Manos Apartments On waterfront ℗22860 23202, www.manos-apartments.gr. Large, cool apartments with kitchens, huge verandas and great views. April–Oct. B&B **7**

Karterádhos

Pension George ℗22860 22351, www .pensiongeorge.com. Great pension with comfortable rooms, pool, and a good welcome, just fifteen minutes' walk from Firá. **3**

The Town

To go along with the views, Firá also has several excellent museums. The **archeological museum** (Tues–Sun 8am–3.30pm; €3 includes entrance to museum of Prehistoric Thira), near the cable car to the north of town, has a collection which includes a curious set of erotic Dionysiac figures. At the other end of town, between the cathedral and bus station, the new **museum of Prehistoric Thira** (Tues–Sun 8.30am–7.30pm; €3 includes entrance to the archeological museum), has interesting displays of fossils, Cycladic art and astonishing finds from Akrotíri. The handsome **Megaro Ghyzi** (Mon–Sat 10.30am–1.30pm & 5–8pm, Sun 10.30am–4.30pm; €3), above the archeological museum in an old mansion owned by the Catholic diocese of Santoríni, has been restored as a cultural centre, and has a good collection of old prints and maps as well as photographs of the town before and after the 1956 earthquake. Further north along the caldera, the **Thíra Foundation**, housed in galleries carved into the cliffside, contains superb life-size colour photo reproductions of the frescoes of Akrotíri (daily 10am–8pm; €3). Towards the back of the town, north of the main square, is the extensive **Lignos folklore museum** (daily 10am–2pm & 6–8pm; €3), which features a completely furnished nineteenth-century house with period winery, cavern, garden and workshops, as well as a gallery and historical archive.

Eating and nightlife

Firá's **restaurants** are primarily aimed at the tourist market, but for dependably good food with a sensational view (and prices to match) find *Aris*, below the *Loucas* hotel, or try the *Flame of the Volcano*, the last of the caldera-side restaurants north past the cable-car station (towards Firostefáni). ✈ *Mama's House*, just north of the main square on the road to Ía, is an excellent, backpacker-friendly spot with cheap, filling dishes and views from its balcony. On Erythroú Stavroú, the first street up from the main square, *Nikolas* is an old and defiantly traditional taverna, but it can be hard to get a table; the best moderately priced choice is *Naoussa*, further north on the same street, upstairs on the right. Nearby *Sphinx* offers exotic pasta dishes with a Greek twist, while *Calderimi*, near the cathedral, serves excellent Italian and Mediterranean food. Otherwise try *Vanilla*, a romantic, candlelit spot in Firostefáni. A good breakfast or afternoon snack can be found at *Corner Crêpes*, near the main square, or at the slightly trendier *Diverso* on the square itself.

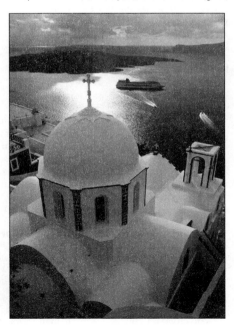

△ Firá, Santoríni

Most of the **nightlife** is northwest of the central square on Erythroú Stavroú: *Murphy's Bar* is an expensive but fun Irish pub with all the obligatory hilarity, while above there's the slightly cooler *Enigma* and *Koo* with chilled-out music and candles to set the scene. The best bars from which to admire the caldera are *Franco's* and *Palia Kameni*, two rather exclusive and pricey cocktail bars with unbeatable locations. More laid-back, but set back from the caldera, is the *Kira Thira* bar, which also offers a wine-tasting package. There is a new open-air **cinema** near the folklore museum.

Northern Santoríni

Once outside Firá, the rest of Thíra comes as a nice surprise. The volcanic soil is highly fertile, with every available space terraced and cultivated: wheat, tomatoes, pistachios and grapes are the main crops (see p.205 for information on Santoríni's wines), all still harvested and planted by hand.

A satisfying – if demanding – approach to **Ía**, 12km from Firá in the northwest of the island, is to walk the stretch from **IMEROVÍGLI**, 3km out of Firá, using a spectacular footpath along the lip of the caldera; the walk takes around two hours. Jutting up from the side of the cliff is the conspicuous conical rock of **Skáros**, once the site of an important settlement and Venetian fortress, the scant remains of which can still be seen; known also as Castle Rock, it can be mounted along a steep but obvious trail for unsurpassed views over the caldera and back to Thíra. Imerovígli is crowded with luxury, caldera-side **apartments** such as *Chromata* (℡22860 24850, @www.chromata-santorini.com; ❼) and *Astra* (℡22860 23641, @www.astra.gr; ❼), requiring reservations well in advance; *Katerina* (℡22860 22708, ℻22860 23398; ❺) is a more moderately priced hotel, with caldera views from the large balcony/bar area only. Between the *Katerina* and *Chromata*, *Altana* is a small **café** whose position and relaxed atmosphere make for a pleasing breakfast spot. Continuing to Ía, you'll pass Toúrlos, an old Venetian citadel on Cape Skáros.

Ía and around

ÍA, the most delightful village on the island, was once a major fishing port of the Aegean, but it has declined in the wake of economic depression, wars, earthquakes and depleted fish stocks. Partly destroyed in the 1956 earthquake, the town has been sympathetically reconstructed, its pristine white houses clinging to the cliff face. Apart from the caldera and the village itself, there are a couple of things to see, including the **naval museum** (Mon & Wed–Sun 10am–2pm & 5–8pm; €3) and the very modest remains of a Venetian castle. Ía is a fine, and quieter, alternative to Firá, with a **post office** and several **bike-rental** offices (of which Motor Fun is particularly good), an **Internet** café, and a good foreign-language bookshop, Atlantis Books. There are also a couple of travel agencies – Karvounis (℡22860 71290, @mkarvounis@otenet.gr), on the pedestrian street, is older and more reliable.

Much of the town's **accommodation** is in its restored old houses, including the traditional *Hotel Lauda* (℡22860 71204, ℻22860 71274; ❺), the popular *Hotel Anemones* (℡22860 71220; ❺), the *Hotel Fregata* (℡22860 71221, @www.fregata.gr; ❺) with its central location and good views; and the luxurious *Perivolas Traditional Houses* (℡22860 71308, @www.perivolas.gr; ❼), which are cut into the cliff near a pool suspended at its edge. Yet another step up are the stunning *Art Maisons* (℡22860 71831, @www.artmaisons.gr; ❽), four self-contained apartments on their own promontory in the heart of the town. Near the bus terminal, and well signposted, is the excellent ⚑ *Oia Youth Hostel*

(☎22860 71465; €13 per person), with a terrace and shady courtyard, a good bar, clean dormitories and breakfast included.

Generally, the further you go along the central ridge towards the new end of Ía, the better value the **restaurants**: the *Anemomilos* and *Laokastri* are two such examples. Slightly removed from the sunset tourist stampede, the pleasant *Karma*, serving Eastern cuisine, is on the road leading down to the youth hostel, while, for a splurge, ✷ *1800* is generally regarded as the finest restaurant on the island, serving a highly refined Mediterranean cuisine. **Nightlife** revolves around sunset-gazing, for which people are coached in from all over the island, creating traffic chaos and driving up prices, though the sunset is no different seen from Ía than from Firá.

Below the town, two sets of 200-odd steps switchback hundreds of metres down to two small harbours: one to **Ammoúdhi**, for the fishermen, and the other to **Arméni**, where the excursion boats dock. Both have decent fish tavernas, the one in Arméni specializing in grilled octopus lunches. **FINIKIÁ**, 1km east of Ía, is a very quiet and traditional little village. *Lotza Rooms* (☎22860 71051; ❸) are located in an old house in the middle of the village, while *Hotel Finikia* (☎22860 71373, ⑤22860 71118; ❺), above the village near the main road, is a smarter option. About 2km north of Ía is **Baxédhes** beach, with a few tavernas including the *Paradhisos*, which has good food and reasonable prices. It's a quiet alternative to Kamári and Périssa (see below), though it's not much of a beach until you reach a secluded cape, about 1km east, where ancient tombs have been discovered carved into the rock.

The east coast

Beaches on Thíra, to the east and south, are bizarre – long black stretches of volcanic sand which get blisteringly hot in the afternoon sun. They're no secret, and in the summer the crowds can be a bit overpowering.

Closest to Firá, **MONÓLITHOS** has a couple of tavernas including the excellent *Mario* and *Galini*. To the south is the pricier *Domata*, serving fusion cuisine that gives Italian food a Greek flair. Further south, **KAMÁRI** is popular with package-tour operators, and hence more touristy. Nonetheless it's quieter and cleaner than most, and is home to a decent diving centre (see box p.122). There's a range of beachfront **accommodation**, including *Hotel Nikolina* (☎22860 32363, €nikolina-htl@hol.gr; ❸), with basic but cheap rooms towards the southern end of the beach, as well as the spacious, if ageing, *White House* (☎69970 91488; ❹) and the friendly *Sea Side Hotel* (☎22860 33403, ⓦwww.seaside.gr; ❹) further along the beach. *Rose Bay Hotel* (☎22860 33650, ⓦwww.rosebay.gr; ❼) is a much pricier option, with a pleasant pool setting, set back away from the noisy beach thoroughfare.

Psistaria O Kritikos, a taverna-grill frequented by locals, is one of the best places to **eat** on the island. It's a long way out of Kamári on the road up to Messariá, and too far to walk, but the bus stops outside. There are plenty of cafés and restaurants behind the beach, though many are expensive or uninspiring. *Saliveros*, in front of the *Hotel Nikolina*, has taverna food at reasonable prices, and *Almira*, next to *Sea Side Rooms*, is a smarter restaurant and only a little more expensive. Kamári is a family resort with little in the way of clubs and nightlife, but there is a good open-air **cinema** near the campsite, and in summer buses run until 1am, so there's no problem getting back to Firá after seeing a film. West of Kamári is **Panayía Episkopí**, the most important Byzantine monument on the island. Built in the eleventh century, it was the setting of centuries of conflict between Orthodox Greeks and Catholics, but is most notable today for its carved iconostasis of light blue marble with a white grain.

Things are scruffier at **PÉRISSA**, around the cape. Because of its attractive situation and abundance of cheap rooms, it's crowded with backpackers. *Camping Perissa Beach* (☎ 22860 81343) is right behind the beach and has plenty of shade but is also next to a couple of noisy late-night bars. There is also a basic youth hostel on the road into Périssa: *Anna* (☎ 22860 82182, ✉ annayh@otenet .gr; €8 per person). There are plenty of cheap rooms in the same area and some upmarket hotels behind the beach; the modern *Meltemi Hotel* (☎ 22860 81325, ⓦ www.meltemivillage.gr; ❻) on the main road, and which also runs the nearby water park, is a good choice. The beach itself extends almost 7km to the west, sheltered by the occasional tamarisk tree, with beach bars dotted along at intervals. *Dichtia* and *Aquarius* are two excellent restaurants here.

Kamári and Périssa are separated by the Mésa Vounó headland, on which stood **ancient Thira** (Tues–Sun 8.30am–2.30pm; free), the post-eruption settlement dating from the ninth century BC. Excursion buses go up from Kamári (€8), staying two hours at the site (ask at Ancient Thira tours, ☎ 22860 31827, at the foot of the hill), but you can also ride a donkey up (€15) or walk the **cobbled path** starting from the square in Kamári by the Argo General Store. The site can also be reached by a path from Périssa; from either it's less than an hour's walk.

The path zigzags up to a whitewashed church by a **cave**, containing one of Thíra's few freshwater springs, before crossing over to meet the road and ending at a saddle between Mésa Vounó and Profitis Ilías, where a refreshments van sells expensive drinks. From here, the path to the site passes a chapel dating back to the fourth century AD before skirting round to the Temenos of Artemidoros with bas-relief carvings of a dolphin, eagle and lion representing Poseidon, Zeus and Apollo. Next, the trail follows the sacred way of the ancient city through the remains of the agora and past the theatre. Most of the ruins (dating mainly from Hellenistic and Roman times) are difficult to place, but the site is impressively large and the views are awesome.

Inland Santoríni

About 2km inland from Périssa, on the paved road west, lies **EMBÓRIO**; though virtually ignored by tourists, it's Santoríni's largest village, with a goldmine of whimsical island architecture and the important remnants of the medieval Venetian fortress that once dominated the landscape.

North of here, **PÝRGOS** is one of the oldest settlements on the island, a jumble of old houses and alleys that still bear the scars of the 1956 earthquake. It climbs to another Venetian fortress crowned by several churches, and you can clamber around the battlements for sweeping views over the entire island and its Aegean neighbours. A thirty-minute hike up the steep, winding road to the south leads to the monastery of **Profitis Ilías**, now sharing its refuge with Greek radio and TV pylons and the antennae of a NATO station. With just one monk remaining to look after the church, the place only really comes to life for the annual Profitis Ilías festival, when the whole island troops up here to celebrate. The views are still rewarding, though, and from near the entrance to the monastery an old footpath heads across the mountainous ridge in about an hour to ancient Thíra.

By way of contrast, **MESSARIÁ** – a thirty-minute stroll north – has a skyline consisting solely of massive church domes that lord it over the houses huddled in a ravine. The **Arhondikó Aryírou** (daily 9am–2pm & 4.30–7pm; €4) is a fully restored nineteenth-century mansion combining Neoclassical elements with island architecture. Southwest of here, **MEGALOHÓRI**, conveniently close to Athiniós, has a few diversions including several tavernas, the hip *Art Café*, and the exclusive *Villa Vedema Hotel* (☎22860 81796, ⓦwww.vedema .gr; ❽), one of the island's finest properties. East of here are scattered a few of Santoríni's most important **wineries**, the largest of which, *Boutari* (just out of Megalohóri), and *Santo* (near Pýrgos) offer the most comprehensive tours (€2–3), complete with multi-media presentations. Slightly more hidden on the road to Kamári are smaller wineries, such as the welcoming *Canava Roussos*, *Antoniou* and *Koutsoyianopoulos* – the last is also home to the **wine museum** (daily noon–8pm; €4 includes tasting) – which offer a more intimate glimpse at the wine-making process. Whatever the scale of the tour, none is complete without a taste of Santoríni's prized dessert wine, **visánto** (reminiscent of the *vin santo* of Tuscan fame), among the finest wines produced in Greece. Tour prices at the smaller wineries (€2–5) usually include tastings, while samples are available from the larger wineries for a nominal fee.

Akrotíri and the south coast

Evidence of the Minoan colony that once thrived here has been uncovered at the ancient site of Minoan Thira at **Akrotíri** (Tues–Sat 10am–3pm, but check times with the prehistoric museum in Firá, see p.207; €5), at the southwestern tip of the island. Tunnels through the volcanic ash uncovered structures, two and three storeys high, first damaged by earthquake, then buried by eruption; Professor Marinatos, the excavator and now an island hero, was killed by a collapsing wall and is also buried on the site. Only a small part of what was the largest Minoan city outside of Crete has been excavated thus far, but progress is being made; a protective roof has been installed and walkways have been constructed, allowing you to walk down an ancient Minoan street. Many of the lavish frescoes that once adorned the walls are currently exhibited in Athens, though you can see excellent reproductions at the Thíra Foundation in Firá (see p.207). Visit early to avoid crowds and heat.

Akrotíri itself can be reached by bus from Firá or Périssa. The newest and best **campsite** on the island, *Caldera View Camping* (☎22860 82010, ⓕ22860 81889), is situated here, as is the excellent *Glaros* **taverna**, on the way to **Kókkini Ámmos** beach, which has fine food, though the equally good *Dolphins Taverna* is better situated on the water. Kókkini Ámmos is about 500m from the site and is quite spectacular, with high reddish-brown cliffs above sand of the same colour (the name means "red sand"). There's a drinks stall in a cave hollowed into the base of the cliff. It's a better beach than the one below the site, but gets crowded in season.

The south coast

More secluded black-sand beaches lie under the surreal, pockmarked pumice stone that dominates the lunar coast around **Cape Exomýtis** at the island's southern extremity. Both **Vlyhádha** to the west and **Áyios Yeóryios** to the east of the cape are accessed by decent roads branching off from the main one to Embório, though no buses run here and there are no amenities to speak of. An hour's walk west of ancient Akrotíri, a lighthouse marks the tip of **Cape Akrotíri**, which offers excellent views of the Kaméni islets and Thirassía.

The Kaméni islets and Thirassía

From either Firá or Ía, boat excursions and local ferries run to the charred volcanic islets of **Paleá Kaméni** and **Néa Kaméni**, and on to the relatively unspoilt islet of Thirassía, which was once part of Thíra until shorn off by an eruption in the third century BC. At Paleá Kaméni you can swim from the boat to hot springs with sulphurous mud, and Néa Kaméni, with its own mud-clouded hot springs, features a demanding hike to a smouldering, volcanically active crater.

To escape Thíra's tourist throngs, **Thirassía** is an excellent destination, except during the lunch-hour, tour-boat rush. At other times, the island is one of the quietest in the Cyclades, with views as dramatic as any on Thíra. The downside is that there is no sandy beach, no nightlife and nowhere to change money, though there is an ATM.

Most tour boats head for **Kórfos**, a stretch of shingle backed by fishermen's houses and high cliffs. It has a few tavernas, including *Tonio* which stays open when the day-trippers have gone, but no rooms. From Kórfos a stepped path climbs up to **MANOLÁS**, nearly 200m above. Donkeys are still used for transport, and stables can be seen in both villages. Manolás straggles along the edge of the caldera, an untidy but attractive small island village that gives an idea of what Thíra was like before tourism arrived there. It has a bakery, a couple of shops and the friendly *Panorama* and *Candouni* tavernas which both do a great octopus *souvláki*, and open for the midday rush. Dhimitrios Nomikos has **rooms** (T22860 29102; ❷) overlooking the village from the south.

The best **excursion** from Manolás is to follow the unmade road heading south; about halfway along you pass the church of Profítis Ilías on a hilltop to the left. From here an old and overgrown trail descends through the deserted caldera-side village of **Kerá**, before running parallel with the road to the **monastery of the Kímisis** above the southern tip of the island. Minoan remains were excavated in a pumice quarry to the west of here in 1867, several years before the first discoveries at Akrotíri, but there is nothing to be seen today.

Ferries run to Thirassía from Órmos Athiniós five times a week; ask at Santo Star (T22860 23082, Wwww.santostar.gr) in Firá for details. There is no problem taking a car or rental bike over, but fill up with petrol first. **Day-tours**, arranged through any of the travel companies in Firá and Ía, take in a hike up to the active crater of Néa Kaméni and a dip in the hot springs at Paleá Kaméni, then stay two or three hours on Thirassía. Prices range from €10 for transport on a large ferry to about €30 for a more intimate guided tour on a traditional *kaïki*. The glass-bottom *Calypso* makes the same excursion for €20 and hovers over the volcanic reefs at the end of each journey to allow passangers a peak at the depths of Santoríni's flooded crater.

Moving on

When it comes to **leaving**, especially for summer evening ferry departures, it's best to buy your ticket in advance. Note, too, that although the bus service stops around midnight, a taxi isn't expensive (about €6 from Firá to Athiniós). Incidentally, **ferry information** from any source is notoriously unreliable on Thíra and rival agencies don't inform you of alternatives – Nomikos Travel (T22860 23660), with seven branches, is the largest, though Pelikan (T22860 22220) is also recommended. In any case, it's wise to enquire about your options at several agencies and triple-check departure times before working your way back to the port. If you do get stranded in Athiniós, there's no place to stay, and the tavernas are pretty awful, though there is Internet access at *@thinios.com café*. With time on your hands, it's probably worth calling for a taxi (T22860 22555) or zigzagging the 3.5km up to the closest village, **Megalohóri** (see p.211).

Anáfi

A ninety-minute boat ride to the east of Santoríni, **Anáfi** is the last stop for ferries and is something of a travellers' dead end, with no high-season ferries on to Crete or the Dodecanese, and no bank. Not that this is likely to bother most of the visitors, who come here for weeks in midsummer to enjoy the island's beaches.

Although idyllic geographically, Anáfi is a harsh place, its mixed granite and limestone core overlaid by volcanic rock spewed out by Thíra's eruptions. Apart from the few olive trees and vines grown in the valleys, the only plants that seem to thrive are prickly pears.

The harbour and Hóra

The tiny harbour hamlet of **ÁYIOS NIKÓLAOS** has a single taverna, *Akroyiali Popi's*, with a few rooms (☏22860 61218; ❸), and a travel agent selling boat tickets next door. In August there are enough Greek visitors to fill all the rooms on the island, so it's a good idea to book ahead. In season a bus runs from the harbour up to Hóra every two hours or so, 9am to 11pm, to stops at both ends of the village.

HÓRA itself, adorning a conical hill overhead, is a stiff 25-minute climb up the obvious old mule path which short-cuts the modern road. Exposed and blustery when the *meltémi* is blowing, Hóra can initially seem a rather forbidding ghost town. This impression is slowly dispelled as you discover the hospitable islanders taking their coffee in sheltered, south-facing terraces, or under the anti-earthquake barrel vaulting that features in domestic architecture here.

For accommodation, try the terraced, purpose-built **rooms** of *Villa Galini* (☏22860 61279; ❸), or the nearby *Ta Plagia* (☏22860 61308; ⓦwww.taplagia .gr; ❹), and welcoming *Panorama* (☏ & ⓕ22860 61292; ❸) at the east edge of the village, with stunning views south to the islets of Ftená, Pahiá and Makriá, and the distinctive monolith at the southeastern corner of Anáfi. Also recommended are the rooms of *Illiovasilema* (☏22860 61280, ⓕ22860 61238; ❸) on the other side of the village (ask at *To Steki* restaurant if you can't find them).

Evening **diners** seem to divide their custom between the simple, welcoming *To Steki*, with reasonable food and barrel wine served on its terrace, and the more upmarket *Alexandhra's* on the central walkway. *Armenaki* is a lively taverna–ouzerí which hosts regular *bouzoúki* nights, whilst the fisherman-owned *Liotrivi* serves up the daily catch. Otherwise, nightlife takes place in *Mylos*, in a converted windmill in the village, and *Argo*, which is also a good spot for breakfast. Anáfi's new roads are best explored by **bike**, and you can rent one at either *Panorama* (see p.213) or Rent Moto-Bikes (☎22860 61280) at the other side of the village. There is also a **travel agency**, Jeyzed Travel (☎22860 61253), who sell boat tickets and arrange excursions around the island. Several shops, a bakery and a **post office** round up the list of amenities.

East along the coast: beaches and monasteries

The glory of Anáfi is a string of south-facing beaches starting under the cliffs at Áyios Nikólaos, and accessible by road; four buses a day ply the route from Hóra, although walking is still a pleasant option. Rough campers head for **Klisídhi**, a short walk to the east of the harbour, which has 200m of tan, gently shelving sand. Above the calamus-and-tamarisk oasis backing the beach, there are two cafés and a taverna, *Margaritas*, which has decent rooms (☎22860 61237, ⓔanafi1@hol.gr; ❷) and accepts credit cards, and the *Villa Apollon* (☎22860 61348; ❹) on the hillside. Klisídhi can be reached by road but it's quicker to take the clifftop path starting behind the power station at the harbour.

From a point on the paved road just east of Hóra, the **main path** skirting the south flank of the island is signposted "Kastélli – Paleá Hóra – Roúkounas – Monastíri". The primary branch of this trail roller-coasters in and out of several agricultural valleys that provide most of Anáfi's produce and fresh water. Just under an hour along, beside a well, you veer down a side trail to **Roúkounas** (also popular with campers and nudists), easily the island's best beach, with some 500m of broad sand rising to tamarisk-stabilized dunes, which provide welcome shade. A single taverna operates up by the main trail in season; the craggy hill of **Kastélli**, an hour's scramble above the taverna, is the site both of ancient Anafi and a ruined Venetian castle.

Beyond Roúkounas, it's another half-hour on foot to the first of the exquisite half-dozen **Katelímatsa** coves, of all shapes and sizes, and 45 minutes to **Monastíri** beach, where the bus stops – all without facilities, so come prepared. Nudism is banned on Monastíri, because of its proximity to the monasteries.

The monasteries

Between Katelímatsa and Kálamos, the main route keeps inland, past a rare spring, to arrive at the **monastery of Zoödhóhou Piyís**, some two hours out of Hóra. A ruined temple of Apollo is incorporated into the monastery buildings to the side of the main gate; according to legend, Apollo caused Anáfi to rise from the waves, pulling off a dramatic rescue of the storm-lashed Argonauts. The courtyard, with a welcome cistern, is the venue for the island's major festival, celebrated eleven days after Easter. A family of cheesemakers lives next door, not far from where the bus stops, and can point you up the start of the spectacular onward path to **Kalamiótissa**, a little monastery perched atop the abrupt pinnacle at the extreme southeast of the island. It takes another hour to reach, but is eminently worthwhile for the stunning scenery and views over the entire south coast. Kalamiótissa comes alive only during its September 7–8 festival; at other times, you could haul a sleeping bag up here to witness the amazing sunsets and sunrises, with your vantage point often floating in a sea of cloud. There is no water up here, so bring enough with you.

Travel details

Ferries

Most of the Cyclades are served by main-line ferries from **Pireás**. Boats for Kéa, and less often Kýthnos, depart from **Lávrio**. There are daily services from **Rafína** to Ándhros, Tínos and Mýkonos, with less frequent sailings to Sýros, Páros, Náxos and Amorgós, and the north and east Aegean. All three ports are easily reached by bus from Athens. From May to September there are also a few weekly sailings from **Thessaloníki** to the most popular islands.

The frequency of sailings given below is intended to give an idea of services from late June to early September, when most visitors tour the islands. During other months, expect departures to be at or below the minimum level listed, with some routes cancelled entirely.

All agents are required to issue computerized tickets, using a computerized booking system. This was designed to conform to EU regulations and prevent the overcrowding of ferries so common in the past. It means that, in high season (particularly August), certain popular routes may be booked up days in advance, so it is important to check availability on arrival in Greece and book your outward and final inbound pre-flight tickets well ahead (particularly those returning to Pireás from the most popular islands). That said, agents are notoriously ill-equipped with advance information on ferry schedules, and purchasing a ticket too far in advance can lead to problems with delayed or cancelled boats. There is usually more space on ferries sailing between islands than to and from Pireás.

Amorgós to: Ándhros (2–3 weekly; 8hr); Astypálea (2–3 weekly; 3hr); Dhonoússa (2–3 weekly; 1hr); Iráklia (2–3 weekly; 1hr); Koufoníssi (2–3 weekly; 1hr); Mýkonos (2–3 weekly; 6hr); Náxos (6–8 weekly; 4hr); Páros (6–8 weekly; 5hr 30min); Pireás (daily; 10hr); Rafína (1 weekly; 12hr); Skhinoússa (2–3 weekly; 1hr); Sýros (3–4 weekly; 7hr); Tínos (2–3 weekly; 8hr).

Anáfi to: Folégandhros (1 weekly; 4hr 30min); Íos (6–8 weekly; 2hr 30min); Náxos (6–8 weekly; 3hr 30min), Páros (6–8 weekly; 4hr); Síkinos (1 weekly; 4hr); Sýros (1 weekly; 10hr); Thíra (6–8 weekly; 1hr

30min & 2 weekly mail boats; 2hr).

Ándhros to: Amorgós (2 weekly; 8hr); Mýkonos (3 daily; 2hr 30min); Náxos (2 weekly; 7hr); Páros (1–4 weekly; 7hr); Sýros (4 weekly; 3hr); Tínos (3 daily; 2hr).

Dhonoússa to: Amorgós (3–4 weekly; 1hr); Iráklia (2–3 weekly; 1hr); Koufoníssi (2–3 weekly; 1hr); Mýkonos (2–3 weekly; 6hr); Náxos (2–3 weekly; 5hr); Páros (2–3 weekly; 5hr 30min); Skhinoússa (2–3 weekly; 1hr); Sýros (2–3 weekly; 7hr 30min); Tínos (2–3 weekly; 6hr 30min).

Folégandhros to: Íos (3–6 weekly; 1hr 30min); Kímolos (2 weekly; 2hr 30 min); Kýthnos (2 weekly; 8hr); Mílos (2 weekly; 2hr 30min); Náxos (3–6 weekly; 2hr 30min); Páros (3–6 weekly; 4hr); Sérifos (2 weekly; 5hr 30min); Sífnos (2 weekly; 5hr); Síkinos (6 weekly; 30min); Sýros (2 weekly; 5hr 30min).

Íos to: Anáfi (4 weekly; 4hr); Crete (1 weekly; 3hr); Folégandhros (4–5 weekly 1hr); Kímolos (1 weekly; 4hr); Mílos (1 weekly; 4hr); Mýkonos (1 daily; 2hr); Náxos (3 daily; 3hr); Páros (3 daily; 5hr); Sérifos (1 weekly; 5hr); Sífnos (1 weekly; 5hr 30min); Síkinos (4–5 weekly; 30min); Sýros (2–3 weekly; 6hr); Thíra (3 daily; 1hr).

Kéa to: Kýthnos (4 weekly; 1hr 30min); Lávrio (1–3 daily; 1hr 30min); Sýros (2 weekly; 3hr).

Kímolos to: Folégandhros (2 weekly; 1hr); Kýthnos (2–5 weekly; 3hr 30min); Mílos, Adhámas (2–5 weekly; 30min); Mílos, Pollónia (4 daily; 30min); Sérifos (2–5 weekly; 2hr 30min); Sífnos (2–5 weekly; 2hr); Síkinos (2 weekly; 1hr 30min); Thíra (2 weekly; 3hr).

Koufoníssi, Skhinoússa, Iráklia to: Amorgós (6 weekly; 2hr); Dhonoússa (6 weekly; 1hr); Mýkonos (1–2 weekly; 1hr 30min); Náxos (2–3 weekly; 1–4hr); Páros (1–2 weekly; 2hr); Sýros (1–2 weekly; 4hr 30min); Tínos (1–2 weekly; 2hr).

Kýthnos to: Folégandhros (3–4 weekly; 8hr 30min); Íos (1–2 weekly; 8hr); Kéa (1–2 weekly; 1hr 30min); Kímolos (4–8 weekly; 3hr 30min); Mílos (2–3 weekly; 4hr); Sérifos (4–8 weekly; 1hr); Sífnos (4–8 weekly; 1hr 30min); Síkinos (1–2 weekly; 8hr), Sýros (1–2 weekly; 3hr); Thíra (3–4 weekly; 10hr).

Mílos to: Crete (Áyios Nikólaos or Sitía; 2 weekly; 8hr); Folégandhros (2–3 weekly; 1hr); Hálki and

Rhodes (1 weekly; 22hr); Íos (2–3 weekly; 2hr); Kárpathos (2 weekly; 16hr); Kássos (2 weekly; 14hr); Kímolos (2–5 daily *kaïkia* & 4–6 weekly ferries; 30min); Kýthnos (1 daily; 3hr); Sérifos (1 daily; 1hr 30min); Sífnos (1 daily; 2hr); Síkinos (2–3 weekly; 1hr 30min); Sýros (2 weekly; 6hr); Thíra (2–3 weekly; 3hr).

Mýkonos to: Amorgós (2–3 weekly; 6hr); Ándhros (at least 2 daily; 2hr 30min); Crete, Iráklion (2 weekly; 9hr); Dhonoússa (1–2 weekly; 2hr); Foúrni (1 weekly; 4hr); Ikaría (3–4 weekly; 2hr); Íos (1 daily; 2hr); Koufoníssi, Skhinoússa and Iráklia (1–2 weekly; all approx. 1hr 30min); Náxos (1 daily; 1hr); Páros (daily; 1hr); Sámos (3–4 weekly; 4hr); Sýros (at least 2 daily; 2hr); Tínos (at least 2 daily; 1hr).

Náxos to: Amorgós (5–7 weekly; 2–6hr); Anáfi (3 weekly; 7hr); Ándhros (2 weekly; 4hr); Astypálea (2–3 weekly; 3hr 30min); Crete, Iráklion (3 weekly; 7hr); Dhonoússa (3–6 weekly; 5hr); Folégandhros (5 weekly; 3hr 30min); Foúrni (1 weekly; 16hr); Ikaría (4–6 weekly; 3hr 30min); Íos (at least 3 daily; 2hr); Iráklia (3–6 weekly; 3hr 30min); Kárpathos (1–2 weekly; 15hr); Kássos (1–2 weekly; 15hr); Kós (1 weekly; 16hr); Koufoníssi (3–6 weekly; 4hr); Páros (at least 3 daily; 1hr); Síkinos (5 weekly; 3hr); Sámos (4–6 weekly; 5hr); Skhinoússa (3–6 weekly; 3hr 30min); Skiáthos (2–3 weekly; 20hr); Sýros (6–8 weekly; 3hr); Thessaloníki (2–3 weekly; 24hr); Thíra (at least 3 daily; 2hr 30in); Tínos (4–5 weekly; 4hr).

Páros to: Amorgós (4–6 weekly; 4hr); Anáfi (4–6 weekly; 9hr); Ándhros (4 weekly; 5hr); Andíparos (hourly from Parikía, 40min; hourly car ferry from Poúnda, 20min); Astypálea (2–3 weekly; 4hr 40min); Crete, Iráklion (4 weekly; 7hr); Dhonoússa (2–4 weekly; 7hr); Folégandhros (2–4 weekly; 4hr 30min); Foúrni (1–2 weekly; 6hr); Ikaría (5–7 weekly; 5hr); Ikaría (3–6 weekly; 5hr); Íos (at least 3 daily; 3hr); Kárpathos (1–2 weekly; 16hr); Kássos (1–2 weekly; 16hr); Kós (1–2 weekly; 16hr); Koufoníssi (2–4 weekly; 6hr 30min); Mýkonos (at least 1 daily; 1hr); Náxos (at least 3 daily; 1hr); Rhodes (2–3 weekly; 17hr); Sámos (3–6 weekly; 6hr); Síkinos (4–6 weekly; 4hr); Skhinoússa (2–4 weekly; 6hr); Skiáthos (2–3 weekly; 10hr); Sýros (6–8 weekly; 2hr); Thessaloníki (2–3 weekly; 14hr); Thíra (at least 3 daily; 3hr 30min); Tínos (6–8 weekly; 1hr 30min); Vólos (1 weekly; 15hr).

Sérifos to: Folégandhros (2–3 weekly; 2hr 30min); Íos (1 weekly; 6hr 30min); Kímolos (2–5 weekly; 1hr 30min); Kýthnos (5–12 weekly; 30min); Mílos (5–10 weekly; 1hr 30min); Sífnos (5–12 weekly; 30min); Síkinos (2–3 weekly; 3hr); Sýros (2 weekly; 6hr); Thíra (2–3 weekly; 7hr 30 min).

Sífnos to: Folégandhros (2–3 weekly; 2hr); Íos (1 weekly; 6hr 30min); Kímolos (2–5 weekly; 1hr);

Kýthnos (5–12 weekly; 1hr); Mílos (5–10 weekly; 1hr); Páros (twice weekly; 5hr); Sérifos (5–12 weekly; 30min); Síkinos (2–3 weekly; 2hr 30min); Sýros (2 weekly; 6hr 30min); Thíra (2–3 weekly; 7hr).

Síkinos to: Folégandhros (6 weekly; 30min); Íos (3–6 weekly; 2hr); Kímolos (2 weekly; 2hr); Kýthnos (2 weekly; 7hr 30min); Mílos (2 weekly; 2hr); Náxos (3–6 weekly; 3hr); Páros (3–6 weekly; 4hr 30min); Sérifos (2 weekly; 5hr), Sífnos (2 weekly; 4hr 30min); Sýros (2 weekly; 5hr); Thíra (3–6 weekly; 2hr).

Sýros to: Amorgós (3 weekly; 7hr); Ándhros (at least 2 weekly; 3hr 30min); Astypálea (2–3 weekly; 5hr); Folégandhros (1 weekly; 4hr 30min); Ikaría (4–7 weekly; 4hr); Íos (2–4 weekly; 7hr); Iráklia (3 weekly; 7hr); Kéa (2 weekly; 4hr); Koufoníssi (3 weekly, 7hr 30min); Kýthnos (2 weekly; 3hr); Lipsí (1 weekly; 5hr); Mílos (2 weekly; 5hr); Kímolos (2 weekly; 5hr); Mýkonos (at least 2 daily; 2hr); Náxos (at least 2 daily; 3hr); Páros (at least 2 daily; 2hr); Pátmos (1 weekly; 5hr); Sámos (4–7 weekly; 6hr); Sérifos (2 weekly; 4hr); Sífnos (2 weekly; 3hr 30min); Síkinos (1 weekly; 6hr); Skhinoússa (3 weekly; 8hr); Skiáthos (1–3 weekly; 12hr); Thessaloníki (1–3 weekly; 15hr); Thíra (2–4 weekly; 8hr 30min); Tínos (at least 2 daily; 1hr).

Thíra to: Anáfi (4–6 weekly; 2hr, 2 weekly mail boats); Crete, Iráklion (5–6 weekly; 5hr); Folégandhros (6–8 weekly; 1hr 30min); Íos (at least 3 daily; 1hr); Kárpathos (1–2 weekly; 12hr); Kássos (1–2 weekly; 10hr); Mílos and Kímolos (2–4 weekly; 2hr); Mýkonos (daily; 2hr 30min); Náxos (at least 3 daily; 2hr); Páros (at least 3 daily; 3hr); Rhodes (2 weekly; 16hr); Sérifos (1–2 weekly; 7hr); Sífnos (4–6 weekly; 7hr); Síkinos (6–8 weekly; 2hr); Skiáthos (3–5 weekly; 14hr); Sýros (6–8 weekly; 8hr); Thessaloníki (5–6 weekly; 18hr); Thirassía (4–6 weekly; 30min); Tínos (3–5 weekly; 5hr).

Tínos to: Ándhros (at least 2 daily; 1hr); Crete, Iráklion (3 weekly; 5hr); Íos (1 weekly; 8hr); Mýkonos (at least 2 daily; 30min); Náxos (3–4 weekly; 2hr); Páros (3–4 weekly; 1hr 30min); Skiáthos (1–3 weekly; 10hr); Sýros (at least 2 daily; 1hr); Thessaloníki (1–3 weekly; 12hr); Thíra (3 weekly; 5hr).

Other services

To simplify the lists above, certain strategic **catamaran** and **small-boat services** have been omitted. Of these, the *Express Skopelitis* plies daily in season between Mýkonos and Amorgós, spending each night at the latter and threading through all of the minor isles between it and Náxos, as well as Náxos and Páros (Píso Livádhi), in the course of a week; however, it's unreliable and often overcrowded – for current info call ☎22850 71256. The *Seajet* catamaran – a small-capacity (and expensive) jet-boat (☎2210 414 1250 for details) – operates daily during summer out of Rafína and connects Sýros, Ándhros, Tínos, Mýkonos, Páros, Náxos and Thíra. The long-haul, full-sized *Blue Star* ships shave a few hours off the travel time to some of the most popular Cyclades (through the hubs of Páros and Náxos) for only slightly more than the price of standard tickets and much less than the cost of catamaran services. Cycladic routes are pretty well mapped out by the three companies – Minoan Flying Dolphins, Speed Lines and Cruises (Santorini Dolphin) and Dolphin Sea Line, with regular services from Pireás, Thíra and Rafína respectively.

Catamaran travel is expensive; however, when time is an issue, or for more regular connections to some of the less commonly serviced routes such as the minor islets around Náxos, these handy high-speed craft are a welcome addition to the conventional fleet.

Flights

There are airports on Páros, Mýkonos, Thíra, Sýros, Mílos and Náxos. In season, or during storms when ferries are idle, you have little chance of getting a seat on any flight at less than three days' notice, and tickets are predictably expensive. Expect off-season (Oct–April) frequencies to drop by at least eighty percent. Flights are on Olympic unless otherwise stated.

Athens to: Mílos (1–2 daily; 45min); Mýkonos (4–5 daily on Olympic; 3–4 daily on Aegean; 40min); Náxos (6 weekly; 45min); Páros (2–3 daily; 40min); Sýros (3–6 weekly; 35min); Thíra (5–6 daily on Olympic; 3–4 daily on Aegean; 50min).

Mýkonos to: Rhodes (2 weekly; 55min); Thessaloníki (2 weekly on Olympic, 1 daily on Aegean; 1hr 20min); Thíra (4 weekly; 30min).

Thíra to: Rhodes (2–5 weekly; 50min); Thessaloníki (2 weekly on Olympic, 1 daily on Aegean; 1hr 20min).

3

Crete

CHAPTER 3 # Highlights

✳ **Archeological Museum, Iráklion** The world's foremost Minoan museum. See p.229

✳ **Minoan sites** Knossos is the most exciting, but Malia, Phaestos, Zakros and other archeological ruins across the island are also worth a visit. See p.249, p.239 & p.262

✳ **Beach resorts** Mátala, Sitía and Paleohóra have bags of charm and excellent strands. See p.240, p.259 & p.292

✳ **Lasíthi Plateau** This green and fertile high mountain plateau has picturesque agricultural villages and unique white cloth-sailed windmills. See p.252

✳ **The Dhiktean cave** Mythological birthplace of Zeus, the Dhiktean cave is stunningly situated on the Lasíthi Plateau. See p.252

✳ **Haniá and Réthymnon old towns** These atmospheric centres display haunting vestiges of their Venetian and Turkish pasts and are a joy to wander around. See p.277 & p.266

✳ **Samariá Gorge** A magnificent gorge: the longest in Europe, offering a chance to see brilliant wildflowers, golden eagles and perhaps a Cretan ibex. See p.285

△ Minoan fresco, Knossos

3

Crete

Crete (Kríti) is a great deal more than just another Greek island. In many places, especially in the cities or along the developed north coast, it doesn't feel like an island at all, but rather a substantial land in its own right. Which of course it is – a precipitous, wealthy and at times a surprisingly cosmopolitan one with a tremendous and unique history. But when you lose yourself among the mountains, or on the lesser-known coastal reaches of the south, it has everything you could want of a Greek island and more: great beaches, remote hinterlands and hospitable people.

In history, Crete is distinguished above all as the home of Europe's earliest civilization. It was only at the beginning of the twentieth century that the legends of King Minos and of a Cretan society that ruled the Greek world in prehistory were confirmed by excavations at Knossos and Phaestos. Yet the Minoans had a remarkably advanced society, the centre of a maritime trading empire as early as 2000 BC. The artworks produced on Crete at this time are unsurpassed anywhere in the ancient world, and it seems clear that life on Crete in those days was good. This apparently peaceful culture survived at least three major natural disasters; each time the palaces were destroyed, and each time they were rebuilt on a grander scale. Only after the last destruction, probably the result of an eruption of Santoríni and subsequent tidal waves and earthquakes, do significant numbers of weapons begin to appear in the ruins. This, together with the appearance of the Greek language, has been interpreted to mean that Mycenaean Greeks had taken control of the island. Nevertheless, for nearly 500 years, by far the longest period of peace the island has seen, Crete was home to a culture well ahead of its time.

The Minoans of Crete probably originally came from Anatolia; at their height they maintained strong links with Egypt and with the people of Asia Minor, and this position as meeting point and strategic fulcrum between east and west has played a major role in Crete's subsequent history. Control of the island passed from Greeks to Romans to Saracens, through the Byzantine empire to Venice, and finally to Turkey for more than two centuries. During World War II, the island was occupied by the Germans and attained the dubious distinction of being the first place to be successfully invaded by paratroops.

Today, with a flourishing agricultural economy, Crete is one of the few Greek islands that could probably support itself without tourists. Nevertheless, tourism is heavily promoted and is making inroads everywhere. The northeast coast in particular is overdeveloped, and though there are parts of the south and west coasts that have not been spoilt, they are getting harder to find. By contrast, the high mountains of the interior are still barely touched, and one of the best things to do on Crete is to rent a vehicle and explore the remoter villages.

Every part of Crete has its loyal devotees and it's hard to pick out highlights, but generally if you want to get away from it all you should head west, towards Haniá and the smaller, less well-connected places along the south and west coasts. It is in this part of the island that the White Mountains rise, while below them yawns the famous Samariá Gorge. The far east, around Sitía, is also relatively unscathed, with a string of isolated beaches worth seeking out to the south of the over-popular Väi beach, which lures crowds attracted by its famous palm grove. However, Sitía's new international airport, opening for international flights in 2007, could change things significantly here in the next few years.

Whatever you do, your first priority will probably be to leave Iráklion (Heraklion) as quickly as possible, having paid the obligatory, and rewarding, visit to the archeological museum and nearby Knossos. The other great Minoan sites cluster around the middle of the island: Phaestos and Ayía Triádha to the south (with Roman Gortys to provide contrast), and Malia on the north coast. Almost wherever you go you'll find a reminder of the island's history, whether it's the superbly preserved Minoan town of Gourniá near the cosmopolitan resort of Áyios Nikólaos, the exquisitely sited palace of Zakros in the far east, or the lesser sites scattered around the west. Unexpected highlights include Crete's Venetian forts at Réthymnon and Frangokástello; its hundreds of frescoed Byzantine churches, most famously at Kritsá; and, at Réthymnon and Haniá, the cluttered old Venetian and Turkish quarters.

Crete has by far the longest summers in Greece, and you can get a decent tan here right into October and swim at least from May until November. The one seasonal blight is the *meltémi*, a northerly wind, which regularly blows harder here and more continuously than anywhere else in Greece – the best of several

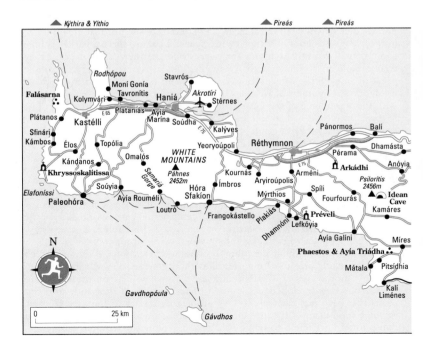

reasons for avoiding an August visit if you can. It's far from an ill wind, however, as it also lowers humidity and makes the island's higher summer temperatures more bearable.

Iráklion, Knossos and central Crete

Many visitors to Crete arrive in the island's capital, **Iráklion** (Heraklion), but it's not an outstandingly beautiful city, and its central zones are often a maelstrom of traffic-congested thoroughfares. However, it does provide a convenient base for visits to an outstanding **Archeological Museum** and nearby **Knossos**. On the positive side, the city does have quite a few plus points – superb fortifications, a fine market, atmospheric old alleys and some interesting lesser museums added to a recent makeover of central areas by the city hall that has improved things considerably.

The area immediately around the city is less touristy than you might expect, mainly because there are few decent beaches of any size on this central part of

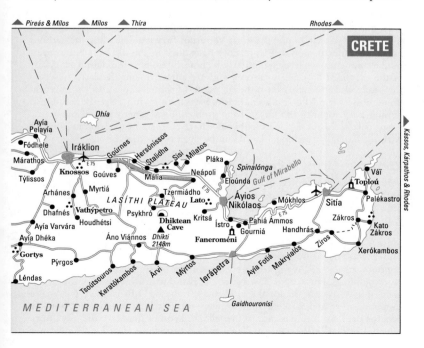

the coast. To the west, mountains drop straight into the sea virtually all the way to Réthymnon, with just two significant coastal settlements: **Ayía Pelayía**, a sizeable resort, and the more attractive **Balí**, which is gradually becoming one as well. Eastwards, the main resorts are at least 30km away, at **Hersónissos** and beyond, although there is a string of rather unattractive developments all the way there. Inland, there's agricultural country, some of the richest on the island, a cluster of Crete's better vineyards and a series of wealthy but rather dull villages. Directly behind the capital rises **Mount Ioúktas** with its characteristic profile of Zeus; to the west the Psilorítis massif spreads around the peak of **Mount Psilorítis** (Ídha) the island's highest mountain. On the south coast there are few roads and little development of any kind, except at **Ayía Galíni** in the southwest, a nominal fishing village which has grown into a popular resort, and beautiful **Mátala** which has thrown out the hippies that made it famous, and, though crowded with package-trippers in high summer, is still an appealing spring and autumn destination. Isolated **Léndas** has to some extent occupied Mátala's old niche, and has a fine beach.

Despite the lack of resorts, there seem constantly to be thousands of people trekking back and forth across the centre of the island. This is largely because of a trio of superb archeological sites in the south: **Phaestos**, second of the Minoan palaces, with its attendant villa at **Ayía Triádha**, and **Gortys**, capital of Roman Crete.

Iráklion

The best way to approach **IRÁKLION** is by sea, with Mount Ioúktas rising behind it and the Psilorítis range to the west. As you get closer, it's the city walls that first stand out, still dominating and fully encircling the oldest part of town; finally you sail in past the great **Venetian fortress** defending the harbour entrance. Unfortunately, big ships no longer dock in the old port but at great modern concrete wharves alongside, which neatly sums up Iráklion itself. Many of the old parts have been restored and are attractive, but these are offset by the bustle and noise that characterize much of the city today. In more recent times, however, Iráklion's administrators have been giving belated attention to dealing with some of the city's image problems, and large tracts of the centre – particularly the focal Platía Eleftherías – have been landscaped and refurbished with the aim of presenting a less daunting prospect to the visitor.

Orientation, arrival and information

Virtually everything you're likely to want to see in Iráklion lies within the northeastern corner of the walled city. The most vital thoroughfare, **25-Avgoústou**, links the harbour with the commercial city centre. At the bottom it is lined with shipping and travel agencies and rental outlets, but further up these give way to banks, restaurants and stores. **Platía Venizélou** (or Fountain Square), off to the right, is crowded with cafés and restaurants; behind Venizélou lies **El Greco Park** (actually a rather cramped garden), with more bars, while on the opposite side of 25-Avgoústou are some of the more interesting of Iráklion's older buildings. Further up 25-Avgoústou, **Kalokerinoú** leads down to Haniá Gate and westwards out of the city; straight ahead, **Odhós-1821** is a major shopping street, and adjacent 1866 is given over to the animated street **market**, perhaps the best on the island. To the left, Dhikeosínis heads for the city's main square, **Platía Eleftherías**, paralleled by the pedestrian alley, Dedhálou, lined with many of the city's swankier fashion stores and the direct link between the two squares. The revamped Eleftherías is very much the traditional centre of the city, both for traffic – which swirls around it constantly – and for life in general; it is ringed by more upmarket tourist cafés and restaurants and comes alive in the evening with crowds of strolling locals.

Points of arrival

Irâklion **airport** is right on the coast, 4km east of the city. **Bus** #1 leaves for Platía Eleftherías every few minutes from the car park in front of the terminal; buy your ticket (€0.70) at the booth before boarding. There are also plenty of **taxis** outside (which you'll be forced to use when the buses stop at 11pm), and prices to major destinations are posted here and in the domestic departures hall – it's about €8 to the centre of town, depending on traffic. Get an agreement on the fare before taking a cab and beware if the driver extols the virtues of a particular place to stay and offers to drop you there – he'll usually be getting a kickback from the proprietors. To avoid such hassles ask to be dropped at the central Platía Eleftherías, from where everything is in easy walking distance.

There are two main **bus stations** (often titled A and B on maps). Bus station A straddles both sides of the main road between the ferry dock and the Venetian harbour, and Station B lies just outside the Haniá Gate. Buses run from here **west** to Réthymnon and Haniá and **east** along the coastal highway to Hersónsissos, Mália, Áyios Nikólaos and Sitía, as well as **southeast** to Ierápetra and points en route. Local bus #2 to Knossos also leaves from here (south side of the main road). Buses for the **southwest** (Phaestos, Mátala and Ayía Galíni) and along the inland roads west (Týlissos, Anóyia) operate out of terminal B, a very long walk from the centre up Kalokerinoú (or jump on any bus heading down this street). From the wharves where the **ferries** dock, the city rises directly ahead in steep tiers. If you're heading for the centre, the Archeological Museum or the tourist office, cut straight up the stepped alleys behind the bus station onto Dhoúkos Bofór and to Platía Eleftherías; this will take about fifteen minutes. For accommodation, though, and to get a better idea of the layout of Irâklion's main attractions, it's simplest to follow the main roads by a rather more roundabout route. Head west along the coast, past the major eastbound bus station and on by the Venetian harbour before cutting up towards the centre on 25-Avgoústou.

Information

Irâklion's **tourist office** (June–Sept: Mon–Fri 9am–9pm; Oct–May: Mon–Fri 9am–2.30pm; ☎2810 246 299) is located just below Platía Eleftherías, opposite the Archeological Museum at Zanthoudhídhou 1. A sub-office at the **airport** (April–Sept daily 9am–9pm) is good for basic information and maps. The **tourist police** – more helpful than most – are at Dhikeosínis 10 (☎2810 283 190), halfway between Platía Eleftherías and the market.

Accommodation

Finding a **room** can be difficult in season. The best place to look for inexpensive places is in the area around Platía Venizélou, along Hándhakos and towards the harbour to the west of 25-Avgoústou. Other concentrations of affordable places are around El Greco Park and in the streets above the Venetian harbour. Better hotels mostly lie closer to Platía Eleftherías, to the south of Platía Venizélou and near the east- and westbound bus stations.

IRÁKLION

N

Natural History Museum

S. VENIZELOU

Koum Kapí

SKORDHILON

Áyios Andhréas Bastion

Priouli Fountain

Netcafé

SAVATHIANON

MAKARIOU

DEDHIOHAKI

SFAKION

AYION THEKON

KALOKERINOU

PLATIA EKATERINIS

Áyios Minas

Pantokratóros Bastion

Cathedral

KARDIOTISSIS

Haniá Gate

South/West Bus Station (B)

PLASTIRA

62 MARTYRON

LOMBAZI

VIANNOU

Haniá & Festós

THERISSOU

THENON

ROMANOU

PLASTIRA

KONDILAKI

Kazantzakis' Tomb

Martinengo Bastion

0   250 m

ACCOMMODATION

Atrion	D
Dedalos	J
Hellas	I
Kris	G
Kronos	A
Lato	C
Mirabello	F
Olympic	K
Rea	H
Vergina	B
Youth Hostel	E

Venetian
Fortress

Venetian Harbour

S. VENIZELOU

Áyios Petros

Historical
Museum

GAZI

Arsenáli

Ferry Dock

East/West
Bus Station (A)

THEOTOKOPOULOU

VYRONOS

EPIMENIDHOU

25-AVGOUSTOU

MINOTAVROU

DHOUKOS BOFOR

El Greco
Park

Áyios Títos

Sabbionera
Bastion

HORTATSON

HANDHAKOS

Lóggia

MIRABELOU

PLATIA
VENIZELOU

Morosíni
Fountain

ANDHROYEO

Archeological
Museum

PSAROMILIGON

MIHELIDHAKI

San
Marco

MILATOU

DHOUKOS BOFOR

Gallery
Games

KORAI

SAPOUTIE

IKAROU

Ayía
Ekateríni

DHIKEOSINIS

ZANTHOUDHIDHOU

Tourist Police

1821

OD. FOTIOU
THEODHOSAKI

VIANARI

PLATIA
ELEFTHERIAS

Airport & the east

Market

1866

SMYRNIS

PLATIA
DHASKALOYIANNI

Bembo
Fountain

AVEROF

PEDHIADHOS

PLATIA
ARKADHIOU

VIKELA

PLATIA
KORNAROU

Public
Gardens

EVANS

PEDHIADHOS

Vitouri
Bastion

Pórta Kenoúria

PLATIA
KYPROU

Southeast
Bus Terminal

Jesus
Bastion

KHRYSSOSTOMOU

KNOSSOU

DHOSOU

DHIMOKRATIAS

RESTAURANTS

40 Kymata	13
Bougatsa Kirkor	10
Fos Fanari	4
Geroplatanos	8
I Avli tou Deikaliona	5
Ippokampos	1
Katsina	2
Loukoulos	9
Pagopoleion	7
Peri Orexeos	11
Ta Asteria	12
Terzáki	3
The Mexican	6

Knossós

There are no **campsites** near Iráklion. The nearest sites both lie to the east of the city: first comes *Creta Camping* at Káto Goúves (☎28970 41400), 16km out, followed by *Caravan Camping* (☎28970 22901) at Hersónissos, 28km from the city.

Atrion Hronaki 9 ☎2810 246 000, ⓦwww.atrion
.gr. Attractive, new central hotel with well-equipped
balcony rooms, satellite TV and free Internet
connection. ❻

Dedalos Dedhálou 15 ☎2810 244 812,
ⓔdaedalos@internet.gr. Recently refurbished hotel
with balcony rooms overlooking a pedestrianized
shopping street which is tranquil at night. All rooms
are en suite and equipped with TV and a/c (€7
surcharge). ❸

Hellas Hándhakos 24 ☎2810 288 851,
ⓕ2810 284 442. Hostel-type place with simple
doubles, and dormitory rooms (❶) favoured by
younger travellers. Also has a roof garden and
snack-bar. ❸

Kris Dhoúkos Bofór 2, near the Venetian harbour
☎2810 285 853. Studio rooms with kitchenette,
fridge, great balcony views and friendly female
proprietor. ❹

Kronos Agaráthou 2, west of 25-Avgoústou
☎2810 282 240, ⓦwww.kronoshotel.gr. Pleasant,
friendly and modern hotel with en-suite, sea-view
balcony rooms. ❹

Lato Epomenídhou 15 ☎2810 228 103, ⓦwww
.lato.gr. Stylish and luxurious hotel where a/c
rooms have minibar, TV and fine balcony views
over the Venetian harbour (the higher floors have
the better views). B&B ❼

Mirabello Theotokopoúlou 20 ☎2810 285 052,
ⓦwww.mirabello-hotel.gr. Good-value, family-run
hotel featuring en-suite balcony rooms, some with
a/c and TV. In a quiet street just north of El Greco
Park. ❸–❹

Olympic Platía Kornárou ☎2810 288 861,
ⓕ2810 222 512. Overlooking the busy platía and
the famous Bembo fountain. One of the many
hotels built in the 1960s, but one of the few that
has been refurbished; facilities include minibar and
strongbox. B&B ❻

Rea Kalimeráki 1 ☎2810 223 638, ⓕ2810 242
189. A friendly, comfortable and clean *pension* in a
quiet street. Some rooms with washbasin, others
en suite. ❷–❸

Vergina Hortátson 32 ☎2810 242 739. Basic but
pleasant rooms with washbasins in a quiet street
and set around a courtyard with a giant banana
tree. ❷

Youth Hostel Vkronos 5 ☎2810 286 281,
ⓔheraklioyouthhostel@yahoo.com. Formerly
Iráklión's official youth hostel, it has been stripped
of its HI status. It is in fact a good place to stay,
family-run and very friendly and helpful. There's
plenty of space and some beds (albeit illegal) on
the roof if you fancy sleeping out under the stars.
Private rooms (❶) as well as dormitories (❶); hot
showers, breakfast and other meals available.

The Town

A good place to start your explorations of the town is the focal **Platía Venizélou**, crowded most of the day with locals patronizing its café terraces, and with travellers who've arranged to meet in "Fountain Square". The **Morosini Fountain**, which gives the square its popular name, is not particularly spectacular at first glance, but on closer inspection is really a very beautiful work; it was built by Venetian governor Francesco Morosini in the seventeenth century, incorporating four lions which were some three hundred years old even then. From the platía you can strike up Dhedhálou, a pedestrianized street full of fashion and tourist shops, or continue on 25-Avgoústou to a major traffic junction at Platía Nikifoúrou Foka. To the right, Kalokerinoú leads west out of the city, the market lies straight ahead along Odhós–1866, and Platía Eleftherías is a short walk to the left up Dhikeosínis.

Platía Eleftherías and the archeological museum

Platía Eleftherías, with seats shaded by palms and eucalyptuses, is very much the traditional heart of the city; traffic swirls around it constantly, and on summer evenings strolling crowds come to fill its café terraces. Most of Iráklion's more expensive shops are in the streets leading off the platía.

The **Archeological Museum** (April–Sept Mon 1–7.30pm, Tues–Sun 8.30am–7.30pm; Oct–March daily 8am–5pm; €7) is nearby. Almost every important prehistoric and Minoan find on Crete is included in this fabulous, if bewilderingly large and unimaginatively presented, collection. The museum tends to be crowded, especially when a guided tour stampedes through, but it's worth taking time over. You can't hope to see everything, nor can we attempt to describe it all (several good museum guides are sold here, the best probably being the glossy ones by J.A. Sakellarakis or Andonis Vasilakis), but highlights include the "**Town Mosaic**" from Knossos in Room 2 (the galleries are arranged basically in chronological order), the famous **inscribed disc** from Phaestos in Room 3 (itself the subject of several books), most of Room 4, especially the magnificent bull's-head **rhyton** (drinking vessel), the **jewellery** in Room 6 (and elsewhere) and the engraved steatite **black vases** in Room 7. Save some of your time and energy for upstairs, where the **Hall of the Frescoes**, with intricately reconstructed fragments of the wall paintings from Knossos and other sites, is especially wonderful. A long-overdue **renovation** of the Archeological Museum is set to start in 2006. When this finally happens it should place the collection at the forefront of museum presentation in Greece. However, once work is under way there will inevitably be some frustration for visitors as rooms are closed and items moved around.

Walls and fortifications

The massive **Venetian walls**, in places up to 15m thick, are the most obvious evidence of Iráklion's later history. Though their fabric is incredibly well preserved, access is virtually nonexistent. It is possible, just, to walk along them from Áyios Andhréas Bastion over the sea in the west, as far as the Martinengo Bastion where lies the **tomb of Nikos Kazantzakis**, Cretan author of *Zorba the Greek*, whose epitaph reads: "I believe in nothing, I hope for nothing, I am free." At weekends, Iraklians gather here to pay their respects and enjoy a free view of the soccer matches played by one of the city's two teams in the stadium below. If the walls seem altogether too much effort, the **port fortifications** are much easier to see. Stroll out along the jetty (crowded with courting couples at dusk) and you can get inside the sixteenth-century **Venetian fortress** (Tues–Sun 8.30am–3pm; €2) at the harbour entrance, emblazoned with the Venetian Lion of St Mark. Standing atop this, you begin to understand how Iráklion (or Candia as both the city and the island were known to the Venetians) withstood a 22-year siege before finally falling to the Ottomans. On the landward side of the port, the Venetian **arsenáli** (arsenals) can also be seen, their arches rather lost amid the concrete road system all around.

Churches and other museums

From the harbour, 25-Avgoústou will take you up past most of the town's other highlights. The **church of Áyios Títos**, on the left as you approach Platía Venizélou, borders a pleasant little platía. Byzantine in origin but substantially rebuilt by the Venetians, it looks magnificent principally because, like most of the churches here, it was adapted by the Turks as a mosque and only reconsecrated in 1925; consequently it has been renovated on numerous occasions. On the south side of this platía, abutting 25-Avgoústou, is the Venetian **city hall** with its famous loggia, again almost entirely rebuilt. Just above this, facing Platía Venizélou, is the **church of San Marco**, its steps usually crowded with sightseers spilling over from the nearby platía. Neither of these last two buildings has found a permanent role in its refurbished state, but both are generally open to house some kind of exhibition or craft show.

Slightly away from the obvious city-centre circuit, but still within the bounds of the walls, there is a clutch of lesser museums worth seeing if you have the time. First of these are the excellent collection of **icons** in the **church of Ayía Ekateríni** (Mon–Sat 10am–1.30pm; €2), an ancient building just below the undistinguished cathedral, off Kalokerinoú. The finest here are six large scenes by Mihaïl Damaskinos (a near-contemporary of El Greco) who fused Byzantine and Renaissance influences. Supposedly both Damaskinos and El Greco studied at Ayía Ekateríni in the sixteenth century, when it functioned as a sort of monastic art school.

The **Historical Museum** (Mon–Fri 9am–4pm, Sat 9am–2pm; €3; @www.historical-museum.gr) lies some 300m north of here, on the waterfront. Its display of folk costumes and jumble of local memorabilia include the reconstructed studies of both Nikos Kazantzakis and Emanuel Tsouderos (the latter both Cretan statesman and former Greek prime minister). There's enough variety to satisfy just about anyone, including the only El Greco painting on Crete, the uncharacteristic *View of Mount Sinai and the Monastery of St Catherine*.

To the west, in a converted old power plant overlooking the bay of Koum Kapí, is the **Natural History Museum** (Sept–June Mon–Fri 9am–3pm, Sun 9am–5pm; July–Aug daily 9am–8pm; €4.50; @www.nhmc.uoc.gr), definitely worth a visit. As well as the usual flora and fauna displays, it has exhibits detailing the island's geological evolution, the arrival of man, and the environment as it would have appeared to the Minoans.

The beaches

Iráklion's **beaches** are some way out, whether east or west of town. In either direction they're easily accessible by bus: #6 heads west from the stop outside the *Astoria* hotel in Platía Eleftherías; #7 east from the stop opposite this, under the trees in the centre of the platía.

Almyrós (or Ammoudhári) to the west has been subjected to a degree of development, comprising a campsite, several medium-size hotels and one giant one (the *Zeus Beach*, in the shadow of the power station at the far end), which makes the beach hard to get to without walking through or past something built up.

Amnissós, to the east, is the better choice, with several tavernas and the added amusement of planes swooping in immediately overhead to land at the nearby airport. This is where most locals go on their afternoons off; the furthest of the beaches is the best, although new hotels are encroaching. Little remains to indicate the once-flourishing port of Knossos here, aside from a rather dull, fenced-in dig. If you're seriously into antiquities, however, you'll find a more rewarding site in the small Minoan villa, known as **Nírou Háni** (Tues–Sun 8.30am–3pm; free) at Háni Kokkíni, the first of the full-blown resort developments east of Iráklion.

Eating

Big city though it is, Iráklion disappoints when it comes to eating, and not many of the central restaurants and tavernas provide good value. The cafés and tavernas of platíes Venizélou and Eleftherías are essential places to sit and watch the world pass, but their food is expensive and mediocre. One striking exception is *Bougatsa Kirkor*, by the Morosini Fountain in Venizélou, where you can sample authentic Cretan *bougátsa* – a creamy cheese pie sprinkled with sugar and cinnamon. For **snacks** and **takeaways**, there's a group of *souvláki* and other fast-food stalls clustering around the top of 25-Avgoústou near the entrance to El Greco Park, which is handy if you need somewhere to sit and eat. For *tyrópita* and *spanakópita* (cheese or spinach pies) and other pastries, sweet or savoury, there is no shortage of zaharoplastía and places such as *Everest* – just north of the Morosini Fountain – which does takeaways of these as well as lots of other savouries. On and around Platía Dhaskaloyiánni (near the archeological museum) are some authentic and inexpensive ouzerís: try *Ta Asteria* or *40 Kymata* on the platía itself for atmosphere and tasty *mezédhes*.

I Avli tou Deikaliona Kalokairinoú 8 at the rear of the Historical Museum (☏ 2810 244 215). Popular taverna with a great little terrace fronting the Idomeneus fountain serving up well-prepared meat and fish dishes. In high summer you may need to book to ensure an outdoor table.

Fos Fanari Marineli 1, opposite the tiny church of Ay. Dimítrios. The first in a row of ouzerís that line this alley off Vironos, sloping down to the harbour. Good fish dishes and *mezédhes*. The similar and neighbouring *Terzáki* is also worth a try.

Geroplatanos in the leafy square fronting the church of Ay. Títos. Taking its name from the great old plane tree beneath which its tables are set out, this is one of the most tranquil lunch spots in town and provides the usual taverna staples.

Ippokampos Sófokli Venizélou, west of 25-Avgoústou, close to the *Kronos* hotel. The best and least expensive fish to be had in Iráklion, served in unpretentious surroundings. Deservedly popular with locals for lunch *mezédhes* as well as dinner, this place is often crowded late into the evening, and you may have to queue or turn up earlier than the Greeks eat. Has a pleasant shaded terrace over the road on the seafront.

Katsina Marineli 12. A simple and friendly ouzerí at the opposite (seaward) end of the alley from *Fos Fanari* (above). Tasty and economical seafood *mezédhes* served at outdoor tables.

Loukoulos on the alley Koraí, parallel to Dedhálou. With a leafy courtyard terrace and an Italian slant to its international menu, this is one of the better tavernas in Iráklion. However, the pricey food and an expensive wine list seem aimed more at luring Iráklion's smart set than the casual visitor.

The Mexican Hándhakos 71. Inexpensive Mexican tacos and beers, complemented by salads and bean dishes.

Pagopoleion Platía Áyios Títos. Iráklion's most original bar has added a mid-priced restaurant serving Cretan and international dishes to a high standard; the wine list includes interesting bottles from little-known but excellent small vineyards around the island. There's also a recommended *mezedhákia* buffet (Sat & Sun 1–4pm).

Peri Orexeos which allows you to fill a plate for €6. A pleasant terrace is also good for lazy breakfasts and snacks.

Koraí 10 almost opposite *Loukoulos* (above). This newly opened taverna is a good bet for traditional Cretan cooking at reasonable prices.

Drinking, nightlife and entertainment

Iráklion is a bit of a damp squib as far as **nightlife** goes, certainly when compared with many other towns on the island. If you're determined, however, there are a few city-centre possibilities, and plenty of options if all you want to do is sit and **drink**. Indeed there is a new breed of **kafenío** emerging in Iráklion, aimed at a younger crowd: the drinks are cocktails rather than *raki*, the music is modern Greek or Western, and there are prices to match. *Andromeda* and *Living Room*, both on Platía Venizélou, are a couple of the most popular. The city's most animated **bars** are located around **Platía Koráï** behind Dhedhálou (up from *Taverna Loukoulos* listed above) and along the alley of the same name to the west.

Bars

To Avgo Platía Koraí. Trendy little bar frequented by students, on a pleasant square just to the north of Dedhálou.

Flash Platía Koraí. This bar has outdoor tables and serves a wide variety of exotic (and expensive)

beers and cocktails. Those on a tight budget can nurse a *frappé* for hours.

Jasmin Ayiostefanitón 6, tucked in an alley on the left midway down Hándhakos. Another good nighttime rendezvous, with jazz, soul and Latin music and an outdoor terrace. Also serves 45 different types of tea, including herbal.

Korais on the alley Koraí, parallel to Dedhálou. Glitzy open-air café with spacious plant-festooned terraces, overhead movie screens and music – highly popular with Iráklion's stylish set.

Mayo Milatou 11, just north of Koraí. This new extravaganza of a bar with spotlights, screens and music under a big canopy terrace is the latest place to be seen if you're part of Iráklion's student set. Its arrival has spawned a whole new set of bars and cafés along the same street.

Orionas Psaromíligon 15. Lively music and drinks bar on two floors with a stylish terrace upstairs; has a varied programme of live music at weekends

in summer, with alternating jazz, blues, reggae and rock acts performing.

Pagopoleion (Ice Factory) Platía Áyios Títos. Stunningly stylish bar created by photographic artist Chryssy Karelli inside Iráklion's former ice factory. She has preserved much of the old building including a lift for hauling the ice from the basement freezer and a fascistic call to duty in German Gothic script on one wall – a remnant of Nazi occupation of the factory in World War II. Make sure to visit the toilets, as they are in an artistic league of their own.

Rebels Perdhíkari 3. A stylish bar which has cloned numerous similar places nearby. On weekends in summer this whole zone is the trendiest place to be if you're under 30.

Clubs and discos

For **discos** and **clubs** proper, there is a large selection, playing Western music, interspersed with Greek tunes (not the type played for tourists). *Privilege* is the most popular, down towards the harbour at the bottom of Dhoúkos Bofór, below the Archeological Museum. The nearby *GDM*, *Megaron* and *Envy* provide competition. Two pleasant and popular music bars with a seafront location are *Loft* and *Caprice* overlooking the western end of Koum Kapí bay near the Natural History Museum. One of the Iráklion beach set's favourite summer venues is at Amnissós beach (see p.230). Here two beach clubs, *Akti* and *Wet Wet*, play host to an under-30 crowd who turn up in their droves to swim, drink and dance to DJ rhythms; night-time is slightly more formal when the dress is smarter and people tend not to swim.

Listings

Airlines Aegean, 25-Avgoústou 34 (℡ 2810 344 324, ⊛ www.aegeanair.com), and Olympic, 25-Avgoústou 27 (℡ 2810 244 802, ⊛ www.olympic-airways.com), are the main scheduled airlines with connecting flights to Athens and other parts of Greece. Charter airlines flying into Iráklion mostly use local travel agents as their representatives.

Airport For airport information call ℡ 2810 397 129. Bus #1 runs from the eastern side of Platía Eleftherías to the airport every few minutes; buy a ticket (€0.70) from a kiosk near the bus stop.

Banks There are ATMs all over town, but the main bank branches are on 25-Avgoústou.

Car and bike rental 25-Avgoústou is lined with rental companies, but you'll often find cheaper rates on the backstreets; it's always worth asking for discounts. For cars and bikes, good places to start include: Blue Sea, Kosmá Zótou 7, near the bottom of 25-Avgoústou (℡ 2810 241 097, ⊛ www.bluesearentals.com), which gives a twenty percent discount to Rough Guide readers, and Sun Rise, 25-Avgoústou 46 (℡ 2810 221 609). For cars try: Reliable, Epimenidou 8 off the east side of the same street (℡ 2810 344 212); Caravel,

25-Avgoústou 39 (℡ 2810 335 900, ⊛ www.caravel.gr); and Ritz in the Hotel Rea, Kalimeráki 1 (℡ 2810 223 638). All offer free delivery to hotels and airport.

Ferry tickets Available from Minoan Lines, 25-Avgoústou 78 (℡ 2810 229 646, ⊛ www.minoan.gr), which handles the islands and Athens; and ANEK Lines, 25-Avgoústou 33 (℡ 2810 222 481, ⊛ www.anek.gr), for Athens only; also try any of the travel agents listed opposite. Another source for tickets and ferry information is the long-established Paleologus Travel, 25-Avgoústou 5 (℡ 2810 346 185); their comprehensive websites (⊛ www.ferries.gr, ⊛ www.greekislands.gr) are excellent.

Hospital Most central is the hospital on Apollónion, southwest of Platía Kornárou (℡ 2810 229 713), between Albér and Moussoúrou.

Internet Iráklion now has a number of Internet cafés located in and around the city centre. Two central places are Netcafé, Odhós-1878 4 (daily 10am–2am) and Gallery Games, Koraï 14.

Laundry Washsalon, Hándhakos 18 (Mon–Sat 8.30am–9pm), is reliable and also does service washes (€6 for 5kg). Laundry Perfect at Malikoúti 32, north of the Archeological Museum, will do the same and has similar prices (Mon–Sat 9am–9pm).

Left luggage Offices in Station A (daily 6.30am–8pm; €1 per bag per day), but not Station B, as well as a commercial agency at Hándhakos 18 (daily 24hr; €1.50 per large locker per day). You can also leave bags at the youth hostel (even if you don't stay there) for €1.50 per bag per day. If you want to leave your bag while you go off on a bike for a day or two, the rental company should be prepared to store it.

Newspapers and books For English-language newspapers and novels, Bibliopoleio, almost opposite the Morosini Fountain on Platía Venizélou, is the most central. The excellent Planet International Bookstore, on four floors behind Platía Venizélou at the corner of Hándhakos and Kydhonías, has the island's biggest stock of English-language titles and is a great place to browse.

Pharmacies Plentiful on the main shopping streets – at least one is open 24hr on a rota basis; the others will have a sign on the door indicating which it is. There are traditional herbalists in the market.

Post office Main office in Platía Dhaskaloyiánnis, off Platía Eleftherías (Mon–Fri 7.30am–8pm).

Taxis Major taxi ranks in Platía Eleftherías and by the Morosini Fountain, or call ☎2810 210 102 or 2810 210 168. Prices displayed on boards at the taxi stands.

Toilets In Platía Kornarou (at the southern end of the market) and the public gardens near the cathedral, or at the bus stations; there's also an excellent one at the Archeological Museum (access without paying the museum entrance charge).

Travel agencies Budget operators and student specialists include the extremely helpful Blavakis Travel, Platía Kallergón 8, just off 25-Avgoústou by the entrance to El Greco Park (☎2810 282 541), and Prince Travel, 25-Avgoústou 30 (☎2810 282 706). For excursions around the island, villa rentals and so on, the bigger operators are probably easier: Creta Travel Bureau, Dhikeosínis 49 (☎2810 300 610), and Adamis Tours, 25-Avgoústou 23 (☎2810 346 202). The latter is also the local American Express agent.

Knossos

KNOSSOS, the largest of the **Minoan palaces**, reached its cultural peak more than three thousand years ago, though a town of some importance persisted here well into the Roman era. It lies on a low, largely man-made hill some 5km southeast of Iráklion; the surrounding hillsides are rich in lesser remains spanning 25 centuries, starting at the beginning of the second millennium BC.

Just over a century ago the palace existed only in mythology. Knossos was the court of the legendary King Minos, whose wife Pasiphae bore the Minotaur, half-bull, half-man. Here the labyrinth was constructed by Daedalus to contain the monster, and youths were brought from Athens as human sacrifice until Theseus arrived to slay the beast and, with Ariadne's help, escape its lair. The discovery of the palace, and the interplay of these legends with fact, is among the most amazing tales of modern archeology. Heinrich Schliemann, the German excavator of Troy, suspected that a major Minoan palace lay under the various tumuli here, but was denied the necessary permission to dig by the local Ottoman authorities at the end of the nineteenth century. It was left for Sir Arthur Evans, whose name is indelibly associated with Knossos, to excavate the site, from 1900 onwards.

The #2 and #4 local **buses** set off every ten minutes from Iráklion's city bus stands (adjacent to the eastbound bus station), proceed up 25-Avgoústou (with a stop just south of Platía Venizélou) and out of town on Odhós-1821 and Evans. This is also the route you should take if **driving** (follow the signs from Platía Eleftherías); there's a free car park downhill on the left, immediately before the site entrance, which will enable you to avoid paying for the private car parks dotting the road before this. A **taxi** from the centre will cost around €6. At Knossos, outside the fenced site, stands a partly restored Minoan caravanserai where ancient wayfarers would rest and water their animals. Head out onto the

PALACE OF KNOSSOS

Royal Road
Theatral Area
N
North Entrance
Lustral Basin
Bull Relief
West Court
Storage Pits
Giant "Pithoi"
Site Entrance
Storerooms
Piano Nobile
Throne Room
Workshops
Statue
West Entrance
Central Court
Grand Stairway
Priest-King Fresco
Royal Apartments
South House
0   25 m
Southeast House

road and you'll find no lack of watering holes for modern travellers either – a string of rather pricey tavernas and tacky souvenir stands.

The British School at Athens has a useful website (Ⓦwww.bsa.gla.ac.uk /knossos/vrtour) dedicated to Knossos, with detail on the history of the site and excavations in addition to a virtual tour.

The site

As soon as you enter the **Palace of Knossos** (daily: April–Sept 8.30am–7.30pm; Oct–March 8.30am–3pm; €6) through the West Court, the ancient ceremonial entrance, it is clear how the legends of the labyrinth grew up around it. Even with a detailed plan, it's almost impossible to find your way around the complex with any success, although a series of **timber walkways** now channels visitors around the site, severely restricting the scope for independent exploration. If you're worried about missing the highlights, you can always tag along with one of the constant guided tours for a while, catching the patter and then backtracking to absorb the detail when the crowd has moved on. Outside the period December to February you won't get the place to yourself, whenever you come, but exploring on your own does give you the opportunity to appreciate individual parts of the palace in the brief lulls between groups.

Knossos was liberally "restored" by Evans, and these restorations have been the source of furious controversy among archeologists ever since. It has become clear that much of Evans's upper level – the so-called *piano nobile* – is pure conjecture. Even so, and putting archeological ethics to one side, his guess as to what the palace might have looked like is certainly as good as anyone's, and it makes the other sites infinitely more meaningful if you have seen Knossos first. Almost as controversial are Evans's designations of the various parts of the palace: he fantasized a royal family living here and in the words of one critic turned the Minoans into "second-millennium BC Victorians". Some sceptical scholars are still not convinced the structure *was* a palace and argue that the building could well have been a religious centre or shrine. Still, without the restorations, it would be almost impossible to imagine the grandeur of the multistorey palace or to see the ceremonial stairways, strange, top-heavy pillars and gaily painted walls that distinguish the site. For some idea of the size and complexity of the palace in its original state, take a look at the cutaway drawings (wholly imaginary but probably not too far off) on sale outside.

Royal Apartments

The superb **Royal Apartments** around the central staircase are not guesswork, and they are plainly the finest of the rooms at Knossos. The **Grand Stairway** itself (now closed to public access) is a masterpiece of design: not only a fitting approach to these sumptuously appointed chambers, but also an integral part of the whole plan, its large well bringing light into the lower storeys. Light wells such as these, usually with a courtyard at the bottom, are a constant feature of Knossos and a reminder of just how important creature comforts were to the Minoans, and how skilled they were at providing them.

For evidence of this luxurious lifestyle you need look no further than the **Queen's Suite** (now viewed behind glass screens), off the grand **Hall of the Colonnades** at the bottom of the staircase (reached by descending a timber walkway). Here, the main living room is decorated with the celebrated **dolphin fresco** (a reproduction; the original is now in the Iráklion Archeological Museum, see p.229) and with running friezes of flowers and abstract spirals. On two sides it opens out onto courtyards that let in light and air; the smaller one would probably have been planted with flowers. The room may have been scattered with cushions and hung with plush drapes, while doors and further curtains between the pillars would have allowed for privacy, and provided cool shade in the heat of the day. Remember, though, that all this is speculation and some of it is pure hype; the dolphin fresco, for example, was found on the courtyard floor, not in the room itself, and would have been viewed from an upper balcony as a sort of trompe l'oeil, like looking through a glass-bottomed boat. Whatever the truth, this is an impressive example of Minoan architecture, the more so when you follow the dark passage around to the queen's **bath-room** (now only partially visible behind a screen). Here is a clay tub, protected behind a low wall (and again probably screened by curtains when in use), and the famous "flushing" toilet (a hole in the ground with drains to take the waste away – it was flushed by throwing a bucket of water down).

The much-perused **drainage system** was a series of interconnecting terra-cotta pipes running underneath most of the palace. Guides to the site never fail to point these out as evidence of the advanced state of Minoan civilization, and they are indeed quite an achievement, in particular the system of baffles and overflows to slow down the runoff and avoid any danger of flooding. Just how much running water there would have been, however, is another matter. Although the water supply was, and is, at the bottom of the hill, the combined efforts of rainwater catchment and hauling water up to the palace can hardly have been sufficient to supply the needs of more than a small elite. The recent discovery of remnants of an aqueduct system carrying water to the palace from springs on nearby Mount Ioúktas (the same source that today provides water for the Morosini fountain in Iráklion) could mean that this was not the only water supply.

The Grand Stairway ascends to the floor above the queen's domain, and a set of rooms generally regarded as the **King's Quarters** (currently not on view). These are chambers in a considerably sterner vein; the staircase opens into a grandiose reception chamber known as the **Hall of the Royal Guard** (or Hall of the Colonnades), its walls decorated in repeated shield patterns. Immediately off here is the **Hall of the Double Axes** (or the King's Room), believed to have been the ruler's personal chamber, a double room that would allow for privacy in one portion while audiences were held in the more public section. Its name comes from the double-axe symbol carved into every block of masonry.

The Throne Room and the rest of the palace

At the top of the Grand Stairway (you will need to retrace your steps up the timber staircase), you emerge onto the broad **Central Court**, a feature of all the Minoan palaces. Open now, this would once have been enclosed by the walls of the buildings all around. On the far side, in the northwestern corner of the courtyard, is the entrance to another of Knossos's most atmospheric survivals, the **Throne Room**. Here, a worn stone throne – with its hollowed shaping for the posterior – sits against the wall of a surprisingly small chamber; along the walls around it are ranged stone benches, suggesting a king ruling in council, and behind there's a reconstructed fresco of two griffins. Just how much rebuilding took place here can be gauged from the fact that when the throne was unearthed the surrounding ruins cleared its back by only a few centimetres: the ceiling and rooms above are all the creation of Evans's "reconstitution", as he preferred to describe his imaginative reconstructions. Anyway, in all probability in Minoan times this was the seat of a priestess rather than a ruler (there's nothing like it in any other Minoan palace), and its conversion into a throne room seems to have been a late innovation wrought by the invading Mycenaeans, during their short-lived domination prior to the palace's final destruction in the fourteenth century BC. The Throne Room is now closed off with a wooden gate, but you can lean over this for a good view, and in the antechamber there's a wooden copy of the throne on which everyone used to perch to have their picture taken, but this is now also off limits.

The rest you'll see as you wander, contemplating the legends of the place which blur with reality. Try not to miss the giant *pithoi* in the northeast quadrant of the site, an area known as the palace workshops; the storage chambers which you see from behind the Throne Room, and the reproduced frescoes in the reconstructed room above it; the fresco of the Priest-King looking down on the south side of the central court, and the relief of a charging bull on its north side. This last would have greeted you if you entered the palace through its north door; you can see evidence here of some kind of gatehouse and a lustral bath, a sunken area perhaps used for ceremonial bathing and purification. Just outside this gate is the **theatral area** (another Evans designation), an open space a little like a stepped amphitheatre, which may have been used for ritual performances or dances. From here the **Royal Road**, claimed as the oldest road in Europe, sets out. At one time, this probably ran right across the island; nowadays it ends after about 100m in a brick wall beneath the modern road. Circling back around the outside of the palace, you can get an idea of its scale by looking up at it; on the south side are a couple of small reconstructed Minoan houses which are worth exploring.

Beyond Knossos

If you have transport, the drive beyond Knossos can be an attractive and enjoyable one, taking minor roads through much greener country, with vineyards draped across low hills and flourishing agricultural communities. If you want specific things to seek out, head first for **MYRTIÁ**, an attractive village with the small **Kazantzakis Museum** (March–Oct daily 9am–7pm; Nov–Feb Sun only 10am–3pm; €3) in a house where the writer's parents once lived. **ARHÁNES**, at the foot of Mount Ioúktas, is a much larger and wealthy farming town that was also quite heavily populated in Minoan times. There are plenty of places to eat on an animated central square, but no places to stay. None of the three archeological sites here is open to the public, but **Anemospiliá**, 2km northwest of the town (directions from the archeological museum cited below), can be visited and has caused huge controversy since its excavation in the 1980s: many traditional views of the Minoans, particularly that of Minoan life as peaceful and idyllic, have had to be rethought in the light of the discovery of an apparent human sacrifice. Close to Arhánes' main square, an excellent **archeological museum** (Wed–Mon 8.30am–3pm; free) displays finds from here and other nearby excavations, including the strange ceremonial dagger seemingly used for human sacrifice. From Arhánes you can also drive (or walk with a couple of hours to spare) to the summit of Mount Ioúktas to see the imposing remains of a Minoan **peak sanctuary** and enjoy spectacular panoramic **views** towards Knossos (with which it was linked) and the northern coast beyond. At **VATHÝ-PETRO**, some 4km south of the mountain, is a **Minoan villa and vineyard** (Tues–Sun 8.30am–3pm; free), which once controlled the rich farmland south of Arhánes. Inside, a remarkable collection of farming implements was found, as well as a unique **wine press**, which remains *in situ*. Substantial amounts of the farm buildings remain, and it's still surrounded by fertile vines (Arhánes is one of Crete's major wine-producing zones) three-and-a-half-thousand years later – making it probably the oldest still-functioning vineyard in Europe, if not the world. Continuing southeast for 2km brings you to another agricultural village, **HOUDHÉTSI**, where you'll find the remarkable **Museum of Musical Instruments of the World** (daily 9am–3pm & 5.30–8.30pm; €3; ⓦ www .labyrinthmusic.gr). Founded by Irish *lýra* player Ross Daly who is famed in Crete and lives in the village, the museum consists of a collection of mainly string and percussion instruments (many very rare) from across the globe. To locate the museum head for *Bar Paranga* at the top (or south end) of the village – the museum is opposite. Should it not be open during these times, ring the English-speaking guardian, Eleni Arvanti, from the public phone alongside the bar, and she will open it up for you (☏ 2810 743 634).

Southwest from Iráklion: sites and beaches

If you take a **tour** from Iráklion (or one of the resorts), you'll probably visit the **Gortys**, **Phaestos** and **Ayía Triádha** sites in a day, with a lunchtime swim at **Mátala** thrown in. Doing it by public transport, you'll be forced into a rather more leisurely pace, but there's still no reason why you shouldn't get to all three and reach Mátala within the day; if necessary, it's easy enough to hitch the final stretch. **Bus services** to the Phaestos site are excellent, with some nine a day to and from Iráklion (fewer Sun), five of which continue to or come from Mátala;

there are also services direct to Ayía Galíni. If you're arriving in the afternoon, plan to visit Ayía Triádha first, as it closes early.

The route to Áyii Dhéka

The road from Iráklion towards Phaestos is a pretty good one by the standards of Cretan mountain roads, albeit rather dull. The country you're heading towards is the richest agricultural land on the island and, right from the start, the villages en route are large and businesslike. In the biggest of them, **Ayía Varvára**, there's a great rock outcrop known as the **Omphalos** (Navel) of Crete, supposedly the very centre of the island.

Past here, you descend rapidly to the fertile fields of the Messará plain, where the road joins the main route across the south near the village of **ÁYII DHÉKA**. For religious Cretans Áyii Dhéka is something of a place of pilgrimage; its name, "The Ten Saints", refers to ten early Christians martyred here under the Romans. The old Byzantine church in the centre of the village preserves the stone block on which they are supposed to have been decapitated and in a crypt below the modern church on the village's western edge you can see the martyrs' (now empty) tombs. It's an attractive village to wander around, with several places to eat and even some **rooms** – try *Dimitris Taverna* (T 28920 31560; ❶), where you can both stay and eat, which has excellent-value en-suite, air-conditioned rooms with views above the restaurant and a splendid new terrace at the rear below.

Gortys and around

Within easy walking distance of Áyii Dhéka, either through the fields or along the main road, sprawls the site of **Gortys** (daily 8am–7pm; €4), ruined capital of the Roman province that included not only Crete but also much of North Africa. After a look at the plan of the extensive site at the entrance, cutting across the fields to the south of the road will give you some idea of the scale of this city, at its zenith in approximately the third century AD. An enormous variety of remains, including an impressive **theatre**, and a couple of **temples** are strewn across your route and more spectacular discoveries are being unearthed by the archeologists who return to dig each summer. Even in Áyii Dhéka you'll see Roman pillars and statues lying around in people's yards or propping up their walls.

There had been a settlement here from the earliest times and evidence of a Minoan site has been unearthed on the acropolis, but the extant ruins date almost entirely from the Roman era. Only now is the site being systematically excavated by the Italian Archeological School. At the main entrance to the **fenced site**, to the north of the road, are the ruins of the still impressive **basilica of Áyios Títos**; the eponymous saint converted the island to Christianity and was its first bishop. Beyond this is the **odeion** which houses the most important discovery on the site, the **Law Code**. These great inscribed blocks of stone were incorporated by the Romans from a much earlier stage of the city's development; they're written in an obscure early Greek-Cretan dialect, and in a style known as *boustrophedon* (ox-ploughed), with the lines reading alternately in opposite directions like the furrows of a ploughed field. At 10m by 3m, this is reputedly the largest Greek inscription ever found. The laws set forth reflect a strictly hierarchical society: five witnesses were needed to convict a free man of a crime, only one for a slave; raping a free man or woman carried a fine of a hundred *staters*, violating a serf only five. A small **museum** in a loggia (also within the fenced area) holds a number of large and finely worked sculptures found at Gortys, more evidence of the city's importance. Next to the museum is a **café** (same hours as site).

Míres

Some 20km west of Gortys, **MÍRES** is an important market town and focal point of transport for the fertile Messará plain: if you're switching buses to get from the beaches on the south coast to the archeological sites or the west, this is where you'll do it. There are good facilities including a **bank**, a few **restaurants** and a couple of **rooms**, though there's no particular reason to stay unless you are waiting for a bus or looking for work (it's one of the better places for agricultural jobs). A useful **Internet** café, *Net Escape*, near the bus stop will allow you to send a few emails while awaiting onward connections. Heading straight for Phaestos, there's usually no need to stop.

Phaestos (Festós)

The **Palace of Phaestos** (daily 8.30am–7.30pm; €4) was excavated by the Italian Federico Halbherr (also responsible for the early work at Gortys) at almost exactly the same time as Evans was working at Knossos. The style of the excavations, however, could hardly have been more different. Here, to the approval of most traditional archeologists, reconstruction was kept to an absolute minimum – it's all bare foundations, and walls which rise at most 1m above ground level. This means that, despite a magnificent setting overlooking the plain of Messará, the palace at Phaestos is not as immediately arresting as those at Knossos or Malia, but no less fascinating.

PALACE OF PHAESTOS

Tourist Pavilion

Lustral Basin · Royal Apartments · Archive

Entrance · Peristyle Hall · Peristyle House

Theatral area and West Court · Grand Stairway · Propylon · Workshops

Storage Pits · Storerooms · Office · Furnace

First Palace Remains · Central Court · Prince's rooms · Steep bank

Classical Temple

Steep bank

N

0 — 25 m

It's interesting to speculate why the palace was built halfway up a hill rather than on the plain below – certainly not for defence, for this is in no way a good defensive position. Psychological superiority over the peasants or reasons of health are both possible, but it seems quite likely that it was simply the magnificent view that finally swayed the decision. The site looks over Psilorítis to the north and the huge plain, with the Lasíthi mountains beyond it, to the east. Towards the top of Psilorítis you should be able to make out a small black smudge: the entrance to the Kamáres cave (see p.251).

On the ground closer at hand, you can hardly fail to notice the strong similarities between Phaestos and the other palaces: the same huge rows of storage jars, the great courtyard with its monumental stairway, and the theatre area. Unique to Phaestos, however, is the third courtyard, in the middle of which are the remains of a **furnace** used for metalworking. Indeed, this eastern corner of the palace seems to have been home to a number of craftsmen, including potters and carpenters. Oddly enough, Phaestos was much less ornately decorated than Knossos; there is no evidence, for example, of any of the dramatic Minoan wall-paintings.

The **tourist pavilion** near the entrance serves drinks and **food**, as well as the usual postcards, books and souvenirs. The nearby village of **ÁYIOS IOÁN-NIS**, along the road towards Mátala, has economical **rooms**, including some at *Taverna Ayios Ioannis* (☎28920 42006; ❶), which is also a good place to eat charcoal-grilled *kounélli* (rabbit) and lamb on a leafy terrace.

Ayía Triádha

Some of the finest artworks in the museum at Iráklion came from **Ayía Triádha** (daily: May–Sept 10am–4pm; Oct–April 8.30am–3pm; €3), about a 45-minute walk (or short drive) from Phaestos. No one is quite sure what this site is, but the most common theory has it as some kind of royal summer villa. It's smaller than the palaces but, if anything, even more lavishly appointed and beautifully situated. In any event, it's an attractive place to visit, far less crowded than Phaestos, with a wealth of interesting little details. Look out in particular for the row of **stores** in front of what was apparently a marketplace, although recent thinking tends towards the idea that these were constructed after the villa had declined, possibly in the Mycenaean period. The remains of a **paved road** that probably led down to a harbour on the Gulf of Messará can also be seen running alongside the royal villa. The sea itself looks invitingly close, separated from the base of the hill only by Timbáki airfield (mainly used for motor racing these days), but if you try to drive down there, it's almost impossible to find your way around the unmarked dust tracks. There's a fourteenth-century **chapel** – dedicated to Áyios Yeóryios – at the site, worth visiting in its own right for the remains of ancient frescoes (key available from the ticket office).

Mátala and around

MÁTALA has by far the best-known beach in Iráklion province, widely promoted and included in tours mainly because of the famous caves cut into the cliffs above its beautiful sands. These are believed to be ancient tombs first used by Romans or early Christians, but more recently inhabited by a sizeable hippie community (including some famous names such as Bob Dylan and Joni Mitchell) in the 1960s and 1970s. You'll still meet people who will assure you that this is *the* travellers' beach on Crete, although today in high season the town is full of package tourists and tries hard to present a more respectable image. The caves have long since been cleared and cleaned up and these days are a fenced-off archeological site (April–Sept daily 10am–7pm; free) and locked up every evening.

The years since the early 1980s have seen the arrival of crowds and the development of hotels, restaurants and even a disco to service them; early afternoon, when the tour buses pull in for their swimming stop, sees the beach packed to overflowing. If you're prepared to accept Mátala for what it is – a resort of some size – you'll find the place more than bearable. The town beach is beautiful, and if the crowds get excessive, you can climb over the rocks in about twenty minutes (past more caves, many of which are inhabited through the summer) to another excellent stretch of sand, known locally as "Red Beach". In the evening,

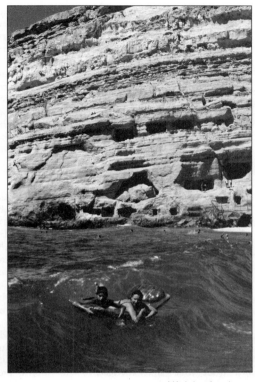

△ Mátala beach and caves

when the day-trippers have gone, there are waterside bars and restaurants looking out over invariably spectacular sunsets. If you are arriving **by car**, park either on the road leading into the town or at the beach car park (€1 per day), on the right as you reach the town proper.

The chief problems with staying in Mátala concern prices and crowds: rooms are relatively expensive and oversubscribed, and food is good but not cheap. If you want **accommodation**, a cluster of places lies near to the *Zafiria* hotel (☏28920 45112, ✉info@zafiria-matala.com; ❸), just beyond the car park turn-off. Here rooms come with a/c but no TV, and there's a pool. For more economical options try looking in the little street to the left just beyond the *Zafiria* signed "Hotels and Rent Rooms". Here you'll find several rooms for rent, such as *Matala View* (☏28920 45114, ⓦwww.matala-apartments.com; ❷), which also rents studios and apartments sleeping two (❸) or up to four (❹). Nearby, the pleasant, modern and good-value *Fantastik* (☏28920 45362, ☏28920 45492; ❶) has airy a/c en-suites with fridge and the equally good and very friendly ⚲ *Hotel Nikos* (☏28920 45375, ⓦwww.kreta-inside.com; ❷) has pleasant a/c rooms off a plant-filled patio. If these are full, then everywhere closer in is likely to be as well, so head back out along the main road where places tend to fill up last, or try the **campsite**, *Camping of Matala* (☏28920 45720), next to the beach above the car park; *Kommos Camping*

(☎28920 45596) is a nicer site, but a few kilometres out of Mátala and reached by heading back towards Pítsidia and turning left along a signed track.

There are places to **eat and drink** all over the main part of town, and it's worth seeking out the *Skala* fish taverna on the south side of the bay for fresh seafood and a great view. Nightlife is confined to a solitary summer **disco**, *Kandari*, plus a couple of music bars on the main square. On the south side of the bay the most popular music bars are the *Marinero*, and *Tommy's Music Bar* above it, plus the nearby *JB Juke Box*. **Internet** access is available inside the stylish *Kafeneio* bar on the main square or at the *Zafiria Café* opposite (and owned by) the hotel of the same name. Impossible to miss are most other facilities, including various stores and a bookshop (with international press) next to *Kafeneio*, currency exchange, car and bike rental, travel agents, post office and a covered market where tourist tat has almost squeezed out the fruit and veg stalls.

Around Mátala: Pitsídhia and Kalamáki

One way to enjoy a bit more peace is to stay at **PITSÍDHIA**, about 5km inland. This has long been a well-used option, so it's not quite as cheap as you might expect, but there are plenty of rooms, lively places to eat and even music bars. If you decide to stay here, the beach at **KALAMÁKI** is an alternative to Mátala. Both beaches are approximately the same distance to walk, though there is a much better chance of a bus or a lift to Mátala. Kalamáki has developed somewhat, with a number of **rooms** – *Psiloritis* (☎28920 45693, ℱ28920 45249; ❷) is a good bet – and a couple of tavernas, but it's still a rather unfinished, soulless little place. The beach stretches for miles, surprisingly wild and windswept, lashed by sometimes dangerously rough surf. At the southern end (more easily reached by a path off the Pitsídhia–Mátala road) lies **Kommos**, once a Minoan port serving Phaestos and now the site of a major archeological excavation. It's not yet open to the public, but you can peer into the fenced-off area to see what's been revealed so far, which is pretty impressive: dwellings, streets, hefty stonework and even the ship sheds where repairs on the Minoan fleet were carried out.

Iráklion's south coast

South of the Messará plain are two more beach resorts, **Kalí Liménes** and **Léndas**, with numerous other little beaches along the coast in between, but nothing spectacular. **Public transport** is very limited indeed; you'll almost always have to travel via Míres (see p.239). If you have your own transport, the roads in these parts are all passable and newly sealed, but most are very slow going; the Kófinas hills, which divide the plain from the coast, are surprisingly precipitous.

Kalí Liménes

While Mátala itself was an important port under the Romans, the chief harbour for Gortys lay on the other side of Cape Líthinon at **KALÍ LIMÉNES**. Nowadays, this is once again a significant port – for oil tankers. This has rather spoilt its chances of becoming a major resort, and there are few proper facilities, but some people like Kalí Liménes: it's certainly off the beaten track and the constant procession of tankers gives you something to look at while beach lounging. There are a couple of places offering **rooms** – the best is the seafront *Taverna Panorama* (☎28920 97517; ❷; April–Nov), which has a decent **taverna** attached. The coastline is broken up by spectacular cliffs and, as long as there hasn't been a recent oil spill, the beaches are reasonably clean and totally empty.

Léndas

LÉNDAS, further east along the coast, is far more popular, with a couple of buses daily from Iráklion and a partly justified reputation for being peaceful (sullied by considerable summer crowds). Many people who arrive think they've come to the wrong place, as at first sight the village looks shabby, the beach is small, rocky and dirty, and the rooms are frequently all booked. A number of visitors leave without ever correcting that initial impression; the attraction of Léndas is not the village at all but the beach on the other (west) side of the headland. Here lies a vast, excellent sandy strand named **Dhytikós** (or Dhiskós) **beach**, part of it usually taken over by nudists, with a number of taverna/bars overlooking it from the roadside. The beach is a couple of kilometres from Léndas, along a rough track; if you're walking, you can save time by cutting across the headland. A considerably more attractive prospect than staying in Léndas itself is **camping** on the beach to the west of the village or, with luck, getting a **room** at one of the few beach tavernas – try ⚓ *Villa Tsapakis* (☏ 28920 95378, ⓦ www .villa-tsapakis.gr; ❷), with sea-view rooms and reductions for longer stays. They will also change money on a credit card here (a useful service in this part of Crete where banks and ATMs are nonexistent) and have their own **taverna**, *Odysseas*, nearby. After you've discovered the beach, even Léndas begins to look more welcoming, and at least it has most of the facilities you'll need, including a couple of minimarkets, both of which will change money, a dual-screen **Internet** café on the main square, and numerous places to **eat and drink**: the outstanding ⚓ *Taverna El Greco* (☏ 28920 95322) with a leafy terrace above the beach on the east side of the village is one of the best restaurants on the whole south coast – their *oktapódhi* (octopus), *kolikythákia* (fried zucchini) or prime Messará beef pepper steak are all recommended.

Once you've come to terms with the place, you can also explore some deserted beaches eastwards, and the scrappy remains of **ancient Lebena** on a hilltop overlooking them. There was an important Asklepion (temple of the god Asklepios) here around some now-diverted warm springs, but only the odd broken column and fragments of mosaic survive in a fenced-off area on the village's northern edge.

East of Iráklion: the package-tour coast

East of Iráklion, the startling pace of **tourist development** in Crete is all too plain to see. The merest hint of a beach is an excuse to build at least one hotel, and these are outnumbered by the concrete shells of resorts-to-be. It's hard to find a room in this monument to the package-tour industry, and it can be expensive if you do. That said, there are one or two highlights amidst the dross, which are well worth a visit. Beyond the teenage-package resort of Mália a fine **Minoan palace** will transport you back three and a half millennia, or, if you're looking for splendid isolation, the twin sea hamlets of **Sísi** and **Mílatos** are refreshingly out of sync with the rest of this coast.

Goúrnes and Goúves

As a general rule, the further east you go, the better things get: when the road detours all too briefly inland, the more alluring Crete of olive groves and stark mountains asserts itself. You certainly won't see much of it at **GOÚRNES**, where an abandoned former US Air Force base still dominates much of the coastline, awaiting a plan for its redevelopment, or at nearby Káto Goúves, where there's a **campsite**, *Camping Creta* (☎28970 41400), sharing a boundary with the former base. From here, however, you can head inland to the old village of **GOÚVES**, a refreshing contrast, and just beyond to the **Skotinó cave**, one of the largest and most spectacular on the island (about an hour's walk from the coast; open all hours; free).

Hersónissos (Límin Hersoníssou)

Heading east from Goúves you'll pass the turn-off for the new E75 Hersónissos bypass (avoiding the beach resort's bottleneck), which cuts inland to rejoin the coast road just before Stalídha (see opposite). Shortly beyond this junction, there's the turning for the direct route up to the Lasíthi Plateau. Carry straight on, though, and you'll roll into the first of the really big resorts, **HERSÓNIS-SOS** or, more correctly, Límin Hersoníssou; Hersónissos is the village in the hills just behind, also overrun by tourists.

Hersónissos was once just a small fishing village; today it's the most popular of Crete's package resorts. If what you want is plenty of video-bars, tavernas, restaurants and Eurodisco nightlife, then this is the place to come. The resort has numerous small patches of sand beach between rocky outcrops, but a shortage of places to stay in peak season.

The focal main street, two-kilometre-long Odhós Elefthériou Venizélou, is a seemingly endless ribbon of bars, travel agents, tacky jewellery and beachwear shops, amusement arcades and – during the daytime at least – nose-to-tail traffic jams. North of here, along the modern seafront, a solid line of restaurants and bars is broken only by the occasional souvenir shop; in their midst you'll find a small pyramidal Roman **fountain** with broken mosaics of fishing scenes, the only real relic of the ancient town of Chersonesos. Around the headland above the harbour and in odd places along the seafront, you can see remains of Roman harbour installations, mostly submerged.

Beach and clubs excepted, the distractions of Hersónissos comprise **Lychnostatis Open-Air Museum** (Mon–Fri & Sun 9.30am–2pm; €4), a surprisingly rewarding "museum" of traditional Crete, on the coast at the eastern edge of the town; a small aquarium, **Aqua World** (April–Oct daily 10am–6pm; €5), just off the main road at the west end of town, up the road almost opposite the *Vibe* style bar. To cool down, there's the watersports paradise **Star Beach Water Park** (daily: April & May 10am–6pm; June–Sept 10am–7pm; free entry) near the beach at the eastern end of the resort or, a few kilometres inland, the competing and more elaborate **Aqua Splash Water Park** (€15 full day, €12.50 half day).

A short distance inland are the three **hill villages** of Koutoulafári, Piskopianó and "old" Hersónissos, which all have a good selection of tavernas, and are worth searching out for accommodation.

Practicalities

Hersónissos is well provided with all the back-up **services** you need to make a holiday go smoothly. Banks, bike and car rental and post office are all on or just off the main drag, Elefthériou Venizélou, as are the taxi ranks. There are a number of **Internet** cafés: *Cafe Neon*, Elefthériou Venizélou 40, and the central *Internet Cafe*, Elefthériou Venizélou 10, alongside the church, both have plenty of screens. **Buses** running east and west leave from the main bus stop on Venizélou every thirty minutes.

Finding somewhere to stay here can verge on the impossible in July and August. Much of the **accommodation** is allocated to package-tour operators and what remains for casual visitors is among the priciest on the island. To check for general availability of accommodation, the quickest and best option is to enquire at one of the many travel agencies along Venizélou such as KTEL Tours next to the bus stop and opposite the petrol station in the centre of town. The town's most reasonably priced central options include *Zorba's Hotel*, Beach Road (☎28970 22134, ⓦwww.hersonissos.com/zorbas; ❸), and *Selena*, Maragáki 13 (☎ & ⓕ28970 25180; ❷), near the sea-front action which can be noisy at night. One place to try on the western edge as you enter the town is *Hotel Ilios* (☎28970 22500, ⓕ28970 22582; ❹), just back from the main road, which has a rooftop pool. There are two good **campsites**: one at the eastern end of town, *Caravan Camping* (☎28970 24718), which also has several reed-roofed bungalows, and *Camping Hersonissos* (☎28970 22902), just to the west of town.

Despite the vast number of **eating places**, there are few in Hersónissos worth recommending, and the tavernas down on the harbourfront should be avoided. One of the few Greek tavernas that stands out is *Kavouri* along Arhéou Theátrou, but it's fairly expensive; a cheaper in-town alternative for some delicious and inexpensive Cretan cooking is ⵊ *Taverna Creta Giannis*, Kaniadhakí 4, just off the south side of Venizélou slightly east of the church. Nearby, and also definitely worth a try, is ⵊ *Passage to India*, an authentic and extremely good Indian restaurant; it lies on Petrákis, another side street just off the main street near the church. Heading out of town on the Piskopianó road, near the junction to Koutoulafári, the friendly *Fegari* taverna also serves good Greek food at reasonable prices. Sitting at your table overlooking the street below you can view the steady trek of clubbers heading down the hill to the bars and night-clubs of Hersónissos. The hill villages have the greatest selection of tavernas, particularly Koutoulafári, where you can have a relaxed evening amongst the narrow streets and small platíes.

Hersónissos is renowned for its **nightlife**, and there's certainly no shortage of it. A night's partying kicks off around the **bars** ringing the harbour, which is packed with promenaders and the overspill from countless noisy music bars from 10pm through to the early hours. After midnight, the larger **disco-clubs** and **pubs** in the streets leading up to and along Elefthériou Venizélou are the places to be seen. Currently the most popular music clubs are *Aria* (open July–Aug only), the island's largest, on the main road at the west end of town, *Cinema*, also on Venizélou, and *Camelot*, *New York* and *Status* (which opens at 4.30am), all near the harbour. Close to *Aria* on Venizélou, the *Hard Rock Café* has transmuted into *Vibe*, with a terrace where clubbers chill out between venues. If you fancy a quiet drink then you've come to the wrong resort, but you could try *Kahluai Beach Cocktail Bar* or *Haris Ouzo & Raki Place* (beneath the *Hotel Virginia*). There is an open-air **cinema** showing original-version films at the *Creta Maris* hotel at the west end of the town and close to the beach.

Stalídha

STALÍDHA is a Cinderella town, sandwiched in between its two louder, brasher and some would say uglier sisters, Mália and Hersónissos, but it is neither quiet nor undeveloped. This rapidly expanding beach resort, with more than sixty tavernas and bars and a few discos, can offer the best of both worlds, with a friendlier and more relaxed setting, a better beach (and usual array of watersports) and very easy access to its two livelier neighbours. The town essentially consists of a single, relatively traffic-free street, which rings the seafront for more than 2km, before the apartment blocks briefly become fewer and further between, until the mass development of Mália begins.

Finding a place to stay can be difficult, since **accommodation** is almost entirely in studio and apartment blocks which are booked by package companies in high season. Out of season, however, you may well be able to negotiate a very reasonable price for a studio apartment complete with swimming pool; ask in the central travel agencies first, as they will know what is available, and expect to pay around ❷–❸ for two. Finding somewhere to **eat** is less difficult as there are plenty of rather ordinary tavernas, the best and most authentic being *Maria's*, the *Hellas Taverna* and the more upmarket *Blue Sea Restaurant*, all at the western end of the seafront.

Stalídha is completely overshadowed by its neighbours when it comes to **nightlife**, though you can dance at *Rhythm*, on the beach; the music bars *Sea Wolf Cocktail Bar* and *Akti Bar* are near each other along the beach nearby.

Mália

Three kilometres east of Stalídha and similar to the other resorts along this stretch of coast, much of **MÁLIA** is carved up by the package industry, so in peak season finding a place to stay is not always easy. The town's focus is a T-junction (where the **bus** drops you) and from where the beach road – a kilometre-long strip lined with bars, clubs, games arcades, tavernas and souvenir shops – heads north to the sea and beaches. South of this junction the older village presents a slightly saner image of what Mália used to be, but even here rampant commercialism is making inroads.

Practicalities

The best **accommodation** options, especially if you want any sleep, are among the numerous **rooms** and **pensions** signposted in the old town, such as *Esperia* (☎28970 31086; ❹), up a side road slightly east of the T-junction. Backtracking from the junction, along the main Iráklion road, there are a number of reasonably priced **pensions** on the left and right, including *Hibiscus* (☎28970 31313, ⓕ28970 32042; ❸), which has rooms and studios with kitchenette and fridge around a pool in a garden behind. If you really want to be in the centre of things, try *Kostas* (☎28970 31101; ❷), a family-run pension incongruously located behind the mini-golf at the end of the beach road. Otherwise, on arrival visit one of the travel companies along the main road – such as the reliable SK-Travel, Venizélou 200 (☎28970 31481) – to enquire about accommodation availability. All the other things you're likely to need – **banks** with ATMs, **post office** and food shops – are strung out along the main street near the junction, but the town's best **Internet** access, *Internet Cafe*, is bang in the middle of the beach road madness (about a third of the way down on the right).

Eating in Mália is unlikely to be a problem as **restaurants** jostle for your custom at every step, especially along the beach road. None is particularly good here, and a few are diabolical. The best places for a meal are around Platía Ayíou Dhimitríou, a pleasant square beside the church in the centre of the old village to the south of the main road. Here, you could try *Kalimera* or *Petros*, or the pleasant *Kalesma* with a delightful terrace, perhaps after an aperitif at *Bar Yiannis* just north of the church or *Ouzeri Elizabeth* alongside it, where they serve local wine from the barrel. A little harder to find, and to the west of the square, *Apolafsi* is a good-quality small family taverna which is slightly less pricey than the others.

The beach road comes into its own at night, when the profusion of **bars**, **discos** and **clubs** erupts into a pulsating cacophony. The aptly named *Zoo* is one of the most frenetic, and once past midnight the internal walls part to reveal an even larger dance area. Other popular venues (many British-owned and -run) along the strip include *Cloud Nine*, *Malibu*, *Zig-Zag*, *Apollo* and *Camelot Castle*. There is also a clutch of "English pubs" with names like *Newcastle* and *Brit's Bar*. Unfortunately, a good night's clubbing is frequently spoilt by groups of drunken youths pouring out of these places and getting into brawls. At one point the situation got so bad that tour operators threatened to pull out of the resort if action wasn't taken to deal with the hooligans – all rather ironic as it was they who were shipping them in by the plane-load on cut-price packages. Recent years have seen a police clampdown on such activities as drinking on the street, and the situation has improved considerably.

The Palace of Malia

Much less imposing than either Knossos or Phaestos, the **Palace of Malia** (daily 8.30am–3pm; €4), 2km east of Mália town, in some ways surpasses both. For a start, it's a great deal emptier and you can wander among the remains in relative peace. While no reconstruction has been attempted, the palace was never reoccupied after its second destruction in the fifteenth century BC, so the ground plan is virtually intact. It's much easier to comprehend than Knossos and, if you've seen the reconstructions there, it's easy to envisage this seaside palace in its days of glory. There's a real feeling of an ancient civilization with a taste for the good life, basking on the rich agricultural plain between the Lasíthi mountains and the sea.

From this site came the famous **gold pendant** of two bees (which can be seen in the Iráklion Archeological Museum or on any postcard stand), allegedly part of a hoard that was plundered and whose other treasures can now be found in the British Museum in London. The beautiful leopard-head axe, also in the museum at Iráklion, was another of the treasures found here. At the site, look out for the strange indented stone in the central court (which probably held ritual offerings), for the remains of ceremonial stairways and for the giant *pithoi*, which stand like sentinels around the palace. To the north and west of the main site, archeological digs are still going on as the **large town** which surrounded the palace comes slowly to light, and part of this can now be viewed via an overhead walkway.

Any passing **bus** should stop at the site, or you could even rent a **bike** for a couple of hours as it's a pleasant, flat ride from Mália town. Leaving the archeological zone and turning immediately right, you can follow the road down to a lovely stretch of clean and relatively peaceful **beach**, backed by fields, scrubland and a single makeshift taverna, which serves good fresh fish. From here you can walk back along the shore to Mália or take a bus (every 30min in either direction) from the stop on the main road.

Sísi and Mílatos

Head **east** from the Palace of Malia, and it's not long before the road leaves the coast, climbing across the hills towards Áyios Nikólaos. If you want to escape the frenetic pace of all that has gone before, try continuing to Sísi or Mílatos. These little shore villages are bypassed by the main road as it cuts inland, and are still very much in the early stages of tourist development. The larger of the two, **SÍSI**, is charmingly situated around a small harbour overlooked by balcony bars and more tavernas. The opening of the resort's first disco bar (*Faros*) and

PALACE OF MALIA

0   25 m

the large holiday complex (*Kalimera Krita*), a couple of kilometres to the east, are a sure sign that more development is on its way; there's even a **post office**, confirming the resort status. **Accommodation** is mainly in studios and apartments; it's best to ask in the travel agencies and bars for details of availability. There's also a small pension, *Elena* ❶), just behind the harbour, and a shady **campsite** with pool and taverna (☎28410 71247) signposted on the way in. Among a cluster of seafront **tavernas** all specializing in freshly caught fish, the *Fisherman's Place* is worth a try.

In quieter **MÍLATOS**, rooms can be found in the old village, 2km inland, but the seaside settlement – despite a rather pebbly beach – is more desirable. A number of the seafront tavernas let out rooms and, outside the peak season when there's little chance of a bed, the friendly ⌁ *Rooms Taverna Sokrates* (☎28410 81375;❷) is worth a try and does decent **food**, especially fish, netted by the village boats. Despite their pebbly main **beaches**, the resorts make for a refreshing change of pace, and there are some fine, deep aprons of sand in the rocky coves beyond the resort centres.

West of Iráklion: around Psilorítis

Most people heading west from Iráklion speed straight out on the **E75 coastal highway**, nonstop to Réthymnon. If you're in a hurry this is not such a bad plan; the road is fast and spectacular, hacked into the sides of mountains which for the most part drop straight to the sea, though there are no more than a couple of places where you might consider stopping. By contrast, the old roads inland are agonizingly slow, but they do pass through a whole string of **attractive villages** beneath the heights of the Psilorítis range. From here you can set out to explore the **mountains** and even walk across them to emerge in villages with views of the south coast.

The coastal route towards Réthymnon

Leaving the city, the **new highway** runs behind a stretch of highly developed coast, where the hotels compete for shore space with a cement works and power station. As soon as you reach the mountains, though, all this is left behind and there's only the clash of rock and sea to contemplate. As you start to climb, look out for **Paleókastro**, hovering beside a bridge which carries the road over a small cove; the castle is so weathered as to be almost invisible against the brownish face of the cliff.

Ayía Pelayía and Fódhele

Some 3km below the highway, as it rounds the first point, lies the resort of **AYÍA PELAYÍA**. It looks extremely attractive from above but, once there, and especially in July and August, you're likely to find the narrow, taverna-lined beach packed to full capacity. This is not somewhere to roll up in high season without reserved **accommodation**, although in quieter times *Zorba's Apartments* (☎ & ℉28102 56072, ✉zorbas@freemail.gr; ❹), along the nameless main street behind the beach, or, on the road above it, the excellent-value ✻ *Danai Rooms* (☎28102 85936; ❷), with air-conditioned, en-suite rooms with kitchenette and fridge, should have space. Opposite *Zorba's Apartments*, the Pangosmio travel agency (☎28108 11402, ℉28108 11424) may be able to come up with something, even at the last minute in high season. Out of season you might find a real bargain apartment and, despite the high-season crowds, the resort maintains a dignity long since lost in Mália and Hersónissos, and even a certain exclusivity; a couple of Crete's most luxurious hotels, including the enormous *Peninsula* (☎28108 11313, ⓦwww.peninsula.gr; ❼), nestle on the headlands just beyond the main town beach. There are plenty of **minimarkets** for buying picnic food, and **Internet** access is available at *Netcafé Atlas*, next door to *Zorba's Apartments*.

Not far beyond Ayía Pelayía, there's a turning inland to the village of **FÓDHELE**, allegedly El Greco's birthplace. A plaque from the University of Valladolid (in Spain) acknowledges the claim and, true or not, the community has built a small tourist industry on that basis. There are a number of craft shops and some pleasant tavernas where you can sit outside along the river. A peaceful one-kilometre walk (or drive) takes you to the spuriously titled **El Greco's House** (May–Oct Tues–Sun 9am–5pm; €1.50), exhibiting a few reprints of his works and not much more, and the more worthwhile and picturesque fourteenth-century Byzantine **church of the Panayía** (Tues–Sun 9am–3.30pm; free) with frescoes, opposite. None of this amounts to very much but it is a pleasant, relatively unspoilt village if you simply want to sit in peace for a while. A couple of **buses** a day run here from Iráklion, and there's the odd tour; if you arrive on a direct bus, the walk back down to the highway (about 3km), where you can flag down a passing service, is not too strenuous.

Balí and Pánormos

BALÍ, on the coast approximately halfway between Iráklion and Réthymnon, also used to be tranquil and undeveloped and, by the standards of the north coast, it still is in many ways. The village is built around a trio of small coves, some 2km from the highway (a hot walk from the bus), and is similar to Ayía Pelayía except that the beaches are not quite as good and there are no big hotels, just an ever-growing proliferation of studios, apartment buildings, rooms for rent and a number of smaller hotels. You'll have plenty of company here and it has to be said that Balí has become a package resort too popular for its own good. The third and best beach, known as "Paradise", no longer really deserves the name; it's a beautiful place to splash about, surrounded by mountains rising straight from the sea, but there's rarely a spare inch on the sand in high season.

Continuing along the coast, the last stop before you emerge on the flat stretch leading to Réthymnon is at **PÁNORMOS**. This makes a good stopover if you're in search of somewhere more peaceful and authentic. The small sandy beach can get crowded when boats bring day-trippers from Réthymnon, but most of the time the attractive village remains relatively unspoilt, and succeeds in clinging to its Cretan identity. There are several decent **tavernas** – try *Taverna Panorama* in the heart of the village or *Sofoklís* near the harbour – and **rooms** places, one large hotel and the very comfortable *Pension Lucy* (☎28340 51328, ❸), which has also sprung a seafront offshoot with balcony studio rooms and apartments.

Inland towards Mount Psilorítis

Of the **inland routes**, the old main road (via Márathos and Dhamásta) is not the most interesting. This, too, was something of a bypass in its day and there are few places of any size or appeal, though it's a very scenic drive. If you want to dawdle, you're better off on the road which cuts up to **Týlissos** and then goes via **Anóyia**. It's a pleasant ride through fertile valleys filled with olive groves and vineyards, a district (the Malevísi) renowned from Venetian times for the strong, sweet Malmsey wine.

Týlissos and Anóyia

TÝLISSOS has a significant archeological site (daily 8.30am–3pm; €2) where three Minoan houses were excavated; unfortunately, its reputation is based more on what was found here (many pieces in the Iráklion Archeological Museum) and on its significance for archeologists than on anything which remains to be seen. Still, it's worth a look, if you're passing, for a glimpse of Minoan life away from the big palaces, and for the tranquillity of the pine-shaded remains.

ANÓYIA is a much more tempting place to stay, especially if the summer heat is becoming oppressive. Spilling prettily down a hillside close below the highest peaks of the mountains, it looks traditional, but closer inspection shows that most of the buildings are actually concrete; the village was destroyed during World War II and the local men rounded up and shot – one of the German reprisals for the abduction of General Kreipe by the Cretan resistance. The town has a reputation as a **handicrafts** centre (especially for woven and woollen goods), skills acquired both through bitter necessity after most of the men had been killed, and in a conscious attempt to revive the town. At any rate it worked, for the place is thriving today – thanks, it seems, to a buoyant agricultural sector made rich by stockbreeding, and the number of elderly widows keen to subject any visitor to their terrifyingly aggressive sales techniques.

Quite a few people pass through Anóyia during the day, but not many of them **stay**, even though there are some good *pensions* and rented rooms in the upper half of the town, including the flower-bedecked *Rooms Aris* (℡28340 31460, Ⓕ28430 31058; ❷) and the nearby *Aristea* (℡28340 31459; B&B; ❷), which has an ebullient female proprietor, en-suite rooms with spectacular views and rates that include breakfast.

The town has a very different, more traditional ambience at night, and the only problem is likely to be finding a **place to eat**: although there are plenty of snack-bars and so-called tavernas, most have extremely basic menus, more or less limited to spit-barbecued lamb, which is the tasty local speciality served up by the grill places on the lower square. If you can face it, a steep hike to the top of the village will bring you to *Taverna Skalomata* offering well-prepared taverna standards, some pretty good barbecued lamb, plus a fine view.

Mount Psilorítis and its caves

Heading for the mountains, a smooth road ascends the 21km from Anóyia to an altitude of 1400m on the **Nídha plateau** at the base of Mount Psilorítis. Here, the *Taverna Nida* (℡28340 31141; April–Sept daily; Oct–May Sat & Sun only) serves up hearty mountain dishes featuring lamb, pork and chicken, and has a couple of simple **rooms** (❶), which makes it a good base for hikes in the surrounding mountains. A short path leads from the taverna to the celebrated **Idean cave** (Idhéon Ándhron), a rival of that on Mount Dhíkti (see overleaf) for the title of Zeus's birthplace, and certainly associated from the earliest of times with the cult of Zeus. The remnants of a major archeological dig carried out inside – including a miniature railway used by archeologists to remove tonnes of rock and rubble – still litter the site, giving the place a rather unattractive prospect. When you enter the cave down concrete steps into the depths, it turns out to be a rather shallow affair, devoid even of natural wonders, with little to see.

The taverna also marks the start of the way to the top of **Mount Psilorítis** (2456m), Crete's highest mountain, a climb that for experienced, properly shod hikers is not at all arduous. The route (now forming a stretch of the E4 Pan-European footpath) is well marked with the usual red dots and paint splashes, and it should be a six- to seven-hour return journey to the **chapel of Tímios Stavrós** ("Holy Cross") at the summit, although in spring, thick snow may slow you down.

If you're prepared to camp on the plateau (it's very cold, but there's plenty of available water) or find rooms at the taverna, you could continue on foot next day down to the southern slopes of the range. It's a beautiful hike and also relatively easy, four hours or so down a fairly clear path to **Vorízia** where there is no food or accommodation, although **KAMÁRES**, 4km west, has both: for **rooms**, the very cheap, very basic and unsigned (you'll need to ask for it) *Hotel Psilorítis* (℡28920 43290; ❶) should have a bed, and the best **place to eat** is the *Taverna Bournelis* at the village's western end. If you're still interested in caves, there's a more rewarding one above Kamáres, a climb of some five hours on a good but aggressively steep path; if you're coming over from Nídha, the cave actually makes a rather shorter detour off the main traverse path. The start of the route is just to the left of the *Taverna Bournelis* and the proprietors here can advise on the ascent (in Greek and German only). There is at least one daily **bus** from here down to Míres and alternative (more difficult) routes to the peak of Psilorítis if you want to approach from this direction.

Eastern Crete

Eastern Crete is dominated by **Áyios Nikólaos**, and while it is a highly developed resort, by no means all of the east is like this. Far fewer people venture beyond the road south to **Ierápetra** and into the eastern isthmus, where only **Sitía** and the famous beach at **Váï** ever see anything approaching a crowd. Inland, too, there's interest, especially on the extraordinary **Lasíthi Plateau**, which is worth a night's stay if only to observe its abidingly rural life.

Inland to the Lasíthi Plateau

Leaving the palace at Malia, the highway cuts inland towards **NEÁPOLI**, soon beginning a spectacular climb into the mountains. Set in a high valley, Neápoli is a market town little touched by tourism. Just off a leafy main square there's an excellent **hotel**, *Neapolis* (☎28410 33967, ⓦ www.neapolis-hotel.gr; ❸), with a/c rooms, some with fine views. On the main square there's a superb little **folk museum** (Mon 9am–2pm, Wed–Sun 9.30am–4.30pm; €1.50) displaying some fascinating photos, utensils and farming equipment from Neápoli's past as well as reconstructions of a bar, schoolroom, cobbler's workshop and domestic kitchen from a bygone age. On the square – and 50m from the museum entrance – *Taverna Yeúseis* is a good place for **food** and has a pleasant shady terrace. Beyond the town, it's about twenty minutes before the bus suddenly emerges high above the Gulf of Mirabéllo and Áyios Nikólaos, the island's biggest resort. If you're stopping, Neápoli also marks the second point of access to the **Lasíthi Plateau**.

Scores of bus tours drive up here daily to view the "thousands of white-cloth-sailed windmills" which irrigate the high plain ringed by mountains, and most groups will be disappointed. There are very few working windmills left, and these operate only for limited periods (mainly in June), although most roadside tavernas seem to have adopted many of those made redundant as marketing features. The drive alone is worthwhile, however, and the plain is a fine example of rural Crete at work, every inch devoted to the cultivation of potatoes, apples, pears, figs, olives and a host of other crops; stay in one of the villages for a night or two and you'll see real life return as the tourists leave. There are plenty of easy rambles around the villages as well, through orchards and past the rusting remains of derelict windmills.

You'll find **rooms** in the main village of **TZERMIÁDHO**, where the *Hotel Kourites* (☎28440 22194; ❸) is to be found on the eastern edge, in **ÁYIOS YEÓRYIOS** – where there's a **folk museum**, and the economical and friendly *Hotel Dias* (☎28440 31207; ❶) – and **PSYKHRÓ**, where the *Hotel Zeus* (☎28440 31284; ❷) lies close to the Dhiktean cave.

The Dhiktean cave

Psykhró is the most visited village on the plateau, as it's the base for visiting Lasíthi's other chief attraction: the birthplace of Zeus, the **Dhiktean cave** (daily 8am–7pm; €4; ask for the free information leaflet on the cave). In legend, Zeus's father, the Titan Kronos, was warned that he would be overthrown by a son, and accordingly ate all his offspring; however, when Rhea gave birth to

Zeus in the cave, she fed Kronos a stone and left the child concealed, protected by the Kouretes, who beat their shields outside to disguise his cries. The rest, as they say, is history (or at least myth). There's an obvious path running up to the cave from Psykhró, near the start of which (beyond the car park) the mule handlers will attempt to persuade you the ascent is better done on one of their steeds (costing a hefty €10 one way). In reality, it's hardly a particularly long or dauntingly steep hike to the cave entrance.

The cave has been made more "visitor friendly" in recent years, with the introduction of concrete steps in place of slippery stones, and electric lighting instead of flashlamps and candles. Inevitably some of the magic and mystery has been lost, and the guides, who used to make the visit much more interesting with their hilarious and preposterous tales, have now been banned, presumably in the interests of accuracy and decorum. Thus you will now have to pick out for yourself the stalactites and stalagmites formed in the image of the breasts of Rhea where the infant Zeus was suckled, as well as the baby Zeus himself – a feat verging on the impossible for someone lacking a Cretan imagination.

One of the cave guardians, Petros Zarvakis, is also a wildlife expert and leads **guided wild-flower and bird-spotting hikes** (April–Sept) into the mountains surrounding the plain, and also to the summit of Mount Dhíkti; if he is not on duty at the cave entrance or at the taverna in the car park, he can be contacted on ☎28440 31600 or 694 56 16 074. **Buses** run around the plateau to Psykhró direct from Iráklion and from Áyios Nikólaos via Neápoli. Both roads offer spectacular views, coiling through a succession of passes guarded by lines of ruined windmills.

Áyios Nikólaos and around

ÁYIOS NIKÓLAOS ("Ag Nik" to the majority of its British visitors) is set around a supposedly bottomless salt lake, now connected to the sea to form an

△ Áyios Nikólaos

inner harbour. It is supremely picturesque and has some style and charm, which it exploits to the full. There are no sights as such, but the excellent archeological museum (Tues–Sun 8.30am–3pm; €3) and an interesting folk museum (Mon–Fri & Sun 10am–4pm; €3) are both worth seeking out. The lake and port are surrounded by restaurants and bars, which charge above the odds, and whilst the resort is still very popular, some tourists are distinctly surprised to find themselves in a place with no decent beach at all.

There are swimming opportunities further north, however, where the pleasant low-key resort of **Eloúnda** is the gateway to the mysterious islet of **Spinalónga**, and some great backcountry inland – perfect to explore on a scooter. Inland from Áyios Nikólaos, **Kritsá** with its famous frescoed church and textile sellers is a tour-bus haven, but just a couple of kilometres away, the imposing ruins of **ancient Lato** are usually deserted.

ÁYIOS NIKÓLAOS

ACCOMMODATION

Angelos	D
Atlantis	I
Coral	A
Hotel Eva	F
Marilena	B
Mediterranean	E
Perla	C
Rooms Mary	G
Sgouros	H

RESTAURANTS & CAFÉS

Auoas	1
Café du Lac	7
Café/Restaurant Migomis	4
Hrisofillís	9
I Pita Tou Riga	2
Itanos	10
La Strada	8
Ofou To Lo	11
Pelagos	3
Peripou	5
Sarri's	12
Twins	6

Áyios Nikólaos practicalities

The **tourist office** (daily: July–Aug 8am–10pm; Sept–June 8am–9.30pm; ☎28410 22357), situated between the lake and the port, is one of the best on the island for information about accommodation. The **bus station** is situated to the northwest end of town near the archeological museum. You'll find the greatest concentration of **stores** and **travel agents** on the hill between the bridge and Platía Venizélou (along the streets 25-Martíou, Koundoúrou and pedestrianized 28-Oktovríou), and the main **ferry agent**, Plora Travel (☎28410 25868), on the corner of 28-Oktovríou and K. Sfakianáki. The **post office** (Mon–Sat 7.30am–2pm) is halfway up 28-Oktovríou on the right. To **hire a motorbike**, **scooter** or **mountain bike** try the reliable Mike Manolis (☎28410 24940), who has a pitch along Modhátsou near the junction with K. Sfakianáki. Good **car-rental** deals are available at Club Cars, 28-Oktovríou 24 (☎28410 25868), near the post office. Various **boat trips** to points around the gulf (such as Spinalónga and Eloúnda; about €12–15 depending on company) leave from the west side of the harbour. **Internet** access is available at *Peripou*, 28-Oktovríou 25 (daily 9.30am–2am), and *Café du Lac* at no. 17 on the same street.

Accommodation

Since many of the package companies have pulled out in recent years the town is no longer jammed solid as it once was, though in the peak season you won't have so much choice. One thing in your favour is that there are literally thousands of **rooms**, scattered all around town. The tourist office normally has a couple of boards with cards and brochures about hotels and rooms, including their prices. If the prices seem very reasonable it is because many are for the low season. The nearest **campsite** is *Gournia Moon*, 17km away (see p.259).

Angelos Aktí S. Koundoúrou 16 ☎28410 23501, ☏28410 25692. Welcoming small hotel offering excellent a/c balconied rooms with TV and fine views over the Gulf. ❸

Atlantis Aktí Atlantidhos 15, near the town beach ☎28410 28964, ✉p.mixalis@mailcity.com. Nothing special, but handy enough for the town beach, offering a/c en-suite balcony rooms with fridge. Also has a snack-bar below serving cheap breakfasts. ❷

Coral Aktí S. Koundoúrou ☎28410 28363, ⊕www.hermes-hotels.gr. One of Áyios Nikólaos's leading in-town hotels offering a/c rooms with sea view, fridge, balcony and satellite TV, plus a rooftop pool and bar. When things are slack, prices can fall by up to 25 percent. In summer you may need to ask for the room-only price as they will quote you half-board. B&B ❻

Hotel Eva Stratigoú Kóraka 20 ☎28410 22587. Decent en-suite a/c rooms with TV in a misnamed *pension* close to the centre. ❷

Marilena Érythrou Stavroú 14 ☎28410 22681, ☏28410 24218. Not the bargain it once was, but it's still a pleasant place to stay; some rooms with sea view and balcony. ❹

Mediterranean S. Dhávaki 27 ☎28410 23611. Clean, economical en-suite rooms with fridges and fans, and close to the lake. ❷

Rooms Mary Evans 13, near the Kitroplatía ☎28410 24384. Very friendly place with a/c (€5 extra) en-suite balcony rooms (some with sea view); access to fridge and use of kitchen. Also has some apartments nearby costing only slightly more. ❶

Perla Salaminos 4, ☎28410 23379. Decent budget option close to the sea, on a hill to the north of the harbour. En-suite rooms with fans and fridge, and front rooms have sea-view balconies. ❶

Sgouros Kitroplatía ☎28410-28931, ⊕www.sgourosgrouphotels.com. Good-value modern hotel with a/c balcony rooms overlooking one of the town's beaches, and close to plenty of tavernas. ❷

Eating

At least when it comes to eating there's no chance of missing out, even if some of the prices are fancier than the restaurants. There are tourist-oriented

tavernas all around the lake and harbour and little to choose between them, apart from the different perspectives you get on the passing fashion show. Have a drink here perhaps, or a mid-morning coffee, and choose somewhere else to eat. The places around the Kitroplatía are generally fairer value, but again you are paying for the location.

Auoas Paleológou 44. This taverna serves good, traditional Cretan dishes in a plant-covered trellised courtyard, where food and wine prices are among the lowest in town.

Hrisofíllis Aktí Themistokléous. Attractive and stylish new eatery with reasonably priced fish, meat and veggie *mezédhes* served on a pleasant terrace fronting the east side of the Kitroplatía beach.

Itanos Kýprou 1, off the east side of Platía Venizélou. Popular with locals, this taverna serves Cretan food and wine and has a terrace across the road.

Café/Restaurant Migomis Nikoláou Plastíra 22 (☎ 28410 24353). Pleasant café high above the bottomless lake with a stunning view. Perfect (if pricey) place for breakfast, afternoon or evening drinks. Their next-door restaurant enjoys the same vista and is pricier than the norm, but perhaps worth it if you've booked a frontline table to feast on that view.

Ofou To Lo Kitroplatía. Best of the moderately priced places on the seafront here: the food is consistently good.

Pelagos Stratigoú Kóraka, just back off the lake behind the tourist office ☎ 28410 25737. A stylish fish taverna with the best garden terrace in town, serving excellent food reflected in the prices.

I Pita Tou Riga Paleológou 24, close to the lake. Excellent Lilliputian snack-bar/restaurant serving imaginative fare – salads, filled pitta breads and some Asian dishes; has a small terrace up steps across the road.

Sarri's Kýprou 15. Great little economical neighbourhood café-diner especially good for breakfast fare and *souvláki*, all served on a leafy terrace.

La Strada Nikoláou Plastíra 5. Authentic Italian fare in swish surroundings serving up good-value pizza and pasta (meat dishes are pricier), should you fancy a change of cuisine.

Twins Fronting the harbour. Handy pizzeria, fast-food outlet and coffee bar, open all hours. Their "small" pizzas measure a giant 40cm in diameter.

Drinking and nightlife

After you've eaten you can get into the one thing which Áyios Nikólaos undeniably does well: **bars and nightlife**. Not that you really need a guide to this – the bars are hard to avoid, and you can just follow the crowds to the most popular places centred around the harbour and 25-Martíou. For a more relaxed drink you could try *Hotel Alexandros* on Paleológou (behind the tourist office), with a rooftop cocktail bar overlooking the lake, which after dark metamorphoses into a 1960s-to-1980s period music bar. A similar pace rules at *Zygos* on the north side of the lake, which serves low-priced cocktails and ices until the small hours. One curiosity worth a look in the harbour itself is *Armida* (April–Oct), a bar inside a beautifully restored century-old wooden trading vessel, serving cocktails and simple *mezédhes*.

Quiet drinking, however, is not what it's all about in the **disco-bars**. *Allou* on the east side of the harbour is the only genuine full-blown dance club, while the nearby *Rule Club* (above the *Creta Café*) doesn't hit its stride until the small hours when the pubs and restaurants close. There are raucous music bars to try at the bottom of 25-Martíou ("Soho Street") where it heads up the hill – *Rififi*, *Royale*, *Oxygen*, *Cellar* and *Cube Club* all get going after sunset, while around the corner on M. Sfakianáki *Santa Maria* is a popular place with locals. Across the harbour *Aquarius* and *Sportz Bar* both get lively, while *Sorrento* is another "golden-oldies" music bar frequented by a north-European crowd.

The coast north of Áyios Nikólaos

North of Áyios Nikólaos, the swankier hotels are strung out along the coast road, with upmarket restaurants, discos and cocktail bars scattered between them. **ELOÚNDA**, a resort on a more acceptable scale, is about 8km out along this road. **Buses** run regularly, but if you feel like renting a **scooter** it's a spectacular ride, with impeccable views over a gulf dotted with islands and moored supertankers. Ask at the bookshop near the post office, on the central square facing the sea, about the attractive *Milos* and *Delfinia* **rooms**, studios and apartments (☎28410 41641, ⓦwww.pediaditis.gr; ❷–❹), which come with sea views and, at the *Milos*, a pool. You could also try the friendly *Pension Oasis* (☎28410 41076, ⓦwww.pensionoasis.gr; ❸), which has en-suite rooms with kitchenette and is just off the square, behind the church. There are quite a few similar places along the same road, or ask at one of the many travel agents around the main square for help finding a room or apartment; try the friendly Olous Travel (☎28410 41324, ⓕ28410 41132), which also gives out **information** and changes money and travellers' cheques. For **eating**, *Britomares*, in a plum spot in the centre of the harbour, the nearby *Poulis* and the even pricier ultra-chic *Ferryman* (tellingly with a menu in English only) are the town's best tavernas, but more economical fish and *mezédhes* are to be had at the simple *Ouzeri Maritsa* below the church tower at the north end of the square. **Nightlife** tends to be generally low-key, and centres around café terraces and cocktail bars. The *Hellas* café, on a backroad behind the beach, has live Greek music at weekends.

Just before the centre of the village, a road (signposted) leads downhill to a natural causeway leading to the ancient "sunken city" of **Olous**. Here you'll find restored windmills, a short length of canal, Venetian salt pans and a well-preserved dolphin **mosaic**, inside a former Roman basilica, but nothing of the sunken city itself beyond a couple of walls in about 70cm of water. Swimming here is good, however – but watch out for sea urchins.

From Eloúnda, boats run half-hourly in high season (€8 return) to the fortress-rock of **Spinalónga**. As a bastion of the Venetian defence, this tiny islet withstood the Turkish invaders for 45 years after the mainland had fallen; in more recent decades and until 1957 it served as a leper colony. As you look around at the roofless shells of houses once inhabited by the unfortunate lepers, and the boat which brought you disappears to pick up another group, an unnervingly real sense of the desolation of those years descends. **PLÁKA**, back on the mainland, and 5km north of Eloúnda, used to be the colony's supply point; now it is a haven from the crowds, with a small pebble beach and a clutch of fish **tavernas**, one of which, *Taverna Spinalonga*, can arrange a boat to take you across to Spinalónga (April–Sept) for about €7 return. This taverna also rents **rooms** (❷) and good-value apartments for the same price for stays of at least two nights. There are **boat trips** daily from Áyios Nikólaos to Olous, Eloúnda and Spinalónga (costing around €12–15), usually visiting at least one other island along the way.

Inland to Kritsá and Lato

The other excursion everyone takes from Áyios Nikólaos is to **KRITSÁ**, a "traditional" village about 10km inland. Buses run at least every hour from the bus station, and despite the commercialization it's still a good trip: the local **crafts** (weaving, ceramics and embroidery basically, though they sell almost everything here) are fair value, and it's also a welcome break from living in the fast lane at "Ag Nik". In fact, if you're looking for somewhere to stay around here, Kritsá has a number of advantages: chiefly availability of **rooms**, better prices and something at least approaching a genuinely Cretan atmosphere; try *Argyro* (☎ & ℱ 28410 51174; ❷), with pleasant rooms – some en suite – around a courtyard on your way into the village. The small platía at the centre of the village is the focus of life and there are a number of decent places **to eat** here, too: the central *Saridhakis* is a cool place to sit out under a plane tree, or you could head for the bakers for tempting *tyrópita* (cheese pies) or currant breads. One of the best-situated tavernas is *Castello*, also in the centre, and there are a few others near where the bus stops.

On the approach road, some 2km before Kritsá, is the lovely Byzantine **church of Panayía Kyrá** (daily 8.30am–6pm; €3), inside which survives perhaps the most complete set of Byzantine frescoes in Crete. The fourteenth- and fifteenth-century works have been much retouched, but they're still worth the visit. Excellent (and expensive) reproductions are sold from a shop alongside. Just beyond the church, a surfaced road leads off for 3km to the archeological site of **Lato** (Tues–Sun 8.30am–3pm; €2), where the substantial remains of a Doric city are coupled with a grand hilltop setting. The city itself is extensive, but largely neglected, presumably because visitors and archeologists on Crete are more concerned with the Minoan era. Ruins aside, you could come here just for the views: west over Áyios Nikólaos and beyond to the bay and Olous (which was Lato's port), and inland to the Lasíthi mountains.

The eastern isthmus

The main road south and then east from Áyios Nikólaos is not a wildly exciting one, essentially a drive through barren hills sprinkled with villas and skirting above the occasional sandy cove. The stretch of the E75 northern highway beyond Ístro is now undergoing major **engineering works** intended to by-pass the archeological site of Gourniá and the coastal town of Pahía Ámmos making the route to Ierápetra more direct. Five kilometres east of Ístro, along a newly completed stretch of the E75, an exit on the left is signed for the **monastery of Faneroméni**. The way bends around to cross the E75 on a viaduct before heading inland along a track (partly asphalted in its early stage) that climbs dizzily skywards for 6km, giving spectacular views over the Gulf of Mirabéllo along the way. The **view** from the monastery over the gulf is one of the finest in Crete. To get into the rather bleak-looking monastery buildings, knock loudly. You will be shown up to the chapel, built into a cave sanctuary, and the frescoes – although late – are quite brilliant.

Gourniá, Pahiá Ámmos and Mókhlos

Back on the coast road, it's another 2km to the site of **Gourniá** (Tues–Sun 8.30am–3pm; €2), slumped in the saddle between two low peaks. The most completely preserved **Minoan town**, its narrow alleys and stairways intersect a throng of one-roomed houses (of which only the ground-floor walls survive – they would have had at least one upper floor) centred on a main square, and the rather grand house of what may have been a local ruler or governor. Although less impressive than the great palaces, the site is strong on revelations about the lives of the ordinary people – many of the dwellings housed craftsmen (who worked with wood, metal and clay), who left behind their tools and materials to be found by the excavators. Its desolation today (you are likely to be alone save for a dozing guardian) only serves to heighten the contrast with what must have been a cramped and raucous community 3500 years ago.

It is tempting to cross the road here and take one of the paths through the wild thyme to the sea for a swim. Don't bother – the bay and others along this part of the coastline act as a magnet for every piece of floating detritus dumped off Crete's north coast. There is a larger beach (though with similar problems), and rooms to rent, in the next bay along at **PAHIÁ ÁMMOS**, about twenty minutes' walk, where there is also an excellent seafront fish taverna, ⚓ *Aiolus*; all the fish (caught with their own boat) plus *kolokithokéftedes* (courgette balls) and *achinosalata* (sea urchin's eggs) are outstanding. In the other direction, there's the campsite of *Gournia Moon* (☎28420 93243; May–Sept), with its own small cove and a swimming pool.

This is the narrowest part of the island, and from here a fast road cuts across the isthmus to Ierápetra (see p.264) in the south. In the north, the route on towards Sitía is one of the most exhilarating in Crete. Carved into cliffs and mountain-sides, the road teeters above the coast before plunging inland at Kavoúsi. Of the beaches you see below, only the one at **MÓKHLOS** is at all accessible, some 5km below the main road. This sleepy seaside village has a few rooms, a hotel or two and a number of **tavernas** – *To Bogazi* is good – squatting along its tiny harbour; if you find yourself needing a **place to stay**, you could try the rooms at the clean and simple *Pension Hermes* (☎28430 94074; ❷) behind the waterfront, which are the cheapest in the village, or there's *Hotel Sofia* (☎28430 94738, 🖷28430 94238; ❷) on the harbour itself for a bit more en-suite luxury. Nearer Sitía the familiar olive groves are interspersed with vineyards used for creating wine and sultanas, and in late summer the grapes, spread to dry in the fields and on rooftops, make an extraordinary sight in the varying stages of their slow change from green to gold to brown.

Sitía

SITÍA is the port and main town of the relatively unexploited eastern edge of Crete. It's a pleasantly scenic if unremarkable place, offering a plethora of waterside restaurants, a long sandy beach and a lazy lifestyle little affected even by the thousands of visitors in peak season. There's an almost Latin feel to the town, reflected in (or perhaps caused by) the number of French and Italian tourists, and it's one of those places that tends to grow on you, perhaps inviting a longer stay than intended. For entertainment there's the **beach**, providing good swimming and windsurfing, and in town a mildly interesting **folklore museum** (Mon–Sat 10am–1pm; €2), a Venetian fort and Roman fish tanks to explore, plus an excellent **archeological museum** (Tues–Sun 8.30am–3pm; €2). As part of a government push to increase tourism at this end of the island, a new **international airport** (set to open to international flights in 2007) is being constructed on a plateau above the town, and will most likely have a big impact on Sitía itself as well as the surrounding area.

Arrival and information

The bus drops you at the **bus station** (actually an office on the street) on the southwest fringe of the centre and close to the town's main **supermarket**, useful for stocking up on provisions. **Internet** access is available at *Enter Café*, Venizélou 95, to the west of Platía Iroón Polytekhniou (daily 8am–midnight).

Should you have problems finding somewhere to stay, the **tourist office** (Mon–Fri 9.30am–2.30pm & 5.30–9pm, Sat 9.30am–2.30pm & 5–8.30pm; ☎28430 28300), on the seafront at the start of the beach road, should be able

Map labels within the image:

SITÍA

Venetian Fortress

Roman Fish Tanks

ODHOS N. PLASTIRA

SFAKIANAKI

I. SFAKIANAKI

E. ROUSELAKI

R. FEREOU

Folklore Museum

METAXAKI

Y. ARKADHIOU

KAZANTZAKIS

N. KONDHILAKI

Pelican House

KAPETAN SITI

EM. FOUNDALIDHOU

V. KORNAROU

EL. VENIZELOU

MYSONOS

PLATIA IROON POLYTEKHNIOU

Zorba's

Enter/Café @

G. VOURLIDAKI

M. KATAPOTI

ELEFTHERIOU VENIZELOU

DIMOKRITOU

4-SEPTEMVRIOU

ANDHREA PAPANDHREOU (ITANOS)

PRAISOU

KONSTANDINOU KARAMANLI

Sitía Development Organisation

Bus Station

Archeological Museum

N

0   100 m

Tourist Police & Áyios Nikólaos

Ferry Port & Airport

Makriyialós & Ierápetra

Váï & Zákros

ACCOMMODATION	
Arhontiko	A
Itano	D
Pension Venus	B
Rooms Apostolis	C

RESTAURANTS	
Chat Noir	1
Creta House	4
Kali Kardia	3
Mikos	2
Symposio	5

to help, or there's the **tourist police** at Therisou 33 (daily 7.30am–2.30pm; ☎28430 24200), who also provide limited tourist information; both can supply a good town map. A colourful weekly **market** takes place on Tuesdays between 7am and 2pm along Odhós Itanou near the archeological museum.

Accommodation

There are plenty of cheap pensions and **rooms** within easy walking distance, especially in the streets around the folklore museum and beyond here towards the ferry port. For economical rooms, try the friendly *Pension Venus*, I.

Kondhiláki 60 (☎28430 24307; ❷) for rooms sharing bath, or *Arhontiko*, I. Kondhiláki 16 (☎28430 28172; ❷) with attractive rooms in a house with a pleasant garden terrace. En-suite accommodation is available at *Rooms Apostolis*, N. Kazantzákis 27 (☎28430 22993; ❷), where balcony rooms come with fridges and fans, or *Nora*, Rouseláki 31 (☎28430 23017, Ⓔnorahotel@yahoo.gr; ❷), near the ferry port with excellent balcony rooms featuring harbour views. An upmarket option in the centre is *Itanos*, Platía Iróön Polytekhníou (☎28430 22146, Ⓦwww.forthnet.gr/internetcity/hotels/itanos; ❹), with balconied sea-view rooms on the town's main square.

Eating, drinking and nightlife

For **food**, the waterside places are relatively expensive; the best-value choices near here are ⚔ *Kali Kardia*, M. Foundalídhou 28, two blocks in from the waterfront, for tasty snail, fish and cheese *mezédhes* served on a pleasant terrace, and *Creta House*, at the start of the beach road (Konstandínou Karamanlí), serving traditional island dishes. The newly arrived *Symposio* almost next door to the latter is also good for fish and meat dishes. Just behind the seafront, the popular *Mikos*, V. Kornárou 117, serves up charcoal-grilled meat and a potent local wine and has a seafront terrace around the corner. At the north end of the seafront *Chat Noir*, Galanáki 3, does the usual standard dishes well and has a small seafront terrace.

Nightlife centres on a few bars and discos near the ferry dock and out along the beach. The town's monster disco-club, *Planitarion*, attracts crowds from all over the east. It's a couple of kilometres beyond the ferry port, and is best reached by taxi. The in-town alternative is *Oasis*, a stylish new bar near the start of the beach road with an attractive terrace, popular with a younger crowd. Sitía's main bash is the summer-long Kornaria **cultural festival** featuring concerts, dance and theatre by Greek and overseas participants (details from the tourist office).

Onward to Váï beach and Palékastro

Leaving Sitía along the beach, the Váï road climbs above a rocky, unexceptional coastline before reaching a fork to the **monastery of Toploú** (daily 9am–7pm, Oct–March closes 4pm; €2.50). The monastery's forbidding exterior reflects a history of resistance to invaders, and doesn't prepare you for the gorgeous flower-decked cloister within. The blue-robed monks keep out of the way as far as possible, but in quieter periods their cells and refectory are left discreetly on view. In the church is one of the masterpieces of Cretan art, the eighteenth-century icon *Lord Thou Art Great* by Ioannis Kornaros. Outside you can buy enormously expensive reproductions.

Váï beach itself features alongside Knossos or the Lasíthi Plateau on almost every Cretan travel agent's list of excursions. Not surprisingly, it is now covered in sunbeds and umbrellas, though it is still a superb beach. Above all, it is famous for its palm trees, and the sudden appearance of the grove is indeed an exotic shock; lying on the fine sand in the early morning, the illusion is of a Carib-bean island – a feature seized upon by countless TV-commercial makers seeking an exotic location on the cheap. As everywhere, notices warn that "camping is forbidden by law", and for once the authorities seem to mean it – most campers climb over the headlands to the south or north. If you do sleep out, watch your belongings, since this seems to be the one place on Crete with crime on any scale. There's a compulsory car park (€2.50), a café and an expensive taverna at the beach, plus toilets and showers. Because of its status as a nature reserve there is **no accommodation** here whatsoever; the nearest place offering a bed for the night is Palékastro. By day you can find a bit more solitude by climbing the rocks or swimming to one of the smaller beaches which surround Váï. **Ítanos**, twenty minutes' walk north by an obvious trail, has a couple of tiny beaches and some modest ruins from the Classical era.

PALÉKASTRO, an attractive farming village some 9km south, makes a good place to stopover. Although its beaches can't begin to compare with those at Váï, you'll find several modest places with **rooms** – among them ⚐ *Hotel Hellas* (☎28430 61240, ⊜hellas_h@otenet.gr; ❷), which offers comfortable en-suite rooms with balcony, TV and fridge and reductions for longer stays; the terrace restaurant below is also excellent. The good-value *Váï* (☎28430 61414; ❶), with rooms above a taverna at the west end of the village, on the Sitía road is another possibility. The extensive **beaches** provide plenty of space to **camp** out without the crowds, but you should respect local sensitivities, keeping away from the main strands and responsibly disposing of any rubbish. Add in a **tourist office** (April–Oct daily 9am–10pm; ☎28430 61546) on the main street, a small **folk museum** (May–Oct Tues–Sun 8.30am–1pm & 5–8.30pm; €1.50), a number of reasonable **tavernas**, a few **bars** and even a **dance-club**, *Design*, and the place begins to seem positively throbbing. The sea is a couple of kilometres down a dirt track, effortlessly reached with a **scooter** hired from Moto Kastri (☎28430 61477), on the eastern edge of the village along the Váï road. Palékastro is also the crossroads for the road south to Zákros and your own transport presents all kinds of beach and exploration possibilities.

Zákros

ÁNO ZÁKROS (Upper Zákros) lies a little under 20km from Palékastro. There are several tavernas and a simple hotel, the *Zakros* (☎ & ⓕ28430 93379; ❷), which has some rooms with bath and great views from its rear rooms; it also offers guests a free minibus service to the Minoan palace and beach. The Minoan palace is actually at Káto ("lower") Zákros, 8km further down towards the sea. Most buses run only to the upper village, but in summer a couple do run every day all the way to the site; it's usually not difficult to hitch if your bus does leave you in the village. Two kilometres along the road you can, if on foot, take a short cut through an impressive **gorge** (the "Valley of the Dead", named for ancient tombs in its sides). The gorge entrance is signed "Dead's Gorge" next to an information board and car-park area with a steep path leading down to the trail, which then follows a stream bed for 4km to reach the sea near the Minoan palace. It's a solitary but magnificent hike, brightened especially in spring with plenty of plant life.

The **Palace of Zakros** (Tues–Sun: July–Oct 8am–7pm, Nov–June 8am–3pm; €3) was an important find for archeologists; it had been occupied only once, between 1600 and 1450 BC, and was abandoned hurriedly and completely. Later, it was forgotten almost entirely and as a result was never plundered or even discovered by archeologists until very recently. The first major excavation began only in 1960; all sorts of everyday objects, such as tools, raw materials, food and pottery, were thus discovered intact among the ruins, and a great deal was learned from being able to apply modern techniques (and knowledge of the Minoans) to a major dig from the very beginning. None of this is especially evident when you're at the palace, except perhaps in a particularly simple ground plan, so it's as well that it is also a rewarding visit in terms of the setting. Although the site is set back from the sea, in places it is often marshy and waterlogged – partly the result of eastern

Crete's slow subsidence, partly the fault of a spring which once supplied fresh water to a cistern beside the royal apartments, and whose outflow is now silted up. In wetter periods, among the remains of narrow streets and small houses of the town outside the palace and higher up, you can keep your feet dry and get an excellent view down over the central court and royal apartments. If you want a more detailed overview of the remains, buy the guide to the site on sale at the entrance.

The delightful village of **KÁTO ZÁKROS** is little more than a collection of tavernas, some of which rent out rooms around a peaceful beach and minuscule fishing anchorage. It's a wonderfully restful place, but is often unable to cope with the volume of visitors seeking accommodation in high season, and as rooms are rarely to be had on spec you'd be wise to ring ahead. You should also be aware that villagers are far more hostile these days to wild camping after years of problems, and you should be sensitive to their concerns. Reliable rooms can be found at *Poseidon* (☎28430 26896; ❶–❷), which has fine sea views, and the friendly *George Villas* (☎ & Ⓕ 28430 26883, Ⓔgeorgevillas@sit.forthnet.gr; ❷–❸), 600m behind the archeological site along a driveable track. Otherwise ask at the *Taverna Akrogiali* (☎28430 26893, Ⓔakrogiali@sit.forthnet.gr; ❷) on the seafront, which acts as an agent for many other room options.

Ierápetra and the southeast coast

The main road from Sitía to the south coast is a cross-country, roller-coaster ride between the east and west ranges of the **Sitía mountains**. One of the first places it hits on the south coast is the sprawling resort of **Makryialós** soon followed by the bustling town and resort of **Ierápetra**. More tranquil hideaways lie further west at the charming pint-sized resorts of **Mýrtos** and **Keratókambos** and the slightly less inviting **Árvi** and **Tsoútsouras**.

Makryialós

Although originally comprised of two distinct villages, the larger **MAKRYIALÓS** (ⓌWww.makrigialos.gr) has gobbled up its neighbour Análipsi to form a single and unfocused resort, whose only real plus point is a long strand with fine sand which shelves so gently you feel you could walk the two hundred nautical miles to Africa. Unfortunately, since the early 1990s it has been heavily developed, so while still a very pleasant place to stop for a swim or a bite, it's not somewhere that's overflowing with cheap **rooms**. The first budget option is *María Tsanakalioti* (☎28430 51557, Ⓔdtsanakalioti@hotmail.com; ❸) on the seaward side as you enter the resort from the east; the friendly proprietor offers pleasant studio rooms – some with sea view and terrace – with kitchenette, a/c and TV. Nearby and up a track inland signed "María Apartments" lies *Stefanos Rooms* (☎28430 52062; ❷) offering decent en-suite rooms with fans. A little before these two and signed up a side road (that soon degenerates into a track) 1km inland is the more upmarket *White River Cottages* (☎28430-51120; Ⓔwrc@sit.forthnet.gr; ❹), where an abandoned hamlet of traditional stone dwellings (originally Áspro Pótamos or "White River") has been restored as a warren of charming a/c studios and apartments with a focal pool. At the western end of town beyond a steep hill (topped with a sign on the left for a Roman villa), *Taverna-Rooms Oasis* (☎28430 51918; ❸) fronts the sea at the end of a short track. Offering sea-view en-suite rooms with a/c and fridge, downstairs there's an outstanding ☨ **taverna** which has based its reputation on using only fresh (never frozen) fish, meat and vegetables, and they claim with some justification that their *moussakás* is the best on the island.

From here to Ierápetra there's little reason to stop; the few beaches are rocky and the coastal plain submerged under ranks of polythene-covered greenhouses. Beside the road leading into Ierápetra are long but exposed stretches of sand, including the appropriately named "Long Beach", where you'll find a **campsite**, *Camping Koutsounari* (☎28420 61213), which offers plenty of shade and has a taverna and minimarket.

Ierápetra

IERÁPETRA itself is a bustling modern supply centre for the region's farmers. It also attracts a fair number of package tourists and the odd backpacker looking for work in the prosperous surrounding agricultural zone, especially out of season. The tavernas along the tree-lined seafront are scenic enough and the EU blue-flagged beach stretches a couple of miles east. But as a town, most people find it pretty uninspiring, despite an ongoing modernization programme, which has cleaned up the centre and revamped the seafront. Although there has been a port here since Roman times, only the **Venetian fort** guarding the harbour and a crumbling Turkish minaret remain as reminders of better days. What little else has been salvaged is in the one-room **Archeological Museum** (Tues–Sun 8.30am–3.30pm; €2) near the post office.

One way to escape the urban hubbub for a few hours is to take a boat to the **island of Gaidhouronísi** (aka Chrissi or Donkey Island) some 10km out to sea. It's a real uninhabited desert island 4km long with a cedar forest, fabulous "**Shell beach**" covered with millions of multicoloured mollusc shells, some good beaches and a couple of tavernas. **Boats** (daily 10.30am & 12.30pm out, 4pm & 7pm return; €20, under-12s €10) leave from the seafront harbour, but you'll need to buy tickets from Iris Travel (☎28420 25423) at the north end of the seafront before boarding. The voyage to the island takes 50min and the boats have an on-board bar.

Practicalities

In the absence of a tourist office the town hall on the main square, Platía Kanoupáki, or the library next door, should be able to provide a copy of the detailed town map (but not much else) which will help you find your way around. If you want to stay, head up Kazantzákis from the chaotic bus station, and you'll find a friendly welcome and good-value, apartment-style **rooms** with kitchenette at *Rooms Popy* at no. 27 (☎28420 24289, ⓕ28420 27772; ❷), or equal comfort in the nearby ⚮ *Cretan Villa*, Lakérdha 16 (☎28420 28522, ⓦwww.cretan-villa.com; ❸) where sparkling a/c rooms with TV and fridge overlook the flower-bedecked patio of a beautiful 180-year-old house. More central and economical is the *Hotel Ersi*, Platía Eleftherías 20 (☎28420 23208; ❷), which will also rent you a seafront apartment nearby for not much more than the cost of a room. The cheapest seafront rooms option is *Katerina* (☎28420 28345, ⓕ28420 28519; ❶–❸) at the eastern end of the strand, offering a/c rooms with TV, fridge and seaview, which also has bargain rooms without a/c or fridge.

You'll find places to **eat** and **drink** all along the waterfront, the better of them, such as *Taverna Napoleon*, *Gorgona* and *Babi's*, being towards the Venetian fort. **Nightlife** centres on a clutch of **clubs**, **bars** and fast-food places along central Kyrba, behind the seafront promenade. The town's most central **Internet café** is *Internet Café* (daily 9am–10pm) inside the *Cosmos Hotel*, Koundoúrou 16, slightly north of Platía Eleftherías.

Beach life

Greece, with some 16,000km of coastline – half on its myriad islands – is extremely well-endowed with beaches. Indeed, despite its great Classical heritage, it's the appeal of stretching out on a sun-soaked strand that draws more visitors than anything else. Varying from idyllic pebble coves to grand sweeps of sand, Greece's beaches offer every kind of seaside entertainment, from windsurfing and all-night parties to bird-watching and calm waters ideal for family holidays. Yet even though foreign sun worshippers descend upon the coast in their hordes during summer, a little legwork can usually find you a secluded spot beside the waves. Alternatively, fleets of water taxis are more than willing to ferry you to remote coves for leisurely day-trips away from the crowds.

Aï Nikítas beach, Lefkádha

For the whole family

All over the country there are **family resorts** filled with Greeks in August, as well as foreign tourists throughout the warm months. These beaches tend to be calm spots, often popular because the sand shelves gently into the water, making ideal swimming conditions for children; as with the rest of the Mediterranean, the lack of a tide also contributes towards **safe swimming**. Often, resorts have grown out of tiny fishing villages or nothing at all, selected for their prime locations such as the long stretch between Ródha and Almyrós on Corfu. Self-sufficient communities like those found across the world, they are usually complete with a plethora of facilities from gift shops to discos.

Windsurfing, Vassilikí Lefkádha

Watersports

With beaches as the focal point of the tourist industry, warm water temperatures throughout the season, and Greece's famous summer winds, it's no surprise that the country offers its visitors a vast and varied selection of **watersports**; inflatable-banana rides, water-skiing and parasailing are almost ubiquitous at the busier spots. Greece also shelters renowned **windsurfing** havens, such as Vromólimnos on Skiáthos and especially Lefkádha's Vassiliki, one of the world's largest windsurf centres. **Scuba-diving** is also increasingly popular on many of the islands – Kassiópi on Corfu is one of the most highly rated locations. Small motorboats and dinghies can be rented on spec almost everywhere, though **yachting** requires a bit more planning and a certain level of expertise.

Nude beaches and naturists

Although **nudity** is officially illegal almost everywhere in Greece, there are pockets where the practice has become a de facto reality that is tolerated by the locals and ignored, if not actually sanctioned, by the authorities. These spots are, unsurprisingly, usually in fairly isolated locations such as beautiful Myrtiótissa on Corfu and the famous gay beach, Super Paradise, on Mýkonos.

Flora and fauna

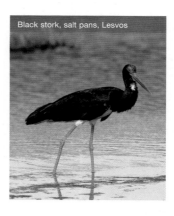
Black stork, salt pans, Lesvos

Greek beaches are often stark and nearly shadeless as the country is too dry to support much lush vegetation. Despite this, you will find some shelter from the sun under pine cover in the western and northern islands and rows of inviting tamarisk trees in the southern Aegean. **Nature-lovers** will find much appeal in Greece's coastal areas: **hikers** will be rewarded after their rural treks with secluded coves, perfect for a refreshing dip; **bird-watchers** will discover that marshy coastal wetlands such as the Korissíon lagoon, and Skala Kallonís on Lésvos, are home to an astonishing variety of species; and conservationists can visit the nesting grounds for the endangered loggerhead **turtle** on the beaches of the Ionian islands.

Blue Flags of Europe

In 2005 no less than 383 Greek beaches were awarded the prestigious **EU Blue Flags**, putting the country in a top-ranking position on the continent. Flags are awarded according to a range of criteria, including **cleanliness** of the sea and coast, organisation and **safety**, and the protection of nature and the environment. Samples are taken to check water quality and litter collection is monitored, as is the amount of information available to the public. If a beach passes muster, it gets to wave its flag prominently for a year, whereupon it must be tested again.

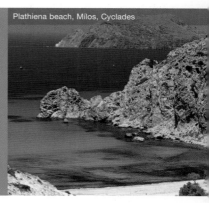
Plathiena beach, Mílos, Cyclades

Volcanic beaches

One unusual phenomenon in Greece is the almost **jet-black sand** that characterizes some island beaches. This effect is owing to the presence of **volcanic activity** in certain areas of the country that has left its mark in incongruously dark lava-scapes. The sole-searing sands on the flat east side of Santoríni are black because of the volcano that erupted three and a half thousand years ago, wiping out the island's Minoan civilisation. Evidence of a tumultuous past can also be seen in the twisted boulders at Thermá Lefkádhos on Ikaría, where thermal waters still bubble away. These **igneous rocks**, almost lunar in their appearance, make for an eerie backdrop to a swim.

Volcanic beach, Santoríni

Top five beaches for relaxing

1   **Triádhes, Mílos** One of the most isolated and deserted beaches in the Cyclades, with a wide strand and a few seaside caves.
2   **Psilí Ámmos, Pátmos** A fine sandy beach backed by shady tamarisks where nude bathing is the norm.
3   **Longás, near Perouládhes, Corfu** The sunsets are breathtaking at this dense red-sand beach set under imposing cliffs.
4   **Yialós, Lefkádha** A stunning coarse-sand beach on the island's west coast.
5   **Mátala, Crete** Now more of a family than a hippy hangout, this beach is a great package destination. It's particularly picturesque in the evening as the sun goes down.

Paleohóra beach, Crete

Top five beaches for activities

1   **Vromólimnos, Skiáthos** An active, youth-oriented beach offering everything from windsurfing to bungee-jumping to the accompaniament of thumping sounds.
2   **Paleohóra, Crete** This all–round tourist beach is in a fine location and has plenty of watersports and dolphin-watching excursions.
3   **Skála Kallonís, Lésvos** An out-of-the-ordinary package resort in that it offers ornithologists ample bird-watching in the gulf behind it.
4   **Thermá Lefkádhos, Ikaría** The perfect place to bathe in bubbling thermal waters beside volcanic rocks.
5   **Super Paradise, Mýkonos** A lively spot for much of the year, this famed gay haunt offers a raft of watersports.

West from Ierápetra

Heading **west** from Ierápetra, the first stretch of coast is grey and dusty, the road jammed with trucks and lined with drab ribbon development and plastic green-houses. There are a number of small resorts along the beach, though little in the way of public transport. If travelling under your own steam, there is a scenic detour worth taking at Gría Lygiá: the road on the right for Anatolí climbs to Máles, a village clinging to the lower slopes of the **Dhíkti range**. Here would be a good starting point for **walking** through some stunning mountain terrain (the E4 Pan-European footpath which crosses the island from east to west passes just 3km north of here). Otherwise, the dirt road back down towards the coast (signposted Míthi) has spectacular views over the Libyan Sea, and eventually follows the Mýrtos river valley down to Mýrtos itself.

Mýrtos and Árvi

MÝRTOS, 18km west of Ierápetra, is the first resort that might actually tempt you to stop, and it's certainly the most accessible, just off the main road with numerous daily **buses** from Ierápetra and a couple direct to Iráklion. Although developed to a degree, it nonetheless remains a tranquil and charming white-walled village kept clean as a whistle by its house-proud inhabitants. There are plenty of **rooms** possibilities, amongst which you could try the central, friendly and good-value ⌓ *Hotel Mirtos* (☎28420 51227, ⓦwww.mirtoshotel.com; ❷) with comfortable en-suite rooms above an excellent taverna. Nearby, *Rooms Angelos* (☎28420 51091; ❶) and *Nikos House* (☎28420 51116, ⓦwww.nikoshouse.cz; ❶) are slightly cheaper options, or there's the even less expensive *Rooms Despina* (☎28420 51524; ❶) at the back of the village near the bus stop. A useful travel agent, Magic Tours (☎28420 51203, ⓦwww.welcometo-magic.com) on the central main street, is a good source of **information**, and also **changes money**, rents **cars**, sells boat and plane tickets and operates a taxi service to Iráklion and Haniá airports. Just off the road from Ierápetra a couple of kilometres east of the village (and signed) are a couple of excavated hilltop **Minoan villas** you might want to explore: Néa Mýrtos (aka Fournoú Korifi) and Mýrtos Pýrgos. Some of the finds from these sites – in addition to a folklore section with tools, kitchen and farming implements once used by the villagers – are displayed in a superb village **museum** (April–Oct Mon–Fri 9am–1pm; €1.50), located to the side of the church. A recent and highly popular addition to the museum is a wonder-fully detailed **scale model** of the Fournoú Korifi site as it would have looked in Minoan days by resident English potter, John Atkinson.

After Mýrtos the main road turns inland towards Áno Viánnos, then continues across the island towards Iráklion; several places on the coast are reached by a series of recently asphalted roads replacing the former rough tracks. **ÁRVI** is a resort of similar size to Mýrtos, although it lacks the latter's charm. The beach, flanked by a new harbour development, hardly justifies it, but it's an interesting little excursion (with at least one bus a day) if only to see the bananas and pine-apples grown here and to experience the microclimate – noticeably warmer than neighbouring zones, especially in spring or autumn – that encourages them. For **rooms** you could try the central *Pension Gorgona* (☎28950 71353; ❷) or, beyond the river at the east end of the beach, the cheaper *Taverna Kyma* (☎28950 71344; ❷).

Beyond Árvi

KERATÓKAMBOS, reached on a side road 4km from Áno Viánnos, has a rather stony beach and, although popular with Cretan day-trippers, is a great

Ierápetra and the southeast coast

place to escape the tourist grind for a spell. It has a range of **rooms**, though they're not easy to come by in August. Try the *Morning Star* taverna (☎28950 51209; ❶) which has a/c rooms with and without bath, or the comparable *Taverna Kriti* (☎28950 51231, ℱ28950 51456; ❷) next door; the **food** at both places is tasty, too.

TSOÚTSOUROS (ⓦ www.tsoutsouros.com), 10km west as the crow flies and now linked by an eleven-kilometre-long asphalted road to the major highway further north, is similar to its neighbour with a line of tavernas, hotels and rooms places arching behind a seafront and yacht harbour, to the east and west of which are a couple of decent if pebbly, grey-sand **beaches**. **Accommodation** may be available here when the other resorts are full: *Rooms Mihalis* (☎28910 92250; ❷) or the good-value *San Georgio Hotel* (May–Sept ☎28910 92322; ❷) further east are both worth trying. There are no facilities for changing money at either place, although both have a couple of **supermarkets**, handy for gathering picnic ingredients.

If you hope to continue across the **south** of the island, be warned that there are no buses, despite completion of the road towards Míres after years of work. It's an enjoyable rural drive, but progress can be slow.

Réthymnon and around

The relatively low, narrow section of Crete which separates the Psilorítis range from the White Mountains in the west seems at first a nondescript, even dull, part of the island. Certainly in scenic terms it has few of the excitements that the west can offer; there are no major archeological sites and many of the villages seem modern and ugly. On the other hand, **Réthymnon** itself is an attractive and lively city, with some excellent beaches nearby. And on the south coast, in particular around **Plakiás**, there are beaches as fine as any Crete can offer and, as you drive towards them, the scenery and villages improve.

Réthymnon

Since the early 1980s, **RÉTHYMNON** has seen a greater influx of tourists than perhaps anywhere else on Crete, with the development of a whole series of large hotels extending almost 10km along the beach to the east. For once, though, the middle of town has been spared, so that at its heart Réthymnon remains one of the most beautiful of Crete's major cities (only Haniá is a serious rival) with an enduringly provincial air. A wide sandy beach and palm-lined promenade border a labyrinthine tangle of Venetian and Turkish houses lining streets where ancient minarets lend an exotic air to the skyline. Dominating everything from the west is the superbly preserved outline of the **fortress** built by the Venetians after a series of pirate raids had devastated the town.

ACCOMMODATION

Atelier	**A**
Barbara Dokimaki	**H**
Byzantine	**G**
Fortezza	**B**
Rooms George	**C**
Ideon	**E**
Leo	**F**
Olga's Pension	**D**
Pension Castello	**J**
Sea Front	**L**
Youth Hostel	**I**
Zania	**K**

RESTAURANTS

Kyria Maria	**6**
Mesostrati	**9**
O Pontios	**4**
O Psaras	**3**
O Zefyros	**10**
Samaria	**11**
Stella's Kitchen	**8**
Taverna Castelvecchio	**2**
Taverna Fanari	**7**
Taverna O Gounakis	**1**
To Pigadi	**5**

Arrival and information

The **bus station** in Réthymnon is by the sea to the west of the town centre just off Periferiakós, the road which skirts the waterfront around the fortress. If you arrive by **ferry**, you'll be more conveniently placed, over at the western edge of the harbour. The **tourist office** (Mon–Fri 8am–4pm; ☎28310 29148, ⓦ www .rethymnon.com) backs onto the main town beach and provides maps, timetables and accommodation lists. To access the **Internet** head for the *Galero Internet Cafe* (daily 9am–midnight), beside the Rimóndi fountain in the old town.

Accommodation

There's a great number of places to stay in Réthymnon, and only at the height of the season are you likely to have difficulty finding somewhere, though you may get weary looking. The greatest concentration of **rooms** is in the tangled streets west of the inner harbour, between the Rimóndi fountain and the museums; there are also quite a few places on and around Arkadhíou and Platía Plastíra.

The nearest **campsite**, *Camping Elizabeth* (☎28310 28694), lies 4km east of town; take the bus for the hotels (marked *Scaleta/ El Greco*) from the long-distance bus station to get there. It's a pleasant, large site on the beach, with all facilities.

Atelier Himáras 32 ☎28310 24440, @atelier@ret.forthnet.gr. Pleasant en-suite rooms run by a talented potter, who has her studio in the basement and sells her wares in a shop on the other side of the building. ❶

Barbara Dokimaki Platía Plastíra 14 ☎ & ☎28310 24581. Strange warren of rooms, with one entrance at the above address, just off the seafront behind the *Ideon*, and another on Dambérgi; ask for the newly refurbished top-floor studio rooms, which have balconies and kitchenettes. ❹

Byzantine Vospórou 26, near the Porta Guora ☎28310 55609, ⊛www.byzantineret.gr. Pleasant en-suite rooms with fans in a renovated Byzantine palace with elegant interior courtyard. ❸

Fortezza Melissinoú 16, near the fortress ☎28310 55551, ⊛www.fortezza.gr. Stylish, top-of-the-range hotel with almost everything you'd expect for the price, including a/c rooms, pool and restaurant. B&B ❹

Rooms George Makedhonías 32 ☎28310 50965. Decent and friendly en-suite rooms (some with fridge), near the archeological museum. ❶

Ideon Platía Plastíra 10 ☎28310 28667, ⊛www .hotelideon.gr. High-class hotel with a brilliant position just north of the ferry dock; little chance of getting one of their balcony, en-suite rooms without pre-booking in high season, though. B&B ❺

Leo Vafé 2 ☎28310 26197. Good hotel with lots of wood and a traditional feel; en-suite rooms come with fans and some have balconies. B&B, and there's a bar. ❷

Olga's Pension Soulíou 57 ☎28310 54896, ☎28310 29851. The star attraction at this very friendly *pension* on one of Réthymnon's most touristy streets is the resplendent flower-filled roof garden. ❶–❷

Pension Castello Karaoli 10 ☎28310 23570, @castelo2@otenet.gr. A very pleasant small *pension* in a 300-year-old Venetian-Turkish mansion; a/c en-suite rooms with fridge and a delightful patio garden. ❸

Sea Front Arkadhíou 159 ☎28310 51981, @lotia@ret.forthnet.gr. En-suite rooms with sea views and balconies in an attractively refurbished mansion with ceiling fans. ❷

Youth Hostel Tombázi 41 ☎28310 22848, ⊛www.yhrethymno.com. The cheapest beds (€8) in town. Large, clean, very friendly and popular, it has food, showers, clothes-washing facilities and a multilingual library. ❶

Zania Pávlou Vlástou 3 ☎28310 28169. *Pension* right on the corner of Arkadhíou in a well-adapted and atmospheric Venetian mansion, but with only a few airy, simple rooms. ❷

The Town

With a **beach** right in the heart of town, it's tempting not to stir at all from the sands, but Réthymnon repays at least some gentle exploration. For a start, you could try checking out the further reaches of the beach itself. The waters protected by the breakwaters in front of town have their disadvantages – notably crowds and dubious hygiene – but less sheltered sands stretch for miles to the east, crowded at first but progressively less so if you're prepared to walk a bit.

Away from the beach, you don't have far to go for the most atmospheric part of town, immediately behind the **inner harbour**. Almost anywhere here, you'll find unexpected old buildings, wall fountains, overhanging wooden balconies, heavy, carved doors and rickety shops, many still with local craftsmen sitting out front, gossiping as they ply their trades. Look out especially for the **Venetian loggia**, which houses a shop selling high-quality and expensive reproductions of Classical art; the **Rimóndi fountain**, another of the more elegant Venetian survivals; and the **Nerandzés mosque**, the best preserved in Réthymnon but currently serving as a music school and closed to the public. When (seemingly endless) repairs are completed it should again be possible to climb the spiral staircase to the top of the **minaret** for a stunning view over the town. Simply by walking past these three, you'll have seen many of the liveliest parts of Réthymnon. Ethnikís Andístasis, the street leading straight up from the fountain, is the town's **market** area.

The old city ends at the Porta Guora at the top of Ethnikís Andístasis, the only surviving remnant of the city walls. Almost opposite are the quiet and shady **public gardens**. These are a soothing place to stroll, and in the latter half of July the **Réthymnon Wine Festival** is staged here. Though touristy, it's a thoroughly enjoyable event, with spectacular local dancing as the evening progresses and the barrels empty. The entrance fee includes all the wine you can drink, though you'll need to bring your own cup or buy one of the souvenir glasses and carafes on sale outside the gardens.

The museums and fortress

A little further up the street from the Nerandzés mosque at M. Vernárdhou 28, a beautifully restored seventeenth-century Venetian mansion is the home of the small but tremendously enjoyable **Historical and Folk Art Museum** (Mon–Sat 9am–2pm & 6–8pm; €3). Gathered within four, cool, airy rooms are musical instruments, old photos, basketry, farm implements, an explanation of traditional ceramic and breadmaking techniques, smiths' tools, traditional costumes and jewellery, lace, weaving and embroidery (look out for a tradi-tional-style tapestry made in 1941 depicting German parachutists landing at Máleme), pottery, knives and old wooden chests. It makes for a fascinating insight into a fast-disappearing rural (and urban) lifestyle, which survived virtu-ally unchanged from Venetian times to the 1960s.

Heading in the other direction from the fountain you'll come to the fortress and **Archeological Museum** (Tues–Sun 8.30am–3pm; €3), which occupies a building almost directly opposite the entrance to the fortress. This was built by the Turks as an extra defence, and later served as a prison; it's now entirely modern inside: cool, spacious and airy. Unfortunately, the collection is not particularly exciting, and really only worth seeing if you're going to miss the bigger museums elsewhere on the island.

The massive **Venetian fortress** (Sat–Thurs 8.30am–7pm; Nov–March closes 6pm; €2.90) is a must, however. Said to be the largest Venetian castle ever built, this was a response, in the last quarter of the sixteenth century, to a series of **pirate raids** (by Barbarossa among others) that had devastated the town. Inside is now a vast open space dotted with the remains of all sorts of barracks, arsenals, officers' houses, earthworks and deep shafts, and at the centre a large domed building that was once a church and later a **mosque** (complete with a surviving but sadly defaced *mihrab*). It was designed to be large enough for the entire population to take shelter within the walls. Although much is ruined, it remains thoroughly atmospheric, and you can look out from the walls over the town and harbour, or in the other direction along the coast to the west. It's also worth walking around the outside of the fortress, preferably at sunset, to get an impression of its fearsome defences, plus great views along the coast; there's a pleasant resting point around the far side at the *Sunset* taverna.

Eating and drinking

Immediately behind the town beach are arrayed the most touristy **restaurants**, the vast majority being overpriced and of dubious quality. Around the inner **harbour** there's a second, rather more expensive, group of tavernas, specializing in fish, though as often as not the intimate atmosphere in these places is spoilt by the stench from the harbour itself.

If you want takeaway food, there are numerous **souvláki** stalls, including a couple on Arkadhíou and Paleológou and another at Petikháki 52, or you can buy your own ingredients at the **market** stalls set up daily on Ethnikís Andistásis below the Porta Guora. The **bakery** *Iy Gaspari* on Mesolongíou, just behind the Rimóndi fountain, sells the usual cheese pies, cakes and the like, and it also bakes excellent brown, black and rye bread. There's a good zaharoplastío, *N.A. Skartsilakos*, at Paleológou 36, just north of the fountain, and several more small cafés which are good for **breakfast** or a quick coffee. The *Cul de Sac* and *Galero* cafés overlooking the fountain are relatively expensive, but great for people-watching.

Taverna Castelvecchio Himáras 29. A long-established family taverna next to the fortress which has a pleasant terrace with view over the town and offers some vegetarian choices.

Taverna Fanari Makedhonías 5, slightly west of Platía Plastíra. A good-value little seafront taverna serving up tasty lamb and chicken dishes.

Taverna O Gounakis Koronéou 6. Hearty, no-frills traditional cooking by a family who leave the stove to perform *lyra* every night, and when things get really lively the dancing starts.

Kyria Maria at Moskhovítou 20, tucked down an alley behind the Rimóndi fountain. Pleasant, unassuming little taverna for good-value fish and meat dishes; after the meal, everyone gets a couple of Maria's delicious *tyropitákia* with honey on the house.

Mesostrati Yerakári 1. Tucked behind the church on Platía Martíron, this is a pleasant little neighbourhood ouzerí/taverna serving well-prepared Cretan country dishes on a small terrace.

To Pigadi Xanthoúdhidhou 31, slightly west of the Rimóndi fountain. In a street containing a cluster of upmarket restaurants with overinflated prices and pretensions, this place stands out for its excellent, reasonably priced food and efficient service; an attractive terrace's main feature – an ancient well (*pigádi*) – has also inspired its name.

O Pontios Melissinoú 34. A good lunchtime stop close to the Archeological Museum, this is a simple place with surprisingly good food, outdoor tables and an enthusiastic female proprietor.

O Psaras corner of Nikiforou Foka and Kironaiou. An economical and unpretentious fish taverna with tables on a terrace beside a church.

Samaria Venizélou, almost opposite the tourist office. One of the few seafront tavernas that maintains some integrity (and reasonable prices) and is patronized by locals.

Stella's Kitchen Great-value little diner serving healthy, home-baked food and six daily specials (at least two of which are vegetarian); there's a leafy terrace roof garden and they also do breakfasts. Closes 9pm.

O Zefyros at the inner harbour. One of the less outrageously pricey fish places here and maintains reasonable standards.

Nightlife

Nightlife is concentrated in the same general areas as the tavernas. At the west end of Venizélou, in the streets behind the inner harbour, the overflow from a small cluster of noisy music bars – *Venetsianako*, *Dimman* and *Xtreme* – begins to spill out onto the pavement as partygoers gather for the nightly opening of the *Fortezza Living Room Club* in the inner harbour itself, which is the glitziest in town, flanked by its competitors *Metropolis*, *ADO Club Rock* and the nearby *Budha Club* a little way down Salamínos. Heading up this street, a string of more subdued cocktail bars – *Ice*, *Aman* and *Aynaia* – caters for those in search of a quieter drink, as does *Notas*, at Himáras 27 near the *Fortezza* and facing the *Atelier* pension, which puts on live (acoustic) guitar and song every night. A relatively new bar scene popular with the local student community has taken root around Platía Plastíra, above the inner harbour, where music bars include *Art*, *Da Cappo*, *Coz*, *Kenzo* and *Aroma*, all with expansive terraces.

Around Réthymnon

While some of Crete's most drastic resort development spreads ever eastwards out of Réthymnon, to the west a sandy coastline, not yet greatly exploited, runs all the way to the borders of Haniá province. But of all the short trips that can be made, the best-known and still the most worthwhile is to the **monastery of Arkádhi**.

Southeast to Arkádhi

The **monastery of Arkádhi** (daily 8am–7pm; €2), some 25km southeast of the city and immaculately situated in the foothills of the Psilorítis range, is also something of a national Cretan shrine. During the 1866 rebellion against the Turks, the monastery became a rebel strongpoint in which, as the Turks gained the upper hand, hundreds of Cretan independence fighters and their families took refuge. Surrounded and on the point of defeat, the defenders ignited a powder magazine just as the Turks entered. Hundreds (some sources claim thousands) were killed, Cretan and Turk alike, and the tragedy did much to promote international sympathy for the cause of Cretan independence. Nowadays, you can peer into the roofless vault where the explosion occurred and wander about the rest of the well-restored grounds. Outside the entrance a modern monument displays the skulls of many of the victims. The sixteenth-century **church** survived, and is one of the finest Venetian structures left on Crete; other buildings house a small **museum** devoted to the exploits of the defenders of the (Orthodox) faith. The monastery is easy to visit by public bus or on a tour.

West to Aryiroúpolis, Yeoryoúpoli and beyond

Leaving Réthymnon to the west, the main road climbs for a while above a rocky coastline before descending (after some 5km) to the sea, where it runs alongside sandy **beaches** for perhaps another 7km. An occasional hotel offers accommodation, but on the whole there's nothing but a line of straggly bushes between the road and the windswept sands. If you have your own vehicle, there are plenty of places to stop for a swim, with rarely anyone else around – but beware of some very strong currents.

One worthwhile detour inland is to **ARYIROÚPOLIS**, a picturesque village perched above the Mousselás river valley and the seat of ancient Lappa, a Greek and Roman town of some repute. The village is famous for its **springs**, which gush dramatically from the hillside and provide most of the city of Réthymnon's water supply. Among a number of **places to stay** try the excellent-value ⚲ *Rooms Mikedaki* (☎28310 81225; ❶) on the right at the foot of the road which climbs to the village; en-suite terrace balcony rooms here have fine views and guests have use of a kitchen. Near the springs *Rooms Argiroupolis* (☎28310 81148, ☎28310 81149; B&B; ❷) has more en-suite rooms in a garden setting. In the upper village there's *Rooms Zografakis* (☎28310 81269; B&B; ❷), or – with great views from its air-conditioned rooms and taverna terrace – the friendly and excellent-value ℣ *Agnantema* (☎28310 81172; ❶). For **places to eat**, you're spoilt for choice, with five tavernas at the springs (try *Vieux Moulin* with an attractive terrace) and a bar (serving tasty *mezédhes*) in the upper village, together with tavernas at *Zografakis* and *Agnantema*, the latter enjoying a spectacular terrace view down the river valley. A shop under the arch in the main square, named Lappa Avocado and selling local products of the region including olive oil and avocado-based skin products, can provide a free **map** detailing a surprising number of churches, caves and ancient remains to see in and around the village, including an outstanding third-century **Roman mosaic**. An interesting **folklore museum** (daily 10am–7pm; free) – signed from the main square – is worth a look for its collection of tapestries, farm implements, photos and ephemera collected by the Zografakis family who have lived here for countless generations. There are numerous fine **walks** in the surrounding hills, on which the proprietor of Lappa Avocado, who speaks English, will advise. Although little over 20km from Réthymnon and easy to get to with your own transport, Aryiroúpolis is also served by **buses** from Réthymnon's bus station (Mon–Fri only), currently leaving at 11.30am and 2.30pm, and in the reverse direction at 7am, 12.30pm and 3.30pm.

Back on the coastal route, if you are looking for a place to relax for a while, probably the best base is **YEORYOÚPOLI** just across the provincial border in Haniá, where the beach is cleaner, wider and further from the road. There's been a distinct acceleration in the pace of development at Yeoryoúpoli over the last few years and it's now very much a resort, packed with rooms to rent, small hotels, apartment buildings, tavernas and travel agencies. But everything remains on a small scale, and the undeniably attractive setting is untarnished, making it a very pleasant place to pass a few days, as long as you don't expect to find many vestiges of traditional Crete. Most of the new beachfront places are exclusively for package tourists, so it's best to head along the roads down towards the beach from the central platía. Here, you'll find *Andy's Rooms* (☎28250 61394; ❷), and *Cretan Cactus* (☎28250 61449, ✉cretancactusge@hotmail.com; ❷), close to the beach and both offering en-suite rooms with fans. On the far side of the bridge across the river, ℣ *Anna* (☎28250 61376; ❶) offers some of the best-value rooms in town in a garden setting and also has a number of apartments (❹) and houses (❺), both sleeping up to five. *Taverna Paradise* (☎28250 61313; ❷), towards the river from the square, has more rooms, studios and apartments plus tasty food. Also for **food** *Taverna Babis*, in the other direction on the main street, is good for standards, as is *Sirtaki*, near the bridge. **Internet** access is on offer at the relaxing *Internet Bar Planet* (9am–midnight) on the main square.

Within walking distance inland – though it can also be visited on the tourist road train from Yeoryoúpoli – is **Kournás**, Crete's only freshwater lake, set deep in a bowl of hills and almost constantly changing colour. There are a few tavernas with rooms to rent along the shore here (bring mosquito repellent), or you could try for a bed in the nearby hill village of **MATHÉS** where the *Villa Kapasa* (☎28250 61050, ⓦwww.villa-kapasas.com; ❷) has some very pleasant en-suite rooms around a garden. *Taverna Mathes*, the village taverna, has great terrace views and good food. A few kilometres uphill from the lake in **KOURNÁS** village, the *Kali Kardia* taverna on the main street is another great place to sample the local lamb and *loukánika* (sausages).

Beyond Yeoryoúpoli, the main road heads inland, away from a cluster of coastal villages beyond Vámos. It thus misses the Dhrápano peninsula, the setting for the film of *Zorba the Greek*, with some spectacular views over the sapphire Bay of Soúdha and several quiet beaches. **Kókkino Horió**, the movie location, and nearby **Pláka** are indeed postcard-picturesque (more so from a distance), but **Kefalás**, inland, outdoes both of them. On the exposed north coast there are good beaches at **Almyrídha** and **Kalýves**, and off the road between them. Both have been discovered by package operators; accommodation is mostly in apartments and rooms are scarce, although there are a few mid-range and more upmarket hotels. Almyrídha is the more pleasant, with a string of good fish tavernas (try *Dimitri's*) along the beach that make for an enjoyable lunch stop. If you want to stay here try *Marilena's Pension* (℡ 28250 32202; ❷), on the seafront to the east, or the more central, modern *Almira Apartments* (℡ 28250 61376; ❸).

South from Réthymnon

There are a couple of alternative routes south from Réthymnon, but the main one heads straight out from the centre of town, an initially featureless road due south across the middle of the island towards **Ayía Galíni**. About 23km out, a turning cuts off to the right for **Plakiás** and **Mýrthios**, following the course of the spectacular Kourtaliótiko ravine.

Plakiás and the south coast

PLAKIÁS has undergone something of a boom in recent years and is no longer the pristine village all too many people arriving here expect. That said, it's still quite low-key, with a satisfactory beach and a string of good tavernas around the dock. There are hundreds of **rooms**, but at the height of summer you'll need to arrive early if you hope to find one; the last to fill are generally those furthest inland, heading towards the youth hostel. Good places to try include *Gio-ma Taverna* (℡ 28320 32003, ⓦ www.gioma.gr; ❷–❸), on the seafront by the harbour with rooms and studios, or the excellent balcony rooms at *Ippokambos* (℡ 28320 31525, ℮ amoutsos@otenet.gr; ❶), slightly inland on the road to the enjoyably relaxed **youth hostel** (℡ 28320 32118, ⓦ www .yhplakias.com; dorms ❶), which is 500m inland and signed from the seafront. *Pension Afrodite* (℡ 28320 31266; ❸) is a quiet spot with pleasant apartments, off the road to the hostel.

Once you've found a room there's not a lot else to discover here. Every facility you're likely to need is strung out along the waterfront or on the few short streets off it, including a **post office** (Mon–Fri 7.30am–2pm), **bike rental**, ATMs and **money exchange**, several **supermarkets** and even a **laundry**. Places to eat are plentiful too. The attractive **tavernas** on the waterfront in the centre are a little expensive; the pick of them – with inviting terraces – are *Sofia* and the adjoining *Christos* and *Gio-ma* for fish. You'll eat cheaper further inland: seek out *Taverna Medousa* at the east end of town, reached up the road inland past the post office and then right. On the way here you'll pass *Nikos Souvlaki* which dishes up the least expensive meals in town – excellent *souvláki* or even fish and chips – often accompanied by live *bouzoúki* music in the evenings. Beyond the harbour at the west end of town *Psarotaverna Tassomanolis* is one of a line of waterfront places enjoying spectacular sunsets and specializes in fish caught by the proprietor from his own boat.

Mýrthios

For a stay of more than a day or two, **MÝRTHIOS**, in the hills behind Plakiás, also deserves consideration. Originally put on the map for legions of younger travellers by a legendary youth hostel (now closed), these days it's distinctly pricey, but there are some great apartments and wonderful views and you'll generally find locals still outnumbering the tourists. To **stay**, check out the classy *Anna Apartments* (T 697 33 24 775, W www.annaview.com; ❷–❹), while for food the long-established *Plateia Taverna* has had a complete makeover but still serves up excellent traditional Cretan cooking. A car is an advantage here, although the Plakiás bus will usually loop through Mýrthios (be sure to check – otherwise, it's less than five minutes' walk uphill from the junction). It takes twenty minutes to walk down to the beach at Plakiás, a little longer to Dhamnóni.

Dhamnóni and Skhinariá

Some of the most tempting **beaches** in central Crete hide just to the east of Plakiás, though unfortunately they're now a very poorly kept secret. These three splashes of yellow sand, divided by rocky promontories, are within easy walking distance and together go by the name **Dhamnóni**. At the first, Dhamnóni proper, there's a taverna with showers and a wonderfully long strip of sand, but there's also a lot of new development including a number of nearby rooms for rent and a huge and ugly Swiss-owned holiday village, which has colonized half of the main beach. At the far end, you'll generally find a few people who've dispensed with their clothes, while the little cove which shelters the middle of the three beaches (barely accessible except on foot) is entirely nudist. Beyond this, **Ammoúdhi** beach has another taverna, *Ammoudi* (T 28320 31355, W www.ammoudi.gr; ❸), with good if slightly pricey rooms for rent, and more of a family atmosphere. **Skhinariá** beach, just around the corner, is a considerable distance by road via the village of Lefkóyia. A popular diving spot, in summer it attracts Greek families, but is otherwise quiet. There's a decent (daytime) taverna here, *Lybian Star*.

Préveli and "Palm Beach"

Next in line along the coast is **PRÉVELI**, some 6km southeast of Lefkóyia, served by two daily **buses** from Réthymnon (check current times with any tourist office). It takes its name from a **monastery** (April & May daily 8am–7pm; June–Oct Mon–Sat 8am–1.30pm & 3.30–8pm, Sun 8am–8pm; in winter, knock for admission; W www.preveli.org; €2.50) set high above the sea which, like every other in Crete, has a proud history of resistance, in this case accentuated by its role in World War II as a shelter for marooned Allied soldiers awaiting evacuation. There are fine views and a new monument – to the left as you approach – commemorating the rescue operations and depicting a startling life-size, rifle-toting abbot and an allied soldier cast in bronze. The evacuations took place from "**Palm Beach**", a sandy cove with a small date-palm grove and a solitary drink stand where a stream (actually the Megapótamos river) feeds a little oasis. The beach usually attracts a summer camping community (now officially discouraged by the authorities due to litter and sanitation problems) and is also the target of day-trip boats from Plakiás and Ayía Galíni. Sadly, these groups between them deposit heaps of rubbish, often leaving this lovely place filthy, and despite an ongoing clean-up campaign it seems barely worth the effort. The easiest way to get to "Palm Beach" from the monastery is to follow a newly asphalted road that leaves the main road 1km before the monastery itself. This leads, after a further kilometre, to a **pay car park** (€1.50) where you'll need to leave any transport. From here, a marked path clambers steeply down over the rocks – about a ten-minute descent to the beach (but a sweaty twenty-minute haul back up). Should you not wish to return this way (although you'll have little option if you've brought transport), you can avoid the arduous, steep climb by taking a track on the east side of the beach which follows the river valley 2km back to a stone bridge, where there are cafés. You should be able to get one of the two daily buses to drop you at this bridge. All this said, **boat trips** from Plakiás and Ayía Galíni will get you here with a great deal less fuss.

Spíli and Ayía Galíni

Back on the main road south, the pleasant country town of **SPÍLI** lies about 30km from Réthymnon. A popular coffee break for coach tours passing this way, Spíli warrants time if you can spare it. Sheltered under a cliff are narrow alleys of ancient houses, all leading up from a platía with a famous 24-spouted **fountain** that replaced a Venetian original. If you have your own transport, it's a worthwhile place to stay, peacefully rural at night but with several good **rooms** for rent. Try the *Green Hotel* (☎28320 22225; ❶), on the main road, or the charming ⚓ *Rooms Herakles* (☎28320 22411, ✉heraclespapadakis@hotmail .com; ❷, reductions for more than one night) just behind; the genial eponymous proprietor can advise on some superb **walks** in the surrounding hills and also rents out **mountain bikes**. There are two **banks** along the main street (with ATMs) and **Internet** access is possible at *Cafe Babis*, close to the fountain.

The ultimate destination for most people on this road is **AYÍA GALÍNI**. If heading here was your plan, maybe you should think again since this picturesque "fishing village" is so busy in high season that you can't see it for the tour buses, hotel billboards and British package tourists. It also has a beach that is much too small for the crowds that congregate here. Even so, there are a few saving graces – mainly some excellent restaurants and bars, a lively nightlife scene, plenty of rooms and a friendly atmosphere that survives and even thrives on all the visitors. Out of season, when the climate is mild, it can be quite enjoyable too, and from November to April, despite competition from immigrant workers, a number of long-term travellers spend the winter packing tomatoes or polishing cucumbers here. If you want somewhere to stay, start looking at the top end of town, around the main road: the economical *Hotel Minos* (☎28320 91292; ❶), with en-suite rooms with superb views, is a good place to start, with the nearby *Hotel Idi* (☎28320 91152, ℻28320 91082; ❶) and *Hotel Hariklia* (☎ & ℻28320 91257; ❷) as back-ups, and close to the foot of the hill leading to the harbour, *Neos Ikaros* (☎28320 91447, ⓦwww .neosikaros.gr; ❸) is a more upmarket option with superb garden pool. There are dozens of other possibilities, and usually something to be found even at the height of summer.

The coastal plain east of Ayía Galíni, hidden under acres of polythene greenhouses and burgeoning concrete sprawl, must be among the ugliest regions in Crete, and **Timbáki** the dreariest town. Since this is the way to Phaestos and back to Iráklion, you may have no choice but to grin and bear it.

The Amári Valley

An alternative route south from Réthymnon, and a far less travelled one, is the road which turns off on the eastern fringe of town to run via the **Amári Valley**. Very few buses go this way, but if you're driving it's well worth the extra time. There's little specifically to see or do (though hidden away are a number of richly frescoed Byzantine churches), but it's an impressive drive under the flanks of the mountains and a reminder of how, in places, rural Crete continues to exist regardless of visitors. The countryside here is delightfully green even in summer, with rich groves of olive and assorted fruit trees, and if you **stay** (there are rooms in Amári, Thrónos, Yerákari and Kouroutes), you'll find the nights are cool and quiet. It may seem odd that many of the villages along the way are modern: they were systematically destroyed by the German army in reprisal for the 1944 kidnapping of General Kreipe and many have poignant roadside monuments commemorating these tragic events.

Haniá and the west

The substantial attractions of Crete's westernmost quarter are enhanced by its relative lack of visitors, and despite the now-rapid spread of tourist development, the west is likely to remain one of the emptier parts of the island. This is partly because there are no big sandy beaches to accommodate resort hotels, and partly because it's so far from the great archeological sites. But for mountains and empty (if often pebbly) beaches, it's unrivalled.

Haniá itself is an excellent reason to come here, but the immediately adjacent coast, especially to the west of the city, is overdeveloped and not particularly exciting; if you want beaches head for the south coast. **Paleohóra** is the only place which could really be described as a resort, and even this is on a thoroughly human scale; others are emptier still. **Ayía Rouméli** and **Loutró** can be reached only on foot or by boat; **Hóra Sfakíon** sees hordes passing through but few who stay; **Frangokástello**, nearby, has a beautiful castle and the first stirrings of development. Behind these lie the **White Mountains** (Lefká Óri) and, above all, the famed walk through the **Samariá Gorge**.

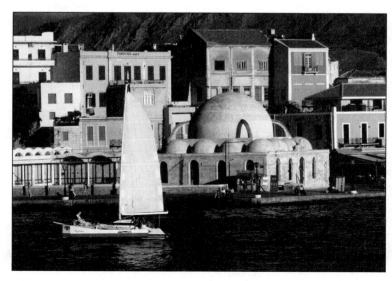

△ Haniá harbour and Mosque of the Janissaries

Haniá

HANIÁ, as any of its residents will tell you, is spiritually the capital of Crete, even if the official title was passed back (in 1971) to Iráklion. For many, it is also by far the island's most attractive city, especially if you can catch it in spring, when the White Mountains' snowcapped peaks seem to hover above the roofs. Although it is for the most part a modern city, you might never know it as a tourist. Surrounding the small outer harbour is a wonderful jumble of half-derelict **Venetian streets** that survived the wartime bombardments, and it is here that life for the visitor is concentrated. Restoration and gentrification, consequences of the tourist boom, have made inroads of late, but it remains an atmospheric place.

Arrival, information and orientation

Large as it is, Haniá is easy to handle once you've reached the centre; you may get lost wandering among the narrow alleys of the old city but that's a relatively small area, and you're never far from the sea or from some other obvious land-mark. The **bus station** is on Kydhonías, within easy walking distance from the centre – turn right out of the station, then left down the side of Platía-1866, and you'll emerge at a major road junction opposite the top of Halídhon, the main street of the old quarter leading straight down to the Venetian harbour. Arriving by **ferry**, you'll anchor about 10km east of Haniá at the port of Soúdha: there are frequent buses from here which will drop you by the **market** on the fringes of the old town, or you can take a taxi (around €8); there are also KTEL buses to Réthymnon and Kastélli meeting most ferries. From the **airport** (15km east of town on the Akrotíri peninsula) taxis (around €10) will almost certainly be your only option, though it's worth a quick check to see if any sort of bus is meeting your flight. The very helpful **tourist office** is in the *dhimarhío* (town hall) at Kydhonías 29 (Mon–Fri 8am–2.30pm ℡28210 36155, Ⓦwww.chania .gr), four blocks east of the bus station.

Accommodation

There are thousands of **rooms** to rent in Haniá and, unusually, quite a few luxurious **hotels**. Though you may face a long search for a bed at the height of the season, eventually everyone does seem to find something. The nearest **campsite** within striking distance is *Camping Hania* (℡28210 31138), some 4km west of Haniá behind the beach, served by local bus. The site is rather small, and hemmed in by new development, but it has a pool and all the facilities just a short walk from some of the better beaches.

Harbour area

Perhaps the most desirable rooms of all are those overlooking the **harbour**, which are sometimes available at reasonable rates: be warned that this is often because they're very noisy at night. Most are approached not direct from the harbourside itself but from the streets behind; those further back are likely to be more peaceful. Theotokopoúlou and the alleys off it make a good starting point. The nicest of the more expensive places are here, too, equally set back but often with views from the upper storeys. In recent years the popularity of this area has led to anyone with a room near the harbour tarting it up and attempting to rent it out at a ridiculously inflated price. You'll often be touted in the street for these and it's wise not to commit yourself until you've made some comparisons.

HANIÁ

N

Firkas & Naval Museum

Byzantine Museum

ANGELOU

AKTI TOMBAZI

Mosque of the Janissaries

LITHINON

AKTI KANARI

THEOTOKOPOULOU

AKTI KOUNDOURIOTOU

Renieri Gate

Café Notos

PLATIA SYNDRIVANI

APOSTOLIDHOU

PIREOS

ZAMBELIOU

SKOUFON

Kathodon

AY. DHEKA

ISODHON

E. DHOUNDOU

PARDHALI

KONDHILAKI

Archeological Museum

Cathedral

PORTOU

HALIDHON

BETOLO

SKRIDHLOF

RESTAURANTS

Akrogiali	5
Amphora	F
Anaplous	7
Apostolis	1
Aroma	6
Doloma	4
Ela	11
Iordanis Bougatsa	12, 13
Karnayio	3
Meltemi	A
Mihalis	2
Rudi's Bierhaus	8
Tamam	9
Tholos	10

METAHAKI

Schiavo Bastion

KYRILOU

Supermarket

SKALIDHI

KISSAMOU

MANOUSOYANAKIDHOU

PLATIA 1866

KRIARI

0   200 m

KYDHONIAS

Bus Station

▼ Plataniás & Kastélli

Amphora 2 Párodos Theotokopoúlou 20 ☎28210 93224, ⓦwww.amphora.gr. Large, traditional hotel in a Venetian mansion, and beautifully renovated; worth the expense if you get a view, but probably not for the cheaper rooms without one. Good restaurant below; see p.282. ❺

Casa Veneta Theotokopoúlou 57 ☎28210 90007, ☞28210 75931. Very well-equipped, comfortable studios and apartments with friendly owner behind a Venetian facade; good value. ❹

El Greco Theotokopoúlou 47–49 ☎28210 94030, ⓦwww.elgreco.gr. Comfortable hotel with nicely furnished if rather compact rooms which include

fridge, a/c and TV. Some have balconies and there's a seasonal roof terrace. B&B ❹

Lucia Aktí Koundouriótou ☎28210 90302 ⓦwww.ellada.net/loukia. Harbourfront hotel with a/c balcony rooms; less expensive than you might expect for one of the best views in town, and – thanks to double-glazing – reasonably soundproof. ❸

Maro B Párodos Porto 5 ☎28210 54981. Probably the cheapest en-suite rooms in the old town, hidden away in a quiet, unmarked alley off Portou not far from the Schiavo bastion. Basic but friendly and clean; a/c €2 extra. ❷

278

▼ New Road, Soúdha, Réthymnon & Iráklion   ▼ Platía Eleftherías   Platía Eleftherías ▼

Meltemi Angélou 2 ☎ 28210 92802. First of a little row of *pensions* in a great situation on the far side of the harbour near the Naval Museum; decent rooms with fans and (some) balcony are perhaps noisier than neighbours, but excellent views and a good café downstairs (see p.282). ❷–❸

Pension Nora Theotokopoúlou 60 ☎ 28210 72265, ⒻΘ 28210 72265. Charming a/c en-suite rooms in an old wooden Turkish house, some with kitchenette and balcony (for the same price which you should ask for). Pleasant breakfast café below. ❷

Rooms Stella Angélou 10 ☎ 28210 73756. Creaky, eccentric old house above an eclectic gift shop, with pleasant en-suite rooms equipped with a/c and fridge. ❸

Thereza Angélou 8 ☎ & Ⓕ 28210 92798. Beautiful old house in a great position, with stunning views from roof terrace and a/c, en-suite rooms (some with TV); classy decor, too. Slightly more expensive than its neighbours but deservedly so; unlikely to have room in high season unless you book. ❹

The old town: east of Halídhon

In the eastern half of the old town, rooms are far more scattered, usually cheaper, and in the height of the season your chances are much better over here. **Kastélli**, immediately east of the harbour, has some lovely places with views from the heights. Take one of the alleys leading left off Kanevárou if you want to try these, but don't be too hopeful since they are popular and often booked up.

To Dhiporto Betólo 41, one block north of Skridhlóf ☎ 28210 40570 ⓦ www.geocities.com/to-diporto. Pleasant, good-value en-suite rooms all with a/c, TV and fridge; some triples and singles. ❸

Fidias Kalinákou Sarpáki 8 ☎ 28210 52494. Signposted from the cathedral, this favourite backpackers' meeting place has been going forever and has the real advantage of offering single rooms or fixing shares. Recently renovated to add some remarkably cheap en suites, but also has the cheapest beds in town. ❶

🏃 **Kastelli** Kanevárou 39 ☎ 28210 57057, ⓦ www.kastelistudios.gr. A comfortable, modern, reasonably priced *pension* that's very quiet at the back. All rooms come with fans or a/c and anti-mosquito machines. The owner is exceptionally helpful and also has a few apartments and a beautiful house (for up to five people) to rent. ❷

Nikos Dhaskaloyiánnis 58 ☎ 28210 54783. Built on top of a Minoan ruin (visible through a basement window), this is one of several rooms places along this street near the inner harbour; good-value, relatively modern rooms, all with a/c, shower, fridge and (the more expensive ones) TV. Same owner has economical studios nearby with fully-equipped kitchens. ❶–❸

Port Sífaka 73, just off Dhaskaloyiánnis ☎ 28210 59484 ⓔ lioliosk@chania.cci.gr. Clean, quiet modern place with good-size, en-suite rooms with a/c. ❸

Vranas Studios Ayíon Dhéka and Kalinákou Sarpáki, near the cathedral ☎ & ⓕ 28210 58618, ⓦ www.vranas.gr. Pleasant, spacious studio-style rooms with TV, a/c, fridge and kitchenette. ❹

The City

Haniá has been occupied almost continuously since Neolithic times, so it comes as a surprise that a city of such antiquity should offer little specifically to see or do. It is, however, fascinating simply to wander around, stumbling upon surviving fragments of city wall, the remains of **ancient Kydonia**, which are being excavated, and odd segments of Venetian or Turkish masonry.

Kastélli and the harbour

The **port** area is as ever the place to start, the oldest and the most interesting part of town. It's at its busiest and most attractive at night, when the lights from bars and restaurants reflect in the water and crowds of visitors and locals turn out to promenade. By day, things are quieter. Straight ahead from Platía Syndriváni (also known as Harbour Square) lies the curious domed shape of the **Mosque of the Janissaries**, built in 1645 (though heavily restored since) and the oldest Ottoman building on the island. It is occasionally open as a gallery, housing temporary exhibitions in the messy structures that adjoin the original mosque.

The little hill that rises behind the mosque is **Kastélli**, site of the earliest habitation and core of the Minoan, Venetian and Turkish towns. There's not a great deal left, but archeologists believe that they may have found the remains of a Minoan palace (logically, there must have been one at this end of the island), and the "lost" city of Kydonia, in the **excavations** being carried out – and open to view – along Kanevárou. It's also here that you'll find traces of the oldest **walls**; there were two rings, one defending Kastélli alone, a later set encompassing the whole of the medieval city. Beneath the hill, on the inner (eastern) harbour, the arches of sixteenth-century **Venetian arsenals**, a couple of them beautifully restored (and one housing a reconstructed Minoan ship), survive alongside remains of the outer walls.

Following the esplanade around in the other direction leads to a hefty bastion which now houses Crete's **Naval Museum** (daily 9am–4pm; €2). The collection consists of model ships and other naval ephemera tracing the history of Greek navigation, plus a section on the 1941 **Battle of Crete** with fascinating artefacts, and poignant photos depicting the suffering here under the Nazis. You might want to wander in through the gate beside the museum anyway for a (free) look at the seaward fortifications and the platform from which the modern Greek flag was first flown on Crete (in 1913). Walk around the back of these restored bulwarks to a street heading inland and you'll find the best-preserved stretch of the outer walls. Just behind the Naval Museum at the top of Theotokopoúlou lies the new **Byzantine Museum** (Tues–Sun 8.30am–3pm; €2, combined ticket with Archeological Museum €3), with a small but interesting collection of mosaics, icons and jewellery from the various periods of Byzantine rule. Continue up Theotokopoúlou and explore the alleys off it to discover some of the most attractive parts of the old town, with widespread restoration and plenty of fascinating small shops.

Halídhon and beyond

Behind the harbour lie the less picturesque but more lively sections of the old city. First, a short way up Halídhon on the right, is Haniá's **Archeological Museum** (Tues–Sun 8.30am–3pm; €3), housed in the Venetian-built church of San Francesco. Damaged as it is, especially from the outside, this remains a beautiful building and it contains a fine little display, covering the local area from Minoan through to Roman times. In the garden, a huge fountain and the base of a minaret survive from the period when the Ottomans converted the church into a mosque; around them are scattered various other sculptures and architectural remnants. The nearby **Folklore Museum** (Mon–Sat 9.30am–3pm & 6–9pm; €2) is worth a look as much for its setting, on a fine courtyard that is also home to Haniá's Roman Catholic church, as for its contents.

The **cathedral**, ordinary and relatively modern, is just a few steps further up Halídhon on the left. Around it are some of the more animated shopping areas, particularly **Odhós Skrídhlof** ("Leather Street"), lined with the shops of traditional leathermakers plying their trade, with streets leading up to the back of the market beyond. In the direction of the Spiántza quarter are ancient alleys with tumbledown Venetian stonework and overhanging wooden balconies; though gentrification is spreading apace, much of the quarter has yet to feel the effect of the city's modern popularity. There are a couple more **minarets** too, one on Dhaliáni, and the other in Platía-1821, which is a fine traditional square to stop for a coffee.

From the top of Halídhon, or beyond the market, spread the broad, traffic-choked streets of the **modern city**. You may venture out here for business – travel agencies and banks lie in this direction, along with the post office, bus station and shops, but few tourists stay long. And in truth there's little reason to linger. On Tzanakáki, not far from the market, you'll find the **public gardens**, a park with strolling couples, a few caged animals (including *krí-krí* or Cretan ibex) and a café under the trees; there's also an open-air auditorium which occasionally hosts live music or local festivities. Locals tend not to hang around this part of town – though they are drawn to the seafront cafés of Aktí Miaoúli, east of the old city, and to the seafood tavernas behind the beach.

The beaches

Haniá's beaches all lie to the west of the city. For the usually crowded and recently cleaned-up **city beach**, this means no more than a ten-minute walk following the shoreline from the Naval Museum, but for more extensive spaces you're better off taking the local bus (#21) out along the coast road. This leaves from the east side of Platía-1866 and runs along the coast as far as **Kalamáki beach**. Kalamáki and the previous stop, **Oásis beach**, are again pretty crowded but they're a considerable improvement over the beach in Haniá itself. In between, you'll find plenty of alternatives, though some of these are quite a walk from the bus stop. Further afield there are even finer beaches at **Ayía Marína** (see p.285) to the west, or **Stavrós** (p.285) out on the Akrotíri peninsula, either of which can be reached by KTEL buses from the main station.

Eating

You're never far from something to **eat** in Haniá: in a circle around the harbour is one restaurant, taverna or café after another. These tend to be pricey, though, and the quality at many leaves a lot to be desired. Away from the water, there are plenty of slightly cheaper possibilities on Kondhiláki, Kanevárou and most of the streets off Halídhon. For snacks or lighter meals, the cafés around the harbour generally serve cocktails and fresh juices at exorbitant prices, though breakfast (especially "English") can be good value. For more traditional places, try around the market and along Dhaskaloyiánnis (*Synganaki* here is a good traditional bakery serving *tyrópita* and the like, with a cake shop next door). Fast food is also increasingly widespread.

Akrogiali Aktí Papanikolí 19, behind the city beach ☎ 28210 73110. Worth the walk, or short taxi ride, to this excellent, reasonably priced seafront fish taverna with a summer terrace. Always packed with locals, so may be worth booking – though there are plenty of alternatives along the same street.

Amphora Aktí Koundourótou, under the *Hotel Amphora*. One of the most reliable places on the outer harbour, with good, simple Greek fare.

Anaplous Sífaka 37. A couple of blocks west of Platía-1821, *Anaplous* occupies a stylishly "restored" ruin of a Turkish mansion bombed in the war. Serves both *mezédhes* and full meals to live guitar music.

Apostolis Aktí Enóseos 6 & 10, inner harbour. The fish tavernas at the inner end of the harbour are rated much higher by locals than those further round – some locals claim *Apostolis 2*, practically the last, and just a couple of doors down from its seemingly identical sister restaurant, is the best of all. The fish is excellent, but pricey.

Aroma Aktí Tombázi 4, next to the Mosque of the Janissaries. Pleasant café with great harbour view to savour over lazy breakfasts or late drinks. *Mousses*, nearby at the corner of Kanevárou, is equally good, and open 24 hours.

Doloma Karsokalyvon 5, near the Arsenali. Excellent little taverna with a nice terrace serving well-prepared and economical Cretan dishes.

Ela Top of Kondhiláki. Standard taverna food with live Greek music accompaniment to enliven your meal in yet another roofless taverna townhouse.

Iordanis Bougatsa Kydhonías 96, opposite the bus station. This place serves little except the traditional creamy *bougátsa*, a sugar-coated cheese pie to eat in or take away. Another branch is at Apokorónou 24, between the market and the tourist office.

Karnayio Platía Kateháki 8 ☎ 28210 53366. Set back from the inner harbour near the port police. Not right on the water, but one of the best harbour restaurants nonetheless. Excellent fish, traditional Cretan cooking and a fine selection of wines – all served on an inviting terrace – make this a winner. The nearby *Faka* is also good.

Meltemi Angélou 2. Slow, relaxed terrace bar beneath the rooms place of the same name; good for breakfast, and where locals (especially expats) sit whiling the day away or playing *tavli*.

Mihalis Akti Tombazi, on the outer harbour ☎ 28210 58330. Near the mosque, this is currently the number-one venue for *haniotes* dining out. Excellent selection of fish and meat dishes appears on a menu featuring many Cretan specialities such as *cóchli* (snails) and *hórta* (wild greens). Throw in a lively terrace, good wine list, attentive service and (very likely) a dessert on the house and you have a memorable place to dine.

Rudi's Bierhaus Sífaka 24 ☎ 28210 50824. Haniá's beer shrine: Austrian – and long-time Hania resident – Rudi Riegler's bar stocks more than a hundred of Europe's finest beers to accompany some outstanding *mezédhes*. **Tamam** Zambelíou. Excellent, fashionable place with adventurous Greek menu including much vegetarian food. Unfortunately only a few cramped tables in the alley outside, and inside it can get very hot. Service can be slow.

Tholos Ayíon Dhéka 36. Slightly north of the cathedral, *Tholos* is another "restaurant in a ruin", this time Venetian/Turkish, with a wide selection of Cretan specialities.

Bars and nightlife

Haniá's **nightlife** has more than enough venues to satisfy most night owls. The majority of the touristy clubs and disco bars are gathered in the area around the harbour, whilst there are plenty of terrace bars along both harbourfronts, with more scattered throughout the old quarter. Young locals, however, tend to start their evenings in the bars and cafés along Aktí Miaoúli, east of the harbour, and Sarpidhónos, which leads from the inner harbour in that direction. Around midnight, most move on to clubs, either in town or out along the coast, especially in Plataniás.

As everywhere, places go in and out of fashion, and names change frequently, but the venues generally remain where they were – in the old town **bars** you're occasionally reminded of the proximity of the Soúdha NATO bases by an influx of rowdy servicemen. Reliable places around the harbour include the *Four Seasons*, a very popular bar by the port police, and several bars, including long-running *Scorpio*, in an alley starting behind the Mosque of the Janissaries. Nearby, on upper floors, is the laid-back *Point* bar (above *Mousses* café). At the opposite or western end of the harbour *Fagotto*, Angélou 16, is a pleasant, laid-back jazz bar, often with live performers.

Most younger *haniotes* get their nightlife kicks by heading out along the coast to the west where a vibrant **club scene** – based around Ayía Marina and Plataniás – goes on all summer. Big out-of-town places here include *Destyle* in Ayía Marina, *Mambo* on the Kató Stalós waterfront (just before Ayía Marina) and *Utopia* in Plataniás. Current boss of the in-town **clubs** scene is *King*, down an alley off the top of Halídhon, under the Schiavo bastion, closely followed by its rival *Premier*, a big, bright place on Tsoudherón behind the market. The most popular drinking locations are the numerous terraces lining **Aktí Míaouli**, the waterfront to the east of the old quarter where dozens of music bars provide lounging chairs and even enormous sofas for their (literally) laid-back clientele. Of the numerous places here, you could try *Ellinikon*, *Mythologia* or *Il Nostro*, though most seem almost interchangeable.

A venue offering more traditional entertainment is the *Café Kriti*, Kalergón 22, at the corner of Andhroyíou, basically an old-fashioned *kafenío* where there's **Greek music** and **dancing** virtually every night. It's also worth checking for events at the open-air auditorium in the public gardens, and for performances in restaurants outside the city, which are the ones the locals will go to. Look for posters, especially in front of the market and in the little platía across the road from there.

For **films**, you should also check the hoardings in front of the market. There are open-air screenings at Attikon, on Venizélou out towards Akrotíri, about 1km from the centre, and occasionally in the public gardens.

Listings

Airlines Olympic, with scheduled daily flights between Haniá and Athens plus frequent flights to Thessaloníki, has an office at Tzanakáki 88 (Mon–Fri 9am–4pm; ☎ 28210 57701–3) opposite the public gardens. Aegean (to Athens only) is at Venizélou 12 (☎ 28210 51100) across from the market. For airport information call ℡ 28210 63264.

Banks and exchange The main branch of the National Bank of Greece is directly opposite the market with two ATMs, and there's a cluster of banks with more ATMs around the top of Halídhon. You'll also find plenty of out-of-hours exchange places on Halídhon, in the travel agencies.

Bike and car rental Possibilities everywhere, especially on Halídhon, though these are rarely the best value. For bikes, Summertime, Dhaskaloyiánnis 7, slightly northeast of the market (℡ 28210 45797, ⓦ www.strentals.gr) has a huge range, including mountain bikes. Bike Trekking, Karaóli 15 (℡ 28210 20143), has organized mountain-biking tours. For cars, look along Halídhon – two reliable local companies are Hermes, Tzanakáki 52 (℡ 28210 54418), or Tellus Rent a Car, Halídhon 108, opposite Platía-1866 (℡ 28210 91500). Good deals for *Rough Guide* readers (25 percent off normal rates) are available from El Greco Cars at the *El Greco* hotel (℡ 28210 60883, ⓦ www .elgreco.gr; see "Accommodation").

Boat trips A number of boats make daily trips from Haniá, mainly to the nearby islands of Áyii Theódori and Lazarétta, for swimming and *krí-krí* (ibex) spotting: you're unlikely to escape the attentions of their stalls around the harbour. The *Evagelos* glass-bottomed boat, for example, makes this trip three times daily, with an all-day alternative on Saturdays to the Rodhópou peninsula (roughly €20; for information call ℡ 694 58 74 283); the *MS Irini* (℡ 28210 52001) is a more traditional vessel.

Diving Blue Adventures Diving, Arholeon 11 near the inner harbour (℡ 28210 40403), runs daily diving and snorkelling trips.

Ferry tickets From any travel agent, or the ANEK line office is on Venizélou, right opposite the market (℡ 28210 27500); Hellenic Sea Ways at Platía-1866 14 (℡ 28210 75444).

Internet There are plenty of Internet cafés including: Kathodon, Isodhíon 10; the more tranquil Vranas, Ayíon Dhéka beneath *Vranas Studios* (see p.280) minimum 1hr, though credit given); and

Café Notos, on the outer harbour under the *Hotel Notos*.

Laundry There are plenty to choose from, including Speedy Laundry (℡ 28210 88411; 9am–2pm & 6–9pm), junction of Koronéou and Korkídhi, just west of Platía-1866, who will collect and deliver your load if you call; Afrodite, Ayíon Dhéka 22 (daily 8.30am–8.30pm) in the old town, and Fidias, Kalinákou Sarpáki 6 (next to the *pension* of the same name; Mon–Sat 9am–9pm). All do service washes (5kg including drying and folding) for around €7.50.

Left luggage The bus station has a left-luggage office open 6am–8.30pm; €1–2 per item per day depending on size.

Market and supermarkets To buy food, head for the entertaining market which has fresh fruit and vegetables, meat and fish, bakers, dairy stalls and general stores for cooked meats, tins, etc; on Saturday mornings there's a wonderful line of stalls along Minóos, inside the eastern city wall, where local farmers sell their produce. Several small stores by the harbour platía sell cold drinks and food; they are expensive but open late. Small supermarkets can be found on Platía-1866, and the larger Champion supermarket is at the top of Pireos, outside the western wall, close to the Schiavo bastion.

Post office The main post office is on Tzanakáki (Mon–Fri 7.30am–8pm, Sat 9am–1pm).

Taxis The main taxi ranks are in Platía-1866. For radio taxis try ℡ 28210 18300, ℡ 28210 94300 or ℡ 28210 98700.

Tourist police April–Sept they man an office in the Mosque of the Janisseries on the outer harbour (℡ 28210 28750). Their inconveniently located main office is at Iraklíou 23 in the southern suburb of Koubés (℡ 28210 53333 or 28210 28708).

Travel agencies El Greco Travel, on Kydhonías near the bus station (℡ 28210 86015), and Tellus Travel, Halídhon 108, opposite Platía-1866 (℡ 28210 91500), are both good for inexpensive bus tickets, flights and standard excursions. For cheap tickets home try Bassias Travel, Halídhon 69 (℡ 28210 44295), very helpful for regular tickets too. They also deal in standard excursions.

Around Haniá: the Akrotíri and Rodhópou peninsulas

Just north of Haniá, the **Akrotíri peninsula** loops around to protect the Bay of Soúdha and a NATO military base and missile-testing area. In an ironic twist, the peninsula's northwestern coastline is fast developing into a luxury suburb; the beach of Kalathás, near Horafákia, long popular with jaded

Haniotes, is surrounded by villas and apartments. **STAVRÓS**, further out, has not yet suffered this fate, and its **beach** is absolutely superb if you like the calm, shallow water of an almost completely enclosed lagoon. It's not very large, so it does get crowded, but rarely overpoweringly so. There's a makeshift taverna/*souvláki* stand on the beach, and a couple of tavernas across the road, but for accommodation you need to search slightly south of here, in the area around **Blue beach**, where there are plenty of apartment buildings but no low-budget accommodation in summer whatsoever. On Blue beach you could try *Zorba's Apartments* (☎28210 52525; ❸).

Inland are the **monasteries** of **Ayía Triádha** (daily 7.30am–2pm & 5–7pm; €1.50) and **Gouvernétou** (daily 7am–2pm & 4–8pm; free). The former is much more accessible and has a beautiful seventeenth-century church inside its pink-and-ochre cloister, though ongoing renovations – the latest has turned one building into an olive-oil factory where the monks produce and bottle their own oil – on occasions make the normally peaceful enclosure more like a building site. Four kilometres north of Ayía Triádha, Gouvernétou – in a far better state of preservation and where traditional monastic life can still be observed – is a tranquil oasis with some fine frescoes in its ancient church. From just beyond the monastery you can clamber down a craggy path to the amazing and abandoned ruins of the **monastery of Katholikó**, built into a craggy ravine, and the remains of its narrow (swimmable) harbour.

West to Rodhópou

The coast to the west of Haniá was the scene of most of the fighting during the German invasion in 1941, and at Máleme there's a big German cemetery; the Allied cemetery is in the other direction, on the coast just outside Soúdha. There are also beaches and considerable tourist development along much of this shore. At **Ayía Marína** there's a fine sandy beach and an island offshore said to be a sea monster petrified by Zeus before it could swallow Crete. Seen from the west, its "mouth" still gapes open.

Between **Plataniás** and **Kolymvári** an almost unbroken strand unfurls, exposed when the wind blows and by no means all sandy, but deserted for long stretches between villages. The road here runs through mixed groves of calamus reed (Crete's bamboo) and oranges; the windbreaks fashioned from the reeds protect the ripening oranges from the *meltémi*. At Kolymvári, the road to Kastélli cuts across the base of another mountainous peninsula, **Rodhópou**. Just off the main road here is a monastery, **Goniá** (summer Mon–Fri & Sun 7am–12.30pm & 4.30–8pm, Sat 4–8pm; winter daily 3.30–5.30pm; free; respectable dress required), with a view most luxury hotels would envy. Every monk in Crete can tell tales of his proud ancestry of resistance to invaders, but here the Turkish cannon balls are still lodged in the walls to prove it, a relic of which the good fathers are far more proud than any of the icons.

South to the Samariá Gorge

From Haniá the **Samariá Gorge** (May–Oct; €5 for entry to the national park) can be visited as a day-trip or as part of a longer excursion to the south. At 16km, it is Europe's longest gorge and is startlingly beautiful. In the June to August period (ring Haniá tourist office or check at the bus station for other times) **buses** leave Haniá bus station for the top at 6.15am, 7.30am, 8.30am and 2pm (this latter service changes to 4.30pm outside school holidays), depositing

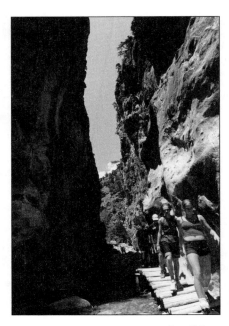

△ Samariá Gorge

you at the gorge entrance and then collecting you at the port of Hóra Sfakíon for the return trip to Haniá. You can also get the boat and bus back via Soúyia or Paleohóra, and if this is your intention you should specify when you buy your ticket: otherwise, for the three early buses, you'll normally be sold a return trip (valid from Hóra Sfakíon at any time). Should you take the last bus you will need to spend a night at Ayía Rouméli (the end of the gorge) as you will not get through the gorge in time for the last boat. It's well worth catching the earliest bus to avoid the full heat of the day while walking through the gorge, though be warned that you will not be alone – there are often as many as five coachloads setting off before dawn for the nail-biting climb into the White Mountains. There are also direct early-morning buses from Iráklion, Réthymnon, Soúyia and Paleohóra as well as bus tours from virtually everywhere on the island, adding up to a couple of thousand plus walkers on most days during high season.

Despite all the crowds, the walk *is* hard work, especially in spring when the stream is a roaring torrent. Early and late in the season, there is a danger of **flash floods**, which are not to be taken lightly: in 1993, a number of walkers perished when they were washed out to sea. For this reason the first and last three weeks of the season are entirely dependent on the weather and you will only be allowed into the gorge if the authorities deem it safe. If in doubt (and to save yourself a wasted journey), phone the Haniá Forest Service's **gorge information number** (☎28210 92287) or the gorge office (☎28210 67179). Should you arrive after 4pm you will only be allowed into the first couple of kilometres from each end of the gorge and the wardens ensure that no one remains in the gorge overnight, where camping is strictly forbidden.

Omalós

One way to avoid an early start from the north coast would be to stay at the elevated village of **OMALÓS**, in the middle of the mountain plain from which the gorge descends. The climate is cooler here all year round and a welcome bonus is the many paths into the hills surrounding the plateau where in season a profusion of wildflowers and birdlife is to be seen. There are plenty of **tavernas** and some ordinary **rooms** for rent – the friendly no-frills *Samaria pension* (☎28210 67168; ❶) is the cheapest – plus a clutch of surprisingly fancy **hotels**; the *Hotel Gigilos* (☎28210 67181; ❶) is good value and its proprietor will drive you the 5km to the top of the gorge in the morning if you stay overnight. However, since the village is some way from the start of the path, and the first buses arrive as the sun rises, it's almost impossible to get a head start on the crowds. Some people sleep out at the top (where there's a bar-restaurant in the *Tourist Lodge* and kiosks serving drinks and sandwiches), but a night under the stars here can be a bitterly cold experience. The one significant advantage to staying up here would be if you wanted to undertake some other **climbs** in the White Mountains, in which case the Kallérgi mountain hut (℡28210 33199 or ℡693 66 57 954; €12 per person including shower) is about an hour's hike (signed) from Omalós or ninety minutes from the top of the gorge; you can also drive up there from Omalós.

The gorge

The **gorge** itself begins at the *xylóskalo*, or "wooden staircase", a stepped path plunging steeply down from the southern lip of the Omalós plain. Here, at the head of the track, opposite the sheer rock face of Mount Gíngilos, the crowds pouring out of the buses disperse rapidly as keen walkers march purposefully down while others dally over breakfast, contemplating the sunrise. You descend at first through almost alpine scenery: pine forest, wildflowers and very un-Cretan greenery – a verdant shock in the spring, when the stream is at its liveliest. Small churches and viewpoints dot the route, and about halfway down you pass the abandoned village of **Samariá**, now home to a wardens' station, with picnic facilities and filthy toilets. Further down, the path levels out and the gorge walls close in until, at the narrowest point (the *sidherespórtes* or "iron gates"), one can practically touch both tortured rock faces at once and, looking up, see them rising sheer for almost a thousand feet.

At an average pace, with regular stops, the walk down takes five or six hours (though you can do it far quicker), and the upward trek considerably longer. It's strenuous – you'll know all about it next day – the path is rough, and walking boots or solid shoes are vital. On the way down, there is plenty of water from springs and streams (except some years in Sept and Oct), but nothing to eat. The park that surrounds the gorge is a refuge of the Cretan wild ibex, the *krí-krí*, but don't expect to see one; there are usually far too many people around.

Villages of the southwest coast

When you finally emerge from the gorge, it's not long before you reach the singularly unattractive village of **AYÍA ROUMÉLI**, which is all but abandoned until you come to the beach, a mirage of iced drinks and a cluster of tavernas with **rooms** for rent. *Livikon* (☎ 28250 91363; ❶) at the back of the village is one of the more tranquil places. On arrival, it's best to buy your boat tickets straightaway to be sure of getting the sailing you want (though in theory they guarantee that no one will be left behind, and that the buses will wait for the boat). If you plan to stay on the south coast, you should get going as soon as possible for the best chance of finding a room somewhere nicer than Ayía Rouméli. From May to October there are three boats daily to Loutró and Hóra Sfakíon (11.30am, 3.45pm and 6pm, plus 9am June–Sept), and a sailing to Soúyia and Paleohóra daily at 4.45pm.

If you are planning on staying down here, bring enough cash – the Visa-only ATM in Hóra Sfakíon is the only one between Paleohóra and Plakías. Drivers heading for Soúyia should also ensure their tanks are full – there's no fuel there.

Loutró

For tranquillity, it's hard to beat **LOUTRÓ**, two-thirds of the way to Hóra Sfakíon, and accessible only by boat or on foot. The chief disadvantage of Loutró is its lack of a real beach; most people swim from the rocks around its small bay. If you're prepared to walk, however, there are **deserted beaches** along the coast to the east which can also be reached by hired **canoe**. Indeed, if you're really into walking there's a **coastal trail** through Loutró which covers the entire distance between Ayía Rouméli and Hóra Sfakíon (now part of the E4 Pan-European footpath), or you could take the daunting zigzag path up the cliff behind to the mountain village of **Anópoli**. Loutró itself has a number of **tavernas** and **rooms**, though not always enough of the latter in peak season. Call the ⚲ *Blue House* (☎28250 91127, Ⓦwww.delftmark.nl/thebluehouse; ❷) if you want to book ahead, where there are comfortable en-suite rooms and a wonderful (slightly pricier) top-floor extension; this is also the best place to eat. Slightly more upmarket accommodation is on offer at the nearby *Hotel Porto Loutro* (☎28250 91433, Ⓦwww.hotelportoloutro.com; ❷–❸), which also hires out canoes and runs full-day **cruises** on its own boat to "Palm Beach" (see p.274) and the island of Gávdhos; prices should be posted outside. There's space to **camp** out on the cape by a ruined fort, but due to a long history of problems, you should be aware that campers are not very popular in the village. If you're determined to camp, head for the **beaches** and coves to the east (such as Sweetwater) and west (Mármara) of the resort which can be reached on foot, or more comfortably by canoe or daily boats from the harbour.

Hóra Sfakíon and beyond

HÓRA SFAKÍON is the more usual terminus for walkers traversing the gorge, with a regular boat service along the coast to and from Ayía Rouméli. Consequently, it's quite an expensive and not an especially welcoming place; there are plenty of **rooms** and some decent **tavernas**, but for a real beach you should jump straight on a bus (currently running at 11am and 6pm April–Sept) going toward Plakiás (see p.273). Plenty of opportunities for a dip present themselves en route, one of the most memorable at **Frangokástello**, named after a crumbling Venetian attempt to bring law and order to a district that went on to defy both Turks and Germans. The four-square, crenellated and imposing thirteenth-century **castle**, isolated a few kilometres below a chiselled wall of mountains, looks like it's been spirited out of the High Atlas or Tibet. The place is said to be haunted by ghosts of Greek rebels massacred here in 1829: every May, these *dhrossoulítes* ("dewy ones") march at dawn across the coastal plain and disappear into the sea near the fort. The rest of the time Frangokástello is peaceful enough, with a superb beach and a number of tavernas and rooms, but there's not a lot to do. The greatest concentration of rooms is immediately below the castle – try *Maria's Studios* (☎28250 92159, Ⓦwww.marias–studios .com; ❷) or *Kali Kardia* (☎28250 92123; ❶), for example. Slightly further east, and less influenced by tourism or modern life, are the attractive villages of **Skalotí** and **Rodhákino**, where basic lodging and food can be found in the villages proper or their seafront offshoots a couple of kilometres to the south.

Soúyia

In quite the other direction from Ayía Rouméli, less regular boats also head to **SOÚYIA** and on to Paleohóra. Soúyia, until World War II merely the anchorage for Koustoyérako inland, is a low-key resort, with a long, grey pebble beach and mostly modern buildings (except for a church with a sixth-century Byzantine mosaic as the foundation). Since the completion in 1990 of the paved road to Haniá, the village has started to expand; even so, except in the very middle of summer, it continues to make a good fall-back for finding a room or a place to camp, eating cheaply and enjoying the beach when the rest of the island is swarming with visitors.

Rooms (slightly more expensive than on the rest of this coast) are scattered around the road on the way in, and in the seafront zone where it hits the sea, although places here tend to be both pricier and noisier. One of the many places on the road as it comes into Soúyia is *Captain George* (☎28230 51133; ❸), where there are some larger apartments, or the peaceful *El Greco*, set further back (☎28230 51186; ②); both offer balcony rooms with fridge and (some) kitchenette. On the seafront, *Hotel Santa Irene* (☎28230 51342, ⓦwww.sougia .info/hotels/santairene; ③) is the fanciest place in town with a/c balcony rooms with marble floors and fridges. Since the local travel agent closed, there's no one centre for **information**. Your hotel should be able to fill you in on how to walk the beautiful **Ayía Iríni gorge** or do a wonderful hour-long hike over to the nearby ancient site of **Lissós** with temples and mosaics. Otherwise, bus tickets are sold at *Snacks Roxana*, near the bottom of the main road, while the two supermarkets opposite can arrange taxi boats to local beaches (get one to bring you home from Lissós, for example). Boat tickets are sold at the *períptero* on the seafront, and the boats leave from the dock at the western end of the beach. For **food**, *Rembetiko* has a pleasant garden terrace just off the main street, while the seafront is packed with possibilities. The German-run *Omikron* taverna has a more northern-European ambience and offers some **vegetarian** choices; *Café Lotos* provides **Internet** access.

Kastélli and the western tip

Apart from being Crete's most westerly town, and the end of the main E65 coastal highway, **KASTÉLLI** (Kíssamos, or Kastélli Kissámou as it's variously known) has little obvious attraction. It's a busy town with a rocky central **beach** (although there's an excellent sandy beach to the west) visited mainly by people using the boat that runs twice weekly to the island of Kathira and the Peloponnese. The very ordinariness of Kastélli, however, can be attractive: life goes on pretty much regardless of outsiders, and there's every facility you might need. The town was important in antiquity, though sadly the recently excavated **mosaics** signed around the centre have all been buried under a layer of earth to protect them, while the new **museum** (located in the refurbished former Venetian governor's residence on the main square), planned to display finds from these digs and others nearby, has yet to open thanks to wrangling over the status of the contents – it will possibly begin operating by May 2006.

As regards **practicalities**, you'll find most of what you need around the main square, Platía Kastellíou. The bus station is here, as are a couple of cafés; banks, shops and travel agencies (for ferry tickets or car rental) lie east of the square along Skalídhi (another group can be found around Platía Venizélou, on the main road through town). The harbour itself is a good 2km west of town – a significant walk if you're heavily laden, or a €5 taxi ride. For **rooms**, *Koutsounakis* (☎28220 23416; ②) and the more basic but clean and friendly *Vergerakis* (aka *Jimmy's*; ☎28220 22663; ①) are both right by Platía Kastellíou. For more facilities and a beachside location, the excellent ⚓ *Hotel Galini Beach* (☎28220 23288, ⓦwww.galinibeach.com; B&B; ③) with sparkling balconies, a/c, sea-view rooms is well worth the extra; it lies at the pebbly, eastern end of the seafront near the sports stadium with easy parking and serves bountiful breakfasts. At the western end of the strand the friendly ⚓ *Maria Beach* (☎28220 22610, ⓦwww.mariabeach.gr; ②–④) has a whole variety of attractive en-suite a/c balcony rooms, plus studios and apartments on the town's sandy western beach.

Heading north from the main square brings you to the beach promenade where there are a number of **tavernas** – *Papadakis* is worth a try and, for its summer *mezédhes* and winter taverna, *Dionysos* is also good. The seafront strip's late-night drinking and music **bars** are also popular with the local younger set, particularly at weekends.

Falásarna to Elafoníssi

To the west of Kastélli lies some of Crete's loneliest and, for many visitors, finest coastline. The first place of note is **Falásarna**, where the scant ruins of an ancient city are ignored by most visitors in favour of some of the best beaches on Crete, wide and sandy with clean water. There's a handful of **tavernas** and an increasing number of **rooms** for rent: *Sunset* (℡ 28220 41204; ❶), at the end of the paved road near the archeological site, is among the better choices for both. Plenty of people **camp** out here too; if you join them, be sure to take any litter away with you. Rubbish, occasional tar and crowds of locals on summer weekends can always be escaped if you're prepared to walk, and the beaches are worth it. The nearest real town is **Plátanos**, 5km up a paved road, serviced by a couple of daily buses; the town has supermarkets and a bank with ATM.

Further south, the western coastline is far less discovered. **SFINÁRI** is a quiet village with a number of rooms to rent on the road down to a quiet pebble beach. At the bottom are a couple of tavernas; try *Captain Fidias,* which offers free camping and sunloungers for the pebbly beach.

KÁMBOS is similar, but even less visited, its beach a considerable walk down a hill (or a very steep drive). **Accommodation** is available at the good-value *Rooms Hartzulakis* (℡ 28220 44445; ❶) on the edge of a long gorge which also leads down to the sea; the same place has a terrace taverna with great views, and you should be able to get information about walking locally. Beyond them both is the **monastery of Khryssoskalítissa**, increasingly visited by tours from Haniá and Paleohóra, but well worth the effort for its isolation and nearby beaches; the bus gets as far as Váthy, from where the monastery is another two hours' walk, although you could try hitching – with a fair chance of success – as many of the tourist cars are bound to be heading for the same destination.

Five kilometres beyond Khryssoskalítissa, the tiny uninhabited islet of **Elafoníssi** lies marooned on the edge of a gloriously scenic turquoise lagoon. It's all too easy to get here now, a fact reflected in the huge number of visitors who do, by car, with coach tours, or on a boat from Paleohóra. The pinky-white sand, the warm, clear lagoon and the islet to which you can easily wade still look magnificent, but you certainly won't have it to yourself. There's a single, inadequate portable toilet and a number of stalls selling cold drinks and basic food, while 1km or so up the road are a couple of taverna/rooms places

---

A round trip

If you have transport, a circular drive from Kastélli, via the west coast and back by the inland route through Élos and Topólia, makes for a stunningly scenic circuit. Near the sea, villages cling to the high mountainsides, apparently halted by some miracle in the midst of calamitous seaward slides. Around them, olives ripen on the terraced slopes, the sea glittering far below. Inland, especially at **ÉLOS**, the main crop is the chestnut, whose huge old trees shade the village streets.

South of **TOPÓLIA**, the chapel of Ayía Sofía is sheltered inside a cave which has been used as a shrine since Neolithic times. Cutting south just before Élos, a spectacular paved road continues through the high mountains towards Paleohóra. On a motorbike, with a sense of adventure and plenty of fuel, it's great: the bus doesn't come this way, villagers still stare at the sight of a tourist, and a host of small, seasonal streams cascades beside or under the asphalt.

– Elafonissi (☎28220 61274; ❷) is the better of them with its own taverna and minimarket. For a day-trip, though, it's best to bring your own supplies.

Kándanos and Paleohóra

The easiest route to the far southwest leaves the north coast at Tavronítis, 22km west of Haniá, heading for Paleohóra; several buses follow this route from Haniá every day, and although this road also has to wind through the western outriders of the White Mountains, it lacks the excitement of the alternatives to either side. **KÁNDANOS**, at the 58-kilometre mark, has been entirely rebuilt since it was destroyed by the Germans for its fierce resistance to their occupation. The original sign erected when the deed was done is preserved on the war memorial in the central square: "Here stood Kándanos, destroyed in retribution for the murder of 25 German soldiers, and never to be rebuilt again." The pleasantly easy-going and once-again substantial village had the last laugh.

When the beach at **PALEOHÓRA** finally appears below, it is a welcome sight. The little town is built across the base of a peninsula, its harbour and a beach known as "Pebble Beach" on the eastern side, the wide sands ("Sandy Beach") on the other. Above, on the outcrop, ruined Venetian ramparts stand sentinel. These days Paleohóra has developed into a significant resort, but it's still thoroughly enjoyable, with a main street filling with tables at night as diners spill out of the restaurants, and with a pleasantly chaotic social life. You'll find a helpful **tourist office** (Mon & Wed–Sun 10am–1pm & 6–9pm; ☎28230 41507) in a cabin on "Pebble Beach", close to the ferry harbour. They have full accommodation lists and provide a decent **map** which is useful for finding food and accommodation locations.

There are plenty of **places to stay** (though not always many vacancies in high season) – try the friendly *Castello Rooms* (☎28230 41143; ❷), at the southern end of Sandy beach; the alleys behind here, beneath the castle, have many more simple rooms places. Just north of here the *Sandy Beach Hotel* (☎08230 42138, Ⓕ08230 42139; ❸) is the town's chicest hotel option for a/c balcony rooms with fridge, TV and sea view. *Villa Marise* (☎28230 42012, Ⓔjetee@otenet.gr; ❹) enjoys one of the best locations in town, right on the sandy beach more or less opposite the post office, and has a variety of well-equipped rooms, apartments and studios for up to six people. Probably the least expensive rooms in town are at *Anonymous* (☎28230 41509; ❶), in a backstreet behind the main street (Odhós Venizélos), with shared bathrooms and kitchen, and a very friendly atmosphere. There's also a fair-sized **campsite**, *Camping Paleohora* (☎28230 41120), 2km north of "Pebble Beach". If you are tempted to sleep on the main "Sandy Beach" – one of the best on the south coast, with showers, trees and acres of sand – be prepared for trouble from police and local residents who are no longer willing to tolerate it. When you tire of beach life there are plenty of alternative entertainments from dolphin-watching trips to excursions into the hills to Azoyirés, or a five-to-six-hour hike along the coastal path to Soúyia.

For **eating** and **drinking**, tavernas, bars and cafés are to be found throughout the resort, particularly along the roads behind the two beaches. A good place to try for some imaginative **vegetarian** specials is *The Third Eye*, just out of the centre towards Sandy beach. Other decent in-town eating places include *Pizzeria Niki*, off the south side of Kondekáki (the road running from east to west at the south end of Venizélou), and *The Wave* at the south end of "Pebble Beach", serving good fish on a seaside terrace. Paleohóra's flagship seafood restaurant, however, is the outstanding ⚓ *Caravella*, with a pleasant waterfront terrace just beyond the harbour at the south end of "Sandy Beach"; the cooking and service are excellent, as is their chilled *hyma* (barrelled wine) from a vineyard in the Kastélli Kissámou area.

As Paleohóra publicizes itself as a "family" resort, there's an unwritten curfew around 11pm when the bars lower their sounds, so if you're looking for some untamed nightlife you've definitely come to the wrong place. Even *Escape Paleohora Club*, at the extreme north end of "Pebble Beach" close to the campsite, has had to close its outdoor **dance** floor, although the authorities recently allowed them a smaller one; but the action still continues till late indoors. In the other direction, just beyond the southern end of the "Sandy Beach", *Nostos* has a more chilled vibe, and opens throughout the day. A great little open-air **cinema**, Cine Attikon, is tucked away in the northern backstreets; most of their films are in English and programmes (which change daily) are posted outside the tourist office and on fliers attached to the odd tree trunk around town.

Almost everything else you're likely to need is located in the centre of town along and around Odhós Venizélos. **Banks** (with ATMs), **travel agents**, a **laundry**, **mountain-bike** and **car-rental** companies and **Internet** access (at *Er@to Cafe* or Notos Travel) are all along Venizélou, while the **post office** is on the road behind "Sandy Beach". There are three **pharmacies** on Kondekáki and there's a **health centre** in the street parallel to Venizélos to the west. When the tourist office is closed, Notos Travel (☎28230 42110), on Venizélou, is a friendly source of information on almost everything to do in Paleohóra and has lots of information on renting apartments, cars, mountain bikes and lots more. PADI-certificated courses in **scuba diving** are on offer at Aquacrete, Kontekáki 4, close to Venizélos (☎28230 41393, ⓦ www.aquacreta.gr).

Boats run from Paleohóra to Elafoníssi, to the island of Gávdhos and along the coast to Soúyia and Ayía Rouméli; Notos Travel (see above), on Venizélos, and E-Motion (☎28230 41755), on Kontekáki by the harbour, are good sources of information and tickets. They also have information about other trips – to walk the **Samariá Gorge**, for example, although you can also do that independently by catching the bus leaving daily at 6am throughout the summer, and a boat back from Ayía Rouméli.

Gávdhos

The island of **Gávdhos**, some 50km of rough sea south of Paleohóra, is the most southerly land mass in Europe. Gávdhos is small (about 10km by 7km) and barren, but it has one major attraction: the enduring **isolation** which its inaccessible position has helped preserve. This may not last much longer, as a big new port is under construction (currently stalled due to the discovery of its Minoan predecessor), together with a new electricity plant and asphalted roads. Providing you avoid the crowds in August, if all you want is a beach to yourself and a taverna to grill your fish, this remains the place for you. For the moment not too much has changed, and it is usually possible to turn up on spec and find a bed, but travel agents in Paleohóra (see above) will arrange a room if you want one and also provide current ferry information. There's a semi-permanent community of campers and would-be "Robinson Crusoes" resident on the island throughout the summer – in addition to the six indigenous families who live here all year round.

Largely because water is often difficult to obtain, most people choose to base themselves near to one of the three largest beaches; at the most popular of all, **SARAKÍNIKO**, there's a slew of beachfront tavernas in addition to a squatters' community spreading a shanty town of unsightly breezeblock summer dwellings behind the beach. For **rooms** *Taverna Gerti & Manolis* (☎28230 41103; ❷) is reliable, while *Sarakíniko Studios* (☎28230 42182, ⓦ www.gavdostudios.gr; B&B; ❸) is a step upmarket. The latter's proprietors will collect you from the harbour and they have a **campsite** for pitching tents. Good **places to eat** at Sarakíniko include *Gerti & Manolis* (see above) for fresh fish, *Karapistolas* for Middle Eastern specialities, and the friendly *Sorolop* with a nice "community" feel when people hang around to play chess or Scrabble after eating. At Áyios Ioánnis, one of the other beach settlements 2km to the northwest (where's there's a thriving "hippy" and nudist community), a solitary and unnamed taverna is also an excellent place for fresh fish. Although many people still bring as much food as they can with them on the boat, there are now well-stocked **minimarkets** at Sarakíniko and Áyios Ioánnis.

Travel details

Buses

The following are the main routes only. For the latest timetables and complete route and fare information for the west of the island, visit the website at ⓦ www.bus-service-crete-ktel.com. There are also plenty of unofficial websites with timetables for the east: the official central timetable at ⓦ www.ktel.org rarely seems to work.

Áyios Nikólaos to: Iráklion (21 daily, 6 via Iráklion Airport 6am–8.30pm; 1hr 30min); Kritsá (9 daily 6.45am–8pm; 30min); Lasíthi plateau (2 daily; 2hr); Sitía (7 daily 6.15am–8.30pm; 1hr 30min).

Haniá to: Hóra Sfakíon (3 daily 8.30am–2pm; 2hr); Omalós (Samariá Gorge; 4 daily 6.15am–2pm; 1hr 15min); Paleohóra (3 daily 8.30am–4pm; 2hr); Iráklion via Réthymnon (21 daily, 2 via old road 5.30am–10pm; 2hr 30min total).

Iráklion to: Ayía Galíni (7 daily 6.30am–4.30pm; 2hr 30min); Áyios Nikólaos (19 daily 6.30am–9.30pm; 1hr 30min); Haniá (21 daily 5.30am–9pm; 2hr 30min); Phaestos (7 daily 7.30am–4.30pm; 1hr 30min); Ierápetra (7 daily 6.30am–7.30pm; 2hr 30min).

Kastélli to: Haniá (14 daily 6.30am–9.30pm; 1hr 15min).

Réthymnon to: Ayía Galíni via Spíli (5 daily 5.30am–2.15pm; 45min–1hr 30min); Haniá (21 daily 7am–10.30pm; 1hr); Iráklion (23 daily 6.30am–10.15pm; 1hr 30min); Plakiás (3 daily 6.15am–2.15pm; 1hr 15min).

Ferries

For the latest timetables for domestic and international ferries to and from Crete visit ⓦ www .cretetravel.com, ⓦ www.ferries.gr or ⓦ www .greekislands.gr.

Áyios Nikólaos and Sitía 3–4 sailings a week to Pireás (12hr); 2–3 ferries a week to Kássos, Kárpathos, Hálki and Rhodes; 2–3 weekly to Mílos.

Haniá Daily overnight to Pireás with ANEK (9–11hr) or Blue Star (5hr 45min).

Hóra Sfakíon 5 ferries daily to Loutró/Ayía Rouméli (1hr/2hr 30min); 3–4 weekly to Gávdhos (1hr 30min) in season.

Iráklion 2 ferries daily to Pireás (12hr); 1 daily fast ferry to Pireás (6hr); 3 ferries weekly to Thessaloníki; 1 daily ferry to Thíra (4hr), also fast boats and hydrofoils (2hr 30min); daily ferries to Páros, Mýkonos, Íos and Náxos in season; twice weekly to Tínos & weekly to Skíathos.

Kastélli (Kíssamos) 2 ferries weekly to Kýthira/ Pireás (3hr 30min/12hr), one of them via Yíthio (6hr); 1 ferry weekly to Kalamáta (7hr 30min).

Paleohóra 2–3 boats a week in season to Gávdhos. Also daily sailings to Elafoníssi and Soúyia/Ayía Rouméli.

Réthymnon Daily ferries to Pireás (11hr 30min); seasonal day-trips to Thíra.

Flights

Haniá to: Athens (5 daily on Olympic; 4 daily on Aegean); Thessaloníki (3 weekly on Olympic).

Iráklion to: Athens (5–7 daily on Olympic; 7 daily on Aegean); Rhodes (4 weekly, summer only, on Olympic; 1–2 daily on Aegean); Thessaloníki (2 weekly on Olympic; 2 daily on Aegean).

Sitía to: Alexandhroúpoli in Thrace (3 weekly on Olympic); Athens (3 weekly on Olympic); Préveza in northwest Greece (3 weekly on Olympic).

The Dodecanese

CHAPTER 4

Highlights

* **Northern Kárpathos** Old walking trails take you between traditional villages. See p.308

* **Ródhos old town** Superbly preserved medieval streets, inextricably linked with the Knights of Saint John. See p.314

* **Lindos Acropolis, Rhodes** A pleasing blend of ancient and medieval culture, with great views over the town. See p.322

* **Thárri monastery, Rhodes** Superb Byzantine frescoes in the oldest religious foundation on the island. See p.325

* **Sými** The officially protected harbour and hillside village teem with trippers during the day, but a stay overnight is rewarding. See p.335

* **Volcano of Níssyros** The craters of the dormant volcano still hiccup, with the most recent activity in 1933. See p.349

* **Brós Thermá, Kós** Relax in shoreline hot springs, which flow into the sea, protected by a boulder ring. See p.357

* **Mount Dhíkeos, Kós** The hike up is worthwhile for the views over the Dodecanese. See p.358

* **Hóra, Astypálea** The windswept island "capital" is perched dramatically above the sea and has a beautiful Venetian *kástro*. See p.364

△ Hóra of Astypálea, with Venetian castle

The Dodecanese

T he furthest island group from the Greek mainland, the **Dodecanese** (Dhodhekánisos) lie close to the Turkish coast – some of them, such as Kós and Kastellórizo, almost within hailing distance of Anatolia. Because of their strategic position, these islands have had a turbulent history: they were the scene of ferocious battles between German and British forces in 1943–44, and were only finally included in the modern Greek state in 1948 after centuries of occupation by Crusaders, Ottomans and Italians. Although relations between Greece and Turkey are currently at their best ever, the Greek army and air force clearly prefer to keep their powder dry, in the form of numerous military bases and smaller watch-points which multiplied after the 1996 incident over the disputed islet-duo of Ímia.

Whatever the rigours of the various occupations, their legacy includes a wonderful blend of architectural styles and of Eastern and Western cultures. Medieval Rhodes is the most famous, but almost every island has some Classical remains, a Crusaders' castle, a clutch of traditional villages and abundant grandiose public buildings. For these last the Italians, who occupied the Dodecanese from 1912 to 1943, are mainly responsible. In their determination to beautify the islands and turn them into a showplace for Fascism they undertook public works, excavations and reconstruction on a massive scale; if historical accuracy was often sacrificed on the altar of visual propaganda, only an expert is likely to complain. A more sinister aspect of the Italian administration was the attempted forcible Latinization of the populace: spoken Greek and Orthodox observance were banned in progressively stricter increments between the mid-1920s and 1936. The most tangible reminder of this policy is the (rapidly dwindling) number of older people who can still converse – and write – as fluently in Italian as in Greek.

Aside from this bilingualism, the Dodecanese themselves display a marked topographic and economic schizophrenia. The dry limestone outcrops of **Kastellórizo**, **Sými**, **Hálki**, **Kássos** and **Kálymnos** have always been forced to rely on the sea for their livelihoods, and the wealth generated by this maritime culture – especially during the nineteenth century – fostered the growth of attractive port towns. The sprawling, relatively fertile giants **Rhodes** (Ródhos) and **Kós** have recently seen their traditional agricultural economies almost totally displaced by a tourist industry focused on good beaches and nightlife, as well as some of the most exciting historical monuments in the Aegean. **Kárpathos** lies somewhere in between, with a lightly forested north grafted on to a rocky limestone south; **Tílos**, despite its lack of trees, has ample water, though the green volcano–island of **Níssyros** does not. **Léros** shelters softer contours and more amenable terrain

Karlóvassi & Vathý (Sámos)

Pythagório

Ikaría

Sámos

Foúrni

THE DODECANESE

0   50 km

Pátmos   Arkí   Agathoníssi

N

Skála
Hóra

T U R K E Y

Lipsí

Farmakoníssi

Léros   Ayía Marína
Lakkí

Xirókambos

Myrtiés   Kálymnos

Télendhos   Psérimos   Bodrum

Póthia

Marmaris

Mastihári   Kós

Kós

Astypálea   Kardhámena

Datça

Astypálea   Kéfalos

Sými

Yialí   Sými

Mandhráki

Nissyros   Ródhos

Megálo Horió

Tilos   Livádhia

Kámiros
Skála

Emborió

Hálki

Monólithos   Líndhos

Yennádhi

Kattaviá   Rhodes
(Ródhos)

Ólymbos   Dhiafáni

Mesohóri   Kárpathos

Rhodes

TURKEY

Kaş

Rhó   Meyísti

Kastellórizo
(Meyísti)

N

0   10 km

Pigádhia

Frý

Kássos

Sitía & Áyios Nikólaos (Crete)

Pireás   Pireás   Pireás   Kastellórizo

than its map outline would suggest, while **Pátmos** and **Astypálea** at the
fringes of the archipelago offer architecture and landscapes more typical of
the Cyclades.

The largest islands in the group are connected by regular **ferries and
catamarans**, and none (except Kastellórizo, Astypálea and Tílos) is hard to
reach. Rhodes is the main transport hub, with connections for Crete, the
northeastern Aegean, the Cyclades and the mainland as well. Kálymnos and
Kós are jointly an important secondary terminus, with a useful ferry based
on Kálymnos, hydrofoil services using Kós and Kálymnos as a focus and

transfer point, and two catamarans based on Rhodes and Pátmos providing a valuable supplement to larger ferries calling at uncivil hours.

Kássos

Like Psará islet in the northeast Aegean, **Kássos** contributed its large fleet to the Greek revolutionary war effort, and likewise suffered appalling consequences. In May 1824, an Ottoman army sent by Ibrahim Pasha, Governor of Egypt, besieged the island; on June 7, aided perhaps by a traitor's tip as to the weak point in Kássos's defences, the invaders descended on the populated north-coastal plain, slaughtered most of the inhabitants and put houses, farms and trees to the torch.

Barren and depopulated since then, Kássos attracts few visitors, despite regular air links with Rhodes and Kárpathos, and being a port of call on ferry lines from those isles to Crete. Numerous sheer gorges slash through lunar terrain, with fenced smallholdings of midget olive trees providing the only visual relief. Springtime grain crops briefly soften the usually empty terraces, and livestock somehow survives on a thin furze of thornbush. The remaining population occupies five villages facing Kárpathos, leaving most of the island uninhabited and uncultivated. Until the millennium, there was little sign here of the wealth brought into other islands by diaspora Greeks or – since Kássos hasn't much to offer them – tourists; amidst the occasional new concrete monster, crumbling houses and disused farmland poignantly recall better days. A long pattern of serving as roving pilots, or residence in Egypt (Kassiots were instrumental in digging the Suez Canal), has been eclipsed by subsequent **emigration to the US**. Thus American-logo T-shirts and baseball caps are *de rigueur* summer fashion, and the conversation of vacationing expatriates is spiked with Americanisms.

Kássos can be tricky to reach, despite the 2002 completion of a proper jetty at Frý (pronounced "free"); in extreme wind conditions, ferries may still not be able to dock. In such cases, you disembark at Kárpathos and fly the remaining distance in a dual-prop, 38-seater aircraft. The air ticket plus a taxi fare to Kárpathos airport isn't much more than the fare charged by Finíki (Kárpathos)-based excursion boats which can manoeuvre into Boúka in most weathers. The airport lies 1km west of Frý, an easy enough walk, otherwise a cheap ride in one of the island's three taxis. Except during summer, when a single scooter/quad rental outfit operates, a Mercedes van provides a regular bus service and boat excursions are offered, the only way of exploring the island's remoter corners is by hiking along fairly arduous, shadeless paths and roads. Place-name signposting tends to be in Greek only, and in Kassiot dialect at that – the islanders clearly aren't expecting many non-Kassiot visitors.

Frý and Emboriós

Most of the appeal of the capital, **FRÝ**, is confined to the immediate environs of the wedge-shaped fishing port of **Boúka**, protected from the sea by two crab-claws of breakwater and overlooked by the cathedral of Áyios Spyrídhon. Inland, Frý is engagingly unpretentious, even down-at-heel in spots; there are no concessions to tourism, though some attempts are now being made to prettify a little town that's quite desolate out of season. Among **accommodation**, there's just one surviving, overpriced seafront hotel, the *Anagenissis* (☎22450 41495, ⓦwww.kassos-island.gr; ❸), run by the eponymous travel agency just below (though Olympic Airways has its own premises two doors down). Better-value, quieter lodgings include the basic, seaside *Flisvos* (☎22450 41430 or 22450 41284; ❷), 150m east of the new harbour, with a shared kitchen, or the *Captain's House* (☎22450 42716, ✉hpetros@otenet.gr; ❹), galleried trad-style studios above Kassian Travel, near the police station. There's no full-service **bank**, but there are two stand-alone **ATMs**, plus an eight-terminal **Internet** café by the police station.

Outside of peak season, Frý supports only one full-service **taverna**: *O Mylos*, overlooking the intermittent harbour works. Luckily it's excellent and reason-able, with a variety of daily-special *mayireftá* at lunch and sometimes fish grills by night. From late June to early September at least one taverna, perched above Boúka, will function, or head for the suburb of Emboriós, fifteen minute's walk east, where *Taverna Emborios* (May–Sept) usually matches *O Mylos* in quality (though exceeds it in price). Failing this, shops in Frý are fairly well stocked for self-catering. Several **bar-kafenía-ouzerí** perched above Boúka – *Zantana* and *To Apangio* being the most durable – are the focus for such nightlife as there is.

Local beaches

Frý's town **beach**, if you can call it that, is at **Ammouá** (Ammoudhiá), a thirty-minute walk beyond the airstrip along the coastal track. This sandy cove, just before the landmark chapel of Áyios Konstandínos, is often caked with seaweed and tar, but persevere five minutes more and you'll find much cleaner pea-gravel coves. The determined can swim off the little patch of sand at **Emboriós**, along with the resident ducks, and there's a more private pebble stretch off to the right. But having got this far, you may as well continue ten to fifteen minutes along the shore, first along an old track, then on a path past the last house, for a final scramble to the base of the **Pouthená** ravine, where there's another secluded pebble cove. Otherwise, it's worth patronizing high-season boat excursions to far better beaches on a pair of islets visible to the northwest, **Armathiá** and **Makrá**.

The villages and Áyios Mámas

At the edges of the agricultural plain just inland from Frý cluster a number of villages, linked to each other by road; all are worth a passing visit, and can be toured on foot in a single day.

Larger in extent and more rural than Frý, **AYÍA MARÍNA**, 1500m inland and uphill, is most attractive seen from the south, arrayed above olive groves; one of its two belfried churches is the focus of the island's liveliest festival, on July 16–17. Some fifteen minutes beyond the hamlet of Kathístres, a further 500m southwest, the cave of **Ellinokamára** is named for the late Classical, polygonal wall completely blocking the entrance; its ancient function is uncer-tain, perhaps a cult shrine or tomb complex. To reach it, turn south at the two restored windmills in Ayía Marína, then right (west) at the phone-box junc-tion; carry on, straight and down (not level and left) until you see a red-dirt path going up the hillside to a crude, stone-built pastoral hut. Some modern masonry walls enclose the start of this path, but once at the hut (the cave is more or less underneath it) you're compelled to hop a fence to visit – there are no gates. From Ellinokamára another, fainter path – you'll probably need a guide, or at least detailed directions – continues for ninety minutes in the same direction to the larger, more natural cave of **Seláï**, with impressive stalactites in the rear chamber.

Generally, walking opportunities on Kássos are poor – trails are few, unmarked and in poor condition, with no shade and few reliable water sources. An exception is the forty-minute path from Arvanitohóri to Póli, which is clearly walled in and enjoyable, shortcutting the road effectively – it starts at the base of the village, where two trees occupy planter-wells. **PÓLI**, somewhat impoverished and resolutely agricultural, is the site of a badly deteriorated ancient and medieval acropolis – a few stretches of fortification remain – and marks the start of a four-kilometre paved-road system leading southeast to **Áyios Mámas**, signposted in dialect as "**Áï Mámas**", one of two important rural monasteries, perched spectacularly overlooking the sea. Alternatively, from Póli you can descend – again on walled-in path for the first twenty minutes, then dirt track – to **PANAYÍA**, famous for its now-neglected mansions (many of Kássos's wealthiest ship captains hailed from here) and for the oldest surviving church on the island, the eighteenth-century **Panayía tou Yióryi**.

Áyios Yeóryios Hadhión and Hélatros

Between Ayía Marína and Arvanitohóri, another road veers off southwest towards the rural monastery of **Áyios Yeóryios Hadhión**. The pleasure of walking this route, however, has been pretty well negated by its having been paved, so you'll want to hire a taxi, rent a scooter if available or hitch a lift in at least one direction. The start of the route skirts the narrows of a fearsome gorge, and from there on you are unlikely to see another living thing aside from goats, sheep or an occasional Eleonora's falcon. Soon the Mediterranean appears to the south, a dull expanse ruffled only by the occasional ship bound for Cyprus and the Middle East. When you finally reach a fork, adopt the upper, right-hand turning, following phone lines towards Áyios Yeóryios Hadhión (signed as "**Áï Yeóryi**"), 12km from Frý. This is busiest at its late-April festival time; there's also cistern water if you need to fill canteens.

From the monastery it's another 2.5km on a paved road to **Hélatros** ("Hélathros" on older maps), a lonely cove at the mouth of one of the larger, more forbidding Kassiot canyons. Only the right-hand 80m of this sand-and-pea-gravel beach is really usable, but the water is pristine and – except for the occasional fishing boat or yacht – you'll probably be alone. The lower, left-hand option at the fork is the direct, dirt-surface track to Hélatros; this is only 700m shorter but perfectly passable to a scooter, and makes an interesting variation of the return to town.

Kárpathos

A long, narrow island between Rhodes and Crete, wild **Kárpathos** has always been an underpopulated backwater, although it's in fact the third largest of the Dodecanese. A habitually cloud-capped **mountainous spine** rises to over 1200m, dividing the more populous, lower-lying south from an exceptionally rugged north. A magnificent, windswept coastline of cliffs and promontories attracts significant numbers of Scandinavian and German package tourists, who pretty well monopolize several resorts in the southern part of the island, pushing independent travellers up to the remote north. Thanks in part to this clientele, Kárpathos' road system has improved no end since the millennium, but food prices (in the south especially) have been pushed to beyond-Rhodes levels, which offsets reasonable room rates. Most island-hoppers come here for a glimpse of the traditional village life in the far north, and for the numerous superb, secluded beaches lapped by proverbial crystalline water.

N

▲ *Rhodes & Hálki*

Saría

Árgos
Palátia

**Áyios
Spyrídhon**

Yaplós
**Ayía
Ekaterína**

Tristomo

Vrykoúnda
Kílios

Avlóna
Vanánda

Dhiafáni

Ólymbos
Fýsses

Papá Miná

**Ayía
Marína**
Forókli

Áyios Minás
Agnóndia

Spóa
Mesohóri
Áyios Nikólaos

2004 fire zone
Ápella

Lefkós
Mértonas
Kyrá Panayiá
Káto Lákkos

Paralía Lefkoú
▲ *Kalilímni
1215m*

Potáli
Voládha
Katódhio
Aháta

Ilioúndas
Epínemo
Stés

Ádhia
Óthos
Apéri

Pylés

Vróndi

Áyios Yeóryios
Kamarákia
Pigádhia

Finíki
Menetés

Áyios Nikólaos
Arkássa
AMFIARTI
Ammopí

Tihiasméni
Trahanamós
Dhamatría

**Áyios
Ioánnis**
Khristoú Pigádhi

Agrilaopótamos
Makrýs Yialós

0   5 km

▲ *Kássos*

▲ *Kássos & Crete*

Kárpathos' **interior** isn't always the most alluring: the central and northern uplands have been scorched by repeated forest fires since the 1980s, while agriculture plays a slighter role than on any other Greek island of this size. The Karpathians are too well off to bother much with farming; emigration to North America and the resulting remittance economy has transformed Kárpathos into one of the wealthiest parts of Greece.

Four local Classical **cities** figure little in ancient chronicles. Alone of the major Dodecanese, Kárpathos was held by the Genoese and Venetians after the Byzantine collapse and so has no castle of the crusading Knights of St John, nor any surviving medieval fortresses of note. The Ottomans couldn't be bothered to settle or even garrison it; instead they left a single judge or *kadi* at the main town, making the Greek population responsible for his safety during the many pirate attacks.

Pigádhia (Kárpathos Town)

The island capital of **PIGÁDHIA**, often known simply as Kárpathos, nestles at the south end of scenic **Vróndi Bay**, whose sickle of sand extends 3km northwest. The town itself, curling around the jetty and quay where ferries and excursion boats dock, is as drab as its setting is beautiful; an ever-increasing number of concrete blocks lend an air of a vast building site, making the Italian-era port police and county-government buildings heirlooms by comparison. Although there's nothing special to see, Pigádhia does offer almost every facility you might need, albeit with a definite package-tourism slant. The name of the main commercial street – Apodhímon Karpathíon ("**Karpathians Overseas**") – speaks volumes about the pivotal role of emigrants and emigration here.

Information

Olympic Airways (book well in advance in summer – **planes** have just 38 seats) is on Platía 5-Oktovríou, corner Apodhímon Karpathíon, but has very restricted hours, so everyone buys tickets from Possi Travel (☎22450 22235) on the front. They're also principal agents for LANE, currently the only **shipping** line to serve Kárpathos. The **post office** is on Ethnikís Andístasis up from Platía 5-Oktovríou, while several **banks** have ATMs. Pigádhia's main **Internet** cafés are Café Galileo (all year), on Apodhímon Karpathíon, and Pot Pourri (summer only), diagonally across the square from Olympic; there's also a fairly useless **tourism information** bureau in a hexagonal booth on the west quay (June–Aug Mon–Fri 9am–2pm).

Accommodation

Most ferries are met by people offering **self-catering studios**, though they may be forbidden from touting on the quay itself. Unless you've arranged something in advance, you might consider such offers – the town is small enough that no location will be too inconvenient, though the best place to stay is on the hillside above the bus terminal and central car park. More luxurious places lie north, behind **Vróndi** beach to either side of the ruined fifth-century basilica of **Ayía Fotiní**, but tend to be occupied by package groups. Better hillside premises include *Amarillis Studios* (☎22450 22375, ✉johnvolada@in.gr; ❸), with enormous suite-sized, air-con units, and the helpful *Elias Rooms* (☎22450 22446 or 697 85 87 924, ⊛http://Eliasroooms.tripod.com; ❷; mid-May to Sept) just above the *Hotel Karpathos*, with variable, mostly en-suite rooms in a converted older house. Up an alley beyond Avis at the start of Vróndi, *Paradise Studios* (☎22450 22949, ⊛www .paradisestudios.gr; ❸ room only) offers seven simple but practical, good-sized

For exploring the island as a passenger, regular **buses** serve Pylés, via Apéri, Voládha and Óthos, as well as Ammopí, Menetés, Arkássa, Finíki and (less frequently) Mesohóri via Paralía Lefkoú; the Pigádhia "station" is a car park at the western edge of town, a block past the post office. Set-rate, unmetered **taxis** have a terminal in the municipal car park two blocks inland from the fountain along Dhimokratías (table of current fares posted), and are affordable as long as you stay off what's left of the island's dirt-track network.

Upwards of ten outfits **rent cars**, though in season you may have to try every one to find an available vehicle, and rates are well over the norm. Reputable agencies include Circle (☎22450 22690) near the post office; Avis (☎22450 22702), at the north edge of town; Drive (☎22450 61249), 2km out behind Vróndi beach; Hertz, inside Possi Travel (☎22450 22235); and Trust, based in Ammopí, which will deliver and collect in Pigádhia (☎22450 81060). You can save €20 return in taxi transfers by car rental from/to the cheerless **airport** (17km distant, no snacks or diversions to hand) which must be arranged in advance with either Hertz or Avis. Moto Carpathos (☎22450 22382), 60m uphill from the town hall (*dhimarhío*), has the largest fleet of scooters for rent. Be warned that the only fuel on the island is to be found at two pairs of stations just to the north and south of town, and that tanks on smaller scooters are barely big enough to permit completing a circuit of the south, let alone head up north. In early 2006 the Spóa–Ólymbos road was finally paved, making hire of a jeep unnecessary except to access certain remote beaches.

Despite this infrastructure improvement, reaching **Northern Kárpathos by boat** is still very much on the agenda. One surviving excursion boat on the jetty, the *Chrisovalandou III*, offers all-in **day-tours** to Dhiafáni and Ólymbos for €15 maximum (pay on board); less well publicized is the fact that you can use this boat to travel **one-way** (1hr 20min journey time) between the north and the south in either direction – the standard rate is €6. Departures are typically 8.30am northbound, 4pm southbound. It's also worth knowing about the tiny **mail kaïki** *Chrisovalandou I*, which reverses this pattern: southbound from Dhiafáni on Mon, Wed and Fri at 7.30am, northbound from Pigádhia on Mon, Wed and Sun at 3pm (one-way fare again €6). Various agents also offer trips to Kássos and to isolated east-coast beaches without facilities (bring lunch if not included).

air-con studios in a quiet, aesthetic orchard setting. The only relatively comfortable hotel that caters in any way to nonpackage guests is the helpful *Atlantis*, opposite the Italian "palace" (☎22450 22777, ✉htatlantis@yahoo.com; B&B; ❹).

Eating, drinking and nightlife

Many of Pigádhia's waterfront **tavernas**, where tacky photo-menus and defrosted *yíros* and chips reign supreme, are undistinguished and overpriced; quality and value improve significantly as you head east towards the ferry dock. Near the end of the strip are two worthy choices: characterful *Anna*, good for non-farmed fish with heaping salads, and the best all-rounder, *Iy Orea Karpathos*, with palatable local bulk wine, *trahanádhes* soup, spicy sausages, marinated artichokes and great spinach pie – you can, as the locals do, use it as an ouzerí and just order *mezédhes*. One block inland, the clear winner is *To Ellinikon*, a *mezedhopolío* that caters all year round to a local clientele with hot and cold *orektiká*, meat and good desserts. If *yíros* and chips it must be, then by far the best place for the fresh kind, own-sourced, is *Ovelistirio tis Erasmias*, inland on Dhimokratías opposite the taxi rank. Trendy, musical **café-bars** such as *Enigma* offer taped sounds from perches overlooking the bay, while *Oxygen* and *Amnesia* are the two most durable indoor midnight-to-dawn **dance clubs**.

Southern and western Kárpathos

The southern extremity of Kárpathos, towards the airport, is extraordinarily desolate and windswept. There are a few relatively undeveloped sandy beaches along the southeast coast in the region known as **Amfiárti**, but many are only really attractive to foreign windsurfers who come to take advantage of the prevailing northwesterlies. The most established surf school here is Pro Center Kárpathos (T 22450 91063 or 697 78 86 289, W www.windsurfen-karpathos .com), which as the web address suggests caters mostly to Germanophones, though all are welcome. They have the advantage of three separate bays near the airport, catering to different ability levels. The most comfortable hotel in the region, though sometimes full with surf packages, is the *Poseidon* (T 22450 91066, W www.hotel-poseidon.gr; B&B; ❸) above sheltered **Dhamatría** beach, also with a full-service taverna open to all.

Most people go no further than **AMMOPÍ** (sometimes transliterated as "Amoopi"), just 7km south of Pigádhia. This, together with development at Arkássa and Paralía Lefkoú, is the closest thing on Kárpathos to a purpose-built beach resort. Three sand-and-gravel, tree- or cliff-fringed coves are bordered by half a dozen tavernas and numbers of **hotels** and **studios**. Quietest of these are the highly recommended, well-designed ⚶ *Vardes Studios* (T 22450 81111 or 697 21 52 901, W www.hotelvardes.com; ❸), with distant sea views and orchard setting. Of the **tavernas**, far and away the best is ⚶ *Esperida* about halfway along the approach road, with such delicacies as local cheese, wine and sausage, roast eggplant, and pickled wild vegetables.

West out of Pigádhia the road climbs steeply 9km up to **MENETÉS**, draped in the lee of a ridge, with some handsome old houses and a spectacularly sited – if hideous – church. The best local **taverna**, east beyond the World War II resistance monument memorial, is ⚶ *Pelayia* in Kritháres district, offering local marinated "sardines" (really a larger fish, *ménoula*) cheese and wild greens; it's open all year, with live music some nights.

Arkássa, Finíki and Ádhia

Beyond Menetés, you descend to **ARKÁSSA**, on the slopes of a ravine draining to the west coast, with excellent views to Kássos en route. A few hundred metres south of where the ravine meets the sea, a signposted cement side-road leads briefly to the whitewashed chapel of **Ayía Sofía**, marooned amidst Classical and Byzantine Arkessia. Its visible remains consist of several mosaic floors with geometric patterns, the best one being inside a vaulted cistern at one corner of the area. The Paleókastro headland beyond was the site of Mycenaean Arkessia; the walk up is again signposted, but scarcely worth it for the sake of a few stretches of polygonal wall and a couple of tumbled columns.

Despite just one good nearby beach, Arkássa has been heavily developed, with hotels and restaurants sprouting along the rocky coastline. Much **accommodation** (and mediocre village-centre tavernas) are aimed squarely at the package market, but independent travellers could try various facilities inland from **Áyios Nikólaos** beach signposted just south, a 100-metre stretch of sand – rare hereabouts. These include the *Montemar Studios* (T 22450 61394; ❹), almost one-bedroom apartments; and – right behind the beach – the *Glaros* (T 22450 61015, F 22450 61016; ❹), five studios and an attached taverna run by a Karpathian-American from Virginia.

The tiny fishing port of **FINÍKI**, just 2km north, offers a minuscule beach, seasonal excursions to Kássos, several tavernas and a few rooms/studios establishments. For value and comfort, top **accommodation** is the well-designed and -built *Arhontiko Studios* up on the main bypass road (℡22450 61473, Ⓕ22450 61054; ❸). Skip the port **tavernas** here in favour of well-loved 🎏 *Under the Trees* (*Kostas*), 1km north under two tamarisks at Áyios Yeóryios monastery above reefy **Kamarákia** beach; it's open all day until two hours after sunset, offering such delights as expertly grilled swordfish, mountainous salads and chips made from home-grown courgettes.

Some 7km north of Finíki along the coast road, Karpathian forest resumes at **ÁDHIA** hamlet, giving rise to the name of the *Pine Tree Restaurant*, which has home-baked bread, lentil soup and octopus *makaronádha* washed down by sweet Óthos wine. There are also six **rooms** and **studios** (plus a basic, free **campsite**) off to one side, overlooking the orchard and the sea (℡697 73 69 948, Ⓔpinetree_adia@hotmail.com; ❷). Ádhia is becoming something of a **walkers' mecca**: easy paths lead twenty minutes west to tiny **Epínemo** beach (and 10min further to larger **Ilioúndas**), whilst a meatier, three-hour (one-way) route up Mt Kalí Límni starts from the main-road bridge.

Paralía Lefkoú and Mesohóri

Dense forest continues much of the way to the turning for the attractive resort of **PARALÍA LEFKOÚ**, shore annexe of the inland hamlet of Lefkós. Unless you **rent a car** locally – there are two agencies here now, Lefkos (℡22450 71057) and Drive (℡22450 71415) – it's not a particularly convenient touring base. But this is a delightful place for flopping on the beach, graced by a striking topography of cliffs, hills, islets and sandspits surrounding a triple bay. There are over two dozen places to stay, and perhaps half as many tavernas, but package companies tend to monopolize the better **accommodation** from June to September. About the only exception is the spartan but en-suite *Sunweek Studios* (℡22450 71025; ❷), on the seaward promontory. You'll have better luck at **Potáli**, the stonier, fourth bay just south of the access road; here go for the excellent, quiet and spacious *Akroyiali Studios* (℡22450 71263, Ⓕ22450 71178; ❸), with balconies overlooking the beach, or the smaller *Lefkosia Studios* close to the road (℡22450 71176 or 22450 71148; ❸). **Tavernas** at the main resort can severely disappoint: best options are *Mihalis* at the base of the point, with lots of vegetarian platters, or the kindly *Blue Sea* with its pizzas, meat-rich *mayireftá* and pancake breakfasts.

Back on the main road, you climb northeast through severely fire-damaged pine forest to **MESOHÓRI**. The village tumbles down towards the sea around narrow, stepped alleys, coming to an abrupt halt at the edge of a flat-topped bluff dotted with three tiny, ancient chapels and separated from the village proper by a vast oasis of orchards. These are nurtured by the fountain (best water on the island) underneath the church of **Panayía Vryssianí**, wedged against the mountainside just east and invisible from the end of the access road. On the stair-street leading to this church is an excellent taverna, the *Dhramoundana*, remarkably reasonably priced for Kárpathos, and featuring local capers, sausages and the local marinated "sardines". The paved main road continues over the island's watershed to Spóa, overlooking the east coast.

Central Kárpathos

The **centre** of Kárpathos supports a group of villages blessed with superb hill-side settings, ample running water – and a cool climate, even in August. Nearly everyone here has "done time" in North America, then returned home with their nest eggs. New Jersey, New York and Canadian car plates tell you exactly where repatriated islanders struck it rich – often fabulously so (the area has the highest per capita income in Greece). West-facing **PYLÉS** is the most attractive, set above another spring-fed oasis, while **ÓTHOS**, noted for its sweet, tawny-amber wine, is the highest (approx 400m) and chilliest, on the flanks of 1215-metre Mount Kalilímni. On the east side of the ridge you find **VOLÁDHA** with its tiny Venetian citadel and a trio of nocturnal tavernas. From the smart track-and-footie stadium below **APÉRI**, the largest, lowest and wealthiest settlement, you can drive 5km along a dirt road to the dramatic pebble beach of **Aháta**, with a spring and reasonable taverna.

Beyond Apéri, the road up the **east coast** passes above beaches often visited by boat trips from Pigádhia. A paved but twisty side road via Katódhio hamlet leads first to a further turning (2km of rough dirt track) to **Káto Lákkos**, 150m of scenic sand and gravel favoured by naturists, and then after 4km on the main pavement to **Kyrá Panayiá**. Here there's a surprising number of villas and rooms in the ravine behind 150m of fine gravel and sheltered, turquoise water; the beach taverna is, alas, mediocre. **Ápella** is the best of the beaches you can reach by road, though there's a final short path from the single, good-value taverna-rooms (the only facility) at the road's end to the scenic 300-metre gravel strand. The end of this route is **SPÓA**, high above the shore just east of the island's spine, with a **snack-bar** and more reliably open *kafenío* at the edge of the village, which might make better meal stops than the overpriced *Votsalo* down at **Áyios Nikólaos**, 5km below, a small port with an average beach.

Northern Kárpathos

Although it's now far easier to reach **northern Kárpathos** from Spóa, sea transport will remain an attractive choice for the immediate future, as there's still no bus service and taxi fares are exorbitant. Inter-island ferries call at Dhiafáni three times a week in season, or passengers can use the above-cited smaller daily *kaïkia* from Pigádhia. The journey time on the excursion boats can be ninety minutes in rough sea, with arrivals met at Dhiafáni eight-kilometre bus transfer up to the traditional village of **Ólymbos**, the main attraction in this

△ Hiking near Ólymbos, northern Kárpathos

part of the island, along with good walking opportunities. The paving of the entire road in from Spóa will, however, pull the rug out from under the day-trip industry, and should encourage a more thoughtful type of tourism than the present commercialized circus. If you can't tear yourself away from the sea, coastal **Dhiafáni** makes a better base, with excellent **beaches** within walking distance to either side.

Ólymbos and hiking

Originally founded as a pirate-safe refuge during Byzantine times, windswept **ÓLYMBOS** straddles a long ridge below slopes studded with mostly ruined windmills. Two restored ones, beyond the main church, grind wheat and barley during late summer only, though one is kept under sail during any tourist season. The village has long attracted foreign and Greek ethnologists, who treat it as a living museum of peasant dress, crafts, dialect and music long since vanished elsewhere in Greece. It's still a very picturesque place, yet traditions are vanishing by the year. Nowadays it's only the older women and those working in the several tourist shops who wear the striking and magnificently colourful traditional dress – an instant photo opportunity in exchange for persistent sales pitches for trinkets mostly imported from China or Bulgaria.

You'll quickly notice the prominent role that the women play in daily life: tending gardens, carrying goods on their shoulders or herding goats. Nearly all Ólymbos men emigrate to Baltimore or work outside the village, sending money home and returning only on holidays. The long-isolated villagers also speak a unique dialect, said to maintain traces of its Doric and Phrygian origins – thus "Ólymbos" is pronounced "Élymbos" locally. Live vernacular music is still heard regularly and draws crowds of visitors at **festival** times, in particular Easter and August 15, when you've little hope of finding a bed.

From the village, the superb west-coast beach at **Fýsses** is a sharp 35-minute drop below, first cross-country, later by path. Most **local hikes**, however, head more gently north or east, many of them on waymarked paths, though you'll have to stay overnight in the area to enjoy them. The easiest option is the ninety-minute walk back down to Dhiafáni, beginning just below the two working windmills. The way is well marked, with water en route. It eventually drops to a ravine amidst extensive forest, though the last half-hour is mostly over bulldozed riverbed. You could also tackle the trail north to the ruins and beach at **Vrykoúnda** ("Vrougoúnda" in dialect), via sparsely inhabited **AVLÓNA**, set on a high upland devoted to grain. From Ólymbos, it's just under three hours' walk one way to Vrykoúnda, which offers traces of Hellenistic/Roman Brykous, the remote cave-shrine of John the Baptist on the promontory and good swimming. **Trístomo**, a Byzantine anchorage in the far northeast of Kárpathos, can also be reached on a magnificent cobbled way beginning above Avlóna (2hr 30min); until the direct Trístomo–Vanánda path is rehabilitated, the return is by the same way. There's also a fine ninety-minute marked path from Avlóna down to Vanánda beach (see opposite).

Among places to **stay** in Ólymbos the friendly *Rooms Restaurant Olymbos* (✆22450 51252 or 22450 51009; ❷), near the village entrance, has rooms with baths or unplumbed ones with traditional furnishings, while the *Café-Restaurant Zefiros*, near the centre and run by two young sisters, manages the eight-room, en-suite *Hotel Astro* (✆22450 51421; B&B; ❸), with breakfast given in the **restaurant**, much the best thing going along with the *Olymbos*. The father of the *Rooms Restaurant Olymbos* management has opened an annexe at Ávlona, *Restaurant Avlona*, on the through road, with four en-suite rooms (✆22450 51046; ❶) in the hamlet centre, an ideal base for committed walkers.

Dhiafáni and beaches

Rooms in **DHIAFÁNI** are inexpensive, and the pace of life slow outside of July and August. Seaonal boat trips are offered to remoter local **beaches**, as well as to the uninhabited islet of **Saría** (most reliably Thur, 10am out, 4.30pm back; €24 with lunch), with passengers hiking the trans-island path to the Byzantine site of Palátia, where a barbeque and opportunity for a swim are provided before the return trip. Among several coves within walking distance, closest is **Vanánda**, a stony beach with an eccentrically managed campsite snack-bar in the oasis behind. To get there, follow the pleasant sign-posted path north through the pines, but don't believe the signs that say "ten minutes" – it's over thirty minutes away, shortcutting the more recent road. **Papá Miná**, with a few trees and cliff-shade, lies an hour's walk distant via the cairned trail taking off from the road to the ferry dock. An ordinary car can just drive the 4.5km there – a jeep's better, with the last 300m on foot in either case; with a jeep you can also confidently reach three other superb beaches below the Spóa–Ólymbos road; the closest, also with path access from Ólymbos, is 250-metre long **Forókli** (clothing optional). Some 7km further towards Spóa, there's the turning for the even worse track down to **Áyios Minás** (seasonal taverna; bear left at fork partway along) or **Agnóndia** (bear right), equally pristine.

Dhiafáni has abundant sleeping and eating opportunities, though the most obvious, aggresively touting ones at mid-quay are well worth avoiding. There's also a small travel agency where you buy ferry tickets and can change money if the stand-alone **ATM** by the waterfront fountain is non-functional. In terms of **accommodation**, top of the heap in all senses is hospitable George and Anna Niotis' ⚜ *Hotel Studios Glaros* (☏22450 51501 or 694 79 44 601, ⓦwww.hotel-glaros.gr; ❸) up the south slope, with some of its sixteen huge, tiered units sleeping four. Worthy alternatives, 300m along the road west more or less opposite each other, are the pleasant, ground-floor *Dolphins/Dhelfinia Studios* (☏22450 51354; ❶) under the eponymous restaurant, or the *Hotel Nikos* (☏22450 51410, Ⓔorfanos-hotel@hol.gr; ❸). As for **tavernas**, *Dolphins/Dhelfinia* does good fish, and vegetables from the garden just below, while vine-shrouded *Iy Anixi* in a backstreet behind the water offers a few inexpensive, homestyle *mayireftá* daily. Behind the fountain, favourite meeting places are Italian-run ⚜ *Iy Gorgona/L'Angolo*, featuring light dishes, wonderful ownmade desserts, proper coffees, and *limoncello* digestif, and ⚜ *Koral* (*Mihalis & Popi's*) across the lane, which serves good grills and salads, Cretan *tsikoudhiá* and doubles as the most atmospheric **nightspot**.

Rhodes (Ródhos)

It's no accident that **Rhodes** is among the most visited of the Greek islands. Not only is its southeast coast lined with numerous sandy beaches, but the capital's nucleus is a beautiful and remarkably preserved medieval city, the legacy of the crusading Knights of St John who used the island as their main base from 1309 until 1522. Unfortunately this showpiece is jammed to capacity with over a million tourists in a good season, as against about 110,000 permanent inhabitants (including many foreigners). Of transient visitors, Germans, Brits, Swedes, Italians and Danes predominate, though they tend to arrive in different months of the year.

Tilos, Nissyros, Astypálea & Kós ◀

Kárpathos, Kássos & Crete ◀

Háilki ◀

Kós, Kálymnos, Léros & Pátmos ◀

Sými ▲ Marmaris (Turkey) ▲

► Kastellórizo

Ródhos Town's medieval Old Town is very much the main event, but the rest of this sizeable island also repays exploration. **Líndhos**, with its ancient acropolis and (occasionally) atmospheric village, ranks second place on most people's lists. The southeastern beaches – particularly near **Afándou** and **Yennádhi** – and isolated monuments of the interior, such as castles near **Monólithos** and **Kritinía**, and frescoed churches at **Thárri** and **Asklipió**, are also worth pointing a car towards. Adrenalin junkies will (literally) want to go to extremes at the far south cape, **Prassoníssi**, one of the best windsurfing venues in Europe.

Some history

Blessed with an equable climate and strategic position, Rhodes was important from earliest times despite a lack of good harbours. The best natural port engendered the ancient town of Lindos which, together with the other city-states Kameiros and Ialyssos, united in 408 BC to found the new capital of **Rodos** (Rhodes) at the windswept northern tip of the island. At various moments the cities allied themselves with Alexander, the Persians, Athenians or Spartans as prevailing conditions suited them, generally escaping retribution for backing the wrong side by a combination of seafaring audacity, sycophancy and burgeoning wealth as a trade centre. Following the failed siege of Demetrios Polyorketes in 305 BC, Rhodes prospered even more, displacing Athens as the major venue for rhetoric and the arts in the east Mediterranean.

Decline set in when Rhodes became involved in the Roman civil wars, and Cassius sacked the island; by late imperial times, it was a backwater, a status confirmed by numerous barbarian raids during the Byzantine period. The Byzantines were compelled to cede Rhodes to the Genoese, who in turn surrendered it to the Knights of St John. The second great siege of Rhodes, during 1522–23, saw Ottoman Sultan Süleyman the Magnificent oust the stubborn knights, who retreated to Malta; Rhodes once again lapsed into relative obscurity, though heavily colonized and garrisoned, until its seizure by the Italians in 1912.

Arrival and information

All international and inter-island **ferries** and the *Dodekanisos Express/ Dodekanisos Pride* **catamarans** dock at the middle of Rhodes' three ports, the commercial harbour of **Kolóna**; the only exceptions are local **boats** to and from Sými, all excursion craft, the small *Sea Star* catamaran and the **hydrofoils**, which use the yacht harbour of **Mandhráki**. Its entrance was supposedly once straddled by the Colossus, an ancient statue of Apollo built to celebrate the end of the 305 BC siege; today two columns surmounted by bronze deer are less overpowering replacements.

The **airport** lies 14km southwest of town, by the village of Paradhísi; public buses returning from Paradhísi, Kalavárdha, Theológos or Sálakos pass the stop (look for the perspex-and-wood kiosk) on the main road opposite the northerly car-park entrance fairly frequently between 6am and 11.30pm (fare €1.70). A taxi into town will cost €14–23, plus bags and airport supplement, depending on the time of day. **Buses** for both the west and east coasts of Rhodes – sleek air-con turquoise-and-blue models displacing the old orange-and-white ones – leave from two almost adjacent terminals on Papágou and Avérof, just outside the Italian-built **New Market** (a tourist trap, to miss without regret except for the wonderful rotunda of the old fish market inside). Between the lower eastern station and the **taxi** rank at Platía Rimínis there's a **municipal tourist office** (June–Sept Mon–Sat 8am–9.30pm, Sun 9am–3pm), while some way up Papágou on the corner of Makaríou stands the **EOT office** (Mon–Fri 8.30am–3pm); both dispense bus and ferry schedules, the latter also providing a list of standard taxi fares, complete with complaint form. Rhodes taxi drivers have a deservedly poor reputation – overcharging of new arrivals is routine, as is refusing to take you to your chosen hotel, while steering you to inconvenient accommodation that gives them kickbacks.

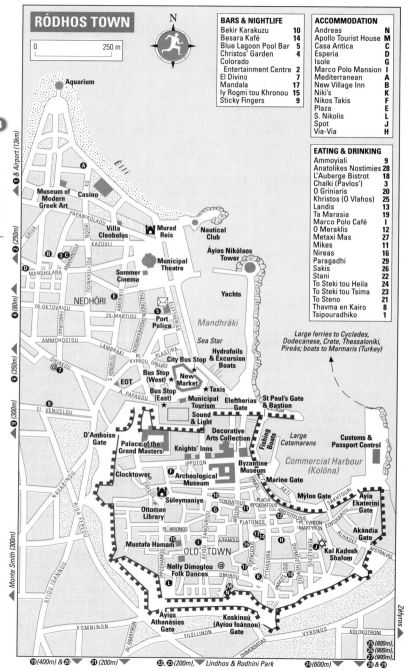

Ródhos Town

Ancient Rodos, which lies underneath nearly all of the modern city, was laid out by Hippodamos of Miletos in the grid layout much in vogue at the time, with planned residential and commercial quarters. Its perimeter walls totalled almost 15km, enclosing nearly double the area of the present town, and the Hellenistic population was said to exceed 100,000 – a staggering figure for late antiquity, as against 50,631 at the 2001 census.

The contemporary town divides into two unequal parts: the compact **old walled city**, and the **New Town**, which sprawls around it in three directions. The latter dates from the Ottoman occupation, when Greek Orthodox residents – forbidden to dwell in the old city – founded several suburb villages or *marásia* in the environs, which have since merged. Commercialization is predictably rampant in the walled town, and in the modern district of Neohóri ("Niohóri" in dialect), west of Mandhráki yacht harbour; the few buildings that aren't hotels are souvenir shops, car-rental or travel agencies and bars – easily seventy in every category.

Accommodation

Hotels and pensions at all price levels abound in the Old Town, mostly in the quad bounded by Omírou to the south, Sokrátous to the north, Perikléous to the east and Ippodhámou to the west. There are also a few possibilities worth considering in Neohóri, especially if you're off to the airport or a ferry at an early hour. During crowded seasons, or late at night, it's prudent to reserve well in advance – only the very lowest standard of unlicensed accommodation is touted by their desperate proprietors at the ferry and catamaran quays.

Old Town

Andreas Omírou 28D ☎ 22410 34156, ⓦ www.hotelandreas.com. Perennially popular (reservations mandatory) and under the dynamic management of Belgian-American Constance Rivemal, this is one of the more imaginative old-Turkish-mansion restoration-*pensions*, thoroughly refurbished in 2003–05. Rooms in a variety of formats (including family-size and a spectacular "penthouse") all have baths, though a few are across a corridor. Terrace bar with views for excellent breakfasts and evening drinks; two-night minimum stay, credit cards accepted, indeed vital for advance bookings. Open all year. ❹–❻

Apollo Tourist House Omírou 28C ☎ 22410 32003, ⓦ www.apollo-touristhouse.com. Six unique, wood-trimmed, centrally heated, en-suite rooms emerged from a thorough overhaul of this old budget standby in 2004–05 by owner Umberto; the self-catering kitchen makes it good for longer stays. Open most of the year. ❸

Isole Evdhóxou 75 ☎ 22410 20682, ⓦ www.hotelisole.com. Simple but salubrious rooms with Hellenic-blue decor in a converted Ottoman house, run by a welcoming, multilingual Italian couple. Pleasant breakfast area at reception, superb roof terrace. Normally open March to mid-Nov, winter by appointment. B&B. ❸ standard rooms, ❹ tower suite.

Marco Polo Mansion Ayíou Fanouríou 42 ☎ & ⓕ 22410 25562, ⓦ www.marcopolomansion.web.com. Superb conversion of another old Turkish mansion, with a *hamam* on site; all rooms are en suite and exquisitely furnished with antiques from the nearby gallery of the same name, plus cotton pillows and handmade mattresses. Large buffet breakfasts are provided by Spyros and Efi in the garden snack-bar, open to all later in the day (see p.317). One-week minimum stay, reservations and credit-card deposit mandatory. B&B. Rates room-dependent ❻–❼

Niki's Sofokléous 39 ☎ 22410 25115, ⓦ www.nikishotel.gr. Some rooms can be on the small side, but all are en suite, most have air con, and upper-storey ones have fine views (three with private balconies). There's a washing machine, two common terraces and very friendly, helpful management to round things off. Someone will wait up for late-night arrivals; credit cards accepted. ❸

Nikos Takis Panetíou 26 ☎ 22410 70773, ⓦ www.nikostakishotel.com. Miniature "fashion hotel" in a restored mansion with just four, somewhat gaudily coloured units (including painted ceilings); junior suites with just CD players are ❻, "honeymoon" suites offer fridge, DVD and TV at ❽. Pebble-mosaic courtyard, with fine views over town, for breakfast and drinks.

S. Nikolis Ippodhámou 61 ☎22410 34561, ⓦwww.s-nikolis.gr. A variety of restored premises in the west of the Old Town. Hotel/honeymoon suite rates (❼) include rooftop breakfast, TV and air con. The self-catering apartments (❺–❻) interconnect to accommodate groups or families. Booking essential, and accepted only with credit-card number. Open April–Nov.

Spot Perikléous 21 ☎ & ☏22410 34737, ⓦwww.spothotelrhodes.com. This modern building has cheerfully painted en-suite rooms of varying formats with textiles on the walls, fridges and air con, representing excellent value (including unlimited buffet breakfast). Internet facilities, rear patio and free luggage storage. Open March–Nov. ❹

Via-Via Lysipoú 2, alley off Pythagóra ☎ & ☏22410 77027, ⓦwww.hotel-via-via.com. Efficiently but congenially run hotel; most one- to four-person rooms are en suite but two share a bath, about half have air con. All are simply but tastefully furnished, with ongoing improvements. Self-catering kitchen, roof terrace for breakfast with an eyeful of the Ibrahim Pasha mosque opposite. Three grades of breakfast offered, from continental to full brunch. Open all year. ❹–❺

Neohóri

Casa Antica Amarándou 8 ☎22410 26206. Double and quad studios in a made-over 150-year-old house, with clean, white-tile decor, courtyard and roof terrace. Near some of the better Neohóri tavernas. ❹

Esperia Yeoryíou Gríva 7 ☎22410 23941, ⓦwww.esperia-hotels.gr. Well-priced, well-run B-class hotel in a quiet location overlooking a little plaza. Small-to-medium size, though salubrious and tasteful rooms with showers. Open all year. ❹

Mediterranean Kó 35 ☎22410 24661, ⓦwww.mediterranean.gr. Beachfront hotel in a superb location; though nominally A-class, it's less expensive than you'd think, especially if booked through the recommended travel agent (see p.320). The street-level snack-bar/café is very popular around the clock with nonresidents as well. ❻ standard, ❽ suites.

New Village Inn Konstandopédhos 10 ☎22410 34937, ⓦwww.newvillageinn.gr. Whitewashed, somewhat grotto-like en-suite rooms (only upper-floor units have balconies), arrayed around a courtyard breakfast-bar; friendly Greek and American management; singles available at a good rate. Open April–Oct. ❹

Plaza Ieroú Lóhou 7, Neohóri ☎22410 22501, ⓦwww.rhodes-plaza.com. One of the best A-class hotel within Rhodes city limits, in the heart of Neohóri. Pool, sauna, jacuzzi, buffet English breakfast, heating/air con. Open all year; substantially discounted rates Nov–April. ❻

The Old Town

Simply to catalogue the principal monuments and attractions cannot do full justice to the infinitely rewarding **medieval city**. There's ample gratification to be derived from slipping through the eleven surviving gates and strolling the streets, under flying archways built for earthquake resistance, past the warm-toned sandstone and limestone walls painted ochre or blue, and over the *votsalotó* (pebble-mosaic) pavements.

Dominating the northernmost sector of the city's fourteenth-century fortifications is the **Palace of the Grand Masters** (summer Mon 12.30–7pm, Tues–Sun 8.30am–7pm; winter Mon 12.30–3pm, Tues–Sun 8.30am–3pm; €6, or joint €10 ticket includes all museums in this section). Largely destroyed by an ammunition depot explosion set off by lightning in 1856, it was reconstructed by the Italians as a summer home for Mussolini and Vittore Emmanuele III ("King of Italy and Albania, Emperor of Ethiopia"), neither of whom ever visited Rhodes. The exterior, based on medieval engravings and accounts, is passably authentic, but inside, free rein was given to Fascist delusions of grandeur: a marble staircase leads up to rooms paved with Hellenistic mosaics from Kós, and the ponderous period furnishings rival many a northern European palace. The ground floor is home to splendid galleries entitled **Rhodes from the 4th century until the Turkish Conquest** and **Ancient Rhodes, 2400 Years** (same hours and admission ticket), together the best museums in town. The medieval collection highlights the importance of Christian Rhodes as a trade centre, with exotic merchandise placing the island in a trans-Mediterranean context. The Knights are represented with a display on their sugar-refining industry and a gravestone of a Grand Master; precious manuscripts and books precede a wing of post-Byzantine icons, moved here permanently from Panayía Kástrou (see below). Across the courtyard in the north wing, "Ancient Rhodes" overshadows the official archeological museum by explaining the everyday life of the ancients, arranged topically (beauty aids, toys, cookware, worship and so on); highlights include a Hellenistic floor mosaic of a comedic mask and a household idol of Hecate, goddess of the occult. On Tuesday and Saturday afternoons, there's supplementary self-guiding access of the **city walls** (one hour starting at 2.45pm; separate €6 admission), beginning from a gate next to the palace and finishing at the Koskinoú gate.

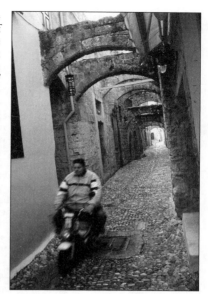

△ Buttressed lanes, Rhodes Old Town

The heavily restored, Gothic **Street of the Knights** (Odhós Ippotón) leads due east from the Platía Kleovoúlou in front of the palace; the "Inns" lining it housed the Knights of St John, according to linguistic and ethnic affiliation, until the Ottoman Turks compelled them to leave for Malta after a six-month siege in which the defenders were outnumbered thirty to one. Today the Inns house various government offices, foreign consulates or cultural institutions vaguely appropriate to their past, with occasional exhibitions, but the whole effect of the Italians' renovation is predictably sterile and stagey (indeed, nearby streets were used in the 1987 filming of *Pascali's Island*).

At the bottom of the hill, the Knights' Hospital has been refurbished as the **Archeological Museum** (summer Tues–Sun 8am–7pm; winter Tues–Sun 8.30am–3pm; €3 or joint ticket), though the arches and echoing halls of the building somewhat overshadow contents – largely painted pottery dating from the ninth through the fifth centuries BC. Behind the second-storey sculpture garden, the Hellenistic statue gallery is more accessible; in a rear corner stands *Aphrodite Adioumene* or the so-called "Marine Venus", beloved of Lawrence Durrell, but lent a rather sinister aspect by her sea-dissolved face – in contrast to the friendlier *Aphrodite Bathing*. Virtually next door is the **Decorative Arts Collection** (Tues–Sun 8.30am–3pm; €2 or joint ticket), gleaned from old houses across the Dodecanese; the most compelling artefacts are carved cupboard doors and chest lids painted in naïve style with mythological or historical episodes.

Across the way stands the **Byzantine Museum** (Tues–Sun 8.30am–3pm; €2 or joint ticket), housed in the old cathedral of the Knights, who adapted the Byzantine shrine of Panayía toú Kástrou for their own needs. Medieval icons and frescoes lifted from crumbling chapels on Rhodes and Hálki, as well as photos of art still *in situ*, constitute the exhibits. The highlight of the permanent collection is a complete fresco cycle from the domes and squinches of Thárri monastery (see p.325) dating from 1624, removed in 1967 to reveal much older work beneath.

If instead you head south from the Palace of the Grand Masters, it's hard to miss the most conspicuous Turkish monument in Rhodes, the rust-coloured **Süleymaniye Mosque**. Rebuilt in the nineteenth century on foundations three hundred years older, it's currently closed like many local Ottoman monuments, though scheduled to emerge soon from a lengthy refit in all its candy-striped glory. The Old Town is in fact well sown with mosques and *mescids* (the Islamic equivalent of a chapel), many of them converted from Byzantine churches after the 1522 conquest, when the Christians were expelled from the medieval precinct. A couple of these, such as the **Ibrahim Pasha Mosque** on Plátonos, are still used by the sizeable **Turkish-speaking minority** here, some descended from Muslims who fled Crete between 1898 and 1913. Their most enduring civic contributions are, opposite the Süleymaniye, the **Ottoman Library** (Mon–Sat 9.30am–4pm; tip to custodian), with a rich collection of early medieval manuscripts and Korans, and the imposing, still-functioning **Mustafa Hamam**, or Turkish bath, on Platía Aríonos up in the southwest corner of the medieval city (Mon–Fri 10am–5pm, Sat 8am–5pm, last admission 3.30pm; €1.50); bring everything you need – soap, shampoo, towel, loofa – to enjoy the separate men's and women's sections. Heading downhill from the Süleymaniye Mosque, you come to **Odhós Sokrátous**, since time immemorial the main commercial thoroughfare, and now the "Via Turista", packed with fur and jewellery stores pitched at cruise-ship tourists. Beyond the tiled central fountain in Platía Ippokrátous, Odhós Aristotélous leads into the **Platía tón Evréon Martýron** ("Square of the Jewish Martyrs"), named in memory of the large local community that was almost totally annihilated during the summer of 1944; a black granite column in the centre honours them. Of the four synagogues that once graced the nearby Jewish quarter, only the ornate, arcaded **Kal Kadosh Shalom** (daily 10am–5pm; donation) on Odhós Simíou, just to the south, survives. It's maintained essentially as another memorial to the approximately 2100 Jews of Rhodes and Kós sent from here to the concentration camps; plaques in French – the language of educated Ottoman Jews across the east Aegean – commemorate the dead. At the rear of the building, a one-room **museum**, set up by a Los Angeles attorney of Jewish Rhodian descent and scheduled to be expanded, features archival photos of the community's life on Rhodes and in its far-flung diaspora in the Americas and Africa.

Neohóri

The pointy bit of **Neohóri** is surrounded by a continuous **beach**, complete with deckchairs, parasols and showers, particularly on the more sheltered east-facing section called **Élli**. At the northernmost point of the island an **Aquarium** (daily: April–Sept 9am–8.30pm; Oct–March 9am–4.30pm; €3.50), officially the "Hydrobiological Institute", offers some diversion with its subterranean maze of seawater tanks. Upstairs is a less enthralling collection of half-rotten stuffed sharks, seals and even a whale. Immediately south of this, on Ekatón Hourmadhiés ("100 Palms") Square, in the Nestorídhio Mélathro, is housed the **Museum of Modern Greek Art** (Tues–Sat 8am–2pm & 6–9pm; €3), one of the most important collections of 20th-century Greek painting and sculpture. East of "100 Palms", the Italian-built Albergo delle Rose (*Hotel Rodon*) has been converted into the **Casino of Rhodes**, Greece's third largest and, unusually, open to locals as well as visitors. Continue in the same direction to the **Murad Reis mosque** and its atmospherically neglected Muslim cemetery, just past the **Villa Cleobolus**, where Lawrence Durrell lived from

1945 to 1947, recently refurbished as home to the Dodecanesian Literature and Arts Club.

About 2km southwest of Mandhráki, the sparse, unenclosed remains of **Hellenistic Rhodes** – a restored theatre and stadium, plus a few columns of an Apollo temple – perch atop Monte Smith, the hill of Áyios Stéfanos renamed after a British admiral who used it as a watchpoint during the Napoleonic Wars.

Eating and drinking

Eating well for a reasonable price in and around Ródhos Town is a challenge, but not an insurmountable one. As a general rule, the further south towards Zéfyros you go, the better value you'll find – so touristy, alas, has the Old Town (and much of Neohóri) become. Unless otherwise stated, the following restaurants are open all year round.

Old Town

L'Auberge Bistrot Praxitélous 21 ☎22410 34292. Genuine, popular, French-run bistro with excellent Frenchified food: allow €21 per person for a starter, meaty main course and dessert; they also feature fish or bouilllabaise, and a "light" menu for a tad less. Wine (extra) from a well-selected Greek list; jazz soundtrack included. Summer seating in the courtyard of this restored medieval inn; inside under the arches during cooler months. Open late March to late Dec for supper Tues–Sun (the place operates with distinguished guest chefs in winter); book in high season.

Landis Sofokléous 5. Hole-in-the-wall ouzerí with sought-after seating out in the lane; big platters of well-fried or -marinated seafood titbits, cheapish ouzo by the carafe.

Marco Polo Café Ayíou Fanouríou 42. What started out as the breakfast venue of the eponymous hotel (see p.313) has become, under Spyros Dedes' stewardship, the sleeper of the old town, open to all. Excellent generic Mediterranean fare – mostly vegetables, salads and seafood – with good wines (Spyros is a fanatic) and in-house desserts. April–Oct.

O Meraklis Aristotélous 30. A *patsatzídhiko* (tripe-soup kitchen) that's only open 3–8am for a motley clientele of post-club lads, Turkish stallholders, nightclub singers and travellers just stumbled off an overnight ferry. Great free entertainment, including famously rude staff, and the soup – the traditional Greek hangover cure – is good too.

Mikes (pronounced "mee-kess") Nameless alley behind Sokrátous 17. Inexpensive but salubrious hole-in-the-wall, serving only grilled fish, a few shellfish appetizers, salads and wine; outdoor tables, galley-like kitchen. April–Nov.

Nireas Sofokléous 22. A kindly proprietor, fair fish prices (for Rhodes Old Town, anyway) and atmospheric indoor/outdoor seating make this a good choice for a last-night-of-holiday treat. If for any

reason *Nireas* doesn't suit, **Sea Star** immediately next door also has its passionate devotees in the seafood sweepstakes.

Neohóri

Ammoyiali Voríou Ipírou 17, cnr Kennedy. 2005-opened, high-end bistro purveying "power breakfasts", salads, pasta dishes like tagliatelle and salmon, accomplished desserts and a decent wine list. Moderately expensive, busiest at night; by day sit outside for the sea view.

Chalki (Pavlos') Kathopoúli 30. Ancient, full bottles of who-knows-what form the eclectic decor of this little ouzerí doing good vegetarian *mezédhes* and a limited daily range of main platters (some cheap seafood), washed down by ouzo and CAIR wine. Average-sized portions, but quite cheap. Evenings only.

O Griniaris Platía Ayíou Ioánni 155. Italian-run "traditional *kafenío*" with superbly executed dishes like cumined chickpeas, grilled aubergine with basil, smoked herring, octopus salad, stewed mussels, and panna cotta for dessert. The organic red Peloponnesian house wine is pricey but worth it. March 15–Nov 15, evenings only.

Ta Marasia Platía Ayíou Ioánni 155. The most daring ouzerí in the town limits, operating out of a 1923-vintage house. The food's excellent, if not always very traditional (grilled oyster mushrooms, red cabbage, yogurt-and-nut salad), though there are more usual seafood platters like urchins and *rengosaláta*. Don't over-order, as portions tend to be generous.

Stani Ayías Anastasías 28, cnr Paleón Patrón Yermanoú, south of the Koskinoú Gate. Most central outlet of a chain of Rhodian Turkish confectioners, scooping out two dozen flavours of the best ice cream on the island – queues at all hours (until 1am) tell you this is the spot.

To Steki tou Tsima Peloponnísou 22, around cnr from *Stani*. Reasonable seafood ouzerí, with the stress on aficionados' shellfish titbits such as *fouskes* (fresh marine invertebrates), *spinialo* (pick-led version of same) and small fish not prone to farming – always ask about off-menu specials. No airs or graces (except for proper table napery), just patently fresh materials. Daily eves only.

To Steno Ayíon Anaryíron 29, 400m southwest of Ayíou Athanasíou Gate. A small, welcoming taverna, with outdoor seating in the warmer months. The menu encompasses sausages, chickpea soup, *pitaroúdhia* or courgette croquettes, stuffed zucchini blossoms and fried little fish; "discovery" means it's oilier and pricer than it once was, but still worth the trek out.

Thavma en Kairo Eleftheriou Venizelou 16–18. ☎ 22410 39805, ⓦ www.restaurantwonder.com. Anders, the Swedish founder of the late, legendary *7.5 Wonder*, has upped sticks and chefs, and migrated to this elegant Belle Époque mansion overlooking parkland. He's repeated his fusion of Asian, Mediterranean and Scandanavian cuisine to good effect, but it – and the four-star wine list – will set you back a minimum €33 per person. Supper only.

Tsipouradhiko Aktí Miaoúli 20. All the meat and seafood ouzerí/*tsipourádhiko* standards in deceptively small but rich platters – six will feed two people – at competitive prices considering the unobstructed sea view. Run by nice folk from main-land Thessaly, who make their own *tsípouro*. Daily noon–3am or so; Tues–Sun in low season.

Zéfyros and around

Anatolikes Nostimies Klavdhíou Pépper 109, Zéfyros beach. The name means "Anatolian Delicacies", and that's what's on offer at this Rhodian-Turkish-run grill: Turkish/Middle Eastern dips and starters, plus a dozen varieties of strictly beef-based kebabs (as opposed to the usual lamb or pork). Beach-hut atmosphere, but friendly and reasonable; post-prandial hubble-bubble provided on request. 1pm–midnight.

Khristos (O Vlahos) Klavdhíou Pépper 165, at the big bend before Zéfyros beach. Enduringly popular *estiatório* where civil servants from the nearby tax office habitually lunch at outdoor seating. Great *tzatzíki*, plus vegetable-strong *mayireftá* (cuttlefish with spinach, pork stew, fish soup, eggplant *imam*) that sell out quickly. Portions have shrunk and prices inched up over the years, but still worth the trek out.

🏃 **Metaxi Mas** Klavdhíou Pépper 113–115, Zéfyros beach. No sign in English – look for the elevated boat – at this excellent-value seafood ouzerí purveying various titbits such as marinated red mullet, a few shellfish, lobster on occasion, vegie starters and meat too for the fish-averse; three can eat well for about €45 – a fraction of Old-Town costs, and with a sea view (and winter fireplace) to boot. Mon–Sat lunch and supper, Sun lunch only.

Paragadhi corner Klavdhíou Pépper and Avstralías. 2004-opened seafood/fish restaurant (as opposed to ouzerí), with fair portions and prices. Their *risótto thalassinoú* is excellent if not puristically authentic. Closed Sun eve & Mon noon.

Sakis Kanadhá 95, corner Apostólou Papaïoán-nou. An old favourite in a new location closer to the beach, with pleasant patio and indoor seating, equally popular with Rhodians and savvy expats. Known for excellent seafood (such as limpets), meat (Cypriot *seftaliés*) and starters; inexpensive by Rhodian standards. Open year round; supper daily, also Sun lunch.

To Steki tou Heila Hatziangélou, corner Episkópi Kyrinías, near Zéfyros. Very popular seafood ouzerí which probably just pips *To Steki tou Tsima* for quality at similar prices, though the street's noisy. Rocket and onion salad, Sými shrimps, squid, mari-nated sardines, *fáva*, shellfish (check price of last). Daily supper only.

Nightlife

In the Old Town, there's an entire alley (Miltiádhou) off Apelloú given over to around ten loud **music bars** and **clubs**, extending into Plátonos and Platía Dhamayítou, and frequented almost exclusively by Greeks; their names and proprietors change yearly, but the locations remain the same. Another, some-what lower-decibel nucleus of activity is around Platía Aríonos. These are just appetizers for the estimated seventy or so suriviving foreigner-patronized bars and clubs in Neohóri, where theme nights and various other gimmicks predominate. They are found mostly along the streets and alleys bounded by Alexándhrou Dhiákou, Orfanídhou, Lohagoú Fanouráki and Nikifórou Mandhilará.

Sedate by comparison, Ministry of Culture-approved **folk dances** (June 15–Oct 1 Mon, Wed & Fri 9.20pm; €12) are presented with live accompani-ment by the Nelly Dimoglou Company, performed in the landscaped Old

Town Theatre off Andhroníkou, near Platía Ariónos. More of a technological extravaganza is the **Sound and Light** show, spotlighting sections of the city walls, staged in a garden just off Platía Rimínis. There's English-language narration nightly except Sunday, its screening time varying from 8.15pm to 10.15pm (€6).

Thanks to a large contingent from the local university, there are year-round **cinemas** showing first-run fare indoors or open-air according to season and air-con capabilities. Choose from among the summer-only outdoor cinema by the Municipal Theatre, next to the town hall in Neohóri; the Metropol multiplex, at the corner of Venetokléon and Výronos, southeast of the old town opposite the stadium; and the nearby Pallas three-plex on Dhimokratías.

Bekir Karakuzu Sokrátous 76. Bags of atmosphere in this, the last traditional Turkish *kafenío* in the Old Town, with an ornate *votsalotó* floor for its Oriental-fantasy interior. Yoghurt, *loukoúmi*, *alisfakiá* tea and coffees on the expensive side, but you are effectively paying admission to an informal museum. 11am–midnight.

Besara Kafé Sofokléous 11–13, Old Town. Congenial breakfast café/low-key boozer run by Australian-Texan Besara Harris, with interesting mixed clientele and live Greek acoustic music some nights Oct–May.

Blue Lagoon Pool Bar 25-Martíou 2, Neohóri. One of the better theme bars, in this case a "desert island" with palm trees, waterfalls, live turtles and parrots, a shipwrecked galleon – and taped music. March–Oct 8.30am–3am.

Christos' Garden Dhilberáki 59, Neohóri. This combination art-gallery/bar/café occupies a carefully restored old house and courtyard with pebble-mosaic floors throughout. Incongruously classy for the area.

Colorado Entertainment Centre Orfanídhou 57, cnr Aktí Miaouli, Neohóri; ⊛www.coloradoclub .gr. Triple venue: "Colorado Live" with in-house band (rock covers), "Studio Fame" with taped sounds, and club, plus chill-out "Heaven" R&B bar upstairs.

El Divino Alexándhrou Dhiákou 5, Neohóri. Upscale, Greek-frequented "music bar" with garden seating and the usual range of coffees and alcohol. June–Oct.

Mandala Sofokléous 38. Part-Swedish-run, enduringly popular snack-café/garden bar where the generic Med-lite salads and pasta dishes are overpriced and incidental to good beer, the crowd, and live Greek acoustic music Sat eve. Open all year 2pm–3am; in winter there's a cozy interior with fireplace.

Iy Rogmi tou Khronou Platía Ariónos, Old Town. Taped proper music (not house or techno) at a reasonable level and a congenial crowd make this established bar worth a look; much the same clientele spills over to **Baduz Loutra** next door, which hosts live rock or jazz one night weekly.

Sticky Fingers Anthoúla Zérvou 6, Neohóri. Long-lived music bar with reasonably priced drinks; live rock several nights weekly from 10.30pm onwards, Fri & Sat only off-season. Typical admission €12.

Listings

Airlines Olympic Airways, Iérou Lóhou 9 ☎22410 24555; Aegean Airlines, Ethelondón Dhodhekanisíon 20 ☎22410 24400.

Bookshop Newsstand at Grigoríou Lambráki 23 is the only (very limited) outlet for any quality foreign-language books.

Car rental Prices at Greek chains are fairly standard at €45–55 per day, but can be bargained down to about €25–35 a day, all-inclusive, out of peak season and/or for long periods. Especially recommended is Drive/ Budget, who change their cars every 12–18 months; they have several premises across the island, including at the airport (☎22410 81011); their central, long-hours reservation number is ☎22410 68243. Other flexible outfits, all in the New Town, include Just/Ansa, Mandhilará 70 ☎22410 31811; Kosmos, Papaloúka 31 ☎22410 74374; and Orion, Yeoryíou Leóndou 36 ☎22410 22137. Major international chains include Alamo/ National, Iraklídhon 41, Ixiá ☎22410 91117 and at the airport ☎22410 81600; Avis, Theodhoráki 3, Neohóri ☎22410 24990 and the airport ☎22410 82896; plus Hertz at Yeoryíou Gríva 16, Neohóri ☎22410 21819 and at the airport ☎22410 82902.

Exchange 8 conventional bank branches are grouped around Platía Kýprou in Neohóri, plus there are various exchange bureaux keeping long hours. In the Old Town, there are two full-service banks with ATMs near the museums, plus a pair of stand-alone ATMs on Sokrátous.

Ferry agents ANES ☎22410 37769, for catamaran and hydrofoil to Sými; Kydon ☎22419 23000, for Agoudimos Lines; Dodhekanisos Navtiliaki ☎22410 70590, for the *Dodekanisos Express/Dodekanisos Pride* catamarans to most Dodecanese islands; Inspiration, Aktí Sakhtoúri 4 ☎22410 24294 (base of main ferry dock), for most GA boats to Dodecanese and Cyclades; LANE ☎22410 33607, to Crete via Hálki, Kárpathos, Kássos; *Sea Star* catamaran to Tílos and Níssyros, booth at Mandhráki port or ☎22410 78052. Weekly tourist office departure-schedule handouts are deeply unreliable; authoritative sailing information is available at the *limenarhío* (port police), on Mandhráki esplanade near the post office.

Internet cafés The most central and competitive of several are EasyInternet, inside El Divino (address p.319), and *Mango Bar* at Platía Dhoriéos 3, Old Town.

Laundries Tornado, Apolloníou Rodhíou 28, Neohóri; Wash & Go, Plátonos 33, Old Town.

Motorbike rental Low-volume scooters will make little impact on Rhodes; sturdier Yamaha 125s, suitable for two people, start at about €25 a day. Recommended outlets in Neohóri include Margaritis, Ioánni Kazoúli 23, with a wide range of late models up to 500cc, plus mountain bikes; or Kiriakos, Apodhímon Amerikís 16, which will deliver to the old town and take you back once you've finished.

Travel agencies In Neohóri, conveniently located Triton Holidays at Plastíra 9 (☎22410 21690, ℮info@tritondmc.gr) is excellent for all local travel arrangements, including car rental, domestic catamaran, ferry and air tickets for every company, plus the catamaran to Turkey or charters to the UK. They also have a network of accommodation across the Dodecanese, and can book you an entire itinerary at attractive rates. French-run Passion Sailing Cruises (☎22410 73006, ⊛www.aegeanpassion.com) offers a bespoke service for skippered cruises, as well as bareboat charter.

The east coast

Heading down the coast from the capital you have to go some way before you escape the crowds from local beach hotels, their numbers swollen by visitors using the regular buses from town or on boat tours out of Mandhráki. You should look in at the abandoned spa of **Thérmes Kallithéas**, a prize example of orientalized Art Deco dating from 1928–29, the work of a young Pietro Lombardi who, in his old age, designed the European Parliament building in Strasbourg. Located 3km south of Kallithéa resort proper, down a paved side-road through pines, the buildings are set in a palm grove, though an EU-funded restoration begun in 1999 has slowed to a snail's pace. The concrete lido beyond the domed structure is popular, as are several secluded coves south of the ex-spa, framed by rock formations which often interpose themselves between the water and the sand. These beachlets are furnished with sunbeds and (in most cases) snack-bars – best of these reckoned to be *Oasis*.

The resort of **FALIRÁKI** has acquired considerable notoriety as the "boozing and bonking" capital of the Dodecanese, a reputation reinforced by a string of rapes and, in August 2003, the fatal stabbing of one British youth and the arrest of several others on charges of public lewdness. This was all fuelled by a culture of pub-crawls organized by tour reps, many of whom were also arrested and charged for taking kickbacks from bar owners. The British press indulged in an orgy of self-flagellation about "ugly Brits", while local authorities made pious noises about cleaning up the resort, with the malefactors subject to (by the standards of any country, let alone Greece) extraordinarily speedy justice *pour encourager les autres*. The clamp-down suceeded far beyond the Rhodian authorities' expectations; since then central Faliráki has all but become a ghost town, with the party action shifted to Laganás on Zákynthos. The cape to the south, **Ladhikó** (45min path from Faliráki), shelters the more scenic bay of

"**Anthony Quinn**", named in honour of the late actor whom Greeks took to their hearts following his roles in *Zorba the Greek* and *The Guns of Navarone* (the latter filmed locally).

South of Ladhikó headland extends the sweeping pebble-and-sand expanse of **Afándou Bay**, the most undeveloped large beach on the east coast, with just a few stretches of sunbeds and showers (laid on by the municipality, as at most beaches). Spare a moment, heading down the main access road to mid-bay, for the atmospheric, frescoed sixteenth-century **church of Panayía Katholikí**, paved with a *votsalotó* floor throughout and incorporating fragments of a much older basilica. Immediately opposite is a very popular, cheap-and-cheerful **taverna**, doing just grills, salad and dips: *Estiatorio Katholiki* (Mon–Sat supper, Sun lunch also).

The enormous promontory of **Tsambíka**, 26km south of town – actually the very eroded flank of a once much-larger mountain – offers unrivalled views from up top along some 50km of coastline. From the main highway, a steep, 1500-metre cement drive leads to a small car park and a snack-bar, from where steps take you to the summit. The little monastery here is unremarkable except for its September 8 festival: childless women climb up – sometimes on their hands and knees – to be relieved of their barrenness, and any children born afterwards are dedicated to the Virgin with the names Tsambikos or Tsambika, which are particular to the Dodecanese. Shallow **Tsambíka Bay** on the south side of the headland (two-kilometre access road) warms up early in the spring, and the excellent beach, protected by its owners, the Orthodox Church, from permanent development – there are just seven *kantínas* – teems with people all summer. For a proper **taverna**, head for *Panorama Tsambikas*, one of a cluster on the grade of the main highway south of the beach turning.

The next beach south is gravelly **Stegná** with its mix of summer cottages for locals and accommodation for Germans, plus a couple of **tavernas** that attract a Greek clientele. Stegná is reached by a steep road east from the less rewarding village of **ARHÁNGELOS**, just inland and overlooked by a crumbling castle. The place is now firmly caught up in package tourism, with a full complement of banks, tavernas, minimarts and jewellery stores. Another overnight base on this stretch of coast, English-dominated this time, is **HARÁKI**, a pleasant if undistinguished two-street fishing port with mostly self-catering accommodation (generally ❸) overlooked by the stubby ruins of **Feraklós Castle**, the last stronghold of the Knights to fall to the Turks. You can swim off the town beach if you don't mind an audience from the handful of waterfront cafés and tavernas, but most people head west out of town, then north 800m along a marked dirt track to secluded **Ayía Agáthi beach**, or down the coast 8km to **Paralía Kaláthou**, with an attractive, and less claustrophobic, stretch of sand and fine gravel.

Líndhos

LÍNDHOS, the island's number-two tourist attraction, erupts from barren surroundings 12km south of Haráki. Like Ródhos Old Town, its charm is heavily undermined by commercialism and crowds. At midday dozens of tour coaches park nose-to-tail at the outskirts; back in the village itself, those few vernacular houses not snapped up by package operators have, since the 1960s, been bought up and refurbished by wealthy British, Germans and Italians. The old *agorá* or serpentine high street presents a mass of fairly indistinguishable bars, crêperies, mediocre restaurants and travel agents. Although high-rise hotels and all vehicular traffic have been prohibited inside the built-up area, the result is a relentlessly commercialized theme park – hot and airless from June to August, but eerily deserted in winter.

Nonetheless, if you arrive before or after peak season, when the pebble-paved streets between the immaculately whitewashed houses are relatively empty of both people and droppings from the donkeys shuttling punters up to the acropolis (see below), you can still appreciate the beautiful, atmospheric setting of Líndhos. The belfried, post-Byzantine **Panayía church** is covered inside with well-preserved eighteenth-century frescoes. The most imposing fifteenth-to-eighteenth-century **captains' residences** are built around *votsalotó* courtyards, their monumental doorways often fringed by intricate stonework, with the number of braids or cables supposedly corresponding to the number of ships owned. A few are open to the public, notably the **Papakonstandis Mansion**, the most elaborate and home to an unofficial museum (erratic hours, nominally daily 11am–2pm).

On the bluff looming above the town, the ancient acropolis with its Doric **Temple of Athena** (restorations ongoing until 2008) and imposing **Hellenistic stoa** is found inside the Knights' **castle** (summer Mon 12.30–6.40pm, Tues–Sun 8am–6.40pm; rest of year Tues–Sun 8.30am–3pm; €6) – a surprisingly felicitous blend of ancient and medieval culture. Though the ancient city of **Lindos** and its original temple dated from at least 1100 BC, the present structure was begun by local ruler Kleoboulos in the sixth century BC after a fourth-century fire.

Líndhos's north beach, once the main ancient harbour, is overcrowded and heavily commercialized; if you do base yourself here, quieter **beaches** are to be found one cove beyond at **Pállas** beach (with a nudist annexe around the headland), or 5km north at **Vlyhá Bay**. South of the acropolis huddles the small, perfectly sheltered **St Paul's harbour**, with excellent swimming; the apostle is said to have landed here in 58 AD on a mission to evangelize the island.

Practicalities

It used to be tempting fate to just turn up and hope for **accommodation** vacancies on spec, but since certain British tour companies abandoned Líndhos, it's something of a buyers' market. If you're not met at the bus stop under the giant fig tree by proprietors touting rooms, Pallas Travel (☎22440 31494) can arrange a room or even a whole villa for a small fee; just watch that you're not shoved into a windowless cell – ventilation is paramount here. The only real **hotel** in Líndhos, the most exclusive on the island, is ✦ *Melenos* (☎22440 32222, ⓦwww.melenoslindos.com; April–Oct; ❽), unimprovably sited on the second lane above the north beach, by the school. No expense has been spared in laying out the twelve suites with semi-private, *votsalotó* terraces, from Kütahya tiles in the vast bathrooms to antiques and wood bed-platforms; all balconies have views, there's an equally pricey on-site garden-bar and restaurant, and by ❽ we mean €200–500 by season.

Most local **restaurants** tend to be exploitatively priced and serve bland fare, with a quick turnover in ownership. You may as well push the boat out at ✦ *Mavrikos* on the fig-tree square, founded in 1933 and in the same family ever since. *Mezédhes* such as *manoúri* cheese with basil and pine-nuts, sweet marinated sardines, or beets in goat-cheese sauce, are accomplished, as are main courses such as cuttlefish in wine sauce, raw tuna with fennel or skate terrine with pine nuts; dipping into the excellent (and expensive) Greek wine list as well will add €18 minimum a bottle to the typical food charge of €23–28 per person. For snacks and desserts, try *Il Forno*, an Italian-run bakery, and *Gelo Blu*, the most genuine of several *gelaterie* here, also offering decadent cakes. The better of two **Internet cafés** is helpful and well-equipped Lindianet; The Link is a unique combination **laundry** and secondhand **bookshop** (Mon–Sat

9am–8pm). Líndhos has one amenity that would be the envy of much larger towns: a **spa** (Mon–Sat 1pm–9pm), offering the full range of services including all-day packages. There are two proper **banks**, each with ATMs. Finally, Lindos Suntours (℡22440 31333) and Village Holidays (℡22440 31486) both may have unclaimed one-way charter seats back to Britain.

The west coast

Rhodes' **west coast** is the windward flank of the island, so it's damper, more fertile and more forested; most beaches, however, are exposed and decidedly rocky. None of this has deterred development and, as in the east, the first few kilometres of the busy main road down from the capital have been surrendered entirely to tourism. From Neohóri's aquarium down to the airport, the shore is fringed by an almost uninterrupted line of generic Mediterranean-*costa* hotels, though such places as Triánda, Kremastí and Paradhísi are still nominally villages, with real centres.

There's not much inducement to stop until you reach the important archeological site of **KAMEIROS**, which together with Lindos and Ialyssos was one of the three Dorian powers that united during the fifth century BC to found the powerful city-state of Rhodes. Soon eclipsed by the new capital, Kameiros was abandoned and only rediscovered in 1859. Thus it's a particularly well-preserved Doric townscape, doubly worth visiting for its beautiful hillside setting (summer Tues–Sun 8am–6.40pm; winter 8.30am–3pm; €4). While none of the individual remains is spectacular, you can make out the foundations of two small temples, the re-erected pillars of a Hellenistic house, a Classical fountain, and the *stoa* of the upper agora, complete with a water cistern. Because of the gentle slope of the site, there were no fortifications, nor was there an acropolis.

At the tiny anchorage of **KÁMIROS SKÁLA** (aka Skála Kamírou) 15km south, there are five rather touristy restaurants, the best being *Loukas* nearest the quay. Less heralded is the daily **kaïki** which leaves for the island of **Hálki** at 2.30pm, weather permitting, returning at 6am the next morning; on Sundays there's a single journey at 9am, returning from Hálki at 5pm. For a taverna alternative, proceed 400m southwest to off-puttingly named **Paralía Kopriá** ("Manure Beach"), where *Psarotaverna Johnny's* has good fish and *mezédhes*; it's been "discovered" and so is pricier than formerly, but still worth a stop.

A couple of kilometres south of Skála, the "Kastello", signposted as **Kástro Kritinías** is, from afar, the most impressive of the Knights' rural strongholds, and the paved access road is too narrow and steep for tour buses. Close up it proves to be no more than a shell, but a glorious shell, with fine views west to Hálki, Alimniá, Tílos and Níssyros. The castle is being restored, with a small museum in the old church, a café, and formal admission tickets foreseen; until then (and afterwards) you should not pay any "toll" to fruit-sellers accosting you illegally on the access road.

Beyond the quiet hillside village of Kritinía itself, the main road winds south through the dense forests below mounts Akramýtis and Atávyros to **SIÁNNA**, famous for its aromatic pine-and-sage honey and *soúma*, a grape-residue distillate similar to Italian *grappa* but far smoother. The tiered, flat-roofed farmhouses of **MONÓLITHOS**, 4km southwest at the end of the public bus line, don't themselves justify the long trip out here, but the view over the bay is striking and you could base yourself at the *Hotel Thomas* (℡22460 61291; ❷), whose fair-sized rooms bely a grim exterior. Best of several **tavernas** is welcoming *O Palios Monolithos*, opposite the church: not bargain-priced but tops for grilled meat and dishes of the day, accompanied by good bread and non–CAIR bulk wine. Diversions in the area include yet another **Knights' castle**, 2km west of town, photogenically perched on its own pinnacle but enclosing very little, and the sand-and-gravel beaches at **Foúrni**, five paved but curvy kilometres below the castle.

The interior

Inland Rhodes is hilly and still mostly wooded, despite the depredations of arsonists. You'll need a vehicle to see its highlights, especially as enjoyment resides in getting away from it all; no single site justifies the tremendous expense of a taxi or the inconvenience of trying to make the best of sparse bus schedules.

Ialyssos and Petaloúdhes

Starting from the west-coast highway, turn inland at the central junction in Tríanda for the five-kilometre ride up to the scanty acropolis of ancient **Ialyssos** (Mon–Sat 8am–6.40pm, Sun 8.30am–2.40pm; €3) on flat-topped, strategic Filérimos hill; from its Byzantine castle Süleyman the Magnificent directed the 1522 siege of Rhodes. Filérimos means "lover of solitude", after the tenth-century settlement here by Byzantine hermits. The existing **Filérimos monastery**, restored successively by Italians and British, is the most substantial structure here. As a concession to the Rhodian faithful, the church alone may be open to pilgrims after the stated hours. Directly in front of the church sprawl the foundations of third-century **temples to Zeus and Athena**, built atop a far older Phoenician shrine. Below this, further towards the car park, lies the partly subterranean church of **Aï-Yeórgis Hostós**, a barrel-vaulted structure with faint fourteenth- and fifteenth-century frescoes. Southwest of the monastery and archeological zone, a **Via Crucis**, with the fourteen stations marked out in copper plaques during the Italian era, leads to an enormous concrete crucifix, a 1995 replacement of an Italian-built one; you're allowed to climb out onto the cross-arms for a supplement to the already amazing view. Illuminated at night, the crucifix is clearly visible from the island of Sými and – perhaps more pertinently – "infidel" Turkey across the way.

The only highly publicized tourist "attraction" in the island's interior, **Petaloúdhes** ("Butterfly Valley") (May–Sept daily 8am–dusk; April & Oct 9am–3pm; admission €3–5 by season), is reached by a seven-kilometre side road bearing inland between Paradhísi and Theológos and is actually a rest stop for Jersey tiger moths. Only in summer do these creatures congregate here, attracted for unknown reasons by the abundant *Liquidambar orientalis* trees growing abundantly in this stream canyon. The moths roosting in droves on the tree trunks cannot eat during this final phase of their life cycle, must rest to conserve energy and die of starvation soon after mating. When sitting in the trees, the moths are a well-camouflaged black and yellow, but flash cherry-red overwings in flight.

Some 2km before Petaloúdhes, the **microwinery** (15,000–20,000 bottles annually) of Anastasia Triandafyllou is worth a stop for its nine varieties, including Athiri whites and Cabernet or Mandhilari reds (daily 8.30am–7pm). There's a popular roadside **taverna** partway up the valley, but for even better fare continue all the way to the edge of **PSÍNTHOS** village, where friendly ⚒ *Piyi Fasouli* serves excellent grills and appetizers as well as a few *mayireftá* at seating under plane trees beside the namesake spring, and is worth the bit extra for the quality.

Eptá Piyés to Profítis Ilías

Heading inland from Kolýmbia junction on the main east-coast highway, it's 4km to **Eptá Piyés** ("Seven Springs"), a lush oasis with a tiny dam created by the Italians for irrigation. A trail, or a rather claustrophobic Italian aqueduct-tunnel, both lead from the vicinity of the springs to the reservoir.

Continuing inland, you reach neglected Rationalist structures at Eleoússa (built as the planned agricultural colony of Campochiaro in 1935–36) after another 9km, in the shade of the dense forest at the east end of Profítis Ilías ridge. From the vast Art Deco pool just west of the village, keep straight on 3km further to the late Byzantine church of **Áyios Nikólaos Foundouklí** ("St Nicholas of the Hazelnuts"). The partly shaded site has a fine view north over cultivated valleys; frescoes inside, dating from the thirteenth to the fifteenth centuries, could use a good cleaning, but various scenes from the life of Christ are recognizable.

Continuing west from the church gets you finally to **Profítis Ilías**, where the Italian-vintage chalet-hotels *Elafos* and *Elafina* (now hosting childrens' summer camps) hide in deep woods just north of the 798-metre peak, Rhodes' third-highest point but out of bounds since it's a military area. However, there's good, gentle strolling below and around the summit, and a snack-bar on the through road is generally open in season. The closest facilities are in **SÁLAKOS** downslope, for example the *Hotel-Café Nymph* (T 22460 22206, W www .nymph.com.gr; ❸) at the top of the village.

Atávyros villages

All tracks and roads west across Profítis Ilías converge on the main road from Kalavárdha bound for **ÉMBONA**, a large and architecturally nondescript village backed up against the north slope of 1215-metre **Mount Atávyros**. Émbona, with a half-dozen meat-oriented **tavernas** (try *Panayiotis Bakis* on the platía, which has its own butcher's), is more geared to handling tourists than you might expect, since it's the venue for summer "folk-dance tours" from Ródhos Town. The village also lies at the heart of the island's most important wine-producing districts, and CAÏR – the Italian-founded vintners' co-operative – produces a choice of acceptable mid-range varieties. However, products of the smaller, family-run Emery **winery** (daily 9am–4.30pm) at the northern outskirts are more esteemed. To get some idea what Émbona would be like without tourists, carry on clockwise around the peak to less celebrated **ÁYIOS ISÍDHOROS**, with nearly as many vines and tavernas, a more open feel and the **trailhead** for the five-hour return ascent of Atávyros. This path, beginning at the northeast edge of the village at a wooden placard and well marked with paint splodges, is the safest and easiest way up the mountain, though you'll find the slopes sullied by a wind-power farm, an air force radar "golf ball" up top and the tracks built to install these.

Thárri monastery

The road from Áyios Isídhoros to Siánna is paved; not so the perennially rough one that curves for 12km east to Láerma, but it's worth enduring if you've any interest in Byzantine monuments. The **monastery of Thárri**, lost in pine forests 5km south, is the oldest religious foundation on the island, re-established as a living community of half a dozen monks in 1990 by the charismatic abbot Amfilohios. The striking *katholikón* (open daily, all day) consists of a long nave and short transept surmounted by barrel vaulting. Various cleanings have restored damp-smudged frescoes dating from 1300 to 1450 to their former exquisite glory. The most distinct, in the transept, depict the Evangelists Mark and Matthew, plus the Archangel Gabriel, while the nave boasts various acts of Christ, including such scenes as the *Storm on the Sea of Galilee*, *Meeting the Samaritan Woman at the Well* and *Healing the Cripple*. In **LÁERMA**, you can dine on the terrace of the aptly named *Psistaria Bella Vista* at the eastern outskirts.

The far south

South of a line connecting Monólithos and Lárdhos, you could easily begin to think you had strayed onto another island. Gone are most of the multi-star hotels, and with them the bulk of the crowds. Only one or two daily buses (in season) ply to the depopulated villages here (Yennádhi has much better services), approaching along the east coast; tavernas dot the village centres and the more popular beaches, but aside from the package enclaves of Lárdhos, Péfki and Kiotári, there are few places to stay.

Despite the shelving of plans for a second airport nearby, new beachfront development mushrooms to either side of **LÁRDHOS**, itself solidly on the tourist circuit despite the village's inland position between Láerma and the Líndhos peninsula. The beach 2km away is gravelly and exposed to southeasterly storms, so you might continue 3km to **Glýstra** cove, a small but delightful crescent which gets crowded in season. Four kilometres east of Lárdhos, **PÉFKI** (Péfkos on some maps) began life as the garden annexe and overflow for Líndhos, but is now a burgeoning package resort in its own right; the sea is clearer than at Lárdhos proper, with small, well-hidden beaches tucked at the base of low cliffs (biggest of these, in western Péfki, is **Lothiáriko**). Among **tavernas**, *Kavos* at the eastern edge of town has the most Greek menu and the pleasantest setting.

Asklipió

Nine kilometres beyond Lárdhos, a side road heads 3.5km inland to **ASKLI-PIÓ**, a sleepy village guarded by a crumbling Knights' castle and graced by the Byzantine church of **Kímisis Theotókou** (daily 9am–6pm, closes 5pm spring/ autumn; €1). The building dates from 1060, with a pebble-floored ground plan nearly identical to Thárri's, except that two subsidiary apses were added during the eighteenth century. Frescoes inside are in better condition than those at Thárri owing to the drier local climate; they are also a bit later, though some claim that the final work at Thárri and the earliest here were executed by the same hand, a master from Híos.

The format and subject matter of the frescoes are equally rare in Greece: didactic "cartoon strips" that often extend completely around the church, featuring extensive Old Testament stories in addition to the more usual lives of Christ and the Virgin. There's a complete sequence from Genesis, from the *Creation* to the *Expulsion from Eden*; note the comically menacing octopus among the fishes in the panel of the Fifth Day, and Eve subsequently being fashioned from Adam's rib. A *Revelation of John the Divine* takes up most of the south transept, while an enormous Archangel Michael dominates the north transept, with sword in right hand and a small soul being carried to judgement in his left. Two adjacent buildings house separate museums: an ecclesiastical exhibit, and a more interesting folklore gallery in an ex-olive mill, full of unlabelled rural craft tools and antiquated, belt-driven machinery.

Kiotári, Yennádhi. Váti and Profýlia

Back on the coast road, the beachfront hamlet of **KIOTÁRI** has mushroomed as a package venue for Germans and Italians since 1995, when the Orthodox

Church elected to sell up its vast holdings here. You could stop for a **meal** in the northern sector at bistro-bar *Mourella*, or in the southerly section at more Greek-feeling *Stefanos*, and have a swim. But there's little local character remaining, so you'll most likely continue 4km to **YENNÁDHI**, the only sizeable settlement on this coast, whose rather drab outskirts mask the attractive older village core inland. Amenities include a **post office**, **car rental** and some **accommodation** – pick of this being *Effie's Dreams* at the northern end of things (☎22440 43410, ⓦwww.effiesdreams.com; ❸), overlooking a fountain-fed oasis. The serviceable studios upstairs have a loyal repeat clientele; returned Greek-Australians Effie and Phillip also keep a lively bar and **Internet** café downstairs. They can also assist in locating the key-keeper for sixth-to-fifteenth-century **Ayía Anastasía**, the village cemetery-church 300m northwest through the oasis, covered inside with naïve post-Byzantine frescoes. Most local **tavernas** (no particular recommendation) stand just behind the dark-sand-and-gravel beach extending for kilometres in either direction, clean and with the usual amenities laid on; on summer Sundays at least one "all-day **beach bar**" sets up shop, to the delight of local youth.

From Yennádhi, a good road heads 7km inland, past baby pines slowly greening up a fire-blasted landscape, to the oasis village of **VÁTI**. Here, the superior of two **tavernas** is *O Petrinos Kafenes*, also doubling as the central *kafenío*; it's pricey for the location, but the quality of country-style offerings like spicy *revíthia* soup, good bread, *hórta* and roast suckling pig is such that many Greeks attend, especially at weekends. If this doesn't suit, the nearby village of **PROFÝLIA** can offer the comparable *To Limeri tou Listi* (closed Mon low season).

The southern tip

Some 10km south of Yennádhi, then 2km inland, **LAHANIÁ** village with its smattering of private **rooms** makes another possible base. Abandoned after a postwar earthquake, since the 1980s its older houses have been mostly occupied and renovated by English and Germans on long-term lease agreements. On the main platía at the lower, eastern end of the village, the ✈ *Platanos* **taverna** has superb home-made *mezédhes* platters like hummus and *dolmadhákia*, and seating between the church and two wonderful fountains, one with an Ottoman Turkish inscription.

From Lahaniá it's also possible to head 9km northwest along a narrow road to the picturesque hilltop village of **MESANAGRÓS**. This already existed in some form by the fifth century AD, judging from foundations of a ruined basilica at the village outskirts. A smaller thirteenth-century chapel squats amidst traces of the larger, earlier church, with a *votsalotó* floor and stone barrel arches (key from the nearby *kafenío*). You can also go directly from Lahaniá to **Plimýri**, an attractive sandy bay backed by dunes, with swimming in the clean, brisk water marred only by strong afternoon winds; the sole facility is an indifferent taverna next to the **church of Zoödhóhou Piyís** (interior open May–Oct Sun only noon–5pm), which has ancient columns upholding its vaulted porch.

Beyond Plimýri the road curves inland to **KATTAVIÁ**, nearly 90km from the capital, lost amidst grain fields; the village, like so many in the far south, is seasonally occupied at best, their owners having emigrated to find work in Australia or North America. There are a few **rooms** to rent, a vital **filling station** and several **tavernas** at the junction that doubles as the platía – most interesting of these being the brightly coloured *Martine's Bakaliko/Mayeriko* (closed Thurs), run by folk from Lahaniá, which has vegetarian dishes and home-made desserts.

From Kattaviá a road continues to **Prassoníssi**, Rhodes' southernmost extremity and a mecca for European **windsurfers**. The sandspit which tethers Prassoníssi ("Leek Island") to Rhodes was breached by currents to form a channel in 1996, but enough remains to create flat water on the east side and up to two-metre waves on the west, ideal for all ability levels. Of the two **windsurfing schools** operating here, Polish-run Prasonisi Center (late April–Oct; ☎22440 91044, ⓦwww.windsurfing-rodos.com) is keener and friendlier. They're geared up for one-week packages, and lodge their clients in one of the half-dozen food and accommodation outfits further inland. One which has been recommended for walk-in service, despite a sizeable allotment to the surf schools, is *Faros/Lighthouse Taverna Rooms to Let* (☎22440 91030; ❹).

West of Kattaviá, the paved island loop road emerges onto the deserted, sandy southwest coast. Only strong swimmers should venture far offshore here, as it's exposed and tricky currents are the rule. The next village is nondescript, agricultural **APOLAKKIÁ**, equipped with **tavernas** but no accommodation. Northwest, the road leads to Monólithos, while the northeasterly bearing leads quickly and pleasantly back to Yennádhi via Váti. Due north, just below an irrigation reservoir, the tiny frescoed Byzantine chapel of **Áyios Yeóryios Várdhas** (unlocked) is well worth the four-kilometre detour if you have your own transport.

Hálki

Hálki, a tiny (20 square kilometres), waterless, limestone speck west of Rhodes, is a fully fledged member of the Dodecanese, though all but about 250 of the former population of three thousand emigrated (mostly to Rhodes or to Florida) in response to Italian restrictions on sponge-fishing in 1916. Despite a renaissance through tourism, the island is tranquil compared with its big neighbour, albeit with a rather artificial, stage-set atmosphere, owing to foreigners in their villas vastly outnumbering locals for much of the year. The big event of the day is the arrival of the regular afternoon *kaïki* from Kámiros Skála on Rhodes.

Hálki first attracted outside attention in 1983, when **UNESCO** designated it the "isle of peace and friendship" and the seat of regular international conferences. Some 150 crumbling houses were to be restored at UNESCO's expense as accommodation for delegates, but by 1987 just one hotel had been completed, and the only sign of "peace and friendship" was a stream of UNESCO and Athenian bureaucrats staging musical binges under the rubric of "ecological seminars". Confronted with an apparent scam, the islanders sent UNESCO packing and engaged two UK package operators to complete restorations and bring in paying guests. There are now in fact two more tour companies present, and most of the ruins have been refurbished to the companies' specifications.

Emborió

The skyline of **EMBORIÓ**, the island's port and only habitation, is pierced by the tallest freestanding clocktower in the Dodecanese and, a bit further north, by the belfry of Áyios Nikólaos church. Emborió's restored houses are pretty much block-booked from May to late September by the tour companies mentioned; independent travellers will be lucky to find anything on spec, even early or late in the season. Non-package **accommodation**, all requiring advance

△ Emborió quayside, Hálki

reservations, includes the delightful, en-suite ⚓ *Captain's House* (☎22460 45201; ❷), which has the feel of an old French country hotel; the house (sleeping four) of Frances Mayes, editor of the local bimonthly newspaper *Halki Visitor* (📠22460 45061, 📧francesm@otenet.gr); and four rather basic, terrazo-floored, sea-view rooms (☎& 📠22460 45295; ❸) at the Póndamos beach taverna (see overleaf). The municipally owned *Hotel Halki* (☎22460 45390; ❹) in the old sponge factory on the south side of the bay was being throughly gutted and rebuilt during 2005; contact Takis on ☎694 621 28 36 for its current status. Of the seven full-service **tavernas** along the field-stoned, pedestrianized waterfront, *Remezzo* is excellent for *mayireftá* and pizzas, *Maria* behind the post office has good grills, *Houvardas* (aka *Asia's*) near the north end of the quay has proven reliable for *mayireftá* and grills, while *Avra* is conscientiously run by Greeks from Caucasian Georgia. Amongst a similar number of quayside **bars** and **cafés**, *Theodosia's* (or "The Parrot Bar" after its resident bird), near the base of the jetty, has puddings and home-made ice cream to die for, while *To Steki* is usually the most musically active, with a sculpted counter outdoors. More formal entertainment is provided through the **Halki Festival** (late June to mid-Sept), with performances by top Greek musical names. There's a **post office**, four well-stocked stores, a bakery, plus two **travel agencies** that sell boat tickets and change money (though there's also a stand-alone **ATM**); one, Zifos Travel (☎22460 45028, 📧zifos-travel @rho.forthnet.gr) often has a few vacancies amongst studios which they hold back from the UK companies.

The rest of the island

Three kilometres west looms the old pirate-safe village of **HORIÓ**, abandoned in the 1950s but still crowned by its Knights' castle. Except during the major August 14–15 festival, the church here is kept securely locked to protect its frescoes. Across the valley, the little monastery of **Stavrós** is the venue for the other big island bash on September 14. There's little else to see or do inland, though you can cross the island on an eight-kilometre road, the extension of the cement "Tarpon Springs Boulevard" donated by the expatriate community in Florida. At the end (best arrange a ride out, and walk back) you'll reach the monastery of **Ayíou Ioánnou Prodhrómou** (festival 28–29 Aug). The terrain en route is monotonous, but compensated by views over half the Dodecanese and Turkey.

Longish but narrow **Póndamos**, fifteen minutes' walk west of Emborió, is the only sandy beach on Hálki, and even this has had to be artificially supplemented. The sole facility is the somewhat pricey *Nick's Pondamos Taverna*, serving lunch daily, plus supper two to three random evenings weekly. A few minutes' well-signposted path-walk behind the *Hotel Halki*, tiny coves of pebbles at **Ftenáya** are also heavily subscribed; a dirt track leads to a decent **taverna-bar** (*Tou Vangelí*) right above the main cove, with good seafood and *ouzomezédhes* on offer.

Small, pebbly **Yialí**, west of and considerably below Horió via jeep track, lies an hour's hike away from Póndamos. A thirty-minute walk north of Emborió is **Kánia**, with a rocky foreshore and a rather industrial ambience from both power lines and the island's only petrol pump to one side.

Since these coves are no great shakes, it's worth signing on at Emborió quay for **boat excursions** to more remote beaches. More or less at the centre of Hálki's southern shore, directly below Horió's castle, **Trahiá** consists of two coves to either side of an isthmus; you can (just) reach this overland by rough path from Yialí. North-coast beaches figuring as excursion-boat destinations include the pretty fjord of **Aréta**, **Áyios Yeóryios** just beyond and the remote double bay of **Dhýo Yialí**. Of these, Aréta is the most attractive, and the only one accessible overland (90min one way) by experienced hillwalkers equipped with the *Chalki, Island of Peace and Friendship* map based on the old Italian topographical survey sheet.

Alimniá (Alimiá) islet

The most promoted boat excursion visits **Alimniá (Alimiá) islet**, roughly halfway between Hálki and Rhodes. Despite more well-water and greenery, and a better harbour than at Hálki, the deserted village here, overlooked by a few palm trees and yet another Knights' castle, was completely abandoned by the 1960s. The locals were initially deported during World War II after they admitted to assisting British commandos sent in April 1944 to sabotage the German submarines who used the deep harbour here. The seven commandos themselves were captured on the spot by the Nazis, bundled off first to Rhodes, then to Thessaloníki, where six were summarily executed as spies rather than regular prisoners of war; future Austrian premier and UN Secretary General Kurt Waldheim allegedly countersigned their death sentences.

Interesting history acknowledged, Alimniá is probably not a place you'd want to be stuck for an entire day. Excursions on offer are overpriced (€25–30, picnic lunch included), beach space very limited, the castle a hot, 45-minute walk up (the best thing to do here) and the crumbling village behind its salt marsh unedifying. If you snorkel beyond little Áyios Minás monastery, you might glimpse outlines of the Italian-built submarine pens to one side of the deep bay. The former inhabitants only show up to graze livestock, or for the annual festival on April 23.

Kastellórizo (Meyísti)

Kastellórizo's official name, Meyísti ("Biggest") refers to its being the largest of a tiny local group of islands. It's actually the smallest of the Dodecanese, over seventy nautical miles from Rhodes but barely more than a nautical mile off the Turkish coast. At night its lights are quite outnumbered by those of the Turkish town of Kaş, which lies across the bay and with whom Kastellórizo generally has excellent relations.

During the island's **heyday** (1860–1910) almost 10,000 people lived here, supported by a schooner fleet that transported timber from the towns on the Anatolian mainland opposite. But the withdrawal of island autonomy after the 1908 "Young Turk" revolution, the Italian seizure of the other Dodecanese in 1912 and period of 1913–15 self-rule sent the island into decline. A French occupation of 1915–21 prompted destructive shelling from the Anatolia, a harbinger of worse to come Shipowners failed to modernize their fleets, preferring to sell ships to the British for the Dardanelles campaign, and the new frontier between the island and republican Turkey, combined with the expulsion of all Anatolian Greeks in 1923, deprived any remaining vessels of their trade. During the 1930s the island enjoyed a brief renaissance as a major stopover point for French and British seaplanes, but events at the close of World War II ended any hopes of the island's continued viability.

When Italy capitulated to the Allies in September 1943, about 1500 Commonwealth commandos occupied Kastellórizo, departing in November once the German capture of the other Dodecanese made their position untenable – and leaving the island vulnerable to looters. In early July 1944, a harbour fuel dump caught (or was set on) fire and an adjacent arsenal **exploded**, taking with it more than half of the two thousand houses on Kastellórizo. Even before these events most of the population had left for Rhodes, Athens, Australia and North America. Today there are just 342 official residents here by the last census (with only about 250 actually living permanently on Kastellórizo), largely maintained by remittances from over 30,000 emigrants and by subsidies from the Greek government, which fears that the island will revert to Turkey should numbers diminish any further.

Yet Kastellórizo has a future of sorts, thanks partly to repatriating "Kassies" who have begun renovating their crumbling ancestral houses as second homes. Each summer, the population is swelled by these returnees, who occasionally celebrate traditional weddings in the Áyios Konstandínos cathedral at Horáfia, which incorporates ancient columns from Patara in Asia Minor. Access has also improved since an airport (domestic flights only) was completed, larger aircraft laid on in 2003, and the harbour dredged to accommodate larger ferries, though the island has yet to be designated an official port of entry to Greece, which causes problems for both yachties and conventional travellers crossing from Turkey.

Perhaps the biggest boost in the island's fortunes, however, was serving as the location for the Italian film **Mediterraneo**, winner of the Oscar for Best Foreign Film in 1992, which has resulted in substantial numbers of Italian midsummer visitors (though the island in fact gets a broad spectrum of tourists). You will either love Kastellórizo and stay a week, or crave escape after a day; detractors dismiss the island as a human zoo maintained by the Greek government for the edification of nationalists, while partisans celebrate an atmospheric, barely commercialized outpost of Hellenism.

Kastellórizo Town

The current population is concentrated in the northern settlements of **KASTELLÓRIZO** – supposedly the finest natural harbour between Beirut and Fethiye on the Turkish coast – and its little "suburb" of **Mandhráki**, just over the fire-blasted hill with a half-ruined Knights' castle. Most of the town's surviving mansions are ranged along the waterfront, their tiled roofs, wooden balconies and blue or green shutters on long, narrow windows having obvious counterparts in the originally Greek-built houses of Kalkan and Kaş just across the water. Just one or two streets back, however, many properties remain derelict – abandonment having succeeded where the World War I shelling, a 1926 earthquake, 1943 air-raids and the 1944 explosions failed; sepia-toned posters and black-and-white postcards on sale of the town in its prime are poignant evidence of its later decline.

The castle's outer bulwark now houses the worthwhile local **museum** (Tues–Sun 7am–2.30pm; free), with displays including plates from a Byzantine shipwreck, frescoes rescued from decaying rural churches and a reconstruction of an ancient basilica on the site of today's gaudy, crumbling Áyios Yeóryios Santrapé church at Horáfia. Just below and beyond the museum, in the cliff-face opposite Psorádhia islet, is Greece's only **Lycian house-tomb**; it's well sign-posted from the shoreline walkway, up some steps beside the first wooden lamp standard. The old **mosque**, also below the castle in waterfront Kávos district, is supposed to open as another museum in 2007.

Arrival, information and transport

A single **bank**, with handy ATM, stands on the east quay; the **post office** is on the far side of the bay. The more reliable and competent of the town's two **travel agencies** is Papoutsis (☎22410 70630), which represents all sea-craft, and sells air tickets. An eleven-seater **minibus** shuttles between town and airstrip at flight times (fare €1.50); excess passengers are accommodated in the lone **taxi**, which may have to make multiple journeys at €5 per passenger.

It is possible to arrange a ride over **to Turkey** on one of four local boats, most reliably on Monday or Friday (8am departure). The standard day-return fee is €15, plus the cost of any visa required on the Turkish side (if you stay overnight), and you have to leave your passport with the authorities the day before. Although Kastellórizo is not yet a legal port of entry to Greece – it lacks a proper Schengen database computer – police here cannot legally deny disembarkation to EU nationals arriving **from Kaş**, which is an official entry/exit point for Turkey.

Accommodation

Kastellórizo is not really geared up for large numbers of visitors, though old-house **pensions** have been upgraded, and prices have climbed sharply, since 2000. Budget options include the large-roomed if basic *Pension Caretta* (☎ & ⓕ22460 49028; ❷), which also has a fine restored apartment (❸) for two, and the *Pension Asimina*, wood-trimmed rooms behind the arcaded Italian market (☎22460 49361; ❷). An excellent mid-range choices is ⚡ *Karnayo* off the platía at the west end of the south quay (☎22460 49225, ⓔkarnayo@otenet .gr); air-conditioned rooms or studios (❹) and an apartment sleeping four spread over two quiet, sensitively restored buildings, all wood and stone with furniture in matching taste. Also in this category, at the end of the northwest quay, *Pension Mediterraneo* (☎22460 49007 or 697 36 76 038, ⓦwww.mediterraneopension.org; ❹) has simple rooms, well furnished with mosquito nets and wall art, half with sea view, plus an arcaded, waterside basement suite (⑥) and optional breakfast with proprietress Marie's home-made marmalade.

Eating, drinking and nightlife

Apart from fish, goat meat and wild-fig preserves, plus fresh produce smuggled over from Kaş, Kastellórizo has to import foodstuffs and drinking water from Rhodes; taverna prices can thus be higher than usual, with the further pretext of the island's celebrity status. Incidentally, do *not* drink the mains water; storage cisterns have become contaminated and you will get very ill. The two most conspicuous central-waterfront **tavernas** are also not recommended – it's best to continue a few steps to *To Mikro Parisi* for affordable, and more likely fresher, seafood and meat grills. Other good quayside choices include *Iy Ipomoni* (dinner only), two doors left from the arcaded market, for simple fish grills; and the inexpensive but savoury *Akrothalassi*, purveying large grills and salads near the west end of the quay, by the church – it's popular at lunch, as they've the only shaded seating. One to dine at inland (still adorned with film posters – it served as the canteen for the *Mediterraneo* film crew) is *Ta Platania* (June to mid-Oct), opposite Áyios Konstandínos in Horáfia, good for daily-changing *mayireftá* and desserts. There are more puddings and good breakfasts at *Zaharoplastio Iy Meyisti*, back on the waterfront.

Nightlife spills out of the half-dozen *barákia* lining the quay, occasionally ending up in the water when tipplers overbalance at their tables. *Faros* near the mosque is a cool place with a roof terrace and music noise levels kept under control; friendly *Mythos* back at centre quay also does cheap snacks – good to know when all the tavernas are booked in mid-summer; and at *Kaz-Bar* (late June–Sept) to the right of the market, host Colin also purveys light snacks appropriate for summer.

The rest of the island

Kastellórizo's austere hinterland is predominantly bare rock, flecked with stunted vegetation; incredibly, three generations ago much of the countryside was carefully tended, producing wine of some quality and in quantity. A rudimentary paved road system links points between Mandhráki and the airport, plus there's an ugly dirt track opened by the army to Áyios Stéfanos, but there aren't many specific places to visit and no scooters for rent. Karstic cliffs drop sheer to the sea, offering no anchorage for boats except at the main town, Mandhráki and Návlakas fjord (see overleaf).

Rural monasteries and ruins

Heat permitting, you can hike up the obvious, zigzag stair-path from town, then south through scrub to the rural **monastery of Ayíou Yeoryíou toú Vouvioú**, 35 minutes away. The sixteenth-to-eighteenth-century church boasts fine rib-vaulting and a carved *témblon*, but its highlight is a crypt, with the frescoed, subterranean chapel of **Áyios Harálambos** off to one side; access is via a steep, narrow passage descending from the church floor – bring a torch and grubby clothes, and get the key first from the annually changing keeper in town. Just beyond, east of the old path (not the new track), there's a sixth-century BC **wine press** carved into the rock strata; another, even better one can be seen by varying the return to town and using a secondary path from the monastery to Horáfia via Avlónia district.

Alternatively, a fifteen-minute track-walk west of the port leads to the peaceful monastery of **Ayías Triádhas**, perched on the saddle marked by the telecom tower, and an army base – one of many strong points which have sprouted here since the Ímia crisis of 1996. The onward path arrives after twenty minutes at the ancient citadel of **Paleókastro**, where you'll find masonry from Classical to medieval times, a warren of vaulted chambers, tunnels, cisterns plus another little monastery with a *votsalotó* courtyard. From any of the heights above town there are tremendous views north over sixty kilometres of Anatolian coast.

The shoreline and Rhó

Swimming is complicated by a total absence of beaches and an abundance of sea urchins and razor-sharp limestone reefs; the safest entries near town lie beyond the graveyard at Mandhráki and the cement jetty below the power plant at road's end – or people just dive from the lidos on the northwest quay. Once away from the shore, you're rewarded by clear waters with a rich variety of marine life. From Ayíou Yeoryíou toú Vounioú, you can continue 45 minutes further on foot, first on a useless modern bulldozer track, then on the original, French-built *kalderími*, to the multi-lobed fjord of **Návlakas**, a favourite mooring spot for yachts and fishing boats. The French built this cobbled way to facilitate offloading the components of a 120-millimetre gun battery here during World War I, safe from Ottoman artillery. Uniquely on Kastellórizo, this bay is sea-urchin-free, with freshwater seeps keeping the temperature brisk; there's superb snorkelling to 25-metre depths off the south wall.

Over on the southeast coast, accessible only by a 45-minute boat ride from town, the grotto of **Perastá** (Galázio Spílio) deserves a look for its stalactites and strange blue-light effects; the low entrance, negotiable only by inflatable raft, gives little hint of the enormous chamber within, with monk seals occasionally nesting in another adjacent cave. Rubber-raft trips (€8–10 depending on passenger numbers) visit only the cave, or for about double that amount on a larger *kaïki*, you can take it in as part of a five-hour tour that includes Rhó islet.

Should you make the trip out to **Rhó**, the tomb of **Iý Kyrá tís Rhó** ("The Lady of Rhó"), aka Dhespina Akhladhiotis (ca.1898–1982) – who resolutely hoisted the Greek flag each day on that islet in defiance of the Turks on the mainland – is the first thing you see when you dock at the sandy, northwestern harbour. From here a path heads southeast for 25 minutes to the islet's southerly port, past the side trail up to the intact Hellenistic fortress on the very summit. The islet has no facilities – just a few soldiers to prevent Turkish military landings or poaching of the hundreds of goats – so bring your own food and water.

Sými

Sými's most pressing problem, lack of fresh water, is in many ways also its saving grace. As with so many dry, rocky Dodecanese islands, water must be imported at great expense from Rhodes, pending completion of a reservoir in the distant future. Consequently, the island can't hope to support more than a handful of large hotels; instead, hundreds of people are shipped in daily during the season from Rhodes, relieved of their money and sent back. This arrangement suits both the Symiots and those visitors lucky enough to stay longer; many foreigners

Map: SÝMI

- Datça (Turkey)
- Large Ferries
- Nímos
- Hydrofoils & Catamarans
- Análipsi
- Áyios Isídhoros
- Dhódheka Spília
- Emborió
- Haráni
- Ayía Marína
- Tolí
- Pondikókastro
- Taxiárhis Mihaïl Roukouniótis
- Pédhi
- Áyios Nikólaos
- Sými
- Áyios Emilianós
- Áyii Anáryiri
- Maróni
- Theológos
- Áyios Yeóryios Dhyssálona
- Áyios Vassílios
- Lápathos
- Áyios Prokópios
- Panayía Staterí
- Nanoú
- Byzantine Wine Presses
- Stavrós Polémou
- Megálos Sotíros (Nerás)
- Marathoúnda
- Taxiárhis Mihaïl Panormítis

- Tilos, Nissyros & Kós
- Rhodes
- Rhodes

0 ————— 5 km

N

return regularly, or even own houses here. Sými, long fashionable amongst Italians in particular, has entered domestic Greek consciousness in a big way by featuring prominently in the 2005–06 Turkish TV serial, *The Frontiers of Love*.

Once beyond the inhabited areas, you'll find a surprisingly attractive island that has retained some forest cover of junipers, valonea oaks and even a few pines – ideal walking country in spring or autumn (though not midsummer, when temperatures are among the highest in Greece). Another prominent feature of the landscape are dozens of tiny monasteries, usually locked except on their patron saint's day, though their cisterns with a can on a string for fetching water are usually accessible.

Sými Town

SÝMI, the island's capital and only proper town, consists of **Yialós**, the excellent natural port, and **Horió**, on the hillside above. Incredibly, just over a century ago the place was richer and more populous (25,000) than Ródhos Town, its wealth generated by shipbuilding and sponge-diving, skills nurtured since pre-Classical times. Under the Ottomans, Sými, like most of the smaller Dodecanese, enjoyed considerable autonomy in exchange for a yearly tribute in sponges to the sultan; but the Italian-imposed frontier, the 1919–22 Greco-Turkish war, the advent of synthetic sponges and the gradual replacement of the crews by Kalymniots spelt doom for the local economy. Vestiges of past nautical glories remain in still-active boatyards at Pédhi and Haráni, but today the souvenir-shop sponges come entirely from overseas and – an ongoing restoration boom notwithstanding – magnificent nineteenth-century mansions still stand roofless and empty.

The approximately 2500 remaining Symiots are scattered fairly evenly throughout the mixture of Neoclassical and more typical island dwellings; despite the surplus of properties, many outsiders have preferred to build anew, rather than renovate derelict shells accessible only by donkey or on foot. As on Kastellórizo, a September 1944 ammunition blast – this time set off by the retreating Germans – levelled hundreds of houses up in Horió. The official Axis surrender of the Dodecanese to the Allies was signed in Yialós on May 8, 1945: a plaque marks the spot at the present-day *Restaurant Les Catherinettes*.

Arrival, information and transport

One of two **catamarans** and a **hydrofoil** run daily to Sými from Ródhos Town, departing at least morning and late afternoon – sometimes evening too – on an *epivatikó* (scheduled service) basis. There are also daily departures on a more expensive *ekdhromikó* (excursion) basis at 8.30–9am, returning 2.30–3.45pm. All ANES craft usually dock at Yialós's south quay, conveniently near the **taxi and bus stops**, while the excursion craft and main-line ferries use the north mooring by the clocktower. The hydrofoil *Aigli* leaves Mandhráki port in Rhodes, takes 55 minutes to arrive, and costs about €14. Both Sými-based catamarans (*Symi II* and *Panormitis*), as well as the *Dodekanisos Express/Pride*, use the central Kolóna harbour of Rhodes, taking about the same time for the crossing and cost rather less (around €7); the *Symi II* carries a few cars. Once or twice weekly there are also mainline ferries in either direction, typically the cheapest and slowest of all (€4, 1hr 40min journey time). Among **ferry** agents, ANES, controlling *Panormitis/Symi II/Aigli* tickets, maintains a booth on the quay and an office in the marketplace lanes (T 22460 71444), while GA and *Dodekanisos Express/Pride* catamarans are handled by Symi Tours nearby (T 22460 71307).

There's no official tourism bureau, but the island's English-language **advertiser-newspaper**, *The Symi Visitor* (free; W www.symivisitor.com), is literate and has current island topics with informative historical and ethnographic features. The **post office** in the official Italian "palace" is open standard hours; both **banks** have ATMs. During the season a small green **bus** (€0.70 flat fare) shuttles between Yialós and Pédhi via Horió on the hour (returning at the half-hour) until 11pm. There are also six **taxis** (allow €3 Yialós–Horió with baggage), and two pricey outlets for **motor-scooter** (minimum €18–24 daily, the better being Glaros on the north quay (T 22460 71926), and **car rental** (a whopping €58–70 daily). **Taxi-boat** fares climbed sharply in 2005, making a scooter – or walking – that much more attractive. A **laundry** operates next to *Pahos'* quayside *kafenío*.

Accommodation

Accommodation for independent travellers is somewhat limited and proprietors tend not to meet arriving boats, though the situation isn't nearly so bad as on Hálki. Studios, rather than simple rooms, predominate, and package operators control most of these, though curiously you may find vacancies more easily in July/August than during spring/autumn, considered the most pleasant seasons here. Despite asphyxiating summer heat, air conditioning and/or fans are not universally present – go for north-facing and/or balconied units when possible.

Albatros Marketplace ☎22460 71707, ⊛www .albatrosymi.gr. Partial sea views from this exquisite, small hotel; pleasant second-floor breakfast salon and air con. **④**

Aliki Haráni quay ☎22460 71665, ⊛www .simi-hotelaliki.gr. A complete overhaul of an 1895 mansion, and Sými's poshest hotel: tasteful rooms with wood floors and some antique furnishings and large bathrooms, though only some have sea views. **⑥** standard, **⑦** suite.

Les Catherinettes Above eponymous restaurant, north quay ☎22460 72698, ⓔmarina-epe@rho .forthnet.gr. Creaky but spotless en-suite *pension* in a historic building with painted ceilings, fridges, fans and sea-view balconies for most rooms. They also offer three studios in Haráni, plus a family apartment. **④**

Fiona At the top of the Kalí Stráta ☎22460 72088. Mock-traditional hotel building whose large airy rooms have double beds and stunning views; breakfast in mid-air on common balcony. Also 2 studios next door. **④**

Jean Manship c/o *Jean & Tonic Bar* ☎ & ⓕ02460 71819 8pm–1am Greek time. Jean manages four traditional houses in Horió, suitable for two to six persons, with stunning views. **③–④**

Katerina Tsakiris Rooms Horió ☎22460 71813. Just a handful of very plain but air-con en-suite rooms with shared kitchen and grandstand view; reservations essential. **③–④**

Kokona Rear of marketplace, beyond main church ☎22460 71549, ⓕ22460 72620. Small hotel with bland if cheerful tile-and-pine, air-con rooms, some with balcony (and some package presence). Breakfast served outdoors, at base of the church belfry. **④**

Niriides Apartments On Haráni–Emborió road, 2km from Yialós ☎22460 71784, ⊛www.niriideshotel .gr. Spacious and quiet if plain units, distributed over four hillside buildings, sleep four and have phone, TV and optional aircon. Friendly father-and-son management; discount for Internet bookings. **⑤**

Symi Visitor Accommodation ☎22460 72755, ⊛www.symivisitor.com. Managed by returned Greek-Australian Nikos Halkitis and partner Wendy Wilcox, who offer a variety of restored houses as double-occupancy studios in prime locations of Horió. Rates range from **④–⑥**; they also have pricier units suitable for four to five persons.

Villa Thalassa Far end of south quay. Contact as for Hotel Albatros. Old mansion divided into two air-con studios for couples (**⑤**), and three larger apartments (**⑥**) accommodating families.

The town

At the lively **port**, an architecturally protected area since the early 1970s, spice and sponge stalls plus a few jewellery shops throng with Rhodes-based trippers between 10am and 2.30pm, and the several excursion craft disgorging them envelop the quay with exhaust fumes. But just uphill, away from the water, the more peaceful pace of village life takes over, with livestock and chickens roaming free range. Two massive stair-paths, the **Kalí Stráta** and **Katarráktes**, effectively deter many of the day-trippers and are most dramatic towards sunset; large, owl-haunted ruins along the lower reaches of the Kalí Stráta are lonely and sinister after dark, though these too are now undergoing restoration one by one.

A series of blue arrows through Horió leads to the excellent local **museum** (Tues–Sun 8.30am–2.30pm; €2). Housed in a fine old mansion at the back of the village, the collection concentrates on Byzantine and medieval Sými, with exhibits on frescoes in isolated, locked churches and a gallery of medieval icons, as well as antiquarian maps and the inevitable ethnographic wing. The nearby **Hatziagapitos mansion** has been refurbished as an annexe; here, wonderful carved wooden chests are the main exhibits, along with fragmentary wall-paintings. On the way back to central Horió, the nineteenth-century pharmacy, with its apothecary jars and wooden drawers labelled for exotic herbal remedies, is worth a look.

At the very pinnacle of things, a **Knights' castle** occupies the site of Sými's ancient acropolis, and you glimpse a stretch of Classical polygonal wall on one side. A dozen churches grace Horió; that of the Assumption, inside the fortifications, is a replacement of the one blown to bits when the Germans detonated the munitions cached there. One of the bells in the new belfry is the nose-cone of a thousand-pound bomb, hung as a memorial.

Eating and drinking

You're best off avoiding most **eateries** on the north and west quays of the port, where menus, ingredients, prices and attitudes have been terminally warped by the day-trip trade. Away from these areas, you've a fair range of choice among *koultouriárika* tavernas, old-style *mayireftá* places, a few genuine ouzerís and even a traditional *kafenío* or two.

Dhimitris South quay, on the way out of town. Excellent, family-run seafood-stressing ouzerí with exotic items such as *hokhlióalo* (sea snails), *foúskes*, *spinóalo* and the miniature local shrimps, along with the more usual dishes and lots of vegetarian starters.

Haritomeni Northeast edge of Horió, about halfway up the hill in kink of the road above Yialós filling station ☎ 22460 71686. Somewhat pricey Greek-patronized ouzerí with such fare as *pastourmá* turnovers, *mydhopílafo* (mussels in rice), artichokes in egg-lemon sauce, assorted aubergine platters. Open all year: lovely terrace with views in summer, fireplace interior in winter. Reserve in peak season.

Lefteris Top of the Kalí Stráta where it levels off into a small platía, Horió. The local characters' *kafenío*, well attended by all. The place for a coffee or an ice cream at any hour.

O Meraklis Rear of the bazaar. Polite service and fair portions of moderate-priced *mayireftá*, fresh fish and *mezédhes* make this a reliable year-round bet. Sample meal: beans, beets, dips, and roast lamb with potatoes as a tender main course.

🏃 **Mythos** South quay between bus and taxi stops, Yialós. Supper-only ouzerí that's reckoned among the best, and best-value, cooking on the island. There is a menu, but let chef Stavros hit you with his Frenchified medley which might include salad, seafood starters (squid in

basil sauce), *poungí* (seafood parcel in fyllo), courgette-and-mushroom mould, and home-made desserts. Budget €23 a head before dipping into the decent wine list. In summer, operations move 150m down the quay to *Aktaion*, a roof-terrace annexe, and *Mythos* becomes a snack-café open at lunch too; otherwise supper only at the main premises spring and autumn. Credit cards accepted.

Pahos West quay (no sign). The old-boys' *kafenío*, in operation since World War II, and still a classic spot for a sundown ouzo and people-watching. Pahos himself has retired and can often be found sitting out front as a customer; otherwise it's unchanged.

🏃 **Syllogos** Just south off Horió platía. Vast but not impersonal place with indoor and outdoor seating, great for taverna standards like *skordhaliá*, *saganáki*, fried fresh fish and eggplant recipes. George Bush (Snr) dined here repeatedly on his visits to the island, as much for the food as for the fact that security arrangements were easy.

Yiorgos Near top of Kalí Stráta in Horió. Jolly, much-loved institution since 1977, with summer seating on a pebble-mosaic courtyard. Service can be slipshod, food quality fluctuates wildly, and prices match Yialós levels, but perennial recipes include feta-stuffed peppers, spinach-rice, chicken in mushroom-wine sauce, and grilled fish when available. Open random lunchtimes in season, supper all year (indoors in winter).

Nightlife and events

Nightlife continues into the early hours and is biased towards Yialós. Convivial *Jean & Tonic* is the heart and soul of the bar scene in Horió, catering to a mixed clientele (visitors and expats until 3am, Greek restaurateurs 3am until dawn) most of the year. Down at Yialós, the *Harani Club* offers a mix of Greek and international music depending on the crowd; in the same alley, *Vapori* was the first outsider-owned bar here (in 1983), and continues the tradition with newspapers draped over chairs, breakfasts and **Internet** access (three terminals). Elsewhere, *Katoi* on the south quay is a no-hassle bar favoured by locals. In terms of more formal **events**, there's a year-round Friday-night **filmthèque** inside the Petrideio mansion, while the July-to-September **Sými Festival** has, since its mid-1990s inception, become one of Greece's more interesting small summer bashes, with a mix of classical and Greek-popular performances.

Around the island

Sými has no big sandy beaches, but there are plenty of pebbly stretches at the heads of the deep, protected bays which indent the coastline. **PÉDHI**, a short bus ride down from Horió, retains some of its former identity as a fishing hamlet, with enough water in the plain behind – the island's largest – to support a few vegetable gardens. The beach is poor, though, and patronage from yachts and the *Pedhi Beach* hotel has bumped up prices at local **tavernas**, of which the most reasonable and authentic is fish specialist *Tolis* (no sign), tucked away by the boatyard at the north corner of the bay. Many will opt for either a taxi-boat or another twenty minutes of walking via a rough but obvious path along the south shore of the almost landlocked bay to **Áyios Nikólaos**. The only all-sand cove on Sými, this offers sheltered swimming, tamarisks for shade and an adequate taverna. Alternatively, a paint-splodge-marked path on the north side of the inlet leads in half an hour to **Ayía Marína**, where there's a minuscule beach, a shingle lido with sunbeds, a rather posh taverna-bar complete with tended lawn, and a monastery-capped islet to which you can easily swim.

Around Yialós, you'll find tiny *Symi Paradise* "beach" (still called **NOS** or Navtikós Ómilos Sýmis by most) ten minutes past the boatyards at Haráni, but there's sun here only until lunchtime – not a bad thing in high summer. You can continue along the cement-paved coast road, with steps leading down to rock slabs favoured by nudists, or cut inland from the Yialós platía past the abandoned desalination plant, to quiet **Emborió** (Nimborió) Bay, with a taverna and a coarse-shingle beach a bit beyond. Inland from this lie Byzantine mosaic fragments under a protective shelter (follow signs to "Early Christian Basilica"), and, nearby, a catacomb complex known locally as **Dhódheka Spília**.

Remoter bays

Plenty of other, more secluded coves are accessible to energetic walkers with sturdy footwear, or those prepared to pay for the taxi-boats (daily in season 10am–1pm, returning 4–6pm. These are the most popular method of reaching the southern bays of Marathoúnda and Nanoú, and the only method of getting to the spectacular fjord of **Áyios Yeóryios Dhyssálona**. Dhyssálona lacks a taverna and lies in shade after 1pm, while **Marathoúnda** is fringed by coarse, often slimy pebbles (though it has a normal-priced, tasty eponymous **taverna**, very popular at weekends), making **Nanoú** the most popular destination for day-trips. The 200-metre beach there consists of gravel, sand and small pebbles, with a scenic backdrop of pines and a reasonable **taverna** (menu of squid, chips and salad) just behind. It's also possible to reach Nanoú overland, via Panayía Strateí chapel up on the main trans-island road, descending a scenic, forested gorge for some forty minutes; most of the old path from Horió to Panayía Strateí still exists, making a marvellous traverse of about three hours in total, leaving time for a meal and swim at Nanóu before the boat trip back to Yialós.

For more hiking adventures, you can cross the island from Horió in ninety minutes to **Áyios Vassílios**, the most scenic of the gulfs with its namesake little monastery and **Lápathos** beach; in about the same time to **Tolí**, a deserted, west-facing cove, also accessible from Emborió; or in three hours, partly through forest, from Yialós to **Áyios Emilianós** at the island's extreme west end, where another little monastery is tethered to the body of Sými by a causeway. On the way to the latter you'll pass near the monastery of **Taxiárhis Mihaïl Roukouniótis** (usually shut, ring current warden on posted mobile number), Sými's oldest, with naïve eighteenth-century frescoes and a peculiar ground plan: the current *katholikón* is actually superimposed on a lower, thirteenth-century structure abandoned after being burnt and pillaged by pirates during the 1400s, though a fine fresco of St Lawrence (Áyios Lavréntios) survives behind the altar screen. However, some of the best frescoes on the island, of early-eighteenth-century vintage, are found at the monastery of **Megálos Sotíros**, on the road south to Panormítis, just before the drop down the escarpment. Frescoes inside the *katholikón*, in the middle of the arcaded, pebble-paved courtyard, are devoted unsurprisingly to the life of the Saviour (*Sotír* in Greek), include a fine *Deposition*, with Joseph of Arimathaea holding a winding sheet to receive the dead Christ, and a *Resurrection* with Jesus all but doing a jig on the sepulchre. Across the road, you can follow a signposted trail to some worthwhile, reconstructed Byzantine **wine presses**.

Panormítis monastery

The Archangel is also honoured at the huge monastery of **Taxiárhis Mihaïl Panormítis** near the southern tip of the island, Sými's biggest rural attraction and the first port of call for some excursion boats from Rhodes (confirm the itinerary if you wish to proceed direct to Yialós – many craft do). These allow only a quick thirty-minute tour; if you want more time, you'll have to come by scooter from Yialós (though the road down from the central escarpment is steep, with nine hairpin bends), or stay the night (€10 minimum donation) in the *xenónas* (inn) set aside for pilgrims. They monopolize it all summer, as Mihaïl has been adopted as the patron of sailors in the Dodecanese.

Like many of Sými's monasteries, Panormítis is of recent (eighteenth-century) vintage and was thoroughly pillaged during World War II, so don't expect much of the building or its treasures. An appealing *votsalotó* courtyard surrounds the central *katholikón*, tended by the Archimandrite Gabriel and lit by an improbable number of oil lamps. It's also graced by a fine *témblon* and of course the cult icon, though the frescoes are recent and mediocre. One of the two small museums (€1.50 each) contains a strange mix of precious antiques, exotic junk (stuffed crocodiles and koalas, elephant tusks), votive offerings, models of ships and a chair piled with messages-in-bottles brought here by Aegean currents – the idea being that if the bottle or toy boat arrived, the sender got their prayer answered. There's a shop/*kafenío*, a bakery and a **taverna** (*Panormion*) popular with passengers of the many yachts calling in. Near the taverna stands a memorial commemorating three Greeks, including the monastery's abbot, executed on February 11, 1944 by the Germans for aiding British commandos.

Tílos

The small, usually quiet island of **Tílos**, with an official population of about five hundred (dwindling to 100 in winter), is one of the least frequented and worst connected of the Dodecanese, though it can (in theory) be visited on a day-trip by catamaran from Rhodes. Why anyone would want to come for just a few hours is unclear: while it's a great place to rest on the beach or go walking, there is nothing very striking at first glance. After a few days, however, you may have stumbled on several of the seven small **castles** of the Knights of St John, which stud the crags, or found some of the inconspicuous medieval chapels clinging to the hillsides.

Tílos shares the characteristics of its closest neighbours: limestone **mountains** resembling those of Hálki, plus volcanic lowlands, pumice beds and red-lava sand as on Níssyros. Though rugged and scrubby on its heights, the island has ample water – from springs or pumped up from the agricultural plains – and clusters of oak and terebinth near the cultivated areas. From many points on the island you've startling views across to Kós, Sými, Turkey, Níssyros, Hálki, Rhodes and even (weather permitting) Kárpathos.

Since the mid-1990s, however, development on Tílos has threatened to reverse the conditions which many visitors have come to enjoy; besides the Dodge City atmosphere of Livádhia, a hyperactive bulldozing programme has scarred virtually every mountain in the east of the island. Thankfully the remotest beaches are located in too steep a terrain to be approached by road without prohibitive expense, and a project is afoot to protect much of coastal and mountain Tílos as a national park (consult Ⓦ www.tilos-park.org).

Getting around and information

Tílos's main road runs 7km from Livádhia, the port village, to Megálo Horió, the capital and only other significant habitation. A public **bus** links the two, and services are theoretically scheduled to coincide with seaborne arrivals; at other times the sleek bus makes up to six runs daily along the Livádhia–Éristos stretch. There are also two **taxis**, or you can rent a **car** from outlets in Livádhia such as Drive (Ⓣ 22460 44173) and Tilos Travel (number below). Stefanakis, also in Livádhia (Ⓣ 22460 44310), has a monopoly on ferry and hydrofoil tickets; Tilos Travel is arguably the more helpful, however (Ⓣ 22460 44294 or 694 65 59 697, Ⓦ www.tilostravel.co.uk), offering an accommodation booking service, used-book swop and scooter as well as car rental. For more active sea-going jaunts with kayaks or windsurfers, contact French-run Tilos Marine at Livádhia beach. The *Sea Star* catamaran has its own office by the church (☎22460 44000). the single **filling station**, keeping odd hours, lies between Livádhia and Megálo Horió.

Many visitors come specifically to **walk**, assisted by the extremely accurate **map** prepared by Baz "Paris" Ward and sold locally – or by certified walking **guides** Iain and Lyn Fulton (☎22460 44128 or 694 60 54 593, ⊜fulton@otenet.gr), who may take you on unusual itineraries not described or mapped in existing literature. A half-dozen sections of deteriorating trail or *kalderími* have been surveyed in preparation for cleaning and consolidation, so quality walking opportunities should improve in the future.

There's a **post office** in Livádhia, a single **bank** with an ATM, **Internet** facilities at Kosmos gift shop and two well-stocked if overpriced **supermarkets**.

Livádhia

Despite an ambitious waterfront improvement programme in 2005 – flagstoned terraces, shoreline walkway, garish 2000-watt lighting – **LIVÁDHIA** with its unfinished building sites and higgledy-piggledy layout makes a poor introduction to the island. Yet it remains the best-equipped settlement to deal with tourists, and is closest to the majority of remaining path-hikes.

Accommodation

There are generally enough beds in the various **studios** and **hotels** to go around, but in peak season it's certainly worth phoning ahead or consulting the Tilos Travel website. Truly budget options are steadily vanishing in favour of newer, better-appointed, sea-view choices like the galleried ⊁ *Blue Sky Apartments* above the ferry dock (apply to Tilos Travel; ❹); *Marina's Studios* (☎22460 44023; ❸), up the hillside from these, large if basic studios arrayed over three buildings; *Pavlos* (☎22460 44011; ❸), four small if well-kept rooms overlooking their own sunbeds at mid-beach; and the *Faros Hotel* (☎22460 44068; ❸) at the extreme end of Livádhia bay, well regarded for its calm atmosphere and hospitable managing family.

Inland, go for the well-appointed *Studios Irinna* (☎22410 44366; ❸), alias *Kula's*; or the *Hotel Irini* (☎22410 44293, ⓦwww.tilosholidays.gr; ❸–❹), 200m inland from mid-beach, with a popular pool, good breakfasts and pleasant gardens making up for somewhat small rooms. The same keen management has the *Studios Ilidi Rock* on the west hillside (❹ for 2, ❺ for 4-person apartments).

Eating, drinking and nightlife

Up to a dozen **tavernas** operate around Livádhia in peak season; of these barely a third merit consideration. At shoulder season, you have to book for timed seatings at the more Anglophilic eateries – unheard of on other islands. Among the more authentic spots for a no-nonsense Greek feed are much-improved *Mihalis* with its popular garden tables, good for roast goat and fish, as well as good vegetable platters and non-CAIR bulk wine; *To Armenon* (alias *Nikos'*) on the shore road, an excellent and salubrious beach-taverna-cum-ouzerí, with octopus salad, white beans and the like; and the restaurant attached to the *Marina Hotel*. French-Vietnamese-run *Calypso* (☎694 72 13 278; supper only) lost its lease at the end of 2005; if it has re-opened elsewhere, it should still excel at Creole-colonial dishes like *Martiniqueois* prawn *acras* or Vietnamese pork-and-mushroom vermicelli.

For **breakfast** (plus evening thin-crust pizzas, home-made desserts and strong cocktails), Anglo-Italian *Joanna's Café*, just inland from the bakery is accomplished but pricey and thus losing business to seaside alternatives. ⚓ *Iy Omonía* (aka *Tou Mihali*), under trees strung with light bulbs, near the post office, is the enduringly popular traditional alternative for a sundowner, breakfast or a tipple while waiting for a ferry, and also does inexpensive, tasty *mezédhes* so generous as to obviate the need for a formal meal. The jetty-café *Remezzo* also does excellent, reasonable ouzo-*mezédhes*.

Organized **nightlife** in or near Livádhia is limited to *Bozi* at the far east end of the bay (nightly in summer, weekends otherwise) and the *Café Aktí* upstairs opposite the Italian "palace", with great views.

Around Livádhia

From Livádhia you can walk an hour north along the obvious trail to the pebble bay of **Lethrá**, or in about the same time south on separate itineraries to the secluded coves of **Stavrós** or **Thólos**. The track to the former begins between the *Tílos Mare Hotel* and the *Castellania Apartments*, becoming a trail at the highest new house in the village; once up to the saddle with its paved road, you've a sharp drop to the beach – ignore over-eager cairning in the bed of the descending ravine, the true path is up on the right bank, indicated by red-painted surveyor's marks. The route to Thólos begins by the cemetery and the chapel of **Áyios Pandelímon**, then curls around under the seemingly impregnable castle of **Agriosykiá**; from the saddle on the paved road overlooking the descent to Thólos (25min; also surveyed in preparation for refurbishment), a route marked with cairns leads northwest to the citadel in twenty minutes. You can use that paved road, heading a couple curves east, to reach the trailhead for **Áyios Séryis** bay, the most pristine of Tílos' beaches but the hardest to get to (30min one-way, path poor but cairned).

It's less than an hour's walk west, with some surviving path sections shortcutting the road curves, up to the ghost village of **Mikró Horió**, whose 1200 inhabitants left for Livádhia during the 1950s. The only intact structures are the church (locked except for the August 15 festival) and an old house which has been restored as a small-hours **music pub** and operates only during July and August, with a rather aggressive house/techno playlist.

Megálo Horió and Éristos

The rest of Tílos's inhabitants live in or near **MEGÁLO HORIÓ**, which enjoys an enviable perspective over the vast agricultural plain stretching down to Éristos (see overleaf), and is overlooked in turn by a prominent castle of the Knights, built on the site of ancient Tílos, whose recycled masonry remains evident. You reach it by a stiff, thirty-minute climb that begins on the lane behind the Ikonomou supermarket before threading its way through a vast jumble of cisterns, house foundations and derelict chapels – the remains of the much larger medieval Megálo Horió. Two more flanking fortresses stare out across the plain: the easterly one of **Messariá** helpfully marks the location of the **Harkadhió** cave (closed), where Pleiocene midget-elephant bones were discovered in 1971; the cave-mouth was hidden for centuries until a World War II artillery barrage exposed it. The bones themselves have been transferred to a tiny, not very compelling **museum** in Megálo Horió, on the ground floor of the town hall (Mon–Fri 8am–2.30pm on application upstairs to the warden).

Best choices for **accommodation** in the village are the central *Milios Apartments* (☎22460 44204, ℻22460 442665; ❷–❸ size-dependent) or

Studios Ta Elefandakia (☎22460 44213; ❷), set among attractive gardens by the car park. The better and friendlier of two **tavernas** is *Iy Kalia Kardhia*, on the downhill one-way street out of the village, with good grills and views. There's a traditional **kafenío** by historic Taxiárhis church, and further up, Athenian-run *Kafenio Ilakati* (late May to early Sept only; opens 7pm), with cakes and drinks.

Below Megálo Horió, signs direct you towards the three-kilometre side road to long, pink-grey-sand **Éristos** beach, allegedly the island's best, though a reefy zone must be crossed entering the water. The far south end, where the reef recedes, is also a designated nudist zone, as are the two secluded, attractive coves at **Kókkino** south beyond the headland (accessible by path only). On the secondary, parallel road down to Éristos, the *En Plo* is the best nearby venue for a snack – also affiliated with the *Nitsa Apartments* (☎694 49 89 437; ❷), while the *Eristos Beach Hotel* (☎22460 44025; ❸) offers some of the highest room standards on Tílos, with a plusher (❹) annexe attracting package clientele.

The far northwest

The main road beyond Megálo Horió hits the coast again at somewhat grim **ÁYIOS ANDÓNIOS**, whose main bright spot is a **taverna**, *Dhelfini*, packed at weekend lunch because of its fresh seafood and frequented otherwise by the local fishermen. At low tide on the exposed, truncated beach you can find more lava-trapped skeletons strung out in a row – human this time – presumably tide-washed victims of a Nissyrian eruption in 600 BC, and discovered by the same archeologists who found the miniature pachyderms. There's better, warm-water swimming at isolated, sandy **Pláka** beach, 2km west of Áyios Andónios, where people camp rough despite a total lack of facilities.

The paved road finally ends 8km west of Megálo Horió at the fortified **monastery of Ayíou Pandelímona** (daily: May–Sept 10am–7pm, Oct–April 10am–4pm), founded in the fifteenth century for the sake of its miraculous spring, still the best water on the island. A fitfully operating drinks café hosts the island's major festival of July 25–27 – as well as several peacocks and Rhodian miniature deer. The monastery's tower-gate and oasis setting, more than two hundred forbidding metres above the west coast, are the most memorable features, though an eminently photogenic inner courtyard boasts a *votsalotói* surface, and the church a fine marble floor. On the south *katholikón* wall, an early eighteenth-century fresco shows the founder-builder holding a model of the monastery, while behind the ornate altar screen, in the conch, hides another rare fresco of the Holy Trinity.

The public bus calls here just once a week as part of a tour, so you'll need transport to get here. To vary the **return to Megálo Horió**, take a taxi out, then walk back much of the way on a signposted path; it's shown correctly on Baz Ward's recommended map, and ends at the minor monastery of Panayía Kamarianí near Áyios Andónios. Committed and experienced hill-walkers can tackle the challenging path which curls around the southwest flank of Profitis Ilías, Tílos's highest mountain, finishing three-plus hours later near Áyios Pétros cove, with a further half-hour track-walking to Éristos (allow 5hr with stops). This begins, as signposted, beside the monastery; it's a well-surveyed route, with no real exposure or sharp drops, but there's only one spring along the way, rather disheartening scree at the start, and the wild feel of a remote traverse on a much larger island.

Níssyros

Volcanic **Níssyros** is noticeably greener than its southern neighbours Tílos and Hálki, and unlike them has proven wealthy enough to retain over eight hundred of its population year-round (down, though, from 10,000 in 1900). While remittances from abroad (particularly New York) are significant, most of the island's income is derived from the offshore islet of Yialí, essentially a vast lump of **pumice** slowly being quarried away by Lava Ltd. The concession fee collected from Lava by the municipality has engendered a huge public payroll and vast per-capita sums available to spend, making Níssyros something of a mini-Kuwait. Under the circumstances, the Nissyrians bother little with agriculture other than keeping cows and pigs; the hillside terraces meticulously carved out for grain and grapes lie fallow, and wine is no longer made here.

The main island's peculiar geology is potentially a source of other benefits: DEI, the Greek power company, spent the years between 1988 and 1992 sinking exploratory **geothermal** wells and attempting to convince the islanders of the benefits of cheap electricity. In 1993, a local referendum went massively against the project, as did (by a closer margin) a 1997 poll, after which DEI and its Italian contractor took the hint and packed up. The desalination plant scarcely provides enough fresh water to spur a massive growth in package tourism; the relatively few tourists (mostly German) who stay the night, as opposed to the day-trippers from Kós, still find peaceful villages with a minimum of concrete eyesores and a friendly if rather tight-knit population.

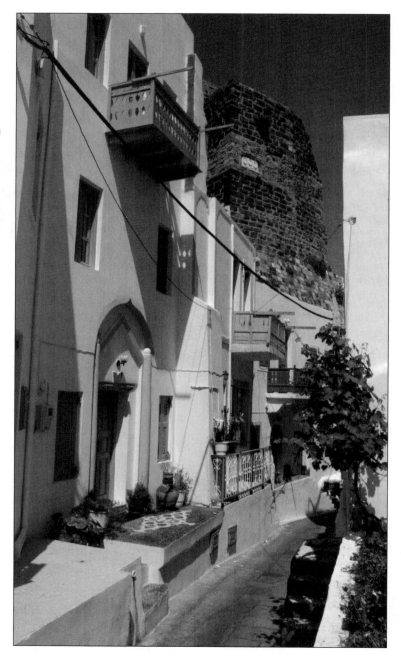

△ Langadháki district, Mandhráki, Níssyros

Níssyros also offers good **walking** opportunities through a countryside planted with oak and terebinth, on a network of trails fitfully marked and maintained; you may hear the contented grunting of pigs as they gorge themselves on acorns from the many oak trees. Autumn is a wonderful time, especially when the landscape has perked up after the first rains; the late-January almond-blossoming is much reduced owing to an early-1990s blight that devastated the trees, which are now making a slow comeback.

Mandhráki

MANDHRÁKI is the deceptively large port and island capital, with blue patches of sea visible at the end of narrow streets lined with tightly packed houses, whose brightly painted balconies and shutters are mandated by law. Except for the tattier fringes near the ferry dock, where multiple souvenir shops and bad tavernas pitched at day-trippers leave a poor first impression, the bulk of the place is cheerful and village-like, arrayed around the community orchard or *kámbos* and overlooked by two ancient fortresses.

Into a corner of the nearer citadel, the fourteenth-century Knights' castle, is wedged the little monastery of **Panayía Spilianí**, built on this spot in accordance with instructions from the Virgin, who appeared in a vision to one of the first Christian islanders. The monastery's prestige grew after raiding Saracens failed to discover the vast quantities of silver secreted here in the form of a rich collection of Byzantine icons. During 1996–97, the Langadháki area just below was rocked by a series of earthquakes, damaging a score of venerable houses (mostly repaired now); the seismic threat is ever present, quite literally cutting the ground out from under those who erroneously dub the volcano "extinct".

As a defensive bastion, the seventh-century-BC Doric **Paleókastro** (unrestricted access), twenty minutes' well-signposted walk out of Langadháki, is infinitely more impressive than the Knights' castle, and ranks as one of the more underrated ancient sites in Greece. Despite lingering scaffolding from a 2002–06 restoration, you can clamber up onto the massive, polygonal-block walls by means of a broad staircase beside the still-intact gateway.

Information and transport

The most useful of Mandhráki's four **travel agencies** are Kentris (℡22420 31227), near the town hall, handling GA and Blue Star ferries, and Dhiakomihalis (℡22240 31459), which acts as a representative for the catamarans and hydrofoils and rents cars; both sell Olympic Airways tickets. There's a **post office** at the port and **Internet** access at *Proveza* café, in Lefkandió district; get money at a single **bank** in town, or an unrelated, stand-alone **ATM** at the harbour. Also at the base of the jetty is the **bus stop**, with (theoretically) up to five daily departures to the hill villages and six to Pálli. Otherwise, there are two set-rate **taxis** and two outlets for **scooter rental**:Yannis (℡693 7234033), on the shore lane, and Manos K (℡22420 31028), by the single filling station, which also **rents cars**.

Accommodation

You'll see a handful of port **hotels** on your left as you disembark, of which the best value and most comfortable are the waterfront *Three Brothers* (℡22420 31344; ❷) and the municipally run *Xenon Polyvotis* (℡22420 31011, ℗22420 31204; ❸), whose biggish, neutral-decor rooms have fans and (mostly) knockout sea views. In the town centre is Mandhráki's best-amenitied accommodation, the *Hotel Porfyris* (℡22420 31376, ℗22420 31176; ❹), with a large swimming pool and breakfast terrace; many rooms, which have air con and fridges, overlook the sea and *kámbos*. Other than this, you're advised to splurge on two excellent restoration projects which are finally making use of Níssyros' considerable architectural heritage. On the shore lane near the windmill are the two comfortable if pricey suites of ⌖ *Ta Liotridia* (☎22420 31580, ✉liotridia@nisyrosnet.gr; ❼), hosting up to four and arguably worth it for the sea views and pointed-volcanic-stone-and-wood decor, though the bar downstairs could be noisy. Near the top of the village stands *Spiliada* (☎22420 31166; ❼), quieter and a tad cheaper, with the same masonry scheme but tile-floored and set up for self-catering.

Eating and nightlife

Culinary **specialities** include *pittiá* (chickpea croquettes), pickled caper greens, honey and *soumádha*, an almond-syrup drink widely sold in recycled wine bottles, which should be consumed within three months of purchase; the latter three specialties are most easily available at To Paradhosiako shop, 250m towards town from the port.

When eating out, give all of the commercialized, shoddy shoreline **tavernas** a miss in favour of more genuine haunts inland. Top of the heap is evenings-only ⌖ *Ouzeri Iy Fabrika* (June–Sept Fri–Wed, Oct–May Thur–Sat), with indoor/outdoor tables by season, *rebétilka* soundtrack and well-priced, hearty fare with plenty for vegetarians. Runners-up include friendly *Irini* on lively, ficus-shaded Platía Ilikioméni, with more involved *mayireftá* unavailable elsewhere as well as fish, or little *Taverna Nissiros*, the oldest eatery in town, always busy despite predictably average grill quality.

Foci of **nightlife** are several cafés on Platía Ilikioméni, and a string of *barákia* on the shore at Lefkandió district, the most popular of these being *Enallax* and the stunning, ex-olive-press bar of the *Liotridia* inn, which also has periodic exhibits.

Pálli and around

Beaches on Níssyros are in even shorter supply than water, so much so that tour agencies have occasionally peddle excursions to a sandy cove on **Áyios Andónios** islet, opposite the Yialí mines. Closer to hand, the short, black-rock beach of **Hokhláki**, behind the Knights' castle, is unusable if the wind is up. It's best to head east along the main road, passing the refurbished spa of **Loutrá** (hot mineral water baths 8–11am; only by doctor's referral), worth a stop for its "snack-bar" at the far end of the building, really an **ouzerí** with a well-chosen soundtrack and fair portions of salads, fried appetizers, seafood and meat – though it's frankly overpriced.

A kilometre or so further, 4km in total from Mandhráki, the fishing village of **PÁLLI** makes an excellent hangout at lunchtime, when the port fills with trippers. **Tavernas** have multiplied, but the newer ones generate reader complaints of price-gouging, so best stick with the two long-term favourites: the less expensive *Ellinis*, with spit-roasted meat by night, grilled fish in season and simple rooms upstairs (☎22420 31453; ❷), or the adjacent *Afroditi* (aka *Nikos & Tsambika*), with big portions of grills and *mayireftá*, Cretan bulk wine and excellent home-made desserts. A scooter-rental outlet, an excellent bakery cranking out brown bread and fine pies (branch in Mandhráki), and modest nightlife make Pálli also worth considering as a base. About the only other **accommodation** is *Frantzis Studios* by the bakery (☎22420 31240; ❸), with well-kept units in slightly scruffy grounds. A tamarisk-shaded, dark-sand **beach**, kept well groomed, extends east of Pálli to the abandoned Pantelídhi spa, behind which the little grotto-chapel of **Panayía Thermianí** is tucked inside the vaulted remains of a Roman baths complex.

To reach Níssyros's best beaches, continue in this direction for an hour on foot (or twenty minutes by bike along the road), past an initially discouraging seaweed- and cowpat-littered shoreline, to the delightful cove of **Liés**, with a snack-bar, *Oasis* (July–Aug only). Just beyond here the paved road ends at a car park 5km beyond Pálli; in summer boat trips from Mandhráki call here too. Walking another fifteen minutes along a trail over the headland brings you to the idyllic, 300-metre expanse of **Pahiá Ámmos**, with grey-pink sand heaped in dunes, limited shade at the far end and a large colony of rough campers and/or naturists in summer.

The interior

Níssyros's central, dormant **volcano** gives the island its special character and fosters the growth of the abundant vegetation – and no stay would be complete without a visit. When excursion boats arrive from Kós, several agency coaches and usually one of the public buses are pressed into service to take customers into the interior. These tours tend to monopolize the crater floor between 11am and 2pm, so if you want solitude, use early-morning or late-afternoon scheduled buses to Nikiá (a few daily continue to the crater floor), a scooter or your own two feet to get there.

The road up from Pálli winds first past the virtually abandoned village of **EMBORIÓS**, where pigs and free-ranging cattle (a major driving hazard) far outnumber people, though the place is slowly being bought up and restored by Athenians and foreigners. New owners are often surprised to discover natural saunas, heated by volcano steam, in the basements of the crumbling houses; at the outskirts of the village there's a signposted public **steam bath** in a grotto, its entrance outlined in white paint. If you're descending to Pálli from here, an old cobbled way starting at the sharp bend below the sauna offers an attractive short cut of the four-kilometre road, while another *kalderími* drops from behind *To Balkoni tou Emboriou* **taverna** (May–Oct; limited, if cheap, menu) to within a quarter-hour's walk of the craters.

NIKIÁ, the large village on the east side of the volcano's caldera, is – with fifty year-round inhabitants – more of a going concern, and its spectacular situation 14km from Mandhráki offers views out to Tílos as well as across the volcanic caldera. The best place to **eat** and **drink** here is *Iy Porta* (all year, but reduced menu Oct–June), serving good salads, dips and variable *mayireftá* on the engagingly round plaza ringed by stone seating, itself called the Pórta and marked out in white paint for the steps of folk dances. By the bus turnaround area, signs point to the 45-minute **trail** descending to the crater floor; a few minutes downhill, you can detour briefly to the eyrie-like **monastery of Áyios Ioánnis Theológos**, which only comes to life at the September 25–26 evening festival. To **drive** directly to the volcanic area you must use the road that veers off just past Emboriós.

The volcano – and walks

However you approach the **volcano**, a sulphurous stench drifts out to meet you as trees and pasture, then clumps of oregano, gradually give way to lifeless, caked powder. The sunken main crater of **Stéfanos** is extraordinary, a striated moonscape of grey, white, brown and sickly yellow; there is another, less-visited double crater (dubbed **Polyvótis**) to the west, arguably more dramatic, with a clear trail leading up to it from the snack-bar. The perimeters of both are pocked with tiny blowholes from which jets of steam puff constantly and around which form little pincushions of pure sulphur crystals. Towards the eastern side of Stéfanos, boiling mud-pots have surfaced since the millennium (not for the first time, and there's a danger of falling through the crater-floor at their edges); anywhere nearby it sounds like a huge cauldron bubbling away below you. According to legend this is the groaning of Polyvotis, a titan crushed here by Poseidon under a huge rock torn from Kós. When there are tour groups around, a small, tree-shaded snack-bar operates in the centre of the wasteland, and a booth on the access road charges admission (€1.50) to the volcanic zone.

Since DEI's 1991 destruction of the old direct *kalderími* between the volcano and Mandhráki, finding pleasant options for **walking** back to town requires a bit of imagination – though paths are marked with red paint-dots and wooden signposts – and possession of Beate and Jürgen Franke's GPS-drawn topographical map (downloadable free from ⓦ www.bjfranke.privat.t-online .de/n1-e.htm). First choice involves backtracking along the main crater access road for about 1km from the admission booth to find the start of a clear, crudely marked path which passes the volcanic gulch of **Káto Lákki** and the monastery of **Evangelístra** on its two-hour-plus course back to the port. You can lengthen the trip by detouring from Evangelístra south to **Profítis Ilías**, the island's summit, a two-hour round-trip – the route is well marked with cairns or white paint. An alternative approach to Evangelístra requires returning to Emboriós and leaving from the top of the village, near the cemetery and small castle, on a 45-minute course to the monastery – an enjoyable link, despite haphazard marking and cleaning. From Evangelístra, the onward route to Mandhráki briefly follows the road down before the marked path resumes, handily shortcutting hairpin bends.

Kós

After Rhodes, **Kós** is the second largest and second most popular island in the Dodecanese, and there are superficial similarities between the two. Here also the harbour is guarded by an imposing castle of the Knights of St John; the streets are lined with grandiose Italian-built public buildings; and minarets and palm trees punctuate extensive Hellenistic and Roman remains. Although its hinterland for the most part lacks the wild beauty of Rhodes' interior, acre for acre Kós is the most fertile of the Dodecanese, blessed with rich soil and abundant ground water.

Mass **tourism** has largely displaced the old agrarian lifestyle amongst the population of just over 28,000; all-inclusive complexes totalling tens of thousands of beds are a spreading blight which contribute nothing to the local economy. Except for Kós Town and Mastihári, there aren't many independent travellers, and from early July to early September you'll be lucky to find any sort of room at all without reservations far in advance, or a prebooked package. The tourist industry is juxtaposed rather bizarrely with cows munching amid baled hay, and Greek Army tanks exercising in the volcanic badlands around the airport. All these peculiarities acknowledged, Kós is still definitely worth a few days' time while island-hopping: its handful of **mountain villages** are appealing, the tourist infrastructure excellent (including such amenities as regular city buses and cycle paths) and swimming opportunities are limitless – about half the island's perimeter is fringed by **beaches** of various sizes, colours and consistencies.

KÓS & PSÉRIMOS

Bodrum (Turkey)

Léros

Kálymnos & Léros

Kálymnos

Nissyros

Nissyros, Tilos & Sými

Rhodes

N

Cape Skandhári

Kós Town

Cape Psalídhi

Cape Áyios Fokás

Lámbi

Áyios Gavríil

Áyios Fokás

Brós Thermá

Platáni (Kermedés)

Asklepíon

Ambávris

Selvéri

Tingáki

Zipári

Evangelístria

Asómatos

Áyios Dhimítrios

Marathoúnda

Vathý

Psérimos

Platý

Graftiótissa

Avlákia

Alykí

Amanioú

Zía

D   I   K   E   O   S

Khristós 846m

A S F E N D H Í O U

Marmári

Pylí

Lagoúdhi

Paleó Pylí

Tolári

Harmýlio

Linópotis

Kardhámena

Troúlos

Mastihári

Áyios Ioánnis

Knights' Castle

Andimáhia

Pláka

Áyios Stéfanos

Limniónas

Kamári

Psilós Grémmos

Langádhes

"Sunny" "Magic"

"Paradise"

"Exotic"

Kamíla "Camel"

Polémi

Kástri

Kéfalos

Panayía Palatiáni

Zíni 362m

Aspri Pétra

Astypalía

Látra 428m

Áyios Mámas

Cape Dhrépano

Áyios Theológos

Áyios Ioánnis Thymianós

Cavo Paradíso

Cape Kríkello

0   5 km

KÓS TOWN

Villages, Airport & Asklepíon

Catholic Cemetery

Ambávris & Platáni

Akti Zouroúdhi (800m) & Lámbi (2km)

⓫ (100m), ⓕ (200m), ⓬ (300m), Campsite (1500m), Psalídhi, Áyios Fokás & Brós Thermá ▲

0   200 m

PLATÍAS
Ayías Paraskevís	D
Dhiagóras	F
'Dolphin'	A
Eleftherías	C
Kazoúli	B
K. Paleológou	E

ACCOMMODATION
Hotel Afendoulis	D
Pension Alexis	A
Hotel Kamelia	B
Hotel Martína	C
Hotel Theodhorou Beach	F
Hotel Thomas	E

EATING
Ambavris	14
Barbas	9
Iy Folia tou Lykou	4
Kanadheza	10
Koakon	13
Pote tin Kyriaki	8
Iy Psaropoula	3

NIGHTLIFE
Cafe Aenaos	6
Apoplous	11
Beach Boys	7
Four Roses	5
Hamam Club	2
Heaven	1
Nostos	12

Yacht Marina

Hydrofoil Jetty

Ferry & Catamaran Dock

Knights' Castle

Hippocrates Park

Excursion Boats

Port Police

Hellenistic Baths

Ancient Stadium

DEAS Terminal

Museum

Winter Cinema

Turkish Fountain

Atik

Nymphaion

Western Excavations

Roman Odeion

Casa Romana

KTEL

Olympic Airways

Airport Coach Stop

Summer Cinema

ITALIAN QUARTER

Loggia · Hippocrates' Plane Tree

Turkish Bath

Old Synagogue

Porta toú Fórou

Agora

Defterdar

Market

Kós Town

KÓS TOWN, home to over half of the island's population, spreads in all directions from the harbour, with most of its charm residing in scattered ancient and medieval antiquities. Apart from the Knights' castle, the first thing you see on arrival, there's a wealth of Hellenistic and Roman remains, many of which were only revealed by an earthquake in 1933, and excavated subsequently by the Italians, who also planned and laid out the "garden suburb" extending either side of the central grid. Elsewhere, vast areas of open space alternate with a hotchpotch of Ottoman monuments and later mock-medieval or Rationalist-Modernist buildings.

Arrival, transport and information

Large **ferries and catamarans** anchor just outside the harbour at a special dock by one corner of the castle; **excursion boats** to neighbouring islands sail right in and berth all along Aktí Koundouriótou. **Hydrofoils** tie up south of the castle at their own jetty, on Aktí Miaoúli. Virtually all ferry and excursion-boat agents sit within 50m of each other at the intersection of pedestrianized Vassiléos Pávlou and the waterfront. Among the more helpful and genuinely representative of ferries and hydrofoils, not just expensive excursions, are Kentriko (for Blue Star) by the DEAS terminal (℡22420 28914); Exas (for most everyone else) opposite the National Bank at Andóni Ioannídhi 4 (℡22420 29900); and Hermes at Vasiléos Pávlou 2 (℡22420 26607) for most hydrofoils.

The **airport** is 24km southwest of Kós Town in the centre of the island; an Olympic Airways shuttle bus (€3) meets Olympic flights for a transfer to the town terminal by the Casa Romana, but if you arrive on any other flight you'll have to either take a taxi, or head towards the giant roundabout outside the airport gate and find an orange-and-cream-coloured KTEL bus – they pass here en route to Mastihári, Kardhámena and Kéfalos as well as Kós Town. The **KTEL bus terminal** in town is a series of stops around a triangular park 400m back from the water, with an info booth adjacent at Kleopátras 7 (tickets on the bus). The municipality also runs a frequent **local bus** service, DEAS, through the beach suburbs and up to the Asklepion, with a ticket and information office at Aktí Koundouriótou 7. Push- or **mountain-bike** rental are popular options for getting around, given the island's relative flatness; if you want a **motor scooter**, try Moto Harley at Kanári 42, or Moto Service at Harmylíou 17. Budget at Vassiléos Pávlou 31 (℡22420 28882 or 694 4500062) and in Psalídhi suburb (℡22420 24853), at both the *Ramira* and *Okeanis* hotels, has a reputation for good-condition **cars**, as does AutoWay at Vassiléos Yeoryíou 22 (℡22420 25326). Major chains, most nearer the marina on Vassiléos Yeoryíou, include Hertz (℡22420 28002) and National/Alamo (℡22420 21722). The main **taxi** stand is at the east end of Koundouriótou.

The municipal **tourist office** at Vassiléos Yeoryíou 3 (May–Oct Mon–Fri 8am–2.30pm & 5–8pm, Sat 9am–2pm; Nov–April Mon–Fri 8am–2.30pm) keeps stocks of local maps, bus timetables and ferry schedules. For more involved information, head for the Newsstand **book shop/newsagent** just behind the archeological museum on Platía Kazoúli. No fewer than seven **banks** have ATMs, while the **post office** is at Vassiléos Pávlou 14. The most central and best-equipped **Internet café** is Cafe del Mare at Megálou Alexándhrou 4. **Laundries** include Happy Wash at Mitropóleos 20 and Laundromat Center at Alikarnassoú 124.

Accommodation

If you're just in transit, you're effectively obliged to **stay** in Kós Town, and even if you plan a few days on the island, it still makes a sensible base, as it's the public transport hub and has the greatest concentration of vehicle rental and nightlife. Be wary of touts which besiege most arriving sea-craft – their rooms are apt to be unlicensed, inconveniently remote and of dubious cleanliness. They may further claim to represent the legitimate establishments listed below, and then take you elsewhere.

Hotel Afendoulis Evrypýlou 1 ☏ 22420 25321, ✉ afendoulishotel@kos.forthnet .gr). Large, air-con, balconied en-suite rooms include a few family quads, but what guarantees a loyal repeat clientele is the way Alexis Zikas, brother Ippokrates and wife Dionysia really look after their guests. Breakfast and mini-fridges on request. April–end Oct; credit cards accepted. ❸

Pension Alexis Irodhótou 9, cnr Omírou ☏ 22420 25594. Deservedly popular budget option across from the Roman agora with wood-floored rooms, which share bathrooms and a self-catering kitchen. Alexis has opted for the *Hotel Afendoulis* (see above), leaving his ebullient sister Sonia in charge here. March to early Nov. ❷

Hotel Kamelia Artemisías 3 ☏ 22420 28983, ⓦ www.geocities.com/kamelia.hotel. Rear-facing rooms at this well-kept C-class have a quiet orchard view; tends to get overflow from the *Afendoulis*. May–Sept. ❸

Hotel Maritina Výronos 19 ☏ 22420 23511, ⓦ www.maritina.gr. Standard mid-town businessmen's hotel with conference facilities and all mod cons in the rooms. Open all year. ❹

Hotel Theodhorou Beach 1200m from the centre, towards Psalídhi ☏ 22420 22280, ⓕ 22420 23526. Generous-sized units renovated in 2004, with disabled access, and now encompassing suites and a wing of self-catering studios. A green environment includes a lawn-pool in back and a small "private" beach. ❹

Hotel Thomas Manoúsi, cnr Artemisías ☏ 22420 24466. Small but adequate heated rooms in 1980s decor, with marble floors and a buffet-breakfast salon. Open all year. ❸

The Town

The **castle** (Tues–Sun 8.30am–2.30pm; €3), called "Nerantziás" locally, is reached via a causeway over its former moat, now filled in and planted with palms (hence the avenue's Greek name, Finíkon). The existing double citadel, built in stages between 1450 and 1514, replaced an original fourteenth-century fort deemed incapable of withstanding advances in medieval artillery. A fair proportion of ancient Koan masonry has been recycled into the walls, where the escutcheons of several Grand Masters of the Knights of St John can also be seen.

Immediately opposite the castle entrance stands the riven trunk of Hippocrates' plane tree, its branches now propped up by scaffolding instead of the ancient columns of yore; at seven hundred years of age, it's not really elderly enough to have seen the great healer, though it has a fair claim to being one of the oldest trees in Europe. Adjacent are two Ottoman fountains (a dry hexagonal one and a working one spilling into an ancient sarcophagus) and the eighteenth-century **mosque of Hassan Pasha**, also known as the Loggia Mosque after the portico on one side; its ground floor – like that of the **Defterdar mosque** on central Platía Eleftherías – is taken up by rows of shops.

Also on Platía Eleftherías stands the Italian-built **Archeological Museum** (Tues–Sun 8.30am–2.30pm; €3), with a predictable Latin bias in the choice of exhibits. Four rooms of statuary are arrayed around an atrium with a mosaic of Hippocrates welcoming Asklepios to Kós; the most famous item, purportedly a statue of Hippocrates, is indeed Hellenistic, but most of the other highly regarded works (such as Hermes seated with a lamb) are Roman.

The largest single section of ancient Kós is the **agora**, a sunken, free-access zone containing a confusing jumble of ruins, owing to repeated earthquakes between the second and sixth centuries AD. More comprehensible are the so-called western excavations, lent definition by two intersecting marble-paved streets and the **Xystos** or restored colonnade of a covered running track. In the same area lie several floor mosaics, such as Europa being carried off by Zeus in the form of a bull; gladiators; a boar being speared; plus gods and muses, all viewable under protective canopies. To the south, across Grigoríou toú Pémptou, are a Roman-era **odeion**, garishly restored both during the 1930s and again in 2000, and the **Casa Romana** (shut for works until early 2006), a third-century-AD house built around three atria with surviving patches of mosaic floors showing panthers and tigers, plus assorted sea creatures.

Kós also retains a thoroughly commercialized **old town**, lining the pedestrianized street running

△ Ancient agora, Kós

from behind the Italian market hall on Platía Eleftherías as far as Platía Dhiagóras and the isolated minaret overlooking the western archeological zone. One of the few areas of town to survive the 1933 earthquake, today it's crammed with expensive tourist boutiques, cafés and snack-bars. About the only genuinely old thing remaining here is a capped **Turkish fountain** with a calligraphic inscription, found where the walkway cobbles cross Odhós Venizélou.

Eating

Despite an overwhelming first impression of Euro-stodge cuisine, it's easy to **eat** well and even reasonably in Kós Town, as long as you search inland, away from the harbour. Koan wine-making has been revived recently, and the Hatziemmanouil label is particularly worth sampling. For **breakfast**, the *Central/Kentriko Café* on Platía Ayías Paraskevís behind the market hall uniquely does American pancakes, French toast and fresh fruit juices.

Ambavris 500m south of the edge of town along the road from near Casa Romana, in eponymous suburb village. To order from their English-only à la carte menu is to miss the point of the place; take the hint about "Mezedes" and let the house bring on their best. This changes seasonally but won't much exceed €20 for six plates – typically *pinigoúri* (bulgur pilaf), *pikhtí* (brawn), little fish, spicy *loukánika*, stuffed squash flowers and *fáva* – drinks extra. May–Oct eves only.

Barbas Evrypýlou 6, opposite *Hotel Afendoulis*. Excellent grills as well as the odd seafood touch like octopus salad, at cozy outdoor seating. April–Oct.
Iy Folia tou Lykou Bouboulína 24. Very reasonable prices for taverna standards, with live *rebétika* music on some weekends. Open all year.
Kanadheza Evrypýlou, cnr Artemisías. Creditable pizzas as well as grills, served at indoor/outdoor tables. Open all year.
Koakon (aka *Andonis*) Artemisías 56. Possibly the best all-rounder in town, purveying grilled meat

and fish, *mezédhes* and a few daily *mayireftá* with equal aplomb, without the usual multinational flags and photo-menus. Open all year.

🏃 **Pote tin Kyriaki** Pissándhrou 9. Kós's sole genuine ouzerí, where the creatively drawn menu (in school copy-books) has delights such as

fried mussels and *dhákos* (Cretan "monk's" salad), as well as grilled chops and *pantsétta*. Mon–Sat (winter Thurs–Sat) eves only.

Iy Psaropoula Avérof 17. Currently the town's best-value fish/seafood specialist, with many Greeks in attendance; open all year.

Drinking and nightlife

Join the largely Greek crowd at *Cafe Aenaos*, right under the Defterdar mosque, and people-watch while refilling your Greek coffee from the traditional *bríki* used to brew it up. For a convivial drink on the water in wicker chairs under a wood gazebo, try *Nostos* on Yeoryíou Papandhréou; doyenne of the beach-bars in this district, it works out of a 1930-vintage house, with occasional live music sessions.

Durable music bars with **dance floors** elsewhere include *Four Roses* on the corner of Arseníou and Vassiléos Yeoryíou, and *Beach Boys* at Kanári 57. Local and touring **live Greek acts** tend to stop at *Apoplous* (mid-June to early Sept) at the start of Psalídhi. If you prefer loud techno and house, look no further than the "**Pub Lanes**" area, officially Nafklírou and Dhiákou; bar identities tend to change each season, and it's gotten very naff. Much the classiest and most stable venue here is *Hamam Club*, installed in an ex-Turkish bath with its original oriental décor and chill-out sofas in the corner rooms; there's a mix of guest and local DJs and live sessions, with outdoor seating before a midnight "curfew" moves everyone indoors. There's a **newer, better nucleus** of nightlife out at Aktí Zouroúdhi, with a more mixed clientele, where *Heaven* (mid–June to early Sept) is the most established club. Otherwise there is one active **cinema**, the Orfeas, with summer and winter (Oct–May) premises as shown on the map; the indoor premises also hosts concerts and other special events.

The Asklepion and Platáni

Native son **Hippocrates** is justly celebrated on Kós; not only does he have a tree, a street, a park, a statue and an international medical institute named after him, but the **Asklepion** (June–Aug Tues–Sun 8am–6.30pm, Sept–May 8.30am–2.30pm; €3), 4km south of town, one of just three in Greece, is a major tourist attraction. A little fake green-and-white train shuttles up to the site regularly; otherwise take a DEAS bus up to Platáni (see opposite), from where the

Hippocrates

Hippocrates (ca. 460–370 BC) is generally regarded as the father of scientific medicine, though the Hippocratic oath probably has nothing to do with him and is anyway much altered from its original form. Hippocrates was certainly born on Kós, probably at Astypalia near present-day Kéfalos, but otherwise details of his life are few and disputed; what seems certain is that he was a great physician who travelled throughout the Classical Greek world, but spent at least part of his career teaching and practising at the Asklepion on his native island. A vast number of medical writings have been attributed to Hippocrates, only a few of which he could have actually written; *Airs, Waters and Places*, a treatise on the importance of environment on health, is widely thought to be his, but others were probably a compilation from a medical library kept on Kós, which later appeared in Alexandria during the second century BC. This emphasis on good air and water, and the holistic approach of ancient Greek medicine, now seems positively contemporary.

ruins are a further 15-minute walk. There's a small snack-bar at the Asklepion, or pause for lunch in Platáni en route.

The Asklepion was actually founded just after the death of Hippocrates, but it's safe to assume that the methods used and taught here were his. Both a temple to Asklepios (god of healing, son of Apollo) and a renowned curative centre, its magnificent setting on three artificial hillside terraces overlooking Anatolia reflects early recognition of the importance of the therapeutic environment. Until recently, two fountains provided the site with a constant supply of clean, fresh water, and extensive stretches of clay piping are still visible, embedded in the ground.

Today, very little remains standing above ground, owing to periodic earthquakes and the Knights' use of the site as a quarry. The lower terrace in fact never had many buildings, being instead the venue for the observance of the Asklepieia – quadrennial celebrations and athletic/musical competitions in honour of the healing god. Sacrifices to Asklepios were conducted at an **altar**, the oldest structure on the site, whose foundations can still be seen near the middle of the second terrace. Just to its east, the Corinthian columns of a second-century-AD **Roman temple** were partially re-erected by nationalistically minded Italians. A monumental **staircase** leads from the altar to the second-century-BC Doric temple of Asklepios on the topmost terrace, the last and grandest of a succession of the deity's shrines at this site.

About halfway to the Asklepion, the village of **PLATÁNI** (also Kermedés, from the Turkish name Germe) is, along with Kós Town, the remaining place of residence for the island's dwindling community of ethnic Turks. Until 1964 there were nearly three thousand of them, but successive Cyprus crises and the worsening of relations between Greece and Turkey prompted mass emigration to Anatolia, and a drop in the Muslim population to currently well under a thousand. Several excellent, Turkish-run **tavernas** are to be found at and around the main crossroads junction, with a working Ottoman fountain: *Arap* (summer only); the slightly less touristy *Asklipios* (aka *Ali's*) and *Sherif*, adjacent across the way (also summer only); and *Gin's Place* (all year), each offering Anatolian-style mezédhes (fried vegetables with yogurt, *bourekákia*, and so on) and kebabs better than most in Kós Town. Afterwards, retire across from *Arap* to *Zaharoplastio Iy Paradhosi* for the best ice cream on the island.

Just outside Platáni on the road back to the port, the island's neglected **Jewish cemetery** lies in a dark conifer grove, 300m beyond the well-kept Muslim graveyard. Dates on the Hebrew-Italian-script headstones stop after 1940, after which none of the local Jews were allowed the luxury of a natural death prior to their deportation in summer 1944. Their former **synagogue** or *hávra*, a wonderfully orientalized Rationalist specimen from 1934, at Alexándhrou Dhiákou 4, has been refurbished as a municipal events hall but also has a plaque commemorating its former use.

Eastern Kós

If you're looking for anything resembling a deserted **beach** near the capital, you'll need to make use of the DEAS bus line connecting the various resorts to either side of town, or else rent a vehicle; push-bikes can take advantage of the cycle paths extending as far east as Cape Psalídhi.

The easterly bus line usually terminates at Áyios Fokás, 8km southeast of Kós Town, but sometimes continues an extra 4km almost to unusual and remote **Brós Thermá** (last service around 6pm); with your own transport be prepared to negotiate a dirt track for the final kilometre. Brós Thermá is known for its massively popular **hot springs** – best experienced at sunset or after – which issue from a grotto and flow through a trench into a shoreline pool protected by boulders, heating the seawater to an enjoyable temperature. Winter storms typically disperse the boulder wall, rebuilt every April, so that the pool changes from year to year. Just uphill, the long-running *Psarotaverna Therma* does affordable fish, though the rest of the menu is unmemorable. There's also a drinks-and-ice-cream café right by the pool.

Tingáki and Marmári

The two neighbouring beach resorts of Tingáki and Marmári are separated from each other by the salt marsh of **Alykí**, which retains water – and throngs of migratory birds, including flamingoes – until June after a wet winter. There's almost always a breeze along this coast, which means plenty of windsurf boards for hire at either resort; the profiles of Kálymnos, Psérimos and Turkey's Bodrum peninsula all make for spectacular offshore scenery. If you're aiming for either of these resorts from town, especially on a two-wheeler of any sort, it's safest and most pleasant to go by the **minor road** which takes off from the southwest corner of town (follow initial signage for the Vassiliadhi supermarket); the entire way to Tingáki is paved, and involves the same distance as using the main trunk road and marked turn-off. Similarly, a grid of paved rural lanes links the inland portions of Tingáki and Marmári.

TINGÁKI, a busy beachside resort popular with Brits, lies 12km west of the harbour. Oddly, there's very little **accommodation** near the beach amongst the dozen or so medium-sized hotels and more numerous studios; most of these are scattered inland through fields and cow pastures. By far the best local **taverna** here, with pleasant seating indoors and out, is ⚘ *Ambeli* (summer daily; winter Fri/Sat eve, Sun lunch), well signposted 2.5km east of the main beachfront crossroads; featured dishes include *pinigoúri* (cracked wheat), pork-based *bekrí mezé*, *pykhtí* (brawn), *yaprákia* (the local *dolmádhes*) and *arnáki ambelourgoú*, washed down with sixty kinds of wine from their cellar. Among **car-rental** outfits, Sevi (☎ 22420 68299) can be recommended, and will even deliver vehicles on request to Kós Town. The beach itself is white sand, long and narrow – it improves, and veers further away from the traffic of the frontage road, as you head southwest.

MARMÁRI, 15km from town, has a smaller built-up area than Tingáki, and the beach itself is broader, especially to the west where it forms little dunes (and supports a wind-surf school). Most hotels here are monopolized by German tour groups, but you might hit on an on-spec vacancy at the B-class *Esperia* on the main access road down from the island trunk road (☎ 22420 42010, ℱ 22420 42012; ❹), in grassy surroundings.

The Asfendhioú villages

The main interest of inland Kós resides in the villages on **Mount Dhíkeos**, a handful of settlements collectively referred to as **Asfendhioú**, nestled amidst the island's only natural forest. Together these communities give a good idea of what Kós looked like before tourism and ready-mix concrete arrived, and all are now severely depopulated by the mad rush to the coast. They are accessible via the curvy side road from Zipári, 8km from Kós Town; an inconspicuously marked minor road to Lagoúdhi; or by the shorter access road for Pylí.

The first Asfendhioú village you reach up the Zipári road is **Evangelístria**, where a major crossroads by the parish church and taverna of the same name leads to Lagoúdhi and Amanioú (west), Asómatos (east) and Ziá (uphill). **ZIÁ**'s spectacular sunsets make it the target of up to six evening tour buses daily, though the village has barely a dozen families still resident, and its daytime tatti-ness seems to increase each tourist season. Best of the dozen **tavernas** here is the secluded ⚓ *Kefalovrissi*, near the top of the village, great for *mezédhes* plus selected daily mains like *pantsétta* or *bakaliáros*, accompanied by Hatziemmanouil red wine; runner-up is the *Olympia*, at the start of the lane up to the church, open all year with such dishes as chickpeas, *spédzofaï* (sausage and pepper stew), dark bread and good bulk wine; there's a good *pikilía* or medley of *mezédhes* off-menu. Ziá is also the trailhead for the ascent of 846-metre **Dhíkeos peak**, a minimum two-and-a-half-hour round-trip, initially on track but mostly by path. The route is fairly obvious, and the views from the pillbox-like summit chapel of Metamórfosis are ample reward for the effort. Up top, you can also ponder the esoteric symbolism of a giant crucifix fashioned out of PVC sewer pipe and filled with concrete.

East of Ziá or Evangelístria, roads converge at **ASÓMATOS**, home to about thirty villagers and a number of outsiders restoring abandoned houses; the evening view from the church of Arhángelos with its pebble mosaic rivals that of Zía, though there's just a single *kafenío*. **ÁYIOS DHIMÍTRIOS**, 2km beyond along a paved road, is marked by its old name of Haïhoútes on some maps, and is today completely abandoned except for a single house next to the attractive church; in the narthex, a small photo display documents a much larger population during the war years, when the village was a centre of resistance to the German occupation. You can continue from here 3.5km more to the junc-tion with the road linking Platáni with the municipal rubbish tip.

Pylí

PYLÍ can be reached via the road through Lagoúdhi and Amanioú, or from the duck-patrolled Linopótis pond on the main island trunk road, across from which *Ouzeri Iy Limni* (aka *Karamelengos*) dishes up excellent seafood *mezédhes*. In the upper of its two neighbourhoods, 100m west of the partly pedestrian-ized square and church, the simple *Iy Palia Piyi* taverna serves inexpensive but appetizing meat grills and fried-vegetable *mezédhes* in a superb setting, beside a giant cistern-fountain (*piyí*). Pylí's other attraction is the so-called **Harmýlio** ("Tomb of Harmylos"), signposted near the top of the village as "Heroon of Charmylos". This consists of a subterranean, niched vault (fenced off), probably a Hellenistic family tomb; immediately above, traces of an ancient temple have been incorporated into the medieval chapel of Stavrós.

Paleó (medieval) **Pylí**, roughly 3km southeast of its modern descendant, was the Byzantine capital of Kós. Head there via Amanioú, keeping straight at the junction where signs point left to Ziá and Lagoúdhi. In any case, the castle should be obvious on its rock, straight ahead; the deteriorating road ends next to a spring, opposite which a stair-path leads within fifteen minutes to the roof of the fort. En route you pass the remains of the abandoned town tumbling south-wards down the slope, as well as three fourteenth-to-fifteenth-century chapels with fresco fragments within; the first church encountered, **Arhángelos**, has the best-preserved ones, mostly scenes from the Life of Christ.

Western Kós

Near the arid, desolate centre of the island, well sown with military installations, a pair of giant, adjacent roundabouts by the airport funnels traffic northwest towards **Mastihári**, northeast back towards town, southwest towards **Kéfalos**, and southeast to **Kardhámena**. Most visitors are after the south-coast **beaches**, reached from the Kéfalos-bound turning.

Mastihári and Andimáhia

The least developed, least "packaged" and least expensive of the north-shore resorts, **MASTIHÁRI** has a shortish, broad beach extending west; at its end, inside a partly fenced enclosure, lie remains of the fifth-century basilica of **Áyios Ioánnis**, one of several on the island. If you want to **stay**, try quieter digs overlooking the west beach such as the simple *Hotel Kyma* (☏22420 59045; ❸) or the *Hotel Fenareti* (☏22420 59024) further up the grade, with rooms (❷) and studios (❸) in a peaceful garden environment. *O Makis*, one street inland from the quay, and ᕢ *Kali Kardia*, at the base of the jetty, are the best of a half-dozen **tavernas**, both well regarded for fresh fish, *mezédhes* and (at *Kali Kardia*) *mayireftá* and desserts. Mastihári is also the port for small roll-on-roll-off **ferries** to Kálymnos; there are three to four well-spaced daily departures in each direction most of the year (current info on ☏22420 59124), timed more or less to coincide with Athens-originating flight schedules – though KTEL buses to or from Kós Town don't (perhaps deliberately) always dovetail well.

The workaday village of **ANDIMÁHIA**, 5km southeast of Mastihári, straggles over several ridges; the only concession to tourism is a line of ouzerís and snack bars at the southwestern edge, easily accessible from the airport (across the road and car park) if your outbound flight is delayed. East of Andimáhia, reached via a marked, 2.8-kilometre side road, an enormous, triangular **Knights' castle** overlooks the straits to Níssyros. Once through the imposing north gateway (unrestricted access), you can follow the well-preserved west parapet, and visit two interior chapels: one with a fresco of Áyios Khristóforos (St Christopher) carrying the Christ child, the other with fine ribvaulting. Gravel walkways, illumination and a ticket booth were installed in 2001, but are never really used aside from the occasional concert held here.

Kardhámena

KARDHÁMENA, on the southeast coast 31km from Kós Town, is the island's largest package resort after the capital itself, with locals outnumbered twenty to one in a busy season by visitors (mostly young Brits) intent on getting as drunk as possible as cheaply as possible. Runaway local development has banished whatever redeeming qualities the place once had, reducing it to a seething mass of off-licences, bars, trinket shops and excursion agencies. Pubs named the *Black Swan*, *Crackers* and *Boozers* dispense imported beer, you can easily find fish and chips and there's even a *McDonalds* now – one of the very few in the islands. A beach stretches to either side of the town, sandier to the southwest, but intermittently reefy and hemmed in by a road towards the northeast as far as Tolári, home to the massive *Norida Beach* all-inclusive complex.

Kardhámena is most worth knowing about as a place to catch a **boat to Níssyros**. There are supposedly two daily sailings in season: the morning tourist excursion *kaïki* at 9–9.30am, and another, less expensive, unpublicized one – either the *Ayios Konstandinos* or the *Nissyros* – at anywhere from 2.30 to 8pm depending on the day.

South-coast beaches

The thinly populated portion of Kós southwest of the airport and Andimáhia boasts the most scenic and secluded beaches on the island, plus a number of minor ancient sites. Though given fanciful English names and shown as separate extents on tourist maps, the south-facing **beaches** form essentially one long stretch at the base of a cliff, most with sunbeds, a rudimentary snack-bar and a jet-ski franchise. "**Magic**", officially Polémi, is the longest, broadest and wildest, with a proper taverna above the car park, no jet skis and a nudist zone (dubbed "**Exotic**") at the east end. "**Sunny**", signposted as Psilós Gremmós and easily walkable from "Magic", has another taverna and jet-skis; **Langádhes** is the cleanest and most picturesque, with junipers tumbling off its dunes and more jet-skis. "**Paradise**", often dubbed "Bubble Beach" because of volcanic gas vents in the tidal zone, is small and over-subscribed, with wall-to-wall sunbeds. Jet-ski-free "**Camel**" (Kamíla) is the shortest and loneliest, protected somewhat by the steep, unpaved drive in past its hillside taverna; the shore here is pure, fine sand, with good snorkelling to either side of the cove.

Uninterrupted beach resumes past a headland at **Áyios Stéfanos**, overshadowed by a huge Club Med complex, and extends 5km west to Kamári (see below). A marked public access road leads down to the beach either side of a small peninsula, crowned with the remains of two triple-aisled, sixth-century basilicas. Though the best preserved on the island, several columns have been toppled since the 1980s, and wonderful bird mosaics languish under a permanent layer of "protective" gravel. The basilicas overlook tiny but striking **Kastrí** islet with its little chapel; in theory it's an easy swim (sometimes wading) across from the westerly beach, with some of the best snorkelling on Kós around the rock formations, but you must run a gauntlet of boats from the local watersports outfit.

The far west

Essentially the shore annexe of Kéfalos, **KAMÁRI** is a sprawling package resort of scattered breeze-blocks, pitched a few notches above Kardhámena; it's a major watersports centre and an alternative departure point for Níssyros in peak season. *Faros* is the most passably authentic, least stodgy **taverna** here, at the far (southwest) end of things near the start of the road up to **KÉFALOS**, 43km from Kós Town. Squatting on a bluff looking down the length of the island, this is the end of the line for buses: a dull village that's a staging point for expeditions into the rugged peninsula terminating dramatically at Cape Kríkello.

Main highlights of a half-day tour here, beginning along the widened ridge road south, include a Byzantine church, **Panayía Palatianí**, built amidst the ruins of a much larger ancient temple, 1km beyond the village; the late Classical theatre (unrestricted access) – with two rows of seats remaining – and Hellenistic temple of **ancient Astypalia**, 500m further at the side-path starting from an unmarked but unlocked gate; and the cave of **Asprí Pétra** (inhabited during the Neolithic period), marked rather vaguely off the ridge road and requiring a half-hour walk to reach. A paved road west from just after Astypalia leads to an often windy beach and small chapel at **Áyios Theológos**, 7km from Kéfalos; the *Ayios Theologos* **taverna** here is popular with locals at weekends especially, despite considerably bumped-up prices (though portions are also generous). Keeping to the main paved road to its end brings you to the appealing (but usually locked) monastery of **Áyios Ioánnis Thymianós**, also 7km from the village; 4km past this on dirt track leads to clothing-optional "**Cavo Paradiso**" beach, 250m of fine sand with sunbeds but no other amenities.

About 1.5km north of Kéfalos on the road tracing the island's summit ridge, a paved side road covers the 2.7km to **Lim(n)iónas**, the only north-facing beach and fishing anchorage on this part of Kós. There's just one surviving fish **taverna** here, the fair-priced *Limionas*; two compact sandy beaches sit either side of the peninsula.

Psérimos

Psérimos could be an idyllic little island were it not so close to Kós and Kálymnos. Throughout the season, both of these larger neighbours dispatch daily excursion boats in such numbers that a second jetty has been built to accommodate them at the small harbour village of **AVLÁKIA**. In midsummer, day-trippers blanket the main sandy beach which curves around the bay in front of Avlákia's thirty-odd houses and huge communal olive grove; even during May or late September you're guaranteed at least eighty outsiders daily (versus a permanent population of 25). There are three other, variably attractive beaches to hide away on during the day: clean **Vathý** (sand and gravel), a well-marked, thirty-minute path-walk east, starting from behind the *Taverna Iy Pserimos*; grubbier **Marathoúnda** (pebble), a 45-minute walk north on the main trans-island track; and best of all **Grafiótissa**, a 300-metre-long beach of near-Caribbean quality at the base of low cliffs. This lies half an hour's walk west of town, more or less following the coast; the way there is cross-country around illegally fenced hillside plots, until a proper trail kicks in at a large, solitary tree by a stone corral.

Even during high season there won't be too many other overnighters, since there's a limited number of beds available. Pick of the several small rooms establishments is *Tripolitis* (☎22430 23196; May–Oct; ❶), upstairs from English-speaking *Anna's* café/snack-bar or the rooms above *Taverna Manola* on the opposite end of the beach (☎22430 51540; ❶). Next door are the slightly higher standard *Studios Kalliston* (❸), though the management is changing and you'll have to contact them on the spot. There's just one small, limited-stock **store**, since most of the island's supplies are brought in daily from Kálymnos. Eating out however, won't break the bank, and there's often fresh fish in the handful of **tavernas**; many of these have contracts with the tour boats, but *Taverna Manola* doesn't, and despite bar-like appearances (it doubles as the main **night spot**) proves adept at ouzerí fare and seafood.

Most **boats** based on Kós and Kálymnos harbour operate triangle tours (approximately €20), which involve departure between 9.30am and 10am, followed by a stop for swimming on either Platý islet or adjacent Psérimos, lunch in Avlákia, or Póthia, the port of Kálymnos (sometimes on board), and another swimming stop at whichever islet wasn't visited in the morning. If you want to spend the entire day on Psérimos, you're much better off departing Póthia at 9.30am daily on the tiny *Nissos Pserimos*, returning at 4pm (€6 round-trip). The islanders themselves use this boat to visit Kálymnos for shopping and administrative business.

Astypálea

Geographically, historically and architecturally, **Astypálea** (alias Astropália) would be more at home among the Cyclades – on a clear day you can see Anáfi or Amorgós (to the southwest and northwest respectively) far more easily than any of the other Dodecanese. Moreover, Astypálea's inhabitants are descendants of medieval colonists from the Cyclades, and the island looks and feels more like these than its neighbours to the east.

Despite an evocative butterfly shape, Astypálea does not immediately strike you as especially beautiful. Many beaches along the bleak, heavily indented coastline have reef underfoot and suffer periodic dumpings of seaweed. The heights, which offer limited walking opportunities, are windswept and covered in thornbush or dwarf juniper. Yet the sage *alisfakiá*, brewed as a tea, flourishes too, and hundreds of sheep and goats manage to survive – as opposed to snakes, which are (uniquely in the Aegean) entirely absent. Lush citrus groves and vegetable patches in the valleys signal a relative abundance of water, hoarded in a reservoir.

In antiquity the island's most famous citizen was Kleomedes, a boxer disqualified from an early Olympic Games for causing the death of his opponent. He came home so enraged that he demolished the local school, killing all its pupils. Things have calmed down a bit in the intervening 2500 years, and today Astypálea is renowned mainly for its **honey, fish and lobster** (which finds its way into the local dish of *astakomakaronádha*); the abundant local catch has only been shipped to Athens since the late 1980s, a reflection of traditionally **poor ferry links** in every direction. Though in theory there are regular high-season links with both Pireás and Rhodes via several intervening islands, in practice arrival/departure times are grim (typically 3am) and berths or bunks are spuriously booked or otherwise not allocated to the island. Outside July or August you risk being marooned here for a day or two longer than intended; all told, you may need or want to take advantage of **flights** to Léros, Kós or Rhodes. There is no conventional package tourism here since Laskarina Holidays dropped the island in 1995, frustrated by chronically unreliable connections to Kós and its major airport.

This isolation and the logistical difficulties discourage casual trade, but motivated people do find their way to Astypálea during the short, intense **midsummer season** (mid-July to first Sept Sun before school starts), when the 1500 permanent inhabitants are vastly outnumbered by their guests. Most arrivals are Athenians, French or Italians, supplemented by large numbers of yachties and foreign owners of second homes in the understandably popular Hóra. At such times you won't find a bed without reserving well in advance, and camping rough is expressly frowned upon.

Péra Yialós and Hóra

The main harbour of **PÉRA YIALÓS** or Skála dates from the Italian era (Astypálea was the first island the Italians occupied in the Dodecanese) and most of the settlement between the quay and the line of nine windmills is even more recent. Its only real bright spot is a small **archeological museum** (June–Sept Tues–Sun 10am–1pm & 6.30–10pm; Oct–May Tues–Sun 8am–2pm; free), a single well-lit room crammed with the best local finds spanning all historical periods from the Bronze Age to medieval times.

As you climb up beyond the port towards **HÓRA**, however, the neighbourhoods get progressively older and more attractive, their steep streets enlivened by the photogenic *poúndia*, or colourful wooden balconies-with-stairways of the whitewashed houses, which owe much to the building styles of Mýkonos and Tínos, the origins of the colonists brought to repopulate the island in 1413. The whole culminates in the thirteenth-century **kástro** (always open; free), one of the finest in the Aegean, erected not by the Knights but by the Venetian Quirini clan and subsequently modified by the Ottomans after 1537. Until well into the twentieth century over three hundred people lived inside the *kástro*, but depopulation and a severe 1956 earthquake combined to leave only a desolate shell today. The fine rib vaulting over the main west gate supports the church of Evangelístria Kastrianí, one of two intact here, the other being Áyios Yeóryios (both usually locked). In 2005 the *kástro* emerged from a three-year consolidation and restoration project, with catwalks and stairs giving you pretty much the run of the place, though some unstable areas are still off-limits.

Information and transport

Two **buses** run along the paved road between Hóra, Péra Yialós, Livádhia and Analípsi, frequently in July and August from 8am until 11pm, at best four times daily out of season. The Análipsi-bound bus usually doesn't dovetail well with arriving/departing aeroplanes, so get your chosen accommodation or rental-car outfit (see below) to come fetch you. There's only one official set-rate **taxi**, incapable of coping with passenger numbers in season; fares are reasonable, for example €6 from Skála to the airport. Around five places offer **scooters**, the most reliable being Lakis and Manolis (☏22430 61263), with branches at Hóra and Skála dock; they also rent out a few pricey **cars** and jeeps, as does Vergoulis (☏22430 61351) near the museum. Also near the museum, Astypalea Tours (☏22430 61571) is the main ticket **agency**, representing GA ferries, the *Nissos Kalymnos* and Olympic Airways; Paradisos under the namesake hotel (☏22430 61224) handles Blue Star. The best island **map** is issued by Road Editions, worth snagging in advance; others sold locally are grossly inaccurate, even by lenient Greek-island standards, though in compensation rural junctions are adequately signposted. The **post office** and most shops are in Hóra, though the island's only **bank**, complete with ATM, is down in Péra Yialós by the port police.

Accommodation

Péra Yialós, and to a lesser extent Hóra, have **accommodation** ranging from spartan, 1970s-vintage rooms to new luxury studios; proprietors tend not to meet ferries unless arrangements have been made, even if they have vacancies. Owing to high-season harbour noise – particularly the sound of ferries dropping anchor at 3am – you might prefer more atmospheric restored studios or entire houses (❹ for two people peak season, ❸ low) up **in Hóra** if uninterrupted sleep is a priority; enquire at Kostas Vaïkousis' antique shop on the quay or reserve in advance on ☎22430 61430 or 697 74 77 800. Rather plusher are the 🕯 *Studios Kilindra* on the quiet west slope of Hóra (☎22430 61966, 📧studioskilindra@otenet.gr; open all year), offering luxury amenities including a swimming pool – units accommodate two to three people, with the smallest at ❻, the suites ❾. About halfway along the road from Hóra to Livádhia, the *Provarma Studios* (☎22430 61096; June to early Sept; ❸), comprise southwest-facing galleried studios with large balconies but no air conditioning.

The better of two not wildly inspiring **hotels in Péra Yialós** is the *Astynea* (☎22430 61040; ❸), though it can get nocturnal noise from bars and cafés just below. On the east shore of the bay, the en-suite *Rooms Australia* above the restaurant of the same name (☎22430 61275 or 22430 61067; ❸) have fans or air con; the same family offers more comfortable studios closer to the water (school hols only; ❹). The remoter *Akti Rooms* (☎22430 61114, 🌐www.aktirooms.gr; ❹) are also well equipped and maintained, with on-site car rental and a popular restaurant on the ground floor. A small, basic, July–August-only **campsite** operates amongst calamus reeds and tamarisks behind Dhéftero Marmári Bay, about 4km along the road to Análipsi, but (like much of the island) it can be mosquito-plagued any year after a wet winter.

Eating, drinking and nightlife

During August, nearly thirty **tavernas** and beach snack-bars operate across the island, few of them memorable and many concerned primarily with turning a quick profit. Among the more reliable Péra Yialós options, *Akroyiali* has somewhat better than average food but fills nightly owing to fair prices and its unbeatable setting with tables on the sand. The *Astropalia* (closes end Sept) on the hillside above the street up to Hóra, does good, if somewhat pricey, fish and not much else. Best of the lot, with even better seafood, and superbly prepared home-grown vegetable dishes, is the homey 🕯 *Australia* (April–Nov), just inland from the head of the bay. Behind the *Hotel Paradhisos*, you'll find more ambitious cooking, polished presentation (and much higher prices) at *Aitherio* and *Maïstrali* (both open into Oct); it's pot-luck as to which is better any given night. Under the *Hotel Astynea*, the *Dapia Café* is good for full **breakfasts**, midday crêpes and novelty teas; a few steps down, on the corner, *O Mihalis* is tops for inexpensive home-made desserts.

Except for the *Yialos* music club near the *Akroyiali*, most **nightlife** happens up in more atmospheric Hóra, where the esplanade between the windmills and the base of the *kástro* seems to be one solid café-bar. Of these, the favourites are the unsigned *Tou Nikola* (*Iy Myli*) on the corner, with the island's characters in residence, the *Ayeri Ouzeri* diagonally opposite, and music bar *Notos* tucked in by the triple chapel, with desserts as well. These are joined in season by the long-lived *Kastro*, good for conversation-level music.

Southwestern Astypálea

A twenty-minute walk (or a short bus journey) from Hóra brings you to **LIVÁDHIA**, a fertile valley draining to a popular, good beach with a generally indifferent collection of restaurants and cafés immediately behind. You can rent a **room or studio** just inland – for example at *Studios O Manganas* (☎22430 61468; ❹), on the frontage road, representing the highest standard here (they've even tiny washing machines in the units), or *Venetos Studios* (☎22430 61490 or 694 43 01 381; ❸; May–Sept), at the base of the westerly hillside, comprising several separate buildings scattered in a pleasant orchard. Among the half-dozen **tavernas**, ☆ *To Yeráni* is the most consistently open (until Oct) and renowned for its excellent *mayireftá*; they also offer equally high standard rooms adjacent, redone in 2005 with modern furnishings and marble floors (☎22430 61484; ❸).

If the busy beach here doesn't suit, continue southwest fifteen minutes on foot to three small single coves at **Tzanáki**, packed out with naturists in midsummer. The third large bay beyond Livádhia, more easily reached by motorbike, is **Áyios Konstandínos**, a partly shaded, sand-and-gravel cove with a good seasonal taverna. Around the headland, the lonely beaches of Vátses and Kaminákia are visited by excursion boat from Péra Yialós; wooden *kaíki* the *Agios Georgios* is the most characterful. By land, **Vátses** has the easier dirt road in, some twenty minutes by scooter from Livádhia; it's one of the sandier island beaches, with a basic *kantína*, but prone to wind. The track to **Kaminákia**, 8.5km from Livádhia, is rough and steep for the final 2km – best to go in a car – but the sheltered, clean and scenic cove, Astypálea's best, makes the effort worthwhile. There's a good, stone-clad **taverna** (July–Sept) here, overseeing a handful of sunbeds and offering honest rustic fare (salads, very fresh fish and a dish of the day).

Northeastern Astypálea

Northeast of the harbour are three coves known as **Próto** (First), **Dhéftero** (Second) and **Tríto** (Third) **Mármari**, and marked as **Marmári A'**, **B'** and **C'** respectively on some maps. The first is home to the power plant and boatyards; the next hosts the campsite, while the third, relatively attractive, also marks the start of the path east to the perfectly decent coves of unfortunately named **Mamoúni** ("bug" or "critter" in Greek). Beyond Tríto Marmári, the main beach at **Stenó** ("narrow", after the isthmus here), with sandy shore and shallows, a few tamarisks and a high-season *kantína*, is the best.

ANÁLIPSI, widely known as **Maltezána** after medieval Maltese pirates, is 9km from Péra Yialós. Although the second-largest settlement on Astypálea, there's surprisingly little for outsiders save a narrow, exposed, packed-sand beach (there are better ones east of the main bay, and west at **Plákes**) and a nice view south to some islets. Despite this, blocks of **rooms/studios** (most open only July & Aug) sprout in ranks well back from the sea, spurred by the proximity of the airport, less than 1km away. A more reliable exception, and the largest **hotel** complex on the island, is the 48-unit *Maltezana Beach* (☎22430 61558, Ⓦwww.maltezanabeach.gr; ❻ high, ❸ low season; Easter to mid-Sept), with large, well-appointed bungalow-rooms and on-site restaurant. There are about five independent **tavernas** here, the most reliably open (Feb–Christmas) being *Analipsi* (aka *Ilias and Irini's*, after the managing couple) by the jetty, which doubles as the *kafenío* for the local fishermen and seemingly every passing worker on the island. The food – fried squid, bean soup – is simple but good; confirm prices and portion size of the often frozen seafood. For meat dishes patronize *Skhinondas* (aka *Tassos*) by the final bus stop, where the road changes to dirt surface. Behind calamus reeds and eucalyptus near the fishing jetty lie the best-preserved mosaic floors on the island: those of the Byzantine **Tallarás baths**, with somewhat crude figures of zodiacal signs, the seasons personified, and a central androgynous figure (Time or Fortune) holding the cosmic orb.

The motorable dirt track ends 23km from Hóra at **Mésa Vathý** (invariably and erroneously shown on most maps as *Éxo Vathý*), a sleepy fishing village with a single **taverna** (*Iy Galini*) and superb small-craft anchorage in what's an almost landlocked inlet. Frankly, though, it's not really worth the long, bumpy trip out overland, and to rub salt in the wound, the fish on the menu is usually frozen (as all too often on Astypálea).

Kálymnos

Most of the 17,000-strong population of **Kálymnos** lives in or around the large port of Póthia, a prosperous but not conventionally beautiful town, famed for its **sponge industry**. Unfortunately, almost all of the eastern Mediterranean's sponges were devastated by a mysterious disease in 1986, related to freak warm currents, and only a few of the fleet of thirty-odd boats are still in use. Warehouses behind the harbour continue to process and sell sponges, but most of these are imported from Asia and the Caribbean. There are also still numbers of elderly gentlemen about who rely on two canes, walking frames or even wheelchairs, stark evidence of the havoc wrought in their youth by nitrogen embolism (the "bends"), long before divers understood its crippling effects.

In response to the sponge blight (and a repeat outbreak in 1999), the island established a tourist industry – confined to one string of beach resorts – and also adapted most of its sponge boats for deep-sea fishing. But **mass tourism** proved as fickle as sponges, and has essentially **collapsed** since the millennium. The nonfunctioning, half-finished airport near Árgos village, two decades a-building, and thus the continuing need for tedious transfers from Kós, was the main excuse for a mass pull-out by most package companies. Given this crash in bucket-and-spade holidays, the island has striven to reinvent itself as an off-season hiking and rock-climbing destination – it has some of the best cliffs in Greece, and a respectable surviving path network – and more recently taken to promoting scuba-diving and sea-kayaking through a late-summer festival.

Kálymnos essentially consists of two cultivated and inhabited valleys sandwiched between three limestone ridges, harsh in the full glare of noon but magically tinted towards dusk. The climate, especially in winter, is purported to be drier and healthier than that of neighbouring Kós or Léros, since the quick-draining limestone strata, riddled with many caves, doesn't retain as much moisture. The rock does, however, admit seawater, which has tainted Póthia's wells; drinking water must be brought in by tanker truck from the Vathýs valley, and there are also potable springs at Kamári, Potamí district of Póthia and Hóra.

Since Kálymnos is the home port of the very useful local namesake ferry (see opposite), a minor hub for hydrofoils, and moreover where the long-distance ferry lines from the Cyclades and Astypálea join up with the main Dodecanesian routes, many travellers arrive unintentionally, and are initially most concerned with how to move on quickly. Yet Kálymnos has sufficient attractions to justify a stay of several days while island-hopping – or even longer, as the vestiges of the package industry at the western beaches suggest.

Póthia

PÓTHIA (sometimes pronounced Pothiá), without being obviously picturesque, is colourful and authentically Greek, its houses marching up the valley inland or arrayed in tiers along the sides of the mountains framing it. Your first and overwhelming impression will be of the phenomenal amount of noise engendered by traffic and the cranked-up sound systems of the half-dozen waterfront cafés. This is not entirely surprising, since with nearly 16,000 inhabitants, Póthia has overtaken Kós Town as the second-largest municipality in the Dodecanese after Ródhos Town. Things get even louder on **Easter Sunday** evening, when competing teams stationed on the heights either side of town engage in an organized dynamite-throwing contest, with feasting and general merriment after the inevitable casualties are carted away.

Perhaps the most rewarding way to acquaint yourself with Póthia is by wandering the **backstreets**, where elegant Neoclassical houses are surrounded by surprisingly large gardens, and craftsmen ply their trade in a genuine workaday bazaar. The Pothians particularly excel in iron-working, and all but the humblest dwellings in the eastern Evangelístria district are adorned by splendidly ornate banisters, balcony railings and fanlights. During the Italian occupation, many local houses were painted blue and white to irritate the colonial overlords, and though the custom has all but died out, the Greek national colours still appear amongst more traditional pink and ochre buildings.

Of the two local museums, priority should be given to the **Municipal Nautical and Folklore Museum** (Mon–Fri 8am–1.30pm, Sat & Sun

10am–12.30pm; €1.50), on the
seaward side of Khristós cathedral.
A large photo in the foyer shows
Póthia as it was in the 1880s, with
no quay, jetty, roads or sumptuous
mansions, and with most of the
population still up in Hóra, while
other photos document sponge
fishing and the Allied liberation of
1945. Three-dimensional exhibits
include horribly primitive divers'
breathing apparatuses, and "cages"
designed to keep propellers from
cutting air lines, a constant fear.
However, in late 2006 or early
2007, a spectacular new annexe to
the rather soporific existing **archeological museum** in Evangelístria
(Tues–Sun 9.30am–2pm) should
open, featuring a dazzling array of
Roman and Byzantine finds.

Information and transport

All **boat** and **hydrofoil** agents,

△ Sponge-seller, Póthia, Kálymnos

plus a municipal **tourist information** booth (sporadic Mon–Fri hours), line
the waterfront as you bear right out of the pier-area gate. Useful agencies
include Mangos (☎22430 28777), for Blue Star, LANE and Agoudimos; Sofia
Kouremeti (☎22430 23700) for the *Dodekanisos Express/Pride*; Kalymna Yachting (☎22430 28200) for GA and the hydrofoils; plus the *Nissos Kalymnos* headquarters (☎22430 29612). Olympic Airways has a helpful represenative agent
at Patriárhou Maxímou 12 (☎22430 29265), 200m inland from the quay. The
Neon Café on the northwest waterfront has a few **Internet** terminals; finally,
four **banks** on or just behind the waterfront have ATMs.

Buses run as far as Emboriós in the northwest and Vathýs in the east, from
two stops beside the municipal "palace", with schedules helpfully posted near
many stops, and departures in season fairly frequent. Tickets must be bought
beforehand from authorized kiosks, and cancelled on board. Otherwise, you can
use shared **taxis** from Platía Kýprou (more than KTEL rates, less costly than a
normal taxi), or rent a **scooter** from reputable Scootermania (☎22430 51780),
just back from the waterfront, near where it bends south. There's plenty of **car
rental** available on the quay (Spiros Kypraios, ☎2430 51470; Budget, phone as
for Scootermania, or ☎697 28 34 628), though the island's compact enough
that only groups would need one.

Accommodation

Accommodation is rarely a problem, with a little high-season booking
office on the quay; as on Kós, beware of *dhomátia* touts as you disembark, since
many of their premises are substandard, unlicensed or remote – often all three.
The town's best, and quietest **hotel**, near the archeological museum, is the
garden-set ☆ *Villa The-melina* (☎22430 22682, Ⓕ22430 23920; open all year;
B&B; ➌), housed in an early-twentieth-century mansion, plus modern studio
and apartment annexes (➍), with breakfast patio and a large swimming pool.

The high-ceiling, bug-screened, wood-floored rooms in the main house make this Kálymnos's most elegant accommodation. The only remotely comparable alternative, on the west quay but fairly quiet, is the *Arhondiko* (℡ 22430 24051, ℻ 22430 24149; ➋), another refurbished mansion whose somewhat plain rooms have TV, fridge and air con; some also have balconies. Places in Amoudhára district (west of the harbour) include the en-suite *Pension Greek House* (℡ 22430 29559; ➊) with volubly friendly management, some studios and kitsch decor; and considerably above this, the well-signposted, well-kept *Hotel Panorama* (℡ 22430 22917, ℻ 22430 23138; April–Oct; ➌), which has balconied rooms with views and a pleasant breakfast salon.

Eating and drinking

The most obvious place for **eating out** is the line of seafood tavernas northeast along the waterfront past the Italian-built municipal "palace", but standards are low and prices inflated. Much the best seafood and Kalymnian specialties are found at ⋇ *Kafenes*, on the esplanade opposite the county "palace", with slightly bumped-up prices justified by generous, savoury portions of salad, seafood, the odd dip and bulk wine; or at *Taverna Pandelis*, tucked inconspicuously into a cul-de-sac behind the waterfront *Olympic Hotel*; this features fresh-gathered shellfish like *foúskes* and *kalógnomes* (related to mussels) and wild scaly fish. Other alternatives include *mayireftá* and grills at *Xefteris*, under new management in 2005 inland from Khristós cathedral, or excellent wood-fired pizzas at *Pizza Imia* at mid-quay. *Dhodhoni*, past the bus stops on the shore, is the main ice-cream outlet, but fans of sticky cakes will want to attend the traditional *Zaharoplastio O Mihalaras* two steps away; they've a more modern annexe near the ferry jetty. Since the crash in tourism, the sole out-and-out **bar** is *Blue Note*, near *Pandelis*; for more ambitious seasonal venues just outside of town, watch for wall posters. A **cinema**, Cine Oasis, operates both summer and winter premises behind the traditional, column-facaded café-tearoom *Ai Musai*, on the front.

Around Póthia

Just over 1km northwest of Póthia, in the suburb of Mýli, is a castle of the Knights of St John, **Kástro Khryssoheriás** (unrestricted access). From the whitewashed battlements there are wonderful views southeast over town to Kós, and north towards Hóra and Péra Kástro. The former Kalymnian capital of **HÓRA** (aka Horió), 1.5km further along the main road, is still a village of nearly three thousand inhabitants, and guards a critical pass in local geography, focus of settlement in every era. Steep steps lead up from its eastern edge to the nocturnally illuminated Byzantine citadel-town of **Péra Kástro** (daily 8.30am–2pm; free), appropriated by the Knights of St John and inhabited until late in the eighteenth century. Inside the gate and recently consolidated perimeter walls you'll find nine little **medieval chapels**, several – in particular Áyios Nikólaos/Pódhromos, Ayía Ánna, Timíou Stavroú and Metamórfosis – containing fifteenth-to-sixteenth-century fresco fragments. A visitors' centre and café should begin operation in the near future.

Some 200m past the turning for Árgos en route to the northwest coast from Hóra, you can detour briefly left to visit two early Byzantine basilicas which are fairly representative, and among the easiest to find, of a vast number on Kálymnos. The more impressive of the two, accessed by whitewashed steps on the left just as the highway begins to descend, is that of **Khristós tís Ierousalím**, probably dating from the late fourth century, with its apse fully preserved; the three-aisled **Limniótissa** church in an adjacent field is larger but considerably less intact.

West coast resorts

From the basilicas, the road dips into a tree-shaded valley leading to the consecutive **beach resorts** of Kandoúni, Myrtiés and Massoúri, collectively referred to as "Brostá" by islanders. **KANDOÚNI**, some 200m of brown, hard-packed sand favoured by the locals, is the shore annexe of the rich agricultural valley-villages of **Pánormos** and **Eliés**. Kandoúni **accommodation** freed up by the departure of the tour companies includes the *Kalydna Island Hotel* (☎22430 47880; ❹), but for both bathing and staying you're probably better off at **LINÁRIA**, the north end of the same bay. A smaller cove set apart from Kandoúni proper by a rock outcrop, this has better sand and the possibility of staying at *Skopellos Studios* (☎22430 47155; ❸), on the slope below the church. Of two shoreline full-service **tavernas** here, *Tò Egeo* is better value for seafood and more locally attended.

The next beach north, **PLATÝ-YIALÓS**, though again a bit shorter than Kandoúni, is arguably the best on the island: cleaner than its southern neighbours, more secluded, and placed scenically at the base of a cliff, opposite Ayía Kyriakí islet. A lone **taverna** (*Kyma/Wave*), right behind the sand at road's end, proves popular for simple, inexpensive lunches or sunset drinks (it closes shortly after). Among a handful of choices for **staying** on spec, long-time budget favourite is the Vavoulas family's *Pension Plati Gialos* (☎ & ⓕ22430 47029), actually overlooking Linária, with spacious balconies, mosquito nets and a terrace bar; choose between simple, fan-equipped rooms (❷) or two family apartments (❸). For more comfort, blue-and-white-decor *Mousselis Studios* (☎22430 48307, ✉mousellis_studios@yahoo.gr; ❸) just down the road towards the beach accommodate two to six people, with half board offered at its acceptable restaurant.

The main road climbs from Pánormos up to a pass, before descending in zigzags to meet the sea again 8km from Póthia at **MYRTIÉS**. Together with **MASSOÚRI** (1km north) and **ARMEÓS** (2km north and end of the line for most buses), Myrtiés has been hardest hit by the Kalymnian tourism slump, so vacant and boarded-up premises abound. Exceptions include 🍴 *Akroyiali* (☎22430 47521 or 693 89 13 210; ❸), seven two-room, beachside apartments in Massoúri sleeping two adults and two kids which require long advance booking; *Bar Babis* on the square in Myrtiés, an Anglophile institution, and jointly operated Avis/Alfa (☎22430 47430) **renting cars and bikes** respectively. No great loss in many other cases, as during their long tenure the package companies had a predictably dire effect on local **tavernas**; much the best survivor, in Armeós, is friendly meat specialist 🍴 *Tsopanakos* (open all year), which has fresh meat and cheese dishes from island-grazed goats, along with the usual grills and appetizers. Armeós is also the local mecca for **rock-climbers**, with many of the most popular cliffs overhead and a small equipment shop (Climber's Nest) catering to them. There's also some Greek-pitched **nightlife**, with live acts at *Kastelli Club*.

The beach at Myrtiés is narrow, pebbly and cramped by development, though it does improve as you approach Massoúri. The closest all-sand beach to Myrtiés lies 500m south, at **Melitsahás** cove (Melitsáhas in dialect), which also has the only locally patronized **taverna** at its fishing anchorage, *Iy Dhrossia* (aka *O Andonis*; open all year), best for oysters, lobster and shrimp as well as scaly fish at affordable rates. On-spec **accommodation** is fairly easy to find here, for example at the spacious *Maria's Studios* (☎22430 48135 or 22430 28528; ❷) up on the hillside. Possibly this coast's most appealing feature is its position opposite the evocatively shaped islet of Télendhos (see overleaf), which frames some of the most dramatic sunsets in Greece. It's also possible to go from Myrtiés directly to Xirókambos on Léros aboard the daily early-afternoon **kaïki**.

Some 5km beyond Massoúri, **ARYINÓNDA** has a clean pebble beach, two **tavernas** and sunbeds. It's also the trailhead for the spectacular two-and-a-half-hour walk inland and over two gentle passes to Metóhi in the Vathýs valley. From the bus stop and gravelled car-park area and small spring, head southeast on a path between rock walls which soon climbs the south flank of the ravine here, sporadically marked by paint dots. Don't believe sources which show the route emerging at Styménia, and be aware that the municipality is bulldozing a road to Vathýs, which will severely disrupt the trail about half an hour along. You'll need a sun hat, stout shoes and a litre or two of water, as the next source is in Plátanos hamlet, beyond Metóhi.

The end of the bus line, **EMBORIÓS**, 20km from the port, offers a gravel-and-sand beach, which gets better as you head west, **accommodation** and a number of **tavernas**, including the long-running *Harry's Paradise*, with attached, air-conditioned garden apartments (☏22430 40061; ❸) in bland white-and-pine decor. If the twice-daily bus service fails you, there is a shuttle boat back to Myrtiés at 4pm (leaving the latter at 10am). There are also better, if unamenitied beaches between here and Skália, such as **Kalamiés** and **Áyios Nikólaos**.

Télendhos

The trip across the strait to the striking, volcanic-plug islet of **TÉLENDHOS** is arguably the best reason to come to Myrtiés; little boat-buses shuttle to and fro regularly (8am–midnight, half-hourly each direction; €1.50), occasionally dodging the sea-kayaks which have become a popular sporting device locally. According to local legend, Télendhos is a petrified princess, gazing out to sea after her errant lover; the woman's-head profile is most evident at dusk. The hardly less pedestrian geological explanation has the islet sundered from Kálymnos by a cataclysmic earthquake in 554 AD; traces of a submerged town are said to lie at the bottom of the straits.

Home to about fifteen permanent inhabitants, Télendhos is car-free and blissfully tranquil, even more so since certain package operators gave up allotments here. For cultural edification you'll find the ruined thirteenth-century **monastery of Áyios Vassílios** and an enormous **basilica of Ayía Triádha** up on the ridge, part way along the flagstoned, ten-minute path to **Hokhlakás** pebble beach, which is small but very scenic, with sunbeds for rent. **Pótha** and nudist **"Paradise"** on the other side of the islet are preferred by some: sandy and with calm water, but no afternoon sun.

There are about eight places to eat and a roughly equal number of **accommodation** establishments, most (but not all) linked to the tavernas. Places to stay that get uniformly positive reviews include *Pension Studios Rita* (☏22430 47914, ℻22430 47927), rooms (❶) and renovated-house studios (❷), managed by the namesake snack-bar/café; the simple but en-suite rooms above *Zorba's* (☏22430 48660; ❶); *Rinio Studios* (☏22430 23851; ❷), set a bit inland and built in 2003 to a high standard; or, north beyond Áyios Vassílios, the Greek-Australian-run ⚓ *On the Rocks* (☏22430 48260, ⓦwww.otr.telendos.com; ❸; April–Nov), three superbly appointed rooms with double glazing, satellite TV, bug screens, fridges and internet access, as well as use of kayaks on the beach out front. If you want more (relative) luxury on Télendhos, it's fairly easy to secure a vacancy at the large *Hotel Porto Potha* (☏22430 47321, ⓦwww.telendoshotel .gr; ❸), set at the very edge of things but with a large pool, "private" beach, some self-catering studios and friendly managing family. Endorseable **tavernas** include *Barba Stathis* (aka *Tassia's*), en route to Hokhlakás, with a few cooked dishes each day; *Zorba's*, doing slightly pricey but excellent goat in tomato sauce or fresh squid; *Plaka*, next to *On the Rocks*, good for inexpensive meat straight from grandpa's flock; and the slightly pricey, full-service taverna at *On the Rocks* itself, with lovely home-made desserts, and a bar that's the heart and soul of local **nightlife**. At one corner of the premises you can visit the chapel of Áyios Harálambos, occupying a former Byzantine bathhouse.

Vathýs and around

The first 4km east from Póthia seem vastly unpromising (power plant, rubbish tip, multiple gasworks, cement quarries, fish farms), until you round a bend and the ten-kilometre ride ends dramatically at **VATHÝS**, a long, fertile valley, carpeted with orange and tangerine groves, whose colour provides a startling contrast to the mineral greys and oranges higher up on Kálymnos. At the simple fjord port of **RÍNA**, more ruined basilicas flank the bay; near the southerly one is the best **accommodation** option, the helpful *Rooms Manolis* (℡22430 31300; ❶), simple but en suite and with sweeping views, set in landscaped terraces and accessible by a lane behind *The Harbors* (see below). Some of the **tavernas** are pricier than you'd expect, owing to patronage from the numerous yachts that call here; the best choice, with shambolic service but good grilled fish, is *The Harbors*, the first place on the right at the road's end.

The steep-sided inlet has no beach to speak of, so people swim off the artificial lido on the south side; the closest pebble-coves reachable overland are **Aktí**, about 3km back towards Póthia, a functional pebble strand with sunbeds and a single snack-bar, and **Pezónda**, a little further north, reached by steep track (and then a 45-minute walk northwest) starting from Metóhi hamlet. At track's end another path heads east in fifteen minutes to the amazingly set little **monastery of Kyrá Psilí**, frequented only on August 15.

Boat excursions sometimes visit the stalactite cave of **Dhaskalió**, inhabited in Neolithic times, out towards the fjord mouth on its north flank, and the remoter, tiny beaches of **Almyrés** and **Dhrasónda**, accessible only by sea.

It's possible to **walk** back to Póthia along the old direct *kalderími* which existed before the coastal highway – a two-hour jaunt that begins in Plátanos hamlet. The route is tricky to find in this direction, however, so most people start in Póthia, at the church of Ayía Triádha behind the *Villa The-melina* hotel – the way is marked initially by red paint splodges.

The southwest

Climbing southwest out of Póthia towards Áyios Sávvas monastery, the most worthwhile halt is the privately run **Folklore Museum–Traditional House of Kalymnos** (daily 9am–9pm; €1.50), a treasure trove of old-time furnishings and costumes. Some 6km southwest of Póthia, the small bay of **Vlyhádhia** is reached through a narrow ravine draining from the nondescript village of Vothýni. The sand-and-pebble beach here isn't really worth a special trip, since the bay is apt to be stagnant and at least some of the locals (who have blotted out all Roman-alphabet road signs) are resentful of foreigners. If you're interested in **scuba diving**, the coast to either side of Vlyhádhia is one of the limited number of legal areas in Greece. A local diver has also assembled an impressive **Museum of Submarine Finds** (Mon–Sat 9am–7pm, Sun 10am–2pm; free), which in addition to masses of sponges and shells offers a reconstructed ancient wreck with amphorae and World War II debris. The best local dive operator,

Pegasus Diving Club (☎694 4180746), works out of Póthia and visits ancient wrecks *in situ*.

Póthia-based *kaïkia* also make well-publicized excursions to the cave of **Kefála** just west of Vlyhádhia, the most impressive of half a dozen caverns around the island. You have to walk thirty minutes from where the boats dock, but the vividly coloured formations repay the effort; the cave was inhabited before recorded history, and later served as a sanctuary of Zeus (who is fancifully identified with a particularly imposing stalagmite in the biggest of six chambers).

Léros

Léros is so indented with deep, sheltered anchorages that between 1928 and 1948 it harboured, in turn, much of the Italian, German and British Mediterranean fleets. Unfortunately, many of these magnificent fjords and bays seem to absorb rather than reflect light, and the island's fertility – there are orchards and vegetable gardens a-plenty – can make Léros seem scruffy when compared with the crisp lines of its more barren neighbours. These characteristics, plus the island's lack of spectacularly good beaches, meant that until the late 1980s just a few thousand foreigners (mostly Italians who grew up on Léros), and not many

Lipsí & Pátmos

LÉROS

N

0   2 km

Kálymnos (Lakki) ▼ Kálymnos (Myrtiés) ▼ Kálymnos (Ayía Marína) & Kós ▼

more Greeks, came to visit each August. The tourist profile is now broader, with a longer season; Scandinavian, British, Dutch and German package operators alternate by season in "discovering" Léros and the company of islanders relatively unjaded by mass tourism. Foreign-visitor numbers have, however, dipped since the millennium, with matters unlikely to change until and unless the airport runway is lengthened to accommodate jets.

Until recently Léros didn't strenuously encourage mass tourism; various **prisons and sanatoriums** dominated the Lerian economy from the 1950s onwards, directly or indirectly employing about a third of the population. During the junta era, the island hosted a notorious detention centre at Parthéni, and for over four decades several mental hospitals served as warehouses for many of Greece's more intractable psychiatric cases and mentally handicapped children. The island's domestic image problem was compounded by its name, the butt of jokes by mainlanders who pounced on its similarity to the word *lerá*, connoting rascality and unsavouriness. In 1989, a major scandal emerged concerning the administration of the various asylums, with EU maintenance and development funds found to have been embezzled by staff, and inmates kept in degrading conditions; a subsequent influx of EU inspectors, foreign psychiatrists and extra funding resulted in drastic improvements. By 1995 the worst wards were closed down, and the inmates placed in sheltered housing around the island, farming and engaging in "work internships" for pocket money; the remaining seven hundred carers now haven't enough to do but legally can't be made redundant. Some of the slack was taken up by tourism, some by the 1999 opening of one of Greece's main nursing colleges, but the institutional identity is not nearly as pervasive as you'd expect.

More obvious is the legacy of the **Battle of Léros** on November 12–16, 1943, when overwhelming German forces displaced a Commonwealth division, which had landed on the island following the Italian capitulation. Bomb nose-cones and shell casings still turn up as gaily painted garden ornaments in the courtyards of churches and tavernas, or have been pressed into service as gateposts. Each year for three days following September 26, memorial services and a naval festival commemorate the sinking of the Greek battleship *Queen Olga* and the British *Intrepid* during the German attack.

Unusually for a small island, Léros has abundant ground water, channelled into cisterns at several points (only the two on the Plátanos upper bypass are potable). These, plus low-lying ground staked with the avenues of eucalyptus trees planted by the Italians, make for a horrendously active mosquito contingent, so come prepared.

Léros is sufficiently compact for the energetic to walk around, but there is a reasonably reliable bus service, plus several motor- and mountain-bike rental outlets, of which Motoland (outlets in Pandélli, ℡22470 24103, and Álinda, ℡22470 24584) has proven reliable on several occasions; Koumbaros in Álinda is by contrast worth avoiding. The island is hilly enough to make motorised wheels a better bet, though the reasonably fit could manage with just a mountain bike between Álinda and Lakkí. If you rent a scooter, take extra care – Lerian roads are particularly narrow, potholed and gravel-strewn, and the low-slung, fat-tyred bikes on offer don't cope well.

Lakkí and Xirókambos

All large **ferries**, the *Nissos Kalymnos* and the *Dodekanisos Pride* arrive at the main port of **LAKKÍ**, originally constructed in 1935–38 as a model town to house 7500 civilian dependents of an adjacent Italian naval base. Boulevards far too wide for today's paltry amount of traffic are lined with some marvellous Rationalist edifices, including the round-fronted cinema, the church, the primary school, a shopping centre with a round atrium and the derelict remains of the Leros Palace Hotel. Their architectural importance has finally been acknowledged and a phased restoration programme should see them all returned to decent condition by 2008.

Buses don't meet the ferries – instead there's a **taxi squadron** that charges set fares to standard destinations. If you arrive during business hours, consider renting a car or bike from Koumoulis (℡22470 22330), near the cinema. Few people stay willingly at any of the handful of drab hotels in Lakkí, preferring to head straight for the resorts of Pandélli, Álinda or Vromólithos (see opposite). There are just two proper **tavernas**: *Marina*, at the base of the yacht jetty, and *To Petrino*, inland next to the **post office**. Other amenities include three ATMs attached to as many **banks**; travel **agencies** are Leros Travel, for GA and the *Nissos Kalymnos* (℡22470 22154); and Aegean Travel a block inland (℡22470 26000), for Blue Star Ferries and the catamaran. The nearest approximation of a **beach** is at sand-and-gravel **Koulóuki**, 500m west, where there's a seasonal taverna and some pines for shade, though it's too close to the ferry jetty for most tastes. You can carry on another kilometre or so to **Merikiá**, a slight improvement, also with a taverna.

XIRÓKAMBOS, nearly 5km from Lakkí in the far south of the island, is the point of arrival for the afternoon *kaïki* from Myrtiés on Kálymnos (it returns early the following morning). Though billed as a resort, it's essentially a fishing port where folk also happen to swim – the beach is poor to mediocre, improving as you head west. Top **accommodation** here is the *Hotel Efstathia* (℡22470 24099; ❹), actually studio apartments with huge, well-furnished doubles as well as family four-plexes, plus a large pool. You've a choice of three evenly spaced **tavernas**, where the road hits the shore. The island's **campsite** (℡22470 23372; May–Oct), with an in-house scuba-diving centre (℡694 42 38 490; ⓦwww .lerosdiving.com), is in an olive grove at the village of **LEPÍDHA**, 750m back up the road to Lakkí. Just north of the campsite, an access drive on the far side of the road (signposted as "Ancient Fort") leads up to a tiny acropolis with stretches of ancient masonry behind the modern chapel on the summit.

Pandélli and Vromólithos

Just under 3km north of Lakkí, Pandélli and Vromólithos together form an attractive and scenic resort, Álinda's (see p.378) only rival.

PANDÉLLI is still a working port, the cement jetty benefiting local fishermen as well as an increasing number of yachts that call here. A small but reef-free, pea-gravel beach is complemented by a relative abundance of nonpackage **accommodation**, such as the *Pension Happiness* (℡22470 23498; ❷), where the road down from Plátanos meets the sea, or the newer *Pension Lavyrinthos*, directly opposite (℡22470 24165; ❷). For a higher standard, try ⚔ *Niki Studios* (℡22470 25600; ❸) at the base of the road up to the castle – air-con double units and quad apartments, Australian-Greek-run and with partial sea views. Up on the ridge dividing Pandélli from Vromólithos in **Spília** district, the *Hotel Rodon* (℡22470 23524; ❸) actually comprises 2005-refurbished studios and larger apartments downstairs, with knock-out views. On summer nights there may be a faint strain of music from *Café del Mar*, perched on a rock terrace below (it operates as a daytime beach-café; May–Oct); the other long-lived local **bar** is the civilized, English-Danish-run *Savana*, at the opposite end of Pandélli, with excellent music (you can nominate your favourite tracks). It stands beyond a row of decidedly uneven waterfront **tavernas**, the best of which are ⚔ *Psaropoula* (open all year), with good, non-farmed fish and *mayireftá*, and *Tou Mihali*, a corner *kafenío* where expertly fried *gópes*, mixed salads and good wine are scoffed by a largely local crowd. Up in Spília, adjacent to the *Hotel Rodon*, *Mezedhopolio O Dimitris O Karaflas* is one of the best-sited ouzerís on the island, scoring highly for delicacies such as chunky local sausages and unusual dips like *xynógalo* and *tsitsíri*.

VROMÓLITHOS boasts the best easily accessible **beach** on the island, car-free and hemmed in by hills studded with massive oaks. The shoreline is gravel and coarse sand, and the sea here is clean, but as so often on Léros you have to cross a rock pavement at most points before reaching deeper water; there's a more secluded, sandier cove southeast at **Tourkopígadho**. Two **tavernas** behind the beach trade more on their location than their cuisine – *To Pigadhi* at the main inland junction is better – but the general standard of **accommodation** here is higher than at Pandélli. Prime choices are *Tony's Beach*, spacious studio units set in equally extensive waterside grounds (℡22470 24743, ⓦwww.tonysbeachstudios.gr; June–Sept; ❹), and the stone-floored *Glaros*, just inland in pleasant grounds (℡22470 24358, Ⓕ22470 23683; May–Oct; ❹).

Plátanos and Ayía Marína

The Neoclassical and vernacular houses of **PLÁTANOS**, the island capital 1km west of Pandélli, are draped gracefully along a saddle between two hills, one of them crowned by the inevitable Knights' castle. Known locally as the **Kástro** (daily 8am–1pm, also May–Oct Wed, Sat & Sun 3–7pm; €1), this is reached either by a zigzagging road peeling off the Pandélli-bound road, or via a more scenic stair-path from the central square; the battlements, and the views from them, are dramatic, especially near sunrise or sunset. The medieval church of **Panayía tou Kástrou** inside the gate houses a small museum (additional €1), though its carved *témblon* and naïve oratory are more remarkable than the sparse exhibits, mostly icons and other liturgical items. The **archeological museum** (Tues–Sun 8am–2.30pm; free), down the road to Ayía Marína, is more interesting, compensating for a dearth of artefacts with a comprehensible gallop through Lerian history.

Plátanos is not really a place to stay or eat, although it's well sown with **shops** and **services**. The latter include Olympic Airways (℡22470 24144), south of the turning for Pandélli; a **post office**, down the road towards Ayía Marína; and a few **banks** with ATMs. The single **bus** (schedule posted at stop, opposite the island's main **taxi** rank) plies several times daily between Parthéni in the north and Xirókambos in the south.

Plátanos merges seamlessly with **AYÍA MARÍNA**, 1km north on the shore of a fine bay, still graced by a small, Italian-built public market building. If you're travelling to Léros on an excursion boat from Lipsí, the *Dodekanisos Express*, or a hydrofoil, this will be your port of entry unless high winds force a diversion to Lakkí. At the western edge of things the superior ⚓ *Ouzeri Neromylos*, out by the wave-lapped windmill, indisputably has the most romantic setting on the island (mid-March–Oct; reservations mandatory July-Aug on ℡22470 24894), the best musical sound-track, and arguably the best food. Host Takis' specialties include *garidhopílafo* (shrimp-rice), superb fresh fish, edible bread and *kolokythokeftédhes* (courgette patties), expertly prepared by his wife and mother-in-law. Lively (for Léros) **nightlife** is provided by several bars near the customs house, such as *Enallaktiko*, with a few **Internet** terminals, and cavernous *Apothiki New Face* on the quay. Kastis Travel nearby (℡22470 22140) handles all ticket sales for hydrofoils and the *Dodekanisos Express*, plus there are two bank **ATMs**.

Álinda and Krithóni

ÁLINDA, 3km northwest of Ayía Marína, ranks as the longest-established resort on Léros, with development just across the road from a long, narrow strip of pea-gravel beach. It's also the first area for accommodation to open in spring, and the last to shut in autumn. Most **hotels** and **pensions** here are partly allotted to tour companies, but worthwhile establishments that keep rooms for walk-ins include *Hotel Gianna* (T 22470 23153; ➌), with fridge-equipped units plus a few studios overlooking the war cemetery, or – set back from mid-beach – the well-kept *Hotel Alinda* (*Xenonas Mavrakis*) (T 22470 23266, W www .alindahotel.gr; ➌), with the very good, affiliated *Taverna Alinda* and sunken Byzantine mosaic out front, plus well-kept rooms with air con and fridges. The other reliable beachfront **restaurant** is *Finikas*. One lodging to avoid is *Studios Diamantis*, whose thoroughly unpleasant management touts aggressively from their taxi and gift shop in Ayía Marína. At **KRITHÓNI**, 1.5km south, more comfort is available at the island's top-flight accommodation: the *Crithoni's Paradise* (T 22470 25120, W www.crithonishotel.com; open all year; rooms ➏, suites ➑), a mock-traditional low-rise complex with decent buffet breakfast, a large pool and all mod cons in the rooms – it's worth the little extra for "superior standard" or a suite.

The **Allied War Graves Cemetery**, mostly containing casualties of the November 1943 battle, occupies a walled enclosure at the south end of the beach; immaculately maintained, with a guestbook, it serves as a moving counterpoint to the beachside life outside. The other principal sight at Álinda is the privately run **Historical and Ethnographic Museum** (May–Sept only, Tues–Sun 9am–1pm & 7–9pm; €3), housed in the unmistakable castle-like mansion of Paris Bellinis (1871–1957). Most of the top floor is devoted to the Battle of Léros: relics from the sunken *Queen Olga*, a wheel from a Junkers bomber, a stove made from a bomb casing. There's also a rather grisly mock-up clinic (mostly gynecological tools) and assorted rural impedimenta, costumes and antiques.

Alternative beaches near Álinda include **Dhýo Liskária**, a series of gravel coves at the far northeast of the bay (one taverna, two cafés), and **Goúrna**, the turning for which lies 1km or so off the trans-island road. The latter, Léros's longest sandy beach, is hard-packed and gently shelving, if wind-buffeted; a few sunbeds are provided by the single taverna.

The far north

Seven kilometres from Álinda along the main route north, a marked side-track leads left to the purported **Temple of Artemis**, on a slight rise just west of the airport runway. In ancient times, Léros was sacred to the goddess, and the temple here was supposedly inhabited by guinea fowl – the grief-stricken sisters of Meleager, metamorphosed thus by Artemis following their brother's death. All that remains now are some jumbled, knee-high walls, which are more likely to have been an ancient fortress, but the view is superb.

The tiny **airport** terminal itself has been expanded for a busier future, but it's still no place to be stuck a minute longer than necessary; if your midday flight to Astypálea or Rhodes is delayed (more likely than not), your only diversion lies across the road at vastly overpriced *Taverna To Arhondiko* – eat elsewhere before you set out, and just have a coffee here.

The onward route skims the shores of sumpy, reed-fringed Parthéni Bay, with its yacht dry dock and dreary, Italian-built army base (the 1967–74 political prison). The camp has, however, left one outstanding cultural legacy: the chapel of **Ayía Kioúra** (always open), reached by a one-kilometre marked access road. During the junta era, certain political prisoners decorated this otherwise unremarkable church with striking murals – squarely in the tradition of Diego Rivera's 1930s Leftist art – rather than conventional frescoes. The Orthodox Church has, of course, always abhorred these images – a resident monk obliterated several in the 1980s – but Ayía Kioúrá is now a protected monument. The paved road ends 11km from Álinda at **Blefoútis** and its huge, almost landlocked bay. The small beach (the rough Lerian norm) has tamarisks to shelter under and an adequate taverna, *Iy Thea Artemi*.

Pátmos

Arguably the most beautiful and certainly the best known of the smaller Dodecanese, **Pátmos** has a distinctive, immediately palpable atmosphere. It was in a cave here that St John the Divine (in Greek, O Theológos or "The Theologian"), set down the New Testament's Book of Revelation and unwittingly shaped the island's destiny. The monastery honouring him, founded here in 1088 by the Blessed Khristodhoulos (1021–93), dominates Pátmos both physically – its fortified bulk towering high above everything else – and, to a considerable extent, socially. While the monks inside no longer run the island unchallenged as they did for more than six centuries, their influence has stopped it going the way of Rhodes or Kós – though Pátmos now has no less than four nudist beaches, something unthinkable a decade or so ago.

Despite vast numbers of visitors and the island's firm presence on the cruise, hydrofoil and yacht circuits, tourism has not been allowed to take Pátmos over completely. While there are several after-hours clubs around the main port town, drunken rowdiness is virtually unknown. Package clients only equal independent visitors in certain years, and are pretty much confined to Gríkou and a handful of larger hotels at Skála and Kámbos. Day-trippers still exceed overnighters, and Pátmos seems an altogether different place once the last cruise-ship passengers have gone after sunset. Away from Skála, touristic development is appealingly subdued if not deliberately retarded, thanks to the absence of an airport. On outlying beaches, little has superficially changed since the 1980s, though "for sale" signs on every seafront field and farmhouse, plus massive villa developments at coves closer in, suggest that such days are strictly numbered.

Skála and around

SKÁLA, where most of the island's three thousand people live, seems initially to contradict any solemn, otherworldly image of Pátmos. The waterside, with its ritzy cafés, arty gift boutiques and clientele, is a bit too sophisticated for such a small town, and certain service staff more than a little world-weary. During peak season, the quay and commercial district swarm by day with trippers souvenir-hunting or being shepherded onto coaches for the ride up to the monastery; after dark there's still a considerable traffic in well-dressed cliques of visitors on furlough from the huge, humming cruisers which weigh anchor around midnight. In winter (which here means by early October), Skála assumes a ghost-town air as most shops and restaurants close, their owners and staff going back to Rhodes or Athens.

Hóra, a brief bus- or taxi-ride up the mountain, would be a more attractive base, but has little accommodation. Yet given time, Skála reveals some more enticing corners in the residential fringes to the east and west, where vernacular mansions hem in pedestrian lanes creeping up the hillsides. The modern town dates only from the 1820s, when the Aegean had largely been cleared of pirates, but at the summit of the westerly rise, **Kastélli**, you can see the extensive foundations of the island's ancient acropolis.

Information and transport

Almost everything of interest can be found within, or within sight of, the Italian-built municipal "palace": all arriving sea-craft anchor opposite, the port police occupy the east end, the **post office** one of its corners, and the main **bus stop**, with a posted timetable, is right in front. There are three **banks**, each with an ATM. **Scooter rental** outfits (such as Billis ☎ 22470 32218 and Aris ☎ 22470 32542) are common, with lowish rates owing to the modest size of the island. **Excursion boats** to Psilí Ámmos and Arkí/Maráthi leave mostly at about 10am (to Léros and Lipsí, sometimes 8am) from just in front of Astoria Travel and Apollon Travel, the two **agencies** handling hydrofoil tickets; Apollon (☎22470 22470) is also the central rep for Blue Star Ferries. GA Ferries (☎22470 31217) and the *Nissos Kalymnos* (☎22470 32575) have separate agencies on, or just off, the central waterfront square; several outlets sell tickets for the *Dodekanisos Express/Pride* catamarans; try Kyriaki Liapi (☎22470 29303) in Konsoláto district to the east. Skála has two **Internet cafés**: one inside the *Blue Bay* Hotel, the other – Millennium – just behind the little park inland from the port-terminal building.

Accommodation

Accommodation touts meet all arriving seagoing craft, and their offerings tend to be a long walk distant and/or inland – not necessarily a bad thing, as no location is really remote, and anywhere near the waterfront, which doubles as the main road between Gríkou and Kámbos, will be noisy. Pátmos vernacular architecture is quite distinctive, but you wouldn't know it from most lodgings; bland if inoffensive rooms thrown up during the 1980s, with institutional (one might even say monastic) furnishings.

Establishments worth reserving in advance (they'll often send a van to fetch you) are scattered across several districts. Unless otherwise stated, assume April-to-October operation. Besides **central Skála**, you could end up in **Konsoláto** district, east of the centre near the fishing anchorage, with fairly high-quality digs, but the worst noise from fishing boats and ferries coming and going from 1 to 4am. **Netiá**, the unglamorous area northwest between the power plant and Mérihas cove, is actually not a bad choice as a base. Pebbly **Hokhlakás** Bay, just a ten-minute walk southwest starting from the central market street, is perhaps the quietest district, with wonderful sunset views. **Melóï** cove, 1.5km northwest, has a good beach and is home to island's well-run **campsite**, *Stefanos-Flowers* (℡22470 31821).

Asteri Netiá, near Mérihas cove ℡22470 32465, ⓔpasca@otenet.gr. The highest standard in this area, unimprovably set on a knoll overlooking the bay, in a well-landscaped environment; guests have own-produced honey, eggs and tomatoes at breakfast. 2003-expanded with a large sea-view lounge and variably sized rooms (including 2 with wheelchair access). B&B ❺

Australis Netiá ℡22470 31576, ⓦwww.patmos _web.gr/australishotel.htm. Somewhat spartan but en-suite hotel owned by a returned Greek-Australian family; full breakfast and an affiliated scooter-rental business saves you traipses into town. There's a better-standard apartment annexe, whose units accommodate 6 people – at ❼ per unit. B&B ❹

Blue Bay About 150m beyond Konsoláto on the Gríkou road ℡22470 31165, ⓦwww .bluebay.50g.com. Probably the best-value, quietest choice for this area, with helpful Australian-Greek management, reasonably furnished air-con, fridged, sea-view rooms piled in tiers, plus Skála's most reliable Internet facilities. Credit cards accepted for stays of over 2 days. ❺

Captain's House Konsoláto ℡22470 31793, ⓦwww.patmosisland.com/captainhouse. The newer wing of much quieter rear rooms overlooks a fair-sized pool and shady terrace. Further pluses are friendly management, above-average furnishings and on-site car rental. ❻

Doriza Bay Hokhlakás, south hillside ℡22470 32702, ⓦwww.portoscoutari.com/doriza_bay.html. Co-managed with the *Porto Scoutari* as a more affordable annexe, this has the best sunsets in Skála, bar none. There's a wing of standard rooms with a breakfast salon, and galleried maisonettes (including some two-bedroom apartments) across the way. Off-street scooter parking. ❻

Effie On hillside above the municipal car park, centre ℡22470 32500, ⓦwww.effiehotel.gr. Two-wing hotel with anodyne, pine-and-tile, heated/air-con rooms and private parking. Unusually, open all year. ❹

Galini secluded cul-de-sac in from ferry dock, centre ℡22470 31240, ⓕ22470 31705. Welcoming C-class hotel that provides excellent value, with the standard of furnishing (including fridges and air con) in the large, terra-cotta-tiled rooms, most with balconies, approaching B-class. ❹

Maria Hokhlakás flatlands, 150m from sea ℡22470 31201, ⓕ22470 32018. Quietly set small hotel where a pleasant front garden, air con and big sea-view balconies make up for tiny bathrooms. ❹

Porto Scoutari Melóï ℡22470 33124, ⓦwww.portoscoutari.com. Pátmos's premier hotel, this bungalow complex overlooks the beach from a hillside setting. Both the spacious individual units, with TV, phone, plus air con, and the vast common areas are furnished with mock antiques and original art, all arrayed around a large pool. A small, on-site spa should commence operation in 2006. But what really makes the place is Elina Scoutari's dedication to her customers' welfare. ❼

Pension Sydney Netiá, up the hill from *Australis* ℡22470 31689. Spartan but adequate balconied rooms with fridge and fan; helpful management. Purified drinking water (a necessity) included. ❸

Yvonni Studios Hokhlakás north hillside ℡22470 32466 or 22470 33066, ⓦwww.12net.gr/yvonni. Basic but salubrious pine-and-tile, medium-sized units with fridges, air con and oblique sea views over a hillside garden. Walk-ins should call at the gift shop next to the *Nissos Kalymnos* agency. ❸

Eating, drinking and nightlife

Restaurant options in Skála have improved from an era of surplus *souvláki/ yíros* joints or snack stalls, and no t enough full-service, sit-down places. Easily the town's most distinctive is seafood-only *Ouzeri To Hiliomodhi* (open all year), just off the start of the Hóra road, with its vegetarian *mezédhes* and delicacies such as limpets (served live, be warned), grilled octopus and salted anchovies and summer seating in a pedestrian lane. The best all-rounder (Easter to early Sept) is reckoned to be 🏃 *Vegghera*, prosaically set opposite the yacht marina, with a VIP clientele, flawless presentation for such as stuffed scorpion fish, vegetarian or seafood salads, superb desserts, and per-head bills of about €40; reservations required on ℡22470 32988. Honourable mentions go to *Yiayia*

△ Mosaic outside the monastery of Ayíou Ioánnou Theológou, Pátmos

in Konsoláto (Thurs–Tues, supper only), which has expanded from several seasons of purveying Indonesian food to generic Southeast Asian fare at slightly elevated prices, and *Pandelis* (all year), one lane inland behind Astoria Travel, where a wide-ranging menu of reliably good *mayireftá* make up for famously dour – if efficient – service.

Aside from these, you're best off heading a bit out of town; this is one island where the beach tavernas excel. **Melöï** has a decent *mayireftá* taverna, *Melloi* (alias *Stefanos*), reasonably priced and open early or late in the season, best at lunch (though it gets coach tours). Just over the hill at **Áspri** cove are two more, *Aspri* and *Kyma*: the former, just inland with a wider-ranging menu, stays open later in the season, but the latter (mid-June to Aug 31 only), fish specialist down on a concrete mole by the water, scores for its romantic setting even though presentation is basic and service often sloppy. At **Sápsila** cove, 2km southeast of Skála, *Benetos* (June–early Oct Tues–Sun supper only; summer reservations mandatory on ☎22470 33089) has since 1998 established a reputation as one of the top eateries on the island due to its Mediterranean and Pacific-Rim fusion dishes, with a stress on seafood. Budget a minimum of €33 for drink and three courses, which may include roast vegetable terrine with balsamic vinegar and raisins, baked fish fillet with risotto and Hubbard squash, *barboúni* sashimi and lemon sorbet.

Back in town, the biggest and most durable **café-bar** is the wood-panelled, barn-like *Café Arion* on the waterside, where all sorts of people sit outside, dance, or prop up the long bar. Other **nightlife** venues include the pricey *Isalos*, inland from the Italian "palace", occasionally hosting live music, and *Celine*, at the opposite end of the quay, beyond the town beach. More perhaps in sync with the tone of the island is the annual **Festival of Religious Music**, held the first two weeks of September in a hillside amphitheatre and featuring performers from Russia, Turkey and the entire Balkans.

The monasteries and Hóra

Top of your sightseeing agenda is likely to be the monastery of Ayíou Ioánnou Theológou (St John), sheltered behind massive defences in the hilltop capital of Hóra. There's a regular KTEL bus up (about 8 daily), or you can do a forty-minute walk along a beautiful old cobbled path. To find its start, proceed through Skála towards Hokhlakás, and once past the telecoms building bear left onto a lane starting opposite an ironmonger's; follow this uphill to its end on the main road – immediately opposite you'll see the cobbled path. Just over halfway, you might pause at the **monastery of Apokálypsis** (daily 8am–1.30pm, also Tues, Thurs & Sun 4–6pm; free) built around the cave where St John heard the voice of God issuing from a cleft in the rock, and where he sat dictating his words to a disciple. In the cave wall, the presumed nightly resting place of the saint's head is fenced off and outlined in beaten silver.

This is merely a foretaste of the monastery of **Ayíou Ioánnou Theológou** (same hours and admission as Apokálypsis). In 1088, the soldier-cleric Ioannis "The Blessed" Khristodhoulos was granted title to Pátmos by Byzantine emperor Alexios Komnenos; within three years he and his followers had completed the essentials of the existing monastery, the threats of piracy and the Selçuk Turks dictating a heavily fortified style. A warren of interconnecting courtyards, chapels, stairways, arcades, galleries and roof terraces, it offers a rare glimpse of a Patmian interior; hidden in the walls are fragments of an ancient Artemis temple which stood here before being destroyed by Khristodhoulos. Off to one side, the **treasury** (same hours; €6) doesn't quite justify its hefty entrance fee with its admittedly magnificent array of religious treasure, mostly medieval icons of the Cretan school. Pride of place goes to an unusual mosaic icon of Áyios Nikólaos, and the eleventh-century parchment chrysobull (edict) of Emperor Alexios Komnenos, granting the island to Khristodhoulos. Coach-tour patrons can crowd out the place at midday, so wisely go early or late. The best time to show up, besides the famous Easter observances, is September 25–26 (Feast of John the Theologian) and October 20–21 (Feast of Khristodhoulos), both marked by solemn liturgies and processions of the appropriate icon.

Hóra

The promise of security afforded by St John's stout walls spurred the growth of **HÓRA** immediately outside the fortifications. It remains architecturally homogeneous, with cobbled lanes sheltering dozens of shipowners' mansions from the island's seventeenth-to-eighteenth-century heyday. High, window-less walls and imposing wooden doors betray nothing of the opulence within: painted ceilings, *votsalotó* terraces, flagstone kitchens and carved furniture. Inevitably, touristic tattiness disfigures the main approaches to the monastery gate, but away from the principal thoroughfares are lanes that rarely see traf-fic, and by night, when the monastery ramparts are floodlit to startling effect, it's hard to think of a more beautiful Dodecanesian village. Neither should you miss the **view** from Platía Lótza (named after the remnant of an adjacent Venetian *loggia*), particularly at dawn or dusk. Landmasses to the north, going clockwise, include Ikaría, Thýmena, Foúrni, Sámos with its brooding mass of Mount Kérkis, Arkí and the double-humped Samsun Dağ (ancient Mount Mykale) in Turkey.

Hóra has several tavernas, but none are really estimable; you'll get better value at *Lotza*, just below the eponymous platía, with light meals, crêpes and desserts as well as creditable hot and alcoholic drinks. There are, however, very few places to **stay**; foreigners here are mostly long-term occupants, who have bought up and restored almost half of the crumbling mansions since the 1960s. Finding a short-term room can be a pretty thankless task, even in spring or autumn; phone well ahead for reservations at the *dhomátia* of Yeoryia Triandafyllou (☎22470 31963; ❸) on the south flank of the village, en suite with a communal terrace and self-catering kitchen, or for more comfort the *Epavli Apartments* at the east edge of Hóra, on the ring road (☎ 22470 31261, Ⓦwww.12net.gr/epavli; ❺), a restored building with superb views, high-stand-ard bathrooms and raised bed-platforms.

The rest of the island

Pátmos, as a locally published guide once memorably proclaimed, "is immense for those who know how to wander in space and time"; lesser mortals get around on foot or by bus, if not a scooter. Unfortunately, most paths have been destroyed by road-building and property development; the single **bus** offers surprisingly reliable service between Skála, Hóra, Kámbos and Gríkou.

After its extraordinary atmosphere and striking volcanic scenery, **beaches** are Patmos's principal attraction. From Konsoláto, a principal road heads east to the average beach at **Sápsila**, home not only to aforementioned *Benetos* but also to ⁂ *Studios Mathios* (☎22470 32119, Ⓦwww.mathiosapartment.gr; ❹), superior rural **accommodation** with creative furnishing and décor, extensive gardens and a lovely managing family. The continuation of this road, and another from Hóra, converge at the sandiest part of rather overdeveloped and cheerless **GRÍKOU**, the main venue for Patmian package tourism – and shut tight as a drum come mid-September. The beach itself, far from the island's best, forms a narrow strip of hard-packed sand, giving way to sand and gravel, then large pebbles at **Pétra** immediately south, whose far end is colonized by nudists – and whose near side features much the best rural **taverna** on Pátmos, ⁂ *Ktima Petra* (Easter to early Oct), where owner Mihalis is likely to personally serve your brown bread, lush salads, good bulk retsina, carefully cooked *mayireftá*, plus grills after dark. Still later, it becomes a bar with a full cocktails list.

En route to Pétra, named for its peculiar volcanic monolith on the shore, you pass hillside *Flísvos* (aka *Floros*), now rather eclipsed by nearby *Ktíma Petra* but going since the 1960s with a limited choice of inexpensive, savoury *mayireftá*, served on the terrace. They also have basic **rooms** (❷) and fancier apartments (❹) – reserve on ☏ 22470 31380, ⓕ 22470 32094.

From Hóra – but *not* Pétra – you can ride a scooter over as far as the car-park beyond the Dhiakoftí isthmus, beyond which a 20- to 25-minute walk south-west on the island's last surviving bona fide path leads to **Psilí Ámmos** beach. This is the only pure-sand cove on the island, with shade lent by tamarisks, nudism at the far south end and a good lunchtime **taverna** that occasionally does roast goat, freshly culled from the surrounding hills. The summer *kaïki* service to here from Skála departs by 10am and returns at 4 or 5pm.

Northern Pátmos

More good beaches are to be found in the **north of the island**, tucked into the startling eastern shoreline (west-facing bays are uniformly unusable owing to the prevailing wind and washed-up debris); most are accessible from side roads off the main route north from Skála. **Méloï** is handy and quite appealing, with tamarisks behind the slender belt of sand, and good snorkelling offshore. The first beach beyond Méloï, **Agriolívadho (Agriolivádhi)**, has mostly sand at its broad centre, kayak rental, and two tavernas, the better being fish specialist *O Glaros* on the south hillside. Hilltop Kámbos is the only other real village on Pátmos, the focus of scattered farms in little oases all around; **Kámbos** beach, 600m downhill, is popular with Greeks, and the most developed remote resort on the island, with seasonal, non-motorized watersports facilities and a durable taverna (*Ta Kavourakia*), though its appeal is diminished by the road just inland.

East of Kámbos are several less-frequented coves, including pebbly **Vayiá**, nudist, double-bay **Liyínou** and long, sand-and-gravel **Livádhi Yeranoú**, the latter with more tamarisks, an islet to swim out to and a very good eponymous **taverna** with something of a cult following, doing simple seafood dishes, chops, *keftédhes*, *hórta* and salads. From lower Kámbos you can also journey north to the bay of **Lámbi**, best for swimming when the prevailing wind is from the south, and renowned for an abundance of multicoloured volcanic stones – as well as another excellent **taverna**, ⚑ *Leonidas* (May to early Oct), up at Koumariá pass overlooking the bay, with terrace seating and massive portions of expertly grilled chops, and maybe a dessert on the house.

Lipsí

Of the various islets to the north and east of Pátmos, **LIPSÍ** is the largest, most interesting, most populated and the one that has the most significant summer tourist trade. The presence of a British package company (Laskarina), on-spec Italian and French travellers, and the island's appearance on minor ferry routes and catamaran/hydrofoil lines means that it's unwise to show up in peak season without a reservation (though rooms proprietors meet arrivals at other times).

During quieter months, however, Lipsí still provides an idyllic halt, its sleepy pace making plausible a purported link between the island's name and that of **Calypso**, the nymph who legendarily held Odysseus in thrall. Deep wells provide water for many small farms, but there is only one flowing spring, and pastoral appearances are deceptive – four times the full-time population of about six hundred live overseas (many in Hobart, Tasmania). Most of those who remain cluster around the fine harbour, as does the majority of food and lodging.

Of late, however, Lipsí has acquired a definite – and unwanted – link with **Dhekaeftá Noemvríou/17 November**, Greece's (and Europe's) longest-lived terrorist organization (see p.624). In July 2002, the national anti-terrorist squad swooped on the island and apprehended the group's supremo, Alexandhros Yiotopoulos (alias Mihalis Ikonomou), in the act of leaving for Sámos, eventual destination exile in Turkey. He had been living quietly here for 17 years in a faded-pink hilltop villa, now abandoned and shuttered (save for occasional visits from his wife) following his December 2003 conviction on all charges and life sentencing; ironically Yiotopoulos was much liked by the islanders for his generosity, sociability and willingness to help with bureaucratic problems.

The port settlement

All **arriving** craft use the same dock at the far west end of the port settlement, the only significant habitation on Lipsí. Among **travel agents**, Laid Back (T 22470 41141) sells tickets for Aegean Hydrofoils, both catamarans and *Nissos Kalymnos*, while Rena's Boats (T 22470 4110) by the port police reps for Samos Hydrofoils, changes money (though there's a free-standing **ATM** nearby) and organizes popular cruises to nearby islets. The **post office** is up a stairway on the attractive cathedral platía, opposite a hilariously eclectic **ecclesiastical museum** (9am–2.30pm daily; free) featuring such "relics" as earth collected from Mount Tabor and water from the Jordan River, as well as archeological finds, medieval glazed ware and two faded letters of 1824 from Greek revolutionary hero Admiral Miaoulis.

Accommodation

A prime **accommodation** choice in all senses is Nikos' and Anna's welcoming *Apartments Galini* (T 22470 41212, F 22470 41012; ❸), the first building you see above the ferry jetty; Nikos may take guests for fishing trips on request. Equally sought after, though less airy, are *Studios Kalymnos* (T 22470 41141, W www.lipsiweb.gr; ❸) in a garden on the road north out of town and run by Laid Back Holidays. Other good options not monopolized by package clients include *Rena's Rooms* (T 22470 41110 or 697 9316512; ❸), overlooking Liendoú beach – ask for room nos. 3 or 4 – and the *Glaros* (T 22470 41360; ❷) on the north hillside, with terrazzo-floored 1980s rooms sharing cooking facilities. Top of the heap is the *Aphrodite Hotel* (T 22470 41000; ❹), a studio-bungalow complex designed to accommodate package clients, though they're not averse to walk-ins at slow times.

Eating and drinking

Among nine full-service **tavernas**, mostly on or just behind the quay, the best are indisputably *O Yiannis* (early May to early Oct), an excellent all-rounder with meat/seafood grills and *mayireftá* – the only one open at lunch out of peak season – and *To Pefko* nearby, with creative oven dishes and *mezédhes*, plus service that copes well with the typical crowds. On the waterfront to either side of the *Kalypso*, *kafenía* and **ouzerís** with idiosyncratic decor (especially *Asprakis*) offer drinks and *mezédhes* outdoors at twilight – an atmospheric and almost obligatory pre-supper ritual – or even a full meal; rivals *Nikos* and *Sofoklis* operate all year. Later on, *The Rock* is the clear winner amongst a handful of **bars** for a congenial crowd and good taped music; after sunrise, *To Limani* (*Stratos*) is the place for breakfast and coffees.

Around the island

The island's **beaches** are scattered, though none is more than an hour's walk distant. Closest to town, and sandiest, are **Liendoú** and **Kámbos**, but many visitors prefer the attractive duo of **Katsadhiá** and **Papandhriá**, adjacent sand-and-pebble coves 2km south of the port by paved road, with a musical taverna-café, ♣ *Dilaila* (June–Sept), which overlooks the left-most bay here and serves such delights as rosemary fish, saffron rice, *fáva* and salad with balsamic dressing. You can **stay** locally at Scottish-run, hillside *Katsadia Studios* (☎22470 41317 or 697 87 09 558; ❸), well designed and with sweeping views.

Another paved road leads 4km west from town to protected **Platýs Yialós**, a small, very shallow, sandy bay with a single taverna (mid-June to late Sept). During this period a pair of white transit vans provides a **minibus** service from the port to all the points cited above (there's also a single **taxi**); otherwise rent a **scooter** from one of two outlets and point them towards isolated east–coast beaches without facilities. Of these, **Hokhlakoúra** consists of rather coarse shingle (finer pebbles at mid-strand); nearby **Turkómnima** is much sandier and shadier, if windy, while **Xirókambos** is calmer if treeless. A final ten-minute path scramble gets you from a rough track's end to **Monodhéndhri**, on the northeast coast, notable only for its lone juniper tree and nudist practice – though there's a superior, nameless cove just to the right.

The road network, paved or otherwise, rather limits opportunities for genuine path **walks** through the undulating countryside, dotted with blue-domed churches. The most challenging route heads west, high above the coast, from the far end of Kámbos bay to the bay of **Kímisi** (3hr round-trip), where the religious **hermit Filippos**, long a cult figure amongst foreign visitors, used to dwell in a tiny monastery above the shore, next to the single island spring. A particularly steep, ugly road was bulldozed in from the north in 1999 and later paved, disturbing his solitude; Filippos moved to town and died, aged 85, in 2002, though a small memorial at the entry to the monastery grounds commemorates him.

Arkí and Maráthi

About two-thirds the size of Lipsí, **Arkí** is considerably more primitive, lacking properly stocked shops or much in the way of a distinct village. Just 45 permanent inhabitants eke out a living here, mostly engaged in fishing or goat/sheep-herding, though catering for yacht parties attracted here by the superb anchorage is increasingly important. Arkí is a frequent stop on the *Nissos Kalymnos*, which you can use to make cheap day-trips from Pátmos; post *kaïkia* (4 weekly) or excursion boats sail right into the main harbour to dock at the inner quay. Of the three **tavernas** on the round harbourside platía, the more frequented two – *Nikolas* (☎22470 32477; B&B; ❸) and *O Trypas* (aka *Tou Manoli*; ☎22470 32230; ❷) – provide **accommodation**; those of *O Trypas* – with fridges and some with stone floors – are perhaps better value. *Nikolas* has home-made puddings, while *O Trypas* doubles as the happening music pub, courtesy of the owner's enormous collection of CDs and tapes – and does very decent fish meals. But perhaps the most accomplished fish grills are to be had at ♣ *Apolavsi*, one inlet southeast at **Dhídhymi Ormí**; yachties (and land-lubbers) in the know come here for the indomitable Angeliki's garden vegetables, slow-cooked fish, octopus and other *mezédhes* at attractive prices.

You can swim at the "Blue Lagoon" of **Tiganákia** at the southeast tip of the island, but other beaches on Arkí take some resourcefulness to find. The more obvious ones are the succession of covelets at **Pateliá** by the ferry jetty, or tiny **Limnári** bay on the northeast coast which fits four or five bathers at a pinch, a 25-minute walk away via the highest house in the settlement.

The nearest large, sandy, tamarisk-shaded beach is just offshore on the islet of **Maráthi**, where more **tavernas** caters to day-trippers who come several times a week from Pátmos or Lipsí. *Marathi* (T22470 31580; all year; ❷) is the more traditional, cosy outfit, with waterside seating and simple, adequate rooms; *Pantelis* (T22470 32609; June–Oct; ❷) is plusher but more commercially minded – and apt to lock the compound's outer gate at 11pm if you go drinking at his rival's bar. In summer 2005, a third taverna between the two began operations.

Agathoníssi

The small, steep-sided, waterless islet of **Agathoníssi (Gaïdharo)** is too remote – much closer to Turkey than Pátmos, in fact – to be a popular target of day-excursions, though a few are half-heartedly offered on Sámos. Intrepid Greeks and Italians form its main clientele, along with a steady trickle of yachts. Even though the *Nissos Kalymnos* (and two weekly hydrofoils) appear regularly, you should count on staying for at least two days, especially if the wind's up. Despite the lack of springs (cisterns are ubiquitous, topped up by tanker shipments from Rhodes), the island is greener and more fertile than apparent from the sea; mastic, carob and scrub oak on the heights overlook two arable plains in the west. Just 146 people live here, down from several hundred before World War II, but those who've opted to stay seem determined to make a go of raising goats or fishing (more accurately fish-farming), and there are almost no abandoned or neglected dwellings.

Most of the population lives in the hamlet of **Megálo Horió**, just visible on the ridge above the harbour of **ÁYIOS YEÓRYIOS**, and eye-level with tiny **Mikró Horió**. Except for two fitfully working café-restaurants in Megálo Horió, all amenities are in the port. Among five **accommodation** choices there, most preferable are *Rooms Theoloyia Yiameou* (T22470 29005; ❷), the vine-patioed *Hotel Maria Kamitsi* (T22470 29003; ❷), or the *Aganandi* above the *Limanaki* taverna (T22470 29019; ❷). Eating out, you'll almost certainly try all three full-service **tavernas**: *George's* for fish, *Seagull/Glaros* for meat dishes, *Limanaki* as the cheap-and-cheerful Greeks' hangout. There is no post office, bank or ATM; ferry and hydrofoil tickets must be bought in advance at a little booth opposite the *Café-Bar Yetoussa*, the best **bar** and also a good source of breakfast.

With no wheeled transport for rent, exploring involves **walking** along the cement- or dirt-road network, or following a limited number of tracks and paths. If you don't swim at the port, which has the largest beach, you walk ten minutes southwest along a track to shingle-gravel **Spiliás**, or continue another quarter-hour along a faint path over the ridge to **Gaïdhourávlakos**, where nudists enjoy a finer gravel cove. Bays in the east of the island, all served by the paved road system (occasionally supplemented by trails), include **Thóli** in the far southeast, with good snorkelling and some morning shade, and **Pálli** on the opposite shore of the same bay, a small but pristine fine-pebble cove reached by fifteen-minute walk down from the trans-island road. Also at **Thóli**, an hour-plus trek away, you can see an arcaded Byzantine structure, probably a combination granary and trading post, and by far the most venerable sight on Agathoníssi.

Travel details

To simplify the lists below, some companies are summarized here. Agoudimos provides a once-weekly link between Rhodes, Kós, Kálymnos, Sámos and Thessaloníki in each direction, while LANE also plies once weekly (north, then south) between Rhodes, Kós, Kálymnos, Sámos, Híos, Lésvos, Límnos and Alexandhroúpoli.

Nissos Kalymnos

The small, slow but reliable **Nissos Kalymnos** (cars carried) is the most regular lifeline of the smaller islands between Kálymnos and Sámos – it visits them all several times weekly between mid-March and mid-January. Its movements are as follows:

Mon, Wed, Fri & Sun Leaves Kálymnos 7am for Léros (Lakkí), Lipsí, Pátmos, Arkí, Agathoníssi, Sámos (Pythagório; arrives 2.30pm). Turns around more or less immediately and retraces steps through the same islands (in reverse order), arriving Kálymnos 10.30pm.

Tues, Thur & Sat Leaves Kálymnos 7am, arrives Astypálea 10am, turns around almost immediately to arrive Kálymnos at 1.30pm.

Large ferries and local services

The following frequencies are only valid for the period mid-June to mid-September.

Astypálea 2 weekly to Kálymnos, Amorgós, Náxos, Dhonoússa, Páros, Kós, Rhodes and Pireás on GA; 1–2 weekly to Kálymnos, Páros and Náxos on Blue Star; 1 weekly to Níssyros, Tílos and Sými on GA.

Hálki 3 weekly to Ródhos Town, Kárpathos (both ports), Kássos, Crete (Sitía & Áyios Nikólaos), Santoríni and Mílos on LANE. Once-daily *kaïki* (6am) to Rhodes (Kámiros Skála).

Kálymnos Similar ferry service to Kós, except no Blue Star service to Rhodes, Pátmos or Léros, plus 3 daily roll-on-roll-off ferries, well-spaced, to Masti- hári; 5 passenger-only speed-boats daily to Masti- hári; daily morning *kaïki* to Psérimos; and a daily *kaïki* (1pm) from Myrtiés to Xirókambos on Léros.

Kárpathos (both ports) and **Kássos** 3 weekly with each other, Hálki, Crete (Áyios Nikólaos & Sitía), Mílos, Santoríni and Ródhos Town, on LANE.

Kastellórizo (Méyisti) 1–2 weekly to Rhodes, then Pireás indirectly, on LANE.

Kós at least daily to Rhodes and Pireás on GA or Blue Star; 6 weekly to Léros and Pátmos on GA or Blue Star; 2 weekly to Tílos, Níssyros, Astypálea and Sými on GA; 3 weekly to Amorgós on Blue Star or GA; 1–2 weekly to Mýkonos and Sýros on Blue star or GA; 1 weekly to Náxos and Páros on GA; 5 weekly (Mon–Fri) *kaïki* to Níssyros; daily islanders' *kaïki* from Kardhámena to Níssyros.

Léros 6 weekly to Pireás, Pátmos, Kós and Rhodes on GA or Blue Star; 4 weekly to Kálymnos on GA or Blue Star; 2 weekly to Sýros on Blue Star or GA; 1 weekly to Mýkonos, Tílos and Níssyros on GA; seasonal daily excursion boats from Ayía Marína to Lipsí and Léros (2pm), and from Xirókambos to Myrtiés on Kálymnos (7.30am).

Níssyros and Tílos 1–2 weekly with each other, Sými, Rhodes, Kós, Astypálea, Amorgós, Náxos, Páros and Pireás on GA. Excursion boats between Níssyros and Kós as follows: to Kard- hámena and Kós Town nearly daily at 3.30–4pm (these are seasonal). The islanders' less expensive "shopping" *kaïkia* the *Panayia Spiliani* leaves Mon–Fri at 7.15am for Kós Town, while the *Ayios Konstandinos* and/or Nisyros goes daily at 7am to Kardhámena. Unless you're bound for the airport it's not cheaper to use Kardhámena services when you consider the cost of a bus to Kós Town.

Pátmos Similar ferry service to Léros, with the addi- tion of tourist *kaïkia* to Sámos (Pythagório), Lipsí and Léros on a daily basis; to Arkí and Maráthi 4 weekly.

Rhodes at least daily to Kós and Pireás on GA or Blue Star; 6 weekly to Léros and Pátmos on GA or Blue Star; 4 weekly to Kálymnos on GA; 3 weekly to Hálki, Kárpathos, Kássos, Crete (Sitía & Áyios Nikólaos), Santoríni and Mílos on LANE; 2–3 weekly to Amorgós on GA or Blue Star; 2 weekly to Astypálea on GA; 2 weekly to Sýros on Blue Star; 1 weekly to Mýkonos on Blue Star; 1–2 weekly to Sými, Tílos, Níssyros on GA; 1 weekly to Náxos, Dhonoússa and Páros on GA.

Sými 1 weekly to Rhodes, Tílos, Níssyros, Kós, Kálymnos, Léros, Pátmos, Astypálea, Amorgós, Náxos, Páros and Pireás on GA; 2–3 daily catama- rans or hydrofoil run by ANES to Rhodes.

Catamarans

Three high-speed, long-distance **catamarans** ply the Dodecanese: The *Dodekanisos Express*, the co- owned *Dodekanisos Pride* and the *Sea Star*.

Dodekanisos Express

The *Dodekanisos Express*, based on Rhodes, can carry 4–5 cars and a slightly larger number of two-wheelers; it's a sleek, 2000-built, Norwegian craft, with a limited amount of aft deck space.

High-season schedules are as follows: Tues–Sun, 8.30am departure from Rhodes to Kós, Kálymnos, Léros, Lipsí and Pátmos; it returns from Pátmos at 1.30–1.45pm, arriving at Rhodes 6.30pm. On Sun & Wed it makes a stop at Sými, in each direction; on Mon it makes a single journey to Kastellórizo, arriving 11am, returning at 4pm. In spring or autumn there is no Kastellórizo service, and services to Lipsí may be infrequent.

Dodekanisos Pride

The *Express's* 2005-built sister ship, *Dodekanisos Pride*, is based on Pátmos but nearly identical in all other respects. Schedule patterns are as follows: departure from Pátmos daily at 6am, arriving at Rhodes via Lipsí, Léros, Kálymnos, Kós and Sými (Panormítis, not Yialós, on Sun), at 10.40am, leaving for Pámos via the same islands at 3.30pm.

Sea Star

The *Sea Star* does not carry vehicles and badly serves only the route Rhodes–Tílos, with occasional extensions to Níssyros or Hálki; it frequently breaks down and may in fact not see the 2006 season through. Schedules are so user-hostile that it's impossible to generalize or predict meaningfully, other than saying it serves Níssyros at best twice weekly (usually Mon and/or Wed), Hálki at weekends, and spends frequent, 24-hour spells idle on Rhodes for maintenance and/or the maximum convenience of the crew.

Hydrofoils

Two **hydrofoil** companies, Aegean Flying Dolphins and Samos Hydrofoils, serve the Dodecanese between mid-May and mid-Oct, operating out of Rhodes, Kálymnos, Kós and Sámos.

Aegean has three remaining active craft; schedules are complicated but fairly predictable. In peak season, there is a daily link from Kós to Rhodes and back, south in the morning and north in the evening; twice a week stops will be made at intervening islands (Sými, Níssyros, Tílos). Another craft leaves Kálymnos at 7.20am for Kós, Kálymnos, Léros, Lipsí, Pátmos and Pythagório on Sámos, returning via the same islands at 1.20pm; while the third craft, based in Pythagório, leaves Kós between 2.15 and 2.45pm, returning to Sámos via Kálymnos, Léros, Lipsí and Pátmos. Twice a week this craft calls at Agathoníssi in each direction as well. For current routes and schedules, phone ☎22420 25551 (Kós), ☎22410 21690 (Rhodes) or ☎22730 25065 (Sámos).

Samos Hydrofoils has just one active craft, which provides an 8am service out of Pythagório as far as Kós and all intervening Dodecanese 3 days weekly,

but goes no further than Lipsí or Léros most other days, owing to extensive detours to Foúrni and Ikaría.

International ferries

NB: In all cases below, the cost of Turkish visas, required by many nationals, is not included.

Kálymnos to Bodrum, Turkey (1hr 45min), departing at 7–8am; €30 day-return, though €20 "specials" 2 days weekly.

Kós 2–14 weekly to Bodrum, Turkey (45min). Greek boat leaves 9am &10am, returns 4pm & 5pm; additional out-and-back 11am/6pm on Tues & Sat, Bodrum market days; €25 return, Greek tax inclusive, no Turkish port tax. Slightly pricier Turkish boat (*Fahri Kaptan*) or hydrofoil departs Bodrum 9am or so, leaves Kós 4.30pm; this provides the only service in winter.

Kastellórizo 2 weekly (Mon & Fri) to Kaş, Turkey; €15 one way or day return; €32 maximum (bargain with boatman if necessary) if you begin travel from the Turkish side.

Rhodes Daily May–Nov to Marmaris, Turkey (1hr) by Greek catamaran at 8–9am, Turkish catamaran at 4pm; €49 day return, €35 plus €19 Greek tax plus €14 Turkish tax open return, €25 plus €19 Greek tax one way. Anka Travel at Gallías 13 in Neohóri (☎22410 26835) is the central agent for the Turkish craft, though most agencies (such as Triton Travel) will readily sell you passage. Also, one daily Turkish hydrofoil to Fethiye in late afternoon; June–Sept; €45 one way.

Sými Up to 3 weekly *kaïkia* (80min, €40 return plus $12 Turkish tax) and 1 hydrofoil or catamaran (40min, €30 return plus Turkish tax); Sat is the most reliable day.

Flights

NB: All are on Olympic Aviation/Olympic Airways unless stated otherwise.

Astypálea 4 weekly to Athens; 3 weekly to Léros, Kós and Rhodes on the same plane.

Kárpathos At least 2 daily to Rhodes; 9 weekly to Kássos; 5 weekly to Athens.

Kássos 9 weekly to Kárpathos and Rhodes.

Kastellórizo (Meyísti) 5 weekly to Rhodes.

Kós 3–4 daily to Athens on Olympic, 3 daily on Aegean; 3 weekly to Astypálea, Léros and Rhodes.

Léros 1 daily to Athens; 3 weekly to Astypálea, Kós and Rhodes.

Rhodes Olympic: 4–5 daily to Athens; at least daily to Iráklion; 3 weekly to Kós, Léros and Astypálea with the same plane; 2 weekly to Sámos and Hios; 5 weekly to Lésvos and Límnos; 8–9 weekly to Thessaloníki. Aegean: 6 daily to Athens; 1 daily to Thessaloníki.

THE DODECANESE | Travel details

The East and North Aegean

Highlights

✳ **Vathý, Sámos** The two-wing archeological museum is among the best in the islands. See p.398

✳ **Ikaría** Western Ikaría has superb beaches and an idiosyncratic lifestyle. See p.414

✳ **Southern Híos** The architecturally unique *mastihohoriá* (mastic villages) have a Middle Eastern feel. See p.423

✳ **Sykiás Olýmbon cave, Híos** Superb formations make this multilevelled cave one of the finest in the islands. See p.425

✳ **Thermal baths, Lésvos** There are four well-kept Ottoman-era spas, ideal for relaxing in. See pp.437, 440 & 447

✳ **Mólyvos, northern Lésvos** This castle-crowned resort village is arguably the most beautiful on the island. See p.444

✳ **Mýrina, Límnos** A characterful port town with a fine castle – and great wines to sample. See p.450

✳ **Samothráki** Remote Samothráki's Sanctuary of the Great Gods is surrounded by natural grandeur. See p.458

✳ **Alykí, Thássos** A beautifully situated beach flanked by ancient and Byzantine archeological sites. See p.466

△ Mýrina harbour, Límnos

5

The East and North Aegean

he seven substantial islands and four minor islets scattered between the Aegean coast of Asia Minor and northeastern Greece form a rather arbitrary archipelago. Although there are some similarities in architecture and landscape, the strong individual character of each island is far more striking. Despite their proximity to modern Turkey, members of the group bear relatively few signs of an Ottoman heritage, especially when compared with Rhodes and Kós. There's the occasional mosque, often shorn of its minaret, but by and large the enduring Greekness of these islands is testimony to the four-millennium-long Hellenic presence in Asia Minor, which ended only in 1923. This heritage has been regularly referred to by the Greek government in an intermittent propaganda war with Turkey over the sovereignty of these far-flung outposts. Tensions here have often been worse than in the Dodecanese, aggravated by potential undersea oil deposits in the straits between the islands and the Anatolian mainland. The Turks have also persistently demanded that Límnos, astride the sea lanes to and from the Dardanelles, be demilitarized, and only since the start of the new millennium has Greece shown signs of complying.

Despite the growth of tourism, large tracts of land remain off-limits as army or air force bases. But as in the Dodecanese, local tour operators do a thriving business shuttling passengers for inflated tariffs between the easternmost islands and the Turkish coast with its amazing archeological sites and busy resorts. Most of these islands' main ports and towns are not quaint, picturesque spots, but urbanized administrative, military and commercial centres; you should suppress any initial impulse to take the next boat out, and press on into the interiors. Bear in mind that the tourist season this far north is short – early July to early September – with many restaurants and lodgings shut down outside this period.

Sámos ranks as the most visited island of the group but, once you leave the crowded resorts behind, is still arguably the most verdant and beautiful, even after a devastating July 2000 fire. **Ikaría** to the west remains relatively unspoilt, if a minority choice, and nearby **Foúrni** is (except in summer) a haven for determined solitaries, as are the Híos satellites **Psará** and **Inoússes**, neither of which has any package tourism. **Híos** proper offers far more cultural interest than any neighbours to the south, but the development of tourism was, until the late 1980s, deliberately retarded. **Lésvos** may not impress initially, though once you get a feel for its old-fashioned Anatolian ambience you may find it hard to leave.

Thessaloníki

Thessaloníki

Kými

Rafína

Lávrio

Pireás

İstanbul

TURKEY

Kavála
Keramotí
Skála Prínou
Thássos
Thássos
Limenária
Alexandhroúpoli

Kamariótissa
Hóra
Samothráki

Gökçeada
(Imbros)
Çanakkale

N

Límnos
Mýrina
Moúdhros

Bozcaada
(Tenedos)

Ay. Efstrátios

Mólyvos
Sígri
Eressós
Ayiássos
Polikhnítos
Plomári
Lésvos
Mytilíni
Ayvalık
TURKEY

Skýros

Psará

Mármaro
Inoússes
Inoússes
Volissós
Híos
Híos
Çeşme
Pyrgí

İZMİR

Ándhros

Efes
(Ephesus)
Kuşadası

Karlóvassi
Vathý
Pythagório
Sámos

Tínos

Áy. Kírykos
Évdhilos
Ikaría

Foúrni

Arkí
Agathoníssi

Mýkonos

Sýros

Pátmos
Lipsí
Farmakónissi

Léros

0   50 km

Páros & Náxos

By contrast, virtually no foreigners and few Greeks visit **Áyios Efstrátios**, and with good reason. **Límnos** to the north is much livelier, but its appeal is confined mostly to the area immediately around the attractive port town. To the north, Samothráki and Thássos are relatively isolated from the others (though the former now has ferry links with Límnos, Lésvos and Híos), and remain easier to visit from northern Greece, which administers them. **Samothráki** (officially in Thrace) has one of the most dramatic seaward approaches of any Greek island, and one of the more important ancient sites. **Thássos** (technically belonging to eastern Macedonia) is more varied, with sandy beaches, mountain villages and minor archeological sites.

Sámos

The lush and seductive island of Sámos was formerly joined to Asia Minor, until sundered from Mount Mykale opposite by Ice Age cataclysms; the resulting 2500-metre strait is now the narrowest distance between Greece and Turkey in the Aegean, except at Kastellórizo. There's little tangible evidence of it today, but Sámos was also once the **wealthiest island** in the Aegean and, under the patronage of the tyrant Polykrates, home to a thriving intellectual community: Epicurus, Pythagoras, Aristarkhos and Aesop were among the residents. Decline set in as the star of Classical Athens was in the ascendant, though Sámos's status improved in early Byzantine times when it constituted its own imperial administrative district. Towards the end of the fifteenth century, the Genoese abandoned the island to the mercies of pirates; following their attacks, Sámos remained **almost uninhabited** until 1562, when an Ottoman admiral received permission from the sultan to repopulate it with Greek Orthodox settlers recruited from various corners of the empire.

The heterogeneous descent of today's islanders largely explains an enduring identity crisis and a rather thin topsoil of indigenous culture. Most of the village names are either clan surnames, or adjectives indicating origins elsewhere – constant reminders of **refugee descent**. Consequently there is no distinctly Samian music, dance or dress, and little that's original in the way of cuisine and architecture. The Samiotes compensated somewhat for this deracination by fighting fiercely for independence during the 1820s, but despite their accomplishments in sinking a Turkish fleet in the narrow strait and annihilating a landing army, the Great Powers handed the island back to the Ottomans in 1830, with the consoling proviso that it be **semi-autonomous**, ruled by an appointed Christian prince. This period, referred to as the *Iyimonía* (Hegemony), was marked by a mild renaissance in fortunes, courtesy of the hemp and (especially) tobacco trades. However, union with Greece in 1912, the ravages of a bitter World War II occupation and mass emigration effectively reversed the recovery until tourism appeared on the horizon during the 1980s.

Today the Samian economy is dependent on **package tourism**, far too much of it in places; Kokkári, and the southeastern and southwestern coasts, have pretty much been surrendered to holiday-makers, although the more rugged northwestern part has retained some of its undeveloped grandeur. The sedate, couples-orientated clientele is overwhelmingly Scandinavian, Dutch, German and Swiss, with a growing number of Brits, Belgians and even Czechs or Slovenians; the absence of an official campsite on such a large island, tame nightlife a world away from that in the Dodecanese and Cyclades, and phalanxes of self-catering villas hint at the forty-something custom expected.

SÁMOS

Kuşadası (Turkey)

Kuşadası (Turkey)

TURKEY

Nissí

Ayía Paraskeví

Kalámi

 Zoödhóhou Piyís

Kamára

Ayía Zóni

Paleókastro

Kérveli

Posidhónio

Kadúna (Klíma)

Vathý

Áno Vathý

Psilí Ámmos

Mykáli

Panayía Spilianí

Pythagório

Roman Baths

Efpalínio Óryma

Hóra

Glyfádha

Potokáki

Heraion

Iréon

Petrokáravo

Kerátos

Kokkári

Tsamadhoú

Lemonákia

Aviákia

Tzaboú

Ayios Konstandinos

Platanákia

Vrondianís

Mytilíni

Timíou Stavroú

Megális Panayías

Mýli

Kyriakoú

Tsópela

Pnáka

Vourliótes

Mt Ámbelos 1153m

Pándhrossos

Mavratzéi

Koumaradhéi

Pagóndas

Spatharéi

Ambelos

Stavrinídhes

Valeondádhes

Manolátes

Pýrgos

Neohóri

Piáki

Kondakéika

Kímisis Theotókou

Idhroússa

Plátanos

Koútsi

Koumêíka

Baláos

Péfkos

Ávios Nikólaos

Karlóvassi

Limáni Paleó

Meséo

Lékka

Kosmadhéï

Kastaniá

Plátanos

Marathókambos

Órmos Marathokámbou

Votsalákia

Psilí Ámmos

Limniónas

Ríva

Metamórfosis

Potámi

Dhrakéï

Mikró Seïtáni

Megálo Seïtáni

Ayía Triádha

Mt Kérkis 1437m

Evangelistrías

Panayía Makriní

Kallithéa

Vársamo

N

0   5 km

Híos & Lésvos

Ikaría & Foúrni

Arkí, Lipsí & Agathoníssi

Pátmos & Foúrni

Pátmos & Foúrni

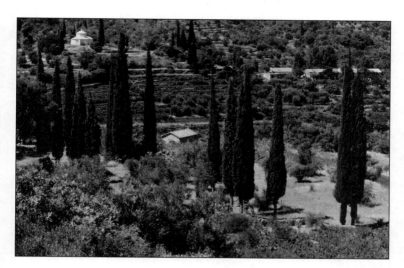

△ Vine and olive terraces, Sámos

The heavily developed areas have unsurprisingly been the most afflicted by **repeated wildfires**, in particular one which lasted a week in July 2000, destroying twenty percent of the island's forest and orchards, and over ninety dwellings; if you take into account other areas that had been torched since 1987, Sámos is indeed about half-scorched. The trees as ever will be a half-century in returning, and the tourist market – admittedly for other reasons also – has not overcome this stigma. Volunteer fire-lookouts with pumper-trucks have now sprouted at critical points, but it does seem a case of locking the stable door after the horse has bolted.

Arrival and getting around

Sámos' 2003-enlarged **airport** (5 car rental booths, no ATM) lies 14km southwest of Vathý and 3km west of Pythagório. There is no airport bus service; **taxi** fares to various points are stipulated on prominent placards, and in high season taxis to the airport or ferry docks must be booked several hours in advance. There are no fewer than three **ferry ports**: Karlóvassi in the west, plus Vathý and Pythagório in the east, making the island a major hub for travel in every direction. All ferries between Pireás and Sámos call at both Karlóvassi and Vathý, as does the small, locally based Samos Spirit, linking the island with Foúrni and Ikaría. Vathý also receives the LANE and/or GA sailings between northern Greece and the Dodecanese, via most intervening islands, the weekly Agoudimos ferry between Thessaloníki and Rhodes, plus small boats from Kuşadasi. Pythagório sees four regular weekly ferry connections from as far south as Kálymnos in the Dodecanese, as well as hosting the **hydrofoil services** to all the Dodecanese down to Kós, and forays over to Foúrni and southern Ikaría.

The **bus terminals** in Pythagório and Vathý lie within walking distance of the ferry dock; at Karlóvassi, you must make your own way the 3km into town from the port. The weekday KTEL service itself is excellent along the Pythagório–Vathý and Vathý–Kokkári–Karlóvassi routes, but poor at weekends or for other destinations; with numerous car- and motorbike-rental outlets, it's easy to find a good deal all year round.

Vathý

Lining the steep northeastern shore of a deep bay, beachless **VATHÝ** (often confusingly referred to as "Sámos", like the island) is a busy provincial town which grew from a minor anchorage after 1830, when it replaced Hóra as the island's capital. It's an unlikely, somewhat ungraceful resort, which has seen numerous hotels gone bankrupt or converted to apartments since the late 1990s, and is minimally interesting aside from tiers of surviving Neoclassical houses and the hill suburb of **ÁNO VATHÝ**, a separate community of tottering, tile-roofed houses.

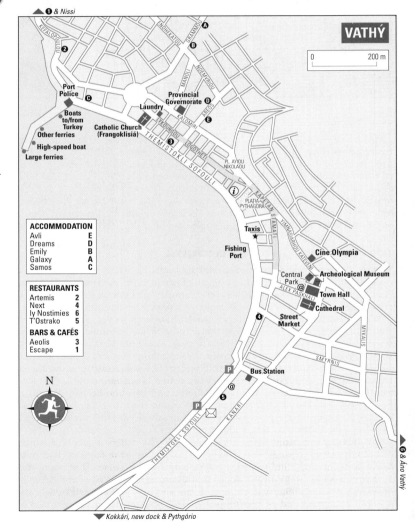

1 & Nissi

VATHÝ

0   200 m

Port Police **C**

Boats to/from Turkey

Other ferries

High-speed boat

Large ferries

Provincial Governorate **D**

Laundry

Catholic Church (Frangoklisiá)

PL. AYIOU NIKOLAOU

THEMISTOKLI SOFOULI

PLATIA PYTHAGORA

Taxis

Fishing Port

Cine Olympia

Central Park

Archeological Museum

Town Hall

Cathedral

Street Market

Bus Station

ACCOMMODATION

Avli	**E**
Dreams	**D**
Emily	**B**
Galaxy	**A**
Samos	**C**

RESTAURANTS

Artemis	**2**
Next	**4**
Iy Nostimies	**6**
T'Ostrako	**5**

BARS & CAFÉS

Aeolis	**3**
Escape	**1**

N

6 & Áno Vathý

Kokkári, new dock & Pythgório

The only real must is the excellent **archeological museum** (Tues–Sun 8.30am–3pm; €3), set behind the small central park beside the nineteenth-century town hall. One of the best provincial collections in Greece is housed in both the old Paskhallion building and a modern wing across the way, specially constructed to house the star exhibit: a majestic, five-metre-tall *kouros* discovered out at the Heraion sanctuary. The *kouros*, the largest free-standing effigy to survive from ancient Greece, was dedicated to Apollo, but found together with a devotional mirror to Mut (the Egyptian equivalent of Hera) from a Nile workshop, one of only two discovered in Greece to date.

In the compelling **small-objects collection** of the Paskhallion, more votive offerings of Egyptian design prove trade and pilgrimage links between Sámos and the Nile valley going back to the eighth century BC. The Mesopotamian and Anatolian origins of other artwork confirm the exotic trend, most tellingly in a case full of ivory miniatures: Perseus and Medusa in relief, a kneeling, perfectly formed mini-*kouros*, a pouncing lion and a drinking horn ending in a bull's head. The most famous local artefacts are the dozen-plus bronze griffin-heads, for which Sámos was the major centre of production in the seventh century BC; mounted on the edge of bronze cauldrons, they were believed to ward off evil spirits.

Arrival, information and transport

From the **ferry dock** the shore boulevard – Themistoklí Sofoúli – describes a 1300-metre arc around the bay. About 400m along is pedestrianized Platía Pythagóra, distinguished by its lion statue; about 800m along there's a major turning inland to the **KTEL** terminal, a chaos of buses at a perennially cluttered intersection by the ticket office. The minimally useful **tourist information** office is at 25-Martíou 4 (May–Oct Mon–Fri 9am–2pm; winter sporadic hours), only worth a stop for bus schedules and accommodation listings. If you've arrived with your own vehicle, use the free **parking lots** shown on the map – there's never any street parking to be had.

The most comprehensive waterfront **ferry/travel agent** for independent travellers is By Ship, with two branches – one at the base of the jetty (☎22730 80445), and one about 300m southeast (☎22730 25065) – selling tickets for most ferry lines, the hydrofoil and airlines. An exception is the Agoudimos ferry, represented solely by Nautica (☎22730 25133). Vathý is chock-a-block with **bike-** and **car-rental** franchises, with supply in excess of demand keeping rates reasonable. Among ten or so agenices, three to try are Aramis/Sixt (☎22730 22682) at Themistoklí Sofoúli 7, Reliable (phone as for By Ship), with branches island-wide, or Hertz (Rhenia Tours) at no. 17 (☎ 22730 24771). Other amenities include the **post office** inconveniently remote on Themistoklí Sofoúli, six waterfront **banks** with ATMs and a self-serve **laundry** on pedestrianized Lykoúrgou Logothéti. The most durable **Internet café** is Dhiavlos, on Themistoklí Sofoúli near the KTEL, though there's another in the café of the central gardens.

Accommodation

Most **accommodation** available to independent travellers is clustered in the hillside district of Katsoúni, more or less directly above the ferry dock; except in August, you'll have little trouble finding affordable vacancies. Budget choices include *Pension Dreams*, up a stair-lane at Áreos 9 (☎22730 24350; ❷), with well-kept en-suite rooms with fridges, or the superior ⚘ *Pension Avli* (☎22730 22939; ❷), a wonderful period piece at Áreos 2, the former convent school of the French nuns who ran the local Catholic church until 1973; affable owner Spyros is an excellent source of information on local eating and drinking opportunities.

For more comfort, go for proper hotels such as the surprisingly affordable *Galaxy* (℡22730 22665; ❸), at Angéou 1 near the top of Katsoúni, set in garden surroundings and with a small pool, though avoid being sent to their lower-standard annexe opposite. If they're full, try the sympathetic *Emily*, just downhill at the top of Grámmou (℡22730 24691; open all year; ❹), a small outfit with a roof garden and plenty of parking out front. The *Samos Hotel* (℡22730 28377; ❹), right by the ferry dock but with double glazing against noise, also works all year, with a plunge-pool in the roof garden.

Eating, drinking and nightlife

The only **waterfront tavernas** worth a second glance, open all year, are *T'Ostrako* at Themistoklí Sofoúli 141, doing shellfish, a few scaly fish of the day and an ample selection of *orektiká*; *Next* at no. 97, reckoned the best of several local pizzerias; and *Artemis* near the dock at Kefalopoúlou 4, good for a pre-ferry lunch or a leisurely supper, though opt for *mezédhes* (especially their *fáva*) and grills rather than their oven dishes. Way up high in Áno Vathý, *Iy Nostimies* (aka *Tassos*; dinner all year, lunch too Oct–May) by the school and community office is well loved for its creative vegetarian dishes, seafood and the odd meat platter.

Vathý's more active **nightlife** revolves around its waterfront bars, the longest lived of these being the ground floor of the *Aeolis Hotel*, where the town's beau monde have their evening *mezédhes* and ouzo, or *Escape*, on a seaview terrace at Kefalopoúlou 9 (north of the jetty). Other, indoor clubs come and go every six months. Cine Olympia, inland on Yimnasiárhou Katevéni, is plushly fitted and operates all year with a variable programme of **films**.

Around Vathý

The immediate environs of Vathý offer some modest beaches and small hamlets, though you'll usually need your own transport to visit them. Two kilometres east and uphill spreads the vast inland plateau of **Vlamarí**, devoted to vineyards and supporting the hamlets of Ayía Zóni and Kamára (plus an increasing number of bad-taste modern villas); from Kamára you can climb up a partly cobbled path to the clifftop **monastery of Zoödhóhou Piyís** (daily except 2–5pm) for superb views across the end of the island to Turkey.

As you head southeast from Vathý along the main island loop road, the triple chapel at **Trís Ekklisíes** marks an important junction, with another fork 100m along the left-hand turning. Bearing left twice takes you through the hilltop village of Paleókastro, where the unassuming-looking *Leonidas* on the square does surprisingly competent snacks. Some 3km beyond is another junction; forking left yet again brings you after another 3km to the quiet, striking bay of **Kérveli**, with a small beach, a pair of **tavernas** by the water (the friendly *Sea and Dolphin* has good *mezédhes* and *soúma*, the local spirit, as well as mains) and another characterful favourite with simple grills only, *Iy Kryfi Folia*, about 500m uphill along the access road. Taking the right fork leads to **Posidhónio**, with an even smaller beach and another taverna, *Kerkezos*, which takes its cooking more seriously, though it's expensive. Bearing right at the junction before Paleókastro leads to the beaches of Mykáli and Psilí Ámmos. **Mykáli**, 1 km of windswept sand and gravel, has three package hotels; the best place to try on spec here is *Villa Barbara* (☏22730 25192; ④), which has apartments behind the *Sirenes Beach* hotel. **Psilí Ámmos**, further east around the headland, is a crowded, sandy cove backed by several tavernas, much the best of which are *Psili Ammos*, on the far right as you face the sea, with good seafood, salads and meat grills. If you swim to the islet, beware of strong currents which sweep through the narrow straits.

Pythagório and around

Most traffic south of Vathý heads for **PYTHAGÓRIO**, the island's premier resort, renamed in 1955 to honour native son Pythagoras, ancient mathematician, philosopher and mystic. Until then it was known as Tigáni (Frying Pan) – in midsummer you'll learn why. The sixth-century BC tyrant Polykrates had his capital here, now subject to sporadic excavations which have forced modern Pythagório to expand northeast and uphill. The village core of cobbled lanes and thick-walled mansions abuts a small **harbour**, fitting almost perfectly into the confines of Polykrates' ancient jetty, but today devoted almost entirely to pleasure craft and overpriced cocktail bars.

Sámos's most complete **castle**, the nineteenth-century *pýrgos* of local chieftain Lykourgos Logothetis, overlooks both the town and the shoreline. Logothetis, together with a certain "Kapetan Stamatis" and Admiral Kanaris of Psará, chalked up decisive victories over the Turks in the summer of 1824. The final battle was won on Transfiguration Day (August 6), and accordingly the church inside the castle precinct is dedicated to this festival. A new **archeological museum** at the start of the road to Vathý was set to open as of writing, featuring finds from the ancient city. Other antiquities include the somewhat dull **Roman baths**, signposted as "Thermai", 400m west of town (Tues–Sun 8.45am–2.30pm; free); considerably more interesting is the **Efpalínio tunnel** (Tues–Sun 8.45am–2.15pm; €4), a 1040-metre aqueduct bored through the mountain just north of Pythagório at the behest of Polykrates. To get there, take the signposted path from the shore boulevard at the west end of town, which meets the vehicle access road toward the end of a twenty-minute walk. Visits consist of traversing a hewn rock ledge used to transport the spoil from the water channel far below; there are guard-grilles over the worst drops, and lighting for the first 650m. Although the slave-labour crews started from opposite sides of the mountain, the eight-metre horizontal deviation from true, about halfway along, is remarkably slight, and the vertical error nil: a tribute to the competence of the era's surveyors.

Practicalities

The **bus** stop lies just west of the intersection of Lykoúrgou Logothéti and the road to Vathý; the taxi rank is at the harbour end of Lykoúrgou Logothéti. A few **bank** ATMs and the **post office** are also along the same street. The flattish country to the west is ideal for cycling, a popular activity, and if you want to rent a **motorbike** several outfits on Logothéti will oblige you. These are interspersed with outlets for every brand of **car rental**, though **parking** in Pythagório is impossible – use the pricey fee lot near the castle, or the free one just west behind the town beach.

Accommodation proprietors meet all arriving ferries and hydrofoils, even in peak season – some of the prices touted seem too good to be true, but it's free to look. The **tourist information booth** (June–Sept daily 8.30am–9.30pm; ☏22730 62274), on the main thoroughfare, Lykoúrgou Logothéti, can also help in finding rooms. Quietly located at the seaward end of Odhós Pythagóra, south of Lykoúrgou Logothéti, the modest *Tsambika* (☎ 22730 61642; ❷) or the more comfortable *Dora*, a block west (☎ 22730 61456; ❸–❹), are two pensions worth contacting in advance. A peaceful area is the hillside north of Platía Irínis, where *Studios Galini* (☎ 22730 61167 or 210 98 42 248 in winter; ❹) has high-quality self-catering units with ceiling fans, balconies and kind English-speaking management. The *Evelin* (☎ 22730 61124, ℱ 22730 61077; ❸) 2km out by the traffic lights isn't brilliantly located – convenient only for the airport – but it's good value and friendly, and has a swimming pool, double glazing against noise and on-site motorbike rental.

Eating out can be frustrating in Pythagório, with value for money often a completely alien concept. Currently the only place the islanders themselves will be caught dead or alive in (especially at weekend afternoons) is also the most atmospherically set: *Varka*, at the base of the jetty, fine for seafood and *orektiká*. Passably authentic Chinese fare at the *Oriental Garden*, two blocks inland from the water behind the town hall, attracts yachties from as far away as Léros; the €13.50 all-you-can-eat buffet is good value. With transport, it's worth heading out 3km east of town to *Yalos* (*Paul's*), the Greek-American-managed seaside taverna of the *Glikoriza Beach Hotel*; though prices are a bit bumped up relative to portion size, the presentation and quality of the fare are also higher than usual. Pythagório's current **nightlife** focus is *Sirius Club* on Dhespóti Kyrílou, which hosts occasional live gigs, while all-year Cine Rex in Mytiliní village, 7km northwest, screens standard first-run **films**; the summer premises at the far edge of town are great fun, with free *loukoumádhes* (sweet fritters) served at intermission.

Around Pythagório

The main local beach stretches for several kilometres west of the Logothetis castle, punctuated about halfway along by the end of the airport runway, and the cluster of nondescript hotels known as **POTOKÁKI**. Just before the turn-off to the heart of the beach sprawls the luxury *Doryssa Bay* complex (☎ 22730 61360, ⓦ www.doryssa-bay.gr; ❻–❽), which includes a meticulously concocted fake village, guaranteed to confound archeologists of future eras. No two of the units, joined by named lanes, are alike, and there's even a platía with a (pricey) café. In early October the *Doryssa Bay's* functions hall hosts an excellent, if poorly publicized, **pan-Mediterranean documentary film festival** (free screenings). Although you'll have to contend with the hotel crowds and low-flying jets, the sand-and-pebble **beach** here is well groomed and the water clean; for more seclusion head out to the end of the road.

Under layers of alluvial mud, plus today's runway, lies the processional Sacred Way joining the ancient city with the **Heraion**, the massive shrine of the Mother Goddess (daily July–Aug 8am–7pm; Sept–June 8.30am–3pm; €3). Much touted in tourist literature, this assumes humbler dimensions – one surviving column and assorted foundations – upon approach. Yet once inside the precinct you sense the former grandeur of the temple, never completed owing to Polykrates' untimely death at the hands of the Persians. The site chosen, near the mouth of the still-active Imvrassós stream, was Hera's legendary birthplace and site of her trysts with Zeus; in the far corner of the fenced-in zone you glimpse a large, exposed patch of the paved Sacred Way.

The modern resort of **IRÉON**, nearby, is a nondescript grid-plan resort behind a coarse-shingle beach, where the water can be cold owing to the outflow of the Imvrassós; nonetheless the place has its fanatical devotees who patronize assorted rooms and small hotels, most within sight of the sea.

Tempting, too, are the handful of waterfront **tavernas**, but for the best eating here follow the locals to *Angyra*, a super-hygienic, seafood-strong ouzerí on an inland corner.

Southern Sámos

Since the circum-island bus only passes through or near the places below once or twice daily, you really need your own vehicle to explore them. Some 5km west of Hóra, a well-marked side road leads up and right to **MAVRATZÉÏ**, one of two Samian "pottery villages", which lost 49 houses to the 2000 fire. The few surviving local potteries specialize in the Koúpa toú Pythagóra or "Pythagorean cup", supposedly designed by the sage to leak over the user's lap if they are overfilled. More practical wares can be found in **KOUMARADHÉÏ**, back on the main road, another 2km along.

From here you can descend a paved road to the sixteenth-century monastery of **Megális Panayías** (theoretically daily 9am–noon & 5–7pm), containing frescoes now very smudged by damp. This route continues to **MÝLI**, submerged in citrus groves and also accessible from Iréon. Four kilometres above Mýli sprawls **PAGÓNDAS**, a large hillside community with a splendid main square (venue for a lively Pentecost Sunday-evening festival) and an unusual communal fountain house on the south hillside. From here, a scenic paved road curls 15km around the hill to **PÝRGOS**, at the head of a ravine draining southwest and the centre of Samian honey production; here the best eating is not on the through road but at *Barba Dhimtris*, in the village centre.

The rugged and beautiful coast south of the Pagóndas–Pýrgos route is largely inaccessible, glimpsed by most visitors for the first and last time from the descending plane bringing them to Sámos. **Tsópela**, a highly scenic sand-and-gravel cove at a gorge mouth, is the only beach here with marked track access and a good taverna in a surviving pine grove, with fish and a dish or two of the day; you'll need a sturdy motorcycle (not a scooter) or a car to get down there. The western reaches of this shoreline are approached via the small village of **KOUMÉÏKA**, with a massive inscribed marble fountain and a pair of *kafenía* on its square. Below extends the long, pebble bay at **BÁLLOS**, with sand, a cave and a naturist area at the far east end. Bállos itself is merely a sleepy collection of summer houses, several simple places to stay and a few tavernas, all on the shore road. The best **accommodation** for walk-ins is the *Hotel Amfilisos* (☎22730 31669; ❹), while the finest **dining** is at *Akrogiali* nearby, with an honourable mention for humbler *Iy Paralia* off to the east. Returning to Kouméïka, the dubious-looking side road just before the village marked "Velanidhiá" is in fact entirely paved – a very useful short cut if you're travelling towards the beaches beyond Órmos Marathokámbou (see p.407).

Kokkári and around

Leaving Vathý on the north coastal section of the island loop road, you've little to stop for until **KOKKÁRI**, Sámos's second major tourist centre after Pythagório. The town's profile, covering two knolls behind twin headlands, remains unaltered, and one or two families still doggedly untangle their fishing nets on the quay, but in general its identity has been altered beyond recognition, given inland expansion over vineyards and the abandoned fields of small boiling-onions that gave the place its name. Since the exposed, rocky beaches here are buffeted by near-constant winds, locals have made a virtue of necessity by developing the place as a successful windsurfing resort – just west of town a windsurf school thrives all season long.

Practicalities

Buses stop on the through road, by the church. Other amenities on the same road include a few **bank** ATMs, branches of all major Samian **travel agents**, and a **newsstand/bookstore**, Lexis; on a seaward lane stands a **post office** in a Portakabin and, next door, a long-hours, self-service **laundry**. We don't usually recommend shops, but Astrid Koumalatsos' Pinokio (opposite the church) has the best stock of olive-wood souvenirs and kitchen ware we've seen in Greece.

As in Vathý and Pythagório, a fair proportion of Kokkári's **accommodation** is block-booked by tour companies; establishments not completely devoted to such trade include *Lemos* (℡22730 92250; ❹), near the north end of the west beach. For a guaranteed view of the fishing port, try the *Pension Alkyonis* (℡22730 92225; ❸) or the *Pension Angela* (℡22730 92052; ❸). If you get stuck, seek assistance from the municipal tourist office (Mon–Fri 8.30am–1.15pm; ℡22730 92217), with premises just east of the main church. If money's no object, then it has to be the A-class *Arion* (℡22370 92020, ⓦwww.arion-hotel .gr; ❼), a well-designed bungalow-hotel complex on an unburnt patch of hillside 2km west.

Tavernas lining the north waterfront have a nice view and little else to recommend them; the area is better regarded as a nightlife venue, with **bars** ringing the little square just west of where the concreted stream meets the sea. By far the best eating is either at *Iy Bira*, opposite the church, packed every night for the sake of proprietor Artemis' mother's cooking, or at ⅜ *Ammos Plaz* on the west beach, one of the oldest (1988) establishments in town, offering very good and fair-priced *mayireftá* and fish – they've a loyal repeat clientele, and you must book days in advance (℡22730 92463) for seaside conservatory tables.

West of Kokkári: the coast

The closest sheltered beaches are thirty to forty minutes' walk away to the west, all with sunbeds and permanently anchored umbrellas. The first, **Lemonákia**, is a bit close to the road, though many *Arion* patrons favour it and the taverna's not too bad; 1km beyond, the graceful crescent of **Tzamadhoú** figures in virtually every tourist-board poster of the island. With path-only access, it's marginally less spoilt, and the far east end of the beach (saucer-shaped pebbles) has become a well-established nudist zone. There's one more pebble bay, 7km west beyond Avlákia, called **Tzaboú**, again with a serviceable snack-bar, but it's not worth a special detour when the prevailing northwest wind is up.

The next spot of any interest along the coast road is **Platanákia**, essentially a handful of buildings at a bridge by the turning for Manolátes (see opposite); here *Iy Apolavsis* **taverna** has a limited choice of very good *mayireftá*. Platanákia is actually the eastern suburb of **ÁYIOS KONSTANDÍNOS**, whose surf-pounded esplanade has been prettified. However, there are no usable beaches within walking distance, so the collection of warm-toned stone buildings, with few modern intrusions, constitutes a peaceful alternative to Kokkári, only getting much trade in spring when Dutch hikers frequent the place. For **accommodation**, try the *Hotel Iro* (℡22730 94013, ℗22730 94610; ❸), or the *Hotel Apartments Agios Konstantinos* (℡22730 94000, ℗22730 94002; ❹), both on the road down to the sea. **Eating** out, you're spoilt for choice; besides *Iy Apolavsis*, there's *To Kyma* at the east end of the quay, with good bulk wine and *mayireftá*, or (best of all) the *Aeolos* at the far west end of the esplanade (June–Sept), with terrific fish or grilled meat and a few well-chosen baked dishes, served at tables on the jetty or by the tiny beach.

Once past "Áyios", as it's locally abbreviated, the mountains hem the road in against the sea, and the terrain doesn't relent until **Kondakéïka**; its diminutive shore annexe of **Áyios Nikólaos** has an excellent venue for fish meals in *Iy Psaradhes* (℡ 22730 32489; Easter–Oct), with a terrace lapped by the waves – booking in season is mandatory as it's appeared (deservedly) in so many guides. There's also the reasonable beach of **Piáki**, ten minutes' walk east past the last studio units.

The next turning inland beyond Áyios Nikólaos, just at the riverbed marking the eastern boundary of Karlóvassi, leads 6km to the little-visited village of Idhroússa, gateway to the Byzantine **church of Kímisis Theotókou**. The oldest and most artistically noteworthy on Sámos, its extensive frescoes are contemporaneous with the building (late 12th or early 13th century). Once in Idhroússa, follow "Petaloúdha" signs from the platía along a dirt-track system for about 3km. The deceptively simple interior (unlocked), a single barrel-vaulted aisle, is covered with frescoes, many still vivid except on the ceiling where damp has blurred them.

Hill villages

Inland between Kokkári and Kondakéïka, an idyllic landscape of pine, cypress and orchards is overawed by dramatic mountains; except for some streaks of damage reaching the sea between Lemonákia and Tzaboú, it miraculously escaped the July 2000 fire. Despite destructive nibblings by bulldozers, some of the trail system linking the various **hill villages** is still intact, and walkers can return to the main highway to catch a bus back to base.

The monastery of **Vrondianís** (Vrónda), directly above Kokkári, was once a popular destination, but between severe fire damage in 2000 and the army's long, hard-wearing use of it as a barracks, it's closed indefinitely for renovations. **VOURLIÓTES**, 2km west of the monastery, has beaked chimneys and brightly painted shutters sprouting from its typical tile-roofed houses. Restaurateur greed has ruined the formerly photogenic central square; it's best to pass over the **tavernas** there in favour of *Iy Pera Vrysi*, at the village entrance, or the *Piyi Pnaka* taverna, in the idyllic hamlet of the same name just off the ascending Vourliótes road.

MANOLÁTES, further uphill and an hour-plus walk away via a deep river canyon, also has several simple **tavernas** (the pick of these being *Iy Filia* near the village entrance), and is the most popular trailhead for the five-hour round-trip up Mount Ámbelos (Karvoúnis), the island's second-highest summit. From Manolátes you can no longer easily continue on foot to Stavrinídhes, the next village, but should plunge straight down, partly on a cobbled path, through the shady valley known as Aïdhónia (Nightingales), towards Platanákia. By far the most characterful base in the area is down in Aïdhónia at the *Hotel Aidonokastro* (℡ 22730 94686, ℻ 22730 94404; ❹). Here the kindly, English-speaking Yannis Pamoukis has renovated half the abandoned hamlet of **Valeondádhes** as a unique cottage-hotel, each former house comprising a pair of two- or four-person units with traditional touches.

Karlóvassi

KARLÓVASSI, 31km west of Vathý and Sámos's second town, is decidedly sleepier and more old-fashioned than the capital, despite having roughly the same population. It's potentially useful as a base for enjoying western Sámos's excellent beaches or taking a number of rewarding walks. The name, despite a vehement denial of Ottoman legacy elsewhere on Sámos, appears to be a corruption of the Turkish for "snowy plain" – the plain in question being the conspicuous saddle of Mount Kérkis overhead. The town divides into five straggly neighbourhoods: Néo, well inland, whose growth was spurred by the influx of post-1923 refugees; Meséo, across the usually dry riverbed, tilting appealingly off a knoll and then blending with the shoreline district of Ríva; and picturesque Paleó (or Áno), above Limáni, the small harbour district.

Most tourists stay at or near **Limáni**, the part of town with most of the tourist facilities. Hotels tend to have road noise and not much view; **rooms**, all on the inland pedestrian lane behind the through road, are quieter – try those of *Vangelis Feloukatzis* (☎22730 33293; ❷). The port itself is an appealing place with a working boatyard at the west end and all the **ferry-ticket agencies** grouped at the middle. **Tavernas** and bars abound on the quay, though the only remarkable one is *Rementzo* (April–Oct), tellingly the locals' hangout, with good fish in season plus *mayireftá*. The local university contingent (a maths and computer science faculty is based here) keeps formal **nightlife** surprisingly lively; try *Popcorn* on the quay.

Immediately overhead is the partly hidden hamlet of **Paleó**, its hundred or so houses draped on either side of a leafy ravine, but with no reliable facilities. **Meséo**, just east, has three **tavernas** on the central platía, of which the most accomplished is *Dionysos* (all year), with a range of creative dishes, equally pleasant indoor/outdoor tables and a wine list aspiring to Athenian sophistication. Following the street linking the central square to **Ríva**, you pass one of the improbably huge, early twentieth-century churches, topped with twin belfries and a blue-and-white dome, which dot the coastal plain here. Just at the intersection with the shore road, you'll find the good-value, sunset-view ouzerí *To Kyma* (April–Oct), where Ethiopian proprietress Berhane adds a welcome Middle Eastern/East African touch (eg *alí saláta*, with sun-dried tomatoes, cashews and courgettes) to the broad variety of seafood and vegetarian dishes – most days you'll fight for a table (no reservations taken). Otherwise, Ríva has little to recommend it besides a wilderness of derelict stone-built warehouses and mansions down near the river mouth, reminders of the vanished leather industry, which flourished here during the first half of the twentieth century. As for **Néo**, you'll almost certainly visit one of several **bank** ATMs, the **post office** or the **bus stop/taxi rank** on the main lower square. The student contingent guarantees some low-key **nightlife** (eg, *Café-Bar Toxotis*) and on the same street helps keep the local **cinema** (Gorgyra) going.

Western Sámos

The closest **beach** to Karlóvassi is **Potámi**, forty minutes' walk away via the coast road from Limáni or an hour by a more scenic, high trail from Paleó. This broad arc of sand and pebbles gets crowded at summer weekends, when virtually the entire town descends on the place. Near the end of the trail from Paleó there are a very few **rooms**, though many folk camp rough along the lower reaches of the river which gives the beach its name. A streamside path leads twenty minutes inland, past the eleventh-century church of **Metamórfosis** – the oldest on Sámos – to a point where the river disappears into a small gorge (a guardrailed but still vertiginous stairway takes you up and left here). Otherwise, you must swim and wade 100m in heart-stoppingly cold water through a sequence of fern-tufted rock pools before reaching a low but vigorous waterfall; bring shoes with good tread and perhaps even rope if you want to explore above the first cascade. You probably won't be alone until you dive in, since the canyon is well known to locals and tour agencies. Just above the Metamórfosis church, a clear if precipitous path leads up to a small, contemporaneous **Byzan-tine fortress**. There's little to see inside other than a subterranean cistern and badly crumbled lower curtain wall, but the views out to sea and up the canyon are terrific, while in October the place is carpeted with pink autumn crocuses.

The coast beyond Potámi ranks among the most beautiful and unspoilt on Sámos; since the early 1980s it has served as a protected refuge for the rare monk seal. The dirt track at the west end of Potámi bay ends after twenty minutes on foot, from which you backtrack 100m or so to find the well-cairned side trail running parallel to the water. After twenty minutes along this you'll arrive at **Mikró Seïtáni**, a small pebble cove guarded by sculpted rock walls. A full hour's walk from the trailhead, through olive terraces, brings you to **Megálo Seïtáni**, the island's finest beach, at the mouth of the intimidating Kakopérato gorge. You'll have to bring food and water, though not necessarily a swimsuit – there's no dress code at either of the Seïtáni bays. If you don't fancy the walk in, during peak season there are a couple of daily **water-taxi** services from Karlóvassi port (€10 return).

Southwestern beach resorts

The first place you reach on the island loop road south of Karlóvassi is **MARATHÓKAMBOS**, an amphitheatrical village overlooking the gulf of the same name; there are no tourist facilities, and by taking the bypass road you'll miss out on the village's traffic bottlenecks – and save about 4km. Its port, **ÓRMOS MARATHOKÁMBOU**, 18km from Karlóvassi, has emerged as a tourist resort since the 1990s, though some character still peeks through in its backstreets. The harbour has been improved, with *kaïkia* offering day-trips to Foúrni and the nearby islet of Samiopoúla, while the pedestrianized quay has become the focus of attention, home to several **tavernas**; best by a whisker is *Lekatis*, though portions aren't huge and seafood freshness can vary. Nearby, *The Mad Pomegranate Tree* is a slightly pricey but tasteful **café-bar** with a good line in piped music. For **accommodation** not monopolized by tours, try *Studios Avra* (☎22730 37221; ❷), unimprovably perched above the jetty.

The beach immediately east from Órmos is hardly the best; for better ones continue 2km west to **VOTSALÁKIA** (officially signposted as "Kámbos"), Sámos's newest, family-pitched resort, straggling a further 2km behind the island's longest (if not its most beautiful) beach. But for most, Votsalákia is still a considerable improvement on the Pythagório area, and the mass of 1437-metre Mount Kérkis overhead rarely fails to impress (see below). For **accommodation**, try Elsa Hiou's rooms behind her sympathetic *Evoinos* taverna near mid-strand (☎22730 37791 or 694 67 92 923; ❸); Emmanuil Dhespotakis has numerous premises towards the quieter, more scenic western end of things (☎22730 31258; ❸–❹). Also in this vicinity is *Loukoullos*, an unusual *koutouriárika* **taverna** overlooking the sea where all food is prepared in a wood oven. Other facilities include branches of nearly all the main Vathý travel agencies, offering **vehicle rental** (necessary, as only two daily buses call here), and a couple of stand-alone ATMs.

If Votsalákia doesn't suit, you can continue beyond for 3km to the 600-metre beach of **Psilí Ámmos**, more aesthetic and not to be confused with its name-sake beach in the southeast corner of Sámos. The sea shelves very gently here, and cliffs shelter clusters of naturists at the east end. Surprisingly, there is still little development: just three small studio complexes in the pines at mid-beach, and two tavernas back up on the approach road. Access to **Limniónas**, a smaller cove 2km further west, passes the *Limnionas Bay Hotel* (☎22730 37057; ❺), much the highest-standard accommodation locally, with its tiered units arrayed around a garden and pool. Yachts and pleasure *kaïkia* occasionally call at the protected bay, which offers decent swimming away from a rock shelf at mid-strand, especially at the east end.

Mount Kérkis and around

Gazing up from a supine seaside position, you may be inspired to climb **Mount Kérkis**. The classic route begins at the west end of the Votsalákia strip, along the bumpy jeep track leading inland towards Evangelistrías convent. After 45 minutes or so on the track system, through olive groves and past charcoal pits (a major local industry), the path begins, more or less following power lines up to the convent. A friendly nun may proffer an ouzo in welcome and point you up the paint-marked trail, continuing even more steeply up to the peak. The views are tremendous, though the climb itself is humdrum once you're out of the trees. About an hour before the top there's a chapel with an attached cottage for sheltering in emergencies, and just beyond, a welcome spring. All told, it's a seven-hour outing from Votsalákia and, back, not counting rest stops.

Less ambitious walkers might want to circle the flanks of the mountain, first by vehicle and then by foot. The road beyond Limniónas to Kallithéa and Dhrakéï, truly back-of-beyond villages with views across to Ikaría, is paved all the way to Dhrakéï, making it possible to venture out here on an ordinary motorbike. The bus service is better during the school term, when a vehicle leaves Karlóvassi (Mon–Fri 1.20pm) bound for these remote spots; during summer it only operates two days a week at best (currently Mon & Fri).

From **DHRAKÉÏ**, a lovely trail – minimally damaged by a track – descends ninety minutes through forest to Megálo Seïtáni, from where it's easy enough to continue on to Karlóvassi within another two-and-a-half hours. People attempting to reverse this itinerary often discover to their cost that the bus (if any) returns from Dhrakéï at dawn or 2.45pm, compelling them to either retrace their steps or stay at one of two unofficial **rooms** establishments (summer only) in Dhrakéï, and dine at one of four taverna-*kafenía*. In **KALLITHÉA**, there's only a simple *psistariá* on the tiny square. From Kallithéa, a newer track (from beside the cemetery) and an older trail both lead up within 45 minutes to a spring, rural chapel and plane tree on the west flank of Kérkis, with path-only continuation for another thirty minutes to a pair of faintly frescoed cave-churches. **Panayía Makriní** stands detached at the mouth of a high, wide but shallow grotto, whose balcony affords terrific views of Sámos's west tip. By contrast, **Ayía Triádha**, a ten-minute scramble overhead, has most of its structure made up of cave wall; just adjacent, another long, narrow, volcanic cavern can be explored with a torch some hundred metres into the mountain.

After these subterranean exertions, the closest spot for a swim is **Vársamo** (Válsamo) cove, 4km below Kallithéa and reached via a well-signposted dirt road. The beach here consists of multicoloured volcanic pebbles, with two caves to shelter in, and a single very friendly **taverna** just inland, run by three generations of women.

Ikaría

Ikaría, a narrow, windswept landmass between Sámos and Mýkonos, is little visited and invariably underestimated by travel writers who don't even bother to show up. The name supposedly derives from the legendary Icarus, who fell into the sea just offshore after the wax bindings on his wings melted. For years

IKARÍA & FOÚRNI

▲ *Pythagório*

▲ *Sámos*

Fourni

Kórakas ▲

Khryssomiliá

Psilí
Ámmos

Fourni

Balli

Vitsiliá

Ayios Ioánnis
Pródromos

Italian
Watchtower

Vlyhádha

Kambí

Aspa

Pelekánia & Eliódhaki

Petrokópio

Kasídhi

Thýmena

Thýmena

Cape
Dhrákano
Hellenistic
Tower

Fáros

Ayía Kyriakí

Thermá

Thermá
Lefkádhos

Ayios Kírykos

Karavóstamo

Aréthoussa

Xylosýrtis

Xylosýrtis

Ikaría

Évdhilos

Kámbos

Khryssóstomos

Dháfni

Koskiná

Playiá

Aváki

Theóktisti

Márátho

Frandáto

Stelli

Kosíkia

Messakhtí

Livédhi

Ayios,
Polýkarpos

Mandriá

Mounté

Vathés
Dam

Seyhélles

Armenistís

Ayios
Dhimítrios

RAHES

Kastaniés

Manganítis

Nás

Hálaris

Loupástra

Kárydhiés

Messakhtí

Profítis Ilías

Megálo
Frágma

Vráhadhes

Langádha

Ayios
Isídhoros

Trapálou

Prospéra

Kálamos

Karkinágri

Mavriánoú

Amálo

Lighthouse

N

▼ *Pátmos*

0 ___ 10 km

the only substantial tourism was generated by a few **hot springs** on the south coast; until the mid-1990s, the Ikarians resisted most attempts to develop their island for conventional tourism. Charter flights still don't land here, as the airport at the northeast tip can't accommodate jets. Since then, however, tourist facilities of some quantity and quality have sprung up in and around Armenistís, the only resort of note.

Ikaría, along with Thessaly on the mainland and Lésvos, has traditionally been one of the Greek Left's strongholds. This tendency dates from the long decades of right-wing domination in Greece, when (as in past ages) the island was used as a place of **exile** for political dissidents, particularly Communists. Apparently the strategy backfired, with the transportees favourably impressing and proselytizing their hosts; at the same time, many Ikarians emigrated to North America, and ironically their capitalist remittances help keep the island going. Of late, the Ikarians tend to embrace any vaguely Left cause; posters urge you variously to attend rallies on behalf of Turkish political prisoners or contribute to funding a Zapatista teacher-training school in Chiapas. Athens has historically reacted to this contrarian stance with long periods of punitive neglect, which has only made the islanders even more profoundly self-sufficient and idiosyncratic, and supportive (or at least tolerant) of the same in others. Local pride dictates that outside opinion matters not a bit, and until very recently Ikarians – mostly dressed in long-out-of-style American garb – seemed to have little idea what "modern tourists" expect. It's this lack of obsequiousness, and a studied eccentricity, which some visitors mistake for hostility.

These are not the only Ikarian quirks, and for many the place is an acquired taste, contrasting strongly (for better or worse) with Sámos. Except for forested portions in the northwest (now a bit fire-denuded near the shore), it's not a strikingly beautiful island, with most of the terrain consisting of scrub-covered schist put to good use as building material. The mostly desolate south coast is overawed by steep cliffs, while the north face is less sheer but nonetheless furrowed by deep canyons creating hairpin road-bends extreme even by Greek-island standards. Neither are there many postcard-picturesque villages, since the rural schist-roofed houses are generally scattered so as to be next to their famous apricot orchards, vineyards and fields.

Áyios Kírykos and around

Passing ferries on the Pireás–Páros–Náxos–Sámos line call at the south-coast port and capital of **ÁYIOS KÍRYKOS**, about 1km southwest of the island's main thermal resort. Because of the spa trade, beds are at a premium here in mid-summer; arriving in the evening from Sámos, accept any reasonable offers of rooms, or – if in a group – proposals of a taxi ride to the north coast, which shouldn't cost much more than €40 per vehicle to Armenistís. A **bus** sets out across the island from the main square (July–Sept 15 Mon–Fri only at noon) to Évdhilos, usually changing vehicles there at 1.30pm for the onward trip to Armenistís.

The spa of **Thérma**, 1km northeast of the port by the direct coastal access road, saw its heyday between the world wars; now distinctly fusty, it relies chiefly on a mostly elderly clientele on limited national-health-insurance stipends. A much better bet for a less formal soak are either the seaside, open-air pool of the **Asklipioú** hot springs in Áyios Kírykos, reached by steps down from the court-house, or the even more natural, shoreline hot springs at **Thérma Lefkádhos**, 2km southwest of Áyios Kírykos. A path opposite a cluster of eucalyptus trees drops to the sea, and then 100m over shoreline boulders brings you to the hot source, which mixes with the sea between giant volcanic boulders to a pleasant temperature.

A more conventional beach – the largest on the south coast – is found at **Fáros**, 10.5km northeast of Áyios Kírykos along a good paved road, which also serves the airport. A considerable colony of summer cottages shelters under tamarisks fringing the mixed sand-and-gravel strand, with a reefy zone to cross before deep water; this rather end-of-the-world place looks across to Foúrni and Thýmena, whose beaches (and landscape) it strongly resembles. But the best reason to make the trip out are two inexpensive **tavernas**, better than anything in Áyios Kírykos: *Leonidas* (open all year), with grilled or fried seafood plus bulk wine, and the more dour, less popular but quality-wise slightly better *O Grigoris* adjacent.

From a signposted point just inland from Fáros beach, a dirt track leads 2km to the trailhead for the round **Hellenistic watchtower** at Cape Dhrákano, much the oldest (and most impressive) ancient ruin on the island.

Practicalities

Hydrofoils, small ferries and *kaïkia* use the small east jetty; large ferries dock at the main west pier. Several **banks** with ATMs, a **post office** on the road out of town and three ferry/hydrofoil **agents** – Ikariadha (☎22750 22277) for hydrofoils, Roustas (☎22750 23691) and Lakios (☎22750 22426) for conventional boats – round up the list of essentials. You can **rent** motorbikes and cars here, too, from Dolihi Tours/Lemy (☎22750 23230) and Glaros ☎22750 23637), both near the east jetty.

There are several **hotels**, most useful (and consistently open) of which is the friendly, air-conditioned, en-suite, spotless *Akti* (☎22750 22694; ❸), on a knoll east of the hydrofoil and *kaïki* quay, with views of Foúrni from the garden. Otherwise, directly behind the base of the large-ferry jetty and two blocks inland there's the *Pension Maria-Elena* (☎22750 22835; ❸), a large modern block in a quiet setting. All in a row above the eastern quay and potentially suffering some noise from the several *kafenía* and snack-bars below are the *Pension Ikaria* (☎22750 22804; ❷), the studios above the *Taverna stou Tsouri* (☎22750 23400; ❸) and the clean *dhomátia* run by Ioannis Proestos (☎22750 23176; ❷).

Eating out, you've less choice than with lodging, with both options operating summer only: grilled dishes served up at the *Estiatorio Tzivaeri* just inland from Ioannis Proestos's rooms, or *Iy Klimataria* just around the corner for less distinguished *mayireftá*. On the front, *Casino* is the last remaining traditional *kafenío*; for further entertainment there's a **summer cinema**, the Rex, and a few summer clubs at the start of the road to Thermá Lefkádhos.

Évdhilos and around

The twisting, 37-kilometre road from Áyios Kírykos to Évdhilos is one of the most hair-raising on any Greek island (especially as a taxi passenger), and the long ridge extending the length of Ikaría often wears a streamer of cloud, even when the rest of the Aegean is clear. Although **ÉVDHILOS** is the island's second town and a regular ferry stop on the Sámos–Mýkonos–Sýros–Pireás line, it's slightly less equipped to deal with visitors than Áyios Kírykos. Évdhilos offers just two **hotels** – the *Evdoxia* on the slope southwest of the harbour (☎22750 31502; ❹) and the low-lying *Atheras* (☎22750 31434, ☎22750 31926; ❹) with a small pool – plus a few **rooms**. A **post office** up on the through road, a pair of **bank ATMs**, and two good **beaches** just to the east, are also worth knowing about, though the nearer beach has been blighted by a massive car park which will in due course become a new, much-needed harbour jetty. The **boat-ticket** trade is divided between the **agencies** Blue Nice (℡22750 31990) and Roustas (℡22750 32293); you can **rent cars** from Aventura ℡22750 31140). Among numerous harbourside sweet shops, *kafenía* and **restaurants**, the wood-signed *Coralli* on the west quay is the most reliable and reasonable option, but for more interesting fare head 1km west of the harbour to **FÝTEMA** hamlet, where just on the roadside *To Inomayerio tis Popis*, alias *Sto Fytema* (open only Easter week & school hols; ℡22750 31928), has lots of options for vegetarians, excellent local wine, low prices and pleasant terrace seating, though opening hours are erratic and it's best to call first.

KÁMBOS, 1.5km west of Fýtema, offers a small hilltop museum with finds from nearby **ancient Oinoe**; the twelfth-century church of Ayía Iríni stands adjacent, with column stumps and mosaic patches of a fourth-century Byzantine basilica defining the entry courtyard. Lower down still are the sparse ruins of a Byzantine palace (visible from the road) used to house exiled nobles, as well as a 250-metre-long sandy beach (unmarked track to it) with a musical *kantína* offering sunbeds. *Rooms Dhionysos* are available from the green-doored store immediately below the church run by Vassilis Kambouris (℡22750 31300 or 22750 31688; 2), who also acts as the unofficial and enthusiastic tourism officer for this part of Ikaría, keeping the keys for the church and museum.

From Kámbos, a twisty road leads up 4km – as does an easier road from Avláki, in 3km – to Ikaría's outstanding medieval monument, the **monastery of Theóktisti**, looking over pines to the coast from its perch under a chaos of slanted granite slabs. The *katholikón* features damaged but eminently worthwhile naïve frescoes dated to 1688; there's also a pleasant *kafenío* on site.

By following the road heading inland from the large church in Évdhilos, you can also visit the Byzantine **castle of Koskiná** (Nikariás), just over 15km south. The road signposted for Manganítis is paved through Kosíkia, 9km away, and for 2km more to the marked side-track. You can get a bike or jeep along this to within a short walk of the tenth-century castle, perched on a distinctive conical hill, with an arched gateway and a fine vaulted chapel.

Beyond this turning, the road creeps over the island watershed and drops steadily towards the south coast; it's completely paved, and with your own vehicle offers an alternative, quicker and much less curvy way back to Áyios Kírykos compared to going via Karavóstomo. The principal potential detour, 2km past the castle turning, is the road right (west) to the secluded pebble beach of **Seyhélles** ("Seychelles"), the best on this generally inhospitable coast, with the final approach by ten-minute hike.

Armenistís and around

Most visitors congregate at **ARMENISTÍS**, 51km from Áyios Kírykos via Évdhilos, and with good reason: this little resort lies below Ikaría's vastest (if slightly diminished) forest, with two enormous, sandy beaches battered by seasonal surf – **Livádhi** and **Mesaktí** – five and fifteen minutes' walk to the east respectively, the latter with no less than four reed-roofed *kantínas* in summer. The waves are complicated by strong lateral currents (as signs warn), and regular summer drownings have prompted the institution of that Greek rarity, a lifeguard service, and the placement of a line of marker buoys beyond which you should not stray. Armenistís itself is spectacularly set, facing northeast along the length of Ikaría towards sun- and moonrise, with Mount Kérkis on Sámos closing off the horizon on a clear day. A dwindling proportion of older, schist-roofed buildings, plus fishing boats hauled up in a sandy cove, lend Armenistís the air of a Cornish fishing village. Despite a 1990s mushrooming it remains a manageable place, even if gentrification (and a noticeable package presence) has definitely set in; the semi-official campsite behind Livádhi beach closed in 2001, though a few tents still sprout in the greenery behind Mesaktí by the river mouth, home to terrapins.

Accommodation

There are easily a score of rooms establishments in the Armenistís area, as well as four bona fide **hotels**. Among the latter, the *Erofili Beach*, right at the entrance to town (☎22750 71058, ⓦwww.erofili.gr; ❻), is considered the best on the island and has a small pool perched dramatically over Livádhi beach. Runners-up include the *Messakti Village* complex (☎22750 71331, ⓦwww .messakti-village.com; ❻) just above Mesaktí beach, with a larger pool, its common areas and private terraces complementing large if minimally furnished self-catering units suitable for families of three to six, or – on the western edge of Armenistís – the *Daidalos* (☎22750 71390, ⓦwww.daidaloshotel.gr; ❺), the less impersonal and less package-dominated of two adjacent hotels, with another eyrie-pool, unusually appointed rooms and a shady breakfast terrace. Among the various **rooms**, the *Kirki* by the *Erofili Beach* (☎22750 71254 or enquire at *Dhefini* taverna; ❸) is spartan but en suite, with large private balconies and sea views; along the shore lane, the *Paskhalia Rooms* (☎22750 71302; Easter–Oct ❷) are on the small side but en suite and good value, with great views east, while at the far end of Livádhi beach, the adjacent 🜋 *Atsahas Apartments* (☎ & Ⓕ22750 71226; April–Oct; ❹) and the *Valeta Apartments* (☎22750 71252; ❹) offer the best standard and setting outside of the hotels.

Eating, drinking and nightlife

Discounting the zaharoplastía and *souvláki* stalls (a pair each), there are a half-dozen full-service **tavernas** in Armenistís, of which two have a consistently good reputation. *Dhelfini*, its terrace hovering right above the fishing cove, is an established favourite – come early or very late for a table, and a mix of grills or *mayireftá*. 🜋 *Paskhalia* (aka *Vlahos* after the helpful managing family) serves similar fare, more expertly prepared at its seaview terrace immediately above, and is the most reliable venue for both breakfast and off-season travellers, open until mid–October. Further afield, the *Atsahas*, attached to the namesake apartments, is acceptable as a beach taverna, with generous portions of slightly oily vegetarian fare. Just east of Mesaktí in the fishing settlement of **Yialiskári**, looking out past pines to a picturesque church on the jetty, there's another cluster of tavernas overlooking the boat-launching slips, of which *Kelaris* (aka *tis Eleftherias*) is the best value for well-executed *mayireftá* and grilled fish. Small clubs like *Casmir* and *Pleiades* operate during summer in the river reeds behind Livádhi, though for the rest of the year **nightlife** is mostly about extended sessions in the line of *kafenía* at the north end of Armenistís quay – or the cafés up in Ráhes, for reasons made clear below.

Information, transport – and getting away

The area's main **Internet café** is Internet Point, at the west edge of the resort. There are at least three **scooter/mountain-bike rental** agencies in Armenistís; among a like number of **car-rental** outlets, Aventura (☎22750 71117) and Dolihi Tours/Lemy (☎22750 71122) are the most prominent, with branches for drop-offs in Évdhilos and Áyios Kirykos respectively, which could be handy for ferry departures towards Sámos at an ungodly hour (typically 4am). Indeed, getting away when you need to is the main drawback to staying in Armenistís, since both taxis and buses can be elusive – with the exception of the fairly frequent (late June to early Sept) shuttle linking Armenistís with Yialiskári and Ráhes. Theoretically, long-distance **buses** head for Évdhilos three times daily mid-July to mid-September, fairly well spaced (though not necessarily coinciding with westbound ferry departures; Áyios Kírykos has only one through service year-round at either 8am or 11am, though this can be full with school kids in term-time. If you've a ferry to catch, it's far easier on the nerves to prebook a **taxi**: a list of all locally based drivers, with their mobile numbers, is posted at the entrance to Armenistís.

Ráhes

Armenistís is actually the shore annexe of four inland hamlets – Áyios Dhimítrios, Áyios Polýkarpos, Kastaniés and Khristós – collectively known as **RÁHES**. Despite the modern, mostly paved access roads through the pines (trails short-cut them), the settlements retain a certain Shangri-La quality, with the older residents speaking a positively Homeric dialect. On an island not short of foibles, Khristós (Khristós Rahón in full) is particularly strange inasmuch as most locals sleep until 11am or so, shop until about 4pm, then have another nap until 8pm, whereupon they rise and spend most of the night shopping, eating and drinking the excellent home-brewed **wine** which everyone west of Évdhilos makes. In fact most of the villages west of Évdhilos adhere to this schedule, defying central government efforts to bring them into line with the rest of Greece. The local festival is August 6, though better ones take place further southwest in the woods at the Langádha valley (August 14–15) or at the Áyios Isídhoros monastery (May 14).

Near the pedestrianized *agorá* of Khristós, paved in schist and studded with gateways fashioned from the same rock, there's a **post office**, plenty of café–bars (4pm–3am) and two sweet shops. In accordance with the above-cited nocturnal habits, lunchtime can offer pretty slim pickings, though two surprisingly expensive, adjacent **tavernas** commence operations at about 8pm.

Walking between Ráhes and the coastal resorts is one of the favourite activities for visitors, and locally produced, accurate if somewhat chatty map-guides are widely available. The black-and-white *Road & Hiking Map of Western Ikaría* shows most asphalt roads, tracks and trails in the west-centre of the island; the more closely focused, colour *Round of Rahes on Foot* details a loop hike taking in the best the Ráhes villages have to offer. The route sticks mostly to surviving paths, and is well marked; the authors suggest a full day for the circuit, with ample rests, though total walking time won't be more than six hours. More advanced outings involve descending the Hálaris canyon, with its historic bridge, to Nás, or crossing the island to Manganítis via Ráhes.

Nás

By tacit consent, Greek or foreign hippies and beachside naturists have been allowed to shift 3km west of Armenistís by paved road to **Nás**, a tree-clogged river canyon ending in a small but deceptively sheltered sand-and-pebble beach. This little bay is almost completely enclosed by weirdly sculpted rock formations, but for the same reasons as at Mesaktí it's unwise to swim outside the cove's natural limits – marked, as at Mesaktí, with a line of buoys. The crumbling foundations of the fifth-century temple of **Artemis Tavropoleio** (Patroness of Bulls) overlook the permanent deep pool at the mouth of the river. If you continue inland along the river past colonies of rough campers defying prohibition signs, you'll find secluded rock pools for freshwater dips. Back at the top of the stairs leading down to the beach from the road are six tavernas, most of them offering rooms. Among **accommodation**, the rambling *Artemis* (℡22750 71485; ❷ rooms, ❸ studios) overlooks the river canyon, while ⚓ *Thea* (℡22750 71491; ❸) faces out to sea. The latter offers much the most accomplished **cooking** in the area, working weekends October to May as well, with lots of vegetarian options like *soufikó* (the local ratatouille).

Satellite islands: Thýmena and Foúrni

The straits between Sámos and Ikaría are speckled with a mini-archipelago of three islets, of which the inhabited ones are Thýmena and Foúrni. More westerly **Thýmena** has one tiny hillside settlement; *kaïkia* call regularly at the quay below on their way between Ikaría or Sámos and Foúrni, but there are no tourist facilities or attractions to speak of, save one large beach south of "town". **FOÚRNI** is home to a huge fishing fleet and one of the more thriving boatyards in the Aegean; thanks to these, and the improvement of the jetty to receive car ferries, its population is stable, unlike so many small Greek islands. The islets were once the lair of Maltese pirates, and indeed many of the islanders have a distinctly North African appearance.

The small ferries *Samos Spirit* and *Samos Sun* are based much of the week at Foúrni, making morning shopping-and-post departures to either Ikaría or Sámos, returning in the afternoon or early evening. The larger main-line ferries which appear every few days in either direction are likewise not tourist excursion boats but exist for the benefit of the islanders. The only way to visit Foúrni on a day-trip is by using one of the few weekly morning **hydrofoils** out of Pythagório on Sámos.

Apart from the remote hamlet of **Khryssomiliá** in the north, where the island's longest (and worst) road goes, most of Foúrni's inhabitants are concentrated in the **port** and Kambí hamlet just to the south. The harbour community is larger than it seems from the sea, with a friendly ambience reminiscent of 1970s Greece.

△ View from Foúrni toward Thýmena and Ikaría

Foúrni port practicalities

The central "high street", fieldstoned and mulberry-shaded, ends well inland at a little platía with two giant plane trees; between them stands a Hellenistic sarcophagus found in a nearby field, and overhead is a conical hill, site of the ancient acropolis. Nearby there's a **post office** and stand-alone **bank** ATM, plus several surprisingly well-stocked shops.

Among several **rooms** establishments, the most popular are the various premises run by Manolis and Patra Markakis (T 22750 51268, F 22750 51355), immediately to your left as you disembark; these range from simple rooms, some with balconies (❷), to fourteen superb hilltop apartments, most sleeping up to four, in a tiered complex (❹). If they're full, try *Kosta-Reli*, just back from the little town beach (T 22750 51481; ❸).

There are three full-service waterfront **tavernas**: local favourite *Rementzo*, better known as *Nikos'*, where, if you're lucky, the local *astakós* or Aegean lobster may be on the menu (except Sept–Jan); shambolically managed *Miltos*, but with good seafood; or newer contender *Ta Dhelfinakia*, a good, hygienic all-rounder with more meat dishes. For breakfast and desserts, repair to the tamarisk terrace at the Markakis family's *To Arhondiko tis Kyras Kokonas*, under their inn. There's surprisingly lively **nightlife** at a half-dozen music bars, clubs and ouzerís, often until 5am.

Around Foúrni

A fifteen-minute trail-walk south from the primary school, skirting the cemetery and then slipping over the windmill ridge, brings you to **KAMBÍ**, a scattered community overlooking a pair of sandy, tamarisk-shaded coves which you'll share with hauled-up fishing boats. There are two cheap and sustaining **tavernas**: the *Kambi* with tables on the sand, and slightly more accomplished *O Yiorgos* clinging to the side of a valley inland. A path system continues south around the headland to other, more secluded bays of varying sizes and beach consistencies which, like Kambí cove, are favourite anchorages for passing yachts, but unlike Kambí have substantial summer communities of rough campers and naturists. One, **Elidháki**, has motorbike-track access, and (like Kambí) taxi-boat service from the port.

Foúrni's only paved road ends at the southerly hamlet and monastery of **Áyios Ioánnis Pródhromos**. Just before arrival, dirt tracks lead to the isolated coves of **Vlyhádha** and **Vitsiliá**, which like most local beaches have no facilities. Overall, southern Foúrni is the most rewarding part of the island; two beaches immediately north of the harbour have been ruined in various ways and, in the extreme north of the island, remote **KHRYSSOMILIÁ** is still easiest approached by the taxi-boat from the port or on the *Samos Spirit* rather than along the atrocious eighteen-kilometre road. The village, split into a shore district and a hillside settlement, has a decent beach flanked by better if less accessible ones. There are two **tavernas** near the jetty and a few **rooms** to be had, though the locals can be less than forthcoming with outsiders.

Híos

"Craggy Híos", as **Homer** aptly described his putative birthplace, has a turbulent history and a strong identity. This large island has always been prosperous: in medieval times through the export of mastic **resin** – a trade controlled by Genoese overlords between 1346 and 1566 – and later by

Lésvos

Psará

Sámos, Ikaría, Foúrni & Pátmos

the Ottomans, who dubbed the place Sakız Adası ("Resin Island"). Since union with Greece in 1912, several shipping dynasties have emerged here, continuing the pattern of wealth. Participation in the maritime way of life is widespread, with someone in almost every family spending time in the merchant navy.

The more powerful ship-owning dynasts, the local government and the military authorities did not encourage tourism until the late 1980s, but the worldwide shipping crisis and the saturation of other, more obviously "marketable" islands eroded resistance. Since then, numbers of foreigners have discovered an Híos beyond its rather daunting port capital: fascinating villages, important Byzantine monuments and a respectable, if remote, complement of beaches. While unlikely ever to be dominated by tourism, the local scene has a distinctly modern flavour – courtesy of numerous returned Greek-Americans and Greek-Canadians – and English is widely spoken.

Unfortunately, the island has suffered more than its fair share of **catastrophes** during the past two centuries. The Ottomans perpetrated their most infamous, if not their worst, anti-revolutionary atrocity here in March 1822, massacring 30,000 Hiots and enslaving or exiling even more. In 1881, much of Híos was destroyed by a violent earthquake, and throughout the 1980s the natural beauty of the island was compromised by devastating forest fires, compounding the effect of generations of tree-felling by boat-builders. Over half of the majestic pines are now gone, with substantial patches of woods persisting only in the far northeast and the centre of Híos (though reafforestation is beginning to have an effect).

In 1988 the first charters from northern Europe were instituted, signalling potentially momentous changes for the island. Nearly two decades on there are still fewer than five thousand guest beds on Híos, the vast majority of them in the capital or the nearby beach resorts of Karfás and Ayía Ermióni. The airport runway was finally lengthened in 2004 to safely accommodate all jets, but there are as yet no direct flights from most countries, including Britain.

Híos Town

HÍOS, the harbour and main town, will come as a shock after modest island capitals elsewhere; it's a brash, concrete-laced commercial centre, with little predating the 1881 quake. Yet in many ways it is the most satisfactory of the east Aegean ports, with a large and fascinating marketplace, several museums and some good, authentic tavernas. Although it's a sprawling place of about 30,000 souls, most things of interest to visitors lie within a hundred or so metres of the water, fringed by Leofóros Egéou.

Arrival, information and transport

Ferries and **kaïkia** large and small dock at various points as shown on the town map. The pokey **airport** (2 car-hire booths) lies 3km south along the coast at Kondári, a €3.50 taxi-ride away; otherwise any blue urban bus labelled "JOMDAQI JAQUAR" departing from the terminal on the north side of the park passes the airport gate, opposite which is a conspicuous stop with shelter. **Ferry** agents cluster along the north end of waterfront Egéou and its continuation Neoríon: NEL (☎22710 23971) is a few paces south of the KTEL station, Traina (☎22710 29292) represents Saos Ferries and local boats to Psará, while Sunrise Tours at Kanári 28 (☎22710 23558) is the central agency for GA and the fast morning boat to Çeşme. Both the Turkish evening ferry to Çeşme, as well as the most regular boat to Inoússes, are represented by Faros Travel at Egéou 18 (☎22710 27240). The helpful municipal **tourist office** (May–Sept daily 7am–10pm; Oct–April Mon–Fri 7am–3pm; ☎22710 44389) is at Kanári 18; quality commercial maps and a limited stock of English-language **books** are at Newsstand, at the first "kink" in Egéou near the Cine Diana. The most reliable **Internet** facilities are at Enter, just seaward of the Fedra Hotel, with upwards of ten terminals upstairs.

The standard green-and-cream **KTEL buses** leave from just behind the passenger waiting-room on Egéou. While services to the south of Híos are adequate, those to the centre and northwest of the island are almost nonexistent, and to explore there you'll need to rent a powerful **motorbike** or a car, or share a **taxi** (which are bright red here, not grey as in most of Greece). Two independent or small-chain **car-rental** agencies sit at Evyenías Handhrí 5–7, behind the eyesore *Chandris Hotel*; of these, Vassilakis/Reliable Rent a Car

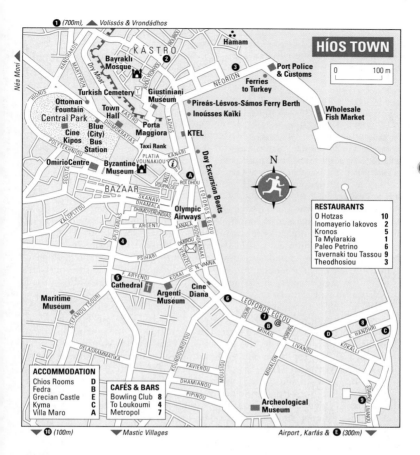

Map labels:

HÍOS TOWN

(700m), ▲ Volissós & Vrondádhos

Néa Moni

KÁSTRO
Hamam
Bayraklı Mosque
Port Police & Customs
Ferries to Turkey
0   100 m
Turkish Cemetery
Giustiniani Muséum
Ottoman Fountain
Town Hall
Pireás-Lésvos-Sámos Ferry Berth
Inoússes Kaïki
Wholesale Fish Market
Central Park
Blue (City) Bus Station
Porta Maggiora
KTEL
Cine Kipos
Taxi Rank
KANARI
PLATIA YOUNAKIOU
OmirioCentre
Byzantine Museum
Day Excursion Boats
ROÏ DHOU
BAZAAR
VOUPALOU
N
Olympic Airways
Cathedral
Argenti Museum
Cine Diana
Maritime Museum
LEOFOROS EGEOU
Archeological Museum
(100m)
Mastic Villages
Airport, Karfás & (300m)

RESTAURANTS

O Hotzas	10
Inomayerio Iakovos	2
Kronos	5
Ta Mylarakia	1
Paleo Petrino	6
Tavernaki tou Tassou	9
Theodhosiou	3

ACCOMMODATION

Chios Rooms	D
Fedra	B
Grecian Castle	E
Kyma	C
Villa Maro	A

CAFÉS & BARS

Bowling Club	8
To Loukoumi	4
Metropol	7

(☎ 22710 29300 or 694 43 34 898, ✉ ivasila@otenet.gr), with a branch at Mégas Limniónas (☎ 22710 31728), is particularly recommended. The **post office** is on Omírou, while numerous **banks** all have ATMs. A final Hiot idiosyncrasy is afternoon **shopping hours** limited to Monday and Thursday in summer.

Accommodation

Híos Town has a fair quantity of affordable **accommodation**, rarely completely full. Most places line the water or the perpendicular alleys and parallel streets behind, and almost all are plagued by traffic noise to some degree – listed are the more peaceful establishments.

Chios Rooms Egéou 110, cnr Kokáli ☎ 22710 20198 or 697 28 33 841, ✉ chiosrooms@hotmail.com. Tile- or wood-floored, high-ceilinged rooms, some en suite and relatively quiet for a seafront location, lovingly restored by proprietors Don (New Zealander) and Dina (Greek), who live on-site. Best is the penthouse "suite" with private terrace. ➋

Fedra Mihaïl Livanoú 13 ☎ 22710 41130, ☏ 22710 41128. Well-appointed *pension* in an old mansion, with stone arches in the downstairs winter bar; in summer the bar operates outside, so ask for a rear room to avoid nocturnal noise. ➍

Grecian Castle Bella Vista shore avenue, en route to airport ☎ 22710 44740, 🌐 www.greciancastle .gr. Occupying the shell of an old factory, and popular with package tourists, this is Híos Town's top-rated (A-class) digs. Lovely grounds and a sea-view pool, but the smallish main-wing rooms, despite their marble floors, wood ceilings and bug screens, aren't worth the rates charged; the rear "villa" suites are far more pleasant. Std rooms ⑥, villa suites ⑧

Kyma East end of Evyenías Handhrí ☎22710 44500, ⓔkyma@chi.forthnet .gr. En-suite hotel rooms in a Neoclassical mansion or a modern extension, with TV, huge terraces on the sea-facing side and Jacuzzi tubs in some rooms. Theo's splendid service and big

breakfasts really make the place. The old wing saw a critical moment in modern Greek history in September 1922, when Colonel Nikolaos Plastiras commandeered it as his HQ after the Greek defeat in Asia Minor, and announced the deposition of King Constantine I. B&B; Aug ⑤, otherwise ④

Villa Maro Roïdhou 15 ☎22710 27003. Modern *pension* tucked onto a tiny plaza just inland from the water; rear rooms unfortunately overlook the public toilets, but all are en suite, tile-floored and well equipped, plus there's a pleasant breakfast/ snack-bar on the ground floor. ④

The Town

South and east of the main platía, officially Plastíra but known universally as Vounakíou, extends the marvellously lively tradesmen's **bazaar**, where you can find everything from parrots to cast-iron woodstoves. Opposite the Vounakíou **taxi rank**, the grandiosely titled "**Byzantine Museum**", occupying the old **Mecidiye Mosque** (closed for renovation), is little more than an archeological warehouse, with a preponderance of Jewish marble gravestones in the courtyard – plus a few Armenian, Genoese and Turkish ones – testifying to Híos' varied population in past centuries.

Until the 1881 earthquake, the Byzantine-Genoese **Kástro** stood completely intact; thereafter developers razed the seaward walls, filled in much of the moat to the south and sold off the real estate thus created along the north waterfront. The most dramatic entry to the citadel is via the **Porta Maggiora** behind the town hall. The top floor of a medieval mansion just inside is home to the **Giustiniani Museum** (Tues–Sun 8.30am–3pm; €2), with a satisfying collection of unusual icons and twelve fourteenth-century frescoes of Old Testament prophets rescued from Panayía Krína church. The old residential quarter inside the surviving castle walls, formerly the Muslim and Jewish neighbourhoods, is well worth a wander. Among the wood and plaster houses you'll find assorted Ottoman monuments in various states of decay: a Muslim cemetery, the minaretless Bayraklı mosque, three ruined *hamams* (Turkish baths) and several inscribed **fountains**, the most ornate of which – with four facets – stands outside opposite the central park.

Further afield, three other museums beckon. The **Maritime Museum** at Stefánou Tsoúri 20 (Mon–Sat 10am–1pm; free) consists principally of model ships and oil paintings of various craft, all rather overshadowed by the mansion containing them. In the foyer are enshrined the knife and glass-globe grenade of Admiral Kanaris, who partly avenged the 1822 massacre by ramming and sinking the Ottoman fleet's flagship. In the centre of town, the **Argenti Folklore Museum** (Mon–Thurs 8am–2pm, Fri 8am–2pm & 5–7.30pm, Sat 8am–12.30pm; €2), on the top floor of the Koráï Library at Koráï 2, features ponderous genealogical portraits of the endowing family, an adjoining wing of costumes and rural impedimenta, plus multiple replicas of Delacroix's *Massacre at Híos*, a painting which did much to arouse sympathy for the cause of Greek independence.

The **archeological museum** on Mihálon (June–Aug daily 8am–7pm; Sept–May Tues–Sun 8.30am–3pm; €3) is a wide-ranging and well-lit collection, arranged both thematically and chronologically from Neolithic to Roman times, demanding at least an hour or so of exploration. Highlights include limestone column bases from the Apollo temple at Faná in the shape of lions' claws;

numerous statuettes and reliefs of Cybele (this Asiatic goddess was especially honoured here); Archaic faïence miniatures from Emborió in the shape of a cat, a hawk and a flautist; terracottas from various eras of a dwarf riding a boar; and figurines (some with articulated limbs) of *hierodouloi* or sacred prostitutes, presumably from an Aphrodite shrine. Most famous of all is an inscribed edict of Alexander the Great from 322 BC, ordering local political changes and setting out relations between himself and the Hiots.

Eating

Eating out in Híos Town can be more pleasurable than the fast-food joints and multiple *barákia* on the waterfront (plus American-style pizza parlours inland) would suggest; it is also usually cheaper than on neighbouring Sámos or Lésvos.

O Hotzas Yeoryíou Kondhýli 3, cnr Stefánou Tsoúri. Oldest (and arguably the best) taverna in town, with chef Ioannis Linos, the fourth generation of his family, presiding. Menu varies seasonally, but expect a mix of vegetarian dishes (black-eyed peas, cauliflower, stuffed red peppers), and *lahanodolmádhes*, sausages, baby fish and *mydhopílafo* (rice and mussels) washed down by own-brand ouzo or retsina. Dinner only, capacious garden in summer; closed Sun.

Inomayerio Iakovos Ayíou Yeoryíou Frouríou 20, Kástro. Iakovos himself has sold up but his chef, now owner, continues to offer a good balance of well-executed fishy dishes, grilled titbits, cheese-based recipes and vegetables; local white bulk wine or ouzo. Atmospheric garden seating in a vine-cloaked ruin opposite, or inside Oct–May. Closed Sun, and no lunch Sept–June.

Kronos Filíppou Aryéndi 2, cnr Aplotariás. The island's best, and own-made ice cream, purveyed since 1929. Limited seating or takeaway; open noon–midnight.

Ta Mylarakia By three restored windmills in Tambákika district, on the road to Vrondádhos ☏ 22710 40412. A large, well-priced seafood selection, every kind of Hiot ouzo and limited

waterside seating make reservations advisable in summer. Dinner all year, lunch also Oct–April.

Paleo Petrino Egéou 80. Standard, no-nonsense ouzerí with such delights as *iliókafto* (sun-dried fish). In the cooler months the interior, with 1950s Greek record and film posters, is more pleasant than quayside seating where you often ingest car fumes with your food.

Tavernaki tou Tassou Stávrou Livanoú 8, Bella Vista district. Superb all-rounder with creative salads, better-than-average bean dishes, dolmádhes, snails, properly done chips, a strong line in seafood and good barrel wine. A bit pricier than usual, but Tassos' and Tsambika's cooking (with son Dhimitris at the grill) is worth it. Open lunch and supper most of the year, with seaview garden seating during warmer months and heated gazebo in winter.

Theodhosiou Ouzeri Neoríon 33. The oldest, least expensive ouzerí on the quay, occupying a domed, arcaded building (though they plan a move to new premises at Kondári in 2007). A fair amount of meat grills for this type of eatery, plus a long list of seafood standards like shrimp-and-onion fry-up. Generally, best avoid fried platters in favour of grilled or boiled ones. Dinner only; closed Sun.

Drinking, nightlife and entertainment

The 1400 or so students at the local technical schools and economics/business management faculties of the University of the Aegean help keep things lively, especially along the portion of the waterfront between the two "kinks" in Egéou. Shooting **pool** is a big thing in Híos Town; many bars have several tables.

Bowling Club East end of Egéou. The seven alleys (and to a lesser extent, five pool tables) are very popular with local youth. Open until at least midnight.

Cine Kipos In central park from early June to mid-Sept only. Quality/art-house first-run fare, two screenings nightly; watch for flyers around town. During winter, the action shifts to Cine

Diana, under the eponymous hotel (two screenings nightly).

To Loukoumi Alley off Aplotariás 27/c. Old warehouse refitted as a café (8am–2pm), ouzerí (8pm–2am) and occasional events centre. Well executed and worth checking out, but closes May–Sept (when a summer premises near the airport operates) & Sun.

Metropolis/Metropol Egéou. The longest-lived
and most civilized of the music bars on this stretch
of the front, always crowded from sunset until the
small hours.

Omirio South side of the central park. Cultural
centre and events hall with frequently changing
exhibitions; foreign musicians often come here after
Athens concerts to perform in the large auditorium.

Beaches near Híos Town

The locals swim at tiny pebble coves near Vrondádhos, north of Híos Town, or from the somewhat grubby town beach in Bella Vista district, but for most visitors the closest decent one is at **Karfás**, 7km south beyond the airport and served by frequent blue buses. Once there you can **rent cars** at MG (booth opposite the Sunset Hotel). Most large Hiot package hotels are planted here, to the considerable detriment of the 500-metre-long beach itself, sandy only at the south end. The main bright spot is a unique **pension**, *Markos' Place* (☎22710 31990 or 697 32 39 706, ⓦwww.marcos-place.gr; April–Nov; ❷), installed in the disestablished **monastery of Áyios Yeóryios and Áyios Pandelímon**, on the hillside south of the bay. Markos Kostalas, who leases the premises from Thymianá municipality, has created a uniquely peaceful, leafy environment much loved by special-activity groups. Guests are lodged in the former pilgrims' cells, with a kitchen available or superior breakfasts laid on by arrangement; individuals are more than welcome (there are several single "cells"), as are families (2 "tower" rooms sleep 4), though reservations are advisable and the minimum stay is four days.

Shoreline **restaurants** aren't brilliant, though *Karatzas* (near mid-beach) and *Giamos* (south end) are striving valiantly to regain credibility after bad patches; *Giamos* has the edge in food quality. *Oasis*, between these two on the sand, is a popular breakfast, juice, snack and drinks café-bar; musical *La Notte*, up on the slope near *Markos' Place*, acquits itself well for **nightlife** into the autumn. Generally, though, it's better to strike inland for eating opportunities. *Ouzeri To Apomero* (open daily all year), in hillside Spiládhia district west of the airport (bear off the Pyrgí road towards Áyios Theodhósios and follow the many luminous green signs) has terrace seating with an eyeful of the Çeşme peninsula and some unusual dishes such as Cretan sausages and battered artichoke hearts. Between Thymianá and Neohóri, *Fakiris Taverna* (open all year but weekends only in winter) offers home-marinated aubergine and artichokes, goat baked in tomato sauce and excellent wood-fired pizzas along with well-executed seafood and pork-based *bekrí mezé* in big portions. The easiest way to find it is to head south on the road to Kalimassiá and then turn west onto the Ayíou Trafonos road, just before Neohóri, and proceed about 1km.

Some 2km further along the coast from Karfás, **AYÍA ERMIÓNI** is not a beach but a fishing anchorage surrounded by a handful of tavernas (none stands out) and apartments to rent. The nearest proper beach is at **Mégas Limniónas**, a few hundred metres further, smaller than Karfás but more scenic where low cliffs provide a backdrop. Both Ayía Ermióni and Mégas Limniónas are served by extensions of blue-bus routes to either Karfás or Thymianá, the nearest inland village. The coast road loops up to Thymianá, from where you can (with your own transport only) continue 3km south towards Kalimassiá to the turning for **Ayía Fotiní**, a 600-metre pebble beach with exceptionally clean water. Cars are excluded from the shore area; the pedestrian esplanade is lined with various blocks of rooms, less monopolized than formerly by tour companies, plus there's car hire locally. A few **tavernas** cluster around the point where the side road meets the sea, but there's far better food, specifically fish, at **KATARRÁKTIS** (return to the Kalimassiá road), where *O Tsambos* is the best and least expensive of several contenders.

Southern Híos

Besides olive groves, the gently rolling countryside in the south of the island is also home to the **mastic bush** (*Pistacia lentisca*), found across much of Aegean Greece but only here producing an aromatic resin of any quality or quantity. For centuries it was used as a base for paints, cosmetics and the chewable jelly beans, which became a somewhat addictive staple in the Ottoman harems. Indeed, the interruption of the flow of mastic from Híos to Istanbul by the revolt of spring 1822 was one of the root causes of the brutal Ottoman reaction.

The wealth engendered by the mastic trade supported twenty *mastihohoriá* (mastic villages) from the time the Genoese set up a monopoly in the substance during the fourteenth and fifteenth centuries, but the end of imperial Turkey and the development of petroleum-based products knocked the bottom out of the mastic market. Now it's just a curiosity, to be chewed – try the sweetened Elma-brand gum – or drunk as a liqueur called *mastíha*. It has also had medicinal applications since ancient times, and high-end cosmetics, toothpaste and mouthwash are now purveyed, most notably at the Mastiha Shop on Egéou in Híos Town. These days, however, the *mastihohoriá* live mainly off their tangerines, apricots and olives.

The towns themselves, the only settlements on Híos spared by the Ottomans in 1822, are architecturally unique, laid out by the Genoese but retaining a distinct Middle Eastern feel. The basic plan consists of a rectangular warren of tall houses, with the outer row doubling as the town's perimeter fortification, and breached by a limited number of arched gateways.

The mastic villages

ARMÓLIA, 20km from town, is the smallest and least imposing of the mastic villages; its main virtue is its pottery industry. **PYRGÍ**, 5km further south, is the most colourful of these communities, its houses elaborately embossed with *xystá*, geometric patterns cut into whitewash to reveal a layer of black volcanic sand underneath; strings of sun-drying tomatoes add a further splash of colour in autumn. On the northeast corner of the central square the twelfth-century Byzantine church of **Áyii Apóstoli** (Tues–Thurs & Sat 10am–1pm), embellished with much later frescoes, is tucked under an arcade. Of late, vast numbers of postcard racks and boutiques have sprung up on every main thoroughfare, detracting somewhat from the atmosphere. In the medieval core you'll find a **bank** (with ATM), a **post office** and an array of cafés and *souvláki* stalls on the central platía. **OLÝMBI**, 7km further west along the bus route serving Armólia and Pyrgí, is one of the less visited mastic villages, but not devoid of interest. The characteristic tower-keep, which at Pyrgí stands half-inhabited away from the modernized main square, here looms bang in the middle of the platía, its ground floor occupied by the community *kafenío* on one side, and a taverna-bar on the other; however, the best **eating** here is found at *Ayioryitiko* by the Káto Pórta, where the menu can encompass game and mushrooms in the right season, otherwise well-executed standards like *melitzánes* imám and various *píttes*.

Sombre, monochrome **MESTÁ**, 4km west of Olýmbi, is considered the finest example of the genre; despite more snack-bars and trinket shops than strictly necessary on the outskirts, Mestá remains just the right side of twee as most people here still work the land. From its main square, dominated by the **church of the Taxiárhis** (the largest on the island), a bewildering maze of cool, shady lanes with anti-seismic buttressing and tunnels, leads off in all directions. Most streets end in blind alleys, except those leading to the six portals; the northeast

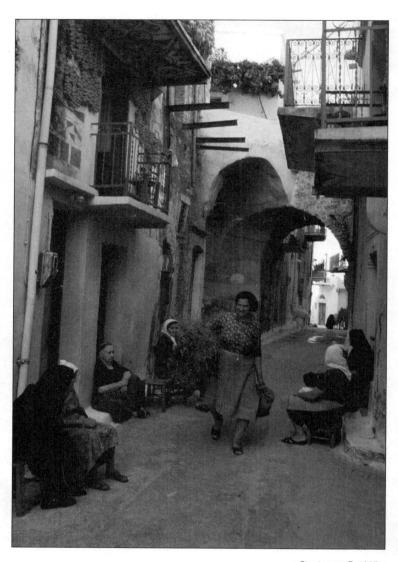

△ Street scene, Pyrgí, Híos

one still has its original iron gate. There are half-a-dozen **rooms** in restored traditional dwellings managed by Dhimitris Pipidhis (☎22710 76029; ❸), or apartments through Dhespina Karambela (☎22710 76065 or ask at *O Morias eis ta Mesta* taverna; ❹). Alternatively, three separate premises managed by Anna Floradhi's gift shop (☎ & ℉22710 76455; ❸) are more modernized. Of the two **tavernas** sharing table-space on the main platía, *Mesaionas* is better value and has the more helpful proprietor (she also has rooms: ☎22710 76494; ❸).

The mastic coast – and the Sykiás Olýmbon cave

The closest good **beaches** to Mestá lie just east of its under used port, Liménas Mestón: **Dhídhyma** (4km away), a double cove with an islet protecting it; **Potámi**, with the namesake stream feeding it; and the least scenic **Ayía Iríni** (8km), which does have a reliable taverna. All of these little bays will catch surf and flotsam when the north wind is up.

From Olýmbi, a paved, six-kilometre road heads to the well-signed **cave of Sykiás Olýmbon** (Easter–Oct Tues–Sun 10am–8pm; admission in groups of 25 or less every 30min; €3), only opened to the public in 2003. For years it was just a small hole in the ground where villagers disposed of their dead animals, but from 1985 on speleologists explored it properly. The cave, with a constant temperature of 18°C, evolved in two phases between 150 million and 50 million years ago, and has a maximum depth of 57m (though tours only visit the top 30m or so). The stalagmite and stalactite formations, with fanciful names like Chinese Forest, Medusa and Organ Pipes, are among the most beautiful in the Mediterranean. Before or after your subterranean tour, you can continue another 1500m on dirt surface to the little cape-top monastery of **Ayía Dhýnami** and two sheltered coves adjacent for a swim: the nearer sandy, the remoter gravel and sand.

Pyrgí village is closest to the two major beach resorts in this corner of the island. The nearest, 6km distant, is **EMBORIÓS**, an almost landlocked harbour with four passable **tavernas**; *Porto Emborios* has the edge with almost year-round operation, fair prices, home-made desserts and seafood like *atherína*-and-onion fry-up or small wild sea bass. British-excavated **ancient Emboreios** on the hill to the northeast and well signposted on the road in, was rehabilitated as an "archeological park" in 2004 – and is closed at the moment for lack of funds; Currently more accessible is the cruciform **early Christian baptistry**, signposted in a field just in from the water; it's protected by a later, round structure (locked but you can see everything through the grating).

For swimming, follow the road to its end at an oversubscribed car park and the beach of **Mávros Yialós** (Mávra Vólia), then continue by flagstoned walkway over the headland to the more dramatic pebble strand (part nudist) of purple-grey volcanic stones, **Fóki**, twice as long and backed by impressive cliffs. If you want sand (and amenities) you'll have to go to **KÓMI**, 3km northeast, also accessible from Armólia via Kalamotí; there are just a few **tavernas** (most reliably open of these are *Bella Mare* and *Nostalgia*, both laying on sunbeds to patrons), café-bars and seasonal apartments behind the pedestrianized beachfront.

Central Híos

The portion of Híos extending west and southwest from Híos Town matches the south in terms of interesting monuments, and good roads make touring under your own power an easy matter. There are also several beaches on the far shore of the island which, though not necessarily the best on Híos, are fine for a dip at the middle or end of the day.

The Kámbos

The **Kámbos**, a vast fertile plain carpeted with citrus groves, extends southwest from Híos Town almost as far as the village of Halkió. The district was originally settled by the Genoese during the fourteenth century, and remained a preserve of the local aristocracy until 1822. Exploring by bicycle or motorbike may be less frustrating than going by car, since the web of narrow, poorly marked lanes sandwiched between high walls guarantees disorientation and frequent backtracking. Behind the walls you catch fleeting glimpses of ornate old mansions built from locally quarried sandstone; courtyards are paved in pebbles or alternating light and dark tiles, and most still contain a pergola-shaded irrigation pond filled by a *mánganos* or donkey-powered waterwheel, used before the age of electric pumps to draw water from wells up to 30m deep.

Many of the sumptuous three-storey dwellings, constructed in a hybrid Italo-Turco-Greek style, have languished derelict since 1881, but an increasing number are being converted for use as private estates or unique **accommodation**. The best and most consistently attended of these are *Mavrokordatiko* (T 22710 32900, W www.mavrokordatiko.com; B&B; ❺), about 1.5km south of the airport, with enormous heated, wood-panelled rooms, and *Arhondiko Perleas* (T 22710 32217; B&B; ❺), set in a huge citrus grove, with ample breakfasts including organic jams.

Not strictly speaking in Kámbos, but most easily reached from it en route to the *mastihohoriá*, is an outstanding rural Byzantine monument. The thirteenth-century **church of Panayía Krína**, isolated amidst orchards and woods, is well worth the challenge of negotiating a maze of paved but poorly marked lanes beyond Vavýli village, 9km from town. It's closed indefinitely for snail's-pace restoration, but a peek through the apse window will give you a fair idea of the intricately frescoed interior, sufficiently lit by a twelve-windowed drum. All of the late-medieval frescoes, as well as some Byzantine work underneath, have been removed, and are sometimes displayed in Híos Town's Giustiniani Museums (see p.420). The alternating brick and stonework of the exterior alone justifies the trip here, though architectural harmony is marred by the later addition of a clumsy lantern over the narthex, and the visibly unsound structure is kept from collapse by cable-binding at the roofline.

Néa Moní

Almost exactly in the middle of the island, the **monastery of Néa Moní** was founded by the Byzantine Emperor Constantine Monomahos ("The Dueller") IX in 1042 on the spot where a wonder-working icon had been discovered. It ranks among the most beautiful and important monuments on any of the Greek islands; the mosaics, together with those of Dháfni and Ósios Loukás on the mainland, are among the finest surviving art of their age in Greece, and the setting – high up in still partly forested mountains 15km west of the port – is no less memorable.

Once a powerful and independent community of six hundred monks, Néa Moní was pillaged in 1822 and most of its residents (including 3500 civilians sheltering here) put to the sword. Since then many of its outbuildings have languished in ruins, though a recent EU grant has prompted massive restoration work, with the exterior cocooned in scaffolding until further notice. The 1881 tremor caused comprehensive damage, while exactly a century later a forest fire threatened to engulf the place until the resident icon was paraded along the perimeter wall, miraculously repelling the flames. Today the monastery, with its giant refectory and vaulted water cisterns, is inhabited by just a couple of lay workers.

Bus excursions formerly provided by the KTEL have been suspended since the main focus of interest, the *katholikón*, is closed to the public until at least late 2007, whilst much-needed restoration proceeds; neither is it worth shelling out specially for a taxi at the moment, but do stop in briefly if touring under your own power.

Just inside the main gate (daily 8am–1pm & 4–8pm, afternoon hours 5–8pm in summer) stands a **chapel/ossuary** containing some of the bones of those who met their death here in 1822; axe-clefts in children's skulls attest to the savagery of the attackers. The **katholikón**, with the cupola resting on an octagonal drum, is of a design seen elsewhere only in Cyprus; the frescoes in the exonarthex are badly damaged by holes allegedly left by Turkish bullets, but the **mosaics** are another matter. The narthex contains portrayals of the various saints of Híos sandwiched between *Christ Washing the Disciples' Feet* and the *Betrayal*, in which Judas's kiss has unfortunately been obliterated, but Peter is clearly visible lopping off the ear of the high priest's servant. In the dome of the sanctuary, which once contained a complete life cycle of Christ, only the *Baptism*, part of the *Crucifixion*, the *Descent from the Cross*, the *Resurrection* and the evangelists Mark and John survived the earthquake.

The west coast

Some 5km west of Néa Moní sits **AVGÓNYMA**, a cluster of dwellings on a knoll overlooking the coast; the name means "Clutch of Eggs", an apt description when it's viewed from the ridge above. Since the 1980s, the place has been almost totally restored as a summer haven by descendants of the original villagers, though the permanent population is just seven. A returned Greek-American family runs a reasonable, simple-fare **taverna**, O Pyrgos (open all year), in an arcaded mansion on the main square. The classiest **accommodation** option here is *Spitakia*, a cluster of small restored houses for up to five people (①22710 20513 or 22710 81200, ⑩www.spitakia.gr; ④), though *O Pyrgos* restaurant also keeps more modernized units in the village (①22710 42175; ③).

A paved side road continues another 4km north to **ANÁVATOS**, whose empty, dun-coloured dwellings, soaring above pistachio orchards, are almost indistinguishable from the 300-metre-high bluff on which they're built. During the 1822 insurrection, some four hundred inhabitants and refugees threw themselves over this cliff rather than surrender to the besieging Ottomans, and it's still a preferred suicide leap. Anávatos can now only muster two permanent inhabitants, and given a lack of accommodation, one mediocre snack bar, plus an eerie, traumatized atmosphere, it's no place to be stranded at dusk.

West of Avgónyma, the main road descends 6km to the sea in well-graded loops. Turning right (north) at the junction leads first to the beach at **Elínda**, alluring from afar but rocky and murky up close; it's better to continue towards more secluded, mixed sand-and-gravel coves to either side of Metóhi – best of these are **Tigáni** and **Makriá Ámmos**, the latter nudist. **SIDHIROÚNDA**, the only village hereabouts (with a competent summer **taverna**), enjoys a spectacular hilltop setting overlooking the sea.

All along this coast, as far southwest as Liménas Mestón, are round **watchtowers** erected by the Genoese to look out for pirates – the second swimmable cove you reach after turning left from the junction bears the name **Kastélla** (officially Trahíli), again mixed sand and gravel. The first cove, more protected and popular, is **Xeropótamos**. A sparse weekday-only bus service resumes 9km south of the junction at **LITHÍ**, a friendly village perched on forested ledge overlooking the sea. There are tavernas and *kafenía* in the older, central core, but most visitors head 2km downhill to **Paralía Lithíou**, a popular weekend target of Hiot townies for the sake of its large but hard-packed, windswept beach. The better of two adjacent, pricey fish **tavernas** here is *Ta Tría Adherfia*.

Some 5km south of Lithí, the valley-bottom village of **VÉSSA** is an unsung gem, more open and less casbah-like than Mestá or Pyrgí, but still homogeneous.

Its honey-coloured buildings are arrayed in a vast grid punctuated by numerous belfries; there's a nameless *kafenío* installed on the ground floor of the tower-mansion on the main through road, while across the square *Kostas* (aka *Froso's*) does excellent *yíros*, *loukániko* and *souvláki*.

Northern Híos

Northern Híos never really recovered from the 1822 massacre, and between Pityós and Volissós the desolation left by 1980s fires will further dampen inquisitive spirits. Since the early 1900s the villages have been left all but deserted much of the year, which means correspondingly sparse bus services. About one-third of the former population lives in Híos Town, returning only during major festivals or to tend smallholdings; others, based in Athens or the US, visit their ancestral homes for just a few midsummer weeks.

The road to Kardhámyla

Blue urban buses run north from Híos Town up to **VRONDÁDHOS**, an elongated coastal suburb that's a favourite residence of the island's many seafarers. Homer is reputed to have lived and taught here, and in the terraced parkland just above the little fishing port and pebble beach you can visit his purported lectern, more probably an ancient altar of Cybele. Accordingly many of the buses heading out here are labelled DARJAKOPESQA, "the Teacher's Rock".

Some 14km out of town, the tiny bayside hamlet of **PANDOUKIÓS** can muster an excellent if pricey waterside **taverna**, the *Kourtesis*, where lobster can sometimes be had. But **LANGÁDHA**, 2.5km beyond, is probably the first point on the eastern coast road where you'd be tempted to stop, though there is no proper beach nearby. Set at the mouth of a deep valley, this attractive little harbour settlement looks across its bay to a pine grove, and beyond to Turkey. Night-time visitors come for the sustaining seafood at two adjacent **tavernas** on the quay: *Tou Kopelou*, better known as *Stelios'*, and second-choice *Paradhisos*.

Just beyond Langádha an important side road leads 5km up and inland to **PITYÓS**, an oasis in a mountain pass presided over by a round castle; people come here from some distance to **eat** at *Makellos* on the southwest edge of the village, a shrine of local cuisine (late June to early Sept daily lunch/dinner; rest of year Fri–Sun evenings only). Continuing 4km more brings you to a junction allowing quick access to the west of the island and the Volissós area (see opposite).

Kardhámyla and around

Most traffic proceeds to **ÁNO KARDHÁMYLA** and **KÁTO KARD-HÁMYLA**, the latter 37km out of the main town. Positioned at opposite edges of a fertile plain rimmed by mountains, they initially come as welcome relief from Homer's crags. Káto, better known as **MÁRMARO**, is larger – indeed, the island's second town – with a bank (no ATM), post office and filling station. However, there is little to attract a casual visitor other than some Neoclassical architecture; the port, mercilessly exposed to the *meltémi*, is strictly business-like, and there are few tourist facilities. A sterling exception is *Hotel Kardamyla* (☎22720 23353, ℱ22720 23354; ❺ Aug, ❹ otherwise), co-managed with Híos Town's *Hotel Kyma*, offering spacious, fan-equipped **rooms** and a few suites. It has the bay's only pebble beach, and the in-house restaurant is a reliable source of lunch (July & Aug) if you're touring. Worthwhile independent **tavernas** include *Ouzeri Barba Yiannis* (run by Irini Tsirigou; all year), beside the port authority, or *Iy Vlyhadha* (summer only), facing the bay of the same name west over the headland.

For better swimming head west 5km to **Nagós**, a gravel-shore bay at the foot of an oasis, which is where the summertime bus line terminates. Lush greenery is nourished by active springs up at a bend in the road, enclosed in a sort of grotto overhung by tall cliffs. The place name is a corruption of *naos*, after a large Poseidon temple that once stood near the springs, but centuries of orchard-tending, antiquities-pilfering and organized excavations after 1912 mean that nothing remains visible. Down at the shore the swimming is good, if a bit chilly; there are two mediocre **tavernas** (there's a better one inland, by the spring) and a few **rooms** to rent. Your only chance of relative solitude in July or August lies 1km west at **Yióssonas**; this is a much longer beach, but less sheltered, rockier and with no facilities.

Volissós and around

VOLISSÓS, 42km from Híos Town by the most direct road (but just 44km by the much easier route via Avgónyma), was once the market town for a dozen remote hill villages beyond. Its old stone houses still curl appealingly beneath the crumbling hilltop Byzantine fort, whose towers were improved by the Genoese. Volissós can seem depressing at first, with the bulk of its 250 mostly elderly permanent inhabitants living in newer buildings around the main square, but opinions improve with longer acquaintance. This back-water ethos may not last; the upper quarters are in the grip of a restoration mania, most of it done in admirable taste, with ruins changing hands for stratospheric prices.

Grouped around the platía you'll find a **post office**, a **bank** ATM and three mediocre **tavernas**. A pair of filling stations operate 2.5km out of town, the only one hereabouts; if reliant on public transport, you should plan on overnighting since the bus only ventures out here on Sundays on a day-trip basis, plus two weekly workdays in the early afternoon (unless you care to travel at 4.30am). This should cause no dismay, since the area has the best beaches and some of the more interesting **accommodation** on Híos. The most reasonable and longest established of a few restoration projects are sixteen old houses, mostly in Pýrgos district, available through ✈ *Volissos Travel* (☎22740 21413 or 693 69 75 470, Ⓦ www.volissostravel.gr; May–Sept; ❹). Units usually accommodate two people – all have terraces, fully equipped kitchens, air conditioning and features such as tree trunks upholding sleeping lofts, reflecting proprietress Stella's past as a sculptor. She often has spring/autumn specials including a hire car.

LIMNIÁ (sometimes Limiá), the port of Volissós, lies 2km south though ferry/*kaïki* service from here to Psará is suspended. The most consistent **taverna** here is *O Zikos* (open all year) at the far end of the quay, with good grills and a superb house salad featuring sun-dried tomatoes, plus occasional seafood. At Limniá you're not far from the fabled beaches either. A 1.5-kilometre drive or walk southeast over the headland brings you to **Mánagros**, a seemingly endless sand-and-pebble beach, though a major resort project here is being debated. More intimate, sandy **Lefkáthia** lies just a ten-minute stroll along the cement drive threading over the headland north of the harbour; amenities are limited to a seasonal snack shack on the sand, and Ioannis Zorbas's apartments (☎22740 21436, Ⓕ22740 21720; ❹), beautifully set in a garden where the concrete track joins an asphalt road down from Volissós. This is bound for **Límnos** (not to be confused with Limniá), the next protected cove, 400m east of Lefkáthia, where *Taverna Iy Limnos* is the better of two tavernas, with fish grills and specials like *kokorás krasáto* (coq au vin), and the spruce *Latini Apartments* (℡22740 21461, Ⅎ22740 21871; ❹) are graced with multiple stone terraces.

Ayía Markélla, 5km further northwest of Límnos, stars in many local post-cards: it's a long, stunning beach fronting the **monastery** of Híos's patron saint (festival July 22), the latter not especially interesting or useful for outsiders, since its cells are reserved for Greek pilgrims. In an interesting variation on the expulsion of the money changers from the temple, only religious souvenirs are allowed to be sold in the holy precincts, while all manner of plastic junk is displayed just outside.

The dirt road past the monastery grounds is passable by any vehicle, with care, and emerges up on the paved road running high above the northwest coast. Turn left and proceed to the remote village of **ÁYIO GÁLA**, whose claim to fame is a **grotto-church** complex, built into a stream-lapped palisade at the bottom of the village. Signs ("Panayía Ayiogaloúsena") point to a lane crossing the water, but for access you'll need to find the key-keeper (ask at the central *kafenío*), and descend via a flight of stairs starting beside a eucalyptus tree. Of the two churches inside the cavern – whose nether depths are being developed as a tourist attraction, so admission will become more formalized – the larger one near the mouth of the grotto dates from the fifteenth century but seems newer owing to a 1993 external renovation. Inside, however, a fantastically intricate *témblon* vies for your attention with a tinier, older chapel, built entirely within the rear of the cavern. Its frescoes are badly smudged, except for a wonderfully mysterious and mournful Virgin, surely the saddest in Christendom, holding a knowing Child.

Satellite islands: Psará and Inoússes

There's a single settlement, with beaches and an isolated rural monastery, on both of Híos's satellite isles, but each is surprisingly different from the other, and of course from their large neighbour. **Inoússes**, the nearer and smaller islet, has a daily *kaïki* service from Híos Town in season; **Psará** has less regular services subject to weather conditions (in theory most days from Híos Town, plus a few weekly subsidized-line ferries), and is too remote to be done justice on a day-trip.

Psará

The birthplace of revolutionary war hero Admiral Kanaris, **Psará** devoted its merchant fleets – the third largest in 1820s Greece – to the cause of independence, and paid dearly for it. Vexed beyond endurance, the Turks landed over-whelming forces in 1824 to stamp out this nest of resistance. Perhaps 3000 of the 30,000 inhabitants escaped in small boats, which were rescued by a French fleet, but the majority retreated to a hilltop powder magazine and blew it (and themselves) up rather than surrender. The nationalist poet Dhionysios Solomos immortalized the incident in famous stanzas:

On the Black Ridge of Psará,
Glory walks alone.
She meditates on her heroes
And wears in her hair a wreath
Made from a few dry weeds
Left on the barren ground.

Today, it's a sad, stark place fully living up to its name ("the mottled things" in Greek), and never really recovered from the holocaust. The Turks burned whatever houses and vegetation the blast had missed, and the official population now barely exceeds four hundred. The only positive recent development was a 1980s revitalization project instigated by a French-Greek descendant of Kanaris and a Greek team. The port was improved, mains electricity and pure water provided, a secondary school opened, and cultural links between France and the island established, though this has not been reflected in increased tourist numbers.

Arrival can be something of an ordeal; the regular small ferry from Híos Town can take up to four hours to cover the 57 nautical miles of generally rough sea. A few times weekly, large ferries on the subsidized Lávrio–Sígri (Lésvos)–Límnos line appear at odd hours; there is currently no *kaïki* service from Límnia.

Since few buildings in the east-facing harbour community predate the twentieth century, it's a strange hotchpotch of ecclesiastical and secular architecture that greets the eye on disembarking. There's a distinctly southern feel, more like the Dodecanese or the Cyclades, and some peculiar churches, of which no two are alike in style.

For **staying overnight**, there's a choice between a handful of fairly basic rooms and three more professional outfits: *Psara Studios* (⊕22740 61233; ④) and *Apartments Restalia* (⊕22740 61201, ⑤22740 61000; ④ Aug, ②–③ otherwise), both a bit stark but with balconies and kitchens, or the EOT *xenónas* (⊕22740 61293; ④) in a restored prison. A few **tavernas**, a **post office**, bakery and shop complete the list of amenities; there's no full-service bank.

Psará's **beaches** are decent, improving the further northeast you walk from the port. You quickly pass Káto Yialós, Katsoúni and Lazarétto with its off-putting power station, before reaching **Lákka** ("narrow ravine"), fifteen minutes along, apparently named after its grooved rock formations in which you may have to shelter – much of this coast is windswept, with a heavy swell offshore. **Límnos**, 25 minutes from the port along the coastal path, is big and attractive, but there's no reliable taverna here, or indeed at any of the beaches. The only other thing to do on Psará is to walk north across the island – the old track there has been paved – to the **monastery of the Kímisis (Assumption)**; uninhabited since the 1970s, this comes to life only in the first week of August, when its revered icon is carried in ceremonial procession to town and back on the eve of August 5.

Inoússes

Inoússes has a permanent population of about three hundred – less than half its prewar figure – and a very different history from Psará. For generations this medium-sized islet, first settled around 1750 by Hiot shepherds, has provided the Aegean with many of her wealthiest shipping families: various members of the Livanos, Lemos and Pateras clans (with every street or square named after the last-named family) were born here. This helps explain the large villas and visiting summer yachts in an otherwise sleepy Greek backwater – as well as a **maritime museum** (daily 10am–1pm; €1.50) near the quay, endowed by various shipping magnates. At the west end of the quay, the bigwigs have also funded a large nautical academy, which trains future members of the merchant navy.

On Sundays in season you can make an inexpensive **day-trip** to Inoússes from Híos with the locals' ferry *Inousses II*; on most other days of the week this arrives at 3pm, returning early the next morning. Otherwise, during the tourist season you must participate in the pricier excursions offered from Híos, with return tickets running more than double the cost of the regular ferry.

Two church-tipped islets, each privately owned, guard the unusually well-protected harbour; the **town** of Inoússes is surprisingly large, draped over hillsides enclosing a ravine. Despite a wealthy reputation, its appearance is unpretentious, the houses displaying a mix of vernacular and modest Neoclassical style. There is just one, fairly comfortable, **hotel**, the recently renovated *Thalassoporos* (☎22720 55475; ❹), on the main easterly hillside lane, but no licensed *dhomátia*. Aside from the restaurant in the hotel, **eating out** is similarly limited; the most reliable option is the simple *Taverna Pateronisso*, conspicuous at the base of the disembarkation jetty, though every season a few simple ouzerís off towards the nautical academy try their luck – the most durable of these is *O Glaros*. Café-bars such as *Naftikos Omilos*, *Karnayio* and (inland uphill) *Trigono* provide a semblance of **nightlife**. Otherwise, be prepared to patronize one of the three shops (one on the waterfront, two up the hill). Beside the museum you'll find a **post office** and a **bank**.

The rest of this tranquil island, at least the southern slope, is surprisingly green and well tended; there are no springs, so water comes from a mix of fresh and brackish wells, as well as a reservoir. The sea is extremely clean and calm on the sheltered southerly shore; among its beaches, choose from **Zepága**, **Biláli** or **Kástro**, respectively five, twenty and thirty minutes' walk west of the port. More secluded **Fourkeró** (Farkeró in dialect) lies 25 minutes east: first along a cement drive ending at a seaside chapel, then by path past pine groves and over a ridge. As on Psará, there are no reliable facilities at any of the beaches.

At the end of the westerly road stands the somewhat macabre convent of **Evangelismoú**, endowed by a branch of the Pateras family. Inside reposes the mummified body of the lately canonized daughter, Irini, whose prayers to die in place of her terminally ill father Panagos were answered early in the 1960s; he's entombed here also, having outlived Irini by some years. The abbess, presiding over about twenty nuns, is none other than the widowed Mrs Pateras; only women are admitted, and casual visits are not encouraged.

Lésvos (Mytilíni)

Lésvos, the third-largest Greek island after Crete and Évvia, is not only the birthplace of Sappho, but also of Aesop, Arion and – more recently – the Greek primitive artist Theophilos, the Nobel laureate poet Odysseus Elytis and the novelist Stratis Myrivilis. Despite these artistic associations, Lésvos may not at first strike the visitor as particularly beautiful or interesting; much of the landscape is rocky, volcanic terrain, dotted with thermal springs and varying between vast grain fields, salt pans or even near-desert. But there are also oak and pine forests as well as endless olive groves, some of these over five hundred years old. With its balmy climate and suggestive contours, the island tends to grow on you with prolonged acquaintance.

Lovers of medieval and Ottoman **architecture** certainly won't be disappointed. Castles survive at the main town of Mytilíni, at Mólyvos, Eressós, Sígri and near Ándissa; most of these date from the late fourteenth century, when Lésvos was given as a dowry to a Genoese prince of the Gattilusi clan following his marriage to the sister of one of the last Byzantine emperors. Apart from Crete and Évvia, Lésvos was the only Greek island where Turks settled significantly in rural villages (they usually stuck to the safety of towns), which explains the odd Ottoman bridge, box-like mosque or crumbling minaret often found in the middle of nowhere. Again unusually for the Aegean islands,

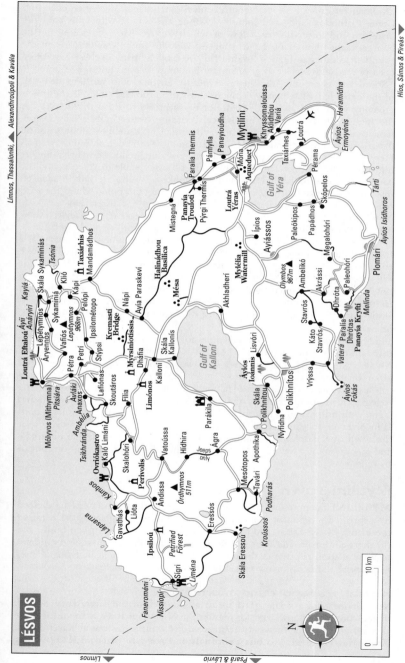

LÉSVOS

Limnos, Thessaloníki, ▲ Alexandhroúpoli & Kavála

Híos, Sámos & Pireás ►

Psará & Lávrio ▲   Límnos ◄

10 km

N

Ottoman reforms of the eighteenth century encouraged the emergence of a Greek Orthodox land- and industry-owning aristocracy, who built rambling mansions and tower-houses, a few of which survive. More common are the bourgeois townhouses of the worthies in Mytilíni town, erected early in the twentieth century to French Second Empire models; many of these have often been pressed into service as government buildings or even restored as hotels.

Social and economic idiosyncrasies persist: anyone who has attended one of the extended village *paniyíria*, with hours of music and tables in the streets groaning with food and drink, will not be surprised to learn that Lésvos has the highest alcoholism rate in Greece. Breeding livestock, especially horses, remains disproportionately important, and traffic jams caused by mounts instead of parked cars are not unheard of – signs reading "Forbidden to Tether Animals Here" are still common, as are herds of apparently unattended donkeys wandering about. Much of the acreage in olives is still inaccessible to vehicles, and the harvest can only be hauled out by those donkeys – who are duly loaded en masse onto the back of trucks to be transported to the point where the road fizzles out. Organic production has been embraced enthusiastically as a way of making Lésvos agricultural products more competitive – *Violoyikó Ktíma* (Organic Plot) or *Violoyikí Kaliéryia* (Organic Cultivation) signs abound.

Historically, the olive plantations, ouzo distilleries, animal husbandry and fishing industry supported those who chose not to emigrate, but with these enterprises relatively stagnant, tourism has made visible inroads. However, it still accounts for under ten percent of the local economy: there are few large hotels outside the capital, Skála Kalloní or Mólyvos. Visitor numbers have in fact dipped since 1996, the result of stalled plans to expand the airport, unrealistic hotel pricing and the dropping of the island from several tour operators' programmes.

Public **buses** tend to observe schedules for the benefit of villagers coming to town on errands, not day-tripping tourists. Carrying out such excursions from Mytilíni is next to impossible anyway, owing to the size of the island – about 70km by 45km at its widest points – and a lingering handful of appalling roads (most others have been improved, along with their signposting). Moreover, the topography is complicated by the two deeply indented gulfs of Kalloní and Yéra, with no bridges across their mouths, which means that going from A to B involves an obligatory change of bus at either Mytilíni, on the east shore, or the town of Kalloní, in the middle of the island. It's best to decide on a base and stay there for a few days, exploring its immediate surroundings on foot or by rented vehicle.

Mytilíni Town

MYTILÍNI, the port and capital, sprawls between and around two bays divided by a fortified promontory, and in Greek fashion often doubles as the name of the island. Many visitors are put off by the combination of urban bustle and (in the traditionally humbler northern districts) slight seediness, and contrive to leave as soon as possible; the town returns the compliment by being a fairly impractical and occasionally expensive place to base yourself.

Arrival, transport and information

The **airport** has a single ATM in arrivals as well as three car rental booths. There's no bus link, so a taxi for the 7km into Mytilíni Town is the usual shuttle method; Olympic Airways is southwest of the main harbour at Kavétsou 44. As on Híos, there are two **bus terminals**: the *iperastykó* (standard KTEL) buses

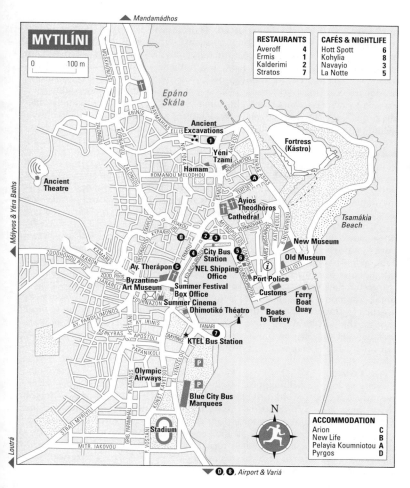

MYTILÍNI

0   100 m

RESTAURANTS	
Averoff	4
Ermis	1
Kalderimi	2
Stratos	7

CAFÉS & NIGHTLIFE	
Hott Spott	6
Kohylia	8
Navayio	3
La Notte	5

Mandamádhos

Epáno Skála

Ancient Excavations

Yéni Tzamí

Hamam

Fortress (Kástro)

Ancient Theatre

Ayios Theodhóros Cathedral

Tsamákia Beach

New Museum

City Bus Station

Ay. Therápon

NEL Shipping Office

Old Museum

Byzantine Art Museum

Summer Festival Box Office

Summer Cinema

Dhimotikó Théatro

Port Police

Customs

Ferry Boat Quay

Boats to Turkey

KTEL Bus Station

Olympic Airways

Blue City Bus Marquees

Stadium

N

Mólyvos & Yéra Baths

Loutrá

ACCOMMODATION	
Arion	C
New Life	B
Pelayia Koumniotou	A
Pyrgos	D

Airport & Variá

leave from a small station near Platía Konstandinopóleos at the southern end of the harbour, while the *astykó* (blue bus) service departs from a marquee at the top of the harbour. If you're driving, use the enormous free public **car park** a few blocks south of the KTEL, or the oval plaza near the new archeological museum – there are no other easily available spaces in the centre. If you're intent on getting over to Ayvalık in Turkey, you've a choice of two boats (Jale or Mytilini); book through the agency at Koundouriótou 78 (☎22510 46668) or Dimakis Tours at Koundouriótou 73 (☎22510 27865). GA ferries is handled by Picolo Travel at no. 73a (☎22510 27000), while Saos Ferries and LANE are handled by Pan Tours at no. 87 (☎22510 46595). NEL Ferries has a dedicated agency at Koundouriótou 47 (☎22510 28480), though in fact nearly everyone sells their tickets.

   Car rental is best arranged through reputable major or local–chain franchises like Payless/Auto Moto at Koundouriótou 49 (☎22510 43555, ✉automoto@otenet. gr), Budget at no. 51 (☎22510 29600, ✉budget@lesvosholidays.com), Just at no. 53 (☎22510 43080), Hertz at no. 87 (☎22510 37355) or Best at no. 89 (☎22510 37337, ⓦwww.best-rentacar.com) – though it can be cheaper to rent at the resort of your choice. Other amenities include the **post office** on Vournázon, behind the central park, and numerous **banks** along Koundouriótou with ATMs. Before leaving town, you might visit the **EOT** regional headquarters at James Aristárhou 6 (Mon–Fri 8am–2.30pm) to get hold of their excellent town and island maps, plus other brochures, or the Newsstand **bookshop** on Kavétsou near Olympic for a limited selection of English literature, including a few Rough Guides.

Accommodation

Finding **accommodation** can be initially daunting: the waterfront hotels are noisy and exorbitantly priced. If you need to stay, it's preferable to hunt down better-value rooms in the backstreets, with supply usually exceeding demand. The friendly if basic rooms of Pelayia Koumniotou at Yeoryíou Tertséti 6 (☎22510 20643; ❷) are partly air-conditioned. *New Life* at the end of Olýmbou, a cul-de-sac off Ermoú (☎22510 42650 or 693 22 79 057; ❸), offers wood-floored, en-suite rooms in an old mansion, or similarly priced ones with wood or mosaic floor, but with bizarre modern murals in the halls, at co-managed *Arion* down the street at Aríonos 4. The most distinctive hotel is pricey *Pyrgos*, Eleftheríou Venizélou 49 (☎22510 25069, ⓦwww .pyrgoshotel.gr; ❼), a converted mansion with utterly over-the-top kitsch decor in the communal areas. However, the rooms – most with a balcony – are perfectly acceptable; the best ones are the three round units in the tower. If you've a car, though, the best local base is probably the ⚓ *Votsala* (☎22510 71231, ⓦwww .votsalahotel.com; ❹), a sophisticated beachfront hotel with well-tended gardens but no TV in the rooms, 13km north in Paralía Thermís.

The Town

Despite its logistical difficulties, Mytilíni offers enough to justify a few hours' stopover. On the promontory sits the Byzantine-Genoese-Ottoman **fortress** (May–Sept Tues–Sun 8.30am–7pm; Oct–April Tues–Sun 8.30am–2.30pm; €2), comprising ruined structures from all these eras and an Ottoman inscription above a Byzantine double-headed eagle at the south gate. Further inland, the town skyline is dominated in turn by the Germanic-Gothic belfry spire of **Áyios Theodhóros** and the mammary dome of **Áyios Therápon**, both expressions of the post-Baroque taste of the nineteenth-century Ottoman Greek bourgeoisie. They stand more or less at opposite ends of the bazaar, whose main street, Ermoú, links the town centre with the little-used north harbour of Epáno Skála. On its way there Ermoú passes several expensive and rather picked-over antique shops near the roofless, derelict **Yéni Tzamí** at the heart of the old Muslim quarter, just a few steps east of a superb Turkish **hamam**, restored to its former glory but now locked unless a special exhibit is being held. Between Ermoú and the castle lies a maze of atmospheric lanes lined with grandiose belle époque mansions and elderly vernacular houses, though most of the ornate townhouses are to be found in the southerly districts of Sourádha and Kióski, on the way to the airport.

Mytilíni's excellent **archeological collection** is housed in **two separate galleries** (May–Sept Tues–Sun 8am–7.30pm; Oct–April Tues–Sun 8.30am–3pm; €3), a few hundred metres apart. The newer, upper museum, at the base of 8-Noemvríou, is devoted to finds from wealthy Roman Mytilene, in particular three rooms of well-displayed mosaics from second/third-century AD villas – highlights are a crude but engaging scene of Orpheus charming all manner of beasts, and two fishermen surrounded by clearly recognizable (and edible) sea creatures. Earlier eras are represented in the older wing (same hours as Roman wing, same ticket admits), located in a former mansion just behind the ferry dock. The ground floor has Neolithic finds from Áyios Vartholoméos cave and Bronze Age Thermí, but the star, late-Classical exhibits upstairs include minutely detailed terracotta figurines: a pair of acrobats, two *kourotrophoi* figures (goddesses suckling infants, predecessors of all Byzantine Galaktotrofoússa icons), children playing with a ball or dogs, and Aphrodite riding a dolphin. A specially built annexe at the rear contains stone-cut inscriptions of various edicts and treaties, plus a Roman sculpture of a drunken satyr asleep on a wineskin.

There's also a worthwhile **Byzantine Art Museum** (Mon–Sat 9am–1pm; €2) just behind Áyios Therápon, containing various icons rescued from rural churches, plus a canvas of the Assumption by Theophilos (see p.overleaf).

Eating, drinking and nightlife

The obvious, if blatantly touristy, venue for a seafood blowout is the cluster of **tavernas** on the southerly quay known as Fanári; *Stratos* at the far end is marginally the best, and doesn't tout aggressively. For *mayireftá* (including early-morning *patsás* or tripe soup), look no further than the *Averoff* on the west quay, popular for lunch before an afternoon ferry departure. Finally, there are two traditional ouzerís at opposite ends of the bazaar. *Kalderími* (closed Sun) occupies two premises around Thássou 2, with seating under the shade of vines; the fare is large-portioned if a bit plainly presented. For a bit less outlay (and with friendlier service), you might be better off at the *Ermis* (open daily), best of a few ouzerís up at Epáno Skála; a 1999 refit didn't much affect its century-old decor (panelled ceiling, giant mirrors, faded oil paintings), or its claimed two centuries of purveying titbits to a jolly, mixed crowd in the pleasant courtyard.

For **snacks and drinks**, *Navayio* at the head of the harbour is the acknowledged favourite, with an unbeatable combo **breakfast** for under a fiver. With an important university in residence, Mytilíni can offer decent **nightlife and entertainment**, especially along the northeast quay, which the trendy contingent has claimed as its own. Here, all in a row, you'll find *La Notte* (a late-night dance club) and the durable *Hott Spott*, interspersed with other bars which change yearly. Out by the airport, the *Kohilia* beach-club has live and DJ'd happenings in summer. Formal live events constitute the Lesviakó Kalokéri, staged in the castle or the waterfront Dhimotikó Théatro during July and August. The summer cinema Pallas is between the post office and the park on Vournázon; there's also a winter cinema, the Arion, near the KTEL station.

Around Mytilíni

Beyond the airport and Krátigos village, the paved road loops around to **Haramídha**, 14km from town and the closest decent (pebble) beach (the fee-entry town "beach" at Tsamákia is mediocre); the eastern bay has a few **tavernas**, best of these by some way being Grioules. The double cove at **Áyios Ermoyénis**, 3km west and more directly accessible from Mytilíni via Loutrá village, is more scenic and sandy, with a single taverna, but small and crowded at weekends. For other pleasant immersions near Mytilíni, make for **Loutrá Yéras**, 8km along the main road to Kallí. These public baths (daily: June–Sept 8am–7pm; April–May & Oct 8am–6pm; Nov–March 9am–5pm; €2.50) are just the thing if you've spent a sleepless night on a ferry, with ornate spouts that feed 38°C water to marble-lined pools in vaulted chambers; there are separate facilities for men and women.

The Variá museums

The most rewarding single targets near Mytilíni are a pair of museums at **VARIÁ**, 5km south of town (hourly buses). The **Theophilos Museum** (May–Sept Tues–Sun 9am–2.30pm & 5–8pm; Oct & April 9am–1pm & 4–6pm; Nov–March 9am–2pm; €2 includes key-catalogue) honours the painter, born here in 1873, with four rooms of wonderful, little-known compositions specifically commissioned by his patron Thériade (see below) during the years leading up to Theophilos' death in 1934. A wealth of detail is evident in elegiac scenes of fishing, reaping, olive-picking and baking from the pastoral Lésvos which Theophilos obviously knew best; there are droll touches also, such as a cat slinking off with a fish in *The Fishmongers*. In classical scenes – Sappho and Alkaeos, a landscape series of Egypt, Asia Minor and the Holy Land, and episodes from wars historical and contemporary – Theophilos was on shakier ground. In *Abyssinians Hunting an Italian Horseman*, the subject has clearly been conflated with New World Indians chasing down a conquistador.

The adjacent, imposing **Thériade Museum** (Tues–Sun 9am–2pm & 5–8pm; €2) is the brainchild of another native son, Stratis Eleftheriades (1897–1983). Leaving the island at an early age for Paris, he Gallicized his name to Thériade and went on to become a renowned avant-garde art publisher, convincing some of the leading artists of the twentieth century to participate in his ventures. The displays consist of lithographs, engravings, wood-block prints and watercolours by the likes of Miró, Chagall, Picasso, Matisse, Le Corbusier, Léger, Rouault and Villon, either annotated by the painters themselves or commissioned as illustrations for the works of prominent poets and authors: an astonishing collection for a relatively remote Aegean island.

Southern Lésvos

The southernmost portion of the island is indented by two great inlets, the gulfs of **Kalloní** and **Yéra**, the first curving in a northeasterly direction, the latter northwesterly, creating a fan-shaped peninsula at the heart of which looms 967-metre Mount Ólymbos. Both shallow gulfs are almost landlocked by virtue of very narrow outlets to the open sea, which don't – and probably never will – have bridges spanning them. This is the most verdant and productive olive-oil territory on Lésvos, and the stacks of pressing-mills stab the skyline.

PÉRAMA is one of the larger places on the Gulf of Yéra, and has a regular **kaïki-ferry** service (no cars) linking it with Koundoroudhiá and blue city buses to/from Mytilíni on the far side. Amongst an oddly attractive townscape of disused olive-oil warehouses, Makis the pelican has been resident in the central square since 1980. A more likely reason to show up is to patronize one of the better **taverna–ouzerís** in the region: ♣ *Balouhanas* (all year; lunch and dinner), northernmost of a line of eateries on the front, with a wooden, cane-roofed balcony jutting out over the water. The name's a corruption of *balıkhane* or "fish-market" in Turkish, and seafood is a strong point, whether grilled or made into croquettes, as are regional starters like *giouzlemés* (cheese-stuffed fried crêpe) and own-made desserts.

Plomári and around

Due south of Mount Ólymbos, at the edge of the "fan", **PLOMÁRI** is the only sizeable coastal settlement hereabouts, and indeed the second-largest municipality on Lésvos. It presents an unlikely juxtaposition of scenic appeal and its famous ouzo industry, courtesy of several local distilleries. Despite a resounding lack of good beaches within walking distance, it's besieged in summer by

Scandinavian tourists, but you can usually find a **room** (they are prominently signposted) at the edge of the old, charmingly dilapidated town, or (better) 1km west in **Ammoudhélli** suburb, which has a small pea-gravel beach. Your best bet for an on-spec vacancy is the welcoming ⚑ *Pension Lida* above the inland Platía Beniamín (☎ & ⓕ22520 32507; ❷), a fine restoration inn occupying adjacent old mansions, with seaview balconies for most units. Rustling up a decent meal presents more difficulties; Ammoudhélli can offer *Tò Ammoudhelli*, perched unimprovably over the beach and under new management; skip the printed menu and ask for dishes of the day (*ambelofásola* – runner beans – and sardines in late summer) or *orektiká* like *tyrokafterí* and grilled octopus.

Áyios Isídhoros, 3km east, is where most tourists actually stay; pick of the **hotels** here, not completely overrun with package tours, is the *Pebble Beach* (ⓣ22520 31651, ⓕ22520 31566; ❹), with many of the large rooms overlooking a slightly reefy section of beach – though avoid those near the in-house bar if you wish to sleep. **Eating** out locally, the clear winner is *Taverna tou Panaï* (all year) at the rear of an olive grove just by the northerly "Áyios Isídhoros" town limits sign; here you'll find big, no-nonsense portions of salubrious meat, seafood and *mayireftá* dishes, and mostly Greeks in attendance.

Melínda, another 700-metre sand-and-shingle beach at the mouth of a canyon, lies 6km west of Plomári by paved road. Here there are several inexpensive **taverna-rooms** outfits, of which *Maria's* (ⓣ22520 93239; ❶) is an endearingly ramshackle place with simple but reasonably priced food and lodging. *Melinda Studios* (ⓣ22520 93282; ❷) near mid-beach presents a better standard (though no meals), as does *Melinda* (aka *Dhimitris Psaros*; ⓣ22520 93234; ❷) at the west end of the strand, with a more elaborate menu. Equally unspoilt (thanks to a formerly dreadful ten-kilometre side road in, now paved for 6km), **Tárti**, some 22km in total from Plomári, is a 300-metre-wide cove sown with three beachfront **tavernas** (sunbeds offered), plus **rooms** lining the final stretch of road (or behind the sand) should you want to stay.

The **bus** into Plomári travels via the attractive villages of Paleókipos and Skópelos (as well as Áyios Isídhoros); the road north from Plomári to Ayiássos has paving and public transport only as far as Megalohóri.

Ayiássos and Mylélia

AYIÁSSOS, nestled in a remote, wooded valley under the crest of Mount Ólymbos, is the most beautiful hill town on Lésvos, its narrow cobbled streets lined by ranks of tiled-roof houses. On the usual, northerly approach, there's no hint of the enormous village until you see huge knots of parked cars at the southern edge of town (where the bus leaves you after the 26-kilometre run from Mytilíni).

Don't be put off by endless ranks of kitsch wooden and ceramic souvenirs or carved "Byzantine" furniture, aimed mostly at Greeks, but continue past the central **church of the Panayía Vrefokratoússa**, originally built in the twelfth century to house an icon supposedly painted by the Evangelist Luke, to the **old bazaar**, with its *kafenía*, yoghurt shops and butchers' stalls. With such a venerable icon as a focus, the local August 15 *paniyíri* is one of the liveliest in Greece, let alone Lésvos. Ayiássos also takes Carnival very seriously; there's a club dedicated to organizing it, opposite the post office. The best **restaurants** are *Dhouladhelli*, on your left as you enter the village from the extreme south (bus stop) end, or the idiosyncratic nocturnal ouzerí *Tò Stavri*, at the extreme north end of the village in Stavrí district.

If you're headed for Ayiássos with your own transport, you might visit the **Mylélia water mill** (ⓦ www.mylelia.gr), whose inconspicuously signposted access track takes off 1km west of the turning for Ípios village. The name means "place of the mills", and there were once several hereabouts, powered by a spring, up-valley at Karíni. The last survivor (open daily 9am–6pm), restored to working order, has not been made twee in the least; the keeper will show you the mill race and paddle-wheel, as well as the flour making its spasmodic exit, after which you're free to buy gourmet pastas at the adjacent shop. Of late, Mylélia has branched out into cheeses, jams, salted fish, even cooking courses – and their products are sold at designated outlets in every Lésvos resort.

Vaterá, Skála Polikhnítou – and spas en route

A different bus route from Mytilíni leads to Vaterá beach via the inland villages of Polikhnítos and Vrýssa. **VRÝSSA** itself has a **natural history museum** (daily 9.30am–5pm; €1) dedicated to local paleontological finds – it's not exactly required viewing at present, but a new, more extensive gallery is planned. Until 20,000 years ago, Lésvos (like all other east Aegean islands) was joined to the Asian mainland, the gulf of Vaterá was a subtropical lake, and all manner of creatures flourished here, their fossilized bones constituting the star exhibits.

If you're after a hot bath, head for the small, vaulted **spa house** 1.5km east of **Polikhnítos**, well restored by an EU programme (daily: July & Aug 9am–1pm & 5–8pm, spring/autumn 9am–1pm & 4–6pm); there are separate, pink-tinted chambers for each sex. Alternatively, there are more **hot springs** at **Áyios Ioánnis**, signposted 3km below the village of Lisvóri; on the far side of the stream here are two pools housed in whitewashed, vaulted chambers – the left-hand one's nicer, and there's no gender segregation or dress code. These baths are under the energetic management of Lazaros (€2 fee when he's around), who also runs a **snack bar** and a few rooms adjacent.

VATERÁ, 9km south of Polikhnítos, is a huge, seven-kilometre-long sand beach, backed by vegetated hills; the sea here is delightfully calm and clean, the strand itself rated as one of the best in the islands. If you intend to stay here you'll probably want your own transport, as the closest well-stocked shops are 4km away at Vrýssa, and the bus appears only a few times daily. Development straggles for several kilometres to either side of the central T-junction, consisting mostly of seasonal villas and apartments for locals; at the west end of the strip is one of the very few consistently attended and professionally run hotels, the Greek- and American-owned *Vatera Beach* (☎22520 61212, @www .vaterabeach.gr; ❺ but ❹ for web bookings), whose rooms offer air conditioning and fridges. It also has a good attached restaurant with own-grown produce and shoreline tables from where you can gaze at the cape of **Áyios Fokás** 3km to the west, where only foundations remain of a temple of Dionysos and a super-imposed early Christian basilica. The little tamarisk-shaded anchorage here has an acceptable fish **taverna**, *Akrotiri/Angeleros*; it's usually better than most eateries east of the T-junction at Vaterá, but not so good as those at **SKÁLA POLIKHNÍTOU**, 4km northwest of Polikhnítos itself, where *T'Asteria*, *Iliova-silema* and *Akroyiali* can be recommended. Skála itself is pleasantly workaday, with only a short, narrow beach but one unusual accommodation option, "Soft Tourism" run by Lefteris and Erika (☎22520 42678; ❷). They generally host walking groups April to June and September, but welcome independent travellers during July and August.

East from Vaterá, a mostly paved road leads via Stavrós, and then Akrássi to either Ayiássos or Plomári within ninety minutes, making day-trips there feasible. When going north towards Kalloní, use the completely paved, fast short cut via the naval base and seashore hamlet at Akhladherí.

Western Lésvos

The main road west of Loutrá Yéras is surprisingly devoid of settlement, with little to stop for before Kalloní other than the traces of an ancient **Aphrodite temple** at **Mésa** (Méson), 1km north of the main road, and signposted just east of the Akhladherí turn-off. At the **site** (may be closed for excavations), just eleventh-century BC foundations and a few column stumps remain, plus the ruins of a fourteenth-century Genoese-built basilica wedged inside; it was once virtually on the sea, but a nearby stream has silted things up in the intervening millennia. All told, it's not worth a special trip, but certainly make the short detour if passing by with your own transport. With more time, you can turn northeast towards **Ayía Paraskeví** village, midway between two more important monuments from diverse eras: the Paleo-Christian **basilica of Halinádhou**, and the large **medieval bridge of Kremastí**.

KALLONÍ itself is an unembellished agricultural and market town more or less in the middle of the island, with various shops and services (including a **post office** and three **banks** with ATMs). Some 3km south lies **SKÁLA KALLONÍS**, a somewhat unlikely package resort backing a long but coarse-sand beach on the lake-like gulf. It's mainly distinguished as a bird-watching centre, attracting hundreds of twitchers for the March–May nesting season in the adjacent salt marshes. Pick of a half-dozen **hotels** is the human-scale bungalow complex *Malemi* (☎22530 22594, Ⓔmalemi@otenet.gr; ⑥), with a variety of units from doubles to family suites, attractive grounds, tennis court and a large pool. **Tavernas** lining the quay with its fishing fleet are generally indistinguishable – though most offer the gulf's celebrated, plankton-fed sardines, best eaten fresh-grilled from August to October (though they're available salt-cured all year round).

Inland monasteries and villages

West of Kalloní, the road winds 4km uphill to the **monastery of Limónos**, founded in 1527 by the monk Ignatios, whose actual cell is maintained in the surviving medieval north wing. It's a huge, rambling complex, with just a handful of monks and lay workers to maintain three storeys of cells around a vast, plant-filled courtyard. The *katholikón*, with its ornate carved-wood ceiling and archways, is built in Asia Minor style and is traditionally off-limits to women; a sacred spring flows from below the south foundation wall. A former abbot established a **museum** (daily 9.30am–6.30pm, may close 3pm off-season; €1.50) in the west wing; only the ground-floor ecclesiastical collection is currently open, with the more interesting upstairs ethnographic gallery off-limits indefinitely. Content yourself with an overflow of farm implements stashed in a corner storeroom below, next to a chamber where giant *pithária* (urns) for grain and olive oil are embedded in the floor.

The main road beyond passes through **VATOÚSSA**, a beautiful landlocked settlement in the heart of Lésvos's westernmost land mass, with a **folk museum** in the ancestral mansion of Grigorios Gogos. Just beyond Vatoússa a paved turning leads 7km to the outskirts of **HÍDHIRA**, where the Methymneos Winery (daily July–Sept 30 9am–6pm, otherwise by appointment on ☎22530 51518; Ⓦwww.methymneos.gr) has successfully revived the local ancient grape variety, decimated by phylloxera some decades ago. Because of the altitude (300m) and sulphur-rich soil (you're in the caldera of Órdhymnos volcano), their velvety, high-alcohol, oak-aged red can be produced organically. Proprietor Ioannis Lambrou gives a highly worthwhile twenty-minute tour of the state-of-the-art premises, in English.

Some 8km beyond Vatoússa, a short track leads down to the sixteenth-century **monastery of Perivolís** (daily 8am–1hr before sunset; donation, no photos), built in the midst of a riverside orchard (*perivóli*). Feeble electric light is available to view the narthex's fine if damp-damaged frescoes. In an apocalyptic panel worthy of Bosch (*The Earth and Sea Yield up their Dead*) the Whore of Babylon rides her chimera and assorted sea monsters disgorge their victims; just to the right, towards the main door, the Three Magi approach the Virgin enthroned with the Christ Child. On the north side you see a highly unusual iconography of *Abraham, the Virgin, and the Penitent Thief of Calvary in Paradise*, with the Four Rivers of Paradise gushing forth under their feet; just right are assembled the Hebrew kings of the Old Testament.

ÁNDISSA, 3km further on, nestles under the arid west's only substantial pine grove; at the western edge of the village a sign implores you to "Come Visit Our Square", not a bad idea for the sake of a handful of tavernas and *kafenía* sheltering under three sizeable plane trees. Directly below Ándissa a paved road leads 6km north to the fishing village of **GAVATHÁS**, with a shortish, partly protected beach (there's a bigger, surf-buffeted one at Kámbos just to the east) and a bare handful of places to eat and stay – among these *Pension Restaurant Paradise* (☎22530 56376; ❷), serving good fish and locally grown vegetables.

Just west of Ándissa there's an important junction. Keeping straight leads you past the still-functioning **monastery of Ipsiloú**, founded in 1101 atop an outrider of the extinct volcano of Órdhymnos. The *katholikón*, tucked in one corner of a large, irregular courtyard, has a fine wood-lattice ceiling but had its frescoes repainted to detrimental effect in 1992; more intriguing are portions of Iznik tile stuck in the facade, and the handsome double gateway. One of a few monks will admit you to the upstairs **museum** (donation), whose exhibits encompass a fine collection of *epitáfios* (Good Friday) shrouds, ancient manuscripts, portable icons and – oddest of all – a *Deposition* painted in Renaissance style by a sixteenth-century Turk. Ipsiloú's patron saint is John the Theologian, a frequent dedication for monasteries overlooking apocalyptic landscapes like the surrounding parched, boulder-strewn hills.

Signposted just west is the paved, five-kilometre side road to the main concentration of Lésvos's rather overrated **petrified forest** (daily: June–Sept 8am–sunset, rest of year closes 3pm; €2), a fenced-in "reserve" which is toured along 3km of walkways. For once, contemporary Greek arsonists cannot be blamed for the state of the trees, created by the combined action of volcanic ash from Órdhymnos and hot springs some fifteen to twenty million years ago. The mostly horizontal sequoia trunks average 1m or less in length, save for a few poster-worthy exceptions; another more accessible (and free) cluster is found south of Sígri.

Sígri

SÍGRI, near the western tip of Lésvos, has an appropriately end-of-the-line feel; the bay here is guarded both by an Ottoman castle and the long island of Nissiopí, which protects the place somewhat from prevailing winds. Until the early 1990s it was an important NATO naval base; battleships have now been replaced by a few weekly ferries on the Lávrio–Psará–Áyios Efstrátios–Límnos line – ring the local agent (☎22530 54430) for current details. The eighteenth-century **castle** (built atop the ruins of an earlier one) sports the reigning sultan's monogram over the entrance, something rarely seen outside Istanbul, and a token of the high regard in which this strategic port with a good water supply was held. The vaguely Turkish-looking **church of Ayía Triádha** is in fact a converted mosque, with a huge water cistern taking up the ground floor by the belfry; this supplied, among other things, the half-ruined *hamam* just south. At the top of town stands the worthwhile **Natural History Museum of the Lésvos Petrified Forest** (daily: May 15–Oct 15 8.30am–8pm, otherwise 8.30am–4.30pm; €2), which engagingly covers pan-Aegean geology with samples and maps (including, ominously, seismic patterns), as well as the expected quota of petrified logs and plant fossils from epochs when the surrounding hills were far more vegetated. Sígri itself presents an odd mix of vernacular and cement dwellings, while the town beach, south of the castle headland, is narrow and hemmed in by the road. There are much better beaches at **Faneroméni**, 3.5km north by coastal dirt track from the northern outskirts of town, plus at **Liména**, 2km south, just below the fifteen-kilometre dirt track to Eressós (passable with care in 35min); neither beach has any facilities.

Some **accommodation** is allotted to two British tour companies (Direct Greece and Sunvil), but on-spec vacancies might be found at *Nelly's Rooms and Apartments* (☎22530 54230; ❸), overlooking the castle. Among several **tavernas**, the best all-rounder, just inland, is Italian-run, ultra-hygienic ⋔ *Una Faccia Una Razza* (April to mid–Oct), with lovely grilled garlicky vegetables, creative salads, pizza, pasta, grilled seafood and an Italian wine list. The *Australia*, a bit seaward, has the Greek standards and an enviable position under the tamarisks. For **nightlife**, look no further than durable *Notia* (June–Sept), with frequent live sessions.

Skála Eressoú

Most visitors to western Lésvos park themselves at the resort of **SKÁLA ERESSOÚ**, accessible via a southerly turning between Ándissa and Ipsiloú. The three-kilometre beach here rivals Vatera's in quality, and consequently the place ranks just behind Mólyvos, Pétra and Plomári for numbers of visitors, who form an uneasy mix of Brits, Germans, Scandinavians, Greek families, neo-hippies and lesbians. Behind stretches the largest and most attractive agricultural plain on Lésvos, a welcome green contrast to the volcanic ridges above.

There's not much to central Skála – just a roughly rectangular grid of perhaps five streets by twelve, angling up to the oldest cottages on the slope of **Vígla hill** at the east end of the beach. The waterfront pedestrian zone (officially Papanikolí) is divided by a café-lined round platía midway along, dominated by a bust of **Theophrastos**, the renowned botanist who hailed from ancient Eressós. This was not, as you might suppose, on the site of the modern inland village, but atop Vígla hill; some of the remaining citadel wall is still visible from a distance. On top, the ruins prove scanty, but it's worth the scramble up for the views – you can discern the ancient jetty submerged beyond the modern fishing anchorage.

Another famous reputed native of ancient Eressós was **Sappho** (ca. 615–562 BC), the ancient poetess and reputed lesbian. There are thus always considerable numbers of gay women here paying homage, particularly in the clothing-optional zone of the beach west of the river mouth, where a small community of terrapins lives. Ancient Eressós endured into the Byzantine era, the main legacy of which is the **basilica of Áyios Andhréas** behind the modern church, merely foundations and a fragmentary if restored floor mosaic; the **tomb** of the saint, an early bishop of Crete (not the patron of Scotland), huddles just beyond the basilica.

Skála has countless **rooms and apartments**, but ones near the sea fill early in the day and can be noisy; in peak season you should aim for something quiet and inland, overlooking a garden or fields. Since the start of the new millennium, most package companies have dropped the resort, usually citing a lack of commitment to "family values" – ie, the radical lesbian contingent was a bit hard for the other tourists to handle – so vacancies are now fairly easy to come by. Still, it's wise to entrust the search to Sappho Travel (T 22530 52202 or 22530 52140, W www.sapphotravel.com). Joanna and her staff are switched-on and helpful, also serving as a car-rental station, ferry agent and air-ticket source; they are happy to place walk-ins in accommodation (②–④). Otherwise, there are just a handful of bona fide **hotels** in the village, and three of these – the remote *Antiopi* (T 22530 53311, W www.antiopi.net; rooms ①, studios ③); the seafront *Sappho the Eressia* (T 22530 53495, E Sappho_sarani@hotmail.com; ③) and *Maskot* (book through Sappho Travel; ③), inland from the preceding – are run exclusively by and for lesbians. The straight alternative is the understandably popular seaview *Kyma* (T 22530 53555, F 22530 53556; ④), at the east end of the front.

Most **tavernas**, with elevated wooden dining platforms, crowd the beach; in the wake of the tourism crash, they've been subjected to a harsh winnowing, with more closures or changeovers likely. The *Kyani Sardhini/Blue Sardine* at the far west end of the front is a creditable seafood ouzerí, while next to *Sappho the Eressia*, *Karavoyiannos* features local traditional recipes (at a price) and bulk wine from the local Methymneos winery; nearby *Soulatsos* is one of the more reliable grill-and-*mezédhes* outfits. In terms of **nightlife**, the gay-women contingent favours *Dhekati Mousa/Tenth Muse*, on the Theophrastos platía, or *Mylos* at the east end of the strip; *Parasol* and *Cooya Caribu* are straighter café-bars. There's also an open-air **cinema** (July to early Sept) in the centre. Skála has a **post office** near the church, as well as a **bank** ATM attached to Sappho Travel, and a small **Internet café**, *Cybersurf*, just east of *Dhekati Mousa*.

If you're returning to the main island crossroads at Kalloní, you can complete a loop from Eressós along the western shore of the Gulf of Kalloní via the hill villages of Mesótopos and Ágra; this route is entirely paved, and quicker than returning via Ándissa and Skalohóri. Just off this route there's an excellent beach at **Kroússos**, with a cult ✴ **taverna** installed in an immobilized bus at the east end; here Kyra-Maria lays on home-style fare (snails, *dolmádhes*, beans, maybe sea urchin roe) a world away from resort platters, at attractive prices.

Northern Lésvos

The main road north of Kalloní winds up a piney ridge and then down the other side into attractive countryside stippled with poplars and blanketed by olive groves. Long before you can discern any other architectural detail, the cockscomb silhouette of **Mólyvos castle** indicates your approach to the oldest-established tourist spot on Lésvos.

Mólyvos (Míthymna)

MÓLYVOS (officially Míthymna), 61km from Mytilíni, is arguably the most beautiful village on Lésvos, with tiers of sturdy, red-tiled houses, some standing defensively with their rear walls to the sea, mounting the slopes between the picturesque harbour and the **Byzantine-Genoese castle** (Tues–Sun: summer 8am–7pm; winter 8am–2.30pm; €2), which provides interesting rambles around its perimeter walls and views of Turkey across the straits. Closer examination reveals a score of weathered Turkish fountains along flower-fragrant, cobbled alleyways, reflecting the fact that before 1923 Muslims constituted over a third of the local population and owned many of the finest dwellings. The **Komninaki Kralli** mansion, high up in the town, is particularly worth getting into (daily 9am–5pm; free); the lower floor houses a **"School of Fine Arts"**

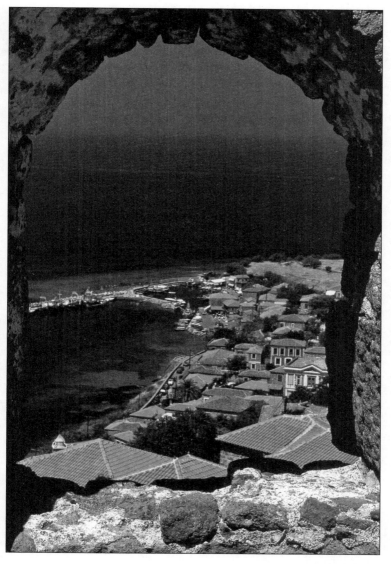

△ View over Mólyvos harbour, Lésvos

(as the building is signposted), but the wall- and ceiling-murals on the upper
storey (dated 1833) compare with those of the Vareltzídena mansion in Pétra
(see p.447). A panel in the smallest room portrays some dervish musicians, while
other murals depict stylized versions of Constantinople and Mytilíni Town; you
can tell the men's and women's quarters apart by the wider recessed "throne"
provided for the latter. Barely excavated **ancient Mithymna** to the northwest

of the village is of specialist interest, though a necropolis has been unearthed next to the bus stop and main car park.

Modern dwellings and hotels have been banned from the municipal core, but this hasn't stopped a steady drain of all the authentic life from the upper bazaar; just one lonely tailor still plies his trade amongst souvenir shops vastly surplus to requirements. Once an exclusive resort, Mólyvos is now firmly middle of the road, with the usual silly T-shirts and other trinkets carpeting every vertical surface of a stage-set, albeit an attractive one, for package tourism.

The shingly **town beach** is mediocre, improving considerably as you head towards the sandy southern end of the bay, called **Pitsiára**, with its clothing-optional zone. Advertised **boat excursions** to remote bays seem a frank admission of this failing; there are also frequent daily bus shuttles in season, linking all points between Ánaxos and Eftaloú.

Arrival and information

The municipal **tourist office** (summer Mon–Fri 9am–3pm & 5–9pm, Sat–Sun 10am–3pm; spring/autumn Mon–Fri 9am–3pm) by the **bus stop**, **taxi rank** and main **car park** at the southeast edge of town keeps lists of rented rooms, but no longer acts as a booking agency. Immediately adjacent you'll find three **bank** ATMs, plus numerous **motorbike and car rental** places, including Kosmos (℡22530 71710), Best (℡22530 72145) and Hertz (℡22530 72471), the latter two offering the ability to pick up here and drop off in Mytilíni or the airport. The main **post office** is near the top of the upper commercial street; Centraal, down near the harbour, is the principal **Internet** café.

Accommodation

The main sea-level thoroughfare of Mihaïl Goútou heads past the tourist office towards the harbour; just below it stand a number of bona fide **hotels** or **pensions** not completely taken over by packages. These include the *Hermes* on the beach (℡22530 71250; ❸), with variable, marble-floored rooms, and the *Molyvos* I next door (℡22530 71496, ℻22530 71640; ❹), with large balconied rooms, and breakfast served on the flagstoned terrace under the palms. For more comfort, you'll need to head 1km south of town to the ⚹ *Delfinia* (℡22530 71315, ⓦwww.hoteldelfinia.com; open all year; ❺ rooms, ❼ bungalows), set in seventy acres of greenery, with friendly staff and direct access to Pitsiára beach.

Rooms are scattered along the lanes leading uphill from the upper market thoroughfare. Best of these are *Studios Voula* below the castle car park (℡22530 72017 or 694 52 41 994), which has studios (❸) and a restored four-person house (❺), both with knockout views. Families should consider the high-standard and restored *Captain's House* offered by Theo and Melinda (℡22530 71241, ⓦwww.lesvosvacations.com), up by the Komninaki Kralli mansion; it sleeps up to six, and seasonal rates vary from €90 to €140 for the entire premises. The official **campsite**, *Camping Methymna* (late June–Sept), lies 2km northeast of town on the Eftaloú road.

Eating, drinking and nightlife

The sea-view **tavernas** on the lower market lane of 17-Noemvríou are all much of a muchness, where you pay primarily for the view; it's far better to head for the fishing port, where ⚹ *The Captain's Table* (with unpainted chairs; supper only) combines the virtues of squirmingly fresh seafood, meat grills and vegetarian *mezédhes*, washed down by their very palatable, own-label wine. *To Khtapodhi*, in the old customs house by the port entrance, attracts a mostly Greek crowd and is best treated as an ouzerí with treats such as salt-cured sardines. *Babis*, at the town approaches with semi-rural seating, is the place to head for good grills and a few *mayireftá* of the day. For snacks, look no further than *Iy Agora* (*To Dhimotiko Kafenío*), just downhill from the converted mosque/conference centre, with a lovely wood interior, view balcony and an excellent ouzo-*mezés* combo for under €2.

Midsummer sees a short **festival of music and theatre** up in the castle, and there's also a well-regarded outdoor **cinema** (June–Sept) next to the taxi rank. **Nightlife** revolves around musical bars: most durable is youth-orientated, tropical-themed *Congas* (May–Sept) down by the shore, with DJ'd events and theme nights; *Opus 6*, just up from the harbour, hosts high-quality live Greek or Western music every evening, while *Molly's Bar* just opposite is the thirty-somethings' preferred hangout, with taped music at a conversational level and a cozy balcony.

Pétra and Ánaxos

Since there are political and practical limits to the expansion of Mólyvos, many package companies have shifted emphasis to **PÉTRA**, 5km due south. The place has sprawled untidily behind its broad sand beach and seafront square, but two attractive nuclei of old stone houses, some with Levantine-style balconies overhanging the street, remain. Pétra takes its name from the giant **rock monolith** located some distance inland and enhanced by the eighteenth-century **church of the Panayía Glykofiloússa**, reached via 114 rock-hewn steps. Other local attractions include the sixteenth-century **church of Áyios Nikólaos**, with three phases of well-preserved frescoes, and the intricately decorated **Vareltzídhena mansion** (Tues–Sun 8am–2.30pm; free), with naive wall paintings of courting couples and a stylized view of a naval engagement at Constantinople.

Most small **hotels** and studios are block-booked, so on-spec arrivals should contact the Women's Agricultural Tourism Cooperative on the south side of the seafront square (T 22530 41238, E womes@otenet.gr), which arranges rooms or studios (❷–❸) in a number of scattered premises. For more comfort, try the *Hotel Michaelia* behind the south waterfront (T 22530 41730, F 22530 22067; ❹). The Women's Coop **restaurant**, under separate management, is excellent and inexpensive with both grills and *mayireftá* served at rooftop seating. Alternatives include *Symposio*, with good starters (though minus points for prefab chips; *Rigas* (evenings only) in the more inland settlement, a characterful ouzerí, the oldest in Pétra; and *Tsalikis Café* on the square for excellent own-made ice cream. You may prefer to head out of town – either to ᴊᴀ *Taverna Petri* (all day May to mid-Oct) in **PETRÍ** village 3km inland, with superb home-recipe *mayireftá* and a view terrace, or to **Avláki**, 1.5km southwest en route to Ánaxos, where there's a competent, signposted taverna/ouzerí behind a tiny beach.

ÁNAXOS, 3km south of Pétra, is a higgledy-piggledy package resort fringing by far the cleanest beach and seawater in the area: 1km of sand well sown with sunbeds and a handful of tavernas. From anywhere along here you enjoy beautiful sunsets between and beyond three offshore islets.

Around Mount Lepétymnos

East of Mólyvos, the villages of 968-metre **Mount Lepétymnos**, marked by tufts of poplars, provide a day's rewarding exploration. The first stop, though not exactly up the hill, might be **Loutrá Eftaloú** thermal baths 5km along the road passing the campsite. Patronize the hot pool under the Ottoman-era domed structure, not the sterile modern tub-rooms (daily: Dec–April unrestricted access; May & Oct 9am–1pm & 3–7pm; June–Sept 10am–2pm & 4–8pm;

€3.50 for group pool). The spa is well looked after, with the water mixed up to a toasty 39–41°C, so you'll need to cool down regularly; outside stretches the long, good pebble beach of **Áyii Anáryiri**, broken up by little headlands, with the remotest two coves nudist. There's a single, fetchingly positioned **taverna** here, the *Khrysi Akti*, which also lets small but en-suite **rooms** (☎22530 71879; ❷), the former cells of the adjacent monastery.

Eftaloú itself has a considerable number of fancy hotels and bungalow complexes, the friendliest and best value (though tour-dominated like the others) being the *Eftalou* (☎22530 71584, ✉parmakel@otenet.gr; ❹), with a pool, well-tended garden and loyal repeat clientele. A highly recommendable **taverna**, within sight of the spa and open all year (except around Christmas), is ⚶ *Iy Eftalou*, where the food (meat/fish grills) and tree-shaded setting are both splendid.

The main paved road around Lepétymnos first heads 5km east to **VAFIÓS**, with its clutch of three fairly comparable view **tavernas** (*Vafios, Ilias, Petrino*; avoid heavy, deep-fried dishes at all three), before curling north around the base of the mountain. The exquisite hill village of **SYKAMINIÁ** (**Sykamiá**) was the birthplace of the novelist Stratis Myrivilis; below the "Plaza of the Workers' First of May", with its two traditional *kafenía* and views north to Turkey, one of the imposing basalt-built houses is marked as his childhood home. A marked trail shortcuts the twisting road down to **SKÁLA SYKAMINIÁS**, easily the most picturesque fishing port on Lésvos. Myrivilis used it as the setting for his best-known work, *The Mermaid Madonna*, and the tiny rock-top chapel at the end of the jetty will be instantly recognizable to anyone who has read the book.

On a practical level, Skála has a few pensions, such as the central, partly air-con *Gorgona* (☎22530 55301; ❸), with a shaded breakfast terrace, and several **tavernas**. The most durable of these is *Iy Skamnia* (aka *Iy Mouria tou Myrivilí*), with seating under the mulberry tree in which Myrivilis used to sleep on hot summer nights, though newer *Anemoessa* (closest to the chapel, open winter weekends also) has overtaken it quality-wise, with good stuffed squash blossoms complementing fresh seafood. The only local beach is the pebble-on-sand-base one of **Kayiá** 1.5km east, where at least one – sometimes two – tavernas operate each season.

Continuing east from upper Sykaminiá, you soon reach **KLIÓ**, whose single main street (marked "*kendrikí agorá*") leads down to a platía with a plane tree, fountain, *kafenía* and more views across to Turkey. The village is set attractively on a slope, down which a six-kilometre road, now half-paved, descends to **Tsónia** beach, 600m of beautiful pink volcanic sand.

South of Klió, the route forks at Kápi, from where you can complete a loop of the mountain by bearing west along a completely paved road. **PELÓPI** is the ancestral village of unsuccessful 1988 US presidential candidate Michael Dukakis (who finally visited the island in 2000), and the main street is now named after him. Garden-lush **IPSILOMÉTOPO**, 5km further along, is punctuated by a minaret (but no mosque) and hosts revels on July 17, the feast of Ayía Marína.

Mandamádhos and Taxiárhis monastery

The main highway south from Klió and Kápi leads back to the capital through **MANDAMÁDHOS**. This attractive inland village is famous for its pottery, including the Ali Baba-style *pithária* (olive-oil urns) seen throughout Lésvos, but more so for the "black" icon of the Archangel Michael, whose enormous **monastery of Taxiárhis** (daily: May–Sept 6am–9.30pm; Oct–April 6.30am–

7pm), in a valley just northeast, is the focus of a thriving cult. The image – supposedly made from a mixture of mud and the blood of monks slaughtered in a massacre – is really more idol than icon, both in its lumpy three-dimensionality and in the methods of its veneration. First there was the custom of the coin-wish, whereby you pressed a coin to the Archangel's forehead – if it stuck, your wish would be granted. This practice (along with candle-lighting next to it) has long been forbidden, with supplicants referred to an alternative icon by the main entrance. It's further believed that while carrying out his errands on behalf of the faithful, the Archangel gets through more footwear than Imelda Marcos. Accordingly the icon used to be surrounded by piles of miniature, votive, gold and silver shoes. The ecclesiastical authorities, embarrassed by such "primitive" practices, removed them all in 1986, though since then several pairs of tin slippers, which can be filled with money and left in front of the icon, have reappeared.

Límnos

Límnos is a sizeable agricultural and military island whose remoteness and peculiar ferry schedules protected it until the 1990s from most trappings of the holiday trade. Conventional tourism was late in coming because the islanders made a reliable living off the visiting relatives of the numerous soldiers stationed here; most summer visitors are still Greek, particularly from Thessaloníki, though the locals are now used to numbers of Danes, Brits, Austrians and Italians flown in by ever-more-regular charter flights. Accommodation tends to be comfortable if overpriced, and **backpackers**

▲ Samothráki & Alexandhroúpoli

LÍMNOS

Gomáti

Pláka

Panayiá

Kabirion
(Kavírio)

Skopiá
470m ▲

Katálakkos

Bourniá
Bay

Hephaestia
(Ifestia)

Atsikí

Salt Marsh

Sardhés

Dháfni

Karpássi

Város

Kótsinas

Áyios
Ioánnis

Kornós

Áyios Dhimítrios

Lýkhna

Repanídhi

Kondopoúli
Kallóipi

Káspakas

Thermá

Livadhohóri

Kallithéa

Romanoú

Kéros

N

Avlónas

Mýrina
(Kástro)

Allied War
Cemetery

Angariónes

Néa
Koútali

Moúdhros
Bay

Roussopoúli

Rihá Nerá

Kákavos
360m ▲

Portianoú

Pedhinó

Tsimándhria

Moúdhros

Kamínia

Kondiás

Fanaráki

Allied War
Cemetery

Polyochni
(Polyókhni)

Paralía
Platý

Platý

Thános

Dhiapóri

Havoúli

Paradhísi
259m

Playiso
Mólos

Evgátis
(Áyios
Pávlos)

Paralía
Thánou

Fyssíni

Skopós
344m ▲

Áyios Sózon

Fakós

Skandháli

0   5 km

▼ Lávrio, Áyios Efstrátios, Lésvos & Híos

are explicitly **discouraged**. Bucolic Límnos has been getting positively trendy of late: there are upscale souvenir shops, village houses restored by mainlanders (and foreigners) as seasonal retreats, and some sort of noon-to-small-hours music bar during summer at nearly every beach.

The island has long been the focus of recurring disputes between the Greek and Turkish governments; Turkey has a perennial demand that Límnos be demilitarized, and Turkish aircraft regularly intrude Greek air space overhead, prompting immediate responses from the Greek Air Force squadron here. Límnos' **garrison** ran to 25,000 soldiers at the nadir of Greco-Turkish relations during the 1980s, though it is now down to about 6,000, and set to fall further when Greece abolishes conscription and most of the remaining army camps (but not the air base) close.

The bays of **Bourniá** and **Moúdhros**, the latter one of the largest natural harbours in the Aegean, divide Límnos almost in two. The west of the island is dramatically bare and hilly, with abundant basalt put to good use as street cobbles and house masonry. Like most volcanic islands, Límnos produces excellent wine – good dry whites, rosés and quality retsina – plus ouzo at Kondiás. The east is low-lying and speckled with marshes popular with duck-hunters, where it's not occupied by cattle, combine harvesters and vast corn fields.

Despite off-islander slander to that effect, Límnos is not flat, barren or treeless; much of the countryside consists of rolling hills, well vegetated except on their heights, and with substantial clumps of almond, jujube, myrtle, oak, poplar and mulberry trees. The island is, however, quite dry, with irrigation water pumped from deep wells, and a limited number of potable springs in the western half. Yet various streams bring sand to several long, **sandy beaches** around the coast, where it's easy to find a stretch to yourself. The bays shelve gently, making them ideal for children and quick to warm up in spring, with no cool currents except near the river mouths, and few of the jellyfish which used to pour out of the Dardanelles to plague bathers.

Mýrina

MÝRINA (aka Kástro), the capital and passenger port on the west coast, has the ethos of a provincial market town rather than of a resort. With about five thousand inhabitants, it's pleasantly low-key, if not especially picturesque.

Arrival, information and transport

The modern civilian **airport** lies 18km east of Mýrina, almost at the exact geographic centre of the island, sharing a runway with an enormous air-force base; there are three car rental booths, a bank ATM, a few taxis outside – and no shuttle bus into town. **Ferries** currently dock at the southern edge of Mýrina, in the shadow of the castle, though a new jetty is being built on the far side of the bay, under the hilltop church of Áyios Nikólaos, ready within the lifetime of this edition. There are separate **agencies** for the sailings of NEL boats (℡22540 22460), GA and LANE ferries (Pravlis Travel, ℡22540 24617) and Saos Ferries (℡22540 29571), as well as a rather glum, useless **tourist information** office on the harbour (Mon–Fri 8am–3pm).

The **bus station** is on Platía Eleftheríou Venizélou, at the north end of Kydhá. One look at the sparse schedules (only a single daily afternoon departure to most points, slightly more frequently to Kondiás and Moúdhros) will convince you of the need to rent a vehicle from one of many agencies clustered around the harbour area. **Cars**, **motorbikes** and **bicycles** can be rented from Limnos Car Rental (℡22540 23777, airport ℡694 54 95 104), Myrina

Rent a Car (☎22540 24476), Petrides Travel (☎22540 22039, airport ☎22540 92700) amd Holiday (☎22540 24347, airport 693 24 81 056); rates for bikes are only slightly above the island norm, but cars are expensive. A motorbike (most obviously from Moto Lemnos, ☎22540 25002) is generally enough to explore the coast and the interior of the closer villages, as there are few steep gradients but many perilously narrow streets, some controlled by traffic lights dictating alternating one-way passage. A new bypass road from Áyios Nikólaos port, probably ready by the time you read this, should relieve most of Mýrina's **traffic** bottlenecks; **parking**, however, will remain nightmarish, with spaces possible only at the outskirts.

All **banks**, most of them along Kydhá, have ATMs; the **post office** and Olympic airlines office are adjacent to each other on Garoufalídhou, with a **laundry** across the way by the *Hotel Paris*. There are **Internet** facilities at *NetPoint*, halfway along Kydhá, and at *Joy*, next to the post office.

Accommodation

Despite Límnos's steady gentrification, you may still be met off the boat with offers of a **room**; there are officially two dozen or so licensed establishments in Mýrina, with the northern districts of Rihá Nerá and Áyios Pandelímonas better bets for **studios**. Otherwise you'll find a pair of decent town **hotels** plus upmarket complexes at nearby beaches. In Romeïkós Yialós a few restored houses serve as small inns, though most are affected by evening noise from the seafront bars. There's **no official campsite**; Greek caravanners and campers have been banished from the north end of Platý beach, though a few tents still sprout furtively at Kéros.

Apollo Pavilion On Frýnis ☎22540 23712, Ⓦwww.apollopavilion.com. Hidden away in a peaceful cul-de-sac about halfway along Garou-falídhou, this offers three-bed studios with air con, TV and mini-kitchen. Most units have balconies, with views of either the castle or the mountains. Open all year; the friendly owner's wine is excellent. ❹

Arhondiko Corner Sakhtoúri and Filellínon, Romeïkós Yialós ☎22540 29800, Ⓦwww.questinn .com. Límnos' first hotel in the nineteenth century, this 1851-built mansion was reopened in 2003 as three floors of medium-sized, wood-trimmed rooms with all mod cons. There's a pleasant ground-floor bar/breakfast lounge. ❺

Ifestos Ethnikís Andístasis 17, Andhróni district, inland from Rihá Nerá ☎22540 24960, Ⓕ22540 23623. Quiet, professionally run C-class hotel, with

pleasant common areas. Slightly small rooms have air con, fridges, balconies and again a mix of sea or hill views. ❹

Porto Myrina Avlónas beach, 1.5km north of Rihá Nerá ☎22540 24805, Ⓦwww.portomyrina.com. The island's best beachfront lodging, though its five-star rating is probably one too many. Standard rooms and free-standing bungalows surround an Artemis temple found during construction; vast common areas include tennis courts, a footie pitch, one of the largest (salt-water) pools in Greece, and summer watersports on the beach. Open May–Oct 15; standard rooms ❼, bungalows ❽.

Romeïkós Yialos Sakhtoúri 7 ☎22540 23787 or 22540 22197. Venerable pension in a Romeïkós Yialós mansion that's quieter than waterfront outfits; just eight good-sized if plain rooms, some with air con. ❸

The Town

Mýrina's main attraction is the Byzantine **castle** (unrestricted access), perched on a craggy headland between the ferry dock and Romeïkós Yialós, the town's chic beach-lined esplanade backed by ornate Neoclassical mansions. In a ruined state despite later additions by the Genoese and Ottomans, the fortress is flatteringly lit at night and warrants a climb at sunset for views over the town, the entire west coast and – in clear conditions – over to Mount Áthos, 35 nautical miles west (which can also be glimpsed from any suitable height east of town). Also worth exploring is the town's core neighbourhood of old stone houses dating from the Ottoman era. Few explicitly Turkish monuments have survived, though an unassuming **fountain** at the harbour end of the main drag, Kydhá, retains its calligraphic inscription and is still highly prized for its drinking water.

The town's shops and amenities are mostly to be found along Kydhá and its continuation Karatzá – which meanders north from the harbour to Romeïkós Yialós – or Garoufalídhou, its perpendicular offshoot, roughly halfway along. As town **beaches** go, Romeïkós Yialós and Néa Mádhitos (ex-Toúrkikos Yialós), its counterpart to the southeast of the harbour, are not at all bad; Rihá Nerá, the next bay north of Romeïkós Yialós, is even better, with watersports on offer.

The **archeological museum** (Tues–Sun 8.30am–3pm; €2) occupies a handsome Ottoman mansion right behind Romeïkós Yialós, not far from the site of partly excavated Bronze Age Myrina. Finds are assiduously labelled in Greek, Italian and English, and the entire premises are exemplary in terms of presentation – the obvious drawback being that the best items have been spirited away to Athens, leaving a collection that's essentially of specialist interest. The south ground-floor gallery is mainly devoted to pottery from Polychni (Polyókhni); the north wing contains more of the same, plus items from ancient Myrina; the upstairs galleries feature post-Bronze Age artefacts from Kabirion (Kavírio) and Hephaestia (Ifestía). The star upper-storey exhibits are votive lamps in the shape of sirens, found in an Archaic sanctuary at Hephaestia, much imitated in modern local jewellery. Rather less vicious than Homer's creatures, they are identified more invitingly as the "muses of the underworld, creatures of superhuman wisdom, incarnations of nostalgia for paradise". Another entire room is devoted to metalwork, of which the most impressive items are gold jewellery and bronze objects, both practical (cheese graters, door-knockers) and whimsical-naturalistic (a snail, a vulture).

Eating, drinking and nightlife

Seafood is excellent on Límnos owing to its proximity to the Dardanelles and seasonal fish migrations; for affordable waterside dining, ✱ *To Limanaki* rates as best of several ouzerís around the little fishing harbour, with good portions and strong ouzo in bulk. About halfway along Kydhá, *O Platanos* serves traditional *mayireftá* to big crowds on an atmospheric little square under two plane trees. Not too surprisingly given the twee setting, most of the restaurants lining Romeïkós Yialós are pretty poor value; the tree-shaded tables of *Iy Tzitzifies* at Rihá Nerá are a far better option. Romeïkós Yialós is, however, where **nightlife** kicks off, with a sunset drink in the shadow of the castle; doyenne of the **café-bars** here is *Karagiozis* at no. 32 (by the bridge, 11am–late). Choices elsewhere in town are limited, for example to stunningly appointed *Alexandros* at the base of the jetty; the closest after-hours beach bars are *Kioski* (July–August) on the sand at Avlónas, and oriental-themed *Al Bazaar/Oasis* just inland by the old Avlónas river bridge. There's also the Maroula **cinema-theatre** on Garoufalídhou.

Western Límnos

Besides Mýrina's respectable town beaches, the closest good sand lies 3km north at Avlónas, with its aforementioned beach-bar, unspoilt except for the local power plant just inland. Just beyond, the road splits: the right-hand turning wends its way through **Káspakas**, its north-facing houses in neat tiers and a potable spring (but no taverna) on its handsome platía, before plunging down to **Áyios Ioánnis**, also reached directly by the newer bypass. There are a fair number of **rooms** to let here, plus a few **tavernas**, most distinctive the one (late June to late Aug) featuring seating in the shade of piled-up volcanic boulders, but the beach beyond is not the best – bearing the brunt of southwesterlies – and the whole area in fact resembles a vast building site.

More unusual immersions and meals are found a short distance east. The old Ottoman baths at **Thermá** have been restored and operate as a contemporary health spa, with all conceivable treatments laid on – or you can just have a hydromassage soak (daily 10am–2pm & 5–9pm; €6). Some 7km north of here, **SARDHÉS** is the highest village on the island, with a celebrated central **taverna**, ⚜ *Man-Tella* (all year, lunch and dinner). Portions are large and the fare rich, so arrive hungry; in season you'll need to book for dinner (☎22540 61349) in the pleasant courtyard.

Beyond Sardhés, via the villages of Dháfni and Katálakkos, 5km below the latter, lies the spectacular, well-signposted **dune environment at Gomáti**, one of the largest such in Greece. There are two zones reached by separate dirt tracks: one at a river mouth, with a bird-rich marsh, and the other to the northwest. Despite the lack of facilities and exposure to the wind, they're a popular outing locally.

Platý to Paleó Pedhinó

PLATÝ, 2km southeast of Mýrina, has had its profile spoilt by the kind of modern villa construction that is blighting many Limnian villages, but it does have two nocturnally popular **tavernas**. Much the better of these is ⚜ *O Sozos*, just off the main platía, where groups should reserve in season on ☎22540 25085. The menu has contracted since Sozos himself was killed in a freak accident, but his daughter carries on with huge, well-priced portions of grills, salads and a few *mayireftá* like dolmádhes, washed down by *tsípouro* and local bulk wine. The long sandy **beach**, 700m below, is popular, with non-motorized watersports available; except for the unsightly Mark Warner compound at the south end, the area still (just) remains rural, with sheep parading to and fro at dawn and dusk. The single **hotel**, low-rise *Plati Beach* (☎22540 23583; ❹), has an enviable position in the middle of the beach, but be sure to get an upper-storey room or attic suite. Nearby, *Grigoris* proves a reliable, popular beachside **taverna**, with fish in season. The highest standard of **studios** in the area, if not the whole island, is ⚜ *Villa Afroditi* (☎22540 23141; ⓦwww.afroditivillasa .gr; mid-May to end Sept; B&B; ❺), with its spectacularly unmissable topiary specimens, a pleasant pool bar, weekly barbecue nights for guests, and one of the best buffet breakfasts in the islands.

THÁNOS, 2km further southeast, seems a bigger, more architecturally characterful version of Platý village, with Nikos Dhimou's high-standard mock-trad **bungalows** at the east edge (☎22540 25284; ❹). **Paralía Thánous**, 1.5km below the village, is perhaps the most scenic of the southwestern beaches, flanked by weird volcanic crags and with views on a clear afternoon to Áyios Efstrátios island. There's good-value **accommodation** at *Villa Thanos Beach* (☎22540 23496 or 697 37 10 543; ❸), with a lush front garden and sunset views, plus good food (if surly service) at *Yiannakaros* **taverna**; their beach bar and one other divide the (complimentary) sunbeds between them. Beyond Thános, the road curls over to the enormous beach at **Evgátis** (Áyios Pávlos), reckoned the island's best, with more igneous pinnacles for definition. Again, a pair of music bar/*kantínas* offer sunbeds, while a full-service taverna across the road has a few comfortable **rooms** (☎22540 51700; ❸).

Some 3km further along (11km from Mýrina), **KONDIÁS** is the island's third-largest settlement, cradled between two hills tufted with Límnos's biggest pine forest. Stone-built, often elaborate houses and a row of sail-less windmills combine with the setting to make Kondiás the most attractive inland village, a fact not lost on the Greeks and foreigners restoring fine old houses with varying degrees of taste. Short-term facilities are nonexistent, however; the closest **tavernas** are 2.5km away at **TSIMÁNDHRIA**, where *O Meraklis* (all year) on the central platía are roast-chicken specialists, or at **PALEÓ PEDHINÓ** 5km northeast, where *Petrino Horio* (dinner only, end June–Aug) offers fine meat and an enchanting setting (if shambolic service) on the flagstoned platía of this mostly abandoned village.

Eastern Límnos

The shores of **Moúdhros Bay**, glimpsed south of the trans-island road, are muddy and best avoided unless you're a clam-digger. The bay itself enjoyed considerable importance during World War I, culminating in the Ottoman surrender aboard the British warship HMS *Agamemnon* here on October 30, 1918. **MOÚDHROS**, the second-largest town on Límnos and the main cargo port, is a dreary place, with only a wonderfully kitsch, two-belfried church to recommend it. There are three **hotels** in Moúdhros, the best of which is the overpriced *Kyma* (☎22540 71333; ❹). Its more reasonable, but run-of-the-mill, **restaurant** is convenient for a lunch break if you're visiting the archeological sites and beaches of eastern Límnos. The closest decent beaches are at **Havoúli**, 4km south by dirt track, and recently cleaned-up **Fanaráki** 4km west, but both have somewhat muddy sand and don't really face open sea.

About 800m along the Roussopoúli road, you pass an **Allied military cemetery** (unlocked) maintained by the Commonwealth War Graves Commission; its neat lawns and rows of white headstones seem incongruous in such parched surroundings. In 1915, Moúdhros Bay was the principal staging area for the disastrous Gallipoli campaign. Of the roughly 36,000 Allied

△ Portianoú World War I Allied cemetery

dead, 887 – mainly battle casualties who died after having been evacuated to the base hospital at Moúdhros – are buried here, with 348 more at another signposted, immaculately maintained graveyard behind the hilltop church in Portianoú.

KALLIÓPI, 8km northeast of Moúdhros via Kondopoúli, has smart **rooms** (*Keros*, ☏ 22540 41059; ❹) at the start of the dirt road down to **Kéros** beach, the best in this part of the island but exposed and often dirty. A 1500-metre stretch of sand with dunes and a small pine grove, plus shallow water, it attracts a number of Greek tourists and foreigners with camper vans and windsurfers; a small *kantína* operates with sunbeds during July and August only.

On the other side of Kondopoúli, reached via Repanídhi village, the hard-packed beach of **Kótsinas** is set in the protected western limb of Bourniá Bay. The nearby anchorage (follow signs to "Kótsinas Fortress") offers a pair of **tavernas**, the better being *Tò Korali* by the water, reliably open all day, with a wide range of *mezédhes* and affordable fish. Up on a knoll overlooking the jetty, there's a corroded, sword-brandishing statue of Maroula, a Genoese-era heroine who delayed the Ottoman conquest by a few years, and a large **church of Zoödhóhou Piyís** (the Life-Giving Spring). This is nothing extraordinary, but beside it 63 steps lead down through an illuminated tunnel in the rock to the potable (if slightly mineral) spring in question, oozing into a cool, vaulted chamber.

Ancient sites

Indications of the most advanced Neolithic civilization in the Aegean have been unearthed at **Polyochni** (**Polyókhni**), 3km from the gully-hidden village of Kamínia (7km east of Moúdhros). The site occupies a bluff overlooking a long, narrow beach flanked by stream valleys. Since the 1930s, Italian excavations have uncovered five layers of settlement, the oldest from late in the fourth millennium BC, predating Troy on the Turkish coast opposite. The town met a sudden, violent end from war or earthquake in about 2100 BC. The **ruins** (Tues–Sun 9am–2pm; free) are well labelled but mostly of specialist interest, though the bouleuterion (assembly hall), a mansion and the landward fortifications are impressive enough. A small but well-presented museum behind the entrance kiosk helps bring the place to life.

Hephaestia and Kabirion, the other significant ancient sites on Límnos, are reached via the village of Kondopoúli; both sites are remote, and only reachable with your own transport. **Hephaestia** (present-day Ifestía; Tues–Sun 9am–3pm), 4.5km from Kondopoúli by rough, signposted track, has been re-excavated since 2001 and can now offer an admirably reconstructed theatre, overlooking its former harbour. **Kabirion**, also signposted as 'Kabeiroi' (modern Kavírion), on the opposite shore of Tigáni Bay and accessed by a paved road, remains more evocative. The **ruins** (Tues–Sun 9am–3pm; free) are those of a sanctuary connected with the cult of the Samothracian Kabiroi (see p.458), though the site here is probably older. Little survives other than the ground plan, but the setting is undeniably impressive. Eleven column stumps stake out a *stoa*, behind eight spots marked as column bases in the *telestirio* or shrine where the cult mysteries took place. A nearby sea grotto has been identified as the Homeric **Spiliá toú Filoktíti**, where the Trojan war hero Philoctetes was abandoned by his comrades-in-arms until his stinking, gangrenous leg had healed. Landward access to the cave is via steps leading down from the caretaker's shelter, though final access (from a little passage on the right as you face the sea) involves some wading.

Áyios Efstrátios (Aï Strátis)

Áyios Efstrátios is indisputably one of the quietest and loneliest islands in the Aegean. Historically, the only outsiders staying here were compelled to do so – it served as a place of exile for political prisoners under both the Metaxas regime of the 1930s and the various right-wing governments that followed the civil war. Before that, it was only permanently settled during the sixteenth century, and its land is still largely owned by three monasteries on Mount Áthos.

ÁYIOS EFSTRÁTIOS village – the only habitation on the island – must be one of the ugliest in Greece. Devastation caused by an earthquake in February 1968, which killed 22 and injured hundreds, was compounded by the reconstruction plan: the contract went to a company with junta connections, who prevented the survivors from returning to their old homes and used army bulldozers to raze even those structures – part of one of the more beautiful ports in these islands – that could have been repaired. From the hillside, some two dozen surviving houses of the old village overlook its replacement, whose grim rows of prefabs constitute a sad monument to the corruption of the junta years.

Architecture apart, Áyios Efstrátios still functions as a traditional fishing and farming community, with the prefabs set at the mouth of a wooded stream valley draining to the sandy harbour beach. Tourist amenities consist of just two basic **tavernas** (one operating July–Aug only), plus a total of four **pensions**. Best of these, in one of the surviving old houses, is the *Xenonas Aï-Stratis* (☎22540 93329; ❹); Andonis Paneras (☎22540 93209; ❸), Stavros Katakouzinos (☎22540 93362; ❸) and Apostolos Paneras (☎22540 93343; ❸) have more conventional **rooms** in the prefabs. These stiff prices for such an out-of-the-way place reflect Aï Strátis' increasing popularity with Greeks, and you may have to ring all four spots for a vacancy in season.

As you walk away from the village – there are few cars and no paved roads – things improve rapidly. The landscape, dry hills and valleys scattered with a surprising number of oak trees, is deserted apart from wild rabbits, sheep, an occasional shepherd, and some good **beaches**. **Alonítsi**, on the north coast – a ninety-minute walk from the village following a track up the north side of the valley – is a two-kilometre stretch of sand with rolling breakers and views across to Límnos.

South of the village, there's a series of grey-sand beaches, most with wells and drinkable water, although, with few real paths in this part of the island, getting to them can be something of a scramble. **Lidharió**, at the end of an attractive wooded valley, is the first worthwhile beach, but again it's a ninety-minute walk, unless you can persuade a fisherman to take you by boat.

Ferries on the Kavála/Alexandhroúpoli–Límnos–Lávrio line call at Áyios Efstrátios several times weekly much of the year; in summer a small Límnos-based ferry, the *Aiolis*, sails every weekday (Mon–Fri) at 3pm from Límnos, returning the next day at 6.30am. Despite harbour improvements, this is still a very exposed anchorage, and in bad weather you could end up stranded here far longer than you bargained for. If an indefinite stay does not appeal, it's best to visit from Límnos on a day-trip (offered once or twice weekly in season).

Samothráki (Samothrace)

Samothráki has one of the most dramatic profiles of all the Greek islands, second only to that of Thíra (Santorini): its dark mass of granite rises abruptly from the sea, culminating in the 1611-metre **Mount Fengári**. Seafarers have always been guided by its imposing outline, clearly visible from the mainland, and, in legend, its summit provided a vantage point for Poseidon to watch over the siege of Troy. Landing is very much subject to the vagaries of the notoriously unpredictable weather, but that did not deter pilgrims who, for hundreds of years in Antiquity, journeyed to the island to visit the **Sanctuary of the Great Gods** and were initiated into its mysteries. The sanctuary remains the main archeological attraction of the island which, too remote for most tourists, combines earthy simplicity with natural grandeur. The tourist season is relatively short-lived – essentially (late) July and August – but you will find some facilities open as early as Easter and one or two all year round.

Kamariótissa

All ferries and hydrofoils dock at the dull village of **KAMARIÓTISSA**, where you're unlikely to want to spend much time. That said, it could be your most convenient base, since some of Samothráki's best **hotels** lie along or just behind the tree-lined seafront and various **rooms** for rent, many of them more than acceptable, can be found in the maze of streets behind; owners often meet incoming vessels. As on most islands with a short season, accommodation can be pricey for what you get, and bargaining is not always productive, especially in midsummer. Along the shore, some way east of your point of arrival, is *Kyma* (☎25510 41263; ❸), where rooms overlooking the pebbly beach can get noise from the string of little bars that constitutes Samothráki's main nightlife; avoid the hotel restaurant – the taverna (see below) is much better. Calmer, but somewhat pricier, is the *Niki Beach* (☎25510 41561; ❹) beyond the far north end of the quay. Above, occupying a bluff and visible from out to sea, is the slightly impersonal *Aeolos* (☎25510 41595, ℻25510 41810; ❺); with a large pool and quiet, spacious rooms, it's the island's most comfortable accommodation and offers good half-board deals out of season. Bars and cafés on the harbour front serve snacks and breakfasts, but the only commendable **taverna** is the *Limanaki*, at the southern end, beyond the docks: excellent Limniot wine from the barrel is perfect with the fish and seafood on offer, which you can watch being unloaded by local fishermen as you order.

Motorbikes and **cars** are in short supply, so it's worth grabbing one immediately on disembarkation – or even reserving a bike in advance from Hanou Brothers (☏ 25510 41511) or a car from Niki Tours (☏ 25510 41465), which sells plane tickets as well; also try Kyrkos car rental (☏ 697 43 71 122). For information about ferries and tickets for **ferries and hydrofoils**, a converted container opposite the docks acts as offices. A fairly reliable timetable for island **buses** is also posted here; these travel up to eight times daily in season (but only twice weekly in deepest winter) along the north coast to Loutrá (Thermá) via Paleópoli, near the site of the Sanctuary, or Karyótes, or directly inland seven times daily to the largest village, Hóra. As with lodging, rented transport is more expensive than on most islands, but if you've the means go for a car, as Samothracian roads are often dangerously windswept for bikes. Note that there is currently only one fuel pump on the entire island, 1km above the port, en route to Hóra. Kamariótissa also has a **bank** with an ATM, but no post office.

Hóra

HÓRA, also known as **Samothráki**, is the island's capital. Far larger than implied by the portion visible from out at sea, it's an attractive town of Thracian-style stone houses, some whitewashed, clustered around a hollow in the western flanks of Mount Fengári. It is dominated by the Genoese Gateluzzi fort, of which little survives other than the gateway. Half an hour or so can be whiled away at the charming **folklore museum**, which is free, but the opening hours are erratic; it contains a motley collection of clothing, domestic items and miscellany.

Hóra has no reliable short-term accommodation, though asking for unadvertised rooms in the various *kafenía* along the winding commercial street can be productive. On the atmospheric, irregularly shaped platía, a couple of **tavernas**, *Iy Platia* and the more down-to-earth *To Kastro*, provide the best suppers on the island, with such delicacies as stuffed squid and *mýdhia saganáki* (mussels with cheese). There have been mutterings of moving the administrative capital down to Kamariótissa, but until further notice the island's **post office** is here.

The Sanctuary of the Great Gods

From Hóra it is 3km to the hamlet of Paleópoli (see opposite) and, in a stony but thickly wooded ravine between it and the plunging northwestern ridge of Mount Fengári, lie the remains of the **Sanctuary of the Great Gods**. Buses from Kamariótissa stop nearby, opposite a small car park on the seashore. From the late Bronze Age until the early Byzantine era, the mysteries and sacrifices of the cult of the Great Gods were performed on Samothráki, indeed in ancient Thracian dialect until the second century BC. The island was the spiritual focus of the northern Aegean, and its importance in the ancient world was comparable (although certainly secondary) to that of the Mysteries of Eleusis.

The religion of the Great Gods revolved around a hierarchy of ancient Thracian fertility figures: the Great Mother Axieros, a subordinate male deity known as Kadmilos, and the potent and ominous twin demons the Kabiroi, originally the local heroes Dardanos and Aeton. When the Aeolian colonists arrived (traditionally ca. 700 BC) they simply syncretized the resident deities with their own – the Great Mother became Cybele, her consort Hermes and the Kabiroi were fused interchangeably with the *Dioskouroi* Castor and Pollux, patrons of seafarers. Around the nucleus of a sacred precinct the newcomers made the beginnings of what is now the sanctuary.

Despite their long observance, the mysteries of the cult were never explicitly recorded, since ancient writers feared incurring the wrath of the Kabiroi (who could reputedly brew up sudden, deadly storms), but it has been established that two levels of initiation were involved. Both ceremonies, in direct opposition to the elitism of Eleusis, were open to all, including women and slaves. The lower level of initiation, or *myesis*, may, as is speculated at Eleusis, have involved a ritual simulation of the life, death and rebirth cycle; in any case, it's known that it ended with joyous feasting, and it can be conjectured, since so many clay torches have been found, that it took place at night. The higher level of initiation, or *epopteia*, carried the unusual requirement of a moral standard (the connection of theology with morality, so strong in the later Judeo-Christian tradition, was rarely made by the early Greeks). This second level involved a full confession followed by absolution and baptism in bull's blood.

The only **accommodation** near the sanctuary is in the tiny hamlet of **PALEÓPOLI**, where the old and basic *Xenia Hotel* (☎25510 41166 or 25510 41230; ❹) offers a downmarket alternative to the smart but overpriced *Kastro Hotel* (☎25510 89400, ⓦwww.kastrohotel.gr; ❺), which comes with pool, restaurant and sea views; there are also some basic but en-suite rooms (❸) down on the seashore below the *kástro*.

The site

The **site** (Tues–Sun 8.30am–8.30pm, or dusk if earlier; €3 combined ticket with museum but no charge for site when museum is closed) is well labelled, simple to grasp and strongly evokes its proud past, while commanding views of the mountains and the sea. You might like to visit the **archeological museum** first (Tues–Sun 8.30am–3pm), and its exhibits spanning all eras of habitation, from the Archaic to the Byzantine, since it explains the significance of the

△ Sanctuary of the Great Gods, Samothráki

sanctuary. Highlights include a **frieze** of dancing girls from the propylon of the Temenos, entablatures from different buildings, and Roman votive offerings such as coloured glass vials from the necropolis of the ancient town east of the sanctuary. You can also see a reproduction of the exquisitely sculpted marble statue, the *Winged Victory of Samothrace*, which once stood breasting the wind at the prow of a marble ship in the Nymphaeum (see below). Discovered in 1863 by a French diplomat to the Sublime Porte, it was carried off to the Louvre, where it is a major draw, and the well-crafted copy was graciously donated to this museum a mere century later.

The **Anaktoron**, or hall of initiation for the first level of the mysteries, dates in its present form from Roman times. Its inner sanctum was marked by a warning stele, now in the museum, and at the southeast corner you can make out the **Priestly Quarters**, an antechamber where candidates for initiation donned white gowns. Next to it is the **Arsinoeion**, the largest circular ancient building known in Greece, used for libations and sacrifices. Within its rotunda are the fourth-century BC walls of a double precinct where a rock altar, the earliest preserved ruin on the site, has been uncovered. A little further south, on the same side of the path, you come to the **Temenos**, a rectangular area open to the sky where the feasting probably took place, and, edging its rear corner, the conspicuous **Hieron**, the site's most immediately impressive structure. Five columns and an architrave of the facade of this large Doric edifice, which hosted the higher level of initiation, have been re-erected; dating in part from the fourth century BC, it was heavily restored in Roman times. The stone steps have been replaced by modern blocks, but Roman benches for spectators remain *in situ*, along with the sacred stones where confession was heard. To the west of the path you can just discern the outline of the theatre, while just above it, tucked under the ridge, is the **Nymphaeum (Fountain) of Nike**, which the *Winged Victory* used to preside over. West of the theatre, occupying a high terrace, are remains of the main *stoa*; immediately north of this is an elaborate medieval fortification made entirely of antique material.

The north coast

With its running streams, giant plane trees and namesake hot springs, **LOUTRÁ** (aka **THERMÁ**), 6km east of Paleópoli, is a pleasant place to stay, although in late July and August it is packed, mainly with an incongruous mixture of foreign hippies and elderly Greeks, here to take the sulphurous waters. Far more appealing than the grim baths themselves, the low waterfalls and rock pools of **Gría Váthra** are signposted 1.5km up the paved side road leading east from the main Thermá access drive.

Loutrá is the prime base for the tough, six-hour climb up the 1611-metre **Mount Fengári** (known to the ancients as **Sáos**, a name found on some maps to this day), the highest peak in the Aegean islands; the path starts at the top of the village, beside a concrete water tank and a huge plane tree. Tell your accommodation proprietors that you're going, but no one else, as the police may try to stop you – army teams have been summoned on occasion to rescue ill-prepared climbers on what can be an unforgiving mountain. Fengári is Greek for "moon" and, according to legend, if you reach the top on the night of a full moon your wish will come true – most of those foolhardy enough to attempt this will just hope to get back down safely.

Loutrá is a rather dispersed place, with its winding dead-end streets, all ghostly quiet in winter, and its miniharbour – built as an alternative to

Kamariótissa, but never used. **Accommodation** includes the *Kaviros Hotel* (☎25510 98277; ❹), just east of the "centre", and, further downhill, 700m from the beach, the *Mariva Bungalows* (☎25510 98258; ❹). Of the tavernas, *Paradhisos* has the best setting, up under the trees, and charges accordingly. About halfway along the track to Gría Váthra, *Safki*, a summer-only café-bar, occupies the delightful old schoolhouse.

Beyond Loutrá and a ford, on the wooded coastline and reached by a road initially signposted "military camp", are two municipal **campsites**: the first, 1.5km from the village, although large, has no facilities except toilets, while the second, 3km from the village, is more expensive but has hot water, electricity, a small shop, restaurant and bar. The Loutrá bus sometimes goes to either site if you ask nicely.

Beaches on Samothráki's north shore are mostly clean but uniformly pebbly and exposed, but it's still worth continuing along the road east from Loutrá for the views and one or two minor sights. At **Cape Foniás** there's a ruined Gateluzzi watchtower and, 45 minutes' walk inland along the stream, there are **waterfalls** and cold pools much more impressive than those at Gría Váthra, though the signposted description of "canyon" is exaggerated. Some 15km from Loutrá along a fine corniche road is **Kípos beach**, a long strand facing the Turkish-held island of Gökçeada (Ímvros to the Greeks) and backed by open pasture and picturesque crags. The water is clean and there's a rock overhang for shelter at one end, a spring, shower and seasonal drinks *kantína*, but no food available.

The south coast

From the warmer south flank of the island, with its fertile farmland dotted with olive groves, there are fine views out to sea – as far as Gökçeada on a clear day. Up to three daily buses go from Kamariótissa via the sleepy village of Lákoma as far as **PROFÍTIS ILÍAS**, an attractive hill village with a number of good **tavernas** – the best being *Paradhisos*, with a wonderful terrace – but no accommodation to speak of, except for some basic **rooms** (❷). From Lákoma it is 8km east to aptly named **Pahiá Ámmos** ("coarse sand"), a long, clean beach with a taverna-rooms outfit (☎25510 94235; ❸) at the west end. The nearest (meagre) supplies are in Lákoma, but this doesn't deter big summer crowds who also arrive by excursion *kaïkia*. These continue east to **Vátos**, a secluded beach (naturism tolerated) also accessible by land, the **Kremastá Nerá** coastal waterfalls, and finally round to Kípos beach (see above).

Thássos

Just 12km from the mainland, **Thássos** has long been a popular resort island for northern Greeks, and since the early 1990s has also attracted a cosmopolitan variety of tourists, in particular from central and eastern Europe, plus plenty of Western Europeans on packages. They are all entertained by vast numbers of *bouzoúkia* (music halls) and tavernas that lay on music at weekends (and during the week in July and August), while nature lovers can find some areas of outstanding beauty, especially inland. Moreover, the island's traditional industries have managed to survive the onslaught of modernity. Thássos still makes a substantial living from the pure-white marble that constitutes two-thirds of the land mass, found only here and quarried at dozens of sites (legal and unlicensed) in the hills between Liménas and Panayía. Olives, honey, fruit and nuts (often sold candied) are also important products. The spirit *tsípouro*, rather than wine, is the main local tipple; pear extract, onions or spices like cinnamon and anise are added to home-made batches.

Inhabited since the Stone Age, Thássos was settled by Parians in the seventh century BC, attracted by gold deposits between modern Liménas and Kínyra. Buoyed by revenues from these, and from silver mines under Thassian control on the mainland opposite, the ancient city-state here became the seat of a medium-sized seafaring empire. Commercial acumen did not spell military invincibility, however; the Persians under Darius swept the Thassian fleets from the seas in 492 BC, and in 462 BC Athens permanently deprived Thássos of its autonomy after a three-year siege. The main port continued to thrive into Roman times, but lapsed into Byzantine and medieval obscurity.

Sadly, the salient fact of more recent history has been a series of devastating, deliberately set **fires** in the 1980s and 1990s. Only the northeastern quadrant of the island, plus the area around Astrís and Alykí, escaped, though the surviving forest is still home to numerous pine martens.

Thássos is just small enough to circumnavigate in one full day by rented motorbike or car. The KTEL will do the driving for you – albeit with little chance for stopping – some four times daily. **Car rental** is dominated by Potos Car Rental (☎25930 23969), with branches in all main resorts, or Rent-a-Car Thassos (☎25930 22535), also widely represented, as are most of the major international chains, such as Budget at Theayénous 2 in the capital, **Liménas** (☎25930 23050). Vigorous bargaining with the local one-off outfits is often productive of 35-percent discounts on official rates – particularly in early June or mid-September. On the other hand, don't bother showing up in Thássos much before or after these dates, as most facilities will be shut, and the weather can be dodgy in any case. Most hotels are closed between October and the end of April, so call ahead to check.

Liménas

Largely modern **LIMÉNAS** (also signposted as Limín or Thássos) is the island's capital, though not the only port. At first glance Liménas seems an unlikely resort, plagued as it is with surprisingly clogged vehicle traffic and often noisy bars, but it is partly redeemed by its picturesque fishing harbour and the substantial remains of the ancient city which appear above and below the streets.

LIMÉNAS (THÁSSOS TOWN)

RESTAURANTS & BARS	
Full Moon	4
Marina's Bar	8
To Perastikon	6
Iy Piyi	7
Platanos	3
Platia Cafe	5
Simi	2
Syrtaki	1

ACCOMMODATION	
Akropolis	G
Alkyon	C
Amfipolis	A
Athanasia	F
Filoxenia Inn	B
Kipos Studios	D
Lena	E
Myroni & Victoria	H

N

◀ Skála Prínou & Nystéri

Ancient Port (Limenáki)

Town Beach

Ancient Theatre

RO-RO Ferry Dock

Hydrofoil Berth

Taxi Stand

Museum (shut)

Temple of Dionysos

Artemis Shrine

Castle & Apollo Temple

MAIN PLATIA

Byzantine Basilica

Agora

ACROPOLIS

Natural Spring

Temple of Athena Polyouhos

Irakleio

Shrine of Pan

Gate of Zeus & Hera

Gate of Hercules

Gate of Silenos

Gate of Parmenon

0   200 m

▼ Panayía & Alykí

Arrival, transport and information

Kavála-based ferries stop down the coast at Skála Prínou, with a KTEL bus always on hand to meet arrivals. Mountain and motorbikes can be rented from Billy's Bikes (☎25930 22490), Thomai Tsipou (☎25930 22815) or Babis (☎25930 22129). The KTEL office is on the front, virtually opposite the ferry mooring; the service is good, with several daily **buses** to Panayía and Skála Potamiás, Limenária via Potós, Theológos, Kínyra and Alykí. The **taxi** rank is just in front of the bus stop. Thassos Tours (☎25930 23250), at the east end of the waterfront, is the principal airline agent (the closest airport is Kavála's Alexander the Great, 14km from Keramotí on the mainland; see p.40). Several **banks** have ATMs.

Accommodation

Few **hotels** enjoy any tranquillity or decent views but there are some worthy finds; if none from the list below suits, there are also some relatively quiet rooms (❷–❸) just behind the town beach. Note that most of the town hotels are shut from October to early May. The closest **campsite** to town is at Nystéri cove, 2.5km west; the beach is reasonable, and its snack-bar has tables out on a lawn, but the site is small, basic and on hard ground.

As formal addresses are nonexistent, see the map opposite for the locations of the following listings.

Akropolis ☎25930 22488, ℱ25930 22441. Occupying a fine traditional house with flagstone floors and a rear garden-bar, though it can get traffic noise; worth a try now that package companies don't use it. ❸

Alkyon ☎25930 22148, ℱ25930 23662. Certainly the most pleasant of the harbour hotels; English tea and breakfast plus friendly, voluble management make it a home away from home for independent British travellers. Open most of the year; ask also about their cottage in Sotíras and beach villa at Astrís. B&B ❸

Amfipolis ☎25930 23101, ℱ25930 22110. Housed in a folly, this atmospheric hotel is the town's most exclusive accommodation outfit – and you pay dearly for the privilege of staying here; it also has a stylish drinks terrace. ❺

Athanasia ☎25930 23247. Giant and eccentrically furnished rooms with balconies; take the lane inland from behind the *Xenia Hotel* to reach it. Run by a friendly fisherman, this place takes the overflow from the *Alkyon*. ❷

Filoxenia Inn ☎25930 23331, ℱ25930 22231. Quietly situated behind the archeological museum, this has immaculate rooms with fridges, designated breakfast areas and a garden with a small pool. ❺

Kipos Studios ☎25930 22469. In a quiet cul-de-sac next to *Iy Piyi* taverna, this has cool lower-ground-floor doubles (❸) and four-person galleried apartments of a fair standard (❹); a pool has been installed in the garden, ostensibly to make the premises attractive to package companies.

Lena ☎25930 23565. Good-value hotel near the post office, with English-speaking management; no packages. ❷

Myroni ☎25930 23256, ℱ25930 22132. Excellent value, well run and allergic to package companies. It's co-managed with the more modest (no air con) *Victoria* (☎25930 23556; ❸) next door, with which it shares a common breakfast room. ❹

The Town

With its mineral wealth and safe harbour, **ancient Thassos** prospered from Classical to Roman times. The largest excavated area is the agora, a little way back from the fishing harbour. The site (free) is fenced but not always locked, and is most enjoyably seen towards dusk. Two Roman stoas are prominent, but you can also make out shops, monuments, passageways and sanctuaries from the remodelled Classical city. At the far end of the site (away from the sea) a fifth-century BC passageway leads through to an elaborate sanctuary of Artemis, a substantial stretch of Roman road and a few seats of the odeion. The nearby archeological museum is closed indefinitely for extensive expansion.

From a **temple of Dionysos** behind the fishing port, a path curls up to a **Hellenistic theatre**, fabulously positioned above a broad sweep of sea. It's currently open, but is a chaos of excavation, with summer-festival performances set to resume in the distant future. On the same corner of the headland as the theatre, you can still see the old-fashioned *kaïkia* being built, and gaze across to the uninhabited islet of Thassopoúla. It's possible to rent boats from the fishing harbour, self-skippered or not, to take you there and elsewhere.

From just before the theatre, the trail winds on the right up to the **acropolis**, where a Venetian-Byzantine-Genoese fort arose between the thirteenth and fifteenth centuries, constructed from recycled masonry of an Apollo temple, which stood here. You can continue, following the remains of a massive circuit of fifth-century walls to a high terrace supporting the foundations of the Athena Polyouhos (Athena Patroness of the City) temple, with Cyclopean walls. From the exit at the southern end of the temple, a short path leads to an artificial cavity in the rock outcrop which was a shrine of Pan, shown in faint relief playing his pipes. Following the path to the left around the summit brings you to a precipitous rock-hewn stairway with a metal handrail, which provided a discreet escape route to the Gate of Parmenon, the only gate in the fortifications to have retained its lintel; it name comes from an ancient inscription ("Parmenon Made Me") on a nearby wall slab. From here a track, then a paved lane, descend through the southerly neighbourhoods of the modern town, completing a satisfying one-hour circuit.

Eating, drinking and nightlife

Given the cheap-and-cheerful-package ethos, cuisine is not Liménas's strong point, and eateries are generally overpriced. The picturesque **tavernas** around the old harbour are predictably touristy – sophisticated *Simi* is marginally the best, and serves memorably good wine. Another good option is *Syrtaki*, at the far eastern end of the overly popular town beach. In the town centre, greasy fast food is all too abundant, though a dependable favourite for *mayireftá* is *Iy Piyi*, up at the south corner of the main square, next to the natural sunken spring of the name. *Platanos*, with a pleasant terrace opposite the ferry docks, is the place to head for breakfast, be it English style or ambrosia-like yoghurt and honey, and its coffee is highly drinkable. Finally, *To Perastikon*, at the northwest corner of the square near *Iy Piyi*, serves the best ice cream on the island. By contrast, there's plenty of choice in local **bars**: *Full Moon* near the *Hotel Amfipolis* is the main Anglophile watering-hole, and comes with a paperback-swap library. *Platia Cafe Bar*, on yet another corner of the basilica square, has good music, while *Marina's Bar* near the *Hotel Alkyon* is the best waterfront night spot, attracting a mainly Greek clientele.

Around the coast

Whether you plan to circumnavigate the island clockwise, or in the opposite direction, plan on a lunch stop at **Alykí**, roughly a third of the way along in the circuit described below, and the most photogenic spot along the coast.

Panayía, Potamiá and Mount Ipsárion

The first beach east of Liménas, **Makrýammos**, is a purpose-built, controlled-access compound for package tourists, so carry on to **PANAYÍA**, the attractive hillside village overlooking Potamiá Bay. It's a large, thriving place where life revolves around the central square with its large plane trees, fountain and slate-roofed houses. Top **accommodation** choice in both senses is the *Hotel Thassos Inn* (☎ 25930 61612, ⊕ 25930 61027; ❹), up in the Tris Piyés district near the Kímisis church, with fine views over the rooftops. Down on the main road, beside the municipal car park, the newish, clean *Pension Stathmos* (☎25930 61666; ❸) is the quietest of several nearby, with stunning views out the back; there are also high-standard rooms (☎25930 61981; ❷) below the school basketball courts. There have been complaints about high-pressure touting tactics from the hotly competing tavernas on the square; for a more low-key approach, try *Iy Thea*, a view-terrace *psistariá* at the southeast edge of town en route to Potamiá.

POTAMIÁ, much lower down in the river valley, is far less prepossessing – with modern red tiles instead of slates on the roofs – and thus little visited, though it has a lively winter carnival. It also offers the **Polygnotos Vayis Museum** (Tues–Sat 9.30am–12.30pm, summer also 6–9pm, Sun 10am–1pm; free), devoted to the locally born sculptor; though Vayis emigrated to America when young, he bequeathed most of his works to the Greek state. Potamiá also marks the start of the preferred route up to the 1204-metre summit of **Mount Ipsárion**. Follow the bulldozer track to the big spring near the head of the valley extending west of the village (the last source of water), where you'll see the first red-painted arrows on trees. Beyond this point, cairns mark the correct turnings in a modern track system; forty minutes above the spring, take an older, wide track, which ends ten minutes later at a narrow ravine with a stream and the current trailhead. The path is steep, strenuous and unmaintained, and you'll be dependent on cairns and painted arrows. Go early in the day or season, and allow four hours up from Potamiá, and nearly as much for the descent.

Skála Potamiás and Khryssí Ammoudhiá

The onward road from Potamiá is lined with rooms for rent and apartment-type accommodation. A side road some 12km from Liménas takes you down to **SKÁLA POTAMIÁS**, at the southern end of the bay, where some fairly uninspired **tavernas** line the harbour front; a road off to the left brings you to sand dunes extending all the way to the far northern end of the bay. An honourable exception amongst the tavernas is *Flor International* (no sign), at the corner where the bus (hourly 7am–8pm to Liménas) turns around; the *Afrodite*, a short way along, is also acceptable for *mayireftá*. Worth a mention is *Eric's Bar* on the main road just outside the village, where one Stratos Papafilippou has made a career of his uncanny resemblance to footballer Eric Cantona; full English breakfast is available, you can watch Premiership matches on satellite TV and there is a heated outdoor swimming pool.

The best places to **stay** are either above the plane-shaded traffic turnaround area by the port, beyond the tavernas – where the *Hera* (☎25930 61467; ❷), just on the left looking inland, or the *Delfini* (☎25930 61275; ❷), 200m straight back, are peaceful but basic – or, if you're prepared to pay more, there's the *Miramare* (☎25930 77209; ❹), which has a swimming pool among well-manicured gardens, further up the same lane. Alternatively, head north along the shore towards the sandy beach, for **rooms** (❷–❸), to either side of the *Arion* (☎25930 61486; ❸) and *Anna* (☎25930 61070; ❷) hotels, which represent the best value hereabouts. The north end of this beach is called **Khryssí Ammoudhiá** ("golden sands"), an increasingly chaotic, built-up cluster of tavernas, hotels and a campsite; a direct road (plied by an infrequent bus service) spirals for 5km down from Panayía. Once there, you can choose between the self-catering *Villa Emerald* (☎25930 61979; ❹) or the *Golden Sand* (☎25930 61771 or 25930 61209; ❸), nearer the sands. The *Golden Beach* campsite (☎25930 61472) is the only official one on this side of the island.

Kínyra and Alykí

The dispersed hamlet of **KÍNYRA**, some 24km south of Liménas, marks the start of the burnt zone which overlooks it, though incipient greenery suggests that recovery is underway; it's endowed with a poor beach, a couple of grocery stores and several small hotels. Those not block-booked include *Villa Athina* (℡25930 41214; ➊) at the north end of things, whose top-floor rooms see the water over the olive trees, and the welcoming *Pension Marina* (℡25930 31384; ➊). *Yiorgos* and Faros are the best tavernas here. Kínyra is convenient for the superior **beaches** of Loutroú (1km south) and partly nudist Paradise (3km along) – officially called Makrýammos Kinýron – both of which can be reached down poorly signposted dirt tracks. The latter ranks as most scenic of all Thassian beaches, with still-forested cliffs inland, a namesake islet offshore beyond the extensive shallows and much cleaner water than at Khryssí Ammoudhiá. A couple of mediocre snack-bars behind the sand overcharge bathers.

The south-facing coast of Thássos has the balance of the island's best beaches. **ALYKÍ** hamlet, 35km from Liménas and just below the main road, faces a perfect double bay, which almost pinches off a headland. Uniquely, it retains its original whitewashed, slate-roofed architecture, since the presence of extensive antiquities here has led to a ban on any modern construction. Those ruins include an ancient temple to an unknown deity, and two exquisite early Christian basilicas out on the headland, with a few columns re-erected. The sand-and-pebble west bay gets oversubscribed in peak season, though you can always head off to the less crowded, rocky east cove, or snorkel in the crystal-clear waters off the marble formations on the headland's far side. Dominating the western inlet on the roadward side, well-established **taverna** *Glaros* serves fresh fish and has decent **rooms** (➌) to let. A lively bar and a row of water-edge tavernas also compete for your custom, with *To Limanaki/The Little Mole* winning, if only for its more varied menu – it also tends to open earlier in the year than the others. One kilometre further along the coast, at secluded **Kékes** beach among a pine grove, traditional taverna *Skidhia* also has **rooms** in plain but comfortable bungalows, with air-conditioning and en-suite bathrooms (℡25930 31528; ➌).

Arhangélou Mihaïl to Potós

Some 5km west of Alykí, the **convent of Arhangélou Mihaïl** (open reasonable daylight hours) clings spectacularly to a cliff on the seaward side of the road. Though founded in the twelfth century above the spot where a spring had gushed forth, the convent has been hideously renovated by the nuns, resident here since 1974. A dependency of Filothéou on Mount Athos, its prize relic is a purported nail from the Crucifixion.

At the extreme south tip of Thássos, 9km further west, **ASTRÍS** (Astrídha) can muster two uninspiring medium-sized hotels, a few rooms and a good beach. Just 1km west is another better but crowded beach, Psilí Ámmos, with watersports on offer. A few kilometres further, **POTÓS** is the island's prime Germanophone package venue, its centre claustrophobically dense, with the few non-block-booked rooms overlooking cramped alleys. However, the kilometre-long beach is still unspoilt. For a less touristy place to eat, the **taverna** *Piatsa*, one of the cheaper and better places, is tucked away at the southern end of the seafront, in a semi-pedestrianized street; next door, *Michael's Place* has great ice cream and breakfasts. Along the harbour front a string of varyingly trendy **bars and cafés** offers viable alternatives. There are plenty of rental outlets for **cars**, scooters and mountain bikes, including the headquarters of Potos Rent a Car. **Pefkári**, with its manicured beach and namesake pine grove,

1km west, is essentially an annexe of Potós, with a few mid-range **accommodation** options such as *Prasino Veloudho* (☎25930 52001, ⓕ25930 51232; ❸) and the rather more upmarket *Thassos* (☎25930 51596, ⓕ25930 51794; ❹). The **campsite**, *Pefkari* (☎25930 51190; June–Sept), with its attractive wooded location and clean facilities, is one of the best on Thássos.

Limenária and the west coast

LIMENÁRIA, the island's second town, was built to house German mining executives brought in by the Ottomans between 1890 and 1905. Their remaining mansions, scattered on the slopes above the harbour, lend some character, but despite attempts at embellishing the waterfront, it's not the most attractive place on Thássos, though it is handy for its **banks** and ATMs, **post office** and seasonal hydrofoil connections. The best **accommodation** is the Hotel George (☎25930 51413, ⓕ25930 52530; ❹), with bright and modern rooms at the lower end of the main street leading down to the harbour front. At the east end of the quay, in some 1960s blocks, are a cluster of very basic hotels such as the *Sgouridis* (☎25930 51241; ❸). There are also plenty of **rooms** on offer (❷–❸). For eating and drinking, choose from among half-a-dozen each of bars and eateries along the front, of which *Mouragio* is the only one that comes close to having some charm.

The nearest good beach is **Trypití**, a couple of kilometres west – turn left into the pines at the start of a curve right. All development – mostly package villas – is well inland from the broad, 800-metre long strand, although there are umbrellas and sun loungers for rent. The cleft that the name refers to (literally "pierced" in Greek) is a slender tunnel through the headland at the west end of the beach, leading to a tiny three-boat anchorage.

Continuing clockwise from Limenária to Limenás, there's progressively less to stop off for as the western coast is the most exposed and scenically least impressive. The various *skáles* (harbours) such as Skála Kaliráhis and Skála Sotíros – originally the ports for namesake inland villages – are bleak, straggly and windy. **Skála Marión**, 13km from Limenária, is the exception that proves the rule: an attractive little bay, with fishing boats hauled up on the sandy foreshore, and the admittedly modern low-rise village arrayed in a U-shape all around. There are **rooms** available (❷–❸), a few tavernas and, most importantly, two fine beaches on either side. **Skála Prínou** has little to recommend it, other than ferry connections to Kavála. Buses are usually timed to coincide with the ferries, but if you want to stay, there are several hotels, numerous rooms, quayside tavernas and an EOT **campsite** (☎25930 71171; June–Sept) 1km south of the ferry dock. **Skála Rahoníou**, between here and Limenás, has more accommodation (including the *Perseus* campsite) and fish restaurants, as well as proximity to **Pahýs beach**, 9km short of Limenás, by far the best strand on the northwest coast. Narrow dirt tracks lead past various tavernas through surviving pines to the sand, partly shaded in the morning.

The interior

Few people get around to exploring inland Thássos – with the post-fire scrub still struggling to revive, it's not always rewarding – but there are several worthwhile excursions to or around the **hill villages**, besides the aforementioned trek up Mount Ipsárion from Potamiá (see p.466).

From Potós you can head 10km along a well-surfaced but poorly signposted road to **THEOLÓGOS**, founded in the sixteenth century by refugees from Constantinople and the island's capital under the Ottomans. Its houses, most with oversized chimneys and slate roofs, straggle in long tiers to either side of the main street, surrounded by generous kitchen gardens or walled courtyards. A stroll along the single high street, with its couple of *kafenía*, a soldiers' bar, sandalmaker and traditional bakery, is rewarding and quickly dispels the off-putting effect of vigorous advertising at the outskirts for "Greek Nights" at local tavernas. Two that eschew musical gimmicks and rely on their good fare are the long-running *Psistaria Lambiris*, at the entrance into town, and *Kleoniki/Tou Iatrou*, in the very centre, on the right-hand side past the bus stop and police station. They're at their best in the evening when the roasting spits, loaded with goat and suckling pig, start turning.

Despite its proximity as the crow flies, there's no straightforward way from Theológos to **KÁSTRO**, the most naturally protected of the anti-pirate redoubts; especially with a car, it's best to descend to Potós before heading up a rough, seventeen-kilometre dirt track from Limenária. Thirty ancient houses and a church surround a rocky pinnacle, fortified by the Byzantines and the Genoese, which has a sheer drop on three sides. Summer occupation by shep-herds is becoming the norm after total abandonment in the nineteenth century, when mining jobs at Limenária proved irresistible. There's only one *kafenío*, on the ground floor of the former school, one telephone therein, no mains elec-tricity and far more sheep than people.

From Skála Marión an unmarked but paved road (slipping under the main highway bridge to the north) proceeds 11km inland through gnarled old olive trees to well-preserved **MARIÉS** at the top of a wooded stream valley; of two tavernas here, the well-signed one to the right, *Bethel*, is preferable. From Skála Sotíros, a very steep road heads 3.5km up to **SOTÍRAS**, the only interior village with an unobstructed view of sunset over the Aegean and thus popular with foreigners, who've bought up about half of the houses for restoration. On the ridge opposite are exploratory shafts left by the miners, whose ruined lodge looms above the church. On the plane-shaded square below the old fountain, *O Plátanos* taverna is congenially run by Maria and Manolis, who offer grills plus one *mayireftá* dish-of-the-day, good bulk wine and sometimes their potent, home-made *tsípouro*, but only in July and August.

From Prínos (Kalýves) on the coast road, you've a six-kilometre journey inland to the Kazavíti villages, shrouded in greenery that escaped the fires; they're (poorly) signposted and mapped officially as Megálo and Mikró Prínos but still universally known by their Ottoman name. **MIKRÓ KAZAVÍTI** marks the start of the track south for **MEGÁLO KAZAVÍTI**, where the magnificent platía, one of the prettiest spots on the whole island, is home to a couple of decent, normal-priced **tavernas**, while *Vassilis*, below in a beautifully restored house, is regarded as a cut above. Some 4km up from its *skála* (harbour), **RAHÓNI** is well set at the head of a denuded valley. The road up to the square has plenty of simple tavernas, such as *Iy Dhrosia*.

Travel details

Ferries

To simplify the lists that follow we've excluded several regular peripheral services on generally north-to-south routes. These are the weekly LANE sailing between Crete, Kárpathos, Rhodes, Kós, Kálymnos, Sámos, Híos, Lésvos, Límnos and Alexandhroúpoli (40hr for the full run, usually over the weekend), the Agoudimos sailing between Crete and Thessaloníki via Kárpathos, Rhodes, Kós, Kálymnos, Sámos and Thessaloníki (39hr for the full run); and the GA sailing linking Kavála with Límnos, Lésvos, Híos, Sámos and Ikaría (total journey time 26hr).

Áyios Efstrátios 4–5 weekly on Saos Ferries to Límnos, Kavála and Lávrio; 1–2 weekly on Saos to Psará, Sígri (Lésvos), Samothráki; 5 weekly by small local ferry to Límnos.

Foúrni 3 weekly to Sámos (northern ports) and Pireás, on GA; daily 7–7.30am except Sun on *Samos Sun* or *Samos Spirit* to Karlóvassi, returning 2pm; 4 weekly on *Samos Spirit* (7am) to Áyios Kírykos (Ikaría) and Vathý, returning 2.15pm.

Híos 11–14 weekly on NEL Lines to Pireás (10hr slow ferry, 5hr high-speed) and Lésvos (3hr 30min/1hr 30min); 3 weekly to Límnos on NEL, 1 weekly on Saos; 2 weekly to Sámos & Ikaría with Saos Ferries and/or *Panayía Psarianí*; 1 weekly to Sýros/Mýkonos & Lávrio on Saos Ferries. Daily 2pm *kaïki* to Inoússes except Sun morning, and Tues in off-season; 5–6 weekly on *Panayia Psariani* – usually at 3pm – from Híos Town to Psará (3hr 30min).

Ikaría At least daily from either Áyios Kírykos or Évdhilos to Sámos (both northern ports) and Pireás, on Hellenic Seaways or GA; 2 weekly to Foúrni from Áyios Kírykos on GA; 5–6 weekly to Mýkonos and Sýros from Áyios Kírykos on GA, 2 weekly to same from Évdhilos on Hellenic Seaways; 2 weekly to Náxos & Páros from Évdhilos on Hellenic Seaways; daily *kaïki* or small ferry from Áyios Kírykos to Foúrni, at either 2pm or 6pm; 3 weekly *kaïkia*, typically Mon, Wed & Fri mornings, from Manganítis to Áyios Kírykos.

Lésvos 11–14 weekly on NEL Lines from Mytilíni to Pireás (10–12hr direct, 13hr via Híos, 7hr high-speed; 10–12 weekly to Híos (3hr 30min, or 1hr 30min high-speed); 2 weekly on NEL from Mytilíni, 3 weekly on Saos Ferries from Sígri, to Límnos (5hr, 2hr 30min high-speed); 2 weekly to Thessaloníki on NEL (13hr, 6hr 30min high-speed); 1–2 weekly to Kavála on NEL (12hr); 1 weekly to Áyios Efstrátios, Samothráki and Alexandhroúpoli on Saos

from Sígri; 1 weekly to Mýkonos, Tínos, Sýros and Lávrio on Saos.

Límnos 3 weekly on NEL Lines to Lésvos (Mytilíni) & Híos, 3 weekly on Saos Ferries; 4–5 weekly to Áyios Efstrátios & Lávrio on Saos Ferries; 2–3 weekly to Sígri (Lésvos) and Samothráki on Saos Ferries; 4–5 weekly to Kavála on Saos, 1 weekly direct on NEL; 2 weekly direct to Thessaloníki on NEL; 2 weekly to Alexandhroúpoli on Saos; 3 weekly to Piraeus on NEL, 1 on Saos; 1 weekly to Sámos and Ikaría on Saos; 1–2 weekly to Kými (Évvia), Alónissos, Skópelos, Skiáthos and Vólos on Saos.

Sámos (Karlóvassi) As for Vathý, but no Agoudimos or LANE service.

Sámos (Pythagório) 4 weekly (Mon, Wed, Fri & Sun afternoon) with the *Nissos Kalymnos* to Agathónissi, Arkí, Lipsí, Pátmos, Léros and Kálymnos, with onward connections to all other Dodecanese (see p.389 for the full schedule).

Sámos (Vathý) 1–2 daily, on GA or Hellenic Seaways, to Ikaría (Áyios Kírykos or Évdhilos) and Pireás (11–14hr); 2 weekly to Páros & Náxos, on GA; 3 weekly to Foúrni on GA; 4–6 weekly to Mýkonos and Sýros on GA or Hellenic Seaways.

Samothráki 2–3 daily to Alexandhroúpoli (2hr 30min) in season, dropping to 5–6 weekly out of season. Also 2 weekly late spring & early autumn, up to 3 weekly in July & Aug, to Kavála (and thence other north Aegean islands). Also during July & Aug, 1 weekly (usually Fri) direct to Límnos.

Thássos At least 7 daily, in summer months only (1 daily Oct–May), between Kavála and Skála Prínou (1hr 15min; 8am–8pm, 6am–7pm to Kavála from the island); 10 daily all year round between Keramotí and Liménas (40min; 7am–10pm, 6am–8.30pm from Thássos).

Hydrofoils

Two companies, **Samos Flying Dolphins** and **Aegean Flying Dolphins**, operate out of Pythagório (Sámos). Full details of Aegean Flying Dolphins' Dodecanese service are given on p.390. The single craft of Sámos Flying Dolphins provides service to the east Aegean as follows: to Foúrni (3 weekly, 1hr–1hr 20min) and Ikaría, Áyios Kírykos (4 weekly, 1hr–1hr 25min).

Samothráki Served by hydrofoil from Alexandhroúpoli April–Nov 4–7 times weekly, usually at 8am (1hr); mid-June to mid-Sept 1–2 extra daily departures at 1 and/or 5pm. 2–4 times weekly the morning or early afternoon sailing may continue on to Límnos, but don't rely on this.

Thássos (Liménas) Service limited to summer: 8–15 times daily, 7am–9pm (6am–8pm from Thássos); in the high season there may also be 2–3 daily departures from Kavála to the west-coast resorts of Skála Kaliráhon, Skála Marión and Limenária.

International ferries

Híos–Çeşme (Turkey) 2–13 boats weekly at 8.30am and/or 6.30pm, depending on season; Thurs evening (Turkish boat) & Sat morning (Greek boat) services tend to run year-round. Passenger fares on the Greek boat (*San Nicholas*, Sunrise Tours) or Turkish vessel (*Ertürk II*) are nominally about €40, including Greek taxes (no Turkish tax), but "special offers" of €30–35 are frequent; one way €25. Small cars €65–70 one way, €110 return, plus small Greek tax. Journey time 30min (*San Nicholas*) or 45min (*Ertürk II*).

Mytilíni (Lésvos)–Ayvalık (Turkey) Daily May–Oct; winter link unreliable. Two Mytilíni-based craft, the Turkish *Jalehan* and the Greek *Mytilinii*, depart Mytilíni 8–8.30am most days. Passenger rates €29 one way or round trip, all taxes inclusive. Small cars (each boat carries two) €60 one way, €90 return. Journey time 1hr 20min.

Vathý (Sámos)–Kuşadası (Turkey) 2 daily, early May to late Oct (at most one weekly in winter). Greek boat at 8am; afternoon (4.45pm) Turkish boats (usually 2 craft in season). Rates are €35–40 one way including taxes on both the Greek and Turkish sides (Turkish boat slightly cheaper),

€45 day return including taxes, €60 open return including taxes. The Turkish boats are not allowed to carry cars owing to deficient insurance; cars are only ferried on the Greek craft Fri, Sat & Sun (€50 one way, €100 return for a small car, plus €10 Turkish tax each way). Journey time 1hr 30min.

Flights

NB: All flights on Olympic Airlines/Aviation unless otherwise specified. Frequencies are for the period June–Sept.

Híos to: Athens (4–5 daily on Olympic, 2 daily on Aegean; 50min); Límnos (2 weekly, both via Lésvos; 1hr 35min); Rhodes (2 weekly, 1 via Sámos; 55min–1hr 45min); Thessaloníki (4 weekly, 2 via Lésvos/Límnos; 1hr 10min–2hr 45min).

Lésvos to: Athens (3–5 daily on Olympic, 3 daily on Aegean; 1hr); to Límnos (5 weekly; 40min); Rhodes (5 weekly, 3 via Híos/Sámos; 1hr 5min–1hr 40min); Sámos (2 weekly, 1 direct; 45min–1hr 30min); Thessaloníki (10 weekly, 5 via Límnos, on Olympic; 1 daily direct on Aegean; 1hr 10min–1hr 50min).

Límnos to: Athens (2–3 daily; 1hr); Lésvos (5 weekly; 35min); Rhodes (5 weekly; 2hr 5min–2hr 50min); Thessaloníki (6 weekly; 45min).

Sámos to: Athens (4–5 daily; 55min); Rhodes (2 weekly; 45min); Lésvos (2 weekly, 1 via Híos; 50min–1hr 30min); Límnos (2 weekly, via Lésvos/Híos; 1hr 35min–1hr 55min); Thessaloníki (2 weekly direct, 2 via intervening islands; 1hr 20min–3hr 45min).

Greek **cuisine**

Although standards like kalamári and moussaka still figure strongly in taverna fare, Greek cuisine is considerably more complex and varied than the ubiquity of these well-loved dishes might suggest. In fact, modern Greeks are busy rediscovering their rich rural culinary heritage, which began as simple and functional, relying on local products, and later expanded under the influence of elaborate, Anatolian-influenced recipes in the 1920s, brought by immigrants from Asia Minor. The result is a rich and wide-ranging cuisine based on fresh, raw ingredients, subtle herbal filips and preparation by charcoal grilling or in wood-burning ovens. You'll find myriad local specialities, all proudly touted: anything from whole pickled caper sprigs to smoked eels, molluscs bottled in brine to soft sheep's cheese or thyme honey to almond syrup.

Market, Keffaloniá

Eat your greens

Wild and cultivated vegetables are the bedrock of Greek cuisine; until the 1950s, most people could afford to eat little else. During the cooler months of the year, street markets will be stocked with leafy greens: purslane and rocket to be eaten raw, or the various chicories, chards and even edible weeds known as *hórta*. These and more usual garden vegetables find their way into salads, *píttes* (baked pies), fritters and casseroles. *Briám* or *tourloú* is, for example, a ratatouille strong on courgettes, potatoes, eggplants and tomatoes; chickpeas are stewed or formed into *revythokeftédhes* (like coarse falafels) and aubergine (eggplant) has numerous uses: fried in slices, stuffed and baked, or even puréed. Greeks are also avid consumers of *toursí* or pickled vegetables – anything from baby cauliflowers, peppers or carrots to terebinth shoots or rock samphire. Finally, hand-cut chips are a staple and any restaurant with an eye to its reputation among local diners prepares them fresh, daily.

Olive oil mill

Olives and olive oil

Olive oil is a universal ingredient in Greek cuisine; traditionally every family made its own supply, if only from a handful of trees on a remote country property. As in most of the Mediterranean, olives are harvested between November and January depending on the locale and variety: beaten off the trees early on, or harvested ripe from the ground at later stages. There are over a dozen Greek varieties, ranging in colour from green to black to purple: some are used mainly for oil, but others – such as the famed Kalamatas and Amfissas – are reserved for eating, particularly as an integral ingredient of the ubiquitous *horiátiki* or "peasant" salad.

Goat's cheeses

Cheeses

Greeks are, perhaps surprisingly, Europe's biggest cheese consumers and every region of the country produces it, with feta merely the most famous. You'll find every consistency, from hard blocks of *kéfalograviéra* suitable for grating over pasta – a habit adopted from Italy – to pyramids of soft cheese, like the sweet *manoúri* or *anthótyro* and the savoury *touloumbísio*, used for spreading or stuffing. Treats to look out for include the Hiot cow's-milk cheese *mastéllo*, served grilled, or the smoked sheep's cheese known as *metsovóne*, from Epirus.

Vineyard near Kavála, Thrace

Meat dishes

Moussaka

In the days when the ownership of animals represented a family's wealth, eating **meat** was reserved for festivals, though it now figures almost daily in the local diet. The legendary *stó héri* (takeway) snack, **souvlaki**, is traditionally pork-based from November to April, but made from lamb the rest of the year. Besides chops and *pansétta* (spare ribs), **pork** appears everywhere as locally made *loukánika* (sausages), or in winter stewed with celery or plums. Many meat dishes are oven-baked casseroles, cooked in the morning and then left to stand and slowly cool throughout the day, a method which enhances the flavour – standards include the perennial favourites *moussaka* and *stifádho*. Another popular meat in Greece is **goat**; whether stewed, baked or grilled, it's the healthiest meat around, free-range and redolent of the herby hillside on which it grazed. Those same herbs reappear at taverna **grills**, where the proprietor bastes the order, sizzling over olive- or oak-wood coals, with a "broom" of thyme or oregano.

Fish and seafood

Seafood Market, Athens

As well as familiar varieties such as bream and bass, there are many indigenous, seasonably available species to choose from. Delicacies of the eastern Aegean, the richest fishing grounds in Greece owing to the nearby Dardanelles and Turkish river mouths, include shrimp and sole in the springtime, and anchovies, *atherína* (silver smelt) and sardines in late summer; these are all best prepared flash-fried. In other regions, fried *gópes* (bogue), *soupiá* (cuttlefish) with rice and spinach, and grilled or wine-stewed octopus are good choices for seafood platters all year round. The truly acculturated will tuck into unusual shellfish such as *petalídhes* (limpets), *yialisterés* (smooth Venus), *kydhónia* (cockles) and *petrosolínes* (razor clams), which must be eaten alive to avoid being poisoned – if they twitch when lemon juice is dribbled on them, they're alive.

Ouzo

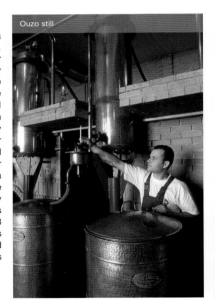

Ouzo still

Ouzo, the quintessential Greek apéritif, is a spirit produced by boiling, in a copper still, the fermented grape-mash residue left after wine-pressing. The resulting liquid, originally known as rakí, grew in popularity during the nineteenth century, when distilleries were established in Smyrna, Constantinople and Lésvos. The word ouzo probably derives from the Italian *uso Massalia*, used to label early *rakí* shipments leaving the Ottoman empire for Marseille. Nowadays it means *rakí* flavoured with various aromatic spices, usually star anise or fennel, both of which contain a compound called anethole. This is responsible for ouzo's harmless property of turning milky white when water is added. Bottled ouzo's alcohol content varies from 40 percent to 48 percent, never higher as the risk of the glass exploding is too great – however you may find home-made ouzo at higher strengths which is kept in barrels to avoid this problem.

Greek coffee

Greek coffee (*ellinikós kafés*), despite its name, is essentially the same drink as prepared across the Middle East and Balkans, though with minor variations in each country. Indeed the term "Turkish coffee" was used in Greece until the Cyprus crises of the mid-twentieth century prompted the renaming. This speciality is made with fine-ground robusta coffee beans (rather than the arabica used to make western filter coffee), sugar to taste and water combined in a long-handled vessel known as a bríki. Allowing it to surge, but not boil, twice before decanting produces the froth or kaïmaki, highly prized and a test of properly made coffee, which is always served with a large glass of cold water.

6

The Sporades and Évvia

CHAPTER 6 # Highlights

* **Skýros** Goaty goings-on, fancy furniture and painted pottery – just some of the attractions of one of the least spoiled islands in the Aegean. See p.492

* **Lalária beach, Skiáthos** This beautiful beach of smooth white stones and turquoise waters, backed by steep cliffs and framed by a famous natural arch, is only accessible by boat. See p.479

* **Skópelos and Glóssa** Pristine facades, slate roofs, bushy palms and luxuri-

ant bougainvillea make these two of the prettiest island towns in the whole of Greece. See p.483 & p.485

* **Convent of Ayíou Nikoláou Galatáki, Northern Évvia** A convent decorated with vivid sixteenth-century frescoes. See p.505

* **Loutrá Edhipsoú** Belle Époque splendours in Greece's top spa town, and an international music festival: all to be found at the remoter end of Greece's second biggest island. See p.506

△ Skýros Town

6

The Sporades and
Évvia

T he **Sporades**, as their Greek name suggests, are a group of islands scattered like seeds in the Aegean, just off the central mainland, their mountainous terrain betraying their origin as extensions of Mount Pílio (see p.371). The three main northern islands are archetypal holiday islands, with fine beaches, transparent waters and lively nightlife – all are very crowded in July and August. **Skiáthos**, nearest to the mainland, is the busiest in the group as it boasts the best beaches and an airport, but **Skópelos**, an emerald isle of thick pine forests, is catching up fast. The quietest and most primitive of the three, **Alónissos**, farthest from the continent, falls within the National Marine Park, a destination more for nature lovers than night-owls.

Skýros, the remotest of the main Sporades, is located some way to the southeast. It retains more of its traditional culture than the others, though tourist development is now well under way. While the dramatically located main town remains a working village rather than a resort, its main street is not without its fast-food and souvenir shops, and a couple of popular beach resorts are situated nearby.

Between Skýros and the continent, the huge island of **Évvia** (classical "Euboea") runs for 150km alongside the mainland. One of the most attractive Greek islands, with a forested mountain spine and long stretches of rugged, largely undeveloped coast, it is explored by few foreign tourists. This is perhaps because it lacks any impressive ruins or real island feel owing to its size and proximity to the mainland. Even so, Athenians and other mainlanders visit the island in force and have erected holiday homes around a handful of seaside resorts.

The northern Sporades are well connected by **bus** and **ferry** with Athens (via Áyios Konstandínos or Vólos), and less often by boat from Thessaloníki; it's easy to island-hop between them. The only connection to Skýros is from Kými on Évvia via a car and passenger ferry. Évvia is linked to the mainland by a couple of bridges at its capital Halkídha, and by local ferries from half a dozen strategic points on the mainland. Only Skiáthos and Skýros have **airports**. Many people come to the Sporades to hike – the pines provide welcome shade. The best **maps** are those published for each island by Anavasi, widely available in Athens and on the islands themselves, for €5–6.

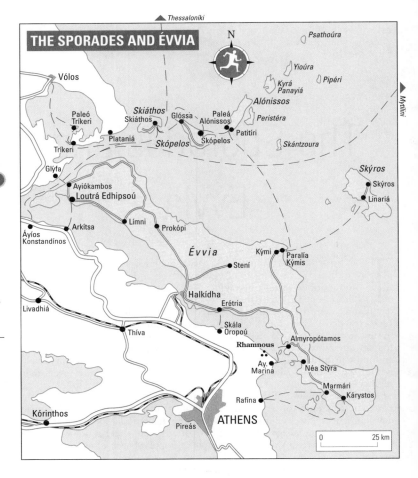

THE SPORADES AND ÉVVIA

Skiáthos

An easy-on-the-eye green landscape, a couple of fine Orthodox monasteries and the labyrinthine streets of the main town are certainly attractions, but the real business of **Skiáthos** is **beaches**: the best, if most crowded, in the Sporades. Tourist literature claims that they number more than sixty, but that's still not enough to soak up the hordes of summer visitors. At the height of season, the island population of four thousand is outnumbered with up to fifty thousand visitors - only Corfu (Kérkyra), Mýkonos and Rhodes (Ródhos) are busier. Along the south and southeast coasts, the road serves an almost unbroken line of villas, hotels and restaurants, and although this doesn't take away the island's natural beauty, it does make it difficult to find anything particularly Greek about it. Nonetheless, you can escape the rush and bustle of the southern coastal strip by heading for the hills: **hiking** through most of northern Skiáthos will bring you to some refreshingly deserted vistas, while an all-terrain vehicle will also get you well off the beaten track. If you're planning to **camp**, bear in mind that pitching your tent outside official sites is strongly discouraged, since summer turns the dry pine-needles to tinder.

Skiáthos Town

SKIÁTHOS TOWN, the main town and port, clambers over two small promontories, dividing the picturesque fishing port from the workaday ferry dock and marina. The western side, with its cubist architecture, maze-like lanes and shady squares rewards aimless exploration while tourist development has scarred the east side of town and main drag Alexándhrou Papadhiamándi, where most services, tackier shops, "English" pubs and eateries are located. Conversely, some pockets of real charm are tucked into the alleys in the older, higher quarter – houses, gardens and flowers galore. As a result, and thanks to some good restaurants and nightclubs, Skiáthos can be fun in a crowded, boisterous sort of way.

Arrival and Information

Buses and **taxis** ply from the area around the **ferry harbour**. Buses run along the main south coast road to Koukounariés, at least hourly in summer (every fifteen minutes at peak times), the last bus returning at 1am; the stops are numbered one to twenty-five.

A large number of competing **rental outlets** in town, most on the front behind the ferry harbour, offer bicycles, motorbikes, cars and motorboats. For an honest and helpful approach, try the efficient Heliotropio (☎24270 22430, @helio@skiathos.gr) opposite the ferry berth, also excellent for accommodation. The cheapest, smallest cars go for around €30 per day for one week's rental, while scooters go for between €15 and €20 per day depending on the length of rental. Several travel agents also organize "round-the-island" mule trips (€20 a day).

Other than using the buses or the various rental outlets in town, you can also get your bearings on a **boat trip** around the island (€20 per person; 5–6hr; leaving 10am daily in high season). Longer excursions, taking in the National Marine Park (see p.491), cost around €30. You could also make a boat trip to the islet of **Tsougriá** (opposite Skiáthos Town), where there's a good beach and a taverna; boats leave from the fishing harbour beyond the Boúrtzi. Boats to the east coast of the island leave from the quay area in front of the bus station, while a bewildering array of tour boats moor at the fishing harbour.

Most other facilities are on Alexándhrou Papadhiamándi, including the **post office** and **banks** (several with **ATMs**); you can check **email** at Internet Zone, Evangelistrías 28.

Accommodation

Much of the island's **accommodation** is in Skiáthos Town. The few reasonably priced hotels or pensions are heavily booked in season, though you can usually find a room (❹–❺), albeit at a slightly more elevated price than on most islands. At other times, supply exceeds demand and you can find very cheap **rooms** with a little bargaining. There is a room-owners' association kiosk on the quay that opens for the best part of the day in high season, but at other times bookings can be made through several tourist agencies.

Good, small **hotels** include the jointly run *Bourtzi* (☎24270 22694, ⓦwww .hotelbourtzi.gr; ❺) on Moraïtou, and *Pothos* (☎24270 22694; ❺), on Evangelistrías, both immaculate with delightful gardens; the former has a swimming pool, the latter only a shady patio. You might also try the *Meltemi* (☎24270 22493; ❺), a pleasant hotel with well-maintained rooms some with balconies, on the waterfront, near the taxi rank. Nearby is the *Akti Hotel* (☎24270 22024, ⓕ24270 22430; ❺) another fine option whose top-floor penthouse, sleeping four, is a good deal if you can land it.

Of the island's three official **campsites**, the closest is that at Xánemos beach, 3km to the northeast of Skiáthos Town next to the airport runway. Apart from being within walking distance of town and close to the beach, there's little to recommend it.

The Town

There aren't many sights to speak of in Skiáthos, but the **Papadiamantis Museum** (Tues–Sun 9.30am–1.30pm & 5–8pm), housed in the nineteenth-century home of one of Greece's best-known writers, Alexandros Papadiamantis, is worth a look. The first floor of the two-storey building has been maintained as the writer's original house, while the ground floor operates as a bookshop-cum-exhibition-area featuring traditional artefacts from the island. The Galerie Varsakis **antique shop** (open usual shop hours), on Platía Trión Ierarhón just inland from the fishing port, has one of the best **folklore displays** in Greece, and many of the older items would do Athens' Benáki Museum proud; the proprietor neither expects, nor wants, to sell the more expensive of these, which include antique textiles, handicrafts and jewellery.

Eating and drinking

There is no shortage of places to **eat**, but nothing is keenly priced apart from the few burger/*yíros* joints, mostly along the main street and nearby. The best fish restaurants tend to be at the far end of the old harbour promenade – their prices reflect this.

1901 En Skiatho In a charming old stone building, close to Platía Trión Ierarhón, this reliable place offers up *bouzoúki*, guitar or jazz to accompany your good-value meal of impeccably prepared traditional Greek fare, accompanied by mellow wine from the barrel.

Alexandros Kapodistríou. This well-signposted taverna is a decent, preferred-by-locals joint with good bulk wine.

Calypso New harbour front. Surprisingly sophisticated Italian-influenced trattoria, serving specials such as black pasta with seafood and wine by the glass.

Dinos Papadhiamándi. One of the most convenient places for breakfast – offering the whole works.

Maria's Syngroú 6. Tucked away up in the back-streets, this is a place to sample excellent pizzas.

Mesogeia Above and to the west of Platía Trión Ierarhón. Of the more traditional and consequently cheaper places to eat, it has excellent moussaka and other home-cooked dishes.

The Windmill Well-signposted, high up overlooking the harbour, this is the decided favourite in the haute cuisine stakes with carefully crafted fish dishes, and commendable pasta and roast vegetables.

Nightlife

In addition to the ultra-trendy waterfront **bars** around the fishing port, with names like Slip Inn, Stay Cool, Bar Fly and Cassa Blanca - **nightlife** centres on the clubs on or near Polytekhníou. The outdoor **cinema**, Refresh Paradiso, on the ring road, shows new releases in their original language. Another source of entertainment is the little offshore Boúrtzi fortress, transformed into an outdoor **theatre** and home to occasional plays and musical performances during the summer.

Adagio Evangelistrías. A bar for those who prefer the softer tones of classical music.

Admiral Benbow Polytekhníou. This very Anglicized and rather small pub plays 1970s and 80s British pop hits to accompany draft cider and English ale.

Borzoi Polytekhníou. The oldest club on the island, playing an eclectic sampling of Latino, blues, rock and jazz.

Kentavros Near the Papadiamantis Museum, on Mitropolítou Ananíou. This long-established and much-loved bar plays jazz and blues.

Around the island

Stopping at two dozen halts along the way, the island bus shuttles between the main town and Koukounariés, a busy resort whose majestic sandy bay of clear, gradually deepening water is backed by acres of pines. Beaches are most people's destination for the day but, with your own transport or if you are prepared to hike, you can escape the crowds, explore the hinterland and visit a monastery or two.

The beaches

The beaches on the northeast coast aren't easily accessible unless you pay for an excursion kaïki: reaching them on foot requires extremely arduous treks. In any case, the prevailing summer meltémi wind blows from the north, so the beaches on the south coast are usually better protected, and you can easily reach a good number of them from the coast road, served by bus. Most of the popular ones have at least a drinks/snacks stall; those at Vromólimnos, Asélinos and Troúlos have proper tavernas.

The famed **Laláxia** beach, featuring on all postcard-stands, is situated almost at the northernmost point of Skiáthos, and can be reached only by taxi-boats from the town. Covered in smooth white pebbles, with steep cliffs rising behind and an artistic natural arch, it's undeniably beautiful and the swimming is excellent, but beware the undertow. Nearby three natural grottoes – Skotiní, Galázia and Halkiní – are included in many of the "round-the-island" trips.

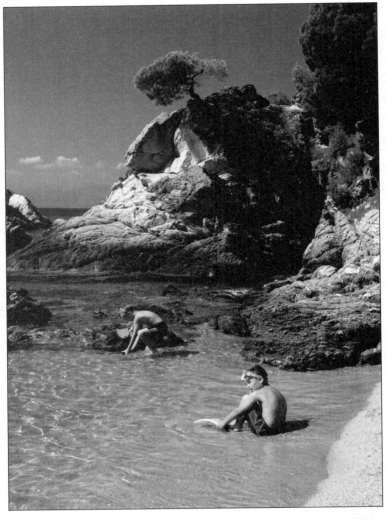

△ Beach on the Kalamáki peninsula, Skiáthos

A short way to the north of Skiáthos town, accessible by road, are the greyish sands of **Mégas Yialós**, one of the less crowded beaches, and **Xánemos**, a nudist beach, but both suffer from airport noise. As you head south, the beaches before the **Kalamáki peninsula** are no great shakes either, but on the promontory itself are the excellent **Tzaneriá** and **Vromólimnos**; Vromólimnos offers windsurfing and water-skiing and is now home to a pumping beach party scene replete with a bungee-jump crane. Overlooking Tzaneriá beach on the eastern side of the Kalamáki peninsula, the Dolphin Diving Centre (☎24270 22599) at the *Nostos* hotel offers **scuba diving**.

Just before Troúlos beach you can turn right up a paved road, which runs 3.5km north to **Megálos Asélinos**, an exposed sandy beach with a bar, reasonable taverna and a decent **campsite**, *Aselinos* (☎24270 49312; April–Oct). A daily bus and excursion boats call here, so it's crowded in season. The fork in the paved road leading to Panayías Kounístras convent (see below) continues to **Mikrós Asélinos**, just east of its larger neighbour and somewhat quieter.

The beaches at **KOUKOUNARIÉS**, the island's second biggest settlement, are excellent if you don't mind the crowds; wooden walkways traverse the sand to a series of *kantínas* selling drinks and light snacks. The approach road runs behind a small lake at the back of the pine trees, and features a string of **hotels**, **rooms** and **restaurants**, as well as a campsite, *Koukounaries* (☎24270 49250; May 15–Sept 15), which is fairly decent with standard facilities. Here, the *Strofilia Apartments* (☎24270 49251, ✉strophilia@n-skiathos.gr; ⊙) are particularly nicely furnished. The prominent *Lake Hotel* (☎24270 49362; ⊙), right opposite the lake itself, is also decent value. Jet-skis, motorboats, wind-surfing and waterskiing are all available off the beach and there's horse-riding at the well-signposted Skiathos Riding Centre.

Signposted across the headland, "**Banana beach**" (officially known as Krasás), is one of the island's trendiest beaches with watersports, a couple of bars and tolerance of nude bathing; named for its crescent of yellow sand, it is divided by rocks into Big Banana and partly gay Small Banana. The turnoff from the coast road for neighbouring **Ayía Eléni** leads 1km to a more accessible, family-oriented beach with a drinks kiosk. Further north, **Mandhráki** and **Eliá** beaches have similar facilities, but are only accessible on foot or by scooter along dirt tracks.

The monasteries and Kástro

Founded at the end of the eighteenth century, the **monastery of Evangelis-trías** (daily 8am–noon & 4–8pm) is exceptionally beautiful, even beyond the grandeur of isolation you find in all Greek monasteries. The Greek flag was raised here in 1807, and heroes of the War of Independence such as Kolokot-ronis pledged their oaths to fight for freedom here. From Skiáthos Town, you can reach Evangelistrías by motorized transport in less than ten minutes or on foot in just over an hour. From the centre, head 500m along the road towards the airport; where the asphalt veers to the right, take a prominently signposted paved side road that veers left; be careful to stick to this and not to wander off onto the dirt roads.

Beyond Evangelistrías, a mule track continues to the abandoned **Ayíou Haralámbou** monastery, from where it's possible to walk northwest to the ruined capital of Kástro (see below) along another dirt road; this takes about two hours. To reach Kástro from Skiáthos Town, it's quicker to take the direct paved road towards it on a motorbike, or take a *kaïki* ride round the island and get off at the beach below.

Continuing west from Evangelistrías, first on track, then on *kalderími*, you reach the paved, Kástro-bound road noted above; turn left, and after 200m or so bear right (west) onto the well-used, signposted dirt track heading towards the abandoned fifteenth-century monastery of **Theotókou Kekhreás**, three hours' walk from town. This is purported to be the oldest monastery on the island and has a colony of bats inside. It's a beautiful walk (or organized donkey-ride), and there are three pebbly beaches below, one with a welcom-ing stream-waterfall that provides a cool shower. Back on the paved road, you can continue on to the **Kástro** in about thirty minutes – a spectacular spot, built on a windswept headland. In the past, the entrance was only accessible by a drawbridge, which has been replaced by a flight of steps. The original settlement was built in the sixteenth century, when the people of the island moved here for security from pirate raids. It was abandoned three hundred years later in 1830, following independence from Turkey, when the population moved back to build the modern town on the site of ancient Skiáthos. The ruins are largely overgrown, and only four churches survive intact, the largest still retaining some original frescoes. From outside the gates, a path leads down the rocks to a good pebble **beach**; with a stream running down from the hills and a daytime café (with slightly overpriced food and drinks), it makes a good place to camp. For an apparently inaccessible spot, though, it does attract a surprising number of people. All the island excursion boats call here, and even when they've gone, there's little chance of having the ruins or beach to yourself.

Finally, the seventeenth-century **Panayías Kounístras** can be reached by taking the right fork along the paved road that runs north across the island from Tróulos to Asélinos beach. It's a very pretty little nunnery, with splendid icons hanging from a beautiful carved screen.

Skópelos

Painted a soothing green by its extensive pine-forests, **Skópelos** is bigger and more rugged than Skiáthos and almost as busy, but its concessions to tourism are lower key and in better taste. Although most of the larger beaches have sunbeds, umbrellas and some watersports, smaller, secluded coves do exist. Inland are prolific olive-groves, and orchards of plums (prunes are a local speciality), pears and almonds. **Skópelos (Hóra)** and **Glóssa**, the two main towns, are also among the prettiest in the Sporades, clambering uphill along paved steps, their houses distinguished by attractive wooden balconies and grey slate roofs.

A number of **nationalities** have occupied the island at various stages of its history, among them the Romans, Persians, Venetians, French and, of course, the Ottomans. The Ottoman pirate-admiral Barbarossa (Redbeard) – actually a Greek renegade from Lésvos – had the entire population of the island slaughtered in the sixteenth century. These days Greeks still manage to outnumber foreign visitors, thanks to the lack of an airport.

Skópelos, especially the pine-clad uplands of its western tract, is prime **walking** territory. Englishwoman and long-time Skópelos resident Heather Parsons runs guided **walking tours** (☎694 52 49 328, ⓦwww.skopelos-walks.com), some ending up at beaches and restaurants.

Skópelos town and around

SKÓPELOS Town (Hóra) slopes down a hill at one corner of a huge, almost circular bay: the tree-lined harbour front, a cascade of handsome mansions and an array of glistening white churches is revealed slowly as the boat rounds the final headland. Though more and more people seem to have discovered Skópelos town, the locals are making a tremendous effort to keep it from going the way of Skiáthos. So while the harbour area is practically wall-to-wall tavernas and cafés, the shops and eateries in the back alleys tend to be imaginative and tasteful, with wooden, hand-painted name signs. Spread below the ruins of a Venetian fortress or **kástro** is an enormous number of

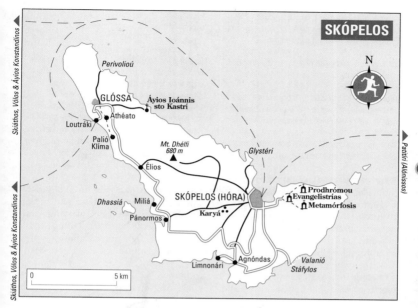

chapels and churches – 123 reputedly, though some are small enough to be mistaken for houses and most are locked except for their annual festival day.

Arrival and Information

The **ferry quay** is at the middle of a long promenade, lined with an array of boutiques, bars, stores and restaurants. Hydrofoil and ferry agencies are opposite the ferry quay; the **bus station** is 100m to the left of the port as you exit. Opposite the harbour entrance, a short road leads into a maze of lanes and signposts to the **post office**, and there are **banks** (with ATMs) about 50m from the ferry quay. You can access the **Internet** at a cybercafé opposite the Metro Club on Doulídhis.

From 7am to 10.30pm, **buses** (6–8 daily) ply the main paved road between Skópelos Town and Loutráki via Glóssa, stopping at the paths to all the main beaches and villages. Among the several **motorbike rental** outlets, friendly service can be had at Panos Wheels (☎24240 23696), near the start of the road towards Glóssa. If you prefer to explore from the sea, day-long **boat cruises** cost around €15 for a trip around the island, or to Alónissos and the National Marine Park (see p.491).

Accommodation

Unless you've booked through a tour operator, you're unlikely to find space in one of the larger, more expensive **hotels** with pools on the hill above the port, but there are dozens of **rooms** (❸–❹) for rent just behind the harbourside promenade or in the backstreets. These can be arranged through the Association of Room Owners office (daily 9am–noon & 6–8pm; ☎ & ℻24240 24567), on the seafront opposite the ferry dock. Madro Travel, by the northern quay (☎24240 22145), is also an excellent place to ask about accommodation, in addition to boat excursions and the like.

Adonis ℡ 24240 22231, Ⓕ 24240 23239. This brightly painted establishment, just above the mid-seafront, is fine though it can be noisy. ❺

Aperitton ℡ 24240 22256, Ⓦ www.aperitton .gr. A modern hotel with pool, up on the ring road, combining contemporary and traditional local architecture. ❼

Dionysos ℡ 24240 23210, Ⓔ dionysco@otenet.gr. This first-rate, neo-rustic hotel, with a palm-fringed pool, is one of the more sophisticated lower-town options. ❻

Georgios L. ℡ 24240 22308, Ⓔ georgios-hotel @skopelos.net. This bland, old-style hotel at the northern end of the promenade is a fair standby, especially if you have a car (parking). ❹

Mando ℡ 24240 23917. Easily the best of accommodation down at Stáfylos (see below); it is extremely friendly and quiet with neat studios set among bowling-green lawns, a short way up from its own rocky beach. ❺

Skopelos Village ℡ 24240 22517, Ⓦ www .skopelosvillage.gr. Located some 500m around the bay from the docks, to the south side of Hóra, these smart bungalows and studios (mostly snapped up by package companies) are set among a green oasis. ❻

The Town and around

Sights include a poorly displayed **folklore museum** (daily 10am–2.30pm & 6–10pm; €2), featuring a motley collection of valuable nineteenth- and early-twentieth-century embroidered cloths, traditional costumes, weaving and decorative artefacts; the highly informative illustrated panels explaining local customs and the religious calendar save the day. High-quality photography exhibitions are held at the **Photographic Centre** (summer: daily 10am–8pm; €1.50) at the eastern end of town.

Outside town, perched on the slopes opposite the quay, are two convents worth visiting for their seclusion and views: **Evangelistrías** (daily 8am–1pm & 4–7pm), which is within view of the town, and **Prodhrómou** (daily 8am–1pm & 5–8pm). Also on this promontory, the monastery of **Metamórfosis**, nestled among lush vegetation, was abandoned in 1980 but is now being restored by the monks and is open to visitors. Access is simplest via an old road behind the line of hotels along the bay to Evangelistrías (an hour's walk). From there it's an extra half-hour's scramble over mule tracks to Pródhromos (with signs to Metamórfosis en route), the remotest and most beautiful of the three. Ignore the new road that goes part way – it's longer, and misses most of the beauty of the walk.

Some 4km south of town, **Stáfylos** is the closest good beach, and is getting increasingly crowded even though rather small and rocky. The road between here and Hóra is lined with more and more places to stay, but these have neither the advantage of Hóra's nightlife and facilities nor Stáfylos' seafront. When Stáfylos beach gets too busy, head a short walk east along the coast to **Valanió**, where you've a better chance of escaping the crowds. Nudity is tolerated and, although the official campsite has long since closed, you shouldn't be hassled if you stay a night or two. There's spring water and a *kantína* here, too.

Eating and drinking

Skópelos Town offers a wide variety of **places to eat**, ranging from acceptable *souvlaki*-joints to truly excellent tavernas serving slightly different food at reasonable prices.

To Aktaion At the northern end of the promenade. One of the most reliable fish tavernas in town.

Anna's Tucked high up in the backstreets behind the port, but well-signposted, this taverna, with a terrace beneath a palm-tree, does Greek food with a slightly Gallic flavour; slow service.

Le Bistro Just behind the seafront near the docks. This sophisticated newcomer offers delicacies such as hare in a red wine sauce, in addition to more conventional seafood pasta and the like; doubles up as a cocktail bar in the early evening.

La Frianderie Opposite the ferry quay. This delicatessen with a range of fresh baguettes, cakes and drinks, plus Greek pies and pastries, is perfect for a quick pre-ferry snack or breakfast.

Klimataria Near the Town Hall. Perhaps the most popular of all the traditional fish tavernas.

Nostos Towards the docks end of the seafront promenade, this taverna has exceptionally pleasant staff and large, delicious and reasonably priced portions of moussaka and the like.

Perivoli Up a narrow street from the square where you'll find the *Platanos* duo of *souvlaki*-joints: an excellent, professionally run taverna in an exquisite garden, preparing good-value Greek food with a cordon bleu twist; wine by the glass.

O Platanos Not one but two *souvláki* places, just inland in the shade of the namesake plane-tree, competing for the distinction of having the best *yíros*; the one with blue chairs has a much wider menu.

Nightlife

Nightlife in Skópelos is increasing, but is more of the late-night-**bar** than the nightclub variety. If you want to head for something more like a **club**, try the enormous, masted, beached galleon, Karavi, reaching out over the harbour perimeter road on the south side. For news of music venues, look for signs around town with their opening days and times.

Anatoli Old rebétika hand Yiorgos Xintaris performs until late on weekends at this small ouzerí on top of the *kástro*.

Bambalo One of two live Greek music clubs up on the ring road.

Platanos Jazz Club A long-standing club on the north side of the harbour, still hanging on (just).

Rembetiki Istoria A popular joint on the ring road which, not surprisingly, features a programme of rebétika music.

Vengera Look out for this classy bar in a restored house in the backstreets; mellow ambience and good music.

Glóssa, Loutráki and around

Skópelos' sleepy second town, **GLÓSSA**, 25km from Hóra at the northern end of the island, seems much further away, and few visitors to the island even bother to explore the place. A fair-sized village of handsome houses, some Cycladic cubes, others Macedonian-style mansions with wooden balconies, it dangles down a steep hillside. Along its winding narrow streets, mostly car-free, you can unearth several *kafenía*, an excellent taverna and a few **rooms** to let, some of which are hot and musty, with erratic water pressure. An exception, *Kostas and Nina's Place* (℡24240 33686; ❸) has simple, clean rooms, some with a view; they also rent out studios longer term. Otherwise you could stay at the *Selinounda Apartments* (℡24240 33570; ❹) on the road down to Loutráki. The well-signposted central **taverna**, justly popular ⌘ *To Agnandi*, serves excellent, innovative food – try the pork with prunes or the almond cake with elderflower syrup - and has a roof terrace with wonderful views.

Hydrofoils and some car ferries call at the diminutive port of **LOUTRÁKI** ("Glóssa" on ferry and hydrofoil schedules), 3km from Glóssa proper down a steep snaking road. It is little more than a narrow pebble beach with a couple of hotels and rooms for rent. If you need to stay over, you could try any of the **rooms** (❸) advertised just in from the seafront. Though most of the quayside **tavernas** don't offer value for money, there are exceptions: the *Orea Ellas* by the harbour is shaded by beautiful chestnut trees and sells a highly recommended, home-made retsina, while the *Flisvos*, on the far west side of the port, is a friendly place with decent pasta dishes.

Ninety minutes' walk up to the north coast from Glóssa will bring you to **Periviolioú beach**. The walk itself is worthwhile: near a stone cairn you will pass a **monastery** containing masses of human bones and skulls. There's also a huge hollow oak tree here, in the heart of which is a small tank of drinking water. The beach, when you get there, is nothing out of the ordinary, but there's pure spring water and a cave for shade.

East of Glóssa, a dirt road leads to the splendidly sited church of **Áyios Ioánnis stó Kastrí**, perched on the top of a rock high above a small sandy cove where you can swim. An unsightly house nearby has spoiled the isolation somewhat, but the walk from Glóssa (again, about ninety minutes) is beautiful and peaceful, with hawks and nightingales for company.

Around the rest of the island

West of Skópelos Town, various jeep tracks and old paths wind through olive and plum groves towards **Mount Dhélfi** and the Vathiá forest, or skirt the base of the mountain northeast to **Revýthi** hill with its fountains and churches, and the site of **Karyá**, with its sendoúkia (ancient rock-cut tombs, possibly early Christian). To the northwest of Skópelos Town, reached by boat trips, **Glystéri** is a small pebble beach with no shade, whose taverna is much frequented by locals on Sundays.

On the other side of the island, some 5km due south of Hóra is the tiny horseshoe-shaped harbour of **AGNÓNDAS**, where you'll find three fish tavernas and rooms to rent. *Pavlina Apartments* (T 24240 23272, E pavlinaskopelos@mail.gr; ❸), just back from the beach, have four high-ceilinged, self-contained and tasteful, wood-furnished apartments on offer. *Pavlos* is the best choice of the restaurants, on the waterfront; count on good, solid grills and fresh fish. Next up and reachable by a paved side road is **LIMNONÁRI**, 300m of fine sand set in a closed, rocky bay. The *Limnonari Beach Restaurant*, right on the beach, serves delicious spiral-shaped local *tyrópites* and rents **rooms** (T 24240 23046; ❹). A little further around the bay, *Ouzeri O Thomas* is another decent option.

Further up Skópelos's southwest coast, **PÁNORMOS** is very much a full-blown, commercial resort, with rooms, tavernas, a campsite, yacht anchorage and watersports. The beach here is gravelly and shelves steeply, but there are small, secluded sandy bays close by. Of places to **stay**, the thirty-room *Panormos Beach Hotel* (T 24240 22711, W www.panormosbeach-hotel.gr; ❻) has a beautiful garden and fine views, and is lovingly looked after; beyond it, the ⚓ *Adrina Beach* (T 24240 23373, W www.adrina.gr; ❻), occupies ivy-clad buildings, with a large pool, its own taverna, fabulous views and relative isolation.

Slightly further on at **Miliá**, there's a tremendous, 1500m sweep of tiny pebbles beneath a bank of pines, facing the islet of Dhassiá. Though this used to be a fairly quiet and secluded getaway, a very popular party scene has developed here in recent years, with a beach bar attracting scores of hedonistic boys and girls bent on a good time.

Further north, **ÉLIOS**, 9km short of Glóssa, is a medium-sized, fairly new resort settled by residents of the earthquake-damaged villages above it; it has a pleasant beach. Beyond here, the renovated village of **Palió Klíma** marks the start of a beautiful forty-minute **trail** to Glóssa, via the empty hamlet of Áyii Anáryiri and the oldest village on the island, **Athéato** (aka Mahalás).

Alónissos

Thanks to its remoteness, the lack of an airport, the infrequency of ferry connections and a slightly negative reputation, **Alónissos** has tended to attract fewer casual foreign visitors than the other Sporades. Arid and ascetic in appearance – the once famed vineyards were wiped out by phylloxera in the 1950s – Alónissos is surrounded by some of the cleanest water in the Aegean, but is

ALÓNISSOS AND PERISTÉRA

N

Koupelousáko

Yérakas

Mourteró

Áyios
Dhimítrios

Kalamákia

Livádhia

Alónissos

Stení Válá

Peristéra

Megáli
Ammos

Miliá • *Kokkinókastro*

Vrysítsa

Khryssí Miliá

Paleá Alónissos
(Hóra)

Vótsi

Roussoúm Yialós

PATITÍRI

Megálos
Mourtiás

Výthisma • Marpoúnda

0 _____ 5 km

▼ Skópelos, Skiáthos, Vólos & Áy. Konstandínos

lacking in photogenic sandy beaches. Nonetheless the number of middle–class Greek visitors has increased sharply in recent years and the island is now considered quite fashionable. Accordingly it can get very crowded from mid-July to the end of August.

Although its harsh, more rugged landscape makes it less congenial to **hiking** than neighbouring Skópelos, you might still consider joining one of the excellent **walking tours** run by Chris Browne (Ⓦ www.alonnisoswalks.co.uk), taking you to churches, beaches and around some of the minor islets nearby.

Patitíri

The island's port and de facto capital, **PATITÍRI**, occupies a pretty cove flanked by pine trees and ringed by busy bars, cafes and restaurants. It is a little soulless – the inhabitants of the old town (Hóra) were forced to move here after an earthquake in 1965 – but it has tried hard to rectify that by means of a paved waterfront and a general tidying up. It's easy, though, to pick up connections here for beaches and Hóra, and it has some good hotels to choose from. Sights include, halfway along the seafront, a huge **wine barrel** (patitíri) of the kind that gave the place its name; and the **Mom Information Centre** (daily 10am–5pm, sometimes open later in midsummer; free; Ⓦ www.mom.gr), on the first floor of a nearby building, whose informative displays include models, photos, videos and slide shows about the endangered **monk seal** (see box). In a splendid stone building on the southern side of the cove, next to the hotel Haravyi, the privately owned **Costas and Angela Mavrikis Museum** (daily 11am–7pm; €3) is crammed with an eclectic set of displays of local artwork, traditional costumes, reconstructed island interiors, war memorabilia, wine-making equipment, piracy and seafaring in general; a drink at the café, whose terrace offers fabulous views, is included in the entrance price.

Practicalities

All Alónissos's important facilities are in Patitíri; **buses** and **taxis** have adjacent terminals on the waterfront. The **post office** is on the Hóra road, while kaïkia leave from the inner ferry quay. You can **rent a scooter, motorbike** or even a car at reasonable prices at I'm Bikes (☎24240 65010). A couple of the rental places on the waterfront also offer out motorboats and dinghies.

Rooms are easy to find here, and you'll probably be approached with offers as you get off the ferry or hydrofoil. If you need help with accommodation, or any other useful travel information, you have a choice of two excellent agencies on the harbour front: Albedo Travel (☎24240 65804, ⊛www.albedotravel .com) and Alonniso Travel (☎24240 66000). The local room-owners' association (☎ & ☎24240 66188), on the waterfront, can also find you a room (mostly ❸) in Patitíri or nearby Vótsi. Other options include the *Ioulieta Pension* (☎24240 65463; ❸) and *Haravyi* (☎24240 65090, ☎24240 65189; ❹). Best in the higher price range is *Liadromia* (☎24240 65521, ⊜liadromia@alonissos .com; ❺), along a raised street above the port.

The **restaurants** along Patitíri's port are reasonably priced, but for the most part the food is nothing special. One exception is *Anaïs*, offering up a selection of ready-made *mayireftá* and grills to order. Recommended ouzerís include *To Kamaki* (July and August only), two blocks up towards the post office from the waterfront, with an amazing selection of seafood *mezédhes*. Heading up to Hóra, you'll pass the family-run *Babis*; the food is good, with a special spin on local pies.

Nightlife is low-key, mostly confined to the seafront bars; for music there are *Enigma* (international) and *Rembetika*, on the road to the old town, for Greek music.

Paleá Alónissos

PALEÁ ALÓNISSOS (Hóra) was damaged by an earthquake in 1965 and virtually the entire population was transferred down to Patitíri, from where it can be reached by a fine but steep fifty-minute walk via a signposted traditional kalderími. Alternatively, there's a frequent bus service (10 min; €1) between the two in the mornings and evenings. Some houses are still derelict, but much of the village has been painstakingly restored, mainly by foreigners. Only a few local families continue to live here, which gives the village a rather odd and un-Greek atmosphere, but it is picturesque and the views make the trip worthwhile.

If you decide **to stay** up here, *Konstantina's Studios* (☎ & ☎24240 66165; ❺) is a small, renovated building with eight studios and one apartment, all enjoying exceptionally good views, while the simple and clean *Fadasia House* (☎24240 65186; ❸) has its own little restaurant. As for **restaurants**, *Astrofengia*, at the entrance to the village, combines the cuisines of Greece

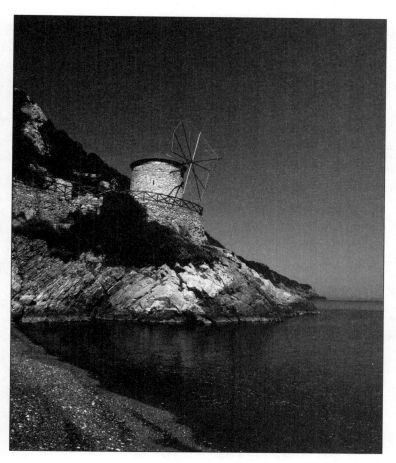
△Windmill, Alónissos

and the Middle East, and the *Paraport*, up on the main square, offers excellent original fish dishes.

The rest of the island

The roads between Patitíri, Stení Vála and the northernmost point on the island are paved, and the dirt roads down to the beaches – with some exceptions – are in good condition: easier to deal with than the twisting, busy roads on Skiáthos and Skópelos. There's a very limited **bus service** along the Hóra–Patitíri–Stení Vála route, but *kaïkia* run half-hourly from Patitíri north to Khryssí Miliá, Kokkinókastro, Stení Vála, Kalamákia and Áyios Dhimítrios, and south around the coast to Marpoúnda, Výthisma and Megálos Mourtiás. *Kaïkia* also sail occasionally to Livádhia on Peristéra islet.

At Patitíri, there's decent swimming from the rocks around the promontory to the north; pick your way along a hewn-out path past the hotels. In

The Mediterranean monk seal

The **Mediterranean monk seal** (*Monachus monachus*) has the dubious distinction of being the European mammal most in danger of extinction – fewer than four hundred survive worldwide, the majority around the Portuguese Atlantic island (ironically) of Madeira. There are other populations along the coasts of Morocco, Algeria, Libya, Croatia and Cyprus. Small numbers survive in the Ionian and Aegean seas of Greece; the largest such community, of around thirty seals, lives and breeds around the deserted islands north of Alónissos.

Monk seals can travel up to 200km a day in search of food, but they usually return to the same places to rear their **pups**. They have one pup every two years, and the small population is very vulnerable to disturbance. Originally, the pups would have been reared in the open, but increasing disturbance by man has led to the seals retreating to isolated sea caves with partly submerged entrances, particularly around the coast of the remote islet of Pipéri.

Unfortunately, the seals compete with fishermen for limited stocks of fish and, in the overfished Aegean, often destroy nets full of fish. Until recently it was common for seals to be killed by fishermen. This occasionally still happens, but in an attempt to protect the seals, the seas around the northern Sporades have been declared a wildlife reserve, the **National Marine Park of Alónissos Northern Sporades**: fishing is restricted in the area north of Alónissos and prohibited within 5km of Pipéri. On Alónissos, the conservation effort and reserve have won a great deal of local support, mainly through the efforts of the **Hellenic Society for the Protection of the Monk Seal** (HSPMS), based at Steni Vála. The measures have been particularly popular with local fishermen, as tight restrictions on larger, industrial-scale fishing boats from other parts of Greece should help restore local stocks, and eventually benefit the fishermen financially.

Despite this, the government has made no serious efforts to enforce the restrictions, and boats from outside the area continue to fish around Pipéri. On a more positive note, the HSPMS, in collaboration with the Pieterburen Seal Creche in Holland, has reared several abandoned seal pups, all of which have been successfully released in the seas north of Alónissos.

For the moment, your chances of actually seeing a seal are remote, unless you plan to spend a few weeks on a boat in the area. It's not recommended that you visit Pipéri – officially prohibited in any case – or approach sea caves on other islands which might be used by seals, or try to persuade boat-owners to do so. If spotted, the seals should be treated with deference; they cannot tolerate human disturbance.

---

the populous south of the island, **MARPOÚNDA** features a large hotel and bungalow complex and a rather small beach. It's better to turn right before Marpoúnda towards **Megálos Mourtiás**, a pebble beach with several tavernas that's also linked by paved track to Paleá Alónissos, 200m above. The island's two best beaches are **Výthisma** and **Vrysítsa** – though the latter is sited a little too close to the island's rubbish dump for comfort, and is on the more exposed north coast. Výthisma, just before Megálos Mourtiás, is best reached by boat, the path here having been washed out. Further north, visible from Paleá Alónissos, Vrysítsa is tucked into its own finger-like inlet. There's a mill, sand and a taverna, but little else.

To the north, above the headlands, Patitíri merges into two adjoining settlements with reasonable beaches, **ROUSSOÚM YIALÓS** and **VÓTSI**. For better beaches, you'll have to get in a boat or on a bike. **Khryssí Miliá**, the first good beach north of Patitíri, has a taverna and pine trees behind the quite decent stretch of sand; there's a couple of new hotels on the hillside above, such as the upmarket *Milia Bay* (T24240 66035, Emilia-bay@forthnet.gr; **7**), and it can get crowded in summer. At **Kokkinókastro**, over the hill further north, excavations have revealed the site of ancient Ikos and evidence of the oldest known prehistoric habitation in the Aegean. There's nothing much to see, but it's a beautiful spot with a good red-pebble beach, and, in July and August, a daytime bar.

STENÍ VÁLA is a haven for the yachts and flotillas that comb the Sporades, and has almost become a proper village, with a shop or two, several houses, a bar, rooms and a handful of tavernas, one of which, the *Kyra Tasia* (offically the *Steni Vála*), stays open more or less throughout the year and is famous for its *tyrópitta*. The **Monk Seal Treatment and Rehabilitation Centre**, housed in a small hut on the beach, can provide information about the endangered mammal and insight into the work of the HSPMS (see box opposite). There's an unofficial campsite (T24240 65258) in an olive grove by the harbour, a long pebble beach – Glýfa, where boats are repaired – and some stony beaches within reasonable walking distance in either direction.

KALAMÁKIA, farther to the north, also has a couple of tavernas and a few rooms, while further on still, at the point where the sealed road ends, **ÁYIOS DHIMÍTRIOS** is rapidly becoming the favourite "remote" beach amongst growing numbers of mainlanders. Backing a curving pebbly beach, the small settlement now has a snack-bar, beach taverna and even a card-phone. There's a good, signposted circular **walking trail** (2hr 30min) from here, that follows the coast for a while before heading up and back to Áyios Dhimítrios via the Kastanórema stream bed.

If you want real solitude you'll need to head north along the paved road that runs the length of the island, though there's nothing in the way of facilities past the turnoff to Stení Vála. At the northernmost point of Alónissos, the old shepherds' village of **YÉRAKAS** is a bit of a disappointment, with only a desultory, seldom-used jetty and a scrappy beach.

The National Marine Park of Alónissos – Northern Sporades

The **National Marine Park**, created in 1992, protects seals, cetaceans and other wildlife, including some rare seabirds, in an area that includes the whole of Alónissos, plus half a dozen tiny **islets** that speckle the Aegean to the northeast: Peristéra, Kyrá Panayiá, Yioúra, Psathoúra, Skántzoura and Pipéri. **Pipéri** lies within the core zone of the park – it is a seabird and monk-seal refuge, visitable only by scientists who've been granted permission from a ministry of the environment representative. Virtually none of the islets has any permanent population, or a ferry service, but Peristéra and Kyrá Panayiá can be visited by excursion *kaïki* (ask at the excursion-boat stands on the harbour in Patitíri), weather permitting. No boats are allowed to take you to the other, more remote islets, as they fall within the restricted zone of the park. Although it is possible to be left for a night or more on Peristéra and Kyrá Panayiá, be sure to bring more supplies than you need: if the weather worsens you'll be marooned until such time as small craft can reach you.

Peristéra, the closest islet to Alónissos, is graced with some sandy beaches and there is rarely anyone around, though some Alonissans cross for short periods to tend the olive groves, and in season there are regular evening "barbecue boats" from the main island. A few unofficial campers are tolerated, but there is only one spot, known locally as "Barbecue Bay", where campfires are allowed. Fertile **Kyrá Panayiá,** the next islet out, belongs to the Meyístis Lávras monastery of Mount Athos, and there are two monasteries here, one still inhabited. There's no other permanent population besides wild goats. Boats call at a beach on the south shore, one of many such sandy stretches and coves around the island. Nearby **Yioúra** boasts a stalactite cave reputed to be the previous abode of Polyphemus, the Cyclops who imprisoned Odysseus, but you won't be able to check its credentials as no one is allowed within 500m of the island; tiny, northernmost **Psathoúra** is dominated by its powerful modern lighthouse, the tallest in the Aegean; and roughly halfway between Alónissos and Skýros, green **Skántzoura**, hosts nothing more than a single empty monastery and a few seasonal shepherds.

Skýros

Despite its airport and natural beauty, the island of **Skýros** has stayed off the beaten track of Aegean tourism, perhaps thanks to a lack of major sites or

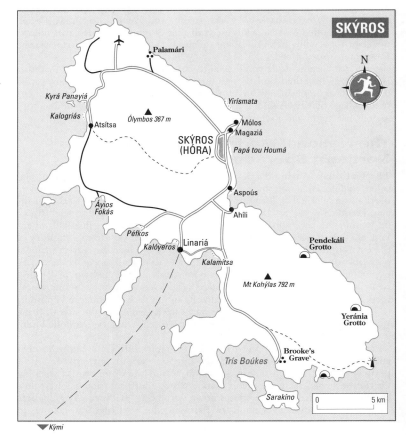

resorts, and its distance from Athens by the land-and-sea route. The popular theory that it was originally two islands seems doubtful, but certainly the character of its two parts is very different. The **north** has a green, gentle landscape and, away from main towns, retains much of its original pine forest, while the sparsely inhabited **south** is mountainous, rocky and barren; there are few trees and the landscape is more reminiscent of the Cyclades than the Sporades.

Compared with the other Sporades, Skýros isn't a great place for beaches. Most of those along the west coast attract a certain amount of seaborne rubbish and, although the scenery is sometimes spectacular, the swimming isn't that good. The beaches along the east coast are all close to Skýros Town, and the best option is probably to stay here rather than head for somewhere more isolated. At the north end of the island the beaches have been commandeered by a big air-force base, which otherwise keeps a low profile.

Considering it is not so far from Athens, Skýros was a very traditional and idiosyncratic island until fairly recently when it began to gain popularity among chic Athenians and foreign visitors, many of whom check into the "New Age" Skyros Centre, to "rethink the form and direction of their lives".

All this notwithstanding, Skýros still ranks as one of the most interesting places in the Aegean. It has a long tradition of painted **pottery** and ornate **wood-carving**, in particular the *salonáki skyrianó* (a handmade set of sitting-room furniture). A very few old men still wear the vaguely Cretan traditional costume of cap, vest, baggy trousers, leggings and *trohádhia* (Skyrian sandals), and some elderly women still wear the favoured yellow scarves and long embroidered skirts, but this is dying out. It's also worth sampling **lobster** in Skýros: it's a local (and expensive) speciality, often served flaked into pasta as *astakomakaronádha*.

Linariá

Ferries dock at the tiny port of **LINARIÁ**, a quiet, functional place on the island's west coast. Less active than Skýros Town, Linariá is certainly a pleasant spot to while away time waiting for the ferry.

△ Wild ponies, Skýros

Skýros has some particularly lively, even outrageous, **festivals**. The *Apokriátika* (pre-Lenten) carnival here is structured around the famous **goat dance**, performed by masked revellers in the village streets. The foremost character in this is the **Yéros**, a menacing figure concealed by a goatskin mask and weighed down by garlands of sheep bells. Accompanying him are **Korélles** and **Kyríes** ("Maidens" and "Ladies" – who are transvestites, as only the men participate) and **Frángi** (maskers in "Western" garb). For further details, read Joy Koulentianou's *The Goat Dance of Skyros*, available in Athens and occasionally on the island.

The other big annual event takes place near Magaziá beach on August 15, when children race domesticated members of the **wild pony** herd, native to Skýros and said to be related to the Shetland pony (if so, it must be very distantly). They are thought to be the diminutive horses depicted in the Parthenon frieze, and at any time of the year you might find some of the tame individuals tethered and grazing near Skýros Town.

A good paved road connects Linariá to Skýros town, 10km away, and then continues round past the airport to Atsítsa, where the Skyros Centre has its main branch; **buses** to Skýros Town, and to Magaziá on the coast below, leave regularly from the quay. Midway up the Linariá–Skýros town route, a paved side-road strikes off east to Ahíli and Kalamítsa. Most other roads are passable by scooter, though the hilly, windswept south does not always lend itself to two-wheeled explorations.

Kalamítsa beach, 7km east of Linariá, reached by a good coastal road, is a narrow strand of pebbles and clear water, but the 🍴 *Mouries* **taverna** between it and Linariá, shaded by the namesake row of mulberry trees, is worth a detour for its famed lamb, delicious wine and delightful setting. In high season, excursion *kaïkia* (€25 including lunch) offer trips from Linariá to the islet of **Sarakíno**, which has a fine beach, stopping at various south coast grottoes. See Monika at the port for details.

If you decide to **stay** (often convenient for catching the morning boat), there are two very reasonable options in Linariá: *King Lykomides* 🍴 (☎22220 93472, 🌐www.inskyros.gr/kinglykomides.htm; ❹), right next to the harbour, has a dozen or so spotless, air-conditioned, standard rooms with little balconies, TV and gleaming bathrooms, while behind and above it, at the start of the Kalamítsa road, the reliable *Linaria Bay Rooms* (☎22220 93274; ❹) has a mixture of rooms and traditional Skyrian studios. For **eating**, try the *Psariotis Ouzeri* or the *Filippeos* fish taverna, down at the harbour. The splendidly situated *Kavos Bar*, a short but steep walk up the main island road, welcomes the arrival of the ferry each evening with a rousing musical fanfare, and is open day and night for **drinks** and snacks; the views down to the village are superb.

Skýros Town

SKÝROS Town (Hóra), with its decidedly Cycladic architecture, sits on the landward side of a high rock that rises precipitously from the coast (according to legend, King Lykomedes pushed Theseus to his death from its summit). With its workaday atmosphere, the town doesn't feel like a resort, but away from the tattier outskirts it's decidedly picturesque. The older and more intriguing parts are higher up, climbing towards the **kástro**, a mainly Byzantine building erected on the site of the ancient **acropolis**. There are few traces of the acropolis, although remains of the classical city walls survive below on the seaward side of the rock. The kástro is open to visitors; to reach its upper parts you pass through a rather private-looking gateway into the monastery, then through an attractive shaded courtyard and up a whitewashed tunnel. There's little to see at the top, apart from a few churches in various states of ruin, but there are great views over the town and the island; the climb up takes you through the quieter, older part of town with its traditionally decorated houses. With their gleaming copper pots, porcelain plates and antique embroideries decorating the hearth, these dwellings are a matter of intense pride among the islanders, who are often found seated in their doorways on tiny carved chairs.

At the northern end of town is the striking and splendidly incongruous **memorial to Rupert Brooke,** the British poet adopted as the paragon of patriotic youth by Kitchener and later Churchill, despite his socialist and internationalist views. The monument is a bronze statue of "Immortal Poetry" whose nakedness caused a scandal among the townspeople when it was first erected. Brooke, who visited the south of the island very briefly in April 1915, died shortly afterwards of blood poisoning on a French hospital ship anchored offshore, and was buried in an olive grove above the bay of Tris Boúkes (see below). He became something of a local hero despite his limited acquaintance with the island.

Just below the Brooke statue, the **Archeological Museum** (Tues–Sun 8.30am–3pm; €2) has a modest collection of pottery and statues from excavations on the island, and a reconstruction of a traditional Skýros house interior. Nearby, in a nineteenth-century house built over one of the bastions of the ancient walls, the privately run **Faltaïts Museum** (daily 10am–noon & 5.30–8pm/6–9pm in summer; €2) is more interesting, with a collection of domestic items, costumes, embroidery, porcelain and rare books.

Practicalities

The **bus** from Linariá leaves you by the school, 200m below the main square; in season, schedules are guaranteed to meet the ferries, but otherwise services can be limited, and you might be better off getting a taxi. The **post office** and **banks** are both near the square. Skyros Travel (℡22220 91600), on the main street north of the square, can provide **information** or advice, and can find a room or hotel, plus **motorbike and car rental**; in high season it's a good idea to phone them in advance. You can access the **Internet** at Meroi on the main street.

You'll probably be met off the bus with offers of **rooms** (mostly ❸). If you'd like to stay in a traditional Skyrian house, those of Anna Stergiou (℡22220 91657) and Maria Mavroyiorgi (℡22220 91440) are clean and cosy (both ❸). A basic option is the *Elena* (℡22220 91738; ❸), near the main square, which has very cheap singles with shared bathrooms. There's a rather scruffy **campsite** nearer the beach, at the bottom of the steps below the archeological museum, with basic amenities. Alternatively, you could try the pleasant, *Nefeli Hotel & Skyriana Spitia* (℡22220 91964, ℻22220 92061; ❻) on the main road before the square offering rooms or traditionally designed studios.

The square and the main street running by it are the centre of village life, with a few noisy pubs and a wide choice of *kafenía*, tavernas and fast-food places, though only a few are outstanding places to **eat**. Top of the list is ⚔ *O Pappous ki Ego*, a very pleasant little ouzerí with a good range of *mezédhes* and quality Greek music on the stereo (and sometimes live); try the local speciality of kid in lemon sauce. *To Metopo*, just below the square, is another decent, reasonably priced ouzerí and is a little cheaper, while *Maryetis* up on the main street above the main square always draws queues for its solid grills, pasta and *mayireftá*. Near the Brooke statue (away from the bustling crowds) and a little more relaxed in style, *Anatolikos Anemos* dishes up Mediterranean and has good sea views from the patio.

The town's **nightlife** is mostly bar-based until very late, when the few clubs get going. The most popular **bars** are the trendy *Kalypso*, playing jazz and blues, as well as dance-oriented *Kata Lathos* and the rockier *Iroön*. Later on, *Iy Stasis* is one of the most popular places. The best **clubs** include the *Skyropoula*, on the coastal road, and, in town, *Mylos* and the *Stone Club*, while you can listen to live Greek music at *Tzivaeri*.

Magaziá and Mólos: the beaches

A direct path, as well as a longer paved road, lead down past the archeological museum towards the small coastal village of **MAGAZIÁ**, coming out by the official campsite. From Magaziá, an 800-metre-long sandy beach stretches to the adjacent village of **MÓLOS**; in recent years, though, a sprawl of new development between the road and the beach has more or less joined the two settlements together. With a villagey feel, Magaziá is still the livelier of the two and has the better selection of rooms; Mólos is more open and scattered, and has a good range of studios plus a more alluring stretch of **beach**, with umbrellas and loungers for hire; the buzzy *Juicy Beach Bar*, attracting a mainly Greek clientele, with its beach volleyball, is located halfway between the two.

The narrow road down to Magaziá beach holds a clutch of very similar **rooms** for rent; of these, the air-conditioned *Georgia Tsakami* (☎22220 91357; ❸), some twenty metres from the beach and opposite a handy car park, is as close as you'll get to the sand and sea. If it's full, try the *Perigiali* (☎22220 91889, ⓔperigiali@skyrosnet.gr; ❹) in Magaziá, a very pleasant mix of studios and air-conditioned rooms with phone, surrounding a large garden. Half-way between Magaziá and Mólos, *Pension Galini* (☎22220 91379; ❸) is a quiet and slightly more expensive choice, while the nearby *Motel Hara* (☎22220 91601; ❹) is another quiet option.

The beachfront **tavernas** often compare favourably with those in town: on the Magaziá side, *Stefanos* is reliable and popular, and overlooks the beach. At Mólos, try the *Kokalenia*, a restaurant in a garden and the ouzerí at *Balabani's Mill*, all at the end of the beach.

For quieter beaches, carry on past Mólos, or try the excellent and undeveloped unofficial nudist beach, **Papá toú Houmá**, directly below the *kástro*. The path down starts 150m beyond the *Skyropoula* disco, and isn't obvious from above. Further along the road south of here, the beaches are disappointing until **Aspoús**, which has a couple of tavernas and rooms to rent, as well as the smart *Ahillion* hotel (☎22220 93300, ⓕ22220 93303; ❺).

Around the rest of the island

In summer, buses visit the more popular beaches, but if you want to branch out on your own, rent a car or a scooter. Tracks and footpaths diverge from the main circular road, leading inward and seaward. Among the most interesting places to head for is **Palamári**, northwest of Hóra, the neglected site of an early Bronze Age settlement set above a fine but exposed beach.

Home to the Skyros Centre, **ATSÍTSA**, in the northwest corner of the island, is set in an attractive bay with pine trees down to the sea, and has a very good fish taverna (✸ *O Andonis*) and an increasing number of rooms. The rocky beach isn't great for swimming, but there are small sandy coves a short way to the north at **Kalogriás** and **Kyrá Panayiá**, with the seasonal taverna at Kalogriás, *O Yiorgos* being the only source of food here. For a taste of the island's wooded interior, you could hike following the dirt track from Skýros Town to Atsítsa; it takes three to four hours, and is too rough for a scooter.

Elsewhere in the coniferous northern half of the island, **Áyios Fokás** and **Péfkos** bays are easiest reached by a turning from the main road near Linariá, though access from Atsítsa is via a reasonable dirt road. Áyios Fokás is home to *Kali Rooms* (☏693 70 90 848; ❸), an excellent, very well-run taverna where you can bed down for the night. In Péfkos, set in a beautiful pine-fringed bay, the best **rooms** option is *Barba Mitsos* (❸).

As for the barren southern half of the island, dominated by the great mountain of **Kohýlas**, exploring is best attempted only if you have a four-wheel-drive vehicle, as the tracks are poor away from the main west-coast road to the naval base at **Tris Boúkes** (where Rupert Brooke is buried). Do not ignore the signs prohibiting photography – this is a military zone.

Évvia (Euboea)

ÉVVIA, the second-largest Greek island (after Crete), seems more like an extension of the mainland to which it was once joined. At **Halkídha**, the gateway to the island, the curious old drawbridge link to the mainland has only a forty-metre channel to span, Évvia reputedly having been split from Attica and Thessaly by a blow from Poseidon's trident (earthquakes and subsidence being the more pedestrian explanations). Besides the newer suspension bridge bypassing Halkídha and also linking Évvia to the mainland, there are ferry crossings at no fewer than six points along its length, and the south of the island is far closer to Athens than it is to the northern part.

Nevertheless, Évvia *is* an island, in places a very beautiful one. But it has an idiosyncratic history and demography, and has largely been kept out of the mainstream of tourism. A marked **Albanian influence** in the south, and scattered Lombard and Venetian watchtowers across the island, lend a distinctive flavour. Indeed, Évvia was the longest-surviving south-mainland outpost of the Ottoman Turks, who had a keen appreciation of the island's wealth. The last **Ottoman garrison** was not evicted until 1833, hanging on in defiance of the peace settlement that awarded Évvia to the new Greek state. Substantial Turkish communities, renowned for their alleged brutality, remained in the northwest half of the island until 1923.

Economically, Évvia has always been prized. By Greek standards, it's exceptionally **fertile**, producing everything from grain, corn and cotton to kitchen vegetables and livestock. The classical name, Euboea, means "rich in cattle", but nowadays cows are few and far between; its kid and lamb, however, are highly rated, as is the local retsina. Greek tourists predominate, especially in the north around the spa of **Loutrá Edhipsoú**. In July and August, Évvia can seem merely a beach annexe for Athens and the mainland towns across the Evvian Gulf.

The rolling countryside of the **north** is the most conventionally scenic part of the island, with grain combines whirling on sloping hay meadows between olive groves and pine forest, echoing the beauty of the smaller Sporades. The **northeast coast** is rugged and largely inaccessible, its few sandy beaches surf-pounded and often plagued by flotsam and jetsam; the **southwest** is gentler and more sheltered, though much disfigured by industrial operations. The **centre** of

ÉVVIA

N

Skýros (Hóra)
Linariá

Skýros

Skiáthos, Skópelos & Alónissos

Psaropoúli
Paralía Kotsikiás
Angáli (Paralía Ayías Ánnas)
Kryá Vrýssi
Kírinthos
Pýli
Prokópi
SaZíniko
Sarakíniko

Ayía
Iríni

Hiliádhou
Stení
Dhírfys
1743 m

Kými
Paralía Kými
Stómio
Platána
Oxýlithos
Avlonári
Ayía Thékla
Basilica of
Áyios Dhimítrios
Neohóri
Alivéri
Amárynthos
Káravos
Kálamos
Lépoura
Dystos

Kavodóro
(Kafiréas)
Dhrakóspito
Óhi, 1399 m
Castel Rosso
Mýli
Káystos
Marmári

Néa
Stýra
Almyropótamos
Panayía
Dhrakóspita
Stýra

Ayía
Márina

Rafína

Skála
Oropoú

Ramnous

Erétria

Fýlla

HALKÍDHA

Néa Artáki

*Paralía
Politikón*

Pagóndas
Dhervéni Gorge
*Kandhíli
1236 m*
Glýfa
Ayíou
Nikoláou
Galatáki
Mandoúdhi
Kírinthos
Limni
Roviés
Strofyliá
Ayía Ánna
Vassiliká
Elliniká
Péfki
Istiéa
Ayiókambos
Loutrá
Edhipsoú
Oreí
Glýfa

Yiáltra

Kaména Voúrla
Áyios Konstandínos

Arkítsa

Lárissa

Kórinthos

ATHENS

0   25 km

the island, between Halkídha and the easterly port of Kými, is mountainous and dramatic, while the far **southeast** is mostly dry and very isolated.

Public transport consists of passable bus services along the main roads to Kárystos in the southeast, and Límni and Loutrá Edhipsoú in the northwest. Explorations are best conducted by rented car; any two-wheeler will make little impact on the relatively great distances involved.

Halkídha

The heavily industrialized island-capital of **HALKÍDHA** (the ancient Chalkis, an appellation still in use today) is the largest town on Évvia, with a population of over 50,000. A shipyard, rail-sidings and cement works do little to make it attractive, but things improve in the old Ottoman quarter, **Kástro**, south of Venizélou, in the area around the Turkish fortress on the mainland and along the waterfront promenade, Leofóros Voudhoúri, backed by tavernas and trendy café-bars. Hardly a trace remains of Halkídha's once-thriving Jewish community, whose presence here dates back around 2500 years.

The entrance to the *kástro* – on the right as you head inland from the old Euripos bridge – is marked by the handsome fifteenth-century **mosque**, nominally a museum of Byzantine artefacts, but permanently locked. Beyond lie the remains of Karababa (the seventeenth-century Ottoman fortress), an arcaded Turkish aqueduct and the unusual **basilica of Ayía Paraskeví** (shut except during services); its oddness is due to its conversion into a Gothic cathedral by the Crusaders in the fourteenth century. In the opposite direction, in the new town, an **archeological museum** at Venizélou 13 (Tues–Sun 8.30am–3pm; €2) has a good display of prehistoric, Hellenic and Roman finds from all over the island.

Halkídha's waterside overlooks the **Évripos** (Euripus), a narrow channel of sea, whose strange currents have baffled scientists for centuries. You can stand on the bridge that spans the narrowest point and watch the water swirling by like a river; every few hours the current changes and the "tide" reverses. Aristotle is said to have thrown himself into the waters in despair at his inability to understand what was happening, so if you're puzzled you're in good company; there is still no entirely satisfactory explanation.

Practicalities

Trains arrive on the mainland side of the channel, beneath the old fortress; given numerous, quick rail links with Athens, there's little reason to stay overnight. Should you want to, though, the basic *Kentrikon* hotel (☏22210 22375; ❸), at Angéli Govíou 5, is a far better deal than the huge waterfront establishments it backs onto. Most other services of interest lie within sight of the old Euripus bridge. The **bus station** is currently 400m from the bridge along Kótsou, then 50m right, but is due to move to the eastern edge of town by 2007; you should get a connection for any corner of the island as long as you show up by 2pm, later for Kými or Límni.

Halkídha is noted for its superior seafood and ouzerís; the waterfront **restaurants** are popular at weekends with Athenians but are not necessarily the best-value options. The exception is *Apanemo* (☏22210 22614), at the northern end of shoreline, in the Fanári district, just before the lighthouse, which has tables on the sand and is so popular that booking is recommended. Inland you might try *Ta Pende Fi* at Evvías 61, a classic fish taverna in a peaceful setting, or the more central, long-running *Tsaf* at Papanastasíou 3, off Platía Agorás, again strong on seafood titbits. *O Yiannis*, at Frízi 8, is an excellent, reasonably priced ouzerí serving up all manner of shellfish. For the truly impecunious or time-pressured, there's also a handful of acceptable grills serving adequate lunches in the immediate vicinity of the old bus station.

Halkídha to Kými

The coast road heading east out of Halkídha offers an exceptionally misleading introduction to the interior of Évvia. The sprawling industrial zone gives way to nondescript hamlets, succeeded between Erétria and Amárynthos by sequestered colonies of Athenian second homes, rather bleak beaches and large hotels frequented by British and German package-tour visitors.

The first town along the main road is modern **ERÉTRIA**, a dreary resort laid out on a grid plan; for most travellers its main asset is the ferry service across to Skála Oropoú in Attica. The site of **ancient Eretria** is more distinguished, though much of it lies under the town. A few scanty remains are dotted around the town centre, most conspicuously an **agora** and a **temple of Apollo**, but more interesting are the excavations in the northwest corner, behind the excellent small **museum** (Tues–Sun 8.30am–3pm; €2), run in collaboration with the Swiss School of Archeology. Here a **theatre** has been uncovered; steps from the orchestra descend to an underground vault used for sudden entrances and exits. Beyond the theatre are the ruins of a **gymnasium** and a **sanctuary**, while the museum guard will be happy to unlock the fourth-century-BC **House of Mosaics**, five minutes' walk from the museum. One of the more affordable and interesting hotels is the municipal tourist complex *Dreams Island* (℡22290 61224, ⓦwww.dreams-island.gr; ❺), on a tiny offshore islet linked by causeway to the end of the bay. The handy and central *Pension Diamando* (℡22290 62214; ❸), right in the middle of the long waterfront promenade, is a less expensive option and a little more convenient for the busy nightlife.

Nine kilometres further east, **Amárynthos** is a smaller and more pleasant resort to stay in. Though the town boasts nothing of particular interest, the seafront square is picturesque and there is an ample selection of good eateries, such as *Stefanos* or *Thodoros*, two reliable fish tavernas on the waterfront, and *To Limanaki* 200m further west. Two good accommodation options are *Iliaktidhes Hotel Apartments* (℡22290 37605; ❹), just off the main road, and the B-class *Stefania Hotel* (℡22290 38382, ⒡22290 38384; ❺), 1km west of the centre right on the beach.

A way east, the enormous modern power plant and virtually intact medieval castle just before dreary **Alivéri** are incongruously juxtaposed, while more Frankish towers look down from nearby hills. The fishing harbour of **KÁRAVOS** has several pleasant watering holes, among them the *Vlahos* taverna. Thereafter the scenery improves drastically as the road heads inland towards the junction village of **Lépoura** from where a road heads southeast towards Kárystos. As you continue north towards Kými, you will cross some of the most peaceful countryside in Greece. With your own vehicle you can detour east after 5km at Neohóri to the secluded beaches at **Kálamos** and **Korasídha**: the selection of places to stay at the former include the very pleasant *To Egeon* (℡22230 41865; ❸), with a downstairs restaurant.

Twelve kilometres north of Lépoura, at Háni Avlonaríou, stands the Romanesque thirteenth- or fourteenth-century **basilica of Áyios Dhimítrios**, Évvia's largest and finest (ask for the key at the café next door). **AVLONÁRI** proper, 2km east, is dominated by a hill crowned by a huge Lombard (or Venetian) tower, rearing above the Neoclassical and vernacular houses that tier the lower slopes. There's a single taverna below the platía, but no accommodation. Avlonári was an archiepiscopal see from the sixth century onwards, and this part of Évvia is particularly well endowed with Byzantine chapels.

Just north of Háni Avlonaríou, you reach a fork in the road: the left fork is the inland road, taken by the bus, direct to Kými. On the way it leads past the hamlet of **Ayía Thékla**, where a small, shed-like **chapel** of that saint, probably slightly later than Áyios Dhimítrios, hides in a lush vale below the modern church. Inside, fresco fragments, depicting large-eyed faces, suggest what has been lost over time.

As for **KÝMI**, the upper part of town is built on a green ridge overlooking the sea, while Paralía Kýmis, the ferry port, is 4km below, via a winding road. All buses from Halkídha deposit you in the upper town, except for the one or two daily that connect with the ferry. In the lower reaches of the town, on the harbour-bound road, the **folklore museum** (daily 10am–1pm and 6–8.30pm; free) houses an improbably large collection of costumes, household and agricultural implements and old photos recording the doings of Kymians both locally and in the US, where there's a huge community. Among the emigrants was Dr George Papanikolaou, deviser of the "Pap" cervical smear test, and there's a statue honouring him up in the upper-town platía, where you might ask about **rooms** (④). Kými boasts some good **tavernas**, the best being *To Balkoni* on the main road towards the shore; it offers a superb view and the chance to sample the produce of the local vineyards.

The right fork north of Háni Avlonaríou is the coast road, taking you past **OXÝLITHOS**, home to the elaborate chapels of **Áyios Nikólaos** and **Ayía Ánna**, both at least a hundred years older than Áyios Dhimítrios. The road hits the coast at **Stómio,** an unappealing strand before the equally dreary seaside village of **PLATÁNA**. Press on to the functional port of **PARALÍA KÝMIS**, for ferry connections to Skýros; despite its name it has no real beach, and is not a particularly congenial place to be stuck overnight waiting for your boat (if you are, move up to Kými proper). The best **taverna** here is *Iy Skyros*, near the docks.

Southeast Évvia

So narrow that you can sometimes glimpse the sea on both sides, the spit of land southeast of Lépoura has a flavour very distinct from the rest of the island. Often bleak and windswept, it forms a geological unit with neighbouring Ándhros to the southeast, with shared slates and marble. Like Ándhros it was heavily settled by Albanian immigrants from the early fifteenth century onwards, and Arvanítika – a **medieval dialect** of Albanian – was until recently the first language of the remoter villages here. Even non-Arvanítika speakers often betray their ancestry by their startlingly fair colouring and aquiline features.

Immediately southeast of Lépoura, Lake Dhýstos is a shadow of its former self, having been mostly drained and reclaimed as farmland; some migratory birds do still frequent its shallow marshes, however. Atop the almost perfectly conical hill in the centre of its flat basin are the sparse fifth-century-BC ruins of **ancient Dystos** and a subsequent medieval citadel, though they're hard to explore because the surroundings are so swampy.

Beyond the Dhýstos plain, the main road continues along the mountainous spine of the island to Kárystos, at the southern end of the paved road and bus line. The nondescript village of **ALMYROPÓTAMOS** lies just off the main road, a couple of kilometres from its namesake port (aka **Panayía**) from where there is an infrequent ferry crossing to Ayía Marína.

If you have your own transport, it's worth stopping off at **STÝRA**, above which is a cluster of **dhrakóspita** ("dragon houses"), signposted at the north edge of the village and reached by track, then trail. So named because only mythological beings were thought capable of shifting into place their enormous masonry blocks, their origins and uses have yet to be definitively established. The most convincing theory suggests that they are sixth-century BC temples built by immigrants or slaves from Asia Minor working in the nearby marble and slate quarries.

The shore annexe of **NÉA STÝRA**, 5km down from the hill village, is a fairly standard package resort, worth knowing about only for its handy ferry connection to Ayía Marína. Much the same can be said for **MARMÁRI**, 19km south, except in this case the ferry link is with Rafina, and now serves as Kárystos's de facto ferry link too. Here there are a few decent places to eat; *Zafiris* has shaded tables right on the waterfront, while if you fancy a walk, head for *To Akriogiali*, at the far southern end of the waterfront on a platform over the water. Stýra and Marmári are linked by an impressive, high corniche road, known as the **Eagles' Road** (Dhrómos tón Aetón).

Kárystos and around

The new road between Marmári and **KÁRYSTOS** completes Évvia's "super-highway", allowing you to enjoy the nether reaches of the island as you cruise down to its last major settlement. Studded with modern buildings, at first sight Kárystos is a rather boring grid (courtesy of nineteenth-century Bavarian town-planners), which ends abruptly to east and west. However, King Otho liked the site so much that he contemplated transferring the Greek capital here, and there are still some graceful Neoclassical buildings dating from the mid-nineteenth century. Though you're unlikely to want to stay for more than a day or two, Kárystos does improve given prolonged acquaintance, with a superb (if often windy) beach to the west, the smaller, sandier **Psilí Ámmos** ten minutes' walk to the east and a lively, genuine working-port atmosphere. Only one plot of fenced-in foundations, in the central bazaar, bears out the town's ancient provenance, and the oldest obvious structure is the fourteenth-century Venetian **Boúrtzi** (locked except for occasional summer-evening art exhibitions) on the waterfront; this small tower is all that remains of once-extensive fortifications. Opposite the Boúrtzi inside the Cultural Centre, a small but interesting **archeological museum** (Tues–Sun 8.30am–3pm; €2) displays finds from the local area – mostly statues and temple carvings, plus a few smaller votive objects. In the evenings, the shore road is blocked by a gate to create an undisturbed promenade.

Practicalities

No passenger ferries serve the town directly: Marmári, 15km back up the road, acts as Kárystos's passenger port. Frequent **buses** link the two centres, arriving at the bus station, a few blocks inland from the waterfront next to the Town Hall on Kotsíka, the street leading directly up from the port. The station (℡22240 26303) displays information on the extremely infrequent (once daily at best) departures to the remote villages of the Kavodóro (Kafiréas) cape to the east.

Finding affordable **accommodation** is not a big problem. The big *Galaxy* (℡22240 22600; ❸) offers air-conditioned rooms on the west side of the waterfront, while in the park beyond the Boúrtzi the excellent ⚡ *Karystion* (℡22240 22391, Ⓦwww.karystion.gr; B&B; ❹) is the best place to stay, with filling breakfasts and living up to its slogan, Relax and Hospitality, Leisure and Serenity.

Good choices for **eating out** include the *Kavo Doro*, a friendly and reasonable taverna one block west of the square on Párodos Sakhtoúri, serving *mayireftá*; *Ta Kalamia*, at the west end of the esplanade by the start of the beach, is a cheap, filling and popular lunchtime option, while 2km east of town at Aetós, the quiet *To Kyma* is an ideal spot for an evening meal or Sunday lunch by the sea. On Kotsíka are several reliable *psistariés*, serving the local lamb and goat for which Kárystos is renowned: *O Panourgias* or the *Karystaki* are two of the better ones.

Mount Óhi

The obvious excursion from Kárystos is inland towards **Mount Óhi** (1399m) Évvia's third highest peak. Some 3km straight inland, **MÝLI**, a fair-sized village around a spring-fed oasis, makes a good first stop with a few tavernas. The medieval castle of **Castel Rosso** beckons above, a twenty-minute climb up from the main church (longer in the frequent, howling gales). Inside, the castle is a total ruin, except for an Orthodox **chapel of Profítis Ilías** built over the Venetians' water cistern, but the sweeping views over the sea and the town make the trip worthwhile.

Behind, the ridges of Óhi are as lunar and inhospitable as the broad plain around Kárystos is fertile. From Mýli, it's a three-hour-plus hike up the largely bare slopes, mostly by a path cutting across the new road, strewn with unfinished granite columns, abandoned almost two thousand years ago. The path passes a little-used alpine club shelter (fed by spring water) and yet another *dhraikóspito*, even more impressive than the three smaller ones at Stýra; built of enormous schist slabs, seemingly sprouting from the mountain, it's popularly supposed to be haunted.

Northwest from Halkídha

Due north from Halkídha, the main road passes a few kilometres of flat farmland and salt marsh before reaching the bustling refugee settlement of Néa Artáki. Here a road served by buses from Halkídha leads up to **STENÍ**, a sprawling alpine village at the foot of Mount Dhírfys. The village has a couple of decent hotels, the *Dirfys* (℡22280 51217; ❸) and the *Steni* (℡22280 51221; ❸). On the main square, in addition to a café and grill, is *Iy Mouria*, a traditional taverna beneath its namesake mulberry tree. This is a fine area for hiking, most notably up the peaks of Dhírfys and Xirovoúni, and beyond to the isolated beach hamlets of Hiliádhou and Ayía Iríni, though you'll need a specialist hiking guide to find the routes (see "Books", p.667).

Beyond Néa Artáki, the main road snakes and climbs steeply through forested hills and the **Dhervéni gorge**, gateway to Évvia's north. The large village of **PROKÓPI** lies beyond the narrows, in a valley defined by the rich and beautiful woods that make it famous. A counterpoint, in the village itself is the unprepossessing 1960s pilgrimage **church of St John the Russian**, which holds the saint's relics. The "Russian" was actually a Ukrainian soldier, captured by the Ottomans in the early eighteenth century and taken to Turkey, where he died. According to locals, his mummified body began to promote miracles, and the saint's relics were brought here by Orthodox Greeks from Cappadocian Prokópi (today Ürgüp) in the 1923 population exchange.

Evvian Prokópi is still referred to by the locals as **Akhmétaga**, the name of the old Turkish fiefdom here that was bought in 1832 by Edward Noel, an English nobleman, a Philhellene and Romantic, and relative of Lady Byron; a direct descendant of his, Philip Noel-Baker, was awarded the Nobel Peace Prize in 1959. Konaki, the main house of the Candili estate, dominating a bluff overlooking the village, is now home to Noel-Baker's namesake grandson, and operates partly as a hotel and creative course centre; comfortable en-suite accommodation (W www.candili.gr; ❻), in the tastefully converted granaries and stables, can usually be booked for a minimum of a week and is intended for groups.

From Prokópi a road leads northeast to **Pýli**, on the coast, and then east to some unspoilt beaches on the way to **Cape Sarakíniko**. The main road, however, follows a shady, stream-fed glen for 8km to **MANDOÚDHI**: at the signposted beach of Paralía Mandoúdhi there's nothing more than abandoned magnesite quarries and crushing plants. The closest serviceable **beach** is at **Paralía Kírinthos**, better known as **KRÝA VRÝSSI** (take a right-hand turning off the main road at the tiny hamlet of **Kírinthos**, 3km beyond Mandoúdhi). At the coast, a river and an inlet bracket a small beach, with the headland south of the river supporting the extremely sparse remains of ancient **Kirinthos**. At the Dutch-run **hotel** Kirinthos (T 22270 23662; ❸), some of whose impeccable rooms enjoy sumptuous sea views, you can also learn crafts such as weaving, pottery and icon-painting.

At a fork at **Strofyliá**, 8km north of Mandoúdhi, a road heads west to Límni (see opposite). Yet another 8km north brings you to **AYÍA ÁNNA** (aka Ayiánna), where most travellers are interested in the prominently marked turn-off for **Angáli beach**, 5km east. Billed as the area's best, it's nothing more than a broad, long and dark swath of sand protected only at the northern end. For **accommodation**, the Agali Hotel (T 22270 97104, F 22270 97067; ❹) is a pretty congenial option, while for **eating**, Armata at the northern end is the only place with tables on the beach. Horseriding on the beach is a well-advertised and popular diversion.

Signs off the next stretch of the main road point to the scruffy, uninteresting beaches of Paralía Kotsikiás and Psaropoúli; **Ellinik, á**, the next signposted beach, lies just 800m below its namesake village inland – it's far smaller than Angáli or Psaropoúli, but is cleaner and certainly the most picturesque spot on this coast, with a church-capped islet offshore as a target to swim to. The approach driveway has a very limited number of facilities: a mini-market and a few **studios** for rent. Motel Egeo (T 22260 42262; ❹) is as good as any if you want to stay, while the O Paradisos taverna is the best of a fairly limited choice of eating options.

Beyond Ellinikká, the road (and bus line) skirts the northern tip of Évvia to curl southwest towards **PÉFKI**, a seaside resort mobbed with Greeks in summer, which straggles for some 2km along a mediocre beach. The best **restaurants**, near the north end of this strip, include Ouzeri Ta Thalassina, Psitopolio O Thomas and O Lambros. **Accommodation** is the usual Evvian mix of self-catering units, and a few seaside hotels such as Galini (T 22260 41208, F 22260 41650; ❺) and Myrtia (T 22260 41202; ❺), both resolutely pitched at mainlanders; the campsite, Camping Pefki, 2km north of town behind the beach, is rather pricey and geared to people with caravans. Excursion **boats** and occasionally **hydrofoils** leave for Skiáthos, during summer months only.

The next resort, 14km southwest, past the major northern settlement of **ISTIÉA** (a dull place but important as the destination shown on many northern road signs), is **OREÍ**, is a low-key fishing village, whose west-facing **cafés** are great places to watch the sunset. In a glass case near the harbourside chapel is a fine Hellenistic statue of a bull, hauled up from the sea in 1965. Nearby **Néos Pýrgos** beach has a selection of **rooms** and restaurants.

Some 7km further along the coast, **AYIÓKAMBOS** is useful for its regular ferry connections to Glýfa on the mainland opposite, from where there are buses to Vólos. Ayiókambos is surprisingly pleasant considering its port function, with a patch of beach, two or three tavernas and a few rooms for rent. Buses from Halkídha continue to Loutrá Edhipsoú, 11km to the south.

Límni and Loutrá Edhipsoú

Low-key Límni, a largely Neoclassical, tile-roofed town, built from the wealth engendered by nineteenth-century shipping prowess, is the most appealing on the island, with serviceable beaches and a famous convent nearby. Farther up the coast, at the island's northwestern tip, Loutrá Edhipsoú has been famous for its spas since antiquity – its water supposedly cures everything from gallstones to depression. Each town is the terminus of bus routes from Halkídha, and both are also linked by bus along the scenic corniche road, via Roviés.

Límni

On the west coast, 19km from Strofyliá, **LÍMNI** is a delightful fishing town, whose small **folk art museum** (Mon–Sat 9am–1pm, Sun 10.30am–1pm; €2) featuring pottery, coins and sculpture fragments, plus local costumes, fabrics and furniture, is well worth a visit. **Buses** from Halkídha stop at the north side of the quay. The **post office** and **banks** are situated inland.

Downtown **rooms** and **hotels** are disappointing, but usually easily available outside August. An outstanding exception, on the main through-road into town from Strofyliá, from where it commands majestic sea and mountain views, is the delightfully welcoming ﹩ *Vateri* (☎22270 32493; ❺), with spacious rooms, traditional furnishings and copious breakfasts based on home-produced breads and preserves. Just over 2km northwest, on the Loutrá Edhipsoú road, is the gravel strand of **Kohýli**, with a basic but leafy **campsite** out on the cape, 500m beyond mid-beach. Other congenial places **to stay** hereabouts include *Dennis House* (☎22270 31787; ❺), down on the shore – the spacious rooms have balconies – and, on the main road, the more luxurious *Ostria* (☎22270 32247; B&B; ❻), with a pool; both are clearly signposted. Every summer the hamlet hosts an **international drama and music festival**, with regular performances mostly of classical music, in a purpose-built amphitheatre surrounded by ancient olive-trees.

Back in Límni itself, the best **place to eat** in terms of setting, menu and popularity is *O Platanos* (under the enormous quayside plane tree), with the adjacent *Avra* not far behind. Other local favourites include the newer *To Fyki*, also on the waterfront, and *Lambros*, 800m along the way to Katoúnia beach to the south of town.

Ayíou Nikoláou Galatáki

Around 7km south of Límni – under your own steam – is the **convent of Ayíou Nikoláou Galatáki**, superbly set on the wooded slopes of Mount Kandhíli, overlooking the north Evvian Gulf. To get there, veer up and left at the unsigned fork off the coast road; there's no formal scheme for visiting, but the gates are shut around sunset. Though much rebuilt since its original Byzantine foundation atop a Poseidon temple, the convent retains a thirteenth-century tower built to guard against pirates, and a crypt. One of a dozen or so nuns will show you **frescoes** in the katholikón, dating from the principal sixteenth-century renovation. Especially vivid, on the right of the narthex, is the Entry of the Righteous into Paradise: the righteous ascend a perilous ladder to be crowned by angels and received by Christ, while the wicked miss the rungs and fall into the maw of Leviathan.

Below Ayíou Nikoláou Galatáki are the pebble-and-sand beaches of **Glýfa**, arguably the best on this part of Évvia's southwest-facing coast. There are several in succession, leading up to the very base of Mount Kandhíli, some reachable by paths, the last few only by boat. The shore is remarkably clean, considering the number of summer campers who pitch tents here for weeks on end; a single roadside spring, 2km before the coast, is the only facility hereabouts.

The coastal road north from Limni glides past **ROVIÉS**, famous for its olives and a medieval tower and with **rooms**, **hotels**, an excellent **campsite** and other services, if you decide **to stay**. It then brings you to the fishing port of **LOUTRÁ EDHIPSOÚ**, better known as one of Greece's most exclusive **spa** towns. Unlike the island's flagship hotel *Thermae Sylla*, the baths themselves are inexpensive (€2 for 20min) and quite an experience; you can always bathe for free at the public beach next to the hotel, where hot spa water gushes out freely into an artificial set of cascades. There are less-regimented **hot springs** at **Yiáltra**, 15km west around the head of Edhipsós bay, where the water boils up on the rocky beach, warming the shallows to comfortable bath temperature.

The vast number of **hotels**, some old and creaky, which service the summer influx means good deals can be had. On the seafront, the classy 1920s-vintage *Egli* (☎22260 22215, ℱ22260 22886; ④) is a good choice, albeit on the old-fashioned side, while the rather flashy *Lito* (☎22260 22081; ⑤), up a quieter sidestreet at Ermoú 25, was refurbished in 2004. You can really push the boat out at the 1897-built ⚘ *Thermae Sylla* (☎22260 60100, ⓦwww.thermaesylla .gr; ⑨), an elegant French-style monument atop what's claimed to be the best thermal spring in Greece; even if you're not a guest you can use the exclusive hotel spa for around €20. For **eating** there is an abundance of tavernas strung along the front; try the leafy restaurant of the *Egli* or the traditional *To Fagadhiko tou Barous*, which offers a wide selection of *mezédhes*.

A frequent **ferry** service links Loutrá Edhipsoú to Arkítsa on the mainland.

Travel details

Ferry services to the northern Sporades run out of Vólos and Áyios Konstandínos; an additional service links Thessaloníki with Iráklion via Skiáthos and a couple of the more popular Cyclades. Hydrofoils from Vólos and Áyios Konstandínos to the Sporades, and the jet ferry between Áyios Konstandínos and the Sporades, run reliably only between early June and mid-September. Hydrofoils are pricier than the ferries, but cut journey times virtually in half, while the jet ferry is noticeably faster than the car-carrying catamaran out of Vólos. The only ferry to Skýros is from Kými on Évvia. NB: Departure frequencies given are for the June-to-mid-Sept period, and may fall sharply at other times. For more details of all services and ferry company websites, visit ⓦwww.gtp.gr.

Skiáthos, Skópelos and Alónissos

Ferries

Skiáthos to: Iráklion (1–2 weekly); Thessaloníki (1–2 weekly); select Cyclades (1–2 weekly).
Vólos to: Skiáthos (2 daily; 2hr 30min); Skópelos (2 daily; 3hr 30min); Alónissos (1 daily; 4hr 20min). Also one weekly service to Límnos and Lésvos via Skiáthos and Skópelos.

Jet Ferry

Áyios Konstandínos to: Alónissos (4–6 weekly; 4hr); Skiáthos (1–2 daily; 3hr); Skópelos (1–2 daily; 3hr 30min).

Hydrofoils

Áyios Konstandínos to: Skiáthos, Glóssa, Skópelos and Alónissos (3 daily).
Vólos to: Skiáthos, Glóssa, Skópelos Town and Alónissos (4 daily).

Flights

Athens to: Skiáthos (mid-June to mid-Sept 1 daily, otherwise 3 weekly; 50min).

Skýros

Ferries

The car ferry from Kými takes 1hr 30min. Services are once or twice daily from mid-June to early Sept (around noon or late afternoon), and once daily (late afternoon) the rest of the year; there may be an additional boat on designated peak travel days in July and August – call ☎ 22220 22020 (Kými) or 22220 91790 (Skýros) for current information. There is a connecting bus service for the late-afternoon boat, from the Liossíon 260 terminal in Athens.

Évvia

Buses

Athens (Liossíon 260 terminal) to: Halkídha (every 30min 5.30am–9.30pm; 1hr 30min); Kými (5 daily; 3hr 15min).
Halkídha to: Kárystos (2 daily; 3hr); Kými (8 daily; 1hr 45min); Límni (5 daily; 1hr 30min); Loutrá Edhipsoú (4 daily; 3hr).

Trains

Athens (Laríssis station) to: Halkídha (20 daily; 1hr 30min).

Ferries

Arkítsa to: Loutrá Edhipsoú (at least hourly July–mid-Sept, every 1–2hr otherwise; 45min).

Ayía Marína to: Néa Stýra (12 daily; 45min); Almyropótamos/Panayía (4-5 weekly; 45min).
Glýfa to: Ayiókambos (12 daily summer, 4 daily winter; 30min).
Rafína to: Marmári (5 daily in summer, 4 in winter).
Skála Oropoú to: Erétria (March–Oct every 30min during the day, hourly in the evening; 30min).
NB: Connecting buses from Athens run to Rafína (every 30min; 1hr), Ayía Marína (5 daily; 1hr 15min) and Skála Oropoú (hourly; 1hr 30min), all from the Mavromatéon terminal, and to Arkítsa and Glýfa from the Liossíon 260 terminal.

7

The Ionian Islands

✳ **Kérkyra (Corfu) Town**
Venetian fortresses, beautiful
churches, fine museums
and appealing architecture.
See p.514

✳ **Perouládhes, Corfu** Shaded
till early afternoon and backed
by sheer vertical cliffs, this
beach is an excellent hangout. See p.234

✳ **Andípaxi** Some of the Ionian's
best swimming and snorkelling is on offer at the exquisite
beaches of Paxí's little sister.
See p.535

✳ **Lefkádha's west coast** The
archipelago's finest beaches
run from Áï Nikítas down to
Pórto Katsíki. See p.541

✳ **Melissáni Cave, Kefalloniá**
See dappled sunlight on the
water amid rock formations
on a boat trip inside this
once-enclosed underwater
cave. See p.546

✳ **Mount Énos, Kefalloniá**
The highest point in the Ionians has stunning vistas of
sea and distant land.
See p.551

✳ **Itháki's Homeric sites** Relive
the myths on Odysseus's
island. See p.554

✳ **Boat tour around
Zákynthos** The best way to
see the impressive coastline
is to cruise from Zákynthos
Town. See p.559

△ Lefkádha's remote Yialós beach

The Ionian Islands

he six Ionian islands, shepherding their satellites down the west coast of the mainland, float on the haze of the Ionian sea, their green, even lush, silhouettes coming as a shock to those more used to the stark outlines of the Aegean. The fertility of the land is a direct result of the heavy rains that sweep over the archipelago – and especially Corfu – from October to May, so if you visit at this time, come prepared.

The islands were the Homeric realm of Odysseus, centred on Ithaca, (modern Itháki) and here alone of all modern Greek territory (except for Lefkádha) the Ottomans never held sway. After the fall of Byzantium, possession passed to the **Venetians** and the islands became a keystone in Venice's maritime empire from 1386 until its collapse in 1797. Most of the population remained immune to the establishment of Italian as the official language and the arrival of Roman Catholicism, but Venetian influence remains evident in the architecture of the island capitals, despite damage from a series of earthquakes.

On Corfu, the Venetian legacy is mixed with that of the **British**, who imposed a military "protectorate" over the Ionian islands at the close of the Napoleonic Wars, before ceding the archipelago to Greece in 1864. There is, however, no question of the islanders' essential Greekness: the poet Dhionyssios Solomos, author of the national anthem, hailed from the Ionians, as did Nikos Mantzelos, who provided the music, and the first Greek president, Ioannis Kapodhistrias.

Today, **tourism** is the dominating influence, especially on **Corfu** (Kérkyra), which was one of the first Greek islands established on the package-holiday circuit, though the recent general downturn means it does not feel as swamped as in the past. Nevertheless, parts of its coastline are among the few stretches in Greece with development to match the Spanish *costas*. Yet the island is large enough to contain parts as beautiful as anywhere in the group. The southern half of **Zákynthos** (Zante) – which with Corfu has the Ionians' most over-subscribed beaches – has also gone down the same tourist path, but elsewhere the island's pace and scale of development is a lot less intense. Little **Paxí** lacks the water to support large-scale hotels and has limited facilities tucked into just three villages, meaning it gets totally packed in season, when connections to Corfu and the mainland peak. Perhaps the most rewarding trio for island-hopping are **Kefalloniá**, **Itháki** and **Lefkádha**. The latter is connected to the mainland by a causeway and iron bridge but still has quite a low-key straggle of tourist centres and only two major resorts, despite boasting some excellent beaches, strung along its stunning west coast. Kefalloniá offers a series of "real towns" and a life in large part independent of tourism, as well as a selection of worthwhile attractions. Finally Itháki, Odysseus's rugged capital, is protected from a tourist influx by an absence of sand. The Ionian islands' claims to

Homeric significance are manifested in the countless bars, restaurants and streets named after characters in the *Odyssey,* including the "nimble-witted" hero himself, Penelope, Nausicaa, Calypso and the Cyclops.

Corfu (Kérkyra)

Dangling between the heel of Italy and the west coast of mainland Greece, green, mountainous **Corfu (Kérkyra)** was one of the first Greek islands to attract mass tourism in the 1960s. Indiscriminate exploitation turned parts into eyesores, but much of the island still consists of olive groves, mountain or woodland. The majority of package holidays are based in the most developed resorts, but unspoiled terrain is often only a few minutes' walk away.

Corfu is thought to have been the model for Prospero and Miranda's place of exile in Shakespeare's *The Tempest*, and was certainly known to writers such

▲ Eríkoussa

▲ Italy

◄ Mathráki & Othoní

Cape Ágias Ekaterínis
Andinióti Lagoon

Longás
Perouládhes
Avlíotes
Sidhári
Astrakerí
Almyrós
Almyrós
Aharávi
Loútses
Kassiópi
Áyios Stéfanos
Áyios Stéfanos
Karousádhes
Ródha
Períthia
Avláki
Kerasiá
Kouloúra
Kalámi
Magouládhes
Siniés
Agrafí
Epískepsi
Mt Pandokrátor
Aríllas
Kraviá
Afiónas
Strinýlas
Agní
Áyios Yeóryios
Spartýlas
Nissáki
Makrádhes
Troumpéta
Pyrgí
Barbáti
Angelókastro
Lákones
Skriperó
Ípsos
Paleokastrítsa
Liapádhes
Dhassiá
Dhafníla
Vídhos
Gouviá
Kondókali

Érmones
Vátos
Potamós
KÉRKYRA TOWN
Myrtiótissa
Glyfádha
Pélekas
Kanóni
Pondikoníssi
Pérama
Achilleion
Gastoúri
Áï Górdhis
Ayii Dhéka
Benítses

Pendáti

Paramónas
Áno Moraïtika
Moraïtika
Pendanísia
Mesongí
Áyios Matthéos
Prasoúdhi
Áno Mesongí
Boúkari
Gardhíki Pýrgos
Halikoúna
Korission Lagoon
Petrití
Línia
Aryirádhes
Lefkími
Íssos
Áyios Yeóryios
Perivóli
Ayía Varvára
Kritiká
Neohóri
Sparterá
Kávos
Áï Górdhis Paleohoríou
Arkoudhílas
Cape Asprókavos

N

ALBANIA

► Igoumenítsa

Igoumenítsa

► Paxí & Pátra

CORFU (KÉRKYRA)

0   10 km

as Spenser and Milton and – more recently – Edward Lear and Henry Miller, plus Gerald and Lawrence Durrell. Lawrence Durrell's *Prospero's Cell* evokes the island's "delectable landscape", still evident in some of the best beaches of the whole archipelago.

The staggering amount of accommodation (over 5000 places) on the island means that competition keeps prices down even in high season, at least in many resorts outside of Kérkyra Town. Prices at restaurants and in shops also tend to be a little lower than average for the Ionians.

Kérkyra (Corfu) Town

The capital, **KÉRKYRA (CORFU) TOWN**, has been one of the most elegant island capitals in the whole of Greece since it was spruced up for the EU summit in 1994. Although many of its finest buildings were destroyed by Nazi bombers in World War II, two massive forts, the sixteenth-century church of Áyios Spyrídhon and buildings dating from French and British administrations remain intact. As the island's major port of entry by ferry or plane, Kérkyra Town can get packed in summer.

Arrival, information and services

Ferries and hydrofoils to and from Italy, the mainland (Igoumenítsa and Pátra) and Paxí dock at the New Port (Néo Limáni) west of the Néo Froúrio (New Fort). The Old Port (Paleó Limáni), east of the New Port, is used only for day-excursions. Most of the ferry offices are on the main road opposite the New Port; ferries to Italy or south towards Pátra become very busy in summer and booking is advisable. The port authority (domestic ☏26610 32655, international ☏26610 30481) can advise on services.

The **airport** is 2km south of the city centre. There are no airport buses, although local **blue buses** #5 and #6 can be flagged at the junction where the airport approach drive meets the main road (500m from terminal). It's a thirty-minute walk on flat terrain into town (follow the road running beside the *Hotel Bretagne* opposite the junction for the shortest route or turn right then follow the sea road). **Taxis** charge at least €6 (but agree the fare in advance) or phone ☏26610 33811 for a radio cab.

The **tourist office** (Mon–Fri 8am–2pm; ☏2661037520, ✉e.o.t.corfu@otenet .gr), housed temporarily inside the Customs Building at the New Port, has accommodation and transport details – the location may well have moved by summer 2006 so phone to check. The **post office** is on the corner of Alexándhras and Zafirópoulou (Mon–Fri 7.30am–8pm). Of the town's several Internet cafés, the best value is *X-plore*, N. Lefteriti 4 (Mon–Sat 9am–2pm & 6–11pm; €4.80 per hour), a couple of blocks north of Plyatía Saróko (often anglicized to San Rocco, though it is officially named Platía Yeoryíou Theotóki).

▲ Vídhos

N

NIGHTLIFE
Au Bar	5
Base	12
Cavalieri	E
Cristal	5
Elxis	5
Hook	12
Privelege	5

RESTAURANTS & CAFÉS
Adherfi Theotoki	13
Aegli	10
Alekos Beach	3
Del Sole	11
Europa	10
Iy Stina	4
Mourayia	1
To Paradosiakon	7
Olympia	10
En Plo	2
Poco Loco	8
Rex	9
Venetian Well Bistro	6

ACCOMMODATION
Astron	A
Atlantis	B
Bella Venezia	E
Cavalieri	D
Corfu Palace Hotel	F
Hermes	C
Phoenix	G
Royal	H

0   200 m

KÉRKYRA (CORFU) TOWN

Ⓖ, Ⓗ & ⑬ ▼   ▼ Mon Repos Estate, Paleópolis & Kanóni

Accommodation

Accommodation in Kérkyra Town is busy all year round, and not always the best value when compared to the rest of the island. Room owners sometimes meet mainland and international ferries, or you can try the Room Owners' Association, near the tourist office at D. Theotóki 2A (Mon–Fri 9am–1.30pm, plus summer Tues, Thurs & Fri 6–8pm; ☎26610 26133, ℮oitkcrf@otenet .gr). Budget travellers might best head straight for the nearest **campsite** at Dhassiá (see p.520).

Astron Dónzelot 15 ☎26610 39505, ℮hotel_astron@hol.gr. Tastefully renovated hotel in the Old Port. Good deals available outside the short peak season. All rooms with fan and optional air con. ❹

Atlantis Xenofóndos Stratigoú 48 ☎26610 35560, ℮atlanker@mail.otenet.gr. Large and spacious

air-con hotel in the New Port; its functional 1960s ambience rather lacks character. ❹

Bella Venezia Zambéli 4 ☎26610 46500, ⒲www.bellaveneziahotel.com. Smart, yellow Neoclassical building just behind the *Cavalieri*, with all the *Cavalieri*'s comforts, but cheaper. ❻

Cavalieri Kapodhistríou 4 ☎26610 39041, ⓦwww
.cavalieri-hotel.com. Smart and friendly, with all
mod cons, great views and a roof bar open to the
public. ❻
Corfu Palace Hotel Leofóros Dhimokratías 2
☎26610 39485, ⓦwww.corfupalace.com. Luxury
hotel with pools, landscaped gardens and excellent rooms, each with a marble bath. The smartest
place on the island. ❽
Hermes Markorá 14 ☎26610 39268, ⓕ26610

31747. An old favourite in a busy part of town. The
cheapest rooms have shared bathrooms. Overlooks
the noisy market. ❸
Phoenix Khryssostómou Smýrnis 2, Garítsa ☎26610
42290, ⓕ26610 42990. Small, stylish hotel between
the airport and the seafront. Good value, B&B ❸
Royal Kanni ☎26610 39915, ⓕ26610 44690.
Splendidly located on a hill 3km south of town and
extremely good value. There's a pool and all rooms
have balconies with bay views. ❹

The Town

Kérkyra Town comprises a number of distinct areas. The **Historic Centre**,
the area enclosed by the Old Port and the two forts, consists of several smaller
districts: **Campiello**, the oldest, sits on the hill above the harbour; **Kofinéta**
stretches towards the Spianádha (Esplanade); **Áyii Apóstoli** runs west of the
Mitrópolis (orthodox cathedral); while tucked in beside the Néo Froúrio are
Ténedhos and what remains of the old **Jewish quarter**. These districts form
the core of the old town, and their tall, narrow alleys conceal some of Corfu's
most beautiful architecture. **Mandoúki**, beyond the Old Port, is the commercial and dormitory area for the port, and is worth exploring as a living quarter
of the city, away from the tourism racket. The town's **commercial area** lies
inland from the Spianádha, roughly between Yeoryíou Theotóki, Alexándhras
and Kapodhistríou streets, with the most shops and boutiques around Voul-
garéos, Yeoryíou Theotóki and off Platía Saróko. Tucked below the southern
ramparts of the Néo Froúrio is the old morning **market**, which sells fish and
farm produce.

The most obvious sights are the forts, the **Paleó Froúrio** and **Néo Froúrio**,
whose designations (*paleó* – "old", *néo* – "new") are a little misleading, since
what you see of the older structure was begun by the Byzantines in the mid-
twelfth century, just a hundred years before the Venetians began work on the
newer citadel. They have both been damaged and modified by various occupiers and besiegers, the last contribution being the Neoclassical shrine of **St
George**, built by the British in the middle of Paleó Froúrio during the 1840s.
Looming above the Old Port, the Néo Froúrio (daily 9am–10pm, closes earlier
off-season; €2) is the more interesting of the two architecturally. The entrance,
at the back of the fort, gives onto cellars, dungeons and battlements, with excellent views over the town and bay; there's a small gallery and café at the summit.
The Paleó Froúrio (Mon–Fri 8am–7pm, Sat & Sun 8.30am–3pm; €4) is not
as well preserved and contains some incongruous modern structures, but has
an interesting Byzantine museum just inside the gate, and even more stunning
views from the central Land Tower. It also hosts daily son et lumière shows.

Just west of the Paleó Froúrio, the **Listón**, an arcaded street built during the
French occupation by the architect of the Rue de Rivoli in Paris, and the green
Spianádha (Esplanade) it overlooks, are the focus of town life. The cricket
pitch, still in use at the northern end of the Spianádha, is another British legacy,
while at the southern end the **Maitland Rotunda** was built to honour the
first British High Commissioner of Corfu and the Ionian islands. The neighbouring statue of Ioannis Kapodhistrias celebrates the local hero and statesman
(1776–1831) who led the diplomatic efforts for independence and was made
Greece's first president in 1827. At the far northern end of the Listón, the
nineteenth-century **Palace of SS Michael and George**, a solidly British
edifice built as the residence of their High Commissioner (one of the last of

whom was the future British prime minister William Gladstone), and later used as a palace by the Greek monarchy. The former state rooms house the **Asiatic Museum** (Tues–Sun 8am–3pm; €3) which is a must for aficionados of Oriental culture. Amassed by Corfiot diplomat Gregorios Manos (1850–1929) and others, it includes Noh theatre masks, woodcuts, wood and brass statuettes, samurai weapons and art works from Thailand, Korea and Tibet. The adjoining **Modern Art Gallery** (Tues–Sun 9am–5pm, special exhibitions 9am–1pm & 6–9pm; €1.50) holds a small collection of contemporary Greek art. It's an interesting diversion, as are the gardens and café-bar secreted behind the palace.

In a nearby backstreet off Arseníou, five minutes from the palace, is the museum dedicated to modern Greece's most famous nineteenth-century poet, **Dhionysios Solomos** (Mon–Sat 9.30am–2pm; €1). Born on Zákynthos, Solomos was author of the poem *Amnos stín Elefthería* (*Hymn to Liberty*), which was to become the Greek national anthem. He studied at Corfu's Ionian Academy, and lived in a house on this site for much of his life.

Up a short flight of steps on Arseníou, the **Byzantine Museum** (Tues–Sun 9am–3pm; €2) is housed in the restored church of the Panayía Andivouniótissa. It houses church frescoes and sculptures and sections of mosaic floors from the ancient site of Paleópolis, just south of Kérkyra Town. There are also some pre-Christian artefacts, and a collection of icons dating from the fifteenth to nineteenth centuries.

A block behind the Listón, down Spyrídhonos, is the sixteenth-century **church of Áyios Spyrídhon** (daily 8am–9pm), whose maroon-domed campanile dominates the town. Here you will find the silver-encrusted coffin of the island's patron saint, **Spyridhon** – Spyros in the diminutive – after whom seemingly half the male population is named. Four times a year (Palm Sunday and the following Sat, Aug 11 and the first Sun in Nov), to the accompaniment of much celebration and feasting, the relics are paraded through the streets of Kérkyra Town. Each of the days commemorates a miraculous deliverance of the island credited to the saint – twice from plague during the seventeenth century, from a famine of the sixteenth century and (a more blessed release than either of those for any Greek) from the Turks in the eighteenth century.

The next most important of the town's many churches, the **Mitrópolis** (orthodox cathedral), perched at the top of its own square opposite the Old Port, also houses the remains of a saint, in this case St Theodora, the ninth-century wife of Emperor Theophilos. The building dates from 1577 and the plain exterior conceals a splendid iconostasis, as well as some fine icons, including a fine sixteenth-century image of *Saint George Slaying the Dragon* by the Cretan artist Mihaïl Dhamaskinos, and three dark, atmospheric Italianate paintings.

Kérkyra Town's **Archeological Museum** (Tues–Sun 8.30am–3pm; €3), just south round the coast, is the best in the archipelago. The most impressive exhibit is a massive (17m) gorgon pediment excavated from the Doric temple of Artemis at Paleópolis, just south of Kérkyra Town; this dominates an entire room, the gorgon flanked by panthers and mythical battle scenes. The museum also has fragments of Neolithic weapons and cookware, and coins and pots from the period when the island was a colony of ancient Corinth.

Just south of Platía Saróko and signposted on the corner of Methodhíou and Kolokotróni, the well-maintained **British cemetery** features some elaborate civic and military memorials. It's a quiet green space away from the madness of Saróko and, in spring and early summer, it comes alive with dozens of species of orchids and other exotic blooms.

The outskirts

Each of the following sights on the outskirts of the city is easily seen in a morning or afternoon, and you can conceivably cover several in one day.

Around the bay from the Rotunda and Archeological Museum, tucked behind Mon Repos beach, the area centered around the **Mon Repos** estate (8am–7pm; free) contains the most accessible archeological remains on the island, collectively known as **Paleópolis**. Within the estate, thick woodland conceals two **Doric temples**, dedicated to Hera and Poseidon. The Neoclassical **Mon Repos villa**, built by British High Commissioner Frederic Adam in 1824 and handed over to Greece in 1864, is the birthplace of Britain's Prince Philip and has been converted into the **Paleópolis Museum** (daily 8.30am–7pm; €3). As well as various archeological finds from the vicinity, including some fine sculpture, it contains period furniture *in situ*, and temporary modern art exhibitions. Other remains worth a peek outside the confines of the estate include the **Early Christian Basilica** (Tues–Sun 8.30am–3pm; free) opposite the entrance, the **Temple of Artemis**, a few hundred metres west, and the eleventh-century church of **Áyii Iáson and Sosípater**, back towards the seafront on Náfsikas.

The most famous excursion from Kérkyra Town is to the islets of **Vlahérna** and **Pondikoníssi**, 2km south of town below the hill of Kanóni, named after the single cannon trained out to sea atop it. A dedicated bus (#2) leaves Platía Saróko every half-hour, or it's a pleasant walk of under an hour. Reached by a short causeway, the tiny white convent of Vlahérna is one of the most photographed images on Corfu. Pondikoníssi (Mouse Island) can be reached by a short boat trip from the dock at Vlahérna (€2.50 return). Tufted with greenery and the small chapel of Panayía Vlahernón, Vlahérna is identified in legend with a ship from Odysseus's fleet, petrified by Poseidon in revenge for the blinding of his son Polyphemus, the Homeric echoes somewhat marred by the thronging masses and low-flying aircraft from the nearby runway. A quieter destination is **Vídhos**, the wooded island visible from the Old Port, reached from there by an hourly shuttle *kaïki* (€1 return, last boat back 1.30am). It makes a particularly pleasant summer evening excursion, when there is live music at the municipal restaurant near the jetty.

Four kilometres further to the south, past the resort sprawl of Pérama, is a rather more bizarre attraction: the **Achilleion** (daily 8am–7pm; €6), a palace built in a (fortunately) unique blend of Teutonic and Neoclassical styles in 1890 by Elizabeth, Empress of Austria. Henry Miller considered it "the worst piece of gimcrackery" that he'd ever laid eyes on and thought it "would make an excellent museum for surrealistic art". The house is predictably grandiose, but the gardens are pleasant to walk around and afford splendid views in all directions.

Eating and drinking

Although there are the inevitable tourist traps, Kérkyra Town offers some excellent, quality restaurants. As well as those listed below, there are several decent *psarotavérnes* on the Garítsa seafront, though you need to be wary of the fish prices.

Adherfi Theotoki M. Athanassíou, Garítsa. By far the best of the several establishments tucked behind the seafront park, this popular family taverna serves excellent *mezédhes*, meat and good-value fish dishes.

Alekos Beach Faliráki jetty. Set in the tiny harbour below the palace, with great views, this place offers simple, mostly grilled meat and fish dishes at good prices.

Del Sole Guildford 17. The town's most authentic Italian food such as smoked salmon antipasti or seafood or meat spaghetti dishes at a little above taverna prices.

Iy Stina Xenofóndos Stratigoú 78, Mandoúki. Quaint traditional taverna one block back from the seafront, serving a fine range of *mezédhes* and main courses, including tasty meat from the oven.

Mourayia Arseníou 15–17. This unassuming, good-value ouzerí near the Byzantine Museum does a range of tasty *mezédhes*, including sausage and seafood such as mussels and shrimp in exquisite sauces. One of the best establishments in town, with views of passing ferries and Vídhos island.

To Paradosiakon Solomoú 20. Behind the Old Port, this friendly place serves good fresh food, especially home-style oven dishes such as *stifádho* and *kokkinistó*.

Poco Loco 1st Párodhos Solomoú 1, Spiliá. At the foot of the steps to the Néo Froúrio, this newly converted Tex-Mex restaurant serves a range of reasonably priced Mexican favourites

and slightly pricier items like ostrich and kangaroo.

Rex Kapodhistríou 66 (the Listón). Pricey owing to its location, but some of the best food in the centre, especially the delicious oven food, mixing Greek with north European.

Venetian Well Bistro Platía Kremastí. A well-kept secret, tucked away in a tiny square a few alleys to the south of the cathedral, this is the nearest you're likely to get to Greek nouvelle cuisine, with large portions, and exotica such as Iraqi lamb and Albanian calves' livers in ouzo. Very expensive.

Cafés and Nightlife

Kérkyra Town has a plethora of **cafés**, most noticeably lining Listón, the main pedestrianized cruising street. None of these popular establishments is cheap, but among the more reasonable are the *Aegli*, *Europa* or *Olympia*, all guaranteed to be packed from morning till late at night. *En Plo* on Faliráki jetty, however, has an unbeatably brilliant and breezy setting and is much quieter, as is the leafy *Art Café*, behind the Palace of SS Michael and George.

Moving on from Corfu Town

Corfu's **bus** service radiates from the capital. There are **two** terminals: the islandwide green bus service is based on Avramíou (also for Athens and Thessaloníki), and the suburban blue bus system, which also serves nearby resorts such as Benítses and Dhassiá, is based in Platía Saróko. Islandwide services stop between 6 and 9pm, suburban ones at between 9 and 10.30pm. Printed English timetables are available for both and can be picked up at the tourist office or the respective terminals.

Frequent **ferries** run throughout the day from the New Port to Igoumenítsa on the mainland, as well as regular services to Pátra and several Italian ports. All the major lines have franchises on the seafront opposite the port: Agoudimos (℡26610 80030, ⓦwww.agoudimos-lines.com), Anek (℡26610 24503, ⓦwww.anek.gr), Fragline (℡26610 38089, ⓦwww.fragline.gr), Minoan (℡26610 25000, ⓦwww.minoan.gr), Superfast (℡26610 32467, ⓦwww.superfast.com), Ventouris (℡26610 21212, ⓦwww.ventouris.gr) and Snav (℡26610 36439, ⓦwww.snav.it). Two companies now run **hydrofoil** services to Paxí: Ionian Lines, managed by the Petrakis agency (℡26610 25155, ⓦwww.ionian-cruises.com), who also operate tours to Albania, Párga and other Ionian islands at much cheaper rates than the travel agents in the resorts; and Paxos Flying Dolphins through International Tours (℡26610 35808).

In late 2004 the much-fanfared **seaplane** service (ⓦwww.airsealines.com) to Paxí finally got off the ground. It now also flies to Ioánnina on the mainland and hopes to expand to other islands and even Brindisi in the near future. It actually takes off from Gouviá marina (see overleaf). For further details on all public transportation see "Travel details" p.574.

Increasing numbers of visitors rent their own vehicles to get round the sizeable island. **Cars** can be rented from international agencies at the airport or in town; try Avis, Ethnikís Andístasis 42 (℡26610 24404, airport 26610 42007), behind the new port, Budget, Venizélou 22 (℡26610 28590; airport 26610 44017) or Hertz, Ethnikí Lefkímis (℡26610 38388, airport 26610 35547). Among local companies, Sunrise, Ethnikís Andístasis 14 (℡26610 44325) is reliable and many agents listed throughout the resorts offer competitive deals. **Motorbikes** and **scooters** can be rented from Easy Rider, Venizélou 4 (℡26610 43026) or Lazy Bone, Venizélou 52 (℡26610 40580) both in the New Port.

The hippest youth **bars** in town are the trio on Kapodhistríou adjacent to the *Cavalieri* hotel, of which *Hook* is the rockiest and *Base* offers a mixture of pop, rock and dance sounds. The rooftop bar at the *Cavalieri* itself is more middle-of-the-road musically but can be heaven at night.

Club action takes place at Corfu's self-proclaimed **disco** strip, a couple of kilometres north of town, past the New Port. This only revs up after midnight, when it becomes classic *kamáki* territory, although in summer many of its macho regulars forsake it for the resorts in order to hunt foreign females. The currently "in" joints are *Privelege*, a standard disco, *Au Bar*, a large indoor club which mixes in some Latin, *Elxis*, which boasts an impressive lightshow for its Euro/Greek sounds, and *Cristal*, whose DJs favour trance and ethnic.

Kérkyra Town's two **cinemas** – the winter Orfeus on the corner of Akadhimías and Aspióti and the open-air summer Phoenix down the side street opposite – both show mostly English-language films.

The northeast and the north coast

The **northeast**, at least beyond the immediate suburbs, is the most typically Greek part of Corfu – it's mountainous, with a rocky coastline chopped into pebbly bays and coves, above wonderfully clear seas. Green **buses** between Kérkyra Town and Kassiópi serve all resorts, along with some blue suburban buses as far as Dhassiá.

Kérkyra Town to Ípsos

The landscape just north of Kérkyra Town is an industrial wasteland, and things don't improve much at the first village you come to, **KONDÓKALI**, overrun by holiday developments. The old town consists of a short street with a number of bars and traditional *psistariés*, the best of which are *Gerekos* and *Takis*, an international restaurant, *Flags*, and the pricey *Lithari* fish taverna.

Neighbouring **GOUVIÁ** is home to Corfu's largest yachting marina. The village boasts a couple of small **hotels**, notably the *Hotel Popi Star* (℡26610 91500, ℡26610 91502; ❸) and great-value *Gouvia View* by the beach (℡26610 9167; ❷). For **rooms**, try Karoukas Travel (℡26610 91596, Ⓔkaroukas@otenet .gr; ❸). There are a number of decent **restaurants**, including all-purpose tavernas *The Captain's* and *Gorgona*, the basic but excellent *Steki psistariá* and pizzerias such as *La Bonita*. The very narrow shingle **beach**, barely 5m wide in parts, shelves into sand; given the sea traffic, the water quality is doubtful.

Two kilometres beyond Gouviá the coastline begins to improve at **DHAF-NÍLA** and **DHASSIÁ**, set in adjacent wooded bays with pebbly beaches. The latter is much larger and contains nearly all the area's facilities, including a trio of **watersports** enterprises. It is also home to the most respected UK-qualified doctor on the island, Dr John Yannopapas (℡26610 97811), whose surgery is on the main road. Two luxury sister **hotels**, the *Dassia Chandris* and *Corfu Chandris* (both ℡26610 97100–3, Ⓦwww.chandris.gr; ❼), dominate the resort, with extensive grounds, pools and beach facilities. Down at the beach the modest but friendly *Spiros Beach* (℡26610 93666; ❸) is the best bet, followed by the twin Dassia Beach/Dassia Margarita (℡26610 93224, Ⓕ26610 93864; ❸). Independent **rooms** can be scarce, the most reliable source being Emka Travel (℡26610 93738, Ⓦwww.emkatravel.com; ❷. Dhafníla does, however, have the best **campsite** on the island, *Dionysus Camping Village* (℡26610 91417, Ⓦwww.dionysuscamping.com); tents are pitched under terraced olive trees. *Dionysus* also has simple bungalow huts, a pool, shop, bar and restaurant, while the friendly, multilingual owners offer a ten-percent discount to Rough Guide readers. Two of the best eateries in Dhassiá are *Andreas*, a pleasant fish taverna on the beach, and *Karydia*, a multi-cuisine restaurant on the main road.

ÍPSOS, 2km north of Dhassiá, can't really be recommended to anyone but hardened bar-hoppers. The thin pebble beach lies right beside the busy coast road and the resort is generally pretty tacky. Most **accommodation** is prebooked by package companies, although Pelais Travel (☎26610 97564, ⓦwww.pelaistravel.com; ❸) can offer rooms. *Camping Ipsos Beach* (☎26610 93246, ⓕ26610 93741) has a bar and restaurant, and offers standing tents. Ípsos is also home to one of the island's major **diving centres**, Waterhoppers (☎26610 93867, ⓔdiverclub@hotmail.com). **Eating** on the main drag is dominated by fast food, though a more traditional meal and a quieter setting can be found in the *Akrogiali psistariá* and *Asteria* taverna, both by the marina to the south of the strip, or you can get a decent curry at the *Viceroy*. The northern end is largely devoted to competing **bars** and **discos** such as *Monte Christo*, *B52* and *Shooters*.

North to Áyios Stéfanos

Ípsos has now engulfed the neighbouring hamlet of Pyrgí, which is the main point of access for the villages and routes leading up to **Mount Pandokrátor** from the south; the road, signposted Spartýlas, is 200km beyond the junction in Pyrgí. A popular base for walkers is the village of **STRINÝLAS**, 16km from Pyrgí. Accommodation is basic but easy to come by: the *Elm Tree* taverna, a long-time favourite with walkers, can direct you to rooms. In summer the main routes are busy, but there are quieter walks taking in the handsome Venetian village of Epískepsi, 5km northwest of Strinýlas – anyone interested in walking the Pandokrátor paths is advised to get the **map** of the mountain by island-based cartographer Stephan Jaskulowski or one of Hilary Whitton-Paipeti's walking books, available locally.

The coast road beyond Ípsos mounts the slopes of Pandokrátor towards **BARBÁTI**, 4km further on. Here you'll find the best beach on this coast, though its charm has been somewhat diminished recently by the construction of the gargantuan *Riviera Barbati* apartment complex. The beach is a favourite with families, and much **accommodation** is prebooked in advance. However, there are some rooms available on spec – try *Paradise* (☎26630 91320, ⓕ26630 91479; ❸) or Helga Travel Agency (☎26630 91547, ⓔhelga@otenet.gr; ❸), both up on the main road.

The mountainside becomes steeper and the road higher beyond Barbáti, and the population thins drastically. **NISSÁKI** is a sprawling roadside settlement rather than a village, with a number of coves, the first and last accessible by road, the rest only by track – the furthest dominated by the gigantic and rather soulless *Nissaki Beach Hotel* (☎26630 91232, ⓦwww.nissakibeach.gr; ❺ half-board). There are a couple of shops and a bakery, and a few travel and **accommodation agencies**. The British-owned Falcon Travel (☎26630 91318, ⓦwww.falcon-travel-corfu.com; ❸) rents out apartments above the first beach, a tiny, white-pebble cove with a trio of fine tavernas – try the quayside *Mitsos*. The *Nissaki Holiday Center* (☎26630 91166, ⓦwww.nissakiholidays; ❷), up by the junction, may have some cheaper rooms.

Three pebbly coves no one visiting this coast should miss are Agní, not far past the *Nissaki Beach Hotel*, Kalámi and neighbouring Koulóura: the first for its trio of fine tavernas, the second for its Durrell connection, the third for its exquisite bay. Crowds flock to **AGNÍ** for the fine eating – *Nikolas* is the oldest taverna and just pips *Toula* and *Agni* for quality; it also runs the peaceful *Nikolas Apartments* (☎26630 91243, ⓦwww.kalamits.com; ❹). **KALÁMI** is on the way to being spoilt, but the village is still small and you can imagine how it would have looked in the year Lawrence Durrell spent here on the eve of World War II. The **White House**, where Durrell wrote *Prospero's Cell*, is now split in two: the ground floor is an excellent taverna; the upper floor is let through CV Travel (see Basics, p.31). Sunshine Travel (☎26630 91170, ⓦwww.sunshineclub.gr) and Kalami Tourist Services (☎26630 91062, ⓦwww.kalamits.com) both have a range of rooms (❷) on their books; see if one's going at *Villa Rita* (☎26630 91030; ❸). The **restaurant** at the White House is recommended, as are *Kalami Beach* and *Thomas' Place*, both above average tavernas on the beach. Two cocktail bars compete for the happy-hour trade.

The tiny harbour of **KOULOÚRA** has managed to keep its charm intact, set at the edge of an unspoilt bay with nothing to distract from the pine trees and *kaïkia*. The fine sole **taverna** here is one of the most idyllic settings for a meal in the whole of Corfu.

Around the coast to Aharávi

Two kilometres beyond Kouloúra, down a shady lane, the large pebble cove of **Kerasiá** shelters the family-run *Kerasia Taverna*. The most attractive resort on this stretch of coast, however, 3km down a lane from Siniés on the main road, is **ÁYIOS STÉFANOS** (officially Áyios Stéfanos Sinión to distinguish it from a namesake in northwestern Corfu). Most **accommodation** here is of the upmarket prebooked villa sort, and the village has yet to succumb to any serious development; the only independent rooms and apartments are managed by the *Kochili* taverna (☎26630 81522; ❸). For food, as well as the friendly *Kochili* itself, try the *Galini* and *Eucalyptus* **tavernas**; the latter, over by the village's small beach, is pricier but serves more adventurous fare such as pork with artichokes. The *Damianos* cocktail bar is the main spot to idle with a drink.

△ Kassiópi harbour and castle

A thirty-minute walk from the coastguard station above Áyios Stéfanos, along a newly surfaced road, stretches the beach of **Avláki**, a pebble bay that provides lively conditions for the **windsurfers** who visit the beach's windsurf club. There are two **tavernas**, the *Cavo Barbaro* and *Avlaki*, but the only accommodation is taken by upmarket package companies.

Further round the coast is **KASSIÓPI**, a fishing village that's been transformed into a major party resort. The Roman emperor Tiberius had a villa here, and the village's sixteenth-century Panayía Kassópitra church is said to stand on the site of a temple of Zeus once visited by Nero. Little evidence of Kassiópi's past survives, apart from an abandoned Angevin *kástro* on the headland – most visitors come for the nightlife and the five pebbly beaches. Most nonpackage **accommodation** in Kassiópi is rented through village agencies; the largest, Travel Corner (T 26630 81220, W www.kassiopi.com; **2**), with offices near the square and the harbour, is a good place to start. An independent alternative, the great-value *Kastro* restaurant-cum-pension (T 26630 81045, E kyrosai@hol.gr; **2**), overlooks the beach behind the castle, while *Panayiota Apartments* (T 26630 81063; **3**) offers bargain studios one block behind Kalamíones beach on the west side. The most popular **restaurants** are multi-cuisine tavernas, which supplement a traditional Greek diet with various international dishes, such as *Janis*, by the corner of Kalamíones beach. Other options include the *Porto* fish restaurant at the harbour and *Sze Chuan* Chinese on the main road.

At night, Kassiópi rocks to the cacophony of its music and video bars: the flashiest is the gleaming hi-tech *Eclipse*, which also shows DVDs, closely followed by the *Jasmine* and *Visions*, all within falling-over distance of the small town square. The *Passion Club* is the liveliest spot down at the otherwise laidback harbour. The village is also home to one of the most reliable diving operations, Corfu Divers (T 26630 81218, W www.corfudivers.com), which is partly British-run. You can get online at Photonet (€4.5 per hr).

The coastline beyond Kassiópi is overgrown and marshy until you get to little-developed **Almyrós** beach, one of the longest on the island, with only a few apartment buildings and one huge new resort dotted sporadically behind it. For a peaceful stay you could try *Villa Maria* (T 26630 63359; **3**) and eat at *Avra*, a pleasant taverna further along the beach. The **Andinióti lagoon**, smaller than Korissíon in the south but still a haven for birds and twitchers, backs Cape Ayías Ekateríni to the east, which marks the northern end of the Corfu Trail. The beach extends east all the way to **AHARÁVI**, whose wide stretch of the main coast road is vaguely reminiscent of an American Midwest truck stop. The village proper is tucked on the inland side of the road in a quiet crescent of old tavernas, bars and shops. Aharávi makes a quieter beach alternative to the southerly strands, and should also be considered by those seeking alternative routes up onto **Mount Pandokrátor**. Roads to small hamlets such as Áyios Martínos and Láfki continue onto the mountain, and even a stroll up from the back of Aharávi will find you on the upper slopes in under an hour.

Accommodation isn't always easy to find, but a good place to start is Castaway Travel (T 26630 63541, W www.corfucastaway.com). One independent hotel is *Dandolo* (T 26630 63557, E dandolo@otenet.gr; **4**), set in lush grounds towards the old village, though it is sometimes booked out to Italian groups in high season. Of the many **restaurants** on Aharávi's main drag the *Pump House* steak and pasta joint and *To Ellinikon psistariá*-taverna are the best. Meanwhile *Neraïda*, which specializes in meat dishes with mushroom or pepper sauces and trout salad, takes the prizes on the beach and the excellent *Theritas* taverna in the old village wins the authenticity award. The main

THE IONIAN ISLANDS | Corfu (Kérkyra)

drag's bar-restaurants tend to get quite rowdy at night, although the light and airy *Captain Aris* is a pleasant watering hole. For a quieter drink, head for, the friendly anonymous *kafenío* or the cosy *Hole in the Wall* pub, both in the old village.

Ródha, Sidhári and Avlíotes

Continuing further west, **RÓDHA** has tipped over into overdevelopment, and can't be wholeheartedly recommended for those after a quiet time. Its central crossroads have all the charm of a service station, and the beach is rocky in parts and swampy to the west. "Old Ródha" is a small warren of alleys between the main road and the seafront, where you'll find the best **restaurants** and **bars**: the *Taverna Agra* is the oldest in Ródha and the best place for fish, while the sadly-named *Opa* and *New Port* are reasonable alternatives. For drinks, try *Crusoe's Pub* or *Maggie's Bar*, both with Sky Sports, or the trendier bar-club *Skouna*. If for some reason you decide **to stay**, the friendly seafront *Roda Inn* (☏26630 63358; ❸) has good value en-suite rooms. Both the Anglo-Greek HN Travel (☏26630 62249, ⓦwww.hntravel.gr; ❷), on the main drag, and Corfu Nostos Travel on the seafront (☏26630 64602, ⓔe.kostaki@otenet.gr; ❷) rent rooms and handle car rental. The smart *Roda Beach Camping* (☏26630 93120) is a little way east of the resort, while even pleasanter *Karoussades Camping* (☏ & ⓕ26630 31415) is to the west, towards Sidhári. Myron's good-rate motorbike rental (☏26630 63477) and Costas horse-riding (☏694 41 60 011; €15 for 2hr) are also based in Ródha. Several kilometres inland from Ródha, just east of Agrafí, the relatively undiscovered ⌖ *Angonari mezedhopolío* serves an excellent range of dishes and great barrelled wine in a relaxed garden with subtle live music.

The next notable resort, **SIDHÁRI**, is constantly expanding and totally dominated by British-package tourists; its small but pretty town square, with a bandstand set in a small garden, is lost in a welter of bars, shops and joints. The beach is sandy but not terribly clean, and many people tend to head just west to the curious coves, walled by wind-carved sandstone cliffs, around the vaunted Canal d'Amour. The biggest accommodation agency is run by young tycoon Philip Vlasseros, whose Vlasseros Travel (☏26630 95695, ⓕ26630 95969) also handles car rental, horse-riding and excursions, including day-trips to the Dhiapóndia islands (see p.531). Sidhári's **campsite**, *Dolphin Camping* (☏26630 31846), is over 1km inland from the junction at the western end of town. Most **restaurants** are pitched at those looking for a great night out rather than a quiet meal in a taverna. The pricey *Olympic* is the oldest taverna here; better value is to be found at *Sea Breeze* or at *Kavvadias*, on the eastern stretch of beach. Asian cuisine, such as the Indian food at *Kohenoor*, and cheap full-on English breakfasts are also readily available. There are no quiet bars in Sidhári, and several **nightclubs** vie for late custom, such as *IQ*, *Mojo* and *Caesar's*. Sidhári also has its own waterpark with free entry, a good place to keep the kids happy.

The Sidhári bus usually continues to **AVLÍOTES**, a handsome hill town with the odd kafenío and tavernas but few concessions to tourism. The town is note-worthy for two reasons: its accessibility to quiet **Perouládhes** in the very northwest and **Áyios Stéfanos** (see p.526) to the southeast, both only a few kilometres away. Stunning **Longás beach**, bordered by vertical reddish layer-cake cliffs that make for shady mornings, lies below Perouládhes. You can stay 200m back from the beach at *Logas Beach Studios* (☏26630 95412, ⓔgiorkou@mailbox.gr; ❸) or enjoy a splendid sunset dinner at the cliff-top *Panorama* taverna.

Paleokastrítsa and the northwest coast

The northwest conceals some of the island's most dramatic coastal scenery, the violent interior mountainscapes jutting out of the verdant countryside. The area's honeypot attraction is **Paleokastrítsa**, the single most picturesque resort on Corfu, which suffers from its popularity. Further north, the densely olive-clad hills conceal better, sandier beaches, such as **Áyios Yeóryios** and **Áyios Stéfanos**. Public **transport** all along the west coast is difficult: virtually all buses ply routes from Kérkyra Town to single destinations, and rarely link resorts.

Paleokastrítsa

PALEOKASTRÍTSA, a small village surrounded by dramatic hills and cliffs, has been identified as the Homeric city of Scheria, where Odysseus was washed ashore and escorted by Nausicaa to the palace of her father Alkinous, king of the Phaeacians. It's a stunning site, as you would expect, though one that's long been engulfed by tourism. The focal point of the village is the car park on the seafront, which backs onto the largest and least attractive of three **beaches**, home to sea taxis and *kaïkia*. The second beach, to the right and signed by flags for Mike's Ski Club, is stony with clear water, and the best of the three is a small unspoilt strand reached along the path by the *Astakos Taverna*. Protected by cliffs, it's undeveloped apart from the German-run Korfu-Diving Centre (T 26630 41604) at the end of the cove. From the first beach you can get a **boat trip** to some nearby seawater caves, known as the "blue grottoes" (€8 for a half-hour trip), which is worth taking for the spectacular coastal views. Boats also serve as a taxi service to three neighbouring beaches, Áyia Triánda, Palatákia and Alípa, which all have snack-bars.

On the rocky bluff above the village, the **Theotókou monastery** (7am–1pm & 3–8pm; free, donations welcome) is believed to have been established in the thirteenth century. There's also a museum, resplendent with icons, jewelled bibles and other impedimenta of Greek Orthodox ritual, though the highlight is the gardens, with spectacular coastal views. Paleokastrítsa's ruined castle, the **Angelókastro**, is around 6km up the coast; only approachable by path from the hamlet of Kríni, it has stunning, almost circular views of the surrounding sea and land. For a drink or snack with tremendous views on the way up, it's worth stopping at the execellent *O Boulis* taverna in Lákones or the *Bella Vista* or *Golden Fox* tavernas, between there and Makrádhes.

Accommodation is not too hard to find but sprawls a long way back from central Paleokastrítsa, often leaving quite a walk to the beach. A good **hotel** is the family-run *Odysseus* (T 26630 41209, W www.odysseushotel.gr; half-board ❹), on the road into town, while the nearby modern *Akrotiri Beach* (T 26630 41237, W www.akrotiri-beach.com; ❼) is upmarket but unpretentious. Along the first turning back from the centre on the north side of the main road, the friendly family-run *Villa Korina* (T 26630 44064; ❷) has great value **rooms**, as does the *Dolphin Snackbar* (T 26630 41035; ❷), further back above Alípa beach. Michalas tourist bureau (T 26630 41113, E michalastravel@ker.forthnet.gr) is another source, as well as offering all the usual services. *Paleokastrita Camping* (T 26630 41204, F 26630 41104) is just off the main road, almost a half-hour walk from the centre.

There isn't a huge choice of **restaurants** in the centre of Paleokastrítsa. The *Astakos Taverna* and *Corner Grill* are two traditional places, while the seafront *Smurfs* has a good seafood menu despite the dreadful name. Also recommended is the very smart *Vrahos*, which offers pricey fish and some unusual dishes like artichokes. **Nightlife** hangouts include the restaurant-bars in the centre, and those straggling back up the hill, such as the relaxing *Petrino* bar. By the Lákones turning is Paleokastrítsa's one nightclub, *The Paleo Club*, a small disco-bar with a garden.

Áyios Yeóryios to Áyios Stéfanos

Like many of the west-coast resorts, **ÁYIOS YEÓRYIOS**, 6km north of Paleokastrítsa, isn't actually based around a village, though it is sometimes referred to as Áyios Yeóryios Pagón after the inland village of Payí to avoid confusion with its southern namesake. The resort has developed in response to the popularity of the large sandy bay, and it's a major **windsurfing** centre, busy even in low season. Contrary to the general trend, more **accommodation** is now blockbooked here than in the past but independent rooms are available at at bargain rates in the cute walled-garden complex of Kóstas Bardhís (☎26630 96219; ❶), towards the north end of the beach, and at the Arista supermarket (☎26630 96350; ❶) or *Studio Eleana* (☎ & ☏26630 96366; ❶), both behind the central section of beach. The *San George* campsite (☎26630 51759) is nearly 1km back from the beach towards Kavvadhádhes. *To Vrahos* at the northern end and *Spiros* halfway along are among the better restaurants, both serving Greek and international cuisine, while gaily-painted *Ostrako* is unbeatable for seafood in the far south. Nearby *Noa Noa* is one of the liveliest nightspots.

On the way north towards Áyios Stéfanos, the pleasant sandy beach of **Aríllas** has given rise to gradual development, including several **tavernas** – try *Kostas on the Beach* or the *Brouklis psistariá*, 200m back inland. Accommodation can be arranged through Arillas Travel (☎26630 51280, ⊛www.arillastravel .gr; ❸), which is very friendly and has a couple of quality hotels on its books, or there is the smart *Akti Arilla* hotel (☎26630 51201, ✉aktiaril@otenet.gr; ❹ half-board).

The northernmost of the west coast's resorts, **ÁYIOS STÉFANOS** is low-key, popular with families and a quiet base from which to explore the northwest and the Dhiapóndia islands, visible on the horizon. Day-trips to Mathráki, Othoní and Eríkoussa (see p.531) run several times a week in season (€15–20 per person), as well as cheaper passenger services (€7–9 return) most days on the Aspiotis lines *kaïki*. Áyios Stéfanos's oldest **hotel**, the *Nafsika* (☎26630 51051, ⊛www.nafsikahotel.com; ❸), has a large restaurant, a favourite with villagers, and gardens with a pool and bar. Also behind the main southern beach are the *Hotel San Stefano* (☎26630 51053, ☏26630 51202; ❸) and **rooms** at the *Sunset* taverna (☎26630 51185, ⊛www.corfusunset.com; ❸), while the *Restaurant Evinos* (☎ & ☏26630 51766; ❸) has small apartments above the northern end of the village. For those on a budget, Peli and Maria's gift shop offers bargain **rooms** (☎26630 51424; ❷) and a number of travel agencies handle accommodation, among them San Stefanos (☎26630 51910, ⊛www .san-stefano.gr; ❷) in the centre. Besides the above-mentioned establishments, good options for **eating** include the *Waves* and very reasonable *Mistral* tavernas above the beach, while O *Manthos* taverna serves Corfiot specialities such as *sofríto* and *pastitsádha*. For **nightlife**, lively *Magnet* and more laid-back *Sundowner* stand out among the handful of music bars.

Central and southern Corfu

Two natural features divide the centre and south of Corfu. The first is the **plain of Rópa**, whose fertile landscape backs on to some of the best beaches on this coast, such as delightful **Myrtiótissa**. Settlements and development stop a little to the south of Paleokastrítsa and only resume around **Érmones** and **Pélekas**

– a quick bus ride across the island from Kérkyra Town. Down to the south, a second dividing point is the **Korissíon lagoon**, the sandy plains and dunes that skirt this natural feature being great places for botanists and ornithologists. Beyond, a single road trails the interior, with sporadic side roads to resorts on either coast. The landscape here is flat, an undistinguished backdrop for a series of increasingly developed beaches and, in the far south, **Kávos**, Corfu's big youth resort.

Érmones to the Korissíon lagoon: the west coast

ÉRMONES, around 15km south of Paleokastrítsa by road, is one of the busiest resorts on the island, its lush green bay backed by the mountains above the Rópa River. The resort is dominated by the luxury *Ermones Beach* **hotel** (℡26610 94241, Ⓦ www.sunmarotelermones.gr; ❽), which provides guests with obligatory full board and a funicular railway down to the beach. Of the two mid-range hotels on the other side of the river, the *Philoxenia* (℡26610 94091, Ⓦ www.hotelphiloxenia.com; ❹) is better value, while cheaper rooms can be found at the *Pension Katerina* (℡26610 94615; ❷) and *Georgio's Villas* (℡26610 94950; ❷), further back on the hillside above the road that leads to the beach. Both the *Maria* and *Nafsica* **tavernas** above the beach provide good, filling *mezédhes* and main dishes. Just inland is the Corfu Golf and Country Club (℡26610 94220), the only golf club in the archipelago, and said to be one of the finest in the Mediterranean.

The nearby small village of **VÁTOS**, on the Glyfádha bus route from Kérkyra Town, has only a shop-cum-café and a quaint church, as all the other facilities are to be found on the main road 1km below. Here, the *Olympic Restaurant and Grill* (℡26610 94318; ❷) has rooms and apartments, as well as the only food, while the *Villa Frederiki* (℡26610 94003; ❸), opposite, consists of two large double studios. The Myrtiótissa turning is signposted just beyond the extremely handy, if basic, *Vatos Camping* (℡26610 94393), 500m further south.

Far preferable to the gravelly sand of Érmones, are the sandy beaches just south of the resort at Myrtiótissa and Glyfádha. In *Prospero's Cell*, Lawrence Durrell described **Myrtiótissa** as "perhaps the loveliest beach in the world"; it was for years a well-guarded secret but is now a firm favourite, especially with nudists, and gets so busy in summer that it supports three *kantínes*, meaning it's at its best well out of high season. Above the north end of beach is the tiny, whitewashed **Myrtiótissa monastery**, dedicated to Our Lady of the Myrtles. There are a few **rooms**, just off the approach road at the friendly *Myrtia* taverna (℡26610 94113, Ⓔ sks_mirtia@hotmail.com; ❸), which serves tasty home-style cooking.

The sandy bay of **GLYFÁDHA**, walled in by cliffs, is dominated by the huge *Louis Grand* hotel (℡26610 94140, Ⓦ www.louishotels.com; ❻), well overpriced despite including half-board. Far more reasonable **accommodation** is available at the extreme north end of the beach at two good adjacent tavernas; *Glyfada Beach* (℡26610 94258, Ⓕ 26610 94257; ❷) and *Glyfada* (℡26610 94224; ❶), whose simple rooms are a real bargain. Nightlife centres on two music bars, the *Kikiriko* and *Aloha*, which pump out heavy-duty sounds all day, as the beach is popular with young Greek and Italian trendies.

PÉLEKAS, inland and 2km south of Glyfádha, has long been popular for its views – the **Kaiser's Throne** viewing tower, just above the town, was Wilhelm II's favourite spot on the island. As the only inland resort, there are some good **room** deals here, including the friendly *Pension Paradise* (℡26610 94530; ❷), on the way in from Vátos, the *Alexandros* pension (℡26610 94215, Ⓦ www.alexandrospelekas .com; ❸) and *Thomas* (℡26610 94441; ❸), both on the way towards Kaiser's

Throne. Among the **tavernas**, *Alexandros*, *Pink Panther* and *Roula's Grill House*, the latter especially good for simple succulent meat, are all highly recommended. Colourful *Zanzibar* is a pleasant spot for a drink by the diminutive square, whose Odhiyítria church, renovated in 1884, is worth a peek.

Pélekas's sandy **beach** is reached down a short path. Here you'll find *Maria's Place*, an excellent family-run **taverna** with **rooms** (℡26610 94601; ❷), serving fish caught daily by the owner's husband. Sadly, the beach has been rather spoilt by the monstrous *Pelekas Beach* hotel that now looms over it.

Around 7km south of Pélekas, **AÏ GÓRDHIS** is one of the key play beaches on the island, largely because of the activities organized by the startling **Pink Palace** complex (℡26610 53103, ⓦwww.thepinkpalace.com), which dominates the resort. It has pools, games courts, Internet access (€3/hr), restaurants, a shop and a disco. Backpackers cram into communal rooms for up to ten (smaller rooms and singles are also available) for €18–26 a night, including breakfast and an evening buffet. Other accommodation is available on the beach, notably at *Michali's Place* taverna (℡26610 53041; ❸); the neighbouring *Alex in the Garden* **restaurant** is also a favourite.

Inland from the resort is the south's largest prominence, the humpback of ** Áyii Dhéka** (576m), reached by path from the hamlet of Áno Garoúna; it is the island's second-largest mountain after Pandokrátor. The lower slopes are wooded, and it's possible to glimpse buzzards wheeling on thermals over the higher slopes. The monks at the tiny monastery just below the summit lovingly tend a bountiful orchard.

Around 5km south by road from Áï Górdhis, the fishing hamlet of **PENDÁTI** is still untouched by tourism. There is no accommodation here, but *Angela's* café and minimarket and the *Strofi* grill cater to villagers and the few tourists who wander in. Another 4km on, **PARAMÓNAS** has slowly evolved over the years but remains a low-key resort with some fine **accommodation** deals: at the beach, the *Sunset* taverna (℡26610 75149, ℱ26610 75686; ❷) and smart *Paramonas* hotel (℡26610 76595, ⓦwww.paramonas-hotel.com; ❹), just behind it, both offer panoramic sea views, while the *Areti Studios* (℡26610 75838; ❸), on the lane in from Pendáti, have a rural air.

The town of **ÁYIOS MATTHÉOS**, 3km inland, is still chiefly an agricultural centre, although a number of *kafenía* and tavernas offer a warm if slightly bemused welcome to passers-by: head for the *Mouria* snack-bar/grill, or the modern *Steki*, which can rustle up tasty *mezédhes*. On the other side of Mount Prasoúdhi, 2km by road, is the **Gardhíki Pýrgos**, the ruins of a thirteenth-century castle built in this unlikely lowland setting by the despots of Epirus. The road continues on to the northernmost tip of splendid and deserted **Halikoúna** beach on the sea edge of the **Korissíon lagoon**, which, if you don't have your own transport, is most easily reached by walking from the village of Línia (on the Kávos bus route) via **Íssos** beach; other, longer routes trail around the north end of the lagoon from Áno Mesongí and Khlomotianá. Over 5km long and 1km wide at its centre, Korissíon is home to turtles, tortoises, lizards and numerous indigenous and migratory birds. For one of the quietest stays on the island, try *Marin Christel Apartments* (℡26610 75947; ❸), just north of Halikoúna beach, or *Logara Apartments* (℡26610 76477; ❹), 500m inland. *Spiros* has the slightly better selection of the two tavernas on this stretch of road. The beach is an idyllic spot for rough camping but only a seasonal canteen operates in the immediate vicinity.

Benítses to Petrití: the east coast

South of Kérkyra Town, there's nothing to recommend before **BENÍTSES**, a once-notorious bonking-and-boozing resort, whose old town at the north end has long since reverted to a quiet bougainvillea-splashed Greek village. There are a couple of minor attractions, namely the modest ruins of a Roman bath-house at the back of the village and the small but impressive **Shell Museum** (March–Oct daily 9am–7pm; €4). **Rooms** are plentiful, as visitor numbers have never returned to heyday levels: try the Best Travel (☎26610 72037, ℱ26610 71036) and Achilles Tourist Centre (☎26610 72228, ℰkapsoandre@ker.otenet .gr) agencies (both ❷). Among **hotels** offering good deals, the central *Hotel Potamaki* (☎26610 71140, ⓦwww.potamakibeachhotel.gr; ❹), is a gigantic 1960s throwback, while the jointly run *Hotel Benitsa/Agis* (☎26610 39269; ❷) offer quiet rooms set back from the main road. Benítses has its fair share of decent **tavernas**, notably *La Mer de Corfu* and the Corfiot specialist *O Paxinos*, as well as the plush Italian *Avra*. Lively **bars** such as *Lacey's* and *Sunshine* are concentrated behind the crescent-shaped park that separates the old village from the coast road, while larger **nightclubs** like *Casanovas 2000* or *Stadium* are at the southern end of the main strip.

   MORAÏTIKA's main street is an ugly strip of bars, restaurants and shops, but its beach is the best between Kérkyra Town and Kávos. Confusingly, the biggest touristic landmark in the area, the *Messonghi Beach* **hotel** complex (☎26610 75830, ⓦwww.messonghibeach.gr; ❻), set in lush landscaped gardens and home to the Nautilus diving centre (daily 5–7pm; ☎26610 83295), actually lies just within the limits of Moraïtika, which is separated from neighbouring Mesongí by the Mesongís River. Other reasonable beachside **hotels** include the *Marga-rita Beach* (☎26610 75267, ⓦwww.corfu-hotel-margarita.com; ❹) and the plusher *Three Stars* (☎26610 75263, ℱ26610 75862; ❹). Budget Ways Travel (☎26610 76768, ☎26610 76769; ❸) offers a range of accommodation and there are **rooms** between the main road and beach, such as those at the *Firefly* taverna (☎26610 75850; ❸). Much of the main drag is dominated by souvenir shops and minimarkets, as well as a range of **bars**, including the village's oldest, *Charlie's*, which opened in 1939, and the lively *Very Coco* nightclub. The *Rose Garden* **restaurant** is just off the main road and has a fair mix of vegetarian, Greek and international food, as does the beach restaurant *Kavouria*, where the seafood and special salads are excellent The village proper, **ÁNO MORAÏ-TIKA**, is signposted a few minutes' hike up the steep lanes inland, and is virtu-ally unspoilt. Its tiny houses and alleys are practically drowning in bougainvillea, among which you'll find two **tavernas**: the *Village Taverna* and the *Bella Vista*, the latter of which has a basic menu but justifies its name with a lovely garden, sea views and breezes.

   Commencing barely a hundred metres on from the Moraïtika seafront, **MESONGÍ** continues this stretch of package-tour-oriented coast but is noticeably quieter and has a range of accommodation deals. Both the *Hotel Gemini* (☎26610 75221, ⓦgeminihotel.gr; ❺) and far better value, British-run *Pantheon Hall* (☎26610 75802, ⓦwww.corfu-summer.com; ❷) have pools and gardens, and en-suite rooms with balconies. Mesongí has a number of good **restaurants**: notably the *Memories* taverna, which specializes in Corfiot dishes and serves its own barrel wine, and the upmarket *Castello*. An alternative is to head for the beachside *Bacchus* and *Spanos* tavernas a short walk south on the road to Boúkari. Try the *Olive Tree Pub* bar for a relaxed drink.

   The quiet road from Mesongí to Boúkari follows the seashore for about 3km, often only a few feet above it. **BOÚKARI** itself comprises little more than a handful of tavernas, a shop and a few small, family-run hotels; the 🏕 *Boukari Beach*, 1km north of the tiny harbour, is the best of the **tavernas**, offering fresh fish and live lobster. The very friendly Vlahopoulos family who run the taverna also offer rooms and own two small hotels nearby, the fully renovated *Penelopi* and *Villa Alexandra* (☎26620 51269, ⓦwww.boukaribeach.com; ❸). Boúkari is out of the way, but an idyllic little strip of unspoilt coast for anyone fleeing the crowds elsewhere on the island, and inland from here is the unspoiled wooded region around **Aryirádhes**, rarely visited by tourists and a perfect place for quiet walks.

Back on the coastline, the village of **PETRITÍ**, only created in the 1970s when geologists discovered the hill village of Korakádhes was sliding downhill, fronts onto a small but busy harbour. It is mercifully free of noise and commerce, with a beach of rock, mud and sand, set among low olive-covered hills. The *Pension Egrypos* (☎26620 51949, ⓦwww.egrypos .gr; ❸) has **rooms** and a restaurant. At the harbour, three **tavernas** serve the trickle of sea traffic: the smart *Limnopoula* guarded by caged parrots, and the more basic but friendly *Dimitris* and *Stamatis*. Back from the village, near the hamlet of Vassilátika, is the elegant *Regina* **hotel**, with gardens and pool (☎26620 52132, ⓦwww.reginahotel.de; ❹), mainly occupied by Germans. Barely 2km south of Petrit, the rocky coves of **Nótos** beach are little visited and conceal a wonderful and friendly place to stay in the shape of *Panorama Apartments* (☎26620 51707, ⓦwww.panoramacorfu.gr; ❷), which also has a fine shady restaurant.

Southern Corfu

Across the island on the west coast, the beach at **ÁYIOS YEÓRYIOS** spreads as far south as Ayía Varvára, and north to encircle the edge of the Korissíon lagoon, around 12km of uninterrupted sand. The resort itself, however, is an unprepossessing seafront sprawl and tourism here has the most mercenary air of anywhere on the island. British package operators dominate the scene, with bars competing to present bingo, quizzes and video nights. The smart *Golden Sands* (☎26620 51225, ⓦwww.corfugoldensands.com; ❸) has a pool, open-air restaurant and gardens, but the best **hotel** bargain is the smaller *Blue Sea* (☎26620 51624, ⓦwww.bluesea-hotel.com; ❸); both are situated midway along the seafront road. The easiest place to look for good **rooms** is at Star Travel (☎26620 52800, ⓦwww.startravel.com; ❷), further north. Most **restaurants** are predictably bland but you can eat well enough at the *Stamatis* and *Splendid* taverna/grill houses. **Nightlife** centres around music and pool bars like the *Gold Hart* and *Bluebell*, although laid-back *Amazona* cocktail bar and lively *Mad Mike's*, one of the few places off the seafront, have a better atmosphere.

A few minutes' walk north of Áyios Yeóryios, **Íssos** is a far better and quieter beach; the dunes north of Íssos towards the Korissíon lagoon are an unofficial nude bathing area. Facilities around Íssos are sparse: one **taverna**, the *Rousellis Grill*, a few hundred metres from the beach on the lane leading to Línia on the main road; the smart new yellow-and-maroon *Vicky's Apartments* (☎26620 53161; ❹), above a bend in the lane; and the *Friends* snack-bar in Línia itself. An English-run **windsurfing school** (ⓦwww.mermanwindsurf.com) operates on the beach and can arrange all-in packages.

Anyone interested in how a Greek town works away from the bustle of tourism shouldn't miss **LEFKÍMI**, towards the island's southern tip. The second-largest settlement after Kérkyra Town, it's the administrative centre for the south of the island as well as the alternative ferry port to or from Igoumenítsa, with half a dozen daily crossings in summer. The town has some fine architecture, including several striking churches: **Áyii Anáryiri** with a huge double belfry, **Áyios Theódhoros**, on a mound above a small square, and **Áyios Arsénios**, with a vast orange dome that can be seen for miles.

There are some **rooms** at the *Cheeky Face* taverna (☎26620 22627; ❷), by the bridge over the canal that carries the Himáros River through the lower part of town, and the *Maria Madalena* apartments (☎26620 22386; ❷) further up. For **food** look no further than the home-cooking at the tiny *Maria estiatório*, on the opposite side of the canal to *Cheeky Face*. A few **bars** are tucked in corners of the upper town and see so few tourists that you are likely to receive a friendly welcome: *Hermes* has a leafy garden, while *Mersedes* and *Enigma* both play Greek and foreign sounds in their dimly lit interiors.

There are no ambiguities in **KÁVOS**, 6km south of Lefkími: either you like 24-hour drinking, clubbing, bungee-jumping, go-karts, video bars named after British sitcoms and chips with almost everything, or you should avoid the resort altogether. Kávos stretches over 2km of decent sandy beach, with watersports galore. This is very much Club 18–30 territory; if you want independent **accommodation**, try Pandis Travel (☎26620 61400, ✉ncpandis@otenet.gr) or Island Holidays (☎26620 61357, ✉vvera@otenet.gr; both ❷). The nearest to genuine Greek **food** you'll find is at the *Two Brothers psistariá*, at the south end of town. Fast food and British-style Asian cuisine are much easier to come by. *Buzz* is the most happening **club**, with imported north European DJs, followed by *The Barn*, *42nd St* and *Sex*. Favourite **bars** include *Time*, *Truants*, *The Face*, *Black Duck* and *Bonkers*, and at night the main drag is one unbroken crowd of young revellers.

Beyond the limits of Kávos, where few visitors stray, a path leaving the road south to the hamlet of Sparterá heads through unspoilt countryside; after around thirty minutes of walking it reaches the cliffs of **Cape Asprókavos** and the crumbling **monastery of Arkoudhílas**. The cape looks out over the straits to Paxí, and down over deserted **Arkoudhílas** beach, which can be reached from Sparterá, a pleasant village 5km by road but only 3km by the signed path from Kávos; its *Fantasia* and *Paradise* tavernas are far more appealing and authentic than any in the resort. Even wilder is **Áï Górdhis Paleohoríou** beach, 3km further on from Sparterá, one of the least visited on the island and not to be confused with the eponymous beach further north; a municipal café provides the only refreshment. The Cape is also the southern starting point for the **Corfu Trail**, inaugurated in 2001, after years of planning by local walkers. Signposted by yellow waymarkers the trail meanders back and forth over 200km of varying terrain all the way to Cape Ayías Ekaterínis on the north coast and is designed to take at least ten days. Those interested should get a copy of Hilary Whitton Paipeti's *Walking the Corfu Trail* or check out ⓦwww .travelling.gr/corfutrail for more details.

Corfu's satellite islands

Corfu's three inhabited satellite islands, **Eríkoussa**, **Othoní** and **Mathráki**, in the quintet of **Dhiapóndia islands**, are scattered up to 20km off the northwest coast. Some travel agencies in the northern resorts offer **day-trips** to Eríkoussa only, often with a barbecue thrown in – fine if you're happy to spend the day on the beach. A trip taking in all three islands from Sidhári or Áyios Stéfanos is excellent value: they are between thirty and sixty minutes apart by boat, and most trips allow you an hour on each (usually longer on sandy Eríkoussa).

Locals use day-trip boats between the islands, so it's possible to pay your way between them. There is also a **ferry** three times a week from Kérkyra Town, the *Alexandros II*, which brings cars and goods to the islands, but given that it has to sail halfway round Corfu first, it's the slowest way to proceed.

Mathráki

Hilly, densely forested and with a long empty beach, beautiful **Mathráki** has the fewest inhabitants of the three islands. Portéllo beach begins at the edge of the tiny harbour, **Plákes**, and extends south for 3km of fine, dark-red sand. A single road rises from the harbour into the interior and the scattered village of **KÁTO MATHRÁKI**, where just one friendly taverna-*kafenío*-shop overlooks the beach and Corfu. The views are magnificent, as is the sense of isolation. However, Mathráki is gradually gearing up towards visitors, and islanders Tassos Kassimis (☎ 26630 71700; ❷) and Khristos Aryiros (☎ 26630 71652; ❸) already rent **rooms** and **studios** on Portéllo beach. At Plákes the *Port Centre* restaurant specializes in freshly caught fish. The road continues to the village of **Áno Mathráki**, with its single, old-fashioned *kafenío* next to the church, but this is beyond walking distance on a day-visit.

❼ Othoní

Eight kilometres northwest, **Othoní** is the largest, and at first sight the least inviting of Corfu's satellite islands. The island has a handful of places to stay and eat in its port, **ÁMMOS**, but the reception from islanders who aren't in the tourism trade is rather cool. Ámmos has two beaches, both pebbly, one on each side of the jetty. The village *kafenío*, *O Mikros*, serves as a very basic shop, and there's one smart **restaurant**, *La Locanda dei Sogni*, which also has **rooms** (☎ 26630 71640; ❸) – though these tend to be prebooked by Italian visitors. Two tavernas, *New York* and tiny *Lakis*, offer decent but fairly limited menus; the owner of the *New York* also offers rooms for rent (☎ 26630 71581; ❷). The number of beds on the island has greatly increased with the opening of the *Hotel Calypso* (☎ 26630 72162, ℱ 26630 71578; ❸), 200m east of the jetty. The island's interior is dramatic, and a road up out of the village leads through rocky, tree-covered hills to the central hamlet, **Horió**, after a thirty-minute walk. Horió, like other inland villages, is heavily depopulated – only about one hundred people still live on the island through the winter – but it's very attractive, and the architecture is completely traditional. On the north coast of the island **Fýki Bay**, accessible via a path from Dhamaskátika, has the longest stretch of sand but there are no facilities and you'll only have time to reach it if you spend at least a night.

Eríkoussa

Some 10km east of Othoní, **Eríkoussa** is the most popular destination for day-trippers. It's invariably hyped as a "desert island" trip, although this is a desert island with a medium-sized hotel, rooms, tavernas and a year-round community. In high season, it gets very busy: Eríkoussa has a large diaspora living in America and elsewhere who return to family homes in their droves in summer, so you may find your *yiásou* or *kaliméra* returned in a Brooklyn accent.

Eríkoussa has an excellent golden sandy beach right by the harbour, with great swimming, and quieter **Bragíni** beach, reached by a path across the wooded island interior. The island's cult following keeps its one **hotel**, the *Erikousa* (☎ 26630 71110; ⓦ www.hotelerikousa.gr; ❹), busy through the season; rooms are en suite with balconies and views. Simpler rooms next door are sometimes available from Theodora Kateni (☎ 26630 71821; ❶). If you're hoping to stay, phoning ahead is essential, as is taking anything you might not be able to buy – the only shop just sells basic groceries and provisions. The *Erikousa* also boasts the only bona fide **taverna**, serving great fish, meat and starters, although a couple of smaller snack-bars, such as the *Oasis*, can rustle up breakfast or simpler meals.

Paxí (Paxos) and Andípaxi

Verdant, hilly and still largely unspoilt, **Paxí (Paxos)** is the smallest of the main Ionian islands. Barely 12km by 4km, it has no sandy beaches, no historical sites, only three hotels and a serious water shortage, yet is so popular it is best avoided in high season. It's a particular favourite of yachting flotillas, whose spending habits have brought the island an upmarket reputation, making it just about the most expensive place to visit in the Ionian islands and lending it a rather cliquey air. Pockets of unauthorized camping, however, are tolerated in the absence of an official site. Most accommodation is block-booked by travel companies, though there are local tour operators whose holiday deals are often a fraction of the price. The capital, **Gáios**, is quite cosmopolitan, with delis and boutiques, but northerly **Lákka** and tiny **Longós** are where hardcore Paxophiles head.

Gáios and around

Most visitors arrive at the new port, 1km north of **GÁIOS**, a pleasant town built around a small square on the seafront overlooking two islands, Áyios Nikólaos and Panayía. Given the shortage of rooms, it's advisable to phone ahead: try Gaïos Travel (☎26620 32033, ⓦwww.gaiostravel.com) or Bouas Tours (☎26620 32401, ⓦwww.bouastours.gr), both situated on the seafront (❸). Paxi's two most established seasonal **hotels** are both near Gáios: the *Paxos Beach Hotel* (☎26620 32211, ⓦwww.paxosbeachhotel.gr; ❻ half-board) which has smart en-suite bungalows on a hillside above a pebbly beach 2km south of town, and the fairly luxurious *Paxos Club* (☎26620 32450, ⓦwww.paxosclub .gr; ❼), nearly 2km inland from Gáios.

Gáios boasts a number of decent **tavernas**, most of which are on the pricey side. The best of the bunch are *Dodo's*, set in a garden inland from the

Anemoyiannis statue, which has a full range of *mezédhes* and main courses; *Apangio*, most reasonable of the seafront establishments; and *Vassilis*, which has the best selection and prices of the trio to the left of the road up towards the bus stop. *The Cellar* at the top of the square is the best place for a tasty *souvláki*. *Gonia*, by the Párga *kaïki* mooring, is the last remaining traditional place for a coffee or drink. Trendier bars include *Remego* on the southern seafront and *Alter Ego* round the quay towards the new port. The *Phoenix* club, out by the new port, opens sporadically after midnight and has a terrace for sublunar fun, while the inland *Castello Music Club*, beyond the bus stop, is a more reliable summer disco.

Inland are some of the island's oldest settlements, such as Oziás and Vellianitátika, in prime walking country, but with few, if any, facilities. Noel Rochford's book, *Landscapes of Paxos*, lists dozens of walks, and cartographers Elizabeth and Ian Bleasdale's *Paxos Walking Map* is on sale in most travel agencies.

The **coast south** of Gáïos is punctuated by the odd shingly cove, none ideal for swimming, until matters improve towards the tip at **Mogoníssi** beach, which shares some of Andípaxi's sandier geology. There is an eponymous taverna and en route you can take a peek at Fiat supremo Agnelli's distinctive hillside mansion, turrets and all.

The north of the island

Paxí's one main road runs along the spine of the island, with a turning at the former capital **Magaziá**, leading down to the tiny port of Longós. The main road continues to Lákka, the island's funkiest resort, set in a breathtaking horseshoe bay. Buses ply the road between Gáïos and Lákka four or five times a day, most diverting to swing through Longós. The Gáïos–Lákka bus (30min) affords panoramic views, and the route is an excellent walk of under three hours (one way). A taxi between the two costs around €8.

Approached from the south, **LÁKKA** is an unprepossessing jumble of buildings, but once in its maze of alleys and neo-Venetian buildings, or on the quay with views of distant Corfu, you do get a sense of its charm. Lákka's two **beaches**, Harámi and Kanóni, are unfortunately prone to high-season pollution from the yachts that cram the bay. **Accommodation** is plentiful (except in high season) from the area's two biggest agencies: local Routsis (☎26620 31807, ⓦwww.routsis-holidays.com) or the British-owned Planos Holidays (☎26620 31744 or UK 01373 814200, ⓦwww.planos.co.uk), both on the seafront (❷). Paxí's third bona-fide hotel is the snooty and overpriced *Amfitriti Hotel* (☎26620 30011, ⓦwww.amfitriti-hotel.gr; ❼). Mercifully, the practise of low-key, freelance camping behind Kanóni has not been affected. There's an embarrassment of good **tavernas**, such as the friendly *Nionios* and neighbouring *Pounentes*, both serving a fine range of Hellenic favourites on the square, the secluded *Alexandros*, great for *gourounópoulo* and fresh fish, and more upmarket seafront *La Rosa di Paxos*, which does risottos and ravioli. There's a similar wealth of bars: the seafront *Romantica* cocktail bar and *Harbour Lights*, *Serano's* in the square, or the friendly *kafenío* of Spyros Petrou – the hub of village life. Lákka is also well situated for **walking**: up onto either promontory, to the lighthouse or Vassilátika, or to Longós and beyond. One of the finest walks – if combined with a bus or taxi back – is an early evening visit to the **Erimítis cliffs**, near the hamlet of Voïkátika: on clear afternoons, the cliffs change colour at twilight like a seafacing Uluru (Ayers Rock), while full moons see the odd party at the sole bar, *Sunset*.

LONGÓS is the prettiest village on the island, and perfectly sited for morning sun and idyllic alfresco breakfasts. The village is dominated by the upmarket villa crowd, making the Planos office here (☎26620 31530) the best place to look for accommodation. Longós has some of the island's best restaurants: the seafront *Vassilis*, which does terrific fish dishes and tasty starters, *Nassos*, also with a wide variety of fish and seafood, and *Iy Gonia*, a much simpler and cheaper *psistariá*. *To Taxidhi* on the quay is a nice spot for coffee or an early drink, while *Roxi Bar* and *Ores* pander to the night-owls.

Longós has a small, scruffy beach, with sulphur springs favoured by local grannies, but most people swim off **Levrehió** beach in the next bay south, which gets the occasional camper. Islanders are touchy about camping for fear of fires so it's politic to ask at the beach taverna if it's acceptable. Longós is at the bottom of a steep winding hill, making **walking** a chore, but the short circle around neighbouring **Dhendhriátika** provides spectacular views and allows access to the small but excellent **Monodhéndhri** beach, and the walk to **Fondána** and **Magaziá** can be done to coincide with a bus back.

Andípaxi

A mile south, Paxí's tiny sibling **Andípaxi** has scarcely any accommodation and no facilities beyond several beach tavernas open during the day in season. It is most easily reached by the frequent shuttle *kaïkia* from Gáïos (€6 return). The glass-bottomed boat (€15 return) also takes you to its sea stacks and caves, the most dramatic in the Ionians. Andípaxi's sandy, blue-water coves have been compared with the Caribbean, but you'll have to share them with *kaïkia* and sea taxis from all three villages, plus larger craft from Corfu and the mainland resorts.

Boats basically deposit you either at the sandy **Vríka** beach or the longer pebble beach of **Vatoúmi**. Vríka has a taverna at each end, of which *Spiros* (☎26620 31172) has great grilled and oven food and can arrange self-catering accommodation up in **Vígla**, the island's hilltop settlement, on a weekly basis.

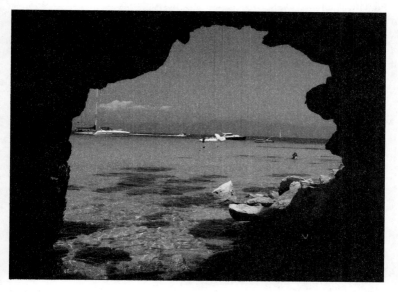

△ Vatoúmi beach, Andípaxi

Vatoúmi also has two restaurants, the justifiably named *Bella Vista* restaurant, perched on a cliff high above the beach, and the newer *Vatoumi*, a little way back from the beach.

For a swim in quieter surroundings the trick is to head south, away from the pleasure-craft moorings, although path widening has made even the quieter bays more accessible. Paths also lead inland to connect the handful of homes and the southerly lighthouse, but there are no beaches of any size on Andípaxi's western coastline and thick thorny scrub makes it difficult to approach. In low season, there's also the risk of bad weather keeping pleasure craft in port and stranding you on the island.

Lefkádha (Lefkas)

Lefkádha is an oddity. Connected to the mainland by a long causeway through lagoons, it barely feels like an island, at least on the busier eastern side – and historically it isn't. It is separated from the mainland by a canal cut by Corinthian colonists in the seventh century BC, which has been re-dredged (after silting up) on various occasions since, and today is spanned by a thirty-metre, pontoon-swivel-bridge. Lefkádha was long an important strategic base, and approaching the causeway you pass a series of fortresses, climaxing in the fourteenth-century castle of **Santa Maura** – the Venetian name for the island. These defences were too close to the mainland to avoid an Ottoman tenure, which began in 1479, but the Venetians wrested back control a couple of centuries later. They were in turn overthrown by Napoleon in 1797 and then the British took over as Ionian protectors in 1810. It wasn't until 1864 that Lefkádha, like the rest of the Ionian archipelago, was reunited with Greece.

At first glance Lefkádha is not overwhelmingly attractive, although it is a substantial improvement on the mainland just opposite. The whiteness of its rock strata – *lefkás* has the same root as *lefkós*, "white" – is often brutally exposed by road cuts and quarries, and the highest ridge is bare except for ugly military and telecom installations. With the marshes and boggy inlets on the east coast, mosquitoes can be a midsummer problem. On the other hand, the island is a fertile place, supporting cypresses, olive groves and vineyards, particularly on the western slopes, and life in the mountain villages remains relatively untouched, with the older women still wearing traditional local dress – two skirts (one forming a bustle), a dark headscarf and a rigid bodice. The rugged west coast also boasts some of the finest beaches in the Ionians.

Lefkádha has been home to various literati, including two prominent Greek poets, Angelos Sikelianos and Aristotelis Valaoritis, and the British writer Lafcadio Hearn. Support for the arts continues in the form of a well-attended international **festival** of theatre and folk-dancing, now extended throughout the summer, with most events staged in the Santa Maura castle. On a smaller scale, frequent village celebrations accompanied by *bouzoúki* and clarinet ensure that the strong local wine flows well into the early hours.

Lefkádha remains relatively undeveloped, with just two major resorts: **Vassi-likí**, in its vast bay in the south, claims to be Europe's biggest windsurf centre; **Nydhrí**, on the east coast, overlooks the island's picturesque archipelago, and is the launching point for the barely inhabited island of **Meganíssi**. The completion of the capital's superb **marina** in 2003, however, with a smart reception centre and ample mooring, refuelling and restocking facilities has increased the island's appeal to yachties.

Lefkádha Town and around

LEFKÁDHA TOWN sits at the island's northernmost tip, hard by the cause-way. Like other (southerly) capitals in the southern Ionian, it was hit by the earthquakes of 1948 and 1953, and the town was devastated, with the exception of a few **Italianate churches**. As a precaution against further quakes, little was rebuilt above two storeys, and most houses acquired second storeys of wood, giving the western dormitory area an unintentionally quaint look. The town is small – you can cross it on foot in little over ten minutes – and despite the destruction, still very attractive, especially around the main square, Platía Ayíou Spyridhónos, and the arcaded high street of Ioánnou Méla. Much of Lefkádha Town is pedestrian-only, mainly because of the narrowness of its lanes. The centre boasts over half a dozen richly decorated private family churches, usually locked and best visited around services. Many contain rare works from the Ionian School of painting, including work by its founder, Zakynthian Panayiotis Doxaras.

The folklore museum has been closed for a number of years but you can catch a glimpse of the old way of life at the quaint little **Phonograph Museum** (daily 10am–2pm & 7–midnight; free), which is dedicated to antique phonographs and bric-a-brac, and sells cassettes of rare traditional music. On the northwestern seafront a modern Cultural Centre houses the newly expanded **archeological museum** (Tues–Sun 8.30am–3pm; €2), which contains interesting, well-labelled displays on aspects of daily life, religious worship and funerary customs in ancient times, as well as a room on prehistory dedicated to the work of eminent German archeologist Wilhelm Dörpfeld. The **municipal art gallery** (daily 10am–1pm & 7–10pm; free) is now also housed in the same complex.

Practicalities

The **bus station** is on Dhimítri Golémi opposite the marina. It has services to almost every village on the island, with extensive daily schedules to Nydhrí, Vassilikí and Káthisma beaches on the west coast. Car and motorbike rental is useful for exploring; try EuroHire, Golémi 5 (℡26450 26776), near the bus station or I Love Santas (℡26450 25250) next to the *Ionian Star* hotel.

All of the half-dozen **hotels** are in busy areas and none is cheap, but the more expensive ones are glazed against the noise and heat. The *Ionian Star* (℡26450 24672, Ⓦwww.ionianstar.gr; ❻), Panágou 2, is the plushest hotel with brand-new fittings and a pool. The best mid-range hotels are the stylish seafront *Nirikos*, Ayías Mávras (℡26450 24132, Ⓦwww.nirikos.gr; ❺), which offers fairly spacious rooms, and the cosy but comfortable *Santa Maura*, Spyridhónos Viánda 2 (℡26450 21308, Ⓕ26450 26253; ❹). The *Pension Pyrofani*, just below the square on Dörpfeld (℡26450 25844, Ⓕ26450 24084; ❹), is just as comfortable and almost as pricey. There are simple **rooms** in the dormitory area northwest of Dörpfeld: the Lefkádha Room Owners Association (℡26450 21266; ❷) can help, or try the *Pinelopis Rooms* (℡26450 24175; ❷) at Pinelópis 20, off the seafront two short blocks from the pontoon bridge. Lefkádha Town has no campsite, although there are decent sites at Karyótes and Epískopos, a few kilometres to the south.

The best **restaurants** are hidden in the backstreets: the *Regantos* taverna, on Dhimárhou Venióti is the local favourite, but only opens in the evenings. At other times, head for the *Eftyhia*, a fine little *estiatório* just off Dörpfeld, or *Romantika* on Mitropóleos, which has nightly performances of Lefkadhan *kantádhes* (a hybrid of Cretan folk song and Italian opera ballad). Tasty meat, fish and *mezédhes* at very fair prices can be enjoyed at *Sto Molo*, on Golémi, although you have to contend with the traffic noise.

The most traditional place for a tipple is the *Cafe Karfakis*, on Ioánnou Méla, an old-style *kafenío* with splendid *mezédhes*. Of the **bars** in the main square, the *Cäsbäh* is the most popular and trendy haunts such as *Excess* and *Il Posto* line the seafront west of the bridge. The town's outdoor **cinema**, Eleni, on Faneroménis, has two showings and programmes change daily.

Around Lefkádha Town

The town has a decent and lengthy shingle-and-sand beach west of the lagoon at **Yíra**, a thirty-minute walk from the centre. Roughly 4km long, the beach is often virtually deserted even in high season; there's a **taverna** at either end, and at the western end a couple of **bars** in the renovated windmills, as well as the trendy *Club Milos*. The beach's western extension, **Aïyánnis**, is growing in popularity and now has several restaurants, including *Tilegraphos* (T26450 24881, Wwww.tilegraphos.gr; ❸), which also lets out some **rooms**.

The uninhabited **Faneroméni monastery** (daily 8am–2pm & 4–8pm; free) is reached by any of the west-coast buses, or by a steep hike on foot from town (45min) through the hamlet of Fríni. There's a small museum and chapel, and an ox's yoke and hammer, used when Nazi occupiers forbade the use of bells. There are wonderful views over the town and lagoon from the Fríni road.

The island's **interior**, best reached by bus or car from Lefkádha Town, offers imposing mountainscapes and excellent walking between villages only a few kilometres apart. **KARYÁ** is its centre, and offers the *Karia Village Hotel* (T26450 41004; ❹), under renovation at the time of writing, and some rooms: try the Kakiousis family (T26450 61136; ❷) or Haritini Vlahou (T26450 41634; ❶). The leafy town square has a popular taverna, *Iy Klimataria*, just below it and two *psistariés* on it, *Ta Platania*, and the smarter *O Rousos*. Karyá is the centre of the island's lace and weaving industry, with a small but fascinating **folklore museum** set in a lacemaker's home (April–Oct daily 9am–9pm; €2.50). The historic and scenic villages of **Vafkerí** and **Englouví** are within striking distance, with the west-coast hamlets of **Dhrymónas** and **Exánthia** a hike over the hills.

The east coast to Vassilikí

Lefkádha's east coast is the most accessible and the most developed part of the island. Apart from the campsite at Karyótes, *Kariotes Beach* (T & F26450 71103), there's little point stopping before the small fishing port of **LIYIÁ**, which has some rooms and the hotel *Konaki* (T26450 71127, Wwww .hotelkonaki.gr; ❻), as well as some restaurants such as *O Xouras psarotavérna* and, as you head south, the inexpensive and excellent garden taverna ❦ *Iy Limni*, which features unique dishes such as *spartiátiko*, a delicious concoction of pork, peppers, mushroom, cheese, wine and cognac. Further on, beyond the *Episcopos Beach* campsite (T26450 71388), lies **NIKIÁNA**, another fishing village where you'll find the hotel *Pegasos* (T26450 71766, Wwww .hotelpegasos.gr; ❸), as well as the *Christina* pension (T26450 25194; ❸). In addition, Nikiána has a selection of fine tavernas, notably *Pantazis psistariá*, which also has rooms to let (T26450 71211; ❸), and *Lefko Akroyiali*, a good fish restaurant further south. Beaches here tend to be pebbly and small.

Most package travellers will find themselves in **NYDHRÍ**, the island's biggest resort by far, with ferry connections to Meganíssi and myriad **boat trips** around the nearby satellite islands. The German archeologist Wilhelm Dörpfeld believed Nydhrí, rather than Itháki, to be the site of Odysseus's capital, and did indeed find Bronze Age tombs on the plain nearby. His theory identifying ancient Ithaca with Lefkádha fell into disfavour after his death in 1940, although his obsessive attempts to give the island some status over its neighbour are honoured by a statue on Nydhrí's quay. Dörpfeld's tomb is tucked away at Ayía Kyriakí on the opposite side of the bay, near the house in which he once lived, visible just above the chapel and lighthouse on the far side of the water.

Nydhrí is an average resort, with some good pebble beaches and a lovely setting, but the centre is an ugly strip with heavy traffic. The best **place**

to stay is the *Hotel Gorgona* (☎26450 95634, ⓕ26450 92268; ❸), set in a lush garden away from the traffic a minute along the Ráhi road, which leads to Nydhrí's very own **waterfall**, a 45-minute walk inland. Rooms are best arranged through any of the resort's many travel agencies – try Nidri Travel (☎26450 92514, ⓕ26450 92256; from ❷). The town's focus is the Aktí Aristotéli Onássi quay, where most of the rather ritzy **restaurants** and **bars** are found. Tourist traps like the *Barrel* taverna are rather pricey but reliable, whereas the *Titanic* on the beach is both quieter and better quality. The cheapest places to eat are predictably on the noisy main drag – try *Agrabeli* or *Ta Kalamia*. Nightlife centres around bars like *No Name* and *The Old Saloon*, and later on *Tropicana* or the *Sail Inn Club*, which claims to be open for 22 hours of the day.

Nydhrí sits at the mouth of a deep inlet stretching to the next village, somnolent **VLYHÓ**, with a few good tavernas and mooring for yachts. Over the Yéni peninsula across the inlet is the large **Dhessími Bay**, home to two campsites: *Santa Maura Camping* (☎26450 95007, ⓕ26450 26087) and *Dessimi Beach Camping* (☎26450 95374, ⓕ26450 95190), one at each end of the beach but often packed with outsized mobile homes. The *Pirofani* beach taverna in between them is excellent.

The coast road beyond Vlyhó turns inland and climbs the foothills of Mount Stavrotás, through the hamlets of Katohóri and Paliokatoúna to **Póros**, a quiet village with few facilities. Just south of here is the increasingly busy beach resort of **MIKRÓS YIALÓS**, more widely known as Póros beach. It boasts a handful of **tavernas**, a few rooms at *Oceanis Studios* (☎ & ⓕ26450 95095; ❸), plus the posh *Poros Beach Camping* (☎26450 95452, ⓦwww.porosbeach .com.gr), which has bungalows (❸), shops and a pool. For food, try the *Rouda Bay* taverna opposite the beach, which also has smart rooms (☎26450 95634, ⓔmanolitsis@otenet.gr; ❺).

A panoramic detour off the main road to quiet **Vournikás** and **Sývros** is recommended to walkers and drivers (the Lefkádha–Vassilikí bus also visits); both places have tavernas and some private rooms. It's around 14km to the next resort, the fjord-like inlet of **SÝVOTA**, 2km down a steep hill (bus twice daily). There's no beach except for a remote cove, but some fine tavernas, mostly specializing in fish: the *Palia Apothiki* is the most attractive and serves giant shrimps wrapped in bacon, but the *Delfinia* and *Ionion* also draw numerous customers. Just above the middle of the harbour there are **rooms** of varying sizes at *Sivota Apartments* (☎26450 31347, ⓕ26450 31151; ❸) or you can ask at any of the seafront supermarkets.

Beyond the Sývota turning, the mountain road dips down towards Kondárena, almost a suburb of **VASSILIKÍ**, the island's premier watersports resort. Winds in the huge bay draw vast numbers of windsurfers, with light morning breezes for learners and tough afternoon blasts for advanced surfers. Booking your **accommodation** ahead is advisable in high season: *Pension Hollidays* (☎26450 31011, ⓕ26450 31426; ❸), round the corner from the ferry dock, is a reasonable option with air conditioning and TV in all rooms. In the centre of town, the two main hotels are the classy *Vassiliki Bay Hotel* (☎26450 31077, ⓦwww.vassilikibay.gr; ❹) and the *Hotel Lefkatas* (☎26450 31801, ⓕ26450 31804; ❹), which operates in high season only. Rooms and apartments are available along the beach road to Póndi: try the smart and purpose-built *Billy's House* (☎26450 31418; ❸) or ask at the central Samba Tours (☎26450 31520, ⓦwww.sambatours.gr; ❸). The largest of the three beach windsurf centres, *Club Vassiliki*, offers all-in **windsurf tuition** and accommodation deals. Vassilikí's only **campsite**, the large *Camping Vassiliki*

Beach (☎26450 31308, ℻26450 31458), is about 500m along the beach road; it has its own restaurant, bar and shop.

Vassilikí's pretty quayside is lined with **tavernas** and bars: the most popular eateries are *Penguins*, specializing in fish and seafood dishes like *marinara*, and *Alexander*, which has pizza as well as Greek cuisine. Quieter spots round the headland include the *Jasmine Garden* Chinese and the leafy *Apollo* taverna. The best place for a **drink** is *Livanakis kafenío* (next to the bakery), now modernized but still genuine and cheap.

The beach at Vassilikí is stony and poor, but improves 1km on at tiny **Póndi**; most non-windsurfers, however, use the daily *kaïki* trips to nearby Ayiófili or around Cape Lefkátas to the superior beaches at Pórto Katsíki and Egremní on the sandy west coast (see overleaf). There's a gradually increasing number of **places to stay** at Póndi, some with great views of the bay and plain behind. One fine spot is the terrace of the *Ponti Beach Hotel* (☎26450 31572, ℻26450 31576; ❺), which is very popular with holidaying Greeks, and has a decent restaurant and bar. The *Nefeli* (☎26450 31378, ✉clubnefeli@hotmail.com; ❹), right on the beach, is much better value though. The *Panorama* **taverna** serves delights such as garlic prawns and steak Diana.

The west coast

Tsoukaládhes, just 6km from Lefkádha Town, is developing a roadside tourism business, but better beaches lie a short distance to the southwest, so there's very little reason to stay here. Four kilometres on, the road plunges down to the sand-and-pebble **Pefkoúlia** beach, one of the longest on the island, with two tavernas towards the north end, one of which, *Pelagos*, has rooms (☎26450 97070, ✉mypelagos@can.gr; ❹) and unofficial camping down at the other end, over 1km away. This part of the island suffered severe structural damage but mercifully no fatalities in the earthquake of summer 2003, which closed the main road, now protected by huge concrete and steel mesh barriers.

Jammed into a gorge between Pefkoúlia and the next beach, Mýlos, is **ÁÏ NIKÍTAS**, the prettiest resort on Lefkádha, a jumble of lanes and small wooden buildings. The back of the village is a dust-blown car park, which has completely taken over the former campsite, but this means that the village itself is now a pedestrian zone. The most attractive **accommodation** is in the ⚓ *Pension Ostria* (☎26450 97483, ℻26450 97300; ❹), a beautiful blue-and-white building above the village, decorated in a mix of beachcomber and ecclesiastical styles. The *Villa Milia* (☎26450 97475; ❷), by the junction offers better rates than most. Other options line the main drag or hide in the alleys running off it; the best bets are the small *Aphrodite* (☎26450 97372; ❸) and quieter *Olive Tree* (☎26450 97453, ⓦwww.olivetreelefkada.com; ❹), which is also signposted from the main road. The best tavernas include the *Sapfo* fish taverna by the sea, the *T'Agnantio*, just above the main street, which serves excellent traditional cuisine, and *O Lefteris*, a good inexpensive restaurant on the main street. *Captain's Corner* near the beach is the liveliest drinking venue, while *En Plo* is a pleasant café-bar overlooking the sea.

Sea taxis (€2 one way) ply between Áï Nikítas and **Mýlos** beach, or it's a 45-minute walk (or bus ride) to the most popular beach on the coast, **Káthisma**, a shadeless kilometre of fine sand, which becomes nudist and a lot less crowded beyond the large jutting rocks halfway along – freelance camping still goes on at this end too. Of the two tavernas on the beach choose the barn-like *Kathisma* (☎26450 97050, ⓦwww.kathisma.com; ❹), with smart apartments. The new *Club Copla* attracts the night-time crowd with house parties. Above the beach

the upgraded *Sunset* has **rooms** (T 26450 97488, W www.sunsetstudios.gr; ⑥),
while the nearby *Hotel Sirius* (T 26450 97025, W www.hotelsirios.gr; ⑤) also
commands fine views. Beyond Káthisma, hairpin bends climb the flank of
Mount Méga towards the small village of **KALAMÍTSI**, a much cheaper base
for this area. Good-value **rooms** or apartments can be found at *Hotel Lenia*
(T 26450 99125; ②), *Hermes* (T 26450 99417; ②), the smart *Blue and White
House* (T 26450 99413, W www.bluewhitehouse.com; ③) and the newer *Pansion
Nontas* (T 26450 99451; ③). There are also a few decent **tavernas**, including
the *Paradeisos*, set in its own garden with fountain, the more basic *Ionio* and, just
north of the village, the aptly titled *Panoramic View*. Three kilometres down a
newly paved road is the village's quiet sandy beach.

South of Kalamítsi, past the hamlets of Hortáta, which boasts the excellent
Lygos taverna with rooms (T 26450 33395, E lola26@ch.gr; ②), and Komíli, the
landscape becomes almost primeval. At 38km from Lefkádha Town, **ATHÁNI**
is the island's most remote spot to stay, with a couple of good tavernas which
both have great-value rooms: the *Panorama* (T 26450 33291, F 26450 33476;
②) and *O Alekos* (T 26450 33484; ②), the latter only open in high season.
Three of the Ionian's choicest **beaches**, where azure and milky turquoise waves
buffet strands enclosed by dramatic cliffs, are accessible from Atháni: the nearest,
reached by a 4km paved road, is **Yialós**, followed by **Egremní**, down a steep
incline unpaved for the last 2km; the former has the *Yialos* café-restaurant and
a couple of *kantínes*, the latter just one *kantína*. Further south an asphalted road
leads to the dramatic and popular twin beach of **Pórto Katsíki**, where there
are several better-stocked *kantínes* on the cliff above.

Keeping to the main road for 14km from Atháni will bring you to barren **Cape
Lefkátas**, which drops abruptly 75m into the sea. Byron's Childe Harold sailed
past this point, and "saw the evening star above, Leucadia's far projecting rock of
woe: And hail'd the last resort of fruitless love". The fruitless love is a reference to
Sappho, who in accordance with the ancient legend that you could cure yourself
of unrequited love by leaping into these waters, leapt – and died. In her honour the
locals termed the place Kávos tis Kyrás ("lady's cape"), and her act was imitated by
the lovelorn youths of Lefkádha for centuries afterwards. And not just by the lovelorn, for the act (known as *katapondismós*) was performed annually by scapegoats
– always a criminal or a lunatic – selected by priests from the Apollo temple whose
sparse ruins lie close by. Feathers and even live birds were attached to the victims
to slow their descent and boats waiting below took the chosen one, dead or alive,
away to some place where the evil banished with them could do no further harm.
The rite continued into the Roman era, when it degenerated into little more than
a fashionable stunt by decadent youth. These days, in a more controlled modern
re-enactment, Greek hang-gliders hold a tournament from the cliffs every July.

Lefkádha's satellites

Lefkádha has four satellite islands clustered off its east coast, although only one,
Meganíssi, the largest and most interesting, is accessible. **Skorpiós**, owned by
the Onassis family, fields armed guards to deter visitors. **Madhourí**, owned by
the family of poet Nanos Valaoritis, is private and similarly off-limits, while
tiny **Spárti** is a large scrub-covered rock. Day-trips from Nydhrí skirt all three
islands, and some stop to allow swimming in coves.

Meganíssi

Meganíssi, twenty minutes by frequent daily ferries from Nydhrí, is a large
island with limited facilities but a magical, if bleak landscape. Ferries stop first

at **Spiliá**, ten minutes by foot below **SPARTOHÓRI**, an immaculate village with whitewashed buildings and an abundance of bougainvillea. The locals – many returned émigrés from Australia – live from farming and fishing and are genuinely welcoming. You arrive at a jetty on a pebble beach with a few tavernas and a primitive but free (for a night or two only) campsite behind the excellent *Stars Taverna*. The village proper boasts three restaurants: a pizza place called the *Tropicana*, which can direct you to **rooms** (☎26450 51486; ❷–❸), as can the simple *Gakias* (☎26450 51050; ❸); the trio is completed by the fine traditional taverna *Lakis*. Further west round the coast at Áyios Ioánnis there is a good beach with the *Il Paradiso* taverna and a makeshift campsite, a great spot to unwind in.

The attractive inland village of **KATOMÉRI** is an hour's walk through magnificent country. It has the island's one **hotel**, the *Meganissi*, a comfortable place with a restaurant and pool (☎26450 51240, ℻26450 51639; ❹), and a few café-bars. Ten minutes' walk downhill is the main port of **VATHÝ**, with some accommodation such as *Different Studios* (☎26450 22170; ❸) and several highly rated restaurants, notably the waterside taverna, *Porto Vathi*, which Lefkadans flock to on ferries for a Sunday fish lunch, and the *Rose Garden*. The *Twins Bar* by the ferry dock is a friendly spot for a drink. After the high-season madness of Nydhrí, Meganíssi's unspoilt landscape is a tonic, and it's easy to organize a **day-trip** from Nydhrí, getting off at Spiliá, walking via Spartohóri to Katoméri for lunch at the *Meganissi* or down at Vathý, from where you can catch the ferry back. Paths lead from Katoméri to remote beaches, including popular **Ambelákia**, but these aren't realistic on a day-trip.

Kefalloniá

KEFALLONIÁ is the largest of the Ionian islands – a place that has real towns as well as resorts. Like its neighbours, Kefalloniá was overrun by Italians and Germans in World War II; the "handover" after Italy's capitulation in 1943 led to the massacre of over five thousand Italian troops on the island by invading German forces, as chronicled by Louis de Bernières in his novel, *Captain Corelli's Mandolin*.

Until the late 1980s, the island paid scant regard to tourism; perhaps this was partly due to a feeling that Kefalloniá could not easily be marketed. Virtually all of its towns and villages were levelled in the 1953 earthquake, and these masterpieces of Venetian architecture had been the one touch of elegance in a severe, mountainous landscape. A more likely explanation, however, for the island's late emergence on the Greek tourist scene is the Kefallonians' legendary reputation for insular pride and stubbornness, plus a good measure of eccentricity.

There are definite attractions here, with some **beaches** as good as any in the Ionian islands, and a fine (if pricey) local wine, the dry white Robola. Mercifully, the anticipated "Corelli factor" did not lead to the island becoming either oversubscribed or over-expensive, despite some predictable theming. Moreover, the island seems able to soak up a lot of people without feeling at all crowded, and the magnificent scenery speaks for itself, the escarpments culminating in the 1632-metre bulk of **Mount Énos**, a national park.

For **airport** arrival see the Argostóli section on p.549. Kefalloniá's **bus** system is basic but reliable, and with a little legwork it can be used to get you almost anywhere on the island. Key routes connect Argostóli with the main tourist centres of **Sámi**, **Fiskárdho**, **Skála** and **Póros**. There's a useful connection

KEFALLONIÁ AND ITHÁKI

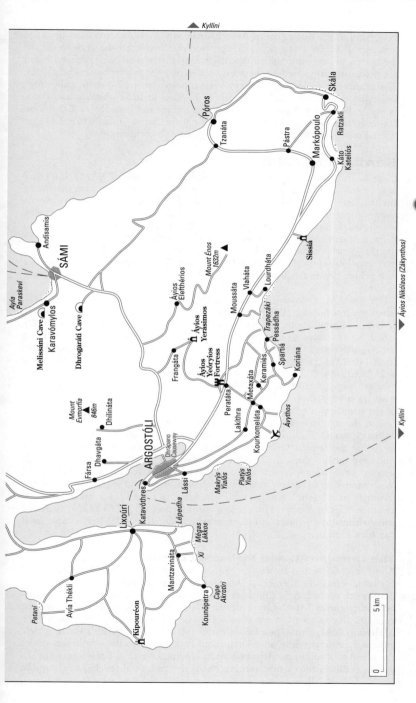

Áyios Nikólaos (Zákynthos)

Kyllíni

7

from Sámi to the tiny resort of **Ayía Efimía**, which also attracts many package travellers. If you're using a motorbike, take care: roads can be very rough off the beaten track – although all the major routes have now been surfaced – and the gradients can sometimes be a bit challenging for underpowered machines. The island has a plethora of **ferry** connections (see p.574) principally from Fiskárdho to Lefkádha and Itháki, and from Sámi to Itháki, Astakós and Pátra, as well as links from Argostóli and Póros to Kyllíni and Pessádha to Zákynthos. Direct sailings between Sámi and one of the Italian ports – usually Brindisi – are offered most years in peak season only, by just one company.

Sámi and around

Most boats dock at the large and functional port town of **SÁMI**, built and later rebuilt near the south end of the Itháki straits, more or less on the site of ancient Sami. This was the capital of the island in Homeric times, when Kefalloniá was part of Ithaca's maritime kingdom: today the administrative hierarchy is reversed, Itháki being considered the backwater. With the only ferry link to Pátra, frequent connections to Itháki and direct (albeit erratic) links to Italy, the town is clearly preparing itself for a burgeoning future. The long sandy beach that stretches round the bay is quite adequate; 2km beyond ancient Sami lies a fine pebble beach, **Andísamis**, with the lively *Andissa Club* providing refreshments.

The town has three big **hotels**: the friendly *Athina Beach* (☎26740 23067, ⓦwww.athinahotel.gr; ❾), is the better of the two at the far end of the beach, actually in Karavómylos, while the *Pericles* (☎26740 22780, ⓕ26740 22787; ❹), which has extensive grounds, two pools and sports facilities, lies over 1km along the Argostóli road. The best mid-range bet is the comfortable seafront *Kastro* (☎26740 22282, ⓦwww.kastrohotel.com; ❹), followed by the *Melissani* (☎ & ⓕ26740 22464; ❹), up behind the main dock. Sámi's **campsite**, *Camping Karavomilos Beach* (☎26740 22480, ⓔvalettas@hol.gr), has over 300 well-shaded spaces, a taverna, shop and bar, and opens onto the beach – it is by far the better of the island's two official sites.

Sámi doesn't have a great many **tavernas** beyond those on the seafront; *Mermaid* and *O Faros*, both with a decent selection of veg and meat dishes, including the famous local meat pie, are the best of the central bunch. Better still, head further along the beach to the *Akroyiali*, where you can sample fresh seafood, or *To Karnayio*, great for succulent home-cooked meat dishes and good local wine. The inevitably renamed *Captain Corelli's* and *Aqua Marina* are the favourite **bars** in the evenings, while the best place for a snack breakfast or ice cream is *Captain Jimmy's*. The seafront Sami Center (☎26740 22254) rents out **motorbikes** at fair rates and Gerolimatos (☎26740 23405) is a reliable local **car hire** company.

The Dhrogaráti and Melissáni caves

Another good reason to stay in Sámi is its proximity to the Drogharáti and Melissáni caves; the former is 5km out of town towards Argostóli, the latter 3km north towards Ayía Efimía. A very impressive stalagmite-bedecked chamber, **Dhrogaráti** (April–Oct daily 9am–8pm; €3.50) is occasionally used for concerts thanks to its marvellous acoustics – Maria Callas once sang here. **Melissáni** (daily 8am–7pm; €5) is partly submerged in brackish water, which, amazingly, emerges from an underground fault that leads the whole way under the island to a point near Argostóli. At that point, known as Katavóthres, the sea gushes endlessly into a subterranean channel – and, until the 1953 earthquake

△ Melissáni cave, Kefalloniá

disrupted it – the current was used to drive sea mills. That the water, now as then, still ends up in the cave has been shown with fluorescent tracer dye. The beautiful textures and shades created by the light pouring through the collapsed roof of the cave make it a must.

Ayía Efimía

AYÍA EFIMÍA, 9km north of Sámi, is a friendly little fishing harbour popular with package operators, yet with no major developments. Its two drawbacks are its beaches, or lack thereof– the largest, risibly named Paradise beach, is a pathetic 20m of shingle, although there are other coves to the south – and its poor transport connections (only two daily buses to Sámi and Fiskárdho). **Accommodation** here is good at two small, smart **hotels**: *Boulevard Pyllaros* (☎26740 61800, ℱ26740 61801; ⊙) and the better-value *Moustakis* (☎26740 61030, ⓦwww.moustakishotel.com; ❸); and there are also apartments offered by Yerasimos Raftopoulos (☎26740 61233, ℱ26740 61216; ❷). The *Paradise Beach* **taverna**, furthest round the headland past the harbour, is the place for moderately priced island cuisine; the *Pergola* and *To Steki Tou Kalofaga* also both offer a wide range of island specialities and standard Greek dishes. Predictably, the café-bar where the film crew and actors used to hang out has been renamed *Captain Corelli's*, while the *Strawberry zaharoplastío* is the place for a filling breakfast. The town's nightclub is *Paranoia*, 700m out of town towards Fiskárdho. If you are making your own way between here and Sámi, the ⚒ *Ayía Paraskeví* taverna, at the tiny cove of the same name, is famous for its delicious spaghetti with mussel marinade and boasts a great setting.

Southeast Kefalloniá

Travel **southeast from Sámi** has been made a lot easier by the completion of the asphalt road to **Póros** and the consequent addition of a twice-daily bus route between the two. Continuing south, Póros is connected to **Skála** by another paved coastal road.

Póros

PÓROS was one of the island's earliest developed resorts, and definitely gives the impression of having seen better days. The town's small huddle of hotels and apartment blocks is almost unique on Kefalloniá, and not enhanced by a scruffy seafront and thin, pebbly beach.

Póros does, however, have a regular ferry link to **Kyllíni** on the Peloponnesian mainland, a viable alternative to the Sámi–Pátra route. Póros is actually made up of two bays: the first, where most tourists are based, and the actual harbour, a few minutes over the headland. There are plenty of rooms, apartments and a few **hotels**. The best deal is at the cosy *Santa Irina* (T 26740 72017, @ maki@otenet. gr; B&B; ❷), by the crossroads inland, whose low rate includes breakfast, while the nearby *Odysseus Palace* (T 26740 72036, W www.odysseuspalace.com; ❺) often gives good discounts. Among **travel agents**, Poros Travel by the ferry dock (T 26740 72476, F 26740 72069) offers a range of accommodation, as well as services such as car rental and ferry bookings. The main seafront has the majority of the **restaurants** and **bars**. The *Fotis Family* taverna serves good food in a pleasant setting and the *Mythos* bar has Internet access.

The aforementioned road twists 12km around the rocky coastline from Póros to Skála at the southern extremity of the island. It's a lovely, isolated route, with scarcely a building on the way, save for a small chapel, 3km short of Skála, next to the ruins of a **Roman temple**.

Skála

In total contrast to Póros, the resort of **SKÁLA** is a low-rise development set among handsome pines above a few kilometres of good sandy beach. A **Roman villa** (daily 10am–2pm & 5am–8pm, longer hours in summer; free) and some mosaics were excavated here in the 1950s, near the site of the *Golden Beach Palace* rooms, and are open to the public.

A faithful return crowd keeps Skála busy until well after Póros has closed for the season, and **accommodation** can be hard to find. There are studios and apartments at *Dionysus Rooms* (T 26710 83283; ❷), a block south of the main street, or a range is available through Etam Travel Service (T 26710 83101, @ etam-kef@otenet.gr; ❷). Of hotels, the cosy *Captain's Hotel* (T 26710 83389, W www.captainshouse.net; ❸), on the road parallel to the main street to the east, is comfortable and friendly, while he more upmarket *Tara Beach Hotel* (T 26710 83250, W www.tarabeach.gr; ❺) has rooms and individual bungalows in lush gardens on the edge of the beach. Skála boasts a number of **tavernas**: *Ta Pytharia* and the *Flamingo* are both good spots with a standard range of Greek and continental cuisine, while, on the beach, *Paspalis* serves fish and home-cooking and *Sunrise* offers pizza as well as Greek food. Drinkers head for *The Loft* cocktail **bar** and the beachside *Stavento* restaurant-bar, which plays the coolest sounds.

Skála to Lourdháta

Some of the finest sandy beaches on the island are just beyond Skála below the village of Ratzaklí, and around the growing micro-resort of **KÁTO KATELIÓS**, which already has a couple of hotels: the smart *Odyssia* (T 26710 81615, F 26710 81614; ❹) and the mostly German-occupied *Galini Resort* (T 26710 81582, W www.galini.de; ❹), which has good deals on **apartments** for four. There are also some rooms and apartments available through the *Light-house* taverna (T 26710 81355; ❸) or the local branch of CBR Travel (T 26710 22770, W www.cbr-rentacar.com; ❸). Of the half a dozen restaurants and cafés at the seafront, the *Blue Sea* taverna is renowned for the freshness and quality of its fish, the *Arbouro* offers a wide selection of dishes, while the *Cozy* bar is the prime drinking location. The coast around Káto Kateliós is also Kefalloniá's key breeding ground for the loggerhead **turtle** (see box, p.563). Camping on the nearby beaches is therefore discouraged.

The inland village of **MARKÓPOULO**, claimed by some to be the birthplace of homophonous explorer Marco Polo, witnesses a bizarre snake-handling ritual every year on August 15, the **Assumption of the Virgin festival**. The church where this ritual is enacted stands on the site of an old convent. The story goes that when the convent was attacked by pirates, the nuns prayed to be transformed into snakes to avoid being taken prisoner. Their prayers were supposedly answered, and each year the "return" of a swarm of small, harmless snakes is meant to bring the villagers good luck. As Mother Nature is unlikely to keep to such a schedule, some discreet snake-breeding on the part of the village priests must be suspected.

The coastline is largely inaccessible until the village of **VLAHÁTA**, which has some rooms and restaurants, but there's little point in staying up here, when you can turn 2km down to **LOURDHÁTA**, which has a kilometre-long shingle beach, mixed with imported sand. *Adonis* (℡26710 31206; ❸) and *Ramona* (℡26710 31032; ❸) have **rooms** just outside the village on the approach road, while the smart new *Thomatos Apartments* (℡26710 31656, ✉critithomas@yahoo .com; ❹), behind the beach, comprise fully equipped kitchen-studios. Of the smattering of **tavernas**, the *Diamond*, on the tiny plane-shaded village square, does a good range of vegetarian items. Further up the hill is the smarter *Spiros* steak-and-grill house and, closer to Vlaháta, *Dionysus*, serving taverna standards; at the beach itself *Klimitis* is good for inexpensive fish. The beachside *Astrabar* is friendly and plays a good mix of English and Greek music into the wee hours. Another fine beach, reached by a turning from Moussáta, west of Vlaháta, is **Trapezáki**, an attractive strand with just one restaurant by the small jetty.

Argostóli and around

ARGOSTÓLI, Kefalloniá's capital, is a large and thriving town – virtually a city – with a marvellous site on a bay within a bay. The stone bridge, connecting the two sides of the inner bay, was initially constructed by the British in 1813. The bridge, known as Dhrépano owing to its sickle shape, was closed to traffic indefinitely in 2005, making it a much more pleasant walk than previously. The town was totally rebuilt after the 1953 earthquake, but has an enjoyable atmosphere that remains defiantly Greek, especially during the evening *vólta* around **Platía Valiánou** (formerly Platía Metaxá) – the nerve centre of town – and along the pedestrianized Lithóstrotou, which runs parallel to the seafront.

Arrival and information

Argostóli's modern **Kefaloniá airport** lies 7km south of town. There are no airport buses, and suburban bus services are so infrequent or remote from the terminal that a taxi (at an inflated flat rate of around €10) is the only dependable connection. Those arriving in Argostóli by bus from Sámi or elsewhere will wind up at the KTEL **bus station**, a minute from the Dhrépano causeway and ten minutes' walk south of the main square, Platía Valianoú. Argostóli's friendly **tourist office** (Mon–Fri 7.30am–2.30pm; ℡26710 22248, ℻26710 24466), on Andoníou Trítsi at the north end of the seafront, next to the port authority, has information about rooms, piles of brochures and trail guides, and can advise on transport, sites and all resorts around the island. The island-wide Sunbird agency

(☎26710 23723, ⓦwww.sunbird.gr) is a reliable outlet for car or motorbike rental. Excelixis (Mon–Sat 9am–2.30pm & 6–10pm; €4 per hour) at Minoös 3, behind the church on Lithóstrotou, has Internet facilities.

Accommodation

Hotels in Argostóli open all year and are mostly mid-range, the best value of these being the ✈ *Ionian Plaza* (☎26710 25581, ⓦwww.ionianplaza.gr; ❺), right on the square. A good option in the opposite corner of the square is the *Mirabel* (☎26710 23454, ⓦwww.mirabel.gr; ❹); one of the best deals going, if you don't mind sharing a bathroom, is the friendly *Chara* (☎26710 22427; ❶), set in a lovely shady courtyard at the corner of Y. Vergóti and Dhevossétou near Dhrépano bridge. The newly upgraded *pension* attached to the *Tsima Cavo* cafeteria (☎26710 23941; ❸), opposite the Lixoúri ferry ramp, is good value, with TV in all the air-conditioned rooms. In a working town with a large permanent population, **private rooms** aren't too plentiful, but you can call the Room-Owners Association (☎26710 29109) to see what's on offer. A number of travel agencies also offer rooms, apartments and villas: try Ainos Travel (☎26710 22333, ⓦwww.ainostravel.gr; from ❷), opposite the Archeological Museum, or Myrtos at A. Trítsi 117 (☎26710 25895, Ⓔmyrtostr@hol.gr; from ❸). The town's **campsite**, *Argostóli Camping* (☎26710 23487), lies 2km north of the centre, just beyond the Katovóthres sea mills; there's only an infrequent bus service in high season, so you'll probably have to walk and it's rather basic with limited shade.

The town

The **Korgialenio History and Folklore Museum** (Mon–Sat 9am–2pm; €3), on Ilía Zervoú behind the Municipal Theatre, has a rich collection of local religious and cultural artefacts, including photographs taken before and after the earthquake. Insight into how the island's nobility used to live can be gained from a visit to the **Focas-Cosmetatos Foundation** (Mon–Sat 9.20am–1pm, plus summer 7–10pm; €3), on Valiánou opposite the provincial government building. It contains elegant furniture and a collection of lithographs and paintings, including works by nineteenth-century British artists Joseph Cartwright and Edward Lear. The refurbished **Archeological Museum** (Tues–Sun 8.30am–3pm; €3), on nearby R. Vergóti, has a sizeable collection of pottery, jewellery, funerary relics and statuary from prehistoric, through Mycenaean to late Classical times. It is well laid out and labelled, rivalling Kérkyra Town's (see p.517) as the best such museum in the Ionians. Island-inspired works by Peter Hemming, a resident British artist, are on display (and for sale) at **The Gallery** (Mon–Sat 10am–2pm & daily 6.30-10pm; free), behind the playground a few blocks north of the square.

Eating, drinking and nightlife

The *Tzivras estiatório* (only open until 5pm), opposite the seafront fruit market on Vandhórou, is one of the best places to try Kefallonian cuisine; the upmarket *Captain's Table* **taverna** just off the main square is worth a splurge for its live *kantádhes*, though they are just about as easily heard from the far more reasonable *Arhontiko* next door. Of the seafront eateries, the friendly ✈ *Kiani Akti*, perfectly located beyond the Lixoúri ferry, has a great, high-quality selection of seafood and *mezédhes*, which can be enjoyed from the wooden deck that juts out above the water. For a change of diet, try *Kohenoor*, 50m towards the front from the square, which dishes up good, authentic Indian food.

Local posers hang out at the café-bars lining the square, while more discerning drinkers head for *Pub Old House*, a relaxed hangout next to The Gallery, or the more modern *Bodega* en route to it. *Bass*, by the museum, is the town's big late-night indoor club. The quayside bars, particularly the *Aristofanis kafenío* by the Dhrépano bridge, are quiet, cheap and have the best views.

South of Argostóli: beaches and Áyios Yeóryios

Many package travellers will find themselves staying in **LÁSSI**, a short bus ride or twenty-minute walk from town. Lássi sprawls unattractively along a busy main road and it cannot be recommended to the independent traveller. At least it has a couple of good sandy beaches, namely **Makrýs Yialós** and **Platýs Yialós**, although they're right under the airport flight path. Further on, **beaches** such as **Ávythos** are well worth seeking out, although if you're walking beyond **Kourkomeláta** there is a real, if occasional, risk of being attacked by farm dogs, particularly during the hunting season (Sept 25–Feb 28). There is very little accommodation in the region, and precious few shops or bars. **Pessádha** has a twice-daily ferry link with Zákynthos in summer, but little else, and be warned that the pathetic bus service from Argostóli is no good for connecting with the boats. You'll have to hitch or take an expensive taxi in most cases.

With a scooter, the best inland excursion is to **ÁYIOS YEÓRYIOS**, the medieval Venetian capital of the island. The old town here supported a population of 15,000 until its destruction by an earthquake in the seventeenth century: substantial ruins of its **castle** (summer Tues–Fri 8.30am–7pm, Sat & Sun 8.30am–3pm; rest of year Tues–Sun 8.30am–3pm; free), now reopened after extensive renovations, churches and houses can be visited on the hill above the modern village of Peratáta. Byron lived for a few months in the nearby village of Metaxáta and was impressed by the view from the summit in 1823; sadly, as at Mesolóngi, the house where he stayed no longer exists. The *Astraia* **café-bar** provides refreshments and great views from near the castle gates. Two kilometres south of Áyios Yeóryios is a fine collection of religious icons and frescoes kept in a restored church that was part of the nunnery of Áyios Andhréas.

Mount Énos

At 15km from a point halfway along the Argostóli–Sámi road, **Mount Énos** isn't really a walking option, but roads nearly reach the official 1632-metre summit. The mountain has been declared a national park, to protect the *Abies cephalonica* firs (named after the island), which clothe the slopes. There are absolutely no facilities on or up to the mountain, but the views from the highest point in the Ionian islands out over its neighbours and the mainland are wonderful. In low season, watch the weather, which can deteriorate with terrifying speed. Not far before the mountain turning, taking a detour towards Frangáta is doubly rewarded by the huge and lively **Áyios Yerásimos monastery** (daily 8am–1pm & 3–7pm), which hosts two of the island's most important festivals (Aug 15 and Oct 20); the most interesting feature is the double cave beneath the back of the sanctuary, where the saint meditated for lengthy periods. Right behind the monastery, the **Robola winery** (April–Oct daily 7am–8.30pm; Nov–March Mon–Fri 7am–3pm), which offers a free self-guided tour and generous wine-tasting.

Lixoúri and its peninsula

Half-hourly ferries (hourly in winter) ply between the capital and **LIXOÚRI** throughout the day until after midnight. The town was flattened by earthquakes, and hasn't risen much above two storeys since. It's a little drab, but has good restaurants, quiet hotels and is favoured by those who want to explore the eerie quake-scapes left in the south and the barren north of the peninsula. **Hotels** are not especially plentiful or cheap, but two comfortable air-conditioned options are the *La Cité* (℡26710 92701, 📠26710 92702; ❹), four blocks back from the front, and a beach hotel just south of town, *Summery* (℡26710 91771, 🌐www .hotelsummery.gr; ❺). Two agencies offer cheaper accommodation (from ❷) in town: A. D. Travel (℡26710 93142, 🌐www.adtravel.gr) on the main road through town, and Perdikis Travel (℡ & 📠26710 92503) on the quay. Among the tavernas, *Akrogiali* on the seafront is excellent and cheap, drawing admirers from all over the island. *Iy Avli*, on the block behind, serves a variety of dishes in a leafy garden, while *Adonis* is a good basic *psistariá* at the back of the square. *Overdose* is the trendy place to drink on the square, while the old seafront *kafenía* have also been replaced by youth-orientated cafés such as *LA Dreams*.

Lixoúri's nearest beach is **Lépedha**, a two-kilometre walk south. Like the **Xí** and **Mégas Lákkos** beaches (served by bus from Lixoúri and both with restaurants and accommodation), it has rich-red sand and is backed by low cliffs. Those with transport can also strike out for the monastery at **Kipouréon**, and north to the spectacular beach at **Petaní**. Here there are two restaurants, the better being the further of the two, *Xougras*, whose friendly Greek-American owner Dina directs those wishing to stay in these relaxing surroundings up the hill to the *Niforo* apartments (℡26710 97350), pending completion of her own rooms.

The west coast and the road north

The journey between Argostóli and Fiskárdho is the most spectacular ride in the archipelago. Leaving town, the road rises into the Evmorfía foothills, where you can detour a short way inland to visit the modest **Museum of Natural History** (daily 9am–1pm, Mon–Sat 6–8pm; €1.50) at **Dhavgáta**. Continuing to rise beyond Agónas, the coast road clings to near-sheer cliffs as it heads for Dhivaráta, which has a smattering of rooms, such as *Mina Studios* (℡26740 61716, 📧markela1@hol.gr; ❸), a couple of restaurants, and is the stop for **Mýrtos** beach. It's a four-kilometre hike down the motorable road, with just one snack-bar on the beach, but from above or below this is the most dramatic beach in the Ionian islands – a splendid strip of pure-white sand and pebbles. Sadly, it's shadeless and gets mighty crowded in high season.

Six kilometres on is the turning for the atmospheric village of **ÁSSOS**, clinging to a small isthmus between the island and a huge hill crowned by a ruined fort. Accommodation is scarce – villagers invariably send you to the chic 🎋 Andhreas Rokos' rooms (℡26740 51523; ❷) on the approach road, which are extremely welcoming and great value, or you can opt for the posher *Kanakis Apartments* opposite (℡26740 51631, 📠26740 51660; ❹). Ássos has a small pebble beach, and three tavernas, notably the *Nefeli* and the *Platanos Grill*, on a plane-shaded village square backed by mansions, mostly now restored after being ruined in the quake. It can get a little claustrophobic, but there's nowhere else quite like it in the Ionians.

Fiskárdho

FISKÁRDHO, on the northernmost tip of the island, sits on a bed of limestone that buffered it against the worst of the quakes. Two **lighthouses**, Venetian and Victorian, guard the bay, and the ruins on the headland are believed to be from a twelfth-century chapel begun by Norman invader Robert Guiscard, who gave the place its name. The nineteenth-century harbour frontage is intact, nowadays occupied by smart restaurants and chic boutiques. There is a new **Environmental and Nautical Museum** (summer daily 10am–7pm;

donations), housed in a renovated Neoclassical mansion on the hill behind the village. The volunteers who curate it conduct valuable ecological research and can also arrange **scuba diving** (☏26740 41182, ⓦwww.fnec.gr).

The island's premier resort, Fiskárdho remains busy through to the end of October, with **accommodation** at a premium. The cheapest rooms are those of Sotiria Tselenti (☏26740 41204, ⓦwww.fiskardo-ellis.gr; ❸), arranged through the bakery 50m back from the tiny square, and *Regina's* (☏ & ⓕ26740 41125; ❸), which has its own café at the back of the village, next to the car park. A splendid if pricey option is the beautifully converted mansion *Archontiko* (☏ & ⓕ26740 41342; ❻), above and behind a harbourfront mini-market. Pama Travel (☏26740 41033, ⓦwww.pamatravel.com; from ❸), on the seafront furthest away from the ferry quay, is another source of rooms and costlier apartments. There's a wealth of good but mostly expensive **restaurants**. Two to try on the seafront are the *Tassia,* which has a vast range of seafood (but check how much fish you are actually ordering), and the *Captain's Table,* serving succulent Greek and Kefallonian fare. On the square, *Alexis* serves pizzas and pastas, while *Lagonderia,* just round the corner, specializes in tasty oven food. *Irida's* and *Theodora's* are two of the most popular harbourside **bars**. The dance spot is *Kastro Club* up at the back of the village. There are two good pebble beaches – **Émblisi** 1km back out of town and **Fókis** just to the south – and a nature trail on the northern headland. Daily **ferries** connect Fiskárdho to Itháki and Lefkádha in season.

Itháki

Rugged **Itháki**, Odysseus's legendary homeland, has yielded no substantial archeological discoveries, but it fits Homer's description to perfection: "There are no tracks, nor grasslands . . . it is a rocky severe island, unsuited for horses, but not so wretched, despite its small size. It is good for goats." In Constantine Cavafy's splendid poem *Ithaca,* the island is symbolized as a journey to life:

When you set out on the voyage to Ithaca
Pray that your journey may be long
Full of adventures, full of knowledge.

Despite the romance of its name, and its proximity to Kefalloniá, very little tourist development has arrived to spoil the place. This is doubtless accounted for in part by a dearth of beaches, though the island is good walking country, with a handful of small fishing ports and inland villages. In the north, apart from the ubiquitous drone of scooters, the most common sounds are sheep bells jangling and cocks (a symbol of Odysseus) crowing.

Itháki's beaches are admittedly minor and mainly pebbly with sandy seabeds, but relatively clean and safe; the real attractions are the interior and sites from the **Odyssey**. Some package travellers will find themselves flying into Kefal-loniá and being bused to Fiskárdho (sit on the left for the bus ride of your life), for a short ferry crossing to **Fríkes** or the premier resort **Kióni**. Most visitors, however, will arrive at **Vathý**, the capital.

Vathý

Ferries from Pátra, Astakós and a minority of those from Kefalloniá land at the main port and capital of **VATHÝ**, a bay within a bay so deep that few realize the mountains out "at sea" are actually the north of the island. This snug town is compact, relatively traffic-free and boasts the most idyllic seafront setting of all the Ionian capitals. Like its southerly neighbours, it was heavily damaged by the 1953 earthquake, but some fine examples of pre-quake architecture remain here and in the northern port of **Kióni**. Vathý has a small **archeological museum** on Kalliníkou (Tues–Sun 8.30am–3pm; free), a short block back from the quay. Near the corner of the quay behind the Agricultural Bank, there is also the moderately interesting **Folklore & Cultural Museum** (summer Tues–Sat 10am–2pm & 5–9pm; €1). There are banks, a post office, police and a medical centre in town.

Vathý now has four **hotels**, the oldest of which is the refurbished and air-conditioned *Mentor* (☎26740 32433, ⊛www.hotelmentor.gr; ❻) in the south-east corner of the harbour. Further on round the bay are the posh *Omirikon* (☎26740 33598, ℱ26740 33596; ❼), and, just beyond it, the much better-value 🍴 *Captain Yiannis* (☎26740 33419, ℱ26740 32849; ❸), complete with tennis court and pool. The small *Odyssey* (☎26740 32268, ℱ26740 32668; ❸) is perched on the hillside a short way up the road to Skínos beach. Room owners rarely meet boats so the best source of rooms, studios or villas is the town's two main quay-side travel agents, Polyctor Tours (☎26740 33120, ✉polyctor@ithakiholidays .gr) and Delas Tours (☎26740 32104, ✉delas@otenet.gr).

Even though it's tiny, Vathý has a wealth of **tavernas** and **bars**. Many locals head off south around the bay towards the friendly, family-run 🍴 *Paliocaravo* (aka *Gregory's*), popular for its lamb and fish and best of the three fine eateries in that direction. In town, the excellent *O Nikos*, just off the square, fills early, while *To Kohili* is by far the best of the half-dozen harbourside tavernas. The *Sirenes Ithaki Yacht Club* is upmarket with a nautical theme but, as usual, the town's ancient *kafenío* one street back from the front is the spot for a quiet and inexpensive tipple with the locals.

There are two reasonable pebble **beaches** within fifteen minutes' walk of Vathý: **Dhéxa**, over the hill above the ferry quay, and tiny **Loútsa**, opposite it around the bay. Better beaches at **Sarakíniko** and **Skínos** are an hour's trek along recently improved roads leaving the opposite side of the bay. In season, daily *kaïkia* ply between the quay and remote coves.

Odysseus sights

Three of the main **Odysseus** sights are just within walking distance of Vathý: the Arethoússa Spring, the Cave of the Nymphs and ancient Alalkomenae, although the last is best approached by **moped** or **taxi** (no more than €15 round-trip).

The Arethoússa Spring

The walk to the **Arethoússa Spring** – allegedly the place where Eumaeus, Odysseus's faithful swineherd, brought his pigs to drink – is a three-hour round trip along a track signposted next to the seafront telecoms office. The unspoilt but shadeless landscape and sea views are magnificent, but the walk crosses slippery inclines and might best be avoided if you're nervous of heights.

Near the top of the lane leading to the spring path, a signpost points up to what is said to have been the **Cave of Eumaeus**. The route to the spring continues for a few hundred metres, and then branches off onto a narrow footpath through gorse-covered steep cliffs. Parts of the final downhill track involve scrambling across rock fields (follow the splashes of green paint), and care should be taken around the small but vertiginous ravine that houses the

spring. The ravine sits below a crag known as **Kórax** (the raven), which matches Homer's description of the meeting between Odysseus and Eumaeus. In summer it's just a dribble of water. You have to return by the same route but you might have time to swim in a small cove a short scramble down from the spring.

The Cave of the Nymphs

The **Cave of the Nymphs** (Marmarospíli) is about 2.5km up a rough but navigable road signposted on the brow of the hill above Dhéxa beach. The cave is atmospheric, but it's underwhelming compared to the caverns of neighbouring Kefalloniá and, these days, is illuminated by coloured lights. The claim that this is the *Odyssey's* Cave of the Nymphs, where the returning Odysseus concealed the gifts given to him by King Alkinous, is enhanced by the proximity of Dhéxa beach, although there is some evidence that the "true" cave was just above the beach, and was unwittingly demolished during quarrying many years ago.

Alalkomenae and Pisaetós

Alalkomenae, Heinrich Schliemann's much-vaunted "Castle of Odysseus", is signposted on the Vathý–Pisaetós road, on the saddle between Dhéxa and Pisaetós, with views over both sides of the island. The actual site, however, some 300m uphill, is little more than foundations spread about in the gorse. Schliemann's excavations unearthed a Mycenaean burial chamber and domestic items such as vases, figurines and utensils (displayed in the archeological museum), but the ruins actually date from three centuries after Homer. In fact, the most likely contender for the site of Odysseus's castle is above the village of Stavrós (see below).

The road (though not buses) continues to the harbour of **Pisaetós**, about 2km below, with a large pebble beach that's good for swimming and popular with local rod-and-line fishermen. There is just one *kantína* here, serving those awaiting the regular ferries from Sámi on Kefalloniá.

Northern Itháki

The main road out of Vathý continues across the isthmus and takes a spectacular route to the northern half of Itháki, serving the villages of **Léfki**, **Stavrós**, **Fríkes** and **Kióni**. There is usually one daily **bus**, which is timed to take kids to school from the north to the capital at 7am, returning at 2pm; out of term the schedule is much more fluid. The north of Itháki is, however, excellent scooter country; the close proximity of the settlements, small coves and Homeric interest also make it good rambling terrain. Once a day a *kaïki* also visits the last two of those communities – a cheap and scenic ride used by locals and tourists alike to meet the mainline ferries in Vathý. As with the rest of Itháki there is only a limited amount of accommodation.

Stavrós and around

STAVRÓS, the second-largest town on the island, is a steep two kilometres above the nearest beach (Pólis Bay). It's a pleasant enough town nonetheless, with *kafenía* edging a small square dominated by a rather fierce statue of Odysseus. There is even a tiny **museum** (Tues–Sun 8.30am–3pm; free) off the road to Platrithriés, displaying local archeological finds. Stavrós's Homeric site is on the side of **Pelikáta Hill**, where remains of roads, walls and other structures have been suggested as the possible site of Odysseus's castle. Stavrós is useful as a base if both Fríkes and Kióni are full up, and is an obvious stopping-off point for exploring the northern hamlets and the road up to the medieval village of Anoyí (see below). Both Polyctor and Delas handle **accommodation** in Stavrós; the traditional *Petra* taverna (℡26740 31596; ❸) offers rooms, or there's the *Porto Thiaki pension* (℡26740 31245, ℻26740 31638; ❸) above the pizzeria. The oldest and best **taverna** is *Fatouros*, and the *Margarita zaharoplastío* is a good place for a drink or to sample the local sweet *rovaní* (syrupy rice cakes).

A scenic mountain road leads 5km southeast from Stavrós to **ANOYÍ**, which translates roughly as "upper ground". Once the second-most important settlement on the island, it is almost deserted today. The centre of the village is dominated by a free-standing Venetian campanile, built to serve the (usually locked) church of the **Panayía**, which comes alive for the annual *paniyíri* on August 14, the eve of the Virgin's Assumption; at other times enquire at the *kafenío* about access to the church, the Byzantine frescoes of which have been heavily restored following centuries of earthquake damage. On the outskirts of the village are the foundations of a ruined **medieval prison**, and in the surrounding countryside are some extremely strange rock formations, the biggest being the eight-metre-high Iraklis (Hercules) rock, just east of the village. The **monastery of Katharón**, 3km further south along the road, has stunning views down over Vathý and the south of the island, and houses an icon of the *Panayía* discovered by peasants clearing scrubland in the area. The monastery celebrates its festival on September 8 with services, processions and music.

Two roads push north of Stavrós: one, to the right, heads 2km down to Fríkes, while the main road, to the left, loops below the hill village of **Exoyí**, and on to **Platrithiés**, where the new *Yefiri* taverna serves a wide range of tasty fare. Just off the start of the road up to Exoyí a signpost points about 1km along a rough track to the supposed **School of Homer**, where excavations still in progress have revealed extensive foundations, a well and ancient steps. The site is unfenced and well worth a detour for its views of **Afáles Bay** as much as the remains. On the outskirts of Platrithiés a track leads down to Afáles, the largest bay on the entire island, with an unspoiled and little-visited pebble-and-sand beach. The landscape around here, thickly forested in parts and dotted with vineyards, provides excellent walking.

Fríkes

At first sight, tiny **FRÍKES** doesn't appear to have much going for it. Wedged in a valley between two steep hills, it was only settled in the sixteenth century, and emigration in the nineteenth century almost emptied the place – as few as two hundred people live here today – but the protected harbour is a natural year-round port. Consequently, Fríkes stays open for tourism far later in the season than neighbouring Kióni, and has a better range of tavernas. There are no beaches in the village, but plenty of good, if small, pebble strands a short walk away towards Kióni. When the ferries and their cargoes have departed, Fríkes falls quiet and this is its real charm: a downbeat but cool place to lie low.

Fríkes's one **hotel** is the upmarket *Nostos* (℡26740 31644, ⓦwww.hotelnostos-ithaki.gr; ❺), which has a pool, or you can try the equally comfy *Aristotelis Apartments* (℡26740 31079, ⓦwww.aristotelis-ithaca.gr; ❸). The Gods souvenir shop (℡ & ℻26740 31021; from ❷) can help find **rooms**, though in peak season chances are slim. Fríkes has a quartet of good seafront **tavernas**, all serving a decent mixture of Greek and international cuisine:

the *Symposium*, the *Rementzo*, the *Penelope* and *Ulysses*. Tucked in the corner of the harbour, *Café Bemenis* often springs into life late at night as the north's main meeting place for youngsters.

Kióni

KIÓNI sits at a dead end 5km southeast of Fríkes. On the same geological base as the northern tip of Kefalloniá, it avoided the very worst of the 1953 earthquakes, and so retains some fine examples of pre-twentieth-century architecture. It's an extremely pretty village, wrapped around a tiny harbour, and tourism here is dominated by British blue-chip travel companies and visiting yachts.

The bay has a small **beach**, 1km along its south side, a sand-and-pebble strand below a summer-only snack-bar. Better pebble beaches can be found within walking distance towards Fríkes. While the best **accommodation** has been snaffled by the Brits, some local businesses have rooms and apartments to let, among them *Captain's Apartments* (℡26740 31481, ℻26740 31090; ❹), *Maroudas Apartments* (℡26740 31691, ℻26740 31 753; ❸) and *Kioni Vacations* (℡26740 31668; ❸). A quieter option, just a short walk uphill on the main road in the hamlet of Ráhi, are the rooms and studios run by Captain Theofilos Karatzis and his family (℡26740 31679; ❸), which have panoramic views.

Kióni's **restaurants** are dotted around the picturesque harbour, but compare unfavourably with those in Fríkes; *Oasis* has a wide selection and is the best of the bunch, the *Avra* fish taverna and *Kioni* pizzeria are adequate, while the upmarket *Calypso* taverna has interesting dishes but is overpriced. Village facilities stretch to two well-stocked shops, a post office and a couple of bars and cafés, of which *Spavento* is the place for eclectic sounds.

Zákynthos (Zante)

Zákynthos, southernmost of the six core Ionian islands, is somewhat schizophrenically divided between underdevelopment and indiscriminate commercialization. Much of the island is still green and unspoilt, with only token pockets of tourism, and the main resorts seem to be reaching maximum growth without encroaching too much on the quieter parts.

The island has three distinct zones: the barren, mountainous northwest; the fertile central plain; and the eastern and southern resort-filled coasts. The biggest resort – rivalling the busiest on Corfu – is **Laganás**, on Laganás Bay in the south, a 24-hour party venue that doesn't give up from Easter until the last flight home in October. There are smaller, quieter resorts north and south of the capital, and the southerly Vassilikós peninsula has some of the best countryside and beaches, including exquisite **Yérakas**.

Although half-built apartment blocks and a few factories are spreading into the central plain, this is where the quieter island begins: farms and vineyards, ancient villages and the ruins of Venetian buildings levelled in the 1948 and 1953 earthquakes. The island still produces fine wines, such as the white Popolaro, as well as sugar-shock-inducing *mandoláto* nougat, whose honey-sweetened form is best. Zákynthos is also the birthplace of *kantádhes*, which can be heard in tavernas in Zákynthos Town and elsewhere. It also harbours one of the key breeding sites of the endangered **loggerhead sea turtle** at Laganás Bay. The loggerhead (see box, p.563) is the subject of a continuing dispute between tourism businesses and environmentalists.

Zákynthos town

The town, like the island, is known as both **ZÁKYNTHOS** and Zante. This former "Venice of the East" (*Zante, Fior di Levante*, "Flower of the Levant", in an Italian jingle), rebuilt on the old plan after the 1953 earthquake, has bravely tried to re-create some of its style, though reinforced concrete can only do so much.

Arrival and information

Zákynthos is a working town with limited concessions to tourism, although there are hotels and restaurants aplenty, and it's the only place to stay if you want to see the island by public transport. The **bus** station is one block back from the seafront, about halfway along it. On the front nearby, the **tourist police** have a fairly welcoming office (May–Oct daily 8am–10pm; ☎26950 24482) in the main police station, which can supply basic information and help people find accommodation.

Accommodation

The Room Owners Association (☎26950 49498) can be contacted for accommodation around town and all over the island. Of the central seafront **hotels**, the *Egli*, on Loútzi (☎26950 28317; ❹) is the best bet, tucked in beside the gargantuan eyesore of the *Strada Marina*. There are quieter hotels in the Repára district beyond Platía Solomoú: try either the *Plaza*, Kolokotróni 2 (☎26950 45733, ℱ26950 48909; ❸), or the classy and surprisingly inexpensive ⚲ *Palatino*, Kolokotróni 10 (☎26950 27780, ⓦwww.palatinohotel.gr; ❹), both near the municipal lido. Cheaper options at the back of town include the cosy *Haravyi pension*, Xanthopoúlou 4 (☎26950 23629; ❷), to the south.

The town

The town stretches beyond the length of the wide and busy harbour, its main section bookended by the grand **Platía Solomoú** at the north, and the church of **Áyios Dhionýsios** (daily 7am–1pm & 5–10pm), patron saint of the island, at the south. The church is well worth a visit for the dazzling giltwork and fine modern murals inside, and a new **museum**, which has some fine paintings and icons (daily 9am–1pm & 5–9pm; €2). The vestments of St Dhionysios are kept in the restored church of Áyios Nikólaos tou Mólou on Platía Solomoú. The **square** is named after the island's most famous son, the poet Dhionysios Solomos, the father of modernism in Greek literature, who was responsible for establishing demotic Greek (as opposed to the elitist *katharévousa* form) as a literary idiom. He is also the author of the lyrics to the national anthem, an excerpt from which adorns the statue of Liberty in the square. There's an impressive **museum** (daily 9am–2pm; €3) devoted to the life and work of **Solomos** and other Zakynthian luminaries in nearby Platía Ayíou Márkou. It

---

Boat trips from Zákynthos

At least ten pleasure craft offer **day-trips** around the island from the quay in Zákynthos Town for around €15. All take in sights such as the **Blue Caves** at Cape Skinári, and moor in **To Naváyio (Shipwreck Bay)** and the **Cape Kerí** caves. You might want to shop around for the trip with the most stops, as eight hours bobbing round the coast can become a bore. Check also that the operators actually take you into the caves.

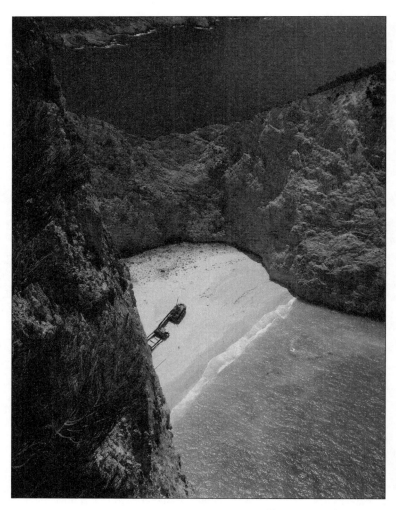

△ Zákynthos's famed Shipwreck Bay

shares its collection with an eponymous museum on Corfu (see p.517), where Solomos spent most of his life. Another local man of letters, who had a museum dedicated to him by the town council in 1998, is novelist and playwright **Grigorios Xenopoulos**. His eponymous **museum** (Mon–Fri 9am–2pm; free), which occupies the small house he inhabited in Gaïta street, not far from Áyios Dhionýsios church, displays a modest collection of manuscripts, books and photographs, as well as the house's original furniture.

Platía Solomoú is home to the town's **library**, which has a small collection of pre- and post-quake photography, and the massive **Byzantine Museum** (Tues–Sun 8am–2.30pm; €3), sometimes referred to as the Zákynthos Museum, most notable for its collection of artworks from the Ionian School, the region's post-Renaissance art movement, spearheaded by Zakynthian painter Panayiotis Doxaras. The movement was given impetus by Cretan refugees, unable to practise their art under Turkish rule. It also houses some secular painting and a fine model of the town before the earthquake.

Zákynthos's other main attraction is its massive **kástro**, brooding over the hamlet of **Bóhali** on its bluff above the town. The ruined Venetian fort (daily 8am–7.30pm in summer, 8am–2pm in winter; €1.50) has vestiges of dungeons, armouries and fortifications, plus stunning views in all directions. Its shady carpet of fallen pine needles makes it a great spot to relax or picnic. Below the *kástro* walls, **Bóhali** has a good though expensive taverna with panoramic views. The ugly new **amphitheatre** on the road up from town sometimes hosts concerts. Further towards the *kástro* the **Maritime Museum** (daily 9am–2pm & 6–9pm; €2.50) contains plenty of naval paraphernalia and presents an interesting chronological history of Hellenic seafaring.

Eating, drinking and nightlife

Most of the **restaurants** and bars on the seafront and Platía Ayíou Márkou are bedevilled by traffic, although the seafront *Psaropoula* does fine meat and fish, and the pricey but elegant *Komis*, across the quay from Áyios Dhionýsios, serves unusual seafood dishes and is far enough away from the bustle. First stop though, should be the friendly ⚡ *Arekia* beyond the lido, which offers a succulent range of dishes and the best nightly *kantádhes* to be heard anywhere. The *Green Boat*, further along, serves up quality fare in a romantic waterside setting. When the bored teens get off their bikes, they go **clubbing** to bars like *Base* on Ayíou Márkou, which plays anything from ethnic to trance, or the *Jazz Café*, on Tertséti which, despite the name, is actually a techno bar with DJs and a token cover charge.

The south and west

The busy southern end of the island comprises the **Vassilikós peninsula**, headed by the package resort of **Argási**, and the large sweep of **Laganás Bay**, whose resort of the same name is a major party destination. At the far southwest end of the bay, the landscape ascends into the mountains around **Kerí**, the first of a series of villages along the sparsely inhabited **west coast**.

Argási

The road heading southeast from Zákynthos passes through **ARGÁSI**, the busiest resort on this coast, but with a beach barely a few feet wide in parts. Although independent travellers would be better off basing themselves at one of the places further down, it could be used as a jumping-off point for the Vassilikós peninsula; there are rooms at the *Pension Vaso* (☎26950 44599; ❸) and *Soula* (☎26950 44864; ❸) just off the main road entering the village, and the seafront boasts some smart hotels, among them the *Locanda* (☎26950 45386, ☏26950 23769; ❹) and the *Iliessa Beach* (☎26950 27800, ☻www.iliessa.com; ❹). Beyond a few indigenous tavernas – try *Three Brothers* or *The Big Plate* restaurant – culture is mainly lowbrow with set-piece "Greek nights", one notable exception being the *Venetsiana*, which accompanies traditional food with nightly *kantádhes*. Argási is also home to some of the island's biggest and most popular discos on the town side, such as *Vivlos* and *Barrage*, and a host of cheap and cheerful bars in the village.

The Vassilikós peninsula

The peninsula that stretches southeast of Argási is one of the most attractive parts of the island, with a happy blend of development and natural beauty.

Various maps vaguely identify different inland spots as **Vassilikós** villages, but the real interest lies in the series of small beach resorts, mainly situated on the east coast. The first two are recently developed **Kamínia**, with the comfortable *Levantino* rooms (℡ 26950 35366, ⓦ www.levantino.gr; ❹), and the more established **Pórto Zóro**, a better strand with the good-value eponymous hotel (℡ 26950 35304, ⓦ www.portozorro.gr; ❸) and restaurant. The only real facilities away from the coast are to be found at the sprawling village of **Áno Vassilikós**, which serves the nearby beaches of **Iónio** and **Banana**. Among accommodation possibilities are the *Vassilikos Apartments* (℡ 26950 35280; ❸), on the main road, and *Angelika* (℡ 26950 35201; ❷), by the church just off it. Among the **tavernas**, on the main road, *O Adherfos tou Kosta* is well worth a try, as is the *Logos Rock Club*. Isolated **Áyios Nikólaos** has a good beach and lures day-trippers from Argási, Kalamáki and Laganás with a **free bus** service in season. Its expanding *Vasilikos Beach* (℡ 26950 35325, ⓦ www .hotelvasilikosbeach.gr; ❺) complex is the focal point of a fast-emerging hamlet with a few restaurants and rooms – the neat white *Christina's* (℡ 26950 39474; ❷) is one of the best deals on the island.

At the very tip of the peninsula is its star: **Yérakas**, a sublime crescent of golden sand. It's also a key loggerhead turtle breeding ground, and is therefore off-limits between dusk and dawn; the excellent open-air **Turtle Information Centre** (ⓦ www.earthseasky.org) provides interesting background on these and other sea creatures. Otherwise, there's little here beyond three tavernas back from the beach – try *To Triodi* – and some pleasant, if remote, cabin accommodation at *Liuba Apartments* (℡ 26950 35372; ❸). The beach does draw crowds, but the 6am bus out of Zákynthos Town should secure you a few hours of Yérakas to yourself. Compared with Yérakas, **Pórto Róma**, back on the east coast, is a disappointment, a small sand-and-pebble bay with a taverna and bar, some rooms on the approach road and occasional hardy campers, although there is a more genuinely Greek flavour to it. The only beach on the west coast of the peninsula really worth visiting, especially in the quieter months, is **Dháfni**; the road to it is now paved and there are a couple of tavernas, such as the fine *Mela Beach*.

Laganás and Kalamáki

The majority of the hundreds of thousands of people who visit Zákynthos each year find themselves in **LAGANÁS**. The nine-kilometre beach in the bay is good, if trampled, and there are entertainments from watersports to ballooning, and even an occasional funfair. Beachfront bars and restaurants stretch for well over a kilometre, the bars and restaurants on the main drag another kilometre inland. Some stay open around the clock; others just play music at deafening volume until dawn. The competing video and music bars can make Laganás at night resemble the set of *Bladerunner*, but that's how its predominantly English visitors like it. If this is your bag, there's no place better; if it isn't, flee. **Accommodation** is mostly block-booked by package companies. There's a basic campsite on the southern edge of town, where there are also quietish private rooms, or you can contact the Union of Room Owners (daily 8.30am–2pm & 5–8pm; ℡ 26950 51590). As for hotels, try the old-fashioned *Byzantio* (℡ 26950 51136; ❸), near the crossroads, *Pension Tasoula* (℡ 26950 51560; ❸), between the beach and the campsite, or the larger *Ionis* (℡ 26950 51141, ⓦ www.hotelionis.com; ❹), on the main drag towards the beach. *Dionysos*, halfway along the main drag, and *Zougras*, just before the river along the Kalamáki road, are among the more authentic **tavernas**, the latter hosting *kantádhes* most nights, and respectable Chinese and Indian food can be had at *Bee Garden* or *Taj Mahal* respectively. Favourite **bars** include *Kamikazi*, *Must*, *Potters Bar* and *Zeros* nightclub.

Neighbouring **KALAMÁKI** has a better beach than Laganás, and is altogether quieter, although it does suffer from some airport noise. There are several sizeable, mostly package-oriented hotels, but the upmarket *Crystal Beach* (T 26950 42788, W www.crystalbeachhotel.info; ⑥) keeps some rooms aside and the islandwide Spring Tours agency (T 26950 43795, W www.springtours.gr; ❸) can also arrange accommodation. The two *Stanis* tavernas have extensive menus of Greek and international dishes, although the beachside version is geared more to lunches and its sibling more to evening meals. Alternatives include the standard *Afrodite* and *Merlis* tavernas or the *Guru* curry house. **Nightlife** centres around bars like the *Rose'n'Crown* and *Down Under* on the Laganás road, and the *Cave Club* or *Byzantio* discos on the hillside above the village, which play the usual mixture of foreign and Greek dance music.

Kerí

The village of **KERÍ** is hidden in a fold above the cliffs at the island's southernmost tip. The village retains a number of pre-quake, Venetian buildings, including the church of the **Panayía Kerioú**; the Virgin is said to have saved the island from marauding pirates by hiding it in a sea mist. A rough path leaving the southern end of the village leads 1km on to the lighthouse, with spectacular

7

THE IONIAN ISLANDS | Zákynthos (Zante)

Loggerhead turtles

The Ionian islands harbour the Mediterranean's main concentration of **loggerhead sea turtles**, a sensitive species which is, unfortunately, under direct threat from the tourist industry. Easily frightened by noise and lights, these creatures lay their eggs at night on sandy coves and are therefore uneasy cohabitants with rough campers and late-night discos. Each year, many turtles fall prey to motorboat injuries, nests are destroyed by bikes and the newly hatched young die, entangled in deckchairs and umbrellas left out at night.

The Greek government has passed laws designed to protect the loggerheads, including restrictions on camping at some beaches, but local economic interests tend to prefer a beach full of bodies to a sea full of turtles. On Laganás, nesting grounds are concentrated around the fourteen-kilometre bay, and Greek marine zoologists are in angry dispute with those involved in the tourist industry. Other important locations include the turtles' nesting ground just west of Skála on Kefalloniá, although numbers have dwindled to half their former strength, and now only about 800 remain. Ultimately, the turtles' best hope for survival may rest in their potential draw as a unique tourist attraction in their own right.

While capitalists and environmentalists are still at, well, loggerheads, the **World Wildlife Fund** has issued guidelines for visitors:

1. Don't use the beaches of Laganás and Yérakas between sunset and sunrise.
2. Don't stick umbrellas in the sand in the marked nesting zones.
3. Take your rubbish away with you – it can obstruct the turtles.
4. Don't use lights near the beach at night – they can disturb the turtles, sometimes with fatal consequences.
5. Don't take any vehicle onto the protected beaches.
6. Don't dig up turtle nests – it's illegal.
7. Don't pick up the hatchlings or carry them to the water, as it's vital to their development that they reach the sea on their own.
8. Don't use speedboats in Laganás Bay – a 9kph speed limit is in force for vessels in the bay.

views of the sea, rock arches and stacks and a taverna. The beach next to **Límni Kérioú** at the southwestern end of Laganás Bay has developed into a laid-back and picturesque resort and is home to the Turtle Beach Diving Centre (℡ 26950 48768, Ⓦ www.diving-center-turtle-beach.com). **Rooms** can be found at the friendly *Pension Limni* (℡ 26950 48716, Ⓦ www.pensionlimni.com; ❸) or through the local Room-Owners Association (℡ & Ⓕ 26950 45105). For **food** there is the *Poseidon* overlooking the bay from the far end and the *Keri* restaurant, which has good daily specials.

Maherádho, Kilíomeno and Kambí

The bus system does not reach the wild western side of the island, but a rental car or sturdy motorbike will get you there. **MAHERÁDHO** boasts impressive pre-earthquake architecture set in beautiful arable uplands, surrounded by olive and fruit groves. The church of **Ayía Mávra** has an impressive free-standing campanile and, inside, a splendid carved iconostasis and icons. The town's major festival – one of the biggest on the island – is the saint's day, which falls on the first Sunday in June. The other notable church in town, that of the Panayía, commands breathtaking views over the central plain.

KILÍOMENO is the best place to see surviving pre-earthquake domestic architecture, in the form of the island's traditional two-storey houses. The town was originally named after its church, **Áyios Nikólaos**, whose impressive campanile, begun over a hundred years ago, still lacks a capped roof. The *Alitzerini* taverna (usually supper only) still occupies a cave-like house that dates from 1630 and dishes up superb traditional food. The road from Kilíomeno passes through the nondescript village of Áyios Léon, from where two turnings lead through fertile land and down a newly-paved loop road to the impressive rocky coast at **Limniónas**, where there is a tiny bay and a taverna.

Further along the main road another turning leads to the tiny clifftop hamlet of **KAMBÍ**, popular with day-trippers, who come to catch the sunset over the sea; there are extraordinary views to be had of the 300-metre-high cliffs and western horizon from Kambí's three clifftop **tavernas**. The best of the three is named after the imposing concrete **cross** above the village, constructed in memory of islanders killed here during the 1940s, either by royalist soldiers or Nazis. The tiny village of **Mariés**, 5km to the north and set in a wooded green valley, has the only other coastal access on this side of Zákynthos, a seven-kilometre track leading down to the rocky inlet of **Stenítis Bay**, where there's a taverna and yacht dock, and another road to the uninspiring **Vrómi Bay**, from where speedboats run trips to Shipwreck Bay (see p.566).

The north

A few kilometres north of the capital the contiguous resorts of **Tsiliví** and **Plános** are the touristic epicentre of this part of the island. Further north they give way to a series of tiny beaches, while picturesque villages punctuate the lush landscape inland. Beyond **Alykés**, as you approach the island's tip at **Cape Skinári**, the coast becomes more rugged, while the mountains inland hide the weaving centre of **Volímes**.

Tsiliví, Plános and around

North and inland from Zákynthos Town, the roads thread their way through luxuriantly fertile farmland, punctuated with tumulus-like hills. **Tsiliví**, 5km north of the capital, is the first beach resort here, and is in effect one with the hamlet of **PLÁNOS** and matches Argási for development. Unfortunately, this part of the coastline suffers from occasional oil pollution, with nothing but the winter storms to clear it. There's a good, basic **campsite**, *Zante Camping* (☎26950 61710), beyond Plános, and, for a prime package-tour location, a surprising variety of accommodation – try the beachside *Anetis Hotel* (☎26950 44590, ⓕ26950 28758; ❸), which has air conditioning and TV in all rooms; *Gregory's* rooms (☎26950 61853; ❷); or contact Tsilivi Travel (☎26950 44194, ⓔakis-125@otenet.gr; from ❷), on the inland road in from town. *The Olive Tree* taverna is the best of a touristy bunch, while the *Mandarin* Chinese is fairly authentic. Pubs such as *The Local* and *Red Lion* tend to be Brit-oriented.

The beaches further along this stretch of coast become progressively quieter and pleasanter, and they all have at least a smattering of accommodation and restaurants to choose from. Good choices include **Pahiá Ámmos**, with the *Pension Petra* (☎26950 61175; ❷) and *Porto Roulis* fish taverna. Also recommended is **Dhrossiá**, where you can find the *Avouris* (☎26950 61716; ❷) and *Drosia* apartments (☎26950 62256; ❸) and eat at another popular fish taverna, *Andreas*.

Alykés and its bay

Órmos Alykón, 12km north of Tsiliví, is a large sandy bay with lively surf and two of the area's largest resorts. The first, **ALIKANÁS**, is a small but expanding village, much of its accommodation being overseas villa rentals; the second, **ALYKÉS**, named after the spooky salt pans behind the village, has the best beach north of the capital. There are **rooms** near the beach, most easily found through the local branch of Spring Tours (☎26950 83035, ⓦwww.springtours.gr; from ❷), and a number of **hotels** set back from it, but with sea views – try the *Ionian Star* (☎26950 83416, ⓦwww.ionian-star.gr; ❹) or the *Montreal* (☎26950 83241, ⓦwww.montreal.gr; ❹), although the best deal is off the crossroads at the chaotic *Eros Piccadilly* (☎26950 83606, ⓦwww.erospiccadilly.com; ❷). There are many eating joints, among the best the *Vineleaf*, which has unusual items such as jalapeño peppers stuffed with cream, and more standard *Fantasia* and *Ponderosa* tavernas. Alykés is the last true resort on this coast, and the one where the bus service largely gives out. **Xygiá** beach, 4km north, has sulphur springs flowing into the sea – follow the smell – which provide the odd sensation of swimming in a mix of cool and warm water. The next small beach of **Makrýs Yialós**, which has a good taverna and makeshift campsite, also makes for an extremely pleasant break on a tour of the north.

Áyios Nikólaos, 6km on, is a small working port serving daily ferries to and from Pessádha on Kefalloniá. Few visitors **stay** here, which perhaps explains why it hosts one of the most exclusive establishments in the Ionian, the classy stone *Nobelos* apartments (☎26950 31131, ⓦwww.nobelos.gr; ❽), as well as the more modest *Panorama* (☎26950 31013, ⓔpanorama@altecnet.gr; ❸). Pre-ferry meals can be had at *La Storia* fish restaurant or *Orizodes* taverna. From here there are trips by **kaïki** (€8) to the extreme northern tip of the island, where the **Blue Caves** are some of the more realistically named of the many contenders in Greece. They're terrific for snorkelling, and when you go for a dip here your skin will appear bright blue. The road snakes onwards through a landscape of gorse bushes and dry-stone walls until it ends at the lighthouse of **Cape Skinári**. With only a taverna and a cafeteria, and a view of the mountainous expanse of Kefalloniá, it's a good spot for unofficial camping, or you could stay in the unique setting of a converted windmill rented out by *To Faros* taverna (☎26950 31132; ❺), whose friendly family also run the cheapest boat trips to the Blue Caves (€7; €15 combined with Shipwreck Bay).

The northern towns and villages are best explored with a car or sturdy motorbike, although there are guided coach tours from the resorts and limited bus services. Two kilometres inland from Alykés, **KATASTÁRI** is the largest settlement after the capital. Precisely because it's not geared towards tourism, it's the best place to see Zakynthian life as it's lived away from the usual racket. Its most impressive edifice is the huge rectangular church of Iperáyia Theotókos, with a twin belfry and small new amphitheatre for festival performances. *Tò Kendro psistariá* does tasty grills at rock-bottom prices. A couple of kilometres south of Katastári, the tiny hamlet of **Pighadhákia** is the unlikely setting for the **Vertzagio Cultural Museum** (summer daily 9am–3pm & 5–7pm; €3), which houses an interesting array of agricultural and folk artefacts. There is also the diminuitive **Áyios Pandeléïmon** chapel, which has the unusual feature of a well, hidden beneath the altar. Just above it the *Kaki Rahi* taverna provides tasty local cuisine.

AYÍA MARÍNA, a few kilometres southwest of Katastári, has a church with an impressive Baroque altar screen, and a belfry that's being rebuilt from the remnants left after the 1953 earthquake. As in most Zákynthos churches, the bell tower stands detached, in Venetian fashion. Just above Ayía Marína is the *Parthenonas* taverna, rightly boasting one of the best views on the island. From here you can see the whole of the central plain from beyond Alykés in the north to Laganás Bay in the south.

VOLÍMES is the centre of the island's embroidery industry and numerous shops sell artefacts produced here. With your own transport, you could make it to the **Anafonítria monastery**, 3km south, thought to have been the cell of the island's patron saint, Dhionysios, whose festivals are celebrated on August 24 and December 17. A paved road leads on to the cliffs overlooking **Shipwreck Bay** (Naváyio), with hair-raising views down to the shipwreck (a cargo ship which ran aground in the Sixties), and a taverna to regain your composure in.

Kýthira and Andikýthira islands

Isolated at the foot of the Peloponnese, the island of **Kýthira** traditionally belongs to the Ionian islands, and shares their history of Venetian and, later, British rule; under the former it was known as Cerigo. Administratively it is part of Pireás in mainland Attica – like the Argo-Saronic islands. For the most part, similarities end there. The island architecture of whitewashed houses and flat-roofs looks more like that of the Cyclades, albeit with an ever stronger **Venetian** influence. The landscape is different, too: wild scrub- and gorse-covered hills, or moorland sliced by deep valleys and ravines.

Depopulation has left the land underfarmed and the abandoned fields overgrown, for, since World War II, most of the islanders have left for Athens or Australia, giving Kýthira a reputation for being the classic emigrant island; it is known locally as "Australian Colony" or "Kangaroo Island", and Australia is referred to as "Big Kýthira". Many of the villages are deserted, their platíes empty and the schools and *kafenía* closed. Kýthira was never a rich island, but, along with Monemvasiá, it did once have a military and economic significance – which it likewise lost with Greek independence and the opening of the Corinth Canal. These days, tourism has brought prosperity (and a few

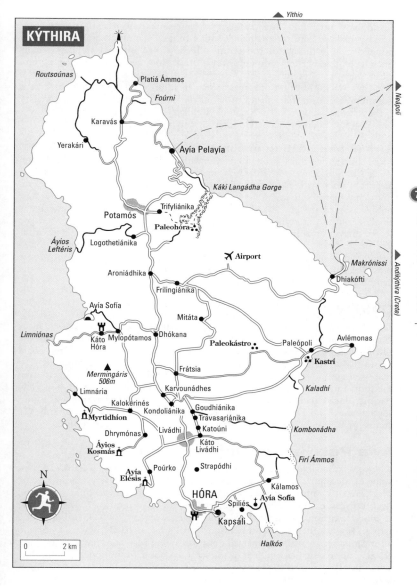

KÝTHIRA

Yíthio

Routsoúnas

Platiá Ámmos

Foúrni

Karavás

Neápoli

Yerakári

Ayía Pelayía

Káki Langádha Gorge

Trifyliánika

Potamós

Paleohóra

Áyios Leftéris

Logothetiánika

✈ **Airport**

Aroniádhika

Frilingiánika

Makrónissi

Dhiakófti

Andikýthira (Crete)

Ayía Sofía

Mitáta

Limniónas

Káto Hóra

Mylopótamos · Dhókana

Paleokástro

Paleópoli

Avlémonas

Kastrí

▲ *Mermingáris 506m*

Frátsia

Kaladhí

Limnária

Karvounádhes

Kalokerinés

Goudhiánika

Myrtidhíon

Kondoliánika

Travasariánika

Kombonádha

Dhrymónas

Livádhi

Katoúni

Áyios Kosmás

Káto Livádhi

Firí Ámmos

Poúrko

Strapódhi

N

Ayía Elésis

Kálamos

HÓRA

Ayía Sofía

Spiliés

Kapsáli

Halkós

0   2 km

luxury hotels), but most summer visitors are Greeks and especially Greek Australians. For the few foreigners who reach Kýthira, it remains something of a refuge, with its undeveloped **beaches** a principal attraction. However, Theo Angelopoulos' film *Taxidhi sta Kýthira* ("Journey to Kýthira"), and, to a much greater extent, a 1998 popular Greek television serial filmed on the island, have attracted a huge amount of domestic attention and, consequently, holiday-makers from the mainland. Much of the accommodation is now fully booked by Christmas for the entire Greek school summer holiday period; outside of this period some accommodation does not open until June and closes early in September. The Association of Rental Room Owners (T & F 27360 31855) has a list of places to stay: in addition to the following, there is accommodation in the villages of Aroniádhika, Dhókana, Dhrymónas, Frátsia, Frilingiánika, Goudhiánika, Kálamos, Kalokerinés, Karvounádhes, Káto Livádhi, Kondoliánika, Mitáta, Mylopótamos, Strapódhi and Travasariánika.

Arrival and getting around

Most large ferries dock at the huge all-weather **harbour** at Dhiakófti, although some Neápoli ferries (W www.atlas-marine.gr) may go into Ayía Pelayía. The airport is deep in the interior, 8km southeast of Potamós, although there are not many flights. The few Olympic Airways flights are met by taxis, as are most high-season boats. The island's **buses** are mostly used for school runs, but a single service runs Ayía Pelayía–Kapsáli–Dhiakófti, starting at 9am Mondays to Saturdays, returning Dhiakófti–Kapsáli–Ayía Pelayía late mornings or mid-afternoon, depending on the ferry times. The only alternative to taxis that often overcharge is to hitch or, more advisedly, hire a **car** or **scooter**. The roads are now well surfaced all over the island and there are reliable petrol stations on the central road at Potamós, Kondoliánika and Livádhi.

Dhiakófti

DHIAKÓFTI, towards the bottom of the northeast coast, was a relatively inaccessible backwater before the opening of the harbour, constructed by joining the islet of Makrónissi to the shore by a causeway. Perched on nearby Prasónisi island – and slightly disconcerting when arriving by sea – is a Greek container ship that went aground in 1999. Dhiakófti has a nice sandy beach, and exploitation of the tourist potential is currently fairly low-key and seasonal; there are just a few **eating places**, including the fish taverna *Manolis*, and **apartments** and rooms such as the *Porto Diakofti* (T 27360 33041, F 27360 33760; April–Oct; ❹–❻). Active (T 27360 33207, F 27360 33911) have an office for **car rental**.

Ayía Pelayía and northern Kýthira

There's a reasonable choice of **rooms** and **tavernas** in **AYÍA PELAYÍA**; best value of the upmarket hotels is *Venardos* (T 27360 34205, W www.kythira.com/greek/venardos.htm; B&B ❻), which is open all year and can offer very good deals off season. The clean and comfortable *Hotel Kytherea* (T 27360 33321; ❺) is more luxurious, as are the *Filoxenia Apartments* (T 27360 33100, F 27360 33610, W www.filoxenia-apartments.gr; April–Oct; B&B ❻), with a pool and an imaginative layout around small courtyards. The *Moustakias* taverna, amongst the seafront eating places north of the jetty, has good, fresh food, including fish, while the *Paleo* ouzerí is also recommended. The main beaches are small, rather scruffy and disappointing, despite the provision of blue-and-white-striped changing huts; the beach at Kalamítsa, a two-kilometre dirt track away to the south, is better.

Potamós and around

From Ayía Pelayía, the main road winds up the mountainside towards **POTAMÓS**, Kýthira's largest village – a pleasant and unspoilt place which, if you have a rented vehicle, makes a good base for exploring the island. It has a few **rooms** with kitchens, such as those at the 🌲 *Xenonas Porfyra* (☎27360 33329, 📠27360 33924; ❹), which has a pretty terrace and courtyard, and the *Alevizopoulos* (☎27360 33245, 🌐www.greek-tourism.gr/kythira/alevizopoulos/ index.htm; ❹) with air conditioning. In addition to **tavernas**, a **bank**, a **post office** and **petrol stations**, facilities include an Olympic Airways office (☎27360 33362). Most of the shops on the island are here, too, as is the **Sunday market**, Kýthira's liveliest regular event. The *Selana* café has **Internet** facilities.

From **Logothetiánika**, just south of Potamós, an unpaved road leads down to Áyios Leftéris beach, where you can **swim** from rocks on the west coast, backed by high cliffs. At Logothetiánika itself, there is a popular taverna, *Karydies* (☎27360 33664), with live music Thursday to Saturday, when booking is advisable.

Paleohóra

The main reason for visiting Potamós is to get to **PALEOHÓRA**, the ruined **medieval capital** (then called Áyios Dhimítrios) of Kýthira, 3km to the east of the town. Few people seem to know about or visit these remains, though they constitute one of the best Byzantine sites around. The most obvious comparison is with Mystra, and although Paleohóra is much smaller – a fortified village rather than a town – its natural setting is perhaps even more spectacular. Set on a hilltop at the head of the **Káki Langádha Gorge**, it is surrounded by a sheer hundred-metre drop on three sides.

The site is lower than the surrounding hills and invisible from the sea and most of the island, something which served to protect it from the pirates that plagued Paleohóra through much of its history. The town was built in the thirteenth century by Byzantine nobles from Monemvasiá, and when Mystra fell to the Turks, many of its noble families also sought refuge here. Despite its seemingly impregnable and perfectly concealed position, the site was discovered and sacked in 1537 by Barbarossa, commander of the Turkish fleet, and the island's seven thousand inhabitants were killed or sold into slavery.

The town was never rebuilt, and tradition maintains that it is a place of ill fortune, which perhaps explains the emptiness of the surrounding countryside, little of which is farmed today. The hills are dotted with Byzantine **chapels**, which suggests that, in its heyday, the area must have been the centre of medieval Kýthira; it is rumoured to have once had eight hundred inhabitants and 72 churches. Now the principal remains are of the surviving churches, some still with traces of frescoes (but kept firmly locked), and the castle. The site is unenclosed and has never been seriously investigated.

The road to Paleohóra is signposted off the main road from Potamós just north of Aroniádhika: the first 2.4km is asphalt, the remainder driveable gravel. By foot, it's more interesting to take the path from the tiny village of Trifyliánika, just outside Potamós – look out for a rusting sign to the right as you enter the village. The path is overgrown in parts and not easy to follow; the ruins only become visible when you join the road above the gorge.

Karavás

KARAVÁS, 6km north of Potamós, has architecture and a setting – above a deep, partly wooded valley with a stream – which are more reminiscent of the Ionian islands. There is nowhere to stay, but there is a popular **café–bar**, *Amir Ali*, providing a large range of *mezédhes* (and sometimes live music) in a shady, streamside setting at the northern end of the village, off the road to Platiá Ámmos.

Platiá Ámmos, at the end of the valley, and en route to the lighthouse at the island's northern tip, is a sandy beach with a seasonal fish **taverna**. There is also an ouzerí, café, the *Modeas* restaurant and several establishments with **rooms**, of which the best is the *Akrotiri* (☎27360 33216; ❸). The little pebble beach at **Foúrni**, 2km south by dirt road, is more attractive.

Kapsáli

KAPSÁLI, on the south coast, in addition to its harbour function, is the one place on Kýthira largely devoted to tourism, although much of it closes down from September to June. Most foreign visitors to Kýthira in summer stay here, and it's a popular port of call for yachts heading from the Aegean to the Ionian islands and Italy, particularly since it is sheltered from the strong north winds of summer. Set behind double pebble-and-sand bays, overlooked by Hóra castle, and backed by high grey cliffs on which the tiny white monastery of Áyios Ioánnis Éngremmos perches, it is certainly picturesque. The larger of its two bays has a line of **tavernas**: *Vlastos* is one of the earliest to open in the season, with fish, local dishes and its speciality, cockerel (*kókoras*) in wine; *Venetsianiko*, halfway along the front, has good food at reasonable prices, but the best is *Idragogio* at the Hóra end of the beach which serves up good veggie options.

The best **accommodation** is in high demand and expensive. Top of the tree is the *Porto Delfino* (☎27360 31940; April–Oct; ❻); a few hundred metres above the bay are *Kalokerines Katikies* (☎ & ☎27360 31265; May–Oct; ❻) and *Hotel Raïkos* (☎27360 31629, ☎27360 31801, ✉raikosho@otenet.gr; May–Sept; ❻). The *Afroditi Apartments* (☎27360 31328; ❹) have more reasonable rates. A basic **campsite** (☎27360 31580; June–Sept) nestles in the pine trees behind the village.

There's a mobile **post office** in summer, and Panayiotis (☎27360 31600, ✉panayoti@otenet.gr) rents **cars**, **motorbikes** and **scooters**, as well as canoes and pedalboats; you can call off season (☎29442 63757) and get wheels when most places are closed.

Hóra

HÓRA (or Kýthira Town), a steep two-kilometre haul above Kapsáli, has an equally dramatic site, its Cycladic-style houses tiered on the ridge leading to the Venetian **castle**. Access to the fortress is up a modern pathway, but, to the right of this, the original narrow tunnel entrance is still usable. Within the walls, most of the buildings are in ruins, except the paired churches of Panayía Myrtidhiótissa and the smaller Panayía Orfáni (these were Catholic and Orthodox respectively, under the Venetian occupation), and the office of the archives of Kýthira opposite. There are spectacular views down to Kapsáli and out to sea to the striking chunk of inaccessible islet known as Avgó (Egg), legendary birthplace of Aphrodite. On the cliffs grow the yellow-flowered everlasting (*sempreviva*), used locally for making small dried flower arrangements. Below the castle are both the remains of older Byzantine walls and, in Mésa Vouryó, numerous well-signed but securely locked Byzantine churches. A small **museum** (Tues–Sun 8.30am–2.30pm; free), at the junction of the Hóra–Kapsáli road, houses modest remnants (labelled only in Greek) of the island's numerous occupiers, in particular Minoan finds from excavations at Paleópoli and an Archaic stone lion, as well as a telling selection of gravestones from the English cemetery. The Stavros bookshop, almost opposite, sells a book of walks (mainly in the southern half of the island).

Compared with Kapsáli, Hóra stays quiet and many places are closed out of season. Facilities include a couple of **banks**, a **post office**, a branch of Panayi-otis vehicle rental (☎27360 31004) and the office of Kýthira Travel (☎27360 31390, ⓔkkmk@otenet.gr), the island's agent for the Neápoli ferry. A few **tavernas** open in summer, of which *Zorba* is by far the best, but the climb from Kapsáli discourages the crowds. A popular café-bar is *Mercato*, which stays open in the winter and also has exhibitions of local art. **Accommodation** is slightly easier to find than in Kapsáli. Options include the *Castello* rooms and studios (☎27360 31069, ⓦwww.castelloapts-kythera.gr; ❹), and the *Hotel Margarita* (☎27360 31711, ⓦwww.hotel-margarita.com; B&B ❺) in a beautiful 1840s house, with air conditioning in the rooms. The *Xenonas Keiti/Keti/Kaiti* (☎27360 31318, ⓕ27360 31558; April–Oct; ❹) has non-smoking rooms in a large 240-year-old characterful house that has seen General Metaxas and George Papandreou as visitors. At **Manitohóri**, 2km further inland, is the more basic pension *Ta Kythera* (☎27360 31563; June–Aug; ❸).

The southeast coast

The beach at Kapsáli is decent but not large and gets very crowded in July and August. For quieter, undeveloped beaches, it's better to head out to the south-east coast, towards Avlémonas.

Firí Ámmos, Kombonádha and Halkós beaches, and Spiliés cave

Firí Ámmos, the nearest good sand beach to Kapsáli, is popular but not overcrowded, even in summer. To get there, you can follow paved roads from Kapsáli or Livádhi as far as the *Filio* taverna with good traditional food and local specialities (June–Sept) in the scattered settlement of Kálamos; the onward road becomes a four-kilometre dirt track to the beach. Firí Ámmos can also be reached by a second dirt track off the Livádhi–Kálamos road, while another, longer, dirt track, off the Káto Livádhi–Frátsia road, leads to **Kombonádha**, the next beach north. There are summer canteens at both beaches. Much smaller, but prettier, pebbly **Halkós** beach near the southeast corner of the island is signposted from the crossroads at the entrance to Kálamos. Between Kálamos and Kapsáli, a short surfaced road leads south to **Spiliés** village; immediately before the village a signed earth road leads down to a small gorge and a large stalagmite cave with an open-roofed church dedicated to Ayía Sofia (not to be confused with the sea cave near Mylopótamos).

Paleópoli and Avlémonas

PALEÓPOLI, a hamlet of a few scattered houses, is accessible by asphalt roads from Aroniádhika, Frátsia and Kondoliánika. The area is the site of the ancient city of **Skandia**, and excavations on the headland of **Kastrí** have revealed remains of an important Minoan colony. There's little visible evidence, apart from shards of pottery in the low crumbling cliffs, but, happily, tourist devel-opment in the area has been barred because of its archeological significance. Consequently, there's just one solitary **taverna**, the *Skandia* (June–Oct), on the two-kilometre sand-and-pebble **beach** that stretches to either side of the headland. This taverna has a great atmosphere, with home cooking and some spontaneous musical evenings.

Paleokástro, the mountain to the west, is the site of ancient Kýthira where there was a sanctuary of Aphrodite, but again, there's little to be seen today. Heading west from Paleópoli, and crossing the river bridge onto the

Kondoliánika road, an unpaved road off to the left leads up to a tiny, white-washed church. From there, a rougher track leads down to **Kaladhí**, a beautiful cliff-backed pebble beach with caves, and rocks jutting out to sea.

AVLÉMONAS, on a rocky shoreline 2km east of Paleópoli beach, is a small fishing port with a bleak end-of-the-world feel as you approach from a distance. It becomes much more attractive once reached, and has a remarkable coordination of colour schemes throughout the village. There is a small, unimpressive Venetian fortress, and two **tavernas**, of which *Sotiris* is particularly recommended for a wide selection of fresh, well-prepared and reasonably priced fish dishes. A number of **rooms**, including the newer apartments of *Popi Kastrisiou* (☎27360 33735; ❹), and the older, air-conditioned *Schina* studios (☎27360 33060; ❹), are available. The Petrohilos family has a number of rooms or studios, including those of *Evdokhia* (☎27360 34069; ❸) opposite the *Sotiris*.

❼ North and west of Hóra

LIVÁDHI, a pleasant but unexciting small town 4km north of Hóra, makes a good base for the southern half of the island if you have transport. It has **accommodation**, including, on the main road, the *Hotel Aposperides* (☎27360 31656, ✉aposperides@freemail.gr; B&B ❹), which makes a good base. Livádhi is also home to one of the most efficient travel agencies on the island, Porfyra Travel, which is the main ANEK/ANEN and Olympic Airways agent (☎27360 31888, ⓦwww.kythira.info), with exchange and car rental; they can also arrange accommodation or transfers. Doufexis Travel (☎27360 34371, ✉douftvl@hellasnet.gr) has recently opened an office and can help with accommodation and car rental for Kýthira and mainland Peloponnese.

At **Káto Livádhi**, 1km to the east of Livádhi, there is a small **museum** of Byzantine and post-Byzantine art (July–Oct Tues–Sun 8am–3pm; Nov–June Mon–Fri 8.30am–2pm; free) next to the large central church. It contains (labelled in Greek only) frescoes, painstakingly removed from island churches, dating from the twelfth to the eighteenth centuries, a seventh-century mosaic floor and some portable icons. Not far away there is also a cooperative pottery workshop (open mornings and evenings, with a 2–4pm break) and, on the road to Katoúni, a multiple-arched bridge, said to be the longest stone bridge in Greece and a legacy of the nineteenth century when all the Ionian islands were a British protectorate; like others on the island it was built by a Scottish engineer called McPhail. The best view of it is from beside *Rena's zaharoplastío* in Livádhi. A popular **taverna** nearby is the *Theofilos*.

From Livádhi, a side road heads west to Kalokerinés, and continues 3.6km further to the island's principal monastery, **Myrtidhíon**, set above the wild and windswept west coast, among a dead forest of pines burned in June 2000. The monastery's main icon is said to date from 1160. Beyond the monastery, a track leads down to a small anchorage at **Limnária**; there are few beaches along this rocky, forbidding shore.

An early left fork off the Myrtidhíon road out of Livádhi brings you through the hamlet of Poúrko and past the unusual Byzantine church of Áyios Dimítrios. From Poúrko, an increasingly steep road leads up to the **Ayía Elésis**, a nineteenth-century monastery marking the martyrdom of the saint on the hilltop in 375 AD, an event depicted in recent wall-paintings inside the church. For many visitors, however, the breathtaking view from the western side of the courtyard is the main reason to visit.

Mylopótamos, Káto Hóra and the Ayía Sofía cave

North of Livádhi, just beyond Dhókana, it is worth making a detour off the main road for **MYLOPÓTAMOS**, a lovely traditional village and an oasis in summer, set in a wooded valley with a small stream. The shady *Plátanos kafenío* makes a pleasant stop for a drink above the village's springs, and the music bar *To Kamari*, in an old restored building, serves snacks and drinks on a lower waterside terrace. Follow the signs for "Katarráktis Neráïdha" to find a waterfall, hidden from view by lush vegetation, next to a long-closed café. The valley below the falls is overgrown but contains the remains of the watermill that gave the village its name.

Káto Hóra (also called Kástro Mylopotamoú), 500m down the road, was Mylopótamos's predecessor, and remains half-enclosed within the walls of a Venetian fortress. The fortress is small, full of locked, well-labelled churches, and has a rather domestic appearance: unlike the castle at Hóra, it was built as a place of refuge for the villagers in case of attack, rather than as a base for a Venetian garrison. All the houses within the walls are abandoned – as are many outside – but are open and accessible. Beyond here, a surfaced but briefly precipitous road continues 5km through spectacular cliffscapes to **Limniónas**, a rocky inlet with a small sand beach, but a fire in June 2000 has left the surrounding countryside exposed and barren.

Most visitors come to Mylopótamos to see the **cave of Ayía Sofía**, the largest and most impressive of a number of caverns on the island. A half-hour signposted walk from the village, or a short drive by a new dirt road being constructed off the Limniónas road, the cave is open regularly from mid-June to mid-September (Mon–Fri 3–8pm, Sat & Sun 11am–5pm; €3). When the cave is closed, you can probably find a guide in Mylopótamos; ask at the village, giving a day's notice if possible. The cave is worth the effort to see: the entrance has been used as a church and has an iconostasis carved from the rock, with important Byzantine frescoes on it. Beyond, the cave system comprises a series of chambers, which reach 250m into the mountain, although the thirty-minute guided tour (in Greek and English) only takes in the more interesting outer chambers. These include some startling formations such as the "shark's teeth", but you have to ask to be shown "Aphrodite's chambers". A minute new species of disc-shaped insect has been discovered there.

Andikýthira island

Thirteen kilometres to the south of Kýthira, the tiny, wind-blown 22-square-kilometre island of **ANDIKÝTHIRA** has, theoretically, a twice-weekly connection with Crete on the Kýthira–Kastélli–Kýthira run (@www.anen.gr), but landings are often impossible due to adverse weather. There are attempts to organize a ferry from Kýthira for the festival of Áyios Mýron on August 17 at Galaniará - an annual reunion jamboree for the Andikytheran diaspora - returning the following day, but these are often thwarted by the wind. Rocky and poor, and a site of political exile until 1964, the island only received electricity in 1984. Attractions include good birdlife (a bird observatory has been built in the old school at Lazi* and flora, but it's not the place if you want company: with only 45 residents divided among a scattering of settlements – mainly in **Potamós**, the harbour, and **Sohória**, the village – people are rather thin on the ground. The only official accommodation is the set of **rooms** run by the local community (☎27360 31390, ✆info@antikythera.gr) at Potamós, which also has a couple of **tavernas**, but you'd be wise to bring plenty of supplies with you. In Sohória the only provisions available are basic foodstuffs at the village shop.

Recent excavation work above Xeropotamos has revealed the site of ancient **Aigila**, a 75-acre fortress city of the Hellenistic period. At the harbour below are the remains of one of ancient Greece's best-preserved warship slipways, a *neosoikos*, carved out of the rock.

The island has one remarkable claim to fame, the **Antikythera Mechanism**, an ancient bronze clockwork "calendar computer" discovered in 1902 in a nearby shipwreck and dated to around 87 BC. It is thought to have been used for calculating the motion and positions of the earth, moon and five other planets, and is the earliest known mechanism with a differential gear by about 1600 years. It is now kept in the National Archeological Museum, Athens.

Travel details

Ferries

The following listings are based on summer schedules, which are often reduced drastically in winter; any services that stop altogether are marked as being summer only. Tourist craft and *kaïkia* are not included below.

Corfu:
Corfu Town to: Eríkoussa/Mathráki/Othoní (3 weekly; 2–4hr); Igoumenítsa (every 10–45min; 1hr 15min); Pátra (6–10 daily; 7–9hr).
Lefkími to: Igoumenítsa (6 daily; 40min).

Ithaka:
Fríkes to: Fiskárdho (Kefalloniá; 1 daily; 1hr); Nydhrí (Lefkádha; daily; 1hr 30min).
Pisaetós to: Sámi (Kefalloniá; 3 daily; 45min).
Vathý to: Astakós (1 daily; 2hr 30min); Pátra (2 daily; 3hr 30min); Sámi (Kefalloniá; 2 daily; 1hr).

Kefalloniá:
Argostóli to: Kyllíni (1 daily; 2hr 15min); Lixoúri (every 30min; 20min).
Fiskárdho to: Fríkes (Itháki; 1 daily; 1hr); Nydhrí (Lefkádha; 1 daily; 2hr 15min); Vassilikí (Lefkádha; 2 daily; 1hr).
Pessádha to: Áyios Nikólaos (Zákynthos; 2 daily May–Sept; 1hr 30min).
Póros to: Kyllíni (3–5 daily; 1hr 15min).
Sámi to: Astakós (1 daily; 2hr 30min); Corfu Town (2 weekly; 5hr); Pátra (1–2 daily; 3hr 30min); Pisaetós (Itháki; 3 daily; 40min); Vathý (Itháki; 1–2 daily; 1hr).

Lefkádha:
Nydhrí to: Fiskárdho (Kefalloniá; 1 daily; 2hr 15min); Fríkes (Itháki; 1 daily; 1hr 30min); Meganíssi (7 daily; 20min).
Vassilikí to: Fiskárdho (Kefalloniá; 2 daily; 1hr); Fríkes (Itháki; 1 daily; 2hr).

Paxí:
Gáïos to: Igoumenítsa (1–2 daily; 1hr).

Zákynthos:
Zákynthos Town to: Kyllíni (7 daily; 1hr 30min).
Áyios Nikólaos to: Pessádha (Kefalloniá; 2 daily May–Sept; 1hr 30min).

International Ferries

Corfu Town is a main stop on many of the ferry routes to Italy from Pátra and a stopover can be added for free with many companies. The frequency and journey time to the various Italian ports is: Ancona (1–2 daily; 14hr); Bari (2–3 daily; 11hr); Brindisi (3–5 daily; 4–9hr); and Venice (2–3 weekly; 25hr).

Hydrofoils

Corfu Town to: Gáïos (Paxí; 3–7 daily; 50min).
Gáïos to: Corfu Town (3–7 daily; 50min).

Buses

Corfu:
Corfu Town to: Athens (3 daily; 10–11hr); Thessaloníki (1 daily; 9–10hr).

Kefalloniá:
Argostóli to: Athens (4 daily; 7–8hr); Pátra (1 daily; 4–5hr).
Póros to: Athens (1 daily; 6–7hr).
Sámi to: Athens (2 daily; 6–7hr).

Lefkádha:
Lefkádha Town to: Athens (1 daily; 2hr 15min); Pátra (2 weekly; 3hr 30min); Préveza (4 daily; 30min); Thessaloníki (2 weekly; 10–11hr).

Zákynthos:
Zákynthos Town to: Athens (5–6 daily; 6hr); Pátra (4 daily; 3hr); Thessaloníki (3 weekly; 11–12hr).

Flights

All domestic flights listed below are on Olympic or Aegean except for the new seaplane service from Corfu to Paxí and Ioánnina. For international flights see "Basics".

Corfu to: Athens (4–8 daily; 1hr); Kefalloniá (1 weekly; 1hr 10min); Paxí (2–3 daily; 20min); Préveza (1 weekly; 25min); Ioánnina (10 weekly; 40min); Zákynthos (1 weekly; 1hr 55min).

Kefalloniá to: Athens (1–2 daily; 1hr); Corfu (1 weekly; 1hr 10min); Préveza (1 weekly; 25min); Zákynthos (1 weekly; 25min).

Zákynthos to: Athens (1–2 daily; 55min); Corfu (1 weekly; 1hr 55min); Kefalloniá (1 weekly; 25min); Préveza (1 weekly; 1hr 15min).

Contexts

Contexts

A History of Greece

The geographical position of Greece on the Mediterranean and at the crossroads of Europe, Asia and Africa has long presented it with unique opportunities and dangers. The Greeks are a people who have suffered calamities, yet they have also achieved the highest reaches of human accomplishment. In the areas of politics, philosophy, literature, science and art, Greece has influenced Western society more than any other nation in history. After four thousand years the Greek language continues to be spoken and remains as vigorous as ever, while the culture and the identity of the Greeks have been forged and tempered by a remarkable history. Now, as Greece enters the twenty-first century, there is much to learn about its present condition, and about our own, from understanding the Greek past.

Prehistoric Greece: to 2100 BC

Evidence of human habitation in Greece goes back half a million years, as demonstrated by the discovery in 1976 of the skeleton of a **Neanderthal** youth embedded in a stalagmite in the **Petralóna Cave**, 50km east of the northern city of Thessaloníki. Cooked animal remains were found amid debris in the floor of the cave at a level corresponding to **500,000 years ago**, which makes this the earliest known site of a man-made fire in Europe.

Only very much later, about **40,000 years ago**, did **Homo sapiens**, the anatomically modern form of man from which we are descended, make his first appearance in Greece after migrating out of Africa. Several sites occupied by Homo sapiens have been identified in **Epirus** in northwest Greece, where they used tools and weapons of bone, wood and stone to gather wild plants and hunt. Even between **20,000 and 16,000 years ago**, when the Ice Age was at its peak, **Stone Age man** continued to make a home in Greece, though it was only when the glaciers finally receded about **10,000 BC** that a considerably warmer climate set in, altering the Greek environment to something more like that of present times.

The Neolithic period

Agricultural communities first appeared in **Macedonia** around **6500 BC** and in **Thessaly** a thousand years later. But whether agriculture developed indigenously or was introduced to Greece by migrants from Asia Minor where animal husbandry and crop cultivation had already been practised for two thousand years cannot be determined conclusively from the archeological evidence. What is certain, however, is agriculture's revolutionary effect.

When leading their hunter-gatherer way of life, the Stone Age inhabitants of Greece had been almost entirely at the mercy of nature; but now for the first time they were able to produce their own food and assure themselves of a more ample and certain supply. They built mud brick houses which they stood on stone foundations as if announcing their intention to stay; they sowed seeds and reaped harvests season after season. Though still reliant on stone technology, this new farming culture was a significant break with the past, so that from 6500 BC a "new stone age" or **Neolithic Period** is said to have begun in Greece.

As the strong variety of flint needed for weapons and tools was rare in Greece, the mainlanders imported obsidian, the hard black glassy stone formed by rapidly cooling volcanic lava, found on the island of **Melos** (Mílos) in the southern Cyclades. This was the earliest **seaborne trade** known anywhere in the world and clearly involved a mastery of building and handling boats.

Cycladic culture and trade

In about **3000 BC** a new people settled in the **Cyclades**, probably from Asia Minor, bringing with them the latest metallurgical techniques. They continued the old trade in obsidian, but they also developed the **trade in tin** and were making prodigious voyages westwards as far as Spain by 2500 BC. The mining of **gold and silver** in the Cyclades may have dated from this period, too. Long before Crete or the Greek mainland, these new inhabitants of the islands became specialists in **jewellery-making**, **metalwork** and **stone-cutting**.

From the marble in which the Cyclades abound, they sculpted statuettes, most of which were female figures. Slender, spare and geometric, these **Cycladic sculptures** are startlingly modern in appearance, and have inspired admiration and imitation from such artists as Epstein, Brancusi, Modigliani and Henry Moore. Usually described as idols, the statuettes were probably used in worship, as well as in burials – where they were perhaps intended as spirit guides. They were exported widely, to Crete and mainland Greece. Indeed during the Early Bronze Age the Eastern Mediterranean witnessed a proliferation in the manufacture and trade of **ritual objects**, probably because ritual itself was becoming more elaborate as societies grew wealthier, more complex and hierarchical.

The beginnings of the Greek Bronze Age

In about 3000 BC, also from the Cyclades, bronze technology was introduced to the mainland, marking the beginning of the **Bronze Age** in Greece. By **2500 BC** the widespread use of bronze and the acquisition of metallurgical techniques had transformed farming and fighting throughout the Eastern Mediterranean and the Middle East.

This rapid spread of bronze technology was due to a well-established network of long-distance trade. Great **palace-cities** had grown up in the Middle East as the culmination of the agricultural revolution and the consequent increase in wealth and population; all political and economic activities were administered from the palace which stood at the centre of these cities, including the trade in precious materials such as gold from Egypt, lapis lazuli from Afghanistan and timber from Lebanon.

To these were added **tin**, which when mixed with copper, a soft metal, created bronze, a tough alloy in demand for tools and weapons. But whereas copper was available locally almost everywhere throughout the Middle East and Europe, tin was a different matter. In the East it could be obtained only in isolated pockets of the Caucasus, Persia and Afghanistan, while in the West sources were confined to Cornwall, Brittany, northwest Spain and northern Italy. The Aegean became an important trade route, accounting for the burst of development that now took place along the eastern coast of **central Greece** and the **Peloponnese**, and on the **Aegean islands** which linked the Greek mainland to Asia Minor and the Middle East.

It is uncertain what **language** was spoken at this time on the mainland and the islands, but one thing is clear: it was not yet Greek. Indeed, when **Greek-speaking people** did arrive on the mainland in about 2100 BC their destructive impact, evident at sites like Lerna, paralysed its development for five hundred years, while the large and secure island of **Crete** – which they did not invade or settle – flourished and dominated the Aegean.

The coming of the Greeks

The destruction of numerous mainland sites in about **2100 BC**, followed by the appearance of a new style of pottery, has suggested to archeologists the violent arrival of a **new people**. They domesticated the horse, they introduced the potter's wheel, and they possessed considerable metallurgical skills. These newcomers replaced the old religion centred on female fertility figures with **hilltop shrines** which, it is believed, were dedicated to the worship of male sky gods like Zeus. And they brought with them a new language, an early form of **Greek**, though they were also obliged to adopt existing native words for such things as olives, figs, vines, wheat and the sea, suggesting that these new migrants or invaders may have come from some distant inland steppes where they had been pastoral highlanders, not farmers, fishermen or sailors.

The shock of domination was followed by five hundred years of adjustment and intermingling. The population increased, new settlements grew up, and there were advances in metallurgy. Yet in comparison with the Cyclades and Crete, which the invaders had never reached, the Greek mainland seems to have been a backward region, its archeological record sparse and unimpressive. Only around **1600 BC**, and then under the influence of Crete, did progress on the mainland quicken – until within little over a hundred years **Crete** itself was conquered by the Greek-speaking mainlanders.

Minoan and Mycenaean civilizations: 2100–1100 BC

The history of the Aegean during the second millennium BC can be seen as a struggle between two cultures, the **Mycenaean culture** of the **Greek mainland** and the **Minoan culture** of **Crete**. Situated halfway between mainland Greece and Asia Minor, Crete was favourably placed to take advantage of the Bronze Age boom in trade, and by the beginning of the second millennium BC it was the dominant power in the Aegean. Its distinctive civilization, called Minoan (a modern term derived from the island's legendary king Minos), and its beneficial economic influence were felt throughout the islands and also on the mainland. The Greek-speaking mainland invaders were "Minoanised", gradually developing a culture known as Mycenaean (after Mycenae, a principal mainland Bronze Age site) which owed a lot to Crete.

Minoan Crete

A large and fertile island with good natural harbours, **Crete**'s coastal plains and highland pastures provided the islanders with an abundance of crops and livestock, producing a surplus in oil and wool that were exported. Among the Cretans' most impressive tools, quite literally at the cutting edge of the new technology, was a four-foot-long bronze saw which readily converted the island's forest-clad mountains into an ample source of **timber for ships**. Some of this timber was probably also exported, most likely to treeless Egypt.

The excellence of Cretan craftsmanship meant that its metalwork, jewellery and pottery were commonly exported to the mainland and beyond. **Kamares ware**, as Cretan pottery of this period is known, was especially valued for its harmony between shape and decoration, its emphatic colours and the boldness of its designs from nature; it has been found all along the Cretans' 1400-mile-long maritime trade route to the East – on the Aegean islands of Rhodes and Sámos, on the coast of Asia Minor at Miletus, and in Syria and Egypt.

On Crete itself, Minoan power was concentrated on three vast **palace complexes** – at **Knossos**, **Phaestos** and **Malia**, all in the central segment of the island. First built around 2000 BC, their similarity of plan and their lack of significant defences suggest that some form of confederacy had by now replaced any regional rivalries on the island, while Minoan sea power induced a sense of security against foreign invasion. Like the palaces of the Middle East, these were all centres of political, economic and religious activity, though Minoan forms of worship also involved communing with the gods of nature at shrines in caves and on mountain tops. Not that prosperity was confined to the palace centres; the numerous remains of villas of the Minoan gentry and of well-constructed villages shows that the wealth generated by the palaces was redistributed among a significant proportion of the island's population. Following an **earthquake** around 1700 BC the palaces at Knossos and Phaestos were rebuilt, and a more modest palace was constructed at **Zakros** on the east coast, this activity coinciding with an apparent centralization of power at Knossos, whose ruler installed a vassal at Phaestos and seems to have united the entire island into a single kingdom, giving rise to a **Minoan golden age**.

Mycenaean dominance

But suddenly around **1500 BC** the Mycenaeans gained control of the palace of Knossos and were soon in full possession of Crete. How this happened is unknown, but probably it marked the culmination of a growing rivalry

△ The so-called "Death mask of Agamemnon", unearthed at Mycenae by Heinrickh Schliemann

between the Mycenaeans and the Minoans for control of the Aegean trade, which perhaps coincided with the effects of a **volcanic explosion** on the island of Thera (Thíra/Santoríni) and its consequent **tsunami**.

Greek now became the language of administration at Knossos and at the other former Minoan palaces, as well as on the mainland – indeed this is the earliest moment that the existence of the Greek language can definitely be identified, as from this point the palace records on Crete are written in a new script known as **Linear B**, which when deciphered in 1953 was shown to be a form of Greek. Having wrested control of the Aegean trade from the Minoans, the **Mycenaeans** enjoyed dominance for another three hundred years, at the end of that period famously laying siege to and destroying yet another rival, the city of **Troy** in about 1220 BC: the events that form the basis of Homer's great poetic narrative, the **Iliad**.

Yet within a generation the Mycenaean world was overwhelmed by a vast **migration** of northerners from somewhere beyond the Black Sea. Probably victims of a catastrophic change in climate which brought drought and famine to their homelands, these **Sea Peoples**, as the ancients called them, swept down through Asia Minor and the Middle East and also crossed the Mediterranean to Libya and Egypt, disrupting trade routes and destroying empires as they went. In Greece, invading marauders, whether Sea Peoples or others taking advantage of the wider disruption, burned and looted the mainland Mycenaean palace sites, causing the administrative and economic systems to collapse. Fleeing the destruction and chaos at home, a first wave of Greeks settled in **Cyprus**.

With the palace-based Bronze Age economies destroyed, the humbler **village-based economies** which replaced them lacked the concentration of wealth and the technological means to make a mark in the world. Instead Greece was plunged into a Dark Age, and knowledge of the Minoan and Mycenaean civilizations slipped into dim and uncertain memory.

The Dark Age and Awakening: 1150–720 BC

Massive migrations and the disruption of trade routes during the late Bronze Age helped undermine the great empires of the Middle East and destroyed the palace organization of Mycenaean civilization, casting Greece into a **Dark Age** of poverty, depopulation and isolation from the world. With the loss of trade, Greece became entirely dependent on agriculture and could no longer support anyone who did not work directly on the land. Many towns and villages were abandoned, and by about 1000 BC the population, which was now entirely illiterate, had fallen by sixty percent to its lowest level in a thousand years. During the next two centuries almost nothing of note was produced in architecture or sculpture, where crudely worked wood was the standard material used for temples and statues, and the backwardness of the times was reflected in the dominant religious image of the **xoanon**, a figure roughly shaped with the minimum of detail from a tree trunk.

Yet the darkness did not extend everywhere. **Athens** was something of an exception to the poverty and isolation that characterized Dark Age Greece, and the reason was **seaborne trade**. Escaping the destruction that accompanied the fall of Mycenaean civilization, Athens maintained trading links abroad and became the route through which the **Iron Age** was introduced to mainland Greece with the importation of iron weapons, implements and technological know-how in about 1100 BC. In Athens too a new cultural beginning was made in the form of pottery painted in the **Geometric style**, a highly intricate and controlled design which would lie at the heart of later Greek architecture, sculpture and painting.

Emigration

At the nadir of Greece's fortunes, many among its desperate population crossed the Aegean. In about 1125 BC Greeks began **emigrating** to the **Dodecanese islands** in the eastern Aegean, others in Cilicia along the south coast of **Asia Minor,** while a further wave of Greeks settled in **Cyprus** which now became Greek-speaking. Later, around 1000 BC, Greeks began settling in large numbers along the western coast of Asia Minor, a remarkable migration which continued for two hundred years until the Aegean became culturally and politically a Greek lake. The desire to escape poverty was probably the cause, though until recently many authorities believed that this second migration was the consequence of an invasion of mainland Greece by a Greek-speaking people from the north called the **Dorians**, who as they pushed their way southwards towards the Peloponnese uprooted the local populations who then fled across the sea. But modern research has turned up no archeological evidence for a Dorian invasion of Greece, and it seems more likely that a pattern of dialects had developed in the broken and mountainous landscape of Greece and was exported in turn to Asia Minor by enterprising migrants.

The Greeks had been a great seafaring people in Mycenaean times, but when the sea lanes were cut by the Sea Peoples, four hundred years of disruption to trade followed. Even during the tenth and ninth centuries BC, after their great migration to Asia Minor, the Greeks inhabited a world of limited horizons, with little evidence that they sailed beyond the Aegean or the Gulf of Corinth. Rather it was the **Phoenicians**, sailing from Sidon and Tyre in present-day

Lebanon, who opened up the old sea trading routes again during the eighth century BC, re-establishing contact between the Middle East and the Aegean world. But soon the Greeks were following in their wake, their ships sailing into the Eastern Mediterranean, where they established a trading station at Al Mina at the mouth of the Orontes as the Mycenaeans had done long before at Ugarit.

The city-state

From 750 BC Greek civilization developed with remarkable rapidity; no other people achieved so much over the next few centuries. The institution most responsible for this extraordinary achievement was the **city-state** or **polis**, where political responsibility belonged to the citizen who nevertheless operated within a disciplined collective ideal. The city-state came into being at a time of rapidly growing populations, greater competition for land and resources, increasing productivity and wealth, expanding trade and more complex relationships with neighbouring states. By mobilising manpower and resources to meet these new conditions, the city-state was expected to protect its citizens, ensure their liberty and provide them with opportunities.

Life not lived in a city-state, the Greeks believed, was semi-barbarous, for it provided the centralized and coordinated **political life** essential for a happy and rational existence. The city-state was small, perhaps only a few square miles and not more than a few hundred, but it was independent in all its affairs. It

Homer and the Iliad and the Odyssey

The **Iliad** and the **Odyssey**, the oldest and greatest works in Greek literature, were the brilliant summation of a long poetic tradition spanning five hundred years or so which had been developed by nameless bards whose recitations were originally accompanied by music. Completed by 725 BC, they are far older than the *Pentateuch*, the first five books of the Old Testament (*Genesis, Exodus, Leviticus, Numbers, Deuteronomy*), which achieved their finished form only in about 400 BC. The admiration of the whole Greek world for the Homeric epics was unique, and their influence upon the subsequent development of Greek literature, art and culture in general cannot be overstated. Few works, and probably none which have not been used in worship, have had such a hold on a nation for so many centuries.

But from time to time the old argument flares up again: did the blind poet **Homer** write the *Iliad* and the *Odyssey*? The best answer came from Mark Twain who said, "The *Iliad* and the *Odyssey* were written by the blind poet Homer or by another blind poet of the same name". For in truth, apart from being the name to which authorship of the poems is ascribed, virtually nothing is known of Homer beyond the tradition that he was blind and was born into the eighth-century BC world of the Asian Greeks, perhaps at Smyrna or opposite on the island of Híos.

The *Iliad* is the story of a few days' action in the tenth and final year of the Trojan War which recalls in its tales of heroic exploits the golden age of the Mycenaeans. The *Odyssey* begins after the war and follows the adventures of Odysseus who takes ten years to return to his island home of Ithaca on the western side of Greece, his voyages showing the new Greek interest during the eighth century BC in the geography to the northeast around the Black Sea and to the west towards Italy and Sicily. Taken together, the epics recover the past and look forwards into the future, and in this they are an Ionian achievement, for it was in Asia Minor that Greek civilization first and most shiningly emerged from the Dark Age. But they are also a celebration of an emerging **panhellenic identity**, of a national adventure encompassing both shores of the Aegean and beyond.

was governed by law, which even if at first unwritten was a guarantee against arbitrary justice, while the intimacy and intensity of city life released a boundless and versatile energy in **literature**, **art** and **philosophy**, while not the least of its achievements was the widescale **Greek colonization** of the **Western Mediterranean** and **Black Sea** which began after 750 BC.

The city-state became the Greek ideal, and by the early seventh century BC it had spread throughout Greece itself and wherever Greeks established colonies overseas. The city-state was a peculiarly Western institution; nothing like it developed in the East either then or later. It put political responsibility in the hands of its citizens; it was the birthplace of **democracy** and of equality before the law.

The revival of commerce with the East restored Greece to prosperity and stimulated the development of the city-state, which would be the foundation of Greek society for nearly a thousand years. Trade also acted as a cultural stimulus. Contact with other peoples made the Greeks aware of what they shared among themselves, and led to the development of a **national sentiment**, notably expressed and fostered by the **panhellenic sanctuaries** which arose during the eighth century BC, of **Hera** and **Zeus** at **Olympia**, where the first **Olympic Games** were held in 776 BC, and of **Apollo** and **Artemis** at **Delos**, as well as the **oracles** of **Zeus** at **Dodona** and of **Apollo** at **Delphi**.

From the Phoenicians the Greeks obtained the basics of the **alphabet**, which they adapted to their own tongue and developed into a sophisticated tool for recording laws, composing literature and chronicling events. **Greek art**, under Eastern influence, saw the Geometric style gradually give way to depicting animals, mythical and real, and finally around 750 BC, for the first time in four hundred years, **human figures** were introduced to vase decorations, most strikingly in group scenes with a story to tell. This was at about the same time as **Homer** was composing his great narrative epics, the **Iliad** and the **Odyssey**, which served not only as witnesses to the glories of the past but reflected also the reawakening of the present.

Expansion and Renaissance: 720–491 BC

The revival of seafaring and commerce in the early centuries of the first millennium BC contributed to the rise of the city-state around 750 BC, which in turn had two dramatic results that were as swift and fundamental as any in human history. One was the Greeks' **colonization movement** throughout the Mediterranean; the other was **radical social and political change** at home.

Colonization

The Greeks began by founding **colonies** in the Western Mediterranean, especially in **Sicily** and **southern Italy** which became known as **Greater Greece**, and a century later, around 650 BC, they began establishing colonies round the shores of the **Black Sea**. By the fifth century BC Greeks seemed to sit upon the shores of the entire world, in Plato's words like "frogs around a pond". Sometimes these colonies were founded on uninhabited land, but otherwise the native inhabitants, usually still living in the Bronze Age, were driven inland.

In any case the colonies were always Greek settlements, not the imposition of Greek rule and ways on non-Greeks.

One cause of the colonization movement was competition between the Greeks and the Phoenicians over trade routes; but there was also competition among the Greek city-states themselves, with **Chalkis**, **Eretria** and **Corinth** the major Greek colonisers in the West, while the **Ionian Greeks**, prevented from expanding into the interior of Asia Minor by Phrygia and Lydia, were the chief colonisers around the Black Sea. When the Spartans needed more land, they conquered neighbouring Messenia in 710 BC, but generally land shortage, and also famine, drove Greeks overseas, notably the colonists from Thera (Thíra) who were sent to found Cyrene in North Africa and were forbidden to return on pain of death. Sometimes the colonizing motive was political, with the aristocracies that ruled Greek city-states during the eighth and seventh centuries BC encouraging emigration to alleviate discontent, just as there were those who were happy to make a new life elsewhere rather than endure discrimination by the aristocracy at home. Yet the colonies, for whatever reason they were founded, usually kept up close relations with their mother cities, while the new city-states of Greater Greece in particular made a major contribution to the literature, philosophy and art of the Hellenic world.

Democracy, tyranny and slavery

In the city-states, which would be the foundation of Greek society for nearly a thousand years, tension arose between the **aristocracy** and the **people**, the one group defending privilege, the other demanding justice. Ultimately wealth from trade undermined the aristocracy and in place of their oligarchic form of government gave rise to **democracy** instead. A new **urban population** developed as commerce became more important relative to agriculture, and this doubtless helped the democratic movement. Ironically, the transition to democracy was often effected by **tyrannies** which were established in many city-states of Greece and Asia Minor around the middle of the seventh century BC. Though tyrants were virtual dictators, they never claimed to rule by divine right, and in theory were always responsible to the public interest, fulfilling the role of professional public servant or statesman. Usually they won power as champions of the people and in some cases were even elected by them; they inaugurated programmes of public works both to give jobs to the poor and to beautify their cities; and like the Renaissance Medicis they were patrons of culture, entertaining poets and seeking out the most brilliant architects and artists to built and adorn the local temples. Their type is illustrated by **Pisistratos**, tyrant of Athens during the sixth century BC, who ensured Athenian prosperity by gaining control of the route into the Black Sea, who ordered that Homer's works be set down in their definitive form and performed regularly at the Panathenaic festival, and who encouraged the theatrical festivals of Dionysus where Greek drama would be born.

Yet at about the same time as they were founding city-states, and faced with a shortage of free men to support the development of trade and manufacturing, Greeks turned to **slavery**, which they organized on a commercial scale from about 700 BC onwards. Previously, household slaves, as found in Homer, were usually war captives; their numbers were not many, nor was Greek society dependent on them. But during the seventh century BC slavery became a widespread, organized and pernicious institution, involving the import of large numbers from Thrace, Asia Minor and the coasts of the Black Sea.

Egypt and Lydia

With the opening up of **Egypt** to Greek traders in about the middle of the seventh century BC, that country was to exercise a profound influence on the culture of Greece, particularly in the fields of stone architecture and sculpture. But immediately more crucial was **Lydia**, on which for better or for worse the Greeks of Asia Minor were largely dependent, prospering on the trade that passed between the two, but always fearing that if Lydia grew too powerful it would threaten the independence of the Greek coastal cities.

Yet the ultimate importance of Lydia was as a buffer between Greece and the great empires of the East; it kept Greece from coming into direct contact with the empire of **Assyria**, and for sixty years it served as a bulwark between the Greeks and the **Persian empire**. But when that barrier was swept away, the course was set for two centuries of conflict between the West and East.

Athens and the Golden Age: 490–31 BC

The **Athenian Acropolis** was inhabited at least as far back as 5000 BC. Men were attracted by its natural springs and the defence provided by its precipitous height. The Mycenaeans fortified it; tyrants later imposed their rule from it. The Acropolis has these associations of primitive succour and power. But with the fall of the Pisistratid dictatorship in 510 BC the Athenians reserved the Acropolis to the exclusive inhabitation of their gods. It was an act of respect to the **deities** but also a shrewd political move by a people bent on democracy. Without tyrants over them and with their gods provided for, down below the citizens could say that they themselves should be the measure of all things. In the century that followed Athens achieved its apotheosis and lived a golden age.

Athenian democracy

Democracy in Athens and its hinterland of Attica was not the mass democracy of today. In all, the population amounted to not more than 400,000 people, of whom about 80,000 were slaves, 160,000 resident foreigners, and another 160,000 free-born Athenians. Out of this last category came the **citizens**, those who could vote and be elected to office, their number amounting to no more than 45,000 adult men.

Yet if the powers of democracy were in the hands of the few, the energy, boldness and creative spirit that it released raised Athens to greatness. Throughout the **fifth century BC** the political, intellectual and artistic activity of the Greek world was centred on the city. In particular Athens was the patron of **drama**, both tragedy and comedy. Whereas the patrons of lyric poetry were tyrants and the aristocracy, drama was the art of a democratic people. Without being necessarily tragic in the modern sense, Greek tragedy, which is to say **Athenian tragedy**, always addressed the great issues of life and death and the relationship of man to the gods. And indeed the Athenians themselves seemed to be conscious of living out a high drama as they fought battles, argued policy, raised temples and wrote plays that have decided the course and sensibility of Western civilization.

A high proportion of the ancient sites that can still be seen in Greece today were built as **shrines and temples to the gods**. They include spectacular sites such as Delphi and the Acropolis in Athens, but also very many other sanctuaries, great and small, in marketplaces and by roadsides, in cities and on islands, on mountaintops and headlands – everywhere, in fact, because the gods themselves were everywhere.

There were many lesser and local gods such as the Nymphs and Pan, but the great gods known to all were the **twelve** who lived on **Mount Olympus**. Ten were already recognised by Homer in the eighth century BC: **Zeus**, the lord of the heavens and supreme power on Olympus; **Hera**, his wife and sister, and goddess of fertility; **Athena** the goddess of wisdom, patron of crafts and fearless warrior; **Apollo** the god of music, of prophecy and the arts; his sister **Artemis**, the virgin huntress and goddess of childbirth; **Poseidon**, the god of the sea and the forces of nature; the beautiful **Aphrodite**, goddess of love and desire; **Hermes**, the messenger who leads the souls of the dead to the underworld, but also the protector of the home and of the market; **Hephaestus**, the lame god of craftsmen and for a while the husband of Aphrodite; and **Ares**, the god of war, who in cuckolding Hephaestus was subdued by the goddess of love. In the fifth century BC these were joined by two deities who had something of a mystical quality of rebirth about them: **Demeter**, the goddess of crops and female fertility; and **Dionysus**, the god of wine and intoxication.

Though limited in number, the Olympian deities could be made to play an infinite number of roles in local cult calendars by the addition of epithets, so that Zeus became "Zeus of the city" or "Zeus of mountaintops", as well as "kindly" or "fulfilling" as place and occasion required. The gods had human form, and they were born and had sexual relations among themselves and humankind, but they never ate human food nor did they age or die. Yet it is notable that whereas the gods of most nations claim to have created the world, the Olympians made no such claim. The most they ever did was to conquer it and then enjoy its fruits, not so unlike mankind itself.

These were the deities, worshipped, feared and admired, who formed the basis for the ancient Greek religion until **paganism** was banned throughout the newly Christianized Roman Empire in AD 391.

The Persian Wars

The wars between Greece and Persia began with a revolt against Persian rule by Ionian Greeks in Asia Minor. They were given support by Athens and Eretria, who in 498 burnt the city of Sardis in Asia Minor. This act of insolence provided a pretext for **Darius**, the Persian king, to launch a punitive expedition against the Greeks. But the **Persians'** unexpected repulse at **Marathon** in 490 BC demanded that Darius hurl his full military might against Greece to ensure its subjection once and for all to the Persian Empire.

When Darius died in 486 BC the execution of this plan was left to **Xerxes** who in 483 BC began preparations that lasted two years and were on a fabulous scale. Bridges of boats were built across the Hellespont near Abydos, modern Çanakkale, for Persia's vast imperial army to parade into Europe, and a canal was cut through the peninsular finger now occupied by the Mount Athos monasteries so that the Persian fleet could avoid the danger of storms while rounding the headlands of the Halkidhikí. Though the Greek historian **Herodotus** claimed that there were one million eight hundred thousand soldiers in Xerxes' army, his figure is probably a tenfold exaggeration. Even so, it was a massive force, an army of forty-six nations under Xerxes' command, dressed and armed according to the ways of their native lands – Persians, Medes

The Battle of Marathon

For the Athenians, victory in the **Battle of Marathon** set the seal on their democracy and marked the beginning of a new self-confident era. And indeed, it was the most remarkable of victories.

Fearing that it would be fatal to attack the larger numbers of Persian infantry supported by cavalry and archers, the Athenian army kept to its position astride the mountain pass leading into the plain of Marathon and waited there for Spartan reinforcements. On the fifth day the Persians gave up hope of joining battle at Marathon and embarked their cavalry to advance on Athens by sea, sending their infantry forwards to cover the operation. With the Persian forces divided, **Miltiades** saw his opportunity, Spartan help or no, and sent his hoplites racing downhill to get quickly under the hail of Persian arrows and engage their infantry in close combat. The Athenian centre was kept weak while the wings were reinforced, so that when the Persians broke through the centre of the charging line, the momentum of the Greek wings soon engulfed them on either side and to the rear. The Persians panicked, fell into disorder, and were beaten into the marshes and the sea. Seven Phoenician ships were lost and 6400 Persians killed. The 192 Athenian dead were buried on the spot, among them Kallimachos, and covered by a mound which can still be seen today. An unrecorded number of Plataeans also died.

The remainder of the Persian force now sailed round Cape Sounion to land within sight of the Acropolis at Phaleron, but Miltiades had brought the army back to Athens by forced march and stood ready to meet the enemy for the second time that day. That astonishing burst of energy – 10,000 men marching 26 miles in full armour after fighting one battle to fight, if need be, another – overwhelmed the Persians' morale, and their expedition returned to Asia.

---

and Cissians; Hyrcanians, Assyrians and Bactrians; Sacae, Indians, Ethiopians, Sarangians and Sagartians; Caspians, Colchians and Thracians, and many more. In addition, Xerxes' fleet of probably eight hundred triremes was furnished by Phoenicians, Egyptians, Cypriots, Cilicians, Pamphylians, Lycians, Carians and subject Ionian Greeks, his ships carrying almost as many sailors as there were soldiers in his army.

Yet both at sea off **Salamis** in 480 BC and on land at **Plataea** the following year, the might of Asia was routed. It was the culmination of that great theme that gives shape to Herodotus's history, the ancient struggle between Europe and Asia which he traced back to the walls of Troy. But it was not at Plataea that Herodotus quite completed his account. Within a few days of that battle came another, near **Miletus**. Following the defeat of his fleet at Salamis, Xerxes had feared a renewed uprising in Ionia, and so leaving his army under the command of Mardonius (who will die at Plataea) he came to Sardis to take charge of his reserves. The Ionians had indeed sent to Greece for help, and now a Greek fleet sailed for **Mycale**, off Samos, where the battle was won when Xerxes' subject Ionians went over to their fellow Hellenes. Xerxes could do no more than return to Susa, his capital deep in Persia, leaving the entire Aegean free.

Though there would be occasional reversals, this sudden shift in the balance of power between East and West would endure, so far as most of Asia Minor was concerned, for the next one thousand five hundred years. Within one hundred and fifty years Alexander the Great would achieve in Asia what Xerxes had failed to achieve in Europe, and the Persian Empire would succumb to a Greek conqueror.

Themistocles

The greatest Athenian statesman, and architect of the victory over Persia, was **Themistocles**. Since the Ionian revolt he understood that a clash between Persia and Greece was inevitable, and he had the genius to recognise that Athens' security and potential lay in its command of the sea. His great achievement was advancing his naval policy in the face of scepticism and opposition. He began the work when he was archon in 493–492 BC by developing **Piraeus** (Pireás) as the harbour of Athens, in place of the open roadstead of Phaleron. He used the hostility of the island of Aegina (Égina) to convince Athenians of his policy, but always his eyes were on the more distant but far greater Persian danger.

When the Persians marched into Attica in the late summer of 480 BC, the oracle at Delphi told the Athenians to trust in their wooden wall, which many took to mean the wooden wall built round the citadel of the Athenian Acropolis, but Themistocles argued that the prophecy referred to the Athenian fleet. Determined to fight at sea, Themistocles warned his Peloponnesian allies against retreating to the Isthmus where they too had built a wall, threatening that if they did the entire citizenry of Athens would sail in their ships to make new homes in southern Italy, leaving the rest of Greece to its fate. On the eve of the Battle of Salamis, as the Persians stormed the walls of the Acropolis, slaughtering its defenders and burning down its temples, the taunt came back from the Peloponnesians that Athens had no city anyway. But Themistocles replied that so long as the Athenians had 200 ships they had a city and a country.

The Greek victory at Salamis cut the Persians' maritime lines of supply and contributed to their defeat at Plataea the following year. Athens and its allies, who now had command of the sea, carried the war across the Aegean, and by the end of 479 BC succeeded in freeing the Greek cities of Asia Minor and the Hellespont from Persian rule. For his pains the Athenians later drove Themistocles into exile. He died at Magnesia on the Maeander, upriver from Miletus, where by way of a pension he was made governor by the Persian king.

The Rise of the Athenian Empire: 478–431 BC

The chronology of the period after the Persian invasion is sketchy: Herodotus ends his history with the capture of Sestos, and Thucydides managed only a scant narrative leading up to his account of the Peloponnesian War. But in outline the trend is clear. The first consequence of the Greek victory against the Persians was not, as might have been expected, the aggrandisement of **Sparta**, the pre-eminent Greek military power, whose soldiers had obediently sacrificed themselves at Thermopylae and had won the final mainland battle at Plataea. Instead, after the repulse of Persia many Greek city-states round the Aegean voluntarily placed themselves under the leadership of Athens.

This confederation was named the **Delian League** – after the island of Delos, sacred to Apollo, at the centre of the Cyclades where the allies kept their treasury – and its first task was to protect the Greeks of Asia Minor against a vengeful Xerxes and to reduce Persia's forward posts. This was the opposite of the policy proposed by Sparta and supported by its Peloponnesian allies, which called for the abandonment of Greek homes across the Aegean and the resettlement of Asian Greeks on the lands of those who had submitted to the Persians in northern Greece.

This policy was in keeping with the attitude shown by Sparta throughout the Persian crisis. Then Sparta had shown no initiative and acted only at the last minute; its policy was provincial, protecting its position in the Peloponnese rather than pursuing the wider interests of Greece. This narrowness and conservatism followed through into the peace. Sparta lacked vision and adventure and experience of the sea; what could not be achieved by land was impossible, it believed. Also Sparta lacked the mercantile ethos; it could not prosper on the widening opportunities presented by the opening of the sea routes to trade. And so over the coming decades Sparta lost prestige to Athens, which Themistocles had established as a maritime power and whose imperial potential was realised under Pericles.

This was the **Athenian golden age**, and in so far as Athens was also "the school of Hellas", as the city's leader **Pericles** said, it was a golden age for all Greece. The fifty years following Salamis and Plataea witnessed an extraordinary flowering in architecture, sculpture, literature and philosophy; men recognised the historical importance of their experience and gave it realisation through the creative impulse. Just as **Herodotus**, the "father of history", made the contest between Europe and Asia the theme of his great work, so **Aeschylus**, who fought at Marathon, made Xerxes the tragic subject of his play *The Persians* and in the process brought the art of drama to life. Indeed in the intoxicating

Aeschylus and Sophocles: The development of Greek tragedy

Tragedy was invented in Athens late in the sixth century BC at a time when peasants were settling in the city but were still in touch with their country traditions. Among these traditions was the fertility ritual celebrating the life and death of Dionysus, the god of the vine, who shed his blood for mankind. Goats were sacrificed in the worship of Dionysus, and so the ritual, in which a chorus danced and sang, was called *trag-odia*, a goat-song. In about 520 BC the story moved away from the Dionysus cycle and an actor was introduced who came and went, changing costumes and playing different roles in a succession of episodes.

Aeschylus changed things greatly by introducing a second actor and increasing the amount of dialogue, while correspondingly reducing the size and role of the chorus, so that tragedy truly became drama, driven by exchanges of words and actions. Aeschylus had fought at Marathon and probably at Salamis too, perhaps explaining the urgency of his play, *The Persians*, the oldest surviving Greek tragedy. Aeschylus was a religious man who believed in the overwhelming power of the gods, but he makes clear that it is man himself, through the free choices he makes rather than as a creature of fate, who steps into the appalling conflicts of the tragic situation.

By tradition four plays were submitted to Athens' annual Dionysian festival, three of them tragedies, the fourth a satyr play providing comic relief, and here too Aeschylus made an innovation, making his three tragedies successive phases of one story – famously in the late work of his maturity, the *Oresteia*, a great drama of revenge and expiation turning on Agamemnon's return home from the Trojan War and his murder. By this time Aeschylus was using a third actor and also painted scenery, ideas taken from **Sophocles**, his younger rival.

Sophocles' innovation of a third actor made it possible to present plots of considerable complexity. He was a man of orthodox piety; he was not in rebellion against the world; but it is a world of inescapable consequences, in his *Oedipus Rex*, for example, where to be unseeing is not enough, or in the *Antigone* which presents the ultimate tragic conflict – between right and right.

The effect of the tragedies of Aeschylus and Sophocles was to leave their audiences with an enhanced sense of pity or of terror; the unspoken moral being "You are in this too", the cathartic experience leaving everyone stronger – as though Athens, democratic, confident and imperial, was preparing itself to meet the blows of destiny.

Athenian atmosphere it seemed that the warriors who turned back the Persian tide had fought in the same cause as Homer's heroes at the walls of Troy. In thanksgiving and celebration the temples upon the Acropolis which the Persians had destroyed were rebuilt, the city ennobling itself as it ennobled the houses of its gods – most notably, of course, with the building of the **Parthenon**.

Yet still Athens was just one among numerous city-states, each ready to come together during a common danger but reasserting its sovereignty as the foreign threat receded. This was illustrated by the ten-year struggle beginning in 461 BC between Athens and various **Peloponnesian states**, which was a warning of a yet greater war to come between Athens and Sparta itself. Perhaps 451 BC marks the fatal moment when Athens passed up the opportunity to create an institution more generous, and more inclusive, than the city-state. Instead Pericles supported the parochial and populist demand that **Athenian citizenship** should not be extended to its allies, thereby stoking up the flames of envy and foregoing the chance of creating a genuine and enduring Greek confederacy.

△ A bust of Pericles, Athens' great statesman, found near Tivoli, Italy

Pericles and his times

Pericles (c.495 BC–429 BC) announced himself on the public stage in 472 BC when he gave his backing to Themistocles by financing the chorus for the *Persians* by Aeschylus; he entered politics during the following decade as prosecutor of the conservative leader, Kimon. In 461 BC, he was elected to the position of *strategos* (general) – the most important elected position in Athens, for the ten strategoi proposed the legislation that was then voted on in the Assembly. Pericles possessed a brilliance in winning over audiences, so that in a society where the people was sovereign the reality was that he governed the state; with only two exceptions, he was annually re-elected *strategos* until his death in 429 BC.

Given the reactionary forces that had to be contended with at home, it is not surprising that after the death of Kimon, head of the conservative pro-Spartan party in Athens, Pericles concluded a **peace with Persia** in 449 BC, the better to turn his attention to **Sparta**, that bastion of reaction in Greece. Pericles believed that Athenian power was not only Greece's best defence against Persia but also the best hope for the unification of Greece under enlightened rule, for he also believed that culturally Athens was "the school of Hellas". The visible expression of this cultural excellence could be seen atop the Acropolis where Pericles was directly responsible for the construction of the Propylaea and the Parthenon, but it was true too in sculpture, painting, drama, poetry, history, teaching and philosophy, their achievement not only celebrated in Athens at the time of Pericles but since then and everywhere informing the values of mankind. Politically, as both Pericles and his enemies understood, the advance of democracy in Greece depended on the success of that Athenian imperialism which grew out of the Delian League.

But whatever the excellence of Athens, whatever the ideals of its power, the jealousies of the Peloponnesians were excited all the more, and it is a testimony to Pericles that he was able to avoid war with Sparta for as long as he did. Thucydides, the historian of the Peloponnesian War, greatly admired Pericles for his integrity and also for the restraint he exercised over Athenian democracy, which never descended into demagoguery under his rule.

The decline of the city-state: 431–338 BC

From about the time of the battle of Eurymedon in 468 BC, association with Athens through the **Delian League** ceased to be voluntary. Allegiances were enforced and contributions became tributes, so that when Sparta and its Peloponnesian allies declared war on Athens in 431 BC, they could claim that they were fighting to restore political independence to all those states, in Greece and across the Aegean, that the Athenians had "enslaved". At war's end, however, when Athens had been defeated, both those who had been subject to its empire as well as others who had been allies of Sparta discovered that a new and far more oppressive power had taken Athens' place: the very Spartans who had proclaimed themselves as liberators. More fundamentally, the **Peloponnesian War**, which had been fought to assert the sovereignty of city-states, in fact left them weaker and more vulnerable in the long term to outside forces, which in the end meant seeing Greece reduced to a province of the new Macedonian empire.

The writing of history began among the Greeks, first with **Herodotus**, then with Thucydides. But with Herodotus there is the feeling that he prefers telling a good story, that he still inhabits Homer's world of epic poetry, whereas with **Thucydides** the paramount concern is to analyse events. In that sense Thucydides is the first modern historian; wherever possible he seeks out primary sources, and his concern is always with objectivity, detail and chronology, for these are the elements of his historical analysis. Not that there is anything dry about Thucydides; the vividness and insight of his writing make reading him as powerful an experience as watching a Greek drama.

Thucydides began writing his history at the outset of the **Peloponnesian War** with the intention of giving an account of its whole duration, but for reasons unknown he abruptly stopped writing in the twentieth year, though he is thought to have survived the war by a few years, living until about 400 BC. He was born into a wealthy and conservative Athenian family in about 455 BC, though he himself was a democrat and an admirer of Pericles, and through his reconstruction of Pericles' speeches he presents the most eloquent expression of the Athenian cause. But when Thucydides was exiled from his city seven years into the war, this was the making of him as a historian, for as he himself said, "Associating with both sides, with the Peloponnesians quite as much as with the Athenians, because of my exile, I was thus enabled to watch quietly the course of events".

However much the statesmen and generals in his history rationalise war, Thucydides was himself a military man who understood war at first hand and knew that there was always the irrational element of chance. He also understood that the best chance for overcoming the hazards of chance came from courage and resourcefulness, from flexibility of mind and clarity of thought. Hence his concern for method in his research and analysis in his writing, for he intended his book to be useful to future generals in conducting war and to future statesmen in forming policy. For these reasons we have a better understanding of the Peloponnesian War than of any conflict in ancient times until Julius Caesar began writing his own first-hand accounts of his campaigns. And for these reasons too, Thucydides' history stands on a par with the greatest literature of ancient Greece.

The Peloponnesian War

The **Peloponnesian War** which began in **431 BC** was really a continuation of the conflict that broke out in 461 BC between Athens and its principal commercial rivals, Corinth and Aegina and their various allies in the Peloponnese. Sparta had at that time stood aside as its interests were not directly affected. But by 432 BC when Corinth again agitated for war, following the bruisings it had received over Corcyra (Corfu) and Potidea, the **Spartans** had become fearful of growing Athenian power. Behind this was their dread that Athens might one day loosen Sparta's hold over the Laconian and Messenian plains; yet they saw no contradiction in joining with their allies of the Peloponnesian League in going to war with the proclaimed aim of "liberating" Greece from the Athenian empire.

The Athenian empire was built on trade. **Piraeus** had grown enormously since the days of Themistocles so that it was now one of the great ports of the Mediterranean, its cosmopolitan population of alien residents controlling most of its manufacturing and mercantile activities. On the initiative of Pericles, the town of Piraeus had been rebuilt by Hippodamus, an architect of Miletus, its streets arranged in a rectangular grid system – the first such layout in Europe and the model for later Greek cities throughout the world. "The fruits of the whole earth flow in upon us", as Pericles said to his fellow Athenians, "so that we enjoy the goods of other countries as freely as of our own." And as well as goods, great wealth and human talent was drawn to Athens, so that Pericles could rightly proclaim that Athens was the centre of Greek culture.

That Athens was a great sea power with 300 triremes while the members of Sparta's **Peloponnesian League** were land powers without significant navies determined the nature of the war. When the Peloponnesians combined with their Boeotian allies they could put 30,000 hoplites into the field without calling on reserves. The Athenians had only half this number and would have to call up reserves to match it. Just as the strategy of Themistocles had been to fight the Persians by sea, so Pericles followed the same plan against Sparta and its allies, avoiding major battles against the superior land forces of the Peloponnesian League. Athens and Piraeus were protected by their walls, but the Peloponnesians and their Boeotian allies were allowed to invade Attica with impunity nearly every year, and there was constant warfare in Thrace. On the other hand the Peloponnesians lacked the seapower to carry the fighting into Asia Minor and the Aegean islands or to interfere with Athens' routes of trade, while the Athenians used their maritime superiority to launch attacks against the coasts of the Peloponnese, the Ionian islands and the mouth of the Gulf of Corinth in the hope that they would succeed in detaching members from the Peloponnesian League. As long as Athens remained in command of the sea, with its trade routes and its prosperity intact, it had every reason to expect that it could wear down its enemies' resolve.

Pericles' death in 329 BC was an early blow to the Athenian cause. **Kleon**, his successor, has received a critical press in the writings of Thucydides and the comic plays of Aristophanes for being an uncouth man of the people who too aggressively pursued the war. But if Pericles' empire was justified, then Kleon's policy of vigorous action was likewise justified, and he served Athens better than the ditherings of Nikias and the peace lobby. A peace party existed at Athens throughout the war, and the city insisted on giving it an audience, not only in political debate but on the stage, for example in the 415 BC production of Euripides' *Trojan Women*, performed on the eve of what proved to be the disastrous Sicilian expedition. By then Kleon was dead, and instead of operational responsibility for the Sicilian expedition being put in the hands of the ablest general, the Assembly divided the command and constantly interfered, so that a bold operation designed to win Sicily to the Athenian cause turned into a catastrophic debacle. The failure, as Thucydides observed, was political, not military, and the same can be said generally about Athens' conduct throughout the second half of the war, where the Assembly's failure to adopt a consistent position led to ultimate defeat.

City-state rivalries

The Peloponnesian War left **Sparta** the supreme power in Greece, but it took very little time for those whom the Spartans had "liberated" to realise that they had simply acquired a new and inferior master, one that entirely lacked the style, the ability and the intelligence of Athens. Nor was it forgotten that Sparta had gained its victory by bargaining away to Persia the freedom of the **Asia Minor Greeks**. Famous for their discipline and incorruptibility at home, the moment the Spartans found themselves in charge of an empire abroad they became avaricious and petty tyrants; they demanded tribute more brutally than Athens had done, and their allies never saw a penny of it.

Isolationist, old-fashioned, autocratic and terrified of overseas commitments, Sparta proved totally inept at playing the leading role in Greece.

Meanwhile Athens had lost its empire but not its trade, which was built on firm foundations, so that not only did Corinth fail in its demands to have its defeated rival razed to the ground, but it faced no less mercantile competition than before. Moreover during the first decade of the fourth century Athens was able to restore much of its naval power in the Aegean. To contain any challenge from Greece, whether from the Spartans or the Athenians, the **Persians** now played one off against the other while giving aid to each, so that for example in 393 BC, just eleven years after they were demolished, the Long Walls between Athens and Piraeus were rebuilt – with Persian money.

Adding to the intrigues between Persia, Athens and Sparta were a bewildering and unstable variety of alliances involving numerous other Greek states. The most important of these was **Thebes**, which had been an ally of Sparta during the Peloponnesian War but came round to the Athenian side, and then for a spectacular moment under its brilliant general **Epaminondas** became the greatest power in Greece. At the **battle of Leuctra** in **371 BC** the Thebans defeated the Spartan army and with it the myth of Spartan invincibility. The following year Epaminondas went further, and after marching through Laconia in a display of strength, he liberated Messenia on which the Spartan economy depended. Sparta suffered an immediate loss of wealth and power from which it never recovered, and its population went into permanent decline.

Almost the whole of Theban energy and power was bound up in the person of Epaminondas, and when he was killed in the **battle of Mantinea** in **362 BC**, Thebes relinquished its ambitions in the Peloponnese. For the first time in over a century Greece found itself free from the dictates of Persia or any overpowerful Greek state. Exhausted and impoverished by almost continuous war, it was an opportunity for Greece to peacefully unite. But along the way the political and moral significance of the city-state had eroded, and with the **rise of Macedonia** came the concept of an all-embracing kingship.

The Macedonian Empire and Hellenistic Greece: 348–146 BC

Despite its large size and population, **Macedonia** had played little role in early Greek affairs. Its weakness was due to the constitutional position of the king who was not assured the throne by primogeniture; rather a member of the royal family who asserted his right to the kingship was subject to approval by a vote of the nobility. Rivalries among potential heirs and fears of usurpation limited royal power. Moreover, the Greeks did not consider the Macedonians to be properly Greek, not in speech, culture or political system. They did not live in city-states, which Aristotle said was the mark of a civilised human being, rather they were a tribal people who were closer to the barbarians.

Philip II and the rise of Macedonia

But towards the middle of the fourth century, and in contrast to the exhaustion and lack of leadership among the Greek city-states, the power of Macedonia grew. This was due to the accession of **Philip II**, who strengthened royal authority by building up the army on the basis of personal loyalty to himself,

The Golden Age of Athens under Pericles, and the period of city-state rivalry after the Peloponnesian War, saw the **birth of Western philosophy** under the towering figures of Socrates, Plato and Aristotle.

Socrates (c.470–399 BC)

Socrates was born the son of an Athenian sculptor and for a time was a sculptor himself. He fought bravely for Athens as a hoplite in the Peloponnesian War, though long before it, in his twenties, he had turned to philosophy, which he practised in his own peculiar style. He promoted no philosophical position of his own but asserted, ceaselessly, the supremacy of reason. Often this was done in the streets of Athens, button-holing some self-regarding Athenian of the older generation, asking him questions, picking his answers to pieces, until he came up with a definition that held water or, more likely, the spluttering victim were reduced to a confession of his own ignorance in front of crowds of Socrates' mirthful young supporters.

By this "Socratic method" he asked for definitions of familiar concepts such as piety and justice; his technique was to argue people into exposing the ignorance that hid behind the bandying about of terms, even as he claimed a similar ignorance for himself. Indeed when the Delphic oracle proclaimed that no man was wiser than Socrates, he explained this by saying wisdom lies in knowing how little one really knows. Because he valued this question-and-answer process over settling on fixed conclusions, Socrates never wrote anything down. Yet his influence was pivotal; before his time philosophical inquiry concerned itself with speculations on how the natural world was formed and how it operates; afterwards it looked to the analysis of concepts and to ethics.

Socrates's method could be irritating, especially when he called into question conventional morality, and his friendships with people associated with oligarchy, like Alcibiades and Kritias, did not put him in good stead with a democratic Athens that had just lost an empire and a war. Probably many factors directed the city's anger, fear and frustration at Socrates, and Athenians wanted to see the back of him. The means used were to try him for impiety and corrupting the young, then to sentence him to death, but to give him the option of naming another penalty, probably expecting that he would choose exile. Instead Socrates answered that if he was to get what he deserved, he should be maintained for life at the public expense. At this the death penalty was confirmed, but even then it was not to be imposed for two months, with the tacit understanding that Socrates would escape. Instead Socrates argued that it was wrong for a citizen to disobey even an unjust law, and in the company of his friends he drank the cup of hemlock. "Such was the end", wrote Plato, who describes the scene in his *Phaedo*, "of our friend; of whom I may truly say, that of all the men of his time whom I have known, he was the wisest and justest and best."

Plato (c.427–c.347 BC)

As a young man, Plato painted, composed music and wrote a tragedy, as well as being a student of Socrates. He intended a career in politics, where his connections would have ensured success; his father could claim descent from the last king of Athens, his mother was descended from Solon, and the family had been close allies of Pericles. But Socrates' death made Plato decide that he could not serve a government that had committed such a crime, and instead his mission became to exalt the memory of his teacher. In Plato's writings, many of them dialogues, Socrates is frequently the leading participant, while at the Academy in Athens, which Plato founded, the Socratic question-and-answer method was the means of instruction.

Plato's philosophy is elusive; he never sets out a system of doctrines, nor does he tell us which of his ideas are most basic, nor rank them in a hierarchical order, nor show how they interrelate. Nevertheless, certain themes recur. He believed that men possess immortal souls separate from their mortal bodies. Also knowledge, he believed, was the recollection of what our souls already know, so that we do not gain knowledge from experience, rather by using our reasoning capacity to draw more closely to the realm of our souls. The true objects of knowledge are not the transient, material things of this world, for these are only reflections of a higher essence which Plato called Forms or Ideas. Forms are objects of pure thinking, cut off from our experience; but also Forms motivate us to grasp them, so that the reasoning part of us is drawn to Forms as a kind of mystic communion.

Plato's notion of a mystic union with a higher essence would play an important role in later religious thought. But more immediately his teachings at the Academy concerned themselves with logic, mathematics, astronomy and above all political science, for its purpose was to train a new ruling class. Prominent families sent him their sons to learn the arts of government, and Plato, an aristocrat born into a calamitous age marked by Athens' imperial defeat, responded by teaching that the best form of government was a constitutional monarchy, at its head a philosopher-king with that higher knowledge of Justice and the Good drawn from the realm of Forms. Though it was a utopian vision, Plato's political philosophy helped prepare the intellectual ground for the acceptance of an absolutist solution to the increasing uncertainties of fourth-century BC Greece.

Aristotle (384–322 BC)

Aristotle grew up in Pella, the capital of an increasingly powerful Macedonia, where his father had been appointed doctor to King Amyntas II; it is therefore not unlikely that Amyntas's son, the future Philip II, and Aristotle were boyhood friends. However, at the age of seventeen, Aristotle was sent to Plato's Academy at Athens to continue his education, and he remained there, first as a student, then as a teacher, a faithful follower of Plato's ideas. His independent philosophy matured later, during the years he spent, again at Pella, as tutor to Alexander the Great, and later still, after 335 BC, when he founded his own school, the Lyceum, in Athens.

Aristotle came to reject Plato's dualism. He did not believe that the soul was of a substance separate from the body, rather that it was an aspect of the body. Likewise with Plato's theory of Forms. Instead of Plato's inward looking view, Aristotle sought explanations of the physical world and of human society from the viewpoint of an outside observer. Essentially a scientist and a realist, he was bent on discovering the true rather than establishing the good, and he believed that sense perception was the only means of human knowledge. Following this vision, his output was vast and covered many fields of knowledge – logic, metaphysics, ethics, politics, rhetoric, art, poetry, physiology, anatomy, biology, zoology, physics, astronomy and psychology. Everything could be measured, analysed and described, and he was the first person to classify organisms into genera and species. He is probably the only person who has ever assimilated the whole body of existing knowledge on all subjects and brought it within a single focus.

The exactitude of Aristotle's writings does not make them easy reading, and Plato has always enjoyed a wider appeal owing to his literary skill. All the same, Aristotle's influence has been enormous on Western intellectual and scientific tradition.

not to tribe or locality. Philip was also determined to hellenise his country. Borrowing from Greek ways and institutions, he founded the city of **Pella** as his capital and lured teachers, artists and intellectuals to his court, among them **Aristotle** and **Euripides**. Philip was an admirer of Athens with which he sought an alliance that would make them joint-masters of the Greek world. But the Athenians opposed him, and he took matters into his own hands.

In **338 BC** Philip brought about the unity of the mainland Greeks, not by their voluntary adhesion that had been envisioned by Isocrates, the Athenian statesman, rather on the battlefield at **Chaironeia**. There, to the east of Delphi, the Theban and Athenian forces were defeated by one of the most formidable fighting units the world has ever seen, the **Macedonian phalanx**. Armed with the *sarissa*, an eighteen-foot pike tapering from butt to tip, its infantrymen were trained to move across a battlefield with all the discipline of a parade ground drill. Instead of relying on a headlong charge, its effectiveness lay in manipulating the enemy line, pinning it down here, advancing obliquely against it there, or by performing that most difficult of manoeuvres, a fighting withdrawal going suddenly over to a forceful and concentrated attack – its purpose always to open up a gap in the enemy line through which the cavalry could make its decisive strike.

Alexander's conquests

After Chaeronia, Philip summoned the Greek states to a meeting at Corinth where he announced his plans for a panhellenic conquest of the Persian Empire. But Philip was murdered two years later and to his son **Alexander** fell his father's plans for an **Asian campaign** – throughout which, it is said, he slept with a copy of the *Iliad* under his pillow.

In the East too there was an assassination, and in 335 BC the Persian throne passed to **Darius III**, namesake of the first and doomed to be the last king of his line. For by using essentially his father's tactics, Alexander would lead his army through a series of astonishing victories, usually against greater numbers, until he reached the heart of the Persian Empire. In May of **334 BC**, with thirty thousand foot soldiers and five thousand horse, Alexander crossed the Hellespont. By autumn all the Aegean coast of **Asia Minor** was his; twelve months later he stood on the banks of the Orontes river in **Syria**; in the winter of 332 BC **Egypt** hailed him as pharaoh; and by the spring of 330 BC the great Persian cities of **Babylon**, **Susa**, **Persepolis** and **Pasargadae** had fallen to him in rapid succession until, at **Ecbatana**, he found Darius in the dust, murdered by his own supporters. Alexander wrapped the corpse in his Macedonian cloak, and in turn he assumed the lordship of Asia.

Hellenistic Greece

No sooner had **Alexander** died at Babylon in 323 BC at the age of thirty-three that Athens led an alliance of Greeks in a **war of liberation** against Macedonian rule. But the Macedonians had built up a formidable navy which inflicted heavy losses on the Athenian fleet. Unable to lift the Macedonian blockade of Piraeus, Athens surrendered and a pro-Macedonian government was installed. The episode marked the end of Athens as a sea power and left it permanently weakened.

Greece was now irrevocably part of a new dominion, one that entirely altered the scale and orientation of the Greek world, for it had been Alexander's strategic vision to see the Mediterranean and the East as two halves of a greater whole. Opened up to Greek settlement and enterprise, and united by Greek learning, language and culture, if not always by a single power, this **Hellenistic Empire** meant an enormous increase in international trade, the creation of unprecedented prosperity, and the establishment of an **ecumene**, the notion of one world, no longer divided by the walls of city-states but a universal concept that was the common possession of all civilized peoples.

"To the strongest", was Alexander's deathbed reply when asked to whom he bequeathed his empire. Forty years of warfare between his leading generals gave rise to three dynasties, the **Antigonid** in Macedonia, which ruled over mainland Greece, the **Seleucid** which ultimately centred on Syria and Asia Minor, and the **Ptolemaic** in Egypt, which ruled from Alexandria, founded by Alexander himself, which in wealth and population, not to mention literature and science, soon outshone anything in Greece.

The emergence of Rome

In the Western Mediterranean, **Rome** was a rising power, its dominance there confirmed in 202 BC when at Zama in North Africa the Carthaginian army under Hannibal was defeated by the legions of Scipio Africanus. **Philip V** of Macedonia had earlier feared the growth of Roman power in the Adriatic and in 215 BC had agreed with Hannibal a treaty of mutual assistance. Now with Hannibal defeated, Rome's legions marched eastwards and at the battle of **Cynoscephalae** in Thessaly in 197 BC they attacked the flanks of the less manoeuvrable Macedonian phalanx and routed Philip's army.

Rome declared Greece liberated and granted autonomy to its **city-states** to order their own affairs. Its actions were marked by a genuine philhellene sentiment, and it was from this time that Rome took on the trappings of **Hellenistic culture**, in architecture, sculpture, literature, philosophy and much else. Continuing eastwards, the Romans first set foot on Asian soil in 190 BC; and as they followed in Alexander's footsteps, it was Rome's generals, and not the Greeks, who first called Alexander "the Great". But Rome's benevolence towards the Greeks ended when Macedonia recovered its former power and found anti-Roman sympathisers among the city-states in Greece. At **Pydna** in 167 the Roman legions again tore into the flanks of the Macedonian phalanx. Macedonia was reduced to a federation of smaller states, and tens of thousands of Greeks who had given it their support were sold into slavery while others were interned for decades without trial in Italy.

The harsh policy stoked up resentment among the Greeks which manifested itself in an **uprising of the Achaean League**, a confederation of city-states in the Peloponnese, which, led by Corinth, raised an army that in 146 BC overran central Greece before it was defeated by Roman legions called in from Italy and the recently annexed province of Macedonia. To guard against further disorder, Rome dissolved the league into its component city-states, turned the Peloponnese and central Greece into the **Roman province of Achaea**, and authorised the Roman governor of Macedonia to interfere whenever necessary to ensure the peace. For good measure they **razed Corinth** and sold off its inhabitants as a warning to any Greeks who might think of resisting Rome again.

Roman Greece: 146 BC–330 AD

With the crushing of the Achaean League in 146 BC, the history of Greece became part of **Roman history**. During the first century BC Rome was riven by a series of civil wars whose climactic battlefields were often in Greece, but Greece was only a bystander in the vaster struggle which determined the shape and mastery of the expanding Roman imperium.

In 49 BC the Roman Republic was in its dying days when **Julius Caesar** defeated his rival Pompey at **Pharsalus** in Thessaly; in 42 BC Caesar's assassins were beaten by **Mark Antony** and **Octavian** at **Philippi** in Macedonia; and in 31 BC **Antony** and his Ptolemaic ally **Cleopatra** were routed by **Octavian** in a sea battle off **Actium** in western Greece before committing suicide in Egypt the following year, Octavian marking the event by changing his name to Augustus and effectively inaugurating the **Roman Empire** – though an empire which in its eastern half continued to speak Greek.

By the first century AD Greece had become a **tourist destination** for well-to-do Romans (and a relatively comfortable place of exile for troublemakers). They went to Athens and Rhodes to study literature and philosophy, and all round the country to see the temples with their paintings and sculpture. They also visited the **Olympic Games** which were by now thoroughly professionalised. When the emperor **Nero** came to Greece in AD 67, he entered the Games as a contestant, the judges prudently declaring him the victor in every competition, even when, as in the case of the chariot race, he was thrown and failed to finish.

Under the Romans there was much **new building** in **Athens** and elsewhere, notably by the emperor Hadrian. The centre of the Athenian Agora, which had long ceased to serve the purposes of a democracy, was filled with an odeon, a covered theatre with seating for a thousand people, the gift of Augustus' general Agrippa. Nearby Hadrian built his public library; he loved Athens and stayed there in 125 and 129, completing the vast **Temple of Olympian Zeus** begun nearly six hundred years before by Pisistratos. **Herodes Atticus**, born into a wealthy Greek family and who served as tutor to the future Roman emperor and philosopher Marcus Aurelius, was a generous patron of the arts in Athens and in the 160s built the odeon that bears his name at the foot of the Acropolis which is still used for plays and concerts today.

Saint Paul and early Christianity

Greece had an early taste of **Christian teaching** when **Saint Paul** came to preach to Jews and Gentiles in 49–52 AD. In Athens he was brought before the Court of the Areopagus, a powerful body that exercised authority over religious affairs, and was asked to defend his talk of the death and resurrection of his foreign god, after which he was dismissed as one of the many cranks who frequented the city. Paul then spent eighteen months in **Corinth** where he made some converts, though as his subsequent Epistles to the Corinthians show, too often their idea of Christianity amounted to celebrating their salvation with carousing and fornication. In the last decades of the century, **Saint John the Divine**, who was proselytising at Ephesus on the coast of Asia Minor, was exiled by the Romans to Patmos where in a cave still shown to visitors today he is said to have written *Revelation*, the apocalyptic last book of the Bible.

Yet though the books of the New Testament were composed in Greek, they were the works of people in the Greek East, while Christianity seems to have made little headway among the inhabitants of Greece itself. Throughout all the **Roman persecutions** of the third and early fourth centuries, in 202 under Septimius Severus, in 249–50 under Decius, in 257 under Valerian and in 303 under Diocletian, in which hundreds of thousands died in Egypt, the Middle East and Asia Minor, there are few recorded martyrs in Greece – probably, it is thought, because there were few Greek Christians.

Barbarian incursions

During the mid-third century the **Heruli**, a tribe in southern Russia associated with the Goths, succeeded in passing through the Bosphorus and into the Aegean where they ravaged far and wide, plundering and burning **Athens** in 267. New city walls were built with the marble rubble from the wreckage, but their circumference was now so small that the ancient Agora, littered with ruins, was left outside, while what remained of the city huddled round the base of the Acropolis. It was a familiar scene throughout Greece, as prosperity declined and population fell, except in the north along the **Via Egnatia**, the Roman road passing through their province of Macedonia, linking ports on the Adriatic with Thessaloniki on the Aegean.

Byzantine and Medieval Greece: 330–1460 AD

That coalescence of Roman authority, Hellenistic culture and the transcendental spirit of the East that we now call the **Byzantine Empire** began in May 330 when the **emperor Constantine** declared that Nova Roma (as he called the city of Byzantium – known today as Istanbul) was the new capital of the Roman Empire. Founded on the banks of the Bosphorus by Greek colonists in the seventh century BC, Byzantium occupied the one supremely defensible and commanding point from where the entire trade between the Black Sea and the Mediterranean could be controlled. But it was only now, a thousand years later, that its full potential was realised. **Constantinople**, the city of Constantine, as it at once became popularly known, was perfectly positioned for the supreme strategic task confronting the empire: the defence of the Danube and the Euphrates frontiers. Moreover the new capital stood astride the flow of goods and culture emanating from the East, that part of the empire richest in economic resources, most densely populated and the home of fertile intellectual and religious activity.

The Christian empire

Constantine's other act with decisive consequences was to **legalise** – and to a considerable extent patronise – the **Christian church**. Here again Constantinople was important, for while Rome's pagan traditions could not yet be disturbed, the new capital was consciously conceived as a Christian city, and within the century Christianity was established as the religion of state, with its liturgies (still in use in the Greek Orthodox Church), the Creed and the New Testament all in Greek.

By allying himself with the Christians, Constantine won the support of the strongest single group in the Roman world. Though perhaps only one in seven of the empire's population were by then admitted Christians, persecution had if anything enhanced their sense of solidarity. Being well organized, their influence extended further than their numbers would suggest, and by preaching the equality and salvation of the individual soul, Christianity could appeal to everyone – men and women, rich and poor, freemen and slaves – while its satisfying synthesis with Greek philosophical thought made it attractive to many of the best intellects of the time. Combining in his person the supreme secular and spiritual authority, Constantine's successors became Christ's vice-regent on earth, while likewise the empire took on a sanctity and a mission that would give it the resilience to survive more than a thousand years to come.

In 391 the emperor **Theodosius I** issued an edict banning all expressions of **paganism** throughout the empire. In Greece the mysteries at Eleusis ceased to be celebrated the following year, and in 395 the Olympic Games were suppressed, their athletic nudity an offence to Christianity. Around this time too the Delphic oracle fell silent. The conversion of pagan buildings to Christian use began in the fifth century. Under an imperial law of 435 the Parthenon and the Erectheion on the Acropolis and the mausoleum of Galerius (the Rotunda) in Thessaloniki and other temples elsewhere were all converted to churches. But even this did not eradicate pagan teaching: in Athens philosophy and law continued to be taught at the Academy, founded by Plato in 385 BC, until prohibited by the emperor Justinian in 529.

Theodosius was the last ruler of a unified Roman Empire, which for much of the past century had seen distinct rulers of its **West and Eastern empires**, and at his death in **395** the split was made permanent, with his sons Honorus and Arcadius appointed Augustus of each respective territory. In 476 **Rome fell** to the barbarians and as the Dark Ages settled on Western Europe Byzantium inherited the sole mantle of the empire. Latin remained the official language of its administration, though after the reign of Justinian (527–565) the emperors joined the people in speaking and writing Greek. Nonetheless they and their people continued to call themselves *Romaioi*, that is Romans.

Plague and invasion

Thessaloníki, the second city of the Byzantine Empire, was relatively close to Constantinople, yet even so the journey by land or sea took five or six days. The rest of Greece was that much farther and, remote from the centre of administration and culture, Attica and the Peloponnese grew decidedly provincial. Conditions worsened sharply in the late sixth century when Greece was devastated by **plague**. In Athens after 580 life came almost to an end, as the remaining inhabitants withdrew to the Acropolis, while at Corinth the population removed itself entirely to the island of Aegina. Only Thessaloníki fully recovered.

Islam and the iconoclastic controversy

The advent of Islam in the mid-seventh century had its effect on Greece. Syria fell to the Arabs in 636 and Egypt in 642, and the loss of these Christian provinces was followed by an attack by an Arab fleet in 677 on Constantinople itself, and again in 717–18 when a combined Arab naval and land force beleaguered the city, while in 823 the Arabs occupied Crete.

The proximity and pressure of Islam helped fuel the great iconoclastic controversy that ignited passions and pervaded many aspects of daily life throughout the Byzantine Empire for over a century. In 730 the emperor Leo III, who was born on the Syrian frontier and earned the epithet "Saracen-minded", proscribed images in the Orthodox Church, claiming they amounted to idolatry. His strongest support came from the farmer-soldiers of Asia Minor, that is those closest to the lands recently conquered by the Muslims, while his opponents, the iconodules, who favoured icons, were found in the monasteries and in Greece. Indeed, it was the empress Irene, an Athenian, who briefly restored the images in 780, though they were again proscribed by imperial decree from 815 to 843, with the effect that almost no representational Byzantine art survives in Greece from before the ninth century.

Following the plague, Greece was invaded by two barbarian tribes, the **Slavs** and **Avars**, who attacked Thessaloníki in 597 and by 600 reached the Peloponnese. Numbering about a hundred thousand in all, the invaders settled throughout the country, and it was not until the tenth century that they were fully pacified by the emperors and converted to Christianity by the Orthodox Church and so assimilated into Greek society.

Meanwhile the **Bulgars** had taken advantage of Byzantine weakness to overrun much of northern Greece. But they were driven out by **Basil II** of the militaristic Macedonian dynasty who in 1018–19 destroyed the Bulgar empire, then celebrated his victory with a visit to Athens, the first in centuries by an emperor, and left magnificent gifts in the Church of the Theotokos Atheniotissa, as the Parthenon had become.

The Crusades

Compared to the Balkans, life in Asia Minor was far more stable and secure. Greeks had been settled on its Aegean shores since the early first millennium BC, and since Alexander's time Greek language and culture had extended eastwards beyond the headwaters of the Euphrates and Tigris rivers. But in 1071 the **Byzantine army** was destroyed at **Manzikert**, a fortress town on the eastern frontier, by the **Seljuk Turks** who went on to occupy almost the whole of Asia Minor.

The Byzantine emperor turned to the West for help to recover his territories from the Muslims, and in 1095 the Roman Catholic Pope replied by launching the **First Crusade**. Together, the Crusaders and the Byzantines won a series of victories over the Seljuks in Asia Minor, but the Byzantines, wary of possible Crusader designs on the empire itself, were content to see their Latin allies from the West advance alone on Jerusalem, which they captured in 1099.

A century later and the worst fears of the Byzantines were borne out when in 1204 the **Fourth Crusade** attacked **Constantinople** itself. Following the recapture of Jerusalem by Saladin, the crusade had embarked from Venice to

---

Plethon replants the seed of Hellas

The encroaching Ottoman threat led to a remarkable reassessment of Byzantine values. Though the Byzantines had never lost sight of their ancient heritage and throughout their history could as readily quote from Homer as from the Bible, now from the first half of the fourteenth century Byzantine intellectuals began to place their hope for regeneration in their classical heritage, in that unconquerable empire of past glory that lay beyond the military and spiritual trespass of the Catholic West and the Muslim East. Among these was **Plethon**, a native of Constantinople, who in the 1420s came to Mystra where he founded a Platonic Academy.

Convinced that Christianity offered no solutions, Plethon proposed instead the salvation of society through a return to the ideals of ancient Greece, supported by a revived Hellenic religion and an ethical system based on Neo-Platonic philosophy. He also supported a new terminology. Until now the word *Hellenes* had been used by the Byzantines to describe the pagan Greeks as opposed to the *Romaioi* of the Christianized Roman Empire. But with the empire reduced to little more than a few city-states, and with a rising admiration in the West for the ancient Greeks, Byzantine intellectuals dropped the word *Romaioi* and began to call themselves Hellenes. And indeed as things turned out, *Rum* became a distasteful appellation, the term applied to subject Greeks of the Ottoman Empire, while as Hellenes they would win independence for the modern state of Greece.

the East. But its purpose was perverted by the **Venetians**, whose aim was to gain the monopoly of the Levant trade from their Byzantine rivals. The Crusaders were indebted for their ships and victuals to the Venetians, who played upon their lust for plunder and their envy of the Greeks to divert them towards the imperial city. After seizing Constantinople and executing the emperor, they installed in his place one of their leaders, **Baldwin**, **Count of Flanders**, while his vassals shared out Greece in a bewildering patchwork of feudal holdings.

In outline, the Peloponnese went to a **Frank** who established himself **Prince of Achaia**; Attica and Boeotia fell to a Burgundian who styled himself **Duke of Athens**; the Lombards set up the **Kingdom of Thessaloníki**; and **Venice**, to ensure its control of the maritime trade, took many of the islands and the chief ports of the Peloponnese. Greeks held only the **Despotate of Epirus** in the northwest of the country, which together with **Nicaea** and **Trebizond** in Asia Minor became the last redoubts of Byzantium.

In 1261 the **Palaeologos dynasty** in Nicaea recovered Constantinople, and the following year the Byzantines made further advances, taking Mistra, Mani and Monemvasiá from which they gradually extended their authority. But a new Turkish dynasty, the **Ottomans**, emerged in the late-thirteenth century and by 1400 controlled Asia Minor and had conquered all of Byzantine Greece except Thessaloníki and the Peloponnese. In 1452 the Ottomans invaded the Peloponnese as a diversion to the main attack on **Constantinople**, which fell to **Sultan Mehmet II** on May 23, 1453.

The Byzantine empire was reduced to a few last enclaves. In 1456 the Ottomans captured **Athens** from the Venetians and turned the Parthenon church into a mosque, and in 1460 Mehmet entered Mistra and conquered the **Peloponnese**. The following year, **Trebizond** fell and the Byzantine empire was no more.

Greece under Turkish occupation: 1460–1821

After 1460 Western possessions in Greece amounted to **Rhodes** – which was held by the Knights of St John – and, under **Venetian rule**, the Peloponnesian ports of **Koróni, Methóni** and **Monemvasiá**, and the islands of **Évvia**, **Crete**, **Corfu**, **Aegina** and (later) **Cyprus**. Outside these areas Greeks lived under **Turkish domination**, the one exception being the **Mani** – the wild mountainous peninsula at the foot of the Peloponnese, where neither Westerner nor Turk dared venture and where the feuding population of Greeks enjoyed a primitive liberty. And the Ottomans continued to extend their power. In 1522 they drove the Knights of St John from Rhodes, and within two more decades they had captured all of the Venetian mainland colonies in Greece, leaving them in control of only Cyprus and Crete.

The nature of Ottoman rule

Sklavía – "slavery" – is the term the Greeks apply to the Turkish occupation, though in exchange for submitting to Muslim rule and paying tribute, the Greeks were free to pursue their religion and were left very much in charge of their own religious and civil affairs. In accordance with Islamic tradition, the

Ottoman sultan regarded his Orthodox Christian subjects as a nation (*millet*) of which the **Patriarch of Constantinople** was both the spiritual and temporal ruler. In effect the patriarch presided over a state within the state, exercising its entire civil and ecclesiastical administration.

The essence of the Turkish administration was **taxation**. The collection of these taxes was often farmed out to the leaders of the Greek communities, to local magistrates for example, who profited from the taxes they collected, enabling some to exercise a dominant role not only within their own region but in the Ottoman Empire at large.

The other important institution within Greece was the **Orthodox Church**. For all its apparent venality and despite the ignorance and bigotry of much of the clergy, the Church preserved the traditional faith, kept alive the written form of the Greek language, and was the focus of Greek nationalism. Also the Orthodox Church was wealthy and powerful; Greeks preferred to give their lands to the monasteries than have them occupied by the Turks, while the Muslims found it easier to allow the Church to act in a judicial capacity rather than have to invent a new administration. Thus Christians took their legal disputes to bishops to decide according to Roman law.

Turks sometimes formed a substantial minority of the population, while in other places there were no Turks at all. Generally the Ottomans controlled the towns and the plains but left the mountains almost entirely to the Greeks. These were controlled by **armatoli**, who were essentially Ottoman-sanctioned Christian militia, and by **klephts** – bandits who exacted contributions from the villages and preyed off Turks whenever they could. The armatoli and the klephts were the counterparts of each other. The *armatoli* were necessary to control the *klephts*, and the *klephts* provided many of the recruits for the *armatoli*. In unsettled times, when the *armatoli* became discontented, the numbers of *klephts* increased. As to the cities, Athens declined, while **Thessaloníki** became comparatively prosperous, particularly after the influx of a large number of **Jewish refugees from Spain** at the end of the fifteenth century. A cosmopoli-

The devshirme

The *devshirme* was an institution of the Ottoman state: a slave levy imposed on the Christian populations living at peace within its borders. Every few years the sultan's commissioners were sent round the villages of Asia Minor and the Balkans where fathers of Christian families were obliged to present for inspection all their male children aged between eight and twenty. Only parents with one child were excepted. Otherwise the commissioners were free to choose, taking away those children, usually one in five, who seemed the fittest and most intelligent.

Denied access to the outside world and subjected to conditions of the strictest discipline, the boys underwent conversion to Islam and were given martial training and an education best suited to their aptitudes. Severed from their families, their homelands and their culture, they owed their fortune to the sultan and, though they were slaves, they could, on the basis of merit, rise to the highest military and official positions in the empire. The most talented, about one in ten, were taken into the sultan's service within the palace itself. The rest became *janissaries*: charging into battle at the critical moment, after the cavalry and the irregulars had done their work, their job was to seize the victory. The *devshirme* both enhanced the authority of the sultan against the hereditary claims of the Turkish aristocracy which in time was all but excluded from key positions, and accounted for much of the vitality of the early Ottoman state. It was a system that remained in operation until the early eighteenth century.

tan outpost, it developed a very mixed population of Greeks, Slavs, Albanians, Vlachs, Armenians, Jews and Turks.

But in fact the term "**Turks**" needs to be qualified, in all these instances, for even before the capture of Constantinople the Ottoman Empire had long since ceased to be run by Turks, rather by Christian youths swept up in the *devshirme* (see box overleaf) who became Muslim converts loyal to the sultan. The ancestors of Mehmet II had so intermarried with Greeks and Serbs or had produced heirs from the women of the harem, Circassians, Georgians, Greeks, Albanians, Serbs and Italians, that Mehmet probably carried no more than one sixty-fourth part of Turkish blood in his veins. And so it was for others of the ruling class, which meant that being an Ottoman had almost nothing to do with ethnic or social origins but was rather to have become a Muslim, to be loyal to the sultan and to practice the complicated system of customs, behaviour and language understood as the Ottoman way. The heights of **Ottoman administration** and society became in fact the preserve of a non-Turkish meritocracy, a great many of whom were Greeks.

Ottoman conquests and the eclipse of Venice

Ottoman troops landed on **Cyprus** in **1570** and, despite the great walls built round Nicosia by the Venetians, the city was taken within the year and 30,000 of its inhabitants were slaughtered. Along with the introduction of Ottoman administration, a large number of Anatolian Turks were settled on Cyprus, the origin of the present minority Turkish population there.

News of Turkish brutality in Cyprus horrified Europe. Under the aegis of the Pope the **Holy League** was formed, Spain and Genoa joining Venice in assembling a fleet led by Don John of Austria, the bastard son of the Spanish king, its lofty aim not only to retake the island but in the spirit of a crusade to recapture all Christian lands that had been taken by the Ottomans. In the event, it was ineffectual to a fault, with no serious attempt made even to launch an expedition to relieve Cyprus. Yet out of it something new arose – the first stirrings of **Philhellenism**, a desire to liberate the Greeks whose ancient culture stood at the heart of Renaissance thought and education.

There was, too, the encouragement of a naval victory, when in 1571 Don John's fleet caught the Ottoman fleet off guard, at its winter quarters at **Lepanto** on the Gulf of Corinth in western Greece. Despite its much greater size, the Ottoman fleet was overwhelmingly defeated. Two hundred and sixty-six of its vessels were sunk or captured, fifty thousand of its sailors died and fifteen thousand Christian galley slaves were freed. Throughout Europe the news of the naval victory at Lepanto was received with extraordinary rejoicing; it was the first time that Europe had won a battle against the Ottomans, and its symbolic importance was profound.

Militarily and politically, however, the Ottomans remained dominant, and the following century **Venice** lost its last outpost in the Eastern Mediterranean, when **Crete** fell to the Ottomans in 1669 after a twenty-year siege. For the Cretans it meant the end of their Byzantine culture which had continued to flourish under Venetian protection since the fall of Constantinople in 1453. Numerous Greek writers, thinkers and painters left the island for the Christian West, mostly to Italy, though Domenico Theotokopoulos preceded them by almost a century, first studying painting in Venice, then by about 1577 settling in Spain where he became known as El Greco. Venice went into terminal decline after the loss of Crete; nothing of its empire was left but the **Ionian islands** which it kept until they were taken by Napoleon in 1797.

Greek nationalist stirrings

Meanwhile during the eighteenth century the islanders of **Ídhra** (Hydra), **Spétses** and **Psará** – most of them Christian Albanian settlers – built up a Greek merchant fleet which traded throughout the Mediterranean where thriving colonies of Greeks were established in many ports. Greek merchant families were also established in the sultan's provinces of **Moldavia** and **Wallachia**, the area of present-day Romania. The rulers of these provinces were exclusively Greeks, chosen by the sultan from wealthy **Phanariot families**, that is residents of the Phanar, the quarter along the Golden Horn in Constantinople and site of the Greek Orthodox Patriarchate which itself enjoyed considerable privileges and was an integral part of the administration of the Ottoman Empire.

These wealthier and more educated Greeks enjoyed greater opportunities for advancement within the Ottoman system than they ever had before, while the Greek peasantry, unlike the Muslim inhabitants of the empire, did not have to bear the burden of military service, nor did they any longer suffer from the *devshirme*, which had fallen out of use. Nevertheless the Greeks had their grievances against the Ottoman government, which mostly concerned the arbitrary, unjust and oppressive system of taxation. But among the Greek peasantry it was primarily their religion that opposed them to their Muslim neighbours – as much as one fifth of the population – and to their Ottoman overlords. Muslim leaders had long preached hatred of the infidel, a view reciprocated by the priests and bishops of the Orthodox Church.

The War of Independence: 1821–32

The **ideology behind the War of Independence** came from the Greeks of the diaspora, particularly those merchant colonies in France, Italy, Austria and Russia who had absorbed new European ideas of nationalism and revolution. Sometime around 1814 a number of such Greeks formed a secret society, the Friendly Society as it was called, **Philiki Etairia**. But their sophisticated political concepts went uncomprehended by the peasantry who assumed that the point of an uprising was the extermination of their religious adversaries. And so when war finally broke out in **spring 1821** almost the entire settled **Muslim population of Greece** – farmers, merchants and officials – was **slaughtered** within weeks by roaming bands of Greek peasants armed with swords, guns, scythes and clubs. They were often led by Orthodox priests, and some of the earliest Greek revolutionary flags portrayed a cross over a severed Turkish head.

The war

While the Greeks fought to rid themselves of the Ottomans, their further aims differed widely. Landowners assumed that their role was to lead and sought to retain and reinforce their traditional privileges; the peasantry saw the struggle as a means towards land redistribution; and Westernised Greeks were fighting for a modern nation-state. Remarkably, by the end of **1823** it seemed that the Greeks had won their independence. Twice the sultan had sent armies into Greece and twice they had met with defeat. Greek guerrilla leaders, above all **Theodoros**

Kolokotronis from the Peloponnese, had gained significant military victories early in the rebellion, which was joined by a thousand or so **European Philhellenes**, almost half of them German, though the most important was the English poet, **Lord Byron**.

But the situation was reversed in 1825 with the invasion of the Peloponnese by formidable Egyptian forces loyal to the sultan. Aid for the Greek struggle had thus far come neither from Orthodox Russia, nor from the Western powers of France and Britain, both wearied by the Napoleonic Wars and suspicious of a potentially anarchic new state. But the death of Lord Byron from a fever while training Greek forces at **Mesolóngi** in 1824 had galvanised European public opinion in the **cause of Greece**, so that when Mesolóngi fell to the Ottomans in 1826, Britain, France and Russia finally agreed to seek autonomy for certain parts of Greece, and they sent a combined fleet under Admiral Codrington to put pressure on the sultan's army in the Peloponnese and the Turkish-Egyptian fleet harboured in Navaríno Bay. Events took over, and an accidental naval battle at **Navaríno** in October 1827 resulted in the destruction of almost the entire Ottoman fleet. The following spring, Russia itself declared war on the Ottomans, and Sultan Mahmud II was forced to accept the existence of an autonomous Greece.

The deal

At a series of conferences from 1830 to 1832, **Greek independence** was confirmed by the Western powers, and borders were drawn in 1832. These included just 800,000 of the six million Greeks living within the Ottoman Empire, and territories, which were for the most part the poorest of the classical and Byzantine lands: **Attica**, the **Peloponnese** and the islands of the **Argo-Saronic**, the **Sporades** and the **Cyclades**. The rich agricultural belt of **Thessaly**, **Epirus** in the west and **Macedonia** in the north remained in Ottoman hands, as did the Dodecanese. Meanwhile after the Napoleonic wars the **Ionian islands** had passed to British control.

The emerging state: 1832–1939

Modern Greece began as a **republic**, and **Ioannis Kapodistrias**, its first president, concentrated his efforts on building a viable central authority and government in the face of diverse protagonists from the independence struggle. Almost inevitably he was assassinated – by two chieftains from the ever-disruptive Mani – and perhaps equally inevitably the "Great Powers" – Brtiain, France and Germany – stepped in. They created a **monarchy**, gave aid and set on the throne a Bavarian prince, Otho (Otto). By 1834, Greece also had a national, state-controlled **Orthodox Church** of its own, independent from the Patriarchate in Constantinople; however, at the same time, two-thirds of the monasteries and convents were closed down and their assets converted to funding secular public education.

Despite the granting of a constitution in 1844, **King Otho** proved an autocratic and insensitive ruler, bringing in fellow Germans to fill official posts and ignoring all claims by the landless peasantry for redistribution of the old estates. In 1862 he was forced from the country by a popular revolt, and the Europeans produced a new prince, this time from Denmark, whose accession was marked by Britain's decision to hand over the **Ionian islands** to Greece, at once increasing the kingdom's population by a fifth. During the reign of the new king, **George I** (1863–1913), the first roads and railways were built in Greece, land reform began in the Peloponnese, and the borders of Greece were extended.

The Great Idea and expansionist wars

From the very beginning, the motive force of Greek foreign policy was the **Megáli Idhéa** (Great Idea) of redeeming ethnically Greek populations outside the country and incorporating the old territories of Byzantium into the new kingdom. There was encouragement all around, as Ottoman control was suddenly under pressure across the Balkans. In 1875 there were revolts by Serbs and Montenegrins, followed by attacks by Russia on Anatolia and Bulgaria. These culminated in the creation of an independent Serbia-Montenegro and autonomous Bulgaria at the 1878 Treaty of Berlin while, as part of the same negotiations, Britain took over the administration of **Cyprus**.

In 1881, revolts broke out among the Greeks of **Crete**, **Thessaly** and **Epirus**, aided by guerrillas from Greece, Britain forced the Ottoman Empire to cede Thessaly and Arta to Greece, but Crete remained Ottoman, and when in 1897 Cretan Greeks set up an independent government and declared *enosis* (union) with Greece, the Ottomans responded by invading the mainland and came within days of reaching Athens. The Great Powers came to the rescue by warning off the Turks and placing Crete under an international protectorate. Only in 1913 did **Crete** unite with Greece.

It was from Crete, nonetheless, that the most distinguished modern Greek statesman emerged: **Eleftherios Venizelos**, having led a civilian campaign for his island's liberation, was elected as Greek prime minister in 1910. Two years later he organized an alliance of Balkan powers to fight the **Balkan Wars** (1912–13), campaigns that saw the Ottomans virtually driven from Europe, and the Bulgarian competition bested in the culmination of a bitter, four-decade campaign for the hearts and minds of the **Macedonian** population. With Greek borders extended to include the **northeast Aegean islands**, **northern Thessaly**, **central Epirus** and parts of **Macedonia**, the Megáli Idhéa was approaching reality. At the same time Venizelos proved himself a shrewd manipulator of domestic public opinion by revising the constitution and introducing a series of liberal social reforms.

Division, however, was to appear with the outbreak of the **First World War**. Venizelos urged Greek entry on the Allied side, seeing in the conflict possibilities for the liberation of Greeks in Thrace and Asia Minor, but the new king, **Constantine I**, who was married to a sister of the German Kaiser, imposed a policy of neutrality. Eventually Venizelos set up a revolutionary government in Thessaloníki, polarising the country into a state of **civil war** along Venezelist–Royalist lines, and in 1917 Greek troops entered the war to join the French, British and Serbians in the Macedonian campaign against Bulgaria and Germany. Upon the capitulation of Bulgaria and the Ottoman Empire, the Greeks occupied **Thrace** (both western and eastern), and Venizelos presented demands at Versailles for the predominantly Greek region of **Smyrna** on the Asia Minor coast to become part of the Greek state.

The Catastrophe and its aftermath

The demand for Smyrna triggered one of the most disastrous episodes in modern Greek history, the so-called **Katastrofí** (Catastrophe). Venizelos was authorized to move forces into Smyrna in 1919, but a new Turkish nationalist movement was taking power under Mustafa Kemal, or **Atatürk** as he came to be known. In 1920 Venizelos lost the elections and monarchist factions took over, at which the Allies withdrew their support for the venture. Nevertheless the monarchists ordered Greek forces to advance upon Ankara in an attempt to bring Atatürk to terms. The Greeks' **Anatolian campaign** ignominiously collapsed in summer 1922 when Turkish troops forced the Greeks back to the coast and a hurried evacuation from **Smyrna**. As the Greek army left Smyrna, the Turks moved in and **massacred** much of the **Armenian and Greek** population before burning most of the city to the ground.

For the Turks, this was the successful conclusion of what they call their War of Independence; already the First World War had cost the Ottoman sultan his empire, and in 1922 the sultan himself was deposed and the borders of modern Turkey, as they are today, were established by the **1923 Treaty of Lausanne**. The treaty also provided for the **exchange of religious minorities** in each country – in effect, the first large-scale regulated ethnic cleansing. Turkey was to accept 390,000 Muslims resident on Greek soil. Greece, mobilized almost continuously for the last decade and with a population of under five million, was faced with the resettlement of over **1,300,000 Christian refugees** from **Asia Minor.** Many of these had already read the writing on the wall after 1918 and arrived of their own accord – from Bulgaria and revolutionary Russia as well as Asia Minor; significant numbers were settled across Macedonia, western Thrace, Epirus and in Athens, as well as on Limnos, Lesvos, Hios, Samos, Evvia and Crete. The Megáli Idhéa had turned in upon itself.

The consequences of the Katastrofi were intense and far-reaching. The bulk of the agricultural estates of **Thessaly** were finally redistributed – completing a program begun in 1909 – both to Greek tenants and refugee farmers, and huge shanty towns grew into new quarters around **Athens**, **Pireás** and **Thessaloníki**, a spur to the country's then almost non-existent industry. Politically, reaction was even swifter. By September 1922, a group of Venízelist army officers under Colonel Nikolaos Plastiras assembled after the retreat from Smyrna, "invited" King Constantine to abdicate and executed six of his ministers held most responsible for the debacle. Democracy was nominally restored with the proclamation of a **republic**, but for much of the next decade changes in government were brought about by factions within the armed forces. Meanwhile, among the urban refugee population, unions were being formed and the **Greek Communist Party** (**KKE**) was established.

The End of Venizelos and the rise of Metaxas

Elections in 1928 **returned Venizelos to power**, but his freedom to manoeuvre was restricted by the Great Crash of the following year. He had borrowed heavily abroad and was unable to renegotiate loan terms in 1931. Late 1932 saw a local crash caused by Britain abandoning the gold standard, with Greek currency heavily devalued and Venizelos forced from office. His supporters under Plastiras tried forcibly to reinstate him in March 1933, but their coup was put down and Venizelos fled to Paris, where he died three years later.

In 1935 a plebiscite restored the king, **George II**, to the throne, and in the following year he appointed as prime minister **General John Metaxas**, who had opposed the Anatolian campaign. But Metaxas had little support in parliament, and when a series of KKE-organized strikes broke out, the king, ignoring attempts to form a broad liberal coalition, dissolved parliament without setting

△ Inhabitants of Smrna (now Izmir) escape by boat after the city is attacked by Turkish forces under Mustafa Kemal Atatürk, September 1922

a date for new elections. It was a blatantly unconstitutional move and opened the way for five years of ruthless and at times absurd **dictatorship**. Metaxas averted a general strike with military force and proceeded to set up a state based on fascist models of the era. Left-wing and trade-union opponents were imprisoned or forced into exile, a state youth movement and secret police were set up and rigid censorship, extending even to passages of Thucydides, was imposed. But it was at least a Greek dictatorship, and though Metaxas was sympathetic to fascist organizational methods and economics, he completely opposed German or Italian domination.

World War II and the Civil War: 1939–1950

Britain and France declared war on Germany in September 1939, but the most immediate threat to Greece was **Italy** which had invaded Albania in April. Even so, Metaxas hoped that Greece could remain neutral, and when the Italians torpedoed the Greek cruiser Elli in Tinos harbour on August 15, 1940, they failed to provoke a response. **Mussolini**, however, was determined to have a war with Greece, and after accusing the Greeks of violating the Albanian frontier, he delivered an ultimatum on October 28, 1940, to which Metaxas famously if apocryphally answered "**ohi**" (no), though in fact he said "This means war". Galvanized by the crisis, the Greeks not only drove the invading Italians out of Greece but managed to gain control over the long-coveted and predominantly Greek-populated area of northern Epirus in southern Albania. ("Ohi Day" is still celebrated as a national holiday.)

The principal Greek minorities – Vlachs, Sarakatsani, Jews, Turks, Slavophones, Catholics and gypsies – are little known, even within Greece. In addition to these traditional groups, recent immigration has introduced new minorities to Greece (see "Immigration" box on p.1104)

Vlachs

The Vlachs' homeland is in the remote Pindos mountains in northwestern Greece near the Albanian frontier, though their range of habitation extends well into the lower hills of western Macedonia. Traditionally they were transhumant shepherds, and they played a major role in Balkan mule-back haulage and running caravanserais where mule convoys halted. They are an ancient community who speak a Romance tongue, possibly acquired through service to the Romans as highway guards along the Via Egnatia which connected Thessaloníki with the Adriatic. Increasingly the Vlachs are abandoning their traditional annual migration with their flocks of sheep; the hardships are too many and the returns too small.

Sarakatsani

The Sarakatsani, celebrated in Patrick Leigh Fermor's *Roumeli* and J. K. Campbell's *Honour, Family and Patronage*, speak an archaic form of Greek. Until the 1940s they were true transhumants, moving between winter quarters well below the snowline and summer pastures in the Pindos mountains. A few still return each summer to the heights, where they pasture their sheep on land rented from the village councils.

Greek Jewry

The Jews of Greece are perhaps the oldest established Jewish community in Europe, dating back to the early Hellenistic period. These original Romaniots, as they are known, were joined in 1493 by Sephardim when Sultan Beyazit II invited Jews expelled from Spain and Portugal to settle in the Ottoman Empire. Thessaloníki in the late nineteenth and early twentieth centuries was one of the largest Jewish cities in the world. Jews made up roughly half the population, and dominated the sailing, shipping and chandlery trades, such that the harbour ceased operations on Saturday but functioned on Sunday. From 1913, however, with a rapid influx of Greek Orthodox into the conquered city, Thessaloniki began to lose its strong Hebraic character; the fire of 1917, emigration to Palestine, the arrival of fiercely nationalistic Greek Orthodox refugees from Anatolia after 1923 and finally the Nazi occupation brought this era to a close.

To make good Mussolini's floundering performance, Hitler determined to send his own troops into Greece, while the British rushed an expeditionary force across the Mediterranean from Egypt where they were already hard-pressed by the Germans. On April 6, 1941 the **Germans invaded**, but while rapidly advancing on Thessaloníki, they simultaneously drove on Belgrade, leading to the swift collapse of the ill-prepared Yugoslav army. Within days the German army was pouring through the Monastir Gap into central Greece, isolating the Greeks on the Albanian front while wheeling round the exposed western flank of the British holding the line along the Aliakmon River. Outmanoeuvered by the enemy's highly mechanized forces and at the mercy of the Luftwaffe's superiority in the air, resistance was soon broken. When the Germans occupied Crete towards the end of May, King George and his ministers fled to Egypt where they set up a government-in-exile in Cairo. Metaxas himself had died before the German invasion.

"Turks"

Greeks talk of "Turks" within Greece when in fact they mean the Muslim remnants of the Ottoman Empire who may have been Greek converts or Albanians and not necessarily ethnic Turks. Even after the 1881 and 1913 acquisitions of Thessaly, Epirus and Macedonia, Muslim villages continued to exist in these regions. Western Thrace was always home to large numbers of Muslims and remained so after the 1919–22 Asia Minor war when the Treaty of Lausanne (1923) confirmed their right to stay in return for a continued Greek Orthodox presence in Istanbul and nearby islands, a bargain the Greeks have honoured but the Turkish government has not. Today Muslims still make up a third of the population of Greek Thrace, where they grow most of the tobacco crop. Additionally there are the Turks of the Dodecanese. Many of the Turks who live in the old town of Rhodes have been there since the sixteenth century and will proudly tell you that they have every right to be considered native Rhodians. In Kos, Cretan Muslims settled both in the port town – where they remain economically active – and at Platani, which still has a mixed Greek Orthodox and Turkish population.

Slavophones

Despite a "voluntary" population exchange between Greece and Bulgaria in 1919, and the flight of many Slavophones abroad after 1948, there remain approximately 40,000 individuals in Greece whose mother tongue is some approximation of Macedonian. They dwell in a ribbon along the northern frontier where some Greeks nervously view them as a potential fifth column for a theoretically expansionist Former Yugoslav Republic of Macedonia (FYROM).

Catholics

The Catholics of the Cyclades, numbering no more than 12,000, are a legacy of Venetian settlement in the Aegean. In Athens there are at least 25,000 more Catholics of Cycladic descent, helping to support a dozen parishes in the city. Often Italianate last names (Dellaroka) or given names (Leonardhos, Frangiskos) distinguish them from their neighbours.

Gypsies

Gypsies – probably from Rajasthan on the Indian subcontinent – first came to the Balkans in about the eleventh century, and were soon well enough established to figure in Byzantine chronicles of the 1300s. The great majority are nominally Greek Orthodox and the rest are Muslim. Generally they offer themselves as transient seasonal labour or drive about Greece in outsize trucks selling cheap goods and agricultural produce.

Occupation and Resistance

The joint Italian-German-Bulgarian Axis **occupation of Greece** was among the bitterest experiences of the European war. Nearly half a million Greek civilians starved to death over the winter of 1941–42, as all available food was requisitioned, principally by the Germans, to feed the occupying armies. In addition, entire villages throughout the mainland, but especially on Crete, were burned at the least hint of resistance and nearly 130,000 civilians were slaughtered up to autumn 1944. In their northern sector, which included Thássos and Samothráki, the Bulgarians demolished ancient sites and churches to support any future bid to annex "Slavic" Macedonia. Meantime, the Germans supervised during the summer of 1944 the **deportation** to extermination camps of the entire **Jewish populations** of Kavála, Ioánnina and Thessaloníki.

No sooner had the Axis powers occupied Greece than a spontaneous resistance movement sprang up in the mountains. The National Popular Liberation Army, known by its initials **ELAS**, founded in September 1941, attracted a wide range of popular support because of its wholehearted commitment to fighting the occupation, and it quickly grew to become the most effective resistance organization. Working in tandem with ELAS was **EAM**, the National Liberation Front, which was founded in September, though with a programme that went beyond resistance and looked towards a radical postwar alteration of the structure of Greek society. Communists formed the leadership of both organizations, but opposition to the occupation and disenchantment with the pre-war political order meant that they won the support of many non-communists. By 1943 ELAS/EAM was in control of most areas of the country and working with the British SOE, Special Operations Executive against the occupiers.

But the Allies – Britain, the United States and the Soviet Union – already had their eyes on the shape of postwar Europe, and British prime minister **Winston Churchill** was determined that Greece should not fall into the communist sphere. Ignoring advice from British agents in Greece that ELAS/EAM were the only effective resistance group, and that the king and his government-in-exile had little support within the country, Churchill gave orders that only rightwing groups like **EDES**, the National Republican Greek Army, which

Greek Jewry and World War II

Following the German invasion of Greece, Jews who lived in the Italian zone of occupation were initially no worse off than their fellow Greeks. But after Italy capitulated to the Allies in September 1943 and German troops took over from the Italian troops, the Jewish communities in Rhodes and Kos in the Dodecanese, as well as in Crete, Corfu, Vólos, Évvia and Zákynthos, were exposed to the full force of Nazi racial doctrine. The Germans applied their "final solution" in Greece during the spring and summer of 1944 with the deportation of virtually the entire Jewish population, about 80,000 in all, to extermination camps in Poland. Thessaloníki alone contained 57,000, the largest Jewish population of any Balkan city, and there were significant populations in all the Greek mainland towns and on many of the islands.

Greek Christians often went to extraordinary lengths to protect their persecuted countrymen. For example, when the Germans demanded the names of the Jews of Zákynthos prior to a roundup, Archbishop Khrysostomos and Mayor Loukas Karrer presented them with a roster of just two names – their own – and secretly oversaw the smuggling of all the island's 275 Jews to remote farms. Their audacious behaviour paid off, as every Zakynthian Jew survived the war. In Athens, the police chief and the archbishop arranged for false identity cards and baptismal certificates to be issued, which again saved large numbers of Jews. Others around the country were warned in good time of what fate the Germans had in store for them, and often took to the hills to join the partisans.

The paltry number of survivors returning from the death camps to Greece was insufficient to form the nucleus of a revival in most provincial towns, and moving to Athens – where about 3000 of today's 5000 Greek Jews live – or emigration to Israel was often a preferable alternative to living with ghosts. In Thessaloníki there are less than a thousand Sephardim, while Lárissa retains about three hundred Sephardim, many of them in the clothing trade. Small Romaniot communities of a hundred persons or less also continue to exist in Halkídha, Ioánnina, Corfu, Tríkala and Vólos. The Kos, Haniá and Rhodes congregations were effectively wiped out, and today only about thirty Jews – many of these from the mainland – live in Rhodes Town, where the Platia ton Evreon Martaron (Square of the Jewish Martyrs) commemorates over 1800 Jews of Kos and Rhodes deported and murdered by the Germans.

opportunistically swung its support to the monarchy, should receive British money, intelligence and arms. In August 1943 a resistance delegation came to Cairo to see the Greek king, George, asking for a postwar coalition government in which EAM would hold the ministries of the interior, justice and war, and asking that the king himself not return to Greece without popular consent expressed through a plebiscite. Backed by Churchill, King George flatly rejected their demands.

The EAM contingent returned to Greece divided, and a conflict broke out between those who favoured working peacefully to gain control of any government imposed after liberation, and the hard-line Stalinist ideologues, who forbade Popular-Front-type participation in any "bourgeois" regime. Armed conflict broke out between ELAS and EDES, with often ferocious actions presaging the civil war that was to come.

Liberation and Civil War

As the Germans began to withdraw from Greece in September 1944, most of the ELAS/EAM leadership agreed to join a British-sponsored interim government headed by the liberal anti-communist politician **George Papandreou** in which it held six ministerial portfolios. Also ELAS/EAM agreed to place its forces under the control of the new government, which effectively meant under General Robert Scobie, commander in chief of the British troops who landed in Greece that October. But many among the ELAS partisans felt that they were losing their chance to impose a communist government and refused to lay down their arms as General Scobie ordered them to do by December 10. On December 3 the police fired on an EAM demonstration in Athens, killing at least sixteen, and the following day vicious **street fighting** broke out between members of the Greek Communist Party (KKE) and British troops which lasted throughout the month, until 11,000 people were killed and large parts of Athens destroyed. In the countryside ELAS rounded up its most influential and wealthy opponents in the larger towns, and marched them out to rural areas in conditions that guaranteed their death.

After Papandreou resigned and the king agreed not to return without a plebiscite, a **ceasefire** was signed on February 12, 1945, and a new British-backed government agreed to institute democratic reforms. Many of these were not implemented, however. The army, police and civil service remained in right-wing hands, and while collaborators were often allowed to retain their positions, leftwing sympathisers, many of them merely Venizelist Republicans and not communists, were excluded. The elections of March 1946 were boycotted by the KKE, which handed victory to the parties of the right, and a **rigged plebiscite** followed which brought the king back to Greece. Rightwing gangs now roamed the towns and countryside with impunity, and by the summer of 1946 eighty thousand leftists who had been associated with ELAS had taken to the mountains.

By 1947 guerrilla activity had again reached the scale of a **full civil war**, with ELAS reorganized into the Democratic Army of Greece (**DSE**). In the interim, King George had died and been succeeded by his brother Paul, while the Americans had taken over the British role and began implementing the **Truman Doctrine**, the beginning of the Cold War against Soviet intimidation and expansion, which involved giving massive economic and military aid to an amenable Greek government. In the mountains American military advisors trained the initially woeful Greek army for campaigns against the DSE, and in the cities there were mass arrests, courtmartials and imprisonments. From their stronghold on the slopes of Mount Grámmos on the border of Greece and Albania, the partisans continued to fight a losing guerrilla struggle. At the beginning of 1948 Stalin withdrew Soviet support, and in the autumn of 1949, after Tito closed the Yugoslav border, denying the partisans the last means of outside supplies, the remnants of the DSE retreated into Albania and the KKE admitted defeat by proclaiming what it called a temporary suspension of the civil war.

Reconstruction and dictatorship: 1950–74

After a decade of war that had shattered much of Greece's infrastructure (it is said that not one bridge was left standing by 1948), and had killed twelve percent of the 1940 population, it was a demoralized, shattered country that emerged into the Western political orbit of the 1950s. Greece was perforce **American-dominated**, enlisted into the **Korean War** in 1950 and **NATO** the following year. In domestic politics, the US embassy – still giving the orders – foisted upon the Greeks a winner-takes-all **electoral system**, which was to ensure victory for the Right over the next twelve years. Overt leftist activity was banned (though a "cover" party for communists was soon founded), and many of those who were not herded into political "re-education" camps or dispatched by firing squads, legal or vigilante, went into exile throughout Eastern Europe, to return only after 1974. The 1950s also saw the wholesale **depopulation of remote villages** as migrants sought work in Australia, America and Western Europe, or the larger Greek cities.

Constantine Karamanlis and Cyprus

The American-backed right-wing **Greek Rally** party, led by **General Papagos**, won the first decisive post-civil-war elections in 1952. After the general's death, the party's leadership was taken over – and to an extent liberalised – by **Constantine Karamanlis**. Under his rule, stability of a kind was established and some economic advances registered, particularly after the revival of Greece's traditional German markets. Health and life expectancy improved dramatically as the age-old scourges of tuberculosis and malaria were finally confronted with American-supplied food and pesticides. Less commendable was Karamanlis's encouragement of the law of *andiparohí*, whereby owners of small refugee shanties or Neoclassical mansions alike could offer the site of their property to apartment-block developers in exchange for two flats (out of eight to ten) in the finished building. This effectively ripped the heart out of most Greek towns, and explains their baleful aesthetics a half-century on.

The main crisis in foreign policy throughout this period was **Cyprus**, where a long terrorist campaign was waged against the British by Greek Cypriots who demanded self-determination with a view to achieving *enosis* (union) with Greece. Turkey adamantly opposed *enosis* and said that if Britain left Cyprus it should revert to Turkish rule. In 1959 a compromise was reached which granted independence to the island and protection for its Turkish Cypriot minority but ruled out any union with Greece.

By 1961, unemployment, the Cyprus issue and the presence of US nuclear bases on Greek soil were changing the political climate, and when Karamanlis was again elected there was strong suspicion of intimidation and fraud carried out by rightwing elements and the army. After eighteen months of strikes and protest demonstrations, during which the leftwing deputy **Grigoris Lamb-rakis** was assassinated in Thessaloníki in May 1963 (an event which became the subject of the Costa-Gavras film *Z*), Karamanlis resigned and went into voluntary exile in Paris.

George Papandreou and the Colonels

New elections held in February 1964 gave the **Centre Union Party**, headed by **George Papandreou**, an outright majority and a mandate for social and economic reform. The new government was the first to be controlled from outside the right since 1935, and in his first act as prime minister, Papandreou sought to heal the wounds of the civil war by **releasing political prisoners** and allowing exiles to return. When King Paul died in March and his son came to the throne as **Constantine II**, it seemed as though a new era had begun.

But soon **Cyprus** was again taking centre stage. Intercommunal fighting between Turkish Cypriots who wanted partition and Greek Cypriots who wanted *enosis* broke out in 1963, and in 1964 it was only the intervention of the United States that dissuaded Turkey from invading the island. In the mood of military confrontation between Greece and Turkey – both of them NATO members – Papandreou questioned Greece's role in the Western alliance, to the alarm of the Americans and the Greek right.

The right was also opposed to Papandreou's economic policies which were having an inflationary effect, and it feared the growing power of the Left, fears that were bolstered in May 1965 when a plot by **Aspida** (Shield), a subversive group of left-wing army officers, was uncovered – and linked, it was claimed, with Papandreou's son Andreas, a minister in his father's government. More serious were indications of rightwing plots within the army against the government, and when Papandreou moved to purge the army of disloyal officers, the Right took this as an attack on their traditional domination of the armed forces. In July, when the king would not support the prime minister in his attempts to dismiss certain officers, Papandreou resigned in order to gain a fresh mandate at the polls, but the king would not order new elections, instead persuading members of the Centre Union to defect and organize a coalition government. Punctuated by strikes, resignations and mass demonstrations, the political situation in Greece became increasingly unstable over the next year and a half until new elections were eventually set for May 1967.

It was a foregone conclusion that George Papandreou's Centre Union Party would win the 1967 poll against the discredited coalition partners. But **King Constantine**, disturbed by the party's leftward shift, was said to have briefed senior generals for a coup. True or not, the king, like almost everyone else in Greece, was caught by surprise when a group of unknown **colonels** staged their own **coup** on April 21, 1967. In December the king staged a counter-coup against the colonels, but when it failed he went into exile.

The junta announced itself as the "**Revival of Greek Orthodoxy**" against corrupting Western influences, not least long hair and miniskirts, which hardly helped the tourist trade. All political activity was banned, independent trade unions were forbidden to recruit or meet, the press was so heavily censored that many papers stopped printing, and thousands of communists and others on the left were arrested, imprisoned and often tortured. Among these were both Papandreous, father and son, the composer Mikis Theodorakis and Amalia Fleming, the widow of the discoverer of penicillin Alexander Fleming.

Thousands were permanently maimed physically and psychologically in the junta's torture chambers. The world famous Greek actress Melina Mercouri was stripped of her citizenship in absentia, and thousands of prominent Greeks joined her in exile. Culturally, the colonels put an end to popular music (closing down most of the live rebétika clubs) and inflicted ludicrous censorship on literature and the theatre, including (as under Metaxas) a ban on the production of classical tragedies. Meantime, the TV and radio broadcast endless speeches by chief colonel **Papadopoulos** – rambling, illiterate texts that became a byword for bad grammar, obfuscation and Orwellian Newspeak. Convinced that he had acquired the job of ruling Greece for life, in 1973 Papadopoulos abolished the monarchy and declared Greece a republic with himself as president.

Restoration of democracy

The colonels lasted for seven years, and whatever initial support they may have met among Greeks, after the first two years they were opposed by the vast majority, including a great many on the right who were embarrassed by their oafishness. Opposition was voiced from the beginning by exiled Greeks in London, the United States and Western Europe, but only in 1973 did demonstrations break out openly in Greece – the colonels' secret police had done too thorough a job of infiltrating domestic resistance groups and terrifying everyone else into docility. On **November 17** the students of the **Athens Polytechnic** began an occupation of their buildings. The ruling clique sent armoured vehicles to storm the Polytechnic's gates and a still-undetermined number of students (estimates range from 34 to 300) were killed. Martial law was tightened and Colonel Papadopoulos was replaced by the even more noxious and reactionary **General Ioannides**, head of the secret police.

The end came within a year when the dictatorship embarked on a disastrous political adventure in **Cyprus**, essentially the last playing of the Megali Idhea card. By attempting to topple the Makarios government and **impose enosis** on the island, the junta provoked a **Turkish invasion** and occupation of forty per cent of Cypriot territory. The army finally mutinied and **Constantine Karamanlis** was invited to return from Paris to again take office.

Karamanlis swiftly negotiated a ceasefire in Cyprus, and in November 1974 he and his **Néa Dhimokratía** (New Democracy) party were rewarded by a sizeable majority in elections, with a centrist and socialist opposition. The latter was the Panhellenic Socialist Movement (PASOK), a new party led by **Andreas Papandreou**.

Europe and a new Greece: 1974 to the present

To Karamanlis's enduring credit his New Democracy party oversaw an effective and firm return to **democratic stability**, even legalizing the KKE (the Greek Communist Party) for the first time in its history. Karamanlis also held a **referendum on the monarchy**, in which seventy per cent of Greeks rejected the return of Constantine II. So a largely symbolic, German-style presidency was instituted instead, which Karamanlis himself occupied from 1980 to 1985, and again from 1990 to 1995.

PASOK comes to power

"Change" and "Out with the Right" were the slogans of the election campaign that swept the socialist party, **PASOK**, and its leader Andreas Papandreou to power on October 18, 1981. PASOK won 174 of the 300 parliamentary seats and the Communist KKE, though not a part of the new government, returned another 13 deputies. The manifesto of Greece's first socialist government was to devolve power to local authorities, nationalize heavy industry, improve the skeletal social services, purge bureaucratic inefficiency and malpractice, end bribery and corruption, and to follow an independent foreign policy after removing US bases and withdrawing from NATO and the European Community.

The new era started with a bang as long-overdue **social reforms** were enacted. Peasant women were granted pensions for the first time; wages were indexed to the cost of living; civil marriage was introduced, family and property law was reformed in favour of wives and mothers; demanding dowries was forbidden (though it still continues informally); and equal rights legislation was put on the statute book. In addition, ELAS was officially recognized and was permitted to take part in ceremonies commemorating the wartime resistance. This prompted fears that the military might again intervene, especially when Andreas Papandreou, imitating his father, briefly assumed the defence portfolio himself. But he went out of his way to soothe military susceptibilities, increasing their salaries, buying new weaponry and being fastidious in his attendance at military functions.

Economically, Papandreou promised a bonanza which he must have known, as an academically trained economist, was strictly fantasy. As a result he pleased nobody. He could not fairly be blamed for the inherited lack of investment, low productivity, deficiency in managerial and labour skills and other chronic problems besetting the Greek **economy**. But he certainly aggravated the situation by allowing his supporters to indulge in violently anti-capitalist rhetoric, which frightened off potential investors. At the same time Papandreou's government

△ Andreas Papandreou rouses the PASOK faithful, 1985

had to cope with the effects of **world recession**. Shipping, the country's main foreign-currency earner, was devastated. Remittances from émigré workers fell off as they became unemployed in their host countries, and tourism diminished. Unemployment rose, inflation hit 25 per cent and the national debt soared.

Under the slogan "Vote PASOK for Even Better Days", backed by a public spending spree intended to buy votes, and a shamelessly nationalistic "Greece-for-the-Greeks" foreign policy, Papandreou won a second term in June 1985. But by October, PASOK had imposed a two-year wage freeze and import restrictions, abolished the wage-indexing scheme and devalued the drachma by fifteen per cent. In the event it was the **European Community**, once Papandreou's bête noire, which rescued him from his follies with a huge two-part loan on condition that an austerity programme was maintained. Increasingly autocratic, Papandreou responded to criticism from the left by firing trade union leaders and expelling three hundred dissenting members of his own party. Fearing that only the presence of US bases in Greece guaranteed protection from Turkish aggression, Papandreou's demand for their removal was dropped. Nor with the European Community – soon to become the European Union – propping up Greece financially would Papandreou now bite the hand that feeds.

Despite Papandreou's many failings and about-turns, it seemed unlikely that PASOK would be toppled in the 1989 elections. But the collapse of Soviet rule in Eastern Europe was reflected by a shift away from the left in Greece, and then there was Papandreou's very public affair with an Olympic Airways hostess half his age and his humiliation of his wife and family, not to mention a whole raft of economic scandals. In consequence, PASOK lost power as a trio of inconclusive elections finally resulted in the New Democracy party winning a tiny majority, its leader **Constantine Mitsotakis** becoming prime minister.

On assuming power, Mitsotakis prescribed a course of austerity measures to revive the chronically ill economy. Little headway was made, though given the world recession that was hardly surprising. Greek inflation was still approaching twenty percent annually, and at nearly ten percent, unemployment remained stubbornly high. Other measures introduced by Mitsotakis included laws to combat strikes, but these were ineffectual, as breakdowns in public transport, electricity and rubbish collection all too frequently illustrated.

The Macedonian problem and return of PASOK

The last thing the increasingly unpopular Mitsotakis needed was a major foreign policy headache. But that was exactly what he got in 1991 when one of the breakaway republics of the **former Yugoslavia** named itself **Macedonia**. Greeks felt threatened because Macedonia was a name historically associated with northern Greece, and the fear was that this new and unstable country was laying claim to a part of Greek heritage and territory. Greek diplomacy and propaganda fought tooth and nail against anyone recognizing the breakaway state, let alone its use of the name Macedonia, but Greece became increasingly isolated, and by 1993 the new country had gained official recognition from both the EU and the UN – albeit under the provisional title of the "**Former Yugoslav Republic of Macedonia**" (FYROM). Salt was then rubbed into Greek wounds when the FYROM started using the Star of Vergina, symbol of the ancient Macedonian kings, as a national symbol on its new flag, as well as having passages in its constitution referring to "unredeemed" Aegean territories.

The Macedonian problem effectively led to Mitsotakis' political demise, after the defection of a senior party figure, Andonis Samaras, and his creation of a new party, Politiki Anixi, based on the issue of Macedonia. When parliament reconvened in September to approve stringent new budget proposals, the government failed to muster sufficient support, and early elections were called for October 1993. On October 11 Papandreou romped to victory; and the youthful Miltiades Evert, ex-mayor of Athens, replaced Mitsotakis as head of the New Democracy party.

So a frail-looking **Andreas Papandreou**, now well into his seventies, became prime minister for the third time. He soon realized that he was not going to have nearly so easy a ride as in the 1980s, with the economy still in dire straits, and nor could PASOK claim to have won any diplomatic battles over Macedonia, despite a lot of tough posturing. The only concrete move was the imposition in October 1993 of a trade embargo on the FYROM, which merely landed the Greeks in trouble with the European Court of Justice – and succeeded in virtually shutting down the port of Thessaloniki. By contrast, alone among NATO members, Greece was conspicuous for its open support of **Serbia** in the wars wracking ex-Yugoslavia, ostentatiously supplying trucks to Belgrade via Bulgaria. In November, Greece lifted its embargo on the FYROM, opening the borders for tourism and trade in return for the former Yugoslav state suitably editing its constitution and removing the offending emblem from its flag. Relations, in fact, were instantly almost normalized, with only the name still a moot point.

Domestically, the emerging critical issue was the 76-year-old Papandreou's obstinate clinging to power despite obvious signs of dotage. Numerous senior members of PASOK became increasingly bold and vocal in their criticism, and in January 1996, after months in hospital intensive care, Papandreou finally resigned the premiership, which went to technocrat **Kostas Simitis**. On assuming office, Simitis vowed *not* to play to the gallery, saying: "Greece's intransigent nationalism is an expression of the wretchedness that exists in our society. It is the root cause of the problems we have had with our Balkan neighbours and our difficult relations with Europe." **Andreas Papandreou** died in June, "a common cheat", as Karamanlis called him in his tart memoirs, when it was discovered that he had accumulated a vast fortune beyond anything he could have earned legitimately as a public servant. But for the time being, Papandreou's death generated a wave of pro-PASOK sentiment which Simitis successfully exploited by quickly calling elections in September and gaining victory. Evert resigned as the New Democracy leader and was succeeded by Karamanlis's nephew Kostas.

Earthquake diplomacy and the Euro

September 1997 saw a timely boost to national morale with the awarding of the 2004 Olympic Games to Athens. Meanwhile, Kostas Simitis, who unlike Papandreou was genuinely pro-European, devoted himself to the unenviable task of getting the Greek economy in sufficiently good shape to meet the criteria for European **monetary union**. The fact that inflation stayed consistently down in single figures for the first time in decades was testament to his ability; indeed his nickname, among both foes and supporters, was "the accountant".

An unexpected and dramatic change in **Greece's relations with Turkey** came when a severe **earthquake** struck northern Athens on September 7 1999, killing scores and rendering almost 100,000 homeless. It came less than a month after a devastating earthquake in northwest Turkey, and proved to be the spur for a thaw between the two historical rivals. Greeks donated massive amounts of blood and foodstuffs to the Turkish victims, and were the earliest foreign rescue teams on hand in Turkey; in turn they saw Turkish disaster-relief squads among the first on the scene in Athens. Soon afterwards, foreign minister George Papandreou (son of Andreas) announced that Greece had dropped its long-time opposition to EU financial aid to Turkey in the absence of a solution to the outstanding Cyprus and Aegean disputes, and further indicated that Greece would no longer oppose Turkish candidacy for accession to the EU.

With his handling of the Turkish detente and progress towards European monetary union the main campaign issues, Simitis called elections five months earlier than required, on April 9, 2000. In the event, PASOK squeaked into office for a third consecutive term by a single percentage point. But the crucial factor was voters' mistrust of new no leader Kostas Karamanlis's manifest inexperience. Simitis capped his election victory by announcing Greece's official entry into the euro-currency zone on June 20, though it later turned out that the conditions were met only by his government falsifying its budget deficit data. Greece adopted **the euro** on January 1, 2002.

The year also saw a strange saga played out with the arrest of apparently the entire operational members of the terrorist group **Dhekaeftá Novemvríou**. This shadowy, leftist organization, named after the Polytechnic uprising against the Colonels, had been a thorn in Greece's security since 1974, killing twenty-four

Immigration – and the Albanian influx

Greece may continue to occupy the EU's economic cellar with Portugal, but it's still infinitely wealthier (and more stable) than many of its neighbours, and this has acted as a magnet for a permanent underclass of immigrants. Since 1990 they have arrived in numbers estimated at 800,000 to well over a million, a huge burden for a not especially rich country of just over ten million citizens. These days your waiter, hotel desk clerk or cleaning lady is most likely to be Albanian, Bulgarian or Romanian, to cite the three largest groups of arrivals. There are also significant communities of Pakistanis, Egyptians, Poles, Bangladeshis, Syrians, Filipinos, Ukrainians, Russians, Equatorial Africans, Kurds and Georgians, not to mention ethnic Greeks from the Caucasus – a striking change in what had hitherto been a homogeneous and parochial culture.

The Greek response to this has been decidedly mixed. The Albanians, making up roughly half the influx, are almost universally detested (except for the ethnic-Greek northern Epirots), and blamed for all manner of social ills. For the first time, crime – especially burglaries – is a significant issue. The newcomers have also prompted the first significant anti-immigration measures in a country whose population is more used to being on the other side of such laws – Greece is a member of the Schengen visa scheme and sees itself, as in past ages, as the first line of defence against the barbarian hordes from the East. The Aegean islands regularly receive boatloads of people from every country in Asia.

In June 2001, as an attempt to cope, legal residence was offered to the estimated half-million illegals who could demonstrate two years' presence in Greece, and pay a hefty amount for retroactive social security contributions. This and a subsequent amnesty legalized about 300,000 residents. Not that the other illegals are likely to be deported en masse, as they do the difficult, dirty and dangerous work that Greeks now disdain, especially farm labour, restaurant work and rubbish collection. From an employer's point of view, they are cheap – thirty to forty per cent less costly than native Greeks – and they are net contributors to the social welfare system, especially to pensions where Greece, like much of Europe, is seeing its population shrinking and aging. The Albanians in particular are also buoying up much of the banking system by their phenomenal saving habits and wiring of funds home.

Though there is much that is positive about immigration, it must also be said that it is having the effect of making Greece less identifiably Greek and of making the native Greeks themselves less welcoming and more self-absorbed than formerly.

industrialists, politicians and NATO military personnel, and bombing the property of foreign corporations in Athens and elsewhere. As with all the best police actions, their demise came through a stroke of luck, when a bomb exploded prematurely in the hands of an operative. After a nine-month trial, fifteen of the group's members received multiple life sentences.

Olympian hurdles and a new Karamanlis

In the October 2002 municipal and prefectural elections, New Democracy took substantial control. PASOK had now been in power nationally for nineteen out of the last twenty-three years, and sentiment was growing for a change. In February 2004 Simitis stood down as party leader, signalling his belief that one of his main reforms had been effected: an end to personality-based politics, and the completed evolution of an issue-based, centrist, technocratic party. That said, both parties had familiar dynastic names in charge, with **George Papandreou** taking over leadership of PASOK, and fighting an election against New Democracy, led by **Kostas Karamanlis**, nephew of Constantine.

New Democracy won comfortably and Karamanlis, who became prime minister, dedicated himself to negotiations over divided **Cyprus** in an attempt to get the entire island into the EU on May 1, 2004 (in the event the internationally recognized Republic of Cyprus did join, but without the Turkish-occupied north). He also took personal responsibility for ensuring completion of all preparations for the **2004 Olympic Games**. In a last-minute rush all facilities were ready in August, in time for the games in Athens, but the cost rose to three times the original estimates, and as a result of poor marketing, jacked-up hotel prices and fears of terrorism, tourism to Greece actually fell during the year and the Games turned in a deficit.

The after effects of Olympic spending, and Greece's joining the euro at too high a level after rigging its accounts, were felt in March 2005 when trade unions launched a wave of twenty-four hour strikes across the country in protest at high inflation and rising unemployment. In April the Greek parliament ratified the EU constitution, but it soon became a dead letter when it was rejected by referendums elsewhere. A further wave of **industrial action** followed in June over the government's plans for labour and pension reforms.

But there was at least some positive economic news, with **shipping** undergoing something of a boom; nearly a fifth of the world's merchant fleet is owned by Greek companies, and their fortunes have a significant impact on the country. And as the dust settled, the Olympics, for all their faults showed enduring benefits to **Greek infrastructure**, particularly in completion of the new **metro system** for Athens, which now speedily and cheaply connects a new airport with the city. These improvements should lay the foundation for the country's future development.

Archeology in Greece

U ntil the second half of the nineteenth century, archeology was a very hit-and-miss, treasure-hunting affair. The early students of antiquity went to Greece to draw and make plaster casts of the great masterpieces of Classical sculpture. Unfortunately, a number soon found it more convenient or more profitable to remove objects wholesale, and might be better described as looters than scholars or archeologists.

Early excavations

The **British Society of Dilettanti** was one of the earliest promoters of Greek culture, financing expeditions to draw and publish antiquities. Founded in the 1730s as a club for young aristocrats who had completed the Grand Tour and fancied themselves arbiters of taste, the society's main qualification for membership (according to most critics) was habitual drunkenness. Its leading spirit was **Sir Francis Dashwood**, a notorious rake who founded the infamous Hellfire Club. Nevertheless, the society was the first body organized to sponsor systematic research into Greek antiquities, though it was initially most interested in Italy. Greece, then a backwater of the Ottoman Empire, was not a regular part of the Grand Tour and only the most intrepid adventurers undertook so hazardous a trip.

In the 1740s, two young artists, **James Stuart** and **Nicholas Revett**, formed a plan to produce a scholarly record of ancient Greek buildings. With the support of the society they spent three years in Greece, principally in and around Athens, drawing and measuring the antiquities. The first volume of *The Antiquities of Athens* appeared in 1762, becoming an instant success. The publication of their exquisite illustrations and the 1764 publication of **Johann Winckelmann**'s *History of Art*, in which the **Parthenon** and its sculptures were exalted as the eternal standard by which beauty should be measured, gave an enormous fillip to the study of Greek sculpture and architecture, which became the fashionable craze among the educated classes; many European Neoclassical town and country houses date from this period.

The Dilettanti financed a number of further expeditions to study Greek antiquities, including one to Asia Minor in 1812. The expedition was to be based in Smyrna, but while waiting in Athens for a ship to Turkey, the party employed themselves in excavations at **Eleusis**, where they uncovered the **Temple of Demeter**. It was the first archeological excavation made on behalf of the society, and one of the first in Greece. After extensive explorations in Asia Minor, the participants returned via Attica, where they excavated the **Temple of Nemesis** at **Rhamnous** and examined the **Temple of Poseidon** at **Soúnio**.

Several other antiquarians of the age were less interested in discoveries for their own sake. A French count, **Choiseul-Gouffier**, removed part of the **Parthenon frieze** in 1787 and his example prompted **Lord Elgin** to detach much of the rest in 1801. These were essentially acts of looting – "Bonaparte has not got such things from all his thefts in Italy", boasted Elgin – and their legality was suspect even at the time.

Other discoveries of the period were more ambiguous. In 1811, a party of English and German travellers, including the architect **C. R. Cockerell**, uncovered the **Temple of Aphaia** on **Égina** and shipped away the pediments. They auctioned off the marbles for £6000 to Prince Ludwig of Bavaria, and, inspired by this success, returned to Greece for further finds. This time they struck it lucky with 23 slabs from the **Temple of Apollo Epikourios** at **Bassae**, for which the British Museum laid out a further £15,000. These were huge sums for the time and highly profitable exercises, but they were also pioneering archeology for the period. Besides, removing the finds was hardly surprising: Greece, after all, was not yet a state and had no public museum; antiquities discovered were sold by their finders – if they recognized their value.

The new nation

The Greek War of Independence (1821–28) and the establishment of a modern Greek nation changed all of this – and provided a major impetus to archeology. Nationhood brought an increased pride in Greece's Classical heritage, nowhere more so than in Athens, which succeeded Náfplio as the nation's capital in 1834 largely on the basis of its ancient monuments, especially those on the acropolis, and its glorious past.

As a result of the selection of Prince Otto of Bavaria as the first king of modern Greece in 1832, the **Germans**, whose education system laid great stress on Classical learning, were in the forefront of archeological activity. One of the dominant Teutonic figures during the early years of the new state was **Ludwig Ross**. Arriving in Greece as a student in 1832, he was on hand to show the new king around the antiquities of Athens when Otto was considering making the town his capital. Ross was appointed deputy keeper of antiquities to the court, and in 1834 began supervising the excavation and restoration of the **Acropolis**. The work of dismantling the accretion of Byzantine, Frankish and Turkish fortifications began the following year. The graceful **Temple of Athena Nike**, which had furnished many of the blocks for the fortifications, was rebuilt, and Ross's architect, Leo von Klenze, began the **reconstruction of the Parthenon**.

The Greeks themselves had begun to focus on their ancient past when the first stirrings of the independence movement were felt. In 1813 the **Philomuse Society** was formed, which aimed to uncover and collect antiquities, publish books and assist students and foreign philhellenes. In 1829 an orphanage on the island of Égina, built by Kapodistrias, the first president of Greece, became the first **Greek archeological museum**.

In 1837 the **Greek Archeological Society** was founded "for the discovery, recovery and restoration of antiquities in Greece". Its moving spirit was **Kyriakos Pittakis**, a remarkable figure who during the War of Independence had used his knowledge of ancient literature to discover the Klepsydra spring on the Acropolis – solving the problem of lack of water during the Turkish siege. In the first four years of its existence, the Archeological Society sponsored excavations in Athens at the **Theatre of Dionysos**, the **Tower of the Winds**, the **Propylaia** and the **Erechtheion**. Pittakis also played a major role in the attempt to convince Greeks of the importance of their heritage; antiquities were still being looted or burned for lime.

The great Germans: Curtius and Schliemann

Although King Otto was deposed in 1862 in favour of a Danish prince, Germans remained in the forefront of Greek archeology in the 1870s. Two men dominated the scene: Heinrich Schliemann and Ernst Curtius.

Ernst Curtius was a traditional Classical scholar. He had come to Athens originally as tutor to King Otto's family and in 1874 returned to Greece to secure permission for conducting the excavations at **Olympia**, one of the richest of Greek sanctuaries and site of the most famous of the ancient pan-Hellenic games. The reigning Kaiser Wilhelm I intended that the excavation would proclaim to the world the cultural and intellectual pre-eminence of his empire. Curtius took steps to set up a **German Archeological Institute** in Athens and negotiated the **Olympia Convention**, under the terms of which the Germans were to pay for and have total control of the dig; all finds were to remain in Greece, though the excavators could make copies and casts; and all finds were to be published simultaneously in Greek and German.

This was an enormously important agreement, which almost certainly prevented the treasure of Olympia and Mycenae following that of Troy to a German museum. But other Europeans were still in very acquisitive mode: **French consuls**, for example, had been instructed to purchase any "available" local antiquities in Greece and Asia Minor, and had picked up the Louvre's great treasures, the **Venus de Milo** and **Winged Victory of Samothrace**, in 1820 and 1863 respectively.

At **Olympia**, digging began in 1875 on a site buried beneath river mud, silt and sand. Only one corner of the **Temple of Zeus** was initially visible, but within months the excavators had turned up statues from the east pediment. Over forty magnificent sculptures, as well as terracottas, statue bases and a rich collection of bronzes, were uncovered, together with more than four hundred inscriptions. The laying bare of this huge complex was a triumph for official German archeology.

While Curtius was digging at Olympia, a man who represented everything that was anathema to orthodox Classical scholarship was standing archeology on its head. **Heinrich Schliemann**'s beginnings were not auspicious for one who aspired to hunt for ancient cities. The son of a drunken German pastor, he left school at fourteen and spent the next five years as a grocer's assistant. En route to seeking his fortune in Venezuela, he was left for dead on the Dutch coast after a shipwreck; later, working as a book-keeper in Amsterdam, he began to study languages. His phenomenal memory enabled him to master four by the age of 21. Following a six-week study of Russian, Schliemann was sent to St Petersburg as a trading agent and had amassed a fortune by the time he was 30. In 1851 he visited California, opened a bank during the Gold Rush and made another fortune.

His financial position secure for life, Schliemann was almost ready to tackle his life's ambition – the **search for Troy** and the vindication of his lifelong belief in the truth of Homer's tales of prehistoric cities and heroes. By this time he spoke no fewer than seventeen languages, and had excavated on the island of **Ithaca**, writing a book, which earned him a doctorate from the University of Rostock.

Although most of the archeological establishment, led by Curtius, was unremittingly hostile to the millionaire amateur, Schliemann sunk his first trench at the hill called Hisarlik, in northwest Turkey, in 1870; excavation proper began in 1871. In his haste to find Homer's city of Priam and Hector, and to convince the world of his success, Schliemann dug a huge trench straight through the mound, destroying a mass of important evidence, but he was able nevertheless to identify nine cities, superimposed in layers. In May 1873 he discovered the so-called **Treasure of Priam**, a stash of gold and precious jewellery and vessels. It convinced many that the German had indeed found **Troy**, although others contended that Schliemann, desperate for academic recognition, assembled it from other sources. The finds disappeared from Berlin at the end of World War II, but in 1994 archeologists discovered that artefacts held by some museums in Russia originated in Troy; most of these are currently on display in the Pushkin Museum in Moscow, with a few items also in the Hermitage collection in St Petersburg. The Germans have requested their return but as the Russian government has since linked this matter to the vexed question of reparations for the damage done to their land and property by the German army, it seems that they are destined to remain in Russia for the foreseeable future.

Three years later Schliemann turned his attentions to **Mycenae**, again inspired by Homer, and once more following a hunch. Alone among contemporary scholars, he sought and found the legendary graves of Mycenaean kings inside the existing Cyclopean wall of the citadel rather than outside it, unearthing in the process the magnificent treasures that today form the basis of the **Bronze Age collection** in the National Archeological Museum in Athens.

He dug again at Troy in 1882, assisted by a young architect, **Wilhelm Dörpfeld**, who was destined to become one of the great archeologists of the following century (though his claim that Lefkádha was ancient Ithaca never found popular acceptance). In 1884 Schliemann returned to Greece to excavate another famous prehistoric citadel, this time at **Tiryns**.

Almost single-handedly, and in the face of continuing academic obstruction, Schliemann had revolutionized archeology and pushed back the knowledge of Greek history and civilization a thousand years. Although some of his results have been shown to have been deliberately falsified in the sacrifice of truth to beauty, his achievement remains enormous.

The last two decades of the nineteenth century saw the discovery of other important Classical sites. Excavation began at **Epidaurus** in 1881 under the Greek archeologist **Panayotis Kavvadias**, who made it his life's work. Meanwhile at **Delphi**, the **French**, after gaining permission to transfer the inhabitants of the village to a new site and demolishing the now-vacant village, began digging at the **sanctuary of Apollo**. Their excavations proved fruitful and continued nonstop from 1892 to 1903, revealing the extensive site visible today; work on the site has gone on sporadically ever since.

Evans and Knossos

The beginning of the twentieth century saw the domination of Greek archeology by an Englishman, **Sir Arthur Evans**. An egotistical maverick like Schliemann, he too was independently wealthy, with a brilliantly successful career behind him when he started his great work and recovered another millennium for Greek history. Evans excavated what he called the "Palace of Minos" at **Knossos** on **Crete**, discovering one of the oldest and most sophisticated of Mediterranean societies, which he christened Minoan.

The son of a distinguished antiquarian and collector, Evans read history at Oxford, failed to get a fellowship and began to travel. His chief interest was in the Balkans, where he was special correspondent for the *Manchester Guardian* during the 1877 uprising in Bosnia. He took enormous risks in the war-torn country, filing brilliant dispatches and still finding time for exploration and excavation. In 1884, at the age of 33, Evans was appointed curator of the Ashmolean Museum in Oxford. He travelled whenever he could, and it was in 1893, while in Athens, that his attention was drawn to Crete. Evans, though very short-sighted, had almost microscopic close vision. In a vendor's stall he came upon some small drilled stones with tiny engravings in a hitherto unknown script; he was told they came from Crete. He had seen Schliemann's finds from

Mycenae and had been fascinated by this prehistoric culture. Crete, the crossroads of the Mediterranean, seemed a good place to look for more.

Evans visited Crete in 1894 and headed for the legendary site of Knossos, which had earlier attracted the attention of Schliemann (who had been unable to agree a price with the Turkish owners of the land) and where a Cretan, appropriately called Minos, had already done some impromptu digging, revealing massive walls and a storeroom filled with jars. Evans succeeded in buying the site and in March 1900 began excavations. Within a few days, evidence of a great complex building was revealed, along with artefacts which indicated an astonishing cultural sophistication. The huge team of diggers unearthed elegant courtyards and verandahs, colourful wall-paintings, pottery, jewellry and sealstones – the wealth of a civilization which dominated the eastern Mediterranean 3500 years ago.

Evans continued to excavate at Knossos for the next thirty years, during which time he established, on the basis of changes in the pottery styles, the **system of dating** that remains in use today for classifying **Greek prehistory**: Early, Middle and Late Minoan (Mycenaean on the mainland). He published his account of the excavation in a massive six-volume work, *The Palace of Minos*, between 1921 and 1936. Like Schliemann, Evans attracted criticism and controversy for his methods – most notably his decision to speculatively reconstruct parts of the palace in concrete – and for many of his interpretations of what he found. Nevertheless, his discoveries and his dedication put him near to the pinnacle of Greek archeology.

△ Sir Arthur Evans holding a Cretan sculpture of a bull's head at an exhibition of relics from Knossos

Into the twentieth century: the foreign institutes

In 1924 Evans gave to the **British School at Athens** the site of **Knossos** along with his on-site residence, the Villa Ariadne, and all other lands within his possession on Crete (it was only in 1952 that Knossos became the property of the Greek State). At the time the British School was one of several foreign archeological institutes in Greece; founded in 1886, it had been preceded by the **French School**, the **German Institute** and the **American School**.

Greek archeology owes much to the work and relative wealth of these foreign schools and others that would follow. They have been responsible for the excavation of many of the most famous sites in Greece: the **Heraion** on **Sámos** (German); the sacred island of **Delos** (French); sites on **Kós** and in southern **Crete** (Italian); **Corinth**, **Samothráki** and the **Athenian Agora** (American), to name but a few. Life as a resident foreigner in Greece at the beginning of the twentieth century was not for the weak-spirited – one unfortunate member of the American School was shot and killed by bandits while on a trip to visit sites in the Peloponnese – but there were compensations in unlimited access to antiquities in an unspoilt countryside.

The years between the two World Wars saw an expansion of excavation and scholarship, most markedly concerning the prehistoric civilizations. Having been shown by Schliemann and Evans what to look for, a new generation of archeologists was uncovering numerous **prehistoric sites** on the mainland and Crete, and its members were spending proportionately more time studying and interpreting their finds. Digs in the 1920s and 1930s had much smaller labour forces (there were just 55 workmen under Wace at Mycenae, as compared with hundreds in the early days of Schliemann's or Evans's excavations) and they were supervised by higher numbers of trained archeologists. Though perhaps not as spectacular as their predecessors, these scholars would prove just as pioneering as they established the history and clarified the chronology of the newly discovered civilizations.

One of the giants of this generation was **Alan Wace** who, while director of the British School at Athens from 1913 to 1923, conducted excavations at **Mycenae** and established a chronological sequence from the nine great *tholos* tombs on the site. This led Wace to propose a new chronology for prehistoric Greece, which put him in direct conflict with Arthur Evans. Evans believed that the mainland citadels had been ruled by Cretan overlords, whereas Wace was convinced of an independent Mycenaean cultural and political development. Evans was by now a powerful member of the British School's managing committee, and his published attacks on Wace's claims, combined with the younger archeologist's less than tactful reactions to Evans's dominating personality, resulted in the abrupt halt of the British excavations at Mycenae in 1923 and the no less sudden termination of Wace's job. Wace returned to Mycenae in 1950, nine years after Evans's death, and found examples of the "Minoan" **Linear B script**, which British architect **Michael Ventris** deciphered in 1952 as the earliest Greek language. This meant that the Mycenaean Greeks had conquered the Minoans in approximately 1450 BC, which vindicated Wace.

Classical archeology was not forgotten in the flush of excitement over the Mycenaeans and Minoans. The period between the wars saw the continuation of excavation at most established sites, and many new discoveries, among them the sanctuary of **Asklepios** and its elegant Roman buildings on **Kós**, excavated by the Italians from 1935 to 1943, and the Classical Greek city of **Olynthos**, in northern Greece, which was dug by the American School from 1928 to 1934. After the wholesale removal of houses and apartment blocks that had occupied the site, the American School also began excavations in the **Athenian Agora**, the ancient marketplace, in 1931, culminating in the complete restoration of the **Stoa of Attalos**.

The advent of **World War II** and the invasion of Greece first by the Italians and then the Germans called a halt to most archeological work, although the Germans set to work again at **Olympia**, supposedly owing to Hitler's personal interest. A few Allied-nation archeologists also remained in Greece, principal among them **Gorham Stevens** and **Eugene Vanderpool**, of the American School, both of whom did charitable work. Back in America and Britain, meanwhile, archeologists were in demand for the intelligence arm of the war effort, both for their intimate knowledge of the Greek terrain and their linguistic abilities, which proved invaluable in decoding enemy messages.

More recent excavations

Archeological work was greatly restricted in the years after World War II, and in the shadow of the Greek civil war. A few monuments and museums were restored and reopened but it was not until 1948 that excavations were resumed with a Greek clearance of the **Sanctuary of Artemis** at **Brauron** in Attica. In 1952 the American School resumed its activities with a dig at the Neolithic and Bronze Age site of **Lerna** in the Peloponnese, and **Carl Blegen** cleared **Nestor's Palace** at **Pylos** in Messenia. Greek archeologists began work at the Macedonian site of **Pella**, the capital of ancient Macedonia, and at the **Nekromanteion of Ephyra** in Epirus.

These and many other excavations – including renewed work on the major sites – were relatively minor operations in comparison to earlier digs. This reflected a modified approach to archeology, which laid less stress on discoveries and more on **documentation**. Instead of digging large tracts of a site, archeologists concentrated on small sections, establishing chronologies through meticulous analysis of data. Which is not to say that there were no spectacular finds. At **Mycenae**, in 1951, a second circle of graves was unearthed; at Pireás, a burst sewer in 1959 revealed four superb Classical bronzes; and a dig at the **Kerameikos** cemetery site in Athens in 1966 found four thousand potsherds used as ballots for ostracism. Important work has also been undertaken on restorations – in particular the **theatres** at the **Athens Acropolis**, **Dodona** and **Epidaurus**, which are used in summer festivals.

A number of postwar excavation were as exciting as any in the past. In 1961 the fourth great **Minoan palace** (following the unearthing of Knossos, Phaestos and Malia) was uncovered by torrential rains at the extreme eastern tip of the island of Crete at **Káto Zákros** and cleared by Cretan archeologist **Nikolaos Platon**. Its harbour is now thought to have been the Minoans' main gateway port to and from Southwest Asia and Africa, and many of the artefacts discovered in the palace storerooms – bronze ingots from Cyprus, elephants' tusks from Syria, stone vases from Egypt – seem to confirm this. Greek teams have found more Minoan palaces at **Arhánes**, **Haniá**, **Galatás** and **Petrás**, and a new generation of scholars believe that these were ceremonial buildings and not the seats of dynastic authority, as Evans proposed. American excavations at **Kommós**, in southern Crete, have uncovered another gateway site, like Káto Zakrós, of the Minoan and Mycenaean periods.

At **Akrotíri** on the island of **Thíra** (Santoríni), **Spyros Marinatos** revealed, in 1967, a Minoan-era site that had been buried by volcanic explosion in either 1650 or 1550 BC – the jury is still deliberating that one. Its buildings were two or three storeys high, and superbly frescoed. Marinatos was later tragically killed while at work on the site when he fell off a wall, and is now buried there.

A decade later came an even more dramatic find at **Vergina – ancient Aegae** – in northern Greece, the early capital of the Macedonian kingdom, which later became its necropolis. Here, **Manolis Andronikos** found a series of royal tombs dating from the fourth century BC. Unusually, these had escaped plundering by ancient grave robbers and contained an astonishing hoard of exquisite gold treasures. Piecing together clues – the haste of the tomb's construction, an ivory effigy head, gilded leg armour – Andronikos showed this to have been the **tomb of Philip II** of Macedon, father of Alexander the Great. Subsequent forensic examination of the body's remains supported historical accounts of Philip's limp and blindness. It was an astonishing and highly emotive find, as the artefacts and frescoed walls showed the sophistication and Hellenism of ancient Macedonian culture. With the background of an emerging, self-styled Slavo-Macedonian state on Greece's northern border, archeology had come head-to-head with politics.

At the beginning of this century the various foreign schools, recently joined by the Australian, Austrian, Belgian, Canadian, Danish, Dutch, Finnish, Georgian, Irish, Norwegian, Spanish, Swedish and Swiss, along with Greek universities and the 25 *ephorates*, or inspectorates, of Prehistoric and Classical Antiquities are still at work in the field, although the emphasis today is equally concerned with the task of **conserving and protecting** what has been revealed as well as unearthing new finds. All too often newly discovered sites have been inadequately fenced off or protected, and a combination of the elements, greedy developers and malicious trespassers – sometimes all three – have caused much damage and deterioration.

The American School continues its work on the **Athenian Agora** and also in excavating **Roman Corinth** and a number of sites in Crete's Mirabello region. The British School maintains its interest in **Knossos**; the **Spartan Acropolis**, **Lefkandí** in Évvia (where **Hugh Sackett**'s team discovered an important Iron Age town and Heroon); and at **Paleókastro** in eastern Crete, the site of the ancient **Diktaion** – the sacred precinct of Cretan Zeus – where a superb Minoan gold and ivory *kouros* was found recently. In Crete too, the French School is carrying out further excavations in the town surrounding the Minoan palace at **Mália**; they are also continuing restoration work in the **Sanctuary of Apollo** on the island of **Delos**.

Meanwhile, and in the footsteps of Curtius, the German Institute continues its long-standing association with excavations at **Olympia** and the **Kerameikos** cemetery in Athens and is still at work on the **Heraion**, the mammoth sanctuary dedicated to the goddess Hera, on the island of **Sámos**. The Italian School is based mainly in Crete where, among other sites, the impressive forum of the island's Roman capital at **Gortys** is being revealed. Italian archeologists have also been busy at the important site of **Polyochni** on **Límnos**.

Since World War II Greek archeologists have also played a leading role and the Greek Archeological Society is involved in excavation and conservation work in all parts of Greece including **Marathon**, **Epidaurus** and **Dodona** as well as at **Akrotíri**, where more of the remarkable Minoan era site with paintings and multistoried buildings is slowly and spectacularly being excavated and protected.

Wild Greece

For anyone who has first seen Greece at the height of summer with its brown parched hillsides and desert-like ambience, the richness of the wildlife – in particular the flora – may come as a surprise. As winter warms into spring, the countryside (and urban waste ground) transforms itself from green to a mosaic of coloured flowers, which attract a plethora of insect life, followed by birds. Isolated areas, whether true islands or remote mountains such as Olympus, have had many thousands of years to develop their own individual species. Overall, Greece has around six thousand species of native flowering plants, nearly four times that of Britain but in the same land area. Many are unique to Greece, and make up about one-third of Europe's endemic plants.

Despite an often negative attitude to wildlife, Greece was probably the first place in the world where it was an object of study. **Theophrastos** (372–287 BC) from Lésvos was the first recorded botanist and a systematic collector of general information on plants, while his contemporary, **Aristotle**, studied the animal world. And during the first century AD the distinguished physician **Dioscorides** compiled a herbal phamacopeia that remained a standard work for over a thousand years.

Some background

In early antiquity Greece was thickly forested: pines and oak grew in coastal regions, giving way to fir or black pine in the hills and lower mountains. But this **native woodland** contracted rapidly as human activities expanded. By Classical times, the pattern of forest clearance was set, followed by agriculture, abandonment to scrub and then a resumption of cultivation or grazing. Huge quantities of timber were consumed for ships and construction work and in the production of charcoal for pottery and smelted metal. Small patches of virgin woodland remain, mostly in the north and northeast, but even these are threatened by loggers and arsonists.

Greek **farming** often lacks the rigid efficiency of north European agriculture. Many peasant farmers still cultivate patches of land, and even city-dwellers travel at weekends to collect food plants from the countryside. Wild greens under the generic term *hórta* are gathered and cooked like spinach. The young shoots of capers, and the fruit of wild figs, carobs, plums, strawberry trees, cherries and sweet chestnuts are harvested. Emergent snails and mushrooms are collected after wet weather. The more resilient forms of wildlife can coexist with these traditions, but for many Greeks only those species that have practical uses are regarded as having any value. Nowadays, access to heavier earth-moving machinery means a farmer can sweep away an ancient meadow full of orchids in an easy morning's work – often to produce a field that is used for forage for a year or two and then abandoned to coarse thistles. Increasingly, the pale scars of dirt tracks crisscross mountainsides, allowing short-termist agricultural destruction of previously undisturbed upland habitats.

During the 1950s the official policy of draining wetlands, for conversion to agriculture, meant important areas were lost to wildlife completely. Those **lakes, lagoons and deltas** that remain on larger islands such as Crete and Kefalloniá are, in theory, now protected for their fragile biodiversity and their environmental and scientific value – but industrial and sewage pollution, disturbance and misuse are unchecked. Four-wheel-drive vehicles and motorbikes race through the dunes destroying the surface stability; military aeroplanes practice low-flying over flamingo flocks; rows of illegally overnighting camper vans disfigure the beaches; and locals drive here to dump unwanted televisions and fridges. On Lésvos, the Kallóni salt-pans, once beloved by rare birds and birdwatchers, are being poisoned by sewage.

The Orthodox Church, whose lands once provided wildlife with a refuge from hunters, is now capitalizing on their value for major tourist developments, with the development of mass tourism and golf courses around the monastery of Toploú in eastern Crete, already one of Greece's most water-deficient areas.

Since the 1970s, tourist developments have ribboned along **coastlines**, sweeping away both agricultural plots and wildlife havens. These expanding resorts increase local employment, attracting inland workers to the coast; the generation that would have been shepherds on remote hillsides now work in tourist bars and tavernas. Consequently, the pressure of domestic **animal grazing** has been significantly reduced, allowing the regeneration of tree seedlings; Crete, for example, has more woodland now than at any time in the last five centuries. However, **forest fires** remain a threat everywhere. Since 1980, fires have destroyed much of the tree cover in Thássos, southern Rhodes, Kárpathos, Híos, Sámos and parts of the Peloponnese; the trees may well regenerate eventually, but by then the complex shade-dependent ecology will have been irrecoverably lost.

Flowers

Whereas in temperate northern Europe plants flower from spring until autumn, the arid summers of Greece confine the main **flowering period** to the spring, a narrow climatic window when days are bright, temperatures not too high and the groundwater supply still adequate. **Spring** starts in the southeast, in Rhodes, in early March, travelling progressively westwards and northwards. Rhodes, Kárpathos and eastern Crete are at their best in March, western Crete in early April, the eastern Aegean from late April, and the Ionian islands in early May, though a cold dry winter can cause several weeks' delay. In the high mountains the floral spring arrives in the chronological summer, with the alpine zones of Crete in full flower in June, and mainland mountain blooms emerging in July.

The delicate flowers of early spring – orchids, fritillaries, anemones, cyclamen and tulips – are replaced as the season progresses by more robust shrubs, tall perennials and abundant annuals, but many of these close down completely for the fierce **summer**. A few tough plants, like thyme and savory, continue to flower through the heat, acting as magnets for butterflies.

Once the worst heat is over, and the first **autumn** showers arrive, so does a second "spring", on a much smaller scale but welcome after the brown drabness of summer. Squills, cyclamen, crocuses and other small bulbs all come into bloom, while seeds start to germinate for the following year's crop of annuals. By the new year, early-spring bulbs and orchids are flowering in the south.

Seashore

Plants on the **beach** grow in a difficult environment: fresh water is scarce, salt is in excess, and dehydrating winds are often very strong. Feathery **tamarisk** trees are adept at surviving this habitat, and consequently often planted to provide shade; they "sweat" away surplus saltwater from their foliage.

Sand dunes in the southern and eastern islands support decreasing numbers of the low gnarled trees of prickly **juniper**. These provide shelter for colourful small plants, while the sandy depressions behind the dunes – where they have not been illegally ploughed for short-term forage crops – are home to a variety of plants. Open stretches of beach sand usually have fewer plants, particularly in resort areas where the bulldozed "spring cleaning" of the beach removes both the winter's rubbish and all the local flora.

Watercourses

Large areas of **freshwater** are naturally scarce, particularly in the warmer south. Many watercourses dry up completely in the summer, and dry river-beds are often simply flood channels; consequently, there are few true aquatic plants. However, species that survive periodic drying-out can flourish, such as the giant reed or **calamus**, a bamboo-like grass reaching up to 8m in height and often cut for use as canes. It frequently grows in company with the shrubby, pink- or white-flowered and highly poisonous **oleander**.

Cultivated land

Arable fields can be rich with colourful weeds: scarlet poppies, blue bugloss, yellow or white daisies, wild peas and gladioli. Small, unploughed **meadows** may be equally colourful, with slower-growing plants such as orchids in extraordinary quantities. In the absence of herbicides, olive groves have an extensive underflora. In the presence of herbicides there is usually a yellow spring carpet of the introduced, weedkiller-resistant Oxalis, now occurring in sufficient quantity to show up in satellite photographs.

Lower hillsides

The rocky earth on some hillsides makes cultivation difficult and impractical; agriculture is often abandoned and areas regenerate to a rich mixture of shrubs and perennials – known as **garigue**. With time, some wet winters, and in the absence of grazing, a few shrubs will develop into small trees, intermixed with tough climbers, forming much denser **maquis** vegetation. The colour yellow often predominates in early spring, followed by the blues, pinks and purples of bee-pollinated plants. An abundance of the pink and white of Cistus rockroses is usually indicative of an earlier fire, since they are primary recolonizers.

A third vegetation type is **phrygana** – smaller, frequently aromatic or spiny shrubs, often with a narrow strip of bare ground between each hedgehog-like bush. Many aromatic herbs such as lavender, rosemary, savory, sage and thyme are native to these areas, intermixed with other less tasty plants such as the toxic euphorbias and the spiny burnet or wire-netting bush.

Nearly 190 species of **orchid** are believed to occur in Greece; their complexity blurs species' boundaries, keeping botanists in a state of taxonomic flux. In particular, the bee and spider orchids have adapted themselves, through subtleties of lip colour and false scents, to seduce small male wasps. Mistaking the flowers for a potential mate, these insects unintentionally assist the plant's pollination. Other orchids mimic the colours and scents of nectar-producing plants, to lure bees. Though all species are officially protected, many are still picked.

Mountains and gorges

The **higher mountains** of Greece have winter snow cover, and cooler weather for much of the year. The **limestone peaks** of islands such as Corfu, Kefalloniá, Crete, Rhodes, Sámos and Thássos hold rich collections of attractive **rock plants**, flowers whose nearest relatives may be from the Balkan Alps or the Turkish mountains. **Gorges** are another spectacular habitat, particularly rich in Crete; inaccessible cliffs act as refuges for plants that cannot survive the grazing or more extreme climates of open areas. Many of Greece's endemic plants are confined to cliffs, gorges or mountains.

Much of the surviving island forest covers **mountainous areas** of Kefalloniá, Évvia, Lésvos and Crete. Depending on the island and altitude, the woodland can include cypress: native to the south and east Aegean, but, in its columnar form, planted everywhere with a Mediterranean climate. The cooler shade of woodland provides a haven for plants which cannot survive full exposure to the Greek summer. Such species include wonderful red, pink or white peonies, and numerous ferns.

With altitude, the forest thins out to scattered individual conifers and kermes oak, before finally reaching a limit at around 1500–2000m on the mainland – much lower on the islands. Above this treeline are **summer meadows**, and then bare rock. If not severely grazed, these habitats are home to many gnarled, low-growing, often splendidly floriferous plants.

Birds

Migratory species which winter in East Africa move north, through the eastern Mediterranean, from around **mid-March to mid-May**. Some stop in Greece to breed; others move on into the rest of Europe. The southern islands are the first landfall after a long sea-crossing, and smaller birds recuperate briefly before moving on. Larger birds such as storks and ibis often fly very high, and binoculars are needed to spot them as they pass over. In autumn, birds return, but usually in more scattered numbers. Although some are shot, such as quail and turtle dove, there is not the wholesale slaughter that occurs in some other Mediterranean countries.

Swallows and martins constantly swoop through the air to catch insects, as do the larger and noisier swifts. Warblers are numerous; other small insect-eaters include stonechats, fly-catchers and woodchat shrikes. At **night**, the tiny Scops owl has a very distinct, repeated single-note call, like the sonar beep of a submarine; the equally diminutive Little owl, with a weird repertoire of cries, may be visible by day in ruined buildings. Near wooded streams, the most evocative nocturnal bird is the nightingale, most audible in the May mating season.

Larger raptors occur in remoter areas, preferring mountain gorges and cliffs. Buzzards are the most abundant, and often mistaken by overoptimistic birdwatchers for the rarer, shyer eagles. Griffon vultures, by contrast, are unmistakable, soaring on broad, straight-edged wings, whereas the lammergeier is a state-of-the-art flying machine with narrow, swept wings, seen over mountain tops by the lucky few; the remaining nine or ten pairs in Crete are now the Balkan's largest breeding population.

Also in the mountains are ravens, and smaller, colourful birds such as alpine choughs, common choughs, black and white wheatears, wallcreepers and the blue rock thrush.

In **lowland areas**, hoopoes are a startling combination of pink, black and white, obvious when they fly, and the only natural predator of processionary caterpillars, a major pest of pine forests. The shy golden oriole has an attractive song but is adept at hiding its brilliant colours among the olive trees. Multicoloured flocks of elegant bee-eaters fill the air with their soft calls as they hunt insects. Brightest of all is the kingfisher, often seen sea-fishing.

In areas of **wetland** that remain undrained and undisturbed – saltmarshes, coastal lagoons, estuaries and freshwater ponds – osprey, egrets, ibis, spoonbills, storks, pelicans and many waders can be seen feeding. Flamingos sometimes occur, as lone individuals or small flocks, particularly in eastern Aegean salt pans between December and May.

Mammals

Greece's small **mammal** population ranges from rodents and shrews to hedge-hogs, hares and squirrels (including the dark-red Persian squirrel on Lésvos). Medium-sized mammals include badgers, foxes and the persecuted golden jackal, but the commonest is the ferret-like stone (or beech) marten, named for its habit of decorating stones with its droppings to mark territory.

In the mainland mountains, mostly in the north, are found the shy chamois and wild boar, with even shyer predators like lynx, wolves and brown bear. Occasionally seen running wild in Crete's White Mountains, but more often as a zoo attraction, is an endemic ibex, known to hunters as the agrími or krí-krí. Formerly in danger of extinction, a colony of them was established on the offshore islet of Dhía, where they thrived, exterminating the rare local flora.

Reptiles and amphibians

Reptiles flourish in the hot dry summers of Greece, the commonest being **lizards**. Most of these are small, agile and wary, rarely staying around for closer inspection. They're usually brown to grey, subtly spotted, striped or tessellated, though in adult males the undersides are sometimes brilliant orange, green or blue. The more robust green lizards, with long whip-like tails, can be 50cm or more in length, but are equally shy and fast-moving unless distracted by territorial disputes.

On some islands, mainly in the central and eastern Aegean, lives the angular, robust, iguana-like **agama**, with rough grey-brown skin, sometimes called the Rhodes dragon. Unlike other lizards, they will stop to study you, before finally disappearing into a wall or among rocks.

Nocturnal **geckos** are large-eyed, short-tailed lizards. Their spreading toes have claws and ingenious adhesive pads, allowing them to cross house walls and ceilings in their search for insects, including mosquitoes. Groups will lie in wait near bright lights that attract their prey; small ones living indoors have very pale, translucent skins. Despite local unpopularity – one Greek name, miaró, means "defiler" after their outsized faeces – they should be left alone. The rare chameleon is a slow-moving, swivel-eyed inhabitant of eastern Crete and some eastern Aegean islands including Sámos. Essentially green, it has the ability to adjust its coloration to match the surroundings.

Once collected for the pet trade, **tortoises** can be found on some islands, though not Crete. Usually their noisy progress through hillside vegetation is the first signal of their presence, as they spend their often long lives grazing it. Closely related **terrapins** are more streamlined, freshwater tortoises which love to bask on waterside mud by streams or ponds. Shy and nervous omnivorous scavengers, usually only seen as they disappear underwater, their numbers have recently declined steeply on many islands.

Sea turtles occur mostly in the Ionian Sea, but also in the Aegean. Least rare are the loggerhead turtles (Caretta caretta), nesting on Zákynthos, Kefal-loniá, and occasionally in Crete. Their nesting grounds are disappearing under tourist resorts, although they are a protected endangered species (see the box on p.563).

Snakes are abundant in Greece and many islands; most are shy and non-venomous. Several species, including the Ottoman and nose-horned vipers, do have a poisonous bite, though they are not usually aggressive; they are adder-like and often have a very distinct, dark zigzag stripe down the back. Snakes are only likely to bite if a hand is put in the crevice of a wall or a rock-face where one

Flora and fauna field guides

In case of difficulty obtaining titles listed below from conventional booksellers, try the UK specialist wildlife bookshop, Summerfield Books (℡ [0044] 17683/41577; ⑩www.summerfieldbooks.com).

Flowers

Hellmut Baumann *Greek Wild Flowers and Plant Lore in Ancient Greece*. Crammed with fascinating ethnobotany, plus good colour photographs.

Marjorie Blamey and Christopher Grey-Wilson *Mediterranean Wild Flowers*. Comprehensive field guide, with coloured drawings; reasonably up to date.

Lance Chilton *Plant Check-lists*. Small booklets which also include birds, reptiles and butterflies, for a number of Greek islands. Available direct: ⑩www.marengowalks.com.

Pierre Delforge *Orchids of Britain and Europe*. A comprehensive guide, with recent taxonomy, though beware small inaccuracies in the translation.

John Fielding and Nicholas Turland *Flowers of Crete* (2005). Large volume with 1900 colour photos of the Cretan flora, much of which is also widespread in Greece.

Oleg Polunin *Flowers of Greece and the Balkans*. Classic, older field guide, with colour photographs and line drawings; good on regional geology, climate and habitats.

Birds

George Handrinos and T. Akriotis *Birds of Greece* (1997) A comprehensive guide that includes island birdlife.

Lars Jonsson *Birds of Europe with North Africa and the Middle East*. The ornithologist's choice for the best coverage of Greek birds, with excellent descriptions and illustrations.

Richard Brooks *Birding on the Greek Island of Lesvos*. Superb guide with colour photos which includes a list of birdwatching sites, with detailed maps, plus an annotated species-by-species bird list. Contact the author directly at email@richard-brooks.co.uk

Stephanie Coghlan *A Birdwatching Guide to Crete* (1996). A fine island guide.

Mammals

Corbet and Ovenden *Collins Guide to the Mammals of Europe*. The best field guide on its subject.

Reptiles

Arnold, Burton and Ovenden *Collins Guide to the Reptiles and Amphibians of Britain and Europe*. A useful guide, though it excludes the Dodecanese and east Aegean islands.

Jiri Cihar *Amphibians and Reptiles* (o/p). Selective coverage, but includes most endemic species of the Dodecanese and east Aegean isles.

Insects

Michael Chinery *Collins Guide to the Insects of Britain and Western Europe*. Although Greece is outside the geographical scope of the guide, it will provide generic identifications for many insects seen.

Lionel Higgins and Norman Riley *A Field Guide to the Butterflies of Britain and Europe*. A thorough and detailed field guide that illustrates nearly all species seen in Greece.

Marine life

B. Luther and K. Fiedler *A Field Guide to the Mediterranean* (o/p). Very thorough; includes most Greek shallow-water species.

of them is resting, or if they are molested. Unfortunately, the locals in some areas attempt to kill any snake they see, thereby greatly increasing the probability of their being bitten. Leave them alone, and they will do the same for you (but if bitten, see the advice on p.48). Most snakes are not only completely harmless to humans, but beneficial since they reduce populations of rats and mice. There are also three species of legless lizards, including glass lizards: equally harmless, but killed when mistaken for snakes.

Frogs and toads are the most obvious amphibians throughout much of Greece, particularly during the spring breeding season. The green toad has a cricket-like trill. Frogs prefer the wettest places, and the robust marsh frog revels in artificial water-storage ponds, whose concrete sides magnify their croaking impressively. Tree frogs are tiny, emerald green jewels, with huge, strident voices at night, sometimes to be found in quantity on the leaves of waterside oleanders. Orange-on-black fire salamanders may be found promenading in mountain woodlands after rain.

Insects

Greece teems with insects: some pester, like flies and mosquitoes, but most are harmless to humans.

Grasshoppers and **crickets** swarm through open areas in summer, with larger species that are carnivorous and can bite if handled. Larger still are grey-brown locusts, flying noisily before crash-landing into shrubs. The high-pitched, endlessly repeated chirp of house crickets can drive one to distraction, as can the summer whirring of cicadas on the trunks of trees.

From spring to autumn, Greece is full of **butterflies**. Swallowtail species are named for the drawn-out corners of the hind-wings, in shades of cream and yellow, with black and blue markings. The unrelated, robust, brown-and-orange pasha is Europe's largest butterfly. In autumn black-and-orange African monarchs may appear, sometimes in large quantities.

Some Greek **hawkmoths** are equally spectacular, and their large caterpillars can be recognized by their tail horn. The hummingbird hawkmoth, like its namesake, hovers at flowers to feed, supported by a blur of fast-moving wings. Tiger moths, with black-and-white forewings and startling bright orange hindwings, are the "butterflies" occurring in huge quantity in sheltered sites of islands such as Rhodes and Páros.

Other insects include the camouflaged **praying mantis**, holding their power-ful forelegs in a position of supplication until another insect comes within reach. The females are notorious for eating the males during mating. Ant-lion adults resemble an ineffectually fluttery dragonfly, but their young are huge-jawed and build pits in the sand to trap ants. Hemispherical scarab beetles collect balls of dung and push them around with their back legs. Cockroaches of varying species live in buildings, particularly hotels, restaurants and bakeries, attracted by warmth and food scraps.

Corfu is famous for its extraordinary **fireflies**, which flutter in quantities across meadows and marshes on May nights, speckling the darkness with bursts of cold light to attract partners; look carefully in nearby hedges, and you may spot the less flashy, more sedentary glow-worm.

Other **non-vertebrates** of interest include the land crabs, which are found in the south and east of Greece. They need freshwater to breed, but cause surprise when seen crawling across remote hillsides. There are plenty of genuine marine creatures, particularly in shallow seawater sheltered by rocks – sea cucumbers, sea butterflies, octopus, starfish and sea urchins.

Greek Popular Music

M usic is ubiquitous in modern Greek culture; even the most indifferent visitor will be aware of it in ferries, tavernas and other public spaces. Like so many aspects of Greece, it is an amalgam of "native" and Anatolian styles, with occasional contributions from points further west, and it survives alongside and often in preference to Western-style pop. In fact, Western music made little impression in Greece until the 1950s, when disputes arose between adherents of indigenous styles and those spurning ethnic roots in favour of jazz, rock or symphonic idioms – a reflection of the broader modernizing-versus-traditionalism debates which preoccupied the country.

Many older songs in Eastern-flavoured minor scales (or more correctly, modes) have direct antecedents in the forms and styles of both **Byzantine religious chant** and the popular music of the **Ottoman Empire**, though more nationalist-minded musicologists claim their original descent from the now-lost melodies of ancient Greece. Almost all native Greek instruments are near-duplicates of ones used throughout the Islamic world, though it's an open question as to whether the Byzantines, Arabs or Persians first constructed particular instruments. To this broadly Middle Eastern base Slavs, Albanians and Italians have added their share, resulting in an extraordinarily varied repertoire.

Regional Folk Music

The best opportunities for hearing live Greek folk music are the numerous summer **paniyíria** (saints' day festivals) or more tourist-oriented **cultural programmes**, when musicians based in Athens or city clubs during winter tour the islands and villages. All too often, alas, traditional instrumentation is replaced by rock instruments, with excess reverb and pick-ups tacked on to string instruments not meant for amplification. However, a number of high-quality revival groups are attempting to recapture the musicianship of the old-timers, which have been well archived on CD in recent years.

Island music

The arc of southern Aegean islands comprising **Crete**, **Kássos**, **Kárpathos** and **Hálki** is one of the most promising areas in Greece to hear live music. The dominant instrument here is the **lýra**, a lap-fiddle directly related to the Turkish *kemençe*. It is played not on the shoulder but balanced on the thigh, with – in the Dodecanese – a loose bow which can touch all three of the gut strings (the middle being a drone) simultaneously, making double chords possible. The contemporary **Cretan lýra** is larger, tuned lower (like a Western violin), played with a much tauter bow, and lacks a drone string. Among outstanding Cretan players are the brothers **Nikos** and **Andonis Xylouris**.

Usually, the *lýra* is backed up by a **laoúto**, which is related to the Turkish/Arab *oud* but more closely resembles a mandolin, with a long fretted neck and four sets of double strings. Usually restricted to percussive chords, these are rarely used to lead or solo, but a virtuoso player will enter a true dialogue with the *lýra*, using well-chosen rhythms and melodic phrases in chime-like tones; poor ones rely more on rhythm.

In parts of the southern and eastern Aegean, most notably **Kálymnos** and northern **Kárpathos**, you also find a simple, **droneless bagpipe** with a double chanter – the **askómandoura** or *tsamboúna*. On most islands, though, this instrument is seen as fit for carnival noise only – played in conjunction with a two-headed, shoulder-strung drum called the *toumbáki*. It seems, sadly, on the way out: Crete, Náxos, Sámos, Ikaría and Tínos each have just one elderly player apiece, with no younger disciples. And much the same goes for the **sandoúri**, or hammer dulcimer – which, if you know Kazantzakis's classic novel, or its film, *Zorba the Greek*, you may recall was played by his Cretan hero. The instrument, which today tends to have a supporting role (at best), was introduced to the islands in the 1920s by Asia Minor refugees.

On most Aegean islands, particularly in the **Cyclades**, the *lýra* is replaced by a more familiar-looking **violí**, essentially a Western violin. Accompaniment was provided until recently by *laoúto* or *sandoúri*, though these days you're most likely to be confronted by a bass guitar and rock drums. Among the better fiddle players, **Stathis Koukoularis** (from Náxos) and younger **Nikos Ikonomidhes** (Skhinoússa/Híos) or **Kyriakos Gouvendas**, are well worth seeking out. Unlike on Crete, where you often catch the best music in special clubs or *kéndra*, Aegean island performances tend to be public, community-based shows, in village squares or monastery courtyards.

Island folk songs – **nisiótika** – feature melodies which, like much folk music the world over, rely heavily on the pentatonic scale. Lyrics, especially on the smaller islands, touch on the perils of the sea, exile and (in a society where long separations and arranged marriages were the norm) thwarted love. The prolific and decidedly uneven **Konitopoulos** clan from Náxos has become virtually synonymous with nisiótika, but older stars like **Anna and Emilia Hatzidhaki**, **Effi Sarri** and **Anna Karabesini** – all from the Dodecanese archipelago – offer a warmer, more innocent delivery.

Lésvos occupies a special place in terms of island music; before the turbulent decade of 1912–22, its "mainland" was Asia Minor rather than Greece, its urban poles Smyrna and Constantinople rather than Athens. As a consequence, its music is far more varied and sophisticated than the Aegean norm, having absorbed melodies and instrumentation from the various groups who lived in neighbouring Anatolia; it is the only island with a vital **brass-band** tradition, and nearly every Greek dance rhythm is represented in local music.

By way of complete contrast, the **Ionian islands** (except for Lefkádha) alone of all modern Greek territory never saw Turkish occupation and have a predominantly Western musical tradition. Their indigenous song-form is Italian both in name – **kantádhes** – and in its instrumentation (guitar and mandolin) and vocalization (major scales, choral delivery); it's most often heard these days on Lefkádha, Kefalloniá and Zákynthos.

Mainland music

In the **Peloponnese** and **central/western Greece**, many of the folk songs – known as **dhimotiká tragoúdhia** – hark back to the years of Ottoman occupation and the War of Independence; others, in a lighter tone, refer to aspects of pastoral life (sheep, elopements, fetching water from the well). Their essential instrument is the **klaríno** (clarinet), which reached Greece during the 1830s, introduced either by Gypsies or by King Otto's Bavarian entourage. Backing was traditionally provided by a *koumpanía* consisting of *kithára* (guitar), *laoúto*, *laoutokythára* (a hybrid in stringing and tuning) and *violí*, with *toumberléki* (lap drum) or *défi* (tambourine) for rhythm.

Many mainland tunes are **dances**, divided by rhythm into such categories as *kalamatianó* (a line dance), *tsámiko*, *hasaposérviko* or *syrtó*, the quintessential circle dance of Greece. Those that aren't danceable include the slow, stately *kléftiko*, similar to the *rizítiko* of Crete, both of which relate, baldly or in metaphor, incidents or attitudes from the years of the Ottomans and the fight for freedom. Stalwart vocalists to look for on old recordings include **Yiorgos Papasidheris** and **Yioryia Mittaki**, the latter actually of Arvanitic (Albanian-speaking) origin, as well as **Tassia Verra**, **Sofia Kollitiri**, **Stathis Kavouras** and **Takis Karnavas** from the 1960s to the 1980s. Among instrumentalists, the violinist **Yiorgos Koros** and clarinetist **Vassilis Saleas** are especially remarkable.

The folk music of **Epirus** (**Ípiros**) exhibits strong connections with that of northern Epirus (now in neighbouring Albania) and the Former Yugoslav Republic of Macedonia, particularly in the **polyphonic pieces** sung by both men and women. The repertoire tends to fall into three categories, also found further south: *mirolóyia* or laments (the instrumental counterpart is called a *skáros*); drinking songs or *tís távlas*; and various danceable melodies as noted above, common to the entire mainland and many islands also. Most notable of the Epirot **clarinettists** are the late **Vassilis Soukas** and **Tassos Halkias**, and the younger (unrelated) **Petros–Loukas Halkias** – all good examples of the (mostly) **Gypsy** or Gypsy-descent musicians who dominate instrumental music on the mainland.

Macedonia and Thrace in the north remained Ottoman territory until early in the twentieth century, with a bewilderingly mixed population, so music here can still sound more generically Balkan. Meriting a special mention are the **brass bands**, introduced in the nineteenth century by Ottoman military musicians, peculiar to western Macedonia. Owing to the huge influx of Anatolian refugees after 1923, these regions have been a treasure-trove for collectors and ethnomusicologists seeking to document the old music of Asia Minor. Noteworthy singers – both still alive and active – include **Xanthippi Karathanassi** and **Khronis Aïdhonidhis**.

Among Thracian instruments, the **kaváli** (end-blown pastoral flute) is identical to the Turkish and Bulgarian article, as is the local drone bagpipe or **gáïda**, made like its island counterpart from a goat-skin. The **zournás**, a screechy, double-reed oboe similar to the Islamic world's *shenai*, is much in evidence at weddings or festivals, together with the deep-toned *daoúli* drum, as a typically Gypsy ensemble. Other percussion instruments like the *daïrés* or tambourine and the *darboúka*, the local version of the *toumberléki*, provide sharply demarcated dance rhythms such as the *zonarádhikos*. The *klaríno* is present here as well, as are two types of *lýras*, but perhaps the most characteristic melodic instrument of Thrace is the **oúti** (*oud*), whose popularity received a boost after refugee players arrived. **Nikos Saragoudas** is its acknowledged living master.

Rebétika

Rebétika began as the music of the Greek urban dispossessed – petty criminals, bar-girls, refugees, drug-users, defiers of social norms in general. It existed in some form in **Greece**, **Smyrna** and **Constantinople** since at least the beginning of the twentieth century – probably a few decades earlier. But it is as hard to define as jazz or blues, with which spurious comparisons are often made. Although rebétika shares marked similarities in spirit with these genres, there's none whatsoever in its musical form. That said, the themes of the earlier songs – illicit or frustrated love, drug addiction, police oppression, disease and death; and their tone – resignation to the singer's lot, coupled with defiance of authority – will be familiar to old time blues fans.

Even the word "rebétika" is of uncertain derivation, most likely from *harabati*, an old Turkish word meaning, variously, "a shanty town", "a privileged drunkard" and "unconventionally dressed bohemian" – all aspects of early *rebétika* culture. Accordingly, searches for its beginnings must be conducted in the Asia Minor of the last years of the Ottoman empire as well as in Greece proper.

Origins: café-aman

Most people equate traditional Greek music with the **bouzoúki**, a long-necked, fretted, three-stringed lute derived, like the Turkish *saz*, from the Byzantine *tambourás*. Early in the twentieth century, however, only a few Greek mainland musicians used it. At the same time, across the Aegean in Smyrna and Constantinople, musical cafés, owned and staffed almost entirely by Greeks, Jews, Armenians, Slavs and even a few Gypsies, had become popular. They featured groups comprising a violinist, a *sandoúri* player and a (usually female) vocalist, who might also jingle castanets and dance. The metrically free, improvisational songstyle became known as **café-aman** or **amanés**, after the frequent repetition of the exclamation *aman aman* (Turkish for "alas, alas"), used both for its sense and to fill time while the performers searched for more articulate lyrics.

Despite sparse instrumentation, the *amanés* was an elegant, riveting style requiring considerable skill, harking back to similar vocalization in central Asia. Among its greatest practitioners were **Andonis "Dalgas" Dhiamandidhis**,

so nicknamed (Dalgas means "Wave") for the undulations in his voice; **Roza Eskenazi**, a Greek Jew who grew up in Constantinople, whose voice inimitably combined innocence and sensuality; her contemporary rival **Rita Abatzi**, from Smyrna, with a huskier, more textured tone; **Marika Papagika**, from the island of Kós, who emigrated to America where she made her career; **Agapios Tomboulis**, a *tambur* and *oud* player of Armenian background; and **Dhimitris "Salonikiyé" Semsis**, a master fiddler from northern Macedonia who in the course of his career travelled across the Mediterranean. This spectrum of origins of these performers gives a good idea of the cosmopolitan influences in the years immediately preceding the emergence of "real" *rebétika*.

△ *Bouzonki* player, Athens

The 1919–22 Greco-Turkish war and the resulting **1923 exchange of populations** were key events in the history of *rebétika*, resulting in the influx to Greece of over a million Asia Minor Greeks, many of whom settled in shanty towns around Athens, Pireás and Thessaloníki. The *café-aman* musicians, like most of the refugees, were far more sophisticated than the Greeks of the host country; many were highly educated, could read and compose music and had even been unionised in the towns of Asia Minor. Such men included the Smyrniots **Vangelis Papazoglou**, a noted songwriter, and **Panayiotis Toundas**, another composer who later ran Columbia Records.

But less lucky refugees lived on the periphery of the new society: most had lost all they had in the hasty evacuation, and many, from inland Anatolia, initially spoke only Turkish. In their misery they sought relief in another Ottoman institution, the **tekés** or hashish den, whose habitués were known as *dervíses* (dervishes). This apparent burlesque of the Islamic mystical tradition was in fact not so flippant as it appears; the Turkish word *harabati*, noted above, is in turn derived from the Arabo-Persian *kharabat*, the Sufi musician's quarter in Afghan or Persian towns, "the place you go to be destroyed (and reborn)" by partaking in the rituals.

The tekédhes and Pireás-style rebétika

In the *tekédhes* of Pireás, Athens and Thessaloníki, a few men would sit around a charcoal brazier, toking from a *nargilés* (hookah) filled with hashish. One of them might improvise a tune on the *baglamás* or the *bouzoúki* and begin to sing. The words would be heavily laced with insiders' argot incorporating Turkish and Venetian words (plus a few Arabic or Albanian ones). As the *taxími* (long, studied introduction) was completed, one of the smokers might rise and begin to dance a **zeïbékiko**, named after the Zeybeks, a warrior caste of western Anatolia. Following an unusual metre (9/8), this would be a slow, intense, introverted performance, danced not for the benefit of others but for himself.

By the early 1930s, various key (male) musicians had emerged from the *tekés* culture. Foremost among them was a Pireás-based quartet: the beguiling-voiced **Stratos Payioumtzis**; composer and lyricist **Anestis Delias** (aka **Artemis**), who succumbed to hard drugs and died in the street of an overdose in 1943; *baglamá*-player Yiorgos Tsoros, better known as **Batis**, an indifferent musician but another excellent composer; and **Markos Vamvakaris**, a Catholic from Sýros who became the linchpin of the group. After a tough childhood, he'd stowed away aged fifteen on a boat for Pireás; within six months of arrival, he had taught himself *bouzoúki* as a way out of a particularly grim job in a slaughterhouse, and was soon playing with the other three. Though an indisputable master instrumentalist, he initially considered that his voice, ruined perhaps from too much hash-smoking, was no good for singing. But he soon bowed to the encouragement of record label Columbia, and his gravelly, unmistakable style set the standard for male *rebétic* vocals until the 1940s. His only close peer as an instrumentalist and composer was **Ioannis Papaïoannou**, with whom he played steadily from 1936 to 1939.

Songs about getting stoned – known as *mastoúriaka* or *hasiklídhika* – were a natural outgrowth of the *tekédhes*. One of the most famous, composed by Batis and first recorded in the mid-1930s with Stratos singing, commemorated the quartet's exploits:

On the sly I went out in a boat
And arrived at the Dhrákou Cave
Where I saw three men stoned on hash

Stretched out on the sand.
It was Batis, and Artemis,
And Stratos the Lazy.
Hey you, Strato! Yeah you, Strato!
Fix us a terrific nargilé,
So old Batis can have a smoke...

Subsequent decades saw such lyrics bowdlerized, for reasons set forth below; the most commonly heard version of this song, from the 1950s, substitutes "Play us a fine bit of *bouzoúki*" for "Fix us a fine *nargilé*", and so forth.

Persecution

This "Golden Age" of rebétika – as indeed it was, despite the unhappy lives of many performers, and necessarily limited audience – was short lived. The association of the music with a drug-laced underworld would prove its undoing. After the imposition of the puritanical **Metaxas dictatorship** in 1936, musicians with uncompromising lyrics and lifestyles were blackballed by the recording industry; anti-hashish laws were systematically enforced, and police harassment of the *tekédhes* was stepped up. In Athens, even possession of a *bouzoúki* or *baglamás* became a criminal offence – thus frequent lyrics about instruments being hidden under coats or smashed by the cops – and several big names did time in jail. Others went to Thessaloníki, where the police chief Vassilis Mouskoundis was a big fan of the music and allowed its practitioners to smoke in private.

For a while, such persecution – and the official encouragement of tangos and frothy Italianate love songs (which always had a much wider audience) – failed to dim the enthusiasm of the *mánges* ("wide boys") who frequented the hash dens. Police beatings or prison terms were taken in stride; time behind bars could be used, as it always had been around the Aegean, to make *skaptó* (dugout) instruments. A *baglamás* could easily be fashioned from a gourd cut in half or even a tortoise shell (the sound box), a piece of wood (the neck), catgut (frets) and wire for strings, and the result would be small enough to hide from the guards. **Jail songs** were composed and became popular in the underworld. The lyrics below, with some literal translation from the 1930s argot, are from a typical, much-recorded song, "Iy Lahanádhes" ("The Pickpockets," or literally "The Cabbage-Dealers") by Vangelis Papazoglou:

Down in Lemonádhika there was a ruckus
They caught two pickpockets who acted innocent
They took 'em to the slammer in handcuffs
They'll get a beating if they don't cough up the loot.
Don't beat us, Mr. Copper, you know very well
This is our job, and don't expect a cut.
We "eat cabbages" and pinch "slippers" so we can
Have a regular rest in jail.
Death don't scare us, it's only hunger we mind,
That's why we nick "cabbage" and get along fine.

The unfortunate *rebétes* incurred disapproval from the puritanical Left as well as the puritanical Right; the growing **Communist Party** of the 1930s considered the music and its habitués hopelessly decadent and politically unevolved. When Vamvakaris was about to join the leftist resistance army ELAS in 1943, he was admonished not to sing his own material; the Left preferred

andártika (Soviet-style revolutionary anthems), although **Sotiria Bellou**, a *rebétissa* (female rebetic musician) and active communist whose career began late in the 1940s, was a conspicuous exception. Despite this, *rebétika* was strangely popular amongst the rank-and-file on both sides of the 1946–49 civil war – perhaps the only taste uniting a fatally polarized country.

Rebétika goes mainstream, declines, then revives

Bellou was one of several important female vocalists to accompany **Vassilis Tsitsanis**, the most significant composer and *bouzoúki* player to emerge after Vamvakaris; the others were **Marika Ninou**, an Armenian refugee from the Caucasus, and **Ioanna Yiorgakopoulou**, the latter also a composer in her own right. From Tríkala in Thessaly, Tsitsanis abandoned law studies to cut his first record in 1936 for Odeon, directed by rebetic composer **Spyros Peristeris**. The war interrupted his – and everyone else's – recording career by closing the studios from late 1940 until late 1945, a period which Tsitsanis spent more comfortably than many, running a musical taverna in Thessaloníki.

When World War II, and the civil war that followed, ended, a huge backlog of songs composed during the interim finally went onto vinyl. The traumatic decade between 1939 and 1949 had erased any lingering fashion for *mastoúriaka*; the Greek public of the 1950s instead craved softer **Neapolitan melodies**, words about love and new heroes. Tsitsanis was happy to oblige on all three counts, and for the first time rebétika enjoyed something like a mass following. But his love lyrics were anything but insipid; the demoralization of the war years led him also to compose darker works, most famous of these "Synnefiasmeni Kyriaki":

Cloudy Sunday, you seem like my heart
Which is always overcast, Christ and Holy Virgin!
You're a day like the one I lost my joy.
Cloudy Sunday, you make my heart bleed.
When I see you rainy, I can't rest easy for a moment;
You blacken my life and I sigh deeply.

Although Tsitsanis performed almost up to his death in 1984 – his funeral in Athens was attended by nearly a quarter of a million people – 1953 effectively marked the end of the original *rebétic* style. In that year, **Manolis Hiotis** added a **fourth string** to the **bouzoúki**, allowing it to be tuned tonally rather than modally; electrical amplification to reach larger audiences, maudlin lyrics and over-orchestration were not long in following. Performances in huge, barnlike clubs, also called *bouzoúkia*, became debased and vulgarized. Virtuoso *bouzoúki* players like **Hiotis**, **Yiorgos Mitsakis** and **Yiorgos Zambetas**, assisted by large-chested female vocalists of little distinction, became immensely rich – the so-called *arhondorebétes*. The clubs themselves were clip-joints where Athenians paid large sums to break plates and watch dancing whose flashy steps and gyrations were a travesty of the simple dignity and precise, synchronized footwork of the old-time *zeïbékiko*.

Ironically, the original *rebétika* material was rescued from oblivion by the **colonels' junta** of 1967–74. Along with dozens of other features of Greek culture, most *rebétika* verses were banned. The younger generation coming of age under the dictatorship took a closer look at the forbidden fruit and derived solace, and deeper meanings, from the nominally apolitical lyrics. When the junta fell in 1974 – even a little before – there was an outpouring of reissued recordings of the old masters.

Over the next decade or so live *rebétika* also enjoyed a revival, beginning with a reunion of old-timers in 1973, and continuing with a clandestine 1978 club near the old Fix brewery in Athens, whose street cred was validated when it was raided and closed by the police. These smoky attempts to recapture pre-war atmosphere, and eventually larger venues, saw performances by revival groups such as the Athens-based **Ta Pedhia apo tin Patra**, **Iy Rebetiki Kompania** and **Iy Opisthodhromiki Kompania**, and from Thessaloníki, **Hondronakos, Maryo** and **Agathonas Iakovidhis** with his **Rebetika Synkrotima Thessalonikis**. Both of the latter are still performing, Agathonas in a new quartet, **Rebetiki Tetras**, with Glykeria, Babis Goles and Babis Tsertos.

A feature film by Kostas Ferris, **Rembetiko** (1983), based loosely on the life of Marika Ninou, attempted to trace the music from Asia Minor of the 1920s to Greece of the 1950s, and garnered worldwide acclaim. Today, however, the *rebétika* fashion has long since peaked in Greece, and hardly any clubs and bands remain from the dozens which existed between 1978 and 1986. Interestingly, *rebétika* has garnered a new lease of life overseas, with a keen following and revival groups in such unlikely countries as Sweden, but the music is now effectively retro and historic.

The éntekhno revolution

The "Westernization" of *rebétika* that had begun with Tsitsanis and been completed by the *arhondorebétes* paved the way for the **éntekhno music** which emerged during the late 1950s. *Éntekhno*, literally "artistic" or "sophisticated", meant an orchestral genre where folk or *rebetic* instruments and melodies would be interwoven into a much larger symphonic fabric, but with a still recognizably Greek sound.

Its first and most famous exponents were **Manos Hatzidhakis** and **Mikis Theodhorakis**, both classically trained musicians and admirers of rebétika. Already in 1948, Hatzidhakis had defended *rebétika* in a lecture, suggesting that Greek composers be inspired by it, rather than bow to the prevailing prejudices against it. At a time when most Greek tunes imitated Western light popular music, he had transcribed *rebétika* for piano and orchestra, keeping only the spirit and nostalgic mood of the original. Theodhorakis, a disciple of Tsitsanis, included *zeïbékika* on his earliest albums, with Grigoris Bithikotsis or Stelios Kazantzidhis on vocals and Manolis Hiotis as *bouzoúki* soloist.

The *éntekhno* of Theodhorakis and Hatzidhakis combined not only *rebetic* and Byzantine influences with orchestral arrangements, but also successfully used the country's rich **poetic tradition**. Among Theodhorakis's first albums was his 1958 *Epitafios/Epifaneia*, settings of poems by **Yiannis Ritsos** and **George Seferis** respectively, and its successor, *To Axion Esti*, a Byzantine-flavoured oratorio incorporating verses by Nobel laureate **Odysseas Elytis**. Hatzidhakis countered with *Matomenos Gamos*, a version of Garcia Lorca's *Blood Wedding* translated by poet-lyricist **Nikos Gatsos**, and also tried his hand at rendering Elytis in song. These early works changed Greek perceptions of *bouzoúki*-based music, popularized Greek poetry for a mass audience and elevated lyricists such as Gatsos and **Manos Eleftheriou** to the status of bards.

The down-side of increased sophistication was an inevitable distancing from indigenous roots, in particular the modal scale which had served Greece so well since antiquity. And with its catchy tunes, *éntekhno* fell prey to the demands of the local film industry – writing a soundtrack became an obligatory rite of passage for composers – and at its worst degenerated to muzak cover versions. Hatzidhakis composed **soundtracks** for various movies starring Melina

Mercouri, most notably *Never on Sunday* (1960); Theodhorakis' international reputation subsequently became distorted by his overplayed and over-covered 1965 soundtrack for *Zorba the Greek*. Soon after this he shunned Byzantine/folk/*rebétic* influence completely in favour of quasi-classical, overtly political symphonic works and film soundtracks dictated by his communist affiliation. Hatzidhakis (who died in 1994) mostly steered clear of political statements; instead he launched, during the 1980s, his own record label, Seirios, to provide a forum for non-mainstream musicians.

Theodhorakis and Hatzidhakis paved the way for less classicizing and more folk-leaning successors such as **Stavros Xarhakos**, most famous for his soundtracks to the films *Ta Kokkina Fanaria* (The Red Lanterns) and *Rembetiko*; Xarkhakos's contemporary **Yiannis Markopoulos** also paid his soundtrack dues (*Who Pays the Ferryman*, 1978) but is arguably the most consistently Greek-sounding of these four composers to emerge from the 1960s. His best work dates from the early-to-mid-1970s – the Indian summer of *éntekhno*.

Laïká: son of rebétika

Diametrically opposed to *éntekhno* was the authentic **laïká** ("popular") music of the 1950s and 1960s, its gritty, tough style a direct heir to *rebétika*, undiluted by Western influences. *Laïká* used not only *zeïbékiko* and *hasápiko* time signatures but also the *tsiftetéli*, another Asia Minor rhythm mistakenly known as belly-dance music overseas. Once again, "debased" oriental influences dominated Greek pop, much to the chagrin of those who objected to the apolitical, decadent, escapist song content.

The most notable *laïká* performer was **Stelios Kazantzidhis** (1931–2001), whose volcanic, mournful style was never equalled. His work, often in duets with **Marinella** and **Yiota Lidhia**, immortalized the joys and sorrows of the Greek working class which emerged from the 1940s faced with a choice of life under restrictive regimes, or emigration. "Stellaras" (as he was nicknamed) inspired fanatical devotion in his fans over a fifty-year career: truck-drivers emblazoned their cabs with a single word, "Yparho" (the name of his biggest hit). On the day he died seemingly every CD player in the land played Kazantzidhis songs in tribute, and his funeral in Elefsína was thronged by thousands.

Top *laïká* star of the next generation has indubitably been **Yiorgos (George) Dalaras**, a musical phenomenon in Greece since he made his 1968 vinyl debut with composer Manos Loïzos. Born in 1952, the son of a *rebétika* musician, Dalaras has featured on well over a hundred recordings, spanning all Greek genres, the works of Theodhorakis, Hatzidhakis and Markopoulos, and collaborations with the flamenco guitarist Paco de Lucia and American blues star Al Di Meola. Dalaras has also been a staunch supporter (through benefit concerts) of progressive causes, enough to forgive him his recent symphonic efforts.

Amongst notable *laïká* composers and lyricists, **Apostolos Kaldharas** was the most prolific during the 1950s and 1960s; he gave singer **Yiannis Parios** his start, and introduced *laïká* star **Haris Alexiou** with his landmark 1972 album *Mikra Asia*. **Khristos Nikolopoulos** was a *bouzoúki* virtuoso who emerged during the 1970s as a composer for Kazanthzídhis, and subsequently went on to mega-selling co-efforts with Dalaras and Alexiou. **Akis Panou** (1934–99) was less prolific and commercially successful – taking time out to be a painter and copper-engraver – but he too produced noteworthy albums with Dalaras, Bithikotsis and Stratos Dhionysiou as well as Kazantzidhis.

Although *laïká* and *éntekhno* represented opposite poles, these extremes sometimes met, with *éntekhno* composers – especially Markopoulos – often hiring *laïká* singers for dates, or trying their hand at writing in *laïká* style. These synthe-ses became increasingly rare as Greek record labels tried to marginalize *laïká* – a trend accelerated under the junta, and a disaster for many types of music. Not only was the greater portion of *laïká* banned from the radio as being too "orien-tal" and "defeatist", but folk music – already disparaged as old-fashioned by a generation coming of age with The Beatles – fell into more disrepute through its use for propaganda purposes. In these conditions, only *elafrolaïká* (literally "light popular songs") and *éntekhno*, with its minority audience and potential for coded messages within oblique lyrics, flourished. But the stage was set for the emergence of singer-songwriters – many of them from Thessaloníki – and groups of folk-rockers, who together arrested the decline of Greek music.

Singer-songwriters and folk-rock

The first significant musician to break out of the *bouzoúki* mould was Thes-salonian **Dhionysis Savvopoulos**, who burst on the scene in 1966 with a maniacal, rasping voice and angst-ridden lyrics, his persona rounded out by shoulder-length hair and outsized glasses. Initially linked with the short-lived **néo kýma** movement – a blend of watered-down *éntekhno* and French *chanson* performed in Athenian *boîtes* soon closed by the colonels – Savvopoulos's work soon became impossible to pigeonhole: perhaps equal parts twisted northern Greek folk, Bob Dylan and Frank Zappa at his jazziest. Though briefly detained and tortured, he resumed performing, and became something of a touchstone for the generation coming of age under the junta.

Out of Savvopoulos's **"Balkan rock"** experiments sprang a short-lived movement whose artists alternated electric versions of traditional songs with original material. The most significant of these were folk "updater" **Mariza Koch**, the Gypsy protest guitarist-singer **Kostas Hatzis**, **Nikos Portokaloglu** at the head of folk-rock group **Fatme**, and folk/*éntekhno* performer **Arletta**, all of whom are still active to various degrees.

Despite a modest discography, it's difficult to overestimate Savvopoulos's effect on younger artists. Credit (or blame) for much Greek rock and fusion can be laid at his door; during his brief tenure as head of Lyra records, and later as an independent producer, Savvopoulos gave breaks to numerous younger artists, many of them also from northern Greece. Among his spiritual heirs were **Nikos Xydhakis** and **Manolis Rasoulis**, whose landmark 1978 pressing, *Iy Ekdhikisi tis Yiftias* (The Revenge of Gypsydom) actually embodied the backlash of *laïká* culture (*laïká*, in Greek, means "common" or "low-class" as well as "popular") against the pretentiousness of 1960s and 1970s *éntekhno* and other "politically correct" music. Its spirited, defiant lyrics – with Nikos Papazoglou on most vocals – and *tsiftetéli* rhythms were both homage to and send-up of the music beloved by Greek truck-drivers, Gypsy or otherwise.

Real **Gypsies** have been disproportionately important in *laïká*, both as performers and composers, though many go to considerable length to conceal the fact; however, for every assimilated personality there are others, such as **Eleni Vitali**, **Makis Khristodhoulopoulos** and **Vassilis Païteris** who make no bones about their identity.

Contemporary roots: the 1980s to the present

After an equally successful 1979 reprise (*Ta Dhithen*) with much the same personnel, **Xydhakis** and **Papazoglou** went on to pursue successful inde-pendent careers, Xydhakis in a notably orientalized style reflecting perhaps his Egyptian childhood. His most successful venture in this vein was the 1987 *Konda sti Dhoxa mia Stigmi* with rising star **Eleftheria Arvanitaki** guesting on vocals. Arvanitaki, who began her career on a Savvopoulos album, and next with the *rebétika* revival group Opisthodhromiki Kompania, went on to try her hand at various genres, and by the millennium was Greece's hottest vocalist, drawing World Music as well as Greek audiences. A Thessalonian like Savvopoulous, Nikos Papazoglou is a more varied, though less prolific, songwriter than Xydhakis; his material, also based on *laïká* and folk, often has a harder electric-rock edge, though he can match Xydhakis for introspection and orientalism. Other performers emerging from the "Salonica Scene" after 1981 included **Himerini Kolymvites** led by Aryiris Bakirtzis, Papazoglou disciple **Sokratis Malamas** and his frequent collaborator Melina Kana.

Back in Athens, Westernizing trends took longer to relax their grip, under the aegis of composers such as classically trained **Thanos Mikroutsikos**, briefly Minister of Culture after Melina Mercouri's death, who despite his high-brow leanings has worked with Alexiou, Dalaras and top vocalist **Dhimitra Galani**. Lyricist **Lina Nikolakopoulou** also made a splash with a number of thoughtful, if somewhat slick, albums stretching into the 1990s, exploring the boundaries between rock, jazz-cabaret and *éntekhno*.

An offshoot of *éntekhno* since the mid-1970s involved combining folk and **Byzantine traditions**. Notable in this was musicologist and arranger **Khristodhoulos Halaris** with his riveting *Dhrossoulites* – featuring Dhimitra Galani with Khrysanthos, a high-voiced male singer of Pontic descent, and with lyrics by Nikos Gatsos – and his version of the medieval Cretan epic *Erotokritos*, showcasing Nikos Xylouris and Tania Tsanaklidou.

Ottoman rather than Byzantine Constantinople was the inspiration for **Bosphorus/Vosporos**, a group co-ordinated in Istanbul from 1986 to 1992 by Nikiforos Metaxas to explore Ottoman classical, devotional and popular music. Since then the group, briefly rebaptized as **Fanari tis Anatolis**, has handled a variety of Greek folk material with Anatolian songs or mystical Alevî ballads. Most recently they've joined forces with **Mode Plagal**, since 1995 Greece's most accomplished funky deconstructors of folk material.

English-born but Irish by background, **Ross Daly** frequently appears live in Athens clubs or tours abroad. He plays a dozen traditional Greek instruments and has absorbed influences not only from Crete, where he was long resident, but from throughout the Near East. Alone or with a group, he offers strikingly contemporary interpretations of traditional pieces, as well as original improvisational compositions. Two other exports from Crete were mandolinist **Loudhovikos ton Anoyeion**, originally one of Hatzidhakis's late-1980s finds at Seirios, and the six-member, all-acoustic group **Haïnidhes**. To foreign ears either can seem more accessible than orthodox, scholarly revivalists such as octagenarian **Domna Samiou**, who ranks as the foremost living collector and interpreter of Greek folk material; since the 1960s, she has also nurtured a generation-plus of young traditional musicians.

A range of other, less durable groups have attempted to explore eastern influences on Greek music with varying success. Often this eclecticism has gone too far, with bells, sitar, ney and synthesizer resulting in a bland, New Agey sound not identifiably Greek. Individuals who have managed to avoid this trap include innovative young clarinettist **Manos Achalinotopoulos**; *oud* player **Haig Yagdjian**; the group **Notios Ikhos**, led by Ahilleas Persidhis; singer **Savina Yiannatou**; and the **Greeks-and-Indians** fusion concerts and recordings coordinated by the visionary **Alexandhros Karsiotis**.

Discography

The following CDs are among the best available for each of the genres detailed in our Greek music article: 🏃 denotes a particular recommendation. Unless another country is specified, all are Greece-based labels. For listings of good Greek record stores, see the Athens shopping section (p.181). Online, you'll find some of our choices at Amazon, but rather more at the London-based specialist Trehantiri (🖥 www.trehantiri.com), which operates a worldwide mail order service. In Greece, look out also for the monthly music magazine *Dhifono* (🖥 www.difono.gr), which includes a covermount CD of Greek roots-oriented music with each issue.

Folk

Compilations

🏃 **Lesvos Aiolis** *Tragoudhia ke Hori tis Lesvou/Songs & Dances of Lesvos* (University Press of Crete, 2 CDs). Two decades' (1974–96) of field recordings of the last traditional music on the island, supervised by musicologist Nikos Dhionysopoulos. The quality and uniqueness of the instrumental pieces, and lavishly illustrated booklet, merit the expense.

Seryiani sta Nisia Mas, vol 1 (MBI). Excellent retrospective of various *nisiótika* hits and artists, mostly from the 1950s; the easiest way to hear the vintage starsRebé. A highlight is Emilia Hatzidhaki's rendering of "Bratsera".

🏃 **Thalassa Thymisou/Sea of Memories: Tragoudhia ke Skopi apo tis Inousses** (Navtiko Mousio Inousson-En Khordais). Superb result of Thessalonian musicologists' "field trip" school to Inoússes, a small islet near Híos; a mix of live sessions in Inoussan tavernas and studio recordings.

Artists

🏃 **Khronis Aïdhonidhis** *TAïd-honia tis Anatolis: Songs of Thrace and Asia Minor* (Minos). This flaw-lessly produced 1990 session features the top singer of material from Thrace and western Asia Minor, plus an orchestra directed by Ross Daly, and guest Yiorgos Dalaras.

🏃 **Petro-Loukas Halkias** *Petro-Loukas Chalkias and Kompania* (World Network, Germany). Halkias is in top form here, as are his *kompanía* (group) of *laoúto*, *violí*, guitar and percussion. Meaty *oud* solos and fiddle-licks realize the true sense of the *kompanía*: tight coordination, yet clearly articulated instrumental voices.

Xanthippi Karathanasi *Tragoudhia ke Skopi tis Makedhonias/Songs and Tunes of Macedonia* (University Press of Crete). A native of Halkidhikí, Karathanasi is a foremost interpreter of northern material – and her side-men are so good they almost steal the show.

Andonis Xylouris (Psarandonis) *Palio Krasi In'iy Skepsi Mou* (Musurgia Graeca) and *Idheon Antron* (Musurgia Graeca). Psarandonis has an idiosyn-cratically spare and percussive *lyra* style, but there is no doubting his musical integrity on these varied collections, with unusual instru-ments well integrated into a densely textured whole. And on *Idheon Antron* daughter Niki does a gorgeous rendi-tion of "Meraklidhiko Pouli".

🏃 **Nikos Xylouris** *Itane mia Fora* (2 CDs, EMI). A thorough selec-tion of Xylouris' best 1970s work, with Yiannis Markopoulos and others, that should give you some idea why he is still worshipped nearly three decades after his tragically early death.

Rebétika

Compilations

The Greek Archives Series (FM Records). This luxuriously pack-aged series has skeletal English notes but they are all well chosen selections. From the first, twelve-volume series, go for no. 1 (*Rembetiko Song in America 1920–1940*); no. 6 (*Women of the Rembetiko Song*); no. 7 (*Unknown Recordings from Smyrna 1922–1940*); no. 8 (*Armenians, Jews, Turks & Gipsies*) and no. 9 (*Constantinople in Old Recordings*). From the second series, *Anthology of Rebetiko Songs 1933–1940, Anthology of Smyrnean Songs 1920–1933* and *Songs of the Sea* are wonderful.

🏃 **Greek Orientale: Smyrneic-Rembetic Songs and Dances** (Arhoolie-Polylyric, US). Superb collection spanning 1911 to 1937, with Roza, Rita, Marika Papagika and Dhimitris Semsis.

🏃 **Rembetika: Songs of the Greek Underground** 1925–1947 (Trikont, Germany). This crammed-full, 2-CD set makes an excellent starter collection, with classics such as Papaïoannou's "Pende Ellines ston Adhi" and Kaldaras' "Nykhtose Horis Fengari".

🏃 **Rough Guide to Rebetika** (World Music Network, UK). The best single introduction to the genre, with performers from its earli-est recorded days to current revivalists.

Artists

🏃 **Agathonas (Iakovidhis)** *Tou Teke keh Tis Tavernas* (Eros). A varied and intimate outing of 1930s material, with a top violinist; *Tis Yerakinas Yios* (Eros, Greece) is typi-cal of his group Rebetiki Tetras, with mostly 1950s material and a more commercial-club sound.

Roza Eskenazi: Rembetissa (Rounder, US/Direct, UK). Ace

renditions of standards and rare gems with her usual sidemen, Semsis, Tomboulis, and Lambros on *kanonáki*.

🏃 **Marika Ninou** *Stou Tzimi tou Hondrou / At Jimmy the Fat's* (Venus-Tzina). Poor sound qual-ity as it was a clandestine recording, but still a classic, and one of the few documents of a live rebetic evening. Ninou performs with Tsitsanis at their habitual club in 1955.

Rebetiki Kompania *Pos Tha Perasi Iy Vradhia* (Lyra-Zodiac) Under lead singers/instrumentalists Dhimitris Kondoyiannis and Manolis Dhimitri-anakis, this is the easiest found offer-ing from a group which spearheaded the late-1970s rebética revival.

Vangelis Papazoglou 1897–1943 (Lyra). Compositions from the 1920s and 1930s, sung by top stars of the era, including Stellakis Perpiniadhis, Roza Eskenazi, Kostas Roukounas and Rita Abatzi. Marred by poor sound quality, but several versions of his classic "Iy Lahanadhes".

Vassilis Tsitsanis *Vassilis Tsitsanis 1936–1946* (Rounder, US/Direct, UK). Mostly male singers, but includes several rare (for him) *mastoúriaka*.) *Ta Klidhia* (EMI Regal) – look for the double keys (*klidhiá*) on the cover – pairs him with such mid-1960s stars as Grigoris Bithikotsis, Panos Gavalas, Poly Panou and Manolis Hiotis.

Markos Vamvakaris *Bouzoúki Pioneer 1932–1940* (Rounder, US/Direct, UK). Excellent sound qual-ity, good notes and unusual material make this a first choice.

🏃 **Stavros Xarhakos** *Rembe-tiko* (CBS). Soundtrack to the namesake film, and virtually the only "original" *rebétika* composed in the last fifty years; lyrics by Nikos Gatsos.

Éntekhno

Manos Hatzidhakis *Matomenos Gamos: Paramythi horis Onoma*

(Columbia). Nikos Gatsos lyrics, with Lakis Pappas singing. *O Megalos Erotikos* (Lyra MBI) has lyrics based on Greek poetry from Sappho to Elytis.

🏃 **Yannis Markopoulos** *Rizitika* (Minos EMI). "La Chante Profunde de Crète" – the French subtitle – says it all: stirring anthems like "Pote Tha Kamei Xasteria", which launched Xylouris' *éntekhno* career. *Thiteia* (Minos EMI), with lyrics by Manos Eleftheriou and enduring hits like "Malamatenia Logia" is also a sentimental favourite.

🏃 **Mikis Theodhorakis** *Epitafios/ Epifaneia* (EMI/HMV) with Bithikotsis and Hiotis, and *To Axion Esti* (EMI/HMV) with Manos Katrakis, are among his most influential, reputation-justifying works, out in white-boxed remasters of the original sessions.

🏃 **Stavros Xarhakos/Nikos Xylouris** *Sylloyi* (Minos EMI). More lyrics by Nikos Gatsos, Xylouris's crystalline voice and orchestra (including funky electric guitar licks) conducted by Khristodhoulos Halaris made this 1973 recording a landmark; the wistful "Itane mia Fora" is particularly loved and still ubiquitously heard.

Laïka

🏃 **Haris Alexiou** *Ta Tragoudhia tis Haroulas* (Minos EMI). From a huge discography, start with this album, with lyrics by Manolis Rasoulis and Manos Loïzos, which secured her position as the queen of 1980s *laïká*. *Ta Tsilika* (Minos EMI) has her *rebétika* interpretations. *Yirizondas ton Kosmo* (Mercury), is a more recent live *éntekhno*/pop disc.

Eleftheria Arvanitaki *Ta Kormia ke ta Mahairia* (Polydor). Best-selling, introspective venture with music by Ara Dinkjian and lyrics by Mihala Ganas; 🏃 *Tragoudhia yia tous Mines*

(Polygram) is more upbeat and *laïká*-based. In *Ektos Programmatos* (Mercury) Eleftheria returns to Greek roots in lively sessions at Athens and Thessaloníki clubs.

Yiorgos Dalaras *Latin* (Minos EMI). A 1987 team-up with Al Di Meola, Glykeria, Alkistis Protopsalti and others, plus Latin rhythms and instrumentalists, resulted in nearly half a million copies sold. *A Portrait: George Dalaras* (EMI, UK) is a "best-of" sampler spanning his career up to the late 1990s.

Glykeria (Kotsoula) *Me ti Glykeria stin Omorfi Nhykhta* (Lyra MBI). Live recording showcases this versatile *laïká* singer and *rebétika/nisiótika* revivalist active from the 1980s on.

Apostolos Kaldharas *Mikra Asia* (Minos EMI) marked Haris Alexiou's 1972 vinyl debut and helped spark the *rebétika* revival.

Stelios Kazantzidhis *Iy Zoi Mou Oli* (2 CD, Minos EMI). A retrospective of all the classic hits that made him a national monument.

Singer-Songwriters

🏃 **Himerini Kolymvites (Lyra).** First and best of their CDs, with surreal lyrics plus rich, drunken melodies.

🏃 **Sokratis Malamas** *Ena* (Lyra MBI). A 2000 release that embodies his mature, confident style, with just voice and guitar.

Lina Nikolakopoulou and Stamatis Kraounakis *Kykloforo ke Oploforo* (Polydor). First and best of their collaborations, featuring Alkistis Protopsalti. Protopsalti and Nikolakopoulou later linked up with Goran Bregovic for the rootsily Balkan *Paradekhtika*, featuring Ferus Mustafov on clarinet.

🏃 **Nikos Papazoglou** *Synerga* (Lyra MBI). A gentle,

mystical album, rather in the mould of Xydhakis, rather than his rock material.

Manolis Rasoulis & Petros Voyiopoulos *Valkanizater* (Eros). Rollicking and accessible acoustic soundtrack to the hit 1995 film, with vocals by Eleni Vitali, Glykeria and Paskhalis Terzis, among others.

Dhionysis Savvopoulos *Trapezakia Exo* (Lyra MBI). The best outing from the man who set off the folk-rock movement.

Nena Venetsanou This female singer has a deep, earthy voice lending itself to a number of genres. *Ikones* (Musrugia Greca) reworks everything from Hatzidhakis to *nisiótika* to chanson; *Zeïbekika* (MBI) is a suprisingly successful recasting of this rebetic style as "profane prayers", performed in French chapels.

Nikos Xydhakis, Thodhoros Gonis, Eleftheria Arvanitaki *Konda sti Dhoxa mia Stigmi* (Lyra MBI). One of the best recordings of the late 1980s, with haunting Xydhakis arrangements and compositions.

Nikos Xydhakis, Nikos Papazoglou, Manolis Rasoulis *Iy Ekdhikisi tis Yiftias* (Lyra MBI). Ground-breaking 1978 outing, still much listened to in Greece; its equally good follow-up *Ta Dhithen* (Lyra MBI) contained the single "Iy Manges Dhen Yparhoun Pia", covered later by Haris Alexiou.

Folk Revival and Fusion

Bosphorus (Fanari tis Anatolis) *Beyond the Bosphorus* (Hitch-Hyke Records). Since 1994, Bosphorus have been alternating vocals in Greek and Turkish, while retaining previous instrumental virtuosity. This album is a tour de force, with guests Mode Plagal working the same transformation on Constantinopolitan melodies as they had done previously on Greek ones.

Ross Daly *Selected Works* (Oriente, Germany). A representative compilation from his many albums. *Mitos* (World Network, Germany) captures 1991 concert recordings.

Haïnidhes *Haïnidhes* (MBI) and *Kosmos ki Oneiro ine Ena* (MBI) are their first two, and arguably best, albums, with folk-influenced original compositions taking precedence over old standards.

Loudhovikos Ton Anoyion *O Erotas stin Kriti ine Melangolikos* (Seirios) helped resurrect the Cretan mandolin from its rhythm-backing ghetto; *Pyli tis Ammou* (Mylos) exemplifies his evolution in a larger group, with Malamas, Papazoglou and Venetsanou as guests.

Mode Plagal *Mode Plagal II* (Lyra MBI). The best of their four solo albums; folk tunes meet funky guitar and saxophone licks à la Coltrane and Miles.

Savina Yiannatou *Anixi sti Saloniki/Spring in Salonika* (Musurgia Graeca). Settings of Ladino Sephardic songs, with crisp backing from Kostas Vomvolos' orchestra; Savina's voice (and trademark vibrato) can take some getting used to, though.

Greeks & Indians (6-vol set on Saraswati label): This series (vols 1 & 5 are highlights) sees top performers of Greek regional music – including Petro-Loukas Halkias, Ross Daly, Nikos and Yiasemi Saragoudhas, Sokaratis Sinopoulos and Yiorgos Koros – joining forces with some of the best North Indian musicians around.

Books

ere is a selection of the most interesting, most informative and most enjoyable books about Greece, and particularly its islands, or books by Greeks, including a selection of modern Greek fiction and ancient classics. The ones we like best are marked with the 𝕶 symbol. Titles currently out of print are indicated as "o/p", while "UP" designates University Press.

Most of our recommended books are readily available online. *Amazon* is an obvious first stop, and for out of print, or secondhand books, sites such as Wwww.abebooks.com or Wwww.bookfinder.com. Better still, try the specialist Greek bookshops *Hellenic Bookservice* (91 Fortress Rd, London NW5 1AG; T 020/7267 9499; Wwww.hellenicbookservice.com), or *Zeno's* (57a Nether St, London N12 7NP; T 020/8446 1985, Wwww.thegreekbookshop.com).

Travel/Impressions

Kevin Andrews *The Flight of Ikaros* (o/p). Intense, compelling account of an educated, sensitive archeologist wandering the backcountry during the civil war, with a fine opening chapter on Páros.

James Theodore Bent *Aegean Islands: The Cyclades*, or *Life Among the Insular Greeks* (Tecla, UK). Originally published in 1881, this remains the most authoritative account of Greek island customs and folklore, and a highly readable chronicle of a year's Aegean travel.

Charmian Clift *Mermaid Singing* (o/p). A narrative of Clift and family's experiences living on Kálymnos during the 1950s; they were amongst the first post-war expats to settle on a Greek island. Last reissued in the early 1990s, it is easily found, often bound with the same author's *Peel Me a Lotus*, about a subsequent sojourn on Ídhra.

𝕶 **Gerald Durrell** *My Family and Other Animals* (Penguin, UK). Funny and entrancing anecdotes of Durrell's childhood on Corfu during the 1930s, where his very odd family settled, and where he developed a passion for the island's fauna – toads, tortoises, scorpions – while elder brother Gerlad entertained Henry Miller and others. Durrell wrote two further books about the time, which have been collected, with *My Family*, as *The Corfu Trilogy* (Penguin, UK).

Lawrence Durrell *Prospero's Cell* and *Reflections on a Marine Venus* (Faber & Faber, UK). The former is the elder Durrell's Corfu book, from his time there with Gerald and the family as World War II loomed. *Marine Venus* recounts his 1945–47 experiences of Rhodes and other Dodecanese islands.

Edward Lear *The Corfu Years* and *The Cretan Journal* (Denise Harvey, Greece). Highly entertaining –and beautifully illustrated – journals from the 1840s and 1850s by the landscape painter and author of *The Book of Nonsense*.

Peter France *A Place of Healing for the Soul: Patmos* (Grove Press, US). A former BBC documentary maker, France settled on Patmos with his Greek Orthodox wife, and slowly moved to adopt her faith. As such, this is more spiritual than travel journey, but the daily life of a Greek island is nicely observed, too.

Elias Kulukundis The Feasts of Memory: Stories of a Greek Family (Peter E. Randall, US). A journey back through time and genealogy by a diaspora Greek two generations removed from Kássos, poorest of the Dodecanese. This is a 2003 re-release, with an extra chapter, of his 1967 classic *Journey to a Greek Island*.

Willard Manus *This Way to Paradise: Dancing on the Tables* (Lycabettus Press, Greece). American expatriate's memoir of nearly four decades in Líndhos, Rhodes, beginning long before its descent into mass-tourist tattiness. Wonderful period detail, including hippie/bohemian excesses and often hilarious cameos from the likes of S.J. Perelman, Germaine Greer and Martha Gellhorn.

Henry Miller *The Colossus of Maroussi* (W.W. Norton). Corfu, Crete, Athens and the soul of Greece in 1939, with Miller, completely in his element, at his most inspired. Funny, sensual and transporting.

James Pettifer *The Greeks: The Land and People Since the War* (Penguin, UK). Useful, if patchy, introduction to contemporary Greece – and its recent past (it was last updated in 2000). Pettifer charts the state of the nation's politics, family life, religion and tourism.

Dilys Powell *The Villa Ariadne* (Efstathiadis, Greece). Powell accompanied archeologist husband Humfry Payne to Greece in the 1930s, and forged a lifelong bond. After his sudden death in 1936, she travelled across the country from Epirus to Crete, which she describes in this enduring book.

Terence Spencer *Fair Greece, Sad Relic: Literary Philhellenism from*

Shakespeare to Byron (Denise Harvey, Greece). A compelling account of how travellers and poets steeped in the classics – culminating in Byron – fueled European support for the 1821 Revolution, despite misgivings about the Greeks themselves.

Tom Stone *The Summer of My Greek Taverna*. (Simon & Schuster, US). An enjoyable cautionary tale for those entertaining fantasies of a new life in the Aegean sun. Moving to Pátmos in the early 1980s, Stone, a rather trusting American, tries to mix friendship and business at the beach, running a taverna.

Richard Stoneman, ed *A Literary Companion to Travel in Greece* (Getty Trust, US). Ancient and medieval authors, plus Grand Tourists – an excellent selection that really does make a good travel companion.

Patricia Storace *Dinner with Persephone* (Granta Books, UK/ Vintage, US). A New York poet, resident for a year in Athens (with forays to the provinces) puts the country's mid-1990s psyche on the couch, while avoiding predatory males. Storace has a sly humour, a fine style, and an interesting take on Greece's "imprisonment" in its imagined past.

Faith Warn *Bitter Sea: The Real Story of Greek Sponge Diving* (Guardian Angel Press, UK). Short, photo-illustrated potted history of the traditional Kálymnos livelihood, as seen some four decades after Clift's experience (see above).

Sofka Zinovieff *Eurydice Street* (Granta Books, UK). An anthropologist and journalist by training, Zinovieff first came to Greece in the early 1980s, then returned in 2001 with her diplomat husband and two daughters to live in Athens. With sharp observations on everything from nationalism to leisure, this is probably the best single account of life in today's Greece.

Photo books

Chris Hellier *Monasteries of Greece* (o/p). Magnificently photographed survey of the surviving, active monasteries and treasures, with insightful accompanying essays.

Constantine Manos *A Greek Portfolio* (W.W. Norton, US). The fruits of a gifted Greek-American photographer's three-year odyssey in the early Sixties through a country on the edge of modernization, still essentially unchanged from the 1930s. The quality and insight you'd expect from a member of the Magnum co-operative, in elegiac black-and-white photos.

Mark Ottaway and Hugh Palmer *The Most Beautiful Villages of Greece* (Thames & Hudson, UK). Greece at its most seductive, charted in 285 mainland and island images.

Clay Perry *Vanishing Greece* (Parkway, UK/Newsstand, Greece). Well-captioned photos depict the threatened landscapes and relict ways of life in rural Greece.

Suzanne Slesin et al *Greek Style.* (Thames & Hudson, UK). This has been in print for nearly twenty years: and rightly so: its images get beyond designer homes, ranging widely through village houses, monasteries, summer villas, and so on.

Yann Arthus-Bertrand *Greece from the Air* (Thames & Hudson, UK). Greece gets the aerial treatment from Arthus-Bertrand – and it looks great, from the Parthenon to the most remote islands and ancient sites.

History and Art

General

Timothy Boatswain and Colin Nicolson *A Traveller's History of Greece* (Weidenfeld & Nicholson, UK/Interlink, US). A well-written overview of the important Greek periods and personalities, from earliest times to the present (last updated in 2003).

Ancient History

This is just a small selection of what is a vast literature on every aspect of Ancient Greek history and culture.

General

A.R. Burn *History of Greece* (Penguin, UK). **Paul Cartledge** *Cambridge Illustrated History of Ancient Greece* (Cambridge UP). These are the two the best general introductions to ancient Greece. Take your pick between brief paperback, or large illustrated tome.

Walter Burkert *Greek Religion: Archaic and Classical.* Superb overview of deities and their attributes and antecedents, rites, the protocol of sacrifice and the symbolism of major festivals; especially good on relating Greek worship to its predecessors in the Middle East.

Mary Lefkowitz *Greek Gods, Human Lives: What We Can Learn from Myths* (Yale UP). Rather than being frivolous, immoral or irrelevant, ancient religion and its myths, in their bleak indifference of the gods to human suffering, are shown as being more "grown up" than the later creeds of salvation and comfort.

William R. Biers *Archeology of Greece: An Introduction* (Cornell UP,

US). A good survey of the subject, published in 1987.

🏃 John Boardman *Greek Art* (Thames & Hudson, UK). This is a classic study, in the *World of Art* series, first published in 1964. Or for more detailed treatment, there are three period volumes: *The Archaic Period, The Classical Period, The Late Classical Period.*

Early Greece

🏃 M.I. Finley *The World of Odysseus* (New York Review of Books, US). Reprint of a 1954 warhorse, pioneering in its investigation of the historicity of the events and society related by Homer. Breezily readable and stimulating.

Oswyn Murray *Early Greece* (Fontana, UK/Harvard UP, US). The Greek story from the Mycenaeans and Minoans through to the beginning of the Classical period.

Robin Osborne *Greece in the Making 1200–479 BC* (Routledge,

UK). Well-illustrated paperback on the rise of the city-state.

Reynold Higgins *Minoan and Mycenaean Art* (Thames & Hudson, UK). A clear, well-illustrated roundup of the culture of Mycenae, Crete and the Cyclades, again in the *World of Art* series.

Colin Renfrew *The Cycladic Spirit* (Thames & Hudson, UK). A fine study, illustrated with the core of the Goulandris Collection in Athens, and convincing on the meaning and purpose of Cycladic artefacts.

Classical

J.K. Davies *Democracy and Classical Greece* (Fontana, UK/Harvard UP, US). Established, accessible account of the Classical period and its political developments.

Simon Hornblower *The Greek World 479–323 BC* (Routledge, UK). An erudite survey of ancient Greece at its zenith, from the end of the Persian Wars to the death of Alexander.

Roger Ling *Classical Greece* (Phaidon,

UK). A survey of the greatest period of Greek civilization, from the 5th to the 1st century BC, taking in the arts, military and political history, and surveying archeoloy on the period.

🏃 James Davidson *Courtesans and Fishcakes* (Fontana, UK). An absorbing book on the politics, class characteristics and etiquette of consumption and consummation – with wine, women, boys and seafood – in Classical Athens.

Hellenistic

Robin Lane Fox *Alexander the Great* (Penguin, UK). An absorbing study, which mixes historical scholar-

ship with imaginative psychological detail.

Paul Cartledge *Alexander the Great: The Hunt for a New Past* (Overlook Press, US). An evocative, meticulous and accessible biography, that stints on neither the emperoror's brutality nor his achievement.

F.W. Walbank *The Hellenistic World* (Fontana, UK/Harvard UP, US). Greece under the sway of the Macedonian and Roman empires.

R.R.R. Smith *Hellenistic Sculpture* (Thames & Hudson, UK). A modern reappraisal of the art of Greece under Alexander and his successors.

Byzantine and Medieval Greece

General

Nicholas Cheetham *Medieval Greece* (o/p). A general survey of the period and its infinite convolutions in Greece, with Frankish, Catalan, Venetian, Byzantine and Ottoman struggles for power.

The classics

Many of the classics make excellent companion reading for a trip around Greece – especially the historians Thucydides and Herodotus. Reading Homer's Odyssey when you're resigning yourself to the vagaries of island ferries puts your own plight into perspective. Here are a few choices for beginners: most of them are published in a range of paperback editions, from Penguin Classics, Oxford University Press, University of Chicago Press, Routledge, Duckworth and others. Where there is an outstanding edition, it is noted.

Mary Beard and John Henderson *The Classics: A Very Short Introduction* (Oxford UP, UK). Exactly as it promises: an excellent overview.

Herodotus *The Histories*. Revered as the father of narrative history – and anthropology – this fifth-century-BC Anatolian writer chronicled both the causes and campaigns of the Persian Wars, as well as the contemporary, assorted tribes and nations inhabiting Asia Minor.

Homer *The Iliad and The Odyssey*. The first concerns itself, semi-factually, with the late Bronze Age war of the Achaeans against Troy in Asia Minor; the second recounts the hero Odysseus's long journey home, via seemingly every corner of the Mediterranean. The best modern prose translations are by Martin Hammond (Penguin), and in verse Richmond Lattimore (Chicago UP). For a vibrant and very loose verse *Iliad*, try also Christopher Logue's version, published as *War Music* (Faber & Faber).

Ovid *The Metamorphoses* (trans A.D. Melville). Collected by a first-century-AD Roman poet, this remains one of the most accessible renditions of the more piquant Greek myths, involving transformations as divine blessing or curse.

Pausanias *The Guide to Greece*. This was essentially the first-ever guidebook – intended for Roman pilgrims to the holy sites of the central mainland and Peloponnese. Invaluable for later archeologists in assessing damage or change to temples over the intervening centuries, or (in some cases) locating them at all. The Penguin edition, annotated by Peter Levi, has notes on modern identifications of sites.

Thucydides *History of the Peloponnesian War*. Bleak month-by-month account of the conflict, by a cashiered Athenian officer whose affiliation and dim view of human nature didn't usually obscure his objectivity.

Xenophon *The History of My Times*. Thucydides' account of the Peloponnesian War stops in 411 BC; this eyewitness account continues events until 362 BC.

Byzantine history and art

John Julius Norwich *Byzantium: The Early Centuries; Byzantium: the Apogee* and *Byzantium: The Decline* (Penguin, UK/US). Perhaps the main surprise for first-time travellers to Greece is the fascination of Byzantine monuments. This is an astonishingly detailed yet readable trilogy of the empire that produced them. There is also an excellent. one-volume abridged version, *A Short History of Byzantium* (Penguin, UK/US).

Steven Runciman *The Fall of Constantinople, 1453* (Cambridge UP, UK). A superb narrative of perhaps the key event of the Middle Ages, and its repercussions throughout Europe and the Islamic world.

Steven Runciman *Byzantine Style and Civilization* (o/p). An out of print Penguin, well worth tracking down for a survey of the empire's art, culture and monuments.

John Beckwith *Early Christian and Byzantine Art* (Yale UP, US/UK). Wide-ranging illustrated study placing Byzantine art within a wider context.

Archbishop Kallistos (Timothy Ware) *The Orthodox Church* (Penguin, UK). A good introduction to what is still the established religion of Greece, by the UK's Orthodox archbishop. Part One describes the history of Orthodoxy, Part Two its currently-held beliefs.

Modern Greece

General

Richard Clogg *A Concise History of Greece* (Cambridge UP, UK). This is the single volume Greek history you need to read: a remarkably clear and well-illustrated account, from the decline of Byzantium to 2000, with the emphasis on recent decades.

C.M. Woodhouse *Modern Greece A-Short History* (Faber & Faber, UK). Woodhouse, long a Conservative MP, was a key figure in liaisons with the Greek Resistance during World War II. Writing from a more right-wing perspective than Clogg, his account – from the foundation of Constantinople to 1990 – is briefer and drier, but scrupulous with facts.

John S. Koliopoulos and Thanos M. Veremis *Greece: The Modern Sequel, from 1831 to the Present* (C. Hurst, UK/New York UP, US). A thematic rather than chrono-

logical study that pokes into corners rarely illuminated by conventional histories, with some tart opinions and debunkings; especially good on Macedonian issues, brigandage and the Communists, on which Koliopoulos is an expert. Best read after you've digested Clogg.

The War of Independence and Unification

David Brewer *The Flame of Freedom: The Greek War of Independence 1821–1833* (Overlook Press, US). Published in 2001, this was the first account for some decades of the War of Independence. Its narrative is strong on the background of Ottoman Greece, as well as the progress of the war.

Michael Llewellyn Smith *Ionian Vision: Greece in Asia*

Minor, 1919–22 (C. Hurst & Co, UK). The subject is the disastrous Anatolian campaign, which led to the exchange of populations between Greece and Turkey. Llewellyn-Smith's account evinces considerable sympathy for the post-1920 royalist government pursuing an unwanted, inherited, unwinnable war.

World War II, Civil War, and its aftermath

David H. Close *The Origins of the Greek Civil War* (Longman, UK). Excellent, readable and impressively even-handed study that focuses on the social conditions in 1920s and 1930s Greece that made the country so ripe for conflict.

C.M. Woodhouse *The Struggle for Greece, 1941–49*. A masterly, well-illustrated account of this crucial decade, exploring all of the so-called "three rounds" of resistance and rebellion, and how Greece emerged without a communist government.

Mark Mazower *Inside Hitler's Greece: The Experience of Occupation 1941–44*. A fascinating, exceptionally well illustrated account of how the demoralization of the country and incompetence of conventional politicians led to the rise of ELAS and the onset of civil war.

Adrian Seligman *War in the Islands*. Collected oral histories of a little-known Allied unit: a flotilla of *kaïkia* organized to raid the Axis-held Aegean islands. Boy's Own stuff, with service-jargon-laced prose, but lots of fine period photos and detail.

Ethnography

Juliet du Boulay *Portrait of a Greek Mountain Village* (Denise Harvey, Greece). An account of the village of Ambéli, on Évvia, during the 1960s. The habits and customs of an all-but-vanished way of life are evoked in an absorbing narrative.

Richard Clogg, ed. *The Greek Minorities* (C. Hurst, UK). Collection of articles on all the various Greek ethnic and religious minorities, current to the mid-1990s – despite its age, error-free and authoritative.

Loring Danforth and Alexander Tsiaras *The Death Rituals of Rural Greece* (Princeton UP, US). Many visitors and foreign residents find Greek funeral customs – the wailing, the open-casket vigils, the disinterment of the bones after five years – the most disturbing aspect of the culture; this book helps make sense of it all.

Gail Holst-Warhaft *Road to Rembétika: Songs of Love, Sorrow and Hashish* (Denise Harvey, Greece). The most intriguing Greek urban musical style of the past century, evocatively traced by a Cornell University professor and long-term observer of the Greek music scene.

John Cuthbert Lawson *Modern Greek Folklore and Ancient Greek Religion: A Study in Survivals* (RA Kessinger, US). Fascinating: the study is exactly as the title states, and still applicable a century after first publication.

David Sutton *Memories Cast in Stone: The Relevance of the Past in Everyday Life* (Berg, UK). A 1990s ethnology of Kálymnos, where vestiges of "traditional" practices such as dynamite-throwing and dowry-collecting confront the new, pan-EU realities.

Fiction

Greek Writers

Artemis Leontis (ed) *Greece:
A Traveller's Literary Companion.*
A nice idea, brilliantly executed:
various regions of the country as
portrayed in (very) short fiction or
essays by modern Greek writers.

Maro Douka *Fool's Gold* (Kedros,
Greece). An upper-class young
woman's involvement, and subsequent disillusionment, with the clandestine resistance to the junta.

Apostolos Doxiades *Uncle
Petros and the Goldbach Conjecture.* (Faber & Faber, UK). One of
the best novels, in any language, of
the past decade. Its central characters, Uncle Petros and his (narrator)
nephew, are mathematicians and the
story inspires a real excitement for
the subject, even for non-initiates.

Eugenia Fakinou *The Seventh
Garment* (Serpents Tail, UK). Greek
history from the War of Independence to the colonels' junta is told
through the life stories (interspersed
in counterpoint) of three generations of women.

Rhea Galanaki *Eleni, or Nobody*
(Northwestern UP, US). Fine
novelization of the life of Eleni
Altamura, Greece's first (nineteenth-
century) woman painter, who lived
in Italy for years disguised as a man.

Panos Karnezis *Little Infamies* and *The Maze* (Vintage,
UK/Farrar, Straus and Giroux, US).
Karnezis is the big new name in
Greek fiction – and these two books
have had deserved success. The
author grew up in Greece, but is
now resident in London, and writes
in English. However, his concerns
and subject matter is utterly Greek.

Little Infamies is a collection of short
stories set in his native Peloponnese
in the late 1950s and early 1960s:
cleverly constructed, with a rather
pleasing love of old fashioned twists.
The Maze is a darker-shaded, more
ambitious novel concerning the Asia
Minor Catastrophe. of 1923, and thus
an interesting counterpoint to Louis
de Bernières' novel (below).

Nikos Kazantzakis *Zorba the Greek;
The Last Temptation of Christ; Christ
Recrucified / The Greek Passion; Freedom
or Death / Captain Michalis; The Fratri-
cides; Report to Greco* (Faber & Faber,
UK/Touchstone, US). Whether in
intricate Greek or somehow not-
quite-adequate English, Kazantzakis
can be hard going, yet the power
of his writing shines through. *Zorba
the Greek* is a dark, nihilistic work,
worlds away from the two-dimen-
sional characters of the film. By
contrast, the movie version of *The
Last Temptation of Christ* provoked
riots amongst Orthodox fanatics in
Athens in 1989. *Christ Recrucified*
(*The Greek Passion* in the US) resets
the Easter drama against the backdrop of Christian/Muslim relations,
while *Freedom or Death* (aka *Captain
Michalis*) chronicles the rebellions of
nineteenth-century Crete. *The Frat-
ricides* portrays a family riven by the
civil war. *Report to Greco* – perhaps
the most accessible of his works – is
an autobiographical exploration of
the novelist's Greekness.

Kostas Mourselas *Red Dyed
Hair* (Kedros, Greece). A
modern picaresque epic – imagine *Zorba* crossed with *Last Exit to
Brooklyn* – of a particularly dysfunc-
tional Pireás *paréa* (the group you
hang out with from youth till

middle age). At its centre stands anti-hero Emmanuel Retsinas, mad, bad and dangerous to know. A particularly good translation of a Greek original which became a popular TV series.

Alexandros Papadiamantis *Tales from a Greek Island* (Johns Hopkins UP, US). Papadiamantis is sometimes compared to Hardy and Maupassant. He lived and wrote on and about the island of Skiathos: quasi-mythic tales of generally grim fate. His novel, *The Murderess* (o/p), has also been translated (by Peter Levi).

Nick Papandreou *Father Dancing/A Crowded Heart* (Penguin, UK/Picador, US). A novel by the late Andreas's younger son. Both are thinly-veiled autobiography, in which Papandreou Senior, not too surprisingly, comes across as a gasbag and petty domestic tyrant.

🏃 **Dido Sotiriou** *Farewell Anatolia* (Kedros, Greece). A perennial favourite since its initial appearance in 1962, this epic chronicles the traumatic end of Greek life in Asia Minor, from World War I to the catastrophe of 1922, as narrated by a fictionalized version of the author's father. In the finale he escapes across the narrow strait of Mykale to Sámos, as so many did during those turbulent years.

Greece in foreign fiction

🏃 **Louis de Bernières** *Captain Corelli's Mandolin* (Vintage, UK/US). Set on Kefaloniá during the World War II occupation and aftermath, this accomplished 1994 tragi-comedy quickly acquired cult, then word-of-mouth bestseller status in the UK and US. But in Greece it was a scandal, after Greek Left intellectuals and surviving Italian partisans woke up to its virulent portrayal of ELAS. It seems the novel was closely based on the experiences of one Amos Pampaloni, an artillery captain on Kefaloniá in 1942–44 who later joined ELAS, and who accused De Bernières of distorting the roles of both Italians and ELAS on the island. The Greek translation was suitably abridged to avoid causing offence, and the movie, watered down to a pallid love story as a condition for filming on the island, sank without trace after a few weeks in 2001. All of which said, the first two parts of the novel are spellbinding.

John Fowles *The Magus* (Vintage, UK/Laurel, US). Fowles' biggest and best novel: a tale of mystery and manipulation – plus Greek island life – inspired by his stay on Spétses as a teacher during the 1950s.

🏃 **Olivia Manning** *The Balkan Trilogy, Volume 3: Friends and Heroes*. A wonderfully observed and moving tale, in which Guy and Harriet Pringle escape from Bucharest to Athens, in the last months before the invasion of 1941.

Evelyn Waugh *Officers and Gentleman* (Penguin, UK/Back Bay, US). This second volume of Waugh's brilliant, acerbic wartime trilogy includes an account of the Battle of Crete and subsequent evacuation.

Steven Pressfield *The Virtues of War: A Novel of Alexander the Great* (Doubleday, US). The emperor tells his warrior's tale to his brother-in-law, Itanes. And he does it well, for Pressfield informs his drama with impressive scholarship.

The Greek myths and legends are fantastic terrain for kids, perfect holiday reading in their original location. And with Terry Deary's "Horrible History" series, the whole of ancient Greek history is an open book.

Terry Deary *Gruesome Greeks* and *Greek Legends* (Scholastic, UK/US). Even decently-read adults will find themselves delving into these very funny, brilliantly conceived books for a refresher on Ancient Greek history and myths and legends. here's a sample from the script for the Trojan War: *Achilles* "Give the girl back, you daft old bat". Irresistible.

Francesca Simon *Helping Hercules* (Orion, UK). If your kid(s) are into *Horrid Henry*, then make a bee-line for this clever retelling of Greek myths by the same author, who has a kid called Susan sort out the not-so-heoric heroes.

Anthony Horowitz *Myths and Legends* (Kingfisher, UK/US). Greece supplies only half of this book, but the storytelling by Horowitz (*Stormbreaker*, etc) is top class.

Ingri and Edgar Parin D'Aulaires *D'Aulaires' Book of Greek Myth* (Doubleday, US). A rather more serious, traditional treatment. Enjoyable nonetheless.

Caroline Lawrence *The Roman Mysteries series* (Orion, UK). This is a great series of Roman-era mystery books for 8–11 year-olds, featuring a group of kids, and full of authentic details. The fifth and sixth books, *The Colossus of Rhodes* and *Fugitive from Corinth* transport the action to Greece.

Mary Renault *The King Must Die; The Last of the Wine; The Masks of Apollo; The Praise Singer* (Arrow, UK/Vintage, US). Mary Renault's imaginative reconstructions are more than the teen reading they're often taken for, with impeccable research and tight writing. But they are great for kids, nonetheless. The quartet above retell, respectively, the myth of Theseus, the life of a pupil of Socrates, that of a fourth-century-BC actor, and the fortunes of poet Simonides at the court of Samian tyrant Polykrates. The life of Alexander the Great is told in *Fire from Heaven*, *The Persian Boy* and *Funeral Games*, available separately or as *The Alexander Trilogy*.

Greek poetry

With two twentieth century Nobel laureates – George Seferis and Odysseus Elytis – modern Greece has an intense and dynamic poetic tradition. Translations of all of the following are excellent.

Anthologies

Peter Bien, Peter Constantine, Edmund Keeley, Karen Van Dyck, eds *A Century of Greek Poetry, 1900–2000* (Cosmos, US). Well produced bilingual volume, with some lesser-known surprises along with the big names.

Nanos Valaoritis and Thanasis Maskaleris, eds *An Anthology of Modern Greek Poetry* (Talisman House, UK). English-only text, but excellent biographical info on the poets and good renditions by two native Greek-speakers.

Individual poets

C.P. Cavafy *Collected Poems* (Harcourt Brace, US). The complete works, translated by Rae dalven, of perhaps the most accessible modern Greek poet, resident for most of his life in Alexandria.

Odysseus Elytis *Collected Poems* (Johns Hopkins UP, US); *The Axion Esti* (Anvil Press, UK). The *Collected Poems* includes virtually everything except *The Axion Esti*, which was cited for his Nobel Prize.

Yannis Kondos *Absurd Athlete* (Arc, UK). One of the best of the latest generation of poets, well translated in a bilingual edition by David Connolloy.

Yannis Ritsos *Repetitions, Testimonies, Parentheses* (Princeton UP, US). A fine volume of Greece's foremost Leftist poet, including work from 1946 to 1975.

George Seferis *Collected Poems, 1924–1955* (Princeton UP, US). Virtually the complete works of the Nobel laureate, with Greek and English verses on facing pages.

Food and wine

Rosemary Barron *Flavours of Greece* (Grub Street, UK). The leading Greek cookbook – among many contenders – by an internationally recognized authority. Contains over 250 recipes.

Andrew Dalby *Siren Feasts: A History of Food and Gastronomy in Greece* (Routledge, UK). This analysis of ancient texts demonstrates just how little Greek cuisine has changed in three millennia; also excellent on the introduction and etymology of common vegetables and herbs.

Konstantinos Lazarakis *The Wines of Greece* (Mitchell Beazley, UK). An excellent, up-to-date overview of what's happening in Greece's eleven recognized wine-producing regions.

Nikos Stavroulakis *Cookbook of the Jews of Greece* (Lycabettus Press, Athens; Cadmus Press, US). Tasty if often fiddly recipes interspersed with their relation to the Jewish liturgical year, plus potted histories of the communities which produced them.

Specific guides

Some specialist guides that you might want to complement this one. See also the Wildlife guides detailed on p.639.

Archeology

A.R. and Mary Burn *The Living Past of Greece: A Time Traveller's Tour of Historic and Prehistoric Places* (Harper Perennial, UK). This wide-ranging guide covers sites from Minoan through to Byzantine and Frankish, with good clear plans and lively text.

Paul Hetherington *The Greek Islands: Guide to Byzantine and Medieval Buildings and their Art* (Quiller, UK). A gazetteer of most significant island sites – readable, authoritative and with useful plans.

Hiking

Lance Chilton Various walking-pamphlets (Marengo Publications, UK). Small but thorough guides to the best walks at various island charter resorts, accompanied by three-colour maps. Available online at ⓦwww.marengowalks. com.

Marc Dubin *Trekking in Greece* (o/p). Though many sections are showing their 1988–92 age (and the depredations of bulldozers), this out-of-print Lonely Planet volume is still a useful walkers' guide, expanding on the hikes covered in this book.

Loraine Wilson *The White Mountains of Crete* (Cicerone, UK). Nearly sixty walks and treks, from easy to gruelling, by the doyenne of foreign trekking guides in Crete; implicitly trustworthy directions and prudent warnings.

Sailing

Rod Heikell *Greek Waters Pilot* (Imray, Laurie, Norie & Wilson, UK). This has taken over from H.M.

Denham's *Aegean* guide as standard reference for Greek waters. It is updated to 2004.

Regional guides

Rough Guides publishes regional Greek guides to: The Ionian Islands, The Dodecanese and East Aegean Islands; Crete; and Corfu. In addition, you might want to check out these...

Oliver Rackham and Jennifer Moody *The Making of the Cretan Landscape* (Manchester UP, UK). It's hard to classify this hugely impressive academic press product written for the casual visitor. It takes in geology, natural history, agricultural practices, place names, architecture and demography, all arranged by topic.

Lycabettus Press Guides (Athens, Greece). This series takes in many of the more popular islands and certain mainland highlights; most, despite decade-long intervals between revisions, pay their way both in interest and usefulness – in particular those on Páros, Kós, Pátmos, Náfplio, Ídhra and the travels of Saint Paul.

Language

Language

Greek

S
o many Greeks have lived or worked abroad in North America, Australia and, to a much lesser extent, Britain, that you will find someone who speaks **English** in the tiniest island village. Add to that the thousands attending language schools or working in the tourist industry – English is the lingua franca of most resorts, with German second – and it is easy to see how so many visitors come back having learned only half a dozen restaurant words.

You can certainly get by this way, but it isn't very satisfying, and the willingness and ability to say even a few words will transform your status from that of dumb *tourístas* to the more honourable one of *xénos/xéni*, a word which can mean foreigner, traveller and guest all rolled into one.

Learning basic Greek

Greek is not an easy language for English-speakers – translators' unions in the UK rate it as harder than German, slightly less complex than Russian – but it is a very beautiful one, and even a brief acquaintance will give you some idea of the debt owed to it by Western European languages. Greek **grammar** is predictably complicated; **nouns** are divided into three genders, all with different case endings in the singular and in the plural, and all adjectives and articles have to agree with these in gender, number and case. To simplify life for beginners, all adjectives are arbitrarily cited in the neuter form in the boxed lists on following pages. **Verbs** are even more complex; they come in two conjugations, in both active and passive voices, with passively constructed verbs often having transitive sense. As a novice, the best thing is simply to say what you know the way you know it, and dispense with the niceties.

Teach-yourself Greek courses

Breakthrough Greek (Pan Macmillan; book and 4 cassettes). Excellent, basic teach-yourself course; no Greek lettering, but good for classicists who need to unlearn bad habits.

Greek Language and People (BBC Publications, UK; book and 2 cassettes available). More limited in scope but good for acquiring the essentials, and the confidence to try them.

Anne Farmakides *A Manual of Modern Greek* (Yale UP; McGill UP; 3 vols). If you have the discipline and motivation, this is one of the best for learning proper, grammatical Greek; indeed, mastery of just the first volume will get you a long way.

Hara Garoufalia *Teach Yourself Holiday Greek* (Hodder & Stoughton, UK; book and cassette available). Unlike many quickie courses, this provides a good grammatical foundation, but you'll need a dictionary to supplement the scanty vocabulary lists.

David Hoton et al *Greek: A Comprehensive Grammar of the Modern Language* (Routledge). A bit technical in terminology, so not for rank beginners, but it covers just about every conceivable construction.

Aristarhos Matsukas *Teach Yourself Greek* (McGraw Hill; book and 2 cassettes).

A complete course, touching on idiomatic expressions too.

Niki Watts *Greek in Three Months* (Hugo, Dorling Kindersley; book and 4 cassettes). Delivers as promised; equals or exceeds *Breakthrough Greek*.

Phrasebooks and dictionaries

Greek, a Rough Guide Phrasebook Up-to-date and accurate pocket phrasebook, full of phrases that you'll actually need. The English-to-Greek section is sensibly transliterated, though the Greek-to-English part requires basic mastery of the Greek alphabet. Feature boxes fill you in on cultural know-how.

The Oxford Dictionary of Modern Greek. A bit bulky in its wide format, but generally considered the best Greek–English, English–Greek paperback dictionary.

Collins Pocket Greek Dictionary. Very nearly as complete as the Oxford and probably better value for money. The inexpensive *Collins Gem Greek Dictionary* (UK only) is palm-sized but exactly the same in contents – the best day-pack choice.

Oxford Greek–English, English–Greek Learner's Dictionary. If you're planning a prolonged stay, this pricey, hardbound, two-volume set is unbeatable for usage and vocabulary. There's also a more portable one-volume *Learner's Pocket Dictionary*, and the even smaller *Oxford Greek Mini Dictionary*.

Katharévoussa, dhimotikí and dialects

Greek may seem complicated enough in itself, but problems are multiplied when you consider that since the early 1800s there has been an ongoing dispute between two versions of the language: **katharévoussa** and **dhimotikí**.

When Greece first achieved independence in the nineteenth century, its people were almost universally illiterate, and the language they spoke – *dhimotikí*, "demotic" or "popular" Greek – had undergone enormous change since the days of the Byzantine empire and Classical times. The vocabulary had assimilated countless borrowings from the languages of the various invaders and conquerors, such as the Turks, Venetians and Slavs, and the grammar had been considerably streamlined since ancient times.

The finance and inspiration for the new Greek state, as well as some of its early leaders, came largely from the diaspora – Greek families who had been living in the sophisticated cities of central and eastern Europe, in Constantinople or in Russia. With their European-Enlightenment notions about the grandeur of Greece's past, and lofty conception of Hellenism, they set about obliterating the memory of subjugation to foreigners in every possible field. And what better way to start than by purging the language of foreign accretions and reviving its Classical purity?

They accordingly created what was in effect a new form of the language, *katharévoussa* (literally "cleansed" Greek). The complexities of Classical grammar and syntax were largely reinstated, and Classical words, long out of use, were reintroduced. To the country's great detriment, *katharévoussa* became the language of the schools and the prestigious professions, government, business, the law, newspapers and academia. Everyone aspiring to membership in the elite strove to master it, and to speak it – even though there was no consensus on how many of the words should be pronounced.

The *katharévoussa/dhimotikí* debate remained a highly contentious issue until the early 1980s. Most writers – from Solomos and Makriyiannis in the nineteenth century to Seferis, Kazantzakis and Ritsos in the twentieth – have championed the demotic, or some approximation of it, in their literature, with advocacy of demoticism became increasingly linked to left-wing politics during the twentieth century. Meanwhile, crackpot right-wing governments forcibly (re)instated *katharévoussa* at every opportunity. Most recently, the **colonels' junta** (1967–1974) reversed a decision of the previous government to use *dhimotiki* as the medium of instruction in schools, bringing back *katharévoussa*, even on sweet wrappers, as part of their ragbag of notions about racial purity and heroic ages.

Dhimiotiki returned once more after the fall of the colonels and now seems here to stay. Perhaps the final blow to the classicizers was the official decision, in 1981, to do away with breath marks (which in fact no longer signified anything) and abolish the three different stress accents in favour of a **single acute accent** (though there are still plenty of pre-1981 road-signs displaying the older system). *Dhimotiki* is used in schools, on radio and TV, and after a fashion in newspapers (with the exception of the extreme right-wing *Estia*). The only institutions which refuse to bring themselves up to date are the church and the legal professions – so beware rental contracts and official documents.

This is not to suggest that there is now any less confusion. The Metaxas dictatorship of the 1930s, elaborating on attempts at the same by previous regimes, changed scores of village names from Slavic, Turkish or Albanian words to Greek ones – often reviving the name of the nearest ancient site – and these official **place names** still hold sway on most road signs and maps – even though the local people may use the *dhimotiki* or non-Greek form. Thus you will see "Plomárion" or "Spétsai" written, while everyone actually says "Plomári" or "Spétses"; Pándhrossos on Sámos, and Platáni on Kós, are still preferably known to locals as Arvanítes and Kermedés respectively.

Dialects and minority languages

If the lack of any standardized Greek were not enough, the islands still offer considerable linguistic diversity, both in their regional variants and minority languages. Ancient **dialects** are alive and well in many remote areas, and some of them are quite incomprehensible to outsiders. The dialect of Sfákia in Crete is one such; those of Náxos and Lésvos are other strong Aegean dialects, influenced by immigration from Crete and Asia Minor respectively. The dialect of Sámos and that of adjacent Híos are completely different from one another, Híos being considered a more pure "Ionian" (and this thousands of years after the Ionians arrived from the mainland), while the rough "Samian" variant owes much to the diverse origins of its settlers. Arvanítika – a form of medieval Albanian – was until well into the twentieth century the first language of many villages of southern Évvia, northern Ándhros, and much of the Argo-Saronic area; it is still (just barely) spoken or at least understood amongst the oldest generation. On Rhodes and Kós there is a dwindling Turkish-speaking population, probably not in excess of six thousand persons as of writing.

The Greek alphabet: transliteration and accentuation

On top of the usual difficulties of learning a new language, Greek presents the additional problem of an entirely separate **alphabet**. Despite initial appearances, this is in practice fairly easily mastered – a skill that will help enormously if you are going to get around independently (see the alphabet box below). In addition, certain combinations of letters have unexpected results. This book's transliteration system should help you make intelligible noises, but you have to remember that the correct **stress** (marked throughout the book with an acute accent or sometimes dieresis) is crucial. With the right sounds but the wrong stress people will either fail to understand you, or else understand something quite different from what you intended – there are numerous pairs of words with the same spelling and phonemes, distinguished only by their stress.

The **dieresis** is used in Greek over the second of two adjacent vowels to change the pronunciation that you would expect from the table below; often in this book it can function as the primary stress. In the word *kaïki* (caique), the presence of the dieresis changes the pronunciation from "cake-key" to "ka-ee-key" and additionally the middle "i" carries the primary stress. In the word *païdhákia* (lamb chops), the dieresis again changes the sound of the first syllable from "pay" to "pah-ee", but in this case the primary stress is on the third syllable. It is also, uniquely among Greek accents, used on capital letters in signs and personal-name spellings in Greece, and we have followed this practice on our maps.

Set out below is the Greek alphabet, the system of transliteration used in this book, and a brief aid to pronunciation.

Greek	Transliteration	Pronounced
Α, α	a	a as in father
Β, β	v	v as in vet
Γ, γ	y/g	y as in yes except before consonants or a, o or ou when it's a breathy g, approximately as in gap
Δ, δ	dh	th as in then
Ε, ε	e	e as in get
Ζ, ζ	z	z sound
Η, η	i	i as in ski
Θ, θ	th	th as in theme
Ι, ι	i	i as in ski
Κ, κ	k	k sound
Λ, λ	l	l sound
Μ, μ	m	m sound
Ν, ν	n	n sound
Ξ, ξ	x	x sound, never z
Ο, ο	o	o as in toad
Π, π	p	p sound
Π, σ	r	r sound

Σ, σ, ς	s	s sound, except z before m or g; single sigma has the same phonic value as double sigma
T, τ	t	t sound
Y, υ	y	y as in barely
Φ, φ	f	f sound
X, χ	h before vowels,	harsh h sound, like ch in loch
	kh before consonants	
Ψ, ψ	ps	ps as in lips
Ω, ω	o	o as in toad, indistinguishable from o

Combinations and diphthongs

AI, αι	e	e as in hey
AY, αυ	av/af	av or af depending on following consonant
EI, ει	i	long i, exactly like ι or θ
EY, ευ	ev/ef	ev or ef, depending on following consonant
OI, οι	i	long i, exactly like ι or θ
OY, ου	ou	ou as in tourist
ΓΓ, γγ	ng	ng as in angle; always medial
ΝΓ, νγ	g/ng	g as in goat at the beginning of a word, ng in the middle
ΜΠ, μπ	b/mb	b at the beginning of a word, mb in the middle
ΝΤ, ντ	d/nd	d at the beginning of a word, nd in the middle
ΤΣ, τσ	ts	ts as in hits
ΤΖ, τζ	tz	dg as in judge, j as in jam in some dialects

Greek words and phrases

Essentials

Yes	Né
Certainly	Málista
No	Óhi
Please	Parakaló
OK, agreed	Endáxi
Thank you (very much)	Efharistó (polý)
I (don't) understand	(Dhén) Katalavéno
Do you speak English?	Miláte angliká?
Sorry/excuse me	Signómi
Today	Símera
Tomorrow	Ávrio
Yesterday	Khthés
Now	Tóra
Later	Argótera
Open	Anikhtó

Closed	Klistó
Day	Méra
Night	Níkhta
In the morning	Tó proï
In the afternoon	Tó apóyevma
In the evening	Tó vrádhi
Here	Edhó
There	Ekí
This one	Aftó
That one	Ekíno
Good	Kaló
Bad	Kakó
Big	Megálo
Small	Mikró
More	Perisótero

Less	Ligótero	With (together)	Mazí (mé)
A little	Lígo	Without	Horís
A lot	Polý	Quickly	Grígora
Cheap	Ftinó	Slowly	Sigá
Expensive	Akrivó	Mr/Mrs	Kýrios/Kyría
Hot	Zestó	Miss	Dhespinís
Cold	Krýo		

Other needs

To eat/drink	Trógo/píno	Bank	Trápeza
Bakery	Foúrnos	Money	Leftá/Khrímata
Pharmacy	Farmakío	Toilet	Toualéta
Post office	Tahydhromío	Police	Astynomía
Stamps	Gramatósima	Doctor	Yiatrós
Petrol station	Venzinádhiko	Hospital	Nosokomío

Requests and questions

To ask a question, it's simplest, though hardly elegant, to start with *parakaló*, then name the thing you want in an interrogative tone.

Where is the bakery?	Parakaló, o foúrnos?	How much?	Póso?
Can you show me the road to . . . ?	Parakaló, ó dhrómos yiá . . . ?	When?	Póte?
		Why?	Yiatí?
We'd like a room for two	Parakaló, éna dhomátio yiá dhy*o átoma	At what time . . . ?	Tí óra . . . ?
		What is/Which is . . . ?	Tí íne /Pió íne . . . ?
May I have a kilo of oranges?	Parakaló, éna kiló portokália?	How much (does it cost)?	Póso káni?
Where?	Poú?	What time does it open?	Tí óra aníyi?
How?	Pós?		
How many?	Póssi, pósses or póssa?	What time does it close?	Tí óra klíni?

Talking to people

Greek makes the distinction between the informal (*essý*) and formal (*essís*) second person, as French does with "tu" and "vous". Young people, older people and country people often use *essý* even with total strangers, though if you greet someone familiarly and they respond formally, it's best to adopt their usage as the conversation continues, to avoid offence. By far the most common greeting, on meeting and parting, is *yiá sou/ yiá sas* literally "health to you". Incidentally, as across most of the Mediterranean, the approaching party utters the first greeting, not those seated at sidewalk *kafenío* tables or doorsteps – thus the silent staring as you enter a village.

Hello	Hérete	Goodbye	Adío
Good morning	Kalí méra	How are you?	Tí kánis/Tí kánete?
Good evening	Kalí spéra	I'm fine	Kalá íme
Good night	Kalí níkhta	And you?	Ké essís?

LANGUAGE

What's your name?	Pós se léne?	I don't know	Dhén xéro
My name is . . .	Mé léne . . .	See you tomorrow	Thá sé dhó ávrio
Speak slower, please	Parakaló, na milísate pió sigá	See you soon	Kalí andhámosi
		Let's go	Páme
How do you say it in Greek?	Pós léyete avtó stá Elliniká?	Please help me	Parakaló, ná mé voithíste

Greek's Greek

There are numerous words and phrases which you will hear constantly, even if you don't have the chance to use them. These are a few of the most common.

Éla!	Come (literally) but also Speak to me! You don't say! etc.	Po-po-po!	Expression of dismay or concern, like French "O là là!"
Oríste!	Literally, Indicate!; in effect, What can I do for you?	Pedhí moú	My boy/girl, sonny, friend, etc.
Embrós!/Léyete!	Standard phone responses	Maláka(s)	Literally "wanker", but often used (don't try it!) as an informal term of address.
Tí néa?	What's new?		
Tí yínete?	What's going on (here)?	Sigá sigá	Take your time, slow down
Étsi k'étsi	So-so	Kaló taxídhi	Bon voyage
Ópa!	Whoops! Watch it!		

Accommodation

Hotel	Xenodhohío	hot water	Zestó neró
Inn	Xenón(as)	Cold water	Krýo neró
Youth hostel	Xenónas neótitos	Air conditioning	Klimatismós
A room . . .	Éna dhomátio . . .	Fan	Anamistíra
for one/two/three people	yiá éna/dhýo/tría átoma	Can I see it?	Boró ná tó dhó?
for one/two/three nights	yiá mía/dhýo/trís vradhiés	Can we camp here?	Boroúme na váloume ti skiní edhó?
with a double bed	mé dhipló kreváti	Campsite	Kámping/Kataskínosi
with a shower	mé doús	Tent	Skiní

On the move

Aeroplane	Aeropláno	Hydrofoil	Dhelfíni
Bus, coach	Leoforío, púlman	Bicycle	Podhílato
Car	Aftokínito, amáxi	Hitching	Otostóp
Motorbike, scooter	Mihanáki, papáki	On foot	Mé tá pódhia
Taxi	Taxí	Trail	Monopáti
Ship	Plío/vapóri/karávi	Bus station	Praktorío leoforíon, KTEL
High-speed, boat catamaran	Tahyplóö, katamarán		

Bus stop	Stássi	Near	Kondá
Harbour	Limáni	Far	Makriá
What time does it leave?	Ti óra févyi?	Left	Aristerá
		Right	Dhexiá
What time does it arrive?	Ti óra ftháni?	Straight ahead	Katefthía, ísia
		A ticket to . . .	Éna isitírio yiá . . .
How many kilometres?	Póssa hiliómetra?	A return ticket	Éna isitírio mé epistrofí
How many hours?	Pósses óres?	Beach	Paralía
Where are you going?	Poú pás?	Cave	Spiliá
I'm going to . . .	Páo stó . . .	Centre (of town)	Kéndro
I want to get off at . . .	Thélo ná katévo stó . . .	Church	Eklissía
		Sea	Thálassa
The road to . . .	O dhrómos yiá . . .	Village	Horió

Numbers

1	énas/éna/mía	30	triánda
2	dhýo	40	saránda
3	trís/tría	50	penínda
4	tésseres/téssera	60	exínda
5	pénde	70	evdhomínda
6	éxi	80	ogdhónda
7	eftá	90	enenínda
8	okhtó	100	ekató
9	ennéa (or more slangy, enyá)	150	ekatón penínda
		200	dhiakóssies/dhiakóssia
10	dhéka	500	pendakóssies/pendakóssia
11	éndheka	1000	hílies/hília
12	dhódheka	2000	dhýo hiliádhes
13	dhekatrís	1,000,000	éna ekatomírio
14	dhekatésseres	first	próto
20	íkossi	second	dhéftero
21	íkossi éna (all compounds written separately thus)	third	tríto

Days of the week and the time

Sunday	Kyriakí	/three o'clock	óra/trís íy óra
Monday	Dheftéra	Twenty minutes to four	Tésseres pará íkossi
Tuesday	Tríti		
Wednesday	Tetárti	Five minutes past seven	Eftá ké pénde
Thursday	Pémpti		
Friday	Paraskeví	Half past eleven	Éndheka ké misí
Saturday	Sávato	In half an hour	Sé misí óra
What time is it?	Tí óra íne?	In a quarter-hour	S'éna tétarto
One/two	Mía íy óra/dhío iy	In two hours	Sé dhýo óres

LANGUAGE

L

Months and seasonal terms

NB: You may see *katharévoussa*, or hybrid, forms of the months written on schedules or street signs; these are the spoken demotic forms.

January	**Yennáris**
February	**Fleváris**
March	**Mártis**
April	**Aprílis**
May	**Maïos**
June	**Ioúnios**
July	**Ioúlios**

August	**Ávgoustos**
September	**Septémvris**
October	**Októvrios**
November	**Noémvris**
December	**Dhekémvris**
Summer schedule	**Therinó dhromolóyio**
Winter schedule	**Himerinó dhromolóyio**

A food and drink glossary

Basics

Aláti	Salt
Avgá	Eggs
(Horís) ládhi	(Without) oil
Hortofágos	Vegetarian
Katálogos, menoú	Menu
Kréas	Meat
Lahaniká	Vegetables
O logariasmós	The bill
Méli	Honey
Neró	Water
Psári(a)	Fish
Psomí....	Bread...
Olikís	Wholemeal
Sikalísio	Rye
Kalambokísio	Corn
Thalassiná	Seafood
Tyrí	Cheese
Yiaoúrti	Yogurt
Záhari	Sugar

Cooking terms

Akhnistó	Steamed
Frikasé	Stew, either lamb, goat or pork, made with celery
Iliókafto	Sun-dried
Kondosoúvli	Any spit-roasted beast, whole or in chunks
Kourkoúti	Egg-and-flour batter
Makaronádha	Any spaghetti/pasta-based dish
Pastó	Marinated in salt
Psitó	Roasted
Saganáki	Cheese-based red sauce; also any fried cheese
Skáras	Grilled
Sti soúvla	Spit-roasted
Stó foúrno	Baked
Tiganitó	Pan-fried
Tís óras	Grilled/fried to order
Yakhní	Stewed in oil and tomato sauce
Yemistá	Stuffed (squid, vegetables, etc)

Soups and starters

Avgolémono	Egg and lemon soup
Bouréki, bourekákia	Courgette/zucchini, potato and cheese pie
Dolmádhes, yaprákia	Vine leaves stuffed with rice
Fasoládha	Bean soup
Fáva	Purée of yellow peas, served with onion and lemon
Féta psití	Baked feta cheese slabs with chili

Galotýri	Curdled creamy dip
Hortópitta	Turnover or pie stuffed with wild greens
Kápari	Pickled caper leaves
Kopanistí, khtypití	Pungent, fermented cheese purée
Krítamo	Rock samphire
Lahanodolmádhes	Stuffed cabbage leaves
Mavromátika	Black-eyed peas
Melitzanosaláta	Aubergine/eggplant dip
Piperiá florínes	Marinated red sweet Macedonian peppers
Plevrótous	Oyster mushrooms
Rengosaláta	Herring salad
Revythokeftédhes	Chickpea (garbanzo) patties
Skordhaliá	Garlic dip
Soúpa	Soup
Taramosaláta	Cod roe paté
Trahanádhes	Crushed wheat and milk soup, sweet or savoury
Tyrokafterí	Cheese dip with chilli, different from **kopanistí**
Tzatzíki	Yogurt and cucumber dip
Tzirosaláta	cured mackerel dip

Vegetables

Ambelofásola	Crimp-pod runner beans
Anginára	Artichokes
Angoúri	Cucumber
Ánitho	Dill
Bámies	Okra, ladies' fingers
Briám, tourloú	Ratatouille of zucchini, potatoes, onions, tomato
Domátes	Tomatoes
Fakés	Lentils
Fasolákia	French (green) beans
Fasóles	Small white beans
Horiátiki (saláta)	Greek salad (with olives, feta etc)
Hórta	Greens (usually wild), steamed
Kolokythákia	Courgette/zucchini
Koukiá	Broad fava beans
Maroúli	Lettuce
Melitzánes imám	Aubergine/eggplant slices baked with onion, garlic and copious olive oil
Patátes	Potatoes
Piperiés	Peppers
Pligoúri, pinigoúri	Bulgur wheat
Radhíkia	Wild chicory – a common **hórta**
Rókka	Rocket, arrugula
Rýzi/Piláfi	Rice (usually with **sáltsa** – sauce)
Saláta	Salad
Spanáki	Spinach
Vlíta	Notchweed – another common **hórta**
Yígandes	White haricot beans

Fish and seafood

Ahini	Sea urchins
Astakós	Aegean lobster
Atherína	Sand smelt
Bakaliáros	Cod or hake, usually latter
Barbóuni	Red mullet
Fangrí	Common bream
Foúskes	Uovo de mare (Italian), violet (French); no English equivalent for this invertebrate.
Galéos	Dogfish, hound shark, tope
Garídhes	Shrimp, prawns
Gávros	Mild anchovy
Glóssa	Sole
Gónos, Gonákia	Any hatchling fish
Gópa	Bogue
Kalamarákia	Baby squid
Kalamária	Squid
Karavídhes	Crayfish
Kefalás	Axillary bream
Koliós	Chub mackerel

Koutsomoúra	Goatfish (small red mullet)
Kydhónia	Warty Venus (!)
Lakérdha	Light-fleshed bonito, marinated
Marídhes	Picarel
Melanoúri	Saddled bream
Ménoula	Sprat
Mýdhia	Mussels
Okhtapódhi	Octopus
Pandelís sykiós	Corvina; also called
Petalídhes	Limpets
Platý	Skate, ray
Sardhélles	Sardines
Sargós	White bream
Seláhi	Skate, ray
Skáros	Parrotfish
Skathári	Black bream
Skoumbrí	Atlantic mackerel
Soupiá	Cuttlefish
Spiníalo or spinóalo	Marinated foúskes
Synagrídha	Dentex
Tsipoúra	Gilt-head bream
Xifías	Swordfish
Yermanós	Leatherback
Yialisterés	Smooth Venus; common ouzerí shellfish

Meat and meat-based dishes

Arní	Lamb
Bekrí mezé	Pork chunks in red sauce
Biftéki	Hamburger
Brizóla	Pork or beef chop
Hirinó	Pork
Keftédhes	Meatballs
Kokorétsi	Liver/offal roulade, spit-roasted
Kopsídha	(Lamb) shoulder chops
Kotópoulo	Chicken
Kounélli	Rabbit
Loukánika	Spicy course-ground sausages
Moskhári	Veal
Moussakás	Aubergine, potato and lamb-mince casserole with béchamel topping
Païdhákia	Rib chops, lamb or goat
Papoutsákia	Stuffed aubergine/ eggplant "shoes" like moussakás without bechamel
Pastítsio	Macaroni "pie" baked with minced meat
Pastourmás	Cured, highly spiced meat; traditionally camel, nowadays beef
Patsás	Tripe soup
Psaronéfri	Pork tenderloin medallions
Salingária	Garden snails
Soutzoukákia	Minced meat rissoles/beef patties
Spetzofáï	Sausage and pepper red-sauce stew
Stifádho	Meat stew with tomato and boiling onions
Sykóti	Liver
Tiganiá	Pork chunks fried with onions
Tziyéro sarmás	Lamb's liver in cabbage leaves
Yiouvétsi	Baked clay casserole of meat and kritharáki (short pasta)

Sweets and dessert

Baklavás	Honey and nut pastry
Bougátsa	Salt or sweet cream pie served warm with sugar and cinammon
Galaktobóureko	Custard pie
Halvás	Sweetmeat of sesame
Karydhópita	Walnut cake
Kréma	Custard
Loukoumádhes	Dough fritters in honey syrup and sesame seeds
Pagotó	Ice cream
Pastélli	Sesame and honey bar

Ravaní	Spongecake, lightly syruped
Ryzógalo	Rice pudding
Smigdhalísios halvás	Semolina-based halva

Fruit and nuts

Akhládhia	Big pears
Aktinídha	Kiwis
Amýgdhala	Almonds
Fistíkia	Pistachio nuts
Fráoules	Strawberries
Himoniátiko	Autumn (cassava) melon
Karpoúzi	Watermelon
Kerásia	Cherries
Krystália	Miniature pears
Kydhóni	Quince
Lemónia	Lemons
Míla	Apples
Pepóni	Melon
Portokália	Oranges
Rodhákino	Peach
Sýka	Figs
Stafýlia	Grapes
Yiarmádhes	Autumn peaches

Cheese

Ayeladhinó	Cow's-milk cheese

Féta	Salty-creamy white cheese
Graviéra	Gruyère-type hard cheese
Katsikísio	Goat cheese
Kasséri	Medium-sharp cheese
Myzíthra	Sweet cream cheese
Próvio	Sheep cheese

Drinks

Alisfakiá	Island sage tea
Boukáli	Bottle
By*ra	Beer
Gála	Milk
Galakakáo	Chocolate milk
Kafés	Coffee
Krasí	Wine
áspro	white
kokkinélli/rozé	rosé
kókkino/mávro	red
Limonádha	Lemonade
Metalikó neró	Mineral water
Portokaládha	Orangeade
Potíri	Glass
Stinyássas!	Cheers!
Tsáï	Tea
Tsáï vounoú	"Mountain" (mainland sage) tea

A glossary of words and terms

Acropolis Ancient, fortified hilltop.

Agora Market and meeting place of an ancient Greek city; also the "high street" of a modern village (**agorá** in modern Greek).

Amphora Tall, narrow-necked jar for oil or wine.

Áno Upper; common prefix element of village names.

Apse Curved recess at the east end of a church nave.

Archaic period Late Iron Age period, from around 750 BC to the start of the Classical period in the fifth century BC.

Architrave Horizontal masonry atop temple columns; same as **entablature.**

Arhondikó A lordly stone-built mansion, often restored as boutique accommodation.

Astykó (Intra) city, municipal, local; adjective applied to phone calls and bus services.

Áyios/Ayía/Áyii Saint or holy (m/f/plural). Common place-name prefix (abbreviated Ag or Ay), often spelled **Agios** or **Aghios.**

Basilica Colonnaded, "hall-" or "barn-" type church adapted from Roman models, found as ruined foundations on Crete, Kós and Kárpathos, among other places.

Bema Rostrum for oratory (and later the chancel) of a church.

Bouleuterion Auditorium for meetings of an ancient town's deliberative council.

Capital The flared top, often ornamented, of a column.

Cavea Seating curve of an ancient theatre.

Cella Sacred room of a temple, housing the cult image.

Classical period Essentially from the end of the Persian Wars in the fifth century BC until the unification of Greece under Philip II of Macedon (338 BC).

Conch Concave semi-dome surmounting a church apse, often frescoed.

Corinthian Decorative columns, festooned with acanthus florettes; a temple built in this order.

Dhimarhío Town hall.

Dhomátia Rooms for rent in purpose-built blocks or (seldomly these days) private houses.

Dorian Northern civilization that displaced and succeeded the Mycenaeans and Minoans through most of Greece around 1100 BC.

Doric Minimalist, unadorned columns, dating from the Dorian period; a temple built in this order.

Drum Cylindrical or faceted vertical section, usually pierced by an even number of narrow windows, upholding a church cupola.

Entablature The horizontal linking structure atop the columns of an ancient temple.

Eparhía Greek Orthodox diocese, also a subdivision of a modern province, analogous to a county.

Exedra Display niche for statuary.

Exonarthex The outer vestibule or entrance hall of a church, when a true **narthex** is present.

Forum Market and meeting place of a Roman-era city.

Frieze Band of sculptures around a temple. Doric friezes consist of various tableaux of figures (**Metopes**) interspersed with grooved panels (**triglyphs**); Ionic ones have continu-ous bands of figures.

Froúrio Medieval citadel; nowadays, can mean a modern military headquarters.

Garsoniéra/es Studio villa/s, self-catering apartment/s.

Geometric period Post-Mycenaean Iron Age era named for the style of its pottery; begins in the early eleventh century BC with the arrival of Dorian peoples. By the eighth century BC, with the development of representational styles, it becomes known as the **Archaic period**.

Hellenistic period The last and most unified "Greek empire", created in the wake of Alexander the Great's Macedonian empire and finally collapsing with the fall of Corinth to the Romans in 146 BC.

Heroön Shrine or sanctuary, usually of a demigod or mortal; war memorials in modern Greece.

Hóra Main town of an island or region; literally it means "the place". An island hóra is often known by the same name as the island.

Ierón Literally, "sacred" – the space between the altar screen and the apse of a church, reserved for priestly activities.

Ikonostási Screen between the nave of a church and the altar, supporting at least three icons.

Ionic Elaborate, decorative development of the older **Doric** order; Ionic temple columns are slimmer, with deeper "fluted" edges, spiral-shaped capitals and ornamental bases.

Iperastykó Long-distance – as in phone calls and bus services.

Kafenío Coffee house or café; in a small village the centre of communal life.

Kaïki (plural **kaïkia**) Caique, or medium-sized boat, traditionally wooden and used for transporting cargo and passengers; now refers mainly to island excursion boats.

Kalderími A cobbled mule-track or footpath.

Kámbos Fertile agricultural plain, usually near a river mouth.

Kantína Shack, caravan or even a disused bus on the beach, serving drinks and perhaps sandwiches or quick snacks.

Kástro Any fortified hill, but most often the oldest, highest, walled-in part of an island hóra, intended to protect civilians.

Katholikón Central chapel of a monastery.

Káto Lower; common prefix element of village names.

Kendrikí platía Central square.

Kouros Nude Archaic statue of an idealized young man, usually portrayed with one foot slightly forward of the other.

Megaron Principal hall or throne room of a Mycenaean palace.

Meltémi North wind that blows across the Aegean in summer, starting softly from near the mainland and hitting the Cyclades, the Dodecanese and Crete full on.

Metope See **Frieze**.

Minoan Crete's great Bronze Age civilization, which dominated the Aegean from about 2500 to 1400 BC.

Moní Formal term for a monastery or convent.

Moreas Medieval term for the Peloponnese; the outline of the peninsula was likened to the leaf of a mulberry tree, mouriá in Greek.

Mycenaean Mainland civilization centred on Mycenae and the Argolid from about 1700 to 1100 BC.

Naos The inner sanctum of an ancient temple; also, any Orthodox Christian shrine.

Narthex Western vestibule of a church, reserved for catechumens and the unbaptized; typically frescoed with scenes of the Last Judgement.

Neolithic Earliest era of settlement in Greece, characterized by the use of stone tools and weapons together with basic agriculture. Divided arbitrarily into Early (ca. 6000 BC), Middle (ca. 5000 BC) and Late (ca. 3000 BC).

Néos, Néa, Néo "New" – a common prefix to a town or village name.

Nomós Modern Greek province – there are more than fifty of them. Village bus services are organized according to their borders (most obviously on Crete with its four provinces).

Odeion Small theatre, used for musical performances, minor dramatic productions or councils.

Orchestra Circular area in a theatre where the chorus would sing and dance.

Palaestra Gymnasium for athletics and wrestling practice.

Paleós, Paleá, Paleó "Old" – again a common prefix in town and village names.

Panayía Virgin Mary.

Pandokrátor Literally "The Almighty"; generally refers to the stern portrayal of Christ in Majesty frescoed or in mosaic in the dome of many Byzantine churches.

Paniyíri Festival or feast – the local celebration of a holy day.

Paralía Beach, or seafront promenade.

Pediment Triangular, sculpted gable below the roof of a temple.

Pendentive Any of four triangular sections of vaulting with concave sides, positioned at a corner of a rectangular space to support a circular or polygonal dome; in churches, often adorned with frescoes of the four Evangelists.

Períptero Street kiosk.

Peristereónes Pigeon towers, in the Cyclades.

Peristyle Gallery of columns around a temple or other building.

Pinakothíki Picture gallery, ancient or modern.

Pithos (plural **pithoi**) Large ceramic jar for storing oil, grain, etc. Very common in Minoan palaces and used in almost identical form in modern Greek homes.

Platía Square, plaza.

Polygonal masonry Wall-building technique of the Classical and Hellenistic period, which used unmortared, closely joined stones; often called "Lesvian polygonal" after the island where the method supposedly originated. The much-(ab)used term "**Cyclopean**" refers only to Mycenean/Bronze Age mainland sites such as Tiryns and Mycenae itself.

Propylaion Monumental columned gateway of an ancient building; often used in the plural, **propylaia**.

Pýrgos Tower or bastion; also tower-mansions found in the Máni or on Lésvos.

Skála The port of an inland island settlement, nowadays often larger and more important than its namesake, but always younger since built after the disappearance of piracy.

Squinch Small concavity across a corner of a columnless interior space, which supports a superstructure such as a dome.

Stele Upright stone slab or column, usually inscribed with an edict; also an ancient tombstone, with a relief scene.

Stoa Colonnaded walkway in Classical-era marketplace.

Távli Backgammon; a favourite café pastime, especially among the young. There are two more difficult local variations (févga and plakotó) in addition to the standard international game (pórtes).

Témblon Wooden altar screen of an Orthodox church, usually ornately carved and painted and studded with icons; more or less interchangeable with ikonostási.

Temenos Sacred precinct, often used to refer to the sanctuary itself.

Theatral area Open area found in most of the Minoan palaces with seat-like steps around. Probably a type of theatre or ritual area.

Tholos Conical or beehive-shaped building, eg a Mycenaean tomb.

Triglyph See Frieze.

Tympanum The recessed space, flat or carved in relief, inside a pediment.

Votsalotó Mosaic of coloured pebbles, found in church or house courtyards of the Dodecanese and Spétses.

Acronyms

ANEK Anónymi Navtiliakí Etería Krítis (Shipping Co of Crete, Ltd), which runs most ferries between Pireás and Crete, plus many to Italy.

EAM National Liberation Front, the political force behind ELAS.

ELAS Popular Liberation Army, the main Resistance group during World War II and the basis of the Communist army during the civil war.

ELTA Postal service.

EOS Greek Mountaineering Federation, based in Athens, controlling a few refuges on Crete.

EOT Ellinikós Organismós Tourismoú, National Tourist Organization.

FYROM Former Yugoslav Republic of Macedonia.

KKE Communist Party, unreconstructed.

KTEL National syndicate of bus companies. The term also refers to individual bus stations.

LANE Lasithiakí Anónymi Navtiliakí Etería (Lasithian Shipping Company Ltd), based in eastern Crete.

ND Conservative (Néa Dhimokratía) party.

NEL Navtiliakí Etería Lésvou (Lesvian Shipping Co).

OA Standard abbreviation and international airline code for Olympic Airlines.

OTE Telephone company.

PASOK Socialist party (Pan-Hellenic Socialist Movement).

Small print and

Index

A Rough Guide to Rough Guides

Published in 1982, the first Rough Guide – to Greece – was a student scheme that became a publishing phenomenon. Mark Ellingham, a recent graduate in English from Bristol University, had been travelling in Greece the previous summer and couldn't find the right guidebook. With a small group of friends he wrote his own guide, combining a highly contemporary, journalistic style with a thoroughly practical approach to travellers' needs.

The immediate success of the book spawned a series that rapidly covered dozens of destinations. And, in addition to impecunious backpackers, Rough Guides soon acquired a much broader and older readership that relished the guides' wit and inquisitiveness as much as their enthusiastic, critical approach and value-for-money ethos.

These days, Rough Guides include recommendations from shoestring to luxury and cover more than 200 destinations around the globe, including almost every country in the Americas and Europe, more than half of Africa and most of Asia and Australasia. Our ever-growing team of authors and photographers is spread all over the world, particularly in Europe, the USA and Australia.

In the early 1990s, Rough Guides branched out of travel, with the publication of Rough Guides to World Music, Classical Music and the Internet. All three have become benchmark titles in their fields, spearheading the publication of a wide range of books under the Rough Guide name.

Including the travel series, Rough Guides now number more than 350 titles, covering: phrasebooks, waterproof maps, music guides from Opera to Heavy Metal, reference works as diverse as Conspiracy Theories and Shakespeare, and popular culture books from iPods to Poker. Rough Guides also produce a series of more than 120 World Music CDs in partnership with World Music Network.

Visit www.roughguides.com to see our latest publications.

Rough Guide travel images are available for commercial licensing at www.roughguidespictures.com

Rough Guide credits

Text editor: Sarah Eno, Alice Park
Layout: Umesh Aggarwal, Diana Jarvis
Cartography: Katie Lloyd-Jones, Ed Wright, Maxine Repath
Picture editor: Mark Thomas
Production: Katherine Owers
Proofreader: Madhu Mohapatra, Janet McCann and David Paul
Cover design: Diana Jarvis

....

Editorial: London Kate Berens, Claire Saunders, Geoff Howard, Ruth Blackmore, Polly Thomas, Richard Lim, Clifton Wilkinson, Alison Murchie, Karoline Densley, Andy Turner, Keith Drew, Edward Aves, Nikki Birrell, Helen Marsden, Alice Park, Sarah Eno, Joe Staines, Duncan Clark, Peter Buckley, Matthew Milton, Tracy Hopkins, David Paul, Lucy White, Ruth Tidball; **New York** Andrew Rosenberg, Richard Koss, Steven Horak, AnneLise Sorensen, Amy Hegarty, Hunter Slaton, April Isaacs, Sean Mahoney
Design & Pictures: London Simon Bracken, Dan May, Diana Jarvis, Mark Thomas, Jj Luck, Harriet Mills, Chloë Roberts; **Delhi** Madhulita Mohapatra, Umesh Aggarwal, Ajay Verma, Jessica Subramanian, Amit Verma, Ankur Guha, Pradeep Thapliyal
Production: Sophie Hewat, Katherine Owers, Aimee Hampson
Cartography: London Maxine Repath, Ed Wright, Katie Lloyd-Jones; **Delhi** Manish Chandra, Rajesh Chhibber, Jai Prakash Mishra, Ashutosh Bharti, Rajesh Mishra, Animesh Pathak, Jasbir Sandhu, Karobi Gogoi, Pradeep Thapliyal
Online: New York Jennifer Gold, Suzanne Welles, Kristin Mingrone; **Delhi** Manik Chauhan, Narender Kumar, Shekhar Jha, Rakesh Kumar, Chhandita Chakravarty
Marketing & Publicity: London Richard Trillo, Niki Hanmer, David Wearn, Demelza Dallow, Louise Maher, Jess Carter; **New York** Geoff Colquitt, Megan Kennedy, Katy Ball; **Delhi** Reem Khokhar
Custom publishing and foreign rights: Philippa Hopkins
Manager India: Punita Singh
Series editor: Mark Ellingham
Reference Director: Andrew Lockett
PA to Managing and Publishing Directors: Megan McIntyre
Publishing Director: Martin Dunford
Managing Director: Kevin Fitzgerald

Publishing information

This 6th edition published May 2006 by **Rough Guides Ltd**,
80 Strand, London WC2R 0RL
345 Hudson St, 4th Floor,
New York, NY 10014, USA
14 Local Shopping Centre, Panchsheel Park, New Delhi 110017, India
Distributed by the Penguin Group
Penguin Books Ltd,
80 Strand, London WC2R 0RL
Penguin Putnam, Inc.
375 Hudson Street, NY 10014, USA
Penguin Group (Australia)
250 Camberwell Road, Camberwell,
Victoria 3124, Australia
Penguin Books Canada Ltd,
10 Alcorn Avenue, Toronto, Ontario,
Canada M4V 1E4
Penguin Group (New Zealand)
Cnr Rosedale and Airborne Roads
Albany, Auckland, New Zealand
Cover concept by Peter Dyer.
Typeset in Bembo and Helvetica to an original design by Henry Iles.

Printed and bound in Italy by LegoPrint

© Andrew Benson, Lance Chilton, Marc Dubin, Nick Edwards, Mark Ellingham, John Fisher, Geoff Garvey and Natania Jansz Rough Guides Ltd, May 2006

712pp includes index

A catalogue record for this book is available from the British Library
ISBN 1-84353-610-2
ISBN 13: 9781843536109

The publishers and authors have done their best to ensure the accuracy and currency of all the information in **The Rough Guide to the Greek Islands**, however, they can accept no responsibility for any loss, injury, or inconvenience sustained by any traveller as a result of information or advice contained in the guide.

1   3   5   7   9   8   6   4   2

Help us update

We've gone to a lot of effort to ensure that the 6th edition of **The Rough Guide to the Greek Islands** is accurate and up to date. However, things change – places get "discovered", opening hours are notoriously fickle, restaurants and rooms raise prices or lower standards. If you feel we've got it wrong or left something out, we'd like to know, and if you can remember the address, the price, the time, the phone number, so much the better.

We'll credit all contributions, and send a copy of the next edition (or any other Rough Guide if you prefer) for the best letters. Everyone who writes to us and isn't already a subscriber will receive a copy of our full-colour thrice-yearly newsletter. Please mark letters: "**Rough Guide Greek Islands Update**" and send to: Rough Guides, 80 Strand, London WC2R 0RL, or Rough Guides, 4th Floor, 345 Hudson St, New York, NY 10014. Or send an email to **mail@roughguides.com**
Have your questions answered and tell others about your trip at
www.roughguides.atinfopop.com

Acknowledgements

Andrew Benson wishes to thank Elias and Dimitris in Athens for their hospitality, Denise for a marvellous evening on Evvia, the Noel-Bakers for a great time, and everyone at the Imaret for their goodwill and impeccable taste; thanks also to Sarah and Geoff, plus all the team back in London, for their confidence, patience and quest for perfection.

Lance Chilton thanks wife Hilary; Chris and Dave Windell in Pyrgiótika; Nick Turland in St Louis; Katerina and Yiannis Katranis in Spárti; Dimitris Papandropoulos of the Láppa Information Centre; Dimitris Pollalis in Arhángelos; the staff at the Byzantion in Monemvasiá; Babis Doufexis and Nicola Dyas of Doufexis Travel in Stoúpa; Nikos Kourtidis and Graham Pond of First Choice in Stoúpa.

Marc Dubin thanks: the Papalexis family in Galaxídhi, the Sakellaris brothers in Náfpaktos, Jill Sleeman in Moúressi, the Boutos family in Karytsá, Anthoula Gouri in Tsepelovo, Kostas and Marianthi Pappas in Ioánnina, Thanassis and Toula Nakas in Metéora, Theo and Melinda Kosmetos in Mólyvos, Markos Kostalas, Theodhore and Güher Spordhilis, and Stella Tsakiri, on Híos, Alexis, Ippokratis and Dionysia Zikas on Kós, David, Lisa, Iain and Lynn on Tílos, Kim Sjögren and his staff at Triton, Constance Rivemale, Efi and Spyros Dedes, Gerald Brisch, Patrick and Anna on Rhodes, Roger Jinkinson, Mihalis, and the Yializis family on Kárpathos, Nikos, Wendy, Adriana and Nicholas on Sými, Andonis and Themelina Andonoglou on Kálymnos, Elina Skoutari on Pátmos, Rena Paradhisi on Lipsí, the managements of the hotels Porphyris (Níssryos), Australia (Astypálea), Crithoni's Paradise (Léros) and Magda's Apartments (Párga) for their support, Panayiotis and Aphrodite Papasotiriou on Límnos, Dudley der Partogh at Sunvil, and Carol Coulter at Skycars, for travel facilities, and last but not least to the

Zdravets for sharing travels to various corners of Greece.

Nick Edwards would like to thank everybody who helped him on the last tour, especially Maria of the Hotel Gorgona in Nydhri*, Panayiotis of the Hara in Argostoli and Kostas of the Boukari Beach. Also thanks to Andronikos of the Kyani Akti in Argosto*li and Kostas of the Angonari near A*grafi for fine feasts. Once more gratitude goes to Mariana, Petros, Orestes and Orfeas for excellent hospitality in Horepískopi. Cheers to Peter Hemming for the Lixouri tour and yiasou to Pam and all at Pub Old House. And here's to the old friends who joined in at various stages: Ann, Steve, Carol & Simon and Gordon. Finally, a huge hug to Maria for minding the homestead.

Mark Ellingham would like to thank Michael Haag (History), George Pissalides (Music) and Sandy MacGillivray (Archeology) for their contributions to the Contexts section of the book; and Sarah Eno, Alice Park and Geoff Howard for their excellent editorial work, overhauling this new edition of the guide.

John Fisher thanks Miranda Rashidian, Kate Donnelly, Nick Edwards and the examination crew, Dimitris Koutoulas and Leonidas Tsagaris; to everyone at Rough Guides especially Sally, Sarah and Ed for a great job on the maps; and as ever to A and the two Js for love and support.

Geoff Garvey would like to thank Nikos Karellis editor of Stigmes magazine, Iráklion, for sharing his encyclopedic knowledge of all things Cretan; a grateful "efharisto pára poli" also goes to Manolis Sergentakis in Kastélli Kissámou, Irene Michaelakis in Haniá, Yiannis & Katerina Hatzidakis in Sitía, Heracles Papadakis in Spili, Lambros Papoutsakis in Thrónos, Froso Bora in Réthymnon, and last but by no means least to the indomitable Stelios Manousakas of Aryiroúpolis (long may his avocados flourish).

Readers' letters

Thanks to all the readers who have taken the time to write in with comments and suggestions (and apologies if we've inadvertently omitted or misspelt anyone's name):

Roger Alsop, Horacio Amarilho, Zaynab Ayub, Thijs Backus, Neil Bailey, Julie Barrie, Tony Birkett, Mario Bottaro, Terence Brace, Sarah Callan, Carlomaria Cairoli, Richard Ciecierski, Martin Coppen, Nuala Crotty, Terence Cuff, Janet Davidson, Barbara Dorf, John Engel, Francesco, Marco Gandini, Stuart Gates, Margaret Gorrie and Barry Williamson, Amanda Gray and Adam Knight, Margaret Green, Averil Harrison and John Sessions, Gordon D. Hillhouse, Steve Hounslow, Jens Erik Jørgensen, Zane Katsikis, Mike Leggett, Mike

Lippman and Laura Gross, Gina and Duncan Langford, Henry Long, Rebecca Macky, Bob Mark, Richard Marks, Debbie Marshall, Andy McCosh, Phil Meade, Daniel Mills, Roger Moorhouse, Michael O'Flaherty, Sue Quinn, Susan Raphael Ben Rees, Julie Reeves, Yizhar Regev, Yoram Regev, Mabel Richmond, Peter Riley, Alan Rooks, Paul Schollmeier, Nic Shannon, Pieter Steine, Pieter Steinz David Tricker, Peter "Pav" Verity, Jeffrey Walter, Peter Watson, Graham Whitehouse, Rachel Williams, Don Wilson, Nick Wurr, Duncan K. Young.

Photo credits

Cover

Front image: Windmill Door, Mikonos, Greece © Jim Zuckerman/CORBIS
Back image: Goat, west coast of Kefalloniá © Alamy
Inside cover image: Longás, near Peroulhádhes, Corfu © Rough Guides Pictures

Title page

Santoríni © Sylvain Grandadam/Getty Images

Full page

Wild flowers overlooking coastline, Crete © Peter Adams/Getty Images

Introduction

Fresco of Dolphins © P. Frillet/Getty Images
Windmill on Santoríni © Todd A Gipstein/Getty Images
Boatyard on Páros © IML Images Group Ltd/Alamy
Fish stall in Crete © Steve Outram/Getty Images
Eye amulet © Helene Rogers/Trip
Wayside shrine, photography by Michelle Grant © Rough Guides
Lefkas Beach © Jochem D Wijnands/Getty Images

Things not to miss

01 Sými Harbour © IML Image Group Ltd/Alamy
02 Hellenistic stoa, Lindos, Rhodes © Marc Dubin
03 Kérkyra Old Town, photography by Michelle Grant © Rough Guides
04 Samaria Gorge National Park, Crete © Alberto Arzoz/Axiom
05 Dhikeos peak, Kós © Marc Dubin
06 View over Firá © Walter Bibikow/Getty Images
07 Patani Beach, Kefallonia, Photography by Nick Edwards © Rough Guides
08 The Queens Megaron, Knossos © Roger Wood/Corbis
09 Sámos landscape © Bob Turner/Alamy
10 View of Mólyvos © IML Image Group Ltd/Alamy
11 Melissáni cave, Kefalloniá © Martin Jenkinson/Alamy
12 Tomatoes drying, Híos © Marc Dubin
13 Woman on boat © Howard Kingsnorth/Corbis
14 Andípaxi, photography by Nick Edwards © Rough Guides
15 Naoússa Village © Glen Allison/Getty Images
16 Loggerhead Turtle © David Boag/Alamy
17 Haniá old town, Crete © Peter M Wilson/Axiom
18 Ídhra © Jose Fuste Raga/Corbis
19 Carpet weaver at work in Crete © Stock Connection Distribution/Alamy
20 Ápella Beach © Gail Mooney/Corbis
21 Vaï Beach, Crete © Peter M Wilson/Axiom
22 Tourists enjoying nightlife © Paul Panayiotou/Alamy
23 Dovecotes on Tínos © IML Image Group Ltd/Alamy
24 View south from Ólymbos village, Karpathos

© Marc Dubin
25 Windsurfing off Vassilikí, Lefkádha © Jack Moscrop/Axiom
26 Monk praying in Pátmos Monastery © Peter Poulides/Getty Images
27 Stéfanos crater floor © Doug Houghton
28 Hozoviotíssas monastery, Amorgos © Pictures Colour Library/Alamy
29 Aphaea Temple © Rainer Hackenberg/Alamy

Black and whites

p.92 Ídhra Town © Marc Dubin
p.105 Póros Town © David Ball/Corbis
p.115 Ayía Paraskeví bay, Spétses © IML Image Group Ltd/Alamy
p.118 Church of Ekatondapliani, Parikía, Páros © Marc Dubin
p.140 Roman amphitheatre and Mílos Bay © Robert Harding Picture Library/Alamy
p.150 Dove House Tínos © Peter M Wilson/Alamy
p.167 Ayios Nikólaos, Ermoúpoli © Terry Harris Just Greece Photo Library/Alamy
p.174 Fishermen in Náoussa, Páros © Yuri Lev/Alamy
p.194 Monastery of Hozoviotíssas, Amorgós © Marc Dubin
p.207 Firá, Santoríni © IML Image Group/Alamy
p.220 Minoan fresco, Knossos © Bob Turner/Alamy
p.241 Matala Beach, Crete © Alberto Arzoz/Axiom
p.253 Ayíos Nikolaos © Peter M Wilson/Alamy
p.276 Hánia harbour and Mosque of the Janissaries © Peter M Wilson/Alamy
p.286 Samariá Gorge © Peter M Wilson/Alamy
p.296 Hóra © Marc Dubin
p.307 Hiking near Ólymbos, northern Kárpathos © Robert Harding Picture Library/Alamy
p.315 Buttressed lanes, Rhodes Old Town © Simon Bracken/Alamy
p.329 Emborió quayside, Hálki © David Trevor/Alamy
p.346 Langadhaki district, Mandhráki, Níssyros © Stefan Auth/Alamy
p.355 Ancient agora, Kós © Jon Arnold Images/Alamy
p.369 Sponge-seller, Póthia, Kálymnos © IML Image Group/Alamy
p.382 Mosaic outside the monastery of Ayíou Ioánnou Theólogou, Pátmos © Terry Harris Just Greece Photo Library/Alamy
p.392 Mýrina harbour, Límnos © IML Image Group Ltd/Alamy
p.397 Sámos landscape © Bob Turner/Alamy
p.415 View from Foúrni toward Thýmena and Ikaría © IML Image Group/Alamy
p.424 Street scene, Pyrgí, Híos © Robert Harding Picture Library/Alamy
p.445 View over Mólyvos harbour, Lésvos © Alan Novelli/Alamy
p.454 Portianoú World War I Allied cemetery © Marc Dubin
p.459 Sanctuary of the Great Gods, Samothráki

Index

Map entries are in colour.

F

G

H

INDEX

Map symbols

maps are listed in the full index using coloured text

▬▬▬	International boundary	▬▬▬	Wall
-----	Chapter division boundary	⊻⊻	Marshland
══════	Motorway	𝕏	Waterfall
═══	Major paved road	⋀⋀	Spring/spa
═══	Minor paved road	●	Cave
───	Unpaved road	♦	Museum
░░░░	Pedestrianized street	⚠	Campsite
-------	Footpath	◉	Accommodation
⊞⊞⊞⊞⊞	Steps	✕	Airport
▬▬▬	Railway	**P**	Parking
── ──	Ferry route	★	Bus/taxi stop
═══	Waterway	ⵙ	Lighthouse
⛫	Mosque	*(i)*	Information office
✡	Synagogue	⊠	Post office
ⵜ	Church	♦	Point of interest
⛩	Monastery or convent	⊞	Hospital
∴	Archeological site	⊠—⊠	Gate
Ⱦ	Castle	⬭	Stadium
	Hill	▬	Building
▲	Peak	⊞	Church
⋀⋀	Mountains	⊹	Christian cemetery
⳾	Gorge	░░	Park
⊻	Viewpoint	░░	Beach
@	Internet		